THE USSR IN 1991:
A RECORD OF EVENTS

Published in cooperation
with Radio Free Europe/Radio Liberty

The USSR in 1991:
A Record of Events

Edited by

Vera Tolz and Melanie Newton

Foreword by Iain Elliot

LONDON AND NEW YORK

First published 1993 by Westview Press

Published 2019 by Routledge
52 Vanderbilt Avenue, New York, NY 10017
2 Park Square, Milton Park, Abingdon, Oxon OX14 4RN

Routledge is an imprint of the Taylor & Francis Group, an informa business

Copyright © 1993 by Radio Free Europe/Radio Liberty

All rights reserved. No part of this book may be reprinted or reproduced or utilised in any form or by any electronic, mechanical, or other means, now known or hereafter invented, including photocopying and recording, or in any information storage or retrieval system, without permission in writing from the publishers.

Notice:
Product or corporate names may be trademarks or registered trademarks, and are used only for identification and explanation without intent to infringe.

Library of Congress Cataloging-in-Publication Data
Tolz, Vera.
  The USSR in 1991 : a record of events / edited by Vera Tolz and Melanie Newton
    p. cm.
  ISBN 0-8133-8717-5
  1. Soviet Union—History—1985–1991—Chronology. I. Newton, Melanie. II. Title.
DK286.T654 1993
947.085'4'0202—dc20
                                                                                        92-42105
                                                                                        CIP

ISBN 13: 978-0-367-29704-6 (hbk)

Contents

Foreword by IAIN ELLIOT	vi
Preface	viii
Acknowledgments	ix
The Month of January	1
The Month of February	72
The Month of March	150
The Month of April	228
The Month of May	302
The Month of June	374
The Month of July	441
The Month of August	517
The Month of September	629
The Month of October	698
The Month of November	781
The Month of December	862
Name Index	925
Subject Index	951

Foreword

On that dramatic day, August 19, 1991, Elena Bonner addressed the citizens of Moscow: "I call on you to defend the freedom we have today. Only in this way can we create a life that is different from the one we and our parents have lived for seventy-three years." Not all who heard such appeals to oppose the attempted coup were prepared to man the barricades, but there were more than enough people all over the USSR for whom a return to the old ways was unthinkable. They rejected the enforced passivity that had allowed an unpopular regime to rule for so long over a greater expanse of territory and greater number of peoples than any tsar. The struggle against authoritarian methods no longer seemed hopeless; at last individual liberty and national sovereignty were more than words.

As the USSR disintegrated, new leaders came into the limelight, and others, already widely known, took on new roles. The rivalry between Mikhail Gorbachev and Boris El'tsin frequently occupied the center of the stage. No doubt Gorbachev believes he was right to oppose the aspirations to independence of the republics, on the grounds that only a strong political union and powerful center could prevent ethnic conflict, territorial disputes, and economic collapse. But the introduction of even limited democracy showed how widespread the demand for national sovereignty was. The year began with Moscow's crackdown in the Baltic republics. On January 13 fourteen people were killed and hundreds injured when Soviet tanks opened fire on a crowd protecting the Vilnius television tower. More blood was shed in Riga on January 20 when Soviet special forces stormed the building of the Latvian Ministry of Internal Affairs. Moscow kept up the pressure in the following months by staging repeated attacks on Baltic customs posts. But this only made the Balts more determined, as their resistance to the August coup testified.

Elsewhere, too, the gulf between the center and the republics was already becoming unbridgeable even before the coup. Only nine republics participated in the March 17 referendum on the preservation of the USSR, and at subsequent negotiations on the Union treaty these nine forced Gorbachev finally to recognize their declarations of sovereignty. Georgia declared its independence on April 9, having rejected, along with Armenia and Moldavia, any new Union state.

That Moscow had suppressed ethnic disputes, not solved them, was underlined once more in 1991. The conflict between Azerbaijan and Armenia over Nagorno-Karabakh flared up again with renewed intensity in April and May, while sporadic clashes between Georgian special units and local forces in South Ossetia left hundreds dead or injured and forced thousands more to flee from their homes. In Moldavia, which declared its independence on August 27, the year ended with fighting between Moldavian units and supporters of the "Dniester SSR."

Amid the general confusion and political uncertainty, the USSR's economic decline accelerated. Industrial and agricultural output continued to fall, and by the end

FOREWORD

of the year the states of the former Union were facing a hard-currency and budgetary crisis. The freeing of some retail prices in April prompted workers in normally conservative Belorussia to stage a protest strike, while in Siberia, Ukraine, and Kazakhstan miners took industrial action to press political as well as economic demands.

The referendum held in Ukraine on December 1 produced a 90-percent majority in favor of independence and put the final seal on the USSR's fate. Leonid Kravchuk, who had demonstrated his political acumen by distancing himself from his Communist Party background to promote the cause of Ukrainian sovereignty, was elected president of Ukraine that same day.

Among other national leaders to emerge from the grey conformity of the Party hierarchy, Nursultan Nazarbaev of Kazakhstan was particularly successful in making his mark as the Central Asian republics strove to forge direct economic links with the outside world.

Gorbachev announced his resignation on December 25, a passing more mourned in the West than in his own country. If indeed he was the best leader the Soviet Union had ever had, his superiority surely lay less in his ability to govern than in his reluctance to use sufficient brutality to prevent the collapse of the system over which he presided. Within two days El'tsin had moved into Gorbachev's Kremlin office, demonstrating his determination, albeit in a somewhat crude manner, to push Russia into a new, non-Communist era. The leaders of the Commonwealth of Independent States, which replaced the USSR, could not be expected to bring their much-suffering populations an immediate transition to democracy, still less instant peace and prosperity. But the end of the USSR did bring a demonstrable freedom, and with it the opportunity to turn hopes for a better future into reality.

This is the third, and last, of the annual *Records of Events* in the USSR expertly produced by Vera Tolz and Melanie Newton with the assistance of their colleagues in the RFE/RL Research Institute. It was not originally seen as a limited series; but as it turns out, their three volumes provide an outstanding chronicle of events so significant for the history of our century as to merit the efforts of many a future Gibbon. These annual records are not, however, merely the raw material for other books. They provide carefully selected but very comprehensive facts, and they succeed admirably in presenting an objective and balanced day-by-day account of three sensational years. Those who have used the first two volumes will find this one equally indispensable for checking who was who and what happened when, in the year that the USSR ended.

IAIN ELLIOT

Preface

The breakup of the Soviet Union makes *The USSR in 1991: A Record of Events* the last of the three annual chronologies of events in and relating to that country. Like its companion volumes, *The USSR in 1989: A Record of Events* and *The USSR in 1990: A Record of Events*, the present work is intended primarily as a reference book whose purpose is to give anyone interested in Soviet affairs easy access to a wealth of detailed information. The volume is organized on a day-by-day basis and divided into chapters for each month. Headlines are used for each entry to facilitate locating information. Entries for a given day have been arranged roughly in descending order of importance. Where a story runs over several days or even weeks—as is often the case with state visits, parliamentary sessions, and ethnic disputes—its sequential parts have been grouped together in a single entry on the day it began.

For its information, *The USSR in 1991: A Record of Events* draws on the wide range of Soviet and non-Soviet media reports at the disposal of RFE/RL. A number of independent media organizations were established in 1991, both in Moscow and in the USSR's constituent republics, and, particularly in times of crisis, they were an important alternative source of information to the central media. In addition, RFE/RL's broadcasting services continued to receive on-the-spot reports from free-lance correspondents in the Soviet Union and to conduct telephone interviews with Soviet politicians and public figures. These circumstances are reflected in the contents of the present volume.

As the Soviet Union began to fall apart, media coverage of developments in individual republics increased dramatically and the quantity of information emanating from the USSR became overwhelming. This inevitably meant that, even more than in the past, some degree of selection had to be exercised in compiling the volume. While priority has naturally been given to covering all the major events in or involving the Soviet Union that were in the public eye during 1991—itself a daunting task—some of the less topical but nonetheless interesting developments that may have escaped notice elsewhere have also been included. The selection of items in the latter category, while taking into account their relative importance and the general scope of the volume, is of course to some extent a matter of predilection.

A comprehensive index is an essential part of any reference work of this kind if users of it are to find information quickly and easily. *The USSR in 1991: A Record of Events* contains two indexes—one of persons only and one of subjects and proper names other than those of persons. Because some persons are mentioned literally hundreds of times in the volume, the index entries of their names are further subdivided into subject categories.

VERA TOLZ AND MELANIE NEWTON

Acknowledgments

Though only the names of the two principals—Melanie Newton and Vera Tolz—appear on the cover of this volume, many other people were involved both directly and indirectly in its preparation. A particularly valuable contribution was made by the analysts on the staff of the RFE/RL Research Institute, whose specialized knowledge and writings helped to make authoritative coverage of such a vast range of topics possible. Their commentaries for the *RFE/RL Daily Report* were drawn on extensively and many of them helped to compile the "Weekly Record of Events," the regular feature of the Research Institute's weekly publication *Report on the USSR* on which *The USSR in 1991: A Record of Events* is based. Of enormous help, too, were the summaries of news agency reports put together by RFE/RL's News and Current Affairs Division, the reports filed by RFE/RL's own correspondents, and the numerous telephone interviews with people in the Soviet Union conducted by members of RFE/RL's broadcasting services.

Without the continuing encouragement of E. Eugene Pell, president of RFE/RL, Inc., *The USSR in 1991: A Record of Events* could not have been produced. Both this volume and its predecessors, *The USSR in 1989: A Record of Events* and *The USSR in 1990: A Record of Events,* manifest his interest in making part of the immense flow of information emanating from the former Soviet Union and being evaluated by RFE/RL in connection with its broadcasts available to the Western public in a convenient, lasting, and usable form.

The idea for the series was conceived by Robert Farrell, former assistant director of the Publications Department of the RFE/RL Institute, who this year undertook the enormous task of proofreading the entire text. Brooke Bessert and Friederike Koos-Molnar typeset and copyfitted the text on a Macintosh® using Microsoft Word® and PageMaker®. The kind help of Rebecca Ritke, acquisitions editor at Westview Press, is gratefully acknowledged. She, Libby Barstow, Connie Oehring, and Jennifer Barrett patiently and conscientiously shepherded the volume through the complicated process of production. Finally, a public expression of gratitude is owed to the indexer, Jane McGraw, whose labors contributed significantly to the volume's usefulness as a reference work.

VT
MN

The Month of January

Tuesday, January 1

A spokesman for the USSR Defense Ministry, Lieutenant Colonel Nikolai Medvedev, told *Izvestia* Soviet soldiers would in future serve in the Transcaucasus on a volunteer basis. He said conscripts from Georgia, Armenia, and Azerbaijan would also be allowed to serve in construction battalions in their own regions. Medvedev explained that the measure was necessary to deal with "difficult conditions" in the area. He said that in 1990 there had been 120 attacks on army installations and property in Armenia alone.

Soviet Soldiers to Serve in Transcaucasus on Volunteer Basis

Kaliningrad Oblast, the most westerly region of the RSFSR, was officially opened to foreigners. TASS said a decree opening the region had been adopted by the Soviet government. Kaliningrad had been a closed area since the end of World War II.

Kaliningrad Opened to Foreigners

Wednesday, January 2

Special forces of the USSR Ministry of Internal Affairs seized the press building in Riga. This action by the "Black Berets," as these MVD units were nicknamed, was intended to bring the press building back under the jurisdiction of the Latvian Communist Party; it also led to a halt in the publication of the principal newspapers and most journals in Latvia (*Radio Riga*, January 2).

On January 7, Colonel General Fedor Kuz'min, commander of the Baltic Military District, announced to Latvian Prime Minister Ivars Godmanis that several thousand USSR Airborne Troops would be sent to Latvia to enforce the draft (only about 25 percent of the Latvian conscripts drafted in the call-up in the fall of 1990 had reported for duty) (*Radio Riga*, January 7).

On January 10, thousands of demonstrators—mostly Russians and other Slavs heeding the call of the International Front of Latvian SSR Workers—gathered outside the Council of Ministers building to demand the resignation of the Latvian government, the dissolution of the

Crackdown in Latvia

legislature, and the institution of presidential rule in Latvia (*Radio Riga*, January 10).

In response to these ominous signs, on January 13, some 700,000 Latvians gathered on the banks of the Daugava River in Riga to show their confidence in the government and their commitment to the peaceful restoration of an independent and democratic Latvia. Fearing Soviet military intervention, they put up barricades near important buildings and bridges in Riga and began a twenty-four-hour watch on these sites. Members of the "Black Berets" tried to intimidate the unarmed volunteer guards.

On January 16, the "Black Berets" opened fire on trucks and other vehicles parked along a bridge and killed Roberts Murnieks, who was behind the wheel of a van. Murnieks was the chauffeur for Minister of Transport Janis Janovskis (*Radio Riga, Reuters*, January 16).

On January 20, a group of "Black Berets" seized five volunteer guards, beat them up, and eventually turned them over to the KGB. That evening they stormed the Ministry of Internal Affairs, killing four people and injuring ten. In the meantime, a self-proclaimed body calling itself the "All-Latvian National Salvation Committee" had announced that it had taken over the reins of government in Latvia. This announcement, made at an antigovernment demonstration on January 15, was widely disseminated by the Soviet media (*Radio Moscow*, January 16).

Shevardnadze Comments on His Resignation

In his first public comment since his resignation on December 20, former USSR Foreign Minister Eduard Shevardnadze told *Moscow News* (No. 1, 1991) he had resigned because he feared the possibility of military crackdowns similar to those in Tbilisi (April, 1989) and Baku (January, 1990). Shevardnadze criticized Soviet President Mikhail Gorbachev's government, saying it was a talking shop that debated problems endlessly, was slow in making decisions, and failed to enforce laws. He characterized the concept of presidential rule as "a punitive sanction" that would not solve problems. Asked by *Moscow News* about his plans for the future, he said he would like to create a foreign-policy association.

Commenting on Shevardnadze's resignation on Central Television on December 31, veteran foreign-affairs journalist Stanislav Kondrashov said Shevardnadze's disagreement with the Soviet Armed Forces was only part of the problem. According to Kondrashov, the main reason for Shevardnadze's resignation was that Soviet foreign policy had lost its impetus. Kondrashov described "new thinking" as a drama in three acts. While in the first act

The USSR in January, 1991

Gorbachev and Shevardnadze had rescued the USSR from international isolation, the second act had seen too hasty a dismantling of the Warsaw Pact, resulting in a humiliating Soviet retreat. Now, in the third act, Soviet society was beginning to free itself from imperial ambitions, Kondrashov said. To illustrate his point, he compared the attacks in 1989 on Andrei Sakharov for his opposition to Soviet involvement in Afghanistan with recent protests by both the armed forces and the public against the possibility of Soviet involvement in the Gulf crisis.

Kondrashov expanded on these statements in a commentary in *Izvestia* on January 3. Arguing that Gorbachev's dependence on military support was the reason why the Soviet president was unwilling to defend his foreign minister against criticism by conservatives, Kondrashov wrote that "today the president needs the army more than ever before, and he does not want the army's patience to run out."

Walesa Speech Criticized in *Izvestia*

In an article published in *Izvestia* of January 3, the Soviet journalist Stanislav Kondrashov criticized Polish President Lech Walesa's inaugural address. Kondrashov complained that Walesa's speech on December 22 had ignored the Soviet Union while mentioning that Poland was developing relations with Ukraine, Belorussia, and Lithuania. The commentator stressed that both Ukraine and Belorussia and, for the time being, even Lithuania were parts of the USSR.

Registration of Political Parties Runs into Problems

The USSR Ministry of Justice began officially registering political parties, as required by the Soviet law on public associations. TASS called the registration the USSR's first practical step towards a multiparty system but noted that the process had immediately run into considerable problems. The agency quoted the Justice Ministry as saying all the applications for registration received so far had been submitted incorrectly.

Priest Investigating Murder of Father Aleksandr Men' Killed

AP quoted the Interfax news agency as saying that Father Lazar', a member of the Church commission investigating the murder of the Russian Orthodox priest Aleksandr Men', had been killed in his Moscow apartment. Interfax quoted the police as saying Father Lazar' had died during an attempted burglary of his apartment; but, the agency went on, unidentified "close associates" of the priest claimed there was no evidence of a burglary. Soviet President Mikhail Gorbachev ordered an official investigation into the murder of Father Men' in September, 1990; the Church had also set up an inquiry of its own.

Curfew Lifted in Dushanbe

Izvestia reported that the curfew imposed in Dushanbe after violence in the city in February, 1990, had finally been lifted. The order removing the curfew noted that the situation in the Tajik capital had stabilized.

Thursday, January 3

Council of Federation Meets

The first session of the Council of the Federation since its powers were increased approved in principle an economic agreement for 1991, TASS reported. The session was attended by representatives of all the Union republics, including those that had refused to sign a new Union treaty; according to the *Los Angeles Times*, however, Lithuanian Prime Minister Kazimiera Prunskiene said Lithuania would not sign the economic agreement, insisting instead on a separate agreement recognizing the republic's independence.

Yanaev to Take Charge of Ministerial Nominations

Soviet President Mikhail Gorbachev announced that Gennadii Yanaev would head a group responsible for nominating members of the new cabinet, according to TASS and "Vremya." The announcement was made following a meeting of the Council of the Federation.

Official Urges Better US–North Korean Ties

USSR Deputy Foreign Minister Igor' Rogachev said the United States should move quickly to improve ties with Communist North Korea in order to help ease regional tension. Rogachev told the South Korean newspaper *Dong-A Ilbo* that the Soviet Union and China had already taken steps to improve ties with South Korea. The United States was lagging behind in this process, he added, saying the USSR would welcome the normalization of US–North Korean ties (*AP*, January 3).

Sale of Missiles to Salvador Investigated

AFP reported that a Soviet-Nicaraguan commission was being created to investigate Nicaragua's sale of thirty Soviet-made antiaircraft missiles to Salvadoran rebels. The USSR sold the missiles to the Sandinista government of Nicaragua in 1986, a time when, according to the United States, the Sandinistas were supplying the rebels with weapons. The Soviet ambassador to Nicaragua,

The USSR in January, 1991

Evgenii Astakhov, said the purchase agreement of 1986 had barred the transfer of the weapons to a third country. He added that the Soviet Union would dispatch a representative to Managua to determine whether Nicaragua had violated the agreement. The USSR suspended arms shipments to Nicaragua in 1989.

Israeli Consul General Ariel Levin said the reopening of the Israeli consulate in Moscow, which took place today, was only the first step in renewing ties between Israel and the Soviet Union (*TASS*, January 3). AP reported that a group of Soviet Jews had "danced for joy" during the official opening celebration.

Israeli Consulate in Moscow Reopens

The Soviet Union criticized Sweden for expelling three Soviet citizens. Sweden had expelled the three—a Soviet diplomat and two other official representatives—on January 2 for "activities incompatible with their status." The Soviet embassy in Stockholm said there was no evidence that they had broken any laws (*Reuters, AP*, January 3).

USSR Criticizes Sweden over Expulsion

---------------- *Friday, January 4*

A commentary by Aleksandr Gol'ts in *Krasnaya zvezda* took a look at the future of Soviet foreign policy and argued that, while the principles of "new thinking" (nonconfrontation and noninterference in other countries' internal affairs) would remain intact, "the content of Soviet foreign policy cannot remain as it is." Gol'ts noted that in the past the country's superpower status had been guaranteed by military might alone, and he questioned whether the USSR would manage to maintain that status by any other means. He also argued that it was the army "that enabled Comrade Shevardnadze to conduct foreign affairs successfully."

***Krasnaya zvezda* Calls for Change in Soviet Foreign Policy**

TASS reported that a new Union of Students of Kirgizia had held a constituent conference at the end of 1990. The new organization proposed to adhere to the principles of the Universal Declaration of Human Rights and to oppose "extremism and chauvinism" (catchwords in Kazakhstan and Kirgizia for, respectively, non-Russian and Russian nationalism). The report did not indicate what the relationship of the new organization to the Komsomol would be but noted that, during interethnic strife in Osh Oblast

Students' Union Set Up in Kirgizia

during the summer of 1990, student demonstrators in Frunze had been able to force the republican government to send a group representing them to Osh to see what was really going on.

Belorussia Permits Hard-Currency Bank Accounts

The Belorussian government issued a decree allowing both Soviet and foreign citizens to establish hard-currency accounts at Belorussian banks. Minsk journalist Yas Voloshka told RFE/RL that the decree specified no limit on the size of the accounts and said depositors would not have to reveal the source of the money (RL Belorussian service, January 4).

USSR Exchanges Ambassadors with Guatemala

The Soviet Union and Guatemala activated diplomatic relations with the exchange of ambassadors. Diplomatic relations between the two countries had been established in 1945 but had never been activated through an exchange of missions, TASS reported on January 9.

Saturday, January 5

Controversy over RSFSR Contribution to Budget

Chairman of the RSFSR Supreme Soviet Boris El'tsin told reporters that the RSFSR had agreed to contribute 77 billion rubles to the Union budget but that this still fell short of the center's demands by some 27 billion rubles. AP quoted RSFSR Mass Media and Information Minister Mikhail Poltoranin as saying the RSFSR was not opposed in principle to contributing funds to the central government but wanted to ensure the money was not wasted.

On January 8, Soviet and Western news agencies provided a breakdown of the RSFSR's contribution. The agreement stipulated that the RSFSR would pay 23.4 billion rubles directly into the budget and, in addition, contribute 38.6 billion rubles from foreign-trade activities and 15 billion rubles from exploitation of natural resources. A major concession on the part of El'tsin was his agreement that the RSFSR would pay an extra .30.6 billion rubles into an "extrabudgetary fund" for economic stabilization. The RSFSR also withdrew its objections to the center's taking a portion of the tax on enterprises.

Gorbachev Issues Decree on Land

In an attempt to boost food production, Soviet President Mikhail Gorbachev called for the redistribution of 3–5 million hectares of farmland by the spring. In a decree

The USSR in January, 1991

issued on January 5, Gorbachev called for the drafting in the first half of 1991 of an inventory of land "not used in a rational manner" (*TASS*, January 5). He said this land would be put into a land bank and distributed to peasant farmers, leaseholders, cooperatives, and individuals. The decree made no mention of private ownership of land. Gorbachev had called for a national referendum on that issue.

Session of Comecon Admits It Has Exhausted Possibilities

Comecon's executive council ended two days of talks in Moscow with a plea to members not to break their traditional economic ties after the dissolution of the Soviet-led trading association scheduled to come about in late February. A communiqué acknowledged that Comecon had exhausted its possibilities but said that economic relations between members could continue. TASS said Comecon would be replaced by a new group called the Organization for International Economic Cooperation.

USSR Grateful for Rescue in Somalia

All staff of Soviet institutions in Somalia were transferred to the US embassy in Mogadishu on January 5, TASS reported. Soviet citizens were said to be at risk because armed groups had invaded the Soviet embassy grounds and food and water supplies were running short. According to TASS, Eduard Shevardnadze expressed his gratitude to US Secretary of State James Baker in a telephone conversation on January 5.

Afghanistan to Resume Supplies of Natural Gas

Afghan officials said natural gas supplies to the Soviet Union would be resumed soon. Supplies were halted in February, 1989, when Soviet troops began withdrawing from Afghanistan (*Reuters*, January 6).

KGB Says Soviet and Western Criminals Cooperate

Deputy Chairman of the KGB Viktor Grushko said the Soviet "mafia" was collaborating with criminal organizations in the West. In an interview with the German newspaper *Bild am Sonntag*, Grushko said the two groups were working together in smuggling works of art, narcotics, and cars.

Yakovlev Says Criticism of Gorbachev Team Justified

In an interview with *Moskovskaya pravda*, former Politburo member Aleksandr Yakovlev said that real *perestroika* was only just beginning in the USSR and that some of the criticism of Soviet President Mikhail Gorbachev and his team was well founded. Yakovlev discounted rumors of a military coup, saying that the only indication of a rebellion was the obstruction of the president's orders by middle-level bureaucrats.

Yakovlev also said that new structures would have to be set up during the course of 1991 to replace the existing ministries. He said coordinating—rather than ruling—bodies should be created; otherwise, he stressed: "Stalin's economic totalitarianism will hold fast."

KGB Requests Funds to Protect Sobchak

The Leningrad KGB organization asked the Soviet KGB to organize personal protection for the chairman of the Leningrad City Soviet, Anatolii Sobchak. Radio Moscow quoted the Postfactum news agency as saying the proposed protection was a response to a death threat against Sobchak. It said the Leningrad KGB had recommended that 60,000 rubles be allocated from the city budget to pay for the service.

Stalin Used Double, Newspaper Reports

Rabochaya tribuna reported that the assassination of Sergei Kirov in 1934 had caused Stalin to fear for his own life and that, subsequently, Stalin had often used a look-alike as a stand-in at public appearances. The man used as Stalin's double was identified as Evsei Lubitsky, a Jewish accountant from Ukraine. The newspaper said that, in order to keep the secret from leaking out, all members of Lubitsky's family had been killed, as well as the team of surgeons, hairdressers, and tailors who worked on Lubitsky's appearance to improve his resemblance to Stalin.

Sunday, January 6

Dzasokhov Says Gulf Policy Unchanged despite Shevardnadze's Resignation

In an interview with TASS, Politburo member Aleksandr Dzasokhov emphasized that Soviet policy on the Gulf crisis had not changed and that the USSR favored a peaceful resolution to the dispute. Dzasokhov told TASS that it was important to stress the invariability of Soviet policy at this time because of speculation in the foreign press that a shift in policy might follow Eduard Shevardnadze's resignation as foreign minister.

The same day, Chairman of the USSR Supreme Soviet Anatolii Luk'yanov asserted that "it would be preferable" for Shevardnadze to remain in his post. Luk'yanov told Central Television that Shevardnadze should continue participating "in all other work, including politi-

The USSR in January, 1991

cal work." He called Shevardnadze "one of the great architects" of *perestroika*.

Filatov Interviewed

In an interview with *The New York Times*, Major General Viktor Filatov, the editor of *Voenno-istoricheskyzhurnal*, said that Soviet President Mikhail Gorbachev was a brilliant leader but that he had underestimated the force of nationalism and had allowed the army and KGB to atrophy. Filatov recommended that Gorbachev "find another Beria." "Now we have means of persuasion," he said, "but no means of compulsion." Filatov, an outspoken nationalist, had been accused of publishing anti-Semitic materials. His journal's circulation had increased tenfold since he took it over in December, 1989.

Official Says Conservative Forces Strong

In an interview with Central Television, USSR Supreme Soviet Chairman Anatolii Luk'yanov said dangerous conservative forces were "quite strong" in the Soviet Union. He said, though, that he did not see any immediate threat of dictatorship. Luk'yanov stressed that the conservatives should be fought unremittingly but that the growing need for law and order should not be confused with a move back to a dictatorship.

Army Units under KGB Control, Newspaper Says

The German newspaper *Morgenpost am Sonntag* reported that certain army units returning to the Soviet Union, especially from Germany, were being placed under the control of the KGB, Reuters reported. The German newspaper quoted Soviet military sources as saying that most of the units coming under KGB control had been redeployed to the Moscow Military District.

Sunday Editions of Central Newspapers Dropped

TASS issued a brief announcement saying that, starting on January 6, Soviet central newspapers would no longer appear on Sundays. TASS said the curtailment was due to a change in operations at the USSR Ministry of Communications, but *Komsomol'skaya pravda* blamed it on higher prices for newsprint. Journalists from that newspaper protested on January 6 against the discontinuation of its Sunday edition, saying it was unfair to subscribers, who were paying higher rates but getting fewer issues.

Soviet Special Envoy in South Korea

Soviet President Mikhail Gorbachev's special envoy, Deputy Foreign Minister Igor' Rogachev, arrived in South Korea to discuss expanded economic cooperation and steps towards peace on the divided Korean peninsula. Talking to reporters in Seoul, Rogachev said Moscow was willing to act as a mediator between North Korea and South Korea. He also said he did not believe mediators between the two were necessary, because there was now a direct dialogue between them (*Reuters*, January 6).

On January 7, South Korean Vice President Yoo Chong Ha asked the Soviet Union to comment on Western press reports that *Izvestia* planned soon to reveal information about the wreckage of the Korean airliner shot down in 1983 (*AP*, January 7). On December 20, *Izvestia* had published an article suggesting that the Soviet authorities knew the location of the wreckage.

In the midst of tension between Moscow and Seoul over potential revelations about the KAL flight, Rogachev extended his stay in South Korea by two days. Rogachev repeated Shevardnadze's formulation of December 17, saying, "We regret that innocent Korean people were killed" (*Reuters*, January 7). Rogachev added, "We will check with the authorities concerned and let you know if there are any new findings."

Meanwhile, on January 7, Reuters reported that Mikhail Gorbachev had requested more cooperation from South Korea. In a personal letter to South Korean President Roh Tae Woo, Soviet President Mikhail Gorbachev made an appeal for more help in revitalizing the Soviet economy.

On January 22, another article on the shooting down of the South Korean airliner in 1983 appeared in *Izvestia*. It contained information about an unofficial investigation that had been going on since the incident. The article said that the plane had been shot down near the Soviet Pacific island of Moneron and that soldiers had found the craft "almost undamaged" in thirty-meter-deep water. The investigation also concluded that the plane could not possibly have been on a spying mission. See *Izvestia*, January 22–25.

Finland Says Number of Soviet and East European Arrivals Increasing

The number of people arriving in Finland from the Soviet Union and Eastern Europe to escape hardship at home was rising. The Interior Ministry said some 24,000 people had been granted residence permits in Finland in 1990, 10,000 more than in the previous year. About 36 percent of the residence permits were granted to Soviet citizens, an eight-fold increase (*Reuters*, January 6).

Moldavia Responds to Gorbachev's Decree

Speakers at a meeting of Communist activists in the largely Russian city of Balti (Beltsy) on January 6 said Moldavia's entry into a renewed Union was of "vital

The USSR in January, 1991

necessity." TASS quoted participants as saying the full implementation of Soviet President Mikhail Gorbachev's decree on Moldavia "would be the first step towards the establishment of civil peace in the republic." (On December 22, Gorbachev had ordered the dissolution of the republics proclaimed by the Gagauz minority and the nonindigenous residents of the Dniester region. He had also called for changes in Moldavia's language law so that the interests of ethnic groups could be respected.) The participants sent an open letter to Gorbachev calling on him to show firmness and to ensure that the decree did not turn into "only [a declaration of] good intentions."

On January 9, TASS reported that the Supreme Soviet of the would-be "Gagauz republic" had rejected Gorbachev's order to dissolve the republic. TASS said the main reason for the refusal was that the Moldavian Supreme Soviet, also affected by Gorbachev's decree, had refused Gorbachev's demand to drop its condemnation of the 1939 Hitler-Stalin pact. TASS quoted the Gagauz Supreme Soviet chairman, Stepan Topal, as saying the Gagauz leadership had decided to seek "a single market of socioeconomic activity" with Ukraine. According to TASS, the Gagauz Supreme Soviet also issued a document asking the USSR to protect the interests of the Gagauz people.

Meeting in Tiraspol on January 22, an extraordinary congress of people's deputies from all levels of the would-be "Dniester SSR" resolved not to accept Gorbachev's ruling that the self-proclaimed republic was illegal. The Russian-dominated congress in Tiraspol justified its decision by pointing to Kishinev's failure to comply with some of Gorbachev's instructions. The congress decided to establish structures of executive power for the would-be republic within the next two weeks, *Izvestia* and Novosti reported.

Monday, January 7

Paratroopers to Enforce Conscription

The USSR Defense Ministry announced on national television that airborne units would be used to enforce the draft in the three Baltic republics; in Armenia, Georgia, and Moldavia; and in some regions of Ukraine. Turnout for the fall draft had been especially low in these areas—a situation the Defense Ministry called intolerable. The announcement appeared to confirm an earlier report from the Baltic republics in which Colonel General Fedor Kuz'min, the district commander, said Defense Minister Dmitrii Yazov had issued such an order on the instructions of Soviet President Mikhail Gorbachev.

The announcement contradicted recent statements by two members of the Soviet High Command. On January 4, Army General Mikhail Moiseev, the chief of the General Staff, had told TASS that Moscow had no plans to station additional troops in the Baltic area and that troop strength there might even be reduced. His comments followed a meeting with President of the Latvian Supreme Council Anatolijs Gorbunovs on January 3. On January 4, Major General Pavel Grachev, the recently appointed commander of Soviet Airborne Forces, had said that his men should not be used to control interethnic conflicts.

On January 7, US Ambassador to the Soviet Union Jack Matlock asked Eduard Shevardnadze about reports that thousands of Soviet paratroopers were being dispatched to the Baltic republics (*Reuters*, January 7).

On January 8, two public officials from Lvov protested against the announced plan to send Soviet paratroopers to enforce conscription in Western Ukraine. Lvov Oblast Soviet Deputy Chairman Ivan Hel' and a deputy of the Ukrainian Supreme Soviet, Yaroslav Kendzior, expressed concern and indignation in an interview with RFE/RL.

The same day, the White House issued a statement on the Soviet troop action, saying: "This action presents a serious step towards an escalation of tension within the USSR and makes the peaceful evolution of relations among the people of the Soviet Union more difficult" (RFE/RL correspondent's report, January 8). Meanwhile, British Foreign Secretary Douglas Hurd asked the Soviet ambassador to London for clarification of the decision to deploy paratroops (RFE/RL correspondent's report, January 8).

Also that day, Moldavian Prime Minister Mircea Druc, who was on a visit to the United States, criticized Moscow's threat to send troops to Moldavia to enforce military conscription and predicted that Moscow's directive would be ignored, *The Washington Post* and Reuters reported on January 9.

On January 9, Boris El'tsin condemned the decision to use Soviet troops in several republics (*Reuters*, January 9).

On January 9, the head of the USSR Defense Ministry's Information Administration told Radio Moscow that the ministry's order regarding the deployment of additional paratrooper units to enforce the draft applied to Lithuania only. Major General Valerii Malinov was responding to the White House criticism.

The same day, Lieutenant General Frants Markovsky told viewers of "Vremya" that the airborne units dis-

The USSR in January, 1991

patched to help with draft enforcement would not perform "gendarme" functions. A senior spokesman for the General Staff, Markovsky said airborne units would be used to make sure that regional commissariats were not blockaded and to protect military personnel conducting draftees to their units. He denied that leaders of the armed forces were planning a military coup in any of the republics seeking independence and said the Defense Ministry actions should in no way interfere with plans for the forthcoming US-Soviet summit.

On January 11, Soviet soldiers stationed in Moldavia started rounding up young men suspected of avoiding the USSR military draft or leaving their military units. News of the roundups came from Sergiu Burca, chief editor of the Moldavian Popular Front's newspaper *Tsara*, and Sorin Bucataru, a spokesman for the Organization of Democratic Youth, in a telephone conversation with RFE/RL. The two men said they had received telephone calls from the mothers of those taken away and from some young men still in hiding. They said some abuse of those apprehended had been reported.

Christmas Day Official Holiday

For the first time in seventy years, the Orthodox Christmas was celebrated as an official holiday in some parts of the USSR. Radio Moscow reported that, at the request of the Orthodox Churches, the parliaments of the RSFSR, Ukraine, Moldavia, Belorussia, and Georgia had revived Christian holidays. In Moscow, thousands crowded into the cathedral where Patriarch Aleksii II celebrated his first Christmas service as leader of the Russian Orthodox Church. The Christmas celebrations were reported extensively by Soviet radio and television.

Gorbachev Offers to Stop Nuclear Weapons Testing

Mikhail Gorbachev said the USSR would stop testing nuclear weapons if the United States did the same, Western news agencies reported. His proposal was made in a message to a UN conference on nuclear testing. Gorbachev's declaration came amid growing controversy in the USSR over nuclear testing. Particularly at issue was the continued use by the USSR Defense Ministry of the testing site at Semipalatinsk in Kazakhstan, which was opposed by local forces.

Protest against Gulf War

A demonstration against military action in the Gulf took place in Leningrad, TASS reported. Organized by the Committee of Wives and Mothers and the group "Otechestvo," the demonstration called for the Gulf conflict to be resolved by peaceful means. Representatives of the Soviet Armed Forces were reported to be present. Participants referred to the losses suffered by the Soviet Union in Afghanistan and issued an appeal to the USSR Supreme Soviet, bearing more than 4,000 signatures, saying a war in the Gulf could still be prevented.

Yavlinsky Named as Aide to Silaev

Radio Moscow reported that Grigorii Yavlinsky had been appointed economic adviser to RSFSR Council of Ministers Chairman Ivan Silaev. Yavlinsky was to perform his work on a voluntary basis. Yavlinsky said his decision was connected with his desire not to leave public service altogether, despite his recent resignation from the post of RSFSR deputy prime minister.

Luk'yanov Meets Japanese Delegation

Chairman of the USSR Supreme Soviet Anatolii Luk'yanov met with a Japanese parliamentary delegation in the Kremlin. They discussed international issues and bilateral relations.

Speaking to the Japanese delegation on January 9, Boris El'tsin said he would like the RSFSR to sign a peace treaty with Japan formally ending World War II without waiting for the USSR as a whole to do so. El'tsin noted that the dispute over the Kurile Islands, part of the Russian Federation, was the main obstacle to signing such a peace treaty. He said an RSFSR-Japanese settlement would add dynamism to relation. "I don't think it would affect the authority of [Gorbachev], because now the sovereignty process is developing rapidly and leading to considerable growth in the role of the republics," Reuters quoted El'tsin as saying.

On January 14, *Izvestia* quoted a Japanese Foreign Ministry spokesman as telling a press conference that Japan did not intend to hold talks on the question of the ownership of "the northern territories"—i.e., the Kurile Islands—solely with representatives of the RSFSR. He said it was necessary to negotiate with the central government over the issue.

Gorbachev Issues Decree on South Ossetia

Soviet President Mikhail Gorbachev issued a decree ordering all armed formations other than those of the USSR Ministry of Internal Affairs to leave the South Ossetian Autonomous Oblast within three days (*Pravda*, January 8). This constituted a demand for the removal of units of the Georgian Ministry of Internal Affairs and the KGB that had been in the oblast to enforce the state of emergency declared on December 12. The decree de-

The USSR in January, 1991

clared unconstitutional South Ossetia's decision of September 20 to proclaim itself a Union republic and Georgia's decree of December 11 abolishing South Ossetia's status as an autonomous oblast. It also called on the Georgian authorities to report to the USSR president within five days on measures to normalize the situation in the oblast.

On January 9, the Georgian Supreme Soviet held an extraordinary session to discuss Gorbachev's decree. Reuters reported that the parliament had rejected the order.

On January 15, Chairman of the Georgian Supreme Soviet Zviad Gamsakhurdia called on Gorbachev to suspend his decree concerning unrest in what Gamsakhurdia called "the former South Ossetian Autonomous Oblast," saying that would be the only way to ease the explosive situation there (*TASS*, January 15).

Situation in South Ossetia Remains Tense

Interfax reported that one person had been killed in South Ossetia and several injured in recent days as a result of clashes between Ossetians and units of the Georgian police. USSR MVD troops tried to prevent the confrontations. The curfew in the autonomous oblast was extended to twelve hours—from 7 P.M. to 7 A.M. Supplies were said to be running short because of an unofficial blockade by the Georgian authorities.

On January 8, "Vremya" and TASS said that the situation in South Ossetia remained very tense, but there were reports that Georgian police units were leaving the autonomous oblast.

On January 9, TASS reported that some Georgian police units had tried to leave the South Ossetian capital, Tskhinvali, but that their departure had been resisted by illegal armed formations. Radio Moscow reported that unofficial talks had taken place in Tskhinvali between representatives of the Ossetian population and leaders of the Georgian Ministry of Internal Affairs. Despite this, there was more shooting, and the Ossetian population refused to give up its weapons until the Georgian police units had been withdrawn.

Meanwhile, the absence of any links with South Ossetia, where many North Ossetians had relatives; rumors of casualties in Tskhinvali; the intention of some young North Ossetians to go to South Ossetia to help their fellow countrymen; and the need to provide constant food assistance to South Ossetia greatly heightened tension in North Ossetia (*TASS*, January 9). On January 9, meetings took place in North Ossetia demanding the unconditional implementation of Soviet President Mikhail Gorbachev's decree. On January 10, the Supreme Soviet of North Ossetia passed a resolution supporting Gorbachev's decree and demanding that Georgia remove its forces from South Ossetia.

TASS reported on January 10 that the rejection of Gorbachev's decree by the Georgian Supreme Soviet had provoked an "extremely negative" response in South Ossetia. It said that there had been exchanges of gunfire in Tskhinvali and that barricades had been erected.

On January 11, Radio Moscow said a Soviet tank "subunit" was being sent into South Ossetia. The radio said the operation was taking place in connection with attempts to seize arms from military facilities located there. Chairman of the Georgian Supreme Soviet Zviad Gamsakhurdia was quoted as saying he believed the Soviet leadership was trying to provoke a confrontation in South Ossetia so that it could impose presidential rule in Georgia. *The Times* quoted him as saying on January 10 that large numbers of Soviet troops were assembled just across the border in the RSFSR.

On January 12, TASS said four Georgian policemen had been killed and at least four others seriously wounded in a shootout in Tskhinvali on January 11. The report quoted a local news agency as saying the deaths came after an attack by unknown persons on the local internal affairs department building in Tskhinvali. The same day, USSR Minister of Internal Affairs Boriss Pugo said Georgia's dispatch of republican police to Tskhinvali had caused violence to escalate there. He said about 1,500 armed Georgians and many armed South Ossetians were in the Tskhinvali area (*TASS*, in English, January 12). On January 18, TASS reported that two more Georgian policemen had been killed in South Ossetia in a car explosion.

On January 23, TASS reported that three more people had been killed in fighting the previous day between Georgian police and Ossetians in Tskhinvali and that the home of an unnamed leader of Ossetian armed groups had been blown up.

On January 25, TASS reported that Soviet troops had mediated a cease-fire between rival militias in South Ossetia and had convinced Georgia to withdraw its police troops from the region. TASS said the agreement had come after a meeting between Georgian Minister of Internal Affairs Dilar Khabuliani and Ossetian representatives.

On January 30, citing Georgian sources in Tbilisi, TASS reported that the chairman of the South Ossetian Oblast Soviet, Torez Kulumbegov, had been arrested by Georgian MVD officials. Georgian MVD troops were being withdrawn from Tskhinvali, and the town was being patrolled by military units, which continued to

The USSR in January, 1991

detain people for curfew violations and confiscate weapons. A Georgian MVD spokesman stated that there had been no shooting in the city for the past three days.

On January 31, an MVD patrol was attacked by an armed group as it tried to remove a roadblock in South Ossetia. According to "Vremya," the troops returned fire, but no mention was made whether anyone had been killed or wounded. The patrol detained the people who attacked it and seized a small quantity of weapons, including guns and grenades.

Radio Kiev reported that Metropolitan of Kiev and Galicia Ioann of the Ukrainian Autocephalous Orthodox Church had in his Christmas message called on the clergy and believers of the Ukrainian Orthodox Church to sever all ties with the Moscow Patriarchate and join with the Ukrainian Autocephalous Orthodox Church in "one Christian family" in unity with Constantinople and other Eastern Churches.

Calls for Ukrainian Orthodox Unity

It was announced that Soviet and foreign citizens would no longer need special permits to visit the city of Magadan and most districts in Magadan Oblast, including Kolyma and Chukotka. The oblast, in the far northeast of the RSFSR, had been closed to visitors for decades. Under Stalin, it was the location of several labor camps and sensitive military installations. Radio Moscow said that the decision to open the oblast had been taken by the government of the RSFSR.

Magadan Declared Open City

Pravitel'stvennyi vestnik reported that the Soviet government had decided to remove the name of Stalin's associate Marshal Kliment Voroshilov from several institutions, including the Academy of the Armed Forces' General Staff and a Defense Ministry sanatorium on the Black Sea.

Voroshilov's Name to Be Removed from Institutions

_____*Tuesday, January 8*

The USSR Supreme Soviet instructed the Vote Counting Commission to investigate allegations made by the Interregional Group of Deputies that there had been irregularities in the election in December, 1990, of Gennadii Yanaev as the USSR's first vice president (*Radio Moscow*, January 8).

Investigation into Alleged Fraud in Yanaev's Election Promised

17

Supreme Soviet Commission for Links with the Public Created

TASS reported that the Presidium of the USSR Supreme Soviet had discussed the mechanics of rotating membership in the Supreme Soviet's permanent committees and commissions and had created a new Commission for Links between the USSR Supreme Soviet and the Public, to be chaired by Boris Oleinik, deputy chairman of the USSR Supreme Soviet Council of Nationalities.

The Presidium also discussed measures to ensure the holding of a referendum on the preservation of the USSR called for by the fourth session of the USSR Congress of People's Deputies and how such a referendum might be organized.

USSR Weapons Sales from 1986 to 1990 Total 100 Billion Dollars

Igor' Belousov, chairman of the USSR State Military-Industrial Commission, claimed that the Soviet Union had sold approximately 56.7 billion rubles' worth of arms abroad between 1986 and the end of 1990. Belousov made his remarks to *Pravitel'stvennyi vestnik* on January 8. About 9.7 billion rubles' worth of weapons were sold in 1990, slightly less than the average for the period. Belousov attributed the shrinking market for Soviet arms to a general warming of international relations and the demilitarization of Eastern Europe.

US Credit Package Complete

After a month of talks, US and Soviet negotiators hammered out the details of a US credit package for the USSR. The package provided US financing for up to 1 billion dollars' worth of agricultural products and the furnishing of credits for financing the shipment of them to the Soviet Union (RFE/RL correspondent's report, January 7).

Controversy over Soviet Freighter in Red Sea

The US Defense Department said a Soviet freighter had been stopped in the Red Sea because its cargo of military equipment was not fully listed on the ship's manifest. Spanish and US ships patrolling to enforce the UN embargo against Iraq stopped the Soviet vessel, the *Dmitrii Furmanov*, on January 4 and inspected the cargo (RFE/RL correspondent's report, January 8). The USSR Ministry of Foreign Economic Relations protested against the action on January 8, saying that the cargo of the *Dmitrii Furmanov* was bound for Jordan and did not violate the UN embargo. A spokesman for the US Defense Department said the ship was told not to head for its planned destination until the situation had been clarified.

The USSR in January, 1991

Bonn Says No Soviet Decision Yet on Honecker Case

Germany said the Soviet Union had not yet replied to Bonn's request to turn over former East German leader Erich Honecker, who was in a Soviet military hospital near Potsdam. A spokesman for the German government said Bonn's position was that the USSR should surrender Honecker to the legal authorities in Berlin, who had issued a warrant for the arrest of the former state and party leader (*DPA*, January 8).

President of World Jewish Congress Meets with Gorbachev and El'tsin

The president of the World Jewish Congress, Edgar Bronfman, met with Mikhail Gorbachev. They discussed the Arab-Israeli conflict, Soviet-Jewish emigration, and the Gulf crisis. Bronfman quoted Gorbachev as saying that Israeli Prime Minister Yitzhak Shamir was welcome to discuss all aspects of the Arab-Israeli conflict with the Soviet leadership. Bronfman also said Gorbachev had assured him that the USSR would not change its Gulf policy, despite Shevardnadze's resignation (*Reuters*, January 8).

On January 10, Bronfman met with Boris El'tsin. El'tsin was quoted by Radio Rossii as telling Bronfman that the RSFSR favored allowing all the federation's minorities to preserve their heritage. He said Russia would not repeat the mistakes made by the central government in refusing people in Armenia, Azerbaijan, and the Baltic republics the right to more self-determination. He also told Bronfman he was "a staunch opponent of anti-Semitism" and would shortly issue a statement pleading for tolerance (*Reuters*, January 12).

New Minister of Internal Affairs in Kirgizia

Izvestia said Feliks Kulov had been appointed Kirgizia's new minister of internal affairs. The newspaper said Kulov, a former deputy minister of internal affairs, had been appointed by decree by Kirgiz President Askar Akaev. Kulov was credited with defusing tensions in Frunze when he was named commandant of the city during the violence in Osh Oblast. A member of the opposition Democratic Renewal group in the republican Supreme Soviet, he was named to Kirgizia's Presidential Council when it was created in November, 1990.

Student Strike Leader Arrested in Ukraine

Radio Kiev reported that the head of the Kiev organization of the Ukrainian Students' Union, Oles' Donii, one of the central figures in the students' hunger strike in October that brought down the head of the Ukrainian government, Vitalii Masol, had been arrested. Donii was charged with instigating the takeover of three Kiev State University buildings during the strike, according to AP. At a press conference on January 9, the Ukrainian Students' Union read a statement charging the Kiev Prosecutor's Office with launching a campaign against the students.

Wednesday, January 9

Shift of Weapons East of the Urals Admitted

Sovetskaya Rossiya admitted that the armed forces had shifted weapons east of the Urals to make them exempt from cuts mandated by the recent Conventional Forces in Europe agreement. V. Litvov, identified as an economist, was quoted as saying that "the armed forces, trying somehow to repair the errors of diplomacy, organized, in the shortest possible time, the transfer east of the Urals of thousands of tanks, weapons, and other equipment—there at least they would not be destroyed." He accused the Foreign Ministry of hustling the armed forces into an early treaty deadline and said the armed forces might not have resented the cuts had the signing of the treaty been delayed.

Bobkov on Gorbachev and KGB

"The KGB understood very well back in 1985 that the Soviet Union would not be able to make further progress without *perestroika*," First Deputy Chairman of the KGB Filip Bobkov told *Nezavisimaya gazeta* (No. 2, 1991). Bobkov added that the KGB had supported Gorbachev then and was continuing to do so. Until 1985, Bobkov was head of the Fifth Main Administration (Ideological Subversion) of the KGB.

RSFSR Foreign-Policy Statement Attacks Enemies of Reforms

The RSFSR Foreign Ministry gave wholehearted support to the USSR's foreign policy of the past few years and said it would oppose attempts to reverse it. TASS said the RSFSR ministry had made this statement in response to concern abroad over possible changes in the USSR's foreign policy and over internal developments following the resignation of Eduard Shevardnadze. The statement said conservative forces were making groundless attacks on "new thinking" in foreign policy. It said these forces were seeking to restore an adversarial image and isolate the USSR again. The ministry declared it would resolutely counter attempts to create an atmosphere of chaos and open the way to reaction and dictatorship.

Aeroflot Suspends Flights to Baghdad

An Aeroflot spokesman said the company was suspending its scheduled flights to Baghdad. Aeroflot was

The USSR in January, 1991

one of the last airlines to fly into the Iraqi capital, AFP said.

The Moscow City Soviet authorized private ownership of shops, cafés, catering companies, and other services. *Izvestia* said large catering companies, supermarkets, and department stores would be transformed into shareholding companies. Priority in the purchase of stock in these holding companies would be given to employees.

Moscow City Soviet Authorizes Private Shops and Cafés

Radio Rossii reported on January 9 that a protest had been held in Barnaul, the administrative center of Altai Krai. Protesters demanded the resignation of the krai leadership and the recall of people's deputies elected from the region to soviets at all levels. On January 3, price increases for meat and some dairy products had been introduced in Altai Krai; the decision was taken by the Presidium of the krai soviet.

Protest in Barnaul against Price Rises

_____ *Thursday, January 10*

Soviet President Mikhail Gorbachev issued a decree ordering central and republican-level authorities to cooperate on exchanges of food supplies during the coming year. The decree also ordered food producers to meet all their delivery obligations to the state for 1991. It said only state prices would be paid for these deliveries. The decree instructed the Union-republican committee supervising a special hard-currency fund to determine how much hard currency would be needed to buy food abroad in 1991 (for the text of the decree, see *Pravda*, January 11).

Meanwhile, Boris El'tsin told the RSFSR Supreme Soviet that food shortages had become acute in several parts of the Soviet Union. He blamed the shortages partly on the refusal of producer regions to make deliveries to consumer regions. He also blamed barter agreements and the collapse of the state distribution system.

Gorbachev Issues Decree on Food Supplies

Soviet President Mikhail Gorbachev issued a statement on Lithuania, saying the situation there had "virtually reached an impasse." He said that the Lithuanian leadership must act in line with Soviet law or face the possibility of presidential rule. He claimed that the problems in Lithuania were rooted in "gross breaches of and departures from"

Gorbachev Issues Statement on Lithuania

the USSR Constitution. He said the Lithuanian leaders had ignored presidential decrees and were attempting to "reestablish a bourgeois regime" that infringed citizens' rights (*Pravda*, January 11).

Soviet Officials on Baker-Aziz Talks

Soviet President Mikhail Gorbachev's military adviser, Marshal Sergei Akhromeev, said he believed there would not be a war in the Gulf. He was quoted by Radio Tallinn as saying he thought an agreement would be reached before January 15, the deadline for Iraq to withdraw from Kuwait. He also expressed the view that the United States and Iraq had proposals they had not yet revealed and that these could mean at least short-term solutions to the Gulf crisis (January 10).

The same day, Foreign Ministry spokesman Vitalii Churkin called for fresh efforts to avert a war in the Gulf (*Reuters, AFP*, January 10). Churkin also voiced regret at the failure of US Secretary of State James Baker and Iraqi Foreign Minister Tariq Aziz to reach a peaceful settlement of the Gulf crisis.

290 Soviet Citizens Remain in Iraq

The Soviet Foreign Ministry said 290 Soviet citizens would remain in Iraq to ensure the operation of Soviet institutions there, TASS reported. It said 151 of them were specialists charged with maintaining Soviet equipment. The Foreign Ministry did not elaborate on the duties of the specialists but said those involved were living in a safe part of the country, far from military and industrial installations. The Foreign Ministry said that the Soviet mission in Baghdad would be pared down to a minimum.

Arbatov Says Military Complex against Reform

Georgii Arbatov, formerly a key adviser to Gorbachev, said in *Izvestia* that the military-industrial complex was fighting reform and imperiling the reform process. Arbatov said that democratization and the well-being of the people were incompatible with militarism, and he contended that Soviet defense spending was far too high given the Soviet Union's domestic and international situation. He also accused the High Command of failing to use its huge budget allocations to improve the living conditions of Soviet soldiers.

Crackdown on Central Television

The popular Soviet television program "Vzglyad," which had been prevented from airing material on Foreign Minister Eduard Shevardnadze's resignation, was taken off the air completely. A moderator of the program,

The USSR in January, 1991

Aleksandr Politkovsky, told RL's Russian service, that the order to stop production of the show had been signed by the deputy head of the USSR State Committee for Television and Radio Broadcasting (Gosteleradio), Petr Reshetov, on January 9.

On January 10, Radio Rossii complained that the head of Gosteleradio, Leonid Kravchenko, was continuing his crackdown on Central Television. Another very popular program, "*Avtorskoe televidenie*," was banned. Several other programs were also scheduled for cancellation. Radio Rossii said this would affect seventy-two employees of Central Television.

On January 12, RSFSR Supreme Soviet Chairman Boris El'tsin offered to take "Vzglyad" under the wing of RSFSR state radio and television when the latter started operations. Radio Moscow reported that the USSR Supreme Soviet had asked Kravchenko, to provide a written explanation of why "Vzglyad" had been dropped.

In a further move in the continuing clampdown on the media, Vladimir Lomakin, a moderator of the television newscast "Vremya," was banned by Kravchenko from appearing on the screen after he had refused to read a biased TASS dispatch on the situation in Lithuania. This was revealed to RL's Russian service by Politkovsky on January 12.

Urals Village to Be Evacuated Because of Radiation

Izvestia reported that residents of a village in the central Urals were to be evacuated because of long-term exposure to radiation. The newspaper said the executive committee of the Sverdlovsk Oblast Soviet had endorsed a decision to evacuate people from the village of Ozreni. *Izvestia* said that uranium was once mined near the village and that much contaminated material, including radioactive sand, had been left there. The mining ended in 1964.

All-Russian Congress of Victims of Repressions

The inaugural congress of the Russian (*Rossiiskaya*) Association of Victims of Political Repressions opened in Moscow, "TSN" reported. Participants in the gathering called on the USSR and RSFSR Supreme Soviets to officially admit that repressions had been going on in the country since 1918. The congress called for legal action to be taken to rehabilitate all the victims of terror. Mikhail Gorbachev's decree on the rehabilitation of victims of political repressions, issued in August, 1990, claimed that repressions had started only in the mid-1920s.

THE USSR IN JANUARY, 1991

Soviet Union Seeks Gold-Mining Deals in Africa

Valerii Rudalov, manager of the state-owned Glavmazzoloto enterprise, said the Soviet Union was investing in gold mining in one African country and hoped to establish joint ventures in four others. Rudalov said the first of the joint ventures would involve gold mining in Sierra Leone. He told Novosti that the Soviet Union would supply experts and technology and that Sierra Leone would provide labor. He said the USSR was negotiating similar arrangements in Mali, Guinea, Nigeria, and Liberia.

Azerbaijani Recruits Protest against Serving in Urals

Sixty-two newly drafted soldiers of Azerbaijani nationality briefly left their units and occupied a train in the south Urals town of Zlatoust. TASS said the recruits were protesting against being stationed so far from their homeland. It said commanding officers' attempts to persuade them to return to their units failed initially but that the protesters gave up when the officers told them their action was illegal and gave a written assurance that their demands would be examined.

Friday, January 11

Soviet Troops Storm Key Buildings in Vilnius

Soviet troops stormed two strategic buildings in Vilnius, after the newly established "Lithuanian National Salvation Committee" had announced that it was taking over control of Lithuania. The troops occupied Lithuania's State Defense Department and the republic's printing house. They fired shots in both takeovers, and several people were reported injured in the clashes. TASS said the troops had been sent in to return the buildings to "their lawful owners"—i.e., the Communist Party Central Committee. Lithuania said these facilities belonged to the republic. TASS said the measures had been taken in keeping with a decree issued by Gorbachev.

On January 10, several thousand supporters of the Lithuanian government gathered at other strategic facilities in Vilnius, including the parliament building, the central telephone exchange, and the broadcasting center, to protect them from Soviet troops. Workers opposed to independence held strikes at several facilities, including Vilnius airport.

The Lithuanian minister of communications, Kostas Birulis, broadcast an appeal from the Lithuanian government urging all Lithuanians to take part in passive civil disobedience if a new "occupation regime and puppet government" were installed in the republic.

The USSR in January, 1991

President of the Lithuanian Supreme Council Vytautas Landsbergis appealed to Western governments to tell Soviet President Mikhail Gorbachev to end the intervention by Soviet troops in Lithuania. In a telephone interview from Vilnius with a French television network, Landsbergis asked: "Why don't Western governments get on the hot line to Gorbachev?"

In a telephone conversation initiated by Gorbachev to discuss the Gulf crisis, US President George Bush said the use of force in Lithuania was counterproductive. The European Community issued a statement saying its member-states were deeply concerned about the situation in the Baltic. It urged the Soviet authorities to refrain from any act of intimidation. NATO called on all concerned to exercise the utmost restraint (*Reuters, AP, AFP*, January 11).

On January 12, the commander of the Vilnius military garrison, Major General Vladimir Uskhopchik, told a news conference that the armed forces had been operating in accordance with directives from Gorbachev (*Reuters, AFP, Radio Vilnius*, January 12).

In the early morning of January 13, fourteen people were killed and more than 150 injured when Soviet troops backed by armored vehicles stormed the radio and television center in Vilnius (*Reuters, AP, AFP*, RFE Lithuanian service, January 13).

On January 12, a meeting of the USSR Federation Council had decided to send a delegation to Lithuania to investigate the Soviet military crackdown. The delegation was led by the chairmen of the Supreme Soviets of Armenia and Belorussia, Levon Ter-Petrossyan and Nikolai Dementei. The delegation held talks with all sides involved in the crisis on January 13 (*TASS, Reuters*, January 12 and 13)

The leaders of Lithuania, Latvia, Estonia, and the RSFSR jointly condemned the military action, while US President Bush said it could harm improved relations between Washington and Moscow. There were also demonstrations in Eastern Europe and the USSR to protest against the Soviet military action. Latvia's parliament met in emergency session to discuss the crisis (RFE/RL correspondent's report, January 13).

On January 14, Gorbachev defended the crackdown in Lithuania but said he had learned about it only after it had happened. He called it "a defensive action" that had been ordered by the local military commander. USSR Defense Minister Dmitrii Yazov said the "Lithuanian National Salvation Committee" had requested help. He said, however, that he did not know who was on the committee. A spokesman for the committee, Juozas

Jermalavicius, told AP that Lithuania was in a state of civil war. He called for the imposition of presidential rule. USSR Minister of Internal Affairs Boriss Pugo told the Supreme Soviet that "no one from the center gave an order" to use force. MVD troops took part in the attack (Western agencies, January 14).

Chairman of the RSFSR Supreme Soviet Boris El'tsin said the army crackdown in Lithuania was only the first step in "a powerful offensive" against democracy in the country. He said the leadership of the RSFSR was on its guard against any similar attempts to undermine its sovereignty and would consider creating a separate Russian army to defend it. El'tsin made the comment in Tallinn, where he had traveled to sign a joint declaration with the leaders of the Baltic republics condemning the attack in Vilnius. He also urged soldiers from the RSFSR who were in the Baltic republics not to use arms against civilians. Officers of the Tallinn garrison called El'tsin's remarks provocative. El'tsin's comments drew fire from Gorbachev, who, in a speech to the USSR Supreme Soviet on January 15, called the idea of creating a Russian army "a gross violation of the USSR Constitution" and "a deliberate act of provocation" (*Reuters, TASS, DPA,* January 15 and 16).

Sharpening its reaction to the Lithuanian events, the United States said it might cancel the US-Soviet summit scheduled to take place in February. White House spokesman Marlin Fitzwater said the United States would also reconsider its agricultural credits and medical and technical aid to the Soviet Union. On January 15, the White House said it held the Soviet government responsible for the crackdown in Vilnius. The sixteen NATO countries said continued use of force in the Baltic would have negative consequences for Europe as a whole and for NATO members' relations with the Soviet Union. German Foreign Minister Hans-Dietrich Genscher said the West should not change its basic policy towards the Soviet Union because of events in the Baltic. The European Community decided to freeze 560 million dollars' worth of technical assistance to the Soviet Union scheduled for 1992 (RFE/RL correspondent's report, January 16)

On January 15, many organs of the Soviet central media continued to blame proindependence Lithuanians for the violence on January 13. *Krasnaya zvezda* said snipers had fired on Soviet troops from nearby buildings, killing an officer and prompting the Soviet attack. Lithuanian officials denied these claims. TASS spoke of Communists' being threatened all over Lithuania.

In Moscow, Soviet Foreign Ministry spokesman Vitalii Churkin said the Soviet leadership was committed to a political solution to the crisis in Lithuania. Churkin told a Moscow news briefing that Gorbachev was actively involved in the effort (*AFP, TASS*, January 15).

Condemnation of the Soviet army action was reported from several other Soviet republics. The Moldavian Supreme Soviet approved a resolution unanimously condemning "the anticonstitutional actions of the Soviet leadership" in Lithuania and saying those actions had led to "the murder of innocent people." In Tbilisi, Chairman of the Georgian Supreme Soviet Zviad Gamsakhurdia told a government-sponsored rally that what had happened in Vilnius could well happen in Georgia, too. He expressed the Georgian government's solidarity with Lithuania (RL Georgian service, RFE/RL Research Institute, January 15).

On January 16, hundreds of thousands of Lithuanians walked in a solemn procession through Vilnius to bury nine of the fourteen people killed on January 13 (RFE Lithuanian service, *Reuters*, January 16). A day of mourning was also declared in Leningrad.

The CPSU Politburo, headed by Gorbachev, issued a statement expressing regret about the deaths and offering condolences to the victims' families. But it also said Lithuania's leaders were trying to avoid responsibility for the events that had led to the use of Soviet troops against civilians in Vilnius ("Vremya," *Central Television*, January 16). The same day, the USSR Supreme Soviet decided to send the head of the parliamentary Commission on Nationalities, Georgii Tarazevich, to Lithuania. His brief was to try to help the Lithuanian government bring the situation in the republic back to normal (*Reuters, TASS*, January 16).

The US Senate called on President Bush to halt moves towards economic cooperation with the Soviet Union until Moscow ended its crackdown against the Baltic republics (RFE/RL correspondent's report, January 16).

On January 17, Radio Riga said a Soviet television program aired on January 16 about the Soviet troop assault in Vilnius was "totally staged terrorist propaganda." The program—which was shown twice—was hosted by Aleksandr Nevzorov, the presenter of the popular Leningrad television program "600 Seconds." The program praised the Soviet army troops for having "saved Lithuania" from the threat of ethnic pogroms. The documentary claimed that those who had died in Vilnius were the victims of heart attacks and road accidents. The Lithuanian government said claims by the Soviet media that soldiers had fired on Vilnius crowds in self-defense were "exceptionally barefaced and shameless lies" (*Radio Kaunas*, January 17).

The same day, Tarazevich said he believed the Soviet leadership had taken "an incorrect approach" over the past year in dealing with Lithuania. Tarazevich spoke in an address to the Lithuanian parliament after talks with Landsbergis that the latter described as constructive (*AP, Reuters, DPA, AFP,* January 17).

In Vienna, the Soviet Union blocked an attempt to call a special meeting of the thirty-four-nation Conference on Security and Cooperation in Europe to deal with recent Soviet actions in the Baltic. AP said all delegations except the Soviet one supported the proposal, which was initiated by Austria, Sweden, and Switzerland. The Soviet side was said to have argued that such a meeting would constitute interference in internal Soviet affairs.

EC foreign ministers meeting in Paris said they would freeze aid to the USSR if Moscow continued repressing the Baltic republics.

On the night of January 29, some thirty to forty truckloads of Soviet soldiers left Vilnius; they were followed the next day by two convoys of Soviet troops, AP reported.

Rabochaya tribuna and *Sovetskaya Rossiya* quoted USSR Internal Affairs Minister Pugo as saying that all extra army paratrooper units and two-thirds of the MVD forces had been withdrawn from the Baltic republics. Presidential spokesman Vitalii Ignatenko confirmed the withdrawal, AP reported.

Landsbergis, however, cautioned that it was too early to say whether a withdrawal was under way, noting that Soviet troops still occupied most of the public buildings they had seized earlier in the month (*AP,* January 31).

Supreme Soviet Approves 1991 Budget

The USSR Supreme Soviet approved a 250-billion-ruble federal budget for 1991 that increased defense spending by slightly less than the government had requested. The budget foresaw a deficit of 26.7 billion rubles. TASS said revenues were expected to be raised from taxes on the income of state enterprises, from foreign operations, and from the newly established 5-percent tax on the sale of goods and services. Defense spending totaled 96.5 billion rubles—2 billion less than the government wanted but a huge increase over the 71 billion allocated for 1990. The KGB's budget amounted to 4.9 billion rubles, about half of which was destined for the KGB Border Troops. The USSR government's foreign aid package of 400 million rubles was to be spread among about thirty countries, with Afghanistan and Cuba receiving the largest share.

The USSR in January, 1991

Regional Newspaper Editor Murdered

A newspaper editor in the RSFSR city of Kaluga was shot dead in what TASS described as a politically motivated murder. TASS said that Ivan Fomin, editor of the regional newspaper *Znamya*, had been killed in his office and that a photographer, Gennadii Golovkov, had also been seriously injured. It reported that a suspect had been arrested who said the attack was politically motivated. In a statement, the RSFSR Press Ministry condemned the shooting as well as recent USSR government actions targeting the press. It said such developments were "a tragic result of a policy of kindling hatred, searching for an internal enemy, and shifting onto the press the blame for all problems."

Interfax Shut Down by Gosteleradio

The USSR State Committee for Television and Radio Broadcasting (Gosteleradio) shut down the independent Soviet news agency Interfax and seized its property and equipment. In a communiqué issued before its transmission lines were cut, Interfax said the shutdown was part of a new Kremlin policy of "liquidating" independent media. Interfax said it was a legally registered organization and would defend its rights in court (*AP, AFP, Reuters*, January 11).

On January 12, Interfax was reported to be back in operation after the intercession of RSFSR Supreme Soviet Chairman Boris El'tsin. Mikhail Komissar, the agency's director, said El'tsin had helped to find Interfax new accommodations after Gosteleradio evicted it from the CPSU Central Committee building (*AFP, ADN, Reuters*, January 12).

Poland Renews Call for Withdrawal of Soviet Troops by 1992

Poland renewed its call for the withdrawal of all Soviet troops from the country by the end of 1991. Polish Foreign Ministry spokesman Wladyslaw Klaczynski said Poland wanted the withdrawal to begin before further trainloads of Soviet troops leaving Germany crossed Polish territory. He said the Soviet pullout from Germany and Poland should be simultaneous and be coordinated by a Polish-Soviet agreement (*PAP*, in English, January 11).

In Prague, a Soviet parliamentary delegation failed to reach agreement with Czech officials on a settlement for the value of assets being left behind by withdrawing Soviet troops. A CTK report said the USSR was asking for about 4,000–5,000 million crowns for the housing, infrastructure, and other assets left behind. But Czechoslovakia's chief negotiator, Major General Rudolf Duchacek, said his country estimated the value of Soviet property left behind at about 1,500 million crowns.

The USSR in January, 1991

Ten Deaths Reported in Nagorno-Karabakh

TASS said ten people including three servicemen had been killed in recent clashes in the Nagorno-Karabakh Autonomous Oblast. It said that the deaths had occurred over the last ten days in more than twenty instances of "extremists'" firing on officials and civilians. The agency said that a curfew would be in force from 6:00 P.M. and that additional highway checkpoints had been introduced.

Two Chernobyl' Reactors Shut Down; Workers Blamed

TASS said two of the three reactors at the Chernobyl' nuclear power station had been shut down owing to a mistake made by workers who were changing the water used to cool electricity generators in the two units. TASS quoted a Chernobyl' shift chief as saying the shutdown was "purely technical" and posed no threat to people or to the environment

Military-Political Organs Re-Created

Gorbachev issued a decree on the creation of "military political organs" within the armed forces, the KGB, and MVD troops. In practical terms this meant that political organs formerly controlled by the CPSU Central Committee would fall under the jurisdiction of the USSR Council of Ministers (for the text of the decree, see *Pravda*, January 12).

Saturday, January 12

USSR to Suspend Nuclear Testing

The USSR said it would suspend all underground nuclear tests for the first four months of 1991 in response to domestic protests. There had been protests against nuclear tests at the USSR's main nuclear testing site at Semipalatinsk in Kazakhstan by local residents; when the USSR proposed to shift its testing program to Novaya Zemlya, it provoked an outcry among residents of the Soviet north. The decision followed the rejection by the United States of a proposed amendment that would have extended a 1963 atmospheric testing ban to underground testing (*TASS*, in English, *Reuters*, January 12).

Sunday, January 13

Primakov on Saddam Hussein

Soviet Middle East expert Evgenii Primakov said in an interview with CNN that Saddam Hussein was convinced there was a conspiracy to surround Iraq as a result of what Saddam described as his defeat of Iran. Primakov said he

THE USSR IN JANUARY, 1991

had known Saddam for twenty-one years and believed that "if Saddam is sure that the only choice is either to die or to stand on his knees only to die afterwards, he would prefer war, where everybody loses" (*Reuters*, January 13). Primakov had repeatedly called on the West to offer Saddam a way of saving face and to provide guarantees that Iraq would not be attacked if it withdrew from Kuwait.

The Estonian Supreme Council ratified a mutual-support treaty with Latvia, Lithuania, and the RSFSR. The treaty was signed by the presidents of the Baltic Supreme Councils and RSFSR Supreme Soviet Chairman Boris El'tsin. It pledged the signatories to recognize each other's inalienable right to independent statehood (RL Estonian service, January 15).

Estonia Ratifies Treaty with Balts and RSFSR

Radio Moscow said the Soviet Union and Albania had signed a trade, economic, and technological cooperation agreement—the first such agreement between the two countries in thirty years. A bilateral trade-economic protocol for 1991 was also signed.

USSR Signs Trade Accord with Albania

Monday, January 14

The USSR Supreme Soviet elected Valentin Pavlov as the new Soviet prime minister by a vote of 279 in favor, 75 against, and 66 abstentions. Pavlov was nominated by Gorbachev, who said he was gifted with profound knowledge of economics and finance. Pavlov had previously been USSR finance minister. He succeeded Nikolai Ryzhkov, who had suffered a heart attack in December, 1990 (*TASS, Reuters, AFP,* January 14). The USSR Supreme Soviet also approved Gorbachev's nominations for four deputies to serve under Pavlov. These included Vitalii Doguzhiev and Vladimir Velichko as first deputy prime ministers and Yurii Maslyukov and Nikolai Laverov as deputy prime ministers.

New USSR Prime Minister Elected

A protest in Red Square by the Radical Party, comparing events in Lithuania over the weekend with the Soviet intervention in Czechoslovakia in 1968, was broken up within three minutes by Moscow police. A spokesman for the party said police had moved in after seven of the party's supporters unfurled banners condemning the

Moscow Police Quickly Break Up Protest over Vilnius Deaths

killing of fourteen people by Soviet troops in Vilnius on January 13 (*Reuters*, January 14).

Bonner Protests to Nobel Committee

Elena Bonner, widow of the Nobel Peace Prize winner Andrei Sakharov, said she wanted the Nobel Prize Committee to delete Sakharov's name from the list of winners. In a letter to the committee, Bonner said she did not want Sakharov's name to appear on the records near that of Soviet President Mikhail Gorbachev. Sakharov, a human-rights activist and dissident, won the prize in 1975. Gorbachev won it in 1990. Bonner said she was acting in protest against the Soviet military action in Vilnius. She said Gorbachev was responsible for the action (*Reuters*, January 14). On January 15, the Nobel Institute said it was impossible to comply with Bonner's demand (*Reuters*, January 15).

Tuesday, January 15

Bessmertnykh Elected Foreign Minister

The USSR Supreme Soviet elected the Soviet ambassador to the United States, Aleksandr Bessmertnykh, as the Soviet Union's new foreign minister by an overwhelming majority (421 in favor, 3 against, and 10 abstentions). Nominated by Soviet President Mikhail Gorbachev, Bessmertnykh replaced Eduard Shevardnadze, who had resigned in December, 1990, warning of moves towards dictatorship in the USSR. Bessmertnykh praised Shevardnadze's foreign policy and said it would be "confirmed and developed." He also said he was opposed to Western efforts to make aid to the USSR conditional on "internal processes." He said Moscow should be able to avoid accepting such conditions, adding that the USSR "will never trade its dignity." He acknowledged, however, that what happened in Lithuania would have an impact on Soviet foreign policy and said the government should work to avert events of this kind (*TASS, AFP*, January 15).

On January 16, Shevardnadze commented on Bessmertnykh's appointment. He said his successor was independent in his thinking, a good colleague, and an excellent diplomat. Shevardnadze said the choice of Bessmertnykh as the Soviet Union's new foreign minister showed continuity in Soviet foreign policy (*Izvestia*, January 16).

US Introduces Legislation to Aid Republics Directly

Legislation was introduced in the US Congress allowing the United States to aid individual Soviet republics,

The USSR in January, 1991

bypassing the central government in Moscow. The proposal was made by Senate minority leader Robert Dole (R-Kansas). Dole said such a move would help the Baltic people, who, he added, faced not only political and military oppression but also economic crises (RFE/RL correspondent's report, January 16).

Coal miners' committees in the Kuzbass region of Western Siberia voted to call a political strike on January 18 to press for the resignation of the Soviet president. Radio Moscow said the miners were angry about the government's failure to honor pledges made to end the nationwide miners' strike in 1989. The miners also called for the nationalization of Communist Party assets and the depoliticization of legal organs (*Radio Moscow*, January 15). A report by the Soviet news agency Postfactum said workers' committees were also demanding an investigation into "the tragic events in Lithuania" and calling for the withdrawal of Soviet troops from that republic. On January 18, however, the Soviet media said the strike call had been ignored by most coal miners and by Kuzbass metal, chemical, and transport workers (*TASS*, "Vremya," *Central Television*, January 18).

Kuzbass Miners Threaten to Stage Political Strike

The commander of the Odessa Military District said he had enough troops and would do everything he could to prevent Moldavia from seceding from the Soviet Union. Colonel General Ivan Morozov made the statement in a radio address. He was speaking in Tiraspol, the capital of the self-proclaimed "Dniester Republic" in Moldavia. He said his troops would not permit Moldavian independence, because too much blood had been shed to obtain the territory in 1940. Most of present-day Moldavia was annexed from Romania as a result of the 1939 Molotov-Ribbentrop Pact.

General Says He Will Keep Moldavia from Seceding

The Soviet Union and Honduras announced at the United Nations that they had established diplomatic relations (Western agencies, January 15).

USSR and Honduras Establish Diplomatic Relations

Wednesday, January 16

The USSR Supreme Soviet rejected a suggestion by President Mikhail Gorbachev that the USSR's law on freedom of the press be suspended. Instead, it approved

Supreme Soviet Rejects Attempt by Gorbachev to Curb Press Freedom

a less drastic proposal by its chairman, Anatolii Luk'yanov, to direct the parliament's Committee on *Glasnost'* to draft a law that would ensure "the objectivity of information [in reporting] on events in the country." The vote on that measure was 275 to 32 with 30 abstentions. Gorbachev's suggestion caused a wave of protest among deputies, but the president backed down by saying that he was "not insisting" on the suspension of the law that ended censorship in the Soviet Union. Gorbachev said he favored allowing all points of view in the media but added that television and newspaper coverage of the Soviet troop actions in Lithuania had not been objective. He singled out for criticism *Moscow News* and *Pravda* (*AFP, Reuters, DPA,* January 16).

The same day, the USSR Ministry of Defense accused three Soviet newspapers of publishing what it called slanderous reports. The ministry released a statement read on Soviet television that rejected reports printed by *Nezavisimaya gazeta, Moskovsky komsomolets,* and *Komsomol'skaya pravda.* One of the reports claimed there had been a mutiny in a Soviet troop unit, another said a Soviet paratrooper had been shot dead by his comrades, and a third said tanks had crushed people ("Vremya," *Central Television,* January 16).

Moscow Keeping Lines of Communication Open with Iraq

The Soviet Union said it was keeping open channels of communication with its former ally Iraq in a bid to avert war, despite the passing of the UN deadline for Iraq to withdraw from Kuwait. Foreign Ministry spokesman Vitalii Churkin told reporters it was now up to Iraqi leader Saddam Hussein to defuse the crisis. Earlier, Deputy Foreign Minister Aleksandr Belonogov said in a report to the Supreme Soviet that Moscow had sought to convince the Iraqi leader that the international alliance against him was serious in its threat to use force. He said the USSR had given Iraq an assurance that its security would be guaranteed if it pulled out of Kuwait and that the way would then be open for launching the mechanism for a Middle East settlement (*Reuters, AP, TASS,* in English, January 16).

Soviet Intellectuals Condemn Crackdown in Lithuania

In a statement published in *Moscow News* (No. 3, 1991), thirty Soviet intellectuals said the violent crackdown in Lithuania had drastically undermined the reforms of President Mikhail Gorbachev. The signatories said the violence in Vilnius amounted to an attack on democracy and could be seen only as a crime. They said there was "almost nothing left" of Gorbachev's previous commit-

The USSR in January, 1991

ments to seek "humane socialism" and "a common European home." The signatories included the reformist economists Stanislav Shatalin and Nikolai Petrakov, sociologist Tat'yana Zaslavskaya, commentator Aleksandr Bovin, and film director Tengiz Abuladze (*Reuters, AP*, January 16).

Interregional Group Calls on Citizens to Fight Dictatorship

A statement addressed by the Interregional Group of Deputies to the USSR Supreme Soviet condemned the use of force in Lithuania and called on citizens of the USSR to unite in their efforts "to fight the approaching dictatorship." The conservative "Soyuz" group of deputies blamed the violence on "political adventurers." It said presidential rule should be imposed in republics not enforcing the USSR Constitution (*Reuters, AP*, January 16).

Another Television Program Banned

The late-night newscast, "TSN," whose coverage of the Baltic events had been more objective than that of "Vremya," was canceled. On January 15, the program had shown tanks on the streets of Vilnius and the corpses of people shot during the violence in Lithuania.

Georgian Foreign Minister Blames Gorbachev for Crackdown

Speaking in Vienna, Georgian Foreign Minister Giorgi Khoshtaria argued that it was impossible for Gorbachev not to have known in advance about the Soviet military action in Vilnius. Khoshtaria further stated that Georgia would resist efforts by the Soviet Armed Forces to round up draft evaders, would establish its own republican military force, and would not comply with Gorbachev's demand to withdraw its forces from South Ossetia (*AP*, January 16).

Czechoslovakia Urges Swift Abolition of Warsaw Pact

The Czechoslovak Federal Assembly condemned the Soviet military crackdown in Lithuania and asked the Czechoslovak government to speed up negotiations on abolishing the Warsaw Pact. The resolutions came at a special session called to discuss the Lithuanian crisis and demands that Prague leave the pact because of the action by Soviet troops in Vilnius. Czechoslovak Foreign Minister Jiri Dienstbier said attempts to dismantle the pact had been delayed since November by the USSR. He said that Moscow had, "for internal political reasons," kept postponing a planned pact summit on the alliance's future (Western agencies, *CTK*, January 16).

Hungarian Defense Minister Lajos Fur said the same day that Hungary wanted to sign a new military agreement with the Soviet Union before the Warsaw Pact was dissolved. He said that, without an agreement, the Hungarian army could drift into a serious crisis, because most of its weapons were imported from the Soviet Union (*Reuters*, January 16).

KGB Says Foreign-Aid Shipments Being Mishandled, Stolen

TASS quoted the KGB as saying tons of foreign-aid shipments had failed to reach the people they were intended for, because of poor organization and theft in Moscow and other cities. The KGB press center said more than seven tons of food aid destined for the Soviet Children's Fund in Minsk had been sitting at Sheremetevo airport for three weeks. The statement also said aid had been stolen and diverted to the black market in Leningrad, Pskov, Zhitomir, Vladimir, and Erevan. It said criminal proceedings had begun in a number of cases.

Controversy over Withdrawal of Soviet Troops from Poland and Germany

Polish officials criticized remarks attributed to the Soviet military commander in Poland about Soviet troop withdrawals. Lieutenant General Vyacheslav Dubinin was quoted by a Soviet army newspaper, *Znamya pobedy*, as saying Poland was trying to portray Soviet soldiers as "occupiers and international criminals" and to send them home in shame. The general was quoted as saying that, if Poland rejected a Soviet proposal on details of the withdrawal, the army would "conduct the withdrawal on its own terms." In that case, he said, "we will answer only for the life and health of Soviet citizens," not for Poles. Dubinin said the army would leave Poland, but not before all Soviet troops were out of the eastern part of Germany. A Polish official called Dubinin's remarks improper (*Reuters, AP*, January 16).

On January 14, German Chancellor Helmut Kohl said he wanted Moscow to withdraw its troops from Germany faster than planned because of the unrest in the Soviet Union. Kohl told Christian Democratic Union parliamentarians that the Soviet army's crackdown in Lithuania had prompted him to support a withdrawal before the agreed pullout deadline of 1994 (*Reuters*, January 15).

Supreme Soviet Decides on March 17 for Referendum

The USSR Supreme Soviet chose March 17 as the date to hold a referendum on whether the Soviet Union should be preserved as an integral state (*TASS*, January 16). The question to be put to voters was: "Do you think it is necessary to preserve the USSR as a renewed federation of sovereign states with equal rights in which the rights

The USSR in January, 1991

and freedoms of an individual of any nationality are fully guaranteed?"

On January 26, the Union of Sociologists suggested that the question should be divided into three parts, Radio Moscow reported. Voters would be asked first whether the federal structure of the state should be preserved; second, whether it should be renamed; and third, whether human rights should be given priority over the rights of nations. Some people had objected to the way the question was formulated, saying that it could cause difficulties for voters who might favor the preservation of the Union but not its Socialist nature.

Sobchak Attacks Party Control over Army

Chairman of the Leningrad City Soviet Anatolii Sobchak told Radio Rossii that attacks by the armed forces against civilians could only be prevented if Communist Party control over the army was ended. Arguing that the army should be an institution of the state and not of the Party, he said that the Communist Party should not give orders to anyone.

Buryat Parliament Rejects Center's Nominee

TASS reported that the Buryat Supreme Soviet had refused to endorse Colonel Veniamin Dolin as chairman of the republican KGB. Dolin was named to the post in November, 1990, by the chairman of the USSR KGB.

USSR Late in Paying for Goods Delivered from Germany

German financial experts said the Soviet Union was late in paying about 1 billion deutsche marks owed to German companies for goods they had delivered. As a result Germany's largest financial institution, the Deutsche Bank, decided to treat the Soviet Union as a less-than-good risk for future loans. The bank's chief executive said, "for us the Soviet Union is a problem country" (*The Journal of Commerce*, January 16).

USSR Publishes Statistics on Death Sentences

The USSR Ministry of Justice for the first time reported the number of death sentences passed in the Soviet Union in a given year (*TASS*, January 16; see also *Komsomol'skaya pravda*, February 26). Minister of Justice Sergei Lushchikov told a press conference in Moscow that in 1989, 276 people had been sentenced to death; 23 of whom were subsequently pardoned. He added that there had been a decline in the number of death sentences since 1985, when 770 people had been sentenced to death, of whom 20 were later pardoned. Lushchikov said the majority of sentences had been handed down for premeditated murder under aggravated circumstances and for rape under aggravated circumstances..

Thursday, January 17

Akhromeev Says No Military Coup

In an interview with the US magazine *Newsweek* (No. 3, 1991), Marshal Sergei Akhromeev, Soviet President Mikhail Gorbachev's military adviser, said he was sure there would never be a military coup in the USSR. He said the Soviet Armed Forces would be "loyal to the president while he is in office and not allow anyone to act against him by unlawful methods." He pointed out, however, that it was the duty of both the president and the armed forces to ensure stability. Akhromeev also said that he saw no danger of a civil war in the Soviet Union and that he supported Gorbachev in opposing regional militias.

Mass Termination of TASS Correspondents

Radio Rossii reported that a mass termination of TASS correspondents had begun in the news agency's Leningrad department. The radio said the correspondents had been accused of gross distortion of information. It said some reports indicated that they would be replaced by former workers of the oblast Party committee.

Gorbachev on Outbreak of War in the Gulf

Soviet President Mikhail Gorbachev said he had taken steps to avert war in the Gulf even in the hour immediately before the attack. In a radio and television speech, Gorbachev said that, after he had received notice of plans to attack, he had tried to get the United States to give Iraq one last chance to pull out of Kuwait. Deputy Foreign Minister Aleksandr Belonogov said the effort had failed for lack of time. Gorbachev also instructed the Soviet ambassador in Iraq to deliver a message to Iraqi President Saddam Hussein. That message was handed to Iraqi Foreign Minister Tariq Aziz inside a bunker in Baghdad. Soviet Foreign Ministry spokesman Vitalii Churkin said the message had urged Saddam to announce the immediate withdrawal of his troops from Kuwait. Gorbachev called the war "a tragic turn . . . provoked by the refusal of the Iraqi leadership to meet the demands of the international community and withdraw from Kuwait" (*AP, Reuters, TASS,* in English, January 17).

Meanwhile, the Soviet Union placed its military forces in the southern USSR on a high state of alert. On January 18, news agencies quoted the USSR Ministry of Defense

The USSR in January, 1991

as saying two Soviet warships were leaving the Gulf region.

Germany and USSR Sign Housing Contract for Returning Soldiers

Germany and the Soviet Union signed a contract for the construction of at least 36,000 apartments in the USSR for troops withdrawing from former East Germany. The agreement was signed in Moscow by Bonn's state credit agency and the USSR Ministry of Defense. The housing scheme was part of a bilateral agreement for the withdrawal of all Soviet forces from eastern Germany by the end of 1994 (*AFP*, January 17).

_____ *Friday, January 18*

Petrakov Leaves Post

Gorbachev's economic adviser Nikolai Petrakov was reported to be "no longer in his job" after signing a letter printed in *Moscow News* (No. 3, 1991) accusing Gorbachev of "stooping to crime" in the attack in Vilnius on January 13. Gorbachev's deputy spokesman, Sergei Grigor'ev, who broke the news, would not say whether Petrakov had resigned or been fired. Petrakov had been considered the top remaining reform economist among Gorbachev's advisers. His departure followed that of other reformers, including Eduard Shevardnadze, Vadim Bakatin, Stanislav Shatalin, and Aleksandr Yakovlev (*AP*, January 18).

On January 19, Petrakov told *Komsomol'skaya pravda* he doubted the new Soviet government would establish a market economy in the country. Petrakov told the newspaper that he had resigned because he was under the impression he was no longer influencing Gorbachev on economic matters. He said that, despite his departure, he remained on cordial terms with the Soviet president.

Moldavia Rescinds Law on Soviet Conscription

The Independent reported that the Moldavian Supreme Soviet had revoked a law passed in September, 1990, ruling that Moldavia's youth were not obliged to obey the draft and could not be punished for refusing to perform military service. The parliament set a new deadline of February 1 for the 40 percent of draft-age Moldavians who had yet to report for service. It also required the government to negotiate an agreement with Moscow whereby no Moldavian conscripts would be used in conflicts of "an interethnic or sociopolitical character." Under the agreement, Moldavia asked for 35 percent of its conscripts to be stationed in Moldavia and the rest in southern Ukraine.

THE USSR IN JANUARY, 1991

Moscow Alarmed over Iraqi Attack on Israel

The Soviet Union expressed serious concern over Iraq's missile attack on Israel, with a senior official saying Moscow feared the strike could have "grave consequences." At the same time, TASS cited Soviet officials as renewing a Kremlin call for Iraq to pull its forces out of Kuwait. There were indications in the hard-line Soviet press, notably *Krasnaya zvezda* and *Sovetskaya Rossiya*, of disagreement with the official stand on the fighting, but television news told viewers that the conflict was "a war against a dictator." *Sovetskaya Rossiya* questioned whether Iraq shouldered the entire blame for the war and demanded to know why world and Soviet opinion were not calling for the destruction of the army of "another aggressor, Israel."

Saturday, January 19

Gorbachev Appeals for Restraint in Gulf Crisis

Mikhail Gorbachev contacted leaders around the world and urged them to call for restraint in the Gulf crisis. He also urged the leaders of Israel, Syria, and other (unidentified) Middle Eastern countries to show restraint. Gorbachev's message, as quoted by Deputy Foreign Minister Aleksandr Belonogov, said, "There are attempts to play on the national interests and feelings of the Arabs . . . these attempts are aimed at fanning the conflict." The message also said Iraq's actions, beginning with its invasion of Kuwait, were leading to disaster (*TASS*, January 19 and 20).

No Army for RSFSR?

Ruslan Khasbulatov, first deputy chairman of the RSFSR Supreme Soviet, told Soviet television viewers that there were no concrete plans to create an RSFSR army. Khasbulatov was answering questions concerning an earlier statement by Boris El'tsin that, in view of developments in Lithuania, the RSFSR would consider forming its own army. Khasbulatov said that in fact the idea had only been raised speculatively by the RSFSR leadership and that no concrete steps towards implementing it had been taken. He implied that El'tsin's opponents were deliberately playing up the issue in order to discredit him.

Qadhafi Says USSR Should Regain Global Role

Libyan leader Muammar Qadhafi said in an interview with Soviet journalists that the USSR had lost confidence in itself and must regain its global role. He said he would like to go out onto Red Square and deliver a speech to boost the population's morale. Qadhafi also said the USSR had

THE USSR IN JANUARY, 1991

a military potential tens of times greater than that of the United States. The interview was carried by *Izvestia* on January 19.

Reuters reported that the Soviet Union had reduced the number of its civilian technicians working in Cuba. The Soviet ambassador to Cuba, Yurii Petrov, said about 1,000 Soviet technical specialists had left Cuba in 1990 and that about 2,000 remained. Petrov said on January 18 that this number would be reduced by half. He did not reveal how many military advisers were in Cuba or whether their number would be reduced.

USSR Reduces Number of Civilian Technicians in Cuba

Krasnaya zvezda published a series of letters bitterly attacking recent statements by Boris El'tsin concerning the Soviet crackdown in the Baltic republics. One of the letters was signed by a group of high-ranking military officers, including former Chief of the General Staff of the Soviet Armed Forces Nikolai Ogarkov. It blamed the Lithuanian government and "hostility towards the armed forces" for the previous week's tragic events there. Another letter, signed by sailors serving in the Baltic Fleet, attacked El'tsin and said servicemen supported the policies of Gorbachev.

On January 22, the military newspaper published another letter criticizing El'tsin. Allegedly signed by more than 800 servicemen stationed in the Baltic region, the letter expressed anger over El'tsin's support for proindependence forces there.

On January 19, *Sovetskaya Rossiya* published a separate letter that deemed El'tsin's position vis-à-vis the Baltic republics "an instigation to civil war." In fact, on January 19, El'tsin issued an open letter to the Baltic people asking all sides to back away from confrontation and to respect elected authorities (*AP, Radio Kaunas*, January 19).

On January 22, Colonel Nikolai Petrushenko, a leading member of "Soyuz," a conservative group of deputies, said in *Sovetskaya Rossiya* that El'tsin's appeals to Russian soldiers carried no authority. El'tsin had earlier called on Russian soldiers to refuse to fire on civilians. Petrushenko also charged that El'tsin's intention to create a Russian army would lead to widespread civil war.

Soviet Press Attacks El'tsin over Baltic

Price increases that went into effect in Kazakhstan at the beginning of the year were temporarily reversed (*Izvestia*, January 19). Prices for several types of foodstuffs had

Price Rises in Kazakhstan Repealed

been doubled and the price of fish raised by 500 percent. No compensatory measures were taken to offset the increases, although Kazakh officials had warned that such measures would be necessary if radical economic reform were to succeed. The increases caused a wave of popular protests, and the trade unions of Karaganda threatened to call strikes. The repeal of the rises provided for compensation to producers who had already introduced the new prices.

Police Chief in Nagorno-Karabakh Attacked

TASS reported that the police chief of the Nagorno-Karabakh Autonomous Oblast had narrowly escaped assassination. The agency said Major General Vladimir Kovalev was driving his car when two gunmen in police uniforms opened fire from an overtaking vehicle. TASS said Kovalev had jumped out of his car and "miraculously" was not hurt. Kovalev told TASS he believed the purpose of the assassination attempt was to escalate tensions in the region.

On January 22, there was a rally in Stepanakert, the capital of Nagorno-Karabakh. The Soviet media said the demonstrators demanded the restoration of the regional government and the withdrawal of Azerbaijani security forces.

On January 23, RSFSR deputy Anatolii Mostovoi told Reuters that a unit of USSR Ministry of Internal Affairs troops (OMON) had intercepted a six-person Russian parliamentary delegation at Stepanakert airport on January 22. The delegation, which had intended to investigate ethnic clashes in the oblast, was roughly handled, detained for several hours, and then sent by bus to Baku, whence it returned to Moscow. On January 24, Azerbaijani President Ayaz Mutalibov and Supreme Soviet Chairwoman Elmira Kafarova apologized to the RSFSR Supreme Soviet delegation for the way it had been treated. The information was passed to RL's Russian service by a member of the delegation, RSFSR people's deputy Sergei Kovalev.

Sunday, January 20

Anti-Gorbachev, Pro-Baltic Demonstration in Moscow

Western agencies reported that at least 100,000 people had attended a demonstration in Moscow. Demonstrators cheered deputies who demanded the resignations of President Gorbachev, Defense Minister Dmitrii Yazov, and Minister of Internal Affairs Boriss Pugo. A strongly worded statement from Boris El'tsin criticizing the crackdown in the Baltic republics was read; Yurii Afanas'ev called for "a decisive condemnation of the bloody attack in Vilnius" and "a decisive 'no' to the reactionary course of Gorbachev and his team." The demonstration was organized by Democratic Russia, the Interregional Group of Deputies, the soldiers' organization "Shield," and other liberal parties and movements. The demonstrators were not allowed to march in Red Square and were warned to stay away from CPSU headquarters.

Soviet Officials Comment on Gulf

In a press briefing, USSR Foreign Ministry spokesman Vitalii Churkin said of the installation of US Patriot missiles in Israel that "any country has the right to take measures it deems necessary to secure its own safety." Churkin also noted that the Soviet embassy in Baghdad had cut its staff to forty-three and that the remaining Soviet technicians working in Iraq would soon return to the USSR (*TASS*, January 20).

Churkin disclosed that Soviet citizens had been advised to avoid for the time being private visits to the Gulf region and to adjacent countries, including Israel. He stressed, however, that the recommendation did not mean the government would stop issuing exit visas to Soviet Jews wishing to resettle in Israel (*TASS*, January 20).

On January 21, Iraqi President Saddam Hussein issued a reply to Gorbachev's message to him of January 17. Saddam rejected Gorbachev's peace plan whereby the Soviet leader offered to intercede with US President George Bush to ensure a suspension of hostilities if Iraq agreed to announce plans to withdraw from Kuwait (*AP*, January 21).

On January 21, former Chief of the General Staff of the Soviet Armed Forces Marshal Sergei Akhromeev said in *Pravda* that the United States had acted prematurely in attacking Iraq. Akhromeev described it as "deeply regrettable that all possibilities for a peaceful solution of the conflict had not been exhausted."

On January 22, Gorbachev said at a Moscow news conference that "events in the Gulf are clearly tending to escalate . . . that is very dangerous. We must do all we can to stop the conflict" (*TASS*, January 22).

TASS said the same day that the USSR Supreme Soviet Presidium had adopted a resolution pledging to pursue a policy "aimed at the quickest possible end to military action and the restoration of peace" in the Gulf.

On January 22, Interfax quoted an unidentified general from the Soviet General Staff as saying that 90 percent of all allied air strikes against Iraq had missed their targets, Reuters and AFP reported. He said most air bases and aircraft had not been hit and that only eleven out of forty-one antiaircraft systems had been knocked out. "Iraqi air bases are very well camouflaged and extremely hard to locate," said the general. He also alleged that the allied leadership was using bad weather as an excuse to ground planes and review its strategy.

On January 23, however, one of the almost 100 Soviet specialists who had fled to Iran on January 22 said that allied bombing attacks had been very accurate, Reuters reported.

On January 23, Colonel General Sergei Petrov, chief of Chemical Troops, was quoted in *Rabochaya tribuna* as saying "in launching strikes against [biological weapons] installations, the anti-Iraqi side would essentially be embarking . . . indirectly on the use of weapons banned under the 1920 Geneva Protocol and the treaty of 1972." While averring that strikes against chemical weapons facilities would not put the Soviet population at risk, he did note that the unleashing of biological weapons could cause epidemics that knew no borders.

On January 24, RSFSR Foreign Minister Andrei Kozyrev said if reactionary forces came to power in the USSR Moscow's policy towards Iraq could change. In an interview in *Komsomol'skaya pravda*, Kozyrev said that a switch to a hard-line policy in Moscow could strengthen totalitarian leaders like Saddam.

On January 24, the USSR denied a BBC report that some Soviet military advisers were still in Iraq helping to maintain sophisticated equipment for the Iraqis. Soviet Defense Ministry spokesman Valerii Myasnikov said, "This report is not true. The last Soviet military adviser left Iraq on January 9." Soviet Foreign Ministry spokesman Vitalii Churkin also rejected the report (*Reuters*, January 24).

On January 27, Aleksandr Dzasokhov, CPSU Secretary for Ideology and a member of the Politburo, said in an interview with the *Los Angeles Times* that the Soviet Union favored a multinational initiative to resolve the Gulf war and saw promise in the idea of "a withdrawal [of Iraqi troops from Kuwait] and a cease-fire that would be tied to a new round of discussions." Dzasokhov emphasized the role of the Arab states and the UN Security Council in the discussions. Dzasokhov was ambassador to Syria from 1986 to 1989.

Soviet Media on Gulf War

TASS reported that six Soviet journalists who were in Baghdad to cover the Gulf war were planning to stay, despite efforts by the USSR to evacuate its remaining citizens from Iraq. Foreign Ministry spokesman Vitalii Churkin said the journalists had originally gone to Baghdad without informing the Soviet embassy there. The spokes-

THE USSR IN JANUARY, 1991

man said two of the journalists were from Lithuania and worked for a press outlet of "Sajudis." He said two others worked for Ukraine's independent television service. The remaining two were a photographer from the Novosti press agency and a journalist from the Russian city of Vologda.

While the main Soviet media organs expressed support for the mission of the anti-Iraqi coalition, some conservative newspapers attacked the United States over the war in the Gulf. On January 11, for instance, conservative Russian nationalists Igor' Shafarevich, Vadim Kozhinov, and Viktor Doroshenko published articles in *Literaturnaya Rossiya* accusing the United States of waging an immoral war for oil and of seeking to extend its military hegemony into the Middle East. They criticized the Kremlin leadership for betraying future Russian interests in the Third World and stressed that the Soviet Union should not participate in an alliance with the West but preserve its strategy as a balancing force between industrialized and developing countries.

On January 22, in its review of the Soviet press, TASS noted that several commentaries appearing that day were critical of the US effort in the Gulf. The *Pravda* correspondent in New York said economic interests were behind the US action, and *Trud* said the war, whose goal "is allegedly limited to the liberation of Kuwait," might turn into a large-scale regional military conflict with unpredictable consequences for the whole world (see also *Pravda*, January 24).

Mass Rally in Baku to Mark First Anniversary of Killings

TASS reported that hundreds of thousands of people had marched through Baku on the first anniversary of the Soviet military action there in which some 150 Azerbaijanis were killed. A message of condolence from Mikhail Gorbachev to the families of those who died was published in the Azerbaijani press. The New York–based Helsinki Watch called for the lifting of the state of emergency declared in Baku after the killings, Western agencies reported.

Unity Day Marked in Ukraine

Ukrainians throughout the republic celebrated unity day, Radio Kiev and Ukrinform-TASS reported. The celebrations were organized by "Rukh" and other anti-Communist groups to mark the unification of the Ukrainian People's Republic and the West Ukrainian People's Republic on January 22, 1919. In Kiev, thousands of people were reported to have gathered in front of St. Sofia's Cathedral, where church services were conducted by the Ukrainian Autocephalous Orthodox Church and the Ukrainian Catholic Church. Unity day was marked for the first time in Ukraine in January, 1990, by a massive human chain stretching through the entire republic.

Monday, January 21

RSFSR Supreme Soviet Discusses Baltic

Addressing the RSFSR Supreme Soviet, its chairman Boris El'tsin accused Soviet President Mikhail Gorbachev of abandoning democracy in favor of "violence and pressure." He said the Kremlin was violating the USSR Constitution by supporting anti-independence "national salvation committees" in an attempt to overthrow legitimate, democratically elected governments in the Baltic republics. Gorbachev's ultimate aim, El'tsin warned, was the establishment of presidential rule throughout the USSR. He said the "national salvation committees" were clearly intended to serve as Gorbachev's agents in this enterprise. Once again, El'tsin said, the Soviet state was placing itself above society.

El'tsin also told the RSFSR Supreme Soviet that it was up to the government of the RSFSR to resist Gorbachev's turn to the right. He said this could best be achieved by speeding up the conclusion of a treaty between the "Big Four" republics (the RSFSR, Kazakhstan, Ukraine, and Belorussia). He told the RSFSR parliament that Prime Minister Ivan Silaev would submit proposals to strengthen the RSFSR's control over enterprises on its territory, including those formally under all-Union subordination (*Radio Moscow*, January 21).

Other speakers at the session called for Gorbachev's resignation. Speaker after speaker attacked Gorbachev, noting that a local military commander could not open fire without orders from the USSR president. No deputy defended the idea of setting up "national salvation committees" to overthrow elected bodies. Despite overwhelming opposition to Moscow's actions in the Baltic, in reporting on the session, TASS highlighted the very few speeches that attempted to justify the use of force there.

On January 24, for lack of a quorum, the RSFSR Supreme Soviet rejected a resolution criticizing Mikhail Gorbachev over events in the Baltic. Deputies supported the draft resolution by a vote of 117 to 51, but it failed to pass, because 117 votes in favor did not constitute a majority of the 250-member parliament (*TASS*, Janu-

The USSR in January, 1991

ary 24). Meanwhile, conservative deputies in the parliament proposed their own resolution criticizing El'tsin for his support of the leaderships of the Baltic republics.

Crimea Votes for Autonomy

Radio Moscow reported that 81 percent of eligible voters in the Crimea had taken part in a referendum on January 20 to decide whether the peninsula should regain its pre-1945 status as an autonomous republic. The proposal was approved by an overwhelming 93.3 percent. In Ukraine, to which the Crimea was transferred under Nikita Khrushchev, the referendum had been criticized as an encroachment on Ukraine's territorial integrity.

On January 28, however, Chairman of the Ukrainian Supreme Soviet Leonid Kravchuk described the results of the referendum in the Crimea as "just" and complimented the residents of the peninsula on their respect for the law in conducting the referendum, Ukrinform-TASS reported.

EC Suspends Economic Aid to USSR

Vice President of the European Community Frans Andriessen announced that, in protest against recent events in the Baltic republics, the EC had decided to "put off until later" a meeting of the EC-Soviet Commission (*Reuters, AP*, January 21).

On January 22, the European Parliament voted to suspend 1.5 billion dollars in food and technical aid to the USSR in response to the crackdown in the Baltic republics (*Reuters*, January 22).

Meanwhile, the US government was considering canceling economic aid to the USSR in view of developments in the Baltic republics, according to government officials and private analysts interviewed by Reuters. Reuters quoted Julius Katz, deputy US trade representative, as saying that developments in the Baltic "are disturbing, and we will watch them carefully."

On January 23, *The Chicago Tribune* said that the USSR had rushed to purchase US grain in an apparent attempt to use up recent credits quickly in case further credits were cut off. Moscow was reported to have bought about 500,000 tons of US wheat on January 22. Of the 900 million dollars in credits approved by President Bush on January 8, only 127 million remained to be spent.

Japanese Foreign Minister Visits Moscow

Japanese Foreign Minister Taro Nakayama arrived in Moscow for talks with the Soviet leadership in preparation for the Soviet-Japanese summit planned for April, TASS reported.

The Soviet crackdown in the Baltic republics cast a shadow over Nakayama's visit. In seeing off Nakayama at Tokyo's Narita airport, Yurii Kuznetsov, chargé d'affaires at the Soviet embassy in Japan, said, "the Soviet government rejects all protests and allegations against Soviet foreign and internal policies that may worsen the situation." Japanese officials expressed deep regret over the USSR's military action in Latvia, AFP reported on January 21.

On January 22, Soviet Foreign Minister Aleksandr Bessmertnykh held talks with Nakayama. Bessmertnykh said after the talks that relations between the USSR and Japan had suffered "a certain lag" and that "this lag cannot be considered normal," Reuters reported. Bessmertnykh said Moscow aimed to normalize fully relations with Japan and pledged that Soviet foreign policy would remain unchanged.

On January 23, the Japanese foreign minister met with Mikhail Gorbachev and USSR Vice President Gennadii Yanaev. The Japanese side said of the talks "there has been nothing, no indication, no hint . . . nothing has emerged from the Gorbachev leadership" on the settlement of the Kurile Islands territorial dispute (Western agencies, January 24).

On January 23, Nakayama met with former Soviet Foreign Minister Eduard Shevardnadze. A television report on the meeting gave no details but said the fact that it had taken place confirmed the high standing that Shevardnadze retained in international politics.

Gorbachev's Position Stable for Now, Aide Says

In an interview published in *Der Spiegel* (No. 4, 1991), presidential aide Georgii Shakhnazarov said Gorbachev's position was stable for the time being. Shakhnazarov warned, however, that, if Gorbachev were to give in to pressure from separatists and democrats to allow the disintegration of the USSR, he could be overthrown and replaced by a military dictatorship. This, he said, would mean the end of *perestroika* and détente, as well as of the Supreme Soviet, democratic guarantees, and the right to criticize the president.

USSR Prosecutor's Office Appeals to Republics over Laws

The USSR Prosecutor's Office appealed to all republican-level authorities to suspend legislation that contradicted the USSR Constitution or violated human rights. The statement also called for the immediate dissolution of all illegal armed groups. The Prosecutor's Office said the primary causes of recent conflicts and clashes in the USSR included "flagrant" violations of the USSR Constitution and disregard for the law. It said "the most resolute

The USSR in January, 1991

measures" would be taken to stop any person or group calling for the violent overthrow of the state and social system. It said the same measures would be used against anyone inciting ethnic or racial hostility (*TASS*, January 21).

Production, Railways Affected by Power Shortage in Georgia

A severe electricity shortage in Georgia caused many factories and a number of passenger railways to suspend operations. TASS reported that practically all machine-building, light industry, and local enterprises in Georgia had ceased operating and would not resume production before the end of the month. The agency said the reason for this was the introduction of energy-saving measures by the Georgian government. It said the government wanted to conserve power so that there would be enough for essential production and community services. The report also said that, beginning on January 22, sixteen passenger train lines would be suspended. The two main reasons given for the shortage were the shutdown of an Armenian nuclear power plant following public protests and a shortage of water to drive hydroelectric stations.

Ukrainian State Program on Language

The Presidium of the Ukrainian Council of Ministers approved a draft program on the development of the Ukrainian language and other national languages of the Ukrainian SSR, Radio Kiev reported. Commenting on the program, First Deputy Chairman of the Council of Ministers Konstantyn Masyk noted that the law on language passed by the Ukrainian Supreme Soviet at the end of 1989 was "not functioning."

Tuesday, January 22

Gorbachev Decrees Monetary Reform

Mikhail Gorbachev decreed a sweeping monetary reform, including a partial freeze on bank accounts and a currency reform. He decreed that, as of January 23, Soviet citizens would be able to withdraw only 500 rubles a month from their savings accounts. The decree also said that, as of midnight on January 22, current-issue 50- and 100-ruble notes would no longer be legal tender It said the old notes would be exchanged for new 50- and 100-ruble notes and also for lower-denomination notes. A decree by the USSR Cabinet of Ministers, also issued on January 22, said workers would be allowed to exchange a maximum of 1,000 rubles in old 50- and 100-ruble notes and pensioners a maximum of 200 rubles.

TASS said the measures were intended to crack down on speculation, corruption, counterfeiting, and unearned incomes, as well as to "normalize money circulation and the consumer market." Prime Minister Valentin Pavlov told Soviet television that the current 50- and 100-ruble notes were one of the main elements of "the shadow economy" and made up more than one-third of the money in circulation.

On January 23, the Soviet and Western media reported widespread chaos and concern during the first of three days allotted for the exchange of 50- and 100-ruble bank notes. Generally speaking, the smarter operators appeared to have been forewarned of the measure and had already disposed of their large-denomination bills, while many banks and post offices had not been informed or had not been provided with the new notes or the necessary forms.

Several deaths and injuries were reported in connection with the public response to Gorbachev's decree, AP said on January 24. Reports from Moscow said large crowds of angry and anxious people had gathered at banks in many cities, trying to exchange rubles. Some people were reported to have been crushed in the crowds. In response to the panic, Armenia, Lithuania, the RSFSR, and Uzbekistan extended the deadline for exchanging rubles, the local republican media reported on January 23 and 24.

The same day, in an interview with Radio Rossii, reformist economist Nikolai Shmelev criticized the monetary reform, saying it would not solve the USSR's financial problems. He said it would affect ordinary people more than black marketers.

On January 25, the chairman of the USSR State Bank, Viktor Gerashchenko, said that the deadline for Soviet pensioners to exchange their 50- and 100-ruble notes for smaller denominations had been extended to January 26. Gerashchenko said people away from home for professional reasons would also get an extension (*TASS*, January 25).

Gorbachev Speaks on Baltic

In a prepared statement aired by Soviet television and radio, Mikhail Gorbachev denied that the USSR was threatened by dictatorship or that the Baltic crisis signaled a swing to the right. The statement was made by Gorbachev at a press conference in the Soviet Foreign Ministry. Expressing his regret over the deaths in Vilnius and Riga, Gorbachev disclaimed responsibility for them and promised an investigation. Gorbachev also stressed that the so-called "national salvation committees" in Lithuania and Latvia were unconstitutional.

The USSR in January, 1991

Shatalin Writes Open Letter to Gorbachev

Radical economist Stanislav Shatalin published an open letter to Soviet President Mikhail Gorbachev in *Komsomol'skaya pravda*. He urged the Soviet president to abandon the post of general secretary and, with it, totalitarian Communist ideology. He called for a center-left coalition and a government of national consensus consisting of representatives of various nationalities, parties, and social groups. Shatalin identified the leadership of the RSFSR Communist Party and "certain members" of the Politburo as "the main leaders" of the conservatives. He stressed that Gorbachev had failed to embark on a policy of radical economic and political reforms because he feared that in the process of their implementation he would lose his power and position.

Newspaper Gives Details of "USSR National Salvation Committee"

Radio Rossii quoted *Nezavisimaya gazeta* as saying the so-called Centrist Bloc had in December, 1990, set up "a USSR National Salvation Committee." The head of the committee was a conservative Centrist Bloc activist, Vladimir Voronin. Members of this bloc, which was believed to be closely connected with the KGB and the conservative Party apparatus, had earlier in the month proposed creating all-Union and republican "national salvation committees" to replace the legally elected parliaments.

On January 23, Voronin was interviewed by the Novosti press agency. He denied that his committee had ties with the "national salvation committees" in the Baltic republics. Voronin had, however, just returned from Vilnius and Riga, where he was supposed to have met with representatives of local "national salvation committees."

South Korea Offers 3 Billion Dollars to USSR

South Korea agreed to extend 3 billion dollars in loans and aid to the Soviet Union over the next three years. The agreement included 1.5 billion dollars for financing Soviet imports of Korean consumer goods and raw materials and 500 million dollars for importing Korean-made industrial products. The remaining 1 billion dollars was to take the form of a cash loan from a consortium of ten Korean banks to help finance Soviet economic development, AP reported.

After signing loan and aid agreements in Seoul, Soviet Deputy Prime Minister Yurii Maslyukov said, "We have the intention of providing South Korea with arms for defensive purposes if necessary." He also said that the Soviet Union had been supplying arms to North Korea since the end of the Korean war but claimed that they were "defensive ones." Alleging that US nuclear weapons existed in South Korea, Maslyukov called for the Korean peninsula to become a nuclear-free zone, Reuters and AP said.

Kuwait Grants 1-Billion-Dollar Loan

TASS reported that the Kuwaiti Foreign Trading Contracting and Investment Company would provide Vneshekonombank in the USSR with a 1-billion-dollar loan. A Kuwaiti foreign-trade official said the agreement reflected the development of relations between the two countries.

Local RSFSR Leaders Meet with El'tsin

Boris El'tsin told the chairmen of the RSFSR's local soviets and executive committees that local authorities would be given wide latitude in dealing with such questions as prices, TASS reported. Anatolii Sobchak, chairman of the Leningrad City Soviet, repeated a point made frequently by his counterpart in Moscow, Gavriil Popov, that the existing system of soviets and executive committees was incapable of carrying out reform. Chairmen of soviets and executive committees from the republican to the district level were in Moscow to participate in a special conference on how best to structure the RSFSR's legislative and executive branches of government in preparation for the drafting of an RSFSR law on local soviets.

Kirgizia Reorganizes Government

TASS reported that the Kirgiz Supreme Soviet had elected a Cabinet of Ministers to replace the former Council of Ministers. The new cabinet was to report directly to republican President Askar Akaev. Nasirdin Isanov, elected republican vice president only a month previously, was named prime minister. His replacement as vice president was a former secretary of the Frunze City Party Committee, German Kuznetsov, presumably a Slav. Few of Akaev's appointees have been Slavs.

Wednesday, January 23

Second Congress of Soviet Jews

Some 1,100 participants representing about 350 Jewish organizations and communities from eighty-two cities of the Soviet Union gathered in Moscow for their second congress, Novosti reported. The congress condemned the use of armed force against the Baltic republics. The press secretary of the congress said the Confederation of Jewish Organizations was not Zionist, was not opposed to the legally elected governments of the republics and the center; and had as its main aim ensuring the survival of the Jewish people. Among the guests attending the congress were Boris Oleinik, deputy chairman of the USSR Council of Nationalities, and various deputies and foreign ambassadors.

Moldavian Law on Ownership

The Moldavian Supreme Soviet passed a law on ownership that codified private, family, cooperative, joint-stock, kolkhoz, and state ownership, as well as permitting ownership combining the above forms. The law enabled foreign citizens and companies to set up joint ventures with Moldavian partners. Land, real estate, transportation, processing workshops, and financial capital may be privately owned. According to the law, however, land would not be treated as a commodity until the year 2001 (*TASS*, January 23).

Thursday, January 24

Leningrad Television Seeking Independence

Leningrad's Radio and Television Committee, run jointly by the USSR State Committee for Television and Radio Broadcasting (Gosteleradio) and the local authorities, said it planned to leave the Soviet state broadcasting system and become an independent republican-level company, TASS reported. Generally liberal, it had already had a series of conflicts with Gosteleradio over broadcasting policy. The move towards independence followed the publication of an open letter by a number of Leningrad intellectuals criticizing the policy of Gosteleradio. The letter was initially published in the Leningrad youth newspaper *Smena* and then reprinted by *Izvestia* on January 11. (The letter was attacked in *Glasnost'*, a weekly publication of the CPSU Central Committee on January 17.)

Soviet Cultural Figures Protest against Television Censorship

About sixty leading Soviet cultural figures said in a letter published in *Komsomol'skaya pravda* that they would boycott Soviet Central Television until censorship imposed on it by Gosteleradio Chairman Leonid Kravchenko was lifted. The letter said that political censorship had been revived and that viewers therefore received an incomplete and distorted picture of events. Criticism of television coverage was also expressed the same day by the moderators of the suspended television show "Vzglyad" (*Izvestia*, January 24).

The USSR in January, 1991

El'tsin Says Gorbachev Should Abandon Dubious Goals or Quit

Boris El'tsin said in an interview with the US television network ABC that Soviet President Gorbachev should resign or abandon "his attempt to set up a dictatorship." El'tsin said that the crisis in the Baltic republics was pushing the USSR to the brink of civil war and that the situation indicated Gorbachev was "losing his common sense." El'tsin also urged the United States to conclude a separate treaty with the Russian Federation.

Military Equipment Auctioned in Moscow

The Soviet army opened an auction in Moscow to sell off tanks, armored vehicles, petrol tankers, and other equipment. Armed forces logistics commander Vladimir Arkhipov said the hardware had been converted for civilian use. He put starting prices for tanks after modification in the range of 65,000 rubles to 120,000 rubles. He said the army hoped to raise about 30 million rubles from the auction (*TASS*, January 24).

Friday, January 25

Army, Police, and MVD Forces to Patrol Major Soviet Cities

"Vremya" announced that on February 1 a new order would go into effect under which regular army troops would join police and MVD forces in armed patrols aimed at securing public order in major Soviet cities. The order had been signed on December 29, 1990, by Defense Minister Dmitrii Yazov and Minister of Internal Affairs Boriss Pugo but was kept secret. The disclosure came after the Estonian government and the RSFSR Supreme Soviet discovered the existence of the order and filed requests to the Soviet leadership to clarify the matter. Under the order the patrols could be used during demonstrations and major political events, and on weekends, and on public holidays.

On January 26, officials from Moscow, Leningrad, and the Baltic republics condemned the order as illegal and dangerous. The deputy chairman of the RSFSR Supreme Soviet, Ruslan Khasbulatov, said such use of the army was "anticonstitutional." Chairman of the Leningrad City Soviet Anatolii Sobchak said the order represented "creeping counterrevolution" (*Reuters*, January 27).

On January 28, Boris El'tsin told Radio Moscow that the order presaged "a state-of emergency-regime" in the USSR and was "a rather serious step" towards dictatorship. He noted that the RSFSR leadership had not been consulted prior to the move. Deputy Chairman of the Moscow City Soviet Sergei Stankevich told RFE/RL the same day that the Soviet had not been officially informed about the

The USSR in January, 1991

order and that he had learned about it from "friends." Stankevich denounced the move as "unconstitutional" and "illegal." Politburo member and CPSU Central Committee Secretary for Ideology Aleksandr Dzasokhov said in an interview with the *Los Angeles Times* of January 29 that the measures taken by Gorbachev were aimed at protecting, not suppressing, democratic reform and were necessary to stabilize the situation during a time of political and economic crisis.

On January 29, Major General Viktor Solomatin, a department head of the USSR Armed Forces General Staff, told TASS the order did not mean that troops would ride in armored vehicles through cities. He said the police would be responsible for preserving public order, while troops would ensure discipline among servicemen. Solomatin said that each garrison would have a permanent reserve of armored vehicle patrols but that these would be stationed only on the territory of the garrisons. He added that the patrols were needed to curb the surging crime rate in the USSR.

The Presidium of the RSFSR Supreme Soviet called the order a crude violation of human rights and Russian sovereignty (*Reuters*, January 29). On January 31, the RSFSR Supreme Soviet voted to ask Gorbachev to suspend the order, Reuters reported.

The Georgian Supreme Soviet voted unanimously to declare the order null and void on Georgian territory.

On January 30, a leader of "Soyuz," Colonel Viktor Alksnis, denounced the order, calling it a measure "to scare dogs" but not to establish proper order in the country. Alksnis told RFE/RL that under the decree the army lacked the legal rights it needed for action. He said martial law should be introduced.

On January 31, the Moldavian Supreme Soviet declared the order a violation of republican law, TASS reported. The Supreme Soviet declared the order legally invalid on Moldavian territory and added that such patrols were unnecessary.

Soviet Economic Report Shows Sharp Decline

The Soviet Union's annual economic report showed a sharp decline in most indicators of the country's wealth and productivity. The report, released by the State Committee for Statistics, showed that the USSR's gross national product had fallen by 2 percent in 1990. (It had risen by 3 percent in 1989.) The report also showed that national income had fallen by 4 percent. The USSR's trade deficit also rose. The only good news was that the government's operating deficit fell by nearly one-third because of cuts in government spending (*TASS*, January 25).

The USSR in January, 1991

Rationing of Meat, Grains, and Vodka to Begin in Moscow

Yurii Luzhkov, the chairman of the Moscow City Soviet Executive Committee, said the soviet had decided to begin issuing ration coupons for meat, lard, sausage, grains, vodka, and wine in the Soviet capital. *Rabochaya tribuna* quoted Luzhkov as saying the rationing would begin on March 1 and that at the beginning of every month Moscow would determine how much of each rationed item it could offer the city's residents. Luzhkov was quoted as guaranteeing consumers that the rationed goods would appear on store shelves.

Bonn and Moscow Agree on Troop Withdrawals for 1991

Bonn and Moscow agreed that 100,000 Soviet troops would withdraw from Germany in 1991. The German Defense Ministry said this had been agreed on by a joint working group on January 24. It said Moscow would also withdraw 50,000 civilians, 1,000 tanks and artillery pieces, 3,000 other armored vehicles, and about 100 aircraft. Germany agreed to give the USSR 15 billion marks to offset the costs of the withdrawal (RFE/RL correspondent's report, January 25).

Latest Statistics on AIDS in USSR

Radio Moscow said an average of ten new cases of AIDS was being diagnosed every month in the Soviet Union. The radio said that 585 USSR citizens and 579 foreigners had been identified as carriers of the AIDS virus. It said twenty-four people had died of AIDS in the USSR, including fifteen children.

Saturday, January 26

Gorbachev Issues Decree on Economic Sabotage

Soviet President Mikhail Gorbachev issued a decree extending to the KGB and the police the right to search virtually every building in the country, except foreign embassies, in order to inspect financial records and confiscate valuables. The decree gave the KGB and the police the authority to enter premises with or without the permission of the owner and without search warrants. The only restriction on the inspections was that they had to be carried out in the presence of a representative of "a public organization."

Natural Population Increase Lowest since 1945

The natural population increase in the Soviet Union in 1990 was the lowest since 1945, according to official statistics for 1990 published in *Ekonomika i zhizn'* on January 26. Deaths were 10.4 per 1,000, up from 10.0 per

The USSR in January, 1991

1,000 in 1989, and births declined from 17.6 to 16.8 per thousand. Some 400,000 Soviet citizens emigrated in 1990.

Congress of Democratic Forces Holds Founding Conference

The founding conference of the Congress of Democratic Forces opened in Khar'kov. Forty-six independent political parties and movements from various Union republics, including Armenia, Azerbaijan, the Baltic republics, Belorussia, Kazakhstan, the RSFSR, and Ukraine, took part in the conference. The meeting's final statement on January 27 said the coalition's purpose was "to carry out joint political actions." It called for the disintegration of the Soviet empire and its replacement by "a voluntary union of sovereign states" (*Radio Moscow*, January 27).

Soviet Evacuees Describe War Experiences

A group of Soviet specialists evacuated from Iraq arrived in Moscow from Baghdad and recounted their experiences of the first days of the Gulf war. *Izvestia* quoted them as saying the bombing of industrial and military targets had been very accurate. They said the allied bombing raids had caused major damage in Baghdad, but they described the Iraqis as calm and very determined and the supply of goods as normal.

Petrakov Provides Insights into Political Machinations

Nikolai Petrakov, who resigned as economic adviser to Soviet President Mikhail Gorbachev on January 18, provided some behind-the-scenes details of the Soviet political swing to the right in an interview with the *Financial Times*. According to him, the conservatives were shocked by the possibility of a Gorbachev–El'tsin coalition and issued Gorbachev an ultimatum. Petrakov said Gorbachev's decision to institute "harsh presidential rule" had come on the night of November 17, after Colonel Viktor Alksnis, a leading member of the parliamentary group "Soyuz," had told him that he had only thirty days to restore order. The decision, Petrakov added, was made without the participation of former Presidential Council member Aleksandr Yakovlev and then Prime Minister Nikolai Ryzhkov.

USSR Prosecutor's Office Says Nuclear Plants Still Dangerous

The head of the Department for Legal Supervision of Economic Operations of the USSR Prosecutor's Office, Lev Baranov, told *Rabochaya tribuna* that disasters like the one that occurred at Chernobyl' could easily happen at many of the USSR's other nuclear plants. He said generators of a type that often had to be shut down because of defects were still in widespread use and were still being built despite their known technological faults. *Izvestia* said the same day, however, that plans for the construction of about sixty nuclear power plants had been scrapped.

Antiwar Rally in Dagestan

In the Dagestan ASSR about 4,000 people attended a rally denouncing the Gulf war, Reuters reported. Abdrashid Saidov, deputy chairman of the Islamic Democratic Party of Dagestan, which organized the rally, said speakers denounced the United States, the Soviet Union, and Israel as aggressors.

Bessmertnykh in Washington

Before leaving Moscow for Washington on January 26, Soviet Foreign Minister Aleksandr Bessmertnykh said that difficulties had emerged in US-Soviet relations because of events in the Baltic but that he hoped to clarify Soviet policy in this area to US leaders. TASS quoted him as saying it would be "extremely dangerous" if the positive trend in US-Soviet relations were to be reversed.

After meeting with US Secretary of State James Baker on January 27, Bessmertnykh said the USSR was in "complete accord" with the multinational force's actions in the Gulf thus far but remained concerned that the conflict was tending towards the destruction of Iraq (*The Washington Post*, January 27).

On January 28, Bessmertnykh spoke to reporters after a two-hour meeting with Baker on arms-control problems. He described the talks as good and constructive (RFE/RL correspondent's report, January 28). After meeting with US President George Bush, Baker and Bessmertnykh announced in a joint statement that the United States and the USSR had agreed to postpone the Moscow summit scheduled for February 11–13. They said that the Gulf war had made it inappropriate for Bush to leave Washington and that the Strategic Arms Reduction Treaty needed more work. The statement did not mention the Baltic crisis, but unidentified US officials were quoted as saying that about half of Bush's meeting with Bessmertnykh was taken up with the Baltic situation. Bush said that he was deeply troubled by the use of force in the Baltic republics and that Moscow had to understand that difficulties would arise in US-Soviet relations if the situation did not improve. According to the same officials, Bessmertnykh said that the events were regrettable but assured Bush that the Soviet leadership had no intention of returning the country to a Stalinist dictatorship (RFE/RL correspondent's report, January 29).

THE USSR IN JANUARY, 1991

Soviet Reaction to Postponement of Summit

On January 29, *Komsomol'skaya pravda* said lack of progress in concluding a strategic arms agreement was the main reason for the postponement of the summit.

The same day, President of the Lithuanian Supreme Council Vytautas Landsbergis expressed concern that failure to mention the Baltic crisis as a reason for the postponement might encourage the Soviet Armed Forces to renew their crackdown against Lithuania (*AFP*, January 29).

Deputy Chairman of the Moscow City Soviet Sergei Stankevich said he considered the postponement of the US-Soviet summit to be a signal to Soviet leaders that the Cold War could be restored if they reversed *perestroika*. If that were to happen, Stankevich told AP in an interview on January 29, almost all of the fruits of the previous period, including the peace dividend, would be sacrificed in favor of an ideological triumph for hard-liners. Stankevich said he believed such an outcome would be "unbearable economically and impossible politically."

On January 30, *Izvestia* said that, by not citing the crackdown in the Baltic republics as the reason for postponing the summit, the White House had given the impression it was fully aware of the unprecedented complexity of Soviet internal problems for which there was no obvious solution. TASS commentator Andrei Orlov, on the other hand, was not impressed by Washington's citation of the Gulf crisis and START agreement as reasons for putting off the summit. He wrote on January 28 that the postponement of the summit was itself a sign that US-Soviet relations had started to deteriorate.

On January 30, *Pravda* published a commentary by its correspondent Tomas Kolesnichenko on the Gulf war and on the postponement of the US-Soviet summit. The article said that it would be naïve to assume that the Soviet Union had conceded the Middle East to the United States. Kolesnichenko said the Soviet Union was not indifferent to the future of Iraq and the entire region, including the matter of how long US troops would remain there.

Tyumen' Officials Warn Gorbachev of Drop in Oil Production

Izvestia carried a letter signed by Tyumen' officials saying that oil production had decreased in 1990 by over 30 million tons (from 589 to 552 million tons) and was expected to drop by a further 30 to 40 million tons in 1991. They warned Gorbachev that the USSR might have to import oil by 1995, and they urged the Soviet president and the Federation Council to take action to avert an economic crisis.

On January 29, AP quoted the chief engineer of the Ministry of Oil and Gas as saying that the USSR risked becoming a net oil importer by 1993. He predicted that only 528 million tons of oil would be produced in 1991. Various estimates put Soviet domestic oil consumption at between 425 and 475 million tons per year.

At a meeting that day of the Cabinet of Ministers, Gorbachev instructed the Cabinet to devise within seven days a series of financial and material-supply measures to immediately improve the situation in the oil- and gas-producing regions. Gorbachev gave the Cabinet six months to address more fundamental problems and to draft plans to halt the decrease in oil and gas production.

Azerbaijan to Create Baku Commodities Exchange

Ragim Guseinov, deputy chairman of the Azerbaijani Council of Ministers and chairman of the republic's State Planning Committee, said the government would soon set up a commodities exchange in Baku (*Radio Moscow*, January 26). The exchange was to be a joint undertaking of the Azerbaijani State Material and Supply Committee, the Baku Executive Committee, and several Azerbaijani banks. It would work according to "classic" market principles but would also deal in auctions and barters. Special exchanges devoted to petroleum, cotton, tobacco, wine, and other Azerbaijani produce would be established when volume allowed.

Ukrainian Parties Discuss Coalition

Representatives of more than ten Ukrainian political parties met at the headquarters of "Rukh" in Kiev to discuss the formation of a new political coalition called Democratic Ukraine, Radio Kiev reported. Among the parties represented were the newly formed Party of Democratic Rebirth of Ukraine, the Ukrainian Republican Party, and the Democratic Party of Ukraine.

Japan and USSR to Increase Air Services

After five days of negotiations in Tokyo, Japanese transport officials announced an agreement with the Soviet Union to increase air services beginning in April, AFP reported. The new routes included a link between the northern Japanese city of Niigata and Irkutsk in Siberia, with Japanese carriers continuing on to points in Europe and the Middle East. Soviet airliners would fly a route between Moscow and Nagoya beginning in July and would also be able to land at Osaka when a new airport opened there.

Branch of Islamic Party Founded in Uzbekistan

A branch of the all-Union Islamic Renaissance Party held a founding congress, a journalist in Tashkent told RFE/RL. Police invaded the congress, detained some participants,

The USSR in January, 1991

and fined them for holding an unauthorized assembly. The journalist said that, in addition to Uzbeks, the congress included participants from other Central Asian and Caucasian republics and from the RSFSR. A branch of the party was set up in Tajikistan in 1990 and had been continually harassed by the authorities there.

------- *Sunday, January 27*

Television Coverage of Baltic Events

The most impressive coverage of recent events in the Baltic republics by Central Television so far was provided by the monthly show "Do i posle polunochi" (Before and after Midnight). The program included film of the seizure on January 13 of the Vilnius television tower by Soviet tanks and airborne troops.

Participating in the program, chief editor of *Moscow News* Egor Yakovlev charged that coverage of events in the Baltic by "Vremya" had been full of outright lies. Moscow film producer Elem Klimov noted he was one of the cultural figures who had just signed a letter announcing a boycott of Central Television. He said he had made an exception for "Do i posle polunochi" because he did not want to miss the opportunity to express his views on the Baltic situation to a large audience.

In the same interview, Yakovlev said that some Soviet journalists did not want to be in the same union as Leonid Kravchenko, the chairman of Gosteleradio, who was widely condemned for providing biased television coverage of the Baltic crackdown.

The majority of Muscovites questioned about *glasnost'* on Central Television said that they had detected heavy censorship in its reporting, "Do i posle polunochi" also reported. In a separate question about the main television newscast, "Vremya," the majority of those polled said that this program lacked objectivity.

Germany Offers Training for Young Soviet Workers

Under an agreement that emerged at the international conference on emigration in Vienna on January 24–25, Germany planned to offer training for 1,500 young Soviet workers in Germany each year. After training, the workers would return to the USSR and train others in new skills that would give them an incentive to remain in their own country (RFE/RL correspondent's report, January 27).

Soviet General on Draft

Deputy Chief of the General Staff of the Soviet Armed Forces Colonel General Grigorii Krivosheev told Soviet television that 84 percent of the fall draft quota had been met. Krivosheev repeated complaints about low turnout rates in the Baltic, the Transcaucasus, and Moscow. He placed blame for draft evasion entirely on republican governments and prodemocracy groups, claiming that low turnouts had left the army undermanned at a time when the United States was mobilizing reserves and endangering Soviet security. Krivosheev also criticized Boris El'tsin for threatening to form a Russian army and charged that the creation of national armies would in general undermine stability.

Soviet Mothers Defend Sons Serving in Baltic

An appeal from a group of mothers in the city of Khabarovsk to mothers in Lithuania, declaring that their sons serving in the army in the Baltic republics were victims of the country's "mindless military machine," was published in *Tikho-Okeanskaya zvezda*, Postfactum reported. Boris El'tsin, who had called on Soviet soldiers in the Baltic to disobey orders to shoot at civilians, was sharply criticized by the Khabarovsk Party organization in the same issue of *Tikho-Okeanskaya zvezda* for "encouraging anti-Communist hysteria."

Alksnis Predicts Civil War

Colonel Viktor Alksnis, a leading member of the parliamentary group "Soyuz," said in an interview with *Argumenty i fakty* (No. 4, 1991) that civil war appeared inevitable, and he hinted that the army could rebel, Reuters reported. Alksnis accused Soviet President Mikhail Gorbachev of betraying political allies by breaking off the army-led Baltic campaign. Alksnis charged that the military action had been intended as a prelude to a declaration of presidential rule but that Gorbachev had switched to a less confrontational course. On January 29, the television news program "TSN" urged Gorbachev to publicly deny Alksnis' assertion if it did not reflect reality.

Moldavian Popular Front Calls for Boycott of Referendum

At a meeting in Kishinev, leaders of the Moldavian Popular Front called for a boycott of the March 17 all-Union referendum on the preservation of the Soviet Union, Novosti reported on January 28. Novosti claimed it was possibly the smallest meeting ever of the front, attended by only about 5,000 of its most radical supporters. The leaders of the front said that, if the referendum were held, the whole Romanian nation should take part.

The USSR in January, 1991

Monday, January 28

Committee for Defense of City Soviet Set Up in Leningrad

A member of the Leningrad City Soviet Presidium, Marina Sal'e, told Radio Rossii that a special committee for the defense of the Leningrad City Soviet and of the RSFSR Supreme Soviet had been set up in Leningrad. In contrast to the "national salvation committees" in the Baltic, the Leningrad committee was open and its main purpose was to defend, not to overthrow, the legally elected state bodies, Sal'e stressed.

Agreement Reached with Donbass Miners

The chairman of the Ukrainian Council of Ministers, Vitol'd Fokin, signed an agreement with coal miners in the Donbass raising coal prices by 6.2 percent, Central Television's "TSN" news program reported. The miners had demanded a doubling of coal prices. Fokin promised that the issue would be reviewed again before mid-February.

Workers' Union Supports El'tsin

Boris El'tsin met with deputies of the RSFSR parliamentary group Workers' Union to discuss recent political developments in the country, Radio Moscow reported. The Russian workers' representatives supported El'tsin's tough stand against the Kremlin's moves in the Baltic and called for a further strengthening of Russian sovereignty. They also asked El'tsin to voice his views on Central Television.

Yakovlev Urges Review of Kirov's Case

In an article published in _Pravda_, Aleksandr Yakovlev urged a review of the assassination in December, 1934, of Leningrad Party leader Sergei Kirov. According to the official version of events, the killer, Leonid Nikolaev, acted alone, and no evidence available suggests that Stalin engineered the crime. As chairman of the Politburo Commission on the Rehabilitation of Stalin's Victims, Yakovlev voiced his doubts about this scenario in the summer of 1990 but was rebuffed by leading KGB and legal officials (see _Pravda_, November 4; and _Trud_, November 25, 1990). In today's article, Yakovlev argued that the question of Stalin's role in this case was not just a matter of curiosity but was connected with the issue of whether the present Soviet regime was reformable and capable of creating a humane society in the USSR.

Firing of Yakovlev and Primakov Denied

Writing in _Izvestia_, Gorbachev's aide Georgii Shakhnazarov denied reports of the resignations of Aleksandr Yakovlev and Evgenii Primakov. Shakhnazarov said that the president had not fired either of them and that allegations to this effect by some media organs were without foundation. He added that Yakovlev and Primakov would soon be entrusted with important new responsibilities.

Moldavian Communist Party Avoids Split

A conference of the Moldavian Communist Party ended on January 28 without the Party splitting, although some of the Trans-Dniestria Communists said they did not want to belong to the Moldavian Communist Party unless the existence of the would-be "Dniester SSR" was recognized, TASS reported. Moldavian Party First Secretary Petru Lucinschi also expressed satisfaction that, in spite of some opposition, the conference had managed to adopt the Party's statutes, thus enabling the Party to apply for registration.

Peasant Bank Set Up in Kazakhstan

TASS reported that a peasants' commercial bank had been established in Chimkent Oblast in Kazakhstan to provide financing to individual farmers, cooperatives, and small enterprises. The new bank, the latest in a number of such financial ventures, was part of a republican program to provide credit to individuals or groups willing to start private economic ventures.

Islamic Institute Opens in Alma-Ata

TASS said thirty young men had begun studies at a new Islamic institute in Alma-Ata that was to train imams for the rapidly growing number of new mosques in the republic. The report noted that the number of mosques in Kazakhstan had almost doubled in 1990, to nearly 150, and that another 20 were under construction.

Tuesday, January 29

Gorbachev Sets Up Anticrime Committee

Reuters reported that Gorbachev had created an Anticrime Coordination Committee to oversee and coordinate the work of law-enforcement agencies, in particular the KGB and the police. Yurii Golik, chairman of the USSR Supreme Soviet Committee for the Struggle against Crime, was named head of the new committee and was asked to make recommendations regarding the body's membership and functions.

Newspaper Reveals Plans to Harass Nationalist Groups

On January 29, *Nezavisimaya gazeta* published secret Party documents calling for the CPSU and the KGB to

The USSR in January, 1991

work together to place KGB military units under the command of the Lithuanian Communist Party and for Communists in prosecutors' offices to organize legal persecution of the leaders of various nationalist and anti-Soviet groups in Lithuania. One document was a report signed by CPSU Politburo member Oleg Shenin after he had met with Lithuanian Communists from August 17 to 19, 1990. A second was a resolution, marked "secret" and dated August 29, approving Shenin's report, signed by Vladimir Ivashko, the CPSU deputy general secretary.

KGB Officer Barred as Diplomat to Vienna

Austrian Foreign Minister Alois Mock told the Vienna daily *Der Kurier* that his country had refused to accredit KGB officer Lev Chapkin as secretary of the Soviet embassy in Vienna. Austrian Interior Minister Franz Löschnak said that Chapkin's task would have been to reestablish the KGB spy network in Eastern Europe, which suffered severe damage after the revolutions in 1989. *Die Welt* reported the same day, without naming Chapkin, that the proposed diplomat was a former KGB deputy chief who had been in charge of the KGB's communications system.

Constitutionality of Order to Be Examined

Radio Rossii reported that the USSR Committee for Constitutional Supervision intended to consider the constitutionality of the order deploying joint army-police patrols in large cities beginning February 1. Committee chairman Sergei Alekseev refused to comment on the inquiry, but the Radio Rossii report said the examination would be difficult.

Justice Minister Criticizes "War of Laws"

In an interview with *Pravitel'stvennyi vestnik*, USSR Minister of Justice Sergei Lushchikov condemned "the war of laws" between the all-Union government and the republics. Lushchikov said the USSR should have one set of laws that applied to citizens of all republics. Lushchikov criticized what he saw as a tendency by republics to focus on how to counteract the laws of the center when drafting their own laws. He also dismissed what he called "the parade of sovereignties," saying that some republics did not correctly understand or define sovereignty and therefore overemphasized their own rights and powers.

Baker Meets with Popov

US Secretary of State James Baker and Chairman of the Moscow City Soviet Gavriil Popov met in Washington, Reuters reported. According to State Department spokeswoman Margaret Tutwiler, the two men discussed Western aid to the Soviet Union, the Baltic events, and the Gulf war. At Baker's request, Popov gave his personal opinion of developments in the Soviet Union.

On January 30, Popov told the *Los Angeles Times* that the West should stop supporting Soviet President Gorbachev and seeing him as a reformer and instead provide direct assistance to republics and cities controlled by democratic forces. He said he believed that Gorbachev would stop all reform efforts during the coming year. Popov also said the crackdown in the Baltic republics had shocked the West because it was inconsistent with the West's image of Gorbachev. He said it was not inconsistent, however, with the real Gorbachev.

Poll on Russian Presidency

Rossiiskaya gazeta published the results of an opinion poll according to which 50 percent of Russian citizens favored the creation of a Russian presidency. Sixteen percent opposed it, and 34 percent did not care or were undecided.

Prosecutor's Office Starts Criminal Investigation into Currency Deal

The USSR Prosecutor's Office started a criminal investigation into a deal between a firm in Chelyabinsk and a British company that provided for the sale of 140 billion rubles for 7.8 billion dollars. TASS reported that the investigation had been launched under Article 170 of the Criminal Code of the RSFSR, which covers abuse of power and official position. In an interview with *Izvestia* on January 25, RSFSR Deputy Prime Minister Gennadii Fil'shin explained that the aim of the deal was to acquire foreign currency for the republic with which to purchase consumer goods and food.

Georgian Supreme Soviet Resolution on Creating National Guard

The Georgian Supreme Soviet unanimously approved the creation of a National Guard intended to replace Soviet forces on Georgian territory and ensure Georgia's security and territorial integrity, Reuters reported. The law on the creation of a National Guard stipulated that service was compulsory for all young men of draft age who were citizens of Georgia.

Georgian Supreme Soviet Restructures Local Government

The Georgian Supreme Soviet reorganized local government structures, setting up a system of local administrative organs called prefectures. These were to be headed by prefects who would report to the Georgian parliament, its Presidium, and the Council of Ministers. Prefects would serve a maximum of two four-year terms. Under the reorganization plan, villages were to be administered by councils (*TASS*, January 29).

Kuibyshev Regains Former Name

A meeting of the RSFSR Supreme Soviet Presidium decided to restore the historical name, Samara, to the city of Kuibyshev. Kuibyshev Oblast was also renamed Samara Oblast. The city is one of the oldest on the Volga River. It was renamed Kuibyshev in 1935 after the Bolshevik leader Valerian Kuibyshev (*TASS*, January 29).

―――――――――――――――――――― *Wednesday, January 30*

Pugo Replaced as Party Control Commission Chairman

USSR Minister of Internal Affairs Boriss Pugo was replaced as chairman of the Communist Party's Central Control Commission (*TASS*, January 30). His former first deputy, Evgenii Makhov, an army lieutenant general and former commander of the Carpathian Military District, replaced him. Commission member Mikhail Kodin was named first deputy chairman in place of Makhov. Kodin was the chairman of the Control and Auditing Commission of the Moldavian Communist Party.

CPSU Central Committee Plenum Opens

The CPSU Central Committee opened a plenary meeting. Issues on the agenda included the USSR's grave economic situation and measures needed to overcome it. On January 31, Politburo member and Party Secretary Aleksandr Dzasokhov said in a statement that the plenum had expressed sorrow about the deaths in the recent clashes in the Baltic republics and in the Transcaucasus and wanted to do everything possible to stop the bloodshed. Dzasokhov also said the plenum considered the creation of illegal armed groups in the republics unacceptable. The statement further stressed the necessity of moving ahead in developing a market economy (*AFP*, January 31).

Deputy Editor of *Izvestia* Fired over Protest

Members of the USSR Supreme Soviet Presidium were asked by telephone to approve the firing of Igor' Golembiovsky, first deputy chief editor of *Izvestia*, Radio Rossii reported. The radio said that the move to fire Golembiovsky had surprised the chairman of the Council of the Union, Ivan Laptev, who, as the former editor of *Izvestia*, oversaw the daily for the Presidium. When

Laptev was elected to his present position in 1990, the staff of *Izvestia* voted to elect Golembiovsky as chief editor. The Presidium, however, bowed to advice from CPSU ideologists and gave the job to Nikolai Efimov, making Golembiovsky his first deputy as a compromise. Golembiovsky recently signed a strongly worded protest published in *Moscow News* (No. 3, 1991) against the Soviet crackdown in Lithuania. The editorial staff of *Izvestia* threatened to strike unless the decision to fire Golembiovsky was reversed (RFE/RL correspondent's report, January 31).

Nina Andreeva for CPSU General Secretary

The reactionary Soviet political group "Edinstvo—za leninizm i kommunisticheskie idealy" (Unity—for Leninism and Communist Ideals) said it wanted to replace Mikhail Gorbachev as CPSU general secretary with Leningrad teacher Nina Andreeva, the author of the 1988 "anti-*perestroika* manifesto." Andreeva is the chairwoman of "Edinstvo." Radio Rossii quoted the group's political adviser as saying "Edinstvo" was working on creating a Bolshevik platform within the CPSU to resist "social democratic efforts" in the Party leadership.

Alksnis Says Gorbachev's and El'tsin's Days Numbered

Colonel Viktor Alksnis told the Finnish daily *Uusi Suomi* that Mikhail Gorbachev's and Boris El'tsin's days were numbered. Alksnis said that Gorbachev collected positions of power the way Leonid Brezhnev collected decorations but that he did not know how to use power and should therefore resign. Alksnis said El'tsin was not an acceptable alternative to Gorbachev, because he was a neo-Bolshevik who had split the Union in order to gain power in the Russian republic. Alksnis also admitted his own involvement in setting up the conservative "national salvation committees" in the Baltic republics.

RSFSR Supreme Soviet Discusses Federal Treaty

The RSFSR Supreme Soviet discussed for the first time in joint session with the RSFSR Council of Nationalities the draft federal treaty for the RSFSR, TASS and Radio Moscow reported. Ramazan Abdulatipov, chairman of the RSFSR Council of Nationalities, who presented the draft, said he hoped it would be signed before the March 17 all-Union referendum. The draft gave the RSFSR Supreme Soviet control over crime fighting, prices, human-rights legislation, banking, taxation, currency, transport, and communications. It also guaranteed all Russian citizens equal rights regardless of religion, party membership, or social status (*TASS*, January 30).

The USSR in January, 1991

RSFSR Economic Performance in 1990

Sovetskaya Rossiya reported disastrous economic results for the RSFSR in 1990. National income decreased by 5.5 percent and labor productivity by 5 percent. Money emissions, on the other hand, almost doubled compared with 1989. Imports and exports declined, with export quotas of gas, oil, coal, and most petroleum products unfulfilled. Agricultural production was 3 percent down from the 1989 level. One of the few bright spots in the report was the news that leased enterprises outperformed state-owned firms.

Georgia to Boycott Referendum

The Georgian Supreme Soviet ruled that Georgia would not participate in the Union-wide referendum scheduled for March 17 on whether the Soviet Union should be preserved as an integral state. Instead, a referendum was to be held on March 31 on the future of the Georgian republic, TASS reported.

Lvov Forms Own Police Patrols

Vyacheslav Chornovil, chairman of the Lvov Oblast Soviet, disclosed a plan to substitute workers' brigades for the proposed army patrols. Reporting from Lvov, *The Independent* quoted Chornovil as saying that, if the plan failed, there would be rallies and that, in an emergency situation, with the soviet stripped of its power, he could call a general strike and cut off water and electricity. *The Times* wrote that Western Ukrainian leaders had also appealed to Kiev to guarantee that there would be no military operations in the region.

Tajik Popular Front Accused of Inciting Disturbances

The head of a group of investigators looking into the disturbances in Tajikistan in February, 1990, for the Tajik Prosecutor's Office accused the leaders of the popular front, "Rastokhez," of having incited the disturbances, TASS reported. The leaders of "Rastokhez" were accused of having spread the rumor—which sparked the disturbances—that Armenian refugees would be given preferential housing in Dushanbe and of having encouraged protesters at unauthorized demonstrations to demand the resignation of republican leaders and to use force if their demands were not met. The investigator indicated that the group's actions would be judged by the republican Supreme Court.

Burlatsky Calls for New Party

Literaturnaya gazeta carried an article by its editor Fedor Burlatsky; Stanislav Shatalin, author of the "500 days" economic program; and Sergei Alekseev, head of the

Committee for Constitutional Supervision, calling for the creation of a new organization, Social Democracy, which could begin as a wing of the Communist Party but later develop into a large party with a social democratic bent. This social democratic party would stand for an economic community, against the Soviet system of power, and for a consistent foreign policy (see also *The Washington Post*, February 1).

Thursday, January 31

RSFSR and Turkmenistan to Allow Foreigners to Compete for Oil

Knight-Ridder Newspapers quoted RSFSR and Turkmen oil officials as saying that foreign firms would be allowed to bid for rights to explore and drill for oil in their republics. An RSFSR official said that budgetary constraints limited the 1991 funds available for oil exploration to 1990 levels. He also asserted that the republic would have exclusive say in concluding oil deals with foreign firms. Leases would be awarded in four oil fields. Foreign investors were given until September to bid on the first two and until December for bids on the second two. Leases for exploration would run for ten years, with another twenty-five years added when production of oil or gas began.

Yanaev Calls for Order

Soviet Vice President Gennadii Yanaev said in an interview with *Glasnost'*, the CPSU Central Committee newspaper, that the Soviet Union had so far failed to achieve its reform goals and that most economic and social problems remained unresolved, TASS reported. He rejected charges that the Soviet leadership had changed its course and was moving back towards a command economy and a centralized state. Commenting on the situation in the Baltic republics, Yanaev said that any attempts by other countries to exert pressure on the Soviet Union were doomed to failure.

Generals Urge Parliament to Act against El'tsin

In an article carried by *Sovetskaya Rossiya*, a group of leading military officials expressed concern over the position taken by RSFSR Supreme Soviet Chairman Boris El'tsin on the situation in the Baltic and on the creation of a Russian army. They urged the USSR and RSFSR Supreme Soviets to take action against El'tsin's "extremely dangerous position."

In reply to the article, El'tsin told the RSFSR Supreme Soviet that some Soviet generals and Party structures were conducting a dirty campaign to discredit him and the RSFSR Supreme Soviet. He retorted that Russian defense and security policy would be made by the Russian Supreme Soviet and not by El'tsin alone. The RSFSR Supreme Soviet appointed Konstantin Kobets, a deputy chief of the General Staff of the Soviet Armed Forces, as head of the RSFSR Committee on Defense and Security. Kobets was the commander of Soviet Communications Forces. Kobets and El'tsin agreed that the RSFSR did not need an army to protect its sovereignty or its policy (*TASS*, January 31).

A group of RSFSR deputies demanded the resignation of Gorbachev, Prime Minister Valentin Pavlov, and their team, saying that it was impossible to cooperate with the Soviet leadership in governing the USSR. The deputies said they wanted the presidential structures abolished and all power handed over to a coordinating council of republican leaders.

Some RSFSR Deputies Demand That Gorbachev Resign

Major Viktor Kutsenko was sentenced by a military court in Moscow to five years imprisonment after being convicted of trying to sell secret documents to a NATO country. According to TASS, Kutsenko, who worked for the Scientific Research Institute of the USSR Ministry of Defense, admitted his guilt. His espionage attempt was said to have been thwarted, however, before it could cause damage to Soviet security.

Soviet Army Officer Convicted of Selling Secrets

The Month of February

Friday, February 1

Joint Patrols in Moscow High-Crime Areas

TASS reported that more than sixty joint army-police units were patrolling the streets in high-crime areas of Moscow. General Nikolai Mirikov of the Ministry of Internal Affairs told AP that each patrol would consist of a policeman, an army officer, and two soldiers armed with bayonets but that there would be no tanks or armored personnel carriers in the city. TASS quoted a senior Moscow police official, Vladimir Vershkov, as saying the patrols were armed with pistols and rubber batons. No joint patrols were reported in Leningrad. The Leningrad City Soviet had condemned them, saying they could become a destabilizing factor (*Radio Moscow*, February 1).

The Armenian Supreme Soviet forbade the use of Soviet army troops for patrols in the republic. The RSFSR Supreme Soviet restated its condemnation of "the illegal involvement" of troops in political conflicts. Moldavia, Georgia, Estonia, Latvia, and Lithuania also barred deployment of the patrols in their cities. Lithuanian Supreme Council deputies, however, said some armored vehicles had been sighted in Vilnius. There was no indication whether the vehicles were part of army patrols or connected with the "Black Beret" (OMON) MVD troops (*Radio Moscow*, February 1).

On February 5, TASS reported that four-man teams of police and soldiers, involving some 12,000 troops, were on the streets in approximately ninety cities. The news agency denied that the patrols were equipped with automatic weapons or armored vehicles.

On February 16, the USSR Ministry of Internal Affairs was quoted by TASS as saying that over 16,000 people had been detained by joint army and police patrols since February 1. The patrols detained 61 people for serious offenses and sent about 3,000 servicemen considered absent without leave back to their units.

RSFSR Supreme Soviet Calls for Stepped-Up Reform of Security Organs

A statement adopted by the RSFSR Supreme Soviet called on the USSR Supreme Soviet and Soviet President Mikhail Gorbachev to accelerate reform in the Soviet army, KGB, and Ministry of Internal Affairs. As reported by TASS, it also called for steps to disband and prevent the emergence of unconstitutional structures seeking the violent overthrow of legally elected bodies of power.

USSR Federation Council Discusses Baltic

The USSR Federation Council met to discuss the situation in the Baltic. Council member and Chairman of the USSR Supreme Soviet Council of Nationalities Rafik Nishanov said the council expressed profound anxiety and concern over the situation in the Baltic republics. TASS quoted him as saying tensions could be eased only by political means.

The Federation Council also discussed the new Union treaty. Council member and Chairman of the Belorussian Supreme Soviet Nikolai Dementei said the current draft was based on the idea that the republics would join the Union only voluntarily, as sovereign states. The powers of the center would be defined by the republics ("Vremya", *Central Television*, February 1).

Gorbachev Appoints High-Ranking Baltic Delegations

Soviet President Mikhail Gorbachev appointed three high-ranking delegations to discuss a range of political, social, and economic questions with each of the Baltic republics, AFP reported. The delegation to Latvia was headed by First Deputy Prime Minister Vladimir Makarovich and included Gorbachev's personal representative, Georgii Tarazevich, and Deputy Defense Minister Valentin Varennikov. The delegation to Lithuania was headed by First Deputy Prime Minister Vitalii Doguzhiev and included the Soviet Armed Forces Chief of Staff General Mikhail Moiseev. Deputy Prime Minister Nikolai Laverov headed the delegation to Estonia. He was accompanied by First Deputy Commander of the Soviet navy Ivan Kapitanets (*TASS*, February 1).

―――――――――――――――――――――――― *Saturday, February 2*

No More Bank Note Exchanges Planned

Responding to a question on Central Television about rumors that 25- and 10-ruble notes would be withdrawn, Prime Minister Valentin Pavlov asserted that the government had no plans to withdraw more currency from circulation or to freeze savings bank accounts.

In two separate interviews on Central Television on February 9, USSR Gosbank officials reported that 41.2 billion rubles' worth of the old 50- and 100-ruble notes had been exchanged, leaving 7 billion rubles' worth to be effectively confiscated. They repeated that no exchange of 25- and 10-ruble notes and no freezing of savings deposits were contemplated.

Decree on Restoration of Soviet German Autonomy

Radio Moscow reported that the RSFSR Supreme Soviet was drawing up a resolution on measures to restore Soviet German autonomy, having concluded that this was the only way to stop Soviet German emigration. Under the resolution a state committee was to be charged with working out a concept and program for restoring the German Volga Republic and would submit it to the RSFSR Supreme Soviet within three months.

Gosteleradio Reduces Radio Rossii Frequencies

The USSR State Committee for Television and Radio Broadcasting (Gosteleradio) reduced the number of frequencies available for use by Radio Rossii, Radio Moscow reported. A spokesman for Radio Rossii said the move deprived the radio of a large part of its audience, since it would now have to stop its broadcasts on frequencies used by Radio Moscow's first and second programs and confine itself to the third program. In addition, on February 3, the broadcasts of Radio Rossii were reduced to one and a half instead of the usual three hours. Radio Rossii said, however, that it had been told the cut in airtime would apply only for one day. The restrictions were imposed after President Gorbachev had complained to Gosteleradio Chairman Leonid Kravchenko about Radio Rossii's coverage of recent events in the Baltic.

A meeting of editors of newspapers published in the RSFSR issued an appeal to the Soviet president, the RSFSR Supreme Soviet, the RSFSR Council of Ministers, and Gosteleradio condemning the restrictions as a violation of the USSR press law and charging that, in the future, only 60 percent of the population of the RSFSR would be able to listen to Radio Rossii. The editors also reiterated a call for the establishment of republican television in the RSFSR and asked Gosteleradio to make the second channel of Central Television available to the All-Russian State Radio Company (*Radio Moscow*, February 3).

On February 4, Radio Rossii announced that its morning program had been eliminated on the orders of Gosteleradio.

Radio Moscow reported the same day that the RSFSR Ministry of the Mass Media and Information had issued a protest saying that the restriction on Radio Rossii's broadcasts had inflicted economic and political damage on Russia by breaking the links between the Russian Supreme Soviet and government and the people.

The USSR in February, 1991

On February 6, Yurii Rostov, a "TSN" presenter, said the RSFSR government had decided to establish its own radio structure, withdrawing the necessary amount of money to finance the project from the RSFSR's contribution to the all-Union budget.

TASS reported that ten people had been hospitalized with typhoid fever after water from a linen factory was mixed with drinking water. The accident occurred in Barysh in Ul'yanovsk Oblast in the RSFSR. A special task force was set up to fight the disease.

Typhoid Reported in Central Russia

Radio Moscow reported that railway stations along the Leningrad lines were jammed with goods awaiting transport. It said some 27,000 tons of goods were waiting to be moved while more than 900 railway cars had yet to be unloaded. The report said the situation was creating a shortage of raw materials in industry and of goods in shops.

Rail Transport Jam in Leningrad

The USSR Ministry of Defense gave permission for foreign airplanes to use the airport of Vladivostok, which was expected to serve as a stopover for airlines from the United States, Japan, South Korea, China, Australia, Hong Kong, and Singapore. A Japanese construction company had submitted a plan to rebuild the airport, adding a high-rise hotel, restaurants, and other facilities (*Radio Moscow*, February 2). Vladivostok was a closed city until recently.

Vladivostok Airport Open to Foreign Planes

Chairman of the Nikolaevsk-on-Amur City Soviet K. Bush was quoted by TASS as saying the city would cut power to a giant gold-mining and -processing plant recently completed on the bank of the Amur River if mining officials tried to begin operations. *Trud* reported that the city had obtained test results showing that the plant's effluent was not being properly filtered and that poisons such as cyanide were draining into the surrounding soil. Bush said the value of the gold mine could not compensate for the damage to health and to the environment expected as a result of the plant's operations.

City Threatens to Cut Power to Environmentally Dangerous Plant

The Belorussian Supreme Soviet adopted a program aimed at reducing genetic birth defects related to the Chernobyl' nuclear disaster of 1986. According to TASS,

Belorussian Program for Chernobyl'-Related Birth Defects

the program would include distribution of condoms, prenatal diagnosis, and comprehensive monitoring of newborns. The occurrence of congenital defects and illnesses such as cancer and heart disease was reported to be on the rise.

Sunday, February 3

Committee Says Decrees Contradict Constitution

The "Avtorskoe televidenie" (Authors' Television) weekly newsreel "Namedni" reported details of a meeting on February 1 of the USSR Committee for Constitutional Supervision devoted to the recent expansion of police powers. Quoting experts present at the meeting, "Namedni" commentator Leonid Miloslavsky said that the decrees extending the authority of the police contradicted not only the USSR Constitution but also "the purposes for which they were issued." Miloslavsky cited experts from the MVD research academy as saying that no financial crime in the USSR in recent years fitted the legal definition of "economic sabotage."

Golik Attacks El'tsin

Yurii Golik, who had recently been appointed head of the new USSR Committee for Coordinating the Work of the Law-Enforcement Organs, attacked RSFSR Supreme Soviet Chairman Boris El'tsin on Siberian television, according to a Postfactum report. Golik called El'tsin "a man with whom it is impossible to agree in principle . . . a lying and inconsistent man."

Ukrainian Army under Discussion

Members of the "Narodna rada" parliamentary faction, "Rukh," the Association of Democratic Soviets of Ukraine, and a previously unknown group called the Committee for the Resurrection of the Armed Forces in Ukraine opened a two-day conference in Kiev devoted to "steps towards the realization of a Ukrainian army."

Radio Kiev reported on February 4 that participants had adopted a four-part appeal to the Ukrainian parliament calling on it to pronounce on the status of the Soviet Armed Forces in Ukraine and to establish a Ukrainian Ministry of Defense.

Zelenchuk-Urup Territorial Okrug Proclaimed

A congress of Cossack deputies of all levels elected from the Zelenchuk and Urup Raions of the Karachai-Cherkess Autonomous Oblast proclaimed the two raions the Zelenchuk-Urup Territorial Okrug, TASS reported. A

The USSR in February, 1991

Cossack ataman had complained earlier that Karachai attempts to regain a separate Karachai national territory would cut the predominantly Russian-speaking Zelenchuk Raion in two and had suggested the raion be subordinated directly to Stavropol Krai. The proclamation was part of the general revival of Cossack national identity in the Northern Caucasus, which was adding to interethnic tensions in the region.

Agreement on Baikonur

The government of Kazakhstan reached agreement with Glavkosmos, the Soviet space agency, about the Baikonur launching facility in Kzyl-Orda Oblast. Republican leaders and journalists had complained that Kazakhstan had no control over, and little knowledge of, what went on at the complex. A Radio Moscow report on the agreement said that the republican government had demanded that the facility directly benefit the republic. Glavkosmos agreed to provide a satellite relay of Kazakh television and accepted two Kazakhs into the cosmonaut program.

Last Synod of Ukrainian Catholic Church in Rome

The last synod of the Ukrainian Catholic Church abroad started in Rome. Myroslav Cardinal Lyubachivs'kyi, the Ukrainian Church leader, said that future synods would take place in Lvov, in Ukraine. The week-long synod brought together all Ukrainian Catholic-Rite bishops from Ukraine and abroad (RFE/RL correspondent's report, February 3). On February 9, AP reported that Lyubachivs'kyi had invited Pope John Paul II to visit Ukraine. No pope had ever visited the Soviet Union, although Gorbachev issued an invitation to John Paul when they met in December, 1989.

Monday, February 4

New Committee to Coordinate Work of MVD and KGB

USSR Minister of Internal Affairs Boriss Pugo said that the newly created Committee for Coordination of the Work of the Law-Enforcement Organs would improve cooperation between the MVD and the KGB, TASS reported on February 4. He noted that the committee would coordinate but not direct the activities of the two institutions. Pugo indicated that, in recent months, problems had arisen in coordinating the activities of the KGB and MVD. He stated that the Soviet leadership would not tolerate the existence of two separate interior ministries in some republics.

The USSR in February, 1991

New Anticrime Decree

Soviet President Mikhail Gorbachev issued a decree ordering the creation of a new main directorate within the Ministry of Internal Affairs, TASS reported. The new directorate would be tasked with fighting organized crime, corruption, and drug dealing. To be set up within a month, it would cooperate with the KGB and was to coordinate the activities of new interregional and local MVD units controlled jointly by Moscow and the republican ministries of internal affairs (see *Pravda*, February 5).

KGB Denies Seeking to Suppress Reforms

In a statement distributed by the KGB public relations center in Moscow, the KGB said that its new powers would not be used to suppress or subvert reforms but exclusively to combat violations of the law, TASS reported. These powers were temporary and aimed at protecting the rights of citizens while the economy was in crisis, the statement said.

Deputy Wins Libel Suit against TASS and *Pravda*

Galina Starovoitova, a liberal USSR and RSFSR people's deputy, won a lawsuit against the CPSU daily, *Pravda*, and against TASS commentator Vladimir Petrunya. According to "TSN," the Moscow Sverdlovsk District Court ordered *Pravda* to publish an apology to Starovoitova on its front page, where it had published Petrunya's articles libeling Starovoitova and other democratic deputies. In a series of articles published in *Pravda* from September 26 to October 2, 1990, Petrunya claimed that the democrats had deliberately created acute food shortages in Moscow with the aim of staging "a counterrevolutionary coup" against the Gorbachev-Ryzhkov leadership.

Russian Information Agency Created

Novosti reported that a Russian (*Rossiiskoe*) Information Agency had been established by a decision of the Presidium of the RSFSR Supreme Soviet. A spokesman for the new agency said it would not attempt to establish any monopoly on disseminating information but would cooperate with other independent agencies already existing in the RSFSR.

Dean of Moscow Church Found Dead

The thirty-two-year-old dean of Moscow's Orthodox Church of the Nativity of the Mother of God, Serafim Shlykov, was found dead in a Moscow apartment where he had been living temporarily. TASS said that he had been murdered and that radio and video equipment, cassettes, and money were missing from the apartment.

Prokof'ev Cites Chile as Model for Economic Reform

First Secretary of the Moscow City Party Committee Yurii Prokof'ev said countries such as South Korea, Spain, and Chile, all of which developed strong market economies during periods of authoritarian rule, offered better models for Soviet economic reform than Western democracies. Prokof'ev told a press conference in Moscow that, whereas the Western democracies had taken centuries to build their market economies, in countries such as Chile "developed market infrastructures were created in a short period of time . . . and in an organized way" (*Reuters*, February 4).

Prokof'ev told the same press conference that newspapers and journals that were organs of government bodies should not be allowed to criticize the Soviet leadership, Novosti reported. Prokof'ev proposed appointing a special official within the new Cabinet of Ministers to control periodicals belonging to the government. He noted that the CPSU had always had such an official.

Shatalin in South Korea

Gorbachev's former economic adviser Stanislav Shatalin flew to South Korea to attend a seminar on Soviet economic reform, AFP reported. Shatalin, who had recently published several articles criticizing Gorbachev's economic policies (*Komsomol'skaya pravda*, January 16 and 22), said the Soviet people had no confidence in their country's economic future.

Dzasokhov Says Gulf War Already Exceeds UN Limits

The Supreme Soviet Committee on International Affairs said that military action in the Gulf had already exceeded the limits imposed by the UN mandate. Committee Chairman Aleksandr Dzasokhov called for measures, including the intervention of the United Nations, to find a political solution.

Syrian Defense Minister in Moscow

Syrian Defense Minister Lieutenant General Mustafa Talas arrived in Moscow for a four-day visit. In a meeting with Soviet Foreign Minister Aleksandr Bessmertnykh on February 5 it was agreed that an Iraqi withdrawal from Kuwait would permit the cessation of military actions and end bloodshed. Bessmertnykh said: "The best path to enduring peace and stability in the [Middle East] region is through an international conference, under UN auspices, and with the participation of all interested parties," TASS reported.

TASS reported that, during his visit, Talas also met with his counterpart Dmitrii Yazov, Minister of

Foreign Economic Relations Konstantin Katushev, and other Soviet officials.

Tourist Trips to Chernobyl'

Komsomol'skaya pravda reported that Kievturist, an excursion association based in Kiev, would arrange trips to "the dead city" of Chernobyl', to a burial site for radioactive waste in a nearby village, to the construction site of the abandoned third reactor, and to the sarcophagus in which the reactor involved in the accident was buried.

New Moldavian Party First Secretary

A plenum of the Moldavian Party Central Committee elected Grigore Eremei first secretary of the Moldavian Communist Party in place of Petru Lucinschi, who the previous week had been elected a secretary of the CPSU Central Committee, TASS reported. Eremei, a Moldavian born in 1935, headed the Moldavian trade-union organization for some years.

Stimulation of Food Production in Kirgizia

TASS reported that a special commission to ensure food supplies and combat "economic sabotage" had been set up by a decree issued by Kirgiz President Askar Akaev. The commission was given until February 15 to inventory existing food resources and create food reserves. The decree also called for measures to stimulate production of food: half of the private cars and television and radio sets available were to be reserved for sale to persons engaged in agriculture. Rationing of food had begun in Kirgizia at the end of 1990 and included sugar, flour, and vegetable oil.

Tuesday, February 5

Gorbachev Declares Lithuanian Poll Illegal

Soviet President Mikhail Gorbachev issued a decree invalidating the decision of the Lithuanian Supreme Council in January to hold a poll on the future of the Lithuanian state on February 9, TASS reported. It instructed the supreme and local bodies of power of Lithuania and the relevant ministries and departments of the USSR to ensure strict fulfillment of the USSR Supreme Soviet resolution of January 16 on the Union-wide referendum on the preservation of the Soviet Union scheduled for March 17. The decree accused the Lithuanian leadership of taking advantage of "the aggravated sociopolitical situation in the republic . . . to organize support for its separatist ambitions" (see *Pravda*, February 6)

President of the Lithuanian Supreme Council Vytautas Landsbergis rejected Gorbachev's decree, declaring that the poll on Lithuania's independence was legal and that the decree constituted political interference in Lithuania's affairs, AP reported.

Seventh Congress of Journalists Opens

Sharp criticism of the policies of Leonid Kravchenko, chairman of the USSR State Committee for Television and Radio Broadcasting, was voiced at the Seventh Congress of Soviet Journalists, which opened in Moscow, Radio Moscow reported. A delegate called on the Journalists' Union to expel Kravchenko. Novosti said on February 6 that Kravchenko would be allowed to address the congress at the insistence of several delegates from Siberia, Volgograd Oblast, and Ukraine.

Delegates at the congress also commemorated the journalists who had recently died while "fulfilling their professional duties," "TSN" reported. Among those honored were two journalists killed during the assault by special police (OMON) troops on the MVD building in Riga on January 20.

Addressing the congress on February 7, Kravchenko defended his position, saying that Soviet television and radio now found themselves at the epicenter of the USSR's political struggle and that taking a neutral stand was impossible. According to Central Television on February 8, Kravchenko added that the very existence of the supreme institutions of state power, including presidential power, was at stake.

The same day, the congress appealed to Gorbachev and the central and republican-level Supreme Soviets not to use the armed forces to settle civilian conflicts, Reuters reported. The journalists also elected Eduard Sagalaev, the forty-five-year-old director general of Soviet television's fourth channel, as the new chairman of the union. After his election, Sagalaev told reporters that the union should work to protect *glasnost'* and objectivity and should provide "social protection" for journalists.

Belonogov Goes to Teheran

Soviet Deputy Foreign Minister Aleksandr Belonogov flew to Teheran for talks with Iranian leaders about the Gulf war. According to AP, Belonogov said before leaving Moscow that the Soviet Union and Iran wanted to stop the conflict because it was close to their borders, and he repeated the demand that Iraq restore Kuwait's independence.

Belonogov met with Iranian President Ali Akbar Hashemi-Rafsanjani. No details of the meeting were reported except an announcement that the USSR Foreign Ministry welcomed the prospect of a meeting between Saddam Hussein and Rafsanjani as long as the meeting would be dedicated to the topic of getting Iraq to withdraw from Kuwait.

On February 6, Belonogov delivered a letter from Soviet Foreign Minister Aleksandr Bessmertnykh to his Iranian counterpart Ali Akbar Velayati. According to an IRNA report cited by AP on February 7, the letter invited Velayati to visit the Soviet Union.

A TASS report of February 7 said that Iran had promised to maintain active neutrality while seeking a political settlement of the Gulf war. The promise was made during talks between Belonogov and Velayati.

On February 8, Belonogov ended consultations in Teheran and went to Turkey to discuss "bilateral relations and international problems of mutual interest," especially the Gulf conflict.

Belonogov held talks in Ankara on February 8 and 9 with Turkish Prime Minister Yildirim Akbulut and First Deputy Foreign Minister T. Ozceri, TASS reported on February 10. Both sides agreed that Iraq's territorial integrity should be preserved after the conflict in the Gulf had ended and that Turkey should not open up a second front unless attacked by Iraq.

Appointment of New Moscow Police Chief Suspended

The Moscow City Soviet appointed a police major general, Vyacheslav Komissarov, as Moscow police chief, replacing Petr Bogdanov, who had been appointed a USSR deputy minister of internal affairs. But the USSR Ministry of Internal Affairs said it would suspend Komissarov's appointment until a new law on the status of Moscow that defines procedures for the appointment of city officials had been approved. The ministry said Bogdanov would stay on as police chief for the time being, adding that it had not been officially informed of Komissarov's appointment. The city soviet answered that it was not legally obliged to inform the ministry about such things. Finally, the Moscow City Soviet said it would appeal to President Gorbachev to intervene to end the dispute (*Reuters*, February 5).

More Cultural Figures Boycott Soviet Television

The Moscow organization of cinema workers was reported to have joined the boycott of Central Television to protest against censorship and disinformation; altogether more than 200 leading Soviet cultural figures were participating in the boycott. The cinema workers said their boycott would apply only to entertainment shows on Central Television, not to Moscow and Leningrad local television or to certain "progressive" political programs. Since some full-time employees of Central Television had opted to join the boycott as well, the filmmakers voted to set up a special Foundation in Defense of *Glasnost'* to help them survive (RL Russian service, February 5).

Ukrainian Radicals Sue KGB Chief

The Ukrainian Republican Party filed a suit against KGB Chairman Vladimir Kryuchkov in the Dzerzhinsky District Court in Moscow, "TSN" reported. The party charged that Kryuchkov had defamed it in an address delivered at the fourth session of the USSR Congress of People's Deputies in December.

Over 72,000 Evacuated from Contaminated Areas in 1990

Viktor Gubanov, head of the Committee for Questions of the Elimination of the Consequences of the Chernobyl' Accident, announced that 72,700 people had been evacuated from contaminated areas of Ukraine and Belorussia during 1990, TASS reported. The evacuees were moved from areas judged to have unacceptably high levels of radiation. According to Reuters on February 6, Gubanov said that a further 140,000 people would be moved from areas of moderate contamination in the course of 1991. Gubanov also announced that funds for the Chernobyl' cleanup would rise from 2.2 billion rubles in 1990 to 10.3 billion rubles in 1991— a nearly fivefold increase.

On February 7, TASS carried a statement by USSR Prosecutor-General Nikolai Trubin, who had begun an investigation into the responsibility of officials in eliminating the effects of the Chernobyl' nuclear disaster. TASS said there were indications of possible abuse of power and suggestions that some high-ranking officials had incorrectly evaluated the dimensions of the catastrophe and had therefore neglected to take necessary measures to protect people in contaminated areas.

More Land to Be Given to Uzbek Peasants

"Vremya" said Uzbek President Islam Karimov had decreed that more than 100,000 hectares of irrigated land should be distributed to peasants to increase the size of their private plots. Karimov told *Izvestia* (January 28) that 170,000 hectares had been distributed in 1990 under a program designed to increase food production in the republic. Village elders quoted by "Vremya" warned, however, that the plots would have to be larger if they were both to feed the villagers and yield enough extra produce to sell in town markets.

Azerbaijani Supreme Soviet Opens Session

The Azerbaijani Supreme Soviet opened a session with President Ayaz Mutalibov calling on deputies to work towards democratic reforms, TASS reported. Elmira Kafarova was reelected as chairman of the Azerbaijani Supreme Soviet. The deputies also discussed Nagorno-Karabakh, the draft of a new USSR Union treaty, and a return to the Latin alphabet, which was in use until 1940, when it was replaced by Cyrillic.

Fazail Agamaliev, a historian and parliamentary secretary of the Azerbaijani Popular Front, reported that about fifty non-Communist deputies who were attending the Supreme Soviet session for the first time had walked out in protest against police action against demonstrators outside the building. Supreme Soviet Deputy Chairman Tofik Bagirov went to the popular front headquarters to convince the deputies to return and was given three demands: one called for either lifting the state of emergency in Baku or moving the Supreme Soviet session to a city not under military control; the other two demands were for unedited television coverage of Supreme Soviet meetings and for the release of the nine demonstrators detained by the police (RL Azerbaijani service, February 6). These demands were later backed by workers in Azerbaijan who staged republican-wide strikes.

According to TASS, on February 6 the Azerbaijani Supreme Soviet voted to drop the words "Socialist" and "Soviet" from the republic's name and adopted a blue-red-green flag containing a white crescent and an eight-point star. The Supreme Soviet also approved a new national anthem and new state symbols.

On February 7, the Supreme Soviet resumed its session with the reelection of Gasan Gasanov as chairman of the Council of Ministers, TASS reported. It also elected a member of the Azerbaijani Popular Front, Tamerlan Karaev, as deputy chairman.

On February 9, strikes ended in Baku after the opposition and the republican Communist Party had reached agreement on a number of issues, including Nagorno-Karabakh. A joint statement called for the Azerbaijani leadership to present concrete proposals to the republican Supreme Soviet within twenty days on measures to ensure the security of Nagorno-Karabakh and of Azerbaijan's border with Armenia. In response to other demands of the strikers, some people who had been detained were released, and several hours a day of

The USSR in February, 1991

unedited television coverage of Supreme Soviet sessions was allowed (RL Azerbaijani service, February 9).

On February 15, the Azerbaijani Supreme Soviet published a resolution saying all issues involving the Nagorno-Karabakh region lay within the exclusive competence of Azerbaijan, TASS reported. The republican Supreme Soviet categorically rejected the possibility of establishing presidential rule in the region, saying it would be viewed as interference by Moscow in the internal affairs of Azerbaijan.

Crackdown on Corruption Snares Millionaire

Among those to come quickly to attention in the crackdown on corruption was the USSR's first legal millionaire, Artem Tarasov, a deputy of the RSFSR Supreme Soviet. Tarasov's foreign-trade company, "Istok," was raided by police on January 28 and its accounts confiscated. "Vremya" announced on February 5 that the Ministry of Internal Affairs would file criminal charges against Tarasov and his company. This was the third occasion on which a business run by Tarasov had been closed down by the police.

The USSR prosecutor-general asked the RSFSR parliament to lift Tarasov's parliamentary immunity so that charges could be brought against him for slandering President Gorbachev, who had threatened to sue Tarasov for alleging that he had reached a secret deal with Japan to return the disputed Kurile Islands in return for Japanese investment in the Soviet economy. TASS reported on February 7 that the charges had been denied by Japan as well as by the USSR. Tarasov had offered to apologize to Gorbachev, but the presidential press service said he was guilty of "an act of glaring political provocation."

Kirgiz Supreme Soviet Restores Frunze's Historical Name

The Kirgiz Supreme Soviet voted to change the name of the Kirgiz capital, Frunze, back to its former name, Bishkek. The city was renamed in 1926 to honor one of the Red Army commanders of the Civil War, Mikhail Frunze (RL Kirgiz service, February 6).

Cofounder of Republican Party Speaks at RFE/RL

Igor' Chubais, one of the leaders of the Republican Party (the former Democratic Platform), told an RFE/RL Research Institute seminar that his 20,000-member organization still relied on the structure of the CPSU throughout the country and therefore had an advantage over other democratic forces. He also stated that the Democratic Russia movement—the umbrella organization of all Russian democrats—had decided to establish its own cells in workers' collectives to challenge the CPSU.

Moldavian Opposition to March 17 Referendum

Novosti reported that Moldavian President Mircea Snegur had failed to obtain consent to his request, submitted during the session of the USSR Presidential Council on February 1, to have the March 17 referendum on the future of the USSR postponed in Moldavia. The Moldavian parliament was considering either calling for a boycott of the referendum or introducing additional questions on the ballot. TASS and Novosti reported, however, that the authorities of the self-proclaimed Dniester and Gagauz "republics" were actively preparing to hold the referendum in the areas of Moldavia under their control.

On February 19, the Moldavian Supreme Soviet voted to reject the holding of the referendum in Moldavia, TASS reported.

On February 28, Snegur said at a meeting of the Moldavian Presidential Council that the decision by the USSR Supreme Soviet to hold the March 17 referendum on the future of the Union was direct interference in the domestic affairs of a sovereign state. The Presidential Council also criticized the Moldavian Communist Party for its efforts to organize the referendum, despite the Moldavian Supreme Soviet's opposition.

Wednesday, February 6

Gorbachev Addresses Nation on Referendum

Soviet President Mikhail Gorbachev delivered a fifteen-minute address on "Vremya" urging participation in the March 17 referendum on the future of the Soviet Union. He rehearsed the arguments for preserving the Union, throwing in for good measure a reference to the "voluntary" unification of many peoples with Russia and a tribute to the Russian people. Gorbachev chided Estonia and Lithuania for ignoring the March 17 referendum and holding their own polls.

CPSU Central Committee Secretary and Chairman of the Party's Nationalities Policy Commission Andrei Girenko held a press conference on the March 17 referendum, TASS reported. Girenko claimed that a recent poll had indicated that about 80 percent of the population would take part in the referendum and that up to three-quarters would vote "yes." He said that, where republican authorities refused to hold the referendum, local authorities should take the initiative. He said it was up to the Central Referendum Commission to decide how the votes of conscripts should be counted.

Leningrad City Soviet Chairman Anatolii Sobchak told *Le Monde* in an interview summarized by Reuters that he would vote "no" in order to avoid reinforcing

The USSR in February, 1991

Gorbachev's concept of a centralized union. In his view, a "yes" vote would encourage Gorbachev to take a hard line, which would only stiffen opposition in the republics. If, however, the referendum results were negative, Sobchak predicted, Gorbachev would be obliged to resign. Sobchak said he was optimistic that the USSR could avoid anarchy and civil war and that the republics could reach agreement among themselves and establish a new system of power that would reduce Gorbachev's role.

Politburo Urges Action against Opponents of Socialism

TASS quoted a CPSU Politburo resolution as saying activities by separatist, nationalist, and anti-Socialist forces must be stopped by the Communists, since these forces were trying to bring about the disintegration of the Soviet Union and were intensifying criticism and slander of the Soviet state and the CPSU. The resolution was entitled "On the Work of Party Organizations on the Eve of the Referendum on the Preservation of the Soviet Union" and was published in *Pravda* on February 7.

Ligachev Calls for Change in Soviet Foreign Policy

Former Politburo member Egor Ligachev called for a complete review of Soviet foreign policy and a return to the priority of class interests over human values. He told *Sovetskaya Rossiya* that democrats were wrongly accusing Soviet President Mikhail Gorbachev of dictatorship. In reality, Gorbachev must be criticized for his liberalism, Ligachev added. He urged Gorbachev to rely more on the Party. He said only the Party and "renewed" soviets could lead the country out of crisis. Ligachev stated that the loss of Eastern Europe had been a heavy blow to the world Socialist movement (*TASS*, February 6).

El'tsin Introduces Members of Advisory Council

RSFSR Supreme Soviet Chairman Boris El'tsin held a press conference in Moscow to introduce the members of his Advisory Council. The council, which began operating in December, 1990, brought together some twenty experts in various fields. (*Nezavisimaya gazeta*, No. 2, December 28, 1990, carried a list of the council's members, who were mainly liberals.)

General Criticizes RSFSR Defense Committee

Lieutenant General Boris Tarasov, an RSFSR people's deputy, told TASS that the new Russian State Committee for Defense and Security was an instrument for weakening, and perhaps even eliminating, the Soviet Armed Forces. Tarasov said that the RSFSR should instead establish a national security committee to deal with oil-pipeline safety, natural disasters, and other matters not related to the activities of the armed forces.

Gamsakhurdia Accuses Moscow of Supporting Ossetians

Chairman of the Georgian Supreme Soviet Zviad Gamsakhurdia told AP in an interview that Moscow was encouraging the separatist movement in South Ossetia in order to have a pretext for imposing presidential rule in Georgia and that Ossetians serving in the Soviet Armed Forces were supplying the separatists with arms and weapons.

Kravchuk Repeats Ukraine's Wish to Be CSCE Member

Speaking at the forty-seventh session of the UN Commission on Human Rights in Geneva, Ukrainian Supreme Soviet Chairman Leonid Kravchuk said his republic was committed to creating a truly democratic society that would conform to international standards of human rights, AP reported. Kravchuk reminded his audience that Ukraine had declared its intention to become a full-fledged member of the Conference on Security and Cooperation in Europe. Kravchuk also called for more foreign investment in Ukraine, saying that foreign investors would enjoy equal rights with local entrepreneurs (*Radio Kiev*, February 6).

Ukraine Adopts Law on Employment

TASS said the Ukrainian Supreme Soviet had adopted a law on employment. The bill was prepared in accordance with International Labor Organization guidelines. Among other things, it defined the legal status of the unemployed, whose numbers were expected to reach 1.5 million people in the industrial sector of the Ukrainian economy alone. According to Radio Kiev on February 7, the law envisaged that about 3 percent of the republican and local budgets should be allocated for unemployment benefits and retraining.

TASS Criticizes EC Reaction to Soviet Actions in Baltic Republics

TASS commentator Al'bert Balebanov accused the European Community's foreign ministers of "ambiguous intervention in the Soviet Union's internal affairs" and of exerting "pressure on Moscow in tackling the problems of its relations with the Baltic Soviet republics." Balebanov was reacting to the EC foreign ministers' decision to hold back aid to the USSR after the Soviet crackdown in the Baltic and to their decision to send observers to Lithuania and Estonia, which were intending to hold polls on independence.

The USSR in February, 1991

On February 22, the European Parliament unfroze the 1-billion-dollar European Community food-aid program to the Soviet Union, AP reported. The package consisted of 350 million dollars in emergency food aid and 700 million dollars in European Community credit guarantees to allow the USSR to buy food. Final approval for the aid was given after Luxembourg's foreign minister, Jacques Poos, had determined that the Soviet Union's attitude towards the Baltic republics had improved.

Centrist Bloc for Presidential Rule in the Baltic

The leader of the conservative Centrist Bloc of political parties and organizations, Vladimir Voronin, said that the fate of the Soviet Union was more important than republican demands for sovereignty. He urged Gorbachev to introduce presidential rule in the Baltic (*TASS*, February 6).

Thursday, February 7

RSFSR to Add Question of Presidency to Referendum

The RSFSR Supreme Soviet voted to add a number of questions to the March 17 referendum on the future of the Soviet Union, AFP reported. Among them was a question on whether the RSFSR should have its own president elected by popular ballot. El'tsin also proposed that a question on ownership of land and property should be included in the referendum.

On February 19, the RSFSR Central Commission for holding the USSR and RSFSR referendums approved the formulation of the two questions to be asked in the RSFSR referendum, TASS reported. The questions were: "Do you consider necessary the preservation of the RSFSR as a single federative multinational state in a renewed Union?" and "Do you consider necessary the introduction of the post of president of the RSFSR elected by universal vote?" These were the only two questions backed by the necessary number of deputies' signatures.

Akhromeev Attacks El'tsin

In an article carried by *Sovetskaya Rossiya*, Soviet Marshal Sergei Akhromeev accused RSFSR Supreme Soviet Chairman Boris El'tsin of conducting an open struggle against President Gorbachev and the USSR Supreme Soviet, TASS reported. Akhromeev wrote that El'tsin had been joined in this by the leadership of the Interregional Group of Deputies and the chairmen of the Moscow and Leningrad city soviets. He accused

Eavesdropping Equipment Found above El'tsin's Office

RSFSR people's deputy Boris Nemtsov told the RSFSR Supreme Soviet that one of the rooms directly above El'tsin's office had been opened during the night of February 6 by people's deputies, public prosecutors, and KGB officials and had been found to contain electronic equipment belonging to the KGB, Reuters and Interfax reported. The search followed the publication in *Komsomol'skaya pravda* of an article alleging that the KGB was eavesdropping on El'tsin. According to TASS, the RSFSR Supreme Soviet opened an investigation.

On February 8, however, the KGB denied that the equipment was being used to spy on El'tsin. It claimed that it was designed to protect RSFSR Prime Minister Ivan Silaev from eavesdropping. According to Evgenii Neskoromnyi, a former KGB officer employed by the RSFSR Supreme Soviet, the equipment could be used either for eavesdropping or to counter it (*AFP*, February 8).

Komsomol'skaya pravda Determined to Stay Independent

The chief editor of *Komsomol'skaya pravda*, Vladislav Fronin, said in an interview published by the *Los Angeles Times* that there had been a shift to the right in the Soviet Union. Fronin said that, if Gorbachev could find a way, he might well reimpose controls on the media but that *Komsomol'skaya pravda* was free of censorship and was determined to compete journalistically, politically, and commercially.

More Than 60,000 Die on Soviet Roads in 1990

More than 60,000 people were killed in road accidents in the Soviet Union in 1990, B. Korekovsky, a senior MVD official, reported on Soviet television. Korekovsky blamed much of the death toll of 63,362 on lax attitudes towards driving and drunkenness. He accused the USSR Supreme Soviet of failing to take road safety seriously by putting off legislation on criminal responsibility for road crashes until completion of a Union treaty.

Shevardnadze Criticized

The Kiev branch of "Edinstvo" attacked former Soviet Foreign Minister Eduard Shevardnadze for his support of the UN resolution supporting military force in the Gulf, TASS reported. According to *Komsomol'skaya pravda*, the Kiev committee distributed leaflets saying that, in supporting the resolution, Shevardnadze had signed a death sentence for Arabs on behalf of the Soviet Union. *Sovetskaya Rossiya* also accused Shevardnadze and the USSR Foreign Ministry of conducting "secret policies" that ignored public opinion and that of elected bodies (*Radio Moscow*, February 7).

Kazakhstan Turns Down Offer for Use of Test Site at Semipalatinsk

The USSR government offered 350 million rubles to Kazakhstan in return for allowing the testing of eighteen more nuclear devices at the Semipalatinsk test range in the period up till 1993, Novosti reported. The chairman of the Kazakh Supreme Soviet Committee for Ecology and the Rational Use of Natural Resources, Marash Nurtazin, was quoted as saying that the Supreme Soviet had decided not to allow military nuclear tests to be conducted at the expense of public health and had turned down the money. Tests of all weapons of mass destruction were banned from the republic following a campaign by environmentalists, who presented evidence of radiation leaks and injuries to people and cattle.

Controversy over Airtime for El'tsin

The RSFSR Supreme Soviet debated the controversy over Boris El'tsin's request to be allowed to speak on Central Television. El'tsin had asked to speak for one hour live on the first channel, but the USSR State Committee for Television and Radio Broadcasting offered him thirty minutes for a prerecorded speech on the second channel (*Central Television*, February 7).

***Pravda* Defends Central Television**

Pravda defended Central Television against criticism over its lack of objectivity, asserting that it succeeded in providing a range of opinion. "No political party can have a monopoly over one channel or a television program," the newspaper stated, accusing democratic forces in the country of trying to monopolize television. In fact, as critics of the USSR State Committee for Television and Radio Broadcasting pointed out, many important television programs, including "Vremya," had returned to the previous practice of expressing just one point of view, that of the CPSU.

Turkmen Supreme Court Rejects Conviction against Nurmyradov

A senior official of the "Agzybirlik" popular front organization, Nurberdi Nurmammedov, said judges of the Turkmen Supreme Court had overturned the conviction of writer and "Agzybirlik" activist Shiraly Nurmyradov. The writer was convicted of defrauding a woman of money on December 1, 1990, but "Agzybirlik" contended that this was a trumped-up charge and that Nurmyradov was really being prosecuted because he had ridiculed Turkmen President Saparmurad Niyazov in his books. The court ruled that there was insufficient evidence to sentence Nurmyradov to seven years in prison. They recommended a new investigation of the case (RL Turkmen service, February 7).

"Rukh" on Referendum

The Ukrainian popular movement "Rukh" requested that the USSR Committee for Constitutional Supervision examine the constitutionality of the USSR Supreme Soviet decree on conducting the March 17 referendum on the preservation of the USSR, Radio Kiev reported. According to the report, "Rukh" also addressed a statement to the Ukrainian Supreme Soviet calling the referendum "illegal."

Ukrainian Property Law Adopted

TASS and Radio Kiev outlined the newly adopted Ukrainian law on property. The law provides for individual, collective, state, and intellectual forms of property and declares the republic the sole owner of its land, natural resources, means of production, and financial resources. It also claims ownership of part of the Soviet gold reserves. The law failed, however, to clarify the status of property belonging to political organizations.

Friday, February 8

Gorbachev Issues Decree on Gosteleradio

Soviet President Mikhail Gorbachev issued a decree turning the USSR State Committee for Television and Radio Broadcasting (Gosteleradio) into a broadcasting company (*Pravda*, February 9). The new company was to take over the functions and funding of Gosteleradio. The decree did not specify how the company would differ from the committee. The decree also ordered the chairman of Gosteleradio, Leonid Kravchenko, who was to head the new company, to set up a national Radio and Television Broadcasting Council and invited the leaders of republic-level broadcasting organizations to join the council.

On February 11, Reuters quoted Kravchenko as saying at a press conference in Moscow that he would be subordinate only to Gorbachev. (Previously, Kravchenko's nomination would have had to be approved by the USSR Supreme Soviet.) Kravchenko rejected a plan to transfer some television and radio equipment belonging to the former Gosteleradio to the newly created RSFSR television and radio system. He suggested, however, that the creation of a new company would broaden the rights of republican television and radio organizations. He said the new company would not attempt to establish control over broadcasting equipment belonging to republican organizations. Asked specifically about the television center in Vilnius, which was still occupied by the armed forces, he said the center belonged to Lithuania, since its creation had been financed from the republican, not the all-Union budget, TASS reported.

At the same conference Kravchenko confirmed that the Soviet media had deliberately distorted coverage of the interethnic clashes in Nagorno-Karabakh to give the impression that casualties on both sides were more or less equal. Both Armenia and Azerbaijan had accused the Soviet media of lacking objectivity in reporting on the situation in Nagorno-Karabakh.

Personnel Changes in the KGB

KGB Chairman Vladimir Kryuchkov announced some personnel changes in the KGB. TASS said the former head of Soviet Counterintelligence, Viktor Grushko, had been appointed first deputy chairman of the KGB and would be replaced in his former position by Gennadii Titov. Grushko replaced Filip Bobkov, who had been assigned to work as a consultant to the USSR Ministry of Defense. Deputy Chairman of the KGB Vladimir Pirozhkov was reported to have retired, but TASS did not say who would replace him.

RSFSR Supreme Soviet to Help North Ossetia

The RSFSR Supreme Soviet approved economic and humanitarian assistance for North Ossetia. Many had fled to North Ossetia to avoid ethnic unrest in South Ossetia, and North Ossetia was said to be in need of food, medicine, and fuel (*Radio Moscow*, February 8).

Alksnis Calls for Authoritarian Rule

A leading member of the "Soyuz" faction in the USSR Congress of People's Deputies, Lieutenant Colonel Viktor Alksnis, declared in an interview published in *The Washington Post* that Gorbachev should establish a period of martial authoritarian rule or resign. Alksnis was quoted as saying that Gorbachev might dissolve the USSR Supreme Soviet as well as the republican Supreme Soviets "by force" to establish "a national salvation committee" to rule the country. Alksnis said he was speaking for "the silent majority" of Soviet people.

Georgian Prime Minister Offers Food in Exchange for Weapons

TASS reported that Georgian Prime Minister Tengiz Sigua had offered food and other products to a weapons plant in Tula in exchange for arms. Sigua requested 10,000 hunting rifles, 500 assault rifles, and 500 other guns. The plant's director, Nikolai Maslennikov refused, however, to consider the offer without a decision by the USSR Ministry of Defense and the Cabinet of Ministers. The Georgian Supreme Soviet voted in January to create a 12,000-person republican National Guard.

Yanaev in Kuzbass

Soviet Vice President Gennadii Yanaev toured the Kuzbass region of Western Siberia and promised coal miners in Novokuznetsk that the government would not raise retail prices "until a law on compensation and other bills protecting the population" had been passed. According to TASS, Yanaev extracted a pledge from the miners not to strike. Following the events in Vilnius in January, leaders of miners' strike committees in the Kuzbass had expressed their willingness to join a general strike calling for Gorbachev's ouster.

Saturday, February 9

Gorbachev Makes Statement on Gulf War

Gorbachev said in a formal statement concerning the Gulf conflict that "the logic of the military operations and the character of the military actions" threatened to go beyond the mandate of UN Resolution 678 on the use of force against Iraq, TASS reported. Gorbachev also appealed to Saddam Hussein to "display realism."

Shevardnadze Creates Foreign-Policy Association

Former Soviet Foreign Minister Eduard Shevardnadze was reported to have created a foreign-policy association to promote links between the USSR and the rest of the world at a nongovernmental level. Interfax said the organizing committee of the research group included some of the USSR's leading political scientists and diplomats. Interfax also said Shevardnadze had turned down offers to teach at US universities and to go on a speaking tour in the West, AFP reported.

In a German television (ZDF) interview on February 12, Shevardnadze said that the USSR's reform process appeared doomed but that it could still be saved if democratically inclined people joined forces. Shevardnadze said he would not withdraw totally from political life.

The USSR in February, 1991

Democratic Russia Forms Own Party Structures

The newspaper *Kuranty* said the Democratic Russia movement had begun to establish its own organizational structures in workers' collectives. It said more than 100 primary Democratic Russia organizations had already been formed in enterprises and institutes in Moscow. A vertical structure of Democratic Russia was also being created.

RSFSR Confirms Composition of Republican Security Committee

RSFSR Supreme Soviet deputy Colonel General Dmitrii Volkogonov confirmed the composition of the republic's Security Committee, TASS reported. He said the fourteen-member committee would focus on ties with the Soviet army and influence the buildup of the armed forces to an extent necessary to ensure Russia's security. Volkogonov stressed that the RSFSR did not need its own army. Besides, he said, it would cost 35–40 billion rubles to maintain such an army.

Named as head of the Security Committee was Sergei Stepashin, chairman of the Subcommission for Army Servicemen's Issues of the RSFSR Supreme Soviet. Stepashin was subsequently interviewed on Central Television on February 12. He said that a major task of the new legislative organ was the creation of an executive body for republican security issues—a Russian KGB—and that his committee would work out a transfer of those structures of the all-Union KGB that were situated on the territory of the RSFSR to the RSFSR leadership. He noted that the concept of a Russian KGB would be based on protecting individual rights, not those of the state, adding that a law on state security would be adopted in the RSFSR legislature.

El'tsin Says Kaliningrad Will Remain Part of Russia

During a weekend tour of Kaliningrad Oblast, RSFSR Supreme Soviet Chairman Boris El'tsin made a series of speeches emphasizing flexibility and his commitment to maintaining the Union. Speaking to officers of the Kaliningrad garrison and the Baltic Fleet, El'tsin said the RSFSR was not planning to set up its own army, although he did not rule out the possibility of a Russian military role in the future. He admitted that a proposal had once been made about the formation of a republican armed force but denied that the matter had been discussed by the RSFSR Supreme Soviet, TASS reported. El'tsin also affirmed that the RSFSR leadership did not seek a confrontation with Soviet President Mikhail Gorbachev or with the USSR government. He sought to reassure his audiences that Kaliningrad would remain part of Russia and that supplies would be guaranteed even if Lithuania, which lies between Kaliningrad and the rest of the RSFSR, became independent.

Fewer Books by Gorbachev to Be Published in 1991

A spokesman for the Politizdat publishers in Moscow told Novosti that the propaganda department of the publishing house had decided to publish fewer books by Soviet President Gorbachev in 1991. He explained that the decision was due to a rise in the cost of paper and to the fact that Gorbachev's books were not selling well. The spokesman added, however, that the publication of a multivolume edition of Gorbachev's selected speeches and articles would be continued.

Soviet-Mongolian Talks

Soviet and Mongolian Prime Ministers Valentin Pavlov and Dashiyn Byambasuren opened talks in Moscow. According to TASS, USSR Minister of Foreign Economic Relations Konstantin Katushev said the talks focused on trade and payments in freely convertible currency and on the working conditions of Soviet construction organizations in Mongolia.

Anti-Communist Rally in Kiev

About 2,000 people attended an unsanctioned rally in Kiev, shouting anti-Communist and antigovernment slogans, TASS reported. Speakers, including leaders of the opposition Ukrainian Republican Party, demanded the release from jail of Stepan Khmara, an opposition deputy in the Ukrainian Supreme Soviet who was arrested in November on charges of attacking a policeman. They also called for a separate Ukrainian poll in advance of the March 17 all-Union referendum on the future of the Soviet Union.

Call for Presidential Rule in South Ossetia

Pravda reported that 700 primary Party organizations in the North Ossetian ASSR had called for the introduction of presidential rule in South Ossetia. Water and power supplies to the blockaded oblast capital, Tskhinvali, were reported to have been cut off, hospitals to be without heat, and the population to be "on the verge of starvation." Some 6,000 Ossetians were said to have fled across the Caucasus through the snow to North Ossetia, some of them dying. TASS reported that a Soviet soldier had been injured when unknown gunmen opened fire on a military vehicle transporting troops to a road that had been blockaded for months by armed civilians.

On February 11, TASS reported that members of the Vladikavkaz City Soviet in North Ossetia had written

The USSR in February, 1991

to Soviet President Mikhail Gorbachev saying the situation demanded decisive and immediate action.

On February 12, Georgian power workers stated their conditions for ending their power blockade of South Ossetia, which had been going on since February 3, TASS reported. They said they wanted two factories in South Ossetia to be opened for inspection by a joint commission from the USSR and Georgian governments. They claimed that the two factories had been illegally manufacturing arms. They also demanded that all weapons in the hands of the Ossetian population be surrendered and that reprisals against Georgian families in the region end. Meanwhile, the Presidium of the Georgian Supreme Soviet again extended the state of emergency in Tskhinvali until March 12 because of the continuing difficult situation in the city (*TASS*, February 12).

On February 12, the USSR Ministry of Internal Affairs forced down a helicopter that was flying a mission for the Georgian Ministry of Internal Affairs. There were twenty-three Georgians on board, and their baggage contained firearms, ammunition, grenades, and sixty kilograms of explosives (*TASS*, February 12).

On February 15, Radio Tbilisi reported that the Georgian Supreme Soviet had sent a letter to the commander of the Transcaucasus Military District saying his troops were encouraging violence in South Ossetia. The letter also said that the Georgian government would continue to do all it could to suppress acts of violence against the republic's population without the interference of outside force. Radio Tbilisi also reported that vandals had burned down the home of Vakhtans Gorgidze, the regional police chief of Tskhinvali.

On February 16, TASS quoted Georgian Foreign Minister Giorgi Khoshtaria as affirming that Georgia would not restore South Ossetia's status as an autonomous oblast. Khoshtaria argued that the Ossetians could claim only "cultural autonomy."

The same day, many thousands of people attended a rally in Vladikavkaz, the North Ossetian capital, to honor the memory of the victims of the past two years of interethnic conflict, TASS reported. Participants adopted appeals to Soviet President Mikhail Gorbachev and to the Supreme Soviets of the USSR and the RSFSR calling for effective and urgent measures to restore law and order in South Ossetia.

On February 17, the Presidium of the Federation Council of Independent Trade Unions of the RSFSR allocated 150,000 rubles in aid to South Ossetia, Radio Moscow reported. The decision was made in response to appeals to help citizens living in the region.

On February 20 the USSR Supreme Soviet voted to impose a state of emergency in South Ossetia if the Georgian authorities did not themselves extend the state of emergency throughout the oblast and take steps to halt fighting there. The Georgian Supreme Soviet was also instructed to end the blockade of Tskhinvali and to restore electricity and fuel supplies to the city, TASS reported.

On February 22, Chairman of the Georgian Supreme Soviet Zviad Gamsakhurdia met with Soviet First Deputy Prime Minister Lev Voronin in Tbilisi to discuss how to end armed clashes in South Ossetia, TASS reported. Voronin toured those regions covered by Georgia's state of emergency and also went to Vladikavkaz.

On February 23, several people were reported to have been wounded in shooting incidents in Tskhinvali, despite MVD troops' efforts to disband nationalist militias in Georgia. Troops seized several kalashnikov submachine guns, seven pistols, ten rifles, hand grenades, and a radio transmitter; forty-three people were detained, Interfax reported.

On February 24, four people were killed and eight wounded in an attack on the village of Avnevi (*TASS*, February 25). Postfactum reported the same day that two ethnic Georgians had also been killed nearby. USSR Minister of Internal Affairs Boriss Pugo told the USSR Supreme Soviet that thirty-three people had died so far in 1991 in ethnic clashes between Georgians and South Ossetians, TASS reported on February 25.

On February 25, Zviad Gamsakhurdia sent a letter to USSR Supreme Soviet Chairman Anatolii Luk'yanov in which he rejected the USSR Supreme Soviet's demand that Georgia declare a state of emergency throughout South Ossetia, TASS reported. Gamsakhurdia did offer to hold talks with South Ossetia, provided Ossetian militants stopped their activities.

One policeman was killed and two others injured in an attack on a police station in the village of Avnevi on February 26, TASS reported. Meanwhile, Georgian Supreme Soviet spokesman Kudzha Rhundadze told Reuters in a telephone interview that electricity was being restored to South Ossetia in an attempt to establish calm. Deputy Chairman of the USSR Supreme Soviet's Council of Nationalities Boris Oleinik was quoted in *Sovetskaya Rossyia* as saying a commission should be sent to Tbilisi and to Tskhinvali to negotiate a settlement (*Reuters*, February 26).

According to an Interfax report, two MVD soldiers, one Lithuanian and one Latvian, deserted from their units in South Ossetia on February 27 and joined Georgian troops to protest against the Soviet army's involvement in South Ossetia. They declared that they wanted to continue their military service as part of the Georgian Ministry of Internal Affairs.

An open letter published in *Rabochaya tribuna* on February 28 and signed by a group of intellectuals from South Ossetia urged Gorbachev to enforce law and order in the region.

Russian Democratic Group Formed in Moldavia

Moldovapres reported that "Demokraticheskaya Moldaviya," "a sociopolitical movement" of Russian-speaking residents of Moldavia had been established in Kishinev. Its program called for "eliminating the consequences of the Communist regime," "a return to authentic democracy," observance of Moldavian laws, and support for the revival of the Moldavian language as a state language. Decrying "the negative effects of Moldavia's remaining part of the USSR," "Demokraticheskaya Moldaviya" declared that "the Romanian population of the republic could find the guarantees for its national development only in the framework of a unified Romanian state."

Overwhelming Vote in Favor of Lithuanian Independence

Residents of Lithuania went to the polls to vote on whether Lithuania should become an independent, democratic state. Radio Moscow reported on February 11 that 2,247,810 of the 2,652,738 eligible voters had participated in the poll, with 2,028,339 voting "yes," 147,040 voting "no" and 66,614 casting invalid votes.

On February 12, presidential spokesman Vitalii Ignatenko said Gorbachev viewed the poll on independence as "a sociological survey," TASS reported. Commenting on the Icelandic parliament's decision to recognize Lithuania's independence, Ignatenko said that Iceland sought to establish diplomatic relations with "an as yet nonexistent entity."

Sunday, February 10

Conservative Groups Demonstrate in Leningrad

Several thousand Leningrad residents participated in protests against Baltic independence movements, the Gulf war, and the reformist city soviet. TASS said 4,000 people were present, but Leningrad police put the figure at between 7,000 and 8,000. The rally was organized by nationalist groups, including war veterans, the Communist Party, and the "Soyuz" faction of the USSR Congress of People's Deputies, AP reported. A resolution adopted by the demonstrators called for the removal of Leningrad administration officials "who have compromised themselves through their action or lack of action" and proposed the formation of a committee to prepare a referendum to gauge popular support for the city soviet.

Democratic Kyrgyzstan Group Holds Congress

The Democratic Kyrgyzstan movement ended its first congress in Bishkek, TASS reported on February 11. Six hundred delegates attended the congress, at which the group's cochairman Kazat Akhmatov, a member of the Kirgiz Presidential Council, said that Kirgizia should join the group of four republics (the RSFSR, Ukraine, Belorussia, and Kazakhstan) that were discussing cooperation among themselves to avoid the dictates of the center. The congress set up organizational structures, including a council with three cochairmen, and elected an editor of the movement's newspaper, *Maidan*.

Monday, February 11

Report of Protest by Soviet Troops in Nagorno-Karabakh Denied

General Yu. Eremeev, chief of staff of the Baku garrison, refuted a Postfactum report that on the night of February 8–9 some 150 servicemen stationed in Stepanakert had marched along the town's Lenin Boulevard shouting "Send us home" and "Down with the Azerbaijani OMON." Azerbaijani special police (OMON) troops had been implicated by the Armenian media in numerous acts of brutality towards the Armenian population of Nagorno-Karabakh (*TASS-Azerinform*, February 11).

Pravda Criticizes Prenatal Care

Pravda criticized the bad state of prenatal care and maternity hospitals in the USSR. The newspaper said that 14,000 women had died in childbirth since 1985 and that 200,000 babies had not survived their first birthday, because of the substandard, unhygienic conditions and the lack of medicine, diagnostic equipment, and disinfectants in maternity clinics. It said that premature births were increasing and that 40 percent of Soviet women went through pregnancy without any medical checkups. *Pravda* said the USSR's infant mortality rate was 24.7 per 1,000.

Primakov in Teheran, Baghdad

On his way to Baghdad, Evgenii Primakov, Gorbachev's special envoy, stopped in Teheran for talks with Iranian

THE USSR IN FEBRUARY, 1991

Deputy Foreign Minister Abbas Maleki. AFP quoted Primakov as saying "we want our diplomatic efforts to be in line and in coordination with Iranian efforts."

According to AFP on February 12, on arrival in Baghdad, Primakov was first given a tour of bomb-hit areas of the city, then had a working lunch with Secretary of State for Foreign Affairs Saad Abdel Majid Al-Faisal, and met afterwards with Iraqi President Saddam Hussein. Members of Saddam's Revolutionary Command Council were present. Primakov delivered a message to Saddam from Soviet President Gorbachev.

On February 13, AP quoted Radio Baghdad as claiming that Iraq was willing to cooperate with the USSR in the interests of finding a peaceful, political solution. Palestine Liberation Organization Chairman Yasser Arafat traveled to Baghdad to meet with Primakov and Iraqi officials, Reuters reported.

On February 13, Primakov held a news conference upon his return to Moscow from Iraq, via Teheran, saying that his talks with Saddam had given cause for optimism about a cease-fire, TASS reported.

The same day, the Moscow City Soviet newspaper *Kuranty*, commenting on the significance of Primakov's mission to Iraq, said that, if the Soviet effort to bring peace in the Gulf were successful, Gorbachev would win needed points on the international level and would boost his image as a world peacemaker, an image tarnished by the crackdown in Lithuania.

Nazarbaev on Preservation of Union

TASS reported that a special session of the Kazakh Supreme Soviet had adopted an appeal for dialogue among those republics that wished to preserve the Union. Kazakh President Nursultan Nazarbaev read out the appeal to the deputies, arguing that the political and economic interests of Kazakhstan required the preservation of the Union and warning that the disintegration of the USSR would lead to economic collapse and a worsening of living conditions.

Ukraine to Mine Its Own Gold

Ukrainian Supreme Soviet Chairman Leonid Kravchuk announced at a press conference in Kiev that, in order to introduce its own currency, Ukraine would mine its own gold, deposits of which he said existed in the Dnepropetrovsk and Transcarpathian Oblasts, Radio Kiev reported. The Ukrainian Supreme Soviet approved a plan in November, 1990, for economic and political independence that called for a separate Ukrainian currency.

Radio Kiev on February 12 claimed that expeditions by the Ukrainian Institute of Geology and Physics had discovered more than ten gold deposits that were economically feasible. One of these, located on the river Mokra Sura (a tributary of the Dnieper in Dnepropetrovsk Oblast), had been discovered some twenty-five years earlier but was kept secret by the USSR Ministry of Geology.

Moldavian Groups Hold Round Table

The Moldavian Popular Front and allied groups held talks for the first time with the pro-Moscow Joint Council of Work Collectives and other Russian groups in Tiraspol, capital of the self-proclaimed "Dniester SSR." TASS reported that the two sides disagreed over the proposed treaty of Union, with the Moldavians declaring support for the position of the republican leadership, which opposed the treaty, and most of the Russian groups demanding that Moldavia sign the treaty in its existing form without delay. Despite the disagreement, the sides pledged to continue the discussions.

Moldavian President in Romania

Moldavian President Mircea Snegur began an official visit to Romania and was received with the full honors reserved for visiting heads of state, according to Radio Bucharest on February 12. Snegur and Moldavian Minister of External Relations Nicolae Tiu held three sessions of talks with Romanian President Ion Iliescu and Prime Minister Petre Roman, covering cultural, economic, and political relations between Moldavia and Romania. Addressing a joint session of the two chambers of the Romanian parliament, Snegur asserted the common Moldavian-Romanian identity and spoke of "a cultural confederation," possibly to be followed in the future by "some other type of confederation" between Moldavia and Romania. Before leaving Bucharest on February 13, Snegur met with Teoctist, the patriarch of the Romanian Orthodox Church.

Tuesday, February 12

French Foreign Minister in Moscow

French Foreign Minister Roland Dumas met in Moscow with Soviet President Mikhail Gorbachev, Soviet Foreign Minister Aleksandr Bessmertnykh, and Soviet Prime Minister Valentin Pavlov, AFP reported. USSR Foreign Ministry spokesman Vitalii Churkin said at a press briefing on February 11 that "the consultations with France will enable the two sides to understand better the situation in the Gulf and the chances of achieving the earliest possible settlement in compliance with the well-known UN Security Council resolutions."

Dumas told reporters in Moscow that France and the USSR had agreed on the aims of the allied campaign against Iraq as well as on the need for a Middle East settlement after the war. Dumas also said Gorbachev had expressed both regret at the lack of Western understanding for the difficulties he faced and his determination to succeed despite everything, AFP reported on February 13. According to Dumas, Gorbachev also rejected suggestions that he had turned to the right in his policies.

Meanwhile, an agreement was signed in Paris at the end of a two-day meeting of the Franco-Soviet Intergovernmental Commission granting about 600 million dollars worth of credits to the USSR. The credits were divided into two parts: one of 200 million dollars for grain purchases totaling 2.5 million tons in 1991; and the other of 400 million dollars for machinery and equipment.

Former RSFSR Finance Minister to Work for EBRD

Boris Fedorov, who resigned as RSFSR finance minister in 1990, was reported to have been recruited by the newly created European Bank for Reconstruction and Development (EBRD) in London, the *Financial Times* reported. He was appointed to head a department of the EBRD, which was set up by forty nations together with the European Commission and the European Investment Bank to support the transition by East European countries to market economies. Fedorov had given up his ministerial post in protest over what he viewed as Chairman of the RSFSR Supreme Soviet Boris El'tsin's unprofessional economic policy.

"Shield" Investigators Detained in Lithuania

Three reserve officers—Lieutenant Colonel Ivan Bichkov and Captains Aleksandr Evstigneev and Gennadii Melkov—were detained by army and KGB officers at the Vilnius railroad station prior to their departure for Moscow, ELTA reported. They were part of a five-member investigative commission from the proreform Soviet military organization "Shield." The commission had spent two weeks in Lithuania investigating the situation there and had concluded that the crackdown in Lithuania in January was a prelude to a planned coup. "Shield" was quoted on February 13 by DPA as saying the results of the investigation, including tape recordings and other documents, had been brought to a safe place. Colonel Sergei Gudinov and Major Nikolai Moskovchenko, members of "Shield," denied that the three detained men possessed weapons or narcotics, as the KGB had asserted (RFE Lithuanian service, February 13).

The Boston Globe on February 13 quoted some Soviet and Lithuanian sources as alleging that a KGB elite unit had led the January 13 attack in Vilnius. But the newly appointed deputy chairman of the KGB, Viktor Grushko, told reporters that the KGB was not involved and that the one casualty among the attacking forces, who was identified as a KGB officer, was alone. Earlier, another KGB officer, Major General Aleksandr Karbainov, had said that a team of about fifteen KGB men had been brought into Vilnius a few days before the attack. He later said, however, that their task was limited to protecting the populace.

The three detained officers were finally released on February 13 and allowed to resume their train journey to Moscow. One of them said they had not been mistreated during their detention (*Radio Vilnius*, February 14).

On February 15, Novosti quoted "Shield" as saying its investigation of the Soviet crackdown in Vilnius had shown that the armed forces had acted with the knowledge of President Gorbachev and other officials. "Shield" blamed Gorbachev, the KGB chairman, and the USSR ministers of defense and internal affairs for approving unconstitutional moves by military units in Lithuania (*TASS*, February 15).

Pavlov Accuses Western Banks of Planning to Annex Soviet Economy

Interviewed by *Trud*, USSR Prime Minister Valentin Pavlov justified the recent withdrawal of 50- and 100-ruble bank notes as a protective measure designed to thwart an international conspiracy, the aims of which were, he said, to flood the USSR with a huge amount of money, bringing about artificial hyperinflation; to annex the Soviet economy; and to topple Soviet President Mikhail Gorbachev. Pavlov claimed the banks involved in the plot were Soviet, Canadian, Austrian, and Swiss but did not name them or say how they had acquired the cash.

The same day, Bryan Griffiths, a senior vice president responsible for foreign exchange at the Royal Bank of Canada, ridiculed Pavlov's allegation as preposterous, Reuters reported. The Union Bank of Switzerland, the Swiss Bankers' Association, and the Federal Banking Commission also rejected the accusation as absurd and said Swiss bankers had no interest in destabilizing the USSR, AP reported on February 13.

On February 14, US State Department spokeswoman Margaret Tutwiler also called the allegation "ridiculous" and said that it would hurt Soviet efforts to attract foreign investment, AP reported.

Grushko Says West Has Stepped Up Spying

At a press conference, First Deputy Chairman of the KGB Viktor Grushko accused the CIA and other Western intelligence agencies of increasing military industrial espionage within the USSR, despite very positive changes in international relations. As reported by TASS and Reuters, Grushko said the KGB Administration for Protection of the Constitutional Order had been created to fight extremist trends in sociopolitical life and "anticonstitutional" organizations and terrorism at home and abroad. The recent reshuffle at the top of the KGB was designed to increase the efficiency of the agency, Grushko said. At the same conference, Grushko and the head of KGB public relations, Aleksandr Karbainov, also repeated denials that the KGB had spied on RSFSR Supreme Soviet Chairman Boris El'tsin.

USSR Signs Antidoping Convention

The Soviet Union signed the Council of Europe's "antidoping" convention against the use of drugs in sports, AFP reported on February 13. The convention called for international laws providing for permanent controls at sports competitions as well as binding standards to limit the use of anabolic steroids. The USSR also signed another convention, which provided for policing of public sporting events and for measures prohibiting the sale of alcoholic beverages near sports stadiums.

Independent Radio Station in Khabarovsk

A radio station independent of both the all-Union State Television and Radio Broadcasting Company and of the local authorities started broadcasting in the Far Eastern city of Khabarovsk. Called Dal'nii Vostok-Rossiya (Far East-Russia), the station received a license from the RSFSR Ministry of Communications for three hours of daily broadcasts on shortwave frequencies.

Ukraine Restores Crimean Autonomy

The Ukrainian Supreme Soviet voted to make the Crimea an autonomous republic within Ukraine, following a referendum in January in which residents of the Crimea supported the restoration of their autonomous republic. Crimean Tatar activists had urged a boycott of the referendum, saying only Tatars had the right to determine the Crimea's future. The Ukrainian opposition movement "Rukh" opposed the vote, arguing that it encroached on the republic's territorial integrity (RFE/RL correspondent's report, February 12).

Ukrainian Miners and Metal Workers Threaten to Strike

Radio Kiev reported that, at a meeting of the Council of Donbass Strike Committees in Donetsk, participants had agreed to stage a warning stoppage of coal deliveries on February 20 and to start a strike on March 1 if the republican government did not meet their demands for a wage increase of 100–150 percent. Metal workers also threatened to go on strike if their demands for wage increases and the freeing of metal prices were not met by the government.

On February 21, Radio Kiev reported that representatives of the Donbass Strike Committees had sent a list of thirteen demands to the Ukrainian Supreme Soviet. The list included demands to halt construction of chemical plants and toxic waste dumps and to stop the dumping of untreated industrial waste into rivers and reservoirs. It also included a call for the Donbass to be declared an ecological disaster area.

On February 27, TASS reported that Ukrainian Prime Minister Vitol'd Fokin had refused to meet Donbass miners' demands for pay rises of 100-150 percent, because the Ukrainian government could not afford to grant them. He stressed that coal prices had been raised from 22 to 99 rubles per ton, thereby allowing miners who worked underground to earn 1,000 rubles or more a month. Furthermore, he added, the coal industry had received 12 billion rubles in subsidies and 1 billion rubles in capital investment in 1991. He said coal production had fallen by 15 million tons in 1990, while miners' salaries had risen by almost 18 percent.

Day of Remembrance in Tajikistan

February 12 was proclaimed a day of remembrance in Tajikistan to commemorate those who died in the violence in Dushanbe that began with demonstrations on February 12, 1990. *Izvestia* reported that the proclamation had been issued by President Kakhar Makhkamov, whose resignation was called for by demonstrators during the disturbances.

Wednesday, February 13

German Economics Minister in Moscow for Talks

German Economics Minister Jürgen Möllemann flew to Moscow for talks on how German-Soviet trade could be maintained despite the shortage of hard currency in the

Soviet Union, DPA reported. After meeting with Soviet Prime Minister Valentin Pavlov, Möllemann said that the USSR would soon order goods worth 9 billion marks from firms in eastern Germany and that the purchases would be financed by German credits.

Gorbachev Calls for "Dictatorship of Law"

Soviet President Mikhail Gorbachev told a conference of prosecutors that only one dictatorship could exist in the USSR during the current critical period—"the dictatorship of law." He added that the Soviet Union needed economic, financial, and legal stability now more than ever (*TASS*, February 13).

Soviet Generals Affirm Party Control

At a press conference in Moscow, General Aleksandr Ovchinnikov, first deputy chief of the Main Political Administration of the Soviet Armed Forces, and Major General Boris Golyshev, a senior member of the KGB Border Troops' Political Administration, said that the Communist Party was the only political organization in the armed forces, TASS reported. The generals noted that all general officers were Party members, as were at least 90 percent of the staff of the military political organs. They said that 37,000 primary Party organizations existed in the armed forces and that servicemen joining the Party exceeded by 19 percent those leaving it; Party membership, they said, had grown by 3.7 percent in 1990.

Gennadii Fil'shin Resigns

Radio Rossii reported that RSFSR Deputy Prime Minister Gennadii Fil'shin had resigned because of pressure from conservative forces. Fil'shin had been accused of involvement in a deal with a British-based trading company, which the USSR State Bank had declared illegal. In his resignation letter, he denied any wrongdoing and accused the KGB and old-style Party officials of working to discredit the democratic RSFSR leadership. He said that his resignation should be understood as "a protest" against "an antidemocratic campaign of provocation." Fil'shin was the third member of Boris El'tsin's RSFSR government, after Grigorii Yavlinsky and Boris Fedorov, to resign in three months.

On February 18, Fil'shin told RFE/RL that, despite his resignation from the RSFSR government, he did not intend to abandon his career as an economist. Fil'shin said he thought the publicity about him had not harmed his prospects but, on the contrary, had made him more popular.

Slander Trial Begins

The trial of Valeriya Novodvorskaya, a leader of the Democratic Union who called Soviet President Mikhail Gorbachev "a red fascist," began in Moscow, AP reported. Novodvorskaya, who was also charged with burning a Soviet flag, said she admitted the charges but did not think her actions should be considered crimes. She added that she saw her case as a duel between a police state and an individual.

On February 27, the USSR prosecutor-general asked for a suspended two-year sentence for Novodvorskaya, AP reported. Novodvorskaya, tried under a law passed in 1990 that outlawed insults against the Soviet president, protested about the leniency of the sentence, saying, "If you are mean enough to pass this law, be mean enough to use it!"

On March 1, Novodvorskaya was acquitted of the slander charge, but she was sentenced to two years of corrective labor for having burned two Soviet flags. A Moscow judge ruled that, although Novodvorskaya had insulted President Mikhail Gorbachev, she had not said anything that could be construed as obscene under Soviet law (*Reuters*, March 1).

Situation of Soviet Soldiers in Baltic Compared with That of Iraqis

Top-ranking political officers representing the Soviet Armed Forces and KGB Border Troops condemned the allied war effort against Iraq at a news conference. The generals said the real goal of the war was the extermination of civilians and the destruction of a former Moscow ally. The deputy head of the Armed Forces Political Administration, Lieutenant General Aleksandr Ovchinnikov, compared the suffering of Iraqi civilians to that of Soviet servicemen in the Baltic republics. He said that US bombing that left peaceful citizens homeless and without food was as unnatural as the Lithuanian government's leaving Soviet servicemen "without homes, without food, without kindergartens and schools" (*Reuters*, February 13).

Gamsakhurdia and Patrikeev Warn against Antimilitary Protests

In separate statements carried by *Krasnaya zvezda* and Radio Tbilisi, Chairman of the Georgian Supreme Soviet Zviad Gamsakhurdia and the commander of the Transcaucasus Military District, Colonel General Valerii Patrikeev, condemned plans by Georgia's unofficial National Congress for a mass protest action against the presence of Soviet troops in Georgia. Patrikeev described the protest, planned for Soviet Army Day, February 23, as either an act of provocation or sheer political puerility.

The USSR in February, 1991

Radio Moscow, quoting the Aziyapress agency, reported that the current session of Kazakhstan's Supreme Soviet had passed a law on priority development of rural villages and the agroindustrial complex. The measure was described as part of an effort to improve food supplies in the republic, which were critically short, despite having been given priority in economic plans since the beginning of 1987. Shortcomings in the supply of food to consumers were officially acknowledged to have been a major contributing factor to the riots in Alma-Ata in December, 1986.

Kazakh Supreme Soviet Takes Measures to Improve Food Supply

Ukrinform/TASS reported that, owing to the closure of the remaining three Chernobyl' reactors by 1995, an energy shortage was expected in Ukraine. Ukrainian Prime Minister Vitol'd Fokin said the republic could produce only 30 percent of its energy needs. Under public pressure, the government adopted a moratorium on the further development of nuclear power.

Closure of Chernobyl' to Lead to Energy Shortages in Ukraine

Thursday, February 14

Nikolai Krasnoshchekov, deputy head of the USSR State Food Committee, told *Pravda* that the Soviet Union was poorly prepared for the spring harvest. He said farm equipment was in a bad state and pointed to persistent problems with spare parts and maintenance affecting tens of thousands of tractors and other types of farm machinery. Krasnoshchekov also said state procurement for meat and milk in January were down 12 percent and 13 percent respectively. He added that there was a serious problem supplying farmers with grain seeds for future planting because deliveries were being held back by Kazakhstan and Ukraine.

Agricultural Official Cites Increasing Problems

The USSR recalled its ambassador to Iceland for "consultations" in Moscow, following a decision by the Icelandic parliament on February 12 to instruct the government to extend diplomatic recognition to Lithuania as an independent state. USSR Deputy Foreign Minister Yulii Kvitsinsky summoned Iceland's ambassador to Moscow and told him the Icelandic parliament's decision was pointless because Lithuania was a Soviet Socialist Republic (RFE/RL correspondent's report, February 14).

The same day, *Pravda* described the recent decision by the United States to send aid directly to the Baltic republics as a formal violation of Soviet sovereignty and

Soviet Ambassador Recalled after Iceland Recognizes Lithuania as Independent State

said it could complicate Soviet-US relations (RFE/RL correspondent's report, February 14).

Sobchak Says USSR's Problems Exaggerated

Chairman of the Leningrad City Soviet Anatolii Sobchak told reporters in Helsinki, where he was on a visit to promote a fund to save Leningrad's historic buildings, that the USSR's problems had been exaggerated by the media and could be solved peacefully by the republican Supreme Soviets, Reuters reported. He said he believed the Soviet economy would stabilize.

El'tsin Again under Attack

RSFSR Supreme Soviet Chairman Boris El'tsin again came under attack from Communist Party publications. The CPSU Central Committee periodical *Glasnost'* said El'tsin had links with a group known as the Chechen mafia, which engaged in black-market trading, while *Sovetskaya Rossiya* claimed that El'tsin would stop at nothing to gain power in the USSR. Pavel Voshchanov, El'tsin's spokesman, commented on the two articles, saying the accusations in them were the "dirtiest" attempt yet by Communists to discredit the RSFSR Supreme Soviet chairman.

El'tsin on Prices Hikes

RSFSR Supreme Soviet Chairman Boris El'tsin told the RSFSR Supreme Soviet that Gorbachev had failed to consult the Soviet people before devising a plan that would cause many consumer prices to rise by 200 percent and more. The plan, detailed in *Izvestia*, said retail prices in the USSR would double or triple under a draft price reform program, Reuters reported. The RSFSR Supreme Soviet later passed a resolution calling on El'tsin not to support the proposed price hikes.

On February 15, Soviet Prime Minister Valentin Pavlov was quoted by Radio Moscow as saying that price reform was inevitable and that the Soviet government would make sure that social protection would be offered to cushion the effects of price rises, TASS reported. Meanwhile, RSFSR Prime Minister Ivan Silaev told the RSFSR Supreme Soviet that price reform would result in lower living standards and that measures planned to offset the effects of the higher prices would only help in the short term (*TASS*, February 15).

"Rukh" Calls for Babii Yar Memorial Day

The Ukrainian popular movement "Rukh" called on the republic's Supreme Soviet to declare September 29 a day to honor the victims of "fascist genocide" at Babii Yar, where Nazi troops massacred more than 100,000 people, most of them Jews, in September, 1941. "Rukh" also called for all those who had took part in the massacre to be brought to account and appealed to the Ukrainian government to institute measures for honoring those who perished during the mass repressions in Ukraine (*TASS*, February 14).

Turkmenistan to Open Foreign Consulates

Turkmen President Saparmurad Niyazov announced Turkmenistan's intention to open consulates in Turkey, Iran, and Afghanistan at a recent congress of the republic's Komsomol. He did not say when the consulates would open (RL Turkmen service, February 14).

Uzbek President Reaffirms Rejection of Draft Union Treaty

Uzbek President Islam Karimov was reported to have said at the Uzbek Supreme Soviet session that the current draft of the USSR Union treaty was unacceptable and that the Uzbeks would not sign it (RL Uzbek service, February 14). On February 15, the Uzbek popular movement "Birlik" called for a boycott of the all-Union March 17 referendum on the future of the Soviet Union by Uzbek residents, the Uzbek Supreme Soviet, and the Uzbek president (RL Uzbek service, February 15).

Ogonek Wins Libel Suit against Military Journal

Ogonek won a lawsuit against the military journal *Voenno-istoricbesky zhurnal*, Radio Moscow reported. In 1990 the journal reprinted from *Ogonek* a declaration by members of the opposition group Democratic Russia who were running for seats in the Congress of People's Deputies, accusing the authors of holding Nazi views. Genri Reznik, *Ogonek*'s lawyer, was quoted by Radio Moscow as saying that the court should have declared the article in *Voenno-istoricbesky zhurnal* a deliberately false political denunciation (a criminal offense punishable by several years in prison). The court, however, found *Voenno-istoricbesky zhurnal* guilty merely of libel and ordered it to apologize in print.

Friday, February 15

Gorbachev Meets Iranian Foreign Minister

Gorbachev met with Iranian Foreign Minister Ali Akbar Velayati in Moscow for talks on the Gulf crisis, Reuters reported. They agreed that it was important to avoid the tragedy of destroying Iraq as a state or dismembering its territory. Commenting on Iraq's conditional offer to withdraw from Kuwait, they said the Iraqi statement was a positive signal (*TASS*, February 15).

Following talks between Velayati and his Soviet counterpart, Aleksandr Bessmertnykh, Soviet Foreign Ministry spokesman Vitalii Churkin said at a press briefing on February 16 that the two countries sought to create a security system in the Gulf that would "guarantee a solid and stable peace," taking into account the overall interests of the states in the region and "observing their independence, their sovereignty, and their territorial integrity," AFP reported.

New Aides to Gorbachev Appointed

TASS said Vladimir Egorov and Oleg Ozherel'ev had become aides to the president. Egorov was appointed a speech writer for the CPSU general secretary, while Ozherel'ev was made deputy chief of the Humanitarian Department of the CPSU Central Committee. TASS said the changes were necessitated by the departure of Gorbachev's former aides, such as the reform-oriented economist Nikolai Petrakov. TASS also reported the appointment of the former head of the Party's press center, Georgii Pryakhin, as a new presidential speechwriter. Egorov, Ozherel'ev, and Pryakhin had all worked in the Ideology Department of the CPSU Central Committee.

Constitutional Supervision Committee on Joint Army-Police Patrols

The chairman of the USSR Committee for Constitutional Supervision, Sergei Alekseev, said Soviet President Mikhail Gorbachev's decree on joint army-police patrols was too vague and opened the way for abuses, TASS reported. Alekseev said it was essential that the demarcation of power between troops, local police, and republican central authorities be clearer in order to prevent misinterpretations. The committee recommended that guidelines be drawn up spelling out the authority of Soviet troop commanders in cases where no official state of emergency existed.

USSR Foreign Ministers Council Planned

USSR Foreign Minister Aleksandr Bessmertnykh and foreign ministers of the Soviet republics agreed to set up a joint council to discuss and coordinate foreign policy, TASS reported. The council would enable republics to help formulate and implement USSR foreign policy. It would also coordinate national and republican foreign-policy interests.

Kvitsinsky Urges Ratification of German Reunification

USSR Deputy Foreign Minister Yulii Kvitsinsky urged the USSR Supreme Soviet to ratify the Treaty on German

The USSR in February, 1991

Reunification. He told *Izvestia* that Germany had to remember that the withdrawal of Soviet troops was directly linked to German pledges to reduce by half the number of men in its forces and that the sooner Germany started the reduction the easier it would be for the USSR to meet the deadline for its withdrawal. If the reduction was not completed on time, he warned, the Soviet Union would have the right "to act in an appropriate manner" regarding the reduction of Soviet forces in Germany. But he also said that he did not believe such a scenario would occur.

Poll of Young Russians on Socialism

A poll, commissioned by *Reader's Digest* and conducted by the USSR Academy of Sciences, interviewed 1,050 residents of the RSFSR aged between eighteen and twenty-five. Almost 50 percent of those polled rejected socialism, saying it had no future in the Soviet Union; 22 percent thought it did. Eighty-five percent favored private ownership of land. Asked about political leaders, 51 percent of those polled said they believed Mikhail Gorbachev was an obstacle to changes and 20 percent were not sure. Given a list of Soviet leaders, only 6 percent chose Gorbachev as their favorite; 39 percent chose Boris El'tsin. By a margin of 70 to 19 percent the young people agreed with El'tsin's view that Soviet republics should be allowed to secede. As for relations with the United States, 86 percent of those polled had a positive attitude towards the United States, and only 3 percent said external threats were the USSR's biggest concern (*The Wall Street Journal*, February 15).

RSFSR Seeks More Control over Defense

Sergei Stepashin, chairman of the Subcommission for Army Servicemen's Issues of the RSFSR Supreme Soviet, told the February 15 issue of *Rossiya* that the RSFSR Supreme Soviet was seeking control over military conscription, troop movements, and appointments of army district commanders on Russian territory. Stepashin said leaders of republican parliaments should become full members of the USSR Defense Council, where these issues were to be decided.

Gorbachev Exempts Creative Unions from Taxes

President Gorbachev decreed "measures of social and economic protection" for Soviet cultural figures during the Soviet Union's transition to a market economy. This meant that Soviet creative unions and their enterprises would pay no tax as of January 1, 1991. The new taxation law adopted by the USSR Supreme Soviet in 1990 was severely criticized by Soviet writers and artists, since it did not take into consideration that such people might earn a large sum of money only once in a number of years.

Saturday, February 16

EC Foreign Ministers Visit Moscow

Three European Community foreign ministers—Jacques Poos of Luxembourg, Gianni de Michelis of Italy, and Hans van den Broek of the Netherlands—arrived in Moscow for talks with Soviet Foreign Minister Aleksandr Bessmertnykh and Soviet President Mikhail Gorbachev on the Gulf war and on EC-Soviet relations, including the situation in the Baltic republics. Gorbachev told the three ministers that he remained committed to *perestroika*. According to TASS, the EC foreign ministers assured Gorbachev of their full support in the pursuit of reforms but expressed concern about the recent Soviet crackdown in the Baltic republics. The issue of EC financial aid to the Soviet Union was not discussed (*TASS*, February 17).

Soviet Reactions to Gulf War

Sovetskaya Rossiya carried an article, presented as a reader's viewpoint, condemning Soviet support for UN Security Council resolution 678 authorizing the use of force against Iraq, saying the resolution was illegal. The article characterized the Soviet Union's vote in favor of the resolution as the personal decision of former Foreign Minister Eduard Shevardnadze. The newspaper said that, by supporting the use of force, the USSR had allowed the United States to assume a leading role in the crisis.

On February 17, Radio Rossii broadcast an interview with the deputy chairman of the Muslim Religious Board for Kazakhstan, Kazi Akhmadzhan, in which the cleric claimed that the goal of the United States in the Gulf war was to destroy Iraq. He said that Saddam Hussein should be condemned for his invasion of Kuwait, but he expressed disquiet over the numbers of Kuwaiti and Iraqi civilian casualties in the air war.

As reported on February 18 by AFP, Marshal Sergei Akhromeev told Interfax that strikes "launched against the Iraqi people" could no longer be tolerated. Warsaw Pact Chief of Staff Vladimir Lobov accused the allied forces of using the UN resolution "to camouflage a massacre on Iraqi territory" and of threatening strategic parity by testing advanced weapons. On February 19, former Warsaw Pact Commander in Chief Marshal Viktor Kulikov charged that US actions indicated the United States had not embraced "new thinking" (*Reuters*, February 18).

The USSR in February, 1991

At the Tajik Communist Party Central Committee plenum held on February 18 a resolution was adopted describing civilian casualties in the Gulf war as unacceptable and calling for a political solution to the conflict (*TASS*, February 18).

The presidents of Kazakhstan and Kirgizia were quoted by Reuters as having stated at a news conference on February 18 that the war should be stopped as soon as possible. Askar Akaev of Kirgizia said that the republic, as part of the Muslim cultural sphere, could not be indifferent to the fate of the world center of Islam. Kazakhstan's Nursultan Nazarbaev said that allied forces were violating the UN mandate and that he feared "this could turn into a demonstration of US might against all of us." Nazarbaev added that Iraqi troops should get out of Kuwait.

Interrepublican Cooperation Agreement

Leaders of the RSFSR, Ukraine, Belorussia, Kazakhstan, and Uzbekistan met in Moscow and established a standing group of senior representatives from each republic to oversee and coordinate the work of enterprises fulfilling interrepublican trade contracts, TASS reported on February 17. The system was to supervise trade flows, in particular of food and consumer goods. Information on interrepublican deliveries was to be published in the republican press.

CPSU Ready to Register as Political Party

Moscow television reported that the CPSU had compiled documents, including a certificate on the formation of the Party in 1898 and a copy of the Party's statutes and was ready to register as a political party. To do so, it was also required to pay a registration fee of 5,000 rubles.

General Denies Increased Role of Defense Ministry in Arms Control

First Deputy Chief of the General Staff Colonel General Bronislav Omelichev said in *Krasnaya zvezda* that all decisions on arms control and the disposition of armaments were taken collegially by an interdepartmental body composed of the relevant ministries, including the Ministry of Foreign Affairs. In comments summarized by TASS, Omelichev tried to dispel Western reports that the Defense Ministry had gained undue influence in the arms control process. He claimed that such reports served those with a Cold War mentality and he also criticized attempts to tie problems connected with the Conventional Forces in Europe Treaty to negotiations on strategic arms reductions.

El'tsin Says Gorbachev Is Moving towards Personal Dictatorship

Speaking on the US television network CNN, RSFSR Supreme Soviet Chairman Boris El'tsin said he thought that Soviet President Mikhail Gorbachev was moving towards a personal dictatorship. El'tsin also criticized what he called "inconsistent actions" by Gorbachev. The withdrawal from circulation of 50- and 100-ruble bank notes, for example, was an insult to every individual in the country, he said. El'tsin added that price increases were totally unreasonable and would drastically reduce living standards. Moreover, he said, such actions could lead to a social explosion (RFE/RL correspondent's report, February 16).

Centrist Bloc Leader Says Gorbachev Will Meet Him

Vladimir Voronin, head of the self-proclaimed Centrist Bloc, a group advocating the introduction of a state of emergency to preserve the Soviet Union, said Gorbachev had promised to meet him formally, Radio Rossii reported. Voronin intended to persuade Gorbachev to admit failure and surrender power to a collective dictatorship to be known as the "National Salvation Committee." According to Voronin, his group would suspend the Supreme Soviets, the presidency, political parties, and the press in order to have absolute power to implement its program.

Western Ukrainian Oblasts to Conduct Parallel Referendums

A joint session of the Lvov, Ivano-Frankovsk, and Ternopol' Oblast Soviets resolved to hold their own referendums on March 17 parallel to the all-Union referendum on the future of the Soviet Union, Radio Moscow reported. Residents of the three Western Ukrainian oblasts were to be asked: "Do you want Ukraine to become an independent state that independently decides all questions of internal and foreign policy and guarantees the equal rights of citizens irrespective of national and religious affiliation?"

At the same meeting, the three oblast soviets decided to consolidate their economies as a first step towards privatization of industry and formed the Galician Assembly to Press for Economic Consolidation (RL Ukrainian service, February 18). First Deputy Chairman of the Ukrainian Supreme Soviet Ivan Plyushch also attended the meeting.

Uzbekistan and Tajikistan Discuss Aluminum Plant

Deputies of the Supreme Soviets of Uzbekistan and Tajikistan studied environmental damage caused by the Tajik aluminum plant and agreed to stop the functioning of 100 electrolysis units at the plant during the summer

The USSR in February, 1991

months in 1991, *Izvestia* reported. Pollution caused by the plant had been a serious cause of friction between the two republics. In January, 1990, *Literaturnaya gazeta* reported that the Party first secretary of Uzbekistan's Surkhandarya Oblast, which adjoins the plant, had demanded 30 million rubles in damages from the plant's director The plant is a major element in Tajikistan's industrialization drive.

--- *Sunday, February 17*

Dzasokhov Convinced There Will Be No Military Coup

CPSU Politburo member and chairman of the USSR Supreme Soviet Committee for International Affairs Aleksandr Dzasokhov dismissed concerns about the possibility of a military takeover in an interview with *Welt am Sonntag*, AFP reported. He said the Soviet army was allied with the people and not an aristocratic armed force.

Reformist Deputies Do Not Support Union Referendum

At a meeting held by the Interregional Group of Deputies in the USSR Supreme Soviet, the deputies called for the cancellation of the nationwide March 17 referendum on the future of the Soviet Union, TASS reported. Deputy Yurii Shcherbak was quoted as saying that, if the referendum went ahead as planned, it should at least carry alternative questions. Shcherbak added that the group had raised the issue of calling to account the organizers of the recent violence in Lithuania and also discussed the worsening of the economy and the increasing "danger from the right." TASS reported on February 18 that the group had adopted a resolution on its attitude towards planned price increases and on the social protection of the working people but it gave no details.

Izvestia Analyses Iraq's Nuclear Capacity

Soviet scientists who helped design and develop Iraq's nuclear facilities told *Izvestia* they believed Iraq had shut down all its nuclear plants, unloaded the fuel, and carried it off to storage facilities before the allied coalition bombing campaign began. The scientists said that there should be no radioactive contamination in the area and that Soviet monitors had recorded no changes in levels of radiation in Iraq. They also said it was unlikely that Iraq could have developed a nuclear bomb. A far more real danger, they affirmed, was that Iraq might try to make use of uranium fuel it had obtained abroad to produce a radiological weapon by packing spent uranium fuel into a conventional bomb, which could cause strong radioactive contamination.

Ukrainian Opposition Leader Arrested

The press center of the Ukrainian Interparty Assembly announced that the cochairman of the Ukrainian People's Democratic Party, Yevhen Chernyshov, had been arrested, Radio Kiev reported. Chernyshov's arrest was connected with an unsanctioned meeting organized by the assembly in Kiev on February 9.

Transition to Market Economy in Ukraine Gaining Speed

Radio Kiev, citing the republican Statistics Committee, reported progress towards a market economy in Ukraine. While every fifth state enterprise was losing money and private farming was still in its infancy, the number of private and cooperative enterprises outside agriculture was steadily growing. There were almost 35,000 cooperatives in Ukraine, while the number of intermediary firms had reached more than 500. The most profitable were those engaged in services and foreign trade.

Sales Tax Introduced in Ukraine

Radio Kiev reported that a 5-percent retail sales tax had been introduced in Ukraine. The proceeds were to go towards creating an extrabudgetary fund for economic stabilization. The Ukrainian Council of Ministers adopted a resolution to this effect on February 11.

Tatar Public Center Expands its Scope

The Tatar Public Center decided at its second congress to reform its organization and expand its scope from Tatarstan to cover the entire Soviet Union. Marat Molukov, one of the nine cochairmen of the organization, was elected its first president. He told RFE/RL that 637 delegates attended the three-day congress held in Kazan'; about 300 observers represented other USSR popular movements (RFE/RL correspondent's report, February 19).

Monday, February 18

Gorbachev Presents Peace Plan

Soviet President Mikhail Gorbachev presented a four-point peace plan for the Gulf to Iraqi Foreign Minister Tariq Aziz and Deputy Prime Minister Saddoun Hammadi during three hours of Kremlin talks. Western agencies said the plan consisted of guarantees that Iraq's borders and state structure would not be changed, that sanctions would be halted, that Saddam Hussein would not be personally punished, and that other regional issues—including the Palestinian question—would be debated. These guarantees were offered in exchange for Iraq's withdrawal from Kuwait. Presidential special envoy Evgenii Primakov and Soviet Foreign Minister Aleksandr Bessmertnykh also attended the meeting.

An adviser to Gorbachev, Andrei Grachev, told Radio Europe-1 that Iraq would accept the Soviet plan's key point— Iraq's unconditional withdrawal from Kuwait: this was confirmed by Aziz at the talks, AP reported on February 19.

During the talks, Gorbachev telephoned German Chancellor Helmut Kohl to discuss the plan and also contacted British, Italian, French, and Iranian officials, Reuters reported on February 19. A summary of the talks was also cabled to Washington.

In an interview on Soviet television, Primakov, indicating the potential long-term value of Gorbachev's peace plan, said that the Soviet Union was working with clean hands now in the Middle East and that, if it managed to bring a peaceful solution to the Gulf conflict and by peaceful means guarantee the Iraqi pullout from Kuwait, it would be of great credit to Gorbachev, TASS reported on February 19.

Komsomol'skaya pravda on February 20 reported details of the Soviet peace plan, quoting well-informed Kremlin sources. The details corresponded with Western press accounts of the plan, although the newspaper added that the plan included a provision for a gradual withdrawal of allied forces from the Gulf and their replacement by Arab or United Nations forces.

Reacting to US President George Bush's assessment that the Soviet peace plan "falls well short" of what was required, Soviet Foreign Minister Aleksandr Bessmertnykh said the plan was addressed to the Iraqi leadership, not to the United States. Bessmertnykh said he did not consider the US statement a rejection. *Izvestia* of February 20 said the UN Security Council, not the United States, should decide whether the war was to continue. *Pravda* on the same day said "certain people" were blind to diplomatic efforts because of their desire to "punish" Iraq.

The Italian government also approved the peace plan proposed by Gorbachev and said it was perfectly in line with United Nations resolutions, AFP reported on February 20.

On February 21, Iraqi Foreign Minister Tariq Aziz returned to Moscow with Iraq's answer to Gorbachev's peace initiative, Reuters reported. But as Aziz left Baghdad, Iraqi President Saddam Hussein said in a television address that Iraq was ready for a ground war and that there would be no withdrawal (*Reuters*, February 21). During the Aziz-Gorbachev talks, a new eight-point plan was announced for Iraq to quit Kuwait, fully and unconditionally, Western agencies reported.

Commenting on Saddam Hussein's speech, Sergei Tarasenko, head of the Soviet Foreign Ministry's Evaluation and Planning Department, told Interfax on February 21 that it was "a kamikaze message with the sole intent of destroying his own people." Tarasenko also said that those critical of allied coalition air raids on Iraq did not understand that a totalitarian regime could only be liquidated if its dictatorship was torn down.

Soviet presidential spokesman Vitalii Ignatenko said on February 22 that Iraq had reacted positively to the Soviet plan calling for Iraq's withdrawal from Kuwait, which should begin on the second day after a cease-fire and would proceed according to a fixed schedule. Although the withdrawal was supposed to be unconditional, further points said that UN sanctions against Iraq would be lifted when the withdrawal was two-thirds complete. It also stipulated that all UN resolutions on the Iraqi invasion and occupation of Kuwait would cease to be in effect after completion of the withdrawal (Western agencies, February 22).

US President Bush told Soviet President Gorbachev that he had serious concerns about several points in the Soviet plan. He thanked Gorbachev for his efforts, however, and said the next step would depend on how the United States and its allies viewed the plan (RFE/RL correspondent's report, February 22).

Although Iraqi Foreign Minister Tariq Aziz confirmed at a press conference in Moscow that Iraq would accept the six-point plan proposed by the Soviet Union for ending the Gulf war, the allied deadline for Iraq to withdraw from Kuwait expired without any indication that Iraqi troops had started to leave Kuwait. In a last-minute effort to resolve the Gulf conflict without a ground offensive, Gorbachev telephoned the leaders of France, Italy, Britain, Egypt, and Syria, appealing to them to find a peaceful solution (Western agencies, February 23).

On February 24, Soviet Foreign Ministry spokesman Vitalii Churkin said the Soviet Union had criticized US President Bush for having ordered a ground war in the Gulf, saying the United States had missed a real chance for peace by rejecting the Soviet peace plan, Western agencies reported.

As many as 5,000 Muslims in the Dagestan ASSR attended a rally on February 24. Speakers in the city of

Makhachkala denounced military actions against Iraq and said they were ready to send volunteers and supplies to Iraq. Interfax said the demonstration was sponsored by the Muslim Religious Board for the Northern Caucasus (*Interfax*, February 25).

On February 25, TASS reported that the Soviet Union had advanced a new peace proposal at the United Nations Security Council. The proposal called on the council to set dates for the start and completion of an Iraqi withdrawal from Kuwait.

Bessmertnykh stressed in an interview with TASS on February 26 that the Soviet Union would play a role in formulating the postwar security structures in the Persian Gulf and the entire Middle East region. The USSR had its own ideas, he said, and considered that a security system could not be established without its participation. He said the Soviet Union would fight to "guarantee the interests of the Arab people of Iraq, the Arab people of Kuwait, and the Arab people of the whole region." In an interview on German television on February 27, German Foreign Minister Hans-Dietrich Genscher also said peace and stability could be created in the Gulf region only with the participation of the USSR (RFE/RL correspondent's report, February 27).

On February 28, Bessmertnykh welcomed the announcement of a cease-fire in the Gulf, saying the world community had for the first time in history joined forces to stop the seizure of one country by another, Reuters reported.

The chairman of the USSR Supreme Soviet Anatolii Luk'yanov told the USSR Supreme Soviet that the end of the Gulf war was a victory for Soviet President Gorbachev's diplomatic initiative (RFE/RL correspondent's report, February 28).

Soviet Defense Minister Marshal Dmitrii Yazov told the USSR Supreme Soviet the same day that the allied victory had prompted the USSR to look again at its air defense capability. He warned that, while it was at present capable of repelling attacks, this might not be true in two or three years. Yazov nevertheless defended the performance of Iraq's Soviet-supplied weaponry, arguing that, particularly in the air, the allies had enjoyed a huge advantage in numbers. (*TASS*, February 28).

USSR Supreme Soviet Opens Session

The USSR Supreme Soviet opened its fifth session. USSR Supreme Soviet Chairman Anatolii Luk'yanov said that the session would be "neither smooth nor easy" but that the stabilization of the USSR depended on its outcome (*TASS*, February 18).

THE USSR IN FEBRUARY, 1991

The USSR Supreme Soviet received a letter from Gorbachev's adviser Marshal Sergei Akhromeev, demanding that television and radio coverage of the USSR and RSFSR Supreme Soviet sessions be stopped. Radio Moscow quoted Akhromeev as saying the broadcasts caused much more harm than good, although he admitted that they were watched by tens of millions of viewers.

Prime Minister Valentin Pavlov outlined the USSR Cabinet of Ministers' price reform plan to the USSR Supreme Soviet. He reiterated that the government did not want to introduce the plan until an implementation agreement had been reached with all fifteen republics, because it was necessary to have a unified system of compensation, Reuters reported.

Pavlov said that prices would rise by about 60 percent in the USSR and that state subsidies to industry would be trimmed by about two-thirds, TASS reported. The government planned to set ceilings on the price of milk, eggs, sugar, and transportation. The prices of medicine, medical supplies, gas, coal, electricity, coffee, and vodka were to remain unchanged. Pavlov also said that the government aimed to provide compensation equal to about 85 percent of the price rises. About 30 percent of all goods would be sold at free market prices determined by suppliers and retailers.

The deputy chairman of the RSFSR Supreme Soviet's Budget and Prices Commission, Aleksandr Pochinok, criticized the plan as "radically wrong." According to TASS, he also said the RSFSR should not block the reforms but instead should use its influence to improve the plan. On February 19, the chairman of the RSFSR Supreme Economic Council, Mikhail Bocharov, said there would be a complete economic collapse if the USSR government did not move faster to free prices, TASS reported. He characterized the reforms announced by Pavlov as insufficient and said that the RSFSR Supreme Economic Council was working on its own reform plans. Pavlov was quoted as saying the same day, however, that "shock therapy" was an unacceptable way to carry out Soviet economic reforms (*TASS*, February 19).

Answering questions from the Supreme Soviet on February 19, Soviet Foreign Minister Aleksandr Bessmertnykh said linkage of the Gulf conflict to the Israeli-Palestinian conflict would be undesirable, TASS reported. When asked when the "slaughter" of innocent Iraqi women and children from allied bombing would cease, Bessmertnykh reminded the deputies not to forget the people of Kuwait, a country suffering from aggression, AP reported on February 20.

THE USSR IN FEBRUARY, 1991

Special Commission Investigates Sale of 140 Billion Rubles

Aleksandr Pochinok, chairman of the special commission of the RSFSR Supreme Soviet investigating the deal involving the sale of 140 billion rubles abroad at a disadvantageous rate in exchange for 7.8 billion dollars with which to purchase large quantities of consumer goods, told "TSN" that it was still possible that the case could bring down the RSFSR government. Pochinok pointed to incompetence on the part of former RSFSR Deputy Prime Minister Gennadii Fil'shin and of the RSFSR minister of trade. In an interview on "Vremya," Pochinok said that it was naïve for members of the government to believe that it could solve all its problems with such a deal, as Fil'shin was still maintaining.

Kitai Gorod to Be Restored in Moscow

TASS reported on a plan to restore an ancient part of Moscow—Kitai Gorod—as a cultural, trade, touristic, and spiritual center. Thirteen churches are situated in Kitai Gorod, among them a cathedral and a monastery. A representative of the Russian Orthodox Church said that the Church would help to restore these churches. The chairman of the Executive Committee of the Moscow City Soviet, Yurii Luzhkov, gave assurances at a press conference that the restoration of churches would continue.

Unofficial Georgian Militia Attacked

Two Soviet soldiers and six members of the unofficial Georgian paramilitary group Mkhedrioni were injured in a clash on the outskirts of Tbilisi, TASS reported, quoting USSR Ministry of Defense sources. Twenty Mkhedrioni members were detained and quantities of weapons and ammunition confiscated. Mkhedrioni leader Dzhaba Ioseliani, who was held by the Georgian authorities, accused Georgian Supreme Soviet Chairman Zviad Gamsakhurdia of masterminding the incident and expressed his intention to join with other Georgian political parties to form "an antifascist union" to oppose Gamsakhurdia's policies, Reuters reported.

Meanwhile, in an interview published in *El Mundo* and summarized by Reuters, Gamsakhurdia predicted that Soviet troops would intervene in Georgia to crush the independence movement. Gamsakhurdia appealed to Western leaders to end their support for Gorbachev, to establish links with those republics seeking independence, and to provide "political and economic aid." He argued that such Western support could put pressure on Gorbachev to withdraw Soviet troops from Georgia.

On February 20, two members of Mkhedrioni were shot dead in the southeast Georgian town of Kvareli by USSR MVD troops sent to detain them. According to

Reuters, one bystander, a priest, also died in the shooting. National Democratic Party Chairman Giorgi Chanturia told a news conference in Tbilisi that sixty Mkhedrioni members had been taken into custody.

TASS quoted a spokesman for the USSR Ministry of Internal Affairs, Aleksandr Rostovtsev, as saying on February 21 that Georgian MVD troops had confiscated a large number of weapons, including machine guns, stolen cars and trucks, and even an armored personnel carrier.

New Georgian Communist Party First Secretary

TASS reported that Avtandil Margiani had resigned two months after his election as Georgian Independent Communist Party first secretary, citing "the complex social and political situation" in the republic and a general decline in Communist Party authority. Margiani had been elected in December, 1990, at a Party congress at which the Georgian Communist Party voted to split from the CPSU.

Margiani was replaced on February 19 by the forty-seven-year-old Jani Migiladze. Migiladze, a police major general, supported Georgian independence (*Reuters*, February 19).

Azerbaijan to Receive Turkish Television

Radio Moscow reported that a satellite television relay station was in operation in Baku and would soon enable Azerbaijanis to receive Turkish television. The satellite facility was one of two donated by Turkey within the framework of increased political, economic, and cultural ties.

Interrepublican Agreements Signed

The presidents of Kazakhstan and Kirgizia signed an agreement on friendship and cooperation, TASS reported. Kazakh President Nursultan Nazarbaev described the agreement as a step beyond the agreement signed in 1990 on developing relations on the basis of mutual recognition of sovereignty. Kirgiz President Askar Akaev said the agreement was important in speeding up the conclusion of a new Union treaty. The two leaders also signed a five-year agreement on economic and cultural cooperation. According to Soviet television, the two republics would help each other in such areas as nuclear safety at the Semipalatinsk weapons testing site and in dealing with the ecological disaster of the Aral Sea. At a press conference, Akaev told journalists that Kirgizia was ready to join the group of four republics (RSFSR, Ukraine, Belorussia, and Kazakhstan) that had signed an agreement on direct

The USSR in February, 1991

relations, bypassing the central government, Radio Moscow reported on February 19.

───────────────────────────────────── *Tuesday, February 19*

RSFSR Deputy Prime Minister Nominated

"Vremya" reported that Al'bert Kamenev had been nominated RSFSR deputy prime minister for economic questions. Kamenev, who had been first deputy chairman of the RSFSR State Planning Committee since 1978, replaced Gennadii Fil'shin, who had stepped down the previous week.

Pugo on Crime Rate

USSR Minister of Internal Affairs Boriss Pugo told a press conference he was worried by both the amount of crime and the aggressiveness of armed elements, Reuters reported. Pugo said the overall crime rate had risen 13 percent from 1989 to 1990. He presented statistics indicating the rate of increase was highest in republics pressing for independence: the greatest increase occurred in Armenia, followed by the Baltic republics. The biggest increases were in drug offenses and misuse of state property. Pugo said the Soviet police needed the help of the population to restore law and order in the country.

Design Flaws Mainly to Blame for Chernobyl' Disaster

The Commission of the USSR State Committee for Safety in the Atomic Power Industry issued a statement saying design flaws in the Chernobyl' nuclear reactor were mainly to blame for the 1986 explosion, TASS reported. Besides the design flaws, the reactor did not have an adequate control and protection system, and workers had violated regulations, the commission said.

Snegur Reports on Visit to Romania

Addressing the Moldavian Supreme Soviet, President Mircea Snegur reported on his visit to Romania the previous week, Moldovapres reported. Snegur announced an agreement with Romanian leaders to coordinate steps towards establishing consulates in each other's countries and to conclude a Moldavian-Romanian intergovernmental treaty setting the framework for economic and cultural cooperation.

The same session of the Moldavian Supreme Soviet approved a document entitled "On the Formation of an Association of Sovereign States" authored by a group of Moldavian experts under Deputy Chairman of the Moldavian Supreme Soviet Victor Puscasu. The document proposed the formation of a confederation giving wide powers to the member-states but practically devoid of a center of power. The Moldavian Supreme Soviet voted to propose this concept to the Union republics.

First Independent Newspaper in Turkmenistan

Ashkhabad journalist Saparmurad Ovezberdev told RFE/RL that publication of an independent newspaper, *Turkmen ili* (The Turkmen People), had started the previous week. The weekly, which appeared in Russian, had a print run of only 999 copies. As long as it remained below 1,000, it was not necessary to register the publication with the authorities, according to Ovezberdev.

Wednesday, February 20

USSR Supreme Soviet Denounces El'tsin TV Broadcast

The USSR Supreme Soviet approved by 280 votes to 31 a resolution denouncing RSFSR Supreme Soviet Chairman Boris El'tsin's televised attack on Soviet President Mikhail Gorbachev. (The previous evening, El'tsin had called for Gorbachev's resignation, accusing him of accumulating too much personal power and bringing the Soviet Union to the brink of dictatorship under the guise of an executive presidency.) TASS reported that the resolution branded El'tsin's call for Gorbachev's replacement "a violation of the constitution" aimed at "the liquidation of the lawfully elected organs of power." The resolution urged Gorbachev to respond directly to El'tsin on television and called on the RSFSR parliament to denounce its leader. El'tsin had also been criticized by the leaders of Ukraine and Kazakhstan, Leonid Kravchuk and Nursultan Nazarbaev. Kravchuk called El'tsin's remarks on Gorbachev "irresponsible," and Nazarbaev described them as "unacceptable."

A number of democrats rose to El'tsin's defense. According to Reuters, the Leningrad City Soviet voted to approve El'tsin's television statement. Its chairman, Anatolii Sobchak, told reporters he "categorically disagreed" with the USSR Supreme Soviet resolution against El'tsin. Vyacheslav Shapovalenko from the Interregional Group of People's Deputies accused the USSR Supreme Soviet of insulting the Russian people by denouncing its leader. El'tsin's military adviser, General Dmitrii Volkogonov, defended the statement as "quite legitimate" but warned that a further confrontation between Gorbachev and El'tsin would "leave only ashes behind."

The Kuzbass Council of Workers' Committees appealed to all Russians to defend El'tsin. Radio Moscow

The USSR in February, 1991

quoted the council as saying that the CPSU *nomenklatura* had launched a campaign aimed at discrediting the RSFSR government and Supreme Soviet in an attempt to shift responsibility away from those who were responsible for the results of seventy-four years of Communist rule.

El'tsin was also criticized in *Pravda* of February 20. The newspaper published a resolution saying that El'tsin had created a confrontation between the RSFSR and the USSR that it called "criminal."

On the same day, Soviet Prime Minister Valentin Pavlov declared on Soviet television that El'tsin's desire to give republican and local governments more power would disrupt all economic links that had been developed over the past several decades.

On February 21, "TSN" news was replaced with an anti-El'tsin broadcast opened by RSFSR Supreme Soviet Deputy Chairman Svetlana Goryacheva, who read a statement attacking all El'tsin's activities in the RSFSR Supreme Soviet. The statement, which blamed El'tsin for the republic's economic problems and for the USSR's disintegration, was signed by two of the three RSFSR Supreme Soviet deputy chairmen and by the chairmen of both chambers of the RSFSR Supreme Soviet and their deputies. The signatories demanded an extraordinary session of the RSFSR Congress of People's Deputies empowered to replace the chairman of the RSFSR Supreme Soviet.

On the same day, a group of 272 deputies from the 1,068-strong Congress of RSFSR People's Deputies also published a call in *Sovetskaya Rossiya* for the holding of a special session of the congress on February 25 at the latest. The idea received only 42 percent of the votes, however, and was rejected (*Central Television*, February 22).

On February 28, some sixty-seven deputies of the Belorussian Supreme Soviet signed an open letter protesting against the campaign unleashed by all-Union officials and the conservative media against El'tsin. Referring to El'tsin's call for Gorbachev's resignation and for the dissolution of the all-Union governing structures, the deputies pointed out that "every statesman is entitled to his own views on the state's problems" and to make those views known to the electorate (RL Russian service, February 28).

In reaction to his critics, El'tsin was quoted by Interfax as saying he was not fighting Gorbachev personally but the old system that would not admit defeat. El'tsin added that the RSFSR had no desire to support the huge central bureaucracy, that the republic was in terrible shape today because it had been plundered by the Soviet Union for years, and that no one wanted to take responsibility for this.

Shevardnadze Holds Press Conference

At a press conference broadcast on "Vremya," former Soviet Foreign Minister Eduard Shevardnadze announced his election as president of the new Foreign Policy Association. Shevardnadze said the aim of his association was not to second-guess the Foreign Ministry but to help create a dialogue on current foreign-policy issues. He stressed that he wanted to communicate the ideas of "new thinking" abroad so that they would be better understood. Shevardnadze criticized the Kremlin's domestic policy and said "if the destabilization process continues, if the Soviet people cannot stabilize the situation and remove social tension, a civil war will come," TASS reported.

Commenting on the Gulf crisis, Shevardnadze, who described USSR policy on the Gulf war as irreproachable, revealed that the Soviet Union had formulated a peace plan for Iraq on January 10–11 but that the plan had never been submitted, owing to problems "of an organizational nature." Shevardnadze also said that, even if there were only a small chance of success, Soviet dialogue with Iraq should continue in the interests of saving human lives, TASS reported. Moreover, Shevardnadze pointed out that not enough attention was being paid to the sufferings of the Kuwaiti people (*AP*, February 20).

New Head of Soviet Women's Committee Elected

The Committee of Soviet Women elected a new chairwoman, Alevtina Fedulova, a fifty-two-year-old teacher from Moscow, TASS reported. She replaced Zoya Pukhova, who had resigned to concentrate on her work in the USSR Supreme Soviet.

RSFSR Supreme Soviet Discusses Nuclear Contamination

The RSFSR Supreme Soviet discussed ways to deal with nuclear contamination of areas of the RSFSR affected by Chernobyl' and passed a number of laws on aid to people exposed to radiation or displaced by the disaster, TASS reported. The chairman of the RSFSR State Committee for the Elimination of the Consequences of the Chernobyl' Disaster, Semen Voloshchuk, said that more than 2 million Russians had been directly affected by nuclear fallout and that the RSFSR expected to spend at least another 2 billion rubles on Chernobyl'-related measures. The RSFSR Supreme Soviet also heard

THE USSR IN FEBRUARY, 1991

a report by USSR people's deputy Aleksandr Penyagin on nuclear contamination in the Chelyabinsk region resulting from years of plutonium production for bombs and missiles. Penyagin reported that, over a forty-year period, more than 500,000 people had been registered as contaminated. Nuclear waste with dangerous levels of radiation had been buried in unsafe dumps, he said (*TASS*, February 20).

Yanaev Election Upheld

The Vote Counting Commission told the USSR Supreme Soviet on February 18 that it had investigated allegations by the Interregional Group of Deputies that there had been irregularities in Gennadii Yanaev's election as USSR vice president. Radio Moscow reported that the commission had admitted that it was itself to blame, since it "gave out more voting slips than were shown in the protocol on the voting on December 27." But, the commission said, this was "a purely technical mistake" that did not invalidate Yanaev's election.

Pavlov Presents New USSR Cabinet of Ministers

Soviet Prime Minister Valentin Pavlov presented a draft law to the USSR Supreme Soviet on the new USSR Cabinet of Ministers, which replaced the former Council of Ministers and was to be directly subordinate to Soviet President Mikhail Gorbachev, TASS reported. Pavlov told the deputies the new Cabinet of Ministers should be able to make decisions about all bodies, organizations, officials, and citizens on Soviet territory. He also criticized proposals by the RSFSR, Ukraine, and Belorussia to delay the formation of the Cabinet until the adoption of a new Union treaty, because this would leave the national economy in a state of anarchy for an indefinite period. Pavlov called on all republics to participate in the transition to an efficient economic system. He proposed the creation of a state council on economic reform, with voting members from administrative bodies of the Union republics.

Uzbek Supreme Soviet Votes to Bar Currency Callbacks

At a special session, the Uzbek Supreme Soviet took measures to bar future callbacks of bank notes by the USSR authorities, Radio Compatriot, the international service of Radio Tashkent, reported. The deputies granted the Uzbek State Bank sole authority to issue and recall bank notes. The purpose of this legislation was to prevent a repetition of the January 23 withdrawal of 50- and 100- ruble notes by the USSR government without consultation with the republics.

Mass Rallies in Nagorno-Karabakh and Armenia

More than half a million people attended a rally in Erevan to mark the third anniversary of the passing by the Nagorno-Karabakh Oblast Soviet of a resolution calling on the Supreme Soviets of Azerbaijan and Armenia to transfer the oblast from Azerbaijan to Armenia "in accordance with the wishes of the workers of Nagorno-Karabakh," Radio Moscow reported. According to TASS, similar demonstrations calling for the transfer of Nagorno-Karabakh to Armenia took place in the oblast capital, Stepanakert, and four other towns.

On February 22, Armenia's permanent representative in the USSR Cabinet of Ministers, Feliks Mamikonyan, called for Armenians and Azerbaijanis to find a compromise solution to the Nagorno-Karabakh conflict. According to TASS, Mamikonyan said it was futile to try to settle the conflict by force. He also declared that Armenia intended to increase economic ties with other Soviet republics and foreign countries, saying that Armenia especially valued its relations with the RSFSR.

Diphtheria Outbreak Reported in Ukraine

Radio Kiev reported that 132 cases of diphtheria had been registered in Ukraine. In an interview, director of the Ukrainian Epidemiology Institute Arkadii Frolov blamed some mass media organs, which, according to him, had widely but incorrectly reported on the harmful effects of diphtheria immunization. Consequently, many adults had not been immunized. He said the medical authorities had not taken the situation seriously.

Commercial Data Bank in Kazakhstan

TASS reported that a computerized data bank had been set up under the auspices of Kazakhstan's new State Supply Committee to provide information on potential business partners to republican enterprises. The bank had assembled data on 4,500 enterprises and information on plants that had unused factory floor space or extra equipment and raw materials. The bank was empowered by a group of firms in the RSFSR to conclude direct agreements to sell their products. The bank was to be connected with similar commercial data banks in Western Europe via an all-Union marketing center.

Amnesty Proposed in Turkmenistan

TASS, quoting *Izvestia*, reported that Turkmen President Saparmurad Niyazov had proposed a partial amnesty for persons who had been imprisoned for their roles in various "cotton affairs" in recent years. A number of Party and government officials, as well as ordinary farm workers, had been arrested for falsifying cotton production figures, for bribery, and for concealing actual amounts of land sown to cotton, a common trick to raise output. The amnesty, Niyazov told the republican Presidential Council, should apply only to those drawn involuntarily into "the cotton affairs."

Bessmertnykh Attends Council of Europe Meeting

Soviet Foreign Minister Aleksandr Bessmertnykh arrived in Madrid for a meeting of the Council of Europe and talks with European ministers, Western agencies reported. On February 21, a statement issued by the German Foreign Ministry said German Foreign Minister Hans-Dietrich Genscher and Bessmertnykh had agreed that an unconditional Iraqi withdrawal from Kuwait was indispensable and that any attempt to play for time had to be rejected (*DPA*, February 21). Speaking at the Council of Europe meeting the same day, Bessmertnykh defended Soviet policy towards the Baltic republics and pleaded for understanding and patience from the West (RFE/RL correspondent's report, February 21).

CPSU Faces Financial Squeeze

CPSU Central Committee Administrator of Affairs Nikolai Kruchina talked at a press conference about the Communist Party's financial problems, TASS reported on February 21. Kruchina said that the Communist Party's income from membership dues had fallen by half in 1990 and that the cutback in the Party's publishing activities, especially the closing of publications designed for young readers, had brought losses amounting to one billion rubles. But, according to Kruchina, the CPSU would be able to maintain its existing structure even if it had to lay off employees in Party schools and institutes.

Thursday, February 21

Shatalin Moves to Quit Communist Party

Moscow News (No. 7, 1991) revealed that Stanislav Shatalin, the former economic adviser to Soviet President Mikhail Gorbachev, had asked to leave the CPSU. A CPSU Central Committee plenum on January 30 decided to study Shatalin's activities, with a view to expelling him from the Party.

Belorussia Reduces Government Work Force

TASS reported that the Belorussian Supreme Soviet had decided to merge a number of the republic's government agencies and to trim the size of its work force by about

30 percent. Belorussian Prime Minister Vyacheslau Kebich was quoted as saying the reform was aimed at reducing the state's role in the economy, breaking up monopolies, encouraging business activity, and improving the republic's finances. Kebich also said that officials would be chosen from among several applicants.

Uzbek Referendum to Ask about Status of Republic

The Uzbek Supreme Soviet Presidium approved the text of an additional question that Uzbeks would be asked to answer during the March 17 referendum on the future of the Soviet Union. Anvar Usmanov, an Uzbek journalist from Tashkent, told RFE/RL that the text of the additional question was formulated as follows: "Do you agree that Uzbekistan should remain part of the restructured Union as a sovereign republic?" (RFE/RL correspondent's report, February 21).

Moldavian Supreme Soviet Rejects Snegur's Resignation

Moldavian President Mircea Snegur announced his resignation at a session of the Moldavian Supreme Soviet, Reuters reported. Snegur accused the Moldavian Communist Party of launching a campaign to discredit him following the election of Moldavian Communist Party First Secretary Grigore Eremei on February 4. He complained of criticism by the Soviet media following his trip to Romania, during which he spoke of the common Moldavian-Romanian national identity. Snegur said he would stay on as acting president if the Supreme Soviet agreed to elect the president by popular vote (Snegur was chosen by the Moldavian Supreme Soviet in September, 1990.) In addition, Snegur said he no longer considered himself a member of the Communist Party. The Moldavian Supreme Soviet refused to accept Snegur's resignation, however, TASS reported.

Sobchak Suffers Political Defeat

Leningrad City Soviet Chairman Anatolii Sobchak suffered a political defeat. According to Radio Moscow, Sobchak asked the chairman of the city's executive committee, Aleksandr Shchelkanov, to resign, but members of the city soviet resisted. They argued that, in the present unstable situation, structural and personnel changes were undesirable. Sobchak had accused Shchelkanov of lack of cooperation with the council's Presidium and with the city's managers and trade unions.

Ukrainian-Kazakh Treaty

Ukraine and Kazakhstan signed a ten-year treaty recognizing each other's sovereignty and covering political, economic, and cultural relations between the two republics (*Radio Kiev*, February 22).

_____ *Friday, February 22*

Pavlov Outlines Plan to Dismantle Gosplan

Soviet Prime Minister Valentin Pavlov outlined at a press conference a plan to dismantle the USSR State Planning Committee (Gosplan) and most ministries involved in industrial production, Reuters reported. The only production-related ministry to remain in its present form would be that responsible for automobiles and tractors. Ministries overseeing railways, engineering, power, and the nuclear industry were to be retained but reformed. Pavlov also said that his government was trying to create a system in which enterprises could be sure that no one would interfere in their business activities. AFP quoted Pavlov as saying that the Soviet Union did not need a Gosplan, but rather "a ministry of economics and forecasts." Pavlov renewed allegations he made on February 12 that some foreign banks were trying to spark high inflation in the USSR, and he expressed regret that those comments had been interpreted as an attack on the USSR's Western trading partners. Pavlov added: "Something like a Columbian mafia has emerged recently" in the Soviet Union, and he vowed to curb speculation (Western agencies, February 22).

El'tsin Visits Novgorod

RSFSR Supreme Soviet Chairman Boris El'tsin visited the city and oblast of Novgorod in the northwestern RSFSR, TASS reported. He discussed with city and oblast officials the social and economic situation and preparations to establish a free-trade zone, toured a video-recorder factory, and attended a meeting of local officials from various political parties. At the meeting, El'tsin declared that he would not run for president of the Soviet Union, even if Gorbachev called a general election and asked El'tsin to oppose him.

USSR to Compensate Poland for Troop Withdrawal

Nikolai Panasyutin, Soviet consul general in Poland, told PAP the USSR was ready to pay Poland more than 1.3 billion dollars in compensation in return for being allowed to use its territory to withdraw troops from eastern Germany. According to a DPA report, the USSR would pay Poland a set rate for each train and vehicle that was used to transport troops across the country. Moreover, according to Panasyutin, the Soviet Union was prepared to give Poland 1 billion dollars to pay for the reconstruction of roads used by the departing troops.

A Hungarian Defense Ministry spokesman, Colonel Gyorgi Keleti, said 30,000 Soviet troops had left Hungary on schedule since agreement on withdrawal was reached, despite a dispute between the two sides over compensation for the pullout, Reuters reported. Hungary wanted the USSR to pay for environmental damage caused by Soviet troops, and the Soviet Union wanted Hungary to pay for the buildings the troops were vacating.

Democratic Russia Group Stages Rally

About 400,000 people rallied outside the Kremlin, calling for democracy and *glasnost'*, as Soviet military leaders gathered inside for the traditional celebration on the eve of Soviet Army Day. At the rally, called by Democratic Russia, people carried signs denouncing the armed forces and the government and praising RSFSR Supreme Soviet Chairman Boris El'tsin (*Radio Moscow*, February 22).

Saturday, February 23

Soviet Armed Forces Day Demonstrations

The USSR ministers of internal affairs and defense, Boriss Pugo and Dmitrii Yazov, as well as KGB Chairman Vladimir Kryuchkov, Armed Forces Chief of Staff Mikhail Moiseev, and Moscow City Communist Party First Secretary Yurii Prokof'ev took part in a demonstration in support of the Soviet army and the integrity of the USSR on Soviet Army Day in Moscow. According to TASS, 300,000 people attended the rally (Western agencies put the size of the crowd at between 30,000 and 100,000), among them Soviet soldiers, war veterans, workers, and civilians. The demonstration, organized by the Moscow City Party Committee, the parliamentary group "Soyuz," and other conservative organizations, expressed support for Gorbachev, for the Soviet army, and for the preservation of the Union. Some of the participants carried anti-American and anti-Israeli placards.

While some hard-line spokesmen, including leading member of "Soyuz" Viktor Alksnis, delivered speeches attacking Soviet democrats and US actions in the Gulf, Western sources characterized the crowd as dispirited. Reuters reported that military personnel had been ordered to attend the rally in civilian clothes so as to increase the number of participants. Other Army Day rallies were held in Leningrad—where some scuffles were reported by Radio Moscow—Kiev, Vladivostok, Vilnius, and Riga. "Black Berets" were present at the Riga rally,

The USSR in February, 1991

Radio Riga reported. President of the Latvian Supreme Council Anatolijs Gorbunovs sent greetings to the staff of the Baltic Military District and veterans, Radio Moscow reported.

The Soviet army repeatedly denied that the rally was meant to intimidate prodemocracy forces in the USSR, but General Konstantin Kochetov, a first deputy defense minister, told Moscow television the same day that the armed forces would resist attempts "to restore capitalism." He said the army would try to ensure that the USSR remained "united, powerful, and inviolable."

Radio Rossii said about 200 people gathered at a counterdemonstration in support of RSFSR Supreme Soviet Chairman Boris El'tsin. No trouble was reported.

Medical Workers to Get Higher Pay

The Presidium of the RSFSR Supreme Soviet approved a salary raise of up to 40 percent for employees in the medical profession, Soviet television reported. Doctors and medical staff had threatened to hold a warning strike the previous week to press for higher pay.

Moldavian Leaders Address Public Rally

Moldavian President Mircea Snegur and Prime Minister Mircea Druc attended a youth rally in Kishinev's athletics stadium. Both pledged to continue "striving for Moldavian state independence." While Snegur indicated that he favored a gradualist approach, Druc did not include that qualification and was clearly the crowd's favorite. The two leaders sought to convey the impression that they were prepared to patch up their differences. Interviewed by Moldavian television the same evening, Snegur backtracked from his demand that Druc resign.

On February 28, the Moldavian Supreme Soviet was forced to adjourn its session after Moldavian Communist, Russian, and most Agrarian Party deputies declared that they would boycott the Moldavian Supreme Soviet's sessions unless Prime Minister Mircea Druc resigned. For three months, Moscow and the pro-Soviet forces in Moldavia had been campaigning to oust Druc. They had been joined by the Agrarians, a large parliamentary group of Moldavian kolkhoz chairmen and other rural officials who supported national demands but opposed the radical agrarian and administrative reforms promoted by Druc. In response, Snegur declared that the Supreme Soviet would suspend its work indefinitely (*TASS*, February 28).

"Kyrgyzstan" against March 17 Referendum

At its first congress, which took place in Bishkek, the capital of Kirgizia, "Kyrgyzstan," the republic's democratic movement, opposed the March 17 referendum on the future of the USSR, Radio Moscow reported.

Sunday, February 24

Rally in Support of El'tsin

A crowd estimated at between 40,000 and 150,000 gathered in Manezh Square near the Kremlin to attend a rally in support of RSFSR Supreme Soviet Chairman Boris El'tsin, Reuters reported. The participants carried some banners praising El'tsin and others denouncing Soviet President Mikhail Gorbachev. Yurii Chernichenko, a USSR people's deputy, told the crowd that "El'tsin represents Russia, we must not betray him," and Father Gleb Yakunin said, "El'tsin spoke the truth" when he denounced Gorbachev on February 19.

Silaev in Turkey for Economic Talks

RSFSR Prime Minister Ivan Silaev flew to Ankara for talks on increasing RSFSR-Turkish economic cooperation. On his arrival in Ankara, Silaev declared to the Anatolian News Agency that the RSFSR's move to a free-market economy should mean expanded economic ties with Turkey (*TASS, Reuters*, February 24). During his four-day visit, Silaev met Turkish President Turgut Ozal, Prime Minister Yildirim Akbulut, and Finance Minister Adnan Kahveci.

Soviet Prisoners in Afghanistan Alive

Zakhir Sattar, secretary of the Afghan Commission for the Search and Release of Prisoners of War, announced that about a hundred Soviet soldiers captured by the resistance during the Afghan war were alive and being held by resistance groups in Afghanistan and Pakistan. According to Sattar, most of the prisoners were being held in villages, some had assumed Muslim names and had families, and most were relatively free to move around, although a degree of supervision and control was exercised over their lives (*TASS*, February 24).

On February 25, Soviet Ambassador-at-Large Nikolai Kozyrev said Soviet aid to Afghanistan was a duty. TASS quoted Kozyrev as saying that, paradoxical as it might seem, Soviet military aid to Kabul was intended to speed up a political settlement in the country and to show the Afghan opposition that attempts to solve the country's problems by military means were futile. Kozyrev added that sending Soviet troops to Afghanistan in 1979 had been a mistake that had caused the deaths of thousands of Afghans. He said aid was a way of paying for that mistake.

The USSR in February, 1991

All-Buryat Congress in Ulan-Ude

A three-day all-Buryat congress ended in Ulan-Ude, TASS reported. The delegates unanimously condemned as unconstitutional the act of 1937 that split the Buryat republic into three but decided for the present to call only for the creation of national-cultural autonomy to consolidate the Buryat people. The congress set up an all-Union association of Buryat culture. Delegates rejected reports on the congress carried in some mass media that the Buryat republic was reorienting itself towards a union with Mongolia and towards Asian culture.

Tajikistan in Favor of Referendum

The Tajik Supreme Soviet voted in favor of participating in the March 17 referendum on the future of the Soviet Union, Soviet television reported. Officials of Tajikistan's Democratic Party, however, announced that they would boycott the poll.

Anniversary of Republic of Estonia Celebrated

For the third year in a row, Estonians celebrated the anniversary of the Republic of Estonia, TASS reported. Rallies and church concerts were held throughout Estonia, and the Estonian tricolor was raised on the Long Hermann Tower in Tallinn. Estonian Prime Minister Edgar Savisaar attended the ceremony and spoke about Estonia's long striving for independence (*Central Television*, February 24). Estonia became independent in 1918 but was incorporated into the Soviet Union in 1940.

_____ *Monday, February 25*

Gorbachev Submits Cabinet of Ministers

Soviet President Mikhail Gorbachev submitted to the USSR Supreme Soviet a list of twenty-three candidates for approval as members of the newly created Cabinet of Ministers, Interfax reported. The list included a number of former USSR ministers, among them Vladimir Kryuchkov (KGB), Dmitrii Yazov (defense), Nikolai Konarev (transportation), Vyacheslav Kolesnikov (electronics industry), Igor' Koksanov (shipbuilding), Vladimir Brezhnev (transport construction), Grigorii Gabrielyants (geology), Yurii Vol'mer (maritime fleet), Sergei Lushchikov (justice), Vladimir Shimko (radio industry), Aleksandr Mikhal'chenko (special construction), and Yurii Semenov (power and electrification).

New nominees included Vladimir Orlov as finance minister, Gennadii Kudryavtsev as communications minister, and Vyacheslav Chernovainov for agriculture, a ministry that had been abolished but was to be revived.

Gorbachev also asked that Vladimir Shcherbakov, Fedor Sen'ko, and Lev Ryabev be reconfirmed as deputy prime ministers. The USSR Supreme Soviet had already approved the nominations of Foreign Minister Aleksandr Bessmertnykh, and Minister of Internal Affairs Boriss Pugo.

On March 1, the USSR Supreme Soviet approved the nominations of Lushchikov, Chernovainov, Shimko, Kudryavtsev, Mikhal'chenko, and Koksanov, TASS reported.

USSR Supreme Soviet Resolution on Referendum

The USSR Supreme Soviet adopted a resolution declaring that the opinion polls on independence being held in various republics did not constitute a legal basis for not holding the March 17 referendum on the preservation of the USSR, and it ordered the republics to take immediate steps to hold the referendum. At the same time, the resolution, reported by TASS, empowered local soviets and labor collectives in republics where no steps had been taken to hold the referendum to set up their own polling stations. The Supreme Soviet did not discuss the question of declaring invalid republican polls being held simultaneously with the all-Union one.

Vladimir Orlov, chairman of the Central Referendum Commission, told the USSR Supreme Soviet that preparations for the referendum were under way in eight of the Union republics and in seventeen of the autonomous republics, Radio Moscow reported. He confirmed that a "no" vote in the March 17 referendum would not be tantamount to secession and that a republic wishing to secede would have to hold a second referendum, as stipulated by the law on the mechanics of secession.

In an article published in *Izvestia*, Rafik Nishanov, chairman of the USSR Council of Nationalities, rejected the argument put forward by a group of scholars that the March 17 referendum was unconstitutional since the question posed lay within the competence of the republics. Nishanov maintained that the question of the preservation of the Soviet Union was not the same as whether or not a given republic should be part of the Soviet Union, as the scholars had tried to argue.

Insurance for Soldiers

Colonel General Vladimir Bab'ev told *Izvestia* that the heirs of soldiers killed performing military service (presumably in peacetime) would receive an insurance payment of 25,000 rubles, TASS reported. Those soldiers who became invalids as a result of military service would

THE USSR IN FEBRUARY, 1991

receive between 5,000 and 15,000 rubles, while those who sustained injuries would be eligible for 500 to 1,000 rubles. Bab'ev said that 285 million rubles had been set aside in the 1991 state military budget for this purpose. Insurance for servicemen was mandated by a presidential decree issued in January.

Moscow Teachers Stage One-Day Strike

Teachers at almost 500 Moscow schools staged a one-day strike to press demands for better funding for education and smaller classes, TASS reported. Vsevolod Lukhovsky, a spokesman for the strike committee, told TASS that the state of public education in Moscow was catastrophic. The city was short 3,500 teachers in 1990, and most school buildings were in a state of decay, with overcrowded classrooms. Furthermore, he added, teachers were overburdened and underpaid. The chairman of the USSR State Committee on Public Education, Gennadii Yagodin, announced the same day that teachers' pay would be increased, but he did not say when or by how much, TASS reported.

Protocol Signed between Lithuania and Ukraine

Radio Vilnius reported that Lithuanian Deputy Prime Minister Vytautas Pakalniskis and Ukrainian Deputy Prime Minister Viktor Kurchyukin had signed an economic and trade cooperation protocol for 1991 in Kiev. The document activated the bilateral agreement on cultural, economic, and trade cooperation signed nearly three months earlier. Each republic expected to obtain goods worth about 900 million rubles from the other. For Lithuania, the Ukrainian goods would amount to about a tenth of all goods purchased from the USSR.

More Chernobyl' Aid Approved by Belorussian Supreme Soviet

The Belorussian Supreme Soviet adopted the first in a proposed package of laws dealing with the consequences of the Chernobyl' accident, TASS reported. Residents in four zones specified in the law were to receive compensation, assuming the government could find the funds. The estimated cost of implementing the law was 6 billion rubles, while the republic's current budget deficit was 3.5 billion rubles. Funds were to be requested from the all-Union authorities.

Statue of Maitreya Returned to Buryat Buddhists

A sixteen-meter-high copper statue of Maitreya, the next Buddha, was returned to the Buddhist datsan (monastery) in Aginskoe in the Aginsky Buryat Autonomous Okrug, TASS reported. The national sacred object of the Buryat people had been removed from the datsan when it was forcibly closed down in 1940. The head of the monastery told TASS that not only believers but also USSR and RSFSR deputies and the local authorities had campaigned for its return.

Sunnah Published in Russian

TASS reported that the *Sunnah* (a collection of traditions about the life and sayings of the Prophet Muhammed) was being published for the first time in Russian. Extracts, translated from the original Arabic, were to appear in each issue for 1991 of the independent newspaper *Uzy* published twice a month in Moscow, and the full text would be published in Moscow by the joint Soviet-Arabic enterprise "Dom Biruni."

Nordic Council Meets

A Baltic delegation of Estonians, led by Supreme Council President Arnold Ruutel; Latvians, led by Supreme Council President Anatolijs Gorbunovs; and Lithuanians, led by Deputy President of the Supreme Council Bronius Kuzmickas arrived in Copenhagen to participate as guests in a session of the Nordic Council (*Radio Riga*, February 26). According to TASS, on February 25 Soviet Foreign Ministry spokesman Yurii Gremitskikh had warned the Nordic Council against adopting positions concerning the Baltic republics that would amount to interference in the internal affairs of the USSR. At the opening meeting, Danish Prime Minister Poul Schlueter said the Soviet warning must be rejected as unacceptable (*AP*, February 26). Anker Joergensen, president of the Nordic Council, declared that the Council regarded its political support of the three Baltic republics as work for democracy.

Gorbunovs and Ruutel called for an international conference to promote the Baltic republics' independence drive, Reuters reported. Gorbunovs said that, without such a conference and without an international declaration on the Baltic issue, the USSR would never officially negotiate with the Baltic republics. Ruutel added that an international conference would help the Baltic republics to bring their issue to the level of the United Nations.

On March 1, the Nordic Council approved a program to increase cooperation with the Baltic republics in economic, cultural, and environmental matters, as well as in "democratic developments." This followed an agreement by the foreign ministers of Denmark and Lithuania to strengthen bilateral ties and to try to reestablish diplomatic relations (*AP*, March 1).

The USSR in February, 1991

Tuesday, February 26

Gorbachev Visits Belorussia

Soviet President Mikhail Gorbachev left Moscow for Minsk on his first domestic trip in six months, AP reported. In a speech at a meeting with Belorussian intellectuals, Gorbachev warned of possible civil war in the Soviet Union. As reported by Soviet television, he accused RSFSR Supreme Soviet Chairman Boris El'tsin and Chairman of the Moscow City Soviet Gavriil Popov of attempting to seize power by force and break up the Soviet Union. Gorbachev denounced "the neo-Bolshevik tactics" of the radical opposition and charged that democratic opposition groups and leaders were being directed by "alien research centers." Gorbachev said the Soviet "left" was in reality "a rightist opposition" because it rejected socialism and favored capitalism. At a meeting with workers at the Minsk Tractor Plant, Gorbachev accused El'tsin of having "diverged from the path of *perestroika*." He dismissed suggestions that he himself had abandoned *perestroika*.

Concerning the Gulf war, Gorbachev declared at the same meeting that the Middle East question should be settled as a whole, AFP reported on February 26. Gorbachev also noted that relations between the United States and Soviet Union were "fragile," and he said Moscow and Washington would have to show "a great sense of responsibility" if they were not to destroy what had so far been achieved in improving ties.

Gorbachev told the Belorussian Supreme Soviet that the proposal submitted by the governments and Supreme Soviets of Belorussia, Ukraine, and the RSFSR for the adoption of a USSR law providing more social and material aid to people affected by the Chernobyl' nuclear power plant explosion in 1986 was justified and logical. He promised that the USSR government would take steps to satisfy them fully, TASS reported on February 26.

On February 27, Gorbachev visited Gomel' Oblast, one of the areas worst hit by the Chernobyl' disaster. He talked to people in the village of Vetka, which was contaminated by radioactivity, and familiarized himself with the situation. During his visit to Gomel', Gorbachev said the USSR needed renovation and improvement, not disintegration and destruction. He also declared that domestic economic relations still threatened the Soviet economy with destabilization and falling production ("Vremya," *Central Television*, February 27).

Speaking in the city of Mogilev on February 28, Gorbachev urged the CPSU to form a centrist coalition with other democratic parties and movements, TASS reported. Gorbachev outlined his centrist position, directed towards reconciling forces on the left and the right, and stressed his commitment to social justice, the separation of powers, and the creation of a state of law and order and a mixed market economy.

Ivashko in Beijing

CPSU Deputy General Secretary Vladimir Ivashko arrived in Beijing to prepare for a visit to Moscow by Chinese Communist Party First Secretary Jiang Zemin (RFE/RL correspondent's report, February 26). On February 27, the two men discussed the role of the Soviet and Chinese Communist Parties in their countries' economic, social and political reforms, as well as Soviet-Chinese contacts and economic cooperation.

USSR and South Africa to Renew Diplomatic Dialogue

For the first time in thirty-five years, the Soviet Union and South Africa agreed to set up a channel for conducting diplomatic dialogue, Reuters reported. Soviet Foreign Ministry spokesman Vitalii Churkin said the decision did not, however, amount to the establishment of diplomatic or consular ties. South African Foreign Minister Roelof Botha said that the new channel would be used for trade, travel, and political contacts. Soviet-South African relations were broken off in February, 1956, after South Africa accused Soviet diplomats of distributing Communist propaganda and maintaining contacts with subversive elements in South Africa.

Ukraine Adds Question to Referendum

Ukrainian Supreme Soviet Chairman Leonid Kravchuk told RFE/RL that, in addition to the official question, Ukrainians would be asked on March 17 whether they favored a restructured union of "sovereign states" to replace the USSR (RL Ukrainian service, February 26).

More Violence in Nagorno-Karabakh

Two Soviet soldiers and an Azerbaijani policeman were killed in the process of trying to free hostages in Nagorno-Karabakh, Radio Moscow reported on February 27.

As reported by TASS, 60 percent of Stepanakert's population was without water because of an explosion at the city's water distribution center.

On February 28, thousands of people gathered in Stepanakert to mark the third anniversary of the 1988 clashes between Armenians and Azerbaijanis in the Azerbaijan city of Sumgait, TASS reported.

The USSR in February, 1991

Uzbek-Turkish Agreement Signed

A treaty was signed in Tashkent, providing for cooperation in public health and medical sciences between Uzbekistan and Turkey, TASS reported. The agreement guaranteed the establishment of joint Turkish-Uzbek pharmacies and pharmacy warehouses in Uzbekistan. The two countries were also to exchange specialists and set up joint ventures for the production of medical equipment and medicines.

Uzbekistan Bans Religious Parties

The Uzbek law on public associations forbade the creation of parties of a religious nature while the corresponding USSR law forbade only the creation of associations whose aim was to provoke religious discord, TASS reported. The authorities in the Central Asian republics had shown themselves hostile to attempts to set up Islamic parties on their territories and had enlisted the official clergy to argue that such parties were incompatible with Islam.

Soviet Germans Meet with Yanaev and Nishanov

USSR Vice President Gennadii Yanaev and Chairman of the USSR Council of Nationalities Rafik Nishanov met with members of the organizing committee of the Congress of Soviet Germans due to convene from March 11 to 15, TASS reported. Yanaev and Nishanov said they would ask the USSR Supreme Soviet to take up the question of annulling all repressive acts against the Soviet Germans and to look into the status of the former members of the labor army in which Soviet Germans served following their deportation from the Volga area. They made no promises, however, on the Germans' main demand, the restoration of their autonomy.

Retail Price Increases in Lithuania

Radio Vilnius announced forthcoming increases in retail prices in Lithuania, together with compensatory supplementary payments for all adult members of the population. The first compensation payments would be made on March 19; the scale of compensation differed from the all-Union rates announced by the central authorities.

Lithuanian Communist Party's Right to Publish Suspended

The Lithuanian government temporarily suspended the Communist Party's license to publish in the republic, AP reported. Unspecified irregularities in the Party's registration of one Lithuanian- and two Russian-language newspapers and several other publications were cited as reasons for the suspension, Baltfax reported. According to TASS, the Lithuanian government decreed that the

Lithuanian Communist Party was an organization "of another state" and therefore had no right to operate in the republic.

Wednesday, February 27

Consumer-Rights Bill Approved by USSR Supreme Soviet

The USSR Supreme Soviet met to discuss a consumer-rights bill, TASS reported. The bill laid down the legal, economic, and social principles of consumer protection, meeting general world standards approved by the UN General Assembly. The bill was approved at its first reading.

RSFSR Supreme Soviet Session

The RSFSR Supreme Soviet called on the USSR to transfer the second television channel to RSFSR authority, TASS reported. It also called on the Soviet broadcasting authorities to let the RSFSR use some of their equipment free of charge.

On the same day, the RSFSR Supreme Soviet debated a bill on the role of the police. Sponsors of the bill believed that the existing structure of the police force did not allow it to properly protect public order or fight crime. According to TASS, speakers said the police performed duties not relevant to police work, such as issuing passports. Therefore, the bill proposed to remove eight such functions from the list of police duties, which would free up about 54,000 policemen for real police work.

Democratic Russia on Referendum

Democratic Russia urged people to cast a "no" vote in the national referendum on the future of the Soviet Union on March 17, TASS reported. Vyacheslav Volkov, coordinator of the work of the faction, said the formulation of the question implied the restoration of Communist and military structures. Democratic Russia adopted a statement calling for the creation of "a commonwealth of sovereign states" on the basis of a confederation. Leaders of Democratic Russia regarded the forthcoming referendum as an opportunity to vote against Gorbachev and his policies.

USSR Wants Germany to Compensate Soviet Victims of War Crimes

Novosti reported that the USSR wanted Germany to compensate Soviet citizens who had been used for forced labor in Germany during World War II. TASS reported on February 26 on a Soviet-German agreement in principle for German payment, and quoted

The USSR in February, 1991

Deputy Foreign Minister Yulii Kvitsinsky as saying an agreement on this point played an important role in Soviet ratification of the treaties on German reunification. Germany also said it planned limited payments to Soviet victims of medical experiments and other similar crimes, Reuters reported.

More Than 500 Parties in USSR

CPSU Central Committee Secretary Valentin Kuptsov told a Moscow news conference that there were more than 500 political parties in the USSR, 20 of which had a nationwide membership, TASS reported. Kuptsov stressed that the CPSU was willing to work with any party that did not reject socialism. He charged, however, that the new parties had no program other than opposition to the CPSU.

Archives on Deportees Opened

Radio Moscow reported that official archives on more than half a million people who were forcibly deported to the Urals region in the 1930s had been opened to the public. Scientists at the Urals branch of the USSR Academy of Sciences had been studying the archives, but access was now to be given to relatives so that they could obtain information on family members who disappeared during that period (RFE/RL correspondent's report, February 27).

Joint Appeal on Referendum

The Central Committees of the Communist Parties of the RSFSR, Ukraine, and Belorussia issued a joint appeal calling on all Communists, workers, and peoples of the USSR to vote "yes" in the March 17 referendum, Ukrinform-TASS reported. The appeal attacked those who, "under the mask of democrats," abused *glasnost'* and pluralism to distort the aims of *perestroika*. It called on the Supreme Soviets and governments of the three republics to be the first to sign the Union treaty.

Soviet Correspondent Tells of Iraqi Valor

Major General Viktor Filatov, who was sent to Baghdad as a special correspondent for *Sovetskaya Rossiya*, gave a different account of the Gulf war to that of his Western counterparts. Even as Iraqi forces retreated in disarray, Filatov wrote on February 27 that the Iraqi army had shown its steadfastness, courage, and valor. Filatov, editor of *Voenno-istoricbesky zhurnal*, also reported that the allied offensive had bogged down, and he compared the Gulf war with US actions in Korea and Vietnam.

Soviet Diplomats Arrive in Albania

Soviet diplomat Vyacheslav Durnev arrived in Albania with his staff members to take up posts as official representatives of the USSR in Tirana, AP reported. Relations were being resumed after a break of thirty years. According to the Albanian daily *Zeri i Popullit*, Durnev was to serve as interim chargé d'affaires until a permanent ambassador was appointed.

Armenia Adopts Law on Political Parties

The Armenian Supreme Soviet adopted a law on social and political organizations, Radio Moscow reported. The law forbade the activity on the territory of the republic of any parties whose headquarters were outside the republic. According to the report, this would apply not only to the CPSU but also to the traditional nationalist parties that until recently had only functioned abroad. The law stated that parties were not allowed to accept funding or donations from outside Armenia and also that they were forbidden to set up organizational structures in state agencies and institutions, in enterprises, or in educational institutions.

Gamsakhurdia Says Gorbachev Issued Ultimatum

Chairman of the Georgian Supreme Soviet Zviad Gamsakhurdia told an emergency session of that body that Soviet President Mikhail Gorbachev had telephoned him on February 25 to threaten to detach Abkhazia and South Ossetia from Georgia unless the republic signed a treaty with the Soviet government. Gorbachev asked him whether he had changed his mind about the Union treaty. Gamsakhurdia replied that his rejection of the treaty was not only his personal position but the position of the whole Georgian nation. A spokesman for Gorbachev said he was unaware of the conversation (*Reuters*, February 27).

On February 28, the Georgian Supreme Soviet accused the USSR of using unrest in South Ossetia to punish Georgia for not participating in the new Union treaty and approved a question to be submitted to Georgian voters in a special March 31 referendum. They were to be asked: "Do you want to restore the state independence of Georgia based on the declaration of May 18, 1918?"

Moldavia Introduces Coupons

The Moldavian government decreed the introduction of coupons to protect the republic's consumers and prevent the flow of scarce goods from Moldavia to other republics. Coupons were to be issued to Moldavia's residents only, for a value equivalent to 70 percent of their salaries.

THE USSR IN FEBRUARY, 1991

Citizens with salaries under 100 rubles would receive 75 rubles' worth of coupons. TASS said the measure would go into effect on March 1.

Moldavian President Mircea Snegur created a Consultative Council consisting of representatives of all political parties, social and political movements and formations, and national-cultural associations legally registered in Moldavia. The council was designed to offer the president a full range of views on all problems affecting the republic and assist in reaching civil accord in Moldavia, TASS reported.

Moldavian President Creates Consultative Council

The Tajik Supreme Soviet decided to return the historical name of Khudzhand to the city of Leninabad in northern Tajikistan, following a referendum in that city in December, 1990, TASS reported. Khudzhand, one of the most ancient Tajik cities, celebrated its 2,500th anniversary in 1989. TASS quoted the city's mayor, Dadodzhon Ashurov, as saying that the city had been renamed to restore historical justice, not to slight Lenin.

Leninabad Regains Historical Name

A conference entitled "Sociopolitical Movements for a Great United Russia" was held in Moscow, TASS reported. Representatives of some eighty political parties, movements, and unions participated, as did First Secretary of the RSFSR Communist Party Ivan Polozkov and the writers Yurii Bondarev and Aleksandr Prokhanov. The conference issued an appeal asserting that "only a strong, patriotic, and active power will be able to lead the people of Russia out of tragedy."

Conference for "A Great United Russia"

―――――――――――――――――――――――― *Thursday, February 28*

Valentin Pokrovsky, head of the USSR Academy of Medical Sciences, told *Trud* that the Soviet Union had halted the spread of AIDS after testing more than 87 million of its 286 million inhabitants. According to statistical trends, Pokrovsky said, 1,600 people should have been infected by 1991, but the number had reached only 1,163, including 274 children who had been infected in a series of incidents in provincial hospitals in the past two years. Pokrovsky added that the creation of an epidemiology service had enabled the Soviet Union to curb any rise in the disease and that a network of

Soviet Medical Expert Says AIDS under Control

The USSR in February, 1991

specialized laboratories and regional centers had been set up to combat it (*Reuters*, February 28).

Ukrainian Supreme Soviet Approves Chernobyl' Relief Legislation

The Ukrainian Supreme Soviet approved legislation designed to provide relief from the effects of the Chernobyl' disaster, TASS reported. The most important part of the legislation concerned aid for the millions of Ukrainians who were affected, and it included resettlement assistance, compensation for material damage, and supplies of noncontaminated food. It was to take effect on April 1. The Ukrainian Supreme Soviet added that the USSR would have to pay for the aid outlined in the legislation out of the funds it had set aside for Chernobyl'.

Clerics Call on Muslims to Fulfill Military Duty

The Muslim Religious Board for Central Asia and Kazakhstan appealed to Muslim servicemen to fulfill their military duty in a fatwa (religious ruling) issued in *Krasnaya zvezda* and summarized by TASS, warning soldiers against "pacific moods." The fatwa said laziness and lack of discipline were a disgrace for defenders of the homeland.

Democratic Bloc of Azerbaijan on Referendum

The opposition Democratic Bloc of Azerbaijan issued a statement calling on citizens not to vote in the March 17 referendum on the future of the USSR. Journalist Elmira Ahmedova told RFE/RL the statement was supported by a number of opposition political and social groups, including three small political parties (RL Azerbaijani service, February 28).

Nordic News for the Baltic

The Norwegian news agency NTB opened a satellite link to Lithuania's ELTA news service to help increase the flow of information to the Baltic republics from the West, AP reported. The service was in Norwegian but included reports from all the news services of the Nordic countries and was to be translated for the Lithuanian media and relayed to wire services in Estonia and Latvia. The Nordic agencies agreed to provide their service free of charge for a one-year trial period.

Right to Nonviolent Resistance Guaranteed in Lithuania

The Lithuanian Supreme Council voted to guarantee the right of nonviolent resistance, AP reported. The Supreme Council said citizens might exercise the right whenever the republic's sovereignty and integrity were threatened. The guarantee was part of a citizens' rights package in which the Supreme Council also reaffirmed the

The USSR in February, 1991

supremacy of republican laws over Soviet ones, declared invalid all decrees by Soviet government structures affecting Lithuania, and warned of the possibility that Lithuania could be further occupied by the Soviet Union.

The RSFSR Supreme Soviet approved the appointment of Colonel Sergei Stepashin as chairman of its Committee on Security, TASS reported. Stepashin had worked in internal affairs organs in Leningrad. Valentin Stepankov was approved as RSFSR prosecutor. Stepankov, a member of the CPSU and an RSFSR people's deputy, was a professional lawyer who until his new appointment had held the post of first deputy prosecutor of the RSFSR.

RSFSR Supreme Soviet Names Security Chief, Prosecutor

The Month of March

Friday, March 1

USSR Supreme Soviet Adopts Law on Currency Regulation

The USSR Supreme Soviet adopted a law on regulation of hard currency, TASS reported. The new law, to take effect on April 1, would provide for a foreign-exchange market open to all domestic and foreign firms. In order to maintain the stability of the ruble's purchasing power, the law banned the use of foreign currency as a means of payment in the USSR and the import and export of rubles. For the text of the law, see *Izvestia*, March 15.

Trade Organizations to Become Independent Companies

Igor' Faminsky, the director of the All-Union Scientific Research Institute of Foreign Economic Relations attached to the USSR Cabinet of Ministers' State Foreign Economic Commission, told Reuters that the nearly one hundred foreign-trade organizations in the USSR were to be dismantled. Faminsky said most of them would be replaced by new, independently operating companies that would have shareholders and would not enjoy monopoly powers. He foresaw the continued transfer of revenue from the all-Union budget to foreign-trade operations by means of an export tax and did not rule out foreign participation in the new companies. He gave no date for the implementation of the measures.

Burbulis on El'tsin-Gorbachev Struggle

Gennadii Burbulis, spokesman for RSFSR Supreme Soviet Chairman Boris El'tsin, told the *Handelsblatt* that the struggle between El'tsin and Gorbachev was not a personal matter but rather a conflict between "new democratic beginnings" and "the old totalitarian structures." He said El'tsin criticized Gorbachev so strongly because it was no longer possible to conceal the differences in opinion between the two men and because Gorbachev was legitimizing a reactionary turnaround in the Soviet Union. El'tsin, for his part, was criticized because he represented a danger to "the totalitarian system of the bureaucracy" (RFE/RL correspondent's report, March 1).

TASS reported the same day that the Leningrad City Soviet had appealed to citizens to support El'tsin in a resolution approved despite opposition from members of the Rebirth of Leningrad movement and many Communists.

The USSR in March, 1991

Armenia to Hold Referendum on Secession

Armenpress-TASS reported that the Armenian Supreme Soviet had reiterated its refusal to take part in the nationwide referendum on the future of the Soviet Union scheduled for March 17, saying it contradicted the right of nations to self-determination. The Armenian Supreme Soviet voted to hold a republican referendum on secession from the USSR on September 21.

Ecology Official Proposes International Commission to Save Aral Sea

Kakimbek Salykov, chairman of the USSR Supreme Soviet Ecology Committee, suggested an appeal be drafted to set up an international commission to save the Aral Sea. He said that 78 percent of the population in the area around the Aral Sea was sick and that death and infant mortality rates had increased. He characterized the destruction of the Aral Sea as the world's largest ecological catastrophe. USSR First Deputy Prime Minister Vitalii Doguzhiev said current efforts to save the Aral Sea were doomed for lack of money (RFE/RL correspondent's report, March 2).

Saturday, March 2

Coal Miners Strike

After a one-day warning strike on March 1, work stoppages at mines in various parts of the Soviet Union continued on March 2 and 3, Western agencies reported. Miners at between twenty and twenty-three of the twenty-six mines in Karaganda in Kazakhstan participated; in Ukraine's Donbass, twenty to twenty-nine of two hundred mines were on strike—these included Ukraine's two largest pits, Krasnolimanskaya and Stakhanov, where strikers held rallies. Soviet television said representatives of the Independent Miners' Union (IMU) from the Kuzbass region of Siberia had arrived in Moscow in anticipation of talks with Soviet Vice President Gennadii Yanaev.

Striking miners in Karaganda decided to resume work after the Soviet and republican governments had agreed to meet them. Kazakh President Nursultan Nazarbaev said neither the republican nor the USSR government could afford to meet their demands. Soviet journalist Karen Agamirov, quoting Bulat Mukhazhanov of the Karaganda Strike Committee, told RFE/RL on March 4 that the Karaganda miners would strike again on March 30 if their demands were not met.

In the Arctic, striking miners decided to extend their strike until at least March 7. Eleven of the thirteen major mines were closed in the region, Radio Moscow reported.

On March 4, twenty-seven of seventy-six mines stopped work for twenty-four hours in the Kuzbass, Vyacheslav

Shapirov, a leader of the IMU said (*Reuters*, March 4). Miners at some Kuzbass pits held three-hour stoppages on each shift, AFP reported. In Prokop'evsk, some 5,000 miners gathered in a rally calling for the resignation of Soviet President Mikhail Gorbachev and his Cabinet, for the transfer of power to the Federation Council, and for higher wages. Six of the 250 pits in the Donbass region, along with one pit of the forty-nine in the Rostov-on-Don region were reported to be continuing their strike (*TASS*, March 4).

By March 5, the number of Donbass coal mines on strike had doubled to twelve, TASS reported. Soviet Prime Minister Valentin Pavlov said on Soviet television the same day that he favored higher wages for miners but that the USSR did not have the money to meet their demands.

The IMU sent appeals to the US Labor Federation—the AFL-CIO—and to the RSFSR Supreme Soviet on March 5, Western agencies reported. The first appeal asked for moral and material support, while the second asked for food and material support. According to IMU spokesman Pavel Shushpanov, the deputy minister of the coal industry had threatened to cut off food and electricity in areas where strikes were under way. Meanwhile, the RSFSR Supreme Soviet agreed to export 60,000 tons of coal to Malta in exchange for consumer goods (*AP*, March 5).

On March 6, the number of mines on strike approximately doubled in both the Donbass and the Kuzbass, according to Western agencies. Figures provided by TASS were lower, however. Miners in Vorkuta went on strike at midnight on March 6 after having refused an offer of talks with Soviet Deputy Prime Minister Lev Ryabev, TASS reported. They said they would meet only with a Cabinet-level official. Representatives of the USSR Prosecutor's Office traveled around the Donbass telling miners that strikes were illegal under the emergency measures adopted by the USSR Supreme Soviet, Reuters reported. USSR Minister of the Coal Industry Mikhail Shchadov said on Central Television that, in contrast to past practice, striking miners would not be paid.

On March 7, a TASS report said that miners in Vorkuta were on strike at twelve of the region's fifteen mines. They demanded talks with Soviet Prime Minister Pavlov, who agreed to meet with them only after all the mines in Vorkuta had resumed operations.

In Kazakhstan, the Karagandaugol coal enterprise began suing miners who had taken part in the previous week's strike in the region, Radio Moscow reported on March 7. The miners were to be charged with absenteeism.

The USSR in March, 1991

On March 10, AP quoted Anatolii Snegurets, spokesman for the Executive Committee of the Independent Miners' Union, as saying forty-eight coal mines were on strike on March 9 in Ukraine, Siberia, Vorkuta, and Kazakhstan. TASS also announced that the Lithuanian Workers' Union had organized the collection of tons of food and other items for the striking miners in the Donbass, Kuzbass, and Vorkuta regions. The donations, collected from private citizens and enterprises from many areas in the republic, amounted to 427 tons and left Vilnius on March 12 in trucks and automobiles, Radio Kaunas reported that day.

On March 10, RSFSR Supreme Soviet Chairman Boris El'tsin met with the leaders of the Kuzbass Strike Committee who had come to Moscow to try to meet with Soviet Prime Minister Pavlov, TASS reported. El'tsin told the miners that only they could decide by what means they should press their demands; the possibility of transferring the mines from national to republican control was also discussed.

On the same day, in response to the appeal made on March 5 by the Independent Miners' Union, the AFL-CIO expressed support for the striking Soviet miners and said it would send a delegation to monitor the strike and seek to counter efforts to violate basic workers' rights (RFE/RL correspondent's report, March 11).

Soviet President Gorbachev refused to meet with miners' representatives, saying such a meeting would be "inexpedient," Central Television reported on March 12. Anatolii Luk'yanov met with them on March 8 and passed on their demands to Gorbachev, Central Television added. The trade unions of the metallurgy, machine-building, defense, timber, and chemical industries complained in *Trud* on March 13 that the miners' actions were aggravating the situation in their industries. The miners' complaints could be resolved only through negotiation, they said, calling on the USSR Cabinet of Ministers to start talks with the striking miners immediately.

News agencies reported on March 13 that five steel mills in Ukraine had been forced to close owing to a lack of coal. In Kemerovo, the oblast soviet voted to seek a meeting with Gorbachev to discuss the miners' demands, TASS reported the same day.

The Latvian Popular Front established a fund to aid striking miners, contributing 10,000 rubles itself, Radio Riga reported on March 13.

On March 14, a Radio Rossii report said that people throughout the USSR were collecting food and other supplies for the striking miners. In Moscow, people collected more than thirty tons of food for the Kuzbass miners and the radio appealed to Muscovites to stop because no more could be transported.

On the same day, a workers' collective of the Donetsk regional railway threatened to end service to some of Ukraine's largest coal mines if strikes were not suspended by March 15, Radio Kiev reported.

A TASS report of March 15 said that the strikes were threatening the production of electricity in the Kuzbass region. Coal deliveries to Kuzbass power plants were some 21,000 tons lower than required. Moreover, stocks of food, including flour, were running out in the region, and the Kemerovo Oblast government met in emergency session to try to deal with the food shortage (*Radio Moscow*, March 15).

On March 19, TASS reported that some 300,000 miners, mostly in the Donbass, the Kuzbass, and Vorkuta, were on strike. Miners at five of the ten mines in Chelyabinsk Oblast were reported to have gone on strike in support of their colleagues in other regions.

Gorbachev met with local officials in Kemerovo in the Kuzbass and promised that wages, tax laws, and food supplies would be adjusted for miners there. Gorbachev and the officials rejected the use of strikes to press "unreasonable" political and economic demands. No representatives of the striking miners were present. Vadim Bakatin, a member of the USSR Security Council, supported Gorbachev's rejection of the Kuzbass miners' political demands. Bakatin told "Vremya" that, if Gorbachev gave in to the miners' demands, he would be violating the USSR Constitution. Bakatin criticized "certain groups of deputies" for raising tensions and abusing the miners' strikes to satisfy their own political ambitions.

In the Donbass, the directors of the Pavlogradugol Association filed a lawsuit against the miners on strike there for ignoring procedures on strikes set out in Soviet labor laws. Miners in Chelyabinsk sent a delegation to Moscow to seek talks. In Moscow, a national strike committee calling for the resignation of Gorbachev and his government was formed.

In Kiev, Ukrainian Deputy Prime Minister Viktor Gladush offered to begin negotiations with Donbass miners. On March 21, about seventy miners' leaders from the Donbass met with Ukrainian Prime Minister Vitol'd Fokin and Gladush for talks on the miners' demand for more pay (*Radio Kiev*, March 21). Miners' representative Yurii Boldyrev told AP that the ministers had agreed to allow early retirement for some miners but had refused to meet their demand for pay raises. As a result, the

The USSR in March, 1991

Donetsk Strike Committee decided to break off the talks and refused to sign a pledge to return to work.

On March 20, Soviet Prime Minister Pavlov agreed to talks with miners in Vorkuta and Inta but only on condition that all mines were working (*Radio Rossii*, March 21). The same day, the strike committee at the RSFSR's largest asbestos combine, Uralasbest, called a twenty-four-hour strike, TASS reported. The strikers were asking for higher pay and more vacation. Gold miners at the Darassunsky pit, the largest gold mine in the Chita Oblast in Siberia, also went on strike, demanding higher salaries and better living conditions (*TASS*, March 21).

On March 21, *Komsomol'skaya pravda* reported that Kazakh President Nazarbaev had persuaded Karaganda miners not to strike for the next three months. Nazarbaev promised to work for a solution to all the miners' problems.

The same day, AFP reported that the USSR Supreme Soviet had approved by a large majority a resolution denouncing the miners' strike and urging the miners to drop their political demands and return to work. USSR Supreme Soviet deputies Nikolai Ivanov and Tel'man Gdlyan announced they would join miners in the RSFSR who had been on a hunger strike since the previous week because the USSR Supreme Soviet had proved it was incapable of dealing rationally with the strikers' demands (RFE/RL correspondent's report, March 21).

Also on March 21, *Rabochaya tribuna* issued an appeal from metal, power, and textile workers to the miners asking them to start working again. The appeal said that, in fighting for their legal rights, the miners were pushing workers of other industries towards starvation.

Later that day, RSFSR Prime Minister Ivan Silaev arrived in the Kuzbass for negotiations with striking miners, TASS reported. On March 22, Silaev told the miners that the RSFSR government wanted foreign help in modernizing the republic's mining industry; foreign participation would make the industry more efficient and allow improvements in social conditions, he said. He also said that the RSFSR government wanted enterprises to be able to withdraw from USSR structures and work independently (*TASS*, March 23).

Also on March 22, a Radio Moscow report said that RSFSR First Deputy Prime Minister Yurii Skokov had gone to the city of Vorkuta to hold talks with miners there. Meanwhile, the strike had spread to 223 of the Soviet Union's 600 coal mines (RFE/RL correspondent's report, March 22). Radio Mayak said that coal production in Ukraine had dropped by about 2 million tons since the strike began three weeks earlier.

Speaking to representatives of the Donbass coal miners in the Ukrainian Supreme Soviet on the same day, Supreme Soviet Chairman Leonid Kravchuk upbraided the strikers for turning to the central government in Moscow for help. According to Ukrinform-TASS, Kravchuk stressed that economic problems were a matter for the Ukrainian government and Supreme Soviet alone. He also asked why mining regions where a large majority had voted in favor of Ukraine's sovereignty in the republican plebiscite on March 17 should now be "bringing the republic to its knees."

Speaking on Central Television on March 23, Soviet Prime Minister Pavlov said several years of work would be needed to repair the economic damage done by the miners' strike. USSR Minister of the Coal Industry Shchadov, also interviewed on television, said the strike was adversely affecting many other sectors of the economy.

Reuters reported on March 25 that the USSR Cabinet of Ministers had agreed to open talks on the strikers' economic demands and that Soviet Prime Minister Pavlov would meet with representatives of the striking miners on March 29. USSR Minister of Justice Sergei Lushchikov proposed that miners be held liable for losses incurred during the strike; according to Shchadov, losses in coal production alone amounted to 443 million dollars at the official exchange rate. Leaders of the striking miners, however, said that they would return to work only if Gorbachev resigned and were replaced by El'tsin or if they were asked by El'tsin to end the strike.

On March 26, citing the USSR Law on Collective Labor Disputes, the USSR Supreme Soviet adopted a draft resolution stating that the strike should be suspended for two months, TASS reported. Strike leaders described the order as antidemocratic but said that miners must decide for themselves whether to comply with it (*Reuters*, March 26). Appearing on Central Television the same day, Gorbachev said he planned to meet with miners' representatives on April 2. A special working group was also being formed by the Ukrainian Supreme Soviet to deal directly with miners' collectives and strike committees in that republic. Chairman of the Ukrainian Supreme Soviet Kravchuk appealed to the strikers, describing their action as a threat to the republic's energy, metallurgical, and agricultural industries. The Lvov Oblast Soviet also urged striking miners in the Lvov-Volyn Basin to return to work, Radio Kiev reported.

Vasilii Romanov, deputy chairman of the RSFSR Federation of Independent Trade Unions, declared on Radio Rossii that his organization was prepared to call a general

The USSR in March, 1991

strike unless Gorbachev met with miners' representatives, and he added that workers in the metal, oil, and construction industries had said they would take part in such a strike.

In Sverdlovsk, workers in several sections of the giant "Uralmash" machine-building plant struck for two hours on March 27 in protest against food shortages in the city and against the Soviet leadership's failure to respond to their economic demands presented two months earlier (*TASS*, March 27). The Vorkuta Strike Committee sent a telegram the same day to Gorbachev and the USSR Supreme Soviet in protest against the latter's order that the miners end their strike and announced that the miners in the region would continue striking. The strike committee appealed to all Soviet workers to hold a one-day strike in support of El'tsin (*TASS*, March 27).

On March 29, representatives of the miners' strike committees met in Moscow to work out a joint position on the USSR Supreme Soviet order to suspend strikes, Radio Moscow reported (*TASS*, March 29). Miners at the Noril'sk nickel mine in central Siberia joined the strike the same day and demanded that their wages be doubled and raised in line with inflation in future and that the Noril'sk nickel mine be privatized. The ten-point package reported by TASS contained—apart from economic demands—a call for Gorbachev and the Soviet government to resign and warned that a general strike might be called at the mine if the workers' demands were not met by April 3. As a result, the price of nickel rose on the London Metal Exchange by 4 percent from 9.32 dollars a ton. A report by AP noted that the Soviet Union supplied about 10 percent of the West's nickel requirements.

Striking miners in the Kuzbass sent a telegram that was read out at the RSFSR Congress of People's Deputies. The miners vowed to continue their month-long strike unless their demands were met, Reuters reported.

Speaking about the strikes at the RSFSR Congress of People's Deputies on March 30, El'tsin said he did not blame the miners for striking, because he knew their living conditions were intolerable. He charged that the central government had often promised to improve miners' circumstances but had done nothing, and he said that both he and RSFSR Prime Minister Silaev welcomed calls by the miners for coal-mining in the RSFSR to be taken out of the jurisdiction of the USSR Ministry of the Coal Industry and henceforth governed by the republican authorities (*TASS*, March 30). Meanwhile, the Voroshilov mine in the city of Prokop'evsk in the Kuzbass agreed to El'tsin's call for the transfer of the coal industry to the RSFSR's jurisdiction, Radio Rossii reported the same day.

THE USSR IN MARCH, 1991

RSFSR Refuses to Strip Deputy of Immunity

The RSFSR Supreme Soviet refused to strip people's deputy Artem Tarasov of his immunity after he was charged with slandering Soviet President Mikhail Gorbachev, TASS reported. In January, Tarasov had referred during a television interview to a secret agreement to return four of the disputed Kurile Islands to Japan in exchange for 200 billion dollars and linked Gorbachev to the deal. USSR Prosecutor-General Nikolai Trubin had requested that the RSFSR Supreme Soviet strip Tarasov of his parliamentary immunity so that criminal proceedings could be instituted against him.

Timetable for Withdrawal from Germany Called Unrealistic

In an interview with Pravda, USSR people's deputy Colonel Nikolai Petrushenko said the four-year schedule for the withdrawal of Soviet troops from Germany was unrealistic; he said that current railroad transport capacity would enable the withdrawal to be completed only over a period of sixteen to nineteen years. He added that the use of naval transport could cut this to ten years. Anticipating German dissatisfaction with his estimates, Petrushenko said it would be better to recognize that the timetable for the withdrawal was a mistake.

In an interview with German television (ZDF) on March 4, liberal war historian Vyacheslav Dashichev said estimates of a ten- to twenty-year timetable for Soviet troop withdrawals from Germany were "nonsense." Dashichev pointed to the Soviet Union's invasion of Czechoslovakia in 1968 and Afghanistan in 1979 as examples of how quickly the Soviet Armed Forces could move from one place to another.

Speaking at a press conference in Berlin on March 5, the Soviet military commander in Germany, Colonel General Matvei Burlakov, declared that the Soviet Union wanted financial compensation for army installations Soviet troops were leaving behind, a DPA report said. He valued the property at 10.5 billion deutsche marks. The money should be used to build apartments for returning Soviet troops, he said, and added that the USSR had demanded similar compensation from Hungary, Czechoslovakia, and Poland.

Democratic Congress Meets

The consultative council of the Democratic Congress held its first meeting in Moscow, Central Television reported. The meeting was attended by at least twenty-two parties and movements from eleven republics, including Democratic Russia, "Rukh," and the Belorussian Popular Front. The meeting expressed support for Chairman of the RSFSR Supreme Soviet Boris El'tsin and

RSFSR Prime Minister Ivan Silaev, denounced the creation of various "national salvation committees" as illegal, called for the creation of a broad-based antitotalitarian coalition, and decided to hold an interparliamentary conference in Moscow from April 21 to 23 to draw up "a treaty of a commonwealth of sovereign states as an alternative to the draft Union treaty." The council adopted a resolution on the situation in Georgia and agreed to accept Chairman of the Georgian Supreme Soviet Zviad Gamsakhurdia's invitation to send a delegation to the republic. It also discussed the creation of an independent news agency and an interrepublican newspaper and called for the abolition of the post of USSR president, the transfer of power to the Federation Council as an interim body, and the dissolution of the USSR Congress of People's Deputies.

At a press conference at the close of the session on March 3, leaders of the Democratic Congress said their supporters in all parts of the country had begun an active campaign aimed at disrupting the March 17 referendum, but they admitted that they were not achieving the desired result everywhere (*TASS*, March 3).

Yurii Bad'zo, a leader of the Democratic Party of Ukraine, spoke to Radio Kiev on March 4 about the session. Bad'zo maintained that, after suffering setbacks recently, the democratic movement in the USSR was picking up again and was moving towards a nationwide coalition. He drew attention to the congress's call to soldiers, officers, and Communist Party members to join forces with democratic movements.

Measures Urged to Improve Kuzbass Ecological Situation

The Kemerovo Oblast Soviet appealed to the USSR and RSFSR Supreme Soviets to declare the Kuzbass region an ecological disaster zone. *Izvestia* did not say when the appeal had been sent but reminded readers that two previous appeals had gone unanswered.

Pravda Gives First Reports of Iraqi Atrocities

Pravda gave readers its first accounts of Iraqi atrocities in Kuwait. The newspaper quoted Kuwaiti survivors who described the horrors of seven months under Iraqi occupation.

In the same issue of *Pravda*, presidential envoy Evgenii Primakov reported on his last meeting with Saddam Hussein in Baghdad on February 12, when the USSR tried to persuade Iraq to agree to a cease-fire. Primakov wrote that Saddam knew that his forces in Kuwait would be crushed by the allied coalition in a ground assault. Saddam told him that he thought the

United States was determined to start the ground offensive, and he complained that the Soviet Union had given its agreement for the assault to begin, Primakov added.

North Ossetia Not to Hold RSFSR Referendum

An extraordinary session of the North Ossetian Supreme Soviet voted not to hold the RSFSR referendum on the institution of the post of president, Radio Moscow reported. Deputies decided that to hold the all-Union and republican referendums the same day would complicate the political situation.

Georgia Appeals to United Nations over South Ossetia

TASS reported that the Georgian Supreme Soviet had sent an appeal to the United Nations calling for the creation of an international commission to investigate the unrest in South Ossetia, TASS reported.

On March 5, the USSR Supreme Soviet began debate on a resolution asking Soviet President Mikhail Gorbachev to declare a state of emergency throughout South Ossetia, TASS reported. Many deputies argued that the resolution was unnecessary, since the president had the power to declare a state of emergency.

On March 6, the Georgian Supreme Soviet issued a statement signed by its chairman, Zviad Gamsakhurdia, offering South Ossetia cultural autonomy, local elections, and a local police force in exchange for the disarming of all illegal armed groups and the establishment of a legitimate authority in Tskhinvali. Georgia refused, however, to allow South Ossetia to restore its status as an autonomous oblast.

On March 7, Gorbachev announced at the USSR Supreme Soviet that a Soviet delegation would be sent to Georgia to try to resolve the conflict between the republic and South Ossetia, Reuters reported.

USSR First Deputy Minister of Internal Affairs Boris Gromov met with regional leaders in South Ossetia on March 14 to discuss ways of ending ethnic violence in the region.

On March 27, RSFSR Supreme Soviet Chairman Boris El'tsin traveled to Vladikavkaz, the capital of the North Ossetian ASSR, where he told a large rally that he would try to send relief for Ossetian refugees from Georgia. Radio Rossii reported that El'tsin then traveled to Georgia, where he met with Supreme Soviet Chairman Gamsakhurdia in Kazbegi. They agreed on measures to halt ethnic clashes in South Ossetia. According to Interfax, these included the creation of a joint police force to disarm illegal national militias and a request for the withdrawal of USSR Defense Ministry units. The two leaders also agreed on an accord between Georgia and the RSFSR to be signed before the end of April.

On March 30, in a telegram to Gamsakhurdia, Gorbachev called for an end to the bloodshed in South Ossetia, TASS reported. Replying to Gorbachev's message on April 1, Gamsakhurdia said that Georgia was taking active measures to end the conflict and that the Georgian police had recently managed to restore relative calm in South Ossetia, TASS reported. But Gamsakhurdia again accused the central Soviet media of bias in coverage of events in Georgia, and he alleged that this was contributing to destabilization.

TASS reported that a resolution had been passed on March 31 by the RSFSR Congress of People's Deputies calling on Georgia to restore South Ossetia's status as an autonomous oblast, lift the blockade, and allow the return of refugees. The congress called on Gorbachev and the Council of the Federation to take urgent measures to normalize conditions in the region.

The Georgian Supreme Soviet rejected the appeal on April 2, calling it "gross interference" in the republic's affairs. According to a report by TASS that day, the presidium of the Georgian Supreme Soviet said that, by making the appeal, the RSFSR Congress shared responsibility for any consequences of actions the USSR might take against Georgia.

Attacks Continue in South Ossetia

On March 1, TASS reported that an intensive gun battle had taken place near Tskhinvali between Georgians and USSR MVD troops. Several of the Georgians were wounded. The same report said that Ossetians had fired shots at the provisional headquarters of the Georgian Ministry of Internal Affairs in Tskhinvali and at USSR MVD troops. One policeman was wounded in the attack.

TASS reported on March 7 that militants had rampaged through Ossetian houses in one village, injuring several Ossetians and taking four others hostage. In another incident, Ossetian militants armed with automatic weapons and grenade launchers attacked villages. Several people were injured.

Three people were reported dead and two wounded in gun battles in the South Ossetian village of Monastyr on March 8; several people were also wounded during an exchange of gunfire in Tskhinvali (*TASS*, March 8).

On March 9, TASS reported that one Georgian had been killed in fighting near Tskhinvali, that Georgian gunmen had killed one Ossetian and ransacked several houses in the village of Khetaguri, and that several more Ossetians had been injured in fighting in the village of

Avneni. Food and other supplies were reported to be critically short in the South Ossetian capital.

On March 12, TASS said the Georgian Supreme Soviet had extended the state of emergency in South Ossetia for another month, after intensive shooting in and around Tskhinvali. Novosti said the same day that Georgian paramilitary groups had looted Ossetian homes and driven residents from twenty-four villages in the region.

Radio Tbilisi reported on March 13 that Georgian militia posts near Tskhinvali had come under machine-gun fire and had fired back. The radio blamed Ossetian extremists for the attack.

Radio Mayak reported on March 15 that 12,000 refugees had arrived in Tskhinvali. The city's health department declared that it was concerned about the possibility of an outbreak of typhoid. It said municipal services had come to a standstill and residents were obtaining water from rivers and wells.

TASS quoted former First Secretary of the South Ossetian Autonomous Oblast Party Committee Anatolii Chekhoev as claiming that four people had been killed in clashes in Tskhinvali on the night of March 16–17 and two more after the closing of the polls on March 17. On March 18, Radio Tbilisi reported that four young Georgians had been burned to death by South Ossetian extremists.

At a meeting on March 20, leaders of both Georgian and South Ossetian armed groups agreed to a cease-fire and to the establishment of a permanent radio link between the two sides in an effort to end clashes, TASS reported. Nevertheless, shooting continued in Tskhinvali. On March 19, the regional hospital again came under fire, and a nurse and a boy were seriously injured.

On March 23, TASS reported that heavy fighting was continuing in South Ossetia for the fourth consecutive day. Residents were beaten in two Ossetian villages on March 24 and homes set ablaze in two further villages. Eight Ossetians were reported to have been wounded. The TASS report contradicted an earlier claim by the Georgian Ministry of Internal Affairs that the cease-fire reported on March 20 was still in force. Three people were killed in a clash between troops of the USSR Ministry of Internal Affairs and Georgians, AP reported. Armed groups of Ossetians and Georgians were engaged in combat operations that involved the use of automatic weapons, heavy machine guns, grenade-launchers, and missiles. Shots were fired on the same day in and around Tskhinvali, seriously wounding an unspecified number of people (*TASS*, March 25).

The USSR in March, 1991

On March 27, while TASS reported intense gunfire around Tskhinvali and casualties in Znauri Raion, Radio Tbilisi claimed there had been no shooting for six days. The radio accused the central Soviet media of spreading slander propagated by North Ossetia.

A TASS report on March 29 quoted the North Ossetian Ministry of Internal Affairs as saying that Tskhinvali was under attack "day and night," with several houses burned down and the city short of food, medicine, electric power, gas, and water supplies. The report added that fighting between Ossetians and Georgians was continuing in some villages.

Stepanakert Left without Drinking Water

More than half of the population of Stepanakert, the capital of Nagorno-Karabakh, was left without drinking water following the sabotage of local reservoirs, Radio Moscow reported. Stepanakert residents appealed to the military commandant of the city to protect the drinking water supply. Fifteen attacks had been made on the local dam in recent months, and efforts to repair it and the pumping system had been unsuccessful.

More Violence in Nagorno-Karabakh

Three Armenians were killed and two Azerbaijanis wounded in Nagorno-Karabakh when gunmen fired automatic weapons near the village of Yukhary Veysaly. In the Armenian village of Artek one person was killed and another wounded when an armed group attacked a farm. In another incident, an Azerbaijani was killed in a gun battle in which automatic weapons and a grenade launcher were used. Three Azerbaijanis were wounded in an attack with automatic weapons on a car near the village of Gevorkavan (*TASS*, March 3)

On March 4, a bomb exploded at a house in Stepanakert where five Soviet MVD officers were staying. The explosion shattered windows and doors but no one was hurt, TASS reported.

The military commissar of Nagorno-Karabakh, Lieutenant Colonel S. Gunko, said that about 100 men had deserted from the Soviet army in the region but that local authorities were not doing anything to round them up. He said the commissar's office had limited powers to bring in deserters. In addition to dealing with deserters and draft dodgers, Gunko added, his office had also put up with provocations, including armed attacks against Soviet soldiers (*TASS*, March 5).

On March 14 TASS reported that three people had been killed and three seriously injured when unidentified gunmen fired at a bus on the border between the Askeran and Agdam Raions. On March 13, several people had been hospitalized after stone-throwing incidents in the Askeran and Khodzhaly Raions.

The news agency Azerinfrom reported on April 3 that armed Armenians had crossed the Azerbaijani border on March 30 and attacked the village of Kheyrimli, in Kazakh Raion. The nighttime attack was repelled. When about five hundred armed Armenians attacked the village again on March 31, they were chased back into Armenia by a combined force of Soviet soldiers and Azerbaijani police. Azerinform said that one Soviet soldier and one Azerbaijani had been injured; Azerbaijani television listed about thirty Armenians as dead, while Interfax said fifteen people had been killed (RL Azerbaijani service, April 3).

Buddhist School Opened

Some 120 candidates from Buryatia, Kalmykia, and Tuva competed for sixty places in a new Buddhist school that had just opened in the Ivolga *datsan* (monastery) in the Transbaikal, *Izvestia* reported. The school was headed by the young rector-lama, Choi Dorzhi Budaev, who had recently graduated from the higher religious school of the Gandan monastery in Mongolia.

Preparations for Referendum in Lithuania

Algimantas Naudziunas, secretary of the pro-Moscow Lithuanian Communist Party, was quoted by TASS as saying preparations were under way in the republic to enable people to vote in the March 17 all-Union referendum on the future of the Soviet Union. The vote was to be held despite the Lithuanian government's decision not to participate.

On March 10, Aleksandr Bobylev, chairman of the Commission on the Referendum in Vilnius, said that twenty-nine precincts had been set up in the city and that people wishing to vote would be able to do so, TASS reported.

On March 12, the Lithuanian Supreme Council declared any attempts to hold the referendum illegal and passed a resolution canceling decisions by two districts (Snieckus and Salcininkai) to carry out the poll on March 17 (*Radio Vilnius*, March 12).

Sunday, March 3

Soviet Television Shows Documentary on Gorbachev

One day after Mikhail Gorbachev's sixtieth birthday, Central Television broadcast a documentary film entitled "The First President." The head of Central Television said the film was a present for Gorbachev. One aim of the documentary was to satisfy widespread curiosity about Gorbachev's home life. The documentary was almost completely lacking in any insights, however. It was the first time such a documentary had been shown on Soviet television.

Estonia Votes for Independence

Some 79 percent of those voting in a plebiscite organized by the Estonian Supreme Soviet opted for independence, Estonian Television reported on March 4. All districts except Kohtla-Järve in northeastern Estonia (encompassing about 5 percent of the population) reported good voter turnout, with an overall turnout of 84 percent of those entitled to vote. Turnout in the largely ethnic Estonian countryside was around 90 percent, with 93 percent voting for independence. The nonbinding vote asked civilian voters in Estonia the question: "Do you want the restoration of the state sovereignty and independence of the Republic of Estonia?"

President of the Estonian Supreme Council Arnold Ruutel said the vote showed that his government was following the right path (*Reuters*, March 4). Estonian Foreign Minister Lennart Meri, told the British daily *The Independent* that the Baltic republics should start making economic arguments to support their drive for independence to show the USSR that it would profit from independent Baltic States.

Latvia Votes for Independence

The vast majority of voters endorsed a democratic and independent Republic of Latvia in a poll held on March 3. Preliminary results, as reported by Radio Riga on March 4, showed that voter participation in Latvia was 87.5 percent, with 73.6 percent voting in favor of independence, 24.8 percent against, and 1.6 percent casting invalid ballots. Latvian officials praised the results of the poll. At a press conference on March 4, broadcast live by Radio Riga, Andrejs Krastins, deputy president of the Latvian Supreme Council, said the poll proved that people of all nationalities living in Latvia were behind the drive for independence. President of the Latvian Supreme Council Anatolijs Gorbunovs said that Moscow should soften its stance on the Baltic now that all three republics had voted in favor of independence, Reuters reported.

Anatolii Alekseev, a deputy to the Latvian Supreme Council and head of the conservative, Russian-dominated "Interfront," told Reuters on March 4 that the Latvian poll was "a grandiose show" and accused the proindependence Latvian Popular Front of rigging the results. Sergei Dimanis, leader of the minority "Ravnopravie" group of deputies at the Supreme Council, claimed: "The popular front has lost. If the parliament uses these results, which show that the nationalities are split down the middle, to try to build an independent Latvia, a civil war could start." Dimanis failed to note that thousands of non-Latvians had voted for Latvian independence.

Latvian representative in Moscow Janis Peters told RFE/RL on March 7 that presidential spokesman Vitalii Ignatenko had confirmed to him that Soviet President Mikhail Gorbachev was taking the results of the March 3 poll seriously. Peters said that, although Gorbachev had declared the poll to be without legal foundation, he did not plan to ignore it.

Bomb Explodes outside Party Building in Vilnius

A bomb exploded outside the Communist Party headquarters in Vilnius, TASS reported. Vilnius military commander Colonel Grigorii Belous said the bomb was a homemade device and that, in his opinion, it had been set off by people wanting to intimidate Communists and to disrupt the March 17 referendum. The explosion damaged six other buildings but no one was hurt.

St. Casimir Church in Vilnius Reopened

Archbishop of Vilnius Julijonas Steponavicius reconsecrated the St. Casimir Church in Vilnius, Radio Vatican's Lithuanian service reported on March 4. The church was closed by the Soviet authorities in January, 1949, and was used as a wine warehouse until 1963, when it was converted into a Museum of Atheism. The church was formally returned to the Catholics in October, 1988, but reconstruction work was so extensive that it took more than two years to complete. President of the Lithuanian Supreme Council Vytautas Landsbergis and a delegation from Aglona, Latvia, attended the service. The church was to be administered by the Jesuits.

Monday, March 4

Gorbachev Reports on Decline in Industrial Production

A statement by the USSR Cabinet of Ministers and an interview on "Vremya" with Soviet President Mikhail Gorbachev testified to a continued fall in industrial production and the food supply during the first two months of 1991. Both ascribed much of the blame to a breakdown in recent agreements between Moscow and the republics.

The USSR Cabinet of Ministers issued an appeal to Union republican governments, workers, and citizens, blaming labor unrest for shortages of coking coal and scrap metal and announcing a halt to exports of both, TASS reported. Shortfalls had amounted to 1.5 million tons of steel and more than 1 million tons of rolled metal since January, 1991. The appeal stated that without metal there would be no oil, gas, energy, heating, machinery, or bread, and that jobs would be lost in practically every branch of the economy.

USSR Supreme Soviet Ratifies "Two-plus-Four" Treaty

In a closed session, the USSR Supreme Soviet ratified the "Two-plus-Four" Treaty on German unification and the Treaty of Good Neighborliness, Partnership, and Cooperation between the USSR and Germany, TASS reported. Deputy Foreign Minister Yulii Kvitsinsky declared that "all provisions of the treaty were accepted by the Germans on the basis of goodwill and that served as the most reliable guarantee of the vitality and soundness of this historic document." Kvitsinsky went on to stress that one of the most important statements of the "Two-plus-Four" Treaty was that "only peace will emanate from German soil."

Provisions for the withdrawal of Soviet troops from German soil were excluded from the ratification and calls were made for additional agreements to be worked out soon. The USSR Supreme Soviet's International Affairs Committee was charged with working out the details of the withdrawal, TASS said.

RSFSR Supreme Soviet Presidium on RSFSR Referendum

The Presidium of the RSFSR Supreme Soviet said that attempts by some local authorities in the republic to prevent the holding of the March 17 RSFSR referendum on the institution of the post of president were unconstitutional, TASS reported on March 5. Mirroring the decision taken at the all-Union level in connection with the refusal of some Union republics to hold the all-Union referendum, the Presidium of the RSFSR Supreme Soviet granted local soviets the right to hold the RSFSR referendum where superior bodies were failing to do so. North Ossetia and Smolensk Oblast had refused to hold the RSFSR referendum.

On March 6, the Left-Centrist Bloc of Political Parties nominated RSFSR Supreme Soviet Chairman Boris El'tsin for the post of RSFSR president, should the post be created by the RSFSR Congress of People's Deputies (*TASS*, March 6).

On March 7, RSFSR Communist Party First Secretary Ivan Polozkov told reporters that he was against elected presidents in the RSFSR and other republics, Radio

Moscow reported. Polozkov declared that one president was enough for the Soviet Union.

On March 8, the Presidium of the Tatar Supreme Soviet announced its decision not to take part in the RSFSR referendum, Radio Moscow reported.

On March 15, El'tsin spoke on Radio Rossii urging his listeners to vote in favor of the direct, popular election of the RSFSR president. He said he would run in such an election because it would give him the popular backing required to introduce the measures he thought the RSFSR needed (*Reuters*, March 15). The same day, El'tsin was granted a ten-minute slot on Central Television, but he designated his first deputy, Ruslan Khasbulatov, to speak in his place, TASS reported. Khasbulatov urged people to vote "yes" in the all-Union referendum because the RSFSR government had never said the Union should be dissolved, and he asked voters to approve the proposal.

British Prime Minister in Moscow for Talks

British Prime Minister John Major arrived in Moscow on his first visit to the USSR since he succeeded Margaret Thatcher as head of the British government, Reuters reported.

On March 5, Major met with representatives of the Baltic republics—Janis Peters of Latvia, Egidius Bickauskas of Lithuania, and Juri Kahn of Estonia, DPA reported. Major urged the Baltic republics to proceed cautiously with their independence drives and avoid conflicts with Moscow, Radio Tallinn reported. During a meeting with Soviet President Mikhail Gorbachev, Major was told that the USSR would seek a solution to the situation in the Baltic republics that was in the interests of the Soviet Union, the republics, and their residents, TASS reported. This would require extra caution and a careful approach, Gorbachev said. The two men also discussed the postwar situation in the Gulf and agreed to establish permanent contacts at foreign-ministry level for consultations on the Middle East (Western agencies, March 5).

The same day, the British prime minister met with Soviet reformers. Among them were Chairman of the Leningrad City Soviet Anatolii Sobchak and former RSFSR Finance Minister Boris Fedorov, TASS reported. Before flying back to London, Major also had talks with Soviet Foreign Minister Aleksandr Bessmertnykh and Defense Minister Dmitrii Yazov.

Kravchuk Urges Unity in Referendum

Ukrainian Supreme Soviet Chairman Leonid Kravchuk met with leaders of Lvov Oblast. Lvov and two other West Ukrainian oblasts were intending to conduct a separate

The USSR in March, 1991

referendum on March 17 on independence from the USSR. Kravchuk, however, brought with him the message that a divided Ukraine would not achieve statehood or national sovereignty. He also urged an end to what he called the war against the Communist Party in the region.

Voters in the Lvov, Ternopol', and Ivano-Frankovsk Oblasts in Western Ukraine were to be asked three questions on March 17: the first about the future of the USSR; the second whether Ukraine should be part of a future Soviet Union; and the third whether Ukraine should become a fully independent state. While all Ukrainians would be asked to answer the second question, the third question would be asked only in these three oblasts (*Radio Moscow*, March 13).

Gagauz to Participate in March 17 Referendum

Stepan Topal, the chairman of the self-proclaimed "Gagauz republic" Supreme Soviet, told Reuters that the republic would take part in the March 17 referendum on the future of the Soviet Union. He said the Gagauz people were treated like second-class citizens in Moldavia and had no choice but to participate in the referendum. Topal predicted overwhelming support for preserving the Soviet Union.

In *Pravda* on March 9, Moldavia's recently elected Communist Party first secretary, Grigore Eremei, called on the Moldavian Supreme Soviet and government to proceed with holding the referendum. Denouncing "destructive forces" for "fanning anti-Communism, anti-Sovietism, and separatism," Eremei said that the Moldavian Supreme Soviet's decision not to hold the referendum had worsened an already bad situation in the republic. Voting began in Moldavia on March 13 in order to allow Soviet servicemen on duty to take part (RFE/RL correspondent's report, March 13).

Iran and Azerbaijan Sign Communications Agreement

The Iranian news agency IRNA said Iran and Azerbaijan had agreed to establish telecommunications links between the border towns of Astara in Azerbaijan and Jolfa in Iran. Iranian technicians would supply and install the equipment.

Tuesday, March 5

Gorbachev Urges Party to Defend Soviet Unity

In a meeting with the first secretaries of the Communist Parties of the republics and autonomous republics, Soviet President Mikhail Gorbachev warned that destructive forces were trying to increase political unrest in advance of the March 17 referendum, *Pravda* reported on March 6. According to *Pravda*, Gorbachev urged Party leaders to step up their efforts to defend the country's unity.

Constitutional Supervision Committee on Referendum

The USSR Committee for Constitutional Supervision ruled that any acts directly or indirectly preventing citizens from exercising their right to take part in a referendum violated the USSR Constitution, TASS reported. The ruling was issued in response to a request from the USSR Supreme Soviet, which had condemned the refusal of some republics to hold the March 17 referendum.

USSR Prosecutor-General Nikolai Trubin told TASS on March 7 that anyone who attempted to prevent the holding of the national referendum would be prosecuted in accordance with the law and could be sentenced to up to five years in prison. In places where the local authorities had decided not to participate in the referendum, citizens had, Trubin declared, been deprived of their right to participate in the governing of the country. Where violations of the law occurred, repeat voting would be organized, he added. Trubin also said that an affirmative answer to the referendum by voters in any republic would not invalidate their constitutional right to secede from the USSR.

Council of Nationalities Annuls Discriminatory Decrees

The USSR Council of Nationalities adopted a resolution to annul all legislative acts infringing the rights of peoples deported under Stalin, TASS reported. The decision made invalid several dozen decrees and resolutions that in practice had ceased to have any effect but that had not been formally annulled. Such a resolution had long been requested by the deported peoples.

Buildup on Kola Peninsula

Space News reported that a Soviet military base at Zapadnaya Litsa on the Kola Peninsula had grown significantly since 1986. It said the base was believed to have the largest cache of nuclear weapons in the world, mostly aboard Typhoon- and Delta-class submarines. The report cited work by Norwegian and Japanese researchers, who also said that the Soviet Union appeared to be building air defenses against cruise missiles throughout the Kola Peninsula. One researcher said the growth virtually ensured that the region would be of strategic importance well into the next century (*Reuters*, March 5).

The USSR in March, 1991

Azerbaijan on Referendum

In an interview with *Izvestia*, Azerbaijani President Ayaz Mutalibov said Azerbaijanis were in favor of the Union, but he implied that they had reservations about the March 17 referendum because the Union had not dealt satisfactorily with the Nagorno-Karabakh question, TASS reported. Mutalibov expressed the fear that, if there should be a flare-up before the referendum, the Azerbaijanis might vote "no" in protest, a vote that they would later regret.

TASS reported that nine out of ten people in Nagorno-Karabakh wanted to take part in the March 17 referendum and wanted to vote for a USSR in which the Nagorno-Karabakh Autonomous Oblast would be an equal member of the federation. There were doubts whether the referendum could be held there, because the activity of the oblast soviet had been suspended and the organizational committee of Azerbaijan for the oblast was not recognized by the Armenian majority and had not taken a public stand on the referendum.

The Azerbaijani Supreme Soviet decided on March 7 that the republic would take part in the referendum (*TASS*, March 7).

Residents of Azerbaijan were also to vote on a second question asking whether the republic might leave the Soviet Union at a later date, AFP reported on March 14.

The editor of the Azerbaijani Popular Front's journal *Azadlyk*, Adalat Tahirzade, told RFE/RL on March 13 that the popular front and the Democratic Bloc of deputies were calling for a boycott of the referendum. The front had scheduled antireferendum rallies for March 16 and had invited foreign observers to monitor the voting. The front and the Democratic Bloc intended to press for the resignation of the Azerbaijani leadership if the voting were falsified (RL Azerbaijani service, March 13).

Moldavia Institutes Presidential Government

The Moldavian Supreme Soviet passed by a large majority a law on reforming executive power and instituting presidential government in the republic, Moldavian deputies told RFE/RL on March 6. The president became the republic's "chief executive authority," with the power to chair the government's sessions, have the final say over the latter's decisions, issue executive decrees, and dismiss ministers, including the prime minister (appointments would be subject to the Supreme Soviet's approval).

Moldavia Limits Military Service to Its Territory

The Moldavian Supreme Soviet decided that conscripts from the republic would perform military service only on the territory of Moldavia. Exceptions could be made only for individual conscripts who requested in writing that they be permitted to serve outside the republic. The decision, which had the force of law effective immediately, reinstated the decision of September 4, 1990, which the parliament had rescinded under pressure from Moscow on January 16, 1991. The Supreme Soviet's decision followed the deaths of two more Moldavian conscripts in Soviet military units, bringing the total for such casualties in 1991 to twelve. The decision also mandated the Moldavian Supreme Soviet's Commission on Military and Security Affairs to submit a draft law on alternative service.

Uoka Receives AFL-CIO Human-Rights Award

The US labor organization, the AFL-CIO, invited Kazimieras Uoka, the founder of the Lithuanian Worker's Union, to the United States to receive its 1991 human-rights award. Uoka was chosen in February to receive the award for his role in promoting free trade unionism in the USSR. The award, named for former AFL-CIO President George Meany, is worth 5,000 dollars. Former winners include Polish President Lech Walesa, Soviet human-rights activist Andrei Sakharov, and Chinese activist Fang Lizhi (RFE/RL correspondent's report, March 5).

Wednesday, March 6

USSR Supreme Soviet Adopts Law on Police

The USSR Supreme Soviet held its last joint session before the March 17 referendum, Radio Moscow reported. Prior to adjourning, it adopted a law regulating the activities of the police throughout the USSR, TASS reported. The law set up "municipal militias" in the Union republics and broadened the republics' powers "to protect public order and combat crime." The law allowed the Communist Party to retain its cells in police departments, although it included a clause stating that "no one but the bodies or officials directly empowered by the law has the right to interfere in police activities." Ernst Ametistov, of the All-Union Research Institute for Soviet State Development and Legislation, said the law "gives the Party the possibility again to have its finger on the police," AP reported. For the text of the law, see *Izvestia*, March 16.

Belonogov in Teheran

USSR Deputy Foreign Minister Aleksandr Belonogov went to Teheran for talks on the postwar situation in the Gulf, TASS reported. Belonogov said he wanted to discuss with Iranian leaders the latest developments

The USSR in March, 1991

in Iraq, the future of the Gulf, and ways to avoid another war in the region.

Soviet Foreign Ministry spokesman Vitalii Churkin said Belonogov's trip to Teheran was undertaken "in the context of wide-scale consultations with many interested parties," TASS reported. Churkin reiterated that the USSR was under no obligation to curtail future arms shipments to the Middle East, including Iraq. Churkin denied the existence of "any direct link" between Belonogov's visit to Iran and the internal situation in Iraq.

On March 7, Belonogov declared on Radio Teheran that the Soviet-Iraqi friendship treaty signed in 1972 would remain in effect even if Iraq's government were toppled, AP reported.

Case Closed on Tbilisi Violence

USSR Prosecutor-General Nikolai Trubin closed the criminal case on the Tbilisi massacre for lack of corpus delicti, "TSN" reported. Nineteen people died when the armed forces used poison gas and shovels to disperse unarmed participants in a nationalist demonstration in Tbilisi in April, 1989. The special commission set up by the USSR Congress of People's Deputies condemned the armed forces and the CPSU leadership for grave violations of legality; its findings were approved by the second session of the Congress in December, 1989, after former Foreign Minister Eduard Shevardnadze threatened to resign if the affair were whitewashed.

Ligachev's Memoirs Published

Excerpts from the memoirs of former CPSU Politburo member Egor Ligachev entitled *V kremle i na staroi ploshchadi* (In the Kremlin and on Old Square—the latter a reference to the address of CPSU headquarters) began appearing in *Sovetskaya Rossiya*. Ligachev said that Gorbachev's election as CPSU general secretary had taken place in "a tense, sometimes dramatic atmosphere." He characterized Konstantin Chernenko as "a virtuoso apparatchik" and claimed that Chernenko's entire thirteen-month reign as CPSU general secretary had been spent "scheming against Gorbachev."

Polozkov Attacks Liberals

Addressing a plenum of the RSFSR Communist Party, its first secretary, Ivan Polozkov, compared the present situation in the Soviet Union to the one that existed at the time of the Nazi invasion in 1941. He also said that the split in Soviet society was "as dangerous as nuclear weapons." Reuters quoted him as saying that "so-called democrats, supported by multinational corporations, which are conducting a cruel struggle for the world's natural resources," were trying to overthrow the country's leadership. Polozkov stressed that stability must take precedence over reform, otherwise "there might indeed be demands for dictatorship."

As reported by *Pravda* on March 7, Polozkov added that the Communist Party had lost more than 1.2 million members in 1990, but still remained the most powerful political force in the republic.

Siberian Television Channel Stops Broadcasting

The commercial television channel "Siberia," which had been on the air for several months in the city of Barnaul, was forced to stop broadcasting because of lack of finances. Representatives of "Siberia" told RFE/RL that, following strong pressure from local oblast Party committees, all the sponsors had withdrawn their financial support. The organizers of the channel were optimistic about finding new sources of income, however, since the channel was reputed to be very popular with local viewers.

Western Companies to Develop Soviet Offshore Oil Fields

With domestic oil output falling at a rate of some 10 percent per annum, the Soviet leadership was reported to have offered foreign companies the opportunity to develop an offshore oil and gas field north of Sakhalin Island (*The Times*, March 6). The fields promised an output of some 200,000 barrels per day, or about 2 percent of current annual Soviet oil production. The USSR was said to have offered a 4.5-billion-dollar contract to a consortium of international companies and asked Mitsui and Co. and Marathon and McDermott International to prepare feasibility studies on the Sakhalin oil fields.

Snegur on March 17 Referendum

Addressing a republic-wide gathering of chairmen of local soviets and economic managers specially convened to discuss Moldavia's boycott of the all-Union referendum, Moldavian President Mircea Snegur warned that local soviets that held the referendum in defiance of the republican Supreme Soviet's decision might be disbanded and the organizers dismissed and held accountable. According to TASS, Snegur said he had issued a similar warning to the leaders of the Moldavian Communist Party "which is conducting propaganda and organizational work for the referendum."

Presidential military adviser Marshal Sergei Akhromeev, who represented a Moldavian constituency in the USSR Congress of People's Deputies, declared on March 7 that

The USSR in March, 1991

Moldavia's leaders should be called to account for their opposition to the referendum, TASS reported.

Speaking after Akhromeev at the USSR Supreme Soviet, Gorbachev warned the Moldavian leadership not to prevent the holding of the referendum, saying he had asked the USSR Prosecutor's Office to investigate "threats against the organizers of the Union referendum" in Moldavia (RFE/RL correspondent's report, March 8).

USSR Referendum without Effect in Latvia

The Latvian Supreme Council ruled that the March 17 referendum would have "no legal effect in Latvia," and it also noted that the election committees that had been set up for the March 3 poll in Latvia would not be involved in the USSR referendum. The attitude of the majority of the legislators, according to Radio Riga, was that Latvia should neither hinder nor aid the USSR referendum.

TASS reported on March 7 that representatives of some seventeen social and political organizations in Latvia had decided to conduct the referendum, despite the Latvian Supreme Council's decision not to participate. Among the organizers were "Interfront," the Council of Workers' Collectives, and deputies belonging to the "Soyuz" group of deputies. Local city councils in Rezekne and Daugavpils and the leadership of the Baltic Military District had also expressed their support for organizing the referendum.

In his March 11 edition of "600 Seconds," Leningrad television journalist Aleksandr Nevzorov said that the "Black Berets" were prepared to hold the referendum at their headquarters in Riga and had invited the civilian population to cast their ballots there, Radio Riga reported on March 12.

Hunger Strike over Occupation of Vilnius Television Center

The workers of Vilnius television and radio whose offices were seized by Soviet troops on January 13 were reported to have organized a hunger strike to demand that their facilities be returned to them (*The Voice of America*, Lithuanian service, March 6).

Three Explosions in Latvia

Radio Riga reported on three explosions that occurred within fifteen minutes of each other in Riga. There were no injuries. The first bomb exploded in the elevator of an apartment house where most of the residents worked at a Soviet military academy. The second bomb went off outside an MVD hostel. The third explosion damaged a bridge leading to a Soviet army base in Adazi, just outside Riga. According to chief investigator Rita Aksenoka, these blasts were part of a series of explosions intended to destabilize the situation in Latvia.

Leningrad Court Refuses to Hear Charges against Nevzorov

The Leningrad City Court refused to accept for consideration criminal charges leveled against the controversial moderator of the popular show "600 Seconds," Aleksandr Nevzorov, Radio Mayak reported. The charge was filed by Leningrad television journalist Gennadii Orlov, whom Nevzorov had called "a coward and a scoundrel" in a show broadcast after Orlov had strongly condemned Nevzorov's program on the events in Vilnius on January 13. (Nevzorov had alleged that the fatalities of January 13 were caused by heart attacks and road accidents.) Deputies of the Leningrad City Soviet and Nevzorov's colleagues at Leningrad television had been complaining for a long time that Nevzorov regularly attacked them in his shows. The authorities had consistently refused to take action against him.

RSFSR-Czech Declaration

The prime ministers of the RSFSR and Czechoslovakia, Ivan Silaev and Petr Pithart, signed a cooperation declaration in Moscow.

The RSFSR and Czechoslovakia were considering paying for imports in rubles and crowns to ease the effect of the move to dollar accounting, Reuters reported on March 7. Pithart and Czech Industry Minister Jan Vrba told reporters in Moscow that the changeover to dollars in 1991 would reduce trade between Czechoslovakia and the USSR to one-fifth of its 1990 level. Pithart and Silaev agreed to establish a joint-stock trading company that could do business in rubles and crowns.

Pithart also met with Soviet Prime Minister Valentin Pavlov for talks on economic cooperation and power-sharing arrangements between central governments and republics (*Radio Prague*, March 7).

Thursday, March 7

USSR Security Council Nominations

Soviet President Mikhail Gorbachev requested the USSR Supreme Soviet to approve the nominations of nine officials to the newly created USSR Security Council, TASS reported. They were Vice President Gennadii Yanaev, Prime Minister Valentin Pavlov, Foreign Minister Aleksandr Bessmertnykh, Minister of Internal Affairs Boriss Pugo, KGB Chairman Vladimir Kryuchkov, Defense Minister Dmitrii Yazov, Foreign Policy Adviser

THE USSR IN MARCH, 1991

Evgenii Primakov, chief of the Office of the President Valerii Boldin, and former Minister of Internal Affairs Vadim Bakatin. The last five were members of the recently dissolved Presidential Council. Aleksandr Yakovlev, the president's former chief adviser on foreign and security questions, was not nominated; nor were any specialists on economic or nationality issues. The Supreme Soviet approved seven of the nominees in the first round of voting. Primakov was elected in a second vote, AFP reported. Boldin was not endorsed, however; his candidacy was sent back to Gorbachev for further consideration.

Addressing a session of the USSR Supreme Soviet, USSR President Mikhail Gorbachev welcomed agreement on the new draft Union treaty by eight of the fifteen Soviet republics but warned of growing dangers to the economy, AFP reported. Gorbachev said that the USSR would remain a federation but that broader powers would be given to the republics. The only unresolved issue, he said, was how the republics would be represented in the USSR Supreme Soviet's nationalities chamber. Gorbachev further declared that an agreement on a price reform had been reached with all Soviet republics and that the government would soon begin introducing it gradually. *Izvestia* quoted him as saying compensation for anticipated price hikes would begin a week before the rise.

Gorbachev Addresses USSR Supreme Soviet

Without mentioning names, Gorbachev went on to strongly criticize republican leaders who hid their political ambitions behind the banner of sovereignty. He said that the deputies of the RSFSR Supreme Soviet were behaving in a "suicidal" way by encouraging miners' strikes. The USSR was slipping towards "feudalism," he claimed, and he criticized the republics seeking to break away from the centralized system for not serving the interests of their people (RFE/RL correspondent's report, March 8).

Pending a final vote on the USSR law on emigration (approved at its first reading in November, 1989), Gorbachev suggested that the USSR Supreme Soviet forbid unauthorized foreign trips by members of the liberal parliamentary opposition on the grounds that certain lawmakers had urged the West to deny credits to the central government. Gorbachev claimed that the activities of these deputies were to blame for the fact that the USSR had received only half of the Western credits that it had expected. Gorbachev added that the Supreme Soviet should work out a rule under which deputies would be allowed to go abroad only when permitted to do so by the Supreme Soviet, its leadership, or its commissions and committees.

Leningrad Barred from Creating Independent Broadcast Company

The USSR State Television and Radio Broadcasting Company said the Leningrad City Soviet had exceeded its jurisdiction by voting to transform Leningrad Radio and Television into an independent company (the city soviet had voted to create an independent broadcasting company, reserving for itself the right to closely control reports broadcast about the activities of the soviet). The decision was declared invalid because it had been taken without the consent of the state and regional broadcasting authorities or of representatives of the Radio and Television Workers' Union. The State Broadcasting Company maintained, moreover, that the Leningrad network belonged to the state, not to the city, since it had been created by the Soviet government to serve central as well as local audiences (*Radio Moscow*, March 7).

The move was also rejected by the workers' collective of Leningrad Television on the grounds that it amounted to interference by the soviet in the functioning of local television and radio, which was prohibited by the USSR Law on the Press. Leningrad Television staffers were asking for financial support and confirmation of their independent status from the RSFSR Ministry for the Mass Media and Information.

El'tsin Complains about Party Apparatus

In an interview with Radio Rossii, RSFSR Supreme Soviet Chairman Boris El'tsin said the main source of tension and confrontation in the Soviet Union was "the struggle for survival" of the Communist Party apparatus. El'tsin also accused Soviet President Mikhail Gorbachev of trying to frighten people by talking about the threat of civil war. He called this a ploy to allow an antidemocratic crackdown.

Interview with Uzbek President

The president of Uzbekistan, Islam Karimov, interviewed in the German weekly *Die Zeit*, said he supported the efforts of all Soviet republics to attain political and economic sovereignty. Karimov said that, at the beginning of their push for sovereignty, the Baltic republics had failed to protect the rights of the nonindigenous nationalities. He added, however, that, the policies of the Baltic leaders had since then become more realistic and constructive. Karimov also said it was time Gorbachev decided to negotiate without preconditions with the representatives of all the Soviet republics, before the

The USSR in March, 1991

Soviet Union became a dictatorship run by those who wanted to strangle republican sovereignty.

Gerasimov Appointed Ambassador to Portugal

Soviet President Mikhail Gorbachev appointed Gennadii Gerasimov Soviet ambassador to Portugal, TASS reported. He replaced Valentin Kasatkin, who had retired. Gerasimov, born in 1930, had worked since 1986 as head of the Information Administration of the USSR Foreign Ministry. From 1983 to 1986 he was first deputy chairman of the press agency Novosti, then chief editor of *Moscow News*.

New Gorbachev Aide Appointed

TASS said Anatolii Lushchikov, head of the chancellery of the CPSU general secretary, had retired at the age of seventy-three. Lushchikov was replaced by Georgii Ostroumov, formerly a speech writer for Mikhail Gorbachev in the latter's function as general secretary.

Khabarovsk Communists Pay 50,000 Rubles for Air Time

The Khabarovsk Krai Party Committee had to pay 50,000 rubles to the local television and radio committee in order to obtain broadcasting time for a monthly show, *Komsomol'skaya pravda* reported. The newspaper also said the television committee had demanded even more money from the regional trade-union council to air its program.

Gamsakhurdia Denies Expulsion of Dagestanis

Georgian Supreme Soviet Chairman Zviad Gamsakhurdia sent a letter to USSR Supreme Soviet Chairman Anatolii Luk'yanov denying allegations that nationalist forces in Georgia were pursuing a policy of expelling Dagestanis, TASS reported. The allegations were made in an appeal by Dagestani Supreme Soviet Chairman Magomedali Magomedov that was circulated among USSR deputies on March 4.

Friday, March 8

Text of Draft Union Treaty Published

The full text of the second draft of the Union treaty was published by TASS on March 8 and by *Izvestia* on March 9. It described the Soviet republics as sovereign and equal states holding the full range of state powers and granted them the right to determine their own form of government and to establish diplomatic, consular, trade, and other relations with foreign states. The draft gave the federal authorities responsibility for defense and foreign policy. Membership was to be voluntary, and republics would be allowed to secede in accordance with guidelines that were still to be drawn up. The draft changed the name of the Union to "Union of Sovereign Equal States." The draft had been given preliminary approval by the Federation Council on March 6.

Shevardnadze Says "Shadow Power" Operating in USSR

Former Soviet Foreign Minister Eduard Shevardnadze said in an interview with ABC Television that he believed there was some kind of "shadow power" operating in the Soviet Union, Reuters reported. Citing the crackdown in the Baltic republics and the introduction of military patrols on city streets, Shevardnadze declared that Soviet President Mikhail Gorbachev did not take all decisions in the Soviet Union and that therefore there must be some shadow power or authority in the USSR.

Leningrad Stock Exchange Established

TASS reported that a stock exchange had been established in Leningrad with 100 founding members, including the executive committee of the Leningrad City Soviet. Stock exchange chairman Igor' Klyuchnikov said there was a charter capital of nearly 30 million rubles. Contacts had been made with foreign firms, and talks were under way for foreign participation in bidding.

USSR Pays Off Most Short-Term Debts

Tomas Alibegov, first vice president of the USSR Foreign Trade Bank, said the Soviet Union had paid off most of its short-term debts. AFP quoted him as saying that, while its financial situation remained difficult, the USSR hoped to restore Western confidence within six months. The short-term debt, which amounted to 18 billion dollars at the start of 1990, was thus reduced to 2 billion. The total Soviet foreign debt was running at about 60 billion dollars. Alibegov added that there was no plan for restructuring the Soviet debt, because it was neither necessary nor desirable. Unpaid commercial invoices amounted to a little less than 5 billion dollars, he said, and measures would be taken to pay them off and to avoid a repetition of the problem.

North Korea Expels *Izvestia* Correspondent

North Korea forced *Izvestia* to withdraw its correspondent for having published articles critical of the North Korean government and to close its Pyongyang bureau, AFP reported. The Yonhap News Agency reported that *Izvestia* had repeatedly published articles urging North Korea to carry out reforms and had recently carried an article saying that North Korea had triggered the 1950-53 Korean War (the official version in the country is that the Korean War was started by a military attack by South Korea across the 38th parallel). After Novosti and *Komsomol'skaya pravda*, *Izvestia* was the third Soviet media organ to close its Pyongyang bureau.

Radio Bucharest reported that Romania and Moldavia had signed an accord on environmental cooperation in the east Romanian city of Iasi. The document called for the two sides to cooperate in fighting sources of pollution in the air, water, and on land, including measures to reverse the deforestation caused by the pumping of waste water into the Prut River.

Romania and Moldavia Sign Environmental Protection Accord

Saturday, March 9

Speaking at a meeting organized by Democratic Russia, RSFSR Supreme Soviet Chairman Boris El'tsin called on democratic movements in the RSFSR to set up a powerful democratic party as an alternative to the CPSU and to declare war on the Soviet leadership for leading the USSR into "a quagmire," AFP reported. El'tsin stressed that the democratic movement must become a single, organized party.

"Vremya" on March 10 and *Pravda* on March 11 accused Radio Rossii of failing to broadcast the entire text of El'tsin's speech: both charged that Radio Rossii had omitted "the most militant passages" from its broadcast of the speech. In response, Radio Rossii rebroadcast the speech on March 11, preceded by an announcement informing listeners that the full text would be read and asking them to judge for themselves whether the speech had been shortened the first time for political reasons or in order to save time and remove repetitions.

On March 11, Central Television broadcast a roundtable discussion in which Sazhi Umalatova, the USSR Supreme Soviet deputy who had called for a vote of no confidence in Gorbachev in December, 1990, criticized El'tsin. This was followed by the appearance on "Vremya" of Vasilii Starodubtsev, who criticized El'tsin's agricultural policies, and then of Vladimir Voronin, the leader of the Centrist Bloc, who criticized leaders of democratic movements for their failure to attend the bloc's recent conference.

The same day, the USSR Supreme Soviet debated whether to censure El'tsin for his remarks in his speech to

El'tsin Calls on Democrats to Unite

Democratic Russia on March 9, news agencies reported. It voted 211-71, with 44 abstentions, against an official condemnation on the grounds that such a move would probably increase popular support for El'tsin.

On March 19, USSR Prosecutor-General Nikolai Trubin sent the USSR Supreme Soviet a legal evaluation of El'tsin's speech. According to TASS, Trubin concluded that El'tsin had not called for the forcible overthrow of the country's leadership. A number of USSR deputies had asked the prosecutor-general to evaluate the legality of El'tsin's comments in light of the constitutional ban on calling for the forcible overthrow of the state.

El'tsin Denies That RSFSR Has Agreed to Sign Union Treaty

Commenting on the draft Union treaty approved on March 6, El'tsin stressed in his speech to the Democratic Russia meeting that, contrary to Gorbachev's statement to the USSR Supreme Soviet on March 7, the RSFSR had not yet agreed to sign the Union treaty. El'tsin said that only the RSFSR Congress of People's Deputies could decide this issue. He added that a number of points in the treaty were unacceptable to the RSFSR, Radio Mayak reported.

In an interview with Radio Rossii on March 13, First Deputy Chairman of the RSFSR Supreme Soviet Ruslan Khasbulatov said El'tsin and the RSFSR commission that had discussed the draft had accepted it as "a working basis" but not as "the basis" of a new treaty. The RSFSR considered that the draft still gave the center too many powers, he said, adding that joint powers were always interpreted in favor of the stronger party. A major cause of concern, Khasbulatov continued, was the question of allowing the autonomous republics to sign the treaty directly, which could lead to the break-up of the RSFSR.

Opinion Polls on Meaning of Union

"TSN" reported the results of a public opinion poll conducted by the All-Union Center for Public Opinion Studies, which asked the question: "What does the Union mean to the average Russian?" According to "TSN," 65 percent of the respondents said that the Union meant shortages, lines, and poverty; 28 percent said it meant arbitrariness and humiliation; 25 percent saw in the Union a guarantee of peace; and 3 percent said it gave them "a sense of pride in the Socialist fatherland."

Shevardnadze Attacked by *Sovetskaya Rossiya*

Former First Deputy Foreign Minister Georgii Kornienko wrote in *Sovetskaya Rossiya* that "the Gulf crisis was hardly the only instance in which former Soviet

The USSR in March, 1991

Foreign Minister Eduard Shevardnadze constructed and implemented our policy without reference to the knowledge and judgment of competent specialists and without the broad consideration of the interests of the Soviet government."

Moldavia Establishes Hard-Currency Fund

Citing the Moldavian Supreme Soviet's newspaper *Sfatul Tsarii*, TASS said the Supreme Soviet had created a republican hard-currency fund at the request of Prime Minister Mircea Druc. The money would be deposited "in places out of the reach" of the USSR government. TASS reported that the Moldavian government and Supreme Soviet felt that republican sovereignty would remain merely declarative without the ability to trade directly with foreign partners.

Explosions in Baltic Allegedly Carried Out by KGB

In an article published in *Lietuvos Aidas*, Audrius Butkevicius, director of Lithuania's Defense Department, affirmed that the explosions in Vilnius on March 3 and in Riga on March 6 could have been carried out only by professionals, Radio Vilnius reported. Butkevicius blamed the blasts on KGB provocateurs, adding that 300 KGB troops had recently arrived in Vilnius.

On March 13, the deputy head of the Military and Political Directorate of Internal Troops of the USSR Ministry of Internal Affairs, General Evgenii Nechaev, denied the Lithuanian charges, saying that no new KGB troops had been deployed in the republic. Nechaev said the only change had been the replacement of several small airborne assault units with MVD forces (TASS, March 13).

Border Crossing to Be Opened between Poland and Kaliningrad

DPA said Poland and the RSFSR had agreed to open a border crossing point and a rail link between Poland and Kaliningrad Oblast for the first time since World War II. The prewar rail link between Gdansk and Kaliningrad would be restored later.

Sunday, March 10

Mass Demonstration in Support of El'tsin

Between 250,000 and 500,000 people were estimated to have marched through Moscow in a rally organized by the Democratic Russia movement in support of RSFSR Supreme Soviet Chairman Boris El'tsin. Demonstrators called for the resignation of Soviet President Mikhail

Gorbachev, Western agencies reported. El'tsin himself did not attend the demonstration, which was addressed by democratic leaders such as Yurii Afanas'ev, Gavriil Popov, Sergei Stankevich, Nikolai Travkin, and Tel'man Gdlyan. Gdlyan proclaimed the creation of a new People's Party of Russia that would support El'tsin's struggle for sovereignty for the RSFSR.

The Main Administration of Internal Affairs for Moscow presented the Moscow City Soviet with a bill for 755,000 rubles in connection with overtime charges accrued by MVD personnel who were on duty during the demonstration in support of El'tsin. The head of the USSR Ministry of Internal Affairs' Public Relations Office, Vladimir Yachenkov, told "Vremya" on March 14 that some 20,000 policemen had been employed to police the demonstration.

Pro-El'tsin rallies were also held in various cities across the RSFSR—in Ulan-Ude, Petropavlovsk-Kamchatsky, and Vladivostok in the Soviet Far East; in Tomsk, Omsk, Novosibirsk, and Tyumen' in Siberia; in Izhevsk, Sverdlovsk, and Chelyabinsk in the Urals; in Orenburg, Kazan', and Volgograd in the heartland; and in Stavropol' and Rostov-on-Don in the south. Crowd estimates in these cities ranged from 4,000 in Chelyabinsk to 10,000 in Volgograd (*Radio Rossii*, March 10).

Georgia Calls for Boycott of Referendum

In a television broadcast to the non-Georgian population of Georgia, Georgian Supreme Soviet Chairman Zviad Gamsakhurdia called for a boycott of the March 17 referendum, Radio Moscow reported. He also said that only those who voted for the restoration of Georgian independence in the republican referendum on March 31 would get Georgian citizenship and land. Since the voting would be by secret ballot, he said, this would be determined by the results in individual raions. Gamsakhurdia expressed regret that the Armenian population of Abkhazia had supported the Abkhaz in deciding to hold the March 17 referendum.

Monday, March 11

USSR Supreme Soviet and Gorbachev on Referendum

The USSR Supreme Soviet warned that any attempt to keep people from voting in the March 17 referendum would be illegal, Reuters reported. The deputies approved a statement ordering all necessary measures to be taken to ensure that every citizen had the opportunity to vote.

The USSR in March, 1991

On March 15, Soviet President Mikhail Gorbachev appealed in a television speech to Soviet citizens to vote "yes" in the referendum. The Soviet president said a positive result would act as a curb on "the destructive processes" taking place in the country (Western agencies, March 15).

Estonia to Allow Referendum

The Estonian Supreme Council voted to allow Soviet citizens living in Estonia to participate in the all-Union referendum if they wished, *Rahva Haal* reported on March 13.

Turkish President Visits USSR

Turkish President Turgut Ozal arrived in Moscow for a five-day visit to the Soviet Union, AP reported. Ozal was greeted at the Kremlin by Soviet President Mikhail Gorbachev and his wife, Raisa. Ozal, the first Turkish head of state to visit Moscow in twenty years, brought with him an entourage of one hundred Turkish officials and businessmen who were interested in improving Soviet-Turkish relations and establishing direct links with Soviet republics.

Soviet Foreign Ministry spokesman Vitalii Churkin said the USSR welcomed Ozal's proposal to create a free-trade zone among countries bordering on the Black Sea, TASS reported.

According to TASS, on March 12 Ozal and Gorbachev signed agreements on trade, economic, scientific, and technological issues, including one to avoid double taxation of profits. They also extended by a year an existing Soviet-Turkish trade agreement. At a dinner given for the Turkish president, Gorbachev declared that the Soviet Union and Turkey should work together to help achieve a postwar settlement in the Middle East (*TASS*, March 13).

Soviet television reported the same day that Ozal had met with RSFSR Supreme Soviet Chairman Boris El'tsin and invited him to visit Turkey. El'tsin accepted the invitation.

On March 13, Ozal held talks in Kiev with Ukrainian Supreme Soviet Chairman Leonid Kravchuk, TASS reported. The Ukrainian government expressed its readiness to join Ozal's project for a Black Sea free-trade zone. After the meeting, Ozal and Kravchuk signed a declaration on the principles and goals of Turkish-Ukrainian relations and an agreement on bilateral cultural cooperation. Ozal left Kiev on March 14 for Alma-Ata where he was welcomed by Kazakh President Nursultan Nazarbaev. Ozal attended prayers on the eve of the Muslim holy month Ramadan at the Alma-Ata mosque, where he was greeted by about 3,000 worshipers (RFE/RL correspondent's report, March 15).

The same day, Ozal signed an agreement for Turkey and Kazakhstan to open consulates on each other's territory (RL Kazakh service, March 15).

Azerbaijan was the last stop on Ozal's visit to the Soviet Union. A member of the Azerbaijani Popular Front's governing board, Hikmet Hadjizedeh, told RFE/RL that the front had issued a statement to Ozal, praising improved economic and cultural relations between Turkey and Azerbaijan but calling on the Turkish president to pay attention to "violations of human rights" in the republic. The statement also asked Ozal to raise his voice in support of the national liberation movement in the republic (RL Azerbaijani service, March 15).

First Anniversary of Reaffirmation of Lithuanian Independence

A special formal session of the Lithuanian Supreme Council celebrated the first anniversary of the reaffirmation of Lithuanian independence, Radio Kaunas reported. The session began with a statement by President of the Supreme Council Vytautas Landsbergis. The "Vytis" Cross was presented posthumously to the fourteen Lithuanians killed in the assault on the television tower in Vilnius on January 13. A delegation of five Norwegians headed by the rector of the University of Oslo, Inge Loenning, gave Landsbergis a peace prize from the Norwegian people worth 2,850,000 kroner (475,000 dollars). Landsbergis said that he would donate part of the prize to help Lithuanian art students to study abroad.

Chechen-Ingush ASSR against RSFSR Referendum

The Chechen-Ingush Autonomous Republic in the RSFSR declared that it would not participate in the March 17 RSFSR referendum, TASS reported. The Chechen-Ingush Supreme Soviet voted to take part only in the all-Union poll.

Over 150 rural and city soviets in Orel Oblast were also reported to have decided not to hold the RSFSR referendum (*TASS,* March 13). Campaigns against the referendum were also going on in Tambov and Ryazan Oblasts, Radio Rossii reported that day.

Romania and USSR End Visa Requirements

In an agreement signed in Bucharest, the Soviet Union and Romania decided to end visa requirements for travel between the two countries, Radio Bucharest reported. The accord allowed Romanians and Soviet citizens with valid travel documents to travel to each other's country for up to ninety days without a visa.

The USSR in March, 1991

On March 22, the newspaper of the Moldavian Supreme Soviet, *Sfatul Tsarii*, criticized the Romanian government for failing to distinguish between residents of Moldavia and other Soviet citizens with regard to visa, residency, border-traffic, and currency-exchange regulations. Complaining that the new Romanian-Soviet agreement did not include any special provisions for Moldavians, *Sfatul Tsarii* argued that Romania was "tacitly failing to recognize the sovereignty of the Republic of Moldavia." The newspaper contended that Romania was negotiating directly with Moscow and bypassing Kishinev on issues of direct interest to Moldavia.

Estonia Calls for Support

The Estonian Supreme Council adopted a resolution calling on the parliaments and governments of all states to recognize the Estonian Supreme Council and government as Estonia's democratically elected state organs, *Rahva Haal* reported on March 13. The resolution said the Supreme Council regarded the results of Estonia's March 3 plebiscite as "the highest expression of the people's will, which, inarguably, forms the foundation for the state organs of the Republic of Estonia to restore independence."

Protest against Soviet Military Activities

Deputy Chairman of the Lithuanian Council of Ministers Zigmas Vaisvila sent a telegram to USSR Defense Minister Dmitrii Yazov and Minister of Internal Affairs Boriss Pugo, protesting about the activities of armed special police (OMON) units in Lithuania. He called their actions "gross interference in the internal affairs of the republic that sought to destabilize the social and political situation in Lithuania." He demanded the immediate return of weapons and other possessions seized from Lithuanian policemen (*Radio Kaunas*, March 11).

Tuesday, March 12

Soviet Germans Hold Congress

A congress of Soviet Germans opened in Moscow with an appeal for the re-creation of their autonomous republic (dissolved by Stalin in 1941) on the Volga River, TASS reported. The congress adopted a resolution condemning the Soviet leadership for delaying the restoration of the autonomous republic. On March 13, a DPA report said the congress had called for the disbandment of the State Committee for the Problems of the Soviet Germans and of the organizational committee for the official Congress of

Soviet Germans, headed by Hugo Wormsbächer, that was to have taken place that week, DPA reported. The 600 delegates unanimously adopted a declaration describing the work of the two committees as unsatisfactory. Volga-German autonomy was the main point of dispute with the state committee, which envisaged only extraterritorial autonomy for the Germans.

All-Union Meeting of Jewish Organizations

The second all-Union meeting of Jewish religious and national organizations opened in Moscow, TASS reported. The chief rabbi of Moscow's Choral Synagogue, Adolf Shaevich, told TASS that participants in the forum were discussing problems connected with coordinating the activities of religious and public organizations whose aim was the revival of the national and cultural traditions of the Jewish population of the Soviet Union.

Another Trial in Uzbek Cotton Affair

TASS, quoting *Izvestia*, reported that the case of Akhmadzhon Odilov, one of the most notorious figures in the so-called Uzbek cotton affair, was going to trial. Odilov was a raion agroindustrial association director who was accused, in a series of spectacular press articles, of having run a private empire, virtually enslaving its inhabitants, and amassing vast quantities of illegally acquired wealth. The charges against him, according to the report, included embezzlement of more than a million rubles and receiving 600,000 rubles in bribes.

Soviet Ambassador on German Support for Baltics

Soviet Ambassador to Germany Vladislav Terekhov told a forum of German Social Democrats in Bonn that support for the Baltic republics could endanger European security, Reuters reported.

Terekhov's speech was severely criticized by President of the Lithuanian Supreme Council Vytautas Landsbergis in a statement issued in Vilnius on March 13. Landsbergis declared that the USSR was now engaged in "open blackmail" to prevent European countries from supporting Baltic independence (RFE Lithuanian service, March 13).

On March 13, Andrejs Urdze suggested to the Social Democratic Party's working group on the USSR at the German Bundestag that the CSCE and other international forums become involved in the resolution of the Baltic independence question. Urdze said the USSR had failed to halt the Baltic independence drive through military intervention and had now started a diplomatic campaign to try to keep the international community quiet on the Baltic question. Urdze was recently appointed spokesman for the Latvian Foreign Ministry in Germany (RFE/RL correspondent's report, March 13).

Wednesday, March 13

Head of European Bank Meets Gorbachev

The president-designate of the new London-based European Bank for Reconstruction and Development (EBRD), Jacques Attali, met Soviet President Mikhail Gorbachev to discuss prospects for possible aid to the USSR. They spoke about the establishment of a new banking system in the Soviet Union and other economic reforms (*Reuters*, March 13).

Commenting on the talks, Attali declared to Reuters that he was convinced the USSR would eventually become a full partner in the world economic system. He added that he had promised Soviet Prime Minister Valentin Pavlov that the EBRD would assist the USSR as long as reforms continued.

Legal Action against Holders of Both Government and Party Posts

In his speech of March 9, RSFSR Supreme Soviet Chairman Boris El'tsin said that the RSFSR Prosecutor's Office would initiate criminal cases against officials who ignored the RSFSR Congress of People's Deputies decree (issued by the RSFSR Supreme Soviet in January) prohibiting individuals from simultaneously holding leading posts in government and party organizations. Valentin Stepankov, the RSFSR public prosecutor, told "Vremya," however, that his office would use "various legal methods" to secure the implementation of that decree rather than initiate criminal cases. He stressed that the decree applied not only to leaders of the CPSU but also to leaders of other political parties.

Military Subunits Dispatched to Moldavia

The Moldavian media reported that additional Soviet military subunits had been dispatched to Moldavia in connection with the March 17 referendum. The republican authorities were informed of the dispatch of 360 armed paratroopers who would guard fifteen military commissariats in which polling centers were being set up. In addition, several columns of armored personnel carriers were reported to be moving into Moldavia from Ukraine. Tent camps prepared by the Soviet military appeared at several locations in fields and forests in Moldavia. Speaking on Moldavian television, Moldavian

President Mircea Snegur declared that Moscow was trying to intimidate the republic and that the dispatch of troops showed an aggressive intent. He also said that he had appealed to Soviet President Mikhail Gorbachev to withdraw the troops.

General on Weapons Production Problems

The head of Missile and Artillery Troops, Marshal of Artillery Vladimir Mikhalkin, told Radio Mayak that weapons technology in the Soviet Union had suffered because of shortcomings in the manufacturing process. The marshal said that the follow-through on good designs was often poor when the production stage was reached, and he suggested that military inspectors in factories might not be doing a good job of quality control. He said he supported current Soviet force reductions but added that cuts should be determined by military professionals.

Soviet Aviation Official Calls for Cooperation

Attending an international aviation symposium in Manila, Aleksandr Gerashchenko, USSR first deputy minister of the aviation industry, offered to share Soviet research with foreign manufacturers in order to develop a new generation of space shuttles and long-range supersonic civilian aircraft, Reuters reported. Gerashchenko said that, although the Soviet Union was one of the leaders in the field of space and aeronautics research, production was so costly that it was difficult for one country to finance it. With the reduction of East-West tensions, the Soviet Union was converting military aircraft factories to civilian use, he added, and the time was ripe to consider joint ventures with foreign companies.

Religious Leaders Favor Maintaining Unity

A group of religious leaders of various faiths met in the Danilov Monastery at the invitation of Patriarch Aleksii II, Radio Mayak reported. The group released a statement expressing "deep concern" about the fate of the Soviet Union and its hope that forces in favor of maintaining unity would become more active in political life.

Godmanis Warns of Economic Problems for Latvia

Latvian Prime Minister Ivars Godmanis warned the Latvian Supreme Council of possible economic problems for Latvia if it did not pay 3.2 billion rubles to the Soviet government. Godmanis said that the USSR was demanding 1 billion rubles as Latvia's share of a fund to stabilize the Soviet economy and another 2.2 billion for a fund to compensate people for forthcoming price increases. *Diena* quoted Latvian Finance Minister Elmars Silins as saying the sum was nearly the entire budget of the republic for 1991. Godmanis proposed seeking a compromise and raised the possibility of paying only part of the sum demanded (RFE Latvian service, March 14).

On March 25, the USSR Finance Ministry sent a telegram to Silins stating that, unless 4 billion rubles were transferred by Latvia to USSR accounts by April 1, retaliatory measures—including dismissal of bank officials and other personnel—would be taken. On March 19, Godmanis had explained in writing to his Soviet counterpart, Valentin Pavlov, the reasons why Latvia could not contribute this sum. Radio Riga reported on March 25 that Latvian leaders were reckoning with the possibility of a Soviet economic blockade.

KGB Declares Bashkiria Ecological Disaster Zone

General Vladimir Podelyakin, chairman of the KGB in Bashkiria, sent a report to the Bashkir Supreme Soviet saying the republic could become uninhabitable unless urgent steps were taken to stop chronic pollution, TASS reported. Podelyakin said that large tracts of land should be declared ecological disaster zones and that the ecological situation had passed the critical point. A spokesman for the ecological department of the Ufa City Soviet said that Podelyakin's report was "all true."

Slovak Prime Minister on First Official Visit to USSR

Slovak Prime Minister Vladimir Meciar arrived in Moscow on March 13 for three days of talks focusing on bilateral economic and trade relations, the Czechoslovak news agency CTK reported. On March 14, Meciar met with RSFSR Prime Minister Ivan Silaev; they agreed to sign a bilateral cooperation treaty within a month. According to TASS, this treaty would cover exchanges in trade, science, education, and culture. The same day, Meciar had talks with Soviet Prime Minister Valentin Pavlov to discuss Czechoslovak-Soviet cooperation and the creation of a joint RSFSR-Slovak commercial bank in Bratislava, to which all payments for goods would be sent and where exchange rates would be agreed to balance price differences (*Radio Prague*, March 14). After the talks, Meciar flew from Moscow to Kiev.

On March 15, according to a CTK report, Meciar and Ukrainian Prime Minister Vitol'd Fokin signed a joint communiqué agreeing on the inviolability of their existing border. They also discussed cooperation and the possibility of immediate barter trade.

Thursday, March 14

Baker in Moscow for Talks

US Secretary of State James Baker arrived in Moscow after a five-country visit to the Middle East and the Persian Gulf, Reuters reported. He met with Soviet Foreign Minister Aleksandr Bessmertnykh for talks that concentrated on the situation in the Gulf.

After a meeting with Soviet President Mikhail Gorbachev on March 15, Baker told journalists that little progress had been made to resolve differences over the existing conventional arms treaty or in advancing a proposed treaty cutting long-range nuclear weapons, AP reported. Baker added, however, that Gorbachev had made progress in reducing tension in the Baltic republics. Later that day, Baker hosted a dinner attended by senior officials of several Soviet republics, including Georgian Supreme Soviet Chairman Zviad Gamsakhurdia and Armenian Prime Minister Vazgen Manukyan, Western agencies reported. Also present were the chairmen of the Moscow and Leningrad City Soviets, Gavriil Popov and Anatolii Sobchak. RSFSR Supreme Soviet Chairman Boris El'tsin, who had also been invited, declined to attend for unknown reasons and sent a representative.

On March 16, Bessmertnykh presented Baker with a six-point plan for stability in the Middle East, TASS reported. According to Soviet Foreign Ministry spokesman Vitalii Churkin, Baker reacted positively to the plan but declared that it needed more study.

The same day, US and Soviet negotiators exchanged new proposals for resolving disputes over the implementation of the Conventional Forces in Europe Treaty, but disagreements remained (*Reuters*, March 16).

Baker also met privately with former Soviet Foreign Minister Eduard Shevardnadze, who called for young political leaders to be given a more active role in running the country and warned that the danger of a dictatorship in the Soviet Union still existed (*Reuters*, March 16).

The same day, Baker met with representatives of the Baltic republics (RFE/RL correspondent's report, March 16).

RSFSR Television to Be Launched

RSFSR Mass Media and Information Minister Mikhail Poltoranin told AFP that the RSFSR would soon have its own television channel and that six hours of programming a day were planned. RSFSR television would broadcast information and cultural programs on the existing second state channel, would maintain its own studio in Moscow, and would hire its own employees.

The USSR in March, 1991

The announcement followed a refusal by Chairman of the USSR Radio and Television Broadcasting Company Leonid Kravchenko to grant RSFSR Supreme Soviet Chairman Boris El'tsin forty minutes of air time on Soviet television to comment on the March 17 referendum on the future of the Soviet Union, AFP reported. Kravchenko said his refusal was based on the popular reaction to El'tsin's speech of March 9, in which he called for "war" on the Soviet government. El'tsin told *Komsomol'skaya pravda* that he regretted his call for "war"; he said he had made a mistake in discarding his prepared text and speaking his mind openly.

First Political Parties Registered in RSFSR

The Democratic Party of Russia, the Social-Democratic Party, and the Republican Party were the first political parties to be officially registered in the RSFSR, TASS reported. Also registered were a number of public groups, including the Chernobyl' Union, the Union of Veterans of the Afghan War, trade unions, charitable organizations, and religious groups.

USSR and South Korea Reach New Aviation Agreement

As reported by AP, the Soviet Union and South Korea reached agreement on gradually increasing the number of commercial flights between the two countries. South Korea would increase its flights over Soviet territory from the current ten per week to fifty by 1994; Soviet flights to Seoul would increase from two a week to thirty in 1994.

Mongolia Stops Trade with Soviet Union

Mongolia's Ministry for Trade and Industry said trade with the Soviet Union had stopped completely because Moscow had failed to pay for 40 million dollars' worth of delivered goods, Reuters reported. The USSR had not paid anything since the two countries agreed to deal in hard currency from the start of 1991. Mongolia retaliated by halting payments for imports of Soviet fuel, and trade then ceased altogether. The ministry complained that cuts in imports of Soviet raw materials had forced Mongolian factories and enterprises, which relied heavily on imported materials, to shut down.

Shevardnadze Visits Italy

Former Soviet Foreign Minister Eduard Shevardnadze arrived in Italy at the invitation of the Italian Society for International Organizations, Lucarini Publishers, and the Soviet-Italian joint venture "Novosti-Italia." According to an AFP report, Shevardnadze appealed in an address at Trieste University for moral and political support for democratic forces in the USSR. Shevardnadze deplored what he called stagnation in East-West relations. He was also awarded an honorary doctorate by the university.

Speaking on Italian television, Shevardnadze said that, without Soviet President Mikhail Gorbachev and *perestroika*, resistance to German reunification could have been strong enough to start a third world war, DPA reported. He repeated that there was still a real danger of a dictatorship in the USSR but that he would always remain a friend of Gorbachev. On March 14, Shevardnadze met with Pope John Paul II.

Gorbachev Appeals for Dialogue on Nagorno-Karabakh

Soviet President Mikhail Gorbachev appealed to Armenians and Azerbaijanis to begin a dialogue on the disputed Nagorno-Karabakh Autonomous Oblast. According to TASS, Gorbachev said he understood that it was not easy to terminate the chain reaction of hurt feelings, wrath, and mutual revenge, but he entreated the two peoples to begin peace talks. Gorbachev added that democratic elections should be held and legitimate organs of power formed. He also said that Nagorno-Karabakh was an inalienable part of Azerbaijan.

Ethnic Armenians held a one-day strike on March 15 to protest against Gorbachev's statement that Nagorno-Karabakh was part of Azerbaijan, TASS reported. Thousands of people rallied in Stepanakert, and workers sent a telegram to Gorbachev protesting his remarks.

Kirgiz-Uzbek Cooperation Treaty Signed

Kirgizia and Uzbekistan signed a friendship and cooperation treaty in an attempt to repair their bilateral relations, which had been strained by violence between ethnic Kirgiz and Uzbeks in Kirgizia in 1990. Over 200 people were killed in the clashes, which began in the southern Kirgiz oblast of Osh (*Central Television*, March 14).

Charges Dropped against Bashkir Poet

TASS said criminal charges had been dropped against former dissident, Bashkir poet Nizemetdin Akhmetov. Akhmetov emigrated to West Germany in 1987 after many years of imprisonment in the Soviet Union. He was detained in November, 1990, when, wishing to return to the Soviet Union, he tried to enter Lithuania from Poland without valid documents. Colonel Anatolii Surkov of the Chelyabinsk Oblast KGB said charges had been dropped because Akhmetov had merely been trying to return to his homeland and had not inflicted any damage on the USSR.

The USSR in March, 1991

Explosion at Gates of Military Command in Vilnius

There was an explosion at the gates of the Soviet military commandant's office in Vilnius, Radio Vilnius reported. The radio quoted Romualdas Venkevicius, an official of the Lithuanian Ministry of Internal Affairs, as saying the explosion, caused by "a device of unknown manufacture," had done no particular damage.

Honecker Moved to Moscow

Former East German State and Party leader Erich Honecker, who faced charges of manslaughter in Germany, was moved from a Soviet military hospital near Berlin to Moscow. The Soviet Union said Honecker had been moved because of his deteriorating health (*AFP*, March 14). German government spokesman Dieter Vogel told a Berlin radio station on March 15 that the move violated the German-Soviet agreement on the status of Soviet forces in Germany. Although Soviet Foreign Minister Aleksandr Bessmertnykh said the Soviet government had informed the Germans about the move, Vogel said the notification had come only about an hour before the event, too late for Germany to take any action, ADN reported. German Foreign Minister Hans-Dietrich Genscher told the German parliament that day that, regardless of the humanitarian and medical grounds cited for the move by Moscow, the removal of Honecker was a violation of international law and of Soviet-German treaties (*Reuters*, March 15). Genscher demanded the immediate return of Honecker, but the Soviet Union said this was impossible (*AP*, March 15).

China Invests in Stability

China granted the USSR a loan of about 730 million dollars to buy meat, grain, tea, peanuts, raw silk, tobacco, and other consumer products from China. China was suffering a glut of these items because of a sluggish economy. Soviet Deputy Prime Minister Yurii Maslyukov, who was on a visit to Peking, called the Chinese loan "very timely." According to AFP, Chinese Prime Minister Li Peng stressed to Maslyukov that China hoped the USSR would regain political stability and develop its economy quickly.

Friday, March 15

RSFSR Banker on Soviet Economic Reforms

Speaking at a conference on Soviet economic reform in Paris, the head of the RSFSR Central Bank, Georgii Matyukhin, declared that Soviet President Mikhail Gorbachev's economic reforms had come to a halt. The Soviet authorities, he said, had no program of economic reform; if they did, Soviet Prime Minister Valentin Pavlov was "keeping it a secret." Matyukhin also said that the RSFSR needed to control its own resources in order to strengthen its economic autonomy.

A representative of the USSR State Bank, Aleksandr Khandruev, told the same conference that splitting up control of precious assets and dividing Soviet economic power would lead to civil war (*Reuters*, March 15).

Gromov Wins Lawsuit

Soviet television reported that Soviet First Deputy Minister of Internal Affairs Boris Gromov had won a lawsuit against Colonel Vilen Martirosyan, who had asserted in the Ukrainian tri-weekly *Komsomol'skaya znamya* that Gromov, who was previously the commander of the Kiev Military District, was one of the men in the Soviet Union capable of initiating a military coup. The Kiev court ruled that such allegations against Gromov were groundless.

Saturday, March 16

Kravchenko Purges Staff of "TSN"

Three editors of the Central Television newscast "TSN," Tat'yana Mitkova, Evgenii Kiselev, and Yurii Rostov, were reported to have been sacked (*Radio Rossii*, March 16). "TSN" was not screened at all on March 15, and on the evening of March 16 it went on the air with new moderators and a much shorter program. On March 17, Radio Rossii announced that "TSN" editor Vitalii Tishin had also been fired. According to Radio Rossii, the purge at "TSN" was ordered by Leonid Kravchenko, chairman of the All-Union State Television and Radio Broadcasting Company.

Rostov told *Komsomol'skaya pravda* on March 18 that a dispute over censorship was the reason for his being fired. Rostov said that "TSN" had begun broadcasting a year ago without censorship but that pressure from the authorities had since increased dramatically. On March 12, 80 percent of the "TSN" newsscript had been cut, and Rostov had refused to appear on the censored program.

Gorbachev Meets with Economists

Pravda reported on March 19 that Soviet President Mikhail Gorbachev had met on with "the country's leading economists" on March 16. *Pravda* printed only Gorbachev's address and did not identify those present, but the television news program "Vremya" showed Valentin Pavlov, Leonid Abalkin, Aleksandr Granberg,

The USSR in March, 1991

and Vadim Medvedev, among others. Gorbachev said a compromise had to be found between what he termed the "Gossnab" approach, in which the entire economy was run by state orders, and a full-blooded market economy based on contracts between enterprises. Both, Gorbachev declared, were wrong for the Soviet Union, adding that the Soviet economy should be based on the Spanish or Brazilian model. He claimed that East Europeans were already regretting their moves towards the market.

Gorbachev also told the meeting that restructuring the defense industries offered one way out of the current economic crisis. According to *Pravda*, Gorbachev said the distortion of the economy in favor of military production had been unfortunate for the Soviet Union, but he added that the military sector offered colossal opportunities. He specifically mentioned "the processing, storage, and transportation of farm produce" as areas where the defense industries could help out.

The first congress of the Peasant Party of Russia opened in Moscow. It was attended by some 300 delegates, who gathered at the headquarters of *Rossiiskaya gazeta*. USSR people's deputy Yurii Chernichenko was elected chairman of the party, which defined itself as a political alliance of like-minded people who advocated agrarian reform and favored fair competition between individually operated farms and kolkhozes and sovkhozes. The congress pointed out that there were 12,000 independent farms starting up in the RSFSR. Complaints were voiced about local authorities that did not permit farmers to acquire small plots of land, gave farmers no assistance, and created artificial obstacles. The congress adopted a program emphasizing that the principal goal of the party was to revive proprietary farming and to protect the economic and social interests of farmers (*TASS*, March 18).

Peasant Party of Russia Holds Congress

Pravda published an interview with former Presidential Council member Aleksandr Yakovlev. Yakovlev said he considered the referendum of March 17 a great step towards democracy, and he criticized the democratic opposition for demanding Gorbachev's resignation. Yakovlev also expressed concern over what he called "the crude methods" of political struggle employed in the drive to create an RSFSR presidency. Commenting on the interview, Radio Rossii said that Yakovlev had initially opposed the introduction of an executive presi-

Yakovlev Gives Interview

197

dency in the RSFSR but had been persuaded to change his mind at a meeting with younger RSFSR politicians.

Congress of Estonia Meets Again

Estonia's alternative parliament, the Congress of Estonia, met for the fourth time. The session, broadcast live on Estonian radio, approved a number of draft resolutions on issues ranging from ownership rights to identification cards for citizens. The plebiscite on Estonian independence held on March 3 and the general economic and political situation were also discussed.

Sunday, March 17

RSFSR Referendum on RSFSR Presidency

In addition to the all-Union referendum, the RSFSR held its own poll asking the population whether it was in favor of a directly elected RSFSR president. The results of the republic-wide referendum from seventy-seven of the eighty-eight electoral districts showed a turnout of 75 percent; 69.86 percent voted in favor of instituting the post of RSFSR president (*TASS*, March 20). The RSFSR referendum was not held in the North Ossetian, Chechen-Ingush, Tatar, and Tuvin ASSRs.

After Chairman of the RSFSR Referendum Commission Vasilii Kazakov had officially announced that the executive presidency had been approved in the Russian Federation, RSFSR Supreme Soviet Chairman Boris El'tsin declared that he would run for the post of president of the republic in a multicandidate popular election (*TASS*, March 21).

Soviet Union Holds Referendum on Its Future

Citizens went to the polls in the Soviet Union's first nationwide referendum on the future of the Union. Voters were asked: "Do you consider necessary the preservation of the Union of Soviet Socialist Republics as a renewed federation of equal sovereign republics, in which the rights and freedoms of an individual of any nationality will be fully guaranteed?"

As the voting took place, both radio and television continued to urge the electorate to vote "yes." This was a violation of the USSR Law on a Referendum, which forbade campaigning of any sort on the day of the vote. "Vremya" carried interviews with a number of people who said attempts to agitate against the referendum were violations of human rights.

Chairman of the Central Referendum Commission Vladimir Orlov announced the results of the referendum to the USSR Supreme Soviet on March 21. According to TASS reports, there was a high overall turnout of 80 percent—about 147 million of the USSR's 184 million eligible voters. Of those who cast ballots, 76.4 percent voted in favor of preserving the Union; 22 percent voted against; and about 2 percent of ballots were spoilt (*TASS*, March 21).

In the RSFSR, 75.4 percent of eligible voters participated in the all-Union referendum, of whom 70.88 percent voted for the preservation of the Union. Turnout in Ukraine was 83 percent, with 70 percent of those voting supporting the Union. At the same time, an even higher percentage—82.8 percent of those who voted—responded positively to the republican opinion poll, which asked whether Ukraine should remain part of the Soviet Union on the basis of its declaration of sovereignty. Voter participation in the all-Union referendum in Belorussia was 83.3 percent, with 82.6 percent registering a "yes" vote (*TASS*, March 21).

In Uzbekistan, turnout was 95.4 percent, with 93.7 percent voting in favor of the Union. In Kazakhstan, 89 percent of eligible voters participated in the referendum, 94.1 percent of whom supported the Union. In Tajikistan, turnout was 94 percent, with 96 percent voting "yes." In Turkmenistan, 97.7 percent of those registered to vote did so, of whom 97.9 percent were in favor of a renewed Union. In Kirgizia, the turnout was also very high—92.9 percent—and 94.5 percent said "yes." In Azerbaijan, 93 percent of those voting were in favor of a renewed Union; turnout was 75 percent (*TASS*, March 21).

The Baltic republics, Armenia, Georgia, and Moldavia boycotted the all-Union referendum, but polling stations were set up by local groups in military installations or other sites guarded by troops. According to Orlov, 800,000 voted in Moldavia, 50,000 in Georgia, and 5,000 in Armenia (*TASS*, March 21).

In Latvia, more than 500,000 people took part in the referendum, and of these about 20,000 voted "no" (*Reuters*, March 21). Pro-Moscow Supreme Council deputy Stanislav Buka told *Diena* on March 18 that 23–30 percent of all eligible voters had participated; 322 polling stations were set up by units of the Soviet Armed Forces, work collectives, and public organizations. In Estonia, 250,000 civilians, representing about 23 percent of civilians eligible to vote in the republic, participated in the referendum, TASS reported on March 18; 95 percent of them supported the preservation of the Union. In Lithuania, 652,000 people voted in the referendum, of whom 96.7 percent voted "yes." The number of voters was less than the majority needed to make the vote official but far in excess of expectations (*TASS*, March 21). In a telephone report to RFE/RL on March 18, a correspondent quoted Lithuanian Communist Party Secretary Algimantas Naudziunas as saying that about 100,000 people had voted at military bases and an additional 500,000 people at civilian polling centers. He also said that about 120,000 people had voted in Vilnius.

On March 21, the USSR Supreme Soviet adopted a resolution declaring the results of the all-Union referendum binding for the whole country, TASS reported. All state bodies and all republics must accept the popular decision on the preservation of a renewed Union, it declared. The Supreme Soviet also asked for a report on efforts by some republics to restrict people's right to vote and asked the USSR prosecutor-general to investigate whether any violations of individuals' constitutional rights had occurred.

USSR Supreme Soviet Chairman Anatolii Luk'yanov declared on Central Television that the referendum would speed up progress towards a new Union treaty (*Reuters*, March 21). He said that, despite being held at a time of social tension, shortages, and worsening interethnic relations, the referendum showed the will of the Soviet people to live within a federation.

Moscow Referendum on Mayor

In Moscow, a separate referendum was held asking residents whether they supported the direct election of the city's mayor. According to AFP on March 18, about 65 percent of eligible voters participated, 80 percent of whom said "yes."

Official Comments on All-Union Referendum

Presidential spokesman Sergei Grigor'ev said the results of the all-Union referendum were good given that the administration's popularity was not very high in the USSR and that price increases were about to take effect, Reuters reported on March 19.

Chairman of the Central Referendum Commission Vladimir Orlov praised the results of the vote at a session of the USSR Supreme Soviet and criticized the authorities in those areas of the USSR where provision had not been made for people to participate in the referendum (*TASS*, March 19).

Grigorii Revenko, an adviser to Soviet President Mikhail Gorbachev, told a press conference in Moscow that the majority vote in favor of preserving the Union had created the basis for further democratic reform (*AFP*, March 20). He said the low pro-Union vote in some big cities, such as Moscow, Leningrad, and Sverdlovsk, was cause for concern for the government, but he also noted that these cities were suffering severe shortages of consumer goods. Revenko added that Gorbachev had reacted calmly to the initial results and had said that republics that had refused to take part in the referendum would not be punished (*TASS*, March 20).

Gorbachev on Soviet Republics' Drive for Independence

USSR President Mikhail Gorbachev compared independence drives in some Soviet republics with the situation that existed in former Soviet satellite countries in 1989. In an interview carried by TASS, he said that, when relations with the Soviet Union's East European allies became tense in 1989, his leadership took "the only correct position" and gave them the opportunity to rethink everything for themselves. Now, Gorbachev claimed, he had difficulty finding the time to meet all the representatives of these countries to discuss future cooperation. The Soviet leader added that a similar development would take place in relations between the center and the republics.

Genscher in Moscow

German Foreign Minister Hans-Dietrich Genscher arrived in Moscow for an official two-day visit, DPA reported. The same day, he started talks with Soviet Foreign Minister Aleksandr Bessmertnykh on the Persian Gulf, the Middle East, and Soviet-German relations—in particular, the agreement on the withdrawal of 340,000 Soviet troops from Germany. During a meeting with Soviet President Mikhail Gorbachev on March 18, Genscher repeated Germany's demand for the return of former East German state and Communist Party leader Erich Honecker, who was abruptly transferred to Moscow from Berlin on March 13 for "humanitarian reasons" (Western agencies, March 18). Gorbachev said he recognized the great importance Germany attached to the Honecker case (*DPA*, March 18).

Genscher told a press conference on March 18 that Gorbachev had accepted his request to meet Soviet ethnic Germans who were pressing for the restoration of the German Volga Republic. For his part, Genscher promised the ethnic Germans that Bonn would do everything possible to improve their lives, but he said that Germany wanted them to stay in the USSR rather than emigrate (Western agencies, March 18).

Addressing a press conference in Leningrad on March 20, Soviet Defense Minister Dmitrii Yazov suggested that Honecker be considered a political refugee, Reuters reported. He compared Honecker's case with that of Soviet soldiers who had deserted in Germany and had been granted political asylum.

Monday, March 18

British Foreign Secretary Visits USSR

British Foreign Secretary Douglas Hurd arrived in Kiev, where he met Ukrainian Prime Minister Vitol'd Fokin, Reuters reported. According to British officials, Hurd began his visit in Kiev in order to gain an alternative perspective on the Soviet Union's future (*Reuters*, March 19). On March 20, Hurd went to Moscow, where he met with Soviet Foreign Minister Aleksandr Bessmertnykh and Soviet President Mikhail Gorbachev on March 21. Talks focused on international topics and Soviet-British relations, TASS reported.

Commenting on the talks at a press conference on March 21, Hurd said that the USSR had no economic reform program that would justify massive aid from the West, Reuters reported. Hurd acknowledged that the European Community had agreed to grant the USSR a 1-billion-dollar aid package, but he said this had been intended for "specific needs" and was not linked to general economic reforms. He also said that foreign businessmen were holding back on large-scale investment in the Soviet Union because of confusion over who was responsible for the Soviet economy. Speaking about arms control, Hurd declared that both the USSR and the West wanted to resolve the current impasse. He said NATO and Warsaw Pact states other than the USSR had agreed that the USSR was violating the terms of the treaty on the reduction of conventional forces in Europe (signed in November, 1990, but pending ratification) and that this had blocked further talks on cutting troop strengths. On the Arab-Israeli conflict, Hurd said both Britain and the USSR believed an international conference involving the United Nations would be necessary, AFP reported. Hurd also said Britain did not intend to establish diplomatic missions in the Baltic republics but had decided to open a consulate in Kiev.

Georgia Reorganizes Government

Central Television reported that the Georgian Supreme Soviet had made some changes in the republic's executive bodies. It said that several ministries and state committees had been abolished or merged and that new departments had been created. The Georgian Council of Ministers would, in future, be called the Government of the Republic of Georgia.

On March 20, the Georgian Supreme Soviet observed a minute of silence for the victims of the South Ossetian conflict, TASS reported. It went on to discuss the poll scheduled to take place in the republic on

The USSR in March, 1991

March 31 and decided that Georgian citizens who would be absent at that time could vote on March 23. The Supreme Soviet also abolished the death penalty for some crimes, including counterfeiting, bribery, and theft of public property.

Kvitsinsky on Soviet-East European Relations

In an interview in *Pravda* on Soviet-East European relations, Deputy Foreign Minister Yulii Kvitsinsky said that Eastern Europe must remain a focal point of Soviet foreign policy. Kvitsinsky said the question of new political agreements between the USSR and East European countries was directly linked to the USSR's own security. He dismissed concerns about NATO's failure to follow the Warsaw Pact's example of dissolving itself, saying that the Warsaw Pact's dissolution was part of a trend towards nonconfrontation in Europe.

Latvian-Danish Agreements Signed

In Copenhagen, the Latvian and Danish foreign ministers signed agreements on cooperation that could lead to the establishment of diplomatic relations between the two countries. Denmark, which never recognized the incorporation of the Baltic States into the Soviet Union in 1940, had already signed identical protocols with Estonia and Lithuania. According to Reuters, agreements on economic, cultural, and educational cooperation were also formalized.

On March 19, Soviet Foreign Ministry spokesman Vitalii Churkin criticized the agreements as a violation of the Helsinki accords, Reuters reported. The USSR said that the protocols could harm its relations with Denmark, but on March 20 the Danish government rejected the Soviet protest and said it would continue to support the Baltic republics in their efforts to break away from the USSR. Danish Foreign Minister Uffe Elleman-Jensen declared that the agreements complied with international law, and he invited Soviet Foreign Minister Aleksandr Bessmertnykh to discuss the issue (*Reuters*, March 20).

Soviet Troops Detain Lithuanian National Defense Department Director

Radio Kaunas broadcast a statement by President of the Lithuanian Supreme Council Vytautas Landsbergis saying that the director of the Lithuanian National Defense Department, Audrius Butkevicius, and his driver had been detained by Soviet MVD troops. When Landsbergis telephoned the Ministry of Internal Affairs to demand Butkevicius' release, MVD General Aleksandr Zhitnikov told him that the matter had been delegated to the Moscow-appointed prosecutor in Lithuania, Antanas Petrauskas and was no longer in his hands.

Butkevicius said on March 18 after his release that he had been interrogated and filmed by Soviet soldiers for twelve hours. He was told that the soldiers who stopped his car had found illegal weapons, but he said he knew nothing about them. Butkevicius added that a member of Lithuania's "National Salvation Committee" had been present during the interrogation (RFE Lithuanian service, March 18).

Tuesday, March 19

Gorbachev Issues Decree on Price Rises

USSR President Mikhail Gorbachev issued a decree introducing new retail state prices for many goods and new tariffs for transportation and communications services as of April 2, TASS reported. Money from the increases would be used to pay tax-free compensation to the population beginning on March 20 and to finance salary increases for workers in education, health, social security, culture, and archives. Prices would not be raised for medicines and medical supplies, coffee, vodka, synthetic materials, gas, coal, firewood, and kerosene. Chairman of the USSR State Committee for Prices Valentin Senchagov said that the central government would set prices but that republican governments would be allowed to make adjustments based on regional considerations.

USSR Supreme Soviet deputy Sergei Ryabchenko declared that Estonia and Lithuania were not on the list of republics that had verbally agreed to the price increases. Ryabchenko reportedly saw the list at a closed meeting with USSR Prime Minister Valentin Pavlov.

Estonian Prime Minister Edgar Savisaar told *Rahva Haal* on March 20, however, that prices would go up in Estonia. He said that, as of April 2, 30 percent of all prices would be fixed by the state, 30 percent would be regulated according to profitability, and the remaining 40 percent would be free-floating.

The text of the agreement on price reform between the USSR and the republics was published in *Pravda* on March 20.

USSR Renews Relations with Dominican Republic

TASS reported the renewal of diplomatic links between the Soviet Union and the Dominican Republic. Such links had been suspended since 1959. There were no plans to exchange ambassadors. Instead, the Dominican Republic would use its mission in Germany to renew ties with the USSR, and the USSR would act through its mission in Venezuela.

Soviet Union Receives Credit from Turkish Bank

Turkey's Eximbank agreed to provide 600 million dollars' worth of credit to the USSR, Reuters reported. Two-thirds of the credit would be used to import Turkish goods.

First Soviet Study of Katyn Massacre

The first major Soviet study of the massacre by the NKVD of Polish officers in the Katyn Forest in 1943 was published in Moscow. In 1990, the USSR officially admitted responsibility for the crime, which it had until then blamed on the Nazis. The book, *Katynsky labirint* (The Katyn Labyrinth), written by *Literaturnaya gazeta* correspondent Vladimir Abarinov, contained new archival materials and interviews with witnesses of the tragedy.

Another Sentence in the Osh Affair

TASS reported that the Kirgiz Supreme Court had sentenced a participant in the violence in Osh Oblast in the summer of 1990 to twelve years of imprisonment. The defendant, Ataman Tashaliev, was accused of leading an attack on Uzbek homes in the town of Uzgen, where some of the worst violence between Kirgiz and Uzbeks took place. According to Aleksandr Frolov, the head of the investigating team sent by the USSR Prosecutor's Office, sixty-five suits arising from the violence in Osh had been filed and about half of these cases had already been heard. At least two death sentences had been handed down.

Latvia Adopts Law to Protect Rights of National Minorities

The Latvian Supreme Soviet adopted a law "On the Free Development of and Rights to Cultural Autonomy of National and Ethnic Groups in Latvia." The law guaranteed the rights of national minorities, who made up about one-half of Latvia's population. It also stated that any acts encouraging discrimination, national superiority, or strife were punishable by law. Deputy Ruta Marjasa noted that the pro-Moscow opposition faction in the parliament, "Ravnopravie," which claimed to represent the Russian-speaking population of Latvia, had not disrupted the work of the deputies during the drafting of the legislation, Radio Riga reported. The text of the law was published in *Vedomosti Verkhovnogo Soveta i Pravitel'stva Latviiskoi Respubliki*, No. 21/22, June 6, 1991.

Wednesday, March 20

USSR Supreme Soviet Adopts Law on Cabinet of Ministers

The USSR Supreme Council adopted a law on the USSR Cabinet of Ministers, TASS reported. The law gave the Cabinet the right to issue decrees that could be abrogated only by the USSR president or the USSR Supreme Soviet. The Supreme Soviet did not give the Cabinet the right to make laws, although Prime Minister Valentin Pavlov had requested it to do so. Under the new law, the USSR Supreme Soviet had the authority to force the Cabinet to resign if at least two-thirds of the total membership supported a vote of no confidence in it.

Bessmertnykh on Republican Foreign Ministries

USSR Foreign Minister Aleksandr Bessmertnykh said that the Council of Ministers for Foreign Affairs, recently established by the central government to coordinate the activities of the foreign ministries of the Union republics, could play a constructive role in resolving ethnic conflicts between republics. He told Radio Moscow that republican foreign ministries were also "essential" for promoting republican economic interests abroad. He indicated that he did not foresee major conflicts between the USSR and the republican foreign ministries as long as their actions were coordinated.

50 Million Soviet People Live in Ecological Disaster Areas

Professor Aleksei Yablokov, deputy chairman of the USSR Supreme Soviet Ecology Committee, said that 40–50 million Soviet citizens lived in ecological disaster zones and that the number of deaths caused by cancer was rising by 2 percent a year. Yablokov, who was interviewed by the Belgian daily *De Morgen*, reported that recent tests of mothers' milk showed that half the samples contained "dangerous concentrations of pesticides." He added that the Soviet Union was plagued by the emission of toxic heavy metals from the metal industry and the unlimited use of pesticides in agriculture (*Reuters*, March 20).

China To Buy Soviet MiGs

DPA reported that the Chinese government had decided to buy an undisclosed number of Soviet MiG-27 fighter planes. The announcement of the purchase came at a four-day air show at a base near Beijing. The show marked the first demonstration of Soviet military technology in China since the two countries normalized relations in 1989.

The USSR in March, 1991

Yazov on Gulf War

At a news conference in Leningrad, USSR Defense Minister Dmitrii Yazov said that the allied ground war in the Gulf had little strategic relevance for the Soviet Union, and he asserted that the Soviet T-72 tank used by Syria had outperformed its US counterpart, Reuters reported. Yazov said that the allies' use of guided missiles and massive air power, electronic warfare, and suppression of enemy command and control systems had provided important lessons for the Soviet Union. He also praised the performance of US General Norman Schwarzkopf, saying it required great skill to manage a coalition of multinational forces.

RSFSR Federation Council Discusses Federal and Union Treaties

The RSFSR Federation Council approved the draft federal treaty, which was to regulate relations between the federal organs of power in the republic and its constituent parts, TASS reported. The draft was then sent to soviets at all levels for examination. At the same session, "stormy debates" took place over whether the autonomous republics should sign the new Union treaty, as most of them wished to do. The meeting came to the conclusion that the Union treaty should be signed by an RSFSR delegation that would include representatives from the autonomous republics and other national-territorial and territorial units of the RSFSR, but the final decision would rest with the RSFSR Congress of People's Deputies, which was due to open on March 28.

Moscow Deputies on Hunger Strike in Protest over Police Chief

Ten members of the Moscow City Soviet were reported to have declared a hunger strike to protest against the refusal by USSR Minister of Internal Affairs Boriss Pugo to replace the present head of Moscow's Main Administration for Internal Affairs, Lieutenant General Petr Bogdanov, with Major General Vyacheslav Komissarov (*Radio Rossii*, March 20). His appointment had been approved by the Moscow City Soviet, but, although the Moscow city police were subordinate both to the city soviet and to the USSR MVD, Pugo insisted that cadres policy came under the jurisdiction of the central authorities.

On March 26, Soviet President Mikhail Gorbachev decreed the creation of a combined Administration of Internal Affairs for Moscow City and Moscow Oblast, Radio Moscow reported. The new administration, which replaced the separate city and oblast administrations that existed previously, was to be headed by the USSR first deputy minister of internal affairs, Lieutenant General Ivan Shilov. Oversight of the Moscow police was taken out of the hands of the Moscow authorities, with Shilov reporting directly to the USSR Ministry of Internal Affairs. At the same time as the proclamation of the decree, Bogdanov was released from his duties. Security Council member Vadim Bakatin said the decree was only a temporary measure (*TASS*, March 26).

The presidium of the RSFSR Supreme Soviet issued a statement on March 27 saying the decree was "a gross violation" of the constitutions of both the USSR and the RSFSR, TASS reported.

Chernobyl'-Related Charges against Kursk Officials

Criminal charges were reported to have been filed against officials in Kursk Oblast in the RSFSR in connection with the Chernobyl' nuclear accident. Radio Moscow said that radioactive fallout had reached five districts of Kursk but that the local authorities had nonetheless allowed the 1986 May Day processions to go ahead.

Shooting Incident in Vilnius

Special police (OMON) troops at a roadblock in Vilnius fired shots at a bus carrying Lithuanian border guards when it refused to stop, Reuters reported. President of the Lithuanian Supreme Council Vytautas Landsbergis told RFE/RL that he regarded the incident very seriously, viewing it as an intentional escalation of force by the Soviet troops. At least three of the guards were injured in the machine-gun fire, and one of the three was reportedly in a serious condition.

The director of the Lithuanian National Defense Department, Audrius Butkevicius, told the Lithuanian Supreme Council in a session that was broadcast live on Radio Kaunas on March 21 that OMON troops in Vilnius had claimed they had tried to stop the bus because the military commissariat in Salcininkai Raion had reported that it contained weapons. Claims that the OMON guards had fired on the bus only after being shot at first were clearly false, he said, since the Lithuanian guards were unarmed and no weapons had been found on the bus. AP reported on March 21 that the deputy head of the OMON garrison had told Lithuanian officials that the troops were "acting on their own."

Baltic Officials at Council of Europe Meeting

The mayor of Tartu, Toomas Mendelson, and Vilnius City Council member Saulius Lapienis attended a local government conference at the Council of Europe in Strasbourg, Reuters reported. The Balts' request for guest status at the council had not been approved, because, a council official explained, "the Council of Europe cannot take the initiative in officially recognizing the

Baltic republics." As an intermediate step, the council invited the Balts to this conference of local and regional authorities.

Thursday, March 21

Romanian Foreign Minister Visits Soviet Union

Romanian Foreign Minister Adrian Nastase left Bucharest for a visit to the Soviet Union, Radio Bucharest reported. On March 22 in Moscow, Nastase and USSR Foreign Minister Aleksandr Bessmertnykh initialed a treaty of friendship and cooperation confirming the positions of both nations on the inviolability of their borders, the territorial integrity of all European states, and the nonuse of force in international relations. The treaty also provided for the development of bilateral economic cooperation at all levels, cooperation in the fight against terrorism and drug trafficking, and environmental protection of the Danube and Black Sea regions. The document was to be signed at a later date by the Soviet and Romanian heads of state (*TASS*, March 22).

On March 24, Nastase held talks in Kiev with the chairman of the Ukrainian Supreme Soviet, Leonid Kravchuk, TASS reported. They discussed how to meet the cultural and spiritual needs of ethnic Romanians and Ukrainians living outside their homelands. Kravchuk told Nastase that Ukraine wanted to establish mutually beneficial relations with all countries, including Romania.

Stopping over in Kishinev on his return to Romania, Nastase met briefly with Moldavian President Mircea Snegur, Moldovapres reported. Snegur commented on the need for special border-crossing facilities for Romanian and Moldavian residents. Rompres cited Nastase as saying he envisaged "a cultural confederation" and eventually "an economic confederation" of Romania and Moldavia—the formula first aired by Snegur on his visit to Romania in February.

Nastase continued his official talks in Kishinev on March 25. With his Moldavian counterpart, Nicolae Tiu, he signed a protocol on cooperation and consultation between foreign ministries on issues connected with Europe, the region, the Danube, and the Black Sea, Radio Bucharest reported. Both sides would seek Moldavia's inclusion in consultations between Romania and Ukraine through their respective foreign ministries, as agreed during Nastase's visit to Kiev on March 23. Nastase inspected possible future sites in Kishinev for the Romanian consulate general, due to open at the same time as a Soviet consulate general in Iasi.

Moldavia had wanted a direct arrangement for Moldavian (rather than USSR) and Romanian consulates.

USSR Government Tries to Ban Rally in Support of El'tsin

The USSR Supreme Soviet passed a resolution saying the rally planned for March 28 by the Democratic Russia movement should be banned by the Moscow City Soviet because it would create an explosive situation (*TASS*, March 21). The rally was scheduled to coincide with the opening of a special session of the RSFSR Supreme Soviet called by the Communists of Russia faction to try to oust RSFSR Supreme Soviet Chairman Boris El'tsin. USSR First Deputy Prime Minister Vitalii Doguzhiev said the Democratic Russia rally would put people's lives in danger.

The USSR Cabinet of Ministers banned street rallies in Moscow from March 25 until April 15, TASS reported on March 25. The government instructed the Moscow City Soviet, the KGB, and the USSR Ministry of Internal Affairs to take all necessary steps to enforce the order. TASS said the order had been issued in response to Soviet President Mikhail Gorbachev's order of March 24 to the government of the USSR to ensure public order and safety in Moscow during the special session of the RSFSR Congress of People's Deputies. Gorbachev was reacting to an appeal for protection by twenty-nine RSFSR people's deputies, who alleged that deputies at past congresses had been psychologically "terrorized" and even physically attacked.

On March 26, the Moscow City Soviet voted at a closed-door session to allow the rally to take place on March 28, *Moskovskaya pravda* reported. According to Reuters, leaders of Democratic Russia said that the USSR government's ban was unconstitutional. (In the fall of 1990, the USSR Committee for Constitutional Supervision had declared unconstitutional a presidential decree, issued earlier in the year, that restricted the right of the Moscow City Soviet Executive Committee to authorize demonstrations in the city center.)

Nikolai Travkin, chairman of the Democratic Party of Russia, told AP on March 26 that he had urged the organizers of the rally to back down, arguing that social tensions had reached a critical point, past which "anger would turn to blood." Obstacles barring access to Red Square and the Manezh were being put into place, AP reported.

Soviet Prime Minister Valentin Pavlov proposed that the ban on demonstrations in Moscow be extended to other parts of the country, saying that industrial action, hunger strikes, and "anticonstitutional" appeals and resolutions could only worsen the USSR's current misfortunes (*TASS*, March 26).

The Presidium of the RSFSR Supreme Soviet issued a statement on March 27 declaring the Soviet government's ban illegal, TASS reported. Meanwhile, Soviet Vice President Gennadii Yanaev, Minister of Internal Affairs Boriss Pugo, and KGB Chairman Vladimir Kryuchkov summoned the chairman of the Moscow City Soviet Executive Committee, Yurii Luzhkov, and Democratic Russia leaders Yurii Afanas'ev and Arkadii Murashov to warn them they would be responsible for "possible breaches" of public order (*Reuters*, March 27). The Moscow City Soviet passed a resolution on the same day saying that the Soviet government would assume all responsibility for the consequences of any use of force against demonstrators (*AP*, March 27).

On March 28, more than 100,000 people rallied in support of El'tsin, Reuters reported. The barricades set up by the security forces prevented the demonstrators from marching to the Manezh, the intended site of the rally, and people gathered instead on the main thoroughfare Tverskaya Street. Radio Moscow also reported demonstrators on Arbat and Mayakovsky Squares. Pugo told the USSR Supreme Soviet that he had 50,000 men under his command in Moscow. Despite the presence of large numbers of riot troops and police armed with water cannons, the demonstrators were calm and peaceful, chanting for the resignation of Gorbachev and carrying signs saying "Save Russia from the Communist Party" and "Say 'No' to the Gorbachev Threat," Western agencies reported. According to AP, Soviet security forces reported that they had made no arrests during the rally, but US Senator David Boren, who witnessed the demonstration from his hotel, said he had seen at least a dozen instances in which men in plain clothes beat protesters and dragged them off to buses.

Earlier that day, a small crowd had gathered spontaneously outside the Hotel Rossiya, Radio Rossii reported. About 200 people were crowded together by the police; some then dispersed, but most remained, holding flags and banners. The police detained 6 persons. Pugo said on March 29 that there had been similar demonstrations in six other Soviet cities, including Voronezh, Novgorod, Cheboksary, and Tbilisi (*TASS*, March 29).

New Appointments

Soviet President Mikhail Gorbachev signed a decree appointing Igor' Prostyakov administrator of affairs for the Cabinet of Ministers. "Vremya" also reported that Kondrat Terekh had been made Soviet trade minister.

THE USSR IN MARCH, 1991

Georgian Supreme Soviet Expels Gumbaridze

The Georgian Supreme Soviet expelled former Georgian Communist Party First Secretary Givi Gumbaridze for dodging the fulfillment of his duties as a deputy, TASS reported. The Supreme Soviet also expelled deputy Guram Kashakashvili for not giving up his job as director of a metallurgical factory. A law had been passed recently stating that deputies must work full-time in the Georgian Supreme Soviet and not hold other positions.

Friday, March 22

El'tsin Makes Speech in Leningrad

RSFSR Supreme Soviet Chairman Boris El'tsin addressed workers at the Kirov heavy engineering works in Leningrad, TASS reported. He said that, if he were elected RSFSR president, he would purge Communist Party officials from local government (*Reuters*, March 22). He also urged factory workers to abandon their ties to the center and to place themselves under the jurisdiction of the RSFSR Supreme Soviet. Speaking about the differences between himself and Soviet President Mikhail Gorbachev, El'tsin said he was convinced that Gorbachev had no desire to accommodate the RSFSR. He repeated his earlier charges that Gorbachev had abandoned reform and blamed him once again for failing to draft a comprehensive program to resolve the Soviet Union's economic problems. El'tsin criticized the price increases that were scheduled to take effect on April 2, and he promised that he would present a Russian program for economic reform to a special session of the republic's Congress of People's Deputies on March 28. El'tsin went on to say that any deal returning the disputed Kurile Islands to Japan would be invalid without the consent of the Russian Federation. He urged Gorbachev to include a senior Russian representative in the Soviet delegation that would accompany him during his visit to Japan in April (*TASS*, March 22).

On March 23, the RSFSR Supreme Soviet debated El'tsin's remarks, TASS reported. El'tsin received both criticism and support. Vladimir Isakov, chairman of the RSFSR Supreme Soviet's Council of the Republic, told *Sovetskaya Rossiya* that El'tsin was establishing a "ruthless" dictatorship and "suppressing all dissent."

Shevardnadze Says Dictatorship Still a Danger

Former Soviet Foreign Minister Eduard Shevardnadze said in an interview on Hungarian Television that there was still a danger of dictatorship in the Soviet Union. He said this was because influential people believed the only alternative to growing chaos was the restoration of an iron-fist policy. Shevardnadze went on to say, however, that democrats in the Soviet Union were now striving to unite and that this, at least, was positive (RFE/RL correspondent's report, March 22).

Krasnaya zvezda on Soviet Military Power

An article published in *Krasnaya zvezda* said the Soviet Union had become a second-rate power in relation to the "hyperpower" of the United States. The author, Captain S. Sidorov, said Washington no longer viewed Moscow as an equal, and he implied that the United States was likely to throw its weight around as a result of the Gulf war. Sidorov argued that the principal reason for the USSR's strategic decline was domestic instability. He said that, until a political consensus was forged, Moscow would obtain nothing from the Americans but "attempted 'diktat' and other manifestations of the Persian Syndrome."

Cossack Squads Help Army and MVD with Joint Patrols

Komsomol'skaya pravda reported that young men in 1913-style Cossacks' uniforms had joined the USSR Ministry of Internal Affairs and army troops in patrolling the streets, airports, and railway stations of eastern Siberian cities. The young men belonged to the Baikal Cossack community, which had decided to form its own squads to maintain public order. The Cossack volunteers were trained by local MVD officers.

Baltic Council Meeting in Jurmala

The Baltic Council, consisting of leading officials from Estonia, Latvia, and Lithuania, met in Jurmala to evaluate the situation in the three Baltic republics. This was the first time they had met since the Soviet crackdown in January in Lithuania and Latvia. The Baltic leaders called for an international conference to discuss ways to restore the independence of their countries, and they appealed for help in gaining membership in the Conference on Security and Cooperation in Europe, Reuters reported on March 23.

Saturday, March 23

Gorbachev Issues Decrees on Taxation and Savings

Soviet President Mikhail Gorbachev issued a decree temporarily changing taxes on businesses and individuals and providing a cut from 45 to 35 percent in the rate of tax on profits made by companies, associations, and organizations, according to *Pravda* of March 24. The 35 percent was to be split so that 17 percent would go to the federal budget and 18 percent to the republican and local budgets. The decree also called for salaries of less than 160 rubles a month to be exempt from tax. Those earning 161 to 1,000 rubles a month would pay 13 percent in taxes on earnings over 160 rubles.

Gorbachev issued a second decree providing compensatory supplements to savings amounting to 40 percent of their level on March 1, 1990. The measure, which was intended to offset price rises on consumer goods, was applicable to 1982 government loan certificates and to government bonds. If the compensation payments did not exceed 200 rubles, they could be cashed in as of July 1. Amounts above 200 rubles would be frozen for three years, and 7 percent interest per annum would be paid on the balance.

Belorussian Popular Front Holds Second Congress

The second congress of the Belorussian Popular Front, held on March 23 and 24 in Minsk, noted that March 25 was the anniversary of the proclamation in 1918 of the independent Belorussian National Republic and said the popular front should strive to continue the unfinished work begun seventy-three years before. The organization's primary goal, speakers said, was the promotion of a free people in a sovereign, independent Belorussia, although some speakers, such as Vasil' Bykau, warned of enormous obstacles ahead. Delegates voted to restructure the front's membership and reelected Zyanon Paznyak as chairman (RFE/RL Belorussian service, March 25).

Moldavia Condemns Campaign as "Slander"

The Moldavian Supreme Soviet Presidium made public a resolution condemning "the slander campaign against Moldavia" conducted by *Pravda*, *Krasnaya zvezda*, Central Television, and other central media organs, as well as by USSR Supreme Soviet deputy Marshal Sergei Akhromeev and the chairman of the "Soyuz" group of deputies, Yurii Blokhin. The Moldavian Presidium expressed concern that the campaign was designed "to prepare the ground for the imposition of exceptional measures in Moldavia, taking the Moldavian people back into a state of vassalage and raising the danger of Moldavia's territorial dismemberment" in retaliation for Moldavia's boycott of the all-Union referendum on March 17.

MVD Troops Dispatched from Estonia

The USSR Ministry of Internal Affairs issued an order dispatching an MVD battalion that included fifty Estonians to a crisis area outside Estonia, ETA reported on March 25. Estonian Minister of Internal Affairs Olev

The USSR in March, 1991

Laanjarv sent his Soviet counterpart, Boriss Pugo, a telegram on March 23 requesting that, in accordance with the agreement of August, 1990, reached by Prime Minister Edgar Savisaar and Pugo's predecessor, Vadim Bakatin, the Estonians not be sent. That agreement stipulated that the MVD in Estonia would remain under local control and that any troop movements should be jointly agreed. On March 25, after receiving no reply from Pugo, Laanjarv received assurances from USSR MVD troops commander, Yurii Shatalin, that men conscripted from Estonia would not be sent outside the republic.

A battalion of MVD troops stationed in Estonia was sent to Nagorno-Karabakh on March 25, *Rahva Haal* reported on March 26. Eleven conscripts from Estonia assigned to the battalion went with them voluntarily.

Ukraine Introduces Private Ownership of Land

The Ukrainian Supreme Soviet approved a resolution on land reform under which individuals were entitled to own and use land and bequeath it to their heirs, Radio Kiev reported on March 28. The resolution was to take effect as of April 19. Under the resolution, sovkhozes and kolkhozes would lose their monopoly on ownership of land, and local officials would be given the authority to allocate land, set charges for leasing, and settle other administrative issues.

―――――――――――――――――――― *Sunday, March 24*

El'tsin Visits Chechen-Ingush ASSR

RSFSR Supreme Soviet Chairman Boris El'tsin visited the Chechen-Ingush Autonomous Republic, TASS reported. In the capital, Grozny, El'tsin met with Chechen-Ingush Supreme Soviet Chairman Doku Zavgaev. In the town of Nazrany, El'tsin addressed a rally at which he demanded the restoration of the autonomous republic of the Ingush people, whose status had been abolished in 1934. The demonstrators also demanded the return of territory transferred to neighboring North Ossetia after the Ingush were evicted from their native land in 1944. According to TASS, El'tsin offered to help restore the autonomy of the Ingush people but suggested that the territorial dispute with North Ossetia be resolved through negotiations involving the RSFSR Supreme Soviet.

Report on Soldiers' Deaths in Peacetime

Knight-Ridder Newspapers reported that a study on peacetime deaths in the Soviet army, which charged that thousands of soldiers had been tortured, beaten, or killed by fellow soldiers, has been suppressed by the military. Written by a commission formed in November, 1990, on the orders of Gorbachev, the study claimed that between 6,000 and 10,000 deaths under suspicious circumstances had occurred between 1986 and 1990. The main causes of violence were rivalry between ethnic groups, hazing of new recruits, and harassment of younger soldiers by older ones. A TASS account on March 23 said only that peacetime deaths were caused by "weak discipline."

The chairman of the USSR Supreme Court's Military Collegium voiced concern in *Krasnaya zvezda* that soldiers rarely reported abuses they suffered in the army. Lieutenant General Nikolai Petukhov said that only a small percent of all cases were reported and that legal action was seldom undertaken. Petukhov said there were violations of regulations by officers as well as indifference towards servicemen and weakness in enforcing discipline.

Monday, March 25

"Soyuz" Calls for Special Congress	The "Soyuz" group of conservative people's deputies issued a statement calling for a special session of the USSR Congress of People's Deputies at which Soviet President Gorbachev would have to explain why he had not used the extra powers granted him to bring the country out of its current crisis, TASS reported. "Soyuz" also charged that the new draft Union treaty violated the USSR Constitution.
Food Supply Commission Set Up	Radio Moscow announced that President Gorbachev had ordered the formation of a special commission to deal with shortages of food supplies. The commission was to be headed by USSR Deputy Prime Minister Fedor Senko.
Turkmen Supreme Soviet Approves Draft Union Treaty	TASS reported that the current session of Turkmenistan's Supreme Soviet had approved the draft Union treaty, although the deputies suggested a number of additions that would give more rights to citizens of the federation.
Half a Million Weapons Confiscated	A Defense Ministry spokesman told TASS that some 513,000 weapons had been handed over to Soviet military units in 1990–91. According to Mikhail Kolesnikov, 73,000 of those weapons came from the Baltic republics, the Transcaucasus, and Central Asia. He claimed that about

The USSR in March, 1991

70 percent of the total had been stolen by "extremists" from arms depots and servicemen. Kolesnikov said that the weapons had been confiscated in accordance with the presidential decree of July 25, 1990.

Gorbachev Discusses Kurile Islands with Ozawa

According to TASS, Soviet President Mikhail Gorbachev told the leader of Japan's ruling Liberal Democratic Party, Ichiro Ozawa, that the Soviet Union was ready to discuss and settle all issues with Japan "in the fairest way possible." Japan had refused to sign a peace treaty and to give economic aid to the Soviet Union until the Kurile Islands were returned to Japan. USSR Foreign Ministry spokesman Vitalii Churkin, questioned at a press briefing on the Kurile Islands issue, said there was too much speculation about the subject, AFP reported.

Transmission of "Vzglyad" to Be Resumed

Deputy Chairman of the All-Union State Television and Radio Company Valentin Lazutkin told Novosti that Central Television planned to put the popular television program "Vzglyad" back on the air. The program had been banned since the end of 1990. Lazutkin said that "Vzglyad" would now differ noticeably in content. Aleksandr Lyubimov, one of the original moderators, would produce the new program.

Zalygin Criticizes Ecology Commission

Sergei Zalygin, the chief editor of *Novyi mir*, wrote a letter published in *Izvestia* criticizing the USSR Supreme Soviet Commission on Ecology and its chairman, Kakimbek Salykov. Zalygin wrote that the commission was not concerned with the rapidly worsening environmental situation in the Soviet Union. He said the Soviet environment was on the verge of a catastrophe, and he urged correspondingly decisive measures.

Food Shortages in Komi ASSR, Tajikistan, and Kazakhstan

Radio Moscow reported severe food shortages in the Komi ASSR. Komi Communist Party First Secretary Yurii Spiridonov ordered all enterprises in the autonomous republic to surrender 15 percent of their output. This would be used to barter for foodstuffs. Rationing was reported to have been instituted.

Kazakh President Nursultan Nazarbaev issued a decree aimed at stabilizing food supplies in the republic, TASS reported on March 27. The decree called on Kazakh citizens to produce food on small private plots. TASS said the decree marked the first step towards privatization of the land: the Kazakh Ministry of Agriculture declared that about a million hectares of land had been given to residents from towns and workers' settlements for market gardens, private gardening, and raising animals.

According to Radio Moscow on March 29, Tajikistan's Council of Ministers set prices for some consumer goods, including foodstuffs, at lower levels than those ordained for the Union as a whole.

Nazarbaev Meets with Industrial Leaders

Radio Moscow reported that Kazakh President Nursultan Nazarbaev had met with heads of enterprises subordinate to all-Union ministries and departments to discuss how these enterprises, which made up the majority of industrial, construction, and transport firms in Kazakhstan, fitted into the republic's program to introduce a market economy. Speakers said that powers would have to be redefined and relations changed between Moscow, Alma-Ata, and the firms themselves. Nazarbaev proposed a fund to finance study abroad, and there was general agreement on the need to reorient the economy towards the production of consumer goods.

KGB Closes Its Office in Prague

In a statement to CTK, Czechoslovakia's Federal Interior Ministry said the KGB had closed its office in Prague on March 15. The last remaining KGB representative, who had been on the Soviet embassy staff, was expected to leave Czechoslovakia in August. In January, the Federal Interior Ministry had decided to cancel a cooperation agreement between Czechoslovak security bodies and the KGB.

Deportees Remembered in Latvia

Throughout Latvia thousands of people attended memorial ceremonies to honor the approximately 50,000 persons, including many children, who were transported to remote regions of the USSR on March 25, 1949. These deportations were ordered by Moscow and sanctioned by the Latvian SSR authorities for the purpose of breaking resistance to the Soviet drive to collectivize agriculture. March 25 had been designated in Latvia as a "Day of Remembrance for Victims of Communist Terror" (*Radio Riga*, March 25 and 26).

Tuesday, March 26

Popov Calls for Creation of Opposition Party

The chairman of the Moscow City Soviet, Gavriil Popov, reiterated calls for the creation of a new party that would constitute a real opposition to the CPSU. Writing in *Komsomol'skaya pravda*, Popov rejected any possibility that a civil war would break out in the USSR.

Gorbachev Attacks His Opponents in Television Interview

Soviet President Mikhail Gorbachev attacked the leaderships of both the RSFSR and the Moscow City Soviet in a ninety-minute interview shown on Central Television, saying that they offered no credible alternative to his government and lacked ideas for ending the USSR's political and economic crises. Gorbachev alleged that the opposition wanted only to exploit the country's troubles to push the people into precipitate action.

USSR Joins European Bank for Reconstruction and Development

The USSR Supreme Soviet ratified the USSR's membership in the European Bank for Reconstruction and Development (EBRD), AP reported. The vote was 380 in favor and 1 against; 11 abstained. USSR State Bank Chairman Viktor Gerashchenko told the assembly that the move would increase the international community's trust in the Soviet Union and its economic policies and would enhance the country's tarnished creditworthiness. As a cofounder of the EBRD, the Soviet Union would have a 6-percent stake in the bank's aggregate capital—i.e., 600 million ECUs. A third of this sum would be payable within the first five years of the bank's operation.

Warning on Dissolution of Warsaw Pact

Krasnaya zvezda warned that new European security structures were emerging too slowly and voiced concern over the dissolution of the Warsaw Pact's military wing. According to a TASS account, the newspaper said NATO's role as a guarantor of European stability had been overstated, and it cautioned against any idea of extending NATO membership to East European nations. The article said a new European system must take into account the state interests of the USSR.

Silaev Presents New RSFSR Economic Reform Plan

RSFSR Council of Ministers Chairman Ivan Silaev revealed parts of his republic's latest economic reform program at a Moscow press conference, TASS reported. Silaev said that the plan represented a realistic program for implementing the basic principles of the "500-Day Program" and that it would run from April, 1991, through December, 1992. It envisaged wide-scale privatization in industry and agriculture, the retention by the republic of most of the hard-currency earnings derived from exports, and lower rates of corporate taxation.

Future of RSFSR Television Uncertain

Deputy Chairman of the All-Union State Television and Radio Broadcasting Company Valentin Lazutkin told Novosti that several (unidentified) Union republics were dissatisfied with plans to transfer Central Television's second channel to the newly created RSFSR Television Company. Lazutkin said that non-Russian republics, including Ukraine, had threatened to stop broadcasting the second channel on their territory if it were given to the Russian Federation.

Islamic Center Founded in Kirgizia

The founding congress of a Kirgiz Muslim Center was held in Bishkek. Sadikjan Kamalov, once the highest-ranking religious official in the republic, was elected to head the center. Kamalov had been removed from his post as kazi of Kirgizia in 1990 after making critical remarks at a meeting of the Muslim Religious Board for Central Asia, but he remained a prominent figure in the republic. (RFE/RL Kirgiz service, March 26).

Soviet Aid to Afghanistan to Continue

Boris Pastukhov, Soviet ambassador to Afghanistan, said on Afghan Radio that Soviet aid to Afghanistan would continue at the level provided in 1990, Reuters reported.

Wednesday, March 27

Soviet Hostages Released from Ethiopia

Eritrean rebels in Ethiopia released three Soviet military advisers captured in 1988 during fighting with the Soviet-backed government, Soviet Foreign Ministry spokesman Vitalii Churkin told AP. Evgenii Churaev, Yurii Kalistratov, and Aleksandr Kuvaldin were released after persistent diplomatic efforts by the Soviet Union and other countries, especially the United States. Churkin gave no details of when and where the three military advisers had been freed, what condition they were in, or when they would return to the Soviet Union. Nor did he say why the rebels had agreed to the release.

Luk'yanov Says USSR Supreme Soviet Supports Gorbachev

USSR Supreme Soviet Chairman Anatolii Luk'yanov wrote in a letter published by *Komsomol'skaya pravda* that the USSR Supreme Soviet always supported Soviet President Mikhail Gorbachev's initiatives at critical moments, TASS reported. In his letter, Luk'yanov expressed regret over the increasing number of articles in the Soviet press that sought to give the impression that the Supreme Soviet opposed the Soviet president.

THE USSR IN MARCH, 1991

Soviet-Cuban Trade Exchanges

The Soviet ambassador to Cuba, Yurii Petrov, told a press conference in Havana that Cuba and the Soviet Union were committed to the trade accord signed on December 29, 1990, which shifted the denomination of bilateral trade in 1991 from rubles to convertible currency. But, despite efforts on both sides, talks to settle practical details of the accord had yet to be completed. Petrov blamed the difficulties in part on the complexity of the reformed Soviet trading system, under which Soviet companies enjoyed more autonomy. The main component of the accord was the exchange of 10 million tons of Soviet oil and oil products for around 4 million tons of Cuban sugar. Petrov declared, however, that delivery of some Soviet oil supplies to Cuba had been delayed because of difficulties with chartering vessels. On the other side, exports of Cuban nickel had been temporarily disrupted (*Reuters*, March 28).

Russian Orthodox Patriarch Visits Israel

The head of the Russian Orthodox Church, Patriarch Aleksii II, arrived in Israel for a five-day visit to Christian holy sites, AP reported. The patriarch, who was accompanied by about fifty people, including fourteen senior Church officials, was welcomed at Tel Aviv airport by Israeli Minister of Religious Affairs Avner Shaki. The Russian patriarch was expected to discuss the status of Church property in Israel, some of which had been in dispute since the 1917 revolution.

Presidential Adviser on Soviet Economy

Soviet President Mikhail Gorbachev's new economic adviser Oleg Ozherel'ev told the *Financial Times* that the Soviet economy had collapsed because of efforts to move too quickly to a market system and that central control should be reimposed to maintain supply contracts between state enterprises. Failing that, he said, overall production could slump by 40 to 50 percent. Ozherel'ev declared that, while the Soviet government remained committed to the transition to a market economy, the changes must be slower than radical economists had demanded. One key constraint, he added, was that most Soviet managers were ignorant of the market economy.

Thursday, March 28

Extraordinary Session of RSFSR Congress of People's Deputies

An extraordinary session of the RSFSR Congress of People's Deputies opened in Moscow with a vote to oppose the ban on demonstrations issued by the USSR government, TASS reported. The proposal, made by RSFSR Supreme Soviet Chairman Boris El'tsin, was passed by 532 votes to 286, with 93 abstentions. The Congress also voted to suspend a decree proclaimed by Soviet President Mikhail Gorbachev to place the Moscow City and Oblast police under the USSR Ministry of Internal Affairs. After Gorbachev's refusal to withdraw troops deployed in central Moscow until March 29, the Congress voted by 615 votes to 354, with 20 abstentions, to adjourn the session until the next day (*AFP*, March 28).

When the session resumed, Ruslan Khasbulatov, the first deputy chairman of the RSFSR Supreme Soviet, who was chairing the meeting, announced that Gorbachev had fulfilled his promise to withdraw the law-enforcement forces from the center of the city (*TASS*, March 29). Addressing the Congress, El'tsin called for a roundtable involving the Communist authorities and opposition leaders as a step towards creating a coalition government of national conciliation to help solve the USSR's economic and social problems, Reuters reported on March 30. El'tsin said that the economic reform plan drafted by the RSFSR government, but not yet made public, would provide a way out of the crisis; but the transition would require hard work, he added. El'tsin also criticized the Soviet leadership, saying that its policies were diverging from the people's interests and that the last six years had had more to do with the end of the period of stagnation than with restructuring (*TASS*, March 29).

The same day, El'tsin lost a key vote on whether to institute a president elected by popular vote in the RSFSR, Western agencies reported. The Congress discussed the RSFSR referendum of March 17, but the deputies voted not to debate a motion on the creation of the post. People's deputy Colonel General Dmitrii Volkogonov called the moves "a very big loss for El'tsin and the democrats."

On March 30, the Congress split over El'tsin's call for a coalition government in the USSR. A deputy told AP that the Congress would remain deadlocked over such key issues as calls by Communist deputies for El'tsin's ouster and calls by reformers for the introduction of a directly elected executive president in the Russian Federation. RSFSR Supreme Soviet Deputy Chairman Vladimir Isakov alleged that El'tsin was plotting to institute "a new dictatorship" and criticized him for failing to accept responsibility for the RSFSR's economic and social crisis and for wrongly laying the blame on Gorbachev, AFP reported.

RSFSR Prime Minister Ivan Silaev told the Congress that the USSR had wasted too much time protecting its "Socialist virginity" to expect a painless transfer to a market economy now. Silaev said his government's plan for quickening the pace of economic transformation called for freeing from the restraints of heavy taxation and bureaucracy those who wished to start their own businesses. The plan called for reducing the tax on company profits to 30 percent and for lower levels of income tax in the RSFSR. Foreign entrepreneurs would be allowed to buy and sell foreign currency on the territory of the RSFSR and their involvement in economic activity in the republic would be encouraged, Silaev said (*TASS*, March 30).

On March 31, the Congress resumed debate on El'tsin's report on the current economic and political crisis, Central Television reported. Supporters and opponents of El'tsin spoke out during the session. Petr Filippov, a El'tsin supporter, called for the ouster of Gorbachev and said that the center was to blame for the economic and political crisis in the RSFSR, adding that the real conflict was not between Gorbachev and El'tsin but between competing economic plans. El'tsin's opponents, on the other hand, said that El'tsin was to blame for the deteriorating conditions in the RSFSR, alleging that he was only interested in amassing power (Western agencies, March 31).

USSR to Consider Asylum for East European Communist Officials

Soviet Foreign Ministry spokesman Vitalii Churkin told reporters that former Communist officials in Eastern Europe were being persecuted for holding views at variance with the present official line and that the USSR would consider their requests for political asylum on a case-by-case basis, Reuters reported. Churkin also said that "witch hunts" were being conducted against these people in the press and in courtrooms.

US Embassy in Moscow Badly Damaged by Fire

A fire seriously damaged the US embassy in Moscow and forced the temporary suspension of operations. More than 180 Soviet fire fighters struggled to contain the blaze for more than eight hours before finally putting it out. The fire started in an elevator shaft, and the flames destroyed part of the roof of the ten-story building, badly damaging the attic. Water and smoke damage were reported to be extensive (RFE/RL correspondent's report, March 28).

Cossacks Elect New Hetman

Cossacks from the Terek River area of the Northern Caucasus elected a hetman at "a grand circle" of 300 people wearing traditional costumes in Vladikavkaz, the capital of the North Ossetian ASSR. According to Radio Moscow, the new hetman was Vasilii Konyakhin.

Estonian Leaders in Washington

On a three-day visit to Washington, Estonian Supreme Council President Arnold Ruutel and Estonian Foreign Minister Lennart Meri met with US Secretary of State James Baker and urged the United States to establish a greater presence in all three Baltic republics, particularly Estonia. Ruutel said, however, that they did not urge immediate diplomatic recognition, because the political situation was not yet ripe (RFE/RL correspondent's report, March 28). In an earlier interview with Reuters, Ruutel declared that US pressure on the USSR had been crucial in preventing a deterioration of the situation after the Soviet crackdown in Latvia and Lithuania in January. Ruutel urged continuation of the strong US support for the Baltic republics, saying that US influence could help lead to negotiations between Moscow and the Baltic republics. At his meeting with Ruutel and Meri on March 29, US President George Bush reiterated the "unequivocal" support of the United States for the right to self-determination of Estonia and the other Baltic republics. He also emphasized his conviction that the only solution was negotiations in good faith between the Baltic republics and Moscow (RFE/RL correspondent's report, March 29).

Friday, March 29

Union Budget Shortfall

USSR Finance Minister Vladimir Orlov told *Pravda* that seven republics—the RSFSR, Ukraine, Georgia, Moldavia, and the Baltic republics—had failed to transfer tax revenue to the central budget. The shortfall for the first two months of 1991 was 75 billion rubles. He said the RSFSR alone had withheld about 66 billion rubles. The USSR Supreme Soviet adopted a national budget of 442 billion rubles in January. Orlov said the USSR Cabinet of Ministers was now looking into ways of forcing the republics to pay their share of the central budget.

Lithuanian State Budget Adopted

The Lithuanian Supreme Council adopted a state budget for 1991 after sharp criticism and cuts in expenditure that averaged 10 percent, TASS reported. The chairman of the standing budget commission, Audrius Rudis, told TASS that Lithuania's budget was now completely separate from the USSR's, that revenue gathered in the republic would not flow into the USSR treasury, and that Lithuania would cover some expenses previously paid by the Soviet Union—for example, for the Ministry of Internal Affairs and the State Prosecutor's Office.

The USSR in March, 1991

Shevardnadze Interviewed by Soviet Television

Central Television's program "Do i posle polunochi" (Before and after Midnight) broadcast an interview with Eduard Shevardnadze in which the former foreign minister criticized the use of military and special MVD units in Moscow on March 28. He said the leadership should trust the people. Shevardnadze said his resignation in December, 1990, had not been unexpected by his family and close associates.

The KGB and the Markov Case

Former KGB officer Oleg Kalugin told RFE/RL that the KGB had provided help in the killing of exiled writer Georgi Markov in London in 1978 at the request of the then Bulgarian minister of the interior, Dimitar Stoyanov. The KGB chairman at that time, Yurii Andropov, had agreed to provide "technical help" on condition that there would be no direct Soviet participation in the murder. The KGB was supposed to have provided the poison that killed Markov and that was contained in a tiny pellet fired from the tip of an umbrella,

Panama and Soviet Union to Establish Diplomatic Ties

AFP reported on March 30 that Panama and the USSR would establish diplomatic relations for the first time after an agreement was signed in New York by their ambassadors to the United Nations, Yulii Vorontsov and Cesar Pereira. Panama's Foreign Ministry announced that consulates would open soon in Moscow and Panama City.

Saturday, March 30

All-Army Party Conference Held

Soviet President Mikhail Gorbachev told the All-Army Communist Party conference in Moscow that the situation in the USSR was tense but that the country had "great chances," TASS reported on March 31. Gorbachev declared that he had not abandoned his line of social renewal but that attempts by opposition forces to destabilize the USSR could lead to the destruction of all state structures. Some opposition groups were aiming to exploit and aggravate social tension at all cost, he added.

Soviet Defense Minister Dmitrii Yazov told the conference that the future of the CPSU depended to a large extent on the vitality of the armed forces' million-strong Party organization. Calling attempts to eliminate the Party's influence in the military "unconstitutional," Yazov accused "liberals" of undermining national security to satisfy their own ambitions.

Yazov on Professional Army

Defense Minister Dmitrii Yazov, while answering viewers' questions during the Central Television program "Who's Who," was asked whether the Soviet Armed Forces should be turned into a professional army. His view was that military recruitment of servicemen should be a mixture of "voluntary and obligatory" in order to sustain numbers and added that recruitment of men for professional service in the navy would start very soon. Yazov rejected allegations that Soviet technology had shown "low combat capability" during the Gulf war, TASS reported.

KGB Deputy Chairman Warns of Threat to USSR

KGB Deputy Chairman Gennadii Titov, head of KGB counterintelligence, told *Rabochaya tribuna* that right-wing forces in the United States, Japan, and other Western countries were encouraging the breakup of the Soviet Union, because they had a direct interest in seeing the disintegration of the USSR. Titov alleged that Western intelligence services were playing a significant role in the confrontation.

South Korea and USSR Sign Loan Agreement

South Korea signed an agreement facilitating a 500-million dollar commercial loan to the Soviet Union. According to AP, the loan was the first part of a 3-billion dollar economic assistance package that South Korea had pledged to the USSR and included other commercial loans, direct aid, and credits for the purchase of Korean goods.

Lyubachivs'kyi Returns to Ukraine

Seventy-seven-year-old Myroslav Cardinal Lyubachivs'kyi returned to his native Ukraine, thus ending fifty-three years of exile. Thousands of Ukrainian Catholics gathered at St. George's Cathedral in Lvov to greet him. On April 1, Cardinal Lyubachivs'kyi told reporters his Church wanted good relations with all other faiths in Ukraine, TASS reported.

Independent Belorussian Confederation of Labor Founded

On March 30 and 31, 115 delegates representing independent labor organizations and strike committees in cities, coalfields, and industrial centers of Belorussia attended the founding congress of Belorussia's Confederation of Labor. In an appeal to workers, a statement released by the congress said that the country could not hope to achieve normality in the absence of free labor unions. Mikhas' Sobol' was elected chairman of the confederation (RL Belorussian service, April 3).

The USSR in March, 1991

_____ *Sunday, March 31*

Warsaw Pact Military Structure Dissolved

The military structure of the Warsaw Pact was officially dissolved, thereby ending its existence as a military alliance, TASS reported. Soviet General Petr Lushev surrendered his powers as commander in chief of the Warsaw Pact's joint forces, while Soviet General Vladimir Lobov gave up the post of chief of staff.

Moldavia and Estonia Sign Cooperation Agreement

The Ministries of Internal Affairs of Moldavia and Estonia signed a treaty on cooperation. According to TASS, Estonian Minister of Internal Affairs Olev Laanjarv said the treaty would help the republics to fight economic crime and to achieve "real rather than declared sovereignty."

Georgia Holds Referendum on Independence

The head of the Georgian Central Electoral Commission, Archil Chirakabze, announced on April 1 that 90.53 percent of the republic's 3.3 million eligible voters had participated in the referendum of March 31 on the restoration of Georgian independence. Of these, 98.93 percent voted in favor; even raions with a predominantly non-Georgian population voted in favor of independence (*TASS*, April 1). Voter participation in Abkhazia was 60 percent, with 97 percent voting for independence. In Adzharia, participation was so high that extra ballot papers had to be printed; in Batumi, participation was over 100 percent, which indicated that nonresidents had traveled there to vote. In South Ossetia, the referendum was boycotted in the raions of Tskhinvali, Dzhava, and Kornisi (*AP*, April 1).

The Month of April

Monday, April 1

Bessmertnykh Arrives in Beijing

Soviet Foreign Minister Aleksandr Bessmertnykh arrived in Beijing. The visit was intended to prepare for Communist Party General Secretary Jiang Zemin's visit to Moscow in May (*TASS*, March 31).

On April 1, Bessmertnykh and his Chinese counterpart, Qian Qichen, discussed the two nations' dispute over the 7,300-kilometer border and international issues, including Korea and Cambodia, Reuters reported. Both sides agreed to work towards a reduction of troops on their common border. Chinese Prime Minister Li Peng told Bessmertnykh that China was concerned about unrest in the Soviet Union but that he believed the country's problems could be resolved (*AP*, April 1).

In Moscow on April 5, the third round of talks about the reduction of Soviet and Chinese forces along their common border opened between Genrikh Kireev, ambassador-at-large at the USSR Ministry of Foreign Affairs, and Liu Guangzhi, deputy chairman of the Chinese Foreign Ministry's Department for Soviet and East European Affairs, TASS reported.

Miners' Strike Continues as Government Tries to Negotiate

Four of the five bauxite mines in Sverdlovsk began a twenty-four-hour strike in support of the coal miners, Central Television reported on April 2. The RSFSR Congress of People's Deputies adopted a motion backing the striking miners on April 2 (*AFP*, April 2).

USSR Prime Minister Valentin Pavlov met in Moscow with about 400 miners representing more than fifty miners' groups to discuss the situation in the mining industry and to try to resolve the crisis, TASS reported on April 2. Both striking miners and those still at work were represented; until this point, Pavlov had refused to meet with the strikers until they returned to work. Pavlov told the miners that their demand for higher pay would be considered only if their productivity increased, and he refused to give any ground on their political demands, saying that these fell outside the mandate of the USSR government negotiators. Aleksandr Sergeev of the Independent Miners' Union declared that economic issues could not be solved without a resolution of political problems and that the strike would continue during the talks; he appealed to workers in other industries to show solidarity. Aleksandr Mrill, from the Donbass coalfield in Ukraine, said it was the government's failure to take the strike seriously that had led to the political demands (*Reuters*, April 3).

On April 3, the USSR Cabinet of Ministers offered to double coal miners' wages by January, 1992, Radio Moscow reported. The pay raise would be in stages: 25 percent in April-June; 50 percent in July-September; and 25 percent in October-December. The deal would be conditional on increased productivity in the mines. The delegates were addressed by Soviet President Mikhail Gorbachev, but the leaders of the strikers refused to talk to him because of his refusal to discuss their political demands, Reuters reported the same day.

Pavel Shushpanov, chairman of the Independent Miners' Union, told a press conference on April 4 that the strike would continue because the Soviet government had made no major concessions on strikers' demands (*Reuters*, April 4).

Radio Moscow reported on April 5 that the workers at the Noril'sk nickel mine had ended a ten-day strike after an agreement on wages had been reached between the Noril'sk City Soviet, the mine management, and the strike committee. Negotiations continued on the implementation of an agreement reached in connection with other social and economic demands.

On April 6, TASS reported that most mining regions remained paralyzed by the five-week-old coal miners' strike. The Kuzbass coalfield in Siberia and the Donbass coalfield in Ukraine were operating at about half capacity. "Vremya" announced on April 7 that coal miners at the Inta coalfield in the north had returned to work but added that mines in the Arctic region of Vorkuta had shut down completely.

On April 9, the coordinating council of strike committees met in Moscow. AP quoted its chairman, Vyacheslav Golikov, as saying the strikers' political demands remained unchanged. The council's deputy chairman, Aleksandr Sergeev, said the council had called for a national system of indexation to raise the wages of all workers to compensate for the rising cost of living. He added that a large number of automobile factories and other enterprises were striking to support the miners' action (*AP*, April 9). Railway workers in Vorkuta were quoted by TASS on April 9 as saying the demands of striking coal miners must not be met at their expense. The railway workers threatened to bring all rail transport, including passenger trains, to a halt if the Vorkuta miners did not start supplying coal.

The head of the Moscow Federation of Trade Unions, Mikhail Shmakov, said on April 9 that his organization supported the economic demands of the striking miners; he called on the RSFSR and USSR Supreme Soviets to take measures to meet them. He added that his federation was calling on the Moscow city authorities to honor earlier agreements reached with his group, including the publication of data on subsistence wages. He said if the demands of his federation were not met, it might have to call a warning strike in the Soviet capital (*TASS*, April 9).

The same day, TASS reported that money, food, and clothing for the striking miners had been collected in Georgia, Armenia, and Irkutsk Oblast.

TASS said bus drivers in the regional center of Kemerovo in the Kuzbass had joined the strike on April 10.

On April 12, striking miners in Donetsk decided to continue their walkout and to call a general strike in the city on April 15. Radio Moscow said this had been decided at a meeting of the Donetsk Strike Committee. According to the radio report, those who spoke at the meeting said the consumer price increases that took effect on April 2 had "very sharply fueled" miners' discontent.

The same day, metal workers in the southern Urals were reported to have expressed solidarity with the striking miners and set a deadline for their own demands for better pay and living conditions to be met (*DPA, AFP*, April 12).

On April 13, striking miners in the Kuzbass coalfield issued a call for an all-Union general strike on April 17 to force the USSR government and Soviet President Gorbachev from power. Radio Rossii reported that the call for the general strike had come from strikers' representatives in Kuznetsk. It was immediately endorsed by strikers in Vorkuta.

The appeal came on the heels of a separate call by striking miners in the Donbass for a one-day general strike and mass rally of all workers in Kiev on April 16. *Nezavisimaya gazeta* quoted Donbass Strike Committee member Leonid Kovalchuk as saying the one-day general strike could serve as a prelude to an unlimited general strike in the republic if negotiations on miners' demands were not opened (*Radio Moscow, Radio Kiev, AP*, April 13).

Also on April 13, a group of executives at mines in the Kuzbass region appealed to the leadership of the RSFSR to begin talks immediately with the striking miners. In a telegram to RSFSR Supreme Soviet Chairman Boris El'tsin and Prime Minister Ivan Silaev, the executives described the situation in their region as "close to catastrophe."

Pravda called the continuation of the miners' strikes "a stab in the people's back."

On April 14, miners in the Vorkuta region were reported to have resumed shipping stockpiled coal to a major metallurgical combine, Cherepovets, although practically all the mines in the area remained on strike. Radio Moscow said the miners had decided to release the coal after receiving telegrams from El'tsin and Silaev.

In response to the Donbass miners' call, workers at several Kiev factories and operators of the city's public transport staged sympathy strikes on April 16. In addition, thousands of people demonstrated demanding the resignation of Gorbachev and the Soviet government, Ukrinform-TASS reported. The formation of a republican strike committee in Ukraine was announced at the demonstration.

The same day, miners in Kursk, in southwest Russia, were reported to have joined the work stoppages (*TASS*, April 16).

Izvestia published statistics showing how the miners' strike was affecting Soviet production. Vladimir Tolkushkin, a deputy chairman of the USSR State Committee for Statistics, was quoted as saying that in March coal extraction was down 18 percent on March, 1990. Production of rolled ferrous metals, which relies on coal, was said to be down 9 percent over March, 1990.

On April 17, miners at the Raspadskaya mine in Western Siberia—the USSR's largest coal mine—called off their strike after winning agreement to transfer the mine from central to RSFSR control. The RSFSR government and miners subsequently reached agreement to run the mine as a joint-stock company. While, according to TASS, forty-six of the seventy-six mines in the Kuzbass remained on strike, there was little response to the miners' call for an all-Union general strike for April 17.

The same day, the independent miners' unions and the Coordinating Council of Strike Committees issued an appeal to republican leaders saying the central authorities were no longer in a position to control political, economic, and social processes. The miners proposed the formation of an interregional parliamentary group made up of strike representatives, republican leaders, and representatives of other political forces (*TASS*, April 17).

Also that day, the RSFSR Federation of Independent Trade Unions called for protest actions throughout the RSFSR on April 26 to support striking miners' demands (*TASS*, April 17).

On April 18, forty-five metallurgy enterprises in the central Urals held a two-hour warning strike in support of the miners, while students and workers held solidarity rallies in Kiev. A Radio Moscow report said miners in Ukraine had agreed to return to work in two days after the authorities had agreed to meet their economic demands. The Interfax news agency said that the miners had won agreement on linking their salaries to the financial situation in the republic but that increases would be limited to 150 percent. The Ukrainian authorities also pledged immunity for the strikers, except for those "involved in illegal action."

On April 20, trade-union leaders representing workers in metallurgy, oil and gas extraction, aviation, the chemical industry, construction, and rail transport sent an appeal to Gorbachev, demanding that he and republican leaders resolve the strikes. They also called on striking miners to return to work to prevent a complete economic breakdown. In the event that the strikes should fail to be resolved, the trade-union leaders called for an extraordinary session of the USSR Congress of People's Deputies to be convened, Radio Moscow reported.

The Vorkuta Strike Committee demanded on April 23 that Soviet Prime Minister Pavlov sign an agreement with the RSFSR government transferring jurisdiction of coal industry enterprises located in the Russian Federation to the RSFSR Cabinet of Ministers, Radio Rossii reported. The committee made this a condition for the miners' ending their strike.

In Leningrad, 10,000 workers from the subway construction company, Metrostroi, went on strike, demanding higher wages, the resignation of Gorbachev, and the dissolution of the USSR Supreme Soviet, AP reported on April 25.

On April 25, miners in the Kuzbass region decided to continue their strike despite an appeal by Gorbachev and nine republican leaders for an end to the action, Reuters reported.

According to TASS, about 50 million people throughout the RSFSR staged a one-hour strike on April 26 to protest against higher prices and worsening living conditions. The strike was called by the RSFSR Independent Federation of Trade Unions.

The same day, several thousand Leningrad students staged a demonstration appealing to the USSR Supreme Soviet and to the local authorities for higher grants, better medical and transportation services, and for job guarantees for graduates. Leningrad City Soviet deputy Yurii Orlov told demonstrators that the situation in Leningrad's higher education system was critical.

The USSR in April, 1991

On April 27, a special commission including representatives of the Vorkuta miners reviewed the conditions of the transfer of the Vorkuta-Ugol mines from USSR to RSFSR jurisdiction. Radio Moscow said miners at eight of the thirteen mines in Vorkuta had resumed work as had miners in Mezhdurechensk in the Kuzbass region.

El'tsin arrived in Novokuznetsk on April 29 and presented the miners with a draft document expected to form the basis of a settlement. TASS quoted El'tsin as saying that the agreement he and eight other republican leaders had signed on April 23 recognized the republics as sovereign states and granted them increased political and economic autonomy. El'tsin declared that these changes should satisfy the miners' political demands.

On April 30, El'tsin met with miners' representatives in Prokop'evsk. He told them he was determined to depoliticize RSFSR state enterprises after he became RSFSR president, Radio Rossii reported. Speaking later that day in the city of Kiselevsk, he declared that it was up to the miners themselves to decide whether to continue their strike, but he said they should not give up their political demands. The radio report also mentioned that signatures were being collected in the Kuzbass supporting El'tsin's bid to become RSFSR president.

Calls for Declaration of State of Emergency in South Ossetia

The USSR Supreme Soviet voted overwhelmingly to ask Soviet President Mikhail Gorbachev to declare a state of emergency in South Ossetia (*TASS*, April 1). TASS reported the same day that three Georgians had been killed and one wounded when gunmen opened fire with automatic weapons on a vehicle in the village of Nuli. In an earlier incident, one person was killed and two wounded in shooting in the village of Nicosia, near the city of Gori. A Radio Moscow report of April 2 said that Georgian forces in armored vehicles had tried to take over the South Ossetian capital, Tskhinvali, but had been repelled by Ossetian volunteers.

On April 3, Chairman of the Georgian Supreme Soviet Zviad Gamsakhurdia sent a telegram to Gorbachev accusing the USSR of continuing its attempt to destabilize Georgia and to deny the republic the right of self-determination, Radio Tbilisi reported. Radio Tbilisi reported the same day that the situation in Tskhinvali was tense and that USSR MVD troops had transported quantities of military equipment into the town. TASS, however, claimed that the night of April 2-3 had been the calmest for months, although the agency went on to cite rumors that an attack on the town by 12,000 Georgians was imminent. TASS further quoted a USSR MVD spokesman as advocating the declaration of a state of emergency throughout South Ossetia to facilitate the work of the MVD troops charged with maintaining order and provide a basis for negotiations between Georgians and Ossetians.

On April 6, intensive gunfire was reported in the village of Tamarasheni, and shots were also fired in the suburbs of Tskhinvali (*TASS*, April 6). On April 7, Soviet television said roads were blocked by armed Georgians, preventing the delivery of humanitarian aid to Tskhinvali, where a shortage of food, medicines, and fuel continued, and disrupting supplies of water, gas, and power. One inhabitant of Tskhinvali was killed and five others injured by gunshot wounds, TASS reported.

On April 7, Gamsakhurdia sent a telegram to Gorbachev threatening to call a general strike in Georgia unless all Soviet army and MVD troops were withdrawn from South Ossetia within an unspecified period, Reuters reported. He claimed that Soviet MVD troops were abetting Ossetians in attacks against Georgian villages in what he termed "flagrant aggression against the Georgian republic." Gamsakhurdia also stated that Georgian workers would join in the demands put forward by striking Soviet miners.

On April 8, the Georgian Supreme Soviet Presidium issued a statement criticizing the deployment of Soviet troops in Tskhinvali to break the three-month blockade of the city, Radio Tbilisi reported. A convoy carrying 700 tons of food had reached the South Ossetian capital on April 7 (*Izvestia*, April 9).

Interfax reported on April 10 that USSR MVD troops had detained twenty-one Georgian policemen in several villages close to Tskhinvali in what a senior MVD officer told TASS was "an attempt to break Georgia's blockade" of the town. Ten Ossetians were also detained and one was killed; quantities of weapons and ammunition were confiscated.

Gamsakhurdia called for a one-day general strike by railway and port workers and by factories subordinate to all-Union ministries to press for the withdrawal of Soviet troops from South Ossetia. He predicted that the strike action, which would disrupt shipments of coal and oil, would be a great blow to the Soviet economy (*Reuters*, April 10).

The leader of the "Soyuz" faction, Yurii Blokhin, said that, during its April 8 meeting with Gorbachev, his group had reiterated its demand that direct presidential rule be instituted in South Ossetia, TASS reported on April 10. Presidential rule in South Ossetia had also been advocated as the only way of stopping the bloodshed by some democrats.

The USSR in April, 1991

On April 11, a TASS report said that more than 15,000 armed Georgians had surrounded Tskhinvali. During the night, Georgians fired weapons into the civilian areas of the city, but no injuries were reported. The report, which came from Vladikavkaz, the capital of North Ossetia, said that Tskhinvali and its suburbs had been without electricity for five days and that there was a danger of epidemics.

As a result of Gamsakhurdia's call of April 10, protest strikes by railway workers shut down rail traffic between Black Sea oil and coal ports and the RSFSR's industrial heartland. Reuters reported that 10,000 auto workers in Kutaisi had also downed tools and had been joined by workers at a metallurgical works and at a wine factory in Tbilisi. Georgia also withdrew its athletes from all Soviet sports teams and competitions (*Reuters*, April 11).

On April 12, the Soviet authorities suspended rail and sea cargo shipments to Georgia after Gamsakhurdia had rejected a request from the USSR Ministry of Railways to lift the strikes, saying they would continue until the USSR withdrew its troops from South Ossetia. TASS said sixty Georgian freight trains were stranded between Georgian depots and their destinations in other parts of the USSR (*Radio Tbilisi, TASS*, April 12).

The same day, officials of the USSR Ministry of Internal Affairs rejected Georgian claims that "unlawful actions" were being committed by MVD troops in South Ossetia. TASS quoted a statement from the MVD's Political Administration as saying that Georgia's version of events in South Ossetia was "ill-intentioned lies." It said the MVD troops were protecting law and order "on behalf of all Soviet people" regardless of their ethnic affiliation.

On April 13, TASS quoted Boris Gromov, USSR first deputy minister of internal affairs, as telling journalists in the North Ossetian capital, Vladikavkaz, after a visit to South Ossetia, that MVD troops in the region "have begun disarming unlawful Georgian and Ossetian groups" and that Georgian claims that MVD troops were committing illegal actions in South Ossetia were untrue.

The same day, the Presidium of the Georgian Supreme Soviet extended for another month the state of emergency first imposed in Tskhinvali in December. Radio Tbilisi subsequently reported several clashes in the town.

On April 14, TASS reported that 100 Georgians and Ossetians had been arrested over the previous twenty-four hours and quantities of ammunition and two armored personnel carriers confiscated.

On April 17, Radio Tbilisi said Ossetian militants had killed a Georgian man the previous day in the Tskhinvali district. It also reported several other incidents, including the burning down by Ossetian militants of a house belonging to a Georgian, also in the Tskhinvali area.

The same day, the USSR Ministry of Internal Affairs said food, medicine, and fuel were reaching Tskhinvali under armored escort. It said MVD troops were continuing to disarm illegal groups and had detained both Georgians and Ossetians. It also said that, according to official data, over fifty Ossetian villages had been burned down and looted in interethnic fighting (*TASS*, April 17).

On April 18, TASS reported that an unspecified number of people had been shot and seriously wounded in the Znaursky Raion of South Ossetia. It also reported that Tskhinvali had come under intense gunfire on the night of April 16, as MVD troops were fired on and returned fire.

According to TASS on April 23, Soviet MVD troops were continuing to disarm militant groups in South Ossetia. More militants from other parts of Georgia had arrived to join Georgians blockading Tskhinvali, where an exchange of gunfire was reported on the night of April 22 between militants and MVD troops.

Meanwhile, Georgian Minister of Internal Affairs Dilar Khabuliani demanded in a letter to USSR Minister of Internal Affairs Boriss Pugo that the USSR MVD forces in South Ossetia begin cooperating with Georgian officials. According to Radio Tbilisi on April 23, Khabuliani also criticized in his letter "unlawful acts" by Soviet troops and the formation of "a national salvation committee" and other local bodies aimed at undermining the Georgian authorities.

The Georgian news agency Sakinform reported on April 23 that Gamsakhurdia had proposed holding a referendum among the Ossetian population of Georgia on whether the autonomous status of the South Ossetian Autonomous Oblast, abolished in December, 1990, by the Georgian Supreme Soviet, should be restored.

On April 25, millions of Georgian workers held a three-minute symbolic general strike to underscore their demand for the withdrawal of Soviet troops from South Ossetia, Sakinform reported. TASS quoted the newspaper of Georgia's social democratic party "Edinstvo" as saying the same day that Georgia should restore "the status quo" in South Ossetia to end the conflict there.

Shevardnadze on Soviet Political Situation

In an interview in the *Los Angeles Times*, former Soviet Foreign Minister Eduard Shevardnadze said Soviet President Mikhail Gorbachev should support the democratic movement more actively and establish a dialogue with its leaders. Shevardnadze said that he believed his resignation had had the desired effect of alerting people to the

THE USSR IN APRIL, 1991

danger of dictatorship and that democrats had begun to consolidate their efforts. In a separate interview with the German magazine *Stern*, Shevardnadze warned that reactionary forces were growing in the country and presented the greatest danger for the Soviet Union.

Tuesday, April 2

El'tsin Survives No-Confidence Motion; Wins Expanded Powers

RSFSR Supreme Soviet Chairman Boris El'tsin survived a political challenge with the help of his former rival Ivan Polozkov, the first secretary of the RSFSR Communist Party. Polozkov told the RSFSR Congress of People's Deputies that it was not the time to change the leadership of the RSFSR. TASS noted that, after Polozkov had spoken, only 121 of the 800 deputies present voted to include a vote of no confidence in El'tsin on the Congress agenda; thus the motion was defeated. Polozkov's support for El'tsin was unexpected and seemed to reflect the split that had emerged in the RSFSR Communist Party. Disagreement came into the open later in that day's session when RSFSR people's deputy Colonel Aleksandr Rutskoi announced the establishment of a new faction in the RSFSR Supreme Soviet called Communists for Democracy, numbering 179 CPSU members. Unlike the Communists of Russia group from which it broke away, Communists for Democracy supported El'tsin.

On April 3, the Congress refused to vote on a motion of no confidence in El'tsin. The Congress also turned down El'tsin's proposal concerning the direct election of an executive president in the RSFSR and, instead, instructed the RSFSR Supreme Soviet to prepare legislation authorizing the election without setting a date for a vote on it (Western agencies, April 3).

On April 4, the Congress voted 588 to 292, with 23 abstentions, for a proposal made by El'tsin to give the chairman of the RSFSR Supreme Soviet expanded powers, including the right to rule by decree, AFP reported. The resolution also allowed the RSFSR Supreme Soviet the right of veto over the chairman's decrees and stated that the expanded powers would only have effect until a constitutional amendment creating a new presidency was adopted. In outlining the proposal, El'tsin said such powers were essential if the RSFSR was to be led towards economic and political reform.

The same day, the RSFSR Congress of People's Deputies ended its work by tentatively setting June 12 as the date for the first direct election of an executive president (*Central Television*, April 5).

In an interview with RSFSR television on April 5, Viktor Sheinis said that, while El'tsin's call for extraordinary powers might appear undemocratic, in fact it had helped the democrats to override opposition from Communist deputies to the setting of a date for the first democratic election of an RSFSR president.

New Regulations on Foreign Currency for Soviet Tourists

With effect from April 2, Soviet tourists traveling abroad were permitted to purchase hard currency equivalent to 200 US dollars per year, for which they had to pay in rubles at the prevailing hard-currency auction rate (27.60 rubles to the US dollar) (*TASS,* April 1). For the previous eighteen months, the regulations had stipulated that a maximum of 2,000 rubles could be changed at the tourist rate of some 6 rubles to the dollar. In a parallel measure, on April 3, the USSR State Bank announced that foreign tourists in the Soviet Union would henceforth receive an exchange rate for their hard currency close to the free-market rate, *The New York Times* reported on April 4. The new tourist rate was to be fixed several times a week, with the initial exchange rate posted at 27.60 rubles to the dollar. The official commercial rates remained unchanged.

Retail Price Increases

Retail price increases went into effect throughout the Soviet Union, Western agencies reported. Prices doubled for milk and eggs, trebled for meat, and quadrupled for rye bread. Large increases were also applied to a wide range of other consumer goods, such as refrigerators, television sets, shoes, and clothing. In many cases, these were the first price increases in thirty years. In Moscow, most food shops and peasants' markets were closed on April 1 so that staff could write new price tags. The chairman of the Moscow City Soviet, Gavriil Popov, said that day that the city had stockpiled staples to help people unable to afford the higher prices (*AP,* April 1). According to Reuters on April 2, Soviet shoppers reacted with shock, despair, and anger when confronted with the new prices. Long queues formed quickly outside Moscow stores, but the shelves were empty. USSR Deputy Minister of Labor and Social Affairs Nikolai Cheshenko was quoted by TASS as saying the price rises should not add to the 80 million people living at or below the official poverty line.

USSR Supreme Soviet Ratifies Final Treaties on German Unification

At a closed session, the USSR Supreme Soviet ratified the final two treaties concerning the unification of Germany. The treaties covered the withdrawal of the more than

The USSR in April, 1991

300,000 Soviet troops stationed in Germany by 1994 and their status in the interim (*TASS*, April 2).

El'tsin Preferred to Gorbachev for President

An opinion poll published in the newspaper *US News and World Report* said 70 percent of Soviet citizens who had responded in a recent survey would like Boris El'tsin to become the president of the USSR. Summarizing the report, AFP said only 14 percent of those polled had expressed a preference for Mikhail Gorbachev's remaining in the post. The survey of 3,000 residents from all fifteen Union republics was conducted between March 1 and 25 by the Center for Sociological and Marketing Research, which was described as a private Moscow-based group.

Bashkir ASSR Seeks Economic Ties with Germany

Interviewed in the *Handelsbatt*, Rail Gasisov, the director of the Bashkir ASSR's State Management Institute, declared that the republic, one of the major Soviet centers for the production of oil and machinery, was seeking close economic ties with Germany. Gasisov said Bashkiria wanted to pass a law designed to attract foreign investors by allowing them rights to use of the land in perpetuity. Bashkiria also hoped to open a trade mission in Germany as a step towards removing its foreign trade from the control of the USSR government.

Turkmen-Uzbek Agreement on Flour Prices

Novosti reported that Turkmen President Saparmurad Niyazov had appeared on the republic's television service to announce the conclusion of an agreement between Turkmenistan and Uzbekistan to keep flour and pasta prices unchanged during 1991. Niyazov was quoted as saying that bread prices would be raised in Turkmenistan but would remain lower than all-Union prices.

Denmark Maintains Economic Links with Baltic Republics

Eric Ovesen, commercial counselor at the Danish embassy in Moscow, told The *Journal of Commerce* that his country was maintaining economic relations with Estonia, Latvia, and Lithuania despite "some opposition from Moscow." In Latvia, there were already joint ventures with Danish fishing, food-processing, and shipping companies.

Oleg Ozherel'ev Interviewed

The *Financial Times* published an interview with Soviet President Mikhail Gorbachev's new economic adviser, Oleg Ozherel'ev, whose policy posture was characterized as one of "caution, withdrawal, and stabilization."

Ozherel'ev said he favored the rapid privatization of small enterprises—i.e., stores and workshops—but for the medium-sized and larger enterprises he advocated using "the old system to reestablish links that will allow them to produce properly once more."

Wednesday, April 3

Belorussian Workers Strike

Factory workers in Minsk expressed widespread popular anger at the government's price increases with a spontaneous strike. RFE/RL was informed that as many as 100,000 workers poured onto the streets to demand "market wages for market prices." A strike committee of six was set up under the leadership of a member of the non-Communist Workers' Union of Belorussia. Activists called for a city-wide strike on April 8 if their demands for higher wages were not met. Radio Minsk reported on April 4 that Belorussian Prime Minister Vyacheslau Kebich had agreed to start talks with the protesters. While he sympathized with their concerns, he said that the republic did not have the funds to meet their demands. Meanwhile, the strike spread to other cities, such as Zhodina, Mogilev, Brest, and Bobruisk (Radio Liberty Belorussian service, April 4).

On April 9, a number of Minsk factories staged a three-hour warning strike to protest about the failure of the Belorussian government to provide the Minsk Strike Committee with daily television time. TASS said that government officials had agreed in principle to give the strikers access to television but that the two sides still disagreed on the format of the broadcasts. The strikers wanted live broadcasts with no state-approved presenters, but the authorities opposed this, TASS reported. The Belorussian Supreme Soviet Presidium and Council of Ministers appealed to work collectives to solve problems through conciliatory measures and not by rallies; they promised to take further steps to soften the impact of economic instability and ease the implementation of market relations (*Radio Minsk*, April 9).

On April 10, an estimated 100,000 workers filled Lenin Square in central Minsk to call for the resignation of the Soviet and Belorussian leaderships. Seventy-nine Minsk enterprises were on strike, AP reported. Speakers condemned the Communist Party, and urged the holding of new multiparty elections to the Belorussian Supreme Soviet and the nationalization of Communist Party property. Vladimir Honcharik, chairman of the official trade unions, was forced by jeering workers to abandon his defense of the Communist record.

According to Western agencies, strikes were also reported in the industrial cities of Zhodina, Borisov, Gomel', Maladechno, and Saligorsk, a potassium mining center. Rallies in support of the Minsk workers were held in Grodno and Lido.

Belorussian First Deputy Prime Minister Mikhail Myasnikovich told strike leaders that the republican government could not meet the workers' economic demands. Strikers were, however, given a chance to appear on republican television. Minsk Strike Committee member Georgii Mukhin used the broadcast to criticize the Party for "the collapse of the economy, lies about Chernobyl', and the annihilation of peoples and their languages" (RL Belorussian service, April 10).

The strikes were suspended on April 11 after First Deputy Chairman of the Belorussian Supreme Soviet Stanislau Shushkevich and Deputy Prime Minister Vladislav Pilyuto had agreed to discuss the strikers' economic and political demands, Western agencies reported on April 12. The strike committee, however, said the suspension was temporary and that workers were ready to resume their action if their demands were not met or if strikers were punished.

Workers' representatives from numerous Belorussian cities met in Minsk on April 13 to vote on the formation of an All-Belorussian Strike Committee. They elected Mikhal Sobal of Minsk to head the new body. Meanwhile, talks continued between the republican government and Supreme Soviet and the Minsk Strike Committee (RL Belorussian service, April 13).

On April 15, the Minsk Strike Committee formally presented its demands to the Belorussian government and set April 22 as a deadline for them to be met. The demands included pay raises to compensate for recent price increases, the abolition of the new 5-percent sales tax, and the resignations of Soviet President Mikhail Gorbachev and the Belorussian government. The Belorussian government promised to tell the strike committee by April 19 which of these demands could be met but rejected the committee's call for it to hold an extraordinary session (*TASS*, April 15; RL Belorussian service, April 16).

On April 17, workers at a potassium mine near Minsk resumed their strike in protest over the mine director's decision to begin court proceedings against the miners (RL Belorussian service, April 17).

On April 18, the Minsk Strike Committee said it had decided unanimously to resume strikes on April 23 because talks with the Belorussian government had stalled after it had rejected their political demands (*Radio Moscow*, RL Belorussian service, April 18).

On April 23, an estimated 200,000 workers took part in a general strike across Belorussia, Western agencies reported. In Minsk, there were work stoppages at forty enterprises, including the city's tractor factory, with its 35,000 employees. According to TASS, some factories, in order not to halt production, delegated workers to represent them at the mass rally on Lenin Square, where up to 50,000 protesters listened to speeches condemning Party rule. Strikes also took place in Vitebsk, Gomel', Mogilev, Orsha, Borisov, and elsewhere. All four potash pits in Saligorsk were shut down, and 5,000 miners gathered on the city square (*Reuters*, April 23).

The political demands voiced by Belorussian strikers included the sale of Party assets, with proceeds to go to Chernobyl' victims; the removal of Party committees from the workplace; the legalization of private property; and the election of a new republican Supreme Soviet. The workers called for an extraordinary session of the Belorussian Supreme Soviet to discuss their agenda, but that demand was rejected by the Presidium (*Reuters*, April 24). Interfax reported on April 23 that the workers had also formally demanded the enforcement of Belorussia's declaration of state sovereignty. Oleg Trizno, press spokesman for the Belorussian Council of Ministers, told AFP on April 23 that broad agreement had been reached on the strikers' economic demands, including a pay increase and a reduction in taxes to allow factories to spend more on canteen food, but that the negotiations on their political demands were deadlocked.

On April 24, thousands of striking workers in the city of Orsha blocked a key railway line from Moscow to the West after the Belorussian government had rejected their call for a special session of the republic's Supreme Soviet, DPA reported. A leader of the Orsha Strike Committee said extra police units and troops with rubber truncheons were patrolling the streets, but no violence was reported.

On April 24, the Presidium of the Supreme Soviet held a joint meeting with the KGB, MVD, and military district commanders. Ales' Susha, editor of the main organ of the proindependence Belorussian Popular Front, was quoted in *The Times* on April 25 as saying that the meeting between the Belorussian Supreme Soviet Presidium and law-enforcement officials had shown that the authorities were working out emergency plans to end the strike.

Minsk strikers added the resignation of the chairman of Belorussian Television and Radio to the list of their demands, citing the republican media's one-sided coverage of events. Radio Rossii said on April 24 that strikers were accusing two television correspondents of openly instigating clashes between workers and police. At a press conference, Minsk Strike Committee representatives said that forty-two enterprises were on strike in the capital, including the Minsk auto works. A total of eighty factories throughout Belorussia were reported to have joined the general strike.

The Minsk Strike Committee suggested on April 25 that Belorussian strikers should go back to work but resume their action on May 21, the day that the Supreme Soviet was scheduled to hold its next session, AP reported. A TASS report said the same day that the USSR had begun legal procedures against the 15,000 transport workers of Orsha, who had blocked the rail route for a second day.

Belorussian Prime Minister Kebich was quoted by *Izvestia* on April 26 as saying that the demands of Minsk workers were justified but that the Belorussian government did not have the money to meet them.

In Orsha, the striking workers ended the railway blockade on April 26, Interfax reported.

Congress Refuses to Lift Tarasov's Immunity

The RSFSR Congress of People's Deputies voted by 458 to 280 to refuse to acquiesce to USSR Prosecutor-General Nikolai Trubin's request that the parliamentary immunity of deputy Artem Tarasov be lifted, TASS reported. Central Television reported that only 280 of the 854 deputies present had voted in favor of a motion to allow Tarasov to be charged with "offending the honor and dignity of the USSR president." Tarasov had alleged in an interview in January that Soviet President Mikhail Gorbachev had offered to return the most southerly of the Kurile Islands to Japan in exchange for 200 billion dollars' worth of Japanese investment in the Soviet economy.

Gorbachev Orders Speedier Land Redistribution

Central Television reported that Soviet President Mikhail Gorbachev had instructed thousands of republican and local governments to accelerate the distribution of plots of farm land to peasants, in accordance with a decree passed in January; he said 3 million hectares of land should be distributed to private farmers by the spring. Gorbachev called on local authorities to take action against anyone obstructing the execution of the order.

Another Financial Scandal Reported

Sovetskaya Rossiya reported a second "ruble scam" involving, among others, Boris El'tsin and Ivan Silaev. The newspaper published a letter purportedly written by Silaev to El'tsin urging a 300-billion-ruble credit line for a shadowy Western group that would allegedly provide in exchange 50 billion dollars in hard currency for imports of consumer goods, food, medicine, industrial equipment, and technology. This allegation followed on the heels of the notorious affair involving Dove Trading International in February, which led to the resignation of RSFSR Deputy Prime Minister Gennadii Fil'shin.

Syrian Foreign Minister in Moscow

Syrian Foreign Minister Farouq al-Shara arrived in Moscow for a working visit, Reuters reported. He held talks with Soviet President Mikhail Gorbachev and Foreign Minister Aleksandr Bessmertnykh about the Middle East, including the situation in the Persian Gulf. TASS quoted Gorbachev as saying that the USSR was determined to develop friendly and cooperative relations with Syria in all areas including defense. Bessmertnykh said the USSR supported Syria's "constructive position" on the creation of a security system in the region (*TASS*, April 4).

Soviet Delegation at Interpol Conference

Gennadii Chebotarev, the head of the Soviet delegation at the Conference of the International Police Organization (Interpol) being held in London, declared that a freer exchange of information between police forces would help the USSR to track down gangs of organized criminals, Reuters reported. He said cooperation with Polish police had already helped to arrest gangs that specialized in the smuggling of cars.

Poll Conducted on Lenin's Popularity

An opinion poll conducted in ten Soviet cities by the Independent Social Forecasting Center with the assistance of the Institute of Marxism-Leninism found that "Lenin's name is still honored in the USSR." Of those polled, 59.1 percent expressed a positive view of the founder of the Soviet state and 10.3 percent a negative view; 66.4 percent condemned "anti-Leninism" in the Soviet press. The organizers of the poll stressed, however, that better-educated people tended to be more critical of Lenin: according to the poll, summarized by Novosti on April 3, negative attitudes towards Lenin were twice as prevalent among scientists and scholars as among other groups.

Committee Declares Party Control "Unconstitutional"

The USSR Constitutional Supervision Committee ruled that the issuing by the Communist Party, in addition to the

The USSR in April, 1991

Soviet government, of military regulations binding the armed forces was unconstitutional. The ruling was announced in *Izvestia* on April 3. TASS reported on April 4 that the ruling was a response to a request by the RSFSR Supreme Soviet for an investigation into the constitutionality of the order on December 29, 1990, calling for joint MVD and army patrols.

Thursday, April 4

Gorbachev Donates Money to Charity

AP reported that Soviet President Mikhail Gorbachev had donated about 1.2 million dollars from royalties on books and the proceeds of his 1990 Nobel Peace Prize to medical institutions. These included the pediatric unit of a hospital in Mogilev Oblast, which is in the area worst affected by Chernobyl'.

USSR Supreme Soviet on Farm Situation

The USSR Supreme Soviet was told of worsening problems on Soviet farms. The report said the central authorities were failing to supply the farms with the equipment they needed. Farms were also being hurt by rising costs for fuel, equipment, spare parts, and labor, the report added. The USSR Supreme Soviet passed a decree on the state of agriculture, Radio Moscow reported.

Gorbachev Meets Polish Prime Minister

Polish Prime Minister Jan Krzysztof Bielecki held talks with President Gorbachev, TASS reported. Soviet Foreign Minister Aleksandr Bessmertnykh and Soviet Prime Minister Valentin Pavlov also attended the meeting. They discussed the withdrawal of Soviet troops from Poland and exchanged views on events in Poland and in the USSR. During the talks, Gorbachev expressed great interest in Poland's economic reforms and said the two countries should cooperate.

Romanian President in Moscow for Official Talks

Romanian President Ion Iliescu arrived in Moscow for official talks and for the signing of a Soviet-Romanian treaty of friendship and cooperation. According to Rompres, the agreement took into account the growing role of the Soviet republics and included provisions for establishing direct relations with the Union republics, especially Moldavia.

On April 22, the Moldavian Popular Front condemned the treaty, saying it "codified a relationship of vassalage" of Romania towards the USSR. Expressing astonishment that the Romanian government had been the first of the former Warsaw Pact member-countries to sign a friendship treaty with the USSR, the Moldavian Popular Front alleged in its statement that Romania had "failed to give a political and legal appraisal" of the Molotov-Ribbentrop Pact and its secret protocols. The front took issue with the treaty's blanket recognition of existing borders, terming it contrary to the aspirations for national independence of the Baltic republics, Georgia, and Armenia.

Soviet Official Calls for Asian-Pacific Security System

Speaking at a session of the United Nations Economic and Social Commission for Asia and the Pacific in Seoul, Igor' Rogachev, a Soviet deputy foreign minister, urged Asian and Pacific countries to develop new security systems aimed at resolving regional disputes. Reuters quoted Rogachev as saying the USSR was prepared to try specific Asian-Pacific methods to deal with regional security and cooperation issues.

Call for Revival of Siberian River Diversion Project

TASS reported that Uzbekistan's Russian-language daily *Pravda Vostoka* had published an appeal in favor of the Siberian river diversion project. Vadim Antonov, the director of the republican association responsible for hydrological design, argued that the diversion scheme, suspended by Moscow in 1986, was needed to save the Aral Sea. He said that, in view of demographic pressure in the Aral basin, reducing irrigation was not feasible.

Helicopter Shot Down in Nagorno-Karabakh

An Azerbaijani government helicopter on a tour of areas in Nagorno-Karabakh primarily inhabited by Azerbaijanis was brought down by gunfire from Galaderesi, a village populated mainly by Armenians. It was carrying Azerbaijan Supreme Soviet Deputy Chairman Tamerlan Karaev, the chairman of the Azerbaijani Popular Front's majilis (assembly), and a Supreme Soviet deputy, Aydin Mamedov, as well as the chairman of the Azerbaijani State Film Production Committee, Ramiz Fataliev. Also among the passengers were Azerbaijani police officers and a correspondent of the Azerbaijani television service. Nobody was injured in the accident (RL Azerbaijani service, April 4).

Friday, April 5

Gorbachev Issues Decree on New Sales Tax

Soviet President Mikhail Gorbachev issued a decree exempting more goods from the 5-percent sales tax

The USSR in April, 1991

because of the impact of price increases, AP reported. The decree recommended that the governments of the USSR and the republics expand the list of consumer products and services to be exempt and warned that revenues from the sales tax would be significantly reduced thereby.

Delegates Protest about Provision in Union Treaty

Some delegates at the RSFSR Congress of People's Deputies criticized the Union treaty, because they objected to the provision allowing Tatarstan, Bashkiria, Yakutia, and other autonomous republics of the RSFSR to sign the treaty in their own right. The declarations of independence by Tatarstan, Bashkiria, and Yakutia were not recognized by the RSFSR (*TASS*, April 5).

Ukrainian Supreme Soviet Deputy Released

The Ukrainian Supreme Court acquiesced to a demand by striking coal miners for the release from detention in Kiev of Stepan Khmara, a deputy to the Ukrainian Supreme Soviet. Radio Kiev reported that Khmara was awaiting trial on charges of attacking a policeman in November, 1990, during celebrations marking the October Revolution.

Kalugin Repeats Markov Charges on Bulgarian Television

Former KGB Major General Oleg Kalugin was interviewed on Bulgarian Television and repeated his charges that the KGB had been involved in the assassination of émigré Bulgarian writer Georgi Markov in London in 1978 and that former Bulgarian state and Communist Party leader Todor Zhivkov himself had wanted Markov murdered. Kalugin, who also acknowledged his complicity in the writer's death, expressed readiness to testify before a Bulgarian or Soviet court about the case. Kalugin told Bulgarian television, moreover, that the umbrella found at the scene was a decoy and not the device that the Bulgarian assassin had used to fire a poison pellet at Markov. Zhivkov and the KGB denied involvement in the affair (RFE Bulgarian service, April 5).

Saturday, April 6

RSFSR Supreme Soviet Presidium Meets to Discuss Economic Situation

The Presidium of the RSFSR Supreme Soviet met to discuss ways of stabilizing the republic's economic situation. The meeting, chaired by RSFSR Supreme Soviet Chairman Boris El'tsin, considered decisions taken by the extraordinary RSFSR Congress of People's Deputies at its session the previous week, including giving El'tsin and the RSFSR Supreme Soviet enhanced powers to stabilize the economy. The Presidium designated reserves from which the population could be supplied with food and consumer goods and discussed measures to protect citizens from the effects of price increases (*TASS*, April 7). These issues were also discussed by the RSFSR Council of Ministers.

Rabochaya tribuna reported that the RSFSR had abolished the 5-percent sales tax imposed by Soviet President Mikhail Gorbachev on most food products.

Soviet Newspapers on Budget Crisis

Izvestia wrote that the failure of the Soviet republics to contribute their agreed portions of the Union budget meant that the country was "facing catastrophe, the actual disintegration of the Union." The daily added that essentially no contributions had been paid into a special fund set up to stabilize the economy. *Krasnaya zvezda* warned that the money in the budget was scarcely sufficient to cover any government expenditure for the April-June period, not even the maintenance of the army.

Aleksandr Orlov, deputy chairman of the USSR Supreme Soviet's Committee on Planning and Finance, elaborated on the budget crisis in *Rabochaya tribuna* on April 10. He said that the RSFSR had withheld all of the 45-percent corporation tax and the 5-percent sales tax levied since January 1. He added that the state budget deficit for the first quarter of 1991 had already climbed to 31.1 billion rubles, whereas a deficit of 26.7 billion rubles had been planned for the entire year. Orlov indicated that the Federation Council might be asked to suspend republican laws that contradicted all-Union legislation and to find ways of forcing the Union republics to pay their dues.

On April 11, TASS published the text of Soviet Prime Minister Valentin Pavlov's speech to a plenary meeting of the USSR Trade-Union Confederation on April 10. Pavlov said Soviet GNP had dropped by 10 percent in the first three months of 1991 and that the economic situation had been made worse by the miners' strikes. Speaking about the price rises, Pavlov said the USSR government was ready to raise wages but only on condition that production also grew.

Soviet Women's Committee Protests over Retail Price Increases

The Committee of Soviet Women complained to Soviet Prime Minister Valentin Pavlov that women who did not work outside the home had not been compensated for the price increases and now found themselves unable to keep their families fed and clothed, TASS reported.

The USSR in April, 1991

Conflict Continues over Moscow Police Chief

The dispute continued between the Kremlin and the RSFSR over control of Moscow's police department. Defying a decree issued by Soviet President Mikhail Gorbachev on March 26 ordering the transfer of supervision of the Moscow police to the USSR Ministry of Internal Affairs, RSFSR Minister of Internal Affairs Lieutenant General Viktor Barannikov named Major General Vyacheslav Komissarov head of the Main Administration of Internal Affairs of the Moscow City Soviet Executive Committee, TASS reported. According to "Vremya," the USSR Ministry of Internal Affairs immediately issued a counterstatement annulling Komissarov's appointment and saying that it was in control of the Moscow police department and that USSR First Deputy Minister of Internal Affairs Lieutenant General Ivan Shilov was police chief in Moscow. On April 8, the Moscow City Soviet approved a resolution to set up a city police force, Radio Rossii reported. Executive Committee Chairman Yurii Luzhkov told USSR Minister of Internal Affairs Boriss Pugo that, if Komissarov were not confirmed, people's deputies and the public would take action. TASS did not specify what the action might involve.

Soviet Deputy Foreign Minister in Morocco

As reported by AFP, Aleksandr Belonogov, a Soviet deputy foreign minister, arrived in Morocco for post–Gulf war discussions and talks on the Arab-Israeli conflict.

Belonogov said on April 8 that the USSR did not have a clear idea of what the United States intended to do in the Gulf. Speaking of the reduction of military forces in the region, Belonogov said the USSR wanted to see the foreign military presence in the region reduced to precrisis levels. He said the creation of a security system in the Persian Gulf must be the concern of the states themselves and that Iraq should be part of it, Reuters reported.

Moiseev on Security

According to Chief of the General Staff of the Soviet Armed Forces Army General Mikhail Moiseev, NATO's "offensive strategy," its unwillingness to disband itself, and its determination to act "as a global policeman" were undermining the positive changes that had taken place in the European security system. Moiseev nevertheless told *Izvestia* that the reduction of tension in Europe, including the Paris agreement to reduce conventional arms, had increased Soviet security. Although he defended controversial Soviet efforts to have certain weapons and troops excluded from the Conventional Forces in Europe treaty, Moiseev urged that the treaty be ratified.

THE USSR IN APRIL, 1991

Kirgiz Communist Party Leader Replaced

TASS reported that Absamat Masaliev, Communist Party First Secretary of Kirgizia since 1985, had been replaced "at his own request" and taken a job in the CPSU Central Committee apparatus. According to the report, Dzhumgalbek Amanbaev, formerly Party first secretary in Issyk-Kul Oblast and a close associate of republican President Askar Akaev, was elected to replace Masaliev.

Six Republics Coordinate Independence Efforts

According to DPA of April 8, representatives of Armenia, Georgia, Estonia, Latvia, Lithuania, and Moldavia met in Kishinev on April 6 and 7 and discussed cooperation in the independence efforts of their respective republics and mutual assistance in case of political, economic, or military pressure from Moscow.

Latvian Property Owners' Association Formed

Radio Riga reported on April 8 the formation of the Lawful Property Owners' Association. The new association, closely affiliated with the Committee of Latvia and the citizens' movement, aimed to protect the rights of those who owned property in prewar Latvia and to ensure that Latvian property rights were not usurped by Soviet institutions. Until June 20, prewar property owners or their heirs would be able to submit claims to ownership of land and buildings to the Latvian authorities. If a claim was recognized, the property would either be returned to the owner or he would receive compensation for it.

Sunday, April 7

Easter Celebrated in USSR

The Easter Orthodox liturgy was celebrated by Patriarch Aleksii II of Moscow and all Russia at the Cathedral of the Epiphany in Moscow. Prominent political figures attended the service, including Boris El'tsin, Sergei Stankevich, and Valentin Pavlov. The service was broadcast live on Soviet television.

Mass was also celebrated on Easter Sunday morning in the Church of the Intercession in Red Square—better known as St. Basil's Cathedral. Parts of the ceremony were shown on "Vremya" on April 7. On April 8, Easter Monday, Patriarch Aleksii said Mass in the Cathedral of the Assumption in the Kremlin.

Kuzbass Deputies Criticize Democratic Union

A group of RSFSR people's deputies from the Kuzbass protested against a call issued by the Kuznetsk branch of the anti-Communist Democratic Union for the disbandment of the soviets and their replacement by "committees of national resistance." The Democratic Union also called on the Kuzbass coal miners to seize control of their mines. According to "Vremya," the deputies called on the USSR prosecutor-general to take action against the Kuznetsk branch of the Democratic Union, saying its call was aimed at the violent overthrow of the constitutional order.

Soviet Television Documentary on Radio Liberty

A forty-minute documentary was shown on Central Television on April 7. The film, called "Alien Voices," attacked Radio Liberty and called on the US government to close the station. The film was made by the public relations department of the KGB and was compiled by Oleg Tumanov. Tumanov, a former acting chief editor of Radio Liberty's Russian service who returned to the USSR in 1986, was identified during the program as a career Soviet intelligence agent.

Ryzhkov Criticizes Soviet Leaders

In an interview with *The Sunday Telegraph*, former Soviet Prime Minister Nikolai Ryzhkov criticized his successor Valentin Pavlov, saying his actions so far had alienated the West—something the USSR could not afford to do. Of Soviet President Mikhail Gorbachev, Ryzhkov said there was no viable alternative to him at the moment. Ryzhkov declared, however, that he was worried because Gorbachev had no strong advisers around him. Ryzhkov saved his strongest criticism for RSFSR Supreme Soviet Chairman Boris El'tsin, saying El'tsin was neither a democrat nor a progressive and that, if El'tsin ever gained supreme powers, he would stop at nothing.

Demonstration for Tatar Sovereignty

Thousands of people demonstrated in Kazan' in support of Tatar sovereignty, which was declared in August, 1990, Radio Moscow reported. The reason for holding the demonstration was the reluctance of the USSR and RSFSR governments to officially recognize Tatar sovereignty.

Armenian-Azerbaijani Conflict Claims More Victims

As reported by TASS, gunmen attacked security forces near the Armenian-Azerbaijani border, killing a military political officer and a local resident and wounding four other people. The situation was also reported tense along the stretch of Azerbaijani railway that crossed Armenia on the way to Azerbaijan's Nakhichevan Autonomous Oblast. The Azerbaijani KGB said that gunmen had fired at two freight trains with automatic weapons on April 7; one man was wounded in the attack. Azerbaijani railway workers called on the Armenian government to officially condemn the attack and to take measures to prevent similar incidents (*TASS*, April 8).

An Armenian boy was killed by shells fired from the Azerbaijani village of Chaikend, near Nagorno-Karabakh, on April 10, TASS reported on April 11. Meanwhile, a Bavarian Red Cross truck left Munich loaded with aid for Nagorno-Karabakh, and another convoy left for Erevan. The 110 tons of aid included food, medicine, medical equipment and various goods for children's homes, a hospital, and other institutions (*DPA*, April 11).

On April 16, two Azerbaijanis were killed and two others seriously wounded when gunmen opened fire on a car passing through Nagorno-Karabakh. A TASS report did not identify the gunmen by nationality, but it quoted Azerbaijani KGB officials as saying that armed citizens of Armenia should be stopped from infiltrating Nagorno-Karabakh.

On April 23, the Azerbaijani Ministry of Internal Affairs said that three people had been wounded when gunfire hit the city of Shusha in Nagorno-Karabakh . The city was inhabited by Azerbaijanis. According to TASS, machine-gun fire came from neighboring villages inhabited by Armenians; three houses were destroyed in the attack.

On April 26, four Azerbaijani policemen were shot dead in a village in Nagorno-Karabakh populated by Armenians, TASS reported. An earlier TASS report said a Soviet MVD soldier guarding Armenian workers in a field in Mardakert Raion had been shot by men wearing police uniforms.

According to the Armenian mission in Moscow, thirty-five people were killed by Soviet troops and Azerbaijani police during an attack on the Armenian village of Getashen in Azerbaijan on April 29, Reuters reported on May 1. Azerinform said Soviet and Azerbaijani troops were disarming local residents, cutting communications with Armenia, and checking passports in several areas.

Armenia Says USSR Government Trying to Provoke Conflict

Armenia accused the USSR government of trying to provoke a large-scale armed conflict in the Transcaucasus. A statement issued by the Armenian government said Moscow was continuing to supply arms to Azerbaijan's special MVD troops and blamed the USSR government for worsening relations between the two republics. It also renewed calls for lifting emergency measures in Nagorno-Karabakh (*TASS*, April 8).

THE USSR IN APRIL, 1991

Monday, April 8

Gorbachev Orders Emergency Agricultural Measures

Three emergency measures were promulgated in an effort to save the 1991 harvest. The USSR Cabinet of Ministers demanded that industry supply the necessary producer goods for the nation's farms and rectify the terms of trade between town and country, TASS reported. The USSR Supreme Soviet passed a resolution along the same lines. In addition, Soviet President Mikhail Gorbachev issued a decree authorizing republican and local authorities to take emergency measures to expedite plowing, sowing, harvesting, and procurement. The decree also called for extra labor, including students, to be mobilized, TASS reported. Other measures concerned tax incentives for construction firms working in rural areas and guaranteed supplies of building materials.

Soviet-Hungarian Agreement Signed on Troop Pullout

Hungary and the USSR signed an agreement on compensation for costs incurred by both sides as a result of Soviet troops' being stationed in Hungary. The pact was to assess the value of Soviet facilities left behind by the departing troops and the costs of environmental damage caused by them during their stay. The USSR wanted compensation for the facilities, and Hungary for the damage.

Pal Nogradi, a department head in the Hungarian commission responsible for the withdrawal of Soviet troops, told RFE/RL that Hungary would make an advance payment of 3.3 billion forints to the USSR for the cost of barracks left behind. According to Nogradi, the Soviet Union would use the money to import Hungarian building materials to construct apartments for Soviet officers and their families withdrawn from Hungary (RFE/RL correspondent's report, April 11).

USSR Concerned about Kurds' Fate

The deputy chief of the Foreign Ministry's Information Department, Yurii Gremitskikh, said the Soviet government was concerned about the fate of Iraqi Kurds and he defended the USSR's support of the UN resolution condemning the repression of the Kurds. Gremitskikh said the resolution did not constitute any type of interference in internal Iraqi affairs, TASS reported.

On April 7, Radio Erevan reported that the Armenian Red Cross Society, the Kurdish section of the Armenian Writers' Union, and the Council of the Armenian-Kurdish Cultural Society had launched a republican-wide appeal for donations for Kurdish refugees from Iraq. The Kurdish population of Armenia numbers approximately 60,000.

On April 12, USSR Foreign Ministry spokesman Vitalii Churkin said the USSR had "serious doubts" about proposals to create "safe havens" for Kurds in northern Iraq. He said such a move would infringe on Iraqi sovereignty. Churkin also said Soviet observers were ready to depart for the Iraq-Kuwait border to monitor the formal ceasefire in the Gulf war (*TASS, AFP*, April 12).

On April 18, however, Soviet Foreign Ministry spokesman Gremitskikh said Moscow regarded the "safe havens" being set up in northern Iraq to protect Kurdish refugees as the most realistic opportunity to save the refugees' lives. (*Reuters, AFP, AP, April 18).*

Bessmertnykh on Tour of Yugoslavia and Greece

Soviet Foreign Minister Aleksandr Bessmertnykh began a two-day visit to Yugoslavia, TASS reported. He met in Belgrade with Yugoslav State President Borisav Jovic and Federal Prime Minister Ante Markovic and also held talks with Foreign Minister Budimir Loncar. Bessmertnykh declared that the USSR advocated the preservation of Yugoslavia's territorial integrity as a vital precondition for European stability. Both sides agreed to take urgent steps to improve their economic ties, Reuters reported on April 9. Bessmertnykh attributed the decline in economic relations to the difference in the pace of reform in Yugoslavia and the USSR and to the changeover to trade in hard currency.

Bessmertnykh went to Greece on April 9 for a two-day visit (*AP*, April 9). Bessmertnykh held consultations in Athens with Greek President Constantine Karamanlis and Foreign Minister Antonios Samaras. The two countries signed a Treaty of Friendship and Cooperation on April 10, agreed to expand business contacts, and talked about direct economic contacts between Greece and regions of the Soviet Union bordering on the Black Sea, TASS reported. According to Reuters, Samaras said steps had been taken to ease emigration for the more than 350,000 ethnic Greeks living in the Soviet Union. The Greek government also agreed to provide teachers of the Greek language and history for ethnic Greeks in the Soviet Union, Radio Moscow reported on April 11.

MVD Officer Murdered

The deputy chief of Internal Troops in the Northern Caucasus and Transcaucasus, Colonel Vladimir Blokhotin, was killed by machine-gun fire outside his house in Rostov-on-Don, Radio Moscow reported.

THE USSR IN APRIL, 1991

Viktor Skrypnikov, chief political officer of the Northern Caucasus and Transcaucasus Internal Troops, told RFE/RL on April 9 he was inclined to believe the murder might be a case of revenge for the activities of the MVD troops in the Transcaucasus (RL Russian service, April 9).

On April 13, the USSR Ministry of Internal Affairs said people had been arrested for Blokhotin's murder.

On April 15, the deputy prosecutor of Rostov Oblast, Vitalii Kalyukin, was quoted by TASS as saying the Armenian National Army may have been behind the killing. The Armenian National Army was an illegal paramilitary group that had been ordered to disband by the Armenian Supreme Soviet.

Religious Holidays Declared Public Holidays in Tajikistan

TASS reported that Tajik President Kakhar Makhkamov had issued a decree declaring the two most important Muslim holidays—*Idi Ramazon*, the holiday that ends the Ramadan fast, and *Idi Kurbon*, the Feast of Sacrifice—public holidays. Muslim religious officials and believers had asked for Friday to become the official day of rest instead of Sunday, but he said that change would cause economic complications.

Independent Moldavian Communist Party Founded

The Democratic Platform faction of the Moldavian Communist Party formed an Independent Moldavian Communist Party at a founding conference in Kishinev. TASS commented that the split "divided the Party along ethnic lines" and "followed the Baltic scenario." Defining itself as "a parliamentary party of Socialist orientation," the new party said it would have no ties with the CPSU and would struggle "for the full sovereignty of Moldavia and against the imperialist policy of the center." The party would also support the formation of a united front among republics seeking to leave the Union. The new party's leadership included Deputy Chairman of the Moldavian Supreme Soviet Victor Puscasu, the main author of Moldavia's concept for a confederated association of sovereign states without a center, which Kishinev had counterposed to the Union treaty.

In an appeal to the people of Moldavia for support, the Independent Moldavian Communist Party denounced "the crimes and errors" of the CPSU, Moldovapres reported on April 9. Urging "the dismantling of totalitarian structures of state socialism," the party pledged to promote "social welfare" within the framework of "democratic socialism" and "the values of Western democracy." The new party said it would recognize internal factions and groupings.

"Soyuz" Leader on Meeting with Gorbachev

On April 10, TASS carried a report by Yurii Blokhin, leader of the "Soyuz" group of USSR people's deputies, on talks between "Soyuz" and Soviet President Mikhail Gorbachev that took place on April 8. Blokhin denied recent reports that the group was demanding Gorbachev's resignation, even though some of the group's leaders, such as Evgenii Kogan, had said that Gorbachev should not stay in power. Blokhin said his group, whose aim was the preservation of the Union, thought that the president was too indecisive but that he had lately begun to move in the right direction. Blokhin added that "Soyuz" had also criticized the draft of the Union treaty on the grounds that it gave too much power to the republics.

Tuesday, April 9

Gorbachev Issues Anticrisis Program

Soviet President Mikhail Gorbachev said the USSR faced the danger of economic collapse, and he proposed a one-year anticrisis program of measures aimed at stabilizing the economy and enforcing law and order, TASS reported. The anticrisis program included the complete transition to free-market prices by October 1, 1992; a reduction in defense spending and the expanded conversion of military factories to the production of consumer goods; and measures to speed up privatization, to encourage entrepreneurs and foreign investment, and to demonopolize the economy. Gorbachev also proposed to suspend republican, regional, and local laws that contradicted Soviet law, and he suggested that sanctions be imposed on republics that refused to sign the new Union treaty or failed to make their full contribution to the state budget.

Included in Gorbachev's measures was a call for a moratorium on all strikes and on demonstrations during working hours. Political strikes would be banned entirely and penalties introduced to ensure that the ban was enforced. Gorbachev did not specify, however, whether he was proposing a legal ban on strikes or merely a voluntary public moratorium (Western agencies, April 9).

On April 18, several prominent Soviet economists met with Soviet Prime Minister Valentin Pavlov and criticized the anticrisis plan proposed by Gorbachev. Soviet television said the working meeting was aimed at eliciting the economists' opinions of the plan. Those attending included Leonid Abalkin, Abel Aganbegyan, Nikolai Shmelev, Nikolai Petrakov, and Grigorii Yavlinsky. The report did not give details of their criticism but said it would be taken into account when the final draft of the plan was prepared ("Vremya," *Central Television*, April 18).

Petrakov asserted in *Rabochaya tribuna* on April 16 that the recent round of price increases smacked of dilettantism and were inflationary because they had not been accompanied by efforts to marketize the economy. Petrakov also said he regretted that the "500 Days" program had not been accepted and implemented.

Yazov on Conventional Forces Treaty

Soviet Defense Minister Dmitrii Yazov told reporters that Moscow had done nothing to contravene the Conventional Forces in Europe (CFE) agreement, TASS reported. Yazov defended the movement of thousands of tanks and other equipment beyond the Urals and the redesignation of three army motor-rifle divisions to naval shore defense. He called the latter step "a purely internal affair" and claimed that all the equipment involved had been accounted for in accordance with the CFE agreement. Yazov also criticized the German press for encouraging an "unhealthy" attitude around Soviet bases in Germany and for encouraging Soviet soldiers to defect.

Sobchak Calls for Alternative to CPSU

The chairman of the Leningrad City Soviet, Anatolii Sobchak, called for the creation of an all-Union social democratic party as a counterweight to the CPSU. The *Financial Times* of April 10 quoted him as telling a meeting in London that such an alternative party should include Eduard Shevardnadze and Stanislav Shatalin. Sobchak said RSFSR Supreme Soviet Chairman Boris El'tsin would use his new powers to rein in the power of local Communist Party structures in the RSFSR.

New Soviet Ambassador to United States Appointed

Viktor Komplektov was named ambassador to the United States by Soviet President Mikhail Gorbachev, TASS reported. Komplektov, a career diplomat specializing in the United States and Latin America, had been a deputy foreign minister since late 1982.

Georgia Adopts Declaration of Independence

At an emergency session in Tbilisi, the Georgian Supreme Soviet unanimously approved a decree presented by Georgian Supreme Soviet Chairman Zviad Gamsakhurdia proclaiming the republic's state independence, AP reported. A joyful crowd filled the streets of Tbilisi to celebrate the event.

Gamsakhurdia stated on April 10 that Georgia's declaration of independence was not a *de facto* withdrawal from the Soviet Union and would have to be followed in the next two to three years by a series of legal steps to establish self-rule, Western agencies reported.

Gamsakhurdia further stated that the autonomous republic of Abkhazia would retain its autonomous status in an independent Georgia and that Adzharia would hold a referendum on its future status, according to AFP. He said the autonomy of South Ossetia, abolished by the Georgian Supreme Soviet in December, 1990, would not be restored, although the 1918 declaration of independence on which Georgia's April 9 proclamation was based specifically guaranteed all minorities in Georgia the right to free development.

Gamsakhurdia sent a personal letter to Soviet President Mikhail Gorbachev on April 10 affirming Georgia's readiness to work out new political and economic relations with Moscow and expressing the hope that Gorbachev would recognize Georgia as an independent state, AP reported.

The same day, President of the Lithuanian Supreme Council Vytautas Landsbergis congratulated the Georgian Supreme Soviet on its decision to declare independence. According to DPA, Landsbergis drew parallels between Lithuania and Georgia, saying both republics had chosen freedom and both faced threats from the central Soviet government.

Russian Citizens to Receive Land

Georgii Matyukhin, chairman of the RSFSR Central Bank, revealed in an interview with *Die Welt* that in the spring of 1991 each citizen in the RSFSR would be entitled to receive 1,500 square meters of land and to purchase an additional 2,500 square meters. Farmers would be eligible for larger plots of land. Matyukhin argued that property owners would be more responsive to real economic pressures than Soviet citizens were to even "the best propaganda."

Political Parties Plan Alliance

Representatives of the moderate faction of the radical Democratic Union, the Russian Christian Democratic Party, and the Liberal Forum held a preliminary meeting in Moscow aimed at establishing an "Independent Russian Alliance." Novosti said the alliance would strive to build an independent Russia, irrespective of the center's position, and would support political trends in the RSFSR Supreme Soviet emphasizing the republic's sovereignty.

THE USSR IN APRIL, 1991

Nazarbaev on Gorbachev

In an interview with the Spanish daily *El Pais*, summarized by Reuters, Kazakh President Nursultan Nazarbaev warned that 1991 would be Soviet President Mikhail Gorbachev's last year in power unless the USSR president made a radical turn, started to direct the situation, and proposed an interesting program acceptable to the people. Nazarbaev complained of "the weakness of Gorbachev and his crowd" in dealing with nationalist violence, citing South Ossetia and Nagorno-Karabakh as cases in point, and recommended the declaration of states of emergency in crisis areas.

Soviet Troops Begin Withdrawal from Poland

Soviet forces began their withdrawal from Poland with the first twenty-car train taking missile launchers, armored cars, trucks, and sixty men from Borne-Sulinowo in Pomerania. General Viktor Dubynin, commander of the Northern Group of Forces, said that Soviet forces should remain in Poland until 1993, when the last of the Soviet troops stationed in the former GDR were scheduled to return home. He argued that it would be inadmissible to leave Soviet forces in Germany completely cut off from the territory of the USSR (*Reuters*, April 9).

Dubynin told a press conference that Moscow had previously stockpiled nuclear weapons on Polish territory. All such arms, he said, had been removed from Poland in the first half of 1990. According to Reuters, the USSR had in the past repeatedly denied that such weapons were ever deployed in Poland. Dubynin added that no Soviet chemical weapons had ever been stationed on Polish soil.

Kravchenko Appears on Soviet Television

Replying to viewers' questions during a live phone-in on Soviet television, the head of the All-Union State Television and Radio Broadcasting Company, Leonid Kravchenko, denied that he had fired the political commentators Vladimir Pozner and Vladimir Tsvetov. Kravchenko said Pozner and Tsvetov had left Central Television of their own free will. He did, however, admit that the two journalists had been displeased with the current situation in Soviet television.

Kravchenko dashed hopes that the television show "Vzglyad" might soon return to the screen. Answering a question from a viewer, Kravchenko said that, for the time being, restoration of the show was still considered undesirable.

The Leningrad television program "Pyatoe koleso" (The Fifth Wheel) also came under attack during the phone-in. Kravchenko read from a hefty pile of letters in which viewers complained that "Pyatoe koleso" was overtly anti-Soviet and that the leadership of Central Television should take action against the show's moderator, Bella Kurkova.

New Aide to Gorbachev Appointed

TASS reported that Valentin Karasev had been appointed aide to Soviet President Mikhail Gorbachev with responsibility for liaison with state and social organizations. Karasev, a candidate of historical sciences, had previously been a member of the USSR Supreme Soviet Committee on the Soviets of People's Deputies, Development of Government, and Self-Government. Before that, he had chaired the department of CPSU History and Scientific Communism at the Kramatorsk Industrial Institute in Donetsk Oblast. Announcing the new appointment, presidential spokesman Vitalii Ignatenko said he himself would remain in charge of ties with the mass media.

Wednesday, April 10

Moscow Was under Pressure to Use Force in Eastern Europe

Former Soviet Foreign Minister Eduard Shevardnadze told *Literaturnaya gazeta* that the USSR government had come under heavy pressure in 1989 to use force to stop anti-Communist movements in Eastern Europe. According to Reuters, Shevardnadze also said in the interview that such measures as erecting barricades at borders or deploying tanks would have led to the brink of a third world war.

Moldavia Sets Immigration Quota

The Moldavian government would limit immigration into Moldavia from other Soviet republics during 1991 to 0.05 percent of Moldavia's current population, Labor Minister Gheorghe Spinei told TASS. The quota amounted to some 2,000 persons. The measure was designed to halt the long-standing practice whereby enterprises of all-Union subordination brought manpower from other republics into Moldavia.

Thursday, April 11

CPSU Registers as Political Party

The CPSU became the first political party to be legally registered under the law on public associations that took effect on January 1, TASS reported. The registration, which was shown on Soviet television, took place

The USSR in April, 1991

at a Moscow ceremony attended by CPSU Central Committee Deputy General Secretary Vladimir Ivashko and Central Committee secretaries Oleg Shenin and Yurii Manaenkov.

Central Television revealed that the second party to be registered was the Liberal Democratic Party—a fringe organization believed to have close links with the KGB. The Soviet government had earlier refused registration to several newly created all-Union political parties on the grounds that they had not submitted all the necessary documents. In the meantime, the RSFSR government had already registered several non-Communist parties active in the Russian Federation.

Akhromeev on NATO and Reforms

Speaking during a live television-satellite link from Moscow to an international conference in Paris, former Chief of the General Staff of the Soviet Armed Forces Sergei Akhromeev, an adviser to Soviet President Mikhail Gorbachev, declared that NATO should follow the Warsaw Pact's example and abolish its military structure. He said there was no justification for NATO to continue as a military organization since the USSR no longer presented any threat to Europe. Akhromeev said that the entire leadership of the Soviet army supported the democratization under way in the USSR and was prepared to defend it (*AFP*, April 11). The military High Command, Akhromeev said, believed in Gorbachev's reforms and would do nothing to stop them.

Landsbergis Speaks to Gorbachev

According to DPA, President of the Lithuanian Supreme Council Vytautas Landsbergis spoke by telephone with Soviet President Mikhail Gorbachev and told him of his objections to the continued Soviet occupation of buildings in Vilnius. Landsbergis said that these actions torpedoed any compromises or negotiations between Lithuania and the Soviet Union. Landsbergis added, moreover, that Gorbachev was misinformed about the situation in Lithuania and offered to meet him personally to clarify it. Gorbachev neither accepted nor rejected the offer but said he would speak to Landsbergis again by telephone.

Ukrainian Communists Ready to Protest

Chairman of the Kiev City Soviet Grigorii Malishevsky said Kiev Communists would be the first to join a protest by those dissatisfied with Soviet government policies, Radio Kiev reported. Malishevsky declared that Gorbachev had deprived the Party of its authority and of the people's trust. Radio Kiev also quoted an open letter sent to Gorbachev by the Communist Party of Dnepropetrovsk saying Gorbachev should show courage and no longer try people's patience.

Tajik KGB Worries about Foreign Muslim Infiltration

Tajik KGB Chairman Vladimir Petkel was quoted by TASS as saying foreign intelligence services, Pakistan's in particular, had stepped up efforts to infiltrate the republic by having Muslim fundamentalists and members of the Afghan resistance establish contacts with Tajik groups. Petkel said he believed the purpose of those contacts was to overthrow the Soviet system and set up an Islamic state in Tajikistan. Eleven groups had recently been caught on the Afghan border trying to smuggle arms, subversive literature, and drugs into the republic, he reported.

Russian Nationalist Writer Attacks Democrats

Speaking on "Vremya," Russian nationalist writer Stanislav Rybas accused Democratic Russia, "Rukh," and "Sajudis" of wrecking the USSR and attacked RFE/RL, calling it a relic of the Cold War. Rybas singled out for criticism one of the leaders of Democratic Russia, Arkadii Murashov. Interviewed by RFE/RL earlier in the week, Murashov had suggested that "if the US Congress stopped funding Radio Liberty, perhaps the RSFSR government ought to take it over." Rybas commented sarcastically that "maybe the Russian government would also like to take over the financing of the CIA."

Moscow Agrees to Latvian Name Change

Latvian and Soviet delegations meeting in Moscow agreed to refer to Latvia in future as the Latvian Republic and no longer as the Latvian Soviet Socialist Republic. Latvian Deputy Prime Minister Ilmars Bisers was quoted by the Latvian press attaché in Moscow, Aris Jansons, as saying, however, that the two delegations remained far apart on most of the other questions raised, including economic relations (RFE Latvian service, April 12).

In an interview with *Pravda* on April 12, the first secretary of Latvia's pro-Moscow Communist Party, Alfreds Rubiks, appealed for the immediate introduction of presidential rule in Latvia. Rubiks said this was the only way to prevent what he termed an impending coup and bloodshed in Latvia. Rubiks said the Latvian Communist Party was ready to negotiate with centrists in the Latvian Popular Front and engage in a dialogue with radicals.

The USSR in April, 1991

Friday, April 12

Gorbachev Issues Decree on Industrial Supplies

With the aim of "preventing chaos and mass unemployment," Soviet President Mikhail Gorbachev issued a decree granting special powers to the newly created USSR Ministry of Material Resources, TASS reported. The ministry was empowered to order new deliveries and redistribute surplus production. The decree exhorted enterprises to adhere to all contracts and economic ties concluded for 1991. To combat growing separatism, the decree also gave republican and local authorities one week to revoke decisions halting the export of goods to other regions and republics. The text did not spell out means of enforcement or penalties for noncompliance.

On April 16, the Ukrainian Supreme Soviet suspended part of the decree, saying it contravened the Ukrainian Constitution and had been issued without the consent of the Ukrainian parliament and government (_TASS_, April 16).

Kravchenko Expelled from Journalists' Union

Leonid Kravchenko, the chairman of the USSR State Company for Television and Radio Broadcasting, was expelled from the USSR Union of Journalists. The decision was taken by the Moscow branch of the union, which accused Kravchenko of reintroducing political censorship on Soviet Central Television (_Radio Rossii_, April 12).

On April 18, the Board of the union issued a statement, which was read out on Soviet television, saying that the union's action was unacceptable. The Board said that the Moscow union had acted without consulting broadcasting journalists and that this would set a precedent for violating the rights of union members ("Vremya," _Central Television_, April 18).

Belorussian Front Leader Says Independence Is Necessary

Zyanon Paznyak, leader of the Belorussian Popular Front, said independence was a necessity for the Soviet republics because the Soviet government no longer had an effective plan to resolve the economic crisis. He told a news conference in Washington that "the Soviet Union as a state structure has fully expended its resources, its ideas, and possibilities. It has become a brake on the path of development" (RFE/RL correspondent's report, April 12).

Call for Strike in Kiev

The Kiev Strike Committee issued a call to work collectives for a strike in the Ukrainian capital, Radio Kiev reported. In addition to the demands put forward by striking Ukrainian miners, the committee also demanded the dissolution of the Ukrainian Supreme Soviet, the release of those arrested in connection with the case of Ukrainian people's deputy Stepan Khmara, the dropping of the case against Khmara, and the initiation of proceedings against the Ukrainian public prosecutor, Mykhailo Potoben'ko.

No Compulsory Soviet Draft in Moldavia in 1991

The general director of Moldavia's State Department for Military Affairs, Colonel Nicolae Chirtoaca, said that, in accordance with republican law, Moldavians would not be forced to serve in the Soviet Armed Forces in 1991. TASS quoted him as saying that those who refused to serve in the Soviet army would not be punished, because Soviet draft law had no legal force on Moldavian territory.

Tokyo Firm to Form Aluminum Joint Venture in USSR

AFP reported that a Tokyo trading firm, Maruichi Shoji, had signed an agreement to form a joint venture with the Soviet Union's largest aluminum smelting plant in Bratsk. It was scheduled to start producing consumer goods, such as pots and frying pans, in 1992, with an annual production target of between 300,000 and 400,000 units.

Poland Offers Surplus Food to Soviet Union

Polish agriculture officials said Poland wanted to sell 4 million tons of surplus food to the Soviet Union in the form of 1.5 million tons of grain, 300,000 tons of sugar, and 2 million tons of potatoes, as well as meat and vegetable oil. The Polish Foreign Trade Ministry said Soviet officials had welcomed the offer but requested credit. Poland told them to find another form of payment (*Reuters*, April 12).

Saturday, April 13

Baltic Leaders Accept Icelandic Offer to Mediate

The leaders of the three Baltic republics decided to accept Iceland's offer to mediate in their independence-related disputes with the USSR central government. The decision was taken at a meeting of the Baltic Council in Riga by Vytautas Landsbergis of Lithuania, Anatolijs Gorbunovs of Latvia, and Arnold Ruutel of Estonia. In March, the Soviet Union had recalled its ambassador to Iceland briefly after the Icelandic parliament had requested the government to extend diplomatic recognition to the Baltic republics (*DPA*, April 13).

The USSR in April, 1991

Georgian Foreign Minister Giorgi Khoshtaria said the West should recognize Georgia's independence because the USSR is an empire that is "bound to collapse." He told AFP in an interview in Paris that Georgia was able to survive on its own and would not be a beggar state or a dictatorship. Khoshtaria was on a week-long visit to France for talks with French and other West European leaders.

Khoshtaria Says West Should Recognize Georgian Independence

The Presidium of the Armenian Supreme Soviet asked Georgia to allow trains bound for Armenia to pass through its territory "as a gesture of goodwill," since Azerbaijan had renewed its rail blockade of Armenia (*Radio Erevan*, April 13). Armenia was said to be completely cut off and facing shortages of petroleum products, food, and construction materials for the earthquake disaster zone. Transport in Georgia had been paralyzed by political strikes aimed at getting Soviet troops removed from South Ossetia.

Armenia ended a railway blockade of its own on April 15, when heavy trucks that had been obstructing the line into the Nakhichevan ASSR in Azerbaijan were removed. TASS said Armenian gunmen were continuing to stage shooting attacks along the tracks, however.

Rail Transit through Georgia Requested by Armenia

Pope John Paul II appointed five Latin-rite Catholic bishops for the USSR in an epoch-making move that would have important consequences for the future development of Catholicism in the USSR. TASS reported that for the first time a residence of a Catholic bishop would be established in Moscow. The pope also announced the formation of three new dioceses and three apostolic administrations in the RSFSR, Belorussia, and Kazakhstan. Churchmen currently serving in the USSR were appointed to head the new units. The Vatican said all the moves were in line with the USSR's postwar borders, a condition insisted upon by Kremlin officials

Vatican Announces Sweeping Changes for Latin-Rite Church in USSR

Sunday, April 14

After amending the Georgian Constitution to create the post, the Georgian Supreme Soviet unanimously elected its chairman, Zviad Gamsakhurdia, as president of the republic. The Georgian president was to be elected for five years. Among other powers, he was authorized to nominate the prime minister and government; declare

Gamsakhurdia Elected Georgian President by Supreme Soviet

war, martial law, and presidential rule; to veto within two weeks any law adopted by parliament; and to grant or revoke Georgian citizenship. Direct presidential elections would be held in Georgia on May 26, the anniversary of the 1918 declaration of Georgian independence.

On April 18, Akaki Asatiani, leader of the Georgian Traditionalists' Union, was elected chairman of the Georgian Supreme Soviet to succeed Gamsakhurdia (*TASS*, RL Georgian service, April 18).

Estonian Popular Front Will Not Be Political Party

At a congress in Tallinn, the Estonian Popular Front adopted a resolution outlining steps for achieving Estonian independence. TASS said that, among other things, the resolution called for winning control over all the territory of Estonia and signing a treaty with the USSR on the status of Estonia's armed forces. The popular front also decided during the meeting not to transform itself into a political party.

Final Draft Figures Revealed

The military television program "Na sluzhbe otechestvu" provided figures on the fulfillment of the military draft in 1990. According to Deputy Chief of the General Staff Colonel Grigorii Krivosheev, the final numbers (as percentages of planned recruitment) were: RSFSR—95.4; Ukraine—95.1; Belorussia—90.4; Lithuania—25.1 Latvia—39.5; Estonia—35.9 Moldavia—96; Georgia—18.5; Azerbaijan—84; Armenia—22.5; Kazakhstan and Kirgizia—100; Tajikistan—93.4; Turkmenistan—96.1; and Uzbekistan—85.6. Krivosheev said that, as a result, the armed forces faced a shortfall of 135,000 men, a situation that he called "critical."

Famous Cathedral in Ufa Returned to Orthodox Church

TASS reported that, for the first time in fifty years, a church service had taken place in one of the most important Russian Orthodox churches—the Kazan' Cathedral of the Mother of God in Ufa, Bashkiria. This church became famous because of its miracle-working icon of the Mother of God.

Monday, April 15

Gorbachev Appeals to Officials to Save the USSR

On his way to Japan, Soviet President Mikhail Gorbachev addressed a meeting of regional soviet, economic, industrial, and public leaders in Khabarovsk. Gorbachev told his audience that political figures at all levels must put aside personal ambition and think solely about saving the country, since time was running out. In response to a question, Gorbachev stressed the importance of the RSFSR within the Soviet Union and appealed to RSFSR Supreme Soviet Chairman Boris El'tsin to "begin constructive cooperation and joint action" with the central government (*TASS*, April 15).

El'tsin in France

RSFSR Supreme Soviet Chairman Boris El'tsin began a three-day private visit to France at the invitation of the International Politics Forum, a Paris-based think tank. The declared aim of the trip was "to bring Russia back into the European fold."

At his first stop, Strasbourg, El'tsin was given a less than enthusiastic reception at a meeting with European Socialists; the chairman of the group introduced El'tsin as "a provocateur" and said many considered him "an irresponsible demagogue." In response to a barrage of questions about "Great Russian nationalism" and his relations with Gorbachev, El'tsin denied that there was any "personal animosity" between himself and Gorbachev and said he was willing to work with him to defeat the conservatives (RFE/RL correspondent's report, April 15).

In an address to conservative and centrist parliamentarians on April 16, El'tsin said that Russia was seeking to establish democracy and a free-market economic system and added that it was turning to Western Europe for help in making this transition. He suggested immediate direct contacts between Russian parliamentary committees and committees of the European parliament. The president of the European parliament, Enrique Baron, however, told El'tsin the parliament would deal directly only with the USSR Supreme Soviet, although the secretary general of the Council of Europe, Catherine Lalumière, informed El'tsin that affiliation with one of its subunits dealing with regional officials was possible. El'tsin also told the parliamentarians that the Soviet government should become "a small coordinating center" with authority only over limited areas, including defense, transport, and energy (RFE/RL correspondent's report, *Reuters*, April 16).

At a news conference in Strasbourg the same day, El'tsin said the time had come for Russia to return to "the heart of Europe" and he proposed that US, Soviet, European, and Japanese leaders hold a meeting "on the future of the world" in the USSR in late 1992. He also proposed "a Euro-Asian economic area." El'tsin added that the RSFSR wanted to send an observer to the United Nations and would ultimately like to become a full member of that body (RFE/RL correspondent's report, *Reuters*, *AFP*, April 16).

The third day of El'tsin's visit was marked by some confusion as he canceled a scheduled trip to Grenoble—to the consternation of the city's mayor—and announced that he intended to meet with French President François Mitterrand. While Mitterrand agreed to a brief meeting with El'tsin, his spokesman Hubert Verdine made clear the French government's attitude towards El'tsin, stating plainly: "There must be no ambiguity. The Soviet Union has one president, and that is Mr. Gorbachev."

El'tsin told reporters after the meeting that he and Mitterrand had discussed Russia's domestic problems and the possibility of contacts between the French and Russian parliaments. El'tsin also said he had expressed his desire to bring Russia into the European Community. He expressed great satisfaction with his trip to France.

European Bank for Reconstruction and Development Inaugurated

The European Bank for Reconstruction and Development was inaugurated in London. Its purpose was defined as helping to promote Soviet and East European advances towards market economies. Soviet President Mikhail Gorbachev said he hoped the bank would support the USSR's integration into Europe (*AFP, Reuters*, April 15).

Addressing the bank's Board of Governors on April 16, Chairman of the USSR State Bank Viktor Gerashchenko urged the removal of limitations on how much the USSR could borrow from the bank. Gerashchenko argued that the USSR's "determination in implementing reforms" should obviate the need for the clause allowing the Soviet Union to borrow only as much as it would have paid in during the first three years of the bank's operation—namely, 220 million dollars. Some Western members first wished to see concrete evidence of more political and economic reform in the USSR

Georgian President Endorses Call for Mass Civil Disobedience

One day after his election as Georgian president, Zviad Gamsakhurdia issued a decree endorsing a call for mass civil disobedience against the Soviet central authorities that was made the same day by the political parties of the Roundtable/Free Georgia coalition. The decree contained provisions for ensuring that the campaign did not harm the Georgian economy and for creating a Media Council to disseminate "correct and verified" information abroad about the situation in Georgia.

Emigration Bill Reported Stalled by Conservatives

Nikolai Neiland, a member of the USSR Supreme Soviet Foreign Affairs Committee, told Reuters that the long-promised law on emigration and freedom of travel had been postponed indefinitely by the "Soyuz" faction and other deputies worried about a possible "brain drain" and the departure of "millions" of Soviet citizens if the law were enacted.

On April 16, the United States told the Soviet Union that failure to ease emigration restrictions would prevent Washington from granting trade benefits. The US State Department cited a US law (Jackson-Vanik amendment) that bars credits to countries that do not allow free emigration. In 1990, US President George Bush waived part of the law when he signed a new US-Soviet trade agreement, but he said at the time that he would not submit the agreement for ratification unless the Soviet Union passed the emigration legislation (*Reuters*, RFE/RL correspondent's report, April 16).

Railways Law

A joint session of the USSR Supreme Soviet adopted a law proclaiming all railways in the USSR to be all-Union property. (Some railways were hitherto under republican administration.) The law forbade any deliberate attempts to block or impede rail traffic (*TASS*, April 15).

Bukovsky Visits USSR

Former Soviet dissident Vladimir Bukovsky returned to the Soviet Union for his first visit since he was freed from prison and exchanged for an imprisoned Chilean Communist in 1976 (*AFP*, April 15).

In an interview with Radio Rossii on April 16, Bukovsky said he supported an all-Union general strike. Bukovsky said Soviet citizens must "rise and tell the Communists: 'Go away'." Otherwise, he said, blood and hunger would ensue. Speaking at a news conference on April 17, Bukovsky had strong praise for El'tsin, "once a populist, now a democrat," and characterized Gorbachev as "too weak to lead the country but still too strong to retire." He faulted the democratic opposition's lack of organization, warning that it could not defeat the Communists without "alternative structures, completely independent of the former system" and he cited Poland's "Solidarity" movement as a model (*AFP*, *Reuters*, April 17).

USSR Warns North Korea of Cutoff of Nuclear Fuel

A senior official of the USSR Academy of Sciences said the Soviet Union had warned North Korea it might face a cutoff of Soviet nuclear fuel and cooperation. Economist Vladlen Martynov said North Korea had been told the action would be taken unless it agreed to international inspection of its nuclear facilities, including two operating reactors. South Korea and other countries were afraid that

North Korea might try to use its nuclear facilities to produce nuclear weapons (*Reuters*, April 15).

Tuesday, April 16

Gorbachev Visits Japan

In the first visit ever by a Soviet leader to Japan, Soviet President Mikhail Gorbachev arrived in Tokyo. Before beginning a series of talks with Japanese Prime Minister Toshiki Kaifu, Gorbachev called on Emperor Akihito (*Reuters, AFP*, April 16).

The first round of talks between Gorbachev and Kaifu was described by Soviet spokesman Vitalii Ignatenko as "businesslike and very serious." Gorbachev was reported to have expressed concern to Kaifu that relations between their nations did not reflect recent changes in the world.

At a banquet the same evening hosted by Emperor Akihito, Gorbachev offered condolences for the deaths of Japanese prisoners of World War II in Soviet camps. Gorbachev said it was time to do everything possible to avoid "the disaster of enmity."

In an address to the Japanese parliament on April 17, Gorbachev urged Japan and the United States to join the Soviet Union in talks aimed at building mutual confidence about the Asia-Pacific region. He also told the parliament about a proposal he had made in a second round of talks with Kaifu for a five-country forum on Asian-Pacific affairs. Kaifu reacted coolly to Gorbachev's proposal, however, saying that Asia did not need such a forum and that Japan preferred to approach regional problems on a case-by-case basis (*Reuters, AFP, Kyodo News Agency*, April 17).

In his address to the parliament and at a lunch with Japanese businessmen the same day, Gorbachev appealed for investment in the USSR to avert an economic collapse that could lead to a dictatorship. He was told, however, that a stable Soviet political and economic environment would be necessary for increased Japanese investment (*AP, AFP*, April 17).

On April 18, Kaifu and Gorbachev held three extra rounds of talks in an attempt to reach a compromise on the Kurile Islands dispute. The deadlock over the issue was reported to have stalled agreement on practically all other bilateral issues (*Reuters, TASS, Kyodo News Agency*, April 18). The talks finally ended late that day with the signing of a joint declaration. The declaration contained Soviet proposals to end visa requirements for Japanese nationals visiting the disputed islands and to reduce the Soviet military presence there. Japan agreed to discuss the points in the future. Gorbachev and Kaifu also agreed to accelerate preparations for a World War II peace treaty. Their declaration said the treaty would include a settlement of the Kuriles dispute (Western agencies, *TASS*, April 18). Gorbachev expressed satisfaction with the talks, which he described as generally good-natured.

Fifteen agreements, memoranda, and notes were signed as a result of the summit, covering such areas as trade and environmental cooperation, cultural exchanges, and Moscow's provision of a list of Japanese POWs who had died in Siberian camps (*Kyodo News Agency*, April 18).

Gorbachev concluded his visit to Japan on April 19, with a tour of western Japan, taking in the cities of Kyoto and Nagasaki. In a meeting with Japanese business leaders in Kyoto, Gorbachev made a strong appeal for aid and investment. But the response of his audience in Kyoto echoed that of their counterparts in Tokyo, making it clear that there could be no mass infusion of money into the Soviet Union until the Kurile Islands dispute was resolved (*Reuters*, April 19).

Draft Law Banning Political Strikes Approved

In a closed session, the USSR Supreme Soviet approved a bill on labor disputes, one article of which banned "political strikes," TASS reported. The Supreme Soviet also adopted a resolution calling on the republican Supreme Soviets quickly to name fully empowered representatives to an interparliamentary commission tasked with devising means of averting strikes.

City Party Leaders Say Motherland Is in Danger

Communist Party leaders from thirteen Soviet cities meeting in Smolensk issued a statement saying forces in the USSR wanted to destroy the country's moral traditions and way of life. Declaring that "our motherland is in danger," the statement said people were being subjected to economic and social experiments leading to the creation of a capitalist society. The statement said a handful of people calling themselves democrats were trying to satisfy their personal ambition and wanted to tear apart a state that had been built over centuries (*AP*, April 16).

Soviet and Israeli Prime Ministers Meet in London

In the first meeting at prime ministerial level since the Soviet Union broke off diplomatic ties with Israel in 1967, Soviet Prime Minister Valentin Pavlov and Israeli Prime Minister Yitzhak Shamir held talks in London. Shamir said he told Pavlov that diplomatic ties would have to be reestablished if Moscow was to take part in a Middle East peace conference (*Reuters, DPA*, April 16).

The USSR in April, 1991

RSFSR Supreme Soviet Chairman Boris El'tsin had told reporters during his trip to France the same week that "the time has come for diplomatic relations between the Soviet Union and Israel" and said that "Russia is prepared either to associate itself [with the Kremlin's efforts to resume ties] or to establish diplomatic relations independently" (*Reuters*, April 17).

South Korea Extends Credits to USSR

The USSR Foreign Trade Bank and the South Korean Export-Import Bank signed an agreement giving the USSR 800 million dollars in credits for purchases of South Korean raw materials and consumer goods. This was part of a 3-billion-dollar package of loans and credits agreed to earlier in the year. The credits were guaranteed by the USSR (*TASS*, April 17).

South Korea Signs Nuclear Cooperation Accord with USSR

South Korea and the Soviet Union agreed to cooperate in the peaceful use of nuclear energy. The agreement, the first of its kind between the two nations on a private level, was signed in Seoul by officials of the USSR nuclear society and two state-funded Korean nuclear research groups (*AP*, April 16).

KGB Plans to Give Its Version of History in TV Series

The KGB was reported to be cooperating in the production of a television series that would cover historical events from the assassination of Leon Trotsky to the defections of British agents. KGB Major General Aleksandr Karbainov said in Rome that the series was designed "to dispel the myth of the KGB as a monstrous giant with tentacles reaching all over the world." The series was to be called "The KGB Tells All."

Wednesday, April 17

Armenia Nationalizes Communist Party Property

The Armenian Supreme Soviet declared all Communist Party assets in the republic to be state property. A resolution issued by the parliament authorized the Armenian government to sell the property. Also nationalized was the property of the Komsomol. The resolution said the Party's wealth had been created at the expense of the state budget (*TASS*, April 17). A government decree issued on April 19 said the assets should be handed over within a week.

On April 19, the CPSU Central Committee issued a statement protesting against Armenia's decision to nationalize Communist Party property. The statement termed the decision a crude violation of both the Armenian and USSR Constitutions and of Soviet laws guaranteeing public organizations the right to own property. It accused Armenia of "pursuing a political course aimed at setting up an antidemocratic and authoritarian regime" and called for the ruling to be reversed.

On April 23, Soviet President Mikhail Gorbachev issued a decree annulling the Armenian ruling (*Reuters*, April 23).

On April 28, a congress of the Armenian Communist Party voted not to hand over the building that houses its headquarters in Erevan in defiance of the Armenian Supreme Soviet resolution, TASS reported.

On May 1, a special commission of the Erevan City Soviet issued an order telling Armenian Communists to leave the Party's Central Committee building.

Armenian Supreme Soviet in Favor of Referendum on Nuclear Plant

The Armenian Supreme Soviet voted overwhelmingly in favor of holding a referendum on whether to recommission the Medzamor nuclear power station near Erevan (*Armenpress*, April 18). The station had been closed in early 1989 following the earthquake there several months earlier; the resulting energy shortfall created serious problems throughout Armenia.

Also on April 17, the Armenian parliament voted to reopen the Nairit chemical plant in Erevan. The Armenian Pan-National Movement, which formed the majority faction in the Armenian parliament, had campaigned for the closure of the plant arguing that pollution from it was causing widespread health problems. This decision was challenged, however, by the plant's management and work force, who argued that the pollution could be eliminated and that the plant's production was vital for the republic's chemical industry (*Armenpress*, April 18).

Central Government to Tighten Control over Local Legislatures

The USSR Supreme Soviet adopted a resolution to ensure that central legislation was enforced locally. The resolution obliged prosecutors at all levels to make local soviets and public groups abide by the USSR Constitution and federal laws. Prosecutors were empowered to start legal action if local authorities ignored calls to revoke acts conflicting with all-Union legislation (see *Pravda*, April 18).

Controversy over Number of Chernobyl' Deaths

A controversy erupted over the number of deaths resulting from the Chernobyl' nuclear accident. In statements to the press in London, Vladimir Chernousenko, a Soviet scientist responsible for monitoring the region around Chernobyl' following the accident in 1986, put the death toll from the accident to date at between 7,000 and 10,000. His estimates were backed by Yurii Shcherbak, a Ukrainian epidemiologist and deputy in the USSR Supreme Soviet, and were apparently based on records kept by the Chernobyl' Union, an organization of veterans of the cleanup operation, which had added up deaths from all causes among its membership. Other scientists maintained that the estimate was flawed, saying there was no proof that the deaths among the group in question had been caused by exposure to radiation. A Swedish authority on the consequences of the disaster, for example, said that the number of deaths among the cleanup workers was "not remarkably high," compared with normal mortality rates for such a large group (660,000 people). There were no official Soviet figures for deaths among cleanup workers and the official death toll from the accident remained thirty-one (*Reuters, AP*, RFE/RL correspondent's report, April 17 and 18).

Fears of Second Chernobyl' Accident

The sarcophagus built to encase the damaged nuclear reactor at Chernobyl' following the explosion there in 1986 was reported to be full of holes and in danger of crumbling. Speaking in London, a spokesman for the scientists monitoring the sarcophagus, Yurii Buzulukov, expressed the fear that, if the structure were to collapse, the impact of the debris could release clouds of radioactive dust still lying in the pit beneath the sarcophagus. He said his team was considering building a second sarcophagus and filling reactor rooms at the lower levels with whisked concrete. He stressed, however, that these might be only short-term measures and said the Soviet Union urgently needed technical assistance from the West to secure the site in the long term (*The Times*, April 17).

Lithuanian Prime Minister in Ottawa

Lithuania Prime Minister Gediminas Vagnorius, on a visit to Canada, held a fifty-minute meeting with Canadian External Affairs Minister Joe Clark during which they discussed the current situation in Lithuania and its relations with the USSR, as well as possible Canadian support for economic reforms. Vagnorius suggested that the West should adopt an active policy of supporting democratic forces in the USSR (RFE Lithuanian service, April 17).

On April 20, Vagnorius met with representatives of the country's financial and banking sector as well as with local Lithuanian communities. In an interview with

The USSR in April, 1991

RFE/RL, Vagnorius said that he was pleased with his visit and that he had signed contracts worth several million dollars with Ontario businessmen. On April 21, Vagnorius met with Alberta government and business officials in Edmonton and Calgary. He completed his visit on April 23 in Montreal, where he held talks with Quebec provincial government officials (RFE Lithuanian service, April 20, 22, and 23).

TASS said Kazakh officials had prepared a draft law setting out rules and regulations for privatizing state property within the republic. The draft, which was to be submitted for public discussion before being considered by the republican Supreme Soviet, aimed to privatize enterprises in all spheres of the Kazakh economy, including a small share of the enterprises in the defense complex. Foreigners, as well as citizens of any republic, would be allowed to purchase Kazakh property.

Kazakhstan to Privatize State Property

―――― *Thursday, April 18*

Reports from Washington said the Soviet Union had asked the United States for 1.5 billion dollars in new credit guarantees to purchase US grain in the hope of forestalling food shortages. The reports said the new guarantees would more than double the Soviet Union's current agricultural credits with the United States. Representative David Nagle, who met with a high-level Soviet trade delegation on April 17, was quoted as saying "there was an atmosphere of desperation" among Soviet officials (*Reuters, The Washington Post*, April 18).

USSR Asks US for New Credit Guarantees for Grain Purchases

The USSR Supreme Court began hearing the case of the former director of an Uzbek agroindustrial association, Akhmadzhon Odilov, who faced charges of abuse of office, misappropriation of more than a million rubles of state property, and taking bribes totaling more than 640,000 rubles (*TASS*, April 18).

Trial of Former Uzbek Director Begins in Supreme Court

The inaugural congress of the newly created Press Association was held in Moscow on April 17 and 18, Radio Mayak and *Izvestia* reported. The association elected Aleksandr Gorkovlyuk, deputy chairman of the USSR State Committee for Publishing and the Press, as its president. Gorkovlyuk said about 500 official and inde-

Official Press Association Set Up

pendent periodicals had already applied for membership in the association. The main issue discussed at the congress was how to set up a fund for helping periodicals threatened with bankruptcy.

Nearly Half a Million People Left USSR in 1990

Almost half a million people left the Soviet Union in 1990, with most emigrating to Israel or Germany. TASS said figures of the Ministry of Internal Affairs reported by the weekly newspaper *Glasnost'* showed that 452,000 Soviet citizens had left the country in 1990—about twice as many as in 1989.

Friday, April 19

Latest Figures Show Soviet Economy in Crisis

Statistics released by the USSR State Committee for Statistics for the first quarter of 1991 showed the Soviet economy in sharp decline. The figures, carried by TASS, showed the gross national product down 8 percent, a drop in productivity of 9 percent, and a decrease of one-third in foreign trade.

Lithuanian Customs Post Seized

Soviet paratroopers occupied the Lithuanian customs post at Medininkai on the Belorussian border for five hours, AP reported. The soldiers broke down the customs barrier, cut telephone wires, and confiscated documents and radio equipment. The unarmed Lithuanians at the post were detained for five hours and warned not to reopen the post. President of the Lithuanian Supreme Council Vytautas Landsbergis telephoned Commander of the Baltic Military District Colonel General Fedor Kuz'min, who agreed that the incident should be investigated "with the cooperation of both sides," Radio Kaunas reported on April 20.

Curfew Lifted in Azerbaijan

TASS and the Azerbaijani news agency ASSA reported that Azerbaijani President Ayaz Mutalibov had issued a decree lifting the curfew imposed in Baku on January 20, 1990, after Soviet troops fought their way into the city following a week of pogroms against ethnic Armenians. The state of emergency imposed at the same time remained in force.

Tatarstan Supreme Soviet Approves Constitutional Changes

In one of a number of constitutional changes made during a session in Kazan', the Supreme Soviet of Tatarstan decided to scrap an article that said it was part of the

The USSR in April, 1991

RSFSR. The Supreme Soviet also approved an amendment creating the post of president. This position would be filled by direct election (RFE/RL correspondent's report, April 19).

The RSFSR Supreme Soviet adopted a law "On Social Guarantees for Working People" that included a new minimum wage of 180 rubles a month effective from October 1, rising to 195 rubles a month from January 1, 1992. Both figures included sixty rubles in compensation ordered by the central government to offset large price rises. The new law also provided for annual paid leave of twenty-four working days. It also said that monthly unemployment benefits ought to equal at least 90 percent of the minimum wage.

Russian Parliament Adopts Law on Minimum Wage

In an interview with Radio Moscow, First Deputy Prime Minister Vladimir Shcherbakov outlined punitive economic measures for those republics that did not intend to sign the Union treaty, saying that in their transactions with the Union they would be treated like foreign countries. "There are world prices . . . . There is world currency. There are export and import duties. Customs posts should be set up."

Shcherbakov Threatens Dissenting Republics

Saturday, April 20

More than 700 delegates representing most of the Soviet republics attended the second congress of the "Soyuz" group of USSR Supreme Soviet deputies, which opened in Moscow for a two-day session, TASS reported. The chairman of "Soyuz," Yurii Blokhin, called for the declaration of an immediate state of emergency across the USSR, to last for six months, during which extraordinary measures should be taken to prevent a drop in the standard of living. He said the state of emergency should include a moratorium on strikes and rallies, suspension of the activities of all political parties, control over the mass media, military control over transportation and communications, and a ban on the uncontrolled privatization of state property. Blokhin added that the declaration of a state of emergency was Soviet President Mikhail Gorbachev's constitutional obligation and that, if he could not meet it, the "Soyuz" faction was ready to take over responsibility for measures to put a state of emergency into force.

"Soyuz" Holds Second Congress

Addressing the congress, Colonel Viktor Alksnis said a special session of the USSR Congress of People's Deputies should be convoked with the aim of ousting Gorbachev. According to Radio Rossii, Alksnis declared that "Soyuz" should begin collecting signatures in order to force the Congress to hold a special session: the signatures of one-fifth of the 2,250 USSR Supreme Soviet deputies were needed in order to convoke an extraordinary session of the Congress, and "Soyuz" claimed to represent 500 deputies (*AP*, April 21).

The delegates approved a resolution saying that the proposed session of the USSR Congress of People's Deputies should require Gorbachev to report on how he had used the powers given him by the previous session of the Congress in December, 1990 (*AP*, April 21). The "Soyuz" congress also rejected the new draft Union treaty, calling it unacceptable because its aim was to abolish the Soviet Union, Radio Moscow reported the same day.

Delegates to the congress also voted to turn the parliamentary group into an all-Union mass movement to be officially registered with the authorities, DPA reported on April 21. Congress delegates described "Soyuz" as "a constructive opposition" to the present leadership of the CPSU.

USSR presidential spokesman Vitalii Ignatenko declared on April 23 that Gorbachev did not want to impose a state of emergency in the country, TASS reported. USSR Supreme Soviet Chairman Anatolii Luk'yanov revealed the same day that he had received a letter from twenty-two "Soyuz" delegates opposing an extraordinary session of the USSR Congress of People's Deputies (*AFP*, April 23).

According to TASS of April 25, a group of Communist deputies of the USSR Supreme Soviet opposed the call for a special session of the USSR Congress of People's Deputies, arguing that it would be unnecessary, expensive, and would keep people from spring sowing.

The Ukrainian Supreme Soviet issued a statement the same day criticizing the "Soyuz" call for the declaration of a state of emergency as an attempt to take the country back to an administrative-command system. The statement added that the Ukrainian Supreme Soviet was in control of its territory; saw no reason for a state of emergency; and, moreover, considered such calls inadmissible and a violation of its sovereignty (*TASS*, April 25).

Yakovlev Warns of Radicalism

In an article published by *Komsomol'skaya pravda*, Aleksandr Yakovlev warned against both right- and left-

THE USSR IN APRIL, 1991

wing radicalism, saying that intolerance and symptoms of authoritarianism and totalitarianism had reappeared in the USSR. Yakovlev wrote that the Soviet government had received a large number of letters protesting against the new authoritarianism, which he said was sometimes more rigid than in the period preceding *perestroika*.

Round-Table Held on Perestroika

A conference entitled "*Perestroika* in the USSR Yesterday, Today, Tomorrow" was held in Moscow, Radio Moscow reported. Political figures attending included USSR Minister of Internal Affairs Boriss Pugo; his predecessor, Vadim Bakatin; former Politburo member Egor Ligachev; radical economist Stanislav Shatalin; Chairman of the Moscow City Soviet Gavriil Popov; former Foreign Minister Eduard Shevardnadze; and Deputy Chairman of the RSFSR Supreme Soviet Ruslan Khasbulatov. The conference was organized by the newspaper *Komsomol'skaya pravda*, an international nongovernmental organization called "The Committee of National Accord," and the independent Washington-Paris-Moscow University.

Shatalin called for the formation of a broad coalition of forces, "a national consensus" body, to lead the USSR out of its economic crisis and to rally the public to accept the unpopular steps necessary to switch to a market economy. He called for cuts in military and KGB spending to control hyperinflation (*AFP*, April 21).

Economist Nikolai Petrakov attacked the USSR Cabinet of Ministers' anticrisis program, saying it offered no concrete way out of the misery. He described the program as a trick to convince the West that the Soviet Union was moving to a market economy, AP reported on April 21.

Bakatin declared that *perestroika* had faltered because there was no unified plan for reforming the economic and political system. Radio Moscow quoted him on April 21 as calling on the Soviet leadership to turn to the democrats and to cooperate in order to remove the mistrust between them and the leadership. Khasbulatov said that the Soviet government had lost the confidence of the people and that a coalition of reformist forces was the only way to restore order peacefully (*Radio Moscow*, April 21).

Ligachev declared that separatism posed the greatest danger to the Soviet Union and that the Communist Party and the soviets were forces that could unite all progressive and patriotic movements in reaching accord (*Radio Moscow*, April 21).

Gorbachev Assesses South Korean Talks

Speaking after ninety minutes of talks with South Korean President Roh Tae-Woo on the island of Cheju,

Soviet President Mikhail Gorbachev stressed that the USSR wanted good relations with both North and South Korea and urged the two countries to reconcile their differences and work towards reunification, Western agencies reported.

Trade issues were discussed in separate talks between USSR Minister of Foreign Economic Relations Konstantin Katushev and South Korean Trade and Industry Minister Lee Bong-Suh. AP reported that the two sides had agreed to step up bilateral trade to 10 billion dollars annually by the mid-1990s. Soviet presidential spokesman Vitalii Ignatenko said that two-way trade was expected to rise to 1.5 billion dollars in 1991 (bilateral trade reached 889 million dollars in 1990).

New USSR Deputy Foreign Minister Appointed

Valerii Nikolaenko, head of the USSR Foreign Ministry's Latin America Department since 1990, was named USSR deputy foreign minister, TASS reported. Nikolaenko, a 1964 graduate of the Moscow State Institute for International Relations, had served in Soviet embassies in Cuba (1964-68), Mexico (1969-74), and the United States (1975-79). From 1980-87 he worked at the Foreign Ministry in Moscow before holding two ambassadorial posts: Colombia (1987-88); and Nicaragua (1988-90).

RSFSR Prime Minister in the United States

RSFSR Prime Minister Ivan Silaev went to the United States to establish contacts between the RSFSR and US political and business circles, TASS reported. On April 22, Silaev met in Washington with US Deputy Secretary of State Lawrence Eagleburger, US Security Adviser Brent Scowcroft, and US Commerce Secretary Robert Mosbacher, to whom he explained the RSFSR's economic reforms and efforts towards democratization. A US spokesman said Silaev did not ask for anything (RFE/RL correspondent's report, April 23).

On April 23, Silaev spoke to an audience of businessmen and members of the US Congress. Later that day, he criticized the Soviet government's anticrisis program but said that Gorbachev's resignation would be contrary to the interests of Soviet democratic forces (*Reuters*, April 24).

Communists of Russia Hold Congress

The conservative group Communists of Russia held its second congress in Leningrad. Among the 750 delegates attending the two-day conference were members of the all-Union society Unity for Leninist and Communist Ideas ("Edinstvo"), the Movement for Communist Initiative, and the Moscow Communist-Leninist Club, TASS reported.

The USSR in April, 1991

The delegates pronounced themselves in favor of the "sovietization" of the economy, improving workers' lives, and lowering prices, according to TASS on April 21. They also seconded the nomination of Aleksei Sergeev for the post of RSFSR president proposed by the United Front of Workers. Sergeev was coauthor of an economic reform plan that would not raise prices or lower workers' living standards.

State of Emergency in North Ossetia

TASS reported that a state of emergency, running from April 19 to May 19, had been imposed in Vladikavkaz, the capital of the North Ossetian ASSR, and in surrounding raions following armed clashes between native Ossetians and the Ingush minority. The unrest first erupted in the village of Kurtat on April 19, when an Ingush began quarreling with an Ossetian kolkhoz worker who was tending his private plot. Tensions between the two nationalities derived from Ingush demands for the revival of their autonomous oblast and the return of land given to the North Ossetian ASSR when the Ingush were deported to Central Asia in 1944. Yurii Bigarov, deputy chairman of the North Ossetian Supreme Soviet, told TASS that armed police had arrived on the scene of the conflict. On April 21, North Ossetian Supreme Soviet Chairman Akhsarbek Galazov confirmed the arrival of additional troops at the request of the government, TASS reported.

TASS quoted USSR First Deputy Minister of Internal Affairs Boris Gromov as telling a press conference in Moscow on April 22 that unresolved interethnic tensions in the Northern Caucasus could lead to "explosions in the entire region." Gromov assessed the situation in the North Ossetian ASSR, where the estimated number of those injured in the fighting had been raised to "dozens," as even more difficult than that in South Ossetia, where more than fifty people had been killed since December, 1990, in fighting between Ossetians and Georgians.

Radio Moscow reported on April 24 that gunfire was continuing despite the state of emergency and that twenty-five violent incidents had been registered since the clashes began.

Some Prices Reduced in Tajikistan

As reported by Radio Moscow, Tajik President Kakhar Makhkamov issued a decree reducing the prices of bread and flour in the republic to the level they were before April 2. Experts estimated that the price reduction would cost the Tajik government between 300 and 350 million rubles.

Demonstration against Future of Lithuania Forum

More than 1,000 people attended a rally in Vilnius protesting against the formation of the Future of Lithuania Forum. Speakers at the rally, organized by the Lithuanian Freedom League, the Lithuanian Independence Party, the Lithuanian Democratic Party, and the Union of Workers of Lithuania, accused the forum, dominated by the Lithuanian Democratic Labor Party (the former independent Lithuanian Communist Party), of being opposed to real independence. A resolution issued at the rally called the forum a stepchild of the CPSU and demanded the resignations of two ministers, the bringing of criminal charges against Algirdas Brazauskas and Kazimiera Prunskiene, and the publication of lists of KGB agents in Lithuania (RFE Lithuanian service, April 21).

Sunday, April 21

Centrist Bloc Ceases to Exist

According to a commentary by Radio Rossii, the so-called Centrist Bloc of political groups set up in 1990 ceased to exist at the end of March. The radio said that nine of the eleven groups that founded the bloc had recently left it. The reason given was "the extreme reactionary nature" of the body. Meanwhile, two leaders of the bloc, Vladimir Voronin and Vladimir Zhirinovsky, had been proposed as candidates for the upcoming presidential elections in the RSFSR.

Interparliamentary Conference of Democratic Forces

The first conference of representatives from the Supreme Soviets of the RSFSR, Ukraine, Belorussia, Uzbekistan, Armenia, and other republics was held in Moscow, Radio Rossii reported. Representatives of Latvia, Lithuania, and Georgia were present as observers. The conference discussed the possibility of creating a permanent interparliamentary committee to coordinate the activities of democrats in various republican parliaments. The conference also discussed the organization of a roundtable of political parties in the USSR.

On April 22, the conference called on all Supreme Soviets to aid the process of "peaceful liquidation of the existing Union structures." The conference also adopted a declaration supporting striking workers. Conference participants expressed their intention to create, together with striking workers, a new "government of people's confidence." The participants also called on all Soviet workers to declare their readiness to strike in response to the April 21 demand by the "Soyuz" group of deputies for the declaration of a state of emergency.

The USSR in April, 1991

Mass Meeting in Kiev

Up to 3,000 people gathered in Kiev in an action organized by "Rukh," Radio Kiev reported on April 22. The gathering approved a list of demands to the Ukrainian Supreme Soviet, including the immediate granting of constitutional force to the republic's declaration of sovereignty, the invalidation of all federal laws and presidential decrees in Ukraine, the subordination of all all-Union enterprises and institutions to republican ownership, and the release of Ukrainian people's deputy Stepan Khmara and his associates from detention.

Uzbekistan and Turkmenistan Sign Agreement

The television newscast "Vremya" reported that an agreement on cooperation in culture, economics, health, the environment, and science had been signed by representatives of Uzbekistan and Turkmenistan. The agreement was cited as an example of the horizontal relations developing between republics; the report noted that the two republics had many problems in common, including a reduction in the subsidies received from the USSR budget.

Monday, April 22

Pavlov Presents Anticrisis Program to Supreme Soviet

Soviet Prime Minister Valentin Pavlov outlined his government's anticrisis program to the USSR Supreme Soviet, following two days of discussion of the program by the USSR Cabinet of Ministers. He warned that failure to adopt it would result in economic collapse and a 25-percent decrease in the national income (*AFP*, April 22).

The main points of the plan were: a ban on strikes and political rallies during working hours; emergency measures to ensure the efficient distribution of essential foodstuffs; financial stabilization measures whereby the USSR State Bank would have the power to control spending by republican governments; and charging republics that refused to sign the Union treaty for the energy and raw materials they consumed (*Financial Times*, April 23).

Pavlov listed a host of shortfalls in the country's economic performance during the first quarter of the year. Compared with the first quarter of 1990 national income was down 10 percent, industrial output was down 5 percent, agricultural production fell by 13 percent, and livestock production dropped 8 to 12 percent. The USSR Ministry of Finance estimated that the Union-wide budget deficit would total around 200 billion rubles (for a total internal government debt of 540 billion) by the end of 1991. In the first quarter, republican payments into the Union budget fell short by over 60 percent of the planned amount.

The anticrisis program was generally well received, with eleven of sixteen speakers coming out in support of it. While Pavlov asserted that his plan could work only if it were backed by the fifteen Union republics, Kazakh President Nursultan Nazarbaev declared that it ignored the rights of the republics.

Dismissing Pavlov's evaluation of the situation as incompetent and vague, Nazarbaev said the government could not impose radical reforms without recognizing the sovereignty of the republics (*Reuters*, April 22).

On April 23, the anticrisis program was approved by 323 votes to 13, with 29 abstentions, AFP reported. Deputies gave Pavlov until May 20 to work out specific details of the plan's implementation. The USSR Supreme Soviet also approved a resolution to create an interrepublican council for economic reform to coordinate the activities of the republics during implementation of the program and to form market relations. The resolution also stipulated that the government should inform the USSR Supreme Soviet in October, 1991, about the progress of the program (*TASS*, April 23).

Government and Trade Unions Reach Agreement

At a press conference in Moscow, Chairman of the USSR Confederation of Trade Unions Vladimir Shcherbakov announced that an agreement had been reached between the government and the official trade unions on a wide range of issues, TASS reported. The agreement foresaw wage indexation, an official subsistence minimum, a wage reform, a change in taxation on many goods, a government unemployment program, compensation for more expensive school and works canteen meals, and other measures. Additional budgetary expenditure for social purposes in 1991 would amount to 47.6 billion rubles. Shcherbakov said that, if the government fulfilled its part of the agreement, the unions would refrain from strikes. He said the agreement was the first of its kind in Soviet history.

Shcherbakov also disclosed that the trade-union confederation had set the subsistence minimum, after the retail price increases of April 2, at 320 rubles a month, "Vremya" reported. Shcherbakov maintained that this subsistence level was considerably higher than the average wage.

Lenin's Birthday Celebrated

The Soviet leadership marked the 121st anniversary of Lenin's birth, TASS reported. The main speech at a traditional meeting was delivered by the CPSU deputy general secretary, Vladimir Ivashko, who said that Lenin's thoughts and deeds had not lost their importance. Soviet President Mikhail Gorbachev, Vice President Gennadii Yanaev, Prime Minister Valentin Pavlov, and other officials attended the ceremonies.

In connection with the occasion, Soviet historians answered questions from Soviet and foreign journalists at a press conference held in Moscow on April 20. Professor of History Vladlen Loginov said that it was former chief ideologist Mikhail Suslov who had personally deleted "unacceptable" passages from Lenin's writings when the fifth edition of Lenin's complete works was being prepared, TASS reported on April 22.

Research Center to Start Work in Chernobyl' Area

An international scientific research center was to start operations in the thirty-kilometer safety zone set up by the Soviet government around the Chernobyl' nuclear power plant. This news was announced by Pavel Pokutny, deputy director of the scientific production association "Pripyat'," located near the damaged reactor. According to TASS, foreign and Soviet specialists would study decontamination, radiation ecology, and radiation epidemiology.

Kravchuk on Visit to Germany

Chairman of the Ukrainian Supreme Soviet Leonid Kravchuk arrived in Bonn at the start of a week-long official visit to Germany, Radio Kiev reported. On the first day of his visit Kravchuk held talks with Foreign Minister Hans-Dietrich Genscher and President Richard von Weizsäcker.

In an address to the Bavarian parliament in Munich on April 23, Kravchuk stressed the importance of Ukrainian sovereignty within the framework of the USSR. He told Bavarian legislators that, although the Ukrainian population had voted to remain part of the Soviet Union, it wanted a qualitatively new arrangement with the central government based on the genuine equality and sovereignty of the USSR's constituent republics. Democratic changes were irreversible, he added, and Ukraine was now pursuing an independent foreign policy and seeking its proper place in Europe as a large and important state. During talks with Kravchuk, Bavarian Prime Minister Max Streibl stressed that Bavaria wanted good-neighborly economic, scientific, and cultural relations with Ukraine (RFE/RL correspondent's report, April 23).

Kravchuk announced at a press conference in Munich on April 25 that he had concluded agreements on technology exchanges with the Bavarian government and on joint ventures with several Bavarian firms for the production of medical equipment, plastic products, gear boxes, and construction materials (*DPA*, April 25).

On April 26, Kravchuk protested about Soviet television coverage of his visit to Germany. He told RFE/RL that he was angered by a report on "Vremya" of April 25, in which a correspondent implicitly criticized the Ukrainian delegation for insisting on speaking Ukrainian, instead of Russian, in talks with German leaders. Kravchuk said he had instructed Ukrainian Foreign Minister Anatolii Zlenko to send a protest to the Central Television authorities demanding the recall of the correspondent (RFE/RL, Ukrainian service, April 26).

Kirgizia Refuses to Sign Union Treaty

The Kirgiz Supreme Soviet decided not to sign the draft Union treaty proposed by the USSR and approved instead a draft Union treaty of its own. *Komsomol'skaya pravda* of April 23 quoted Kirgiz President Askar Akaev as criticizing virtually all points of the USSR Union treaty at a session of the Kirgiz Supreme Soviet.

Kirgiz President Proposes Anticrisis Measures

Kirgiz President Askar Akaev told the Kirgiz Supreme Soviet that an anticrisis program was needed in the republic to avoid a food crisis and social unrest. Akaev said that agricultural reforms should be implemented immediately to stop the present "slide towards hunger," and he called on deputies to implement land reform that would allow peasants to make more efficient use of the land, TASS reported. He also said peasants should be allowed to sell 20 percent of their produce at market prices. Akaev also said he favored launching industrial and agricultural ventures that would increase barter trade.

Arabic Cultural Center Set Up in Uzbekistan

TASS reported that an Arabic cultural center had been set up in Tashkent to help Soviet Arabs revive their culture and traditions. It planned to offer Arabic classes and publish a newspaper; its library would have a large stock of books in Arabic. The center also planned to establish links with Arab countries.

Press Building in Riga to Remain Communist Property

It was decided that the press building in Riga, seized by Soviet MVD troops in January, would remain the property of the Latvian Communist Party. *Diena* reported on April 22 that the State Board of Arbitration had decided

The USSR in April, 1991

that the base funds of the building belonged to the Communist Party and that the joint-stock company Press House had been founded illegally without taking the interests of the Communist Party into account. Latvian Deputy Prime Minister Ilmars Bisers called the decision "vague and lacking many essential facts."

Dockers' Strike in Klaipeda Wins Wage Raise

Dockworkers in the port of Klaipeda began a strike demanding higher wages, Radio Kaunas reported. The workers complained that the port administration had ignored their attempts to negotiate and that the last straw had been the nonpayment in April of the 105-ruble compensation that the Lithuanian parliament had approved to offset the increase in prices. Port manager Nikolai Berezhnoi announced on April 24 that an agreement ending the strike had been signed on April 23 between the striking workers and the port management, who decided to double the dockworkers' pay (*Reuters*, April 24).

─────────── *Tuesday, April 23*

Gorbachev and Republican Leaders Sign Pact

Soviet President Mikhail Gorbachev and representatives of nine Union republics, including RSFSR Supreme Soviet Chairman Boris El'tsin, met in Novo-Ogarevo and signed a five-point joint statement on measures to stabilize the crisis situation in the country (the text of the agreement was published in *Pravda* on April 24). The session was also attended by representatives of Ukraine, Belorussia, Kazakhstan, Uzbekistan, Azerbaijan, Tajikistan, Kirgizia, and Turkmenistan. The agreement primarily emphasized the speedy conclusion of a new Union treaty and the adoption of a new USSR Constitution. It also recognized the right of the three Baltic republics and of Moldavia, Armenia, and Georgia to decide independently whether to sign the Union treaty and contained an economic package that reversed several elements of the USSR government's anticrisis measures.

Lev Ponomarev, a leader of the Democratic Russia movement, declared he was concerned about some elements of the declaration, including a one-year ban on strikes, Reuters reported on April 25. Such wording, he said, "smells of 1937." El'tsin called the declaration a tremendous victory and said that, by signing the document with the leaders of the nine republics, Gorbachev had recognized them as sovereign states (*TASS*, April 25).

The USSR in April, 1991

Soviet-Cambodian Talks

Soviet Foreign Minister Aleksandr Bessmertnykh and his Cambodian counterpart Hor Namhong opened talks in Moscow to discuss the Cambodian conflict. Talks on Soviet-Cambodian bilateral relations continued on April 24 between Hor and USSR Deputy Foreign Minister Igor' Rogachev, TASS reported.

New University To Be Opened in Moscow

TASS reported that an independent university for studies in the humanities would be opened in Moscow soon. The main organizer of the university would be Moscow's Institute of Historical Archives. The institute's rector, Professor Yurii Afanas'ev, would serve as rector of the new university as well. The new university, whose aim was to improve the level of research and teaching in the humanities in the USSR, would employ specialists from foreign countries as well as Soviet scholars.

Law on Religion Passed in Ukraine

The Ukrainian Supreme Soviet passed a law "On Freedom of Conscience and Religious Organizations," Ukrinform-TASS reported. The law reaffirmed the separation of church and state and the equality of all faiths, simplified registration procedures for religious groups, and allowed religious education. It permitted the Ukrainian Catholic Church, the Autocephalous Orthodox Church, and the Jehovah's Witnesses to operate publicly.

Protest Demonstrations in Adzharia

TASS reported that thousands of workers had gathered in Batumi, the capital of the Adzhar ASSR in Georgia, for the second consecutive day, to protest religious discrimination against the largely Muslim population and to demand the resignation of the republic's prime minister and minister of internal affairs and the replacement of prefects sent from Tbilisi by local officials. The Georgian National Guard opened fire on protesters on April 22, when they approached the local Supreme Soviet building but no injuries were reported. Local journalists told Reuters on April 23 that the protesters had invaded the Supreme Soviet building and evicted the prime minister from his office. Tensions in the region derived from Georgian President Zviad Gamsakhurdia's desire to abolish local autonomy.

Ter-Petrossyan Complains to Gorbachev about Treatment of Armenians in Azerbaijan

TASS said Chairman of the Armenian Supreme Soviet Levon Ter-Petrossyan had written to Soviet President Mikhail Gorbachev expressing his concern over the treatment of ethnic Armenians in Azerbaijan. Ter-

The USSR in April, 1991

Petrossyan stated his objections to the recent mass deportation of Armenians from several settlements in Azerbaijan. He also said that the Shushinsky and Shaumyansky districts and the village of Berdadzor in Nagorno-Karabakh were completely cut off and that the people there were without water, electricity, or food. Ter-Petrossyan proposed that all troops of the Azerbaijani Ministry of Internal Affairs be withdrawn from regions populated by Armenians.

New Soviet Baltic Port

Viktor Kharchenko, the head of the Baltic Shipping Line, told a news conference that Soviet specialists were studying the possibility of building a new port near the village of Ust-Luga, 150 kilometers from Leningrad, TASS reported. The port would take over the work of the ports of Tallinn, Klaipeda, and Ventspils. The plans called for the creation of a new city with some 25,000–30,000 inhabitants. It was hoped that the necessary funding of 5 billion rubles would be supplied by Soviet and foreign investment.

Wednesday, April 24

CPSU Central Committee Plenum Rejects Gorbachev's Resignation Offer

A plenum of the CPSU Central Committee opened in Moscow, TASS reported. Deputy General Secretary Vladimir Ivashko told reporters before the meeting that the CPSU Politburo was unanimously opposed to calls for General Secretary Mikhail Gorbachev's resignation (*Reuters*, April 24). Addressing the plenum, Gorbachev said that it was still necessary for the same person to hold the posts of USSR president and CPSU general secretary because destruction of the present constitutional order would result in a power vacuum that would in turn lead to clashes and the overthrow of democratic institutions. Defending his policies, he said *perestroika* had helped the country rid itself of totalitarianism and that, even though the way towards reform was difficult, it should not give rise to panic (*TASS*, April 24).

On April 25, the plenum rejected an offer by Gorbachev to resign as general secretary after numerous Central Committee members, including RSFSR Communist Party First Secretary Ivan Polozkov, had blamed his policies for the USSR's economic and political crisis, Western agencies reported. The plenum ended after passing a resolution ordering the Central Committee Secretariat to invite political parties and movements for bilateral and multilateral political consultations (*TASS*,

April 25). The resolution followed an offer by Soviet Prime Minister Valentin Pavlov to include members of rival political groups and representatives of the republics in his government, and it expressed unconditional support for the declaration signed by Gorbachev and the leaders of nine republics on urgent measures to stabilize the Soviet economic and political situation (*TASS*, April 25).

Changes in CPSU Politburo

Personnel changes were approved at the plenum of the CPSU Central Committee held on April 24 and 25, TASS reported on April 26. Dzhumgalbek Amanbaev, appointed in early April to head the Communist Party in Kirgizia, was coopted to the Central Committee and elected to the Politburo; his predecessor, Absamat Masaliev, was dropped. The head of the Moldavian Communist Party, Grigore Eremei, appointed to lead the Moldavian Communist Party in February, and Major General Mikhail Surkov, appointed secretary of the All-Army Party Committee at the end of March, were also elected to the Politburo.

Oleg Baklanov lost his post as Central Committee secretary because of his appointment as deputy chairman of the Defense Council under the USSR president. Central Committee Secretary Valentin Falin was appointed chairman of the Central Committee's Commission for International Policy Issues. Finally, Stanislav Shatalin was deemed to have lost his Central Committee membership in view of the fact that he had left the CPSU (*TASS*, April 26).

Law on Election of RSFSR President Adopted

The RSFSR Supreme Soviet adopted a law on election of the RSFSR president, TASS reported. The law stipulated that any citizen of the RSFSR between the ages of thirty-five and sixty-five could be elected president. RSFSR political parties, trade unions, and public organizations could nominate candidates. According to Radio Mayak, these candidates would be officially registered once they had proved that they had the support of 100,000 voters and one-fifth of the deputies in the RSFSR Congress of People's Deputies. The president would be elected for a five-year term and would be allowed to serve no more than two terms. Any republican citizen over the age of eighteen would be eligible to vote. A 50-percent voter turnout was required to validate the election, and the candidate who received over 50 percent of the votes cast would be considered elected.

Debate on the draft of the law on the RSFSR presidency itself began on the same day, TASS reported. The draft stated that the president was the chief executive in the republic but did not have the right to dismiss the republican Supreme Soviet or the Congress of People's Deputies or suspend their activities.

Democratic Russia Registered

TASS reported that the Democratic Russia movement had been officially registered by the RSFSR Ministry of Justice. TASS said the movement had millions of supporters in Russia and was represented in almost all the republic's major cities.

Armenian Genocide Commemorated

Tens of thousands of Armenians marched through Erevan to the monument commemorating the victims of the 1915 genocide. For the first time, representatives of all political parties in the Armenian Supreme Soviet took part, as did representatives of the diaspora and the republican leadership, including Supreme Soviet Chairman Levon Ter-Petrossyan and Catholikos Vazgen I. A similar ceremony took place in Stepanakert, the capital of Nagorno-Karabakh, and in Moscow, where a requiem was held that day at the Armenian Apostolic Church to mark the anniversary of the Armenian genocide and in memory of Armenians killed by Azerbaijanis over the past three years. The ceremony was attended by members of the USSR and RSFSR Congresses of People's Deputies and by representatives of the Russian and Armenian intelligentsia (*TASS*, April 24).

Soviet Troops Take Over Bank Building in Vilnius

Radio Kaunas reported that Soviet MVD troops had taken over, without violence, a building in Vilnius housing the Naujoji Vilnius district branch of the Republic of Lithuania's Agroindustrial Bank and a commercial bank registered as a branch of the USSR Bank. The soldiers controlling the entrance to the building said they were following directives of USSR Minister of Internal Affairs Boriss Pugo to protect Soviet banks. President of the Lithuanian Supreme Council Vytautas Landsbergis telephoned USSR Deputy Prime Minister Vitalii Doguzhiev after the seizure. Doguzhiev told him there could be no question of the use of force and that all disputes had to be resolved by political means and economic agreements.

On April 25, Soviet troops occupied at least ten sites in Lithuania, all of them sports facilities formerly owned by the Soviet Armed Forces.

On April 26, the Lithuanian government accused the Soviet Armed Forces of perpetrating "terrorist acts" in seizing the buildings, Radio Vilnius reported. Landsbergis told a press conference that the government would not be able to guarantee that citizens would not retaliate if such actions continued (*AP*, April 26).

On April 29, Radio Independent Lithuania reported that the Naujoji Bank was conducting business illegally because it was not registered with the Lithuanian authorities. The Lithuanian government said that the bank was issuing credits and supplying funds to organizations and enterprises not registered in Lithuania and exacerbating inflation in the republic. The government warned that, if the USSR government did not halt these illegal activities, Lithuania would be forced to introduce its own currency.

Thursday, April 25

Soviet Leaders Commemorate Chernobyl' Disaster

In a statement issued on the eve of the fifth anniversary of the nuclear catastrophe at Chernobyl', Soviet President Mikhail Gorbachev declared that the world was just beginning to realize the seriousness of the social, medical, and psychological problems caused by the nuclear explosion. He thanked the United Nations for its work on the problems arising from the catastrophe and called on all nations to contribute what they could to efforts to remedy its effects (*TASS*, April 25).

Addressing the RSFSR Supreme Soviet, its chairman, Boris El'tsin, said that the disaster had been made worse by the irresponsible attitude of the Soviet authorities to those exposed to radiation, which, he said, showed the traditional Soviet indifference to people's fates, Radio Rossii reported. El'tsin also said that cooperation between the RSFSR, Ukraine, and Belorussia was essential in overcoming the consequences of Chernobyl', and he suggested that a resolution on the social protection of Chernobyl' victims be adopted by the RSFSR Supreme Soviet.

On April 26, the Ukrainian government expressed gratitude to all those who had offered solidarity and help in dealing with the consequences of the Chernobyl' disaster, Western agencies reported. The statement was issued as about 5,000 people, some wearing gas masks, marched by candlelight to the Cathedral of Saint Sofia in Kiev, where a commemoration service was held. In Belorussia, rallies were held in Minsk, Vitebsk, Gomel', Orsha, and Mogilev, Reuters reported. The RSFSR Supreme Soviet interrupted its session in Moscow to observe a minute of silence for the victims of Chernobyl' (*AP*, April 26).

US-Soviet Talks in Kislovodsk

Soviet Foreign Minister Aleksandr Bessmertnykh held talks with US Secretary of State James Baker in the

The USSR in April, 1991

Caucasus town of Kislovodsk, Western agencies reported. In an announcement issued after the meeting, Bessmertnykh said the Soviet Union was willing to cosponsor a Middle East peace conference with the United States. Bessmertnykh also said that the USSR and the United States had come closer to agreement on some important issues blocking US ratification of the Conventional Forces in Europe Treaty, such as the issue of redesignation.

Pugo Replaced as Head of Control Commission

TASS reported that USSR Minister of Internal Affairs Boriss Pugo had been replaced as head of the CPSU's Central Control Commission by his former first deputy, Evgenii Makhov. Pugo had asked to be relieved of the post because of his ministerial commitments.

Kvitsinsky Speaks of Soviet Interests in Eastern Europe

Addressing a conference on future European security in Prague, USSR Deputy Foreign Minister Yulii Kvitsinsky spoke of a natural Soviet zone of interest in Eastern Europe. While pledging that there could be no return to a policy of Soviet domination of Eastern Europe, he added: "The Soviet Union's legitimate interests in this region have historical and geopolitical roots and must be taken into account." Kvitsinsky also warned the conference that Europe could be heading for a fresh era of confrontation unless NATO responded "adequately" to the dissolution of the Warsaw Pact. Georgii Arbatov, the leading Soviet expert on the United States, who was also attending the conference, spoke of the dangers of "a fortress Soviet Union" emerging as a result of dissatisfaction in the Soviet Armed Forces about "losing" the satellite states (*The Guardian*, April 26).

Friday, April 26

Lushev Released

Soviet President Mikhail Gorbachev issued a decree releasing Army General Petr Lushev from his posts as first deputy defense minister and commander in chief of the Warsaw Pact Armed Forces.

RSFSR Cities Form League to Coordinate Policies

Eighty RSFSR cities, including Moscow, were reported to have formed a league to coordinate policies and defend their interests in dealing with higher and lower-level authorities, TASS reported. The foundation had been endorsed by the RSFSR Supreme Soviet.

THE USSR IN APRIL, 1991

German Defense Minister and Soviet General Meet

Commander in Chief of the Western Group of Forces General Matvei Burlakov and German Defense Minister Gerhard Stoltenberg discussed the problem of Soviet deserters and other issues, Reuters reported. Burlakov asked Germany not to give political asylum to some people whom he referred to as "criminals" who had deserted Soviet army units stationed on the territory of the former GDR. Some 200 Soviet soldiers had asked for political asylum in Germany since October, 1990.

Supreme Soviet Resumes Debate on Labor Amendment

The USSR Supreme Soviet decided to review an amendment to the Soviet Labor Code after Soviet President Mikhail Gorbachev had refused to sign it, TASS reported. The amendment, approved in March by the USSR Supreme Soviet, would have allowed management to dismiss employees without trade-union approval. Gorbachev rejected it on the grounds that it conflicted with the existing Soviet law on trade unions in accordance with which employees could be dismissed only with union consent.

The Supreme Soviet also adopted a law on safety in the workplace, which made managers responsible for breaches of safety regulations at enterprises run by the USSR ministries of defense and nuclear energy (*Radio Moscow*, April 26).

Uzbek Popular Front's Headquarters Closed

The headquarters of the Uzbek Popular Front "Birlik" in Tashkent were reported to have been closed by the Soviet authorities on the grounds that they represented a fire hazard. Bekjan Tashmuhammadov, a cochairman of "Birlik," told RFE/RL that he believed the authorities were using the issue of fire safety as a method of hindering the popular front's operations (RL Uzbek service, April 26).

Smirnov-Ostashvili Commits Suicide

Konstantin Smirnov-Ostashvili, who headed a radical faction of the "Pamyat'" organization, committed suicide, TASS reported on April 29. Smirnov-Ostashvili was serving a two-year sentence at a labor camp near Tver' following his conviction for violating a law prohibiting the incitement of interethnic enmity. He and a group of "Pamyat'" members shouted anti-Semitic slogans and smashed furniture during a meeting of the "April" society at the Central House of Writers in Moscow in January, 1990.

Surkov on Army's Communists

Major General Mikhail Surkov, secretary of the All-Army Party Committee, told Novosti that the number of service-

The USSR in April, 1991

men joining the Communist Party exceeded the number of those leaving. According to Surkov, in 1990 34,616 servicemen left the Party. Of those, roughly a third were officers, while 51 percent were soldiers from the ranks. During the same period, however, 41,474 servicemen joined the Party. Of those, according to Surkov, 40 percent were officers, 45 percent were cadets from military academies, and only 3 percent were from the ranks.

Saturday, April 27

Government Invites Political Parties for Consultations

The USSR Cabinet of Ministers ended two days of discussions on its anticrisis program and the Union treaty with members of various political parties, Radio Rossii reported. A wide range of groups participated, from Democratic Russia to the United Front of Workers and the Orthodox Monarchist Union.

Photographs of Riots in Novocherkassk Published

Komsomol'skaya pravda published photographs of the workers' riots in Novocherkassk in June, 1962, and a copy of a written promise from a soldier "to keep as a state secret" what he had witnessed during the suppression of the riots. Details of the riots and their violent suppression had been withheld from the public until June, 1989, when *Komsomol'skaya pravda* published an article about them giving a death toll of twenty-two to twenty-four persons..

El'tsin Formally Nominated for RSFSR Presidency

The Democratic Russia movement formally nominated RSFSR Supreme Soviet Chairman Boris El'tsin as its candidate for the RSFSR presidential elections to be held on June 12, TASS reported. While nominating El'tsin, several leaders of the movement criticized him for signing a joint declaration with Soviet President Mikhail Gorbachev on April 23.

Former Prime Minister Nikolai Ryzhkov told *Komsomol'skaya pravda* on April 30 that he had been urged by representatives of various industrial and agricultural enterprises as well as by public groups to challenge El'tsin for the post. Ryzhkov said he also had support from the CPSU.

On April 29, an estimated 15,000 people gathered in Moscow's Manezh Square to show support for El'tsin, AP reported. The rally was organized by Democratic Russia. The demonstrators also expressed support for the striking miners, and many people donated money to help them.

THE USSR IN APRIL, 1991

Members of Democratic Party of Russia Quit after Congress

A congress of the Democratic Party of Russia, which ended in Moscow on April 28, was marked by sharp debates and ended with the departure of several leading members of the party. The leadership of the party and an opposition group within the party, led by chess champion Gary Kasparov, proposed two different party programs for adoption at the congress. After the majority voted for the leadership's program, Kasparov and another opposition leader, Arkadii Murashov, announced their decision to leave the organization.

Soviet Democrats Favor Round-Table Talks

Writing in *The Independent*, the leader of the Russian Social Democratic Party, Oleg Rumyantsev, called for a coalition government and roundtable talks between Communists and democrats to prevent chaos. He criticized radical democrats and reactionary Communists for rejecting such a coalition, which, he said, could become an umbrella to replace the Communist Party monopoly, thus ensuring a peaceful transfer of power. Viktor Aksyuchits, leader of the Russian Christian Democratic Movement, also welcomed the idea of a roundtable (*Radio Rossii*, April 29).

Vladimir Pozner Criticizes Broadcasting Company

Soviet television commentator Vladimir Pozner strongly criticized the policies of the USSR State Company for Radio and Television Broadcasting chaired by Leonid Kravchenko. Pozner told the *Los Angeles Times* that Kravchenko had tried to make Soviet television into "presidential" television, which Pozner called unacceptable. He said that, for democracy to develop, alternative views were needed rather than a return to a government monopoly on broadcasting. Pozner, who had quit the company earlier in the year, also said that to have stayed would have meant betraying the principles of journalism.

Damage Caused by Spring Floods

Floodwaters covering 50,000 square kilometers of land in Volgograd Oblast caused estimated losses of 35 billion rubles and affected the lives of 40,000 people, Soviet television reported. It said 50,000 cattle would have to be moved ("Vremya," *Central Television*, April 27).

Tskhinvali Raion to Be Abolished

Radio Tbilisi reported that the Georgian Supreme Soviet had voted to abolish Tskhinvali Raion in the former South Ossetian Autonomous Oblast. The territory of the raion would be subsumed into the neighboring Gori Raion, which lies outside the borders of the South Ossetian Autonomous Oblast.

The USSR in April, 1991

Latvian-USSR Agreement on Budget

Radio Moscow quoted Latvian Prime Minister Ivars Godmanis as saying agreement had been reached with the Soviet authorities on Latvia's contribution to the Soviet budget. Latvia agreed to pay 350 million rubles and not the 4.2 billion that the USSR had previously demanded.

Baltic Communist Parties Hold Congress in Riga

TASS reported that a Congress of Baltic Communist Parties had been held in Riga. The congress called for the creation of a single body to help unite Communists against "concentrated pressure" from the state authorities in Lithuania, Latvia, and Estonia. It approved a document protesting against attempts by Western states to interfere in the affairs of the Baltic republics and asked the Soviet authorities to take preventive measures to limit "the diplomatic aggression from outside."

People's Front on Restoration of Latvian Independence

The council of the Latvian Popular Front drafted a plan providing for the transition period leading to the restoration of Latvian independence to be concluded and for *de facto* independence to be achieved in 1992. According to *Diena* of April 29, the plan called for the annulment of the declaration of July 21, 1940, establishing Soviet rule in Latvia; the revocation of the Latvian SSR Constitution and its replacement by legislation for the transition period; the reinstatement of the code of civil laws adopted in 1937; the reestablishment of citizenship of the Republic of Latvia; and the registration of Latvia's residents.

Sunday, April 28

Secret Memorandum Alleged to Have Been Signed

Kommersant reported that a secret memorandum had been signed at the joint meeting between Soviet President Mikhail Gorbachev and nine republican leaders on April 23, in which Gorbachev agreed to respect the precedence of republican law over all-Union law in the future. He allegedly also agreed that the Union treaty would be negotiated among the republics themselves, with the center playing a minimal role in the negotiations. The president's press center denied the existence of a secret memorandum in a separate statement broadcast by TASS on April 29.

Soviet Prime Minister in Brussels

Soviet Prime Minister Valentin Pavlov arrived in Brussels for talks with President of the European Commission

Jacques Delors to discuss European Community aid to Moscow, TASS reported. A meeting on April 29 focused on the general question of opening the doors of "the European House" to the Soviet Union (*Central Television*, April 30). Addressing reporters in Brussels, Pavlov said the Soviet economic crisis was an artificial one and not the result of misdirection. He added that he believed it was in the interests of both the West and the USSR to help end the crisis (*AFP*, April 29).

Soviet Foreign Trade in 1990

Ekonomika i zhizn' published foreign-trade statistics for 1990. The value of exports dropped from 68.8 billion rubles in 1989 to 60.9 billion rubles, while imports fell from 72.1 to 70.7 billion. In an accompanying commentary, it was noted that Soviet machinery exports were hopelessly uncompetitive on the world market and that in the mid-1980s only 29 percent of Soviet mass-produced fabricates corresponded to world norms.

Ethnic Clashes in Chechen-Ingushetia

Eight people were killed in clashes between Chechen-Ingush and Cossacks in a Cossack settlement eighty kilometers from Grozny in the Chechen-Ingush ASSR, TASS reported. Sixteen others received stab or bullet wounds. The incident took place outside a hospital where two Chechen-Ingush youths were recovering from injuries received in a fight with Cossacks the previous day.

Violence Reported in Nakhichevan

Renewed violence was reported in the Nakhichevan ASSR, where the raion center of Sadarak was shelled, causing injuries to thirteen people and damaging some houses. The republic's MVD forces repelled the attackers, who were not identified (*Radio Moscow*, April 30).

Monday, April 29

Earthquake Hits Georgia

An earthquake measuring 7.2 on the Richter scale hit central Georgia killing more than 144 people, injuring 300, and rendering 67,000 homeless. The epicenter was near Kutaisi, the second largest city in the republic. Georgian officials stated that seven villages had been completely destroyed as had more than 75 percent of buildings in Dzhava and in the small towns of Oni, Sachkhere, and Ambrolauri. The earthquake was also felt in Erevan (RFE/RL correspondent's report, April 29).

The USSR in April, 1991

A spokesman for the Brandenburg state police said that an eighteen-year-old Soviet sentry had been found shot dead near a military exercise zone outside the village of Schweinichen, about sixty miles northwest of Berlin. According to Reuters, the sentry's automatic rifle and sixty rounds of ammunition were missing, but there were no clues to the killer's identity.

Soviet Sentry Shot Dead in Germany

The Lithuanian government issued orders granting guards of the Lithuanian Defense Department, who were protecting the Supreme Council, the government building, the Bank of Lithuania and its branches, and other sites considered vital by the government, the same rights to use firearms when under attack as troops of the former Lithuanian Ministry of Internal Affairs, Radio Independent Lithuania reported.

Lithuanian Defense Department Guards Can Use Firearms

Tuesday, April 30

Yurii Balagurov, head of the section of the USSR State Bank responsible for money circulation, said in an interview with the German economic news service Ostwirtschaft Intern that Soviet government debts to the State Bank had passed a critical point. According to Balagurov, more than 50 percent of the State Bank's credits had had to be used for the budgets of the USSR central and republican governments, which had a negative effect on granting credits to companies. He also said that Soviet gold reserves were legally supposed to be controlled by the State Bank but were now in the hands of the USSR Finance Ministry (*DPA*, April 30).

Soviet Government Debts

The Soviet Union gained observer status on a committee of the General Agreement on Tariffs and Trade (GATT) charged with monitoring government action against the dumping of foreign imports at prices below those charged on the world market, Reuters reported. The USSR already had observer status on GATT's ruling council and had to apply separately for admission to individual committees.

USSR Gains Observer Status on GATT Committee

Addressing a press conference in Moscow, Yurii Blokhin, the chairman of the "Soyuz" group in the USSR Supreme Soviet, stated that his group had softened its critical opinion of Soviet President Mikhail Gorbachev after the signing of the April 23 declaration between Gorbachev

"Soyuz" Less Critical of Gorbachev

and the leaders of nine Soviet republics, AP reported. Blokhin said the joint statement conformed with the proposals of "Soyuz" and the group would support Gorbachev's efforts.

Shevardnadze Continues to Warn of Dictatorship

Former Soviet Foreign Minister Eduard Shevardnadze told journalists that the threat of dictatorship had grown recently, AP reported. He maintained that there were plans to "double or triple the size of the army" and to impose a nationwide state of emergency. Shevardnadze said a coup was possible if the government did not succeed in stabilizing the economy. He indicated that Soviet President Mikhail Gorbachev was not capable of keeping the army under firm control, and he did not exclude the possibility that military units could be used against Soviet citizens, even in Moscow, without Gorbachev's approval.

Drilling Starts at Tengiz

The Journal of Commerce said operations had started at a dozen wells in the Tengiz oil field in Kazakhstan. The Tengiz operation, which had been the subject of negotiations for several years, was expected to be a joint venture between the Chevron Corporation and the Kazakh SSR and was anticipated eventually to yield between 30 and 35 million tons of oil a year as well as natural gas.

Ukraine Votes to Lift Sales Tax on Consumer Goods

The Ukrainian Supreme Soviet voted to lift the national 5-percent sales tax on some food products and on basic consumer goods in the republic, Radio Moscow reported. The change was to take effect on May 1.

Roundtable/Free Georgia Official Killed in Adzharia

The leader of the Adzhar branch of the Roundtable/Free Georgia organization, Nodar Imnadze, was shot dead by security guards in the Adzhar Supreme Soviet building in Batumi, where he was attending a session of a task force set up to assist earthquake victims in Georgia. TASS reported that two other people had been wounded in the incident but gave no further details.

Moldavian Agreement on Social Protection

The Moldavian government and the republic's Trade-Union Council signed a second agreement on social protection, Radio Moscow reported. The government obligated itself to set a guaranteed minimum living standard for all categories of wage earners and to increase allocations for state-subsidized meals in educational and social institutions in proportion to price increases. This agreement supplemented the general agreement for 1991 signed by the republic's government and trade unions on April 15.

Last Independent Lithuanian Foreign Minister Dies

Juozas Urbsys, the last foreign minister of independent Lithuania, died at the age of ninety-five in Kaunas. He served as Lithuanian foreign minister from 1938 to 1940. He was arrested in 1940 and imprisoned in Siberia until Stalin's death. In 1988 he published his memoirs on the events of 1940, which became a best-seller. In 1989 he expressed his support for Lithuania's bid for independence and served as an example of the continuity between the prewar Republic of Lithuania and the current efforts to reestablish it (RFE Lithuanian service, May 1).

The Month of May

Wednesday, May 1

May Day Celebrations

The May Day celebrations on Moscow's Red Square, organized for the first time by official trade-union organizations alone rather than by the CPSU, were perfunctory and joyless. Western agencies reported on May 2 that about 50,000 workers had attended, carrying slogans reflecting the country's dire economic straits. Soviet President Mikhail Gorbachev was present atop the Lenin Mausoleum, together with Supreme Soviet Chairman Anatolii Luk'yanov, but he did not speak. Radio Moscow noted that security was tight. The USSR's democratic opposition boycotted the rally. Marchers included members of the conservative group "Edinstvo," who carried portraits of Stalin and anti-Semitic placards, Radio Rossii reported.

Chairman of the All-Union Confederation of Trade Unions, Vladimir Shcherbakov, addressed the parade and criticized the Soviet government for ineffective policies in dealing with the economic crisis (Western agencies, May 1).

Radio Rossii reported that Chairman of the Moscow City Soviet Gavriil Popov had been invited to attend the May Day rally in Red Square together with Gorbachev but had declined on the recommendation of the coordinating council of Democratic Russia.

Thousands of people gathered in Leningrad, carrying slogans criticizing the government's economic policies. A branch of "Pamyat'" also organized a demonstration parallel to the rally (Western agencies, May 1).

In Kiev, a crowd of tens of thousands, including many striking miners, marched through the center of the city shouting anti-Communist and proindependence slogans. They later gathered in front of the Lukyanivska prison to demand the release of Ukrainian Supreme Soviet deputy Stepan Khmara (*Radio Kiev*, May 1).

Kazakhstan, Uzbekistan, Tajikistan, Turkmenistan, and other parts of Central Asia also celebrated May Day with parades and rallies, TASS reported.

In Lithuania, where the authorities had earlier decided that May Day should not be a public holiday, 2,000–3,000 people gathered in Vilnius by the Lenin monument and heard Lithuanian Communist Party First Secretary Mykolas

THE USSR IN MAY, 1991

Burokevicius criticize the Lithuanian authorities, TASS reported. According to Radio Independent Lithuania, the Lithuanian Communist Party organized a rally in Klaipeda, but it was attended by considerably fewer people than in the past.

Three political parties marked May Day in Riga, TASS reported. The city Party committee held a meeting on the banks of the Daugava River; the Latvian Democratic Labor Party convened near the monument to the 1905 revolutionaries; and members of the Latvian Social Democratic Workers' Party gathered around the monument to the poet Janis Rainis, a leading personality in the party prior to and during Latvia's independence.

May Day commemorations in Estonia were quiet and uneventful, according to a report from Tallinn. Mart Linnart told RFE/RL that only about 2,000 demonstrators had gathered on Tallinn's Freedom Square.

A rally organized by the Moldavian Popular Front and allied groups in Kishinev on May 1, with 20,000 attending, expressed support for the demands of the striking miners in the RSFSR and Ukraine, Moldovapres reported. The rally also denounced the proposed Union treaty, which Moldavia had rejected, and expressed support for RSFSR Supreme Soviet Chairman Boris El'tsin.

Mines Transferred to RSFSR Jurisdiction

RSFSR Supreme Soviet Chairman Boris El'tsin signed a resolution transferring the jurisdiction of mines in the Kuzbass, Rostov, and Komi regions from the USSR government to the RSFSR government. The resolution had been approved by regional leaders and the Kuzbass Strike Committee. El'tsin said the resolution aimed to inject new life into the industry, and he described it as a sign of solidarity between the RSFSR and the miners (*Reuters*, May 1). Under the accord, El'tsin added, Kuzbass miners would be given full independence to choose their own forms of management and ownership, Western agencies reported on May 2. He said that mines would have to remit taxes and license fees for the coal they produced but could keep 80 percent of any hard currency they earned and use it to improve their working and living conditions. He also addressed a May Day rally of workers in Novokuznetsk, Reuters reported.

On May 2, miners in Donetsk decided to end their nine-week-old strike and to resume work on May 4 to prevent a further deterioration of the economic situation in the Soviet Union. But they also reserved the right to resume their strike if they were not satisfied with the results of a forthcoming session of the Ukrainian Supreme Soviet. The Donetsk miners favored a more autonomous government in Kiev (RFE/RL correspondent's report, May 2).

On May 3, RSFSR First Deputy Prime Minister Yurii Skokov said in Kemerovo that the USSR government had also agreed to place coal mines in Vorkuta, metallurgical enterprises in Cherepovets and Lipetsk, and the Uralmash machine-building enterprise under RSFSR jurisdiction.

The USSR Ministry of the Coal Industry and the official coal miners' trade union were shocked by the news of the transfer of mining enterprises from all-Union to RSFSR jurisdiction, Radio Rossii reported on May 7. A trade-union official told Radio Rossii that the news undermined the talks, which were nearing completion, between the ministry and the union over labor and social guarantees for miners in 1991. The official said that, if other republics followed the RSFSR's example, there would be no money to implement the agreement, and the existence of the all-Union ministry would be threatened.

Miners at six of Vorkuta's thirteen mines were still on strike, as were miners at thirty-four mines in the Kuzbass, AP reported on May 7. The chairman of the Vorkuta Strike Committee told Interfax that the strike had "practically failed to achieve anything," because it was clear that Soviet President Mikhail Gorbachev and the government would not resign. According to Radio Rossii, Kuzbass miners were waiting to see the document confirming the transfer of the mines to RSFSR jurisdiction. Interfax reported, however, that miners were demanding that control of all enterprises in the Kuzbass owned by the USSR Ministry of the Coal Industry be transferred to the RSFSR government.

On May 8, forty-one of the fifty-three mines in the Kuzbass voted in favor of returning to work. The remaining twelve mines, in Berezovo and Leninsk-Kuznetsky, proposed to hold a meeting on May 9 to decide whether to prolong their walkout, AP reported. In Vorkuta, all but two mines agreed to resume work on May 10, AP reported. On May 10, all but three pits in the Kuzbass resumed work.

In Donetsk, workers at a large cotton mill ended a twenty-day strike after being promised 150-percent wage increases (*Radio Moscow*, May 10).

Agreement on Social Protection Signed in Ukraine

The Ukrainian government and the council of the Ukrainian Independent Trade-Union Federation signed an agreement on social protection, Radio Moscow reported. The agreement called for the government to establish a new minimum living standard, to index wages to price increases by the end of the month, and to guarantee a plan

The USSR in May, 1991

for the distribution of goods in case supplies worsened. According to the radio report, wage increases were expected in 1991 for workers in the health, education, cultural, and social security sectors.

Soviet Troops Intervene as Armenian-Azerbaijani Conflict Worsens

The Armenian Supreme Soviet issued a statement accusing the central authorities of trying to draw Armenia into a war with Azerbaijan and of waging "state terrorism" against the republic, Radio Moscow reported.

Azerinform reported that Armenian forces had taken fourteen Soviet and Azerbaijani troops hostage in the village of Chaikend, not far from Getashen. The fourteen troops were in an armored vehicle, which was surrounded by Armenians when it became separated from a larger force conducting raids in the Khanlar Raion aimed at disarming illegal forces.

Postfactum reported on May 2 that at least fifty people had been killed in the recent clashes between Armenians and Azerbaijanis. The village of Getashen was attacked again and burned down. Soviet MVD troops were able to break through to a second village to which some of the inhabitants of Getashen had escaped, TASS reported. The troops brought out five dead and seven wounded.

Armenian Supreme Soviet Chairman Levon Ter-Petrossyan said that he had spoken about the situation with Soviet President Mikhail Gorbachev on May 1 and that Gorbachev had promised to try to stop the armed clashes, Reuters reported.

Ter-Petrossyan also spoke on Armenian television on May 2, saying that the USSR central government had been tardy in acting to prevent the conflict between Armenians and Azerbaijanis. He said he had repeatedly warned that something should be done about the plight of ethnic Armenians in Nagorno-Karabakh and in other parts of Azerbaijan. He told Reuters the same day that he had evidence that the attacks on April 29 had been planned by the Azerbaijani government and the USSR Ministry of Internal Affairs to hinder Armenian moves towards independence and to support Azerbaijani President Ayaz Mutalibov, who was using ethnic conflict to distract attention from social discontent in his republic.

David Vardanyan, chairman of the Armenian Supreme Soviet's Foreign Relations Commission, told reporters in Moscow that Azerbaijani forces were preventing doctors from reaching victims in the villages of Getashen and Martunashen (*AP*, May 2).

The coordinating committee of the Democratic Russia movement issued a protest over the use of Soviet MVD troops in the Armenian-Azerbaijani conflict. A member of the coordinating committee, RSFSR Supreme Soviet deputy Anatolii Shabad, told RFE/RL that the protest had called the use of Soviet troops on the Azerbaijani side "a crime" and claimed that responsibility for the deaths in the conflict lay with the USSR president and his subordinates (RFE/RL correspondent's report, May 2).

DPA quoted Postfactum on May 2 as reporting that the radical Armenian Union for National Self-Determination, headed by Paruir Airikyan, together with the Armenian Republican Party, had responded to the latest violence by calling for Armenia's immediate secession from the USSR. The call was made at a rally in Erevan on May 1 attended by 400,000 people.

Gorbachev convened a meeting in Moscow on May 3 between Armenian Supreme Soviet Chairman Ter-Petrossyan and Azerbaijani President Mutalibov to discuss the situation, Reuters reported.

Meanwhile, violence spread in Azerbaijan. The deputy head of Azerbaijan's mission in Moscow, Manaf Agaev, told a press conference that Armenian combatants had attacked villages near the Armenian border with Azerbaijan and destroyed many houses, killing one Azerbaijani and injuring two others. Armenpress denied the report and said that Azerbaijanis had fired on several villages in the early hours of the morning (*AFP*, May 3).

Reporting on two meetings with Gorbachev, Ter-Petrossyan stated that the Soviet president had ordered military sweeps along the Armenian-Azerbaijani border in an effort to end the killings provoked by the ethnic conflicts between the two republics (*Reuters*, May 4).

A joint statement issued by the USSR Ministry of Internal Affairs and Ministry of Defense claimed that the situation on the Armenian-Azerbaijani border and in Nagorno-Karabakh had deteriorated sharply. It condemned "terrorist acts by Armenian nationalists against military personnel" and laid the blame for the current crisis on Armenia. *Izvestia* quoted USSR MVD officials as describing the Armenian-Azerbaijani conflict as "civil war".

The Russian Information Agency reported that between 400 and 700 Soviet paratroopers had been airlifted to Armenia in fifteen helicopters to protect military personnel and installations. AP quoted Colonel General Yurii Shatalin, commander of the USSR MVD forces in the area, as telling *Izvestia* that his troops were guarding the Medzamor nuclear power station near Erevan against a possible attack by Armenian nationalists.

Meanwhile, up to 200,000 Armenians gathered in Erevan to mourn the victims of the fighting in Azerbaijan on April 29; funeral services were held for five of the dead, and a national day of mourning was observed in the republic, TASS reported.

On May 5, Ter-Petrossyan spoke by telephone with RSFSR Supreme Soviet Chairman Boris El'tsin, who promised to "follow carefully the course of events" in Azerbaijan and dispatched a group of RSFSR people's deputies to Armenia and Azerbaijan to investigate the circumstances of the previous week's violence, TASS reported.

On May 6, the USSR Supreme Soviet began debating an Armenian call for the convoking of a special session of the USSR Congress of People's Deputies to debate the deteriorating situation on the Armenian-Azerbaijani border, TASS reported. Azerbaijani Supreme Soviet Chairwoman Elmira Kafarova argued that the request should be rejected because it constituted "gross interference in Azerbaijan's affairs."

An Armenian deputy read a statement by Ter-Petrossyan to the USSR Supreme Soviet session, accusing Moscow of "waging war" on Armenia by attacking the village of Voskepar in northeastern Armenia on May 6. He claimed that helicopters, tanks, and heavy artillery had been used to attack the village and that dozens of people had been killed and homes burned by units of the Fourth Soviet Army. Moreover, he stated, helicopters had begun shooting at settlements near the town of Goris in southeastern Armenia. Armenpress, however, quoted the Soviet military commander in the Transcaucasus, General Valerii Patrikeev, as telling the Armenian MVD that the attack had been carried out by USSR MVD troops (*AP*, May 6).

Addressing a press conference on May 7, Ter-Petrossyan said that twenty-three people had died in the May 6 attack on the village of Voskepar, agencies reported. The regional police chief, Major Tigran Sarkisyan, told AP the death toll was fifteen, including eleven of his officers who had been attacked on a bus by Soviet and Azerbaijani forces; a Soviet army lieutenant told AP that the Armenians had fired first.

USSR First Deputy Minister of Defense Konstantin Kochetov denied in *Izvestia* that Soviet army units had used tanks, helicopters, and heavy artillery in the attack on Voskepar, explaining that the army units were not waging a war against the population but against illegally armed groups and that the helicopters had been used for reconnaissance flights.

Meanwhile, the USSR Supreme Soviet rejected Armenia's call for a special session of the USSR Congress of People's Deputies, TASS reported on May 7. It did decide, however, to send a special group from the USSR Prosecutor's Office to the border areas of Armenia and Azerbaijan to investigate the latest clashes. Kafarova told a news conference in Moscow that war had been declared on Azerbaijan and that all military action to date had taken place on Azerbaijani territory, Reuters reported.

On May 8, Azerbaijani President Mutalibov ruled out talks with Armenia to end the ethnic conflict, saying that there could be no compromise on the question of territorial claims and that the clashes had been caused by armed Armenian groups repeatedly launching attacks into Azerbaijan, Reuters reported. He also denied Armenian claims that Azerbaijani forces had attacked villages on the Armenian side of the border. On the same day, the Armenian Ministry of Internal Affairs said Armenian police troops were withdrawing from the border with Azerbaijan pursued by Azerbaijani MVD troops.

Meanwhile, the USSR redeployed its forces in the border region and issued new, more aggressive rules of engagement to Soviet troop commanders in the field, *Izvestia* of May 9 reported. According to Colonel General Shatalin, the troops were told to meet fire with fire. The newspaper report also said Soviet MVD troops would be concentrated in and around Nagorno-Karabakh; the Soviet army would cover the 700-kilometer-long Armenian-Azerbaijani border, and KGB border troops would be responsible for the border between Armenia and Azerbaijan's autonomous republic of Nakhichevan.

Krasnaya zvezda of May 9 said the military council of the Transcaucasian Military District had called on the Armenian leadership to stop "attacks by bandits on military personnel." The same day, the Armenian Ministry of Internal Affairs said Soviet troops had attacked the Armenian villages of Manashit and Uzlu in Azerbaijan, Reuters reported. Minister Arshot Manucharian added that the troops had also surrounded the Armenian village of Artzvashen, AP said.

One Soviet soldier was killed and eight wounded when they were ambushed on May 10 by Armenian extremists in Azerbaijan, the Azerbaijani Assa-Irada news agency reported. The Armenians, armed with grenades and machine guns, opened fire on a group of fourteen soldiers between the settlements of Kehen Gishlak and Tatli in the Akstafa area, near the Armenian border.

A spokeswoman for the Armenian Ministry of Internal Affairs, Bella Harutyunyan-Kozak, stated the same day that Soviet troops had threatened to destroy the Armenian village of Paravakar unless villagers surrendered arms hidden there (*Reuters*, May 10).

Meanwhile, the Presidium of the Armenian Supreme Soviet issued a statement expressing concern over the fate of Armenian villagers arrested during combat actions in the border area, TASS reported on May 10. The Armenian Communist Party Central Committee urged Gorbachev to call a full meeting of the CPSU Politburo to discuss the current crisis.

In an interview with Reuters on May 11, Armenian Prime Minister Vazgen Manukyan said that during the first three months of 1991 Armenia had received only 30 percent of the food supplies expected from Moscow and that over the past month the supply had deteriorated even further. Manukyan compared Moscow's action to the economic blockade imposed on Lithuania in 1990.

Spokeswoman Harutyunyan-Kozak said one person had been killed in a helicopter attack by Azerbaijanis on the Armenian village of Seisulan in Nagorno-Karabakh. She also stated that Soviet troops had withdrawn from the village of Paravakar after disarming the inhabitants and firing warning shots from tanks and helicopters (*AP*, May 11).

Speaking at a press conference in Moscow on May 12, Armenia's permanent representative Feliks Mamikonyan accused the USSR government of "trying to bring the Armenian people to their knees." He said that Armenia was putting its case to the UN but that, since many countries viewed Armenia as part of the USSR, any such request "would meet with a cold response" (*AP*, May 12).

TASS reported on May 12 that a Ukrainian Supreme Soviet delegation had arrived in Erevan to assess the situation there and attempt to find a way to stabilize it.

More violence was reported that day in Stepanakert, the capital of Nagorno-Karabakh, where a hotel used to lodge USSR troop commanders arriving in the city from Moscow came under fire twice. According to TASS, the situation there had deteriorated so sharply that the region's commander banned all motor traffic from the roads, except for vehicles with special passes, and extended the curfew by two hours.

Radio Moscow's World Service reported on May 13 that Manukyan and the Azerbaijani prime minister, Gasan Gasanov, had discussed the possibility of holding talks during a telephone conversation the previous day. TASS on May 13 quoted Azerbaijani Supreme Soviet Deputy Chairman Tamerlan Karaev as calling for negotiations between the two republics on condition that Armenia renounce its territorial claims to Nagorno-Karabakh.

In an interview in the May 13 issue of *Libération*, Armenian Supreme Soviet Chairman Ter-Petrossyan claimed to have proof that the Soviet troop actions in Armenia were part of an overall plan that was approved in advance by Gorbachev and that was aimed at strengthening the position of Azerbaijani President Mutalibov and demoralizing the Armenian population. He claimed that Armenia's land privatization program was already yielding results and that, whereas food prices were rocketing elsewhere in the USSR, in Armenia they remained stable. Ter-Petrossyan also reaffirmed that the only solution to the Nagorno-Karabakh issue was peaceful negotiation.

Mutalibov was said by Western agencies to have threatened to deport the Armenian population of Nagorno-Karabakh if they "turned their villages into bastions of resistance against the Azerbaijanis." TASS quoted an unnamed spokesman for the special military command in Nagorno-Karabakh as denying that USSR MVD troops planned to deport the Armenian population and that troops were guilty of brutality towards civilians.

TASS quoted USSR Deputy Minister of Internal Affairs Ivan Shilov as saying on May 15 that 112 civilians had been killed and 311 wounded in ethnic clashes in Armenia, Azerbaijan, and Georgia since the beginning of the year and that the number of refugees from those regions had reached 700,000.

Leaders of the Governing Council of Nagorno-Karabakh called on the UN and foreign governments to grant political asylum to Armenians to save their lives, according to TASS of May 15. The appeal claimed that Soviet and Azerbaijani units were engaged in "genocide" against the Armenian people. TASS said that 200 people had been detained during the previous twenty-four hours by Soviet army and Azerbaijani MVD units.

A TASS report of May 17 said a court in Azerbaijan had sentenced three people to up to fifteen years in prison for attacks on Armenians in Baku in January, 1990.

Ter-Petrossyan talked by telephone with USSR KGB Chairman Vladimir Kryuchkov, who admitted that Armenians were being dealt with harshly in Azerbaijan and along the border with Armenia. Ter-Petrossyan quoted Kryuchkov as saying the Azerbaijani police would not participate in any further action in the region with Soviet forces, RSFSR television reported on May 16.

On May 17, Ter-Petrossyan said that more than 1,000 Armenian women, children, and old people had been rounded up and deported from Nagorno-Karabakh's Gadrut Raion to Goris Raion on the Armenian border, where there was no housing available (*Izvestia*, May 18). A TASS report the same day said an Azerbaijani policeman had been killed and two others wounded by ethnic Armenian paramilitary forces during a raid by Azerbaijani police and Soviet forces in Martuni and Mardakert Raions in Nagorno-Karabakh.

The USSR in May, 1991

The head of the Armenian government mission in Moscow, Mikit Kazaryan, claimed on May 18 that thousands of Armenians were being forcibly deported from Nagorno-Karabakh. He said 1,500 Armenians had been deported at gunpoint to Armenia; another 1,200 Armenians had been forced to leave their homes in Nagorno-Karabakh and were now living in tents. Shahen Karamanoukyan, an adviser to Ter-Petrossyan, said residents of sixteen predominantly Armenian villages had been deported (RFE/RL correspondent's report, May 19).

On May 18, Radio Erevan read out a statement adopted by the Latvian Supreme Council Presidium that expressed alarm over the bloodshed in Nagorno-Karabakh, Armenia, and Azerbaijan; condemned the use of force by the Soviet military against Armenians in Nagorno-Karabakh; and called for the establishment of an international commission under UN auspices to seek to resolve the conflict between Armenia and Azerbaijan.

Armenia's State Security Committee protested about the way in which several organs of the Soviet media, in particular *Pravda* and the television news program "Vremya," had reported on developments in Nagorno-Karabakh, saying their reports were intended "to hide the truth from the public" (*TASS*, May 19).

On May 22, TASS reported that Armenia and Azerbaijan had started forming special units to prevent violence along their common border. The groups were being set up with the assistance of the USSR KGB and included local officials as well as police and KGB officers from both republics.

The same day, the Azerbaijani Supreme Soviet accused the RSFSR of trying to interfere in the dispute with Armenia over Nagorno-Karabakh. A statement in Baku professed "bewilderment" at the decision of the RSFSR Congress of People's Deputies to discuss the issue during its current session (*Central Television*, May 22).

Gorbachev discussed the conflict in the Transcaucasus with the Communist Party first secretaries of Armenia and Azerbaijan and told them that the USSR central leadership would support every effort to find constructive solutions within the framework of the law, TASS reported on May 22. Gorbachev added that illegal armed groups in the conflict region were a serious obstacle to a settlement.

On May 22, First Deputy Chairman of the Latvian Supreme Council Dainis Ivans and Chairman of the Latvian Supreme Council's Commission on Defense and Internal Affairs Talavs Jundzis reported to the Council on their visit to Armenia. Both men stressed the role of the Soviet Armed Forces in the violence in Azerbaijan and Armenia and expressed concern that such conflicts might be provoked in the Baltic area. Jundzis said he had learned that Azerbaijani OMON detachments, rather than the Soviet military, had been responsible for "the most despicable actions against the Armenians in Nagorno-Karabakh," Radio Riga reported on May 23.

TASS reported on May 24 that four Soviet soldiers had been involved in an exchange of fire when more than twenty people attacked an Armenian village in Nagorno-Karabakh; one soldier and two of the attackers were killed.

Thursday, May 2

Yazov Visits China

Soviet Defense Minister Marshal Dmitrii Yazov arrived in Beijing for the first official visit to China by a USSR defense minister in the history of Sino-Soviet relations, Reuters reported. TASS quoted the head of the Soviet Defense Ministry's Information Directorate, General Valerii Manilov, as saying Yazov's visit marked a normalization of relations.

Yazov met on May 3 with Chinese Defense Minister Qin Jiwei. TASS reported that they had discussed ways of continuing the positive trend towards closer Sino-Soviet contacts and resolving outstanding problems concerning the Sino-Soviet border.

On May 4, Yazov spoke about Soviet military reforms and issues relating to security and peace in the Asia-Pacific region during a speech to the Chinese Defense Academy in Beijing, TASS reported (*AP*, May 6). Yazov met on May 7 with Chinese Prime Minister Li Peng and Communist Party General Secretary Jiang Zemin, TASS reported on May 8.

USSR Joins World Conservation Union

The USSR joined the World Conservation Union, an environmental protection group composed of governments and private groups based in the Swiss city of Gland. The union's members include fifty-four countries and some 500 bodies, such as the World Wide Fund for Nature and Greenpeace (*Reuters*, May 2).

Soviet Oil Production Declines in April

The International Energy Agency said that Soviet oil production had dropped 1.1 million barrels a day, nearly 10 percent, in April. Soviet oil production problems were attributed to outdated equipment, transportation problems, and extraction difficulties in some areas (*AFP*, May 2).

THE USSR IN MAY, 1991

A ferry service between Japan's Hokkaido Island and Sakhalin resumed for the first time since World War II. According to a TASS report, the service to the Soviet port of Korsakov first began in the 1920s but was discontinued at the end of the war, when Korsakov became a Soviet naval port closed to foreign ships. The port was reopened in February, 1991.

Japanese-Soviet Ferry Service Resumes

Uzbek President Islam Karimov, who in February rejected a draft of the USSR Union treaty, accepted the latest draft for Uzbekistan. He declared in an interview with *Izvestia* that his position had changed after many debates between republican leaders and the USSR government over the treaty. In his opinion, there was a new consensus that the Union treaty should be built around the powers of the republican governments, with the central government being given certain powers and all others falling to the republics.

Uzbek President Favors Union Treaty

The German government said Soviet troops stationed in eastern Germany had polluted the bases they would leave behind by 1994. German newspaper reports described pollution at over 1,000 Soviet-held sites as "catastrophic." Oil and ammunition had been dumped on the ground, and, according to *Die Welt*, Soviet troops had been ordered to cover up the damage in an attempt to minimize Soviet costs.

Pollution at Soviet Bases in Eastern Germany

TASS reported that a Russian National Party, headed by monarchist Aleksei Brumel', had been created and had urged the RSFSR Supreme Soviet to invite Grand Duke Vladimir Kirillovich to the USSR. The agency quoted Brumel' as saying the party's aim was to introduce a constitutional monarchy in Russia and to make Vladimir Kirillovich Russian tsar.

Russian National Party Set Up

Friday, May 3

RSFSR Supreme Soviet Chairman Boris El'tsin declared on Soviet television that introducing a state of emergency or direct presidential rule under current conditions would be "political madness" and would only produce chaos. El'tsin said what was needed was the implementation of joint "crisis measures." Referring to the joint declaration signed by nine republican leaders and Soviet President

El'tsin Speaks on Television

Mikhail Gorbachev on April 23, El'tsin noted that the declaration had recognized that Latvia, Lithuania, Estonia, Georgia, and Armenia should be able to choose freely whether to join the Union (*TASS*, May 4). El'tsin also hailed the striking Soviet coal miners, saying that the movement had provided a counterweight to rising reactionary forces (*Reuters*, May 5)

Pavlov Meets with Rupert Murdoch

Soviet Prime Minister Valentin Pavlov met with international media tycoon Rupert Murdoch, TASS reported. Murdoch, who owns several major newspapers and television organizations in a number of countries, was visiting the USSR at the invitation of the All-Union Copyright Agency. The two men discussed opportunities for Murdoch's news corporation and Soviet organizations to work together. Murdoch also met with Soviet President Mikhail Gorbachev.

More People Killed in South Ossetia

TASS reported that armed Georgians had killed seven more people in South Ossetia. The population of South Ossetia also protested against the decision taken by the Georgian Supreme Soviet on April 27 to abolish the Znauri and Tskhinvali Raions.

On May 8, TASS reported that violence was continuing in the region and that people with gunshot wounds were still arriving at hospitals. TASS also confirmed a Radio Tbilisi report of May 8 according to which Georgian President Zviad Gamsakhurdia and the Presidium of the Georgian Supreme Soviet had sent letters to Soviet President Mikhail Gorbachev, to RSFSR Supreme Soviet Chairman Boris El'tsin, and to the USSR Supreme Soviet rejecting an effort by the South Ossetian Supreme Soviet to restore the autonomous status of the republic and make it part of the RSFSR.

On May 15, the Georgian Supreme Soviet declared a state of emergency in Tskhinvali. Sakinform said the measure would be in effect for one month and would include a nightly curfew in effect from 2200 to 0700 local time.

TASS also said fourteen people had been injured by gunfire in the village of Nikozi and in small villages in the Tskhinvali, Znauri, and Leningori Raions.

On May 31, an officer of the USSR MVD troops was killed in an ambush by unknown gunmen in South Ossetia, TASS reported on June 2. The head of an investigatory group of the USSR Prosecutor's Office, Aleksei Vinogradov, told TASS that Lieutenant Andrei Pitin had been shot when a vehicle carrying him and other

The USSR in May, 1991

USSR MVD troops was fired on as it moved through the outskirts of the South Ossetian capital, Tskhinvali.

Latest AIDS Count

The chairman of the Soviet Association to Combat AIDS told Radio Moscow that to date there were 623 reported cases of Soviet citizens carrying the AIDS virus and 586 reported carriers among foreign residents of the USSR.

Georgia Sets Fixed Prices

Georgian President Zviad Gamsakhurdia issued a decree setting fixed prices for some basic goods and lifting the national 5-percent sales tax on some food and services (*Sakinform*, May 3).

Rally in Vilnius

About 200,000 people gathered in Vingis Park in Vilnius for a rally called by "Sajudis." The rally adopted an appeal read by "Sajudis" Chairman Juozas Tumelis, calling on leaders of the world's nations, parliaments, and political parties and movements to realize that the question of Lithuanian independence was not an internal matter of the USSR and that silence would only encourage Soviet troops to perpetrate new acts of repression. It declared that Lithuania's political and civic determination to achieve independence was unshakable. The affairs of Lithuania should be discussed at the United Nations, in which Lithuania should be entitled to membership as in all international organizations, the appeal stated.

Lithuanian Social Democratic Congress

The Lithuanian Social Democratic Party held its second congress in Vilnius following its reestablishment in 1989. The congress amended the party's program and discussed at length its relations with the Lithuanian Democratic Labor Party (the former independent Lithuanian Communist Party). It elected a thirty-four-member council with Lithuanian Supreme Council deputy Aloyzas Sakalas as its chairman (RFE Lithuanian service, May 6).

Attack on Former OMON Chief in Riga

TASS reported that Cheslav Mlynnik, former head of the OMON unit in Riga, had been shot in his apartment. His wounds were not life-threatening. Initial reports by investigators did not reveal whether the shooting was politically motivated, though it occurred on the first anniversary of Latvia's independence declaration.

Sunday, May 5

RSFSR KGB Created

Agreement on the creation of an RSFSR KGB was reached during a meeting between RSFSR Supreme Soviet Chairman Boris El'tsin and USSR KGB Chairman Vladimir Kryuchkov, TASS reported. The Presidium of the RSFSR Supreme Soviet appointed Major General Viktor Ivanenko acting chairman of the RSFSR KGB. Until recently, Ivanenko had been deputy head of the USSR KGB Inspectorate. The chairman of the RSFSR Supreme Soviet Committee on Security, Sergei Stepashin, said the RSFSR KGB would initially have 350–400 officers. The complete delineation of duties between the USSR KGB and the RSFSR KGB would be defined after the Union treaty had been signed, he added. The main functions of the RSFSR KGB would be control over the situation in the republic, prevention of anticonstitutional activity, and the fight against organized crime (see *Kommersant*, No. 19).

Gorbachev Meets Commission on Army Deaths

Soviet President Mikhail Gorbachev discussed the results of work completed by a commission investigating the causes of "death and traumatism" suffered by servicemen in peacetime, TASS reported. Gorbachev recommended that the drafting of legislation on military reform and on ensuring the social security of servicemen be speeded up. It was also decided that an oversight body should be created to ensure proper observance of soldiers' rights (*TASS*, May 5).

Landslide in Uzbekistan

A landslide in the village of Chigiristan, fifteen kilometers from Uzbekistan's coal-mining center Angren, killed sixty-four people. May 6 was declared a day of mourning in the republic. Uzbek President Islam Karimov pledged aid to the victims of the landslide, which occurred after torrential rain in the area (*TASS*, May 5).

Press Day Observed

Interviewed by "Vremya" in connection with the Day of the Press, Chairman of the USSR State Committee for Publishing and the Press Mikhail Nenashev said he would ask Soviet President Mikhail Gorbachev and the Cabinet of Ministers to review the problems of the Soviet press. These included a sharp rise in the price of paper and the doubling of prices for deliveries of periodicals; the resulting increase in prices for periodicals meant that the Soviet press had lost 33 percent of its subscribers. "Vremya" stressed, however, that the number of new periodicals had still increased. In 1991 alone 500 new newspapers and journals had been created. Radio Rossii marked the Day of the Press by broadcasting several commentaries on how the central Soviet leadership had made it difficult for the RSFSR to create its own media network.

Gorbachev Meets Japanese Delegation

A Japanese delegation headed by Michio Watanabe, a member of Japan's ruling Liberal Democratic Party, met with Soviet President Mikhail Gorbachev, who declared after the talks that, despite a lack of concrete results from his visit to Tokyo in April, he was happy about the political dialogue, which had been conducted in a spirit of goodwill, TASS reported. TASS quoted Watanabe as saying Gorbachev's visit was viewed in Japan as an event of historical importance, but he also expressed regret that no agreement had been reached on the dispute over the Kurile Islands.

RSFSR Supreme Soviet Chairman Boris El'tsin met with the Japanese delegation on May 6 and stressed that the RSFSR was ready to cooperate directly with Japan, "TSN" reported on May 7. He said such cooperation could only help the RSFSR and the country as a whole to emerge from the current crisis.

Baltic Leaders in the United States

President of the Lithuanian Supreme Council Vytautas Landsbergis arrived in Washington for a visit aimed at gaining support for Lithuania's independence drive and at discussing the problems of the Baltic republics at the international level (*TASS*, May 5). Speaking at the US Chamber of Commerce, Landsbergis called for expanded economic ties between the United States and Lithuania to aid the latter's efforts to implement economic and political reform. Landsbergis expressed the hope that Lithuania would reach agreement with the USSR on joint control of borders and acceptance of Lithuanian-issued visas (RFE Lithuanian service, May 6).

On May 7, Landsbergis, Estonian Prime Minister Edgar Savisaar, and Latvian Prime Minister Ivars Godmanis spoke at a hearing of the US Commission on Security and Cooperation in Europe. The leaders pleaded for more US support for their efforts to restore full independence and for the holding of an international conference on the Baltic question. Godmanis stressed the importance of "internationalizing" the Baltic question, especially through the Conference on Security and Cooperation in Europe. He requested aid to improve the industrial infrastructure in Latvia so as to preclude the possibility of major strikes and help achieve economic independence from Moscow, Radio Riga reported on May 8.

The presence of the Baltic leaders affected the debate on a Senate resolution to extend a 1.5-billion-dollar credit to the USSR to purchase US grain. The Baltic leaders urged that economic aid should go not to the center but to the republics, since they faced the threat of an economic blockade by the Soviet government. Landsbergis said the United States should refuse to sign any agreements with the USSR until Moscow kept its promise to hold independence talks and pledged not to use force (RFE/RL correspondent's report, May 7).

The same day, members of the US Congress and the three Baltic leaders signed a charter establishing an Interparliamentary Group to Support Human Rights and Democracy in the Baltic States.

On May 8, the leaders of the three Baltic republics met with US President George Bush, Reuters reported. After the talks, Godmanis said they had asked Bush to support them if Moscow imposed an economic blockade after signing the Union treaty with nine other republics. US Secretary of State James Baker, who also attended the meeting, suggested that a new mechanism for resolving the independence question should be found that would enable the USSR to "save face." Bush promised to tell Soviet President Mikhail Gorbachev that it would be very useful for the USSR to have three very good neighbors on its border. Landsbergis, Godmanis, and Savisaar also declared that the meeting was of great importance, "perhaps symbolical," because it defined the three countries as a specific region in which the United States had an interest (*Reuters*, May 8).

On May 8, Landsbergis flew to Los Angeles where he met on May 9 with former US President Ronald Reagan and spoke by telephone with Richard Nixon (*The Voice of America*, Lithuanian service). Speaking at the Los Angeles World Affairs Council on May 10, Landsbergis expressed his disappointment that the United States and other Western governments were dragging their feet in recognizing Lithuania's independence because they were concerned about Gorbachev's position.

Kalinin Monument Dismantled in Estonia

TASS said a monument to Mikhail Kalinin had been dismantled in Tallinn and his name removed from a street and an administrative district there. Kalinin was chairman of the USSR Supreme Soviet from 1938 to 1946.

THE USSR IN MAY, 1991

CPSU Secretariat Meets

CPSU Deputy General Secretary Vladimir Ivashko was quoted by Radio Moscow as saying at a meeting of the CPSU Secretariat that the Central Committee plenum of April 24–25 had shown that Communists were alarmed at "intensifying ideological confrontation, incipient factionalism, and the existence of a tangible threat to Party unity." Ivashko went on to say that at present the main danger to the CPSU came from "the growing pressure to oust Party organizations from the workplace." Ivashko also told the Secretariat that, whereas 1.8 million Communists had left the CPSU in 1990, a total of 587,000 had quit in the first three months of 1991; he also revealed that 108,000 people had joined the Party in 1990 and 46,000 had joined in the first three months of 1991.

Monday, May 6

USSR Supreme Soviet Adopts Law on Chernobyl' Compensation

The USSR Supreme Soviet unanimously passed a law to compensate citizens affected by the Chernobyl' nuclear accident. TASS said the law provided money and other benefits for people whose health had suffered or who had had to be evacuated from contaminated areas. The chairman of the USSR Supreme Soviet's Ecology Committee declared that the new law was in line with similar legislation already adopted by Ukraine and Belorussia. For the text of the law, see *Izvestia*, May 21, 1991.

127,000 Imprisoned under Antispeculation Law

An article carried by *Novaya stroitel'naya gazeta* said that about 127,000 people were in prison in the USSR after being convicted of engaging in illegal private business activities, including speculation and black-marketeering. It added, however, that some of them had been unjustly convicted. The article also observed that, instead of carrying out a policy of promoting free trade, the Soviet government was actually discouraging it by imposing restrictions and bans. It said an organization had been formed to defend the rights of private businessmen and to try to change the Soviet population's negative attitude towards the market.

Shevardnadze on US Tour

Former Soviet Foreign Minister Eduard Shevardnadze began a speaking tour of the United States in Washington, where he met with US President George Bush and appealed for US financial aid for the USSR. Shevardnadze reassured Bush that the threat of dictatorship in the Soviet Union was decreasing, AP reported.

At a luncheon meeting with *The Washington Post* on May 8, Shevardnadze stressed that his decision to resign had been the result not only of attacks by his adversaries but also of the failure of anybody to defend him or reject these criticisms.

Soviet-German Treaty on Troop Withdrawal in Force

The treaty covering the Soviet troop withdrawal from Germany went into force with the exchange of ratification documents in Moscow, DPA reported. German Foreign Minister Hans-Dietrich Genscher said in Bonn that the move laid the groundwork for the orderly withdrawal of Soviet troops by the end of 1994. Genscher added that more than 30,000 of a total of 380,000 Soviet soldiers had already left German territory and that 100,000 military personnel and 50,000 civilian dependents would have left by the end of 1991. Genscher said he hoped the troops would leave with feelings of friendship.

Moiseev on East-West Relations

Chief of the General Staff of the Soviet Armed Forces General Mikhail Moiseev told TASS that, despite some complications, East-West relations were moving from confrontation to cooperation. Moiseev nevertheless cautioned that the practical realization of "the Soviet model of security" had been problematic, and he pointed to the dissolution of the Warsaw Pact and the fact that the Soviet Union now faced the NATO alliance alone. Moiseev said that Moscow had completed its unilateral troop reduction of 500,000 men, and he called for a further easing of the arms race and improved relations between East and West.

Threat of Strike in Latvia

Radio Riga said pro-Soviet representatives of forty-two work collectives in Latvia who opposed an independent Republic of Latvia were threatening to stage a strike on May 14 unless the government agreed to their demands. These included signing the new USSR Union treaty and withdrawing recently instituted price increases. The Latvian Communist Party was behind the strike call, the radio report said.

On May 8, the representatives of the forty-two collectives, strike committees, and public organizations presented their demands to the Latvian government and parliament, Radio Moscow reported. In addition to their other demands, they also called for the reversal of the government's decision to return land to those dispossessed by the USSR's Communist government since 1940.

THE USSR IN MAY, 1991

RSFSR Supreme Soviet Discusses Media Coverage of Its Activities

The RSFSR Supreme Soviet opened a session with criticism of central Soviet media coverage of its debates, especially television coverage, "Vremya" reported on May 7. RSFSR deputies recommended that in future the press center of the RSFSR Supreme Soviet prepare its own reports on parliamentary sessions for subsequent dissemination by the media. Many journalists present at the session criticized the suggestion on the grounds that it amounted to an attempt to introduce media censorship. The RSFSR Supreme Soviet also approved in principle a draft law on the procedure for recalling deputies. According to the law, a deputy would lose his position in the Supreme Soviet if more than half of the electorate participating in the voting supported the recall, "Vremya" reported.

A commission was set up to investigate "blackmail and threats" made against Deputy Chairman of the RSFSR Supreme Soviet Svetlana Goryacheva, "Vremya" reported. In February, Goryacheva had prepared a formal statement demanding the replacement of RSFSR Supreme Soviet Chairman Boris El'tsin for his attack on Soviet President Mikhail Gorbachev. This action provoked sharp criticism from El'tsin's supporters. Goryacheva claimed that in the course of this criticism threats were made against her and members of her family (see *Sovetskaya Rossiya*, May 1).

Tuesday, May 7

USSR Gives Building Contracts for Troop Housing to Turkish and Finnish Firms

The Soviet Union announced that contracts for the building of the first 3,000 apartments for Soviet troops returning from Germany had been given to three Turkish firms and a Turkish-Finnish consortium, DPA reported on May 8. Germany, which was financing the construction at a cost of 7.8 billion marks, had hoped that the contracts would go to companies in the former GDR, and an economic spokesman for the opposition Social Democrats called on Foreign Minister Hans-Dietrich Genscher to intervene immediately in the situation. The state secretary of the German Economics Ministry, Klaus Beckman, said Germany might withhold the money if the contracts did not go to German firms. German government spokesman Dieter Vogel said the cabinet had in fact decided not to accept Moscow's plan and had made a counterproposal involving four German companies (*DPA*, May 9).

On May 20, German and Soviet officials opened talks in Moscow on the dispute, DPA reported. On May 22, Bonn announced the project would now include German firms, which would be awarded a 60-percent share in the building of the first three sites, at Zhaikovka and Vladikavkaz in the RSFSR and at Krivoi Rog in Ukraine. More than half of the contracts awarded to German firms would go to concerns in the former GDR. The value of the first phase of the plan was put at 570 million deutsche marks (RFE/RL correspondent's report, May 22).

Gorbachev Appoints Advisers

TASS reported the appointment by Soviet President Mikhail Gorbachev of six advisers. They were: jurist and Vice President of the USSR Academy of Sciences Vladimir Kudryavtsev; former Presidential Council member and likewise Vice President of the USSR Academy of Sciences Yurii Osipyan; Director of the Institute of World Economics and International Relations Vladlen Martynov; Ukrainian writer and Vice President of the Council of Nationalities of the USSR Supreme Soviet Boris Oleinik; and economists Leonid Abalkin and Yurii Yaremenko.

USSR Railways Minister Resigns

Radio Moscow reported the resignation of Nikolai Konarev, USSR minister of railways since November, 1982, without giving any reason for it. The USSR Supreme Soviet approved the appointment of Leonid Matyukhin, a USSR people's deputy and CPSU member who had been head of the Nizhnii Novgorod Railways Administration, to replace him.

Army General Lobov Relieved of Duties

TASS reported that Army General Vladimir Lobov had been relieved of his duties as Warsaw Pact chief of staff. Lobov, who assumed the Warsaw Pact post in January, 1989, had long been known as a hard-liner.

Ryzhkov Enters Race for RSFSR Presidency

Former Prime Minister Nikolai Ryzhkov officially entered the race for the RSFSR presidency. He told a press conference that his election platform would be largely based on his former government's program, which had been rejected by Soviet President Mikhail Gorbachev as being too cautious on reform.

USSR-Vietnam Talks

Soviet President Mikhail Gorbachev expressed satisfaction with the state of Soviet-Vietnamese relations during talks with Vietnamese Prime Minister Do Muoi. TASS reported that the talks were characterized by "benevolence and mutual understanding."

The USSR in May, 1991

Nguyen Van Linh, head of the Vietnamese Communist Party, arrived in Moscow on May 8. He held talks with Gorbachev on economic and foreign-policy cooperation, the civil war in Cambodia, and Sino-Soviet and Sino-Vietnamese relations. The main focus of the talks, however, was the roles of the two countries' Communist Parties and their adaptation to "new realities," TASS reported.

Reform Fund Created in Kazakhstan

TASS, quoting *Trud*, reported the creation in Kazakhstan of a republican fund for economic and social reform. The objective of the fund, which was set up on the initiative of Kazakh President Nursultan Nazarbaev, was to ensure financial support for projects to introduce market mechanisms and attract Soviet and foreign expertise. Among the creators of the fund were major industrial enterprises, which were expected to supply financing.

Council of Cossack Atamans Discusses Conflict with Ingush

At a press conference, Aleksandr Martynov, ataman of the Union of Cossacks, called the recent clashes between Cossacks and Ingush in the Sunzha Raion of Checheno-Ingushetia part of a deliberate attempt on the part of the Ingush "to dislodge the Cossacks from their historic territory," TASS reported. The press conference was held to report on an extraordinary session of the Council of Atamans held in Moscow on May 6 and 7 to discuss the clashes. The session adopted a resolution calling on the all-Union government to declare a state of emergency in the area and start disarming "Ingush bandit formations."

The resolution also suggested that former Cossack conscripts should be called up to serve as USSR MVD troops in the area of conflict and stated that the Cossacks would seek the restoration of the Sunzha Autonomous Cossack Okrug, which was abolished after the revolution, and compensation for the material damage suffered by families during the recent clashes.

Law on Rehabilitation of Deported Peoples Adopted

The RSFSR Supreme Soviet adopted a law on the rehabilitation of deported peoples, recognizing their right to restore any national-state formations that existed prior to their deportation. The text of the law was published in *Sovetskaya Rossiya*.

Congress of Deputies of Peoples of North

The first congress of deputies of the peoples of the North, Siberia, and the Far East ended on May 7, TASS reported. The congress, held with the active assistance of the USSR and RSFSR Supreme Soviets, decided to set up a deputies'

Zyuganov Attacks Yakovlev

assembly of the numerically small peoples of the region and a special fund for their survival and development.

Gennadii Zyuganov, Politburo member of the RSFSR Communist Party, attacked presidential adviser Aleksandr Yakovlev in an open letter published in *Sovetskaya Rossiya*. Yakovlev had previously accused the conservative RSFSR Communist Party of undermining reform. Zyuganov held Yakovlev responsible for the rise of nationalism and criticized him for having destroyed the ideological basis of Soviet society and for abolishing censorship. He charged that during Yakovlev's tenure as head of the crime-fighting group in the Presidential Council crime had increased in the country.

Wednesday, May 8

Pavlov on Importance of Meeting Consumer Demand

Soviet Prime Minister Valentin Pavlov told the USSR Cabinet of Ministers that economic performance in 1991 had to be measured by how well consumer demand was satisfied and not on the basis of meeting a plan. Radio Moscow quoted him as saying that the USSR's strongest enterprises should be the engine of reform and that the Soviet government should begin to rely on decisions made by these enterprises' leaders, not on those made by economic bureaucrats.

Bessmertnykh on Tour of Middle East

Soviet Foreign Minister Aleksandr Bessmertnykh arrived in the Syrian capital, Damascus, on the first leg of a tour of the Middle East aimed at persuading Israel and its Arab neighbors to engage in peaceful negotiations. Bessmertnykh held talks with Syrian President Hafiz al-Assad and Syrian Foreign Minister Farouq al-Shara. He declared after the meeting that the USSR would not abandon its traditional support for Arab causes and that his government still supported the rights of the Palestinian people (*AFP*, May 8). On May 9, Bessmertnykh went to Amman for talks with Jordan's King Hussein. He declared there that Israel's settlements in the occupied Arab territories were blocking efforts to convene a Middle East peace conference and that he could not foresee any conference as long as the Jewish settlements existed (*Reuters*, May 9).

Bessmertnykh held talks on May 10 with Israeli Prime Minister Yitzhak Shamir and Israeli Foreign Minister David Levi during the first visit to Israel by a Soviet foreign minister since the Jewish state was founded in 1948. The two foreign ministers declared after the talks that their countries had agreed to maintain close contact while working towards peace in the Middle East, AP reported. Bessmertnykh also said the talks with Levi had helped him to understand better Israel's position with regard to the Middle East peace process, and he promised that free emigration from the Soviet Union would continue as part of the Soviet democratization policy. He suggested that Soviet Jewish emigrants might be allowed to retain their Soviet citizenship (*Reuters*, May 10). Bessmertnykh left Israel the same day for Cairo.

On May 11, Bessmertnykh met in Cairo with Egyptian President Hosni Mubarak to discuss efforts to reach peace in the Middle East, AFP reported. Bessmertnykh declared after the talks that he saw some small movement towards the start of a peace process. On May 12, Bessmertnykh met for ninety minutes with US Secretary of State James Baker in Cairo (*AFP*, May 12). During their second round of talks, on May 13, Baker and Bessmertnykh discussed the prospect of replacing the US forces in northern Iraq with a UN-sanctioned relief force.

On May 13, Bessmertnykh went to Riyadh, Saudi Arabia, where he had talks with Saudi Foreign Minister Prince Saud al-Faisal and King Fahd. He urged patience in resolving the Arab-Israeli dispute (*AP*, May 13). Before leaving Riyadh on May 14, Bessmertnykh attended the formal opening of the new Soviet embassy there, Reuters reported. Bessmertnykh returned to Damascus to give Syrian President Assad and other officials a briefing on his talks in Jordan, Israel, Egypt, and Saudi Arabia as well as on his talks with Baker, TASS reported on May 14. He then flew to Geneva to meet with Palestine Liberation Organization (PLO) Chairman Yasser Arafat (Western agencies, May 15).

Bessmertnykh told Soviet journalists accompanying him on his flight home that the leaders of Saudi Arabia, Jordan, Egypt, Israel, Syria, and the PLO supported an active Soviet role in the peace process for the region, TASS reported. Bessmertnykh also noted that a special working group had been set up at the USSR Ministry of Foreign Affairs to study questions relating to the Middle East peace process.

Thursday, May 9

Soviet President Mikhail Gorbachev and other USSR Communist Party and government leaders attended cer-

USSR Marks Victory Day

emonies in Moscow commemorating the forty-sixth anniversary of the victory over Germany at the end of World War II, AP reported. In an article marking Victory Day, Soviet Defense Minister Dmitrii Yazov wrote in *Pravda* that the creation of republican armed forces could violate international disarmament treaties and that, moreover, the fragmentation of the USSR would make it militarily weak. Yazov also said that the end of the Warsaw Pact as a military organization had not resulted in "a bloc-free system of European security" and that the USSR Armed Forces continued to be confronted by "the huge NATO military machine." His sentiments were echoed by Soviet Marshal Sergei Sokolov and Admiral Vitalii Ivanov, commander of the Soviet Baltic Fleet, who complained that NATO was increasing its troops and conventional weapons strength while the Soviet Union was making cuts in these areas (*Reuters*, May 9).

Pavlov Calls for Western Economic Aid

Soviet Prime Minister Valentin Pavlov told *The New York Times* that Western help was needed in the Soviet Union to make the ruble convertible. He said that without this the country could either return to former practices or collapse.

Friday, May 10

Stalinist Group Promotes Candidate for RSFSR Presidency

Members of the group "Edinstvo" rallied in Moscow, carrying portraits of Stalin, and laid flowers at Lenin's tomb and Stalin's grave, Radio Moscow reported. The demonstrators called for support for the candidacy of Colonel General Al'bert Makashov, the commander of the Volga-Urals Military District, for the RSFSR presidency.

Cossack Units to Be Restored in Soviet Army

Soviet Defense Minister Dmitrii Yazov approved a plan to form Cossack units in the Soviet army. Radio Rossii, quoted by Postfactum, said that the Soviet military oath would be changed for Cossacks so as to eliminate references to the CPSU.

Tatarstan Protests about Republican Agreement

In a statement published in newspapers in Tatarstan, government and Party leaders in Tatarstan criticized the agreement signed by Soviet President Mikhail Gorbachev and nine republican leaders on April 23 for not recognizing Tatarstan's sovereignty. The statement said this pre-

The USSR in May, 1991

cluded Tatarstan from signing a new Union treaty as a sovereign state—something it was determined to do (RFE/RL Tatar-Bashkir service, May 8).

Saturday, May 11

Interviewed by the British newspaper *The Sunday Times*, Soviet President Mikhail Gorbachev said the USSR was on the verge of chaos because it was abandoning a command economy in favor of a market system. He added, however, that stopping this process would lead to the reimposition of the command system. Gorbachev also said that, while implementing these changes, the USSR could not allow the collapse of its political system or the breakup of its multiracial society.

Gorbachev Says USSR on Verge of Chaos

RSFSR Supreme Soviet Chairman Boris El'tsin said that he had put personal matters aside and now regarded Soviet President Mikhail Gorbachev as an ally of the democrats. Interfax quoted El'tsin as saying that Gorbachev was clearly in favor of reforms. El'tsin emphasized that he and Gorbachev, as leaders of two state structures, the RSFSR and the USSR, had to join forces to prevent the disintegration of the Union.

El'tsin Calls Gorbachev an Ally

Former USSR Prime Minister Nikolai Ryzhkov declared in an interview published in *Krasnaya zvezda* that his campaign for the RSFSR presidency would be fought on a moderately radical platform, especially concerning price reform. At a meeting on May 12, the "Soyuz" group of people's deputies agreed to support Ryzhkov's candidacy, TASS reported.

Siberian farm and transport workers were reported to be collecting signatures to nominate RSFSR people's deputy Aman Tuleev as a candidate for the RSFSR presidency (*TASS*, May 11). Tuleev, who was chairman of the Kemerovo Oblast Soviet, criticized the coal miners for their two-month strike and faulted the stance taken by RSFSR Supreme Soviet Chairman Boris El'tsin during the conflict.

The former USSR minister of internal affairs, Vadim Bakatin, announced on Soviet television his intention to run for the RSFSR presidency. Bakatin said he felt he had no moral right to refuse the nomination and so applied for registration.

On May 13, the RSFSR Communist Party endorsed Ryzhkov as its official candidate for the RSFSR presi-

Campaign for RSFSR Presidency Gets Under Way

dency. But many speakers also supported the candidacy of General Boris Gromov. The Initiative Congress of Russian Communists also rejected Ryzhkov and endorsed its own candidate, economist Aleksei Sergeev, who favored a radical return to a planned economy. (*TASS*, May 13).

A plenum of the RSFSR Communist Party called on the RSFSR Congress of People's Deputies to postpone the presidential election for two or three months in order to give El'tsin's opponents more time to conduct their campaigns, TASS reported on May 13. RSFSR Communists also objected to the provision in the RSFSR law on the presidency that stipulated that the president should not be a member of any party.

General Al'bert Makashov, whose candidacy had been endorsed by several military units in the RSFSR, indicated that his platform would emphasize not the sovereignty or wealth of Russia but the preservation of a strong Soviet Union and its armed forces (*TASS*, May 14).

Leaders of Democratic Parties Meet

Radio Moscow reported that a meeting of leaders of democratic parties in the Soviet Union had started in Dushanbe. It cited Postfactum as saying that the participants, who included the leaders of the Democratic Party of Tajikistan, the Democratic Kyrgyzstan movement, and the Democratic Party of Russia, were discussing whether to create a unified all-Union Democratic Party.

Although the congress failed to reach agreement on this, the democratic movements in the Central Asian republics did decide to establish a Regional Congress of Democratic Forces in which democratic groups from all five Central Asian republics would participate.

Moiseev on Visit to Canada

A five-day visit by Soviet Chief of the General Staff Mikhail Moiseev to Canada concluded with the signing of a military cooperation pact by Moiseev and his Canadian counterpart, General John de Chastelain, Reuters reported. The agreement was the result of over a year of negotiation and provided for better communication between military authorities in the two countries to avoid dangerous military incidents. In comments to the press, Moiseev defended the use of Soviet army units "to resolve internal problems" in the Transcaucasus and the Baltic republics. He also said that the Lithuanian military port of Klaipeda would never become "an open area."

The USSR in May, 1991

Sunday, May 12

Pavlov Calls for Western Investment

In an interview with Interfax, Soviet Prime Minister Valentin Pavlov reiterated the necessity for a long-term program to encourage Western investment in the Soviet economy. He restated the concept of an all-European investment project to exploit and develop Soviet energy sources for the benefit of consumers in Western and Eastern Europe. Pavlov referred to this latter proposal as a new kind of Marshall Plan.

Naval Service Cut to Two Years

The USSR Supreme Soviet voted to cut military service in the navy from three years to two and approved a plan to staff several ships with volunteers instead of conscripts on an experimental basis. The reduction in naval service had been long awaited and brought the navy into line with the other services. Reuters quoted Deputy Chief of the General Staff Grigorii Krivosheev as telling the USSR Supreme Soviet that the experiment with voluntary service would run from 1991 to 1994. Under the plan, seamen and petty officers in four large naval units would be recruited on a contract basis, signing three-year contracts; Krivosheev said the experiment would help determine the feasibility of switching to professional armed forces.

Gorbachev Meets with El'tsin and Leaders of Autonomous Republics

Soviet President Mikhail Gorbachev met with RSFSR Supreme Soviet Chairman Boris El'tsin and the chairmen of the Supreme Soviets of fourteen of the sixteen autonomous republics of the RSFSR to discuss the status of the republics, how they should sign the Union treaty, and how they should be represented in the USSR Supreme Soviet (*TASS*, May 12).

Ramazan Abdulatipov, chairman of the RSFSR Council of Nationalities, confirmed to TASS on May 13 that all the autonomous republics of the RSFSR except Tatarstan had agreed at the meeting to sign the Union treaty as part of the RSFSR delegation. He said that this would not infringe their statehood or sovereignty and that they would sign as "equal subjects of both the USSR and the RSFSR."

Gorbachev's adviser Grigorii Revenko confirmed at a press conference on May 14 that republics not signing the Union treaty would have to abide by the Law on the Mechanics of Secession. Those republics would be free to leave the Soviet Union after a five-year transitional period. In the meantime they would have a special status, and each would be entitled to establish "special relations of its own in the Union and with the Union."

Khmara Released; Trial Begins

Ukrainian people's deputy Stepan Khmara, who had been arrested in November, 1990, and charged with assaulting a police colonel, was released at the request of the Presidium of the Ukrainian Supreme Soviet. The move followed the refusal by the Ukrainian parliamentary opposition, "Narodna Rada," to attend the current session of the Ukrainian Supreme Soviet unless Khmara was released.

Khmara addressed a rally called by the Ukrainian opposition movement "Rukh" on May 13. He again rejected the charges against him and called for the dissolution of the Ukrainian Supreme Soviet and for parliamentary elections (*TASS*, May 13). Khmara went on trial as scheduled on May 14 in Kiev, but the proceedings had to be adjourned twice (RL Ukrainian service, May 14 and 15).

Tajik Government Reduces Retail Prices

Radio Moscow reported that the Tajik Cabinet of Ministers had passed a resolution to reduce retail prices on many goods produced in the republic by up to 50 percent and to cover the resulting budget deficit by raising the retail prices of alcoholic beverages by an average of 70 percent. Officials in Tajikistan and in the other Central Asian republics had sought to avoid social unrest by setting lower prices for food and consumer goods.

Monday, May 13

El'tsin in Prague

Boris El'tsin arrived in Prague for a two-day visit, his first to an East European country as chairman of the RSFSR Supreme Soviet. He told reporters that he considered the Soviet invasion of Czechoslovakia in 1968 to have been a big mistake. He and Czechoslovak President Vaclav Havel discussed plans to strengthen economic ties (Western agencies, May 13). On May 14, El'tsin met with the Czechoslovak parliamentary chairman, Alexander Dubcek, and with Czech National Council Chairman Dagmar Buresova and Prime Minister Petr Pithart (*CTK*, May 14). In an address to an informal meeting of some 200 Czechoslovak parliamentarians, El'tsin said he was convinced the country's challenge to totalitarianism in 1968 had affected the fate of the whole world. The Prague Spring, he said, had provided an impulse to people like

Andrei Sakharov and Aleksandr Solzhenitsyn. Later that day, El'tsin and Dubcek signed a joint declaration on fundamental relations and cooperation, Reuters reported. The same day, El'tsin went on to Bratislava to meet with Slovak Prime Minister Jan Carnogursky. The two men held a press conference after their talks: Carnogursky told reporters that social changes should not disturb mutual ties and that Slovakia was interested in links with the RSFSR that would make these ties more profitable (*CTK*, May 14).

Pithart declared on Czechoslovak Television on May 17 that he had offered 1 million tons of grain to the RSFSR. El'tsin also welcomed the offer of 70,000 tons of beef, CTK reported. Pithart added that the RSFSR would pay for those goods at world-market prices in hard currency or oil.

Gorbachev Targets Key Economic Sectors

Soviet President Mikhail Gorbachev signed a decree establishing "a special regime" in key sectors of the Soviet economy. Interfax said the decree allowed increased autonomy in basic industries such as mining, steel and chemical production, and energy as well as in the transport sector. It aimed to introduce a special regime to supply enterprises with raw materials and other resources and would permit them to retain 10 percent of income earned on domestic or foreign markets, including hard currency. A sharp increase in production would be rewarded by considerable pay raises. Local and republican governments would control a negotiated share of revenue (*Financial Times*, May 14).

Decree on Compensation for People with Children

Soviet President Mikhail Gorbachev issued a decree ordering that more compensation be given to people with children in order to offset higher retail prices, "Vremya" reported on May 14. Families with children under the age of thirteen would receive an annual payment of 200 rubles and those with children over that age 250 rubles. The compensation was designed to offset the two- and threefold increases in the prices of school uniforms and other items of children's clothing.

Russian Television Launched

The RSFSR launched its own television channel, called the All-Russian State Television and Radio Broadcasting Company, "Vremya" reported. It was to be carried on the second channel of Soviet Central Television three times a day—from 11:30 A.M. to 1:00 P.M., from 5:00 P.M. to 7:00 P.M., and from 10:00 P.M. to midnight, Moscow Time. In an interview broadcast on the occasion of the channel's inauguration, RSFSR Supreme Soviet Chairman Boris El'tsin said it was a vital element in the republic's struggle for full political sovereignty. El'tsin pledged that it would provide balanced and impartial coverage of life in the republic. A director of RSFSR television, Sergei Podgorbunsky, said his news team would strive to produce objective reports on the USSR's ethnic disputes.

Belorussian Government Signs Agreement with Trade Unions

The Belorussian government signed an agreement with the republic's trade unions, TASS reported. The government pledged to guarantee living standards, full employment, public health, and a sound environment; the trade unions promised in return not to strike. Agreement was also reached on taxation, but TASS gave no details.

Ukrainian Government Restructured

The Ukrainian Supreme Soviet approved the restructuring of the government, replacing the Council of Ministers with a streamlined Cabinet of Ministers, Ukrinform-TASS reported. In accordance with Ukraine's declaration of sovereignty, the republican KGB would be subordinated to the Supreme Soviet and its chairman would have ministerial rank. Radio Kiev and Ukrinform-TASS also reported that additional ministries of higher, specialized, and secondary education; foreign trade; commerce; transport; internal affairs; and the environment would be established. In addition, a state television and radio company would be created. The Ukrainian Supreme Soviet declined, however, to transfer jurisdiction over the republican bank to the Cabinet of Ministers.

Moldavian Supreme Soviet Begins Session

The Moldavian Supreme Soviet began a session expected to consider draft laws on changing the name of the republic, republican citizenship, alternative military service, republican referendums, freedom of the press and the operation of the mass media, administrative reform, banking, privatization of state property, and agrarian reform, among other bills prepared mostly by popular front deputies and the Presidium of the Supreme Soviet, which was dominated by the popular front (RFE/RL correspondent's report, May 13).

The same day, the Moldavian government permitted the breakaway Independent Moldavian Communist Party–Democratic Platform to register legally, Moldovapres reported on May 15.

On May 14, President Mircea Snegur reiterated Kishinev's goal of achieving "full sovereignty and independence," Moldovapres reported. In line with the existing consensus among non-Communist Moldavian groups, Snegur envisaged "two independent Romanian states," Romania and Moldavia, existing alongside each other in close economic and cultural cooperation. Snegur also called for intensified efforts by Moldavia to establish its own economic and political contacts with other countries.

The session voted down a proposal by popular front deputies to submit a declaration of independence to a parliamentary vote, Moldavian journalists told RFE/RL on May 15. Supreme Soviet Chairman Alexandru Mosanu, a popular front supporter, argued that the measure was "premature" in the absence of a law on republican referendums and that a declaration of independence should first be put to a referendum and be adopted by the parliament afterwards.

Protest in Vilnius Marks Four Months' Occupation of Television Tower

About 2,000 people gathered in Vilnius to mark the fourth month of the occupation of the Vilnius television tower, Western agencies reported. Lithuanian Prime Minister Gediminas Vagnorius said that the Soviet Armed Forces wanted to silence Lithuania but that Lithuanian voices were louder than before. A hunger strike in front of the tower by Lithuanian journalists and technicians who had lost their offices in the occupation continued. Meanwhile, the programs of the army-protected television station had a rating of only 3 percent.

USSR–North Korean Trade Accord

In an interview with Radio Moscow, Aleksandr Kachanov, USSR first deputy minister of foreign economic relations, said that the USSR and North Korea had agreed in their trade accord for 1991 on a list of commodities to be delivered to the USSR in return for the cancellation of North Korea's debts to the Soviet Union. Kachanov noted that the USSR had agreed to provide loans to North Korea and cooperate in the construction of the East Pyongyang thermal power plant.

Tuesday, May 14

Negotiations on Anticrisis Program

Soviet and republican deputy prime ministers from all the republics other than Georgia and Estonia met near Moscow to try to resolve differences over the provisions of the anticrisis program, according to Interfax. Discussions focused on the right to exploit mineral and other natural resources, on the privatization of property, and on republican liabilities for the USSR foreign and domestic budget deficits. It was agreed that a commission would be formed to work out the debt figures. The meeting issued a draft economic program for joint action and presented it to the USSR Cabinet of Ministers on May 15, Radio Moscow reported. Addressing the session, Soviet President Mikhail Gorbachev said that the key goal of the program was to attract foreign investment (*Reuters*, May 16).

While USSR Deputy Prime Minister Vladimir Shcherbakov warned of harsh measures and sacrifices ahead, Ukrainian Prime Minister Vitol'd Fokin complained that the program offered all stick and no carrot. RSFSR Prime Minister Ivan Silaev reported that several questions remained unresolved, including the division of hard-currency earnings (*Moscow Television*, May 15).

Belorussian Prime Minister Vyacheslau Kebich shared some of those concerns and wanted to see the large state enterprises in his republic converted to joint-stock companies. He also wanted a policy included to support the Central Asian republics. Other republican leaders, including Kirgiz Prime Minister Nasirdin Isanov and Kazakh Prime Minister Uzakbai Karamanov, supported the quick adoption and implementation of the plan, though Karamanov shared concerns over who "owns" the enterprises on republican territory and who would control their privatization.

RSFSR Communist Party Plenum Inconclusive

A plenum of the RSFSR Communist Party produced no constructive results and was devoted largely to the leveling of accusations at reform Communists, such as Aleksandr Yakovlev and Aleksandr Rutskoi, TASS commented. Russian Communists failed to agree on a transition to a market economy, and speakers expressed wonder at why the Communists found themselves on the other side of the barricades, opposed to the striking miners.

Crime Rises in USSR

USSR First Deputy Minister of Internal Affairs Ivan Shilov was quoted by Interfax as saying the crime rate in the USSR had reached its highest level since the end of World War II. According to Shilov, economic crime had become especially serious: 265,000 cases of economic crime were reported in 1990, 20 percent more than in 1989. The annual volume of black-market trade had grown to an estimated 70 billion rubles, Shilov added.

Russian Military Union Founded

The Russian All-Army Union, founded in Leningrad and dedicated to protecting the rights of Russian servicemen, appealed for recognition from the Soviet Armed Forces, the KGB, the MVD, and the law-enforcement agencies of the RSFSR. According to Radio Rossii, the union stood for a sovereign, democratic Russia, advocated a strong Russian executive and the nationalization of Communist Party property, and refused to execute "criminal orders."

Oil Producers to Market Part of Production

Tyumen' oil producers were given permission to sell 1 million tons of oil on the free market, Western agencies reported. Most of this would be sold through a local commodity exchange that opened in April. It was not specified whether the sales would be in rubles or in hard currency; some seats on the Tyumen' exchange were bought by foreigners.

Tatarstan Supreme Soviet Deputy on Hunger Strike

Favzia Bairamova, a deputy of the Tatarstan Supreme Soviet and chairman of the Tatar National Party "Ittifak," began a hunger strike in Kazan' to protest the decision of the republican Supreme Soviet to allow citizens of Tatarstan to vote in the RSFSR presidential elections on June 12. The decision was reached on May 13. It also provided that Tatarstan would hold elections for its own president on the same day. The opposition democratic movement claimed that allowing RSFSR elections in the republic would be an infringement of Tatarstan's sovereignty (RFE/RL correspondent's report, May 14).

An antielection rally sponsored by the National Democratic Movement of Tatarstan was attended by some 15,000 people in Kazan' on May 20.

Bowing to public pressure, the Tatarstan Supreme Soviet decided on May 28 that Tatarstan would not officially take part in the elections of the RSFSR president on June 12 but that, "in accordance with human rights," assistance would be given to those who wished to vote (*TASS*, May 28).

Checheno-Ingushetia Proclaims National "Justice Day"

The Chechen-Ingush Supreme Soviet proclaimed April 26, the day the RSFSR Supreme Soviet adopted a law on the rehabilitation of repressed peoples, "Justice Day." According to *Pravda* of April 23, the law adopted by the USSR Supreme Soviet in March, 1991, annulling various decrees affecting deported peoples was the cause of the recent armed clashes between Ingush and Ossetians in North Ossetia, which occurred when some Ingush interpreted the law as entitling them to repossess their former homes.

Wednesday, May 15

New Permanent USSR Representative to European Community

Soviet President Mikhail Gorbachev appointed Lev Voronin, a former first deputy chairman of the USSR Council of Ministers, as the USSR's permanent representative to the European Community, TASS reported. He replaced Vladimir Shemyatenkov, who had been transferred to another job. Voronin served from 1979 to 1980 as first deputy minister of the defense industry and then spent five years as a deputy chairman of the USSR State Planning Committee. He became deputy chairman of the USSR Council of Ministers in 1985 and was promoted to first deputy chairman in 1989.

Chinese Communist Party General Secretary in Moscow

Chinese Communist Party General Secretary Jiang Zemin arrived in Moscow for a five-day visit, TASS reported. This was the first visit to the USSR by a Chinese Party leader since Mao Tse-tung's last trip in 1957. A written statement released upon Jiang's arrival said the purpose of the visit was to further the process of normal development of relations between the two countries, and it expressed confidence that the bilateral talks would promote deeper mutual understanding (*TASS*, May 15). Jiang held talks with Soviet President Mikhail Gorbachev, who declared that the new Sino-Soviet relationship would become a pillar of stability, security, and development in Asia and the world. Both Gorbachev and Jiang stressed the importance not only of stability in international relations but, more pertinently, of domestic political stability in both their countries.

Jiang met on May 16 with USSR Prime Minister Valentin Pavlov, who showed interest in how the Chinese had combined the market mechanism and state management. In a ceremony attended by Gorbachev and Jiang, USSR Foreign Minister Aleksandr Bessmertnykh and his counterpart, Qian Qichen, signed a document settling most elements of the two countries' border dispute, excluding only "the difficult parts," such as the disputed islands in the Amur River, TASS reported.

On May 17, Jiang declared in a nationwide address on Soviet television that he was sure the people of the Soviet Union would be able to overcome their temporary difficulties. Asked at a Moscow news conference whether China was pursuing an arms deal with the Soviet Union, Jiang remarked only that military exchanges were proceeding normally.

On May 18, Jiang went to Leningrad, where he met with the chairman of the city soviet, Anatolii Sobchak,

The USSR in May, 1991

TASS reported. A joint communiqué issued in Moscow on May 19 said China and the USSR believed that reforms were necessary to open up the potential of socialism but that there was not necessarily just one route to such reforms. It also said that differences in their respective social systems, ideologies, economic models, and paths of development should not be allowed to hinder normal relations (*Reuters*, May 20). *Pravda* and the official Chinese Communist Party newspaper, *The People's Daily*, both praised the results of Jiang's visit.

Kvitsinsky Promoted

USSR Deputy Foreign Minister Yulii Kvitsinsky was appointed USSR first deputy foreign minister, TASS reported. Kvitsinsky worked in the Soviet embassy in East Germany in the 1960s and was counselor in the Soviet embassy in West Germany from 1978 to 1981. Before his appointment to the post of deputy foreign minister in 1990, Kvitsinsky was Soviet ambassador to West Germany.

RSFSR Presidential Election Campaign Budget

The chairman of the RSFSR Central Electoral Commission told TASS that the republic had set aside 155 million rubles for financing the RSFSR presidential campaign. Most of the money would be spent on operating the 98,000 polling stations and on printing and distributing ballot papers. Candidates for the post would also receive equal financial support from the state for campaign expenses.

Soviet Statistics on Fall in Production

The USSR State Committee for Statistics published statistics in *Izvestia* showing that production was down in many sectors of the economy. During the first four months of 1991, production declined by more than 5 percent compared with the same period in 1990. Of the 156 items monitored, the production of 115 was lower in April, 1991.

Armenian Communist Party First Secretary Resigns

TASS reported that Stepan Pogosyan had resigned from the post of Armenian Communist Party first secretary, to which he had been elected in November, 1990. The resignation of the second secretary was rejected. After debating and then rejecting a proposal to expand the Buro and create a collective Party leadership, the plenum drew up a list of six provisional candidates for first secretary, of whom four declined to run.

USSR Gives Official Figures on Refugees

Trud quoted Petr Rudev, head of the Migration and Resettlement Department at the USSR Ministry of Labor and Social Affairs, as saying the number of refugees in the Soviet Union had reached 665,000. Azerbaijan had provided asylum for 237,000 refugees, most of them either Azerbaijanis who had fled from Armenia or Meskhetians who had fled from Central Asia. Armenia had 237,000 refugees, most of them Armenians from Azerbaijan. Rudev added that there were also 150,000 refugees in the RSFSR, about 20,000 in Ukraine, 2,500 in Kazakhstan, and 1,500 in Belorussia.

Dagestan Declares Sovereignty

The Congress of People's Deputies of Dagestan declared the autonomous republic to be the Dagestan SSR, Radio Moscow reported. At the same time, it confirmed that the republic was still part of the RSFSR. Dagestan was the last of the sixteen autonomous republics of the RSFSR to adopt a declaration of sovereignty.

Border Post Incidents in Baltic Republics

Lithuanian Public Prosecutor Arturas Paulauskas told the press in Vilnius that earlier that day several members of the MVD special forces had fired shots over the heads of Lithuanian border guards near a customs post close to the Belorussian border. The Soviet authorities did not recognize the Lithuanian border posts.

Soviet soldiers set up checkpoints along highways in Lithuania and attacked another customs post on May 16 on the road to Grodno, Belorussia: about twenty Soviet soldiers armed with machine pistols opened fire with plastic ammunition and signal flares, Lithuanian parliamentary spokesman Audrius Azubalis told RFE/RL. One customs officer was slightly injured (RFE Lithuanian service, May 16).

On May 18, AFP reported that a Belorussian had been killed during an incident at a border checkpoint along the Belorussian-Lithuanian border, an event that Lithuanian Prime Minister Gediminas Vagnorius made public in a telegram addressed to the Belorussian government and Ministry of Internal Affairs. Radio Vilnius reported on May 19 that about thirty Soviet troops had attacked and burned down a checkpoint at Kalvarija near the Polish-Lithuanian border the day before, injuring two people.

Another incident occurred at the Lithuanian border post at Krapunai on May 19, during which a Lithuanian border official was killed in his office by bullets fired from a hunting rifle, Radio Vilnius reported.

On May 20, Vagnorius told RFE/RL that he and Belorussian Prime Minister Vyacheslau Kebich had decided to form a joint commission to investigate the recent attacks (RFE Lithuanian service, May 20). Vagnorius said Belorussia had arrested three people in connection with the attacks.

On May 23, Latvia and Lithuania protested to the USSR government that seven of their border posts had been destroyed, AP reported. Lithuanian Defense Department Chairman Audrius Butkevicius told the Lithuanian Supreme Council that Lithuanian border officials had been beaten up during the attacks and that four Lithuanian border posts on the Latvian border had been burned down, two by OMON detachments and two by Soviet paratroopers (RFE Lithuanian service, May 23). Radio Riga reported the same day the burning down of three Latvian border posts, all of them at the hands of OMON troops from Riga.

Two Estonian border posts, located in the towns of Luhamaa and Murati on the border with Latvia, were burned down on May 24, Estonian radio reported. According to Baltfax, the Estonian government sent a telegram to the USSR government protesting what it termed "provocations."

During the night of May 24 and 25, five posts along the Lithuanian-Latvian border were attacked, Reuters reported. A meeting of the Presidium of the Supreme Council and of the Council of Ministers of Latvia adopted a resolution calling for urgent self-defense measures to prevent the further use of violence by the Soviet Armed Forces and also ordering the reconstruction of the demolished border posts and the strengthening of police posts on the border (*Radio Riga*, May 24). Also on May 24, Lithuanian Prime Minister Vagnorius met with USSR Minister of Internal Affairs Boriss Pugo in Moscow; the latter promised to send an envoy to Lithuania to discuss the border incidents (*AFP*, May 25).

On May 25, the presidents of the Supreme Councils of the three Baltic republics issued a joint statement protesting Soviet attacks on border posts in the Baltic republics during the previous two nights and appealing to the international community to "resolutely protest the new acts of coercion perpetrated by the Soviet Union." The statement described the attacks as "reminiscent of the period prior to the tragic events of January, 1991." "As long as such attacks continue," the statement went on, "it is impossible to rely on assertions about the continuation of reform and the process of democratization in the Soviet Union" (*Radio Vilnius*, May 26).

The same day, Pugo said he had no evidence that the MVD was involved in the attacks, and he described the Latvian and Lithuanian protests as "provocations" (*Radio*

Moscow, May 25). RSFSR Supreme Soviet Chairman Boris El'tsin said Gorbachev had assured him that no orders had been given by the Kremlin for Soviet troops to attack the Baltic border posts (*AP*, May 25).

The Baltfax news agency reported that a further post—on the border between Lithuania and Belorussia—had been burned down on May 25 by Soviet MVD troops stationed in Vilnius.

On May 27, the Lithuanian Supreme Council adopted two resolutions. The first declared that "the USSR MVD OMON and any other formations not provided for by the laws of the Republic of Lithuania are illegal." It also called on the Lithuanian government to strengthen control over the Lithuanian border and reestablish the customs posts that had been destroyed. The second resolution was an appeal to the citizens and inhabitants of Lithuania that urged OMON troops to refuse to participate in criminal activities against the people of Lithuania (*Radio Independent Lithuania*, May 28).

On May 28, USSR Prime Minister Valentin Pavlov denied that the USSR had known of or planned recent raids on border posts in the Baltic republics. According to the Estonian newspaper *Paevaleht*, Pavlov told his Estonian counterpart Edgar Savisaar that the attacks "are not consistent with the central government's strategic interests."

On May 29, Lithuania said Soviet soldiers had set fire to another of its border posts the night before. Parliamentary press spokesman Azubalis told a press briefing in Vilnius that Soviet soldiers had beaten up two Lithuanian guards and then set fire to the post at Lavoriskes on the Belorussian border. He said the two border guards had been hospitalized. The radio report did not make clear whether the attackers were army or MVD troops (RFE Lithuanian service, May 29).

After hedging for several days on who had ordered the OMON attacks on Baltic customs posts, on May 29 Pugo finally provided a formal explanation. In a statement circulated in the USSR Supreme Soviet, Pugo said the attacks were aimed at enforcing Soviet law, which he said still applied in Lithuania, Latvia, and Estonia and forbade the establishment of non-Soviet customs posts. He also said the attacks had been carried out without the knowledge or orders of the MVD, and he described them as "offensive behavior against republican employees" and as "destruction of property." He said he would "take steps to regulate the work of OMON" (RFE Latvian service, May 29).

On May 30, USSR Prosecutor-General Nikolai Trubin said he would start criminal proceedings against the

OMON units involved in the attacks. The Interfax news agency quoted him as saying that, to the best of his knowledge, the troops had acted on their own initiative in carrying out the attacks.

Also on May 30, the Lithuanian government issued a statement declaring that members of the USSR MVD OMON had until June 7 to quit their jobs or be considered elements of a criminal group. The government offered to assist them in finding new employment. The commander of the Vilnius OMON, Boleslaw Makutinowicz, said in an interview on Soviet army-controlled Vilnius television that OMON only obeyed the orders of the USSR MVD and did not plan to disband (*Radio Vilnius*, May 31).

Thursday, May 16

Gorbachev Issues Decree Banning Strikes

Soviet President Mikhail Gorbachev issued a decree banning strikes in key industries such as energy, coal, oil, gas, chemicals, petrochemicals, metallurgy, and railways in order to prevent economic chaos, TASS reported. The decree also mandated "administrative prosecution" of people who organized strikes in those industries.

USSR Prime Minister Valentin Pavlov told a news conference that the recently ended miners' strike might result in some mine closures and the layoff of miners. According to AP, Pavlov said that many mines were damaged beyond repair and that there was an enormous amount of work to be done before full production could resume.

The Russian Federation of Independent Trade Unions rejected the decree, TASS reported on May 17. The chairman of the federation, Igor' Klochkov, told a news conference in Moscow that bans were "not a cure for an illness. . . . They could only drive it deeper inside an organism."

USSR Government Appointments

The USSR Supreme Soviet appointed Vladimir Shcherbakov as USSR first deputy prime minister with responsibility for the economy and forecasting, by a vote of 373 to 17, with 6 abstentions, TASS reported. Shcherbakov had been a deputy prime minister since March, 1991.

The USSR Supreme Soviet also endorsed Bikhodzhal Rakhimova as a USSR deputy prime minister; she had been a secretary of the Tajik Communist Party Central Committee. Deputy Prime Minister Nikolai Laverov was appointed chairman of the USSR State Committee for Science and Technology. In addition, the Supreme Soviet created an agency called the USSR Control Chamber to oversee the Soviet Union's budget and use of Union property and to operate under the authority of the Supreme Soviet. Aleksandr Orlov, former deputy chairman of the USSR Supreme Soviet's Planning, Budget, and Financial Commission, was named chairman of the new chamber (*TASS*, May 16).

USSR Supreme Soviet Adopts Law on Security Agencies

The USSR Supreme Soviet adopted a law regulating the KGB and other security agencies by a vote of 352 to 1, with 10 abstentions. TASS called the law "the first unclassified act pertaining to state security in Soviet history." It defined the agencies' duties and rights and set up a system to monitor their activities. The law required the KGB to ensure state security in accordance with all-Union and republican laws. It permitted citizens to appeal against injustice at the hands of state security bodies and officials and said these officials were not bound by decisions of political parties or mass movements in pursuing political objectives. USSR KGB Chairman Vladimir Kryuchkov told the Supreme Soviet after the vote that the law was a powerful weapon and that the KGB would use it only in legal ways to defend Soviet values, the main one being the preservation of a single Union. For the text of the law, see *Izvestia*, May 24, 1991.

RSFSR Cancels Sales Tax on Food Products

The RSFSR Supreme Soviet was told by its chairman, Boris El'tsin, at a plenary session that the 5-percent sales tax introduced by presidential decree in December, 1990, had been canceled on almost all food products in the republic. A tax on spirits, tobacco products, coffee, and chocolate remained in force, however (*TASS*, May 16).

El'tsin told the same session that he had given the USSR Cabinet of Ministers two weeks to suspend any USSR laws hindering the development of free enterprise in the RSFSR. TASS reported that El'tsin had signed a resolution, to be published within a week, aimed at stimulating entrepreneurial activity. According to the resolution, dormant production projects in the RSFSR worth 253 billion rubles would be restarted.

USSR Signs Over Uranium Mines to Germany

The USSR signed over to the German government the Wismut uranium mines in former East Germany. The agreement, signed by German Economics Minister Jürgen Möllemann and Soviet Atomic Energy Minister Vitalii Konovalov, absolved the USSR of all responsibility for cleaning up radioactive material accumulated during the forty-five years of mining operations. The cost of the cleanup was estimated at more than 10 billion deutsche marks. Wismut supplied the USSR with more than 220,000 tons of uranium from 1945 until the end of 1990 and played a key role in the start-up of the Soviet nuclear-weapons program (*AP*, May 16).

Explosion at Democratic Russia Headquarters

An explosion damaged the headquarters of the Democratic Russia movement in Moscow, blowing a hole through the roof and shattering windows in surrounding buildings (RFE/RL correspondent's report, May 16). A member of Democratic Russia, Vladimir Bokser, told a press conference on May 17 that the group regarded the explosion as an act of terrorism (*AP*, May 18).

On May 18, *Sovetskaya Rossiya* reported that the Libertarian (Radical) Party of the USSR had claimed responsibility for the explosion. According to the newspaper, the party's reason for staging the attack was that its candidate for the RSFSR presidential elections, Roman Kalinin, had been beaten up by supporters of RSFSR Supreme Soviet Chairman Boris El'tsin, the candidate of the Democratic Russia movement. Russian Television quoted a representative of the Libertarian Party as denying the report by *Sovetskaya Rossiya*, calling it a provocation.

Journalists Protest Restrictions on Press Freedom in Lithuania

The USSR Union of Journalists expressed concern over restrictions on press freedom in Lithuania. The union stated that the continuing presence of Soviet troops at the republic's television center and the Vilnius press house had denied hundreds of journalists the chance to work. It also said press laws were being flouted and international agreements violated (*TASS*, May 16).

Vandalism in Tatar Oil Fields

Some sixty automatically controlled oil wells had been put out of action in Tatarstan, TASS reported, citing *Trud*. The loss from each well was approximately 300 tons of oil a day. The authorities were investigating whether the vandalism was politically motivated. Recently, activists of the Tatar Public Center had tried to shut off the "Druzhba" pipeline in the republic to demonstrate the republic's sovereign ownership of its oil wealth.

Friday, May 17

Gorbachev Approves Plans for Wage Indexation

Soviet President Mikhail Gorbachev proposed linking incomes to the cost of living to help compensate for the effects of price rises. According to Reuters, Gorbachev gave his approval to a plan that would give pensioners, students, the unemployed, and others on low incomes compensation in accordance with a schedule worked out by the central and republican governments and trade unions.

RSFSR Adopts Law on Emergency Measures

The RSFSR Supreme Soviet adopted a law prescribing the circumstances in which a state of emergency could be proclaimed in the republic, TASS reported. The law empowered the president of the RSFSR or the Presidium of the RSFSR Supreme Soviet to declare a state of emergency if the constitutional order were threatened or in the event of a natural disaster or an industrial accident. If the RSFSR wanted to declare a state of emergency in one of its constituent republics, however, the consent of the Supreme Soviet of that republic would be required.

Food Supply in the RSFSR

Deputy Chairman of the RSFSR Supreme Soviet Boris Isaev, who was also deputy chairman of the RSFSR Emergency Commission on Food, told a session of the RSFSR Supreme Soviet that April's price increases had not resulted in any significant improvement in the supply of goods to the market. Isaev also noted persistent shortages of meat, milk, and butter; he added that the RSFSR considered farm privatization very important in the program to improve food supplies (*Russian Television*, May 18).

Air Traffic Controllers Gain Wage Increase after Threatening to Strike

Soviet air traffic controllers and pilots announced their intention to begin an indefinite strike on May 21 in support of demands for more pay and other improvements in their working conditions, AFP reported.

The television news program "Vremya" reported on May 18 that the Soviet government had offered concessions to the air traffic controllers. The USSR Cabinet of Ministers proposed that the retirement age for air traffic controllers be reduced to fifty for men and forty-five for women; that annual vacation be increased to 48–50 days; and that salaries be raised by 50 percent. The air traffic controllers wanted their salaries tripled. USSR Civil Avia-

The USSR in May, 1991

tion Minister Boris Panyukov said on May 19 that military personnel would be asked to stand in for their civilian colleagues in the event of a strike ("Vremya," *Central Television*, May 20).

A last-minute concession by the Soviet government on May 21 averted the strike. Thirty minutes before the deadline, the government agreed to give pilots and air traffic controllers pay raises averaging 60 percent. On May 22, Soviet media reported that all airports were operating normally.

Large Gas Field Discovered in the Barents Sea

Large reserves of natural gas were reported to have been discovered in the Barents Sea off the Arctic port of Murmansk; the find was thought to be large enough to satisfy Soviet and Western demand for decades. TASS said, however, that it would be hard to prospect, because the sea was 300 meters deep where the gas had been found. Contacts had been made with foreign companies with experience in deep-sea gas extraction.

USSR Appoints Ambassador to Albania

Soviet President Mikhail Gorbachev appointed the first ambassador to Tirana from Moscow since Albania broke off relations with the USSR in 1961, TASS reported. Viktor Nerubailo worked at the USSR embassy in Tirana in the years immediately preceding the break and later held various posts in the Soviet diplomatic service and the Communist Party.

Gorbachev Meets with Bulgarian Prime Minister

Soviet President Mikhail Gorbachev told Bulgarian Prime Minister Dimitar Popov at a meeting in Moscow that the USSR and Bulgaria had to remake their relationship in the knowledge that both countries had "freedom of choice" in all matters. A joint communiqué quoted by TASS said financial, political, and cultural relations now had to be grounded on mutual advantage and common interest. Popov, who also met with Valentin Pavlov and Ivan Silaev, the prime ministers of the USSR and the RSFSR respectively, handed Gorbachev a message from Bulgaria's president, Zhelyu Zhelev.

Landsbergis Meets with German Officials

Lithuanian Supreme Council President Vytautas Landsbergis stopped briefly in Bonn on his way home from the United States. He met with Bundestag President Rita Süssmuth, German Foreign Affairs Committee Chairman Hans Stercken, and Minister of State at the Chancellery Lutz Stavenhagen. Landsbergis said Lithuania hoped to open an information bureau in Bonn to handle economic and diplomatic relations and added that he expected that Germany and Lithuania would one day reestablish full diplomatic ties. At a press conference, a member of the Bundestag, Wolfgang von Stetten, said that the parliamentary Foreign Affairs Committee had voted to urge the reciprocal establishment of information bureaus with the Baltic republics (RFE/RL correspondent's report, May 17).

Jewish Autonomous Oblast Declares Independence

The Jewish Autonomous Oblast declared itself independent of Khabarovsk Krai, TASS reported. Deputies in the oblast soviet in the capital, Birobidzhan, said they wanted to be administered directly by the RSFSR instead of by Khabarovsk Krai.

Saturday, May 18

Russian Party of the RSFSR Holds Founding Congress

The founding congress of the Russian Party of the RSFSR took place in Moscow, Russian Television reported. The party's draft program called for the rebirth of the state of Russia, which was to be made up of the RSFSR and predominantly Russian areas in other republics—namely, northern Kazakhstan and the city of Alma-Ata, northern Kirgizia together with the city of Bishkek, the left bank of the Dniester in Moldavia, and the Crimea. It also called for the creation of Russian autonomous formations within the Union republics, a unitary state structure for the RSFSR without autonomous national formations, and "the repatriation of Jews from Russia."

Sakharov Honored

A museum devoted to the human-rights activist and Nobel laureate Andrei Sakharov was opened in Nizhnii Novgorod in the apartment where the academician served his enforced exile from 1980 to 1986, TASS reported. Thousands of Muscovites gathered in Moscow on May 20 to honor his memory (*DPA*, May 20).

On May 21, to mark the anniversary of Sakharov's birth, a five-day international conference on human rights and Sakharov's legacy, entitled "Peace, Progress, and Human Rights," opened in Moscow with the support of Sakharov's widow, Elena Bonner, AP reported. Soviet President Mikhail Gorbachev attended the opening session of the conference, together with RSFSR Supreme Soviet Chairman Boris El'tsin, former Czechoslovak President Alexander Dubcek, and Portuguese President Mario Soares (*AP*, May 21).

The USSR in May, 1991

The same day, the deputy chairman of the Moscow City Soviet, Sergei Stankevich, unveiled a memorial plaque at the house where Sakharov had been living at the time of his death in December, 1989, Reuters reported.

Krasnaya zvezda Criticizes Shevardnadze

Former USSR Foreign Minister Eduard Shevardnadze, who was on a lecture tour of the United States, was criticized in an article published in *Krasnaya zvezda* for his "private diplomacy," for the fee he received for speaking, which the newspaper judged too high, and for visiting his granddaughter at an American university. The daily also complained that Shevardnadze was trying to obtain a credit of 1.5 billion US dollars for Soviet grain purchases.

Military Budget Squandered

Nearly 1 percent of the USSR's military budget may be wasted because of fraudulent or unwarranted use of military transport by high-ranking military leaders, *Komsomol'skaya pravda* reported. According to Western agencies, a USSR Supreme Soviet commission investigating such abuses said that heavy transport planes made thousands of flights without cargo. Among those singled out for criticism were Marshals Sergei Sokolov and Viktor Kulikov, Generals Valentin Varennikov and Konstantin Kochetov, and Leonid Sharin, chairman of the Supreme Soviet Defense and State Security Commission.

Gromov on "Black Berets"

USSR First Deputy Minister of Internal Affairs General Boris Gromov said on Central Television that there were thirty special police units (OMON) operating across the USSR, with a total strength of 8,000 men. Gromov denied that OMON troops, also known as the "Black Berets," were occupying the Lithuanian Television Center in Vilnius. He said that the building was being guarded by regular MVD troops. He added that the MVD considered the government of Vytautas Landsbergis to be a legally elected body that had adopted illegal practices.

Earth Tremors Cause Damage in South Ossetia

Fifty-five people were killed and more than 3,000 homes destroyed as the result of earth tremors in South Ossetia on May 14 and 15, a report by a committee of the North Ossetian Supreme Soviet stated. It also said that some 10,000 people were without shelter because of the damage caused by the tremors (*TASS*, May 18).

The USSR in May, 1991

Sunday, May 19

Russian People's Party Founded

A new opposition party in the RSFSR, the Russian People's Party, adopted statutes and a program at its founding congress, Radio Rossii reported on May 20. USSR people's deputy Tel'man Gdlyan was elected as cochairman with Oleg Berezin. The congress of the new party also endorsed RSFSR Supreme Soviet Chairman Boris El'tsin's bid for the RSFSR presidency.

Lithuanian Bishops Consecrated

In Kaunas Cathedral, Vincentas Cardinal Sladkevicius was ordained as the rector of the Kaunas Seminary; Sigitas Tamkevicius was made the suffragan bishop of the archdiocese of Kaunas and chancellor of the archdiocese of Vilnius; and Juozas Tunaitis was made the suffragan bishop of the archdiocese of Vilnius (RFE Lithuanian service, May 20).

Monday, May 20

USSR Supreme Soviet Adopts Law on Entry and Exit

The USSR Supreme Soviet approved the Law on Entry and Exit from the USSR by 320 votes to 37, with 32 abstentions, Central Television reported. The law gave Soviet citizens the right to leave the USSR and to return, as well as the right to possess documents allowing them to go abroad valid for five years rather than for a single journey. Full implementation of the law was, however, delayed until January 1, 1993. Supreme Soviet deputies agreed that some provisions of the law could be implemented before this date.

Law on Labor Disputes Amended

The USSR Supreme Soviet amended a 1989 law on settling labor disputes by stiffening sanctions against wildcat strikes. TASS quoted Nikolai Gritsenko, the chairman of the USSR Supreme Soviet's Commission on Labor and Social Policy, as saying the law would conform with another on trade unions adopted a few months earlier. Under the trade-union law, unions were authorized to organize and hold strikes. That provision was incorporated into the law on labor disputes. The amendments also made it illegal to strike for political reasons and provided for fines and other penalties for those who organized or participated in wildcat strikes. The amended law also contained a provision stipulating that the USSR president and certain government bodies could postpone a strike or suspend it for two months.

Compensation for Farms

RSFSR Supreme Soviet Chairman Boris El'tsin told a meeting of agrarian specialists that farms would receive compensation for the higher costs of industrial products and that the RSFSR Finance Ministry had ordered a 3-billion-ruble advance payment to be made in the first six months of 1991. El'tsin said there were also plans for compensation to be paid to farmers for the increased price of domestic and imported agricultural equipment (*TASS*, May 20).

Popov Loses Vote in Moscow City Soviet

The majority of deputies of the Moscow City Soviet declined to endorse the body's chairman, Gavriil Popov, in his candidacy for the mayoral elections in June. About 100 of the 450 deputies left the chamber just before the vote, Western agencies reported. Of those who stayed, only 189 voted in favor of Popov's candidacy. In order to register as a candidate, the law did not require that Popov have the approval of the deputies, merely 10,000 signatures of eligible voters. Radio Rossii said that nearly 200,000 signatures supporting Popov's nomination had been collected. Interfax reported that Popov had himself proposed the vote, saying that, if he did not receive the endorsement of the soviet, he would not run. On May 24, however, he declared that he had decided to run after all, Reuters reported.

Kozyrev on Minorities Convention

Speaking on behalf of the Soviet delegation at the United Nations, RSFSR Foreign Minister Andrei Kozyrev called on the UN Economic and Social Council to enact an international convention on the rights of people belonging to national, ethnic, religious, and linguistic minorities. Kozyrev said the United Nations should ensure that states acted in the interests of the individual, and he advocated the creation of national institutions to protect human rights as well as the formation of nongovernmental organizations to help disseminate information in the USSR on human rights (RFE/RL correspondent's report, May 21).

Casualties of Interethnic Conflicts in 1991

USSR MVD officials told TASS that, since the beginning of 1991, about 200 civilians and more than 40 law-enforcement officers and MVD troops had been killed in interethnic conflicts and 700 civilians injured. Over the preceding three years, more than 1,200 people, including at least 131 MVD personnel, had been killed and 10,000 wounded, TASS reported. Direct material damage exceeded 6 billion rubles.

Moldavian Ministry of Internal Affairs under Republican Control

As part of a reorganization of the republican government, the Moldavian Supreme Soviet voted to place Moldavia's Ministry of Internal Affairs under exclusive republican subordination, Moldovapres reported. Previously, the ministry had been subordinated to both the Union and the republican governments, which meant that crime fighting and traffic control had come under republican jurisdiction but that all activities with political implications had come under the jurisdiction of the USSR Ministry of Internal Affairs.

Lithuanian Government Supports Anticrisis Program

Radio Independent Lithuania reported that Lithuanian Prime Minister Gediminas Vagnorius had sent a telegram to Soviet President Mikhail Gorbachev, Prime Minister Valentin Pavlov, and First Deputy Prime Minister Vitalii Doguzhiev stating that the Lithuanian government supported the USSR's economic anticrisis program. He said that Lithuania would participate in work on it, normalize economic relations with the USSR, and spur international economic activities after the preparation and signing of an agreement between the Lithuanian and USSR governments.

Tuesday, May 21

RSFSR Congress of People's Deputies Approves Law on Presidency

The Fourth RSFSR Congress of People's Deputies opened in Moscow to discuss the legislation enabling direct presidential elections on June 12, TASS reported. In his opening speech, Supreme Soviet Chairman Boris El'tsin welcomed Soviet President Mikhail Gorbachev's recent moves towards conciliation with the RSFSR and other republics, Radio Moscow reported. El'tsin further noted that under his leadership major steps to strengthen the RSFSR's sovereignty had been taken. While recognizing that Russia's legislature had been successfully reformed, El'tsin nonetheless admitted that almost nothing had been achieved in the economic sphere. He blamed the central authorities, which, he said, had controlled the entire economy until recently. El'tsin said that, if elected RSFSR president, he would strengthen executive power at all levels by enhancing the role of the chairmen of the city soviets.

The USSR in May, 1991

Communist deputies tried unsuccessfully to resist debate on the RSFSR presidency at the first session of the Congress. The majority of deputies approved the proposed agenda, which ensured that the Congress would first vote on the law on election procedures and powers of the president, rather than, as conservatives had suggested, on amendments to the constitution, Western agencies reported.

North Ossetian deputies to the Congress walked out after demanding that a statement by their Supreme Soviet declaring the recent RSFSR law on the rehabilitation of oppressed peoples unconstitutional be read to the Congress, Radio Rossii reported. El'tsin proposed that the matter be submitted to the constitutional court due to be set up at the Congress. The law called for the restoration of frontiers that existed prior to the deportation of peoples in the 1940s, which would mean that North Ossetia would lose territory to Checheno-Ingushetia.

On May 22, the Congress adopted a law establishing an executive presidency for the RSFSR by 615 votes to 235, Reuters reported. The law gave the RSFSR president the power to issue decrees and to appoint and dismiss ministers but required him to suspend his membership of political parties and other public organizations and barred him from holding other state office. It also gave the RSFSR Supreme Soviet the power to overrule the president.

Among presidential hopefuls who spoke on May 22, General Al'bert Makashov was quoted by TASS as having promised in a speech to establish order in society, preserve the USSR within its 1945 borders, and wipe out profiteering if elected president. Vadim Bakatin told the Congress that he rejected attempts to justify poverty for the sake of principles, according to Western reports, and denounced those radicals who wanted to send Communists "to the firing squad." Vladimir Zhirinovsky also addressed the Congress, but deputies later referred to his speech as "a shameful comedy," according to the *Financial Times* of May 23.

RSFSR Communist Party First Secretary Ivan Polozkov, addressing the Congress, criticized the creation of the presidency, saying it contradicted "the very idea of *perestroika*." He said he believed that the office would lead to a regime of personal power and to the destruction of all democratic principles and would turn the RSFSR from a popular democracy into a kind of monarchy.

On May 24, the Congress gave final approval for the creation of an executive presidency. According to AFP, 894 deputies voted in favor of a president for the RSFSR, 6 voted against, and 16 abstained. Reuters reported that the Congress had also passed an amendment that would ban the president from dismissing regional executive officials. A TASS report that day said that El'tsin had greeted the Congress's decision as "a great victory."

USSR Supreme Soviet Discusses Union Treaty

The draft Union treaty was discussed in closed session by the USSR Supreme Soviet after Georgii Tarazevich, chairman of the USSR Supreme Soviet's Commission on Nationalities Policy, had reported on the substance of discussions of the draft in the parliamentary committees and commissions, TASS reported. Tarazevich said that the draft had been approved in the main but that more than 200 comments and suggestions had been made. Chairman of the Supreme Soviet Anatolii Luk'yanov argued that the USSR president and parliament had a right to take an active part in the elaboration of the text because the question was not one of creating a new state but of renewing an existing one.

On May 22, the USSR Supreme Soviet adopted a resolution on the Union treaty that called for the text of the draft to be brought into line with the results of the March 17 referendum and for representatives of the supreme organs of state power of the USSR to take part in the signing of the treaty, TASS reported. Some deputies objected to the latter. Sergei Ryabchenko, a leader of the Interregional Group of Deputies, said that an attempt by the center to meddle in the signing process would only hamper conclusion of the treaty.

Five-Percent Sales Tax Selectively Repealed

The USSR central government repealed the 5-percent sales tax on consumer goods and some services, TASS reported. The decision was said to be a consequence of "social stabilization" in the USSR following the joint declaration on April 23 by Soviet President Mikhail Gorbachev and the leaders of nine Union republics. The tax would be lifted on meat, milk, bread, potatoes, pasta, fruit, vegetables, beer, and baby food but remain on wine; it would also be lifted on coal, gas, petrol, and telephone and postal services but would continue in restaurants, luxury shops, and shops dealing in hard currency.

Prosecutors Told to Keep Close Watch on Political Activity

A session of the collegium of the USSR Prosecutor's Office was held in Moscow, including for the first time representatives of the republics, TASS reported. The session called on republican public prosecutors to keep a tighter watch on political parties and movements; to observe whether the activities of political groups were legal; and, if not, to issue official warnings, prosecute individuals, and seek the disbanding of offending groups when necessary. The collegium also called on prosecutors to rein in local legislators who ignored federal laws and to give priority to the enforcement of measures designed to promote the anticrisis program and other economic laws.

A report presented at a four-day conference in Vienna organized by the International Atomic Energy Agency on the 1986 nuclear catastrophe at Chernobyl' suggested that the disaster's impact on the physical health of the Soviet population had been exaggerated, AP reported. The year-long study, conducted by the International Chernobyl' Project at the USSR's request, involved about 200 doctors and scientists from twenty-five nations and investigated an estimated 825,000 people in an area of 25,000 square kilometers in Belorussia, the RSFSR, and Ukraine. Viktor Gubanov, head of the Soviet committee responsible for dealing with the Chernobyl' accident, criticized the investigation for failing to consider the 116,000 people evacuated from within the thirty-kilometer zone around Chernobyl' immediately after the accident or the estimated 600,000 people who worked on cleaning up the area. Nonetheless, he and other Soviet scientists expressed satisfaction that the study had vindicated their own conclusions. The vice president of the Ukrainian Academy of Sciences, Viktor Bar'yakhtar, said he was very dissatisfied with the study.

Officials from both Ukraine and Belorussia objected to the report, AP reported on May 24. They presented formal statements at the conference asking for more detailed study of the effects on health and the environment. A spokesman for the Soviet mission in New York, Yurii Chizik, said that "calming the Soviet people down was not a solution" for dealing with the aftermath of Chernobyl' (RFE/RL correspondent's report, May 24).

International Study Says Impact of Chernobyl' Exaggerated

Italian Prime Minister Giulio Andreotti arrived in Moscow, TASS reported. On May 22, he met with USSR Prime Minister Valentin Pavlov to discuss Soviet-Italian economic relations and, later that day, with Soviet President Mikhail Gorbachev, who briefed him on the political situation in the USSR and expressed gratitude to the Italian government for its solidarity with the USSR government on reform. TASS also said the two men discussed the Middle East, the Mediterranean region, and Eastern Europe. Gorbachev described the talks as "very useful" and very important. The two leaders signed an agreement establishing a direct link between the Kremlin and Italy's

Italian Prime Minister in Moscow

seat of government to facilitate the rapid exchange of information.

Soviet Union Launches More Submarines

The latest edition of *Jane's Fighting Ships* reported on May 20 that the Soviet Union had launched ten submarines in 1990, six of them nuclear-powered and equipped with the latest weapons and sensing equipment. According to a summary published by *The Times* on May 21, the book also warned that after five years of *perestroika* the rate of buildup in the Soviet navy had not declined enough to justify "the partial unilateral naval disarmament which is affecting the West." By the mid-1990s, the report said, the Soviet navy was expected to introduce new generations of ballistic missiles and of nuclear- and conventionally-powered submarines.

Japanese Banks Suspend Credits to USSR

According to TASS, Japanese banks suspended further credits to the Soviet Union. A representative of Vneshekonombank, Vladimir Sterlikov, said that the credit suspension would mainly affect Japanese companies whose Soviet clients were not paying their bills. Japanese banks also warned that hard-currency shortages had reduced the USSR's creditworthiness. Soviet firms were some 450 million US dollars behind in payments to Japanese creditors.

Strike Leaders Put Pressure on Belorussian Deputies

The fourth session of the Belorussian Supreme Soviet opened with heated debate over the question of whether to include the political and economic demands of Belorussian strike committees on the session's agenda. The deputies, according to Belta-TASS, agreed in the end to put the following issues on the agenda: ridding state enterprises and organizations of Party influence, nationalization of property belonging to the CPSU and the Belorussian Communist Party, the performing of military service in Belorussia, and proposed measures to guide the republic through the transition to a market economy.

Strike leader Sergei Antonchyk, a Belorussian people's deputy, announced that 80 percent of the republic's strike committees were ready to call a strike on May 22 because not all their demands concerning the agenda had been met (*Reuters*, May 22).

Workers from the Minsk Truck Factory and one or two other large enterprises walked off the job on May 22 but were back at work by the afternoon, according to Belta-TASS.

The USSR in May, 1991

Seven major factories were reported to be on strike on May 23 in the city of Mogilev. They timed their action to coincide with the opening of a session of the Mogilev Oblast Soviet. A spokesman for the Minsk Strike Committee said that four members of the strike committee in one defense industry factory had been fired and that nearly all the members of other strike committees had been summoned by the public prosecutor's office and warned that court action might follow if work stopped at their factories. Viktor Rasosnykh said that labor protests would continue but not in the form of a general strike and that it would be for each factory to decide what action to follow (RFE Belorussian service, May 23).

Ter-Petrossyan in Paris

Armenian Supreme Soviet Chairman Levon Ter-Petrossyan arrived in Paris for a four-day visit (RFE/RL correspondent's report, May 21). He met with French President François Mitterrand to discuss the Armenian-Azerbaijani conflict and told him that Armenia was committed to independence within a democratic framework, AP reported.

After talks between French Foreign Minister Roland Dumas and Ter-Petrossyan on May 23, the French government declared that it wanted "concrete" cooperation with Armenia regarding the establishment of democratic institutions in the republic and of direct relations between French and Armenian economic enterprises. According to AFP, officials at the French embassy in Moscow would travel regularly to Erevan to foster such contacts.

Speaking at a press conference in Paris, Ter-Petrossyan said he was convinced that France recognized the necessity of dealing with the rising republican forces, and not with Moscow alone, in its relations with the USSR. He reaffirmed Armenia's decision to move towards independence in conformity with the USSR Constitution and other laws and observed that, in choosing the constitutional path, Armenia knew Moscow could pose no legal obstacles (RFE/RL correspondent's report, May 24).

Moldavian Prime Minister Ousted

The Moldavian Supreme Soviet voted by 207 to eleven for a motion of no confidence in Moldavian Prime Minister Mircea Druc and in his government, which was dominated by the Moldavian Popular Front, accusing him of mismanaging the economy and of links with an enterprise found to be embezzling money, Reuters reported. The move came after Moldavian President Mircea Snegur had accused a number of leading figures in the popular front of trying to whip up disorder to prevent the constitutional changes he had proposed. Snegur wanted the republic's prime minister to be subordinated to the president and not responsible to the Supreme Soviet as he was under the existing arrangement. TASS reported later that day that around 1,000 people had gathered in the center of Kishinev to protest against Druc's ouster and that clashes between Druc's supporters and Moldavian police had resulted in casualties.

The Moldavian Supreme Soviet decided on May 23 to drop the words "Soviet" and "Socialist" from the republic's name and adopted the official title "Republic of Moldova," Reuters reported. According to TASS, the deputies also refused to reopen Druc's case.

On May 28, the Moldavian parliament approved Snegur's nomination of Valeriu Muravschi as prime minister in place of Druc. Muravschi, an economist, had been minister of finance since June, 1991, and concurrently deputy prime minister since March, 1991. His nomination was supported by the Moldavian Popular Front and opposed by Russian Communist deputies. Presenting his program to the parliament the same day, Muravschi assessed the state of the republic's economy as "chaotic." He urged parliament to expedite the adoption of laws on privatization, the establishment of a national bank, and local self-government. He also pledged to pursue Moldavia's "integration with European countries and horizontal ties with Union republics." His agenda was similar to Druc's (*Moldovapres*, May 28).

USSR General Says Soviet Forces Damaged Mongolia's Environment

Major General Vyacheslav Mezun, leading the third phase of a troop withdrawal from Mongolia, said Soviet forces had done serious damage to the country's environment, TASS reported. He said that the current phase of the withdrawal had begun on May 15 and would include up to 8,000 troops and that support personnel were repairing the damage done to Mongolia's desert and steppes by troop exercises.

Wednesday, May 22

USSR Supreme Soviet Adopts Consumer-Rights Law

A consumer-rights law adopted by the USSR Supreme Soviet was the first attempt in Soviet history to enforce minimum standards of service and quality for consumers, TASS reported. It would go into effect on January 1, 1992, and would give consumers the right to file official

The USSR in May, 1991

complaints and seek compensation if they were abused or sold defective goods. For the text of the law, see *Izvestia*, June 8, 1991.

Referendum Planned for Ukraine

The Ukrainian Supreme Soviet decided to hold a referendum in September on the political future of the republic, Ukrinform-TASS reported. Citizens would be asked to decide on a name for the state, its symbols, form of state administration, and whether or not the notion of "Socialist choice" was to be enshrined in the constitution.

The Ukrainian Supreme Soviet also confirmed ministers proposed by Ukrainian Prime Minister Vitol'd Fokin. According to TASS, they confirmed Konstantin Masik as Fokin's first deputy and Aleksandr Masel'sky as a deputy prime minister. Viktor Antonov became minister of defense and the conversion of defense industries, Anatolii Minchenko became economics minister, and Aleksandr Tkachenko became minister for agriculture and food.

Pskov Paratroopers Return to Lithuania

Lithuanian Prime Minister Gediminas Vagnorius sent a telegram to Soviet President Mikhail Gorbachev and USSR Defense Minister Dmitrii Yazov, Radio Independent Lithuania reported. Vagnorius expressed regret that paratroopers from Pskov who had participated in the attack on the Vilnius television tower on January 13 had been sent to Lithuania and Belorussia on May 21 without informing the Lithuanian authorities. He wrote that sharing information on troop movements could help ease tension.

Thursday, May 23

Publishers Ask for Tax Break

The publishers of several leading Soviet periodicals called on the USSR government to establish a preferential taxation system for the print media and for activities associated with print production. The request was made in a letter to Soviet President Mikhail Gorbachev published in *Pravda* in which Gorbachev was asked to issue a decree fixing prices for paper, communications services, and transportation charges associated with the production and the delivery of print. The publishers suggested that, if fixed prices exceeded certain limits, the difference should be subsidized by the state. The request came after *Pravda* had announced that the prices of newspapers and other periodicals would soon double in the USSR, attributing the rises to increased costs for paper, communications, and other services.

USSR Ready to Join US in Destruction of Chemical Arms

Soviet delegate Sergei Batsanov told the thirty-nine-nation Disarmament Conference in Geneva that the Soviet Union welcomed the new US proposals to ban chemical weapons and was prepared, together with the United States, to destroy all chemical weapons stocks after conclusion of an international treaty, Reuters reported.

Soviet Official on Western Aid

USSR Deputy Foreign Minister Ernest Obminsky, attending talks in Brussels on the distribution of European Community food aid to the USSR, declared that no amount of Western aid would help the Soviet Union if its political problems persisted. DPA quoted him as saying that development in the USSR depended not on aid but on the successful distribution of power from the central government to the republics. The European Community announced the same day its intention to deliver 300 million dollars in aid in July, 1991.

Leningrad Stock Exchange Reopened

A stock exchange first founded by Tsar Peter the Great in 1705 officially reopened for business in Leningrad after an interruption in trading of seven decades, Reuters reported. The oldest Russian bourse was to be run by an association of 250 Soviet enterprises, banks, private entrepreneurs, and brokers, and had an initial capital of 25 million rubles. Its president, Professor Aleksandr Kartashov, told reporters the exchange had in fact been trading for the past six weeks and that some 150 deals worth a total of 50 million rubles had been made. He added that, although the bourse planned to develop conventional securities and commodities trading with uniform contracts, at present its main role was to auction scarce goods, such as building materials.

Ukrainian Cardinal Meets Republican Leaders

Myroslav Cardinal Lyubachivs'kyi, the leader of the Ukrainian Greek-rite Catholic Church, told Ukrainian Supreme Soviet Chairman Leonid Kravchuk and Prime Minister Vitol'd Fokin in Kiev that his Church expected full rehabilitation and the return of its former property, TASS reported. The Church lost its property to the Russian Orthodox Church when it was forced to merge with it by Stalin. Since its rehabilitation in 1990, the Ukrainian Catholic Church had been trying to reclaim its property, which led to friction with the Russian Orthodox

The USSR in May, 1991

Church. Kravchuk asked Lyubachivs'kyi to use his authority to end the conflict.

Friday, May 24

Republican Leaders Meet to Discuss Union Treaty

A meeting intended to produce a draft of a new Union treaty was held in Novo Ogarevo, outside Moscow. It was chaired by Soviet President Mikhail Gorbachev and attended by the premiers and speakers of the supreme soviets of most of the Union republics and by the leaders of eighteen autonomous republics. (An outline agreement on the fate of the Union had been reached in Novo Ogarevo on April 23 between Gorbachev and the representatives of nine Union republics.) Radio Rossii reported that the main items of discussion were the conditions under which republics could join the Union and the principles for the establishment of the central organs of power.

On May 25, both Mikhail Gorbachev and Boris El'tsin expressed satisfaction with progress made at the meeting. Both made plain that what was envisaged was a federation, not a confederation. El'tsin noted, however, that there was still disagreement on issues such as taxation, control of local defense industries, and ownership of Russia's oil and gas reserves (*TASS*, May 25).

Soviet Budget Figures Show Deficit

The USSR State Committee for Statistics reported that the USSR had spent 27 billion rubles more than it had collected in the first quarter of 1991. The figures, which were presented to the USSR Supreme Soviet, showed that the country's budget deficit for the first quarter of 1991 was more than five times higher than the planned deficit for the entire year. Most of the blame for the problem was put on the failure of the republican governments, in particular the RSFSR and Ukraine, to contribute their share to the Union budget, as a result of which the central government had been forced to cut spending on the economy drastically and to curb spending on defense, science, and foreign activities, TASS reported.

Soviet-German Agreement on Fighting Crime

USSR Minister of Internal Affairs Boriss Pugo and Eduard Lintner, state secretary of the German Interior Ministry, signed an agreement in Moscow intended to increase cooperation in fighting organized crime, the narcotics trade, illegal arms dealing, the trade in human beings, illicit gambling, fraud, blackmail, and economic crime.

According to DPA, a joint commission of officials from the German and Soviet interior ministries would meet annually to coordinate actions. The cooperation would include the exchange and training of experts and the provision of technical assistance, Lintner said. Moreover, the accord should pave the way for the permanent stationing in the USSR of German police officers to help fight the drugs trade.

Sobchak Meets German President

The chairman of the Leningrad City Soviet, Anatolii Sobchak, held talks in Bonn with German President Richard von Weizsäcker, AFP reported. Weizsäcker expressed Germany's interest in further steps towards reform in the USSR and the RSFSR and said that the next century's task would be to bring Europe and the Soviet Union closer together. Sobchak also met later that day with the Eastern Committee of German Business to discuss promoting cooperation in the electrical and textile industries. Sobchak elaborated his concept of an economic and cultural opening to the West and his ideas on the resettlement of ethnic Germans from Central Asia to Leningrad (RFE/RL correspondent's report, May 24).

New Conservative Group Created

A new conservative group organized inside the RSFSR Supreme Soviet was reported to have been joined by more than 150 deputies. Lieutenant General Boris Tarasov told RFE/RL that the group, called "Otchizna," would be similar to the "Soyuz" faction in the USSR Supreme Soviet and would seek to unite deputies who were concerned about such issues as the RSFSR's sovereignty and integrity and the preservation of national pride and the dignity of the state.

***Izvestia* on Secret Organs of Power in Ukraine**

An article published by *Izvestia* reported that unconstitutional organs of power had been uncovered in the Kiev City Soviet and in other governing bodies in Ukraine. According to the author, who was a deputy in the Kiev City Soviet and a member of its executive committee, groups of officials had been making decisions among themselves but passing them off as the decisions of elected organs. This practice had started in 1984 and was authorized by the then Ukrainian Communist Party first secretary, Vladimir Shcherbitsky, and then prime minister, Aleksandr Lyashko. The article also suggested that analogous secret organs functioned in all the republics of the Soviet Union.

The USSR in May, 1991

Saturday, May 25

Independence-Seeking Republics Set Up Coordinating Body

Delegates of popular movements in six republics seeking independence from the USSR conferred in Kishinev on May 25 and 26. Initiated by the Moldavian Popular Front, the meeting was attended by delegates from Lithuania's "Sajudis," from the Latvian and Estonian Popular Fronts, from the Georgian Round Table, and from the Armenian Pan-National Movement. The delegates signed the founding documents of a coordinating body, the Assembly of Popular Fronts and Movements from Republics Not Joining the Union Treaty, also to be known as the Kishinev Forum. According to the documents, the Kishinev Forum was to be based on the principles of the UN Charter; on the right of peoples to self-determination as defined in UN resolutions on decolonization; and on international covenants on human, civil, and political rights. The document also said that normalization of the situation in the USSR and stability in the world were impossible without recognition and observance of the rights of the republics that had chosen to set up independent states.

In separate telegrams to Soviet President Mikhail Gorbachev and UN General Secretary Javier Perez de Cuellar, the Kishinev Forum protested about the USSR's use of military force in the Baltic republics and in Armenia and Nagorno-Karabakh and about what it called the fanning of interethnic conflict in Georgia by the center. It demanded legal prosecution of those responsible for the use of violence against civilians and the withdrawal of Soviet troops from six republics.

The forum said it would meet once a month to coordinate activities and plan joint political action (RFE/RL Research Institute, Western press reports, May 26 and 27).

El'tsin Sees Momentum Shifting Back towards Reform

RSFSR Supreme Soviet Chairman Boris El'tsin said he believed momentum in the USSR was shifting back towards reform and away from conservatives who favored dictatorship. He said it was remarkable that his meeting with Soviet President Mikhail Gorbachev the previous day had been conducted in a business-like fashion and without conflict (*TASS, Radio Rossii*, May 25).

Soviet Minister Confirms Increased Reliance on Nuclear Power

In an article published in *Pravda*, USSR Minister of Atomic Energy Vitalii Konovalov said the Soviet government intended to triple the country's nuclear energy capacity by the year 2000 and boost sales of uranium on world markets. He said his ministry was counting on the construction of some 20,000 megawatts in capacity—or about twenty reactor units—in the next decade to make up for shortfalls in other energy sources. The figures confirmed recent forecasts by nuclear industry officials and were part of a long-awaited national energy program for the period up to 2005 to be presented soon to the USSR Supreme Soviet. Konovalov also said sales of uranium on the free market would average no less than 5,000 tons a year in the coming five years.

Pravda Says West Will Suffer Unless It Helps USSR

In a commentary written by Tomas Kolesnichenko, *Pravda* warned the West that it would suffer greatly unless it helped the Soviet Union avert economic disaster. It said Western reluctance to help economic recovery in the Soviet Union could plunge the world back into the dark days of the Cold War. Kolesnichenko suggested that such reluctance might encourage the rise of hard-line forces opposed to Soviet President Mikhail Gorbachev's reforms, a process that he said could eventually cost Western countries much more than the 100 billion dollars they had spent on evicting Iraqi troops from Kuwait.

Ter-Petrossyan Sees Link between Accord and Military Action

Armenian Supreme Soviet Chairman Levon Ter-Petrossyan said there was a direct link between attacks by Soviet troops on Armenian settlements and Soviet President Mikhail Gorbachev's accord with nine Soviet republics signed in April. In an interview with *Le Monde*, Ter-Petrossyan said Azerbaijani President Ayaz Mutalibov had justified signing the accord by saying that Moscow had allowed "the liberation" of several Armenian villages in exchange for his signature. Armenia did not sign the accord. Ter-Petrossyan alleged that Gorbachev expected the military action to dissuade Armenians from voting for independence in the republican referendum to be held on September 21. Similar allegations about a link between the signing of the accord and the commencement of the violence in the Transcaucasus were made by Aleksandr Yakovlev in *la Repubblica* of May 12–13.

Sunday, May 26

Presidential Elections in Georgia

Zviad Gamsakhurdia was elected Georgian president by a majority of 87 percent in what was the first direct popular contested election of a republican leader in the USSR. Voter turnout was given as 84 percent, according to *The New York Times* of May 28. During an emotional election campaign, Gamsakhurdia's opponents accused him of being a dictator, while the fifty-two-year-old former political prisoner charged that the other five candidates were all Kremlin agents. Gamsakhurdia's main rival, Valerian Advadze, who received 6 percent of the vote, predicted that the vote would be rigged, that Gamsakhurdia would initiate reprisals against himself and other rivals, and that Gamsakhurdia would face a rebellion within six months if he did not change his political course. International observers said there was no evidence of malpractice at the polling stations they monitored in Tbilisi. There was no voting in South Ossetia or Abkhazia.

Gamsakhurdia celebrated his victory on May 27 with a march-past by the newly created Georgian National Guard. He pledged to ensure the security of the Georgian people and to fight "provocateurs, criminals, and the Communist mafia" (Western press reports, May 26 and 27).

Myroslav Cardinal Lyubachivs'kyi, Ukrainian Catholic Church leader, was prevented from conducting a mass at St. Andrew's Church in Kiev. Several hundred jeering Russian Orthodox protesters blocked the entrance to the church. Kiev city officials had given their approval for the church service. Later, the service was conducted in another church in the Ukrainian capital (Western press reports, May 26).

Controversy over Ukrainian Cardinal

The new law on the KGB gave state security officers the right to enter public and private premises without the sanction of the prosecutor's office, people's deputy Galina Starovoitova told Radio Rossii. She criticized the USSR Supreme Soviet for adopting a law that legally extended the KGB's functions. As examples, Starovoitova cited provisions of the law allowing postal censorship and eavesdropping and KGB control over the army and the MVD. She expressed the hope, however, that the newly created RSFSR KGB would not be involved in political surveillance and ideological control.

Starovoitova Comments on KGB Law

―――――――――――――――――――――――――――――― *Monday, May 27*

German Economics Minister Jürgen Möllemann held talks with USSR Prime Minister Valentin Pavlov in Moscow. The two ministers focused their attention on the further development of Soviet-German economic relations and

Möllemann Meets Pavlov

discussed the maintenance of "traditional business ties" between Soviet enterprises and their partners in the former GDR, TASS said. They also grappled with the issue of housing construction for the Soviet troops returning from Germany. Western press reports quoted Möllemann as saying that Pavlov had agreed to award firms in the former GDR 1.2 million deutsche marks in contracts for investment goods, in addition to 9 billion deutsche marks in orders for which the USSR had already contracted.

Thatcher Tells Soviet Students to Support Reform Path

Former British Prime Minister Margaret Thatcher spoke to Soviet students in Moscow and strongly supported the reform efforts of Soviet President Mikhail Gorbachev. In a lecture at the Institute for International Relations, she said there had been "enormous advances" in the USSR, including moves to protect the freedoms of speech, religion, and travel. She also spoke in favor of inviting Gorbachev as a guest to the economic summit of industrial nations to be held in London in July. Although some of the Soviet students did not share Thatcher's high opinion of Gorbachev, they gave her a rousing welcome. Thatcher was in Moscow at the personal invitation of Gorbachev with whom she met later in the day. TASS quoted her as saying the world wanted *perestroika* to succeed (Western press reports, *TASS*, May 27).

The same day, Thatcher met with USSR Prime Minister Valentin Pavlov and Defense Minister Dmitrii Yazov. They discussed Soviet reforms and international issues (*TASS*, May 27). On May 28, she met with representatives of the Baltic republics (*Radio Riga*, May 28).

On May 29, Thatcher arrived in Leningrad and defended Gorbachev in talks with Chairman of the Leningrad City Soviet Anatolii Sobchak. She said she did not agree with Sobchak's assertion that Gorbachev presented an obstacle to private land ownership (Western press reports, May 29).

Ministry of Finance Takes a Loan

The USSR Supreme Soviet approved a presidential order for the USSR State Bank to lend 5 billion rubles to the USSR Ministry of Finance, TASS reported. The loan would run until October 1, 1991, and carry an annual interest rate of 6 percent. The loan would go to the extrabudgetary fund for economic stabilization established by agreement between the center and republics in 1990. The Baltic republics subsequently refused to contribute to the fund, and other republics reduced the size of their contributions. Of an expected 12 billion rubles of deposits, only 1.8 billion had been received by May 1.

The USSR in May, 1991

Green Party Founded in RSFSR

TASS reported that ecological groups in the RSFSR had joined forces to form a Green Party. At its founding conference in Leningrad, the new party called for the replacement of all nuclear power plants in the USSR with "ecologically clean" sources of energy.

Testing to Be Resumed at Semipalatinsk?

Nevada-Semipalatinsk, Kazakhstan's antinuclear movement, said that it had learned testing was soon to be resumed at the testing site in Semipalatinsk Oblast and that the movement's Siberian chapter was appealing to the population of Altai Krai to protest. A TASS report of May 27 quoted the Siberian appeal as warning that the Altai was downwind of the testing site and that tests were conducted only when the wind was blowing in that direction. The appeal also said if tests are resumed, the movement would have to resort to extreme measures; it did not specify what these might be.

Last Soviet Unit Pulls Out of Czechoslovakia

The last unit of Soviet troops stationed in Czechoslovakia as a result of the 1968 Soviet-led invasion left the country. A Czechoslovak television report said a battalion that had been guarding Soviet troop headquarters at Milovice near Prague was the last unit to move out. The only troops left were 350 officers and 450 enlisted men who were to hand over the remaining Soviet military installations by June 20.

Ukraine Intends to Take Over Defense Industries

At a conference in Kiev, Ukraine's newly appointed minister of the military industry and conversion, Viktor Antonov, said he believed "100 percent of the military-industrial complex located on the territory of Ukraine will come under direct Ukrainian control as of January 1, 1992." Ukraine held roughly 13 percent of the USSR's defense and defense-related industry (Western press reports, May 27).

USSR Protests about Lithuanian Attendance at Cracow Conference

The Soviet Union protested to Poland about its extension of an invitation to four Lithuanians to attend the Cracow Cultural Symposium. Symposium officials said the Soviet culture minister, Nikolai Gubenko, had threatened not to attend the symposium unless the invitation was withdrawn. The symposium was part of the follow-up to the 1975 Helsinki accords, which established the meetings of the Conference on Security and Cooperation in Europe (CSCE). Lithuania, along with Estonia and Latvia, was seeking membership in the

CSCE as a sovereign state. The Soviet Union had blocked their attempts to send representatives as observers to previous meetings of the conference (RFE/RL correspondent's report, May 28).

On May 29, Gubenko sharply criticized Polish Prime Minister Jan Krzysztof Bielecki for comments he made in a speech opening the symposium. Gubenko accused Bielecki of "dancing on the grave of socialism" when he referred to communism as a forty-year aberration in Poland's thousand years of cultural history (RFE/RL correspondent's report, May 29).

On May 30, Poland officially complained about Gubenko's remarks, saying that he had "insulted" Bielecki (Western press reports, May 30).

Tuesday, May 28

Center Sets Tough Terms for Independent Republics

Western and Soviet reports said the USSR government had proposed strict economic sanctions against republics that did not sign the new Union treaty. The measures, designed by the State Planning Committee, would apply to the Baltic republics, Georgia, Armenia, and Moldavia. According to the document, these republics would have to pay their share of internal and external debt, pay the full price for all-Union factories, and then either lease them back to the USSR on favorable terms or create joint ventures, with the USSR as majority stockholder. Further, terms of trade between the USSR and the independent states would be set strongly in the USSR's favor, and the USSR would plan to reduce sharply the volume of goods and services it would import from them.

New Restrictions on Commercial Activities

The USSR Supreme Soviet approved a government decree banning commercial activities in certain sensitive sectors of the economy. Also approved was a decree requiring state licenses for trade in other sensitive sectors. Soviet Deputy Prime Minister Yurii Maslyukov said the measures applied to those activities that concerned "the defense capabilities of the country, the maintenance of state and social security, the environment, and the health of the population." Sales of precious and radioactive materials, of weapons, and of military technology were forbidden. Enterprises were obliged to obtain a license to develop and produce military equipment and spare parts, exploit minerals, and to transport, process, and store uranium and other similar substances as well as oil and gas (*TASS*, May 28).

THE USSR IN MAY, 1991

Primakov in Washington in Search of Aid

Kremlin envoy Evgenii Primakov held talks in Washington with officials of the US administration, the World Bank, and the IMF in a bid to win aid for the struggling Soviet economy. An official at the Soviet embassy in Washington, Yurii Khomenko, said that, in his meetings at the World Bank and the IMF, Primakov had discussed but had not formally applied for Soviet membership in these organizations.

On May 29, Primakov had talks with US Senate Republican leader Robert Dole and with US Secretary of State James Baker to whom he outlined the latest Soviet program for economic reform. While Baker declared that the United States was "strongly interested" in helping the Soviet Union move to a market economy, US officials said on May 30 that the Soviet anticrisis program needed substantial work. The unnamed officials told reporters that the United States remained unconvinced that the USSR was either willing or able to confront the painful political problems brought on by reform (Western press reports, *AFP*, May 29 and 30).

On May 31, Primakov and other Soviet officials had a meeting with US President George Bush at the White House. After the meeting, Bush said he felt "more positive" about the Soviet request for Western aid, adding that he had gained the impression the USSR had embarked on radical economic reform. The same day, sources at the IMF revealed that Primakov had told IMF Managing Director Michel Camdessus earlier in the week that the Soviet Union would require 30–50 billion dollars a year in foreign finance over the next five or six years if its economic reform program was to succeed (Western press reports, May 31).

Law Privatizing Apartments Passed in Lithuania

The Lithuanian Supreme Council passed a law on the privatization of apartments. Apartments were to be sold to current residents, with up to 80 percent of the cost covered by investment checks that would be given only to citizens of the Republic of Lithuania as compensation for losses suffered under Soviet rule (*Radio Independent Lithuania*, May 28). A plenum of the Vilnius Communist Party sent appealed to Soviet President Mikhail Gorbachev not to allow implementation of the law, because it discriminated against Soviet citizens, TASS reported.

Gorbachev in Kazakhstan

"Vremya" showed Soviet President Mikhail Gorbachev's arrival in Kazakhstan and his meeting with inhabitants of Kokchetav. A television correspondent asked him if he was visiting Kazakhstan because it had a reputation for being one of the most stable republics. Gorbachev answered that he was pleased with Kazakhstan's stability and also its adherence to the Union and that he wanted to support its leadership, which he characterized as highly responsible.

On May 29, Gorbachev arrived in Alma-Ata, where he was greeted by banners urging him to prevent the resumption of nuclear testing at Semipalatinsk. In a public speech on May 30, Gorbachev said the testing range would be converted to a scientific research center after a few more tests (*TASS*, May 29 and 30).

Gorbachev also addressed a meeting of Communist Party officials and economic managers. He told them that after being "on the brink of social upheaval" in March and April, the Soviet Union was now seeing "the first glimmer of political accord." He also listened to criticism by Kazakh President Nursultan Nazarbaev of the command-administrative system of economic management. According to TASS, Nazarbaev said the Soviet Union needed a market economy, civil accord, and democratization in all spheres of life.

El'tsin's Campaign in Full Swing

RSFSR Supreme Soviet Chairman Boris El'tsin kicked off his campaign for the RSFSR presidency with a visit to Murmansk. There, according to Western press reports, he was mobbed by crowds waving the flag of prerevolutionary Russia and shouting "We love you, Boris Nikolaevich!" As on previous trips to far-flung areas of the RSFSR, El'tsin promised the local population that his administration would devolve enough powers to the regions to enable them to solve their problems themselves. His itinerary also included Petrozavodsk in Karelia, where he signed an agreement stipulating, among other things, that deductions from general state revenue generated in the Karelian ASSR and subject to transfer to the RSFSR republican budget would remain in the autonomous republic (*TASS*, May 29).

On May 30, El'tsin addressed a rally of 12,000 enthusiastic supporters in Tula. He skipped a planned meeting with political and industrial leaders, however, claiming his back was bothering him. His press secretary told AP, "We don't need those people. They are factory directors. These [the people at the rally] are the people we need."

Latvian Deputy Says USSR Owes Latvia Money

The Latvian Supreme Council discussed economic relations with the USSR and Latvian contributions to the USSR budget. Valentina Zeile, head of the budget commission, pointed out that an assessment of the financial value of the exchange of goods and services between Latvia and the USSR indicated that Latvia had provided 90 billion rubles' worth of goods and services more than it had received. Thus, she said, "it is not Latvia that is in debt to the USSR but the Union that it is in debt to Latvia" (*TASS*, May 28).

Belorussian Strike Leaders Facing Charges

Some of the leaders of the protest strike in April in Belorussia were reported to be facing charges of unsanctioned labor activity. A Minsk journalist told RFE/RL that the latest person to be charged was Mikalai Razumau, the chairman of the strike committee in the town of Orsha, east of Minsk. The journalists said Razumau was being charged in connection with the temporary blockade of the Minsk-to-Moscow railway during the strike. Three leaders of the strike committee in Gomel' also faced charges in connection with the strike, and four members of the strike committee at a Minsk defense industry factory had been fired.

Wednesday, May 29

Pavlov Presents Legislation on Foreign Investment

USSR Prime Minister Valentin Pavlov presented radical draft legislation allowing wholly Western-owned firms to operate in the USSR as part of a plan to save the Soviet economy by means of large-scale foreign investment. Pavlov told the Supreme Soviet that the country needed investment of 500 billion rubles to modernize industry. He said he planned to give priority to direct foreign investment rather than credits, which he said were not used effectively enough. He said foreign companies would be guaranteed the right to export products and profits and be allowed tax concessions. Foreign investment would be barred or restricted only in specific sensitive areas, he said, apparently referring to armaments and related industries. The Supreme Soviet approved the legislation at its first reading by 291 votes to 11 (Western press reports, May 29).

Gidaspov Says Leningrad Should Retain Its Name

Leningrad Communist Party First Secretary Boris Gidaspov said the campaign to change the name of Leningrad back to St. Petersburg dishonored the people who had fought to protect it from the German army during World War II. Speaking at a news conference in Leningrad, Gidaspov said the June 12 referendum on restoring the city's old name was merely an opinion poll and would not be binding. He predicted that it was "doomed to fail."

Kaliningrad Port Reopened to Foreign Vessels

The Soviet Baltic port of Kaliningrad, which had been off-limits since 1945, was reopened to foreign shipping. TASS reported the arrival of the first foreign vessel, a Danish freighter sailing under a Panamanian flag. The port manager, Arkadii Mikhailov, said the port's handling facilities would be modernized to make cargo handling more efficient.

Soviet Commander Criticizes Poland over Troop Pullout Talks

The commander of Soviet troops in Poland, Colonel General Viktor Dubynin, said Poland was showing an uncompromising attitude in talks about the Soviet troop withdrawal. Dubynin told *Pravda* that recent talks between Soviet and Polish negotiators in Moscow had ended in an impasse. The two sides disagreed on the timing of the withdrawal and other issues, including environmental damage caused by Soviet troops. Polish experts estimated the damage at 3 billion dollars.

Thursday, May 30

Honecker Says USSR Has Granted Him Political Asylum

Former East German State and Party leader Erich Honecker revealed in an interview with German television that the USSR had granted him political asylum. In the interview, Honecker also spoke about orders to shoot East Germans trying to flee to the West and the events that had led to his departure for the USSR. Honecker was wanted in Germany on manslaughter charges linked to the alleged shooting orders (*DPA, AFP*, May 30).

US Jewish Group Supports One-Year Waiver for USSR

The US National Conference on Soviet Jewry said it supported a one-year waiver of the Jackson-Vannik amendment for the Soviet Union. In a statement, the group cited "the unprecedented numbers of Soviet Jews who have received permission to emigrate to Israel and elsewhere." The Jackson-Vannik amendment links the granting of most-favored-nation trading status to the USSR to free emigration.

Bessmertnykh Welcomes Bush's Middle East Plan

Soviet Foreign Minister Aleksandr Bessmertnykh welcomed a US plan to curb the spread of arms in the Middle East. Bessmertnykh said the plan included some

THE USSR IN MAY, 1991

positive ideas that merited serious study, but he said some points needed further clarification. On May 29, US President George Bush had outlined a plan to halt the spread of weapons of mass destruction and restrict conventional forces in the Middle East. Speaking in Rome, Bessmertnykh said the five permanent members of the UN Security Council must face the fact that they supplied 90 percent of the Middle East's arsenal (Western press reports, May 30).

Armenia Replaces Head of News Agency

TASS said the Armenian government had replaced the director of the republic's official news agency, Armenpres, with a man with longtime links to the Communist Party. TASS said the new director, Gevork Oganesyan, had served as an aide to all three Party first secretaries over the past four years. The former director of Armenpres, Artak Vartazaryan, had been in the job for just over six months.

Explosion on Baku-Bound Train

Eleven people died and eight were injured in an explosion on a train traveling from Moscow to the Azerbaijani capital, Baku. The explosion occurred in the Dagestan Autonomous Republic between the town of Gudermes and the Dagestani capital, Makhachkala. It was caused by a powerful explosive that had been placed in one of the train's compartments (*TASS*, "Vremya," *Central Television*, May 31).

***Moscow News* Calls Chevron-Tengiz Deal a Sellout**

Moscow News (No. 21) denounced the multimillion-dollar deal with the US corporation Chevron to develop the Tengiz oil field near the Caspian Sea, saying it amounted to "giving away" an oil field that some experts said could provide almost 10 percent of the Soviet Union's oil output. The weekly said the cost of the deal for the Soviet side was unacceptably high by comparison with the benefits it would provide. President of Chevron Overseas Petroleum Richard Matzke was quoted as criticizing the *Moscow News* report, saying the newspaper had misunderstood the business arrangement.

Friday, May 31

Democratic Communists to Set Up Own Party

The leader of the Communists for Democracy group in the RSFSR Congress of People's Deputies, Colonel Aleksandr Rutskoi, was quoted by the Russian Information Agency as saying that his group intended to convene a founding congress of a new party. Rutskoi, who had already called on reformists to set up a strong party to oppose the CPSU was running for vice president of the RSFSR on El'tsin's ticket. Rutskoi's initiative was the second attempt (after the creation of the Democratic Platform of reformist Communists of the CPSU) to split the CPSU.

MVD Prepares for Market Transition

Minister of Internal Affairs Boriss Pugo told *Ekonomika i zhizn'* (No. 22) that law-enforcement agencies must institute preemptive policies during the introduction of market relations in order to catch every new form of economic crime. He suggested legislation imposing criminal and administrative penalties for creating "front" cooperatives, claims of false bankruptcy, intentional shortages, unjustified raising of prices, and the distortion of recruitment and employment rules. Pugo advocated a single system of declaring and controlling income.

Georgian Journalists Demand Press Freedom, End to Harassment

Five Georgian journalists were reported to have complained to Georgian President Zviad Gamsakhurdia and to the International Organization of Journalists about poor working conditions and harassment. The journalists, some of whom had reported for RFE/RL, said they had been denied information from official sources and subjected to attacks in the official Georgian media. Two of the journalists said they had been expelled from a press conference given by Gamsakhurdia on May 26 (*TASS*, May 31).

Kravchuk Says Hungarian Pacts Are "Real Recognition"

Hungary and Ukraine signed nine accords, and Ukrainian Supreme Soviet Chairman Leonid Kravchuk called them "real recognition" of Ukrainian sovereignty. The documents were signed in Budapest, where Kravchuk was on an official visit. Radio Budapest quoted Hungarian President Arpad Goncz as saying the accords were special because Ukraine was the first Soviet republic with which Hungary had been able to establish basic ties of this kind.

Soviet Troops on Kurile Islands to Be Cut 30 Percent

A Soviet general was quoted as saying Soviet troop strength on four of the disputed Kurile Islands would be reduced by 30 percent by the end of 1991. The commander of the Far East Military District, Colonel General Viktor Novozhilov, was quoted in the Japanese daily *Yomiuri Shimbun* (*TASS*, May 31).

The USSR in May, 1991

TASS said a social protection fund had been set up for discharged servicemen and invalids of the Soviet Armed Forces. Its founders included the USSR ministries of defense and internal affairs and the KGB. Its president was Major General Kim Tsagalov (*Izvestia*, May 31).

USSR Sets Up Fund to Help Discharged Soldiers

The Month of June

Saturday, June 1

Baltic Leaders Conditionally Endorse Western Aid for USSR

The presidents of the Supreme Councils of the three Baltic republics endorsed the idea of Western aid for the USSR on condition that Moscow refrained from violence and did not use the aid against them. President of the Lithuanian Supreme Council Vytautas Landsbergis told a news conference in Brussels that aid should only be granted in conjunction with Western political support for the Baltic republics' campaign for independence. Landsbergis, along with Anatolijs Gorbunovs of Latvia and Arnold Ruutel of Estonia, was in Brussels at the invitation of the Benelux Interparliamentary Consultative Council (*AFP*, June 1).

El'tsin Promises to Improve Living Conditions within Two Years

RSFSR Supreme Soviet Chairman Boris El'tsin announced his presidential program at a meeting of the Democratic Russia movement. According to TASS, he promised to improve living conditions within two years. El'tsin said he wanted to obtain ultimate control over financial policy on RSFSR territory and to transfer all RSFSR industries, including military plants, to RSFSR government jurisdiction. He also promised to ban Party organizations from the workplace and said that, if elected president, he would conduct a sovereign foreign policy.

Ryzhkov's Election Platform

Former Prime Minister Nikolai Ryzhkov stressed during an electoral campaign meeting in Bashkiria that he supported the Socialist path and rejected capitalism for Russia. TASS quoted him as saying that, if elected president, he would prevent a sellout of Russia's factories to millionaires and foreigners. He said factories should be modernized using state funds. Ryzhkov emphasized that not he, but Vadim Bakatin, former minister of internal affairs, was Soviet President Mikhail Gorbachev's candidate for RSFSR president. He criticized the Gorbachev-El'tsin alliance and said it would last only until June 12—the day of the RSFSR presidential election.

First Congress of Russian Popular Front

The first congress of the Russian Popular Front, set up in 1988, opened in Moscow, TASS reported. The front

The USSR in June, 1991

initially included people supporting democratic reforms, but then nationalists close to the extremist organization "Pamyat'" gained the upper hand in the forum. TASS quoted the front's secretary as telling the congress that the front advocated "a confederation of sovereign states with different social systems" on the territory of the USSR.

El'tsin Meets with Patriarch Aleksii

RSFSR Supreme Soviet Chairman Boris El'tsin met with the patriarch of Moscow and all Russia, Aleksii II, to discuss the return of Church property seized by the Soviet state. TASS said the two men held an informal conversation about eliminating atheism from Russia's schools and about the recently enacted law on freedom of conscience and religious organizations.

Armenian CP Elects New First Secretary

The Armenian Communist Party elected Aram Sarkisyan to the post of first secretary in place of Stepan Pogosyan, who had resigned on May 14 (*TASS*, June 2). Sarkisyan was formerly a correspondent of *Pravda* in Armenia.

Moldavian Prime Minister Gives Television Interview

In his first interview with the Soviet central media as prime minister of Moldavia, Valeriu Muravschi told Central Television that "the center completely failed to take our position seriously" in preparing the Union treaty and that, partly as a result of this, Moldavia "has moved, and is trying to move further, in the direction of independence." Indicating that any decision on independence would be made by popular consultation, Muravschi added that Kishinev considered economic links with Soviet republics to be vitally necessary, irrespective of Moldavia's future political status.

In an interview with the Romanian agency Rompres on June 2, Muravschi said of Moldavian links with Romania, "we have the same language, history, and destiny . . . we must now strive to integrate our economies." Echoing his predecessor Mircea Druc, Muravschi called for "100 joint ventures" to be set up by Romania and Moldavia.

Sunday, June 2

Novocherkassk Marks Deaths of Protesters

A memorial plaque was unveiled in the southern Russian city of Novocherkassk to honor demonstrators killed by security forces there twenty-nine years earlier. On June 2, 1962, residents of Novocherkassk demonstrated to protest against food price rises and demand better living standards. Army troops opened fire, killing twenty-two protesters and injuring thirty-nine others. Fourteen people were later convicted of having organized the Novocherkassk protest, and seven of them were executed. RSFSR Supreme Soviet Chairman Boris El'tsin sent a message to the gathering. He called the Novocherkassk killings "a terrible warning to those who attempt to solve social problems by using military force."

RSFSR to Privatize 20 Percent of Economy by 1993

According to RSFSR Deputy Prime Minister Mikhail Malei, the RSFSR planned to begin privatizing its food, light industry, transportation, public works, and commerce sectors in the near future. The first stage of the privatization scheme was intended to raise some 200–250 billion rubles for the RSFSR government. In comments carried by Western and Soviet media, Malei said that each of the 150 million RSFSR citizens would receive 7,000 rubles in coupons that would be redeemable for stocks in privatized companies.

On June 3, Radio Rossii reported that Gorbachev had stressed in comments regarding the new Union treaty that the defense, oil, and gas industries should remain under all-Union subordination. These industries, the primary hard-currency earners in the USSR, would apparently not be eligible for privatization.

Scientists Oppose Leningrad Dam Project

A group of Soviet scientists was reported to be demanding an immediate halt to the construction of a dam meant to protect Leningrad from annual floods. Radio Moscow said the scientists believed that miscalculations in the blueprints for the project had already brought the delta of the Neva River to the verge of ecological disaster. They said construction so far had caused vast areas of still water to form in the Gulf of Finland, causing heavy metals and carcinogens to accumulate in deposits in the river delta.

Monday, June 3

Soviet Prosecutor Exonerates Soviet Troops

USSR Prosecutor-General Nikolai Trubin issued a preliminary report on the activities of Soviet troops in Vilnius on the night of January 12–13, 1991 (*TASS,* June 3). Trubin said his office had found no evidence that Soviet troops were responsible for the deaths at the Vilnius television center that night. Rather, he declared, the tragic events were "the result of the Lithuanian leadership's anticonstitutional activities." According to Trubin, statements by witnesses and the results of expert forensic examinations had shown that the fourteen people who died had been shot by Lithuanian militants or crushed by cars. When attacked by militants "using knives, sticks, and metal rods," he said, the soldiers had only "defended themselves with rifle butts, firing shots with blanks and some live cartridges into the air." His report contradicted reports by witnesses and foreign journalists at the scene who saw civilians run over by Soviet tanks and shot by Soviet paratroopers.

Trubin's report was immediately attacked by Lithuanian officials. President of the Lithuanian Supreme Council Vytautas Landsbergis told RFE/RL's Lithuanian service that Nazi Propaganda Minister Josef Goebbels "would be envious" of the report. Landsbergis said he believed that the USSR prosecutor was "sacrificing himself to save Gorbachev" before the latter's Nobel Peace Prize acceptance speech. The Lithuanian parliament issued a statement declaring that the report was full of "impudent and boundless" lies, *The Washington Post* reported on June 4.

On June 4, US State Department spokeswoman Margaret Tutwiler denounced Trubin's report, saying that it appeared to be "at odds with the facts." She also commented on the Soviet troop deployments in Vilnius on June 3, noting that it was unclear how the latest Soviet display of force in Lithuania "can be consistent with the expressed intentions of Moscow to avoid violence" (RFE/RL correspondent's report, June 4).

Soviet Troops Set Up Checkpoints in Vilnius

Soviet army troops set up about fifteen checkpoints in Vilnius around important sites in the city, including three around the parliament building, and forced passers-by to show identification documents, Radio Independent Lithuania reported on June 4. Some soldiers said they were searching for army deserters, but they even stopped women. Two members of the National Defense Department were briefly detained. President of the Lithuanian Supreme Council Vytautas Landsbergis appeared several times on Lithuanian television calling on the people to go to the parliament to be "witnesses" if the parliament were attacked. Thousands of Lithuanians gathered around the parliament, and the troops withdrew at about midnight.

On June 4, Radio Independent Lithuania read an appeal to the people of Lithuania issued by "Sajudis" calling for vigils around the parliament building in Vilnius to help prevent an army attack.

On June 6, the Soviet military commander in Vilnius said his men had had no intention of seizing the Lithuanian parliament building on June 3. Major General Vladimir Uskhopchik said the 160 men who had started checking documents in Vilnius were carrying weapons but had no ammunition. He said they had been looking for draft dodgers and deserters and had found seven of the latter. Uskhopchik said the idea of a small group of "practically unarmed" soldiers seizing the parliament was "not serious, to put it mildly" (*TASS*, June 6).

More Attacks on Baltic Border Posts

Six Soviet armored military vehicles surrounded the Lithuanian customs post at Medininkai on the Lithuanian-Belorussian border. The troops pointed their guns at the customs post but withdrew without incident eight hours later (*Radio Vilnius*, June 3).

On June 8, OMON forces attacked another customs checkpoint in Latvia in the early hours of the morning. The post was in the Ludza Raion near the RSFSR border. The OMON forces beat up the guards, undressed them, and burned their uniforms. They then seized money and equipment and set fire to the customs post. The Latvian authorities informed the MVD in Moscow of the attack (*Radio Riga*, June 8).

The same day, fifteen plainclothes men with submachine guns attacked the Luhamaa post on the Estonian-RSFSR border. The men, who arrived in vehicles said to have been used two weeks earlier by Soviet military officers, destroyed the trailer being used as a border post. They left after threatening to destroy another border post some twenty kilometers away (*Baltfax, Radio Riga*, June 8).

Following the raid on the Estonian border post, the Estonian Supreme Council was reported on June 10 to be considering a proposal to permit border guards to carry firearms. The parliament was also said to be considering creating an elite police force of former Soviet paratroopers and Afghan war veterans to protect border posts from further OMON raids (*ETA*, June 10).

Soviet troops raided seven Baltic customs posts early on June 14, injuring at least five people. Radio Riga reported that day that four Latvian posts—at Skaistkalne, Bauska, Ainazi, and Ezere—had been attacked and burned. According to Radio Tallinn (June 14), an Estonian border post at Ikla was attacked by troops "armed with submachine guns, grenades, and signal rockets." Radio Independent Lithuania reported that two Lithuanian customs posts—at Germaniskis and Salociai—had been hit.

An OMON detachment raided a Latvian customs post in the Riga central railway station on the night of June 16

The USSR in June, 1991

(*Radio Riga*, June 17). The troops demolished the office, confiscated documents, and beat up the customs official on duty. The injured official was brought to the Latvian SSR Prosecutor's Office and charged with violating Soviet law, but was later released.

On June 18, twelve armed OMON troops coming from Latvia attacked the Lithuanian customs post at Vegeriai in Akmene Raion and the neighboring Latvian customs post, Radio Vilnius reported. Both posts were burned down and the two customs and four National Defense Department officials, including one woman, at Vegeriai were beaten up. The OMON troops forced the officials to take off their uniforms, which they confiscated. Lithuanian Prime Minister Zigmas Vaisvila sent a telegram to USSR Minister of Internal Affairs Boriss Pugo protesting about the attack.

The same day, a Soviet border guard who had recently been treated in a psychiatric hospital killed two Lithuanians near Klaipeda, Radio Independent Lithuania reported. Later that day, President of the Lithuanian Supreme Council Vytautas Landsbergis received a telephone call from the border commander of the Baltic Military District apologizing for the tragedy and saying the officer in charge of protecting weapons at the Palanga base had been relieved of his duties.

On June 21, four armed men, three of them dressed in OMON uniforms, attacked and burned down the Lithuanian customs post at Salociai in the Pasvalys Raion and the corresponding Latvian customs post, Radio Independent Lithuania reported on June 22. There were no reports of injuries.

On June 22, OMON troops forced Lithuanian customs officials out of their office at Vilnius airport, tore off the sign on the office, confiscated documents and keys, and told the officials never to return to work. This was the first time a Lithuanian customs post had been attacked that was not on the Lithuanian border (*Radio Independent Lithuania*, June 22).

"Socialist" to Be Dropped from Title of Soviet Union

At a meeting in Novo-Ogarevo, the preparatory committee working on the final draft of the Union treaty reaffirmed its decision to drop the word "Socialist" from the name of the USSR and replace it with the word "Sovereign," TASS reported. Gorbachev aide Georgii Shakhnazarov said some participants had argued that the word "Socialist" should be retained in the name in accordance with the results of the March 17 referendum. Shakhnazarov said the name change did not mean the rejection of Socialist ideals.

THE USSR IN JUNE, 1991

Law on Recall of Deputies Adopted

The USSR Supreme Soviet approved a law on the recall of people's deputies, TASS reported. Deputies could be recalled for failing to fulfill their duties, for violating the USSR Constitution, for breaking the law, or when they no longer enjoyed the trust of their constituents. The recall process would begin with a petition that had to be signed by at least 10 percent of the voters in the deputy's electoral district and would then be reviewed by the local soviet. If the petition were approved, voters would go to the polls to vote for or against the deputy. For the text of the law, see *Izvestia*, June 13.

Only Volunteers to Serve in "Hot Spots"

The USSR Defense Ministry announced that military units deployed in areas of social unrest would be staffed only by volunteers, Radio Mayak reported. Conscripts who agreed to serve in such areas would receive three to four times normal pay, a further two months' pay upon discharge, and twenty days vacation a year. Units composed of "draftee-volunteers" were reportedly already being formed in Leningrad for deployment to the Transcaucasus, including the border regions between Armenia and Azerbaijan.

Bessmertnykh Warns of "New Risks" to Europe

In a letter to European Community foreign ministers meeting in Dresden, USSR Foreign Minister Aleksandr Bessmertnykh warned that Europe faced "new risks" following the end of the Cold War. According to Western agency reports, Bessmertnykh cautioned Europeans to be aware of rising nationalism, ideological revanchism, the widening gap between rich and poor countries, and population growth in countries on Europe's borders. Bessmertnykh told the EC ministers that these risks required "a joint response."

USSR on Situation in Ethiopia

Soviet Foreign Ministry spokesman Vitalii Churkin announced that the Soviet Union wanted "constructive dialogue" with the United States, Italy, and other interested countries to bring about a speedy normalization of the situation in Ethiopia, TASS reported. He stressed that the USSR remained "a reliable friend of the people of Ethiopia" and supported "peaceful, democratic reconstruction of the country . . . in conditions of freedom of choice and respect for human rights."

Zhirinovsky's Election Platform

Vladimir Zhirinovsky, leader of the Russian Nationalist Liberal Democratic Party, said at a meeting in Perm that only he could save Russia from the danger of civil war. TASS quoted him as saying that, if elected president, he would change the country's foreign policy. He pointed out that the East-West conflict was over and said the focus of world politics should shift to North-South relations. He said his main aim would be to defend the interests of the Russian people, who were currently discriminated against. He promised to lift all economic barriers. He also stressed that he would not touch the privileges of the military-industrial enterprises in Perm, because the export of weapons remained an important source of hard-currency income.

Defense Ministry Forbids Campaigning by Democrats

A directive issued by the USSR Defense Ministry to commanders in the city of Arkhangel'sk forbade "spy-democrats" to campaign for the RSFSR presidency in military units, Radio Rossii said. The directive—first picked up by the Russian Information Agency from Arkhangel'sk—was reportedly announced to troops stationed at the local garrison. At the same time, according to Radio Rosii, campaigning in support of former Prime Minister Ryzhkov was taking place without restriction.

Shatalin Joins Democratic Party of Russia

Radio Mayak reported that Academician Stanislav Shatalin, former economic adviser to Soviet President Mikhail Gorbachev, had joined the Democratic Party of Russia headed by Nikolai Travkin. Shatalin was quoted by the radio as saying the Democratic Party represented the interests of Russia better than any other political organization. For his part, Travkin (a worker) said Shatalin's membership in his party refuted the myth, spread by its critics, that it was not suitable for intellectuals.

Nagorno-Karabakh Armenians Ready for Dialogue?

TASS reported that a group of Nagorno-Karabakh officials had dispatched a telegram to Soviet President Mikhail Gorbachev, USSR Supreme Soviet Chairman Anatolii Luk'yanov, and Azerbaijani President Ayaz Mutalibov expressing their readiness for dialogue with the Azerbaijani leadership in the presence of USSR Supreme Soviet representatives. The signatories demanded an end to the ongoing bloodshed and forced deportation of Armenians and called for the release of hostages.

Speaking in Paris on June 4, former Soviet Foreign Minister Eduard Shevardnadze offered to mediate between Armenia and Azerbaijan. Arguing that the conflict between the two republics "has reached its apogee," Shevardnadze advocated contacts between the leaderships of the two republics on a weekly or even a daily basis in order to hammer out a compromise. If such measures failed, he said, UN Secretary-General Javier Perez de Cuellar should be asked to mediate in the conflict (Western agencies, June 4).

Makashov's Election Platform

General Al'bert Makashov promised to establish law and order in Russia if elected president. According to TASS, Makashov, who was supported by neo-Stalinists, said that enterprises should not be sold but handed over to workers' collectives. Makashov also spoke in favor of changing the political system so that the RSFSR parliament and the local soviets would be elected by workers' collectives, not through popular elections. He maintained that his goal was to preserve Russia as a strong and wealthy power.

Chernobyl' Victims Start Hunger Strike in Riga

Representatives of the organization "Chernobyl'" began a hunger strike in the Dom Square in Riga, Radio Riga reported. Many of the organization's 6,000 members had participated in the cleanup after the Chernobyl' nuclear accident, and the deaths of fifty-eight people in Latvia were linked to Chernobyl'. The hunger strikers were demanding that Latvia ratify recently approved Soviet laws providing compensation for Chernobyl' victims. This demand was problematic, and some members of "Chernobyl'" did not support it, saying that, as an independent state, Latvia could not adopt or ratify laws of another state.

The group ended their hunger strike on June 13 after the Latvian Supreme Council had adopted a resolution on a program of aid for them. The resolution did not include ratification of the USSR decision of May 12 concerning compensation for Chernobyl' victims but instead called on the Latvian delegation taking part in the Latvian-USSR consultations to deal with the issue at the next meeting. It also set up a special working group under the Latvian Council of Ministers to deal with more immediate problems (*Radio Riga*, June 13).

Tuesday, June 4

US Nominates New Ambassador to Moscow

US President George Bush nominated Robert Strauss, a prominent member of the Democratic Party, to succeed Jack Matlock as US ambassador to the Soviet Union. Bush said he was certain Strauss was the right man to represent the United States during this period of "fantastic change" in the USSR. The seventy-two-year-old Strauss was a former Democratic Party chairman and a long-time friend of Bush (*AP*, June 4).

Yakovlev Says No Way to Hold Back Six Republics

In an interview with the Vienna daily *Die Presse*, Soviet presidential adviser Aleksandr Yakovlev said "nobody has the strength to hold back" the six Soviet republics that were seeking independence. He added that he was most interested in the future of the 90 percent of the Soviet population that would remain in the USSR after the six republics left. Asked why in the fall of 1990 Gorbachev had given the impression of shifting towards the conservatives, Yakovlev said he had done this because the reformers were calling for his resignation, adding "when Gorbachev goes, dictatorship will follow immediately." He said, "the left has now understood this." Yakovlev also said he did not believe the Communist Party had a strong future in the USSR.

Yakovlev made further comments about the future of the USSR in a television debate with former US Secretary of State Henry Kissinger on Austrian television on June 4. He expressed his conviction that the USSR would eventually have a democratic regime and said he did not believe that any forces in the USSR had an interest in staging a coup d'état or inciting civil war.

Moiseev Warns Latvians about Military Draft

In a letter sent to Latvian Supreme Council President Anatolijs Gorbunovs, USSR First Deputy Defense Minister Mikhail Moiseev warned that all possible measures would be taken in order to fulfill the spring draft (*Radio Riga*, June 4). Spokesmen for the Military Commissariat in Latvia told Supreme Council deputies that, although the draft had been met by only about 20–25 percent, force would not be used to complete it. The deputies were skeptical about these assurances, recalling Soviet attempts to enforce conscription in Latvia in January.

Georgia Criticized for Human-Rights Violations in Ossetia

TASS summarized a statement issued by the Federation Council condemning as "a gross violation of the USSR Constitution and international accords on human rights" what it termed a campaign to drive ethnic Ossetians out of Georgia. The outflow of Ossetians from Georgia, which began in January, was said to be increasing.

Moldavia Founds National Bank

Moldavian President Mircea Snegur issued a decree founding a Moldavian National Bank by means of what in effect amounted to a takeover of the Moldavian branch of the USSR State Bank. The bank was empowered to implement the republic's financial policy and was due to become operational by December, 1991.

Wednesday, June 5

Gorbachev Delivers Nobel Peace Prize Speech in Oslo

In his speech in Oslo accepting the 1990 Nobel Peace Prize, Soviet President Mikhail Gorbachev stated that the creation of "a new world order" hinged on the success of *perestroika* in the USSR. He cautioned that, if *perestroika* failed, "the prospect of entering a new peaceful period in history will vanish, at least for the foreseeable future." Gorbachev asserted that the West therefore had a vital interest in ensuring that his policies succeeded. Regarding the issue of secession, Gorbachev said republics could decide to leave the Soviet Union by means of an "honest" referendum and with an agreed transitional period. He expressed optimism about the conclusion of a new Union treaty, saying that, after "the euphoria of sovereignization," a healthy acceptance of existing realities was prevailing (*TASS*, Western press reports, June 5 and 6).

Gorbachev Blames Latvia and Lithuania for Baltic Tension

Clearly losing his temper at a news conference after his Nobel Peace Prize address, Soviet President Mikhail Gorbachev blamed Latvia and Lithuania for increasing tension in the Baltic region, Western agencies reported. Raising his voice and gesticulating, Gorbachev said those two republics had started the trouble by setting up their own customs posts. Gorbachev also criticized Western reporters for misrepresenting the situation in the Baltic republics, accusing them of exaggerating events and applying double standards.

Pavlov again Accuses West of Economic Subversion

Addressing a meeting of industrial and farm managers in Moscow Oblast, USSR Prime Minister Valentin Pavlov again accused Western banks of subverting the Soviet economy. An account of his speech appeared in *Leninskoe znamya* on June 7 and was widely cited by Western agencies. Pavlov was quoted as asserting that unnamed banks were conducting a credit blockade against the Soviet Union. Referring to credit quotas set by the Bank for International Settlements, Pavlov charged that "as soon as this quota has been drawn, the red light glows. Not one bank will give money." In February, Pavlov alleged that Western banks were planning to flood the USSR with money in order to bring about hyperinflation.

Pope Supports Lithuanian Independence

Speaking at a service in Lomza in Poland attended by some 16,000 Lithuanian pilgrims, Pope John Paul II expressed support for Lithuania's "just national aspiration," saying "the pope is with you." He told the worshipers that "his meeting with Lithuanians will bring closer the day when Lithuania will be on the papal pilgrimage trail." Before the Mass, the pontiff met with Lithuanian Vincentas Cardinal Sladkevicius and Lithuanian government officials. They said the pope condemned the Hitler-Stalin pact of 1939 as "a historic injustice." Polish television, which could be seen in many parts of Lithuania, broadcast the Mass live.

Farmers Reluctant to Grow or Sell Grain

The chairman of the USSR State Committee for the Procurement of Food Supplies, Mikhail Timoshishin, told *Pravda* that many farmers were reluctant to grow grain. Among the reasons he cited were the poor security of the ruble and the lack of machinery, chemicals, and other goods needed for production. Several recent articles in the Soviet press had complained about the adverse terms of trade for the agricultural sector—i.e., that prices of goods needed for production had risen far faster than procurement prices for farm produce.

Afghanistan Apologizes for Bombing

Afghanistan apologized to the USSR and Tajikistan for the accidental bombing of a Tajik village by an Afghan air force jet on June 4. A spokesman for the Afghan Foreign Ministry said that the plane had accidentally strayed across the border and mistaken the village for a resistance hideout. The Afghan authorities offered to pay compensation to the injured and to the families of the four people killed in the attack (Western agencies, June 5).

Moldavia Bars Dual Moldavian-USSR Citizenship

The Moldavian Supreme Soviet passed legislation banning residents of Moldavia from holding dual Moldavian and USSR citizenship. The law also contained a provision allowing citizens of other states to obtain Moldavian citizenship. This was designed to permit the hundreds of thousands of Moldavians living in Romania to become Moldavian citizens while retaining their Romanian citizenship and continuing to live in Romania (*Radio Moscow*, June 5).

Thursday, June 6

Gorbachev Tells Swedes Not to Interfere over Baltic Republics

Soviet President Mikhail Gorbachev told Sweden not to let concern for the neighboring Baltic peoples cause them to interfere in internal Soviet affairs. The Soviet leader was speaking at a press conference in Stockholm after talks with Swedish Prime Minister Ingvar Carlsson. Reports said the Baltic independence issue was a dominant topic at the talks. Carlsson later told a news conference that he had insisted to Gorbachev that the Baltic peoples had the right to self-determination and that political dialogue, not force, was the way to proceed. Carlsson also criticized the Soviet prosecutor-general's report denying that Soviet troops had killed Lithuanians at the Vilnius television tower in January. He said Swedes had difficulty accepting that view since they had seen television pictures of the events in Vilnius. At a demonstration in Stockholm, leaders of all the larger Swedish opposition parties emphasized their support for independence for Estonia, Latvia, and Lithuania (Western press reports, *TASS, Central Television*, June 6).

KGB Comments on Terrorism, Disarming Illegal Groups

A spokesman for the KGB told reporters in Moscow that Soviet security forces had disarmed more than thirty illegal groups in the USSR since the beginning of 1991 and confiscated nearly 45,000 firearms and more than 1 million rounds of ammunition. Major General Valerii Vorotnikov also said that the use of terrorism as a means of political struggle had increased in the USSR recently. He said this had happened as institutions of state power had grown weak and ethnic conflicts had escalated (*TASS*, June 6).

Bakatin Says He Was Fired because He Favored Compromise

Former USSR Minister of Internal Affairs Vadim Bakatin said he had been fired in 1990 because he was trying to reach a compromise with the elected leaders of some republics. Bakatin said he had wanted to find "a sensible compromise" under which the republics would have a say in the activities of the USSR MVD troops on their soil. In an interview with the *Frankfurter Allgemeine Zeitung*, Bakatin said this approach had been opposed by forces over whom Soviet President Mikhail Gorbachev had insufficient control. He did not name the forces.

Central Asian Movements Avow to Oppose Communists

Leading figures of the democratic movements of Central Asia and Kazakhstan said their new umbrella organization would work to end Communist control of their republics and aimed to replace the Communist regimes with free, democratic governments. The cochairman of the Uzbek Popular Front "Birlik," Abdurrakhim Pulatov, told RFE/RL the decision had been made at a meeting of the coordinating council of the democratic movements and political parties in Bishkek, Kirgizia, in May (RL Uzbek service, June 6).

--- *Friday, June 7*

Interrepublican Commission Rejects Division of Republics into Two Categories

Participants in the third session of the Interrepublican Economic Commission, set up to control implementation of economic agreements between the USSR and the republics, rejected a proposal to divide the republics into those willing to sign the Union treaty, which would be granted "most-favored" trading status, and those not signing, which would be treated like foreign countries (*TASS*, June 7).

Ukraine Votes to Take Control of Soviet Enterprises

The Ukrainian Supreme Soviet voted overwhelmingly to take control of all Soviet enterprises and organizations in the republic. Ukrainian Prime Minister Vitol'd Fokin told parliament that the takeover was necessary because some USSR ministries had been creating joint-stock companies out of their enterprises in Ukraine. Fokin said these moves were designed to prevent the properties from being transferred to republican ownership and ran counter to Ukraine's declaration on state sovereignty and its law on economic autonomy (*TASS, Izvestia,* June 8).

In an interview with "Vremya" on June 16, Fokin said Ukrainian law on jurisdiction over Union enterprises in Ukraine had been misunderstood. He said his government had no intention of owning such enterprises, as the center had thought, but simply wanted to exercise control over decisions, especially those concerning joint ventures and privatization, made by the present owners. Fokin said every government in the world exercised such control. He claimed that his government had had a bad experience with the transfer of the coal industry to republican ownership and that it now realized it simply could not afford to "own" all industries on Ukrainian soil. (Moscow's reaction to such transfers was to cut off the industry's access to central resources, research, and technology.) As a result, Fokin said, his government was now negotiating very carefully the transfer of the metallurgical industry to the republic.

Supreme Soviet Approves Law on Work Safety

The USSR Supreme Soviet approved in principle a bill designed to increase work safety in the USSR. The legislation was proposed by the General Confederation of USSR Trade Unions. Its deputy chairman, Vladimir Kuzmenok, said more than 14,000 people died at work in the Soviet Union every year. Kuzmenok also said that there were about 700,000 industrial accidents a year and that some 7 million workers suffered from gas or dust poisoning or exposure to radiation or were harmed by poor lighting or excessive noise. Previously, labor unions had enforced safety in the workplace. The legislation approved would make it a state responsibility (*TASS, Radio Moscow*, June 7).

RSFSR Economic Performance in May

The RSFSR's economy continued to slide in May, according to *Ekonomika i zhizn'* (No. 23). Industrial production for the month was more than 3 percent lower than in May, 1990, largely owing to the effect of widespread strikes in RSFSR coal mines in the first part of the year. Production of oil was down 11 percent in May (as it was in April). Production trends in most sectors pointed to a slowdown in economic activity since April.

EC Official Says Aid to Be Shared among Republics

Moldavian President Mircea Snegur conferred in Kishinev with EC official Helmut Lohan, who was quoted as saying that the EC's planned aid to the USSR, worth 500 million dollars "will be equitably apportioned among republics" both to support the transition to the market and to provide food aid (*Moldovapres*, June 7).

Kirgizia Establishes Its First Free Economic Zone

Kirgizia was reported to have established its first free economic zone in Naryn Oblast on the border with China. TASS said the region was rich in minerals, including gold, and had a plentiful supply of electricity from power stations on the Naryn River. It also said the region was underdeveloped socially and economically and had no major factories. Under Soviet law, Soviet and foreign investors who established businesses in a free economic zone were entitled to reductions in taxes and customs fees.

Saturday, June 8

Latvia Would Retaliate for Soviet Economic Pressure

Latvian Foreign Minister Janis Jurkans said if the USSR should exert economic pressure on Latvia by charging world market prices for oil and gas, Latvia would retaliate by charging the USSR world market prices for the use of Latvian harbors and airspace. He also said there would be major problems if Latvia stopped delivering food to Moscow and Leningrad. Jurkans made the remarks in an interview with the *Süddeutsche Zeitung*.

Landsbergis Accuses USSR of "Constitutional Aggression"

President of the Lithuanian Supreme Council Vytautas Landsbergis said the USSR was pursuing "constitutional aggression" against Lithuania, adding that the Soviet government was becoming confused by its own contradictions. In a statement broadcast by Radio Vilnius, Landsbergis cited protests by the USSR's Committee for Constitutional Supervision against Lithuania's citizenship law and other acts deemed not to comply with the USSR Constitution. Landsbergis pointed out that, while the committee objected to the possibility of Soviet citizens' choosing another citizenship on the grounds that this constituted a violation of rights, the Soviet citizenship law actually guaranteed people the right to change their citizenship.

USSR OMON Troops Sent to Moldavia

Supplementary units of the USSR MVD's OMON troops arrived in Tiraspol', the center of the would-be "Dniester SSR" in eastern Moldavia, on June 7 and 8. Some units crossed the Dniester into the city of Bendery on the western bank, where the self-proclaimed republic was seeking to establish a bridgehead. The Moldavian government was not notified of the action. Moldovapres reported on June 8 that Moldavian President Mircea Snegur had responded by sending a telegram on the matter to Soviet President Mikhail Gorbachev and USSR Minister of Internal Affairs Boriss Pugo protesting the violation of Moldavian sovereignty and "the intrusion into the republic's internal affairs" and demanding the immediate recall of the units.

On June 11, Moldavian deputies told RFE/RL by telephone that the command of the Odessa Military District had cabled the Moldavian leadership that day announcing the withdrawal of the OMON units from Moldavia. The command claimed that the units were merely in transit through Moldavia as part of an exercise.

Congress of Chechen People

A congress of the Chechen people that resumed work on June 8 reaffirmed its decision to rename Chechnya the Chechen Republic of Nakhichichi in keeping with its historical frontiers (*Radio Moscow*, June 9). The decision had been taken at the first stage of the congress in November, 1990, but the Chechen-Ingush Supreme Soviet had subsequently refused to divide Checheno-Ingushetia into two republics or change its name.

Sunday, June 9

ILO Says Unemployment "Set to Reach 20 Million" in USSR

In a new book, the International Labor Organization (ILO) predicted that, in the event of a market reform, Soviet unemployment could grow to 20 million within a year or two. It warned that inadequate social security arrangements and lack of employment services could result in social and political chaos, widespread poverty, and mass emigration to the West (RFE/RL correspondent's report and *The Independent*, June 10).

Romanians in Ukraine Set Up Umbrella Body

Representatives of Romanian/Moldavian associations from northern Bukovina and southern Bessarabia—areas transferred to Ukraine following their annexation by the USSR from Romania—decided at a meeting in the capital of northern Bukovina, Chernovtsy, to set up a Democratic Union of All Romanian Associations in Ukraine. The meeting issued an appeal for "the observance of the sacred rights to national history and culture . . . , an end to intimidation and oppression by local and all-Union authorities," the reestablishment of Romanian-language schools, and equitable representation of Romanians/Moldavians in state and public bodies. The meeting also made public an appeal to the office of the secretary-general of the United Nations complaining of "grave violations of the human and nationality rights of the Romanian population" in Ukraine. The meeting was reported by the Romanian and Moldavian media on June 10.

Monday, June 10

"Soyuz" Statement on Union Treaty

In a statement read out in the USSR Supreme Soviet, the conservative "Soyuz" group of deputies said the decision to send the draft Union treaty to the republican parliaments before it had been examined by the USSR Supreme Soviet was "unconstitutional," TASS reported. USSR Supreme Soviet Chairman Anatolii Luk'yanov told the deputies Soviet President Mikhail Gorbachev had agreed that as soon as the draft had been signed by the members of the preparatory committee it would be sent to the

The USSR in June, 1991

USSR Supreme Soviet as well as the republican parliaments. At a press conference, presidential adviser Grigorii Revenko said the USSR Congress of People's Deputies and Supreme Soviet should be involved; "however, they are not the ones forming the Union," he added.

El'tsin Gives Interview to RFE/RL

In an exclusive interview with RFE/RL, RSFSR Supreme Soviet Chairman Boris El'tsin said the center was resisting demands by the RSFSR that weapons-manufacturing plants situated in the RSFSR should be transferred to its jurisdiction. El'tsin stressed that, while the RSFSR intended to insist on the transfer, it would not enter the arms trade. El'tsin went on to caution Soviet President Mikhail Gorbachev that the Soviet army must not be used against Russian civilians once the new Union treaty had been signed. If the Soviet president used the army in this way, El'tsin said, he would himself be violating the Union treaty, and this could lead to the breakup of the new Union outlined in it. El'tsin also said that, although the RSFSR could not yet afford financially to join the United Nations, agreement had been reached with UN Secretary-General Javier Perez de Cuellar that the Russian republic would have a permanent representative there.

Newspapers Attack El'tsin on Eve of Election

In a preelection profile, *Pravda* described RSFSR Supreme Soviet Chairman Boris El'tsin as unpredictable, authoritarian, and incompetent. Calling El'tsin a weak man who was power-hungry, the Communist Party newspaper went on to say that El'tsin's emotional side dominated his rational side and that his views changed so rapidly that it was hard to identify his convictions. The newspaper also carried remarks by El'tsin, who said if elected RSFSR president, he could offer the republic a secure and healthy future.

On June 11, *Sovetskaya Rossiya* printed a front-page article in which USSR Prosecutor-General Nikolai Trubin accused El'tsin of involvement in an illegal attempt to sell rubles for dollars at several times the official rate. The deal was never implemented, although RSFSR Deputy Prime Minister Gennadii Fil'shin resigned in February because of his involvement in it.

USSR Needs 20 Billion Dollars in 1991 Alone

The chairman of the International Bank for Economic Cooperation, Vitalii Khokhlov, told Western agencies that the Soviet Union would require Western financial aid in excess of 20 billion dollars in 1991 alone. Khokhlov, who was attending a meeting of the Bank for International

Settlements in Basel, added, "Of course, foreign bankers are fairly cautious, and we understand them. We must first pull ourselves out of the current chaos." He also said the Soviet Union's current foreign debt was 60–70 billion dollars.

EC Official Says Aid to USSR Should Be Linked to Reform

Frans Andriessen, European commissioner for external affairs, said that a strong commitment to reform by the Soviet leadership should be a precondition for Western aid to the USSR. Speaking at a conference of international industrialists in Dobris, Czechoslovakia, Andriessen was quoted by Western agencies as saying that reform in the USSR was "a prerequisite for stability and peace in Europe and in the whole world." He said the EC would like the USSR to continue trading with East European countries, and he warned that a sudden loss of the Soviet market could spell disaster for efforts towards economic reform in Eastern Europe.

At the same meeting, East European ministers also called on the West not to give aid to Moscow in a way that would reduce Soviet purchases of East European goods.

Formation of Broad-Based Democratic Party Urged by Shevardnadze

Speaking in Vienna, former Soviet Foreign Minister Eduard Shevardnadze advocated the formation of a broad-based democratic party in the USSR to accelerate economic and social reform. According to Western agencies, Shevardnadze appealed to democratic forces in the USSR to come together to create "a strong, organized, democratic party." Such a party, he said, would rejuvenate the Soviet parliament so that it could work for "the spiritual and economic rebirth" of the USSR. "People must be brought into parliament who are more progressive . . . , who have no fear of the new," Shevardnadze said.

In reaction to the call, the CPSU on June 12 ordered an investigation of Shevardnadze, who was still a Communist Party member. TASS said that the decree had been issued by the Presidium of the CPSU Central Control Commission and that the results of the Party investigation would be reviewed by that body.

Black Market in Hard Currency Undercut

Izvestia reported that, since the official rate for changing hard currency into rubles was raised in April, banks had been changing ten to twelve times as much money. This suggested that the state was succeeding in cutting the flow of hard currency to black marketeers.

The USSR in June, 1991

New Violence Reported in and Near Nagorno-Karabakh

Azerinform and Interfax, quoting MVD sources, reported shooting incidents in and near the Nagorno-Karabakh Autonomous Oblast. In the village of Kapanly, near Nagorno-Karabakh, two farmers were killed and two wounded by shots fired from automatic weapons. Azerinform said the attackers had arrived by car from the neighboring Mardakert Raion in Nagorno-Karabakh. On June 9, a Soviet army unit killed two Azerbaijanis and wounded two others during a clash in a village inside the Mardakert Raion, Interfax reported. The report, quoting the local MVD office, said the Azerbaijanis were members of an armed group that had attacked the village.

TASS reported on June 19 that USSR MVD Major Aleksei Khomich had been ambushed and killed by unidentified gunmen while driving from the Nagorno-Karabakh capital, Stepanakert, to the town of Shusha on June 18. A senior lieutenant traveling with him was severely wounded.

On June 27, three men and three women were found shot dead in the village of Karadagly near the raion center of Martuni in Nagorno-Karabakh. TASS said the victims had been shot with automatic weapons and their bodies burned. The agency said the attackers had fired on the village for more than an hour with mortars, grenade launchers, and other weapons. The ethnic origin of the attackers and the victims was not clear from the TASS report, but the agency said the attack had been directed from a nearby Armenian village, Kendhurd.

Yazov Defends Soviet Military Presence in Baltic

Soviet Defense Minister Dmitrii Yazov defended the Soviet military presence in the Baltic republics, saying Moscow would like to see the Baltic issue resolved in a constitutional way. He rejected reports that Soviet troops had intimidated citizens in the Baltic republics, saying there was "a lot of loud talk" in the area (*AP*, June 10).

USSR Supreme Soviet Rejects Law on Intellectual Property

TASS reported that the USSR Supreme Soviet had refused to approve a bill on scientific and intellectual property. Opposing views of the purpose of the bill were heard. Speaking in defense of the original draft, Deputy Prime Minister Nikolai Laverov said it should "prevent cooperatives and foreign firms from pumping the ideas of Soviet scientists to the West and stop the members of the shadow economy from waxing rich." The law was never adopted, but on May 31 the Soviet parliament adopted a law on "Discoveries in the USSR," the text of which was published in *Izvestia* on June 14.

Tuesday, June 11

Pavlov Claims Economy Has Stabilized

In what was described as an unscheduled address to the USSR Supreme Soviet, USSR Prime Minister Valentin Pavlov claimed that the slump in output had been halted, TASS reported. He attributed the purported stabilization to his anticrisis program, although the program was not yet technically in force. Pavlov promised that "state-set retail prices for basic food and nonfood goods" would not be raised again in 1991.

United States Approves Grain Credits for Moscow

White House spokesman Marlin Fitzwater announced that US President George Bush had approved 1.5 billion dollars in farm credit guarantees for the Soviet Union. The credits, which had been requested by Soviet President Mikhail Gorbachev, would allow the USSR to buy US agricultural products. Fitzwater said the credits, to be made available in three installments over the next nine months, had been granted after the United States had received assurances that the food would be "fairly distributed" among the Union republics (Western agencies, June 11).

On June 16, Gorbachev was reported to have welcomed the approval of the grain credits. In a letter to Bush, Gorbachev said the move was a sign of "solidarity at a difficult moment." Gorbachev also said the credits reflected what he saw as the new character of the US-Soviet relationship (*TASS*, June 16).

USSR Supreme Soviet Cuts Income Taxes to Stimulate Investment

The USSR Supreme Soviet decided to cut income tax rates in an attempt to stimulate the growth of business and thus increase budget revenues. The cuts came in amendments to an income tax law. TASS said the amendments would raise the minimum amount of nontaxable income to 160 rubles a month and reduce the tax rate on earnings of up to 1,000 rubles a month to 12 percent. The amendments would establish a maximum tax rate of 30 percent on incomes over 1,000 rubles a month (*TASS*, June 11).

Izvestia Journalists Plan to Leave

Russian Television reported that up to thirty journalists were planning to quit their jobs at *Izvestia*. The report said this would be a logical end to the conflict between the newspaper's staff and its founder, the USSR Supreme Soviet Presidium, and also between the staff and the newspaper's chief editor, Nikolai Efimov. The conflict began in February when the staff resisted Efimov's appointment. The latest bone of contention was the appointment of Vladimir Sevruk as chief editor of *Nedelya*, the weekly supplement to *Izvestia*. Sevruk headed the CPSU Central Committee Propaganda Department in the Brezhnev era.

On June 18, *Izvestia* staffers again called for the ouster of Efimov and Sevruk (*Russian Television, Radio Rossii*, June 18). Yurii Markov, a staff member of *Izvestia*, said he and his colleagues had considered withholding one issue of the newspaper in protest but then decided against this course of action because they were afraid it would hurt the newspaper's circulation.

European Bank Agrees to Help Set Up New Soviet Bank

The new European Bank for Reconstruction and Development (EBRD) signed an agreement with the USSR State Bank to help set up "an investment bank" in the Soviet Union. *The Wall Street Journal* said the bank would finance projects to develop a free market. EBRD head Jacques Attali, who spoke at a press conference in The Hague, also said he would like to see limits lifted on EBRD lending to the USSR. His bank's statutes limited lending to about 70 million dollars a year (Western agencies, June 12).

More Soviet Soldiers Apply for Asylum in Germany

A spokesman for the German Interior Ministry said that fourteen more Soviet soldiers had sought political asylum in Germany since the middle of May, bringing to 206 the total number of Soviet soldiers seeking asylum over the past eighteen months (RFE/RL correspondent's report, June 11).

Barter Trade with Cuba

The Russian Information Agency (RIA) said the Soviet Union and Cuba were preparing an agreement to shift trade to a barter basis as an interim measure until trading in hard currency could begin. Products to be bartered included Soviet oil, food, wood, and machinery parts in exchange for Cuban sugar and other food products. The RIA made no mention of the terms on which Cuban nickel would be sold to the Soviet Union. Trade between the two countries had been virtually halted for six months owing to Cuba's lack of hard currency (*AP*, June 11).

Shevardnadze Says United States Has Vital Role in New World Order

Former Soviet Foreign Minister Eduard Shevardnadze said the United States was such a pioneer that no one could discuss a new world order without taking the US experience into account. In an interview broadcast by

RFE/RL, Shevardnadze praised the unique way in which Americans had created democratic institutions and material wealth. He said Soviet people could learn from this example. He warned, however, against simply copying the US model. He said it was more reasonable to adapt such models to national characters, adding that nothing had come of Eastern Europe's copying the old Soviet system.

Lithuanian Deputy Foreign Minister Meets with Soviet Officials

Lithuanian Deputy Foreign Minister Valdemaras Katkus held talks with USSR Deputy Foreign Minister Valentin Nikiforov and the leader of the Soviet delegation to the Conference on Security and Cooperation in Europe, Yurii Deryabin. On June 13, Katkus briefed the Lithuanian parliament on the USSR Foreign Ministry's position on Lithuania, explaining that the USSR still considered Lithuania to be part of the Soviet Union and that secession could be achieved only by following the provisions of the USSR Constitution. During the meeting, Nikiforov raised doubts about whether the majority of Lithuanians in fact supported the republic's independence drive (*Radio Independent Lithuania*, June 13). Katkus criticized Soviet negotiating tactics, saying the Soviet Union was trying to hold "endless talks" with Lithuania while avoiding genuine negotiations. He also said Soviet officials were pursuing different negotiating tactics with each of the Baltic republics "in order to destroy their political unity."

Prospects for Iranian-Azerbaijani Cooperation

Azerbaijani Prime Minister Gasan Gasanov met in Teheran with Iranian President Ali Akbar Hashemi-Rafsanjani and called for an expansion of bilateral relations. On June 12, Gasanov and Iranian Energy Minister Bijan Namdar-Zangeneh signed an agreement on possible gas exports to Azerbaijan and cooperation in the fields of shipping, railway and road construction, and communications. IRNA reported that Gasanov had told Iranian Foreign Minister Ali Akbar Velayati that Azerbaijan wished to join the Iran-Turkey-Pakistan economic group.

Wednesday, June 12

El'tsin Elected RSFSR President

Chairman of the RSFSR Supreme Soviet Boris El'tsin was elected president of the RSFSR, winning 57.3 percent of the vote. His main rival, Nikolai Ryzhkov, received 16.85 percent. The leader of the Liberal Democratic Party,

The USSR in June, 1991

Vladimir Zhirinovsky, who ran on a Russian nationalist platform, came third with almost 8 percent; Siberian Aman Tuleev got just over 6 percent; Soviet army General Al'bert Makashov won 4 percent; and former USSR Minister of Internal Affairs Vadim Bakatin, 3 percent. More than 74 percent of the electorate participated in the election. El'tsin did poorly in many rural areas, where he generally received around 30 percent, but in urban areas 70 percent and more of the electorate gave him their vote. Some predominantly military electoral districts showed strong support for El'tsin (*TASS, Central Television, Russian Television*, June 13).

Interfax reported that El'tsin had won 90 percent of the vote in Sverdlovsk, his home city; 85 percent in Leningrad; 70–75 percent in Moscow; and 70 percent in major cities of the Far East. Ryzhkov received support in rural areas. Russian Television reported that the KGB had supported Zhirinovsky. Soviet President Mikhail Gorbachev told reporters after casting his vote that he was prepared to cooperate with whoever was elected RSFSR president.

The White House hailed El'tsin's election as a historic step and invited him to meet with President George Bush on June 20 (Western agencies, June 13 and 14). El'tsin expressed satisfaction with the invitation and said he hoped to develop "direct relations" between Russia and the United States (*ZDF*, June 13).

Former Soviet Foreign Minister Eduard Shevardnadze said the election of El'tsin could only be positive. He told a news conference in Bonn that El'tsin had the support of a broad majority of Russians and now had to justify this confidence (RFE/RL correspondent's report, *AFP*, June 13).

In his first public statement following the elections, El'tsin said he was satisfied with his election as RSFSR president but worried about the responsibilities he would have to bear for the republic's future. He also reiterated his commitment to radical political and economic reform but warned that Russians should not expect quick results (*AP, AFP*, June 14).

Popov and Sobchak Elected Mayors of Moscow and Leningrad

Soviet and Western news agencies reported that Gavriil Popov and Anatolii Sobchak had been elected mayors of Moscow and Leningrad respectively. Popov received more than 60 percent of the votes and Sobchak about 70 percent. Both thus received the necessary mandate to enhance executive power in their cities. In Moscow, only around 60 percent of eligible voters went to the polls, according to some Soviet news reports.

THE USSR IN JUNE, 1991

Leningrad Votes to Rename City St. Petersburg

About 54 percent of Leningraders voted to change the city's name back to St. Petersburg—the city's name from 1703 to 1914. The vote was a nonbinding referendum.

The Leningrad City Soviet formally endorsed the name change on June 25, TASS reported. The agency also said the soviet had asked the RSFSR Supreme Soviet to make the name change legal.

Shaimiev Elected President of Tatarstan

Mintimer Shaimiev was elected the first president of a sovereign Tatarstan, winning some 73 percent of the votes cast. Shaimiev, chairman of the Tatarstan Supreme Soviet, was the only candidate. Kazan' journalist Damir Gismetdinov told RFE/RL that 63 percent of eligible voters had cast ballots in the Tatarstan presidential election but that no more than 40 percent had participated in choosing a president for the RSFSR (RL Tatar-Bashkir service, June 13).

El'tsin Rejects Reconsideration of Kuriles Issue for Now

Asked about Japan's demand for the return of four islands in the Kurile chain occupied by the USSR since World War II, RSFSR Supreme Soviet Chairman Boris El'tsin said "reconsidering the borders is out of the question for now. It would be blood again" (*AP*, June 12). Prior to and during Soviet President Mikhail Gorbachev's visit to Japan in April, El'tsin had stressed that the RSFSR (the republic of which the islands are a part) must play a part in negotiations over the return of the islands. He had also proposed a plan for resolving the dispute. The plan included the establishment of a free-enterprise zone on the islands and the removal of Soviet troops and bases. He had given a time frame of fifteen to twenty years for the program.

Pay Increase Awarded to Oil and Gas Workers

USSR Prime Minister Valentin Pavlov agreed to boost the pay of Soviet oil and gas workers by 40 percent, backdated to June 1, the *Financial Times* reported. It added that the pay increase was gradually to grow to 75 percent by the fourth quarter of the year and would be accompanied by large investments in the oil and gas industries' infrastructure.

Head of Ukrainian Catholics Announces End of Exile

It was announced that the head of the Ukrainian Catholic Church, Myroslav Cardinal Lyubachivs'kyi, had decided to end more than half a century of exile and return to live in Ukraine. Lyubachivs'kyi's office in Rome said he had made the decision during his visit to Ukraine in April, his first in fifty-two years.

The USSR in June, 1991

TASS said Kirgiz President Askar Akaev had vetoed an article of a new land law approved by the republic's parliament in April. The article, which said that the land in the republic belonged to the Kirgiz people, led to a flood of protest letters. Akaev asked for it to be amended to stipulate that "the land is the property of citizens of Kirgizia and all other nationalities making up the republic's people."

Kirgiz President Vetoes Land Law

USSR Supreme Soviet Chairman Anatolii Luk'yanov reiterated that Moscow had not ordered the recent wave of attacks on Soviet customs posts in the Baltic republics. Luk'yanov told the Royal Institute of International Affairs in London that the Soviet Union had no interest in such clashes. He said the trouble was "quite independent of the Union itself" (RFE/RL correspondent's report, June 12).

Luk'yanov Reiterates Moscow Did Not Order Attacks in Baltic

Radio Vilnius said the Lithuanian and Belorussian Ministries of Internal Affairs had signed a treaty of cooperation. The report quoted Lithuanian Minister of Internal Affairs Marijonas Misiukonis as saying the treaty was needed in light of recent attacks on border posts between the two republics.

Belorussia and Lithuania Sign Agreement

It was reported that Germany was sending seven special trucks to the Soviet Union to conduct radiation tests on people in the RSFSR. An estimated 100,000 people would be tested through October in the Bryansk, Kaluga, and Tula areas as part of an effort to measure the effects of the Chernobyl' nuclear disaster. German Environment Minister Klaus Töpfer said the purpose of the program, whose estimated cost would be 7 million deutsche marks, was to inform individuals about their exposure to radiation (*DPA*, *AFP*, RFE/RL correspondent's report, June 12).

Bonn Sends Mobile Radiation-Measuring Units to USSR

Thursday, June 13

British Prime Minister John Major was reported to have formally invited Soviet President Mikhail Gorbachev to London for talks with leaders of the Group of Seven leading industrial democracies after their summit on July 15–17. Major said he had decided to extend the invitation after consulting with the participants in the summit and after meeting with USSR Supreme Soviet

Gorbachev Formally Invited to G-7 Meeting

Chairman Anatolii Luk'yanov. He said Luk'yanov had delivered a message from Gorbachev reaffirming his commitment to reforms (Western agencies, June 13).

Soviet Nuclear Weapons Still in Germany

Soviet Foreign Minister Aleksandr Bessmertnykh said there were still Soviet nuclear weapons in the former GDR. Bessmertnykh was speaking at a news conference in Bonn after talks with German Foreign Minister Hans-Dietrich Genscher. The Bonn government said it had asked Moscow to clarify the situation after USSR Defense Minister Dmitrii Yazov had told German Environment Minister Klaus Töpfer earlier in the month that there were no nuclear weapons in the former GDR. Bessmertnykh said he had told Genscher that Moscow would inform the German government when the withdrawal of the nuclear weapons had been completed (RFE/RL correspondent's report, June 12 and 13).

Zhirinovsky Files Election Protest

Vladimir Zhirinovsky, the Liberal Democratic Party's candidate for the RSFSR presidency, filed a protest seeking the annulment of all votes received by Boris El'tsin. *Rabochaya tribuna* quoted Zhirinovsky as saying El'tsin had used his post as chairman of the RSFSR Supreme Soviet to give himself an unfair advantage in the election. Zhirinovsky came third in the RSFSR presidential elections, winning some 8 percent of the vote. The Russian Television news show "Vesti" characterized him as a dangerous populist and compared his emergence on the political scene with the rise of Hitler and Stalin in the 1920s.

Three Former Deputy Prime Ministers Investigated

A Soviet official said three former USSR deputy prime ministers were being investigated on charges that they had bought state-owned dachas at discount prices. The three were Lev Voronin, Aleksandra Biryukova, and Igor' Belousov. The investigations were revealed in an interview with Chairman of the USSR Supreme Soviet Commission on Privileges Mikalai Ihnatovich published by Novosti press agency. The commission was responsible for the investigation.

New Supreme Soviet Chairman Elected in Uzbekistan

Shavkat Yuldashev, chairman of the Uzbek Communist Party Central Control Commission since 1990, was reported to have been elected chairman of the republic's Supreme Soviet. He replaced Mirzaolim Ibragimov, who had retired for health reasons (*TASS*, June 13).

The USSR in June, 1991

Human-Rights Group Finds Abuses against Armenians

An international commission that visited the Armenian-Azerbaijani border area said Soviet troops and local police had been directly involved in violating the human rights of the Armenian people in April. The International League for Human Rights, a nongovernmental organization based in New York, said the inquiry also covered the disputed Nagorno-Karabakh region in Azerbaijan. The group said the inquiry had the personal authorization of Soviet President Mikhail Gorbachev (RFE/RL correspondent's report, June 13).

Izvestia Reports Investigation of Border Attacks

Izvestia reported that the USSR Prosecutor's Office in Lithuania had started an investigation to determine whether the people who raided Lithuanian customs posts had exceeded their authority. *Izvestia* said the Prosecutor's Office "indirectly acknowledges" that Soviet MVD OMON troops were involved in the raids.

Joint Saudi-Soviet Bank Set Up in Kazakhstan

Radio Moscow carried a report saying that the first bank in the Soviet Union in which foreign capital had a half share had begun operations in Kazakhstan. The bank, which is known as the Islamic Soviet-Saudi International Commercial Bank, intended to take part in restoring the Great Silk Route, financing an international airport in Alma-Ata, building medreses and mosques, renovating hotels, and constructing motels and camping sites along the silk route.

State of Emergency Declared in Makhachkala

Warning shots were fired in Makhachkala against a crowd of several hundred Muslims who had been demonstrating for ten days against the high cost of making a pilgrimage to Mecca ("Vremya," *Central Television, Radio Moscow,* June 13). The crowd tried to storm the Council of Ministers building and threw stones at the police. The Muslims were demanding that all those who had applied to go to Mecca (estimates varied between 3,000 and more than 10,000) should be allowed to do so and that the cost should be reduced from 30,000 to 3,000 rubles. At a late-night sitting, the Dagestan Supreme Soviet declared a state of emergency in the city for a month (*TASS,* June 14). According to Interfax on June 15, one person was killed and at least four people were injured in the clashes. Russian Television, reporting on June 14, said that five people had been hospitalized but that there were no dead.

Russian Television reported on June 17 that the Saudi king had offered to pay all the expenses of the pilgrimage to Mecca for 5,000 Soviet Muslims. In 1990, the

Saudi king had paid all the expenses in Saudi Arabia for about 1,500 Soviet pilgrims. Meanwhile, Makhachkala was reported quiet.

Sunken Soviet Submarine Could Start Leaking Radiation

A Soviet expert said a Soviet nuclear-powered submarine that sank in the Arctic Ocean off Norway in 1989 might start leaking radiation as early as 1992. Academician Igor' Spassky was quoted by the newspaper *Rossiiskaya gazeta* as saying experts believed the protective seal around the submarine's nuclear reactor could be wearing out. The submarine caught fire and sank in April, 1989, killing more than forty sailors. It was armed with two nuclear-tipped torpedoes. The crew shut down the reactor after the accident.

US Oil Company Wins Caspian Sea Drilling Rights

TASS said the US oil company Amoco had been awarded a contract over several other contenders to develop a large oilfield in the Caspian Sea. The agency said officials from the USSR Ministry of the Petroleum and Gas Industry and from Azerbaijan had chosen Amoco's bid because it was the best technically, ecologically, and socially. Western estimates said the field could contain up to 1 billion barrels of oil (Western press reports, June 13).

French Consulate Opened in Kiev

French Foreign Minister Roland Dumas arrived in Kiev for the opening of the French consulate there. Dumas met with Ukrainian Supreme Soviet Chairman Leonid Kravchuk and Prime Minister Vitol'd Fokin (RFE/RL correspondent's report, June 13).

Kirgizia Approves Law on Employment

Kirgizia was reported to have approved a law establishing a benefit program for jobless citizens. Radio Bishkek said the law directed all enterprises and state agencies in the republic to contribute to an unemployment fund. The report said the benefits would be available to anyone who applied for them until he or she found work. The program would go into effect on July 1.

Friday, June 14

Harvard Plan Unveiled

A team of Soviet and US scholars said the USSR could have a free-market economy and broad democracy within seven years if the West sustained it with large amounts of aid. The assertion came in a draft proposal unveiled at

The USSR in June, 1991

Harvard University. Two of the plan's main authors, US scholar Graham Allison and former RSFSR Deputy Prime Minister Grigorii Yavlinsky, said the aid would not be charity but rather an investment program aimed at reducing the risk of chaos in the USSR and any related security risk to the West. The two men declined to say how much the plan would cost, although the previous day, another member of the team, US economist Stanley Fischer, had said it could cost the West as much as 140 billion dollars over four years.

The plan would begin with implementation of the "Nine-plus-One" agreement signed between Soviet President Mikhail Gorbachev and nine republics in Novo-Ogarevo on April 23. A rapid sequence of price and trade liberalization, privatization, and fiscal and monetary reform would follow. Initially, the West would provide technical assistance, commodity credits, and money to finance imports—all needed to stave off politically intolerable shortages of goods and to make the ruble convertible. Later, Western aid would finance development of the infrastructure and assist the private sector (Western agencies, RFE/RL correspondent's report, June 14 and 15, and *The Washington Post*, June 15).

At a seminar on changes in the USSR on June 22, Soviet First Deputy Prime Minister Vladimir Shcherbakov said Soviet society would not survive an attempt to implement the Harvard plan. According to Western reports, Shcherbakov said people in the USSR still equated capitalism with exploitation. He said, "There is enormous resistance to change on the part of the population . . . it would not survive shock therapy."

KGB Head Meets with Victims of Repressions, Gives Figures

KGB Chairman Vladimir Kryuchkov met in Moscow with representatives of three groups working on behalf of victims of Stalinist repression. According to TASS, he used the occasion to reveal some new figures. Kryuchkov said his organization had established that 4,200,000 people had fallen victim to repressions between 1920 and 1953. (This figure is regarded by many specialists as too low.) He said that 1,200,000 victims of repressions had been rehabilitated between 1988 and October, 1990, and that the process was continuing. Some 100 mass graves of victims of repressions had been found so far in the USSR., Kryuchkov disclosed. He emphasized the KGB's current role in the rehabilitation of the victims.

CFE Compromise Approved

The Soviet Union pledged to eliminate roughly a quarter of the military equipment it had moved beyond the Urals and to adhere to limits set by the Conventional Forces in Europe Treaty signed in November, 1990 (Western agencies, June 15). The Soviet declarations, made by Oleg Grinevsky, were formally accepted by the twenty-one other parties to the treaty (sixteen NATO states and five former Warsaw Pact members). In a legally binding declaration, Moscow pledged to count disputed coastal defense and naval infantry within the original treaty provisions. It also made a political commitment to destroy or convert 14,500 tanks, armored personnel vehicles, and artillery systems deployed beyond the Urals.

USSR Offering MiG-31s for Sale

The Soviet Union displayed its frontline MiG-31 "Foxhound" fighter for the first time in the West on June 14, offering to sell it for 40 million dollars to any interested country except Iraq, Western agencies reported. The MiG-31 is a long-range interceptor that carries an advanced phased array radar (which one Soviet official said was capable of tracking "stealth" aircraft) and can land on grass or snow strips. Soviet representatives at the Paris Air Show said that talks were under way to sell the plane to the United Arab Emirates and that Libya and India were also interested. They added that a successor to the MiG-31 was already in the air.

Minister of the Aviation Industry Apollon Systsov denied Western reports that the Soviet Union had offered to sell advanced MiG–31 fighters to Israel. His comments appeared in *Izvestia* on June 24. "The MiG-31 was demonstrated only as an example of Soviet scientific and manufacturing potential," Systsov said. "No other country has this aircraft, and we are not offering it for sale." He called such reports "sheer fiction." Foreign Ministry spokesman Vitalii Churkin also denied that Moscow intended to sell the planes.

USSR to Keep Foothold in Vietnam

Rear Admiral Vladimir Kasatkin, a General Staff officer with responsibility for the Asia-Pacific region, said that Soviet forces would continue to use Cam Ranh Bay as "a support point" for naval operations in southeast Asia, the Indian Ocean, and the Gulf. In an interview with the *International Herald Tribune* published on June 14, Kasatkin stressed that the residual Soviet force in Vietnam was nonoffensive and would not take part in regional disputes. Aleksandr Panov, director of the Foreign Ministry's Department of the Pacific and Southeast Asian Countries, told the *International Herald Tribune* that a number of countries in the region wanted a "reduced but conspicuous" Soviet presence, along with

The USSR in June, 1991

the US military presence, to ward off possible encroachments by Japan, China, or India.

On June 18, Andrei Levin, a counselor at the Soviet embassy in Hanoi, contradicted the statement that the USSR would retain a support base at Cam Ranh Bay. According to Western agency reports, Levin said the USSR had already moved about 75 percent of its ships and aircraft from the base and that the withdrawal should be complete by 1994.

The Soviet government daily *Izvestia* said that its issue for June 12 had not been published in Georgia, because it contained an article that local printers considered slanderous to Georgia. While investigating the case, the newspaper's representatives were told that other Soviet periodicals critical of Georgia would be suppressed in the republic. *Izvestia* also said that Georgian television had stopped showing the main Central Television news program "Vremya" to "prevent the spreading of slander about Georgia and its people."

Issue of *Izvestia* Not Published in Georgia

Gavriil Popov issued his first decree following his election as mayor of Moscow. It stipulated that the city's pensioners could use all kinds of public transport free of charge starting July 1. Popov also told reporters that a consultative council of mass movements should be set up to provide jobs for everybody in the city and to improve the economic situation (*Radio Moscow*, June 14).

Moscow Pensioners to Ride Public Transport for Free

Saturday, June 15

At least eight people were killed and more than 100 injured when an earthquake hit central Georgia. Two villages were destroyed and six others severely damaged. The epicenter of the earthquake, which measured 6.3 on the Richter scale, was the resort of Bakuriani, 100 kilometers west of Tbilisi. In the South Ossetian Autonomous Oblast, where several towns were devastated and 144 people were killed in an earlier tremor in late April, the earthquake destroyed several villages and 80 percent of the buildings in Gori and Tskhinvali left standing after the April tremor (*TASS*, June 16).

Eight Killed in Georgian Earthquake

Soviet Prime Minister Valentin Pavlov said radical change in the Soviet economy had been delayed because

Pavlov Says Change Delayed by Hard-Liners

Soviet President Mikhail Gorbachev had had to maneuver around hard-liners. In an interview published in *Izvestia*, Pavlov said Gorbachev had had to avoid confrontation with former Politburo members Egor Ligachev and Mikhail Solomentsev or risk being ousted by them. Ligachev was dropped from the Politburo in 1990, Solomentsev in 1988. Pavlov said people who blamed Gorbachev for wasting time during his first six years in power did not understand how cautious he had had to be to avoid "political suicide." Pavlov also said he favored foreign investment rather than loans to help the Soviet Union convert to a market economy.

Sovetskaya Rossiya Attacks Shevardnadze

Sovetskaya Rossiya blamed former Soviet Foreign Minister Eduard Shevardnadze for turning the USSR from a great power into "a second-rate country." The newspaper accused Shevardnadze of "seeking success at the cost of giving up positions, making concessions, and sometimes directly capitulating as the only way to stay at the center of attention." The article equated Shevardnadze's legacy as foreign minister with "the results of defeat in an unfought . . . third world war." In a separate press review the same day, TASS described the article as containing "fierce and insulting attacks."

EC Protests about Baltic Attacks

The EC delivered a verbal protest to Moscow about Soviet troop attacks on customs posts in the Baltic republics. TASS said Luxembourg's ambassador to Moscow, Hubert Wurth, had delivered the complaint to Soviet First Deputy Foreign Minister Yulii Kvitsinsky. Kvitsinsky responded by saying there was no legal basis for the protest, as events in the Baltic republics were a purely internal matter. TASS quoted Kvitsinsky as saying that Moscow's evaluation of events in the Baltic "does not depend on any recognition or approval from abroad."

Gamsakhurdia Says Georgia Wants EC Membership

Georgian President Zviad Gamsakhurdia said Georgia wanted eventual membership in the EC and the United Nations. Gamsakhurdia made the comment in an interview with Saarländische Rundfunk. He said membership in international organizations and recognition of Georgia by Western Europe and the United States were his primary foreign-policy goals. He also said he wanted good economic, political, and cultural relations with the Soviet Union—but as a foreign state.

The USSR in June, 1991

Sobchak Outlines Restructuring of Leningrad City Soviet

Speaking to deputies of the Leningrad City Soviet, the city's first popularly elected mayor, Anatolii Sobchak, enumerated a number of changes in the structure of the city soviet: the abolition of the soviet executive committee and its replacement by a new executive apparatus; and the abolition of some commissions and other structures within the soviet. Sobchak said that all deputies wanting to work within the new executive apparatus would have to give up their status as deputies (*Radio Rossii*, June 15).

Sunday, June 16

USSR Offers to Sell Missiles to Israel

Western agencies reported that officials from ALMAZ—identified as a Soviet state industrial corporation with some 55,000 employees—had offered to sell Israel an antimissile defense system during the Paris Air Show. An Israeli representative identified the Soviet missiles as AF-300s. The USSR claimed that the missiles—with a range of ninety kilometers and an altitude of 25,000 meters—were superior to the US Patriot system. The unprecedented offer would help Israel defend itself against Soviet-made systems like the SCUD. An Israeli official was reported as saying: "The Soviet Union needs cash, and they're ready to sell those systems."

Iranian Oil Minister in Moscow

A high-ranking Iranian delegation, led by Oil Minister Gholam Reza Aqazadeh-Kho'i, arrived in Moscow for talks with Soviet officials about cooperation on oil and gas issues. IRNA quoted Aqazadeh-Kho'i as saying Iran believed the USSR was eager to increase its imports of natural gas from Iran. He said the talks would also deal with the transit of Iranian natural gas through the USSR to Europe and with bilateral cooperation in international oil markets, particularly the East European market.

New Political Groups Meet

The hard-line political group "Edinstvo," headed by Leningrad teacher Nina Andreeva, held a congress in Odessa at which it announced the creation of the Leninist Workers' Party. The party would unite members of the CPSU who rejected "the revisionist course" of its current leadership, "TSN" reported. "TSN" also said that a new political movement, "Rus' monarkhicheskaya" (Monarchist Russia), had been set up the same day in Moscow. The movement demanded a criminal investigation into the 1918 murder of the tsar and his family. The party of Constitutional Democrats also held a congress in Moscow, "TSN" reported. The Constitutional Democrats claimed to continue the activities of the Kadet Party, which was outlawed after the October Revolution.

Alaska Airlines Begins Service to Soviet Far East

The Seattle-based Alaska Airlines became the first US airline to operate a regular service to the Soviet cities of Magadan and Khabarovsk. Alaska Airlines extended its service from the US West Coast to the Soviet Far East via Anchorage, Alaska (*AP*, June 16).

Moldavians and Romanians Celebrate Cross-Border Festival

At least half a million Moldavians crossed the border into Romania at eight crossing points for prearranged festivities on Romanian territory, the Moldavian media reported. Deliberately nonpolitical, the festivities featured religious, musical, and literary events. The festival was held for the second consecutive year to mark the end of isolation between compatriots on the two sides of the border.

Monday, June 17

Pavlov Asks for More Powers

At a Supreme Soviet session, USSR Prime Minister Valentin Pavlov asked the legislature for expanded powers for the central government to enable it to tackle the country's economic problems. Pavlov said the cabinet needed powers such as those already enjoyed by the president to initiate legislation and issue decrees. He said that efficient government required the power to take quick decisions and that it was physically impossible for Soviet President Mikhail Gorbachev to handle all the responsibilities he had. Pavlov said, for example, that, in order to save the harvest, the government had to be able to draft manpower and machinery from industrial enterprises for use in the fields (*Financial Times*, June 18).

Pavlov also attacked the economic and political proposals put forward by Grigorii Yavlinsky and a group of Harvard scholars to reform the Soviet economy using Western aid. He said, "The American program undermines trust in the anticrisis program of the Cabinet of Ministers."

On June 18, a number of Supreme Soviet deputies supported Pavlov's request for expanded powers. Yurii Blokhin, a deputy of the "Soyuz" faction, said Pavlov had "the will and desire to take resolute measures" to bring about real reform. Gorbachev, on the other hand, lacked "the civil courage" to take firm measures to lead the country out of its crisis, Blokhin maintained. Sergei Ryabchenko, of the Interregional Group of Deputies, said Pavlov's request was "a coordinated campaign to remove the USSR president from power" (*TASS,* June 18). A decision on the matter was delayed until June 21. Later reports said Gorbachev was responsible for the delay.

On June 19, the chairman of the USSR State Committee for Constitutional Supervision, Sergei Alekseev, rejected Pavlov's demand on the ground that it would create three power centers—the presidency, the prime minister, and the USSR Supreme Soviet—in opposition to one another (*Central Television,* June 19).

Russian Television on June 19 disclosed that Pavlov's proposal was supported in the USSR Supreme Soviet by the heads of the army, Ministry of Internal Affairs, and KGB—Dmitrii Yazov, Boriss Pugo, and Vladimir Kryuchkov, respectively. One of the security chiefs was reported to have described Soviet President Gorbachev's policy of dismantling the Union as coinciding with the plans of US intelligence.

On June 21, the USSR Supreme Soviet rejected Pavlov's request. The vote was 264–24 in favor of removing the question from the agenda. Western agencies reported on June 22 that Gorbachev had attacked the leaders of the "Soyuz" faction, accusing them of plotting behind his back and being "completely divorced from reality." Gorbachev told reporters that he was not afraid of hard-liners and that "society will reject them."

The rejection of Pavlov's demands was not, however, a clear victory for Gorbachev. Not only did the prime minister keep his job, but Gorbachev even admitted that Pavlov had acted "within the framework of *perestroika* in requesting new powers." He also promised Pavlov he would merge his economic plan with the more radical Harvard one. In turn, Pavlov told the Supreme Soviet that his demands for more power had been "misinterpreted" and that in reality there were no disagreements with Gorbachev. The leaders of "Soyuz" were surprised by Pavlov's retreat (Western agencies, June 21; *The Boston Globe,* June 22).

Supreme Soviet Reviews Anticrisis Program

The USSR Supreme Soviet heard a presentation by USSR Prime Minister Valentin Pavlov of the "final" version of the government's anticrisis program (*TASS,* June 17). The program was first presented in April. Signing the document were the USSR and the leaders of Belorussia, Uzbekistan, Kazakhstan, Azerbaijan, Kirgizia, Tajikistan, Armenia, and Turkmenistan. The RSFSR and Ukraine were prepared to sign it after a few changes had been made concerning taxes and property rights. Lithuania, Moldavia, and Latvia abstained from signing, and Estonia and Georgia did not take part in the preparation of the document.

The document emphasized that the USSR government and the republics would enforce strict monetary and fiscal policies aimed at reducing the budget deficit. The Council of the Federation was to divide up internal and external debt among the USSR and the republics by the end of June. Gold, diamonds, and hard-currency resources were also to be divided up. As of July 1, it was envisaged that the republics would conduct their own foreign trade independently of the center. This included securing and using new commercial debt and foreign government credits and other types of foreign assistance. The document gave republics the legal right to engage in barter trade. Finally, the plan called for "internal ruble convertibility" to be achieved by January, 1992.

Final Draft of Union Treaty Sent to Republican Parliaments

The Preparatory Committee set up by the Fourth USSR Congress of People's Deputies to complete work on the draft Union treaty met again on June 17 in Novo-Ogarevo, the Soviet media reported. It approved the draft and sent it to the republican and all-Union parliaments for approval. The parliaments were asked to review it before the end of June.

Gorbachev presented the new draft Union treaty to the public during the main television news program on June 18. He told his audience that the treaty "broadened the possibilities for the republics" but that there was still a need "to keep the center alive."

Grigorii Revenko, adviser to Gorbachev, told reporters in Moscow on June 20 that no republic would be dragged into the reconstituted Soviet Union and that those that did not sign the new Union treaty would be able to decide independently the question of their presence in the USSR (RL Russian service, June 20).

The text of the latest draft of the Union treaty was published in *Nezavisimaya gazeta* on June 22. It stated that the new Union was the successor state to the old Union as a subject of international law, which seemed to make the position of the republics not signing the treaty even more anomalous; that the adoption of the constitution was the exclusive prerogative of the Union, and not a joint Union-republican matter, as had been stated in an earlier draft; that the armed forces might be used inside the country only to deal with natural disasters or as stipulated in legislation on a state of emergency; and that control of defense enterprises was a joint Union-republican matter. The article on federal taxes, one of the main sticking points, remained virtually unchanged. The draft abolished the Council of the Federation and proposed yet another structure for the Supreme Soviet.

Zhurnalist under Attack

Radio Rossii said the main journal of the USSR Journalists' Union was being put under economic pressure by its founder, the "Pravda" publishing house. The radio said "Pravda" had revoked its status as the journal's founder and thereby deprived the periodical of access to the publishing house's printing equipment. The reason for this was that *Zhurnalist* had recently abandoned its previously conservative stance and started to publish data on violations of the press law by CPSU officials. Commenting on the development, Radio Rossii said that CPSU officialdom was attempting to replace political censorship (banned by the press law) with economic sanctions against "disobedient periodicals."

Kazakhstan Signs Agreement with All-Union Ministries

In what was regarded as an important precursor to the signing of the new Union treaty, Kazakh President Nursultan Nazarbaev met with the ministers of the coal industry (Mikhail Shchadov), metallurgy (Oleg Syskovets), and the radio industry (Vladimir Shimko) to organize the transfer of these ministries' enterprises to Kazakhstan's jurisdiction, Radio Mayak reported. Nazarbaev said he wanted full authority to work on problems in these areas, saying that Moscow had been weak and ineffective.

Latvia Says Prosecutor Illegal

The Latvian Supreme Council Presidium was reported to have passed a resolution saying the operations of the Latvian SSR Prosecutor's Office were illegal and ordering it to stop its work. The report, which did not say when the resolution was passed, also quoted the Latvian SSR prosecutor, Valentin Daukshis, as telling Postfactum in an interview that he intended to continue his work (*Radio Moscow*, June 16).

Tuesday, June 18

El'tsin Visits United States

RSFSR President-elect Boris El'tsin said after his arrival in the United States that "Russia has suffered through a Marxist experiment but is now determined to follow the Western road to democracy" (Western agencies, June 19). He emphasized at a meeting at the Soviet embassy that

Russia would travel the road the West traveled some time ago. Before his departure for the United States, El'tsin said that "Russia has become very independent in foreign policy as well" (*The New York Times*, June 19). He promised to create conditions in Russia that would have foreigners "rushing over with great willingness." He also said that an aim of his visit to the United States was to study how to organize executive power.

On his arrival in Washington, El'tsin praised Soviet President Mikhail Gorbachev, saying that the USSR president had been the father of democracy in the Soviet Union (Western agencies, June 19). He told journalists that he and Gorbachev backed the Yavlinsky economic reform plan in principle. He urged the West to hold a dialogue with both Gorbachev and himself. Gorbachev welcomed El'tsin's trip to the United States.

On June 19, El'tsin held private meetings with members of the US House of Representatives and Senate and attended a luncheon held in his honor by the US Congressional leadership, Western agencies reported. He declared there that he was not seeking money from the United States but closer ties between it and the RSFSR and a series of "cooperative programs" to aid his reforms; he mentioned agriculture, privatization, and a Russian-American Bank, as well as a management training program and the conversion of military industries to civilian production as areas of potential cooperation.

El'tsin ended his three-day visit to Washington on June 20 with detailed discussions of his proposed reform program with US President George Bush. He told reporters after the talks that the meeting had been interesting, with "lots of specifics" focusing primarily on cooperative programs between the United States and the RSFSR. National Security Adviser Brent Scowcroft said Bush had made clear that the United States was prepared to cooperate with individual Soviet republics in fields allowed under the new Union treaty but that any US cooperation of this kind would require the acquiescence of the central Soviet government (Western agencies, June 21).

Speaking at New York University on June 21, El'tsin predicted the creation of a common political and economic system in which the United States and Russia would play a leading role, Western agencies reported on June 22.

On June 26, El'tsin told the RSFSR Supreme Soviet that the most important result of his trip to the United States was the fact that the Bush administration had agreed to establish independent ties with the Russian Federation. Stressing that a renewed Russia would have to convince its new partners that it wanted to play a stabilizing role in world politics, El'tsin said he did not want, in his foreign policy, to act in opposition to Gorbachev (*TASS*, June 26).

Gorbachev Promises to Reassess Agricultural Prices

Soviet President Mikhail Gorbachev faced an angry congress of peasant farmers in Moscow and promised to consider raising the prices the government paid for their produce. TASS said Gorbachev spoke to the farmers after a speech by Prime Minister Valentin Pavlov had enraged them so much that they had threatened to hold a protest strike to press their demands. There was no word of what Pavlov said. TASS said Gorbachev promised he would put pressure on the government not only to raise procurement prices but also to ensure that farmers had access to the agricultural equipment and consumer goods they needed.

Miners Hold Underground Strike to Protest against Closure

Ninety workers at copper mines in Chelyabinsk Oblast in the Urals began a hunger strike 850 meters underground to protest against the planned closure of their mine. TASS said that the mine had gone bankrupt and that the Soviet government had failed to fulfill promises to give the mine the necessary equipment to clean up industrial pollution. Part of the facility had had to be closed down in 1990. A third of the miners had subsequently been laid off, and those remaining had not been paid for a month. TASS said the miners were demanding a meeting with USSR Minister of Metallurgy Oleg Syskovets to discuss their situation.

The hunger strike ended on June 24 after RSFSR people's deputy Gennadii Sereda had promised the miners that the USSR Ministry of Metallurgy would keep the mine open until the end of the year.

Peacetime Deaths in Soviet Armed Forces

A commission of the RSFSR Supreme Soviet charged with investigating peacetime deaths in the armed forces said that some 310,000 Soviet soldiers had died during peacetime since the end of World War II, "Vesti" reported. The commission said that half of the deaths were the result of suicide, some 20 percent had been caused by beatings, and only 10 percent were related to accidents. *Ogonek* (No. 22) carried an article on the difficulties faced by parents and investigators in their efforts to uncover the extent of, and reasons for, noncombat deaths among conscripts. Author Gennadii Zhukovets concluded that the USSR Defense Ministry had stonewalled the investigation and that a presidential commission appointed to investigate had been ineffective. He said, however, that a USSR Defense Ministry statement suggested that some 8,000 conscripts had died annually over the last fifteen years and that letters to the presidential commission implied that some 75–80 percent of all deaths, and 70 percent of serious injuries, were related to violence in army life (See also *Kuranty*, No. 67).

Belorussian Chernobyl' Commission Abolished

Belorussian people's deputy Syarhei Navumchyk told RFE/RL that the Belorussian Supreme Soviet commission on Chernobyl' had been abruptly abolished on June 14 after it became known that its members had incriminating evidence of official misdeeds perpetrated after the nuclear plant explosion in 1986. According to Navumchyk, a report by the commission described the actions of former Party First Secretary Nikolai Slyun'kov and Prime Minister Mikhail Kovalev as "irresponsible and even criminal" and called for an investigation by the Belorussian Public Prosecutor's Office. The Communist-controlled Supreme Soviet also turned down a proposal to account for funds spent on Chernobyl' victims.

Belorussian Communists for Democracy

Radio Rossii reported that a group called Communists for Democracy had been formed in the Belorussian Supreme Soviet. It was composed of Party members who were dissatisfied with the policies of the Belorussian Communist Party leadership. They intended to push for implementation of the republic's sovereignty declaration and to transform the Communist Party into a parliamentary party.

Belorussian Strikers' Demands Rejected

The Belorussian Supreme Soviet voted to reject demands put forward in May by Belorussian strikers on the grounds that "departification" of enterprises, "depoliticization" of law-enforcement agencies, and the nationalization of Communist Party property would be unconstitutional and in violation of international laws (*Belta-TASS*, June 18).

Ukraine to Mark "Independence Day"

Radio Kiev announced that the Ukrainian Supreme Soviet had proclaimed a new official holiday in the republic, Ukrainian Independence Day. It would be celebrated on July 16, the anniversary of the declaration of state sovereignty. USSR Constitution Day would no longer be observed in Ukraine.

The USSR in June, 1991

Wednesday, June 19

CSCE Agrees on Crisis Mediation Measures

The thirty-five-state Conference on Security and Cooperation in Europe (CSCE) met in Berlin to discuss ways to prevent conflicts and manage crises on the European continent, DPA reported. The USSR differed with most members of the conference over a crisis-mediation process that would permit mediation to take place without the agreement of all member-states, insisting that member-states should be able to veto the use of emergency procedures in disputes involving them.

US Secretary of State James Baker told the Baltic representatives of US efforts to win observer status for the Baltic republics at CSCE meetings. Under the existing arrangement, the Baltic republics were participating as guests of other countries, which denied them entry to the closed-door sessions. Baker said that the USSR was blocking the US effort (*AFP*, June 19).

Before concluding on June 20, the conference approved an agreement on crisis mediation. Under the agreement, a panel of twelve members could be convened to discuss a crisis and make recommendations. Member-states involved in the crisis could not block the discussions; yielding to Soviet objections, though, the ministers agreed that the state in question could veto any decision or mediation attempts recommended by the panel. The meeting also decided to create a conflict prevention center in Vienna (Western press reports, June 20).

Cuts in Soviet Ministries Announced

According to TASS, the USSR Cabinet of Ministers announced that it planned to cut one-third of all jobs in central Soviet ministries as the USSR made the transition to a market economy. About 36,000 jobs would be eliminated overall, with some ministries being cut by 50 percent and their functions transferred to the republican level. The only ministries to escape cuts would be the defense and railway ministries, which would remain firmly under the center's jurisdiction.

Soviet Union Prepares for War Anniversary

Marking the fiftieth anniversary of the German attack on the USSR on June 22, 1941, Chief of the General Staff of the Soviet Armed Forces Mikhail Moiseev took issue with the idea that losses early in the war were the result of ineptitude on the part of the High Command and that the army had relied on numbers rather than skill. He admitted, however, that the General Staff had made serious errors (*Pravda*, June 19). Moiseev also addressed a conference in Moscow on the early period of the war, and USSR Defense Minister Dmitrii Yazov addressed a conference jointly sponsored by the Defense Ministry and the USSR Union of Writers.

In a joint article devoted to World War II in *Die Welt* of June 20, Soviet Marshal Sergei Akhromeev and German Christian Democratic Party deputy Alfred Dregger stressed the importance of good relations between the USSR and Germany. Akhromeev used the occasion to call for the dissolution of NATO and for a definition of the role to be played by the West European Union. Dregger said these organizations were the basis for the success of the Helsinki process.

Head of Military History Institute Dismissed

Dmitrii Volkogonov, the director of the USSR Defense Ministry's Institute of Military History, was dismissed from his post after being called "a crying anti-Communist" by Soviet Marshal Sergei Akhromeev. *Nezavisimaya gazeta* quoted Volkogonov, who was also chief editor of a new ten-volume *History of the Great Patriotic War* due to be published on June 22 to mark the fiftieth anniversary of the German invasion, as saying he had lost his job because Akhromeev disagreed with his views on the war and on current Soviet politics (*Radio Rossii*, June 19).

Akhromeev told reporters on June 20 that he had decided to ban the publication of the new history because the book was full of lies and inaccuracies that would hurt the USSR and the Communist Party (*Radio Moscow*, June 20).

On June 21, Volkogonov defended his history of the war, saying that it was entirely truthful and that the Soviet people did not need "sugary patriotism." He accused the military leadership of trying to control history and said that criticism of his work had prompted him to resign as editor of the history and from his post as head of the Institute of Military History.

Experimental Creative Center Publishes Magazine

The interdisciplinary Experimental Creative Center, headed by political scientist Sergei Kurginyan, started a bimonthly magazine, *Polis*, published under the aegis of the USSR Academy of Sciences. Founders of *Polis* also included the association "Save the World and Nature," the Soviet Committee for the Defense of Peace, the Council of the All-Union Confederation of Trade Unions, the Institute of the International Workers' Movement, and "Progress" publishers. USSR Deputy Foreign Minister Ernest Obminsky, Chairman of the State Committee for the Press and Publishing Mikhail Nenashev, rector of the former CPSU Central Committee Institute of Social Sciences Yurii Krasin, leading consultants from the CPSU International Department, and experts from the USA and Canada Institute and the Institute of the World Economy and International Relations were on the editorial board.

Number of Death Sentences Rises

An interview in *Rabochaya tribuna* with the director of the clemency appeals department of the USSR Supreme Soviet, Gennadii Cheremnykh, revealed that the number of death sentences in the USSR had increased in 1990. According to agency reports, Cheremnykh said 445 people had been convicted of capital crimes in the USSR in 1990. Of those, 29 had since been pardoned, and 29 had already been executed. Statistics on capital punishment were a state secret in the USSR until, on February 26, 1991, *Komsomol'skaya pravda* published figures for 1985–89. These showed the numbers of death sentences dropping from 770 in 1985 to 526 in 1986, 344 in 1987, and a low of 271 (of whom 72 were pardoned) in 1988. The figures began to rise again in 1989, when 276 people were sentenced to death (of whom 23 were pardoned).

RSFSR Supreme Soviet Discusses Languages Bill

The RSFSR Supreme Soviet approved a draft law "On the Languages of the Peoples of the RSFSR," the first in the republic's history, TASS reported. Some deputies objected to the provision in the bill declaring Russian the state language only in the republic's krais and oblasts and leaving it up to the local authorities to decide what the situation should be in the autonomous formations. In fact, in their declarations of sovereignty, the autonomous formations had already given both the vernacular and Russian the status of state language.

RSFSR Cities Rated According to Living Standards

A new sociological survey concluded that Moscow and Leningrad had the best overall living standards of cities in the RSFSR, *Argumenty i fakty* (No. 21) reported. Leningrad's Voznesensky Finance and Economics Institute said the lowest living standards were found in Elista (Kalmyk ASSR), Groznyi (Checheno-Ingushetia), Makhachkala (Dagestan), Ulan-Ude (Buryatia), and in Tambov (RSFSR). The highest dietary standards after Moscow were in Leningrad, Murmansk, and Kaliningrad, with the poorest in Groznyi and Kyzyl. Rates of infant mortality, illness, and industrial accidents were the lowest, however, in Makhachkala and Groznyi, and the highest in Yakutsk and Kemerovo. The least polluted cities were Kurgan, Tyumen', Chita, and Pskov, while the most polluted were Groznyi, Lipetsk, and Nalchik in Kabardino-Balkaria.

Delors Arrives in Moscow

President of the European Commission Jacques Delors arrived in Moscow for two days of talks on cooperation between the Soviet Union and the European Community, Reuters reported. After meeting with Soviet President Mikhail Gorbachev on June 20, Delors told reporters that Soviet economic reforms could not succeed without institutional changes. Gorbachev was quoted as saying during the meeting that it was now necessary to speed up the pace of Soviet reforms so as to complete the dismantling of the old system and create a new one. He added that he hoped cooperation would increase between the Soviet Union and Western countries so that the USSR could join the world economy.

Shcherbak Elected Ukrainian Minister for Environment

Writer and physician Yurii Shcherbak was elected to the post of Ukrainian minister for the environment, TASS announced. Shcherbak has written extensively on the effects of the Chernobyl' disaster and is also chairman of the Ukrainian Green Party.

Ukrainian and Belorussian Foreign Ministers on Chernobyl'

At a press conference in Berlin, the foreign ministers of Ukraine and Belorussia, Anatolii Zlenko and Petr Krauchanka, said the world still did not know the truth about the impact and scale of the Chernobyl' disaster. The two ministers took issue with the recently issued and highly controversial report by the International Atomic Energy Agency, stating that its findings would lead to unjustified optimism. Zlenko and Krauchanko were in Berlin as members of the Soviet delegation to the Conference on Security and Cooperation in Europe. Their comments were summarized by TASS.

Return of Crimean Tatars to Crimea

TASS quoted the chairman of the Crimean ASSR Committee for Deported Peoples, Lentun Bezaziev, as saying more than 130,000 Crimean Tatars had returned to the Crimea. Those coming by invitation had their expenses paid and were given plots of land and credit, but members of the intelligentsia had difficulty finding work in their specialities, Bezaziev said, adding that efforts were being made to revive the national culture and that work was under way to restore local monuments. Novosti reported on June 18, however, that members of the National

THE USSR IN JUNE, 1991

Movement of Crimean Tatars were not satisfied with the progress made and wanted the matter raised at the fifth session of the USSR Congress of People's Deputies.

General Viktor Shilov, commander of the Southern Group of Soviet Forces, was the last Soviet soldier to leave Hungary, MTI reported. His departure ended over forty years of Soviet military presence in the country, where 100,000 Soviet servicemen and their families were stationed.

Last Soviet Soldier Leaves Hungary

President of the Lithuanian Supreme Council Vytautas Landsbergis began a ten-day trip to France, Norway, Germany, and Finland. In Paris he met on June 20 with French President François Mitterrand, who assured him that the problems of the Baltic republics would be discussed at the European Community summit meeting on June 28–29 in Brussels, AFP reported. French officials said an agreement in principle had been reached between Paris and Vilnius to open a French cultural center in the Lithuanian capital. Landsbergis met later with the presidents of the French National Assembly and Senate, Laurent Fabius and Alain Poher, before flying to Lyon.

On June 22, Landsbergis flew to Norway on the second leg of his European tour. There he opened a Lithuanian music festival in Tundsburg. On June 23, he traveled to Kiel, in Germany, for the annual meeting of representatives of the parliaments of North European countries. President of the Estonian Supreme Council Arnold Ruutel and Landsbergis told journalists that day that they trusted and supported RSFSR President-elect Boris El'tsin, Radio Independent Lithuania reported on June 24.

Landsbergis visited the European Parliament in Strasbourg on June 25, Radio Independent Lithuania reported. Landsbergis expressed hope that the European Community would go a step beyond its previous declarations and offer the Baltic republics "concrete help." The EC invited Landsbergis to attend the next session of the European Parliament beginning on July 8.

Landsbergis on European Tour

Estonian Prime Minister Edgar Savisaar avoided an attempt by some parliamentary deputies to force a vote of no confidence in his government, Radio Tallinn reported. The Supreme Council voted to approve the suggestion by its president, Arnold Ruutel, not to put the no-confidence motion on the day's agenda.

Estonian Prime Minister Avoids No-Confidence Vote

Thursday, June 20

New Chairman of Moscow City Soviet Elected

Nikolai Gonchar was elected chairman of the Moscow City Soviet, replacing Gavriil Popov, who was elected mayor of Moscow on June 12. Gonchar's election was announced at a meeting of the Moscow City Soviet, TASS reported.

Prokof'ev Comments on June 12 Elections

The first secretary of the Moscow Communist Party, Yurii Prokof'ev, said Moscow Communists would not become "an obscure opposition" despite severe losses in the elections of June 12. According to TASS, Prokof'ev discussed the election results with Moscow Mayor Gavriil Popov, and both agreed that Communists would continue to take part in governing the city.

Special Police to Find Undeclared AIDS Sufferers

Izvestia reported that USSR Minister of Internal Affairs Boriss Pugo had issued an order authorizing special police units to find and prosecute people anywhere in the Soviet Union who were suffering from AIDS but concealing their illness.

Bonn and Moscow Agree on Housing Contracts

The Soviet Union and Germany agreed to give German companies preference in contracts for the more than thirty remaining housing projects for Soviet soldiers withdrawn from Germany. The agreement stipulated that enterprises in eastern Germany would be given at least 20 percent of all work to be done regardless of who was the main contractor; it also said that 70 percent of building materials bought with a special 120-million-mark German emergency aid package for the USSR must be bought from German firms (RFE/RL correspondent's report, June 20).

Ivan Polozkov in China

RSFSR Communist Party First Secretary Ivan Polozkov arrived in China on a ten-day visit. He declared on his arrival that the USSR should study closely the work of the Chinese Communist Party, which was playing the leading role in China's current successful economic transformation at a time when the Communist movements in Europe had been annihilated (*AFP*, June 20).

Belorussia Creates Post of President

The Belorussian Supreme Soviet voted to follow the lead of the RSFSR and other republics and to opt for a presidential form of government, TASS reported. The

THE USSR IN JUNE, 1991

Supreme Soviet would draft a law on the presidency specifying the powers of the new post.

The US House of Representatives passed a foreign-aid bill with an amendment linking aid to the USSR with the situation in the Baltic republics, Western agencies reported on June 21. According to the amendment, the United States would withhold aid pending a USSR pledge to distribute the aid equally among the Baltic and other Soviet republics. The USSR would also have to return property seized in the Baltic republics since January 1, 1991. Half of the proposed 30 million dollars in technical aid for 1992 and 1993 would go directly to the Baltic republics and the other half would be sent to democratically elected local governments in the USSR and to other organizations deemed "eligible" for aid.

Pro-Baltic Amendment to US Foreign Aid Bill

Friday, June 21

In a television address marking the fiftieth anniversary of Nazi Germany's attack on the Soviet Union, Soviet President Mikhail Gorbachev said the Soviet Union was "firmly set on the path of reconciliation with Germany." Gorbachev also said that good relations between the two former adversaries "constitute a true example of good-neighborliness and partnership." Gorbachev's address was also broadcast on German television.

Gorbachev Hails Soviet-German Relations

Radio Rossii reported that the Political Committee of the Russian National Monarchist Party had demanded that the Holy Synod of the Russian Orthodox Church canonize Tsar Nicholas II and the members of his family immediately. The tsar and his family were among several thousands of "new martyrs" canonized in 1981 by the US-based Russian Orthodox Church Abroad.

Demand for Canonization of the Last Tsar

Saturday, June 22

Gatherings were held throughout the Soviet Union to mark the fiftieth anniversary of the German invasion on June 22, 1941. According to Western and Soviet reports, President Mikhail Gorbachev, together with Prime Minister Valentin Pavlov and Defense Minister Dmitrii Yazov, laid a wreath at the Tomb of the Unknown Soldier, while

USSR Marks Fiftieth Anniversary of German Invasion

many Soviet newspapers devoted full pages to the first days of the German-Soviet conflict. *Pravda* carried a four-page supplement to mark the anniversary.

In a speech on June 21 devoted to the anniversary, Gorbachev said the Soviet victory had been the result of the solidarity of the Soviet people. He said that ethnic and national differences had been overcome and that people with different social backgrounds, as well as varying political and religious beliefs, had been able to unite. He also praised Allied cooperation during the war and lamented the breakdown of East-West relations during the Cold War years.

In Lithuania, USSR war veterans gathered at the Chernyakhovsky monument in Vilnius for "an antifascist meeting." Speakers at the meeting, including Lithuanian Communist Party First Secretary Mykolas Burokevicius, denounced the current Lithuanian government, especially Supreme Council President Vytautas Landsbergis, claiming that his father had collaborated with the Nazis during the war (*Radio Independent Lithuania*, June 23).

Kryuchkov Says CIA Plotting to Destroy Soviet Economy

In a hard-line speech to a closed session of the USSR Supreme Soviet on June 18, KGB Chairman Vladimir Kryuchkov said the West was trying to undermine the Soviet system by pretending to support *perestroika*, and he accused the CIA of plotting to destroy the Soviet economy. Kryuchkov's statements were aired on Soviet television on June 22 by the controversial Leningrad journalist Aleksandr Nevzorov. Kryuchkov said that Soviet plans for economic reform and attempts to gain Western aid amounted to capitulation and that they would give the West leverage over Soviet internal affairs. He also claimed that the West wanted Moscow to make "intolerable" defense cuts.

Yazov on Army's Problems

USSR Defense Minister Dmitrii Yazov said in an interview with *Komsomol'skaya pravda* (June 22) that the army's biggest problem was managing the withdrawal from Eastern Europe. Yazov complained that the Germans had not met all their commitments with respect to housing. Yazov also criticized living conditions for soldiers in the Baltic and Transcaucasus regions and said that the Nagorno-Karabakh conflict could be solved if all forces "observed the law and constitutional order." He appeared to criticize the reestablishment of Cossack troop units.

On June 27, *Sovetskaya Rossiya* quoted Yazov as telling a closed session of the Supreme Soviet on June 18 that the armed forces were falling apart because many republics were withholding conscripts. He said that the armed forces were already about 353,000 conscripts short because of recruitment problems. He claimed that only 6 percent of eligible conscripts had been drafted in Georgia, Armenia, and the Baltic republics. Yazov's speech was also published in *Politika*, the newspaper of the "Soyuz" faction in the USSR Supreme Soviet.

Chilean Economy Minister in Moscow

Chilean Minister of Economy Carlos Ominami left for the USSR on June 22 together with a group of thirty-five Chilean business leaders, according to Western reports. The aim of the visit was to increase exports to the USSR and to expand technical cooperation in the fields of fishing, textiles, metallurgy, and agriculture. This was the first official Chilean visit to the USSR at such a level since 1972. Relations between Chile and the USSR were suspended between 1973 and 1990. Soviet trade statistics through the end of 1990 reported no trade with Chile.

RSFSR Reports Marked Increase in Inflation

Consumer prices in the RSFSR rose by an average of 96 percent in May compared with May, 1990, according to Western and Soviet reports of official RSFSR statistics. Food prices went up by 127 percent on average, while the price of textiles and clothes increased by 166 percent and that of building materials by 132 percent.

New Data on Uzbek Joint Venture Deals

In remarks carried by TASS, Uzbek Vice President Shukurulla Mirsaidov said that there were some thirty joint ventures in Uzbekistan, capitalized at about 377 million hard-currency rubles. The joint ventures had already produced some 2.4 billion hard-currency rubles' worth of consumer goods. At a five-day international business seminar in Tashkent, which ended on June 22, contracts worth 65.8 million dollars were signed.

Sunday, June 23

Protest in Kiev against Union Treaty

Thousands of people demonstrated in Kiev to demand that Ukraine reject the proposed Union treaty, according to agency reports. Speakers at the rally, which was organized by "Rukh," said the treaty would deprive Ukraine of its independence.

Reports by the Soviet and Ukrainian media on June 23 and 24 said the Coordinating Council of Oblast Soviets of Ivano-Frankovsk, Lvov, and Ternopol' had forwarded a protest to the republican Supreme Soviet concerning the draft Union treaty. The West Ukrainian people's deputies asserted that neither the examination nor the signing of the treaty at this time was appropriate, reminding the parliament that 90 percent of voters in the three oblasts had voted in favor of an independent Ukrainian state in a referendum on March 17.

Chairman of the Ukrainian Supreme Soviet Leonid Kravchuk raised serious objections to the draft Union treaty in an article in *Trud*. Kravchuk argued that the draft posited the new Union as a sovereign state, which he said was unacceptable. In his view, the new formation should be "a state union."

On June 27, the Ukrainian parliament voted to delay further discussion of the Union treaty in order to allow experts to assess whether it contradicted the republic's sovereignty declaration issued in 1990. Kiev journalist Svetlana Ryaboshapka told RFE/RL that the parliamentary commission had until September 1 to complete its review.

Ukrainian police and USSR OMON troops used tear gas and batons to prevent several thousand people who were protesting against the treaty from forcing their way inside the parliament building. There were no reports of serious injuries.

On June 28, at the start of a visit to Canada, Deputy Chairman of the Ukrainian Supreme Soviet Ivan Plyushch said his republic had to become a fully independent and sovereign state before deciding what its relations with other states should be (RFE/RL correspondent's report, June 28).

USSR MVD Troops Detailed to Kishinev

During Moldavian President Mircea Snegur's absence abroad, special troops of the USSR MVD were sent to central Kishinev on June 23 to prevent the planned relocation of the Lenin monument from the central square. Kishinev's Communist Party organization had attempted to exploit ethnic tensions by calling on local Russian residents and Communists to block the planned relocation of the monument, thus allowing it to justify the presence of troops on the grounds that they were needed to prevent clashes.

On June 26, the chairman of the Kishinev City Soviet, Nicolae Costin, told Moldovapres that the planned relocation of the Lenin monument from Kishinev's central square was being resisted by the CPSU, the USSR MVD, and the command of the Southwestern Military District. Costin said he had met with the district command to reassure it that "conservative forces and all those who worship Lenin will have the opportunity to lay as many

The USSR in June, 1991

flowers as they wish at the monument" at its new location, in a park on the outskirts of Kishinev. The statue of Lenin was removed from Kishinev's main square on June 28.

New Group within Democratic Movement to Be Created

A conference was held over the weekend in Moscow to discuss the creation of a new organization to be called the Liberal-Conservative Union, AP reported on June 26. Participants included leading members of the Democratic Russia movement—Yurii Afanas'ev, Gary Kasparov, and Arkadii Murashov. AP gave few details, but another Democratic Russia leader, Galina Starovoitova, revealed that radical members of Democratic Russia had for some time been considering setting up their own group, which would have a broader aim than merely supporting the policies of Boris El'tsin. Starovoitova explained that, now that El'tsin has been elected RSFSR president, he needed "a constructive opposition."

Adzhar ASSR Holds Parliamentary Elections

The ruling Roundtable/Free Georgia coalition won 47.5 percent of the vote in elections to the Supreme Soviet of the Adzhar ASSR, the Iberia News Agency announced on June 26. The Adzharia bloc won 19.3 percent, and the independent Georgian Communist Party, 17.6 percent. The elections had been postponed three times as a result of domestic tension, specifically opposition to Georgian President Zviad Gamsakhurdia's proposal to hold a referendum on whether or not to preserve the republic's autonomous status within Georgia.

Ukrainian "Solidarity" Formed

A three-day congress of workers ended in Kiev with a decision to form an All-Ukrainian Association of Solidarity with Workers. People's deputy Larisa Skoryk told AP the group would use Poland's "Solidarity" movement as a model and would aim to defend workers' rights and fight for an independent Ukraine. Donetsk coal miner Oleksandr Ivashenko was elected to lead the new association.

_____ *Monday, June 24*

Pugo Complains about Rising Crime

Politika, the newspaper of the "Soyuz" group of deputies, published excerpts from a speech by Minister of Internal Affairs Boriss Pugo to the Supreme Soviet on June 18 in which he criticized Gorbachev's indecisiveness and came out in favor of a partial transfer of Gorbachev's powers to Prime Minister Valentin Pavlov. Pugo complained in his speech about rising crime and said the police had confiscated 52,000 firearms and 4.5 tons of explosives since August, 1990.

"Soyuz" against Draft Union Treaty

The "Soyuz" group of deputies denounced the third draft of the Union treaty, which, it said, called for the elimination of the USSR as a single, federal state. TASS quoted a leading member of "Soyuz," Yurii Blokhin, as saying the draft was in conflict with the results of the March referendum on the preservation of the USSR. Blokhin stated that his faction supported Prime Minister Valentin Pavlov and regarded Soviet President Mikhail Gorbachev's policies as "inadequate" to solve the country's problems.

Executive Structure of Moscow Revamped

The mayor of Moscow, Gavriil Popov, issued instructions outlining a new administrative structure for the city. A member of the Moscow City Soviet, Andrei Bondarenko, told Radio Rossii that a city duma, a city assembly, a mayoral department, an administrative affairs department, and a city government would be established.

Battle over Television Continues

In the continuing battle over control of television, Soviet President Mikhail Gorbachev issued a decree making Leningrad Television a branch of the All-Union State Television and Radio Company. Boris Petrov, formerly of the Leningrad Television and Radio Committee, was appointed deputy chairman of the all-Union company. The news was announced in Leningrad on June 24 by the head of the all-Union Company, Leonid Kravchenko, the central and RSFSR media reported. Earlier in the year, the Leningrad City Soviet in cooperation with employees of Leningrad Television had decided to make Leningrad Television a shareholding company, a decision in effect annulled by Gorbachev's decree. Radio Rossii said Leningrad Mayor Anatolii Sobchak had protested strongly against Gorbachev's decree.

Center to Suspend Supplies to Leningrad

Leningrad Mayor Anatolii Sobchak went to Moscow on June 24 to meet with the central Soviet authorities to discuss a resolution of the USSR Cabinet of Ministers stipulating that, from 1992 on, Leningrad would stop receiving any food supplies from all-Union stocks. Radio Rossii said the resolution was one of the first responses of the central government to the victory of democratic forces in the June 12 elections of the RSFSR president and the mayors of Moscow and Leningrad.

THE USSR IN JUNE, 1991

Four More Republics Approve Union Treaty

Kazakh President Nursultan Nazarbaev, presenting the third draft of the Union treaty to the Kazakh Supreme Soviet on June 24, said it was "the most democratic" so far, but he had a number of critical comments, TASS reported. He wanted the participants in the treaty to be confined to republics directly forming the Union—i.e., the present Union republics. The representation of the autonomous formations in the Supreme Soviet needed sorting out, he said. Nazarbaev objected further to the concept of "joint property" on the territory of the republics and to the mechanism proposed for levying federal taxes. The Kazakh Supreme Soviet approved the draft in principle and set up a delegation headed by Nazarbaev to oversee final amendments.

The treaty was approved in principle by the Tajik, Kirgiz, and Azerbaijani Supreme Soviets on June 26. Also that day, a spokesman for the USSR Supreme Soviet, Arkadii Maslennikov, told TASS that the USSR Congress of People's Deputies was not expected to debate the treaty until the end of August at the earliest. The Russian news agency RIA said the treaty would be discussed at a special meeting of the RSFSR Congress of People's Deputies on August 27. Final approval of the treaty would thus be delayed until at least the end of August. Soviet President Mikhail Gorbachev had hoped that it could be signed in July. For the text of the third draft, see *Izvestia*, June 27.

German National Raion Created in Altai Krai

Radio Mayak reported that the Altai Krai Soviet had decided to create a German national raion in the krai. The radio described the decision as the first concrete step towards solving the Soviet German problem in the USSR. It was hoped this move would at least slow down the massive emigration of Germans. Recommendations by scholars to local politicians and the decision to create a free economic zone in the Altai were said to be behind the decision to establish the raion in Altai Krai rather than elsewhere. The recent RSFSR decree on repressed peoples also played a role.

Compensation for Invalid Care

The USSR Cabinet of Ministers adopted a resolution on paying compensation to those caring for invalids (*Radio Moscow*, June 24). Able-bodied individuals who were looking after invalids of the first category, disabled children up to the age of sixteen, or elderly persons over the age of eighty would receive 60 rubles a month to offset the retail price increases that took effect on April 2.

Germany to Open Consulate General in Alma-Ata

It was announced that the German government planned to open a consulate in Alma-Ata in 1991. A German Foreign Ministry spokesman said the consulate would be responsible for dealings with the Kazakh, Kirgiz, Uzbek, Tajik, and Turkmen republics and for the Omsk, Novosibirsk, and Altai areas of the RSFSR. The main concentrations of the Soviet German population are in Kazakhstan and in the areas of southern Siberia to be covered by the new consulate (RFE/RL correspondent's report, June 24).

Finnish President in Moscow

Finnish President Mauno Koivisto, who was visiting Moscow, expressed concern about a sharp decline in Finnish-Soviet trade. Speaking at a dinner hosted by Soviet President Mikhail Gorbachev, Koivisto said that political cooperation between the two states was "stable, good, and substantive" but that the situation regarding economic links "has been causing concern." Koivisto attributed the problems to the USSR's internal economic troubles, but TASS said the two leaders expressed confidence that the difficulties could be overcome.

RSFSR President-elect Boris El'tsin met with Koivisto in Moscow on June 25, Radio Moscow reported. They agreed to develop closer economic and cultural ties between Russia and Finland. Koivisto expressed hope that Finland could have the same kind of beneficial relations with the republics as it had with the Soviet Union. El'tsin informed his guest about the new cooperation between the center and the republics.

Islands Turned Over to China

Soviet Foreign Ministry spokesman Vitalii Churkin confirmed the transfer of Damansky Island to China as a result of documents signed during the recent Sino-Soviet summit, TASS reported. Damansky Island, which lies in the Ussuri River, was the site of violent clashes between Soviet and Chinese troops in 1969. Churkin portrayed the settlement not as a concession of Soviet territory to China but as the arbitrary result of the newly drawn border now falling north of the island. According to a separate Soviet television report (June 25), other islands in the vicinity were also turned over to China, but they were not named.

Tuesday, June 25

Soviet Protest to Council of Europe Dismissed

The president of the Parliamentary Assembly of the Council of Europe, Anders Bjoerk, rejected Soviet complaints about a hearing on the Baltic republics scheduled for June 27 (RFE/RL correspondent's report, June 25). Speaking at a press conference following the opening of the assembly's session in Helsinki on June 25, Bjoerk justified international discussion of Baltic affairs by saying that "in today's Europe, human-rights questions are never strictly internal." The USSR had warned the Council not to "meddle" in what it considered an internal matter. Bjoerk also said that the Council of Europe would protest if Soviet violence continued in the Baltic republics.

The text of the Soviet Union's protest to the Council of Europe was made available to RFE/RL on June 26. In it the USSR stated that it considered "unacceptable all attempts to internationalize the problem by involving [the USSR] in a discussion of the future status of the Baltic republics. We intend in the future to reject all such attempts categorically."

Following the hearing on June 27, the leaders of the three Baltic republics said it was a major help in publicizing Baltic issues. RFE/RL's correspondent in Helsinki quoted President of the Estonian Supreme Council Arnold Ruutel as saying the hearing "took the Baltic issue to an international level, even though Moscow has declared this a domestic issue."

Saudargas in London

Speaking at a discussion with British parliamentarians in London, Lithuanian Foreign Minister Algirdas Saudargas said that Lithuania needed a stable Soviet Union, Radio Independent Lithuania reported on June 26. Saudargas warned that, if Gorbachev were to be ousted before the signing of the Union treaty, the resulting instability could lead to a clash between conservative forces and RSFSR President-elect Boris El'tsin. Saudargas also drew attention to the continued Soviet violence in Lithuania, calling the periodic OMON attacks on customs posts "very clever," since they "keep our society tense but have not resulted in any serious response from the West."

Lithuania to Sign Nuclear Nonproliferation Treaty

The Lithuanian Supreme Council voted to join the signatory nations of the Nuclear Nonproliferation Treaty, Radio Independent Lithuania reported. The Supreme Council, acting under Section 9 of the treaty, requested its president, Vytautas Landsbergis, to send the necessary documents to the governments of the United States, Britain, and the USSR, the original signatories of the 1968 treaty.

USSR Damage to Lithuania Estimated

Soviet damage inflicted on Lithuania from January to May, 1991, totaled about 80 million rubles, Radio Independent Lithuania reported on June 26. According to a government study released to the parliament on June 25, the sum covered property damage caused by the Soviet army and USSR MVD OMON troops. The parliament resolved to submit a bill to the USSR. A parliamentary commission would produce an estimate of Soviet damage to Lithuania over fifty years of occupation in preparation for talks on independence with the USSR.

Conference Held on Entrepreneurship

"Vremya" reported on the opening in Moscow of a two-day conference on the development of entrepreneurship in the USSR. The conference was being held under the auspices of the Soviet employers' association, the League of Scientific and Industrial Associations. Its aim was to work out ways of resolving problems arising "during the transition from an administrative-command to a normal economy."

In an address delivered to the conference, Grigorii Yavlinsky disclosed some more details of his "Window of Opportunity" program, Interfax reported that day. The program was to cover a five-year period, broken down into six-month stages. For each of these, detailed economic and political reform targets were set, together with coordinated Western responses. The massive inflow of Western goods was scheduled for the outset of the program only. Western aid would be in the form of credits, rather than grants, and would be tied to specific projects, such as conversion, ecology, and employment.

Economist Leonid Abalkin told the conference that Western financial aid would only serve a purpose if the Soviet Union developed alternative economic structures, Interfax reported on June 25. Abalkin announced that national income in May was 11 percent lower than one year earlier. The state budget deficit had grown to 32.3 billion rubles by May, although the deficit planned for the entire year was 27.6 billion rubles.

Incomes Indexation Law

The USSR Supreme Soviet passed fundamental legislation on indexing incomes, TASS reported. The state budget would finance the indexation of pensions, stipends, other transfer payments, and the salaries of employees of "budget organizations." The indexation of salaries of employees of "profit-making" enterprises would have to be negotiated in collective agreements. USSR Minister of Labor and Social Issues Valerii Paul'man ruled out 100-percent indexation for all incomes within the minimum

THE USSR IN JUNE, 1991

consumer budget as "hyperinflationary." Indexation would cost 3.55 billion rubles for each percentage point of growth in the retail price index.

Protocol Signed on Abolition of Comecon

The USSR Supreme Soviet gave its assent to the signing of a protocol on the abolition of Comecon, TASS reported. The USSR's representative at Comecon, Stepan Sitaryan, told the assembly that the council had been inactive for a year. He said that all the member-countries were in favor of seeking new forms of multilateral cooperation but that the European members wanted this cooperation to be limited to "a regional context," excluding such countries as Cuba, Mongolia, and Vietnam.

Atomic Energy Council Established

An interrepublican council, with representatives from all fifteen republics, was set up to oversee safety issues in industry and atomic energy. The Interrepublican Council for Safety in Industry and Atomic Energy was confirmed by the USSR State Industrial and Atomic Energy Inspectorate. The council would have mainly consultative functions.

Georgia Publishes Draft Law on Citizenship

TASS reported that the long-awaited draft of the Georgian citizenship law had been published. Georgian citizenship would be open to all persons who had lived in Georgia for the previous ten years, knew the language, recognized the Georgian Constitution, and had a legal source of income. Residents of Abkhazia were required in addition to speak the local language. The draft represented a considerable modification of Georgian President Zviad Gamsakhurdia's previous pronouncement; he had formerly argued that only those persons whose ancestors were resident in Georgia prior to its annexation by tsarist Russia in 1801 should be eligible for citizenship.

Armenia to Hold Direct Presidential Elections

The Armenian Supreme Soviet voted to create the post of president of the republic and scheduled direct presidential elections for October 16, Radio Moscow reported.

Moldavian President on Independence Referendum

In an interview with *Asahi Shimbun*, reported by Interfax on June 24 and Rompres on June 25, Moldavian President Mircea Snegur said that Moldavia would hold a referendum on the republic's independence in the fall. "Moldavia never agreed to join the USSR . . . and was included in the USSR under the Molotov-Ribbentrop Pact, not by the will of its people," Snegur was quoted as saying. An independent Moldavia would seek to maintain economic links with individual republics of the present USSR and, he hoped, also with the Union as a whole. Moldavia would also seek cultural and economic "integration" with Romania but would do so as an independent state under the formula "one nation, two states," Snegur was further quoted as saying.

Taxation Law Adopted by Ukrainian Supreme Soviet

Radio Kiev reported that after heated debates the Ukrainian Supreme Soviet had rejected a proposal by its Economic Commission to tax total sales income of enterprises and had decided instead to adopt the government's proposal to tax profits only. Volodymyr Pylypchuk, chairman of the Economic Commission, said that its proposal was based on the need to fight hyperinflation. He said the government's version of the law would be ineffective in fighting inflation and would bankrupt the republican budget, which was already suffering from a 40-billion-ruble deficit. The law on taxation would become effective on October 1 and contained clauses on rent for the use of land, ecological and forest taxes, and customs dues.

On June 26, the Ukrainian Supreme Soviet approved a bill claiming exclusive tax-collection rights for the republic, according to TASS. The bill flew in the face of the provision in the draft Union treaty allowing for separate republican and all-Union taxes.

Imprisoned Minsk Journalist Appeals for Help

Radio Liberty's Belorussian service learned on June 25 that journalist Valerii Sedov had appealed to the US embassy in Moscow for help. Sedov was imprisoned on May 7 without trial for his part in an anti-Communist rally in Minsk in November, 1990, and faced up to five years in jail for "hooliganism." The letter protested about the conditions in the prison. In addition, the Belorussian Public Prosecutor's Office had circulated a letter asking that the republican Supreme Soviet strip Belorussian Popular Front leader Zyanon Paznyak of his parliamentary immunity so that he could be charged with leading the November demonstration.

Wednesday, June 26

OMON Raids Vilnius Telephone Exchange

At 4:48 P.M. about fifty OMON troops stormed the central telephone exchange in Vilnius, Radio Independent Lithuania reported. Telephone and telefax communications between Lithuania and the outside world were severed. Radio Independent Lithuania went off the air briefly but resumed broadcasting from Kaunas. The heavily armed OMON troops withdrew from the building at 6:50 P.M. Normal telecommunications were restored in about two hours. OMON activity continued in Latvia as well—the customs office in the Riga railway station was raided the same evening

Explanations for the OMON action in Vilnius were contradictory. OMON commander Boleslaw Makutinowicz said his troops' mission was to search the telephone exchange for weapons and ammunition allegedly stored there illegally, Radio Independent Lithuania reported on June 27. According to Makutinowicz, a pistol and some cartridges were found in a ventilation shaft. Jonas Jagminas, the director of the exchange, said that any weapons found must have been planted as a provocation. A duty officer at the USSR Ministry of Internal Affairs told the Lithuanian representation in Moscow that OMON troops had confiscated rifles, pistols, and explosives. Deputy Chairman of the Lithuanian Supreme Council Ceslovas Stankevicius called the attack "a rehearsal" for the overthrow of the Lithuanian government.

Speaking after a meeting with French Prime Minister Edith Cresson in Paris on June 26, Lithuanian Supreme Council President Vytautas Landsbergis condemned the OMON attack, citing it as proof of the Kremlin's "terrorist policies" against Lithuania, Radio Independent Lithuania reported on June 27. Landsbergis said the USSR was trying to provoke Lithuania into armed conflict.

On June 27, Soviet President Mikhail Gorbachev ordered an investigation into the raid. Presidential spokesman Vitalii Ignatenko said the attack appeared to be a provocation aimed at discrediting Gorbachev as he prepared to meet with the leaders of the seven leading industrialized nations after their summit in London in July. Ignatenko did not say who might be trying to discredit Gorbachev (*Radio Moscow*, Western agencies, June 27).

The White House sent a telegram to Gorbachev calling the raid "an unwarranted and unacceptable level of intimidation, which we condemn." The US Commission on Security and Cooperation in Europe also lodged a protest, saying the action appeared to be "a deliberate provocation to intimidate Lithuania's democratically elected leadership" (RFE/RL correspondent's report, June 27).

Slowdown in Troop Withdrawal from Germany

General Matvei Burlakov, the commander of Soviet forces in Germany, announced that the withdrawal of Soviet troops would slow down starting in July and might also be temporarily suspended, Western agencies reported. The justification given was that Germany had not yet started to build the 36,000 apartments in the USSR for returning Soviet forces and their families. The statement added that Moscow still wanted to withdraw its troops from Germany by the end of 1994 in line with treaty obligations. Bonn expressed surprise at the announcement, noting that construction of the housing had already begun.

The same day, the German government summoned Soviet Ambassador Vladislav Terekhov and pointed out that the German-Soviet transitional agreement covering the troop withdrawal called on Germany to provide funding for but not to implement housing projects in the Soviet Union. Furthermore, the ministry pointed out that the Soviet-German agreements signed in 1990 contained no provisions for the synchronization of the Soviet troop withdrawal and the housing construction program (*DPA*, June 26).

NATO Concerned about Soviet High Command

Sources within NATO were concerned that top Soviet generals, embittered by Moscow's loss of power in Eastern Europe, were starting to cut back contacts with the West and to speak increasingly in hard-line terms (Western press reports, June 27). One source said that the General Staff was no longer "being open" with Western officials and that it had also closed itself off from the rest of Soviet society. The NATO sources pointed especially to a very harsh article written by former Warsaw Pact Chief of Staff Vladimir Lobov that was published in issue No. 2 of *Voennaya mysl'*. In it, Lobov denounced the Conventional Forces in Europe Treaty and demanded qualitative military superiority over the West.

RSFSR TV News Program More Popular than "Vremya"

The flagship of Russian Television, the news program "Vesti," was more popular than Central Television's main news show, "Vremya," an opinion poll conducted by the All-Union Center for the Study of Public Opinion demonstrated. According to Radio Rossii (June 26), the poll showed that 57 percent of those questioned preferred the RSFSR television newscasts, while 43 percent were still loyal to "Vremya."

Deputy Belozertsev Files Suit against Luk'yanov

Radio Rossii reported that a leader of the RSFSR democratic movement, USSR people's deputy Sergei Belozertsev, had filed a lawsuit against the chairman of the USSR

The USSR in June, 1991

Supreme Soviet, Anatolii Luk'yanov. Belozertsev accused Luk'yanov of abusing his powers and of harassing prodemocratic deputies in the Soviet parliament. The radio quoted the Moscow City Soviet newspaper, *Kuranty*, as saying the court hearing of the case had opened in the Moscow City Court.

Legislation on Ukrainian Presidency Approved

Draft legislation on the institution of a presidency in Ukraine was approved on June 26 by the republican Supreme Soviet, Radio Kiev reported. The president would be the highest executive in Ukraine and "the guarantor of state sovereignty." The president and vice president would be chosen simultaneously by universal ballot, with a limit of two five-year terms in office. The draft legislation was opposed by both leaders of the Communist majority bloc in the parliament—Oleksandr Moroz and Communist Party First Secretary Stanislav Hurenko—who absented themselves during the discussion and voting.

Azerbaijan Sets Date for Presidential Elections

The Azerbaijani Supreme Soviet scheduled direct presidential elections for September 8. Ayaz Mutalibov, named president by the parliament in May, 1990, announced that he would run for the post, TASS reported. A spokesman for the Independent Azerbaijan Democratic Bloc told RL's Azerbaijani service that it would nominate a candidate only on condition that the state of emergency in Baku be lifted, that an independent, non-Communist commission be created to monitor political developments in Azerbaijan, and that an international commission oversee the election itself.

Amoco Joint Venture with Azerbaijan

AP and *The Wall Street Journal* reported that an Amoco subsidiary had received permission for joint development of an offshore oil field in the Caspian Sea off the coast of Azerbaijan. A feasibility study was to be undertaken over the next eighteen months.

Moldavia Hosts Conference on Molotov-Ribbentrop Pact

An international conference on "The Molotov-Ribbentrop Pact and its Consequences for Moldavia" opened in Kishinev. It was sponsored by the Moldavian parliament, and the participants included Western and East European scholars and parliamentarians. Chairman of the Moldavian parliament Alexandru Mosanu told a press conference that Kishinev's decision to organize the conference had come in response to Gorbachev's decree of December 22,

1990, on normalizing the situation in Moldavia; that decree ordered Kishinev to rescind its appraisal of the Molotov-Ribbentrop Pact and the ensuing Soviet annexation as illegal.

Addressing the opening session of the conference, Moldavian President Mircea Snegur said that a truly new, integrated and democratic Europe could not exist until the consequences of the Molotov-Ribbentrop Pact and of Stalinism had been eliminated from the Baltic republics and Moldavia. Snegur said Moldavia and the Baltic republics had for the past fifty years been "excluded from international life" and "had an alien form of statehood, hostile to and incompatible with their civilizations," imposed on them by the USSR, which "cut them off from the progress of mankind." The Baltic and Moldavian issues were not local but international problems, he said.

On the second day of the conference, Valentin Aleksandrov of the CPSU Central Committee International Relations Department presented Moscow's official position. Although he reiterated the highly critical assessment of the pact and its secret protocols, Aleksandrov—who was the secretary of the USSR Congress of People's Deputies ad hoc commission to assess the pact—added that the accession of Bessarabia and northern Bukovina to the USSR was a result not of the pact but of subsequent events. The accession was valid under international law, and the present status of the territories had legal force under the USSR Constitution and the constitutions of Moldavia and Ukraine, he asserted.

Thursday, June 27

New CPSU Draft Program Published

A draft of a new CPSU Program was published in *Moskovskaya pravda*. The new program was only slightly less critical of the failures and mistakes of the Gorbachev leadership than of the crimes of the Stalin period. The draft was prepared by a commission chaired by Soviet President Mikhail Gorbachev and had been expected to be reformist in tone.

Foreign Ministry Statement on Yugoslavia

The USSR Foreign Ministry said in a statement published in *Pravda* that the documents adopted by the Slovenian and Croatian parliaments "have not been recognized by the state bodies of the Socialist Federal Republic of Yugoslavia and cannot be regarded as promoting the resolution of Yugoslavia's complex problems." The ministry said "the Soviet Union continues to advocate the unity and territorial integrity of Yugoslavia, the inviolability of its borders (including internal borders), and the right of the peoples of Yugoslavia to decide their own future. It also supports the federal structures of authority that are striving to preserve the Yugoslav state."

Tajik Supreme Soviet Approves Citizenship Law

The Tajik Supreme Soviet approved a new law on citizenship. TASS said the law specified that anyone living in the republic could become a citizen, regardless of racial or national origin, material situation, or the amount of time spent in Tajikistan. The agency said Tajik citizens would simultaneously be citizens of the USSR.

El'tsin to Earn the Same as Gorbachev

The RSFSR Supreme Soviet set the salary for Russian President-elect Boris El'tsin at 4,000 rubles a month and put his vice president's salary at 3,200 rubles a month. El'tsin's salary raise would put him on a par with Mikhail Gorbachev, who received 4,000 rubles a month as Soviet president (2,300 rubles after tax) (*Radio Moscow, TASS,* June 27).

German License to Build Buses in USSR

The German car producer Mercedes-Benz said a Soviet company, Avtrokon, would soon produce buses under a license given by the German company. A spokesman for Mercedes-Benz told RFE/RL that the financing of the project, worth about 200 million deutsche marks, had been secured by German bank credits backed by the German government. The spokesman said that Avtrokon would build a new bus factory near Moscow and that the annual output would reach 2,500–3,000 buses in about three years.

Georgian President Asks Gorbachev to Help Stop Economic Blockade

Georgian President Zviad Gamsakhurdia asked Soviet President Mikhail Gorbachev for help in stopping what he called "a severe economic blockade" of Georgia. In the appeal, Gamsakhurdia said all goods coming into or out of Georgia were being "illegitimately" stopped in Krasnodar and Stavropol' Krais and, after customs inspections, were usually readdressed or sold among the local population. Gamsakhurdia also said USSR departments and services had refused to transport Western medical supplies donated to Georgia following recent earthquakes there.

The USSR in June, 1991

Friday, June 28

Crimean Tatars Vote for Sovereignty

Delegates at a congress of Crimean Tatars voted overwhelmingly to declare sovereignty over the Crimean Peninsula. A document issued at the congress said the Crimean Tatars would work for the creation of a sovereign national state in the Crimea. The document also claimed Tatar control over natural resources and holiday resorts, including Yalta, which is among the most popular vacation spots in the Soviet Union. According to TASS, about 130,000 Crimean Tatars had returned to the region, which is part of Ukraine. Several hundred thousand Tatars were still scattered across the USSR. They had been deported by Stalin in 1944 for allegedly collaborating with Nazi Germany. Moscow acknowledged in 1987 that the deportation had been illegal.

Abortion Increasing in the Soviet Union

Komsomol'skaya pravda reported that Soviet women were now having 137 abortions for every 100 live births. The newspaper cited price increases, economic decline, and the worsening of living standards as reasons for the increase. It said the number of abortions had risen to "monstrous proportions." The newspaper said that more than one in ten Soviet women between the ages of fifteen and forty-nine had an abortion every year.

Saturday, June 29

Yakovlev Says He Is Target of Party Investigation

Presidential adviser Aleksandr Yakovlev told *Rabochaya tribuna* that he was under investigation by the CPSU Central Control Commission, which intended to look into his "social and political activity" and even "to expel [him] from the Party." In his statement, Yakovlev complained that the Party press, especially *Sovetskaya Rossiya*, had demonstrated "brutal rage" towards him. According to *Rabochaya tribuna*, Yakovlev reserved the right to decide whether to resign from the CPSU, but he denied having made statements to the media about his forthcoming resignation from the Party.

Orthodox Communists Open Congress in Moscow

A two-day congress of the Communist Initiative Movement—a group of orthodox Communists from across the USSR—opened in Moscow. TASS said more than 800 delegates attended. "TSN" quoted speakers who accused Soviet President Mikhail Gorbachev and presidential adviser Aleksandr Yakovlev of being "puppets of Washington." The movement called for holding an extraordinary congress of the CPSU before the end of the year.

Republican Party of Russia Splits

The second congress of the Republican Party of Russia opened in Moscow, TASS reported. (The party was created in November, 1990, by radical members of the Democratic Platform in the CPSU.) Speaking at the congress, Moscow Mayor Gavriil Popov called for the creation of an all-Union democratic party in opposition to the CPSU that would unite reformist forces throughout the country. Despite the call for unity, however, the congress of the Republican Party ended with a split in its ranks. "TSN" reported on June 30 that a group of delegates had announced its break with the Republican Party and the creation of a more leftist (Socialist) organization.

General Criticizes Military Conversion

The chief of the Military Political Directorate of Soviet Space Troops told TASS that, as a result of conversion, "the defense industries have lost significantly more than the civilian economy has gained." General Igor' Kurinnyi said he was disturbed by deteriorating production in the military-industrial complex and added that reductions in defense funding had led to a halt or significant slowdown in the work of many research institutes and design bureaus, as well as negative trends in serial production. With respect to space-based industries, Kurinnyi encouraged production of "dual-use" items that had both a civilian and military application.

Democratic Party of Ukraine Registered

Radio Kiev said the Ukrainian Ministry of Justice had registered the Democratic Party of Ukraine. The party held its constituent congress in December, 1990, and was the fourth political party in Ukraine to be officially registered.

Armenian Legislator's Family Attacked

The family and bodyguards of Armenian Supreme Soviet Chairman Levon Ter-Petrossyan were attacked by "hooligans" while traveling by car from Lake Sevan to Erevan, TASS reported on June 30. Four construction workers were arrested in connection with the incident.

Deportation Costs 500 Rubles

Armenians were being charged 500 rubles per head for the dubious privilege of being deported by military helicopter from Nagorno-Karabakh to Armenia, according to Interfax. More than 3,000 Armenians were reported to have been deported from Nagorno-Karabakh and from Khanlar Raion during the first half of May.

Sunday, June 30

Fire in Donbass Kills Thirty-One

A fire broke out at the Yuzhno-Donbasskaya mine, TASS reported, causing thirty-one fatalities. The fire was reported to be burning 335 meters below ground, and there was concern that large amounts of methane gas could explode there. TASS said that clouds of poisonous gas had been released into the air and that a nearby electric substation was threatened. The fire started on a conveyor belt.

Molchanov Leaves Central Television

Vladimir Molchanov became the latest television moderator to leave Central Television in protest against attempts by its head, Leonid Kravchenko, to reimpose political censorship, according to Radio Rossii. Since 1987, Molchanov had moderated "Do i posle polunochi" (Before and after Midnight), one of the most widely viewed political shows. On June 30, it was broadcast for the last time. Radio Rossii reported that when Molchanov informed the leadership of Central Television of his intention to leave no attempt was made to dissuade him.

Over 20 Million KGB Collaborators

Retired KGB Lieutenant Colonel Valentin Korolev told Russian Television that "there are more than 20 million citizens who cooperate with the KGB by working as secret informers, 'trusties,' providers of 'safe houses,' and in other capacities." The former chief of the KGB station in Denmark, Mikhail Lyubimov, appeared on the same program. He maintained that he respected those who collaborated with the KGB on patriotic grounds, but he added that the Soviet system had also led many to cooperate merely to enhance their social status. Both retired officers called for reform of the KGB, and both sharply criticized its chairman, Vladimir Kryuchkov, as well as the new law on state security organs.

The Month of July

Monday, July 1

New Democratic Movement Launched

Nine leading political figures and officials—former Politburo members Eduard Shevardnadze and Aleksandr Yakovlev; Gorbachev's former economic advisers Stanislav Shatalin and Nikolai Petrakov; RSFSR Vice President-elect Aleksandr Rutskoi; RSFSR Prime Minister Ivan Silaev; the head of the USSR Scientific-Industrial Union, Arkadii Vol'sky; and the mayors of Moscow and Leningrad, Gavriil Popov and Anatolii Sobchak—issued a formal statement calling on all democratic and reformist forces in the USSR to unite. Russian Television reported that the authors of the statement had announced plans to set up a committee to organize an inaugural conference of a new democratic movement—the Movement for Democratic Reforms—in opposition to the CPSU. The conference was to be held in September and would decide whether a real opposition party should be created. *Nezavisimaya gazeta* reported on July 2 that the nine officials had in fact already signed "a declaration on the formation of a united democratic party of the USSR." There were widespread rumors in Moscow that the new movement had been created with the approval of Soviet President Mikhail Gorbachev, RFE/RL was told.

On July 2, *Izvestia* published excerpts from the statement, which called for the return to Soviet citizens of "what has been taken away from them." Specifically mentioned was the return of land to the peasants. The statement also emphasized the necessity of privatizing the Soviet economy and demilitarizing both the economy and society. In an interview with "TSN," Shevardnadze called the statement "a landmark" in the country's history.

Izvestia of July 2 also published an article by Yakovlev, who said there was an urgent need for the USSR to create an effective multiparty parliamentary system because, unless the USSR moved ahead with major reforms, it would retreat into dictatorship and violence. He criticized the CPSU for not keeping up with the pace of reforms. Presidential spokesman Vitalii Ignatenko said Gorbachev considered the creation of the new movement to be "a positive step," Western agencies reported on July 3. Sobchak told reporters that the movement hoped to force a meeting of the CPSU Central Committee at which hard-liners would be expelled from the Party.

RSFSR President-elect Boris El'tsin said he would like to see the newly created Movement for Democratic Reforms develop as a party, not as a broad political movement. In an interview with Russian Television, El'tsin said those who wanted to participate in the movement should leave the CPSU.

The initial response of liberal Ukrainian Communists and non-Communists to the new democratic reform movement was largely negative, according to interviews conducted on July 4 for Radio Liberty's Ukrainian service. Mykola Shul'ha, a Central Committee member who headed the Ukrainian Supreme Soviet Commission on Internationality Relations, said that the Shevardnadze-Yakovlev initiative had been coolly received but noted that the Ukrainian Party was itself wracked by internal divisions. A copy of the new movement's platform received in Kiev referred to the USSR as "a Union of sovereign peoples"—a designation not calculated to please Ukrainian democrats.

On July 5, the CPSU Central Committee issued a statement on the creation of the Movement for Democratic Reforms. TASS quoted the statement as saying the Party did not rule out cooperation with the movement, provided its proclaimed goals were matched by "practical deeds." The statement said several public movements had claimed to support *perestroika* but had "fallen down on their stated goals." Meanwhile, *Pravda* and *Sovetskaya Rossiya* (July 5) criticized the founders of the movement. *Pravda* first deputy chief editor and CPSU Central Committee member Gennadii Seleznev expressed doubts about the founders' sincerity and their ability to achieve their stated goals. *Sovetskaya Rossiya* said the Communist Party would have to pay for many years for the actions of the movement's founders.

The same day, the main opposition group in the RSFSR, Democratic Russia, said it was open to cooperation with the Movement for Democratic Reforms but considered it "inexpedient" to participate in the movement's organizational committee. The leader of Democratic Russia, Yurii Afanas'ev, expressed some concern that his organization and the new movement could become rivals, TASS reported. Kazakh President Nursultan Nazarbaev reacted positively to the movement, saying he agreed with its humanistic goals, Radio Moscow reported. In contrast, an Uzbek opposition leader said he was skeptical about the movement. Muhammad Salih, chairman of the "Erk" Democratic Party and an Uzbek Supreme Soviet deputy, told RFE/RL on July 5 that he did not particularly trust the new organization, because it was mostly made up of "old Communists" and advocates of the preservation of the Union.

Shevardnadze told the latest issue of *New Times* that he hoped the movement would act as "a constructive opposition" to the current Soviet government. In a separate interview with *Komsomol'skaya pravda* (July 5), Shevardnadze, who had just quit the CPSU, said that he did not urge anyone else to leave the Party but that he hoped "for mass entries into the ranks of the new movement."

Aleksandr Vladislavlev, chairman of the executive committee of the Soviet employer's association, the Scientific-Industrial Union, was quoted by Interfax on July 2 as saying his organization supported "all democratic forces, including the Movement for Democratic Reforms."

In Central Asia, the reaction to the establishment of the Movement for Democratic Reforms was mixed. One of Turkmenistan's best-known writers, poet Rakhim Esenov, told RL's Turkmen service on July 7 that a group of Communist Party members in Turkmenistan, including himself, had formed an initiative group to support the new movement. A journalist in Alma-Ata told RL's Kazakh service that "Azat," Kazakhstan's largest and most influential political opposition party, had condemned the establishment of the movement, describing it as a stratagem to preserve the CPSU under another name.

Elena Bonner, human-rights activist and widow of Andrei Sakharov, also criticized the new movement. In an interview with RFE/RL on July 8, Bonner said the movement was merely an attempt to save Gorbachev and was aimed mainly at impressing the West.

On July 9, the chairman of the Council of the Union of the USSR Supreme Soviet, Ivan Laptev, said he wanted to join the Movement for Democratic Reforms. Radio Moscow and Russian Television quoted Laptev as saying that he did not intend to leave the CPSU for the time being and that he thought membership in both organizations was compatible, since the newly created group was a movement, not a party. The same day, thirty-two USSR Supreme Soviet deputies set up a group "in support of the movement," *Izvestia* reported on July 10. (Radio Moscow and TASS reported on July 9 that only twenty deputies had joined the group.) According to *Izvestia*, the support group included such well-known figures as reformist economist Pavel Bunich and Academician Evgenii Velikhov.

Radio Moscow reported on July 9 that the Buro of the conservative Latvian Communist Party had contacted the founders of the movement. The report noted that the

Latvian Communist Party wanted to learn more about the movement, its activists (former CPSU members), and their interest in forming a political party and becoming involved in the struggle for power.

Interviewed in the German daily *Handelsblatt* on July 10, the chairman of the Democratic Party of Russia, Nikolai Travkin, said the movement did not have the answers to the USSR's problems. Travkin said what was needed was a new party, and he added that he feared the new movement might turn out to be "a reconstructed Communist Party" and just a vehicle for Gorbachev.

The same day, Chairman of the Executive Committee of the Democratic Party of Russia Valerii Khomyakov told Novosti that there was a provisional agreement between Travkin and the nine founding members of the movement that they would all leave the CPSU immediately. Three members of the movement—Rutskoi, Yakovlev, and Vol'sky—had violated that agreement, Khomyakov said. (Shevardnadze and Silaev left the CPSU within a few of days after the creation of the movement.) Khomyakov said that, because the agreement had been violated, the Democratic Party of Russia had refused to be a founding member of the new movement.

On July 11, Shevardnadze was named chairman of the organizational committee of the Movement for Democratic Reforms. Interfax said Yakovlev, Vol'sky, and Laptev had been elected deputy chairmen of the committee.

On July 12, *Pravda* and *Sovetskaya Rossiya* reported that the bureau of the All-Army Party Committee had condemned the Movement for Democratic Reforms. A statement by the army's Party leadership said that the actions of the reform group would split the Communist Party and increase tension within Soviet society.

On July 15, TASS said the Democratic Party of Communists of Russia, set up on the basis of the faction Communists for Democracy in the RSFSR Supreme Soviet, intended to join the Movement for Democratic Reforms. Both the faction and the party were headed by RSFSR Vice President Rutskoi, a founding member of the Movement for Democratic Reforms. Rutskoi hoped that his new party would oppose the conservative RSFSR Communist Party and eventually drive it out of the republican political arena. TASS also reported that another group, the Republican Party of Russia, had also decided to join the Movement for Democratic Reforms. The Republican Party was set up in 1990 on the basis of the radical wing of the Democratic Platform within the CPSU.

TASS carried a report on a Moscow press conference held on July 16 at which a founding member of the

The USSR in July, 1991

Movement for Democratic Reforms, Academician Stanislav Shatalin, said the movement's main aim was "to change the country's social and political system through new elections and other parliamentary means, as well as to create a real opposition to the CPSU." Shatalin was quoted as saying the movement would probably be transformed into a centrist party.

Employment Law Comes into Effect

With the coming into effect of the USSR Law on Employment, the registration of unemployed citizens and payment of benefits began for the first time in Soviet history (*Radio Moscow*, Western agencies, June 30). For the texts of the USSR Law on Employment and its RSFSR counterpart, see *Izvestia*, January 25, and *Sovetskaya Rossiya*, May 18, 1991.

Privatization Law Passed

The USSR Supreme Soviet approved 303 to 14, with 26 abstentions, the new law on privatization, Radio Moscow reported. The bill provided for the state to relinquish direct control over 40–50 percent of its enterprises by the end of 1992, with this figure rising to 60–70 percent by 1995. It exempted certain, unspecified enterprises from privatization, and not all of its provisions were compatible with those already approved by several republican parliaments. For the text of the law, see *Izvestia*, June 24.

Mass Media Censorship Administration Closes

The Main Administration for Safeguarding State Secrets in the Mass Media (GUOT SSSR) ceased to exist as of July 1, Radio Mayak reported. Its functions were transferred to the newly created USSR Ministry of Information. GUOT was created in 1990 on the basis of the previous censorship body Glavlit, which had existed since the 1920s. There had been complaints that the existence of GUOT/Glavlit violated provisions of the new law on the press that forbade censorship of the mass media (see *Moscow News*, No. 22).

Supreme Soviet Defends Old Comrades

The USSR Supreme Soviet passed a declaration urging East European parliaments to defend former leaders, Communist party functionaries, and officers of "law-enforcement organizations" against persecution. "The open harassment of people simply because they fulfilled their constitutional duty and alliance obligations in the past is a direct infraction of human rights," TASS quoted the declaration as saying.

THE USSR IN JULY, 1991

Oil Output Continues to Decline

An official of the USSR State Committee for Statistics noted that oil output in the first five months of 1991 was 220.5 million tons—i.e., 9 percent down on the same period in 1990, Western agencies reported. The director of the USSR Academy of Sciences Oil and Gas Institute, Anatol Dmitrievsky, told Interfax that oil output in 1991 would not exceed 528 million tons (compared with 570 million tons in 1990). Dmitrievsky said up to one-sixth of all oil wells were idle because of shortages of pumps or compressor pipes and declared, "The Soviet Union cannot go it alone without foreign investment to modernize its gas and oil industry."

***Pravda* Links Balts and Yugoslavs**

An unsigned commentary in *Pravda* drew a connection between the crisis in Yugoslavia and the Western position on the Baltic republics. "On the one hand, [the Western politicians] loudly advocate keeping the Soviet Union as a single state, and on the other they support the separatist bids of the Baltic leaders. Is it not on such double standards that the Yugoslav separatists rely?" the commentary asked. The article likened the Slovenian and Croatian declarations of independence to "a separatist virus reaching epidemic proportions." Western support for Baltic independence, *Pravda* said, encouraged Balkan separatism.

Kravchuk on Union Treaty

Chairman of the Ukrainian Supreme Soviet Leonid Kravchuk, who was visiting Khar'kov, once again affirmed his opposition to any Union treaty if it conflicted with the republic's declaration on state sovereignty, Radio Kiev reported. "If we want to join the Union," Kravchuk told a crowd in Khar'kov, "we have to know what kind of a Union it is, what rights it gives us, what is positive about it and what is negative, [and] whether it corresponds to the interests of the people, our declaration, and our society." See also an article in *Pravda* by Kravchuk on July 15.

First Congress of Repressed Peoples Opens

The first Congress of Repressed Peoples opened in Moscow, TASS reported. It was called on the initiative of the Confederation of Repressed Peoples of the RSFSR. Delegates intended to draw up proposals for a just solution to their problems, which they would send to the Supreme Soviets of the USSR, the RSFSR, and other republics with the demand that they be taken into account in the new Union treaty. The congress was attended by representatives of the Union and Russian governments, by various parties, and by social and religious organizations.

The USSR in July, 1991

Ukrainian Coupon System Abolished

Effective July 1, the special coupons that Ukrainian workers had been receiving as part of their pay for the previous nine months were abolished, Ukrinform-TASS reported. Ukrainian Prime Minister Vitol'd Fokin said that the coupons had helped to stabilize the republican economy but that it was now time to move on to other means of protecting the internal Ukrainian market.

Tuesday, July 2

Economic Crisis Management Conference

Representatives from all the Union and autonomous republics attended a one-day economic development conference in Moscow. The event was widely covered by Radio Moscow, Central Television, and Interfax. USSR Prime Minister Valentin Pavlov repeated his recent assessments that the slump was stabilizing, with national income down 11 percent compared with that in mid-1990.

Pavlov again offered the choice of three ways out of the crisis: a no-change variant; his anticrisis program; or a rapid transition to the market. Gorbachev warned the assembly that they were all in the soup together and that no republic could manage to extricate itself on its own. With the G-7 meeting coming up, he reminded them that no Western nation would have any dealings with them if the stability and unity of "the single economic area" were not restored.

Nazarbaev Says G–7 Will Not Subsidize Individual Republics

In an interview published in *Izvestia*, Kazakh President Nursultan Nazarbaev said the most important current issue was the Union treaty. The republics could not enter the market without the Union, he argued, because no "Group of Seven" would subsidize individual republics. He added that leaders who really wished their people well should give up politicking and concern themselves with the economy.

Union Treaty and Union Property

In an interview in *Pravitel'stvennyi vestnik*, Igor' Tsyganenko, first deputy head of the Legal Department of the USSR Cabinet of Ministers, complained that the latest draft of the Union treaty did not recognize the existence of Union property. He argued that unless the Union owned property it would have no credibility on the world market or as a partner in international agreements. He pointed out that it was the Union that would have to guarantee the convertibility of the ruble and bear responsibility for the nonfulfillment of international agreements.

Democratic Russia on the Union Treaty

A draft statement adopted by a conference of the council of representatives of Democratic Russia noted with concern that the "Nine-plus-One" agreement set no date for the replacement of the unpopular Pavlov cabinet, Novosti reported. The conference participants also objected to the reference in the draft Union treaty to special courts in the armed forces and to the fact that the draft treaty did not spell out how a republic could secede. They supported El'tsin's opposition to federal taxes and said the present USSR Congress of People's Deputies had no right to adopt the constitution of the new state.

Top KGB Officer Rejects Colleagues' Revelations

A top KGB officer, writing under the pen name Vyacheslav Artemov in *Moskovskie novosti* (No. 25), said the publications of former KGB officers and journalists about the present role of the KGB either were ill informed or were pursuing political aims. In particular, he rejected the notion that the KGB had played a major role in the preparation of *perestroika*. He also noted that the KGB did not have a monopoly on information and could, therefore, not disinform the USSR president or manipulate him.

First Congress of Dukhobors

The Times carried a report from Tselina (near Rostov-on-Don) on the first congress of Dukhobors, a religious denomination heavily persecuted under the tsars and by the Soviet authorities. More than 300 people attended the congress, which reunited long-separated families and friends. A Soviet journalist was quoted as saying that the Dukhobors had asked for permission to establish communes in the area but that local kolkhozniks had objected because they could make more money by renting land to Georgian and Armenian melon growers.

Yugoslav Crisis "Close to Heart"

Soviet presidential spokesman Vitalii Ignatenko said at a briefing that the situation in Yugoslavia was "close to the Soviet Union's heart," TASS reported. Commenting on the election of Stipe Mesic to the post of Yugoslav president, Ignatenko expressed the hope that it would help bring about stabilization in the country. "The Soviet Union is prepared to see a dynamic development of relations with Yugoslavia and to give Yugoslavia maximum friendly support," Ignatenko concluded.

Deliveries to Cuba Cut

Cuban President Fidel Castro said in a speech to chemical and mining engineers on July 2 that Cuba had received neither raw materials nor spare parts for its Soviet-made automobiles and agricultural machinery from the Soviet Union during the first five months of 1991, Western agencies reported. He added that, although Moscow had honored its promise to ship 10 million barrels of crude oil for 1991, this amount was 30 percent lower than previous annual levels.

After three inconclusive rounds of voting, the Leningrad City Soviet finally elected Aleksandr Belaev, the former chairman of the soviet's finance and budget commission, as chairman of the city soviet to replace Anatolii Sobchak, who was elected mayor in June, TASS reported.

New Chairman for Leningrad City Soviet

Ekspress khronika (No. 27) reported that Russian leaders of the would-be "Dniester SSR" in eastern Moldavia were staging celebrations to mark the anniversary of Moldavia's annexation by the USSR. The rallies were addressed by the self-proclaimed republic's president, Igor' Smirnov, and other leaders who proclaimed their "adherence to the Socialist course and a unitary Soviet Union" and "support for the 'Soyuz' group of deputies."

"Dniester SSR" Celebrates Anniversary of Moldavia's Annexation

---

Wednesday, July 3

The RSFSR Supreme Soviet passed two laws on denationalization on July 3 and 4—the first providing for the denationalization of most industry, trade, and services, and the second handing over state housing to tenants (*TASS, RIA*, July 3 and 4). The bulk of denationalized state property was to be sold at auctions during the period 1992–95 to RSFSR residents for bonds that would be issued in 1992. Employees of an enterprise would get a 30-percent discount on any purchase of its shares. Both of the RSFSR laws appeared to be uncoordinated and incompatible with the all-Union legislation already passed or under deliberation. For the text of the laws, see *Sovetskaya Rossiya*, July 3.

RSFSR Passes Denationalization Law

The Belorussian Supreme Soviet rejected a request from the office of the republican prosecutor to strip Belorussian Popular Front leader Zyanon Paznyak of his deputy's immunity, Radio Moscow reported. Prosecutor Ryhor Tarnausky, a hard-line Communist, wanted to institute a criminal case against Paznyak in connection with an anti-Communist demonstration on November 7, 1990.

No Criminal Case against Paznyak

Thursday, July 4

Shevardnadze Quits CPSU

Former USSR Foreign Minister Eduard Shevardnadze was reported to have resigned from the CPSU (*Russian Television*, Western agencies, July 4). Shevardnadze sent his resignation letter to the CPSU Central Control Commission, which had initiated disciplinary action against him in connection with his support for the creation of the Movement for Democratic Reforms. In his letter, a copy of which Shevardnadze forwarded to Interfax, he wrote that the Party apparatus' attempt to punish him amounted to a return to "repressive methods of suppressing alternative views."

Gorbachev Attacks Party Conservatives

In a speech reported in *Pravda*, Soviet President Mikhail Gorbachev said that, if conservatives within the Party continued to "cannibalize" it from within, the Party would "lose all future political battles and elections." Commenting on the various platforms within the CPSU, Gorbachev said that "arbitrarily affixing such labels goes beyond any boundary of Party, civil, or even human morality."

Gorbachev-Salinas Talks

Soviet President Mikhail Gorbachev and Mexican President Carlos Salinas held talks to discuss the creation of "a new economic and political order in the world," TASS reported. Gorbachev stressed the importance of the Soviet Union's dialogue with Mexico and said he hoped to be able to accept Salinas' invitation to visit the country.

Churkin on Rapid Deployment Force

Soviet Foreign Ministry spokesman Vitalii Churkin expressed concern during his July 4 briefing about the notion of stationing a rapid deployment force (currently being discussed by NATO) in Turkey near the Iraqi border, TASS reported. Churkin noted, "It is a question of a region directly adjacent to the borders of the USSR."

State of Emergency Lifted in Parts of Azerbaijan

Soviet President Mikhail Gorbachev exempted Azerbaijan's Dzhebrail and Geranboi Raions from the state of emergency declared in the Nagorno-Karabakh Autonomous Oblast, the Azerbaijani raions adjacent to it, and Armenia's Goris Raion on January 15, 1990, on the grounds that the situation there had normalized, TASS reported. Gorbachev pointed to assurances given by Azerbaijani President Ayaz Mutalibov that "all measures will be taken to ensure the safety of the people living in the zone of conflict and to preclude cases of unlawful settlement of local inhabitants."

In the early morning of July 6, however, Azerbaijani special troops (OMON) attacked three Armenian villages in the two raions, Western news agencies reported on July 7. Armenian Supreme Soviet Chairman Levon Ter-Petrossyan was quoted by Interfax on July 7 as stating that two Azerbaijanis and one Armenian had been killed in the fighting and fourteen persons injured.

On July 9, Western news agencies reported that Ter-Petrossyan was heading for Moscow to discuss the latest escalation of tension. Ter-Petrossyan was reported to have warned KGB Chairman Vladimir Kryuchkov that Armenia would not permit Azerbaijani troop patrols to enter Armenian villages on Azerbaijani territory. Interfax reported on July 8 that four Azerbaijanis had been burned to death in Nagorno-Karabakh the previous day.

On July 29, seven members of OMON units and two civilians were killed in fighting in the Armenian village of Erkech on the Azerbaijani side of the Armenian-Azerbaijani border, TASS reported on July 31, quoting Armenian officials. Ten other persons were wounded. On July 31, fifteen people were killed in an explosion on a train traveling from Moscow to Baku. The explosion occurred approximately forty kilometers from Makhachkala in Dagestan; an Azerbaijani official accused Armenian militants of planting a bomb on the train.

Gorbachev Meets Kohl in Kiev

Ukrainian demonstrators greeted Mikhail Gorbachev with chants and boos as he drove through Kiev with German Chancellor Helmut Kohl, according to Western news agencies. When Kohl and Gorbachev stopped their car on Kiev's main boulevard, the Kreshchatik, to meet the crowd, protesters shouted "Down with Gorbachev." Several hundred people also demonstrated at Kiev airport as Gorbachev waited for Kohl to arrive. One banner read "Tsar Gorbachev is violating the sovereignty of Ukraine."

During their five-hour meeting on July 5, Kohl urged Gorbachev to provide a concrete program of economic and political reforms when he met with the leaders of the seven leading industrialized nations later in the month, *The New York Times* reported on July 6. Kohl said he backed plans for massive aid to the Soviet Union, adding: "I will try to make my colleagues understand that the success of reforms in the Soviet Union is important not only for the Soviet people but for all of us in Europe." Gorbachev stressed "the solidarity of the two countries." On July 6, Kohl called for full Soviet membership in the International Monetary Fund in the near future. At a joint press conference, Gorbachev replied to a question about Yugoslavia by saying that the crisis was a warning for the USSR, the disintegration of which would bring huge risks with unpredictable consequences.

Ukrainians Protest about Central TV Programming

Ukrainian people's deputy Roman Lubkivs'kyi raised the question of tendentious coverage by "Vremya" of developments in Ukraine, Radio Kiev reported. Lubkivs'kyi proposed to the Supreme Soviet that it prepare a resolution on the subject, that the Ukrainian state prosecutor institute criminal proceedings against the "Vremya" editors for inflaming interethnic and interconfessional passions, and that the accreditation in Ukraine of those journalists responsible for "political provocations" be canceled.

Crimean ASSR Approves Union Treaty

Radio Kiev reported that a session of the Supreme Soviet of the Crimean ASSR had approved the draft Union treaty "in the main." The session affirmed that the Crimean ASSR was a constituent part of Ukraine and delegated the parliament's chairman, Mykola Bahrov, to sign the treaty.

Ukrainian Anticrisis Program Passes Second Reading

Radio Kiev reported that the Ukrainian Supreme Soviet had adopted Prime Minister Vitol'd Fokin's anticrisis program, after making minor amendments. In order to implement the program, some Ukrainian and USSR laws, among them the presidential decree on hard-currency taxes on Soviet foreign-trade participants, had to be suspended. Under the new law 70 percent of Ukraine's hard-currency earnings would go to the republican rather than the all-Union hard-currency fund.

Moldavia Commemorates Holocaust

Moldavia observed a "Day of Remembrance" for the Jewish victims of the holocaust on the territory of Romania (which included Bessarabia, northern Bukovina, and Trans-Dniestria) during World War II. The observances were cosponsored by the Moldavian government and the Jewish communities of Moldavia and Romania. Moldavian government and parliamentary leaders participated in the observances.

Friday, July 5

Law on Foreign Investment Passed

The USSR Supreme Soviet passed the general principles of legislation on foreign investment by 340 to 11, TASS reported. The law permitted 100-percent foreign ownership of certain Soviet enterprises; granted foreign investors the right to export and import without licenses; freed them from paying export taxes and customs duties on imports; and guaranteed them the right to export hard-currency profits and to purchase hard currency with ruble earnings. It excluded foreign ownership of land and restricted access to property sold by the state under the provisions of the new law on privatization. For the text of the law, see *Izvestia*, July 24.

USSR presidential adviser Aleksandr Yakovlev had agreed to serve as chairman of the new Moscow City Assembly, Radio Rossii reported. The Moscow City Assembly, a consultative body, brought together representatives of a broad cross-section of society.

Yakovlev to Chair Moscow City Assembly

The Ukrainian Supreme Soviet set December 1 as the date for Ukraine's first multicandidate election for the newly created post of president, TASS reported on July 6.

Ukraine to Elect President on December 1

Saturday, July 6

A threatened strike by Leningrad port workers was called off after Prime Minister Valentin Pavlov agreed to give them a pay increase of 50 percent, *Komsomol'skaya pravda* reported.

Dockers Granted Big Pay Increase

One person of Caucasian nationality was killed and twenty people were hospitalized, some with gunshot wounds, after clashes between the local population and Caucasians in Kashino in Tver' Oblast at the end of June, *Rabochaya tribuna* reported. Sixteen Caucasians and five local inhabitants were arrested. The trouble started when the Caucasians bought up large consignments of food and vodka.

Disturbances in Kashino

USSR First Deputy Foreign Minister Yulii Kvitsinsky, in the capacity of special presidential envoy to Yugoslavia, visited Belgrade on July 6 and Zagreb and Ljubljana on July 7, TASS said. Tanjug quoted Kvitsinsky as telling federal Prime Minister Ante Markovic that the Yugoslav crisis was "of direct interest" to Gorbachev because it could have repercussions for the USSR. "We support

Kvitsinsky in Yugoslavia

democratic solutions but not those that threaten European borders," Kvitsinsky said. He added that the USSR opposed international attempts to intervene in the crisis and would veto any attempt to convoke the United Nations Security Council to discuss it.

RSFSR Supreme Soviet Finishes Discussion of Union Treaty

A session of the RSFSR Supreme Soviet, attended by RSFSR President Boris El'tsin, approved in principle the third draft of the Union treaty, Radio Moscow said. The radio quoted deputies as saying that the republican parliament still wanted some corrections to be made in the final text (see *Izvestia*, June 27). Russian Television said the previous day that many "democrats" in the parliament were very critical of the treaty. The report said that El'tsin found himself in a difficult position because he knew very well that Russia could not avoid signing the treaty—if it refused to do so, the RSFSR (which consists of many autonomous state units) would also disintegrate. TASS said on July 9 that eight of the nine republics that had signed the "Nine-plus-One" agreement with Soviet President Mikhail Gorbachev on April 23 had already approved the draft Union treaty in principle. The only exception was Ukraine, which had postponed debate on the matter until September.

Meanwhile, the parliaments of the RSFSR's autonomous republics also discussed the draft Union treaty. On July 6, the Tatar Supreme Soviet voted to approve the draft in principle. The parliament decided, however, that the autonomous republic would sign the treaty as an independent state (RL Tatar service, July 6). A similar position was adopted by the Bashkir Supreme Soviet, Radio Rossii reported on July 11. On July 7, the Karelian Supreme Soviet decided that it would sign the Union treaty and send deputies to participate in the RSFSR delegation (*Radio Moscow*, July 7). On July 8, the Udmurt Supreme Soviet decided that the republic would sign the Union treaty as a sovereign entity within the RSFSR (*Radio Mayak*, July 8).

RSFSR Communists Criticize CPSU

Twelve members of the RSFSR Communist Party—ten of whom were also members of the RSFSR Supreme Soviet—circulated an appeal on July 6 blaming the RSFSR Communist Party leadership for "ruinous decisions and the actual discrediting of the Party" and "political deafness," TASS reported. The authors of the appeal also charged the CPSU Central Committee with "political suicide and the murder of the Party" and said that Soviet President Mikhail Gorbachev was "incapable of ensuring the observance of the constitution" and "cannot hold the post of Party leader any longer." See *Kommersant* (No. 26)

New Lithuanian Holiday Celebrated

Lithuania celebrated for the first time the Day of Statehood, a new holiday marking the anniversary of the coronation of Mindaugas as king of Lithuania in 1253, Radio Independent Lithuania reported. One reason for introducing the holiday was to remind people that Lithuania joined Western Europe more than 700 years ago.

Servicemen in Baltic Republics Defend OMON

A letter written by the information center of the Union of Servicemen in the Baltic Military District defended the ongoing actions by USSR MVD special troops (OMON) in Lithuania and accused Soviet President Mikhail Gorbachev of "doublethink" regarding the operations, Central Television reported. "The Lithuanian OMON was carrying out the presidential order of July 25, 1990, on the seizure of illegally stored weapons," the letter said. It went on to complain that "this operation was not carried to its logical conclusion, largely thanks to the ambiguous policy of the USSR Ministry of Internal Affairs." According to the letter, Gorbachev's recently ordered investigation of the OMON troops following their seizure of the Vilnius telephone exchange raised tension both among the OMON and in Lithuania as a whole.

―――― *Sunday, July 7*

Nevzorov's Staff Members Leave "600 Seconds"

Several producers and correspondents resigned from the controversial Leningrad television program "600 Seconds," moderated by Aleksandr Nevzorov. (Nevzorov's reputation was seriously undermined by his support of the military crackdown in Lithuania in January.) Russian Television said on July 7 that Nevzorov's staff members had left the program because of political disagreements with him. On July 9, Russian Television and Radio Rossii reported that those who had left "600 Seconds" were planning to set up their own current affairs program and were supported in this undertaking by the Leningrad branch of the All-Union Television and Radio Broadcasting Company. Radio Rossii said the head of the branch, Boris Khitrov, had asked Nevzorov to resign. Nevzorov had refused, however.

On July 15, Radio Rossii reported that armed Afghan veterans had taken up positions at Nevzorov's office. The irregular guards reportedly also accompanied film crews working on "600 Seconds" and guarded the apartments of the program's staff. The head of the All-Union Television and Radio Broadcasting Company, Leonid Kravchenko, was reported to have questioned Nevzorov about the posting of the guards. Nevzorov was quoted as saying that he was not going to remove the guards, since he and his program were under threat from "envious people and other riffraff."

CPSU CC Calls for Measures against Economic Crimes

A resolution adopted by the CPSU Central Committee Secretariat said corruption, bribe-taking, extortion, organized crime, smuggling, and illegal hard-currency operations were spreading to all sectors of the economy. A special danger was posed by growing links between regional and national economic officials and organized criminals, the report said. It also expressed concern that newly created commercial banks were operating beyond state control. The banks, which were involved in large-scale financial and credit transactions with cooperative and joint-venture enterprises, were engaging in severe violations of the law, the resolution charged. It called for the quick adoption of legislation to rectify the situation and for measures to increase the authority of law-enforcement agencies (*TASS*, July 7).

Monday July 8

Gorbachev Wins Republican Backing for G-7 Summit

Mikhail Gorbachev won backing for his approach to the G-7 summit from the nine republics that participated in the "Nine-plus-One" agreement in Novo Ogarevo, according to TASS and Western reports. The agreement would allow Soviet President Mikhail Gorbachev to show that the USSR was not disintegrating to a degree that would make aid to the center ill advised.

Japan Has Doubts about Soviet Reform

Japanese officials in Tokyo and Washington expressed doubts about the USSR's reform efforts and the advisability of extending large amounts of aid to the USSR, TASS and Western agencies reported. In Tokyo, Prime Minister Toshiki Kaifu said there was confusion over which reform plan (Pavlov's, Yavlinsky's, or Gorbachev's) was the one that would guide reform in the future. Kaifu seemed to play down the importance of the dispute over the Kurile Islands, but other Japanese officials said that the islands were still a major stumbling block. Japanese officials also stated their belief that, while Soviet foreign policy towards

The USSR in July, 1991

Europe and the West had improved, the USSR had strengthened its military capability in Asia. For the time being, Japan would continue to provide technical assistance to the USSR but was not expected to help with large financial aid programs.

Constitutional Committee Approves Draft Union Treaty

The USSR Committee for Constitutional Supervision ruled that the draft Union treaty did not contain any violations of the USSR Constitution or of republican constitutions. The ruling, which was presented to the USSR Supreme Soviet, said the draft as a whole merited approval. The committee stressed, however, the necessity of clarifying certain legal aspects of the draft treaty, particularly contradictions with regard to Union and republican sovereignty (*TASS*, July 8)

The same day, Ukrainian Supreme Soviet Chairman Leonid Kravchuk was quoted by Reuters as saying that his republic would not sign the Union treaty in its present draft form, stating that "we . . . would like a treaty that provides for a real union of sovereign states—not only in words." In even sharper terms, Ihor Yukhnovskyi, leader of the radical "Narodna Rada" faction in parliament, said that, if Ukraine signed the current version of the treaty, the opposition would "mobilize the people."

OMON Attacks in Latvia

The customs post at Riga airport was attacked by MVD special troops (OMON). The Russian Television newscast "Vesti" identified the attackers as members of the OMON troops based in the Latvian capital.

On July 17, Radio Riga reported that four "Black Berets" (OMON troops) had broken into the customs post at the main railroad station in Riga and confiscated documents. This was the second attack on the post in recent weeks.

At a press conference reported by Radio Riga, Latvian Minister of Internal Affairs Aloizs Vaznis told of another OMON assault a few days earlier in which twelve armed "Black Berets" had attacked two policemen unloading boxes of cartridges and taken both the policemen and the cartridges to their base in Vecmilgravis. There the two policemen were interrogated for six hours by an official of the Latvian SSR Prosecutor's Office and roughed up by the "Black Berets." Vaznis said the Ministry of Internal Affairs in Moscow was disregarding Latvian protests concerning OMON assaults and probably supported these efforts to destabilize the situation in Latvia and undermine efforts of the Latvian police to enforce the law.

An representative from the MVD in the Baltic area, N. Goncharenko, told *Diena* that "if complaints from citizens about thefts and affronts to human dignity by Latvian customs officials continue, then [the MVD] will continue its action against the customs posts." He claimed that there were alcoholics and men with "a shady past" working at the customs posts.

On July 19, Vitalii Sidorov, USSR deputy minister of internal affairs, said that problems with the OMON unit stationed in Riga must be resolved in Latvia, since it is "a strictly republican formation, in which residents of Latvia serve." He recommended that members of the OMON be used for law enforcement in the republic and that OMON members found guilty of criminal acts be brought to justice (*Novosti*, July 19).

On July 23, Radio Riga reported that, at 1:15 A.M., five armed men had attacked the Latvian customs post at Grebnevo in Ludza Raion, which borders on the RSFSR. The report did not identify the attackers but gave the license number of their car, which indicated that the car was registered in Latvia. The attackers assaulted not only the customs officials and a policeman but also travelers. They took 5,000 rubles from one traveler and damaged his car. Before departing, they threw a grenade at the customs post.

On July 29, Radio Riga reported on two attacks carried out on the Rainis customs post (Bauska Raion) near the Lithuanian border on July 28. The first assault took place shortly after midnight and the second one around midday. The customs officials were beaten up, equipment and money were stolen, and hand grenades were thrown at the post. The eleven attackers, dressed in civilian clothes, were believed to be members of the Riga-based OMON unit.

CPSU Conservatives Want Shenin to Replace Gorbachev

The ultraconservative movement Communist Initiative demanded the convening of an extraordinary CPSU Congress in order to remove Mikhail Gorbachev from the post of general secretary and to oust him from the CPSU, according to Novosti on July 8, quoting *Kommersant*. The newspaper reported that conservative Communists wanted to replace Gorbachev with Politburo member and CPSU Central Committee Secretary for Cadres Oleg Shenin or alternatively with Novosibirsk Party First Secretary Vladimir Mindolin.

Deaths of Soviet Servicemen

Eight Soviet soldiers were killed and another five were wounded by two servicemen who had stolen submachine guns from a barracks in the RSFSR, Interfax reported. According to a Western news agency account, the two had attacked an MVD guard on July 6 in Yakutia and stolen the weapons. They were reported to have escaped.

In Ul'yanovsk Oblast on the Volga River two Soviet soldiers shot dead ten of their fellow soldiers while they slept, Western news agencies reported on July 14. The two soldiers then fled, taking two submachine guns and 600 cartridges with them.

Fourth Round of Sino-Soviet Talks Completed

The fourth round of talks devoted to military reductions and confidence-building measures on the Sino-Soviet border concluded in Beijing on July 8, TASS reported on July 9. The talks were said to have been constructive, but no further details were provided.

ELTA-PAP Agreement Signed

The Lithuanian news agency ELTA signed an agreement with its Polish counterpart, PAP, Radio Independent Lithuania reported. The agreement would facilitate cooperation between the two agencies through a regular exchange of correspondents in Vilnius and Warsaw. ELTA depended on PAP for information during the economic blockade imposed on Lithuania by the USSR in 1990.

Baltic States Committee Protests to UN

In a letter to UN Secretary-General Javier Perez de Cuellar, the Committee on Cooperation with the Baltic States protested about the United Nations' unwillingness to discuss the Baltic question. According to ELTA, the Swedish-based group's letter pointed to plebiscites carried out in the Baltic republics as evidence of popular support for independence and reminded the United Nations of treaties concluded with the RSFSR in 1920 recognizing the independence of Estonia, Latvia, and Lithuania.

Tuesday, July 9

Landsbergis in Strasbourg

Lithuanian Supreme Council President Vytautas Landsbergis urged the EC to pay as much attention to the Baltic republics as it had to the Balkans. Speaking at a press conference in Strasbourg, where he was visiting the European Parliament during its regular monthly session as a guest of the European People's Party, Landsbergis said he would invite all members of the European Parliament who were "interested in our fate" to visit the

Baltic republics in August (RFE/RL correspondent's report, July 9).

On July 10, Landsbergis met with members of the parliament's Socialist Group and had brief meetings with the Greens, the Rainbow Group, and the European Democratic Group. He invited them to come to Vilnius on August 23, the anniversary of the Molotov-Ribbentrop Pact, Western agencies reported.

Anticrisis Program Signed by Ten Republics

The anticrisis program prepared by the USSR Cabinet of Ministers was signed by representatives of ten Union republics (the nine republics that participated in the "Nine-plus-One" agreement and Armenia). TASS said that the RSFSR and Ukraine had signed the program only after the Union government had agreed that the two republics could determine independently how much of their republican taxes should go into the Union budget. In the case of the other republics that signed the program, the center would have a say in the level of federal taxation.

Soviet-Spanish Treaty Signed

The Soviet Union and Spain signed a treaty of friendship and cooperation—the first treaty of its kind between the two countries. The signing took place during a visit by Spanish Prime Minister Filipe Gonzalez to Moscow. Soviet President Mikhail Gorbachev described the document as "a reliable link in the common European area" during a dinner speech on July 8.

Journalist on Hunger Strike in Belorussian Prison

A correspondent for *News of the Belorussian Popular Front* who was in prison awaiting trial on charges of hooliganism was reported to have gone on a hunger strike (*Radio Rossii*, RL Belorussian service, July 8). Valerii Syadou, who had recently sent a letter to the US embassy in Moscow protesting against his detention, also published a statement in the Belorussian Supreme Soviet organ *Narodnaya bazeta* describing conditions in the prison where he was being held. He complained of unsanitary and overcrowded cells, mandatory AIDS blood tests using one common needle, and health hazards that he alleged could lead to tuberculosis. Syadou was not allowed visitors. On July 17, RL's Belorussian service was told that Syadou had been transferred to a Minsk hospital.

Moscow Accused of Delaying Negotiations with Lithuania

Lithuanian Minister without portfolio Aleksandras Abisala said in an interview with *Lietuvos aidas*, reported by Radio Vilnius on July 9, that his two meetings with Soviet

THE USSR IN JULY, 1991

officials had convinced him Moscow was unwilling to begin negotiations on Lithuanian independence. Lithuania had expected the meetings (in Vilnius in late June with the USSR Ministry of Defense and in Moscow on July 4 with KGB officials) to be between groups of experts on defense and state security matters, but the Soviet officials whom Abisala met said they had no authorization to conduct genuine negotiations and only discussed some local matters.

Silaev Quits the CPSU

Citing unofficial reports, Russian Television's newscast "Vesti" said on July 9 that RSFSR Prime Minister Ivan Silaev had requested he be allowed to resign from the CPSU. A member of the CPSU Central Committee, Silaev was one of the nine cofounders of the Movement for Democratic Reforms.

No Funds for Retraining Unemployed

The chairman of the RSFSR State Committee for Employment, Anatolii Arzamastsev, told a news conference in Moscow that the RSFSR government could not fund the retraining of the unemployed, agencies reported. He reported that 3,000 persons had qualified for unemployment benefits since the new law on unemployment took effect on July 1. If registration continued at that rate, the authorities could finance compensation at 160 rubles a month through the end of 1991 but could not pay for retraining.

Latest Popularity Poll in Lithuania

The results of the latest public opinion poll in Lithuania showed that 83 percent of the residents of Lithuania supported independence, with only 4 percent opposed to it, Radio Vilnius reported on July 9. The most popular political figure was Supreme Council President Vytautas Landsbergis, followed by deputy Eduardas Vilkas and former Deputy Prime Minister Romualdas Ozolas.

Wednesday, July 10

El'tsin Sworn In

Boris El'tsin was sworn in as president of Russia in the Kremlin, the Soviet media reported. Six thousand guests attended the ceremony. El'tsin took the presidential oath with his hand on the RSFSR Constitution and declaration of sovereignty rather than on a Bible, which had been suggested by some of his aides. Soviet President Mikhail

Gorbachev and Moscow Patriarch Aleksii II took part in the event.

The same day, the fifth RSFSR Congress of People's Deputies opened with the announcement that the seat of the RSFSR president would be in the Kremlin. El'tsin would, therefore, share the premises with Gorbachev.

In his address to the opening session of the RSFSR Congress of People's Deputies, Gorbachev described the election of the RSFSR president as a major positive step in the reform process, saying that it satisfied the need to strengthen executive power in the USSR as a whole. Gorbachev also welcomed the end of "the war of laws" between the all-Union and RSFSR legislatures and thanked El'tsin and the RSFSR deputies for their contribution to his efforts to preserve the Soviet Union.

Soviet Journalist Links KGB to Vilnius Attack

Yurii Shchekochikhin, a correspondent for *Literaturnaya gazeta*, claimed that the KGB had been directly involved in the attack on the Vilnius television tower on January 13. Basing his conclusions on transcripts that were part of the Lithuanian prosecutor's report on the attack, Shchekochikhin wrote that the KGB had planned the operation well in advance but kept its involvement secret so as not to undermine reports about "the unknown Committee of National Salvation and about everything happening so suddenly."

USSR Law on Profits Tax

The USSR Supreme Soviet amended the law of July 14, 1990, on taxes on enterprise profits reducing the standard rate from 45 percent to 35 percent, TASS reported. This implemented the presidential edict of March 22, which lowered the profits tax rate to 35 percent with effect from second-quarter profits. The reduction of tax rates on profits resulted, first, from the proliferation of republican tax laws that set the rates of taxation on profits at below 45 percent (many enterprises previously subordinate to the Union had been "taken over" by the republics), and, second from the difficulty enterprises had had in paying wage supplements to their workers since the price rises. Joint ventures were taxed under separate legislation.

Soviet Chemical Weapons in Former East Germany?

Reports that US satellites had detected Soviet chemical weapons being removed from eastern Germany (*Stern*, July 11; *The Washington Post*, July 8) were denied by the press center of the Soviet Union's Western Group of Forces (*TASS*, July 10). The Soviet Union officially admit-

The USSR in July, 1991

ted on June 13 that not all nuclear arms had been removed from the former GDR. The Soviet army source pointed out that Bundeswehr specialists had visited eight Soviet military sites of their own choosing in the former GDR in summer, 1990, and found no trace of chemical weapons there.

Leningrad Free Enterprise Zone Begins Operating

The chairman of the Leningrad City Soviet's Economic Reform Committee, Anatolii Chubais, announced that the Leningrad free enterprise zone had begun operations (*TASS*, July 10). The zone offered special tax and customs regimes, as well as special social amenities and a system for hard-currency repatriation.

Tatar President on Union Treaty, Federal Taxes

In an interview on Radio Mayak, Tatar President Mintimer Shaimiev said it was not only the leadership of the republic but also public opinion that was insisting Tatarstan sign the Union treaty independently of the RSFSR. This had been shown by the RSFSR presidential elections in which only 36 percent of the electorate chose to vote. Shaimiev added that there must be federal taxes. Many Union enterprises in Tatarstan found themselves without funds because all taxes were going into the RSFSR bank and not being handed over to the center. Shaimiev said Tatarstan would have to set up its own bank to collect the federal taxes.

Democratic Party of Tajikistan Registered

Izvestia reported that the Democratic Party of Tajikistan had been formally registered as a public organization. The group was reported to have some 15,000 members, making it the second-largest political organization in the republic, after the Communist Party. The republican authorities seemed to have decided to tolerate the Democratic Party, which they initially harassed, because it posed less of a threat to their power than the Islamic Renaissance Party, which was banned.

Dashnak Party Registered in Armenia

The Armenian Ministry of Justice registered the main Armenian émigré party, the Dashnak Party. (The Dashnaks emerged in Armenia in the early twentieth century and held Menshevik views. They were driven into emigration after the establishment of Bolshevik power in Armenia.) Novosti said the Dashnak Party was critical of the current political course in Armenia; and the chairman of the Armenian Supreme Soviet, Levon Ter-Petrossyan, in turn, criticized the Dashnaks.

Thursday, July 11

CPSU Central Control Commission Attacks Shevardnadze

The CPSU Central Control Commission issued a statement in response to a letter addressed to the commission on July 3 by former USSR Foreign Minister Eduard Shevardnadze announcing his resignation from the CPSU. (The CPSU Central Committee initiated an investigation of Shevardnadze after he proposed during a visit to Vienna on June 10 to set up a new political party parallel to the CPSU. Shevardnadze refused to attend a hearing of his case in the commission, calling it "an inquisitorial court.") In its statement, cited by TASS, the commission alleged that, in contrast to rumors that it was planning to expel Shevardnadze from the CPSU, the commission just wanted to discuss with Shevardnadze his views on a possible new party. The statement claimed that Shevardnadze had left the CPSU in order to avoid responsibility for the current crisis in the Party.

El'tsin's First Decree Calls for Higher Pay for Teachers

Boris El'tsin issued his first presidential decree, which called for higher pay for republican teachers and other educational employees as well as for higher grants for students. TASS said the decree foresaw a state program of educational development being completed before the end of 1991.

Sobchak Criticizes USSR Supreme Soviet

Leningrad Mayor Anatolii Sobchak said he believed the present USSR Supreme Soviet should cease operating. Russian Television quoted Sobchak as telling a Leningrad press conference that "it is now clear that its current membership will obstruct the signing of the Union treaty and the country's new constitution." On July 10, the Russian Information Agency quoted Soviet President Mikhail Gorbachev as telling the USSR Supreme Soviet that it had only six months to live. The report said Gorbachev had informed legislators that neither parliament nor the USSR Congress of People's Deputies would adopt a new constitution or Union treaty. But he said that they would adopt a new election law and that elections would be held in 1992 for new deputies.

USSR and China to Hold Talks with ASEAN for First Time

The Soviet Union and China accepted invitations to hold their first talks with the Association of Southeast Asian Nations (ASEAN), Reuters and AP reported. Soviet and Chinese representatives would attend the formal opening of the meeting of ASEAN foreign ministers on July 19. The

The USSR in July, 1991

USSR would be represented by Deputy Prime Minister Yurii Maslyukov.

Melor Sturua Leaves the CPSU

Radio Rossii reported that *Izvestia*'s foreign correspondent Melor Sturua had left the CPSU. He was quoted as saying: "The CPSU is now the main obstacle on the path of the country's development towards democracy and a market economy." In the pre-*perestroika* period Sturua was one of the main political correspondents who wrote articles highly critical of the West, especially of the United States.

"Soglasie" Press Conference

Fedor Burlatsky, one of the members of the coordinating council of the "Soglasie" (Agreement) group of people's deputies, told a press conference in Moscow that the best way to resolve the divisive issues separating the center, the republics, and the various nationalities and groups was on the basis of treaties and a new parliamentary structure, "Vremya" reported. The group supported a Union formed on the basis of agreements with sovereign republics, destatization, privatization, and free enterprise, with the corresponding social protection.

―――――――――――――――――――――――――――― *Friday, July 12*

USSR Supreme Soviet Approves Union Treaty

The USSR Supreme Soviet supported "in the main" the third draft of the Union treaty by a vote of 307 in favor, 11 against, and 18 abstentions, TASS reported. The Supreme Soviet appointed a delegation headed by Soviet President Mikhail Gorbachev to sign the treaty on behalf of the Union after appropriate amendments had been agreed with the republics. The delegation was instructed to point out to republican Supreme Soviets the USSR Supreme Soviet's views that: the treaty should designate both the Union and autonomous republics as subjects of the federation; that it should provide for Union property and federal taxes; that neither the Union nor the republics should be entitled to suspend each other's laws; that both chambers of the future Supreme Soviet should be elected by direct vote; and that the composition of the cabinet and other bodies should be approved by both chambers. Some or all of the Union republics opposed many of these points. For the text of the third draft, see *Izvestia*, June 27.

An attempt by the influential "Soyuz" faction to have the treaty ratified by the USSR Congress of People's Deputies failed. Chairman of the USSR Supreme Soviet

Anatolii Luk'yanov reiterated that the Congress had no right to do this, since final agreement on the treaty was a matter for the republics. The resolution did, however, state that the treaty should be signed at the USSR Congress of People's Deputies. The Supreme Soviet also adopted an appeal to the six republics not participating in the treaty to study the text and find ways of taking part in the creation of the new state, TASS reported.

El'tsin Nominates Silaev as RSFSR Prime Minister

RSFSR President Boris El'tsin nominated Ivan Silaev to be reelected as prime minister of the RSFSR, Radio Rossii reported. Silaev resigned from his post following El'tsin's inauguration in accordance with the RSFSR Constitution, which entitled the president to name a new head of government. On July 13, the RSFSR Congress voted for Silaev's reelection (*TASS*, July 13).

Gorbachev on Land Ownership

Speaking at a Kremlin news conference, Soviet President Mikhail Gorbachev again displayed hesitation on the crucial question of the private ownership of land. As reported by *The New York Times* (July 13), he said: "I support transferring the land to private individuals with the right to inherit it, so a person would feel the master of his own land." He felt the question of land ownership could be solved in different ways in the fifteen Soviet republics but that, sooner or later, "it will be decided by the people." He apparently remained opposed to the individual sale and purchase of land in a free market.

Supreme Soviet Approves Information Minister

The USSR Supreme Soviet confirmed Mikhail Nenashev to fill the new post of USSR minister of information and the press, TASS reported. He had headed the ministry's predecessor, the USSR State Committee for the Press. Nenashev served as editor of the daily *Sovetskaya Rossiya* from 1978 to 1986 and also served briefly as chairman of the USSR State Committee for Television and Radio Broadcasting.

Supreme Soviet Calls for End to Secret Privileges

After hearing revelations by its Committee on Privileges that former leading government officials had purchased state-owned dachas at rock-bottom prices, the USSR Supreme Soviet approved a resolution aimed at ending secret privileges for top Communist Party and government leaders (*Radio Rossii*, July 12). The measure reinforced an order by Gorbachev instructing Prime Minister Valentin Pavlov to find and punish guilty officials by July 25. Observers noted, however, that the Soviet parliament had approved the new measure only after excluding from the text virtually all mention of the possibility that illegal privileges might be enjoyed by the parliamentarians themselves.

On July 31, the Soviet government ordered all state agencies to halt the sale of country dachas to officials, Western agencies reported on August 1. The order decreed that all such sales should cease until new regulations on the privatization of state property came into operation.

Calls for Referendum on Confiscation of CPSU Property

Nezavisimaya gazeta said the last Communist chairman of the Moscow City Soviet, Valerii Saikin, had given thirty-three city buildings to the CPSU during his last few weeks in office. On July 12, AP quoted Nikolai Kruchina, the CPSU Central Committee administrator of affairs, as admitting that the Party had acquired 2,000 of its 5,000 buildings wholly or partly with government funds. It was also reported that a group had been set up in Moscow to collect signatures for a petition calling for an all-Union referendum on confiscation of CPSU property.

Law on RSFSR Constitutional Court Adopted

The RSFSR Congress of People's Deputies adopted a law on the republican constitutional court. Unlike most judges in the USSR, those serving in the Constitutional Court would be appointed for life. The role of the RSFSR constitutional judges would be crucial, since their verdicts would enable the RSFSR president to fire republican executives found by the court to be violating the RSFSR Constitution and laws. The judges were to be nominated by the chairman of the RSFSR Supreme Soviet, not by the president. See *Rossiiskaya gazeta*, July 13.

RSFSR Reform Plan

Some details of the RSFSR reform plan were given in *Kommersant* (No. 26). The main architect of the plan was economist Evgenii Saburov, who was also RSFSR deputy education minister. The plan, which was intended to cover the period up to the end of 1993, emphasized privatization, with a strategy that would adjust over time to the population's response in terms of savings rates. Free privatization vouchers would be issued to the population, but shares would be sold preferentially to people offering money as well as vouchers; then 10–25 percent of the unsold shares would be offered to foreign investors.

Saturday, July 13

CPSU Bolshevik Platform Meets

The Bolshevik Platform within the CPSU, composed of hard-line Communists, met in the Belorussian capital, Minsk, over the weekend. Addressing the congress, the platform's leader, Nina Andreeva, denounced "'Gorbostroika,' revisionism, and capitalist-roaders," TASS reported. The gathering, attended by some 500 people, adopted a declaration officially forming a CPSU Bolshevik Platform and passed a motion of no confidence in CPSU General Secretary Mikhail Gorbachev. Andreeva was elected head of an organizational committee given the task of garnering support for the convoking of an extraordinary congress of the CPSU.

Picketing the oblast Party committee building where the Bolshevik Platform met, Belorussian Popular Front activists and leaders of non-Communist political parties carried signs reading "Stalinists Get Out of Minsk!" In an interview on July 13 with Radio Rossii, Mikhas' Tkachou, a prominent Belorussian social democrat, said that, in allowing the Bolshevik Platform to hold a conference, the Central Committee of the Belorussian Communist Party had "covered our . . . guiltless Belorussia in shame."

Troops Attack Armenian Villages

The inhabitants of three Armenian villages in the Geranboi Raion of Azerbaijan, which borders on Nagorno-Karabakh, were ordered by unidentified troops to leave their homes. On July 14, units of the twenty-third division of the Soviet Fourth Army launched an attack on the villages, according to Western news agencies on July 14 and 15. USSR KGB Chairman Vladimir Kryuchkov was quoted as having assured Armenian Supreme Soviet Chairman Levon Ter-Petrossyan that the situation in the region was quiet. Chairman of the Azerbaijani KGB Vagif Guseinov claimed that MVD troops had been deployed to protect the Armenians.

Congress of Lutherans in Leningrad

TASS reported that a congress of Lutherans of Russia was meeting in Leningrad for the first time in sixty-seven years. This forum planned to discuss the problems of reviving the Evangelical-Lutheran Church, pass Church statutes, and elect its leadership.

Nazarbaev in China

TASS reported that, during Kazakh President Nursultan Nazarbaev's visit to China, he had met with the general secretary of the Chinese Communist Party, Jiang Zemin,

THE USSR IN JULY, 1991

as well as with government leaders. Upon his return to the Soviet Union on July 15, Nazarbaev told a TASS correspondent that learning firsthand about the Chinese experience with special economic zones was particularly valuable, because Kazakhstan had decided to establish such zones itself. Nazarbaev also said that developing relations between Kazakhstan and Xinjiang must be seen in the context of relations between the USSR and China.

Sunday, July 14

Kasparov Criticizes El'tsin

A former member of the Democratic Party of Russia, Gary Kasparov, said RSFSR President Boris El'tsin had made a mistake in siding with Soviet President Mikhail Gorbachev. He told *The Sunday Times* that "in trying to save Gorbachev, he [El'tsin] will probably go down with him." Kasparov criticized El'tsin for having nominated as his deputy the Communist Aleksandr Rutskoi. He also stated that, by trusting Gorbachev's word on economic reform and reshaping the USSR, "El'tsin has condemned himself." Kasparov said the greatest obstacle to renewing the Union would be Ukraine.

Estonian Foreign Minister in London

Estonian Foreign Minister Lennart Meri arrived in London for a seven-day visit planned to coincide with the G-7 summit, an RFE/RL correspondent reported. The Estonian Foreign Ministry told RFE/RL that Meri hoped to meet with senior representatives of the G-7 nations "to explain the position of the Baltic States on Western financial aid to the Soviet Union."

On July 15, Meri told reporters that any Western aid to the Soviet Union should target the republics, RFE/RL's correspondent in London reported.

Jewish Summer School in Donetsk

Ukrinform reported from Donetsk about the opening there of a Jewish summer school. The classes, which would be free, were being organized by the new society of Jewish culture, Revival, and the local synagogue. Rabbis from New York would be teaching children modern Hebrew, and Jewish history, and culture.

Monday, July 15

Japan Raises Kuriles Question at G-7 Talks

During the first round of G-7 talks, Japanese Prime Minister Toshiki Kaifu called on the Soviet Union to provide specific "proof of the application of new global thinking" by resolving the Kurile Islands dispute with Japan. Kaifu also noted that Soviet President Mikhail Gorbachev's elaboration of his reform plans had come too late for the G-7 to consider a massive aid package during the London summit, Western agencies reported.

Landsbergis Demands Withdrawal of OMON Troops

President of the Lithuanian Supreme Council Vytautas Landsbergis called for the withdrawal of the MVD special troops (OMON) from Lithuanian territory, Radio Independent Lithuania reported. In a telegram sent to Soviet President Mikhail Gorbachev, Landsbergis expressed his fear that OMON troops would be used to stage provocations that could be used as "a pretext for new Soviet army actions in Lithuania."

KGB Criticizes OMON, Blames Baltic Republics

Lieutenant General Bruno Steinbrik, chief of the KGB Special Department of the Baltic Military District, told *Sovetskaya Latviya* that the creation of customs posts by the Baltic republics directly violated all-Union laws. While attacks by MVD special troops (OMON) on the customs posts must also be condemned, he said, lawlessness could not be fought with lawlessness. Steinbrik added that the OMON troops were not guilty, since they had not made the decision to stage the attacks themselves.

Grain Procurement Target Reiterated

The USSR Cabinet of Ministers reminded Union republics of the need to meet the grain procurement target of 77 million tons, Radio Moscow and TASS reported. This was considered to be an unrealistic goal, being well above the 1990's procurement level of around 70 million tons from a record harvest. Farms that would sell more than their allotted quota of grain to the state were being offered a variety of scarce consumer and producer goods, ranging from passenger cars to cement and sewing machines, at state retail prices. Similar offers of goods and hard currency had been largely ineffective over the previous two years, owing to poor administration of the scheme and unavailability of products.

In a related move, the USSR Ministry of Defense was reported to have allocated the troops and vehicles of sixty motorized battalions to help bring in the harvest, (*Pravda*, July 15). Some 30,000 army vehicles would be involved.

Problems with Registration of CPSU

Argumenty i fakty (No. 26) reported that the CPSU had been officially registered under the law on public associations despite the fact that its rules had not yet been revised in accordance with this law. In January, a CPSU Central Committee plenum had promised to revise the rules, adding a required chapter regulating the procedure for disbanding the Party. *Argumenty i fakty* emphasized that the CPSU had not yet published even a draft of the chapter.

"Soyuz" Still Aiming at Vote of No Confidence in Gorbachev

At a press conference, the leaders of the "Soyuz" faction in the USSR Supreme Soviet reiterated their criticism of the draft Union treaty and accused Soviet President Mikhail Gorbachev of pursuing a consistent policy of breaking up the country, TASS reported. Yurii Blokhin, chairman of the "Soyuz" Coordination Council, said the faction was delaying the convocation of the USSR Congress of People's Deputies for a vote of no confidence in Gorbachev only because it wanted to be sure it had the necessary majority to carry the motion.

Moscow Rejects Use of Force against Iraq

Presidential spokesman Vitalii Ignatenko said Moscow was opposed to the use of military action to force Iraq to abandon its nuclear weapons development. Speaking at a London news conference, Ignatenko said that every method except military action should be used to influence Iraq (Western agencies, July 15).

TASS observer Yurii Tyssovsky said in a July 15 commentary that it "does no honor to US diplomacy" to take "a selective approach" towards Iraq with respect to its nuclear weapons building potential. "Israel already has . . . at least hundreds of nuclear warheads with their means of delivery, and on the banks of the Potomac they aren't planning to impose sanctions against Tel Aviv."

On July 16, Soviet Ambassador to the United Nations Yulii Vorontsov stressed that the Iraqi nuclear program should not exist. "This a serious matter," he said; "[Iraq] should not have such a program." Vorontsov also called for a special resolution of the UN Security Council to assist the work of UN inspection groups, TASS reported.

Bessmertnykh Warns Yugoslavia's Neighbors against Intervention

The Austrian magazine *Profil* published a letter from Soviet Foreign Minister Aleksandr Bessmertnykh warning against intervention in the Yugoslav crisis by the country's neighbors. He deplored recent arms deliveries allegedly made to Yugoslavia without the knowledge of "the legitimate government" of Yugoslavia. Bessmertnykh also condemned "the numerous overtures" of "supporters of the disintegration" of Yugoslavia and concluded,

"Unless a stop is put to attempts to meddle in the Yugoslav internal crisis, all the conditions will be present to bring about the same situation that existed at the beginning of the century."

Sobchak Orders Joint Police-Military Patrols

The new mayor of Leningrad, Anatolii Sobchak, ordered joint patrols by police and military personnel to handle growing crime in the city, Radio Mayak reported. When Soviet President MikhailGorbachev ordered such joint patrols throughout the country by presidential decree in December, 1990, the decree was denounced as a step towards dictatorship. Sobchak's order provided for about twenty-five police and seventy-five military servicemen to participate in joint patrols everyday. The crime rate in Leningrad had risen by 15 percent since the beginning of the year, and the local police were not technically equipped to deal with the problem.

On July 16, the Presidium of the Leningrad City Soviet voted down the decree on joint police-military patrols, Interfax reported. Sobchak protested against the vote and stressed that his decree accorded with Gorbachev's decree of December, 1990. Sobchak also stated that the RSFSR government supported his decree. He declared the Presidium's decision invalid and said that he would not adhere to it.

Tajik Supreme Soviet Forbids Defamation of President

TASS reported that the Tajik Supreme Soviet had passed a law calling for up to six years' imprisonment for individuals who defamed the president of the republic by disseminating "slanderous materials." The report added that public criticism of the president's actions and policies was not subject to prosecution. The Tajik law appeared to be modeled on the USSR law passed in 1990.

Tajik Research Reactor to Be Closed

TASS reported that the Dushanbe City Soviet had decided to dismantle a nuclear reactor in one of the city's research institutes after an investigation, demanded by city residents, found that the facility had been built without the approval of seismologists, although the area was subject to severe earthquakes. In addition, groundwater had often flooded the area where the reactor's fuel was stored.

Morals Police Set Up in Moldavia

The Moldavian MVD told journalists that a morals police force was being set up in Moldavia to protect young people from the cult of violence, cruelty, and pornography, TASS and Novosti reported. An MVD spokesman

The USSR in July, 1991

said the rapid growth of prostitution and the pornography business had made the creation of the new force necessary. The number of prostitutes in Kishinev had risen from 200 to 800 in three years. Units of the morals police were to be created in all major population centers and on international routes through the republic.

Tuesday, July 16

Group of Seven on USSR

A political declaration issued in London by leaders of the G-7 countries expressed their hope that "the negotiations between the USSR and the elected governments of the Baltic countries would resolve their future democratically and in accordance with the legitimate aspirations of the people." It welcomed "efforts to create a new Union based on consent, not coercion, which [would] genuinely respond to the wishes of the peoples of the Soviet Union." The leaders declared themselves committed to support for Soviet efforts "to create an open society, a pluralistic democracy, and a market economy." In a nod to Japan's security concerns, they expressed hope that "the new thinking" in Soviet foreign policy would be "as fully reflected in Asia as in Europe." The leaders reiterated that their "support for the process of fundamental reform in the Soviet Union remains as strong as ever."

Vagnorius Sends Telegrams to London

Lithuanian Prime Minister Gediminas Vagnorius sent telegrams to the G-7 meeting in London and to Soviet President Mikhail Gorbachev, Radio Independent Lithuania reported. In the telegrams, Vagnorius asked for the return of the buildings in Vilnius seized by the Soviet Armed Forces in January. Vagnorius expressed the hope that the G-7 leaders would raise the Baltic question in their talks with Gorbachev, stressing that Lithuania was willing to solve all existing problems in its relations with the USSR through interstate discussions in a spirit of good-neighborliness and cooperation.

New Lithuanian Deputy Prime Minister

The Lithuanian Supreme Council voted to approve Lithuanian Minister of Social Security Algis Dobravolskas as the republic's third deputy prime minister, Radio Independent Lithuania reported.

USSR State Bank Publishes Balance Sheet

With the declared aim of "showing that the Soviet Union seriously wishes to move towards a market economy," the USSR State Bank published its first balance sheet since 1936 in *Izvestia*, TASS reported. Thenceforth, balance sheets were to be published four times a year. The figures showed a balance of 638 billion rubles. The bank's gold reserves were given as 374 tons—an amount previously disclosed at a Vienna conference (see the *Financial Times*, June 25)—in addition to holdings of other precious metals and foreign currency valued at nearly 1.2 billion rubles. (Reserves of gold and other precious metals were also held by other Soviet institutions.)

Agreement between Turkmenistan and Kirgizia

Radio Moscow reported that the presidents of Kirgizia and Turkmenistan had signed an agreement on economic and cultural cooperation between the two republics for the years 1991–95. The document was the latest in a series of bilateral agreements between various republics in Central Asia.

Wednesday, July 17

Gorbachev at G-7 Meeting

Gorbachev presented his case for Western aid to the USSR to the leaders of the G-7 nations in London. In addition to addressing them as a group, he held individual talks with each of the seven. The Soviet president got kind words but no money from the G-7 nations (*The New York Times*, *The Washington Post*, *The Journal of Commerce*, July 18). The seven pledged special associate member status in the International Monetary Fund (IMF) and World Bank for the USSR: this meant access to IMF expertise but not IMF or World Bank loans. Beyond that, the seven said they would each provide technical assistance (which they were already doing); urge the European Bank for Reconstruction and Development (EBRD) and the Organization for Economic Cooperation and Development (OECD) to help (but not raise the low ceiling on EBRD finance for the USSR); and monitor progress.

Four members of the Ukrainian parliament sent a letter to the leaders attending the G-7 summit stating that, if the G-7 nations really wanted to help, they should give aid directly to the republics, not to the center. Radio Kiev reported that a member of the parliament, Dmytro Pavlychko, pointed out that Ukraine currently had to relinquish 100 billion dollars a year to the center. He said this money could be used to repay any assistance it received from the West.

The USSR in July, 1991

Gorbachev Compares Nonsigners of Union Treaty with Former Allies

Presidential spokesman Vitalii Ignatenko told reporters in London that Soviet President Mikhail Gorbachev had spoken at length to the G-7 leaders about the relationship between the republics, including the Baltic republics, and the center, RFE/RL's correspondent in London reported. According to Ignatenko, Gorbachev said the USSR's relations with the countries of Eastern Europe "remind one of a family . . . where partners live together for a long time, then divorce, then live separately, then realize that they can't live without each other." Gorbachev was reported to have said that "something similar" might occur with those republics that wanted to leave the Union.

RSFSR Congress Postpones Election of Supreme Soviet Chairman

The RSFSR Congress of People's Deputies postponed the election of a Supreme Soviet chairman until the fall after failing to approve a new leader for the body. The congress decided to temporarily charge First Deputy Chairman Ruslan Khasbulatov with the duties of Supreme Soviet chairman, TASS reported. The congress had tried six times since July 12 to elect a chairman, but no candidate received the required majority of 531 votes. TASS commented that, although RSFSR President Boris El'tsin strongly supported Khasbulatov's candidacy, up to 100 pro-El'tsin democrats in the congress had consistently voted against Khasbulatov, whom they accused of "authoritarian methods" of leadership.

Appeal to Supreme Soviet from Minorities in Republics Not Signing Union Treaty

Representatives of minority areas in four of the republics that had refused to sign the Union treaty sent an appeal to the USSR Supreme Soviet insisting that they be allowed to sign it. The appeal, published in *Izvestia*, came from the Abkhaz ASSR and the South Ossetian Autonomous Oblast in Georgia, the self-styled Dniester and Gagauz "republics" in Moldavia, the Interregional Council of Estonia, and the predominantly Polish Salcininkai Raion of Lithuania. The appeal cited the law on the mechanics of secession of April, 1990, which allowed autonomous territories and areas inhabited primarily by minorities in republics wishing to secede to remain part of the USSR and suggested that a commission be set up to determine their rights under this law and the draft Union treaty.

Half-Yearly Economic Results

Chairman of the USSR State Committee for Statistics Vadim Kirichenko outlined preliminary data for economic performance during the first half of 1991 to a press conference in Moscow, TASS and Western agencies reported. Compared with the first half of 1990, there were declines of 10 percent in GNP, 12 percent in national income, 6.2 percent in gross industrial output, 11 percent in labor productivity, and 10 percent in oil output. Wholesale prices in June, 1991, were 120 percent higher and retail prices 90 percent higher than in June, 1990.

Gidaspov Comments on CPSU and Capitalism

At a press conference, First Secretary of the Leningrad Party Committee Boris Gidaspov supported the idea of holding an emergency CPSU congress in the fall, Radio Rossii reported. He rejected, however, a proposal to replace Soviet President Mikhail Gorbachev as the Party's general secretary and condemned the Bolshevik Platform in the CPSU for advancing this proposal. Gidaspov was also skeptical about the Movement for Democratic Reforms. He said it had been set up by representatives of the CPSU apparatus and alleged that the movement's program was almost identical to the resolutions of the Twenty-eighth Party Congress.

At the same press conference, Gidaspov made some controversial remarks about Germany. Commenting on the situation in the USSR, he said that Marxist-Leninist ideology was currently being replaced in the Soviet Union by Darwinism, with weaker individuals being pushed aside by stronger ones. He said that a similar situation was to be observed in all Capitalist countries and cited Germany as an example. Gidaspov said that in Germany it was not a chancellor or federal government that ruled the country, but dynasties of industrialists, who, although they had already twice initiated world wars, remained in power. Radio Rossii reported that the German consulate in Leningrad had already expressed dissatisfaction about Gidaspov's statement and was intending to pursue the issue further.

Explosion in Riga

A blast caused by explosives placed in a lavatory rocked the premises of the Prosecutor's Office of the Republic of Latvia. One man was seriously injured and hospitalized, according to Radio Riga.

Joint Military Commissions in Baltic Republics

Radio Vilnius reported that Chief of the General Staff of the Soviet Armed Forces General Mikhail Moiseev had sent a telegram to Lithuanian Prime Minister Gediminas Vagnorius proposing the creation of joint commissions in the Baltic republics to control civilian-military tensions in the region. Moiseev was reported to have ordered commanders of the Baltic Military District and the navy to work with republican and local governmental bodies in

The USSR in July, 1991

all three Baltic republics towards that end. Similar telegrams had been sent to Latvian and Estonian leaders, the report said.

Human-Rights Delegation Confirms Armenian Deportations

An international delegation that had just visited Nagorno-Karabakh told Western journalists at a Moscow press conference that, since late April, 10,000 Armenians had been forcibly deported from the area by Soviet army and Azerbaijani special police troops (OMON). Armenians had also been illegally detained, beaten, and tortured, and Armenian villages had been resettled by Azerbaijanis. The Azerbaijani authorities had persistently maintained that Azerbaijani troops were merely enforcing passport controls to identify Armenian guerrillas and that Armenians who left Azerbaijan were doing so voluntarily.

Regulations for Kuzbass Free Economic Zone Signed

Radio Moscow and Russian Television reported that RSFSR Prime Minister Ivan Silaev had signed regulations setting up a free economic zone in the Kuzbass. This would affect all enterprises in Kemerovo Oblast. They would be allowed to pay wages in hard currency, and the creation of joint ventures in the sphere of banking and insurance would be permitted. A free customs enclave would also be created. Joint ventures and participants in external trade could register with the oblast executive committee, which would establish quotas for the extraction and exploitation of mineral resources.

Legislator on Trial in Uzbekistan

Supreme Soviet deputy Shovruk Ruzimuradov was reported to have been put on trial in Karshi for his role in fomenting unrest in the town of Yakkabag in connection with the April price increases, according to TASS, quoting *Vechernyaya Moskva*. The report said that the trial of Ruzimuradov, who was identified as a leader of "Birlik," the Uzbek Popular Front organization, was closed to the public and that the police had sealed off all access to the town. Uzbek President Islam Karimov stated in an interview published in *Rabochaya tribuna* on July 3 that the Yakkabag disturbance had been minor and that there had been no casualties.

Poll on Moldavian Popular Front

A recent opinion poll in Moldavia showed that the Moldavian Popular Front could count on the votes of only 15 percent of the electorate but was still the most popular party or movement, Novosti reported. Only about 8 percent of voters supported the Social Democrats, 7.5 percent supported the Communists, and 6.7 percent favored "Edinstvo." Forty-seven percent of those interviewed said they disliked the popular front. On the other hand, about 60 percent (a few percentage points less than the Moldavian share of the population) said they wanted full independence, and only a quarter were in favor of signing the Union treaty.

Thursday, July 18

El'tsin and Landsbergis Meet

President of the Lithuanian Supreme Council Vytautas Landsbergis met for two hours in Moscow with RSFSR President Boris El'tsin, Radio Independent Lithuania reported. They decided that a treaty establishing bilateral relations between the two "sovereign" republics would be signed in Moscow on July 29. They expressed their readiness to expand cooperation in political, economic, scientific, and cultural areas and to guarantee the rights of Russians in Lithuania and Lithuanians in the RSFSR. Representatives' offices would be opened in Vilnius, Moscow, Leningrad, and Kaliningrad. Another agreement would be signed guaranteeing the RSFSR access to Kaliningrad Oblast.

USSR Supports US Proposal at Minorities Conference

The chief Soviet delegate at the Geneva Minorities Conference, Georgii Tarazevich, told reporters in Geneva that the Soviet Union supported the US proposal on international mediation to help resolve ethnic crises, RFE/RL's correspondent in Geneva reported. Tarazevich, who was chairman of the Council of Nationalities Commission on Nationalities Policy and Interethnic Relations, said the various parties in a conflict might find it easier to trust international mediators. Asked specifically if they could be used in the Soviet Union in conflicts such as that over the Nagorno-Karabakh Autonomous Oblast, he said "yes."

New Joint Oil Venture in Komi ASSR

British Gulf and Gulf Canada Resources announced that they were in the final stages of setting up a joint venture to develop a new oilfield and to boost output at a nearby existing field in the Komi ASSR, Western agencies reported. The reports said that the sites had estimated reserves of 2.2 billion barrels and that the Western share of investment would be nearly 900 million dollars.

The USSR in July, 1991

Spring Draft Figures

Deputy Chief of the General Staff of the Soviet Armed Forces Colonel General Grigorii Krivosheev told *Krasnaya zvezda* the spring military draft was proceeding in an "unsatisfactory" manner. Krivosheev said that as of mid-July only 91.4 percent of the total draft contingent had been inducted. In Georgia, he said, the figure was 8.2 percent; in Lithuania, 12.3 percent; in Armenia, 16.4 percent; and, in Estonia, 30 percent. Krivosheev blamed the low turnout primarily on the uncooperative actions of republican governments.

Demonstration for Independence of Leningrad TV

A demonstration was held in Leningrad to protest about the decision in June by the central broadcasting authorities to put Leningrad Television firmly under the supervision of the All-Union State Television and Radio Broadcasting Company. (In contrast, the Leningrad City Soviet wanted to make Leningrad Television a shareholding company.) Radio Rossii reported that the demonstrators carried slogans attacking the head of the all-Union company, Leonid Kravchenko.

Romanovs' Remains Uncovered?

TASS reported from Sverdlovsk that nine skeletons had been discovered at the site where the remains of the last tsar of Russia and his family were said to have been hidden. The Russian Orthodox Church, which in 1991 commemorated for the first time the day the tsar and his family were killed, was reported to have opened a bank account for the construction of a memorial temple on the site of the shooting. At present there is only a crucifix.

Khmara Arrested Again

Ukrainian people's deputy Stepan Khmara was arrested again, Radio Kiev reported on July 20. A special police division arrived at the Ukraina Hotel where Khmara was staying and, after a confrontation with Khmara's supporters and bodyguards, took him away. The confrontation, which included the use of tear gas and police batons, left a total of twenty-three people injured—twelve members of the police force and eleven Khmara supporters. More than two thousand people gathered on one of Kiev's main streets later that evening to protest against the action. Khmara was scheduled to go on trial in July charged with attacking a police officer.

Ukraine Protects Its Grain Harvest

Central Television quoted Chairman of the Ukrainian Supreme Soviet Leonid Kravchuk as saying that, while Ukraine intended to supply grain to fulfill state orders and bilateral agreements with other regions, it had "taken measures to protect its harvest from massive purchases by other republics." Both the all-Union and Ukrainian governments were offering a variety of incentives in exchange for additional grain deliveries, including sewing machines, refrigerators, and other scarce goods.

Lvov against Party Organs in Police

Radio Kiev reported that the Lvov Oblast Soviet had passed a resolution recommending that the police be purged of Communist Party organs. The resolution was adopted by a large majority, including deputies who were Communist Party members. Ukrainian Communist Party First Secretary Stanislav Hurenko, had, however, stated his opposition to such a move.

Nishanov Makes Appeal to Gamsakhurdia to Permit Meskhetians to Return

The chairman of the USSR Council of Nationalities, Rafik Nishanov, appealed to Georgian President Zviad Gamsakhurdia to allow those Meskhetians who wished to do so to return to Georgia, from where they were deported en masse to Central Asia in November, 1944 (*TASS*, July 19). Following violent clashes with local Uzbeks in the Fergana Valley in June, 1989, many Meskhetians fled from Uzbekistan to the RSFSR, and some 40,000 settled in Azerbaijan. Gamsakhurdia opposed the return of the Meskhetians to Georgia because they were Muslims and the majority did not speak Georgian.

Plea for Moderation in Kirgizia

A number of prominent intellectuals and political figures in Kirgizia published an appeal to their fellow citizens to eschew extremism and to support a moderate democratic movement called Popular Unity, TASS reported. The signatories, who included republican Vice President German Kuznetsov, complained that "the superradicals" often put national interests before democratic ones (the reference was apparently to the primarily Kirgiz Democratic Kyrgyzstan group). But they were most worried about the machinations of conservatives in the republican Communist Party, who were trying to undermine recent moves towards democracy.

Friday, July 19

Gorbachev Admits Possibility of Non-Communist President

Soviet President Mikhail Gorbachev acknowledged the possibility that a non-Communist could be elected USSR president. When asked during an interview with Britain's

THE USSR IN JULY, 1991

Independent Television News whether he could foresee such a possibility, Gorbachev replied elliptically. Noting that some republics had already elected non-Communist presidents, he went on to say that the USSR presidential election "has to be a competition of programs, a competition of parties, a competition of leaders. . . . The winner will have the support of the people, and naturally the winner in the elections will be the leader of reform in the Soviet Union."

Prokof'ev Forecasts Split in CPSU

The first secretary of the Moscow City Party Committee, Yurii Prokof'ev, told a Moscow press conference that a two- or possibly three-way split in the CPSU, whose members had made demands ranging from the creation of a capitalist society to a return to Stalinism, was "inevitable," TASS reported. Prokof'ev also said that Mikhail Gorbachev should resign as general secretary, because he could not do justice to both his presidential and Party duties. Prokof'ev suggested Gorbachev could perhaps serve in a ceremonial capacity as Party chairman.

Democratic Congress Adopts Position on New Reform Movements

An extraordinary session of the Consultative Council of the Democratic Congress—an umbrella organization of democrats—met in Kiev to adopt a position regarding the new reform movements in the country (the Movement for Democratic Reforms, the United Democratic Party of the USSR, and the Democratic Party of Communists of Russia), Ukrinform-TASS and Radio Kiev reported. Anatolii Zhivotnyuk, cochairman of the United Democratic Party of Belorussia, was quoted as saying that, although the Democratic Congress supported the new Movement for Democratic Reforms, it could not agree with its approach to the reform of the national-state structure of the USSR—specifically, its appeal only to those national movements and parties that supported preservation of the unitary state.

Minister of Education Dismissed

"Vesti" reported that USSR Education Minister Gennadii Yagodin had been dismissed, possibly at the behest of Defense Minister Dmitrii Yazov. Yagodin reportedly opposed a Defense Ministry initiative that would end draft deferments for university students.

El'tsin Sees KGB as Crime-Fighting Force

RSFSR President Boris El'tsin told a conference of KGB territorial officers that the time when the KGB violated human rights was past. Today, he said, the KGB's task was to ensure citizens' personal security and rights. Among the RSFSR KGB's other tasks were protecting Russia's economic security, safeguarding Russian businessmen's interests in their transactions with foreign partners, and combating economic crimes. El'tsin said its most important activity was the struggle against organized crime, terrorism, and corruption. The KGB must also guarantee the stability and security of legally elected bodies and of the state structure, El'tsin added (*TASS, Russian Television*, July 19).

Aliev Resigns from CPSU

Interfax reported that former Politburo member Geidar Aliev had resigned from the CPSU on the grounds that "the Communist experiment and the choice of socialism have not proved themselves in our country, and the Union of republics that was created by brute force has outlived itself." On July 21, Radio Rossii quoted Aliev as stating that the Communist Party in his native republic, Azerbaijan, had lost all authority and should give up its monopoly on power. He further charged that the Azerbaijani Communist Party, with the backing of the CPSU Central Committee, was suppressing a broad democratic movement in Azerbaijan.

On July 25, TASS quoted a statement by the Party Control Commission of the Azerbaijani Communist Party as claiming that Aliev's resignation from the CPSU had been prompted not by ideological considerations but by his responsibility for widespread corruption in Azerbaijan during his tenure as Party first secretary there.

Armenians Overwhelmingly Support Secession

Radio Moscow said a poll conducted in Armenia earlier in the month by the Armenian Public Opinion Poll Center had indicated that 80 percent of Armenians supported the idea of Armenia's secession from the USSR. The size of the poll sample was not stated.

Ukrainian Miners Organize

A conference of representatives of miners' collectives met in Krasnoarmeisk in Donetsk Oblast to discuss the formation of an independent miners' trade union, Radio Kiev reported. The miners were dissatisfied with the official trade-union organization, the Federation of Independent Trade Unions, which was said to have taken a neutral position regarding the miners' strikes in the spring. The miners complained that the federation had supported only certain economic demands put forward by the strikers and totally ignored their political demands.

The USSR in July, 1991

The Ukrainian Supreme Soviet issued a resolution calling for the creation of a special commission to investigate violence in army life. According to Radio Moscow, the document also contained a number of other measures related to military service.

Ukrainian Resolution on Violence in Army Life

Saturday, July 20

In his second decree since assuming the office of RSFSR president, Boris El'tsin banned the activities of political parties and public organizations in state agencies, Radio Rossii reported. Organizational structures or cells representing any new or existing political party or public organization would not be tolerated either in executive organs attached to soviets at any level, in state enterprises, or in any other state body. Participation in the activities of any political party or public organization could not be used as a basis for discrimination against individuals so long as they did not break the law. State employees were to be guided by RSFSR law in the execution of their duties and were permitted to participate in the activities of political parties and public organizations only outside working hours.

El'tsin's decree also instructed the RSFSR Supreme Soviet to prepare a bill banning political activity in the USSR Supreme Court, the USSR Prosecutor's Office, the Soviet Armed Forces, the USSR Ministry of Internal Affairs, and the KGB. These agencies were not administered solely by republican authorities, so neither the RSFSR Supreme Soviet nor El'tsin had the power unilaterally to eliminate party activities in them. Instead, the RSFSR Supreme Soviet planned to use its right of legislative initiative to submit the bill to the USSR Supreme Soviet. For the text of the decree, see *Sovetskaya Rossiya*, July 20.

RSFSR Minister of Justice Nikolai Fedorov told Radio Moscow on July 23 that fines of up to 10,000 rubles might be imposed on those who did not comply with the decree and that any organization that proclaimed its intent not to comply might find itself barred from operating entirely.

On July 23, the CPSU Politburo and Secretariat, the RSFSR Politburo and Central Control Commission, and the Party committees of the USSR Supreme Soviet, the USSR KGB, and the USSR Ministry of Internal Affairs all issued similar statements condemning El'tsin's decree, TASS reported. All charged that the decree violated Articles 48 and 51 of the USSR Constitution, Article 48 of the RSFSR Constitution, and Articles 10 and 15 of the law on public associations. The Communists argued that the abolition of

El'tsin Issues Decree Banning Party Organizations from State Agencies

Article 6 of the USSR Constitution had been all that was needed to eliminate the CPSU's right to guide state activities. All requested that constitutional authorities at the all-Union and RSFSR level review the decree for constitutional compliance.

Presidential spokesman Vitalii Ignatenko told reporters in Moscow Gorbachev was concerned that "this decree contains elements of tension and confrontation," Western news agencies reported.

RSFSR Vice President Aleksandr Rutskoi told a news conference that the decree "makes all political parties equal and allows officials to work guided only by the constitution and the law," TASS reported on July 22.

On July 24, USSR Minister of Justice Sergei Lushchikov told Radio Moscow that the decree contained many internal contradictions and ran counter to the Helsinki accords on human and political rights.

The same day, the deputy chairman of the Federation of Independent Trade Unions of Russia, Vasilii Romanov, told TASS he was confident that the trade unions would continue to operate as fully empowered organizations and that he did not think the decree gave employers the right to decide whether trade unions should be formed within their enterprises.

Also on July 24, Novosti reported "the full support" of the Democratic Party of Russia for the decree. Sergei Vvedensky, an aide to the party's leader, Nikolai Travkin, said the party would comply with the decree and dissolve some twenty party committees that currently existed in state enterprises.

Both the Russian Television newscast "Vesti" and Central Television's "TSN" news presented El'tsin's decree on "the departification" of state bodies as the top news story on both July 20 and 21. In sharp contrast, the main forty-minute "Vremya" newscast did not report on the decree on either day. This was not, however, the first time "Vremya" had failed to note a major political event that could displease the CPSU establishment. Late on July 23 "Vremya" finally carried a TASS dispatch on the decree. In the ensuing flurry of reaction, "Vremya" gave coverage only to opponents of the decree without bothering to mention that it also had support.

On July 30, El'tsin was cited by Interfax as saying he had deliberately timed the publication of his decree banning political parties from workplaces in the RSFSR to coincide with the CPSU Central Committee plenum in order to help Gorbachev ward off conservative opposition.

The same day, First Secretary of the Novosibirsk Oblast Party Committee Vladimir Mindolin, one of the architects of the preplenum anti-Gorbachev campaign,

The USSR in July, 1991

told TASS that up to half of the oblast's Party members might leave the Party after El'tsin's decree took effect. A district secretary predicted that two-thirds of the local Communists would quit the Party; neither he nor Mindolin explained why. Mindolin said the Party's task now was to form cells based on profession, age, and other criteria.

Popov and Shevardnadze Call for Centrist Party

At a meeting of members of the Movement for Democratic Reforms, Eduard Shevardnadze and Moscow Mayor Gavriil Popov called for the formation within the movement Democratic Russia of a centrist parliamentary party, TASS reported.

Moscow Workers' Union Holds Congress

A new organization, the Moscow Workers' Union, held a congress, TASS and Radio Moscow reported. Delegates came from approximately 700 Moscow enterprises to establish the statutes of the union. The organization opposed the transition to the market, privatization of state property, and individual ownership of land. It supported neither the RSFSR nor the USSR Supreme Soviet, whose laws, it claimed, did not serve the interests of the working class.

Soldiers' Mothers Appeal to El'tsin

A group representing the All-Union Council of Soldiers' Mothers told Radio Rossii that it had met with RSFSR President Boris El'tsin earlier in the day and asked him to create a commission attached to the RSFSR Prosecutor's Office to investigate violence in army life. A spokeswoman said the group had already had fruitless meetings on the matter with Soviet President Mikhail Gorbachev, USSR Prime Minister Valentin Pavlov, and USSR Defense Minister Dmitrii Yazov. She claimed that, according to official figures provided by the USSR Cabinet of Ministers, some 310,000 Soviet soldiers had suffered noncombat deaths since 1945. She also said that a special commission appointed by Gorbachev in the fall of 1990 had done virtually nothing to investigate this violence.

New Rail Line Opens between China and USSR

Freight service started on a trial basis on the new railroad linking Xinjiang and Kazakhstan, Western agencies reported on July 22. The Xinhua news agency said the new rail link would greatly decrease travel time from the Pacific to Europe, as well as reducing transport costs. Passenger service was due to start in June, 1992, with full freight service beginning later.

Sunday, July 21

El'tsin Praises Gorbachev's Performance at G-7 Summit

El'tsin said that Soviet President Mikhail Gorbachev had fulfilled the mandate of the Soviet republics not to go "cap in hand" to Western leaders. Radio Rossii, reporting on a press conference El'tsin gave in Bishkek, Kirgizia, quoted him as saying the G-7 meeting had in general demonstrated a high degree of maturity in international relations.

El'tsin Signs Agreement with Kirgizia

RSFSR President Boris El'tsin and Kirgiz President Askar Akaev signed a treaty on relations between the two republics in the Kirgiz capital, Bishkek, TASS and Radio Moscow reported. The treaty laid particular stress on the defense of the interests of the large Slav minority in Kirgizia and of Kirgiz in the RSFSR. Akaev said the Kirgiz did not want people of other nationalities to leave their republic. A special feature of the treaty was that it provided for financial aid to Kirgizia.

Maslyukov Arrives in Indonesia

Soviet First Deputy Prime Minister Yurii Maslyukov arrived in Indonesia for an official visit, during which he was scheduled to hold talks on cooperation in technical and commercial spheres. Upon arrival, Maslyukov said the USSR and Indonesia could cooperate in space technology, transportation, communications, electronics, energy, and aviation. Maslyukov reiterated the Soviet Union's interest in setting up a forum to discuss Asian-Pacific security, TASS reported.

Platinum Marketing Talks Reported

The Sunday Telegraph reported that the giant pan-African trading conglomerate Lonrho was sending a team to Moscow to discuss the marketing of platinum. It was thought that Lonrho would like to arrange a platinum-marketing deal similar to the accord De Beers concluded with Moscow in 1990, which gave De Beers exclusive rights to the marketing and sale of Soviet rough diamonds for a period of five years. South Africa and the Soviet Union produce more than 95 percent of the world's platinum.

Demonstrators Demand Novodvorskaya's Release

Several dozen protesters took part in a demonstration demanding the release of Democratic Union leader Valeriya Novodvorskaya and the disbandment of the USSR and RSFSR KGBs, TASS reported. Novodvorskaya was arrested by the KGB on May 16 and accused of calling for the violent change of the Soviet constitutional order.

Russian Democratic Groups Oppose Azerbaijan's Signing Union Treaty

Several democratic groups within the RSFSR Congress of People's Deputies stated their opposition to Azerbaijan's signing the Union treaty on the grounds that "union with a state that widely violates human rights is unacceptable," Interfax reported. The groups proposed a peace treaty between Azerbaijan and Armenia, a stop to the deportations of Armenians from Azerbaijan, and measures to guarantee the rights of minority groups in Azerbaijan, including Russians, as preconditions for Azerbaijan's participation in the new Union treaty.

Congress of Jehovah's Witnesses in USSR

Novosti (July 23) reported that a local congress of Jehovah's Witnesses had taken place on July 20 and 21 in Usole-Sibirskoe in Irkutsk Oblast. The report noted that, until recently, the adherents of this branch of Christianity had been persecuted and the center of their religious organization in Brooklyn branded "a nest of the CIA."

―――――― *Monday, July 22*

El'tsin Creates Presidential Apparatus

RSFSR President Boris El'tsin issued a decree creating three new bodies, all attached to the RSFSR presidency, Radio Rossii reported. The Council of State would serve as an advisory body to the president; Gennadii Burbulis, a member of El'tsin's advisory staff, was appointed its secretary. The Council for Federation Affairs and Territories of the RSFSR would also serve as an advisory body and would examine questions of internal republican economic activity; its secretary was Yurii Skokov. The third body was the Commission for Drafting Proposals on Procedures of the Russian Security Council.

Khasbulatov Studies British Parliamentary System

Ruslan Khasbulatov, acting chairman of the RSFSR Supreme Soviet, began a five-day visit to Britain for talks with British parliamentarians. Khasbulatov's visit was reported to have been arranged to enable him to learn about the British parliamentary system. He was also to meet with trade officials to discuss prospects for trade between Britain and the RSFSR (RFE/RL correspondent's report, July 22).

THE USSR IN JULY, 1991

Colin Powell Visits USSR

Chairman of the US Joint Chiefs of Staff General Colin Powell arrived in Moscow at the start of a nine-day official visit. In a busy first day, Powell met with Soviet Defense Minister Dmitrii Yazov, Chief of the General Staff of the USSR Armed Forces Mikhail Moiseev, and Foreign Minister Aleksandr Bessmertnykh. According to Western and Soviet reports, talks centered on increasing contacts between the Soviet and US Armed Forces, on the START agreement, and on European and regional security.

On July 23, Powell met with Soviet President Mikhail Gorbachev, and the two discussed military conversion. Yazov and Moiseev were also present. Later that day, Powell attended a Soviet military exercise. He reportedly commiserated with Soviet generals over the difficulties of coping with defense budget cuts.

Speaking at a military training center near Moscow on July 25, Powell said that the size of the Soviet Armed Forces remained "much bigger than we think is justified," and he complained that military conversion was progressing more slowly than expected, according to Western reports.

In a joint appearance with Moiseev on ABC television on July 25, Powell said joint military exercises between the Soviet Union and the United States were possible in the near future. Moiseev said US-Soviet military relations were now at their closest since World War II. Powell ended his trip to the Soviet Union on July 28, following his attendance at a Soviet Navy Day celebration in Vladivostok.

Greek Prime Minister Visits USSR, Signs Treaty

Greek Prime Minister Constantine Mitsotakis arrived in Moscow at the start of a five-day visit, TASS reported. He held talks with Soviet President Mikhail Gorbachev on improving bilateral relations. In his dinner speech, Gorbachev highlighted "the old traditions" and "the enduring attraction of our peoples for one another." A bilateral treaty was signed on July 23. Gorbachev raised the Cyprus dispute with Mitsotakis, calling for an international conference to resolve the issue.

At the invitation of the All-Union Public Association of Greeks, Mitsotakis visited the Soviet Greeks in Anapa and Gelendzhik on July 26, "Vremya" reported on July 27. A growing number of Soviet Greeks emigrating to Greece were encountering difficulties because of their ignorance of Greek and lack of housing and jobs. Mitsotakis said that Soviet Greeks would receive concrete assistance in the near future. He discussed the possibility of strengthening economic ties and creating joint enterprises in areas where there were concentrations of Soviet Greeks, "Vremya" added.

The USSR in July, 1991

Talks on Compensation for Soviet Victims of Nazism

Germany and the Soviet Union began official negotiations in Bonn on the question of compensation for Soviet citizens who were victims of Nazism. German government spokesman Dieter Vogel told Berlin television that the amount paid to Soviet victims would not be as high as the amount received by Israel (an estimated 100 billion marks over the past four decades), Western agencies reported.

Shevardnadze Interview in *Le Figaro*

Former USSR Foreign Minister Eduard Shevardnadze gave a wide-ranging interview to *Le Figaro*'s Moscow correspondent. Concerning the new Movement for Democratic Reforms, of which he was a founder, Shevardnadze predicted that the movement would probably encompass several parties that would keep their autonomy.

Asked about criticism of his performance as foreign minister, particularly his role in German unification, Shevardnadze told *Le Figaro* that, given his time again, he would not do things differently. About "the German affair," Shevardnadze said: "We knew it would happen. But, in fact, the acceleration of the process was spontaneous . . . . Nothing was decided in Moscow." In response to a question about the genesis of "the new thinking," Shevardnadze said that, at the time of the invasion of Afghanistan, he and Gorbachev had agreed that it was necessary to change everything. He maintained that he and Gorbachev had learned about the invasion from the radio.

Regarding the G-7 summit, Shevardnadze said, "It is not a matter of asking for credits but of organizing our cooperation with the West." He stressed that the USSR must "create favorable conditions for foreign investment: it is the only way to accelerate our transition to the market, and we have no other path."

Patriarch Aleksii Interviewed by *Der Spiegel*

In an interview in *Der Spiegel*, Patriarch Aleksii II warned that the process of Westernizing the Soviet way of life had little to do with either humanization or Christianization. The patriarch discussed relations with the Vatican and expressed the view that, for the approximately 200 Catholics living in Novosibirsk, a parish would suffice; the pope had assigned an archbishop to the city. The patriarch speculated that Catholic missionary work was planned among the Russian Orthodox population, and he said that this would seriously impair relations between the Moscow Patriarchate and the Vatican.

Latvian Elected Vice President of Lutheran World Federation

Karlis Gailitis, archbishop of the Evangelical Lutheran Church of Latvia, was elected one of seven vice presidents of the Lutheran World Federation. This, according to *Diena*, was the first time a Lutheran Church leader from Eastern Europe had been elected to such a high position in the federation.

Communist Party of Ukraine Registered

The Communist Party of Ukraine was officially registered, Ukrinform-TASS reported. With a membership of 2.7 million, it became the fifth political party in the republic to be given legal status.

Draft Crimean Constitution Considered

A draft of a new constitution for the Crimean ASSR was adopted by its Supreme Soviet, Ukrinform-TASS reported. The question of the peninsula's name would be decided by a referendum. The deputies decided against a presidential form of government and proposed that Russian be the official language and that citizenship of the Crimean republic be established. The new constitution was not subject to ratification by the Ukrainian Supreme Soviet.

Poland Signs Agreement with Kaliningrad Oblast

An unprecedented treaty of economic cooperation between an oblast of the RSFSR and a foreign state was signed in Kaliningrad, Radio Moscow reported on July 23. The agreement—between Kaliningrad Oblast and Poland—provided for the creation of joint enterprises, the restoration of the prewar Königsberg-Berlin railway line, and the opening of customs posts on the frontier.

Tuesday, July 23

Talks on Union Treaty; Surprise over Armenian Participation

Soviet President Mikhail Gorbachev and republican leaders met again in Novo-Ogarevo to discuss the Union treaty. Early on July 24, Gorbachev said that Armenia was preparing to sign the new Union treaty, Western agencies reported. Gorbachev also said that he hoped Moldavia would come to the same decision. The attendance of Chairman of the Armenian Supreme Soviet Levon Ter-Petrossyan at the meeting was a surprise, since only a couple of days earlier it had been reported that the presidium of the Armenian Supreme Soviet had decided he should not attend.

In implicit contradiction to Gorbachev's assertion that Armenia was preparing to sign the Union treaty, Western agencies quoted the Armenian permanent representative in Moscow, Feliks Mamikonyan, as stating later that day that Ter-Petrossyan had attended the Novo-Ogarevo meeting "as an observer" to take part in political consultations and that Armenia's stance on the Union treaty would be decided by means of the referendum on secession scheduled for September 21.

Ter-Petrossyan himself told *Le Monde* on July 25 that Armenia had not agreed to sign the Union treaty and that the referendum scheduled for September 21 would prove that the Armenian people favored secession. Ter-Petrossyan confirmed that he had attended the Novo-Ogarevo meeting "as an observer" and complained that Moscow was violating Soviet law by imposing trade restrictions on those republics that wished to secede.

Nazarbaev on Union Treaty

"Vesti" augmented its report on the Novo-Ogarevo meeting with an interview with Kazakh President Nursultan Nazarbaev. Nazarbaev told "Vesti" the negotiations had not been easy, since participants had suddenly been burdened with as many as three alternative drafts of the Union treaty written by various central bodies. The participants put them aside, however, and concentrated on their original draft, he added. If the center continued to interfere in the Novo-Ogarevo process, Nazarbaev warned, republican leaders would meet in Alma-Ata to discuss the Union treaty among themselves. They could save Soviet President Mikhail Gorbachev [from his conservative opponents] without his actually being present, Nazarbaev continued, adding that the leaders needed Gorbachev and supported him but would not tolerate any tricks.

USSR Seeks Full Membership of IMF

Western agencies reported that the Soviet Union had applied for full membership of the International Monetary Fund, the International Bank for Reconstruction and Development, the International Development Association, and the International Finance Corporation. According to *The New York Times*, the letter of application was dated July 15—i.e., before Soviet President Mikhail Gorbachev's meeting with the G-7 leaders—but was delivered only on July 22 and its receipt made public on July 23. The application for full membership did not exclude the granting of "special associate" status, as was recommended by the G-7 summit.

Yavlinsky Speaks Out

Economist Grigorii Yavlinsky, whose draft economic reform plan was difficult to discern in Gorbachev's presentation to the G-7 summit, confirmed in an interview with the *Financial Times* that he had stayed away from London because he could not support the official Soviet reform plan. He told the *Financial Times* that Western countries should not give aid to the USSR as long as the government continued to adhere to the present anticrisis program. In his view, USSR Prime Minister Valentin Pavlov and First Deputy Prime Minister Vladimir Shcherbakov "are still thinking with the mentality of the 1970s."

Hard-liners Call for Patriotic Front

Twelve ultraconservatives issued an appeal in *Sovetskaya Rossiya* calling for the creation of a national-patriotic movement to "save the homeland." According to TASS and Western reports, the signatories of "A Word to the People" included Yurii Bondarev, Boris Gromov, Valentin Rasputin, Valentin Varennikov, and Yurii Blokhin. "We are convinced, the manifesto said, "that the army and the navy will prevent fratricidal war and the destruction of the motherland and will be a safe guarantee of security." The manifesto also argued that the Communist Party was being destroyed by its own leaders.

El'tsin Gets Support on Stance against Federal Taxes

RSFSR President Boris El'tsin met with the leaders of the RSFSR's autonomous republics and won their support for a "one-channel" tax system whereby all taxes would be paid into the republican budget, Radio Rossii reported. Tatarstan had recently refused to pay taxes to the RSFSR, because the RSFSR was not making its obligatory payments to the federal budget. The center could therefore not finance the all-Union enterprises in Tatarstan, which made up some 80 percent of the republic's economy. The rest of the RSFSR's autonomous republics, however, seemed to think they would have more control over their economies if they paid all taxes to the RSFSR Ministry of Finance, which would then transfer a predetermined amount to the all-Union budget.

US Points to Violations of INF Treaty

The US State Department demanded that the Soviet Union "account fully" for intermediate-range nuclear missiles that may still be located in Eastern Europe, Western news agencies reported. The United States contended that Moscow had not disclosed the deployment of SS-23 missiles in East Germany, Czechoslovakia, and Bulgaria, although it should have done so to comply with the INF treaty of 1987.

Soviet Foreign Ministry spokesman Vitalii Churkin denied charges that Moscow had in any way violated the

THE USSR IN JULY, 1991

INF treaty, Western agencies reported on July 24. Churkin told reporters that SS-23 missiles located in Czechoslovakia, East Germany, and Bulgaria were owned by those countries and that they did not fall under the 1987 treaty. Churkin also accused the West of using Cold War tactics by bringing up the issue just as a treaty on long-range missiles was about to be signed.

On July 26, *Izvestia* carried a commentary on the question of Soviet violations of the INF treaty. Noting that German Chancellor Helmut Kohl and Czechoslovak President Vaclav Havel had provided the United States with information about SS-23 missile transfers, *Izvestia* lamented: "Things are serious. . . . They could hardly be more serious." The report went on to stress that "many specialists agree that creating a verification system that would provide a 100-percent guarantee of the punctilious observance of such agreements is practically impossible." It concluded that, in the light of the recent conclusion of the Conventional Forces in Europe Treaty and the approaching settlement of START, "now is not the time to be getting engaged in wrangling and morbidly suspicious recriminations."

Soviet TV Portrays Yugoslav Crisis as Warning to USSR

A Central Television report portrayed the Yugoslav crisis as a warning of what could happen in the USSR. The report laid heavy blame on Western countries for "encouraging separatist tendencies" through "inflammatory policies." The report said the Yugoslav crisis was rooted in "conditions of a prolonged, bitter political struggle against the center [whereby] the republics achieved a considerable expansion of their powers, which . . . led to a growth in national egoism and separatism." Austria, Hungary, Italy, and Albania were named as countries that had pursued misguided policies. The report congratulated the USSR for its efforts to calm the situation, saying Moscow had "temporarily succeeded in taking the heat out of the crisis."

Soviet Barter Agreement with Poland

The Soviet Union and Poland agreed on a 325-million-dollar barter agreement whereby Poland would supply the Soviet Union with medicines in exchange for Soviet oil and natural gas, Western agencies reported on July 24.

Moscow Party Committee Losing Members

First Secretary of the Moscow City Party Committee Yurii Prokof'ev said the city Party organization had 870,000 members. Prokof'ev told Central Television that 200,000 members had left the Party in 1990 and that 90,000 had left so far in 1991. Forty-seven percent of those who turned in their Party cards were workers, 33 percent were classed as members of the intelligentsia, and 17 percent were pensioners. So far, 9,500 people, most of whom Prokof'ev said were under thirty-five, had joined the Moscow city Party organization in 1991.

Agreement in Principle on Copyright Law

The Journal of Commerce reported that US and Soviet officials had reached agreement in principle on changes in the Soviet copyright law. Among US objections to the original Soviet law, passed on May 31, were its lack of criminal penalties and its failure to regulate the use of videotapes played for public audiences. The agreement in principle increased the chances that the US-Soviet trade agreement would soon be sent to Capitol Hill. Once this had been approved, the way would be clear for the United States to grant most-favored-nation trading status to the Soviet Union.

Workers' Errors Cause Shutdowns of Nuclear Power Plants

Trud reported that mistakes by workers at Soviet nuclear power plants were to blame in many cases for temporary shutdowns of the power stations. According to a TASS summary of the article, twenty out of fifty-nine recent shutdowns were caused by human error. *Trud* said that, in the first half of 1991, Soviet nuclear power plants were utilized at only 67 percent of their capacity. The report quoted Anatolii Mazalov, chief of supervision of the Soviet nuclear industry, as saying that nuclear plant personnel were applying safety measures incorrectly in operating the reactors.

New International Association Created in Uzbekistan

TASS reported that Uzbeks living abroad who took part in a recent conference of foreign businessmen and their Soviet counterparts in Tashkent had set up an international association, "El." Its aim was to develop cultural and economic cooperation between Soviet Uzbeks and Uzbeks abroad. Its main emphasis would be on boosting the economy by attracting foreign investment, creating joint enterprises, and holding charity events for the benefit of Uzbekistan.

Wednesday, July 24

Democrats Support Gorbachev

"Vesti" quoted RSFSR Vice President Aleksandr Rutskoi as saying that Soviet democratic movements "will stick up

The USSR in July, 1991

for Gorbachev." In turn, RSFSR President Boris El'tsin told "Vesti" that his decree on "departification" had not damaged his relations with the CPSU general secretary and that the two leaders had achieved consensus in Novo-Ogarevo. The reports indicated that, in sharp contrast to the militantly anti-Gorbachev mood that prevailed among democrats earlier in the year, El'tsin's supporters were now having something of a honeymoon with the USSR president.

Committee for Constitutional Supervision Considers "Departification" Decree

Chairman of the USSR Supreme Soviet Anatolii Luk'yanov, responding to numerous requests, instructed the USSR Committee for Constitutional Supervision to examine RSFSR President Boris El'tsin's decree on banning political parties from state organizations in order to determine whether it conflicted with the USSR and RSFSR Constitutions, the USSR law on public associations, the USSR law on trade unions, and various other laws and international agreements, TASS reported.

On July 27, Sergei Alekseev, chairman of the USSR Committee for Constitutional Supervision, told a Moscow press conference that the committee had appealed to El'tsin to suspend implementation of his decree of July 20 on "departification" until the committee had completed its review, Radio Moscow reported. At the CPSU Central Committee plenum, a resolution calling the decree "an illegal act" was adopted (*TASS*, July 26). Meanwhile, the RSFSR Council of Ministers issued a statement declaring that El'tsin's decree complied fully with all constitutional norms and USSR and RSFSR laws, TASS reported.

At the press conference, Alekseev hinted strongly that the committee would not declare the decree null and void. Changes in Article 6 of the USSR Constitution (which cleared the way for a multiparty system in the USSR) made it necessary to "deideologize" or to "departify" certain state offices, Alekseev said, adding that his committee had already been "departified," since its members had decided to refrain from establishing a primary Party cell ("Vremya," *Central Television*, July 27). "We shall probably find an unusual way out," Alekseev said. Meanwhile, Soviet President Mikhail Gorbachev told the CPSU Central Committee plenum that he would nullify El'tsin's decree with a presidential decree only if the Committee for Constitutional Supervision ruled El'tsin's decree illegal.

Cabinet of Ministers Rejects Draft Law on Consumer Budget

The USSR Cabinet of Ministers discussed the draft law on a minimum consumer budget or "consumer basket," "Vremya" reported. The draft valued the basket for one person at 210 rubles a month, including 113 rubles for foodstuffs, 24 rubles for consumer services, and 62 rubles for clothing, medicines, and other goods. The consumer basket would be used as the basis for setting minimum wages, stipends, pensions, and other transfer payments. It was to be adjusted once a year. The draft was rejected apparently because retail prices were changing too quickly for any specific norms to be established.

USSR to Sell Part of Volga Auto Plant

The USSR was reported to be looking for a way to sell part of its Volga auto plant to foreign investors, according to Western reports. *The New York Times* cited Soviet reports as saying that the USSR would like to sell at least 30 percent of the plant and had hired a Wall Street firm to help with the deal, which could total over a billion dollars.

Western reports of Soviet radio broadcasts on July 25 noted that workers in the Volga auto factory wanted shares in the company if it were privatized. The workers also want to be involved in direct talks with the relevant Soviet and foreign authorities. Some reports said that 30–40 percent of the factory would be sold to Fiat, some 20 percent retained by the Soviet state, and the remainder sold to VAZ workers. The plant made about 750,000 of the 1.3 million autos built in the USSR each year.

Japanese Loan Extended

Japan's Ministry of International Trade and Industry would underwrite 200 million dollars of a 350-million-dollar bridging loan to the USSR that would be provided by Japanese commercial banks, Western agencies reported. The bridging loan would be used to refinance part of the outstanding Soviet trade debt of some 500 million dollars to Japanese companies.

Yazov Addresses CPSU Commission

The CPSU Central Committee Commission for Military Policy met in Moscow to discuss conversion of military industries, Novosti reported. The meeting was addressed by Defense Minister Dmitrii Yazov, who focused on cuts in Soviet military forces. Yazov said that the unilateral force reduction announced by Soviet President Mikhail Gorbachev in December, 1988, was complete. He also claimed that over the past three years the Soviet Union had cut its tanks by 44 percent, rockets by 33 percent, planes by 38 percent, and submarine-based ballistic missiles by 54 percent. The report provided no specifics on these figures.

The USSR in July, 1991

Ukrainian Volunteers to Fight for Slovenia and Croatia

The Zagreb newspaper *Vecernji list* reported that fifty volunteers had come forward in Kiev "to defend with arms the independence of Slovenia and Croatia." The initiator of this display of Ukrainian solidarity with the two republics was named as reserve army Captain Vladimir Filatov. The newspaper cited as its sources Tanjug and *Moscow News*.

Northeastern Estonia Wants Special Status

The mayors of northeastern Estonia's three major cities were calling for the Estonian government and Supreme Council to grant the region special status, *Paevaleht* reported. The mayors of Kohtla-Jarve, Sillamae, and Narva made the demand in a memorandum sent to Prime Minister Edgar Savisaar and Supreme Council President Arnold Ruutel. The memorandum said that conflicts between the region and the republic might become insoluble if talks did not take place, and it pointed out that, in the all-Union referendum, the people of the region had voted to stay in the USSR. The demand came in the midst of an escalating crisis in Narva over the economic border.

Thursday, July 25

CPSU Central Committee Plenum Opens

The CPSU Central Committee began a plenary session to discuss the draft Party program. General Secretary Mikhail Gorbachev delivered the opening address, after which twenty-seven people spoke. According to TASS, the majority supported the draft program (*Nezavisimaya gazeta* published some excerpts from and an analysis of the CPSU's draft program on July 22.)

Gorbachev dwelt at length on the USSR's economic backwardness and ascribed the primary cause to the Party's ideological rejection of the market. After reviewing the benefits of the market as an economic tool, Gorbachev proclaimed that "socialism and the market are not only linked, they are indivisible." On ideology, Gorbachev said one of the main achievements of the new Party program was its "decisive break with obsolete dogmatism and stereotypes." The Party should draw on "all the riches of our country's and the world's Socialist and democratic thought," he said. With regard to the CPSU, Gorbachev reported that in eighteen months the Party had lost 4.2 million members, only 2–3 percent of whom had joined some other political group. He criticized both the Bolshevik Platform and the Communist Initiative Movement and mentioned plans to form "an alternative democratic Russian Communist Party." He advised all the CPSU's factions to reexamine their positions and cautioned that Party periodicals that "discredit the Party day in, day out" can hardly be considered Party publications.

Gorbachev spoke in favor of convoking an extraordinary Party congress in November or December, 1991, in response to the many calls from Party organizations for such a congress. The declared purpose would be to adopt the final version of the Party Program. USSR Minister of Information Mikhail Nenashev observed that an extraordinary congress would solve nothing by adopting a program so general that most CPSU members could support it, while the leader of the Marxist Platform, Aleksandr Buzgalin, observed that the only change it would bring would be a switch from "bureaucratic politics under the rubric of communism to bureaucratic politics under the rubric of social democracy."

Commenting on the plenum proceedings, Central Committee member Otto Latsis, the deputy editor of *Kommunist*, told TASS that the discussion had been heated and that Gorbachev clearly did not have the full support of the Central Committee. Nikolai Stolyarov, head of the RSFSR CP Central Control Commission, predicted, however, that the program would be adopted by a majority and reported that no one had called for Gorbachev's resignation. The president of the USSR Union of Leaseholders and Entrepreneurs, Pavel Bunich, said Gorbachev had the Central Committee well in hand, noting that even Yurii Prokof'ev, first secretary of the Moscow City Party Committee, had adopted a more conciliatory position. Leningrad Party leader Boris Gidaspov expressed surprise at the calmness with which the plenum was proceeding.

Nearly every speaker commented on El'tsin's "departification" decree, and the agenda was amended to include discussion of a Central Committee resolution on the decree. Gorbachev said the decree "could destroy the consensus only now beginning to take shape" and added: "Nobody has the right to forbid the Party to work with the collectives." He also voiced his support for the review of the decree being conducted by the USSR Constitutional Supervision Committee.

On July 26, the Central Committee gave its preliminary approval to the draft Party program. Some amendments would be made prior to publication for debate, and another plenum was scheduled to be held in September to review the program before the Party congress. The problem areas included the Party's stance on property and on the all-Union and republican Party structure.

The USSR in July, 1991

Before the plenum ended, Vladimir Kalashnikov and Ivan Mel'nikov were elected to the Secretariat.

Chernavin Announces Fleet Cuts

Admiral Vladimir Chernavin, commander in chief of the Soviet navy, announced that the Soviet fleet would be cut by 20–25 percent by the year 2000, according to TASS and the *Los Angeles Times*. His comments came in anticipation of Soviet Navy Day and during US General Colin Powell's stay in Moscow. Chernavin said the fleet would maintain its combat capabilities "thanks to the qualitative renewal of all branches of the service." The cuts reflected a decision to decommission older vessels, and Chernavin said the latest Soviet ships, including the Typhoon-class guided missile submarines, the third-generation attack submarines, the Kirov-class cruisers, and the Sovremennyi-class destroyers would form the basis of the new fleet.

Moiseev Calls for CFE Ratification

During a joint press conference with visiting US General Colin Powell, Chief of the General Staff of the Soviet Armed Forces Mikhail Moiseev denied rumors that the Conventional Forces in Europe Treaty would run into opposition when considered for ratification by the USSR Supreme Soviet, TASS reported. Moiseev said the treaty did not favor the West, as some Soviet critics had charged, and that in fact it was fully consistent with Soviet military doctrine and allowed Moscow sufficient forces to guarantee national security. Moiseev also claimed that he had received a similar evaluation from the USSR Supreme Soviet Committee for Defense and Security. He predicted that ratification would come at the next Supreme Soviet session.

Commodities Exchange Reopens in Riga

After fifty years of inactivity, the commodities exchange resumed operations in Riga. On offer were more than 700 types of commodities, worth about 250 million rubles, from various parts of the USSR. On the first day, some 100 contracts worth about 11 million rubles were signed (*Radio Riga*, July 25).

Military Cutbacks in Vietnam to Continue

Rashid Khamidoulin, the Soviet ambassador to Vietnam, told reporters in Hanoi that the USSR would proceed with cutbacks at the Soviet base at Cam Ranh Bay announced in 1990, Western agencies reported. He did not, however, give a timetable for the withdrawal of Soviet forces from Vietnam. In other remarks, Khamidoulin said the USSR supported Vietnamese rapprochement with the

Association of Southeast Asian Nations (ASEAN) and the United States, although he complained that the United States was "too slow in . . . normalizing relations with Vietnam." He doubted that any concrete moves towards warmer relations between Vietnam and ASEAN would come in the near future, despite the ASEAN foreign ministers' proposal the previous week for regional cooperation with Vietnam, Cambodia, and Laos.

Kaganovich Dies

The last of the "Old Bolsheviks," Lazar Kaganovich, died in Moscow at the age of ninety-eight, Western agencies reported on July 26. Kaganovich rose through Bolshevik ranks to become one of Stalin's closest associates and oversaw the brutal policy of forced collectivization during the 1930s. He was dropped from the CPSU Central Committee in 1957 after an abortive attempt to depose Khrushchev and was expelled from the Party in 1962.

Kaganovich may have missed a political comeback: on July 29, Radio Rossii broadcast a session of the second congress of the Stalinist movement "Edinstvo" held in Minsk on July 13 and 14 at which a delegate suggested that Kaganovich be elected honorary president of the movement.

Lithuanian Land Reform Law Passed

The Lithuanian Supreme Council passed a law on land reform in Lithuania and a resolution implementing it, Radio Independent Lithuania reported. The law, to go into effect no later than November 1, provided for two types of ownership, private and state, but did not include a third type, collective, that the left wing had advocated.

RSFSR and Uzbek Justice Ministers Sign Agreement

The RSFSR and Uzbek ministers of justice signed an agreement on mutual legal assistance and the exchange of information, Russian Television reported. This was the first agreement of its kind. The RSFSR planned to sign similar agreements soon with other republics.

Cheboksary Steelworkers on Strike

Some steelworkers at the Cheboksary Aggregate Plant in Chuvashia went on strike demanding a two- to three-fold increase in their wages, TASS reported. On the eve of the strike, the management agreed to double the workers' wages, but the strike went ahead nonetheless.

The strike was halted on July 26 for two months by an order of the republican authorities, TASS reported. The order was issued on the grounds that the plant's output was important for agriculture.

The USSR in July, 1991

Friday, July 26

Gorbachev Adviser Says El'tsin Agrees to Federal Taxes

Soviet President Mikhail Gorbachev's senior adviser on nationalities affairs, Grigorii Revenko, said RSFSR President Boris El'tsin had agreed to a federal taxation system, the *Financial Times* reported on July 27. Revenko said El'tsin had approved a long-debated compromise on taxation during talks on July 25. Under the agreement, a fixed percentage of revenues from the taxation of enterprises in the republics would go to the federal government. Revenko added, though, that the percentage going to the federal budget had not yet been fixed and that it had yet to be decided who would collect the taxes. Revenko forecast that the Union treaty could be signed in the fall.

Japanese White Paper on Soviet Military Threat

In its annual report on the status of the Soviet military threat, the Japanese Defense Agency said that Soviet forces in East Asia remained formidable but that the Soviet Union would now find it difficult to stage aggressive action against other countries because of its domestic situation. The report made no mention of a potential Soviet threat to Asia but did argue that the political-military situation in Asia was "much more complicated" than in Europe. The report noted further that the USSR had deployed its most modern military equipment in the Asian region, Western news agencies reported.

Tajikistan and Kirgizia Try to Solve Land Dispute

TASS reported that Tajikistan and Kirgizia were making a new attempt to resolve a long-standing dispute between villages on their common border over land and water. The dispute erupted into violent clashes in 1989. TASS said the two republics were launching land and river reclamation work to counter environmental degradation that had caused a decline in living standards in the region. According to the report, the two republics recently concluded an agreement on water use in the border area.

Saturday, July 27

Yakovlev on Movement for Democratic Reforms and CPSU

At a press conference of the Movement for Democratic Reforms, Aleksandr Yakovlev said he supported RSFSR President Boris El'tsin's decree on "departification." Yakovlev said that he did not approve of the new draft Party program, because it was not radical enough, but that he had nevertheless not yet quit the CPSU. Yakovlev also revealed that the Movement for Democratic Reforms intended to become a political party at its founding congress in September. This party, Yakovlev explained, would be based on a philosophy completely different from that of the CPSU. "The ideology that has ruled in our country," Yakovlev said, "has taught us to mistrust each other, to suspect each other, and, on occasions, to inform on each other." In order to live in a truly lawful, democratic society, Soviet people must adopt an entirely different morality, he added ("TSN," *Central Television*, and Western news agencies).

Admiral Sees Western Naval Threat

In an interview in *Sovetskaya Rossiya* marking Soviet Navy Day, Admiral Konstantin Makarov warned that the USSR faced an increasing threat from Western naval forces and sea-based missiles, which, he said, more than offset any gains from arms reduction treaties. According to TASS and Western reports, the deputy commander of the Soviet Navy said that "the massive deployment" of sea-based cruise missiles by Western navies had nearly doubled the threat to Soviet security. His remarks, coming only days before the signing of the START treaty in Moscow, reflected the Soviet military leadership's dissatisfaction over the failure to negotiate cuts in naval forces.

Tajikistan to Have Own Agricultural Academy

TASS said Tajik President Kakhar Makhkamov had signed a decree on the creation of a republican Academy of Agricultural Sciences. It would be headed by Akbar Maksumov, an academician of the all-Union Academy of Agricultural Sciences, who had been a vocal opponent of cotton monoculture and the submission of Central Asian agriculture to Moscow's dictates. Other Central Asian republics had also set up their own agricultural academies, seeing this as an important step in gaining control over agricultural policy.

"Birlik" on Democracy in Uzbekistan

In an interview with *Komsomol'skaya pravda*, two leaders of the Uzbek Popular Front, "Birlik," Abdurrakhim Pulatov and Pulat Akhunov, said that, despite their long-term goal of independence for Uzbekistan, they believed it should remain part of the USSR for now because the republic had a better chance of absorbing democracy from the rest of the country. If Uzbekistan were independent, the present corrupt and conservative leadership would remain in control, they said. Pulatov and Akhunov traveled to Moscow to be interviewed after a *Komsomol'skaya pravda* correspondent was expelled from Uzbekistan in June for trying to interview them there.

On July 30, Radio Mayak reported that the Presidium of the Uzbek Supreme Soviet had accused *Komsomol'skaya pravda* of contributing to the destabilization of the republic by publishing an article claiming that publicist and Supreme Soviet deputy Erkin Vahidov had been the target of an assassination attempt. The authorities in Uzbekistan were angry at the progressive daily for claiming that the head of the Muslim Religious Board for Central Asia had been dislodged from his post. An attempt was made to remove him, but it was unsuccessful.

Belorussian Sovereignty Day

The first anniversary of Belorussia's declaration of state sovereignty was celebrated in a way reminiscent of the Brezhnev era, according to Radio Rossii. Raion Party secretaries and token representatives of society were invited to attend an official ceremony, the high point of which was a speech by the unpopular Supreme Soviet chairman, Nikolai Dementei. Opposition leader Zyanon Paznyak complained to Radio Rossii that nothing had changed in Belorussia in the year since sovereignty was declared. He said the republic had the most reactionary leadership in the country.

Auction of Moscow Residence Permits

The *Los Angeles Times* of July 28 provided a description of Moscow's first auction of residence permits. Two out-of-towners acquired permits for 1.5 million rubles apiece. A bystander noted it would have been cheaper for the bidders to pay the going rate of 30,000 rubles for a marriage of convenience to a Moscow woman.

Sunday, July 28

OMON Attacks Resume in Lithuania

The Salociai customs post on the Lithuanian border with Latvia suffered two attacks, Radio Independent Lithuania reported. In the first incident, five gunmen attacked the post at 1:00 A.M. stealing the Lithuanian guards' money and some radio equipment. After setting fire to one of the post's customs booths, the men fled in a car identified by the customs officers as one used by special MVD troops (OMON) in the past. More than a dozen OMON troops attacked the post again at 2:10 P.M., stealing Lithuanian uniforms and more money, and destroyed a second booth with hand grenades. The two attacks brought to twenty-five the total number of border incidents in Lithuania instigated by OMON.

On July 29, the Lithuanian government called on the USSR to take "decisive measures to halt the illegal actions of OMON divisions on Lithuanian territory," Radio Independent Lithuania reported on July 30. The statement demanded that the USSR either disband the OMON units or withdraw them from Lithuania.

Soviet and US Polls Focus on Economic Issues

The results of two separate polls conducted in the USSR and the United States were written up in *The New York Times* and the *Los Angeles Times*. The Soviet poll, held in April and May under the auspices of the Institute of Sociology of the USSR Academy of Sciences, showed a majority opposed to the private ownership of basic industries. Farming was the only one of thirteen economic activities that most respondents agreed should be "mainly run privately." In the Gallup poll, most Americans interviewed from July 18 to 21 felt that Soviet economic problems were "very serious" and that Gorbachev's efforts at reform would fail; most were opposed to outright grants to the USSR.

Zaslavsky Appointed Adviser to Popov

A prominent member of Democratic Russia, former Chairman of the Oktyabr'sky Raion Soviet Il'ya Zaslavsky, was reported to have become an adviser to Moscow Mayor Gavriil Popov ("Avtorskoe televidenie," *Central Television*, July 28).

Monday, July 29

START Treaty Initialed

After nine years of negotiations, the US-Soviet treaty limiting strategic weapons was initialed in Geneva, paving the way for Presidents George Bush and Mikhail Gorbachev to sign it at their summit meeting in Moscow.

Generals Back START

A first deputy chief of the General Staff of the Soviet Armed Forces, Colonel General Bronislav Omelichev, told TASS that the START agreement would lower the level of confrontation between the United States and the USSR, strengthen strategic stability, and improve the military-political situation in Europe. Chief of the General Staff Mikhail Moiseev, who participated in the START negotiations, had spoken of the treaty in similar terms.

The USSR in July, 1991

Bessmertnykh and Baker Discuss New Arms Agreements

With the START treaty not yet signed, Soviet Foreign Minister Aleksandr Bessmertnykh said that he and US Secretary of State James Baker had already begun to talk about new agreements on limiting weapons. In an interview with Novosti, Bessmertnykh said the two had talked about pursuing a continuous process of arms control. Among the issues they touched upon were the reduction of conventional arms in Europe, the US "Open Skies" proposal, the limitation of nuclear testing, and the nonproliferation of missiles and missile technology.

Lithuania and RSFSR Sign Treaty

Lithuanian Supreme Council President Vytautas Landsbergis met in Moscow with RSFSR President Boris El'tsin to sign a treaty regulating Lithuanian-RSFSR relations, Radio Independent Lithuania reported. The treaty stated that Lithuania and the RSFSR recognized each other as "sovereign states," specifically mentioning the Lithuanian independence declaration of March 11, 1990. Two other documents were also signed, one on the establishment of representative offices in the two countries' capitals and another guaranteeing the RSFSR access to Kaliningrad Oblast. Under one of the treaty's provisions, recent immigrants to Lithuania from the RSFSR previously ineligible for local citizenship would be able to apply for it and thus be enabled to participate in the privatization process. During a press conference following the signing, Landsbergis urged other states to follow the RSFSR's example and said he hoped the USSR would "start real negotiations with Lithuania." El'tsin said the treaty had "great historical significance."

Germany Displeased with Pace of Soviet Troop Withdrawal

According to an internal report of the German Defense Ministry, excerpts from which were published in *Die Welt*, Bonn was disappointed with the slow pace of the Soviet troop withdrawal and with efforts by the Soviet Armed Forces to use the withdrawal to fight their own domestic battles. Specifically, the report lamented attempts by Soviet military officials to blame the slow pace of the withdrawal on the absence of housing for returning soldiers. The report claimed that Bonn had made it clear to the Soviet side that agreements between the USSR and Germany were binding.

Higher Fees for Passports and Visas

With retroactive effect to July 1, many of the fees for issuing passports and a variety of visas and citizenship papers for Soviet citizens and foreigners were raised, TASS reported. The fee for a Soviet passport for foreign travel was increased to 1,000 rubles (i.e., by a factor of five). The charge for the acquisition or relinquishment of Soviet citizenship rose to 500 rubles. Foreign visitors would in future have to pay 100 rubles for tourist visas. According to Western agencies, details of the new charges appeared in *Izvestia*.

Congress of Officers of Ukraine Ends

A congress of officers of Ukraine, which took place in Kiev over the weekend, was attended by approximately 320 people, half of whom were reserve officers, according to TASS. In addition to discussing the idea of a Ukrainian national army and the general political situation in the republic, participants sharply criticized the CPSU, the Union treaty, and the Soviet army, which was termed an "occupation" force serving "imperial ends." The congress voted to create a committee of Ukrainian officers. In *Novoe vremya* (No. 26), a member of the Republican Party estimated that Ukraine would save 70 billion rubles a year by maintaining its own professional army of 300,000 men or fewer.

Estonia Sets Own Ruble Rate

Estonia set its own ruble exchange rate at 33 rubles to the dollar, Radio Moscow reported. The internal exchange rate, which in effect devalued the currency within Estonia, was intended to attract a greater share of the Soviet export transit business to its ports. The official Soviet exchange rate was just over 27 rubles to the dollar for foreign transactions.

Suspected Outbreak of Meningitis in Soviet Far East

TASS quoted doctors in Komsomol'sk-on-Amur in the Soviet Far East as saying they suspected that meningitis was to blame for the hospitalization of about 100 children in the city. The doctors said they believed poor-quality drinking water had caused the outbreak of illness among children at several kindergartens. According to TASS, Komsomol'sk-on-Amur suffers from a chronic lack of drinking water and an inadequate water purification system.

Joint-Stock Company to Build Power Plant in Kazakhstan

TASS reported that a joint-stock company had been established to build a hydroelectric station to provide power for agriculture in the Alma-Ata region after the Kazakh Ministry of Power and Electrification said that it had no money to finance the project. According to the report, half of the new company's capital was being supplied by local food-processing enterprises. This

The USSR in July, 1991

appeared to be the first new enterprise to be established under the law on privatization adopted by the Kazakh Supreme Soviet in June.

Apple to Enter Soviet Computer Market

The US computer company Apple planned to enter the personal computer market in the USSR, Western news agencies reported. Apple's director, Greg Borovsky, said that, as of October, the company would be offering a Russian-language Macintosh PC at a base price of around 1,050 dollars. (This was about the same price as a similar model sold in the United States; Apple planned to charge hard currency for its products sold in the USSR.) Borovsky also said Apple planned to launch a massive advertising campaign. The main pitch would be to Soviet newspaper publishers. Borovsky said even *Pravda* had expressed interest in buying Apple computers.

Tuesday, July 30

Summit Opens

US President George Bush and Soviet President Mikhail Gorbachev began a two-day summit meeting in Moscow, RFE/RL's correspondent in Moscow reported. In welcoming Bush to the Kremlin, Gorbachev said, "A great deal in world politics will continue to depend on how the Soviet Union and the United States interact with each other. For the first time ever, our two countries have a chance to build their relations on the natural basis of universal human values and national interests. We are beginning to realize that we need each other, that the security, internal stability, and dynamic development of each of our two countries benefits both of them."

The first day of talks between Bush and Gorbachev yielded few surprises. Both presidents were upbeat about "the new age" in US-Soviet relations. Economic concerns appeared to have predominated in the talks. In a speech at a Kremlin banquet, Gorbachev appealed for still more economic assistance for the USSR. On July 31, Bush told a group of Soviet and US businessmen that the United States wanted to expand economic cooperation with the USSR (*TASS* and Western agencies, July 30 and 31).

On July 31, Bush and Gorbachev wrapped up their two-day summit by signing the START treaty and discussing prospects for future cooperation. To underline their declared partnership in international affairs, Bush and Gorbachev issued several joint statements on regional conflicts. Citing "a historic opportunity" for peace in the Middle East, they announced that the United States and the USSR would act as "coinitiators" in trying to bring about a Middle East peace conference in October. They said USSR Foreign Minister Aleksandr Bessmertnykh and US Secretary of State James Baker would work to prepare such a conference (*TASS*, Western media, July 31).

Bush and Gorbachev agreed on a statement on the situation in Yugoslavia, which TASS issued on July 31. It expressed "deep concern" over the dramatic events in Yugoslavia, condemned the use of force to settle political disputes, and called upon all sides to observe a cease-fire. The statement stressed that a solution must be found "by the peoples of Yugoslavia themselves, on the basis of democratic principles."

The summit also produced a declaration on US-Soviet cooperation in Central America, which noted that this cooperation had enhanced stability in the region, TASS reported on July 31. Baker and Bessmertnykh specifically called for a cease-fire and a definitive settlement in El Salvador.

While seeing Bush off on August 1, Gorbachev outlined his view of "the most important recent gains" in US-Soviet relations. "The reduction of nuclear arms has begun and is gathering momentum. The European process has been brought to a qualitatively new level. We have helped to resolve a number of regional conflicts and have brought others closer to a settlement. A major step has been taken towards a new type of international economic relations."

El'tsin and Nazarbaev in Summit Delegation

In a nod to their pivotal role in hammering out the new Union treaty, Soviet President Mikhail Gorbachev invited RSFSR President Boris El'tsin and Kazakh President Nursultan Nazarbaev to attend a working meeting with US President George Bush as part of the Soviet delegation. They were also to attend an official reception for Bush. According to *The Washington Post*, Foreign Ministry spokesman Vitalii Churkin said the USSR was "a new country, a country where we have a different attitude towards republics and where they are going to have a higher profile, including a higher foreign-policy profile." Gorbachev's spokesman Vitalii Ignatenko was quoted in the *Los Angeles Times* as saying "an important meeting like this should have really important representation."

El'tsin did not, however, appear as planned for the meeting and working lunch as part of the Soviet delegation but instead met with Bush later as RSFSR president in his Kremlin office. An RSFSR government spokesman said El'tsin had informed Gorbachev the previous evening that he preferred to meet Bush on those terms; Igor' Malashenko, deputy presidential spokesman, played down El'tsin's absence from the joint meeting. After meeting with Bush, El'tsin announced that the RSFSR intended to establish formal links with the United States, which would be spelled out in a document to be signed after the Union treaty had been signed, Western agencies reported.

Baker and Bessmertnykh Sign Bilateral Agreements

US Secretary of State James Baker and Soviet Foreign Minister Aleksandr Bessmertnykh signed several agreements expanding bilateral US-Soviet cooperation, RFE/RL's correspondent in Moscow reported. Among the agreements were a protocol on technical and economic exchange, a memorandum of understanding on disaster relief, a memorandum on security cooperation to prevent hijacking and terrorism in aviation, an agreement on assistance in housing development, and an agreement on medical emergencies. According to Western agencies, the protocol on technical and economic cooperation would permit the United States to extend aid to Soviet republics as well as to the central government.

Bush's Address to IMEMO

In his speech to the World Economics and International Relations Institute in Moscow, US President George Bush raised the Baltic issue as an obstacle to further improvement in US-USSR relations, RFE/RL's correspondent in Moscow reported. According to Bush, "only good-faith negotiations with the Baltic governments can address the yearnings of their people to be free." The brief remark followed Bush's announcement of plans to extend most-favored-nation (MFN) trading status to the USSR.

In the same speech, Bush referred to "conflicts and quarrels rooted in a world war fought fifty years ago . . . disputes like Japan's claim, which we support, for the return of the northern territories." Bush's comments were headline news in Japan. Before his first round of talks with Gorbachev, Bush had noted that Moscow's territorial dispute with Tokyo "could hamper [Soviet] integration into the world economy."

The US president also spoke on the subject of Cuba, noting: "The United States poses no threat to Cuba; therefore, there is no need for the Soviet Union to funnel millions of dollars in military aid to Cuba, especially since a defiant Castro, isolated by his own obsolete totalitarianism, denies his people any move towards democracy.

Castro does not share your faith in *glasnost*. Castro does not share your faith in *perestroika*."

Lithuania Recognizes Slovenia and Croatia

The Lithuanian parliament adopted a resolution recognizing "the independent republics of Slovenia and Croatia," Radio Independent Lithuania reported on July 31. "The legal aspirations of these republics are an expression of the sovereign will of their people," the resolution read, and empower the Lithuanian government to "establish relations with the governments" of Slovenia and Croatia. The resolution drew parallels between the Baltic and Balkan independence drives, formalizing earlier Lithuanian declarations of support for Slovenia and Croatia.

The USSR Ministry of Foreign Affairs issued a statement on July 31 declaring Lithuania's recognition of Croatia and Slovenia invalid, TASS reported on July 31. The statement said that the move could not have any legal effect, insofar as Lithuania had no separate status under international law.

Gorbachev and El'tsin Reach Compromise on Taxation

The last major obstacle to the RSFSR's signing the Union treaty was removed on the night of July 29 when Soviet President Gorbachev, RSFSR President El'tsin, and Kazakh President Nazarbaev agreed to a compromise on the question of taxation, the Western media reported on July 30, citing Interfax and the Russian Information Agency. Gorbachev yielded to El'tsin's insistence that all taxes should be paid to the republics rather than some taxes being paid directly to the center. At the same time, El'tsin conceded that a fixed percentage of the taxes should be paid by the republics to the center rather than a lump sum, as he had earlier demanded. It was not clear from the reports how this percentage would be decided. The compromise was clearly a setback for Gorbachev, who had been insisting on federal taxes.

Stankevich Named El'tsin Adviser

"Vesti" reported that Sergei Stankevich, former deputy chairman of the Moscow City Soviet, had been appointed a state adviser to the RSFSR president.

Latvian Official Holds Talks with Pugo

Latvian Deputy Prime Minister Ilmars Bisers met for two hours with USSR Minister of Internal Affairs Boriss Pugo on July 30, *Diena* reported. The meeting was proposed by Pugo to inform Bisers about MVD proposals related to the Latvian-USSR consultations. The principal topic of discussion was the status and activities of OMON troops in Latvia. Pugo admitted that the existing situation, in which OMON troops were apparently not answerable to any government or lawmaking institution, was abnormal.

A *Pravda* commentary praised US work towards convoking Middle East peace talks and said it had "long been time to talk to all the countries of the Middle East without any exceptions." The commentary also criticized the Palestine Liberation Organization for "having miscalculated badly in its uninhibited 'romance' with Baghdad," Western agencies reported.

Pravda **Commentary on Middle East**

Interfax reported that the USSR State Bank had introduced measures to tighten the money supply. The bank disclosed that the money supply had risen by 41.6 percent during the first half of 1991 and that the budget deficit had grown to 60 billion rubles—i.e., roughly twice the planned level. Most of the money in circulation had been used to repay the national debt of around 800 billion rubles, while only one-third of the amount had been utilized for new lending. The bank was reported to have limited the interest rate on credits for financing the budget deficit to 6 percent and to have placed a ceiling of 600 billion rubles on credits intended to finance medium- and long-term debt.

Gosbank Tightens Money Supply

The USSR Cabinet of Ministers issued a decree on the organization of public works programs for the unemployed. TASS said contracts would be concluded with enterprises on a two-month basis with the possibility of extension. Public works projects would be financed by local authorities or, if necessary, through state subsidies. Among the types of jobs listed were those in construction, a whole range of agricultural operations, and care of invalids and the elderly. The decree was part of a package of measures connected with the law on unemployment that took effect on July 1.

Public Works Programs Initiated

"Vesti" reported on a rally organized near the Moscow City Soviet headquarters by the backbone of the Democratic Russia movement, the Voters' Club of the USSR Academy of Sciences. The demonstrators protested against the appointment by Mayor Gavriil Popov of Boris Nikol'sky as one of his deputies. (Nikol'sky was

Democrats Up In Arms against Popov

believed to have been primarily responsible for the Tbilisi massacre of April, 1989, in his then capacity as second secretary of the Georgian CP.) The rally of the Voters' Club was not the first occasion on which activists of Democratic Russia had rallied in protest against the appointment by Popov of discredited CPSU officials to crucial positions in the Moscow administration (see *Kuranty*, July 11; *Nezavisimaya gazeta*, July 9). Popov, a cochairman of Democratic Russia, justified his choices in the past by pointing out that the appointments were not political ones and that these people had proved to be good economic managers.

Georgian President Receives New Powers; Appeals to Bush

Radio Moscow reported that the Georgian Supreme Soviet had amended the Georgian Constitution to give the republican president the power to suspend legislation enacted by the Supreme Soviets of Georgia's autonomous republics but at variance with the Georgian Constitution.

The same day, the Georgian presidential press service released to RFE/RL a copy of a letter from Georgian President Zviad Gamsakhurdia to US President George Bush requesting that the United States take a stand against what he termed Soviet government "provocations" in the form of small-scale military operations against Georgia.

Meskhetians Demand Right to Return to Georgia

Western news agencies reported from Moscow that up to 1,000 Meskhetians—the Muslim ethnic Georgians deported by Stalin from their homeland in southern Georgia in November, 1944—had demonstrated outside the Kremlin in the hope of bringing their plight to US President George Bush's attention. Many Meskhetians fled Uzbekistan following the violence there in 1989, but they were not allowed to resettle in Georgia. "Vremya" cited a Georgian presidential decree permitting Georgians made homeless by the earthquake that shook the republic on April 30 to settle in the raions formerly populated by Meskhetians.

Wednesday, July 31

Killings in Lithuania

Six dead and two injured Lithuanian border guards were found at the Medininkai customs post on the Belorussian border early in the morning, Radio Independent Lithuania reported. Travelers passing through the post at 5:00 A.M.

The USSR in July, 1991

discovered the guards, who were apparently victims of an armed attack. In another incident, a bomb exploded outside a Soviet army building in Vilnius at 2:50 A.M. No injuries were reported in the blast, which shattered some windows in the area.

The Lithuanian parliament met in an extraordinary session to discuss "the terrorist and repressive structures of the Soviet Union in Lithuania," Radio Independent Lithuania reported. The Lithuanian Supreme Council Presidium condemned the attack as an escalation of the USSR's "aggressive actions" against Lithuania. The Lithuanian government announced that it was offering a 500,000-ruble reward for bringing the killers to justice.

Speaking at a press conference in Vilnius, Lithuanian Supreme Council President Vytautas Landsbergis called the Medininkai attack "a brutal act of coercion," Radio Independent Lithuania reported that day. Placing the attack in the context of the continuing violence Lithuania had experienced since January, Landsbergis drew attention to "a repeatedly occurring coincidence": whenever the United States "shows a greater benevolence" to the USSR, Landsbergis said, "the Baltic States, especially Lithuania, suffer blows from the Soviet Armed Forces." Landsbergis did not specifically accuse OMON troops of complicity, but he did say that "this thought strikes every citizen of Lithuania."

According to a TASS report, USSR Minister of Internal Affairs Boriss Pugo denied that his OMON troops had been involved in the attack, adding that he was "shocked to the depths of [his] heart by the tragedy." Pugo also pledged his ministry's support in investigating the attack. In Vilnius, an OMON spokesman claimed that all troops had been in their barracks at the time of the killings, contradicting a Lithuanian report that an OMON vehicle had been sighted in the Medininkai area during the night of the attack.

During a joint press conference in Moscow, US President George Bush and Soviet President Mikhail Gorbachev briefly addressed the subject of the Medininkai attack, TASS reported. Both leaders expressed their sympathy for the victims' families and called for a peaceful settlement of differences. Gorbachev said that "we are making every effort to avoid such excesses." Bush threw his support behind Gorbachev's plans for an investigation and said he hoped it would "lead to cooperation between Lithuania and Belorussia." An RFE/RL correspondent in Washington reported that the Lithuanian-American community was calling for a more forceful reaction, saying that Bush's comment made the attack seem like a local ethnic dispute.

RSFSR President El'tsin also expressed sympathy for the victims' families but went a step further, RIA reported. "To avoid possible future incidents, I insist that OMON subdivisions be withdrawn from the Lithuanian republic," El'tsin said, echoing a Lithuanian government statement of July 29 demanding the same. El'tsin called the attack "a crime that I sharply condemn."

In sharp contrast to the widespread condemnation in Latvia of OMON attacks and killings in the Baltic republics, Andris Reinieks, deputy prosecutor of the Latvian SSR, said that OMON actions against the customs posts and customs employees were justified, Radio Riga reported. He said that such measures on the part of OMON stemmed from a rightful desire to uphold Soviet law, which did not allow Baltic customs posts. Reinieks was speaking in Daugavpils, a stronghold of Soviet conservatism, where Latvians made up less than 12 percent of the population.

The Estonian Foreign Ministry issued a statement condemning the attack and calling for international observers to be stationed at the Baltic-Soviet borders to prevent further attacks.

In a statement carried by TASS on August 1, the Baltic Military District disavowed the Medininkai attack, demanding "a swift and objective investigation" of this "terrorist act." The statement said the district's Military Council resented Lithuanian suspicions of army or OMON involvement in the killings, considering them an attempt to "ignite anti-Soviet hysteria and antiarmy psychosis, not only in the Baltic region, but also in other republics."

Lithuanian parliamentary deputies spent August 1 in an emergency session discussing "terrorist and repressive structures of the Soviet Union in Lithuania," Radio Independent Lithuania reported that day. The parliament appealed to CSCE member states, asking that the CSCE crisis-control mechanism be applied to normalize relations between Lithuania and the USSR. Another resolution requested that Denmark and Iceland, two of the most vocal supporters of Lithuania, raise the issues of Soviet aggression and Lithuanian independence with the UN Security Council.

On August 2, the Lithuanian parliamentary information bureau announced that a seventh border guard had died in a Vilnius hospital. In a report to the parliament, Lithuanian State Prosecutor General Arturas Paulauskas said that "there are five or six possible versions of the crime," but he did not elaborate. The victims were apparently forced to lie on the floor and were shot point-blank in the head. There was no indication of an armed struggle, Paulauskas said.

The USSR in July, 1991

Goncharenko Proposes New Oversight Body for OMON

Colonel Nikolai Goncharenko, identified by Radio Riga as coordinator of OMON forces in the Baltic republics, proposed to the Ministry of Internal Affairs that the units be made directly answerable to Moscow via a newly created interregional oversight body. Goncharenko also wanted OMON to concentrate on fighting organized crime. His proposal reportedly had the backing of Vitalii Sidorov, a USSR deputy minister of internal affairs.

Lamont Arrives in Moscow

Britain's chancellor of the exchequer, Norman Lamont, arrived in Moscow for a four-day visit, TASS reported. TASS said Lamont's trip was the first in a series of visits by Western finance ministers in accordance with an agreement reached during Gorbachev's talks at the G-7 summit. Lamont was scheduled to meet Gorbachev and a number of all-Union and republican officials, as well as Soviet businessmen. He would also visit enterprises and commercial centers and would travel to Kiev at the end of his stay. As quoted by TASS, Lamont told the BBC that his aim was to acquaint himself with the situation in the USSR. He stressed the importance of integrating the USSR into the world economic system but ruled out any immediate Western aid.

Customs Posts on Moldavian-Ukrainian Frontier

"TSN" reported that the government of Moldavia had decided to set up twenty-five customs posts on the Moldavian-Ukrainian frontier to control the export of agricultural produce and consumer goods. TASS reported that, because of torrential rain earlier in the summer, the Moldavian grain harvest was expected to amount to little more than 1.2 million tons, which was much lower than had been previously estimated. The government had therefore banned the trading of agricultural produce on the exchange and its export from the republic—except for deliveries to all-Union consumers and those covered by interrepublican agreements—until state orders had been fulfilled.

Paper Shortage Threatens Newspapers

At a press conference kicking off a subscription drive for about 8,000 newspapers and periodicals, V. Leont'ev, director of "Pravda" publishers, cautioned that, "strictly speaking, we do not have the moral right to announce today subscriptions for 1992, since we aren't assured of paper even for this year." Novosti reported concern that, if the present level of state distribution of paper at fixed prices were not maintained, "then not a single Party paper will be able to support itself."

THE USSR IN JULY, 1991

New CPSU Secretary Speaks Out

Vladimir Kalashnikov, who was elected a CPSU secretary at the previous week's Central Committee plenum, told TASS he would be dealing with "ideological problems." Kalashnikov said he favored a mixed economy and market relations but with the state strongly oriented towards defending workers' interests. He defined socialism as "a society of social equality, in which man's condition depends on the results of his work."

The Month of August

Thursday, August 1

Markovic in Moscow

Yugoslav Prime Minister Ante Markovic arrived in Moscow for a two-day working visit at the invitation of the USSR Cabinet of Ministers (*TASS*, August 1). Markovic held talks with his Soviet counterpart, Valentin Pavlov, TASS and Western agencies reported. Pavlov reiterated the Soviet position that Yugoslavia should not break up. Markovic also met with Soviet President Mikhail Gorbachev and with RSFSR President Boris El'tsin.

Upon returning to Belgrade on August 2, Markovic said his visit to the USSR had exceeded his expectations, both politically and economically. According to a Tanjug report issued the same day, Markovic predicted that an agreement on Soviet-Yugoslav relations signed during his trip would ease the burden on Yugoslavia's economy.

Soviet Military Spring Draft in Latvia

Diena reported that the quota for the spring draft in Latvia had been fulfilled by only 15 percent and that about 75 percent of the draft-age youths had opted for alternative service. Latvian SSR Military Commissar Janis Duda claimed, however, that the draft had been fulfilled by 33 percent. In a related development, Radio Riga reported on August 3 that the local draft office in Balvi was coercing young men already performing alternative service to switch over to regular military service.

Bush Visits Kiev

US President George Bush arrived at Kiev's Borispol Airport, where he was met by Ukrainian Supreme Soviet Chairman Leonid Kravchuk. From there he went to the Supreme Soviet for a private talk with Kravchuk and a meeting with the highest-ranking members of the Ukrainian parliament. After lunch, Bush addressed the Supreme Soviet on the subject of US relations with the Soviet republics and then went on a sightseeing tour, which included the St. Sofia Cathedral and the Babii Yar Memorial. Bush was the first incumbent US president to visit Kiev since Richard Nixon went there in May, 1972, after the signing of the SALT agreement.

President Bush's visit to Kiev was acclaimed in the Ukrainian media as a further step on the road to Ukrainian sovereignty. Ukrainian opposition leaders expressed regret, however, that the US president would not meet with representatives of the opposition (*Ukrinform-TASS*, July 31).

Bush's address to the Ukrainian Supreme Soviet sent a message of both support and caution to his audience. He said the United States supported "the struggle in this great country for democracy and economic reform" and "those in the center and the republics who pursue freedom, democracy, and economic liberty." Bush assured his audience that the United States was not interested in meddling in internal Soviet affairs but did want "good relations, improved relations, with the republics." He further stated that "the 'Nine-plus-One' agreement holds forth the hope that the republics will combine greater autonomy with greater voluntary interaction—political, social, cultural, and economic—rather than pursuing the suicidal course of isolation." He ended his speech by saying "we support those who explore the frontiers of freedom."

Vyacheslav Chornovil, chairman of the Lvov Oblast Soviet, said the part of Bush's speech he liked best was when the president spoke of democracy, "which it won't hurt the Communists to hear." On the eve of Bush's visit, Ivan Drach, chairman of "Rukh," issued a statement saying that Bush, seemingly "hypnotized by Gorbachev," appeared to believe that Moscow was the source of stability.

Air Traffic Controllers Win Concession

A Soviet trade-union official was quoted by Western agencies as saying the Soviet government had agreed to the union's demand that the retirement age of air traffic controllers be lowered. This was a partial victory for the new, independent trade union of air traffic controllers, which had threatened strike action on August 10 in support of demands for higher pay, shorter working hours, and longer vacations.

"Soyuz" Delegation in Iraq

A delegation of USSR Supreme Soviet deputies from the hard-line "Soyuz" faction began talks with members of the Iraqi National Assembly in Baghdad. A press release issued by the official Iraqi news agency quoted the leader of the Soviet delegation, Evgenii Kogan, as saying Soviet experts were ready to return to Iraq to participate in reconstruction after the war. The Iraqi agency also reported that Kogan had pledged to press for the lifting of the embargo against Iraq (Western agencies, August 1).

The USSR in August, 1991

After its return from Iraq on August 8, the delegation called at a press conference for the restoration of close Soviet-Iraqi ties. TASS quoted Kogan as saying that Iraqi officials, businessmen, and ordinary citizens had emphasized the need for the USSR to revive its contacts with Iraq and to strengthen cooperation, above all in the economic sphere. Kogan accused the USSR Foreign Ministry of "insufficient activity and even political myopia" in its seeming reluctance to broaden ties with Iraq. "Soyuz" was highly critical of Soviet support for the Gulf war.

The United Nations announced a global plan to spend 646 million dollars to combat the effects of the Chernobyl' disaster. Countries would be asked to pledge funds for the project at a conference to be held in conjunction with the opening of the UN General Assembly on September 20. The plan would address issues ranging from health and reconstruction to the environmental consequences of the accident and would involve the all-Union authorities as well as the RSFSR, Ukraine, and Belorussia. (Western agencies, August 1)

UN Plan for Chernobyl' Aid

Armenian Prime Minister Vazgen Manukyan, together with three supporters, announced the creation of a new political organization, the Armenian National-Democratic Union (*TASS*, August 1). The aim of the new organization, according to a statement issued by its founders, was to unite the existing political groups in Armenia "on the basis of a common national ideology," since the current preoccupation of many parties "with a social rather than national struggle" could be "fatal" for Armenia.

New Political Union Created in Armenia

Friday, August 2

"Vremya" started with a fifteen-minute address by Soviet President Mikhail Gorbachev on the Union treaty. Gorbachev said that the RSFSR, Kazakhstan, and Uzbekistan would sign the treaty on August 20, with the other republics following later. The timetable would allow Ukraine to finish its examination of the draft, Armenia to hold its referendum on secession, and Moldavia to make a decision on the treaty. The peoples of Georgia, Latvia, Lithuania, and Estonia would also "be able to determine their position on this vital matter."

Gorbachev Addresses Nation on Union Treaty

Bush Seeks Separate Trading Status for Baltic Republics

US President George Bush sent to Congress the US-Soviet trade agreement, which foresaw separate trade benefits for the three Baltic republics, *The Journal of Commerce* reported on August 3. He requested separate "most-favored-nation" trade benefits for Estonia, Latvia, and Lithuania, initially on a temporary basis but becoming permanent once the United States recognized their independence from the USSR. In a related move, the US customs service planned to start recording separate data on trade with each of the Baltic republics instead of including them in statistics for trade with the USSR as a whole.

Yakovlev Disenchanted with Socialism

"More and more I am coming to the conclusion that our tragedy stems from Marxist dogma," Aleksandr Yakovlev told TASS. Stalin practiced Marxism, albeit in a distorted way, Yakovlev said, adding that he was disenchanted with socialism. Yakovlev explained that three months ago he had submitted to Gorbachev a letter of resignation as the president's senior adviser. Yakovlev said that, unlike Gorbachev, he no longer believed that the CPSU could renew itself. He added that, while some provisions of the new Party Program approved by the CPSU Central Committee in July might be good, it was now too late, because people had lost faith in the CPSU. A former Politburo member and Party secretary, Yakovlev had publicly criticized the Marxist concepts of violence and dictatorship since at least 1989.

Officials Defend Cooperation with Cuba

During a joint press conference with visiting Yugoslav Prime Minister Ante Markovic, Soviet Prime Minister Valentin Pavlov declared that "Cuba was, is, and will be our friend and . . . partner." He added, "No one has the right to interfere in our bilateral relations," TASS reported. Meanwhile, General Mikhail Surkov, the top CPSU official in the Soviet Armed Forces, criticized US President George Bush's suggestion during the summit that the USSR stop aiding Cuba. The *Los Angeles Times* of August 3 quoted Surkov as saying Bush's statements were "disrespectful."

USSR and EC Sign Protocol on Technical Cooperation

TASS reported that the European Community had signed a program of technical cooperation with the USSR designed to promote reforms. The agreement was signed by EC External Relations Minister Frans Andriessen and Soviet permanent representative to the EC Lev Voronin. TASS said the protocol provided for technical

THE USSR IN AUGUST, 1991

cooperation in energy, transport, food distribution, financial services, and management training.

Chinese Worried That CPSU May Abandon Marxism

Western agencies reported that the *Beijing Youth News* had published an article expressing concern about the new CPSU Program, which would eliminate references to Marxism. The article reportedly viewed the revised CPSU Program as a revision of "the nature of the Soviet Communist Party, [its] guiding ideology and guiding principles." It went on to charge that the West was putting pressure on the USSR to "become a member of the Western camp" in return for economic aid.

Moldavia and RSFSR Sign Cultural Agreement

The ministers of culture of Moldavia and the RSFSR, Ion Ungureanu and Yurii Solomin, signed an agreement on cultural cooperation between the two republics, Russian Television reported. The agreement provided for the setting up of cultural centers and various forms of cultural exchanges to serve the needs of Russians residing in Moldavia and of Moldavians residing in the RSFSR.

――――― *Saturday, August 3*

Decree on Supplies Issued

A presidential decree on foodstuffs and consumer goods published on August 4 stipulated that priority in supplies be granted to consumer-goods industries. It allocated hard currency for the import of grain, medicine, building supplies, and spare parts for consumer durables. Farms were promised additional incentives, including imported consumer goods and relevant producer goods if they met and overfulfilled their procurement quotas (*TASS*, August 4).

Democratic Party of Communists of Russia Holds Organizing Conference

Concluding a two-day organizing conference in Moscow attended by more than 800 delegates from all republics and regions of the RSFSR, the Democratic Party of Communists of Russia announced that it had decided to form a political party "within the CPSU," Soviet news agencies reported. A founding congress would be held in October; Aleksandr Rutskoi would head the temporary organizing committee but, because he was RSFSR vice president, would not stand for election as leader of the party. More than 7,000 applications for membership had already been received, which was enough to permit the party to apply for registration as a republican political organization. The conference also adopted a resolution demanding that the CPSU form a commission to preserve and make accessible its archives.

The same day, the CPSU Secretariat issued a statement declaring the resolutions adopted by the Democratic Party of Communists of Russia invalid, TASS reported. Explaining its decision, the Secretariat said that delegates to the founding conference had not been chosen in accordance with CPSU rules and that non-Party members had also participated. The Secretariat also said that forming a party within a party was a violation of CPSU rules and that CPSU members were not allowed to hold simultaneous membership in two political parties.

Sovetskaya kul'tura Attacks Party Reactionaries

Sovetskaya kul'tura published a long article by I. Zaramensky, deputy head of the CPSU Central Committee Department for Ties with Sociopolitical Organizations. The article criticized recent publications by highly placed Party reactionaries, such as RSFSR CP Politburo member Gennadii Zyuganov and Leningrad ideologue Yurii Belov. Zaramensky argued that a split in the CPSU would be better than "the slow death and disintegration" that the Party was currently undergoing. Zaramensky believed that the CPSU should support the Movement for Democratic Reforms and he defended Aleksandr Yakovlev against "populist hunting" by Party reactionaries who, he said, were lacking in "ideological intellect."

"Shield" Says KGB Responsible for Medininkai Killings

Russian Television carried a statement issued by the military reform group "Shield" saying it believed the KGB was responsible for the Medininkai killings. The statement said a preliminary investigation by independent military experts had shown KGB involvement in "planning and leading the operation" at Medininkai. "Shield" called for an international commission of experts to carry out an objective investigation of the crime.

On August 7, the USSR Ministry of Internal Affairs and the KGB issued a joint statement denying responsibility for the murders, TASS reported. "The leadership of these agencies categorically declares that they had absolutely no involvement in the tragedy," the statement read, adding that the MVD and the KGB were cooperating with the Lithuanian law-enforcement authorities in investigating the killings.

Croatia Recognizes Lithuania

The Croatian parliament voted "overwhelmingly" to recognize the Republic of Lithuania, Tanjug reported. The vote reciprocated a Lithuanian resolution of July 30 recognizing Slovenian and Croatian independence. Croatian Assembly President Zarko Domljan was quoted as saying Croatia would attempt to "establish comprehensive cooperation with the Republic of Lithuania."

Sunday, August 4

Departification Decree Comes Into Force

RSFSR President Boris El'tsin's decree of July 20 banning formal party activity in state institutions and enterprises came into force. RSFSR presidential press secretary Pavel Voshchanov told Radio Rossii on August 2 that no specific period of time for the fulfillment of the decree had been set but that El'tsin expected departification to be essentially complete by the end of 1991.

"Vesti" quoted the Leningrad Oblast Party Committee as reporting that every third head of state-owned enterprises in the region had requested Party cells to leave the premises. "Vesti" commentator Aleksandr Gurnov observed that this was not a bad result if compared with how Soviet President Mikhail Gorbachev's presidential decrees were implemented.

Western news agencies reported on August 5 that managers who failed to close down Party cells at their enterprises would be liable to a fine of 10,000 rubles. CPSU leaders, such as Leningrad Party leader Boris Gidaspov, had ordered implementation of the decree and the relocation of Party organizations outside factories in electoral constituencies. Some managers decided, however, to wait for the decision of the Committee on Constitutional Supervision, which they hoped would nullify the decree. Others still thought that Gorbachev might challenge El'tsin with a decree of his own.

While the army was resisting implementation of El'tsin's decree, the KGB was obeying it. RSFSR KGB Chairman Viktor Ivanenko was reported to have assured El'tsin that the KGB in the RSFSR would be depoliticized (*Financial Times*, August 5). Meanwhile General Mikhail Surkov, head of the Party organization in the armed forces, stressed that the armed forces were subordinate only to the Union and would ignore El'tsin's decree until Gorbachev issued his own, *The Guardian* reported.

The president of Tatarstan, Mintimer Shaimiev, declared that he would not carry out the decree and that Communists would continue to play a dominant role in the enterprises in his republic, according to the *Financial Times* (August 5). According to an opinion poll published in *Moskovskie novosti* on August 4, 73 percent of RSFSR citizens supported El'tsin's decree, 13 percent objected to it, and 14 percent were undecided.

In a telegram of August 7 to the RSFSR Communist Party leadership, the Secretariat of the Ukrainian Communist Party Central Committee expressed solidarity with Communists in the RSFSR, TASS reported. The telegram condemned "the actions of people calling themselves democrats who are blatantly denying the legitimate rights of the working people and trying to destroy the foundations of the Communist Party." The Ukrainian Communist Party appealed to Gorbachev to adopt laws protecting the rights of Communists and mass movements.

Speaking on "Vesti" on August 14, RSFSR Communist Party leader Valentin Kuptsov said his party would remove its cells from state enterprises within a year in compliance with El'tsin's edict on "departification," if the USSR Committee for Constitutional Supervision approved the decree. Kuptsov said he and El'tsin had agreed on this during a meeting the previous day.

The CPSU Secretariat met on August 15 to discuss the implementation by the RSFSR Communist Party of El'tsin's decree on depoliticization, TASS reported that day. CPSU Secretary Yurii Manaenkov reported that a survey of 450 enterprise directors in Moscow had revealed that only two thought they did not need a CPSU organization in their enterprise.

Shcherbakov on Customs Duties

During a Central Television interview, USSR First Deputy Prime Minister and Minister of the Economy and Forecasting Vladimir Shcherbakov announced that the government planned to reduce the high customs duties levied on consumer goods brought into the country by Soviet citizens returning from abroad. Customs duties on these goods were sharply raised with effect from July 1, but at an informal meeting on July 26 all fifteen republics drafted a letter to Prime Minister Valentin Pavlov asking for the higher tariffs to be rescinded. Shcherbakov was quoted as saying the customs authorities had raised the duties on their own initiative and without prior government approval.

Semipalatinsk Testing Site to Be Closed

Radio Moscow reported that the Kazakh Supreme Soviet had decided to hold a referendum among residents of raions near the nuclear testing site in Semipalatinsk Oblast on whether to accept an offer of 5 billion rubles in compensation from the USSR Ministry of Defense. The ministry wanted to conduct three more tests at the site. The chairman of Kazakhstan's antinuclear movement, poet Olzhas Suleimenov, had called on area residents to vote against accepting the offer. The radio report suggested that the USSR Supreme Soviet should take a close look at the finances of the Ministry of Defense.

On August 6, Radio Moscow reported that, for the first time, the Politburo of the Kazakh Communist Party had issued a declaration formally demanding the immediate closure of the testing site.

On August 29, TASS reported that Kazakh President Nursultan Nazarbaev had signed a decree shutting down the testing facility. Nazarbaev left the USSR Supreme Soviet session in order to attend an antinuclear demonstration in Alma-Ata.

Moldavia Sponsors Gagauz Cultural Celebrations

The Moldavian authorities opened the "Days of Gagauz Culture" in Kishinev, Moldovapres reported. Gagauz artists, ethnologists, and folk ensembles from Moldavia and the neighboring Odessa Oblast and guests from Azerbaijan, Central Asia, and Turkey participated. The celebrations were scheduled to move to the Gagauz-inhabited raions of southern Moldavia later in the week.

Monday, August 5

Vol'sky and Alksnis Interviewed on Television

Central Television's "Who's Who" phone-in featured interviews with "the black colonel," Viktor Alksnis, and the president of the Soviet employers' association, Arkadii Vol'sky. Alksnis said the "Soyuz" parliamentary group, which he leads, still wanted to see Soviet President Mikhail Gorbachev replaced by a collegial body. As members, Alksnis proposed two liberals—Vol'sky and former Deputy Chairman of the Moscow City Soviet Sergei Stankevich—and two conservatives—Second Secretary of the Russian Communist Party Aleksei Il'in and Colonel General Igor' Rodionov, notorious for his role as commander of the troops who used gas and shovels to disperse peaceful demonstrators in Tbilisi in April, 1989.

Asked whether it was true that he was "Gorbachev's secret adviser," Vol'sky said his role was so secret "that even Gorbachev doesn't know about it." Vol'sky was known to have come to Gorbachev's defense in April when the general secretary came under fire from conservatives at a plenum of the CPSU Central Committee. But on "Who's Who" Vol'sky revealed that he had also criticized Gorbachev at that plenum for his "mistaken personnel policy." No such criticism appeared in accounts of the plenum at the time.

RSFSR Supreme Court Judges Quit the CPSU

The judges of the RSFSR Supreme Court held their last Party meeting, *Izvestia* reported. The meeting was devoted to RSFSR President Boris El'tsin's edict banning organized political activity from workplaces. The judges decided not merely to remove their primary Party cell from the court premises, as the RSFSR president had decreed, but also to suspend their membership in the CPSU as long as they were members of the court. This move was to prevent interference by CPSU officials in court proceedings. The RSFSR justices cited the decision of the members of the USSR Committee for Constitutional Supervision, "who suspended their membership in the CPSU long ago despite the lack of any direct order [from President Gorbachev]."

Measures to Boost Oil and Gas Production

A decree of the USSR Cabinet of Ministers published by TASS provided a series of incentives to encourage an increase in the production and export of oil and gas. It raised the producer price of crude oil from 60 to 74 rubles per ton (compared with about 200 rubles a ton on the commodities exchanges and a world price of some 155 dollars a ton). The decree also cut the share of hard currency earned from oil and gas exports that must be converted to rubles at the unfavorable official rate from 40 percent to 3 percent. A levy on negotiated hard-currency sales would go to the stabilization fund for boosting output.

Landsbergis Sends Telegram to Gorbachev

Lithuanian Supreme Council President Vytautas Landsbergis sent a telegram to Soviet President Mikhail Gorbachev calling for urgent talks, Radio Independent Lithuania reported. "Mr. President, We don't have much time," the telegram read. "The OMON must be withdrawn without delay, and we must meet." Landsbergis warned that "terrorists will continue to kill, and events will become unpredictable." Landsbergis told Gorbachev, "I cannot believe that this is what you want."

Workers Strike in Support of Belorussian Labor Leader

Workers at the Minsk Tractor Factory staged a one-hour strike to protest about the trial of Belorussian labor leader Mikalai Razumau. An independent journalist in Minsk told RL's Belorussian service by telephone that the factory's management had apparently called out the police to prevent the strike but that the policemen—armed with rubber truncheons—had stood aside while workers walked off the job. Razumau went on trial in Mogilev on August 1 charged with organizing a blockade of the main east-west railway line in Orsha in April in order to press for democratic reforms.

Seventy Belorussian workers from Orsha traveled by bus to Mogilev on August 7 and entered the courtroom where Razumau was on trial. Independent Minsk journalist Yas Valoshka told RFE/RL's Belorussian service that the workers had carried Razumau out of the courtroom and back to their bus in a protective cordon and then driven back to Orsha without incident. The workers vowed to protect Razumau until his trial was moved from Mogilev to Orsha, and they also demanded that non-Communist judges be appointed to hear his case.

Razumau's trial resumed in Mogilev on August 12, but the defendant was absent. Razumau told RFE/RL's Belorussian service that he would not attend the trial unless forced to do so. He said he planned to remain in his home town, Orsha.

Judicial sources in Rome reported that Soviet President Mikhail Gorbachev had sent a letter to Italian Prime Minister Giulio Andreotti saying he had no evidence of KGB involvement in the attempt to assassinate Pope John Paul II in 1981. The Italian sources said Gorbachev told Andreotti that he had ordered trusted investigators to go through all relevant KGB files but that they had found no evidence of any KGB involvement in the attack.

Gorbachev Asserts KGB Not Involved in Shooting of Pope

TASS reported that the building of a former religious Jewish school had been returned to the Jewish community in Moscow. The school was confiscated in the summer of 1941 to be used as a military hospital but was never given back to the believers. Rabbi Arthur Schneier from New York had appealed to the Soviet authorities to return the building, which would in future be used as a religious and cultural center.

Former Jewish School Building Returned to Community

Tuesday, August 6

First Deputy Chairman of the Ukrainian Supreme Soviet Ivan Plyushch told Ukrainian television viewers that Soviet President Mikhail Gorbachev's remarks about the new Union treaty's being ready for signing were incorrect, Radio Kiev reported. Moreover, Plyushch said he had attended the latest meeting at Novo-Ogarevo only as an observer. Ukraine, Plyushch reminded viewers, had not yet formed a commission empowered to sign the treaty.

Objections to Signing Union Treaty

In a populist concession that could delay the signing of the Union treaty, RSFSR President Boris El'tsin promised to negotiate new prices for energy and raw materials with other republics after the treaty had been signed (*TASS* and Western agencies, August 7). The move was considered likely to spark a trade and price war with republics that were important exporters to the RSFSR.

On August 8, *Nezavisimaya gazeta* published an appeal to El'tsin from a group of parliamentarians and public figures, including Yurii Afanas'ev and Elena Bonner, calling on him not to sign the Union treaty until the final text had been made available to the population of the RSFSR. The authors of the appeal complained that the latest published text, "prepared in secret and not subjected to detailed discussion either in the press or by the RSFSR Supreme Soviet," was unsatisfactory and suggested that the main theses of the treaty be the subject of an RSFSR referendum. The fourth draft of the Union treaty was published in *Izvestia* on August 15.

El'tsin replied to the appeal in a statement published in *Nezavisimaya gazeta* on August 13. El'tsin argued that any delay would play into the hands of conservative forces and that Gorbachev had promised that, as soon the treaty was signed, he would issue a decree handing over the whole economic potential of the RSFSR to the republic. El'tsin also rejected the argument that he had no right to sign the treaty, maintaining that the RSFSR Supreme Soviet had discussed it more than once and that the draft had been published. He chose to ignore the resolution of the RSFSR Supreme Soviet of July 5 stipulating that it must discuss the final text before the treaty was signed.

RSFSR Communist Party Central Committee Holds Plenum

The RSFSR Communist Party Central Committee began a closed plenary session, TASS reported. Both RSFSR Vice President Aleksandr Rutskoi, head of the new Democratic Party of Communists of Russia, and Vladimir Lipitsky, leader of the Democratic Movement of Communists (in the CPSU), lost their membership on the RSFSR Central Committee and were expelled from the CPSU for having violated the Party rules on factionalism. Yurii Protasenko was removed from the RSFSR Central Committee for the same reason.

The plenum also saw the resignation of RSFSR Communist Party First Secretary Ivan Polozkov. Polozkov's opening speech contained no hint that he might resign. Later in the day, however, after speakers representing both conservative and reform factions had criticized him, Polozkov tendered his resignation. He was replaced by

The USSR in August, 1991

Valentin Kuptsov, who also replaced Polozkov on the RSFSR CP Politburo.

Rutskoi told reporters in Moscow on August 7 that the RSFSR CP Central Committee was not empowered to expel him from the CPSU. (Rutskoi had been elected to the RSFSR Congress of People's Deputies from a district in Kursk; after he formed the Communists for Democracy faction in April, the Kursk Oblast Party Committee said it would have expelled him from the Party if he had joined it in Kursk.) Rutskoi also said RSFSR President El'tsin, with whom he met on August 3, approved of the plans to form the Democratic Party of Communists of Russia.

Rutskoi told Radio Rossii on August 8 that the RSFSR Party's aim in expelling him was to intimidate other Party members who supported the Democratic Party of Communists of Russia, and he said he planned to appeal the decision to the CPSU Central Committee.

On August 7, Kuptsov told a press conference broadcast by "Vremya" that the RSFSR Communists would seek cooperation with the El'tsin administration and with other political parties. He stressed the need for RSFSR Communists to restructure their work and learn how to operate under conditions of depoliticization of enterprises and the transition to a market economy.

On August 9, the Movement for Democratic Reforms condemned the expulsion of Rutskoi and Lipitsky, from the CPSU, *Izvestia* reported. "While paying lip service to cooperation, consensus, consolidation, and dialogue, the leadership of the Russian Communist Party behaves in the old Stalinist way, in the traditions of the worst times of the past," the Movement for Democratic Reforms complained.

Yurii Petrov Returns

Radio Rossii reported that Yurii Petrov had been selected to head the RSFSR president's administration. Petrov hails from Sverdlovsk, where he succeeded Boris El'tsin as oblast Party first secretary in April, 1985. Petrov graduated from the Urals Polytechnic Institute, the alma mater of many of the early members of Soviet President Mikhail Gorbachev's team, and seemed to be a Party leader cast in the new mold. In 1988, though, *Pravda* published a critical account of a Sverdlovsk Party plenum, and shortly thereafter Petrov was named Soviet ambassador to Cuba.

MVD on Crime Increase

USSR Deputy Minister of Internal Affairs Ivan Shilov told a press briefing that law-enforcement bodies had been unable to halt the continued rise in crime overall, although violent crimes had decreased. According to TASS, Shilov said 1.5 million "serious" crimes had been reported in the first half of the year, a 20-percent increase over the same period in 1990. Crimes involving firearms had increased three fold.

Germany Reluctant to Return Soviet Deserters

The German government said it would not return deserters from the Soviet army unless their applications for political asylum were rejected, RFE/RL's correspondent in Bonn reported. A Western agency report noted, moreover, that, according to German officials, Soviet deserters in the former GDR were being transferred out of the area to protect them from alleged Soviet attempts to capture and repatriate them. The report said that between five to ten Soviet deserters were applying for asylum in Germany each week.

USSR Cabinet Decree on Repatriation of Crimean Tatars

TASS reported on a decree of the USSR Cabinet of Ministers "On Organizing the Return of Crimean Tatars to the Crimean ASSR and Guarantees for Their Settlement There." The decree recommended that the governments of the RSFSR, Ukraine, Kazakhstan, Uzbekistan, Tajikistan, and Kirgizia set up commissions where there were concentrations of Crimean Tatars to deal with problems connected with their return to the Crimea. The decree stated that Tatars who had left a house or apartment behind would be reimbursed so that they could build or purchase housing in the Crimea. Survivors of the deportation from the Crimea in 1944 would be given 2,000 rubles each from the all-Union budget upon their return to the Crimea.

Georgia Criticizes US Support for Union Treaty

The Georgian government issued a four-page statement criticizing US support for the draft Union treaty as "extremely dangerous," inasmuch as the Soviet Union "is ruled by force" and the republics "compelled by violence" to remain in the Union, Western news agencies reported. The statement accused the United States of preaching the virtues of justice, freedom, and democratic self-determination while failing to support the republics in their drive for independence, and it described President George Bush's statements in Kiev on August 1 as "exceeding all the unpleasant expectations we had."

Moldavian-Romanian Intergovernmental Agreements

Moldavian and Romanian Prime Ministers Valeriu Muravschi and Petre Roman signed an intergovernmental agreement in Kishinev on economic cooperation and trade. On the same occasion, high-ranking officials of the two governments signed an agreement establishing a joint commission on economic, commercial, and scientific cooperation. The two prime ministers, accompanied by their economics ministers, discussed ways to finance bilateral trade and prospects for joint ventures in the areas of food processing, telecommunications, and electronics, the Romanian media reported.

Limited to only six hours and deliberately low-key, Roman's visit was the first official visit to Moldavia by a Romanian prime minister since the Soviet annexation. He observed at the signing ceremony that the undertaking "would have been unthinkable only eighteen months ago." Muravschi, in turn, termed the visit "a psychological threshold that we have now crossed." In an address to mark the occasion, Moldavian President Mircea Snegur said that progress in the relationship "faced many obstacles inherent in the political situation in the USSR" and that Moldavia was seeking "to advance along this road at a deliberate pace and with dignity."

"Dniester SSR" Defies Moldavia

Unspecified bodies of the would-be "Dniester SSR," organized by Russian Communists in eastern Moldavia, issued an edict "ensuring the study of the Moldavian language in the Cyrillic script," TASS reported. Exceptions would be permitted only in individual cases upon written request. The measure, which defied the republican law on language, meant that those Moldavian schools in the area that had managed to switch to the Latin script were likely to be forced back to using the Cyrillic script. The same day, the "Dniester SSR" leaders called a congress of people's deputies of all levels from the area for September to adopt state symbols and a constitution for the would-be republic.

The "Dniester SSR" also began forming OMON detachments of its own. According to Novosti of August 7, the Joint Council of Work Collectives and the Bendery City Executive Committee were recruiting "non-Moldavians" into these detachments, offering "high pay." The recruitment drive was being conducted through the military commissariat, reflecting the known links between the leaders of the "Dniester SSR" and the Soviet Armed Forces in Moldavia.

Conversion Throws Thousands Out of Jobs

Soviet First Deputy Prime Minister Vladimir Shcherbakov made public data gathered by the USSR State Committee for Statistics that showed significant increases in unemployment resulting from the conversion of Soviet defense industries, according to TASS. Of some 300,000 workers who lost their jobs in defense plants in 1990, 76 percent were reassigned to civilian production while the rest entered the growing ranks of the Soviet unemployed. The expectations for 1991 were similar. Shcherbakov said current trends made it likely that another 380,000 people would be "freed" from defense production, with some 70,000 of those becoming unemployed.

Fil'shin Expelled from Party

Novosti reported that RSFSR Deputy Minister of Foreign Trade Gennadii Fil'shin had been expelled from the CPSU by the Buro of the Irkutsk Oblast Party Committee. Fil'shin was expelled for nonpayment of Party dues and nonparticipation in the primary Party organization of the Irkutsk Department for Regional Economics of the USSR Academy of Sciences, where he once worked. Novosti reported that Fil'shin had submitted his resignation from the Party before the Buro expelled him and that "informed circles" thought Fil'shin had been expelled as part of a campaign to prevent his nomination for election as governor (*gubernator*) of Irkutsk.

End of Radical Soviet

Moscow Deputy Mayor Yurii Luzhkov told the Moscow government that the executive committee of the Oktyabr'sky Raion Soviet had been disbanded for "complete disruption of work" (*razval raboty*), "Vesti" reported. Headed by the radical Il'ya Zaslavsky, the Oktyabr'sky Raion Soviet, along with its executive committee, had been lionized by the liberal Soviet media as the vanguard of economic and political reform. A year after they were elected, however, both Zaslavsky and the chairman of the executive committee, Georgii Vasil'ev, resigned owing to a split in Democratic Russia that was reflected among the soviet's deputies.

Wednesday, August 7

New Censorship Agency Set Up

Novosti reported that a new government agency was being set up to "advise" the Soviet media on how to avoid divulging state and commercial secrets. This "Agency for the Protection of State Secrets in the Mass Media" was clearly yet another incarnation of the notorious Glavlit censorship agency founded in the 1920s. (Glavlit was abolished in 1990 in line with the new USSR Law on the Press, which forbids political censorship, but the former censors immediately found a home in a new body, the Main Administration for Safeguarding State Secrets [GUOT].

GUOT in turn was reported to have been abolished as of July 1, 1991.) Statutes for the new body were being drafted, according to Deputy Chairman Nikolai Glazatov, who added that the agency would check the all-Union mass media for commercial or state secrets, but only after, not before, publication.

Finnish and Soviet Prime Ministers Discuss Trade

Soviet Prime Minister Valentin Pavlov met with his Finnish counterpart, Esko Aho, in Soviet Karelia to discuss trade between the USSR and Finland, which Pavlov described as having been suffering from "serious obstacles" of late, TASS reported. Pavlov announced after his four-hour meeting with Aho that the USSR Cabinet of Ministers had decided to allow Soviet enterprises to conduct barter trade with Finnish firms. Aho welcomed the decision, saying that it would help stimulate Soviet-Finnish trade and economic relations but that Finnish enterprises still had to find Soviet partners for the plan to work. Officials from Karelia participated in the talks, and both Pavlov and Aho expressed hope that Karelia would play an enhanced role in future bilateral relations.

Proposed Law on Weapons

The USSR Ministry of Internal Affairs was reported to have drafted a proposed law on the control of weapons, including a section on "weapons of self-defense." The ministry was said to have stated that it was necessary to give citizens "the right to defend themselves from crime independently, with the aid of weapons of self-defense." According to *Izvestia*, the law would give Soviet citizens new rights that would demonstrate that "individual security is becoming no less important than state security." Weapons would be sold in special shops to citizens over sixteen years of age.

Moldavians for Two Independent Romanian States

The Romanian Institute for the Study of Public Opinion and the Moldavian Academy's Institute of Social Studies conducted a joint poll in July on political preferences in Moldavia, using a representative sample of 2,200 residents. In the poll's most important finding, 71 percent of those asked agreed with the proposition that Moldavia and Romania "should form two independent states in the period ahead"; 17 percent disagreed; and 12 percent had no opinion. The finding reflected the low level of support in Moldavia for the idea of reunification with Romania and a consensus behind the Moldavian leadership's concept of "two independent Romanian states." The results of the poll were reported by Radio Bucharest.

THE USSR IN AUGUST, 1991

National Independence Front Formed in Lithuania

A new political association, the National Independence Front, was founded in Kaunas, Radio Independent Lithuania reported. The Kaunas branch of the Lithuanian Freedom League, the Kaunas Workers' Union, the national youth union Young Lithuania, the Republican Party, the Lithuanian Landowners Union, and the Political Prisoners Club 58 (all extreme right-wing groups) expressed interest in forming the association, whose avowed purpose was to further the implementation of Lithuanian independence.

Up to 25 Percent of Siberian Energy to Be Sold at World Prices

TASS reported that RSFSR President Boris El'tsin was granting various Siberian energy producers the right to sell up to 25 percent of their products at world market prices as of September 1. The rights were extended to a group of seventeen local governments. The increased revenues were to be targeted at developing the region's social infrastructure. The energy could be sold internally or abroad. Many energy producers had asked for permission to sell 50 percent of their output at world market prices, but El'tsin rejected that proposal.

Thursday, August 8

Changes in CPSU Draft Program

Pravda published the revised version of the CPSU draft Program with several significant changes. One was that Party members would be required to pay dues and to participate in local Party organizations. In addition, a sentence noting that Communist deputies owed first allegiance to their voters had been struck out, as had a paragraph critical of Bolshevism. The new version also contained a call for a united armed forces under a central leadership and stated that the CPSU "rejects interference by state bodies in the activities of public groups" that adhere to the USSR Constitution—a clear reference to El'tsin's decree on departification.

Communist Party Facing Bankruptcy?

Secret Party documents published in *Nezavisimaya gazeta* showed the CPSU facing a budget deficit in 1991 of 1.1 billion rubles—five times greater than the shortfall in 1990. The deficit was blamed on sharp drops in membership dues and sales of Party newspapers. The fall in revenue came at a moment when RSFSR President Boris El'tsin's determination to oust the CPSU from enterprises in the RSFSR threatened to involve the Communist Party in the expense of paying local officials and hiring office space—previously such bills had been footed by the enterprises, not the Party. *Nezavisimaya gazeta* predicted that, if things continued this way, the CPSU would face bankruptcy within a few years.

New Estimates of Poverty Level

In the absence of regular, comprehensive, and authoritative data on living standards from the USSR State Committee for Statistics, various agencies and media were offering their calculations on how many Soviet citizens were living below the poverty level, Novosti reported. It contrasted the official estimate that some 90 million Soviet citizens might fall below the poverty line in 1991 with the trade unions' projection of one-half the population.

Latvian Opposition Faction No Longer Endorses Union Treaty

Sergei Dimanis, opposition leader in the Latvian Supreme Council, told Radio Riga that he and other deputies of the "Ravnopravie" faction no longer endorsed the USSR Union treaty—until then a fundamental tenet of the faction's political program. He said the treaty did not serve a useful purpose at this time and would not prevent the USSR from sliding into chaos. He proposed instead an economic accord among the USSR republics along the lines of the agreement serving as a foundation for the European Common Market.

Mutalibov Rejects Russian Mediation in Transcaucasus

Moscow independent journalist Dmitrii Volchek told RFE/RL that three Russian people's deputies had met in Baku with Azerbaijani President Ayaz Mutalibov and Viktor Polyanichko, head of the Organizing Committee administering Nagorno-Karabakh, to propose plans for a settlement of the conflict between Armenia and Azerbaijan over the autonomous oblast. Mutalibov was reported to have rejected the deputies' proposals, however, and told them that their presence in Baku was undesirable.

Romanian Minister for Reunification with Moldavia in Stages

Interviewed in Tokyo by the Kyodo News Agency, Romanian Foreign Minister Adrian Nastase said Romania expected to achieve reunification with Moldavia in three stages: formation of a cultural confederation, formation of an economic confederation, and finally a merger "on the German model." Nastase added that "if the Soviets want to have a friendly nation on their border, they must take into account that nation's concerns, wishes, and expectations." This was the first time that a senior Romanian official had publicly outlined a strategy for reunification with Moldavia. Previously, Bucharest had professed unconditional adherence to Moldavia's concept of "two independent Romanian states."

State of Islam in Kazakhstan TASS quoted the mufti of Kazakhstan, Ratbek Nysanbaev, as saying there were more than 230 Muslim religious communities in Kazakhstan, five times as many as five years ago. Mullahs now took part in all aspects of public life; several translations of the Koran into Kazakh had been made; an Islamic institute was functioning in Alma-Ata; there were courses for Muslim clergy in several cities in southern Kazakhstan; and an independent newspaper, *Islam shapagaty*, had begun to appear. At the same time there had been an increase in the number and influence of adherents of "pure Islam," who on some questions opposed the Muslim Religious Board.

Yakovlev Interviewed on "Vesti" "Nothing imaginable could be worse than Bolshevism except Bolshevism," said Aleksandr Yakovlev in an exclusive interview carried by "Vesti." Yakovlev was interviewed in his new office in the Moscow City Soviet with his Kremlin phone line cut off, but he said his relations with Soviet President Mikhail Gorbachev remained "normal"—the two disagreed only on the CPSU's potential for reform. Yakovlev said he would quit the CPSU if the Movement for Democratic Reforms, of which he was a cofounder, were transformed into a political party at its next congress.

Friday, August 9

Soviet-Indian Treaty Renewed The Treaty of Peace, Friendship, and Cooperation between the USSR and India was renewed automatically, TASS reported. A joint Soviet-Indian declaration on the prolongation of the treaty stated that the accord formed the basis of "the particularly friendly relations between India and the USSR" and that the two countries had decided to extend the treaty for another twenty years.

Grain Procurements Lagging Chairman of the USSR State Committee for the Procurement of Foodstuffs Mikhail Timoshishin told *Pravda* that, with the grain harvest half completed, farms had sold the state only about one-fourth of the grain planned. Farms were protesting about adverse terms of trade, whereby the procurement prices they received for state deliveries had risen appreciably less than the prices of producer goods that they must buy from industry. Despite colorful lures of imported and domestic consumer and producer goods on offer to farms that fulfilled and overfulfilled their procurement quotas, farms were refusing to take rubles for their produce.

Gerashchenko Interview

In an interview with the *Financial Times*, Chairman of the USSR State Bank Viktor Gerashchenko warned that he would start cutting off funds to spendthrift republican banks after the first republics signed the Union treaty on August 20. He named the RSFSR central bank as the main culprit and charged that it had declined all effective cooperation with the USSR State Bank. Gerashchenko estimated that the USSR State Bank would issue 80 billion rubles' worth of bank notes in 1991 instead of the 35 billion rubles' worth planned. He said the income of the population had risen by 71 percent during the first half of the year.

Gerashchenko also confirmed that the USSR State Bank's reserves of 374.56 tons of gold represented only a small part of total Soviet gold reserves. He claimed that he was urging the Soviet government to end its secrecy concerning the country's gold production, sales, and reserves and suggested that Soviet gold be used as collateral for making the ruble convertible. Gerashchenko said he had proposed to the IMF and World Bank that Western countries extend further credits to the USSR but maintained that the Soviet Union could honor its debt repayments—which he estimated at 20 billion dollars—"at least until December."

In an overview of current problems, Gerashchenko said pay was running way ahead of productivity, taxation was too low, the budget deficit was uncontrolled, the printing of money continued unabated, the internal convertibility of the ruble—planned for January, 1992—was impossible, and government and presidential decrees and exhortations had no effect.

Ukrainian Premier on Draft Union Treaty

At a press conference in Kiev, Ukrainian Prime Minister Vitol'd Fokin said that the latest draft of the Union treaty showed a clear desire on the part of the center to defend old formulations, Ukrinform-TASS reported. Fokin complained that under the draft about 45 percent of Ukraine's industrial potential would remain under centralized management and that the center wanted to retain control of road, sea, and air transport. He also disagreed with the proposed retention of a single financial, credit, and insurance policy.

THE USSR IN AUGUST, 1991

Tajikistan Takes Steps to Control Cross-Border Trade

TASS reported that the republican Cabinet of Ministers had taken steps to limit the amount of fruit and vegetables leaving Tajikistan by forbidding cross-border barter trade unless it enabled Tajikistan to receive goods that were in extremely short supply in the republic. Nonstate traders (cooperatives, and private persons, for example) would be charged a 30-40 percent export tax on produce they shipped out of the republic.

Moldavian President Reaffirms Support for Proindependence Stand

In a speech broadcast on Radio Kishinev, Moldavian President Mircea Snegur dismissed as "fabrications" and "provocations" recent claims by the Soviet media and the Moldavian Popular Front that the Moldavian leadership was inclined towards signing the Union treaty. Accusing Moscow and the Moldavian Communist Party of "putting pressure on Moldavia" and "bombarding us with demands in connection with the Union treaty," Snegur said "the idea of independence has seized the broadest masses of the people."

Kirgizia's Privatization Project Published

A project for transforming Kirgizia's economy was published in the republican press for public discussion. The centerpiece of the project, according to Kirgiz President Askar Akaev, was large-scale privatization of state holdings. First to be privatized would be retail trade, service, and public catering firms; small construction organizations; and some highway transport. It was recommended that some enterprises under construction should be sold or given to work collectives so the new owners could complete them at their own expense. The reform was also to include laws to encourage foreign investment. See *Slovo Kirgizstana*, August 9 and 13.

Saturday, August 10

Three-Day Protest against OMON

Thousands of Lithuanians spent the weekend protesting outside the headquarters of police special troops (OMON) in Vilnius, demanding the withdrawal of the troops from the republic, Radio Independent Lithuania reported on August 11. "Sajudis" organized the three-day demonstration, which began on August 9. Estimates of the size of the crowd ranged from 1,000 to 5,000 throughout the weekend. No incidents were reported. Demonstrators also marched to a Soviet army building and the local KGB headquarters. On August 11, they sent an open letter to Soviet President Mikhail Gorbachev, demanding that he

THE USSR IN AUGUST, 1991

withdraw the OMON from Lithuanian territory and asserting that the notion the Soviet president was not responsible for the OMON was "a myth" (RFE Lithuanian service, August 12). The organizers of the rally also sent a letter to USSR Deputy Prime Minister Vitalii Doguzhiev, the official charged with conducting negotiations with Lithuania, calling for the return of Lithuanian property seized by Soviet forces in January. The demonstrators presented the OMON with a petition asking the servicemen to "reconsider and desert this criminal structure."

Shakhrai on Union Treaty

Sergei Shakhrai, chairman of the RSFSR Supreme Soviet Committee on Legislation and adviser to RSFSR President Boris El'tsin on legal questions, warned El'tsin that he should either call an urgent session of the RSFSR Supreme Soviet to approve the latest draft of the Union treaty or postpone signing it. Shakhrai maintained that a number of articles in the treaty could be interpreted in such a way as to pose a threat to the RSFSR's statehood. Shakhrai suggested that the signing of the treaty should be accompanied by a declaration by the president of the RSFSR and its constituent republics stating that their aim was not to bring about the disintegration of the RSFSR (*Russian Television*, August 10).

Did El'tsin Do a Deal with Gorbachev over the Union Treaty?

In an interview published in *Rossiiskie vesti* of August 10, Evgenii Ambartsumov, deputy chairman of the RSFSR Supreme Soviet Committee for International Affairs and Foreign Economic Ties, said that a large degree of dissatisfaction with the text of the draft Union treaty remained. Ambartsumov said he thought El'tsin had agreed to sign the treaty with all its shortcomings in exchange for Gorbachev's silent assent to El'tsin's decree on depoliticization.

El'tsin on New Power Structures

"Vesti" reported that RSFSR President Boris El'tsin would soon sign a decree establishing presidential administrations in all oblasts and raions of Russia, including the autonomous republics. The heads of the administrations would be elected later; in the meantime, El'tsin would send personal envoys to the periphery to watch over the implementation of his decrees. In a meeting with the independent trade unions of Russia on August 10, El'tsin said that his newly created State Council would consist of fifteen people—nine of them heads of the most important republican ministries and the rest state councilors with various areas of responsibility. El'tsin said the RSFSR

Security Council would maintain ties with the USSR KGB and MVD and with the Soviet Armed Forces (*Radio Rossii*, August 10).

USSR and Poland Officially Confirm Murders near Khar'kov

A joint Soviet-Polish commission officially confirmed that several thousand Polish army officers were shot by the NKVD in Khar'kov in April and May, 1940, and buried in a nearby forest. The exact number of Polish army officers was not given, but Radio Moscow said the remains of about 8,000 people, including Soviet citizens, had been found at the burial site (*Radio Moscow*, August 10; *TASS*, August 12).

Kaliningrad-Berlin Rail Link Reestablished

On August 8, the first train with German tourists arrived in Kaliningrad from Berlin, Radio Moscow reported on August 10. The notice that had hung in the station in West Berlin for forty-six years saying "Trains to Königsberg have been temporarily canceled" was transferred to a museum.

Head of North Ossetian Parliament Replies to Gamsakhurdia

The chairman of the North Ossetian Supreme Soviet, Akhsabek Glazov, rejected the demand of Georgian President Zviad Gamsakhurdia that North Ossetia should rename itself Ossetia, according to TASS. Glazov described Gamsakhurdia's demand as gross interference in the affairs of a sovereign republic and said that North Ossetia alone would decide what it wanted to call itself. Glazov also rejected Gamsakhurdia's assertion that the conflict in South Ossetia had been provoked by the Ossetians.

Sunday, August 11

Airikyan Registers as Presidential Candidate

Former Armenian dissident Paruir Airikyan was nominated by the Council for National Self-Determination as a candidate for the Armenian presidential election on October 16 (*TASS*, August 11). The Council for National Self-Determination advocated Armenia's immediate secession from the USSR. Airikyan was stripped of his Soviet citizenship and expelled from the USSR in the summer of 1988; he returned to Armenia, where he is a member of the Supreme Soviet, in November, 1990.

Temporary Ban on Exports from Ukraine

Ukrainian Prime Minister Vitol'd Fokin announced on Central Television on August 11 that Ukraine had imposed a temporary ban on the export of sixty scarce consumer goods, including foodstuffs, with effect from August 10. Fokin justified the measure on the grounds that large amounts of goods that "we badly need ourselves" were being taken out of the republic. He said farms were sending grain and other produce to other republics where the wholesale prices were higher. The Ukrainian government also reintroduced ration coupons. (These had been withdrawn following large-scale forgeries.)

International Israeli Organization Opens Branch in Kiev

Testifying to the growing ties between Ukraine and Israel, an official branch of the international Israeli organization "Sokhnut" was opened in Kiev. The purpose of the organization was to promote Jewish culture, tradition, and customs in Ukraine and also to answer inquiries regarding immigration to Israel (*Radio Kiev*, August 11).

--- *Monday, August 12*

Gas Concession for Anglo-Soviet Group

The *Financial Times* reported that an Anglo-Soviet trading company, Orbicom, had been granted a concession to exploit gas reserves on the Western side of the Yamal Peninsula. Reserves in the two specified areas were believed to exceed 150 million tons of gas condensate. Orbicom has a 50-percent stake in the corporate vehicle set up to handle the operation, and the balance is held by Tyumen' Geologiya and Yamalneftegaz Geologiya.

RSFSR Communist Party Sponsors New Newspaper

The RSFSR Communist Party Central Committee and the Leningrad Oblast Party Committee were reported to have founded a new newspaper called *Narodnaya pravda*, with a print run of 200,000 copies. Among the forty-four members of the editorial board were Yurii Bondarev, General Al'bert Makashov, and Viktor Tyul'kin, a member of the RSFSR CP Central Committee. TASS reported on August 12 that the tone of the articles was "sharp and uncompromising" and that it contained material critical of Mikhail Gorbachev, Aleksandr Yakovlev, and Eduard Shevardnadze.

Riga Railroad Customs Post Suffers Another Attack

Six armed men attacked the customs post at the Riga railroad station at 11:40 P.M. on August 12, Baltfax reported on August 13. They broke the door and windows of the office and beat up a customs official who was on duty at the time. One of the attackers was wearing an OMON uniform.

Georgia Recognizes Slovenia

TASS reported that the Georgian Supreme Soviet had officially recognized Slovenia as an independent state and had affirmed its readiness to begin talks immediately on setting up diplomatic relations. The Georgian move was condemned by a USSR Foreign Ministry spokesman who argued that it had no legal force as Georgia was itself not an independent state.

Zhirinovsky Backs Would-Be Dniester and Gagauz Republics

At the end of a visit to the self-proclaimed Dniester and Gagauz "SSRs" in eastern and southern Moldavia, Vladimir Zhirinovsky, the hard-liner who ran for RSFSR president, was interviewed by TASS's chief correspondent in Moldavia. Zhirinovsky said that Moldavia's "other peoples" would be justified in breaking away from Moldavia if the latter sought independence from the USSR. On July 29, Zhirinovsky was given a triumphant reception at a mass rally in Tiraspol', capital of the "Dniester SSR."

Criminal Charges Brought against Azerbaijani Social Democrat

TASS reported from Baku that Social Democrat Araz Ali-Zade, brother of presidential candidate Zardusht Ali-Zade, had been charged with insulting Azerbaijani President Ayaz Mutalibov in election campaign speeches in Geranboi Raion. Zardusht Ali-Zade was the sole candidate opposing Mutalibov in the Azerbaijani presidential election, which was to take place on September 7.

Kirgizia Takes Over All-Union Enterprises

Radio Moscow reported that Kirgiz President Askar Akaev had signed a decree transferring to republican subordination enterprises in Kirgizia that were previously subordinate to all-Union ministries. The decree asserted jurisdiction over all enterprises and organizations within the republic, with the exception of those (presumably military installations) whose activities fulfilled certain all-Union functions.

Helsinki Watch Blames Makhkamov

The US Helsinki Watch Group issued a report blaming Tajikistan's president, Kakhar Makhkamov, for the deaths of more than twenty unarmed demonstrators during violence in Dushanbe in February, 1990, because he asked Soviet President Mikhail Gorbachev to send troops from outside the republic to put down the disturbances. The conclusions in the report were based on the findings of two Helsinki Watch missions to the Tajik capital. The report recommended to the USSR and Tajik governments that the armed forces not be used for policing functions.

The USSR in August, 1991

Mujahidin on Soviet Border

Novosti quoted an officer of the Central Asian Border District on the taking over by the Afghan resistance of three districts on the border with Tajikistan. According to the officer, more than 90 percent of the area on the Afghan side of the Tajik border was under the control of the Mujahidin, but he said that incursions by the Afghan resistance into Soviet territory were unlikely.

Moldavia and Russian Federation Sign Economic Agreement

The prime ministers of the RSFSR and Moldavia, Ivan Silaev and Valeriu Muravschi, signed an agreement in Kishinev dealing with economic cooperation and trade for 1992, the Soviet, Moldavian, and Romanian media reported. Silaev declared that the agreement would stand regardless of Moldavia's position on the Union treaty. The agreement made international law the basis for economic relations between the two republics. Commodities were to be traded at world prices, but payments could be made through ruble-denominated clearing. Enterprises and organizations in the two republics would be free to establish direct contractual relationships. Both sides would encourage joint ventures.

_____ *Tuesday, August 13*

Pavlov Warns of Power Vacuum after Union Treaty Signed

Speaking at a press conference in Moscow, USSR Prime Minister Valentin Pavlov warned of the risk of a power vacuum after the Union treaty was signed unless the center retained some control over the economy, Western agencies reported. Pavlov appeared to be reacting to RSFSR President Boris El'tsin's remarks to leaders of the Federation of Independent Trade Unions of Russia on August 10 in which he said that the power of the Union ministries would end after August 20 and that "neither Pavlov, nor Petrov, nor Sidorov" would any longer be able to dispose of property on a given territory. Pavlov maintained that in certain key sectors republics would still have to take the central authorities into account when making important decisions. For the text of the fourth draft of the Union treaty, see *Izvestia*, August 15.

USSR Government Proposes Wage Freeze; RSFSR Resists

USSR Prime Minister Valentin Pavlov said his first deputy, Vladimir Shcherbakov, had proposed a nationwide wage freeze. He said the RSFSR representative had agreed in principle to the idea but had requested a delay while the republic implemented wage increases that had been granted since April. The other fourteen republics asked to be given a week to consider the pay freeze. Pavlov characterized the RSFSR's objections as being "of a purely populist character." He criticized the RSFSR government for promising pay increases to coal miners, claiming that Kuzbass wages were now four to five times higher than in Karaganda, and for agreeing to wage increases that would put the republican budget a further 25 billion rubles in the red in addition to its existing deficit of 81 billion rubles. He also criticized the RSFSR's decision to raise oil and coal producer prices.

The prime minister stated that a wage freeze was needed in order to stabilize the ballooning money supply. Reporting on the deliberations of the USSR Cabinet of Ministers on August 12, Pavlov said that the grain harvest would be "considerably" lower than in 1990 but that such emergency measures as mobilizing labor and trucks had been rejected; instead a new body named Agrosnab had been created to help with harvesting and distribution. Pavlov also said widespread and chronic shortages of electricity were anticipated for "at least five years" because of a freeze on the construction of new nuclear stations, the coal miners' strike, and the dilapidated state of the energy sector.

An account of Pavlov's press conference carried in *Izvestia* of August 14 revealed that a draft presidential decree calling for the introduction of a state of emergency and the universal mobilization of transport had been prepared but that the USSR Cabinet of Ministers had decided against its adoption.

Pavlov on "Real" Economic Reform

In an interview published in *Rabochaya tribuna*, USSR Prime Minister Valentin Pavlov warned readers not to expect any real economic reform in 1991. Pavlov insisted, on the other hand, that a noticeable stabilization in economic performance had begun. Pavlov reiterated his goal of restructuring the economy towards social needs, using the market as a tool but not as an end in itself.

Lushchikov on Registration of Public Organizations

USSR Minister of Justice Sergei Lushchikov told *Izvestia* that only two political parties—the CPSU and the Liberal Democratic Party—were among the more than 200 public organizations that had so far been registered at the all-Union level. No other political party had been able to satisfy all the requirements for registration as a national party. He also noted that many organizations could not be registered, because they violated Article 17 of the USSR

The USSR in August, 1991

law on public organizations, which forbade such groups from pursuing commercial aims. Asked why the CPSU and Komsomol had been registered despite the fact that they engaged in commercial activity, Lushchikov replied that making money was not the raison d'être of either the CPSU or the Komsomol.

"Patriots" Unite against Elected Governments

The leadership of the RSFSR Communist Party, members of the armed forces, and ultranationalist Russian writers were reported to be trying to establish a mass movement of all "patriotic" forces to replace the present state power, probably by violent means. The movement was to embrace hard-core Orthodox Marxists as well as anti-Communists, such as "Pamyat," known for their illiberal and anti-Semitic convictions. On August 13, "TSN" broadcast an interview with the movement's organizers, writers Aleksandr Prokhanov and Eduard Volodin, who signed the notorious "Word to the People," published in *Sovetskaya Rossiya* on July 23, calling on all true Russian patriots to join ranks against Gorbachev and El'tsin. Prokhanov told "TSN" that they planned to hold a founding congress in September or October.

Conflict between Sobchak and City Soviet

Leningrad's mayor, Anatolii Sobchak, was facing a serious conflict with the Leningrad City Soviet over privatization of the city's property. *Izvestia* reported that the Presidium of the Leningrad City Soviet had questioned Sobchak's right to conduct the privatization of the city's property through the mayor's office alone, without the participation of the city soviet. Sobchak responded that questions of privatization of city property were not within the competence of the Presidium of the city soviet and that he intended to defend the sovereignty of his office.

Moscow Students Protest against the Draft

Moscow students were reported to have set up a strike committee to protest against proposed legislation on military service, under which all students under the age of twenty-seven would have to serve in the army for two years (*TASS*, August 13.) The army had argued against preferential treatment for students, citing the need for more draftees. According to a member of the strike committee, Nikolai Pakhomov, the students' goal was "real reform of the army."

Zhirinovsky Questions Finnish Independence

The USSR Ministry of Defense distanced itself from remarks made by the leader of the Liberal Democratic

Party, Vladimir Zhirinovsky, who, in an interview with the Finnish newspaper *Iltalechti*, questioned Finland's independence. Zhirinovsky, who had started a personal campaign for the post of USSR president, asserted that Finland should be part of a Russian empire and added that his views corresponded with those of the USSR Ministry of Defense. On August 13, Novosti quoted Valerii Manilov, chief of the Defense Ministry's information service, as saying that Zhirinovsky's statement was the latter's personal view and was by no means supported by the Defense Ministry.

Dissension over Idea of Siberian Republic

A proposal to create a Siberian Soviet Federal Republic with its capital in Novosibirsk recently published in the Tomsk newspaper *Narodnaya tribuna* became the subject of heated argument, TASS reported from Novosibirsk. The new republic would embrace nineteen krais, oblasts, and national-state formations. The idea was said to have been fiercely rejected by the acting chairman of the RSFSR Supreme Soviet, Ruslan Khasbulatov, and by RSFSR Prime Minister Ivan Silaev. According to TASS, the idea of proclaiming a Siberian republic was first expressed publicly in 1990 by some Siberian leaders but did not receive support.

Armenian Prime Minister on Union Treaty

TASS quoted Armenian Prime Minister Vazgen Manukyan as proposing at a news conference in Erevan that Armenia could become "an associate member" of the Soviet Union. Manukyan said that it would make sense for Armenia to sign the Union treaty only if it contained a provision on the procedure for secession from the Union.

Central Asian Presidents Meet

TASS reported on August 13 that the heads of state of the five Central Asian republics were meeting in Tashkent to assess the results of the cooperation agreement they had signed a year earlier in Alma-Ata. They were also to discuss the new Union treaty. Interfax on August 14 quoted Kazakh President Nursultan Nazarbaev as saying on his arrival in the Uzbek capital that all republics planning to sign the treaty should ask whether it would be the prelude to fundamental changes that would end the country's economic crisis.

TASS reported on August 14 that the meeting had ended with the signing of several documents, the most important of which created an interrepublican council to oversee the implementation of agreements among

The USSR in August, 1991

the Central Asian republics. The prime minister of Azerbaijan, who attended the meeting as an observer, declared that Azerbaijan wanted to become integrated into the Central Asian economy. An article in *Nezavisimaya gazeta* of July 27 had noted the progress of Central Asian leaders towards regional unification and speculated that "a Greater Turkestan" could be in the process of formation.

Ukraine and Kirgizia Expand Economic Cooperation

Radio Kiev reported that Ukrainian Prime Minister Vitol'd Fokin was in Kirgizia to sign an agreement on economic cooperation between Ukraine and that republic for 1992.

Moldavia Moving towards Own Financial System

Moldavia's law on "The National Bank and Banking in the Republic" went into effect, Moldovapres reported. Under the law, the Moldavian National Bank was empowered to "work out the unitary state policy of the Republic of Moldavia with respect to monetary circulation" and set the exchange rate "of Moldavia's currency in relation to foreign currencies."

Wednesday, August 14

Bush Replies to Vagnorius

US President George Bush replied to a letter from Lithuanian Prime Minister Gediminas Vagnorius about the murders at the Medininkai customs post on July 31, Radio Independent Lithuania reported. Bush expressed his condolences to the families of the victims and wrote: "We will continue to press the Soviet government to exercise control over the actions of its forces in the Baltic States and to make clear our belief that Moscow is ultimately responsible for acts committed by its personnel." Bush also noted that he had told Gorbachev "the United States attaches great importance to progress towards freedom for the Baltic States and that our support for the people of the Baltic States will remain constant."

Nazarbaev Refuses to Sign Chevron Contract

In the latest development in the Tengiz-Chevron oil saga, *Moscow News* stated that Kazakh President Nursultan Nazarbaev had refused to sign the contract giving Chevron development rights at the Tengiz oil fields, Novosti reported. Nazarbaev was quoted as saying that the USSR government had not been conscientious in negotiating the transaction. He was drafting a decree declaring the oilfields to be Kazakh property. This meant that the Kazakh government would conduct all further negotiations on developing the Tengiz and other oilfields in Kazakhstan.

Low Draft Turnout in Lithuania

The Soviet military commissar in Lithuania, Major General Algimantas Visockis, told journalists in Vilnius on August 14 that in Lithuania only 13 percent of young men drafted for the Soviet Armed Forces had actually joined, Radio Independent Lithuania reported on August 15. Visockis also repeated that the USSR did not recognize duty in the Lithuanian National Defense Department as alternative military service.

Treaty Signed between Lithuania and Armenia.

Armenian Supreme Soviet Chairman Levon Ter-Petrossyan and Lithuanian Supreme Council President Vytautas Landsbergis signed a bilateral five-year treaty in Vilnius recognizing each other as sovereign states and calling for the development of mutually beneficial cooperation in the economy, culture, health care, ecology, and other sectors (Radio Independent Lithuania, August 14).

Soviet Economic Performance in July

Contrary to recent claims by USSR Prime Minister Valentin Pavlov that the economy had begun to stabilize, figures issued by the USSR State Committee for Statistics for July indicated simply that the pace of deterioration had slowed somewhat and only in a few sectors. The strongest recovery seemed to have been in the mining and natural resources industries, according to a TASS review of August 14. Industrial production was off by 6.2 percent compared with the first seven months of 1990.

Ford Dealerships in the USSR

Western agencies reported that the Ford Motor Company had opened a joint venture dealership in Dnepropetrovsk and planned to open a second in Tallinn later in the year. Further Ford service centers were planned for Moscow and Leningrad. These centers would sell and service European-made Ford cars and trucks for hard currency only.

Sofia Cathedral in Novgorod Returned to Russian Orthodox Church

Novgorod's Sofia Cathedral and its icons were returned to the Russian Orthodox Church (*Radio Rossii*, August 15). Two monasteries that housed museums were also returned, but an agreement was reached under which these buildings may continue to be used as museums.

The USSR in August, 1991

Thursday, August 15

Soviet Pilgrims at World Youth Day

Western agencies reported on the participation of Soviet young people in the World Youth Day celebrations in Czestochowa, Poland. Church sources estimated that 50,000–70,000 pilgrims from the Soviet Union had followed the invitation of Pope John Paul II to attend the youth rally.

Catholic Cathedral Returned to Believers

Ukrinform-TASS reported on August 15 that the first festive mass had been conducted in the Catholic cathedral in Odessa to celebrate its return to the community by the local authorities after forty years. In recent years, more than 100 church buildings in Odessa Oblast alone have been returned to believers.

Nuclear Disarmament Conference in Moscow

A cochairman of the Uzbek Women's Association "Tomaris" informed the RL Uzbek service that the tenth European Conference on Nuclear Disarmament was being held in Moscow for the first time. The majority of the Soviet participants, according to the "Tomaris" spokeswoman, were members of democratic movements from across the USSR, including Memorial, the Russian Social Democratic Party, and the Uzbek Popular Front, "Birlik," as well as her own organization.

Travkin for Preservation of the Soviet Union

The leader of the Democratic Party of Russia, Nikolai Travkin, said at a meeting in the Moldavian city of Tiraspol' that his party was in favor of the preservation of the Soviet Union. Travkin stated that his party sought to become an all-Union democratic party that would challenge the CPSU for power. Travkin had initially cooperated with Eduard Shevardnadze and other reform Communists in setting up the Movement for Democratic Reforms but later quit the organizational committee.

Yakutia Claims Ownership of State Enterprises

The Supreme Soviet and Council of Ministers of the Yakut-Sakha republic passed legislation transferring all enterprises and organizations in the republic to Yakut ownership, according to TASS and Novosti reports. This transfer involved about 900 enterprises. Yakutia would continue to fulfill state orders for diamonds, gold, and other resources. Yakutia intended to work with the RSFSR on the basis of negotiations and long-term agreements.

Georgia Nationalizes Banks

TASS reported that the Georgian parliament had ordered the nationalization of all local branches of all-Union banks on Georgian territory. Georgian branches of the USSR State Bank would constitute a national Bank of Georgia, while branches of other federal banks would be transformed into state banks or Georgian-owned commercial banks.

Armenia Lifts State of Emergency

The state of emergency imposed in Armenia on August 29, 1990, after the shooting of a member of parliament in Erevan by informal paramilitaries was lifted at midnight on August 15 by order of the Armenian Supreme Soviet, TASS and Interfax reported. The Armenian parliament's decision was prompted by the need "to guarantee democracy and normal social conditions" in the lead-up to the referendum on secession from the USSR scheduled for September 21.

"Dniester SSR" Claims Jurisdiction over Enterprises

The leadership of the would-be "Dniester SSR" in eastern Moldavia ordered all enterprises, institutions, and organizations of republican subordination in the area, effective immediately, to pass from Kishinev's jurisdiction to the jurisdiction of the "Dniester SSR," TASS reported. The move by the Russian Communist leaders of the would-be republic appeared calculated to exert pressure on Kishinev to reconsider its opposition to the Union treaty.

Friday, August 16

Azerbaijani President Visits Iran

Azerbaijani President Ayaz Mutalibov began an official visit aimed at improving economic and cultural ties between Iran and Azerbaijan, RL's Azerbaijani service was informed on August 15 by a presidential spokesman.

Mutalibov met in Teheran on August 17 and 18 with Iranian President Ali Akbar Hashemi-Rafsanjani and Foreign Minister Ali Akbar Velayati (*TASS*, August 18). Mutalibov described the talks on expanding Soviet-Iranian cooperation as "extremely positive."

Yakovlev Quits the CPSU

Aleksandr Yakovlev announced his resignation from the CPSU. His statement was published in *Izvestia* on August 16, the day after the Soviet media had reported the recommendation by the Buro of the Presidium of the CPSU Central Control Commission that Yakovlev be expelled from the CPSU. Yakovlev was accused of making "statements intended to split the CPSU as well as to remove the CPSU from the political scene"—i.e., participating in the creation of the Movement for Democratic Reforms. Yakovlev wrote that no one had talked to him before the decision was made and that he had found out about it by chance. Yakovlev termed the way he had been treated by the Central Committee "a personal insult and violation of a Party member's rights." In such a situation, Yakovlev concluded, he considered it "no longer possible, and indeed, immoral to serve the cause of democratic reforms within the framework of the Soviet Communist Party."

Yakovlev Warns of Stalinist Coup d'Etat

In the same statement in *Izvestia*, Yakovlev wrote that "an influential Stalinist group has formed within the Party's leadership core" and that reactionaries are planning a vindictive Stalinist coup d'état. Despite their liberal declarations, Yakovlev wrote, the leadership of the CPSU is ridding the Party of its reformist "democratic" wing in order to be prepared "for social revenge—a Party and state coup." In an interview with RSFSR radio and television, Yakovlev said the "revanchist, Stalinist" movement consisted of top Party officials as well as commanders of the military and law-enforcement bodies. "I cannot name a single regional Party secretary who is not participating in it," Yakovlev told "Vesti."

Gorbachev Does Not Control the Party, Yakovlev Says

Asked whether his old friend CPSU General Secretary Mikhail Gorbachev had been aware in advance that the Party Control Commission was going to expel Yakovlev from the CPSU, Yakovlev said that he did not know ("Vesti," *Russian Television*, Radio Ro*ss*ii, *Moskovsky komsomolets*, August 16). "I feel," Yakovlev added, that in his capacity as USSR president, Gorbachev "does exercise control in the country" but as general secretary he controls the Party "only to a very small extent."

State Television Seized by CPSU

The popular youth show "VID" was interrupted for a forty-minute roundtable discussion by three CPSU leaders of the draft of the new Party Program. This discussion was not in the program schedule, nor was there an interview with the new leader of the RSFSR Communist Party, Valentin Kuptsov, which was to have been broadcast in prime time, after the "Vremya" newscast on August 15. At the same time, elected officials—including RSFSR President Boris El'tsin and the mayors of Moscow and Leningrad—were not allowed to air their views on Central

Television, except on the news. Moreover, "Vremya," which on August 15 had broadcast the CPSU Control Commission's statement recommending that Yakovlev be expelled from the Party, did not bother to mention Yakovlev's own statement the following day.

Movement for Democratic Reforms Supports Yakovlev

Yakovlev's concern over the purge of reformers from the CPSU was echoed on August 16 in a statement by the Movement for Democratic Reforms and in an interview with Eduard Shevardnadze broadcast on "Vesti." The decision to expel Yakovlev, whom Shevardnadze called "a war hero and a hero of *perestroika*," was indeed an unusual development. Since Nikita Khrushchev rid himself of an "anti-Party" group of Stalin's accomplices in the late 1950s, no former Politburo member had been expelled from the CPSU, despite the charges of corruption and abuse waged against some of them in the Soviet media.

Communist Party Counterattacks in Kirgizia

TASS reported that the leadership of the Kirgiz Communist Party had declared invalid a decision by the Party organization of the republican Ministry of Internal Affairs to end Party work in the ministry. The Party leadership complained that the "departification" decision had been taken under pressure from Minister for Internal Affairs Feliks Kulov. The minister was well known for his support of democratization in the republic.

Moldavia's Jewish Community Gets More Cultural Facilities

Moldavian President Mircea Snegur approved by a decree issued on August 16 the republican government's "special program for the development of Jewish culture and meeting the social needs of the Jewish population" (*Novosti*, August 16; *TASS*, August 17). The republican-financed program created a Department of Jewish Studies at Kishinev University to teach Jewish history and culture and the Hebrew and Yiddish languages; mandated the opening of a Jewish high school in Kishinev and the introduction of Jewish classes in high schools in several other Moldavian cities; and provided financial support for the Society for Jewish Culture and its publication.

Saturday, August 17

USSR Cabinet Criticizes Union Treaty

The Presidium of the USSR Cabinet of Ministers met to discuss the impact on the center of the signing of the

The USSR in August, 1991

Union treaty (*TASS*, August 17). The Presidium issued a statement calling for changes in the draft of the Union treaty, warning that the present draft would deprive the center of power and destroy the economic and political integrity of the USSR. In an interview published the same day in *Sovetskaya Rossiya*, Chairman of the USSR State Bank Viktor Gerashchenko also expressed serious reservations about the latest draft of the Union treaty and complained that the provisions of the treaty concerning monetary issues were inadequate.

El'tsin and Nazarbaev Set To Sign Union Treaty

RSFSR President Boris El'tsin and Kazakh President Nursultan Nazarbaev met in Alma-Ata to ratify a cooperation agreement that would reduce the role of Moscow in the economies of their two republics (*Central Television, Radio Moscow, TASS*, August 17 and 18). Talks centered on the revamped Union treaty, which the two leaders were scheduled to sign in Moscow on August 20 together with Soviet President Mikhail Gorbachev and the leaders of Uzbekistan, Tajikistan, and Belorussia (other republics were due to sign in September). El'tsin told a press conference that he and Nazarbaev were still dissatisfied with some of the clauses of the Union treaty and hoped to cut back the power of the center still further. Nazarbaev added that he and El'tsin had worked out a proposal for a single economic entity that would embrace all fifteen republics. On August 18, El'tsin returned to Moscow. For the text of the fourth draft, see *Izvestia*, August 15.

Sunday, August 18

Georgian Government Shake-Up

Georgian Prime Minister Tengiz Sigua resigned after President Zviad Gamsakhurdia had criticized his government for failing to reverse the economic crisis in the republic (*TASS*, August 18). Gamsakhurdia subsequently appointed former Deputy Minister of Culture Vissarion Gugushvili as acting prime minister (*Interfax*, August 22). Gamsakhurdia also fired Foreign Minister Giorgi Khoshtaria and Deputy Prime Minister Otar Kvilitaya. First Deputy Prime Minister Murman Omanidze was named to succeed Khoshtaria.

Coup d'Etat Mounted: Gorbachev Put under House Arrest

Late on August 18, Soviet President Mikhail Gorbachev was placed under house arrest in the Crimean villa where he and his family were vacationing. During the first two days of the coup, Gorbachev's whereabouts were unknown. Only later did it become known that Gorbachev was visited at 4:50 P.M. (local time) on August 18 by a four-man delegation consisting of his own chief of staff, Valerii Boldin; First Deputy Chairman of the USSR Defense Council Oleg Baklanov; CPSU Central Committee Secretary Oleg Shenin; and Chief of the Soviet Ground Forces General Valentin Varennikov. The visitors were accompanied by KGB General Yurii Plekhanov, chief of the state security-guard organization. Smelling a rat, Gorbachev tried to put through a call to Moscow, only to discover that all his telephone lines had been cut and the villa surrounded by KGB troops. The delegation demanded, in the name of the "State Committee for the State of Emergency in the USSR" (*Gosudarstvennyi Komitet po chrezvychainomu polozheniyu v SSSR*), that Gorbachev declare a state of emergency and turn power over to USSR Vice President Gennadii Yanaev. Gorbachev told them to "Go to hell." He was then placed under detention by Colonel General Igor' Mal'tsev, commander of Air Defense Troops.

The first details of Gorbachev's detention were made available in a speech delivered in Moscow on August 20 by RSFSR State Secretary Sergei Stankevich; the text of his speech was made available to RFE/RL's Russian service. Further details of Gorbachev's detention were provided in a special investigative edition of the Soviet television program "Vzglyad," screened on Soviet Central Television on August 25.

What Happened to the Nuclear Codes?

Vladimir Lysenko, a member of the RSFSR parliament, claimed after Gorbachev's release that those who placed the president under house arrest had seized from him the briefcase containing the secret codes for launching Soviet nuclear weapons (*The Washington Post*, August 23; *The Guardian*, August 24). According to *Time* (September 2, 1991), Moscow's strategic nuclear "button" is a two-part system, of which the USSR president controls one part and the USSR minister of defense the other. If, therefore, the conspirators took away Gorbachev's half of the system, General Dmitrii Yazov would, at least in theory, have had the wherewithal to order the launching of nuclear missiles. The new RSFSR defense minister, Konstantin Kobets, sought on August 24 to allay fears on this account, saying there had never been any danger of nuclear weapons being used. The Pentagon also discounted the possibility (*CNN*, August 27).

On August 28, the new chief of the General Staff, Vladimir Lobov, told TASS that "the Strategic Nuclear Forces of the USSR—the Rocket Forces, the fleet, and

The USSR in August, 1991

strategic aviation—as well as the tactical nuclear weapons of the Ground Forces" remained under "firm and constant" control during and after the coup attempt. His comments followed similar assurances by the new defense minister, Evgenii Shaposhnikov.

Monday, August 19

Shortly after 6:00 A.M. (Moscow time), TASS and Radio Moscow announced that Soviet President Mikhail Gorbachev was prevented by "ill health" from executing his duties and that, in accordance with Article 127-7 of the USSR Constitution, Soviet Vice President Gennadii Yanaev was assuming power as acting president.

It was announced that Yanaev headed an eight-man "State Committee for the State of Emergency in the USSR." Its other members were First Deputy Chairman of the USSR Defense Council Oleg Baklanov; Chairman of the USSR KGB Vladimir Kryuchkov; USSR Prime Minister Valentin Pavlov; USSR Minister of Internal Affairs Boriss Pugo; Peasants' Union Chairman Vasilii Starodubtsev; President of the USSR Association of State-Owned Industrial, Construction, Transport, and Communications Enterprises Aleksandr Tizyakov; and USSR Minister of Defense Dmitrii Yazov. As was repeatedly pointed out during the following days, the majority of these men had been appointed by Gorbachev personally.

Gorbachev Deposed

Yanaev and the Emergency Committee immediately issued a number of declarations. These were read hourly throughout the day on all channels of Soviet television by somberly attired announcers. They included "An Address to the Soviet People," which began, "Fellow Countrymen! . . . Mortal danger hangs over our great homeland! The policy of reform initiated by M. S. Gorbachev . . . has, for a number of reasons, come to a dead end." There followed "A Declaration of the Soviet Leadership" imposing a six-month period of emergency rule "in certain [unspecified] parts of the country." (The original text, as issued by TASS, spoke of a state of emergency "throughout the country," but TASS quickly issued a correction. The reason was that the Emergency Committee tried hard to give its actions a semblance of legality. Under the USSR Law on a State of Emergency of April, 1990 [see *Izvestia*, April 9, 1990] the USSR Supreme Soviet had the exclusive right to declare a state of emergency throughout the country. The president

State of Emergency Declared

555

had the right to do so only in "individual areas" and even then must refer the matter to the USSR Supreme Soviet for ratification "without delay.")

The sixteen-point Resolution No. 1 of the Emergency Committee placed a ban on strikes, demonstrations, and rallies and imposed press censorship. The activities of political parties and mass movements were banned if they "prevented the normalization of the situation." The Ministries of Defense and Internal Affairs, the Prosecutor's Office, and the KGB were instructed to ensure public order and state security. Special measures were promised against mismanagement, the shadow economy, corruption, and speculation.

Finally, Acting President Yanaev issued an address to foreign heads of state and governments and the UN secretary-general, assuring them that the introduction of emergency rule in the USSR would in no way alter the USSR's international obligations, treaties, or agreements. (For the texts of these declarations, see *Izvestia*, August 20.)

Coup Precipitated by Imminence of Union Treaty

The coup's timing seemed to have been determined not so much by Soviet President Gorbachev's absence from Moscow on vacation as by mounting opposition to the new Union treaty. Gorbachev and RSFSR President El'tsin were both, for different reasons, determined to push ahead with the signing of the treaty on August 20, even though the document bore the hallmarks of an unsatisfactory compromise. Among its first statements, the Emergency Committee promised to hold a Union-wide discussion of the draft "in which everyone would have the right to consider the document in a calm atmosphere and determine their attitude towards it" (*TASS*, August 19).

Luk'yanov Denounces Union Treaty

Sharp criticism of the draft Union treaty was contained in a statement by Anatolii Luk'yanov, chairman of the USSR Supreme Soviet, which was distributed by TASS early on August 19 (and published in *Izvestia* on August 20). Luk'yanov complained that the text of the Union treaty did not reflect the results of the all-Union referendum of March 17, 1991, and that, although the text had been approved by the USSR Supreme Soviet, subsequent alterations did not take account of the Supreme Soviet's objections. Luk'yanov warned that the text would allow the republics to suspend the operation of all-Union laws, thus perpetuating "the war of laws," and proposed that there should be another referendum in connection with the adoption of a new USSR Constitution.

THE USSR IN AUGUST, 1991

Cabinet Supports Coup

The USSR Cabinet of Ministers met on August 19 and expressed support for the decisions of the organizers of the coup, which were, the Cabinet said, "aimed at pulling the country out of its deep political and economic crisis" (*Pravda*, August 21). (On August 23, El'tsin forced Gorbachev to read the minutes of this meeting to the RSFSR Supreme Soviet; the account revealed that all but two of about twenty ministers had either approved the coup or failed to oppose it [*Russian Television*, August 23].) Also on August 19 Supreme Soviet Chairman Anatolii Luk'yanov announced that the USSR Supreme Soviet would meet on August 26 to endorse the state of emergency (*TASS*, August 19).

Mass Media Muzzled—But Not For Long

The Emergency Committee introduced an immediate ban on the independent media. All channels of Soviet television and radio carried identical programs—classical music, football, and ballet—interspersed with the solemn reading and rereading of the Emergency Committee's edicts. Western news agencies reported on August 19 that the independent Moscow radio station "Ekho Moskvy" had been occupied by KGB officers and ordered to stop broadcasting. RFE/RL's Russian service was informed that the armed forces had placed censors in the offices of independent newspapers such as *Moskovsky komsomolets*, *Megapolis-Ekspress*, and *Kuranty*.

TASS reported on August 19 that the Emergency Committee was banning all but nine national newspapers. Permitted to publish were: *Trud, Rabochaya tribuna, Izvestia, Pravda, Krasnaya zvezda, Sovetskaya Rossiya, Moskovskaya pravda, Leninskoe znamya*, and *Sel'skaya zhizn'*.

The Emergency Committee's attempts to clamp down on the mass media were only partially successful. No attempt was made to jam Western radio broadcasts. Independent newspapers banded together to put out a joint edition—*Obshchaya gazeta*. *Moscow News* defied the ban and managed to bring out a limited circulation issue. "Ekho Moskvy" quickly set up an office in the Russian White House—the headquarters of the RSFSR parliament on Moscow's Krasnopresnenskaya embankment—and resumed local broadcasting. Radio Mayak, taken off the air on August 19, resumed broadcasting on August 20. Even Central Television's "Vremya," generally noted for its conservatism, screened film in its evening newscast on August 19 of demonstrations in Moscow and Leningrad; interviewed protesters; and, by broadcasting the questions posed by journalists at the press conference given by Yanaev on August 19, informed Soviet viewers of El'tsin's call for a general strike.

Tanks on the Moscow Streets

At 9:00 A.M. (Moscow time) columns of military vehicles began to move towards the center of Moscow. Armored vehicles and tanks took up positions outside key state buildings, on the squares, and along the main thoroughfares of the capital. That morning, CNN showed what Soviet television (initially) did not—Moscow being entered by tanks and armored personnel carriers. Observers noted that three hours elapsed between the announcement of the coup and the appearance of the tanks in Moscow and interpreted this delay as yet another sign of the bungling and indecisiveness that dogged the coup. Civilians pleaded with the soldiers not to obey the orders of the coup organizers, and there were frequent reports of fraternization between troops and the population throughout the crisis. Protesters threw up the first barricades outside the Russian White House. Shouting "Fascism Shall Not Pass!" and waving the white, blue, and red tricolor of prerevolutionary Russia, the demonstrators tore up paving stones, reinforced them with girders and planks, and formed human chains to block the path of the armored vehicles. These early acts of defiance set the scene for what was to follow.

Scarce Goods Appear in Moscow Stores

Scarce food items that had not been available in Moscow for months reappeared almost immediately after the coup. Western agencies reported on August 20 that state stores were stocked with sausage, cheese, coffee, candy, poultry, tea, cookies, and smoked salmon. Gasoline also became available.

El'tsin Defiant, Calls for General Strike

CNN reported (which Soviet television did not) a press conference given by Boris El'tsin at the headquarters of the RSFSR government at 11.00 A.M. (Moscow time). Describing the coup as "madness" and "an illegal act," El'tsin said he would "never be removed by anyone but the people of Russia." El'tsin called for Gorbachev's reinstatement and appealed to the Moscow population to stage protest demonstrations in defense of democracy.

At 12:50 P.M. (Moscow time), El'tsin climbed atop an armored truck outside the Russian White House to address the people who had gathered to protect the building, Western agencies reported. El'tsin called for an immediate general strike to protest against Gorbachev's unconstitutional ouster. The crowd outside the building soon swelled to thousands.

Izvestia Joins the Opposition

Although *Izvestia* was one of the central newspapers allowed to publish, it did not appear on August 19, RFE/RL's Russian service was informed. The issue of *Izvestia* that appeared on August 20 gave extensive coverage to El'tsin's views and to resistance. In this, *Izvestia* distinguished itself from the other central Soviet dailies permitted to publish. *Sovetskaya Rossiya* was the toughest in propagating the position of the Emergency Committee. On August 21, however, even *Pravda* and *Sovetskaya Rossiya* carried a short TASS report reflecting the position of the El'tsin leadership.

El'tsin Assumes Control

El'tsin issued a presidential edict declaring the Emergency Committee illegal, its members guilty of treason under the RSFSR Criminal Code, and its orders invalid on the territory of the RSFSR. El'tsin ordered all army and KGB units involved in Gorbachev's overthrow to stand down and declared that he was assuming control throughout the territory of the RSFSR. El'tsin's edict, copies of which were distributed by hand outside the Russian parliament building and which was published in *Rossiiskaya gazeta* on August 23, ordered all officials in the RSFSR to obey only the commands of the RSFSR government, not those of the Emergency Committee. The following day, this and other edicts issued by El'tsin were declared unconstitutional and legally invalid by Acting President Gennadii Yanaev ("Vremya," *Central Television*, August 20).

Strike Calls

The Ukrainian popular movement "Rukh" called for a general strike to protest against Gorbachev's ouster, RFE/RL's Ukrainian service was informed by telephone from Kiev on August 19. Chairman of the Ukrainian Supreme Soviet Leonid Kravchuk, however, appealed to workers not to join the strike (*The Guardian*, August 20). Also on August 19, RFE/RL's Russian service reported that coal miners in the Kuzbass region of Western Siberia had declared a strike of indefinite duration, starting on August 20.

Yanaev Gives Press Conference

At 5:00 P.M. (Moscow time), Yanaev addressed a press conference at the Press Center of the USSR Foreign Ministry. The conference was screened live on Soviet television and attended by the world's press corps.

The USSR in August, 1991

Flanked by the other members of the Emergency Committee, Yanaev said the declaration of a state of emergency had been necessary because the country had become "ungovernable" and faced "a slide into catastrophe" following "the emergence of multiple power centers." Yanaev said he hoped "my friend President Gorbachev" would eventually return to his post. He said Gorbachev was "undergoing treatment in the south of our country." Gorbachev was, Yanaev added, "very tired after all these years and will need some time to get better," but newsmen noted that Yanaev's own hands were trembling as he spoke. Yanaev went on to caution the citizens of the RSFSR that their acts of resistance—in particular, the manning of barricades—could provoke a military response, the responsibility for which, he said, would rest with the leaders of the RSFSR.

Gorbachev Makes Home Video

Gorbachev subsequently revealed (in a speech to the RSFSR parliament, shown live on Russian Television on August 23) that, thanks to his bodyguards, who fixed up a makeshift television connection, he was able to watch Yanaev's press conference. Only then did Gorbachev learn of Yanaev's claim that he (Gorbachev) was too sick to do his job. At 2:00 A.M. that night, with the help of his son-in-law, Gorbachev made a home video in which he rebutted Yanaev's claims. Copies of the film were smuggled to Moscow, and it was shown on Soviet television's "Vzglyad" on August 25.

Constitutional Watchdog Challenges Seizure of Power

In a statement read on the evening edition of "Vremya," the USSR Committee for Constitutional Supervision queried the Emergency Committee's right to introduce emergency legislation, pointing out that only the USSR Supreme Soviet had the right to declare a state of emergency throughout the country. The statement went on to say that such measures as the removal of Gorbachev as head of state and the creation of the Emergency Committee could be legally justified only under the condition of "strict observance" of the constitution and other Soviet laws. The watchdog body, whose recommendations had advisory force only, accordingly counseled the Emergency Committee to consult the USSR Supreme Soviet.

El'tsin Appeals to Russian Orthodox Church

RFE/RL's Russian service reported that El'tsin had issued a personal appeal to the Patriarch Aleksii II of the Russian Orthodox Church, urging him to speak out against the coup. On August 20, the Moscow Patriarchate replied

THE USSR IN AUGUST, 1991

with a statement in which the patriarch sharply criticized the fact that Gorbachev had been detained and that his whereabouts remained, at that time, unknown. The patriarch appealed to the Soviet Armed Forces to remain calm and "not to permit fraternal blood to be shed." On August 21, the patriarch anathematized all those who took part in organizing the coup. (Anathema is the strongest means at the Church's disposal of publicly displaying its disapproval of an individual's behavior or beliefs.)

Hard-liners Express Satisfaction

Interviewed by RFE/RL's Russian service on August 19, the leader of the hard-line "Soyuz" group of deputies, Colonel Viktor Alksnis, expressed satisfaction with Gorbachev's ouster. On August 20, Vladimir Zhirinovsky, chairman of the Liberal Democratic Party, gave an interview to Central Television in which he, too, supported the coup. As an international lawyer, Zhirinovsky asserted, he felt able to state that the Emergency Committee consisted of "ministers currently in office" and therefore represented legitimate authority. Those who believed otherwise, Zhirinovsky went on, were "rabble" and "state criminals." The interview with Zhirinovsky was screened by Central Television on August 23.

Leningrad under Military Rule

The Soviet Armed Forces were reported to have taken control of Leningrad. Interfax reported that the commander of the Leningrad Military District, Lieutenant General Viktor Samsonov, had addressed Leningrad residents on local radio to say he had declared a state of emergency in the city and ordered a curfew. Samsonov banned all strikes and demonstrations and threatened to disband certain political parties and mass media organs, warning that the leaders and members of banned organizations would be "forcibly employed at factories, enterprises, and kolkhozes." Samsonov described himself as chairman of the Leningrad State of Emergency Committee, whose other members included the first secretary of the Leningrad Communist Party organization, Boris Gidaspov, and Deputy Mayor Vyacheslav Shcherbakov. RFE/RL's Russian service was informed on August 19, however, that Shcherbakov had called the RSFSR Supreme Soviet to deny his membership and declare his support for El'tsin.

Thousands of demonstrators gathered in St. Isaac's Square outside the headquarters of the Leningrad City Soviet as the soviet met in emergency session and deputies expressed support for El'tsin (*Central Television*, "Vremya," August 19). Interviewed by RFE/RL's Russian service, Leningrad Mayor Anatolii Sobchak said that Gorbachev was not ill and that the "coup d'état" against him was illegal. Sobchak called for an immediate emergency session of the USSR Congress of People's Deputies. Speaking later that evening on Leningrad television, Sobchak called on soldiers to hand over for trial all those officers who had helped organize the coup. Late that night, Sobchak held a press conference at which he said the Emergency Committee did not have wide support in the armed forces and was not as strong as it claimed to be (*Interfax*, August 20).

Moldavia Condemns Coup

Sources in Moldavia told RFE/RL that the republic's leadership had condemned "the military putsch and coup d'état in Moscow" and rejected a demand by the Soviet Armed Forces that would have led to the takeover of the capital, Kishinev. A mass rally was held that evening on Kishinev's central square, and Moldavian President Mircea Snegur appeared on Moldavian television to denounce the coup.

Reaction in Ukraine

Chairman of the Ukrainian Supreme Soviet Leonid Kravchuk appeared on republican television and appealed to citizens to remain calm. Kravchuk's address, which was also carried by radio, noted that there was no state of emergency in Ukraine. He said the appropriate evaluation of the situation would be made by the Ukrainian Supreme Soviet. Such serious political matters, Kravchuk declared, precluded hasty reactions.

Reactions in the Transcaucasus

Georgian President Zviad Gamsakhurdia appealed to the population to stay at their workplaces and perform their duties "without yielding to provocation or taking unauthorized action." Armenian President Levon Ter-Petrossyan warned in an address on Radio Erevan that any self-motivated act or unconsidered step might cause distorted interpretations and "short-sighted reaction." IRNA quoted Azerbaijani President Ayaz Mutalibov as stating that he welcomed Gorbachev's removal as "the natural consequence of the policies that have brought chaos to the Soviet Union over the past few years." IRNA subsequently reported that Mutalibov had cut short his official visit to Teheran and flown home to Baku.

Situation in Kazakhstan and Central Asia

During his press conference on August 19, Yanaev cited Uzbekistan and Kazakhstan as examples of regions where there was no need to declare a state of emergency. TASS reported on August 19 that Kazakh President Nursultan Nazarbaev had appealed to the people of the republic for calm. There was increased danger in Kazakhstan of a confrontation with the armed forces because of a peace march moving towards Semipalatinsk, intent on preventing the Ministry of Defense from conducting a nuclear test planned for August 29. In his appeal, Nazarbaev assured his listeners that no state of emergency would be introduced in Kazakhstan by outside forces.

TASS reported on August 19 that Kirgiz President Askar Akaev, probably the most convinced democrat among Central Asian leaders, had issued an appeal to the people of Kirgizia, calling for calm, unity, and respect for the constitution.

Islam Karimov, the conservative president of Uzbekistan, was, on the other hand, quoted by TASS on August 20 as having told a meeting of Communist Party and government leaders in Tashkent on August 19 that things were functioning normally in Uzbekistan and that there was no need to declare a state of emergency. Karimov was quoted as comparing the implementation of *perestroika* to tearing down one's house before a new one was built and as claiming that, without order, democracy could bring no good. He also took a swipe at the opposition, criticizing it for using democracy and *glasnost* as a cover from which to grab power. But Karimov reportedly told the meeting that he remained a proponent of the text of the Union treaty agreed on in Novo-Ogarevo.

State of Emergency in Moscow

In the early evening, Acting President Yanaev declared a state of emergency in Moscow. His edict, summarized by TASS, appointed Colonel General Nikolai Kalinin as city commandant. TASS said the state of emergency was declared because of the failure of citizens to obey the edict issued earlier in the day banning rallies, demonstrations, and strikes. Tanks and other armored vehicles took up positions around the Russian White House, where El'tsin's supporters had erected barricades that kept the tanks at bay. Reuters reported that some 5,000 people had braved heavy rain overnight to keep vigil outside the building. Bonfires were lit, and the Russian tricolor fluttered from a small air balloon overhead. El'tsin himself spent the night inside the Russian White House. His press spokesman, Pavel Voshchanov, told AP the next day (August 20): "El'tsin feels OK. He worked until 3:00 A.M., slept a little, and was up at 5:00 A.M. to begin work again."

THE USSR IN AUGUST, 1991

El'tsin Appeals to Soldiers Not to Shoot; Tanks Defect

During the evening, El'tsin appealed to Soviet soldiers and KGB officers not to shoot people (*Russian Information Agency, AP*, August 19). "Soldiers, officers and generals!" the appeal read, "You can build a throne out of bayonets, but you cannot sit on it long."

During the evening, RFE/RL's Russian service learned that tanks from the elite Taman' Motor Rifle Division, the 106th Airborne Division, and the Kantemirov Tank Division had disobeyed orders and arrived to help defend the Russian White House. The tanks, flying the Russian tricolor, were cheered on by the crowds. By the morning of August 20, ten friendly tanks encircled the Russian parliament. Among those joining El'tsin was Colonel General Konstantin Kobets, chairman of the RSFSR State Committee for Defense (*The Washington Post*, August 20).

Landsbergis Addresses Lithuania

In an address broadcast by Radio Independent Lithuania, Lithuanian Supreme Council President Vytautas Landsbergis warned that the new Soviet leadership posed a threat to Lithuanian independence. "Our greatest weapon is our spirit," Landsbergis said, calling for civil disobedience and noncollaboration in the event of a dictatorship. Whatever happens, he went on, "we know that the darkest hour of the night is before the dawn."

Lithuanian Supreme Council Session

At an emergency session on August 19 and 20, the Lithuanian parliament unanimously ratified the treaty signed between Lithuania and the RSFSR on July 29. The session issued a statement addressed to RSFSR President Boris El'tsin vigorously condemning the attempt to overthrow the democratically elected RSFSR government and expressing solidarity with "all progressive Russian forces." It also issued an appeal to the parliaments and governments of the world's democratic states calling on them to officially recognize the Republic of Lithuania and establish diplomatic relations with it. The appeal called on the Conference on Security and Cooperation in Europe to apply the conflict-resolution mechanism envisaged by the Paris Charter and send a fact-finding mission to Lithuania.

The session adopted a resolution "inviting the people of Lithuania to begin a political strike for an unlimited period of time in enterprises and organizations" (except for health care, agriculture, communications, energy, the food industry, and transport) if the government was impeded in executing its duties. (A similar appeal was issued by "Sajudis.") It also issued an appeal asking "all soldiers and officers of the Soviet Armed Forces stationed in Lithuania not to make encroachments on the residents of Lithuania or their democratically elected leadership" (RFE Lithuanian service, August 19).

Soviet Military Activities in Lithuania

The Lithuanian Information Center reported that Soviet troops had moved against media and communications facilities in Lithuania. They seized the Lithuanian television and radio broadcasting center in Kaunas and disconnected lines to the Juragiai television transmitter and the Sitkunai radio relay station. Soviet soldiers also raided the main telephone exchange in Vilnius but apparently did not sever communication links. The port of Klaipeda was reported to be under blockade, with Klaipeda garrison commander Colonel Chernykh declaring himself in charge. Shortly after 11:00 P.M., about eighty tanks threatened the Lithuanian parliament, where deputies were meeting in an emergency session. Some 5,000 Lithuanians were massed outside. The tanks withdrew after twenty minutes (RFE Lithuanian service, August 19).

Gorbunovs Addresses the People of Latvia

Addressing the people of Latvia on Radio Riga, Latvian Supreme Council President Anatolijs Gorbunovs said that a coup d'état had taken place in the USSR, that power had been seized by an unconstitutional Emergency Committee, and that this unlawful committee had no authority in Latvia. He urged the people not to cooperate with unlawful groups but to maintain peace and order and, should the need arise, to engage in peaceful protest. In conclusion, he emphasized that all rightful power and authority belonged to the people of Latvia.

The leadership of the Latvian Democratic Labor Party (formed by liberal Communists who split from the conservative, pro-Moscow Latvian Communist Party in the spring of 1990) announced its support for Gorbunovs' speech.

Rubiks Calls for New Government in Latvia

In a previously scheduled morning press conference broadcast by Radio Riga, Alfreds Rubiks, leader of the pro-Moscow Latvian Communist Party, expressed satisfaction with the events in Moscow. He said that a new government would be formed in Latvia and that all political parties, except the Latvian Communist Party, would be disbanded. He added that the radical deputies of the Supreme Council would be recalled and an Emergency Committee formed in Latvia.

THE USSR IN AUGUST, 1991

Luk'yanov Says No State of Emergency in Latvia

Gorbunovs telephoned Chairman of the USSR Supreme Soviet Anatolii Luk'yanov to clarify the situation in Latvia. He was told by Luk'yanov that no state of emergency had been declared in Latvia by the authorities in Moscow. When asked to explain the work of the Emergency Committee, Luk'yanov advised Gorbunovs to talk to Yanaev and said that he (Luk'yanov) wanted the USSR Supreme Soviet to look into the legal underpinnings of the committee.

Troops Surround Riga

Soviet troops, tanks, and armored vehicles started to take up key positions in and around Riga. Radio Riga reported late in the afternoon that there were concentrations of troops at the main intersections on the outskirts of the Latvian capital and in the evening noted that a column of tanks was moving from the base at Adazi to Riga. Unusual military activity was noted around a communications center in Sigulda.

Appeal to Local Governments

The Latvian Supreme Council called on local governments in Latvia not to cooperate in any way with the USSR Armed Forces, KGB, MVD, CPSU, or groups under the orders of the USSR Emergency Committee; to distance themselves from any illegal entities of state power and their activities; to consider the orders and decisions of the formations stemming from the Emergency Committee as having no legal force in Latvia; and to obey under all circumstances the laws and decisions of the Supreme Council and the Council of Ministers of Latvia.

Latvian Television and Radio Silent

The Latvian radio and television building was taken over by OMON units and Soviet paratroopers during the afternoon of August 19 and consequently all programming stopped, Radio Riga reported that day. Radio Riga stopped shortwave broadcasts at around 2:15 A.M. on August 20.

Latvian Ministry of Internal Affairs Seized

Radio Riga reported late in the afternoon that Soviet forces had taken over the Latvian Ministry of Internal Affairs as well as the Riga Department of Internal Affairs. Western reports indicated that the main telephone and telegraph office in Riga had been seized by Soviet troops.

Estonian Government Supports El'tsin's Strike Call

The Estonian Government issued a statement condemning the coup and supporting RSFSR President Boris

THE USSR IN AUGUST, 1991

El'tsin's call for a general strike. The government called on all democratic forces "in the current and former republics of the Soviet Union" to defend democracy and freedom (*Estonian Radio*, August 19).

Estonia Condemns Coup, Grants Powers, Appeals to World

The Estonian Supreme Council condemned the coup in Moscow, saying that the Emergency Committee was illegal and that any attempts to implement its program should be rebuffed. In a separate resolution, the Supreme Council granted emergency powers to a three-member Emergency Defense Council of the Republic of Estonia. The Emergency Defense Council, set up in January and consisting of Prime Minister Edgar Savisaar, Speaker Ulo Nugis, and Supreme Council President Arnold Ruutel, was empowered to act on the state's behalf in restoring Estonian state independence "should the activities of the Supreme Council be obstructed." The Estonian Foreign Ministry sent RFE/RL the Supreme Council's resolutions.

Kuz'min "Only Following Orders"

Colonel General Fedor Kuz'min, commander of the Baltic Military District, informed Gorbunovs that he would be assuming control of Estonia, Latvia, and Lithuania on behalf of the Emergency Committee. Subsequently, however, according to a *Diena* dispatch of August 20, Kuz'min told the Latvian government that he was not a member of the Emergency Committee and was simply following orders from above.

Emergency Committee Says It Will Not Force Republics to Sign Union Treaty

The leader of the Emergency Committee, Gennadii Yanaev, said the committee would respect the will of the people in the Baltic republics, Moldavia, Georgia, and Armenia with regard to the draft Union treaty.

―――――――――――――――――――――――― *Tuesday, August 20*

El'tsin Issues Ultimatum, Assumes Military Command

In an ultimatum addressed to the chairman of the USSR Supreme Soviet Anatolii Luk'yanov, Boris El'tsin made the following demands: that he be allowed to meet with deposed President Mikhail Gorbachev within twenty-four hours in the presence of Acting President Gennadii Yanaev; that Gorbachev be given a medical examination, at the expense of the Russian government, within three days by doctors from the World Health Organization; that the results of the examination be made public; and that, if Gorbachev were found to be in good health, he be restored to power; that all restrictions on the RSFSR media be lifted; that troops be withdrawn from Moscow and Leningrad; and that the Emergency Committee be disbanded. El'tsin's demands were reported by CNN on August 20. They were conveyed to Luk'yanov later that day by Acting Chairman of the RSFSR Supreme Soviet Ruslan Khasbulatov (*Izvestia*, August 21).

El'tsin Assumes Command of Armed Forces, Appoints Defense Minister

El'tsin promulgated a presidential edict announcing that he was taking immediate control of all units of forces on the territory of the RSFSR. He ordered all units to remain at their permanent bases and called upon those currently deployed to return to base. El'tsin also declared all orders signed by Defense Minister Dmitrii Yazov and KGB Chairman Vladimir Kryuchkov invalid and ordered RSFSR Vice President Aleksandr Rutskoi to prepare proposals for the formation of an RSFSR National Guard. El'tsin said his edict would remain in effect only until constitutional order was restored in the USSR. (The edict was read on Moscow's Radio Triana, broadcasting from inside the RSFSR parliament building, on August 20.) Later in the day, Western agencies reported that El'tsin had appointed General Konstantin Kobets as RSFSR defense minister.

Ban on Public Rallies Defied

Former Politburo members Aleksandr Yakovlev and Eduard Shevardnadze were among those who addressed a rally against the coup that was held in front of the Moscow City Soviet. The official estimate of the size of the crowd was 200,000 people. Interviewed by RFE/RL's Russian service, Yakovlev branded the coup as "in the tradition of the banana republics." Shevardnadze later addressed the crowd of at least 50,000 people who had gathered outside the Russian White House. The crowd was also addressed by El'tsin, who vowed, "We will remain as long as is necessary to block this junta from power and to bring it to justice" (*AFP*, August 20).

Komsomol Condemns Coup

The Central Committee of the Komsomol issued an appeal calling on young people and soldiers to refrain from acts that could be considered provocative. Independent journalists in Moscow told RFE/RL's Russian service, however, that the summary of the text of the appeal carried by the official media omitted its main points. The journalists, who obtained the full text of the appeal, said it strongly condemned the change of power in Moscow as unconstitutional and criticized the ban on

THE USSR IN AUGUST, 1991

publication of the main Komsomol newspaper, *Komsomol'skaya pravda*.

US President George Bush telephoned El'tsin and repeated US support for restoring President Gorbachev to power (*AFP, AP*, August 20). The US president told reporters he had tried to call Gorbachev but had been unable to reach the deposed leader. Bush promised El'tsin that Moscow would not have normal relations with the United States or receive Western aid until the coup ended.

Bush Telephones El'tsin, Supports Gorbachev

Coal miners in Vorkuta in the Arctic and in the Kuzbass in Western Siberia began a strike in protest against the coup, Western agencies reported. In Vorkuta, strike committee member Yurii Kovalenko said five out of thirteen pits were on strike. Twenty-six pits stopped work in the Kuzbass, according to unnamed union spokesmen from Kemerovo quoted by Western agencies; but, while the strike call was heeded in Sverdlovsk, it was ignored in Petropavlovsk, Volgograd, and Vologda. Response in Ukraine's Donbass was also said to be patchy (*The Guardian*, August 20). In all, about half the mines in the USSR stopped work. Workers in the giant Tyumen' oilfield ignored the strike call.

Strike Call Heeded by Coal Miners, Ignored by Oil Workers

RSFSR Foreign Minister Andrei Kozyrev arrived in Paris and told Western newsmen he was empowered by his government to form a government-in-exile in France if necessary (*DPA, AFP*, August 20). CNN reported that Kozyrev would travel on to Washington, DC, where he would put the case of the Russian government to the Bush administration.

Kozyrev Travels to Paris and Washington, DC

TASS reported that Leningrad Mayor Anatolii Sobchak had declared his support for a general strike. Interfax said Sobchak addressed a meeting of 200,000 people in Leningrad's Palace Square, where he said he had reached an agreement with the commander of the Leningrad Military District, Lieutenant General Viktor Samsonov, as a result of which Samsonov ignored the orders he had been given by his military superiors, and two armored columns turned back and did not occupy the city center. Sobchak assured the crowd that the situation in the city was "fully under the control of the lawful authorities." The rally was also addressed by, among others, Academician Dmitrii Likhachev. The meeting adopted a resolution in

Sobchak Supports Strike

support of the RSFSR leadership. RFE/RL's Russian service was informed by a source in Leningrad that workers at many enterprises in the city were ready to stay on strike until the organizers of the coup were arrested. Sobchak said twenty factories had stopped work, including the giant Kirov plant, which produces tractors and tanks.

Leningrad Media Ignore Ban With the exception of the newspaper of the city soviet, *Vechernii Leningrad*, all the Leningrad papers appeared on August 20, a local journalist told RFE/RL's Russian service. These included such outspoken newspapers as the Komsomol periodical, *Smena*, and the newly created organ of the local soviet, *Nevskoe vremya*. The independent Leningrad radio station, "Svobodnyi gorod," was also able to resume broadcasting on August 20 and broadcast the documents issued by the RSFSR leadership.

Ukrainian Parliament Issues Statement on Coup The Presidium of the Ukrainian Supreme Soviet issued a statement saying that a full analysis of the situation would be made by the Ukrainian Supreme Soviet after its extraordinary session scheduled for August 26; that a state of emergency had not been introduced in Ukraine and the Presidium of the Ukrainian Supreme Soviet saw no justification for its introduction; that the decisions of the Emergency Committee would have no legal force in the republic prior to resolutions' being adopted by the USSR Supreme Soviet; and that the Presidium of the Ukrainian Supreme Soviet would continue to defend the state sovereignty of Ukraine, human rights, and the democratic achievements initiated in 1985 (*Radio Kiev*, August 20).

Soviet Troops Move towards Kiev The presence of troops was largely restricted to Moscow and Leningrad, but on August 20, as Ukraine's parliamentary leadership was meeting in emergency session, a column of more than 30,000 Soviet troops was reported moving towards Kiev (Western agencies, August 20).

Moldavians Vow to Resist Coup, Call for Independence A rally attended by an estimated 50,000 people in Kishinev's central square was addressed by President Mircea Snegur, parliament Chairman Alexandru Mosanu, government and parliamentary officials, and representatives of political parties and movements. Snegur vowed "not to budge one iota from the policy line aiming for complete independence." He and the other speakers attacked the Emergency Committee and vowed to resist any attempt by its representatives or the armed forces to take control in Moldavia. A resolution adopted by acclamation contained the following demands: dissolution of "the reactionary junta" and criminal prosecution of those responsible for the coup; the release of Gorbachev and his reinstatement as USSR president; an early declaration of independence by the Moldavian parliament; and a ban on the CPSU in Moldavia and confiscation of its assets.

Moldavian Government Bans Distribution of Emergency Committee Documents

The government of Moldavia displayed its contempt for the coup by banning the sale and distribution in the republic of the very nine newspapers the Emergency Committee had sanctioned, Western agencies and Interfax reported on August 20. The government also warned that newspapers published on the territory of the republic would be closed if they published documents issued by the Emergency Committee. Later in the day, the Moldavian Supreme Soviet expressed support for El'tsin, Western agencies and Interfax reported.

"Gagauz SSR" and "Dniester SSR" Support Coup

On the initiative of the Joint Council of Work Collectives (OSTK), an organization of Russian Communists that was the main political force in the self-proclaimed "Dniester SSR" in eastern Moldavia, special sessions of raion and city soviets were held in the area. The sessions sent messages of support to the Emergency Committee and resolved to set up an Emergency Committee in the "Dniester SSR" headed by OSTK President Vladimir Rylyakov and subordinated to the USSR Emergency Committee, Moldovapres reported on August 20. For their part, the Communist leaders of the would-be "Gagauz SSR" in southern Moldavia held similar sessions in their raions and cabled messages of support to the Emergency Committee, Novosti reported.

Georgian President Appeals to West

In an appeal received by RFE/RL on August 20, Georgian President Zviad Gamsakhurdia called on the West to support democracy, pluralism, and democratically elected presidents and parliaments in the USSR and to recognize the independence of republics, such as Georgia, that have democratically elected governments and now face "direct military aggression."

Nazarbaev Denounces Coup

Kazakh President Nursultan Nazarbaev issued a statement on August 20 denouncing the Emergency Committee as illegal and its coup as a betrayal of the USSR's efforts to become a law-based state; apart from anything else, Nazarbaev said, the actions of the Emergency Committee "flout republican declarations of sovereignty" (*TASS*, August 20). Nazarbaev acknowledged that he had been impatient with Gorbachev's unwillingness to intervene decisively to end the economic crisis in the country but made clear that he had wanted Gorbachev to take more radical steps, not return the USSR to conservative policies. Nazarbaev demanded to hear the opinion of Gorbachev and called not only for a session of the USSR Supreme Soviet but also for the USSR Congress of Peoples' Deputies to meet within ten days to set a date for the popular election of the president of the USSR.

Akaev Removes KGB Chairman

TASS reported that the Kirgiz capital, Bishkek, was quiet and that all shops, enterprises, and transport were working normally. On the evening of August 19, liberal republican President Askar Akaev had issued a decree retiring the chairman of the Kirgiz KGB, Dzhumabek Asankulov, ostensibly at his own request. The duties of Asankulov, who had not been a visible supporter of democratization in the republic, were taken over by republican Vice President German Kuznetsov, founding member of a political group supporting the aims of the Movement for Democratic Reforms. Minister of Internal Affairs Feliks Kulov, a prominent member of the liberal Democratic Renewal faction in the Kirgiz Supreme Soviet, declared that he would act in accordance with republican and USSR law and the orders of Akaev, TASS said. MVD units were reported to be protecting important buildings. Akaev and his liberal supporters appeared determined to forestall any attempt to use local law-enforcement or security forces to institute a state of emergency, which would certainly have been supported by conservative Communists in Kirgizia.

Kirgiz Democrats Support El'tsin

The Kirgiz Democratic Movement, Kirgizia's largest democratic group, informed the RFE/RL Kirgiz service on August 20 that it had sent a telegram to El'tsin, condemning the unconstitutional removal of Gorbachev and supporting El'tsin's position. The same day, the Kirgiz Democratic Movement issued an appeal to the people of Kirgizia. A representative read the text to RFE/RL's Kirgiz service. The appeal demanded the reinstatement of Gorbachev and the implementation of the Union treaty and called on the republican government to ignore the orders of the Emergency Committee.

THE USSR IN AUGUST, 1991

Niyazov Sits on the Fence

RFE/RL's Turkmen service learned on August 21 that Turkmenistan's conservative president, Saparmurad Niyazov, had chosen to wait and see what would happen in Moscow before committing himself. Neither he nor the Presidium of the republican Supreme Soviet made any public statement either in favor of or against the coup. A leader of the opposition Turkmen Popular Front "Agzybirlik," on the other hand, told the Turkmen service that his group condemned the overthrow of Gorbachev.

On August 27, Turkmen people's deputy Maral Amanova told the USSR Supreme Soviet session that Turkmenistan's leadership had done nothing about the Moscow coup because it had had too little information about what was going on. El'tsin's appeal of August 19 reached the republic only on the evening of August 20. The Turkmen media stopped disseminating the orders of the junta the following day. Amanova boasted that the government of Turkmenistan had not carried out any of the junta's orders and that Niyazov had kept military units out of Ashkhabad. Amanova said Niyazov had resigned from the CPSU Politburo.

RSFSR Regions Support El'tsin

Local governments in the Far Eastern oblasts of Kamchatka, Magadan, and Sakhalin declared their support for El'tsin, Interfax reported. Radio Vilnius reported that deputies in Volgograd, Smolensk, Kirov, and Chelyabinsk Oblasts had also expressed support for El'tsin, as did the city soviets of Leningrad, Moscow, Petrozavodsk, and Novgorod.

Tatarstan Supports Coup

The president of Tatarstan, Mintimer Shaimiev, was quoted by Interfax as telling Acting President Gennadii Yanaev that Tatarstan would comply with the orders of the Emergency Committee.

Luk'yanov Meets "Soyuz" Deputies

The chairman of the USSR Supreme Soviet, Anatolii Luk'yanov, met with ten USSR deputies of the conservative "Soyuz" faction early in the evening, RFE/RL's Russian service was informed from Moscow. Deputy Oleg Borodin, who was present, said Luk'yanov claimed that, when Oleg Baklanov and other members of the Emergency Committee visited Gorbachev's villa on the eve of the coup, Gorbachev had agreed to the committee's program, provided all its actions and its creation were sanctioned by the USSR Supreme Soviet. (This version of events was subsequently denied by Gorbachev.) Luk'yanov said Gorbachev had changed his mind about the Union treaty and decided to postpone its signing after receiving an "extremely offensive" reply from El'tsin to his invitation to attend a meeting of the Federation Council on August 21, the day after the Union treaty was to be signed.

Luk'yanov professed to believe that Gorbachev was ill. He told the "Soyuz" deputies that he thought the creation of the committee was a necessary measure brought on by the crisis into which the RSFSR leadership, and El'tsin in particular, had brought the country. Luk'yanov added that he did not support all the committee's actions and thought troops should be removed from the cities, above all from Moscow. Luk'yanov said he had declined to be a member of the committee.

The Coup Unravels

As popular opposition grew stronger, the cohesion of those who had organized the coup began to break. This was due partly to the failure of the CPSU leadership to give the coup full backing (see below) and partly to the disagreements that arose within the Emergency Committee over the advisability of using military force against those barricaded inside the Russian White House. A clear sign that the coup was unraveling came with the epidemic of "coup flu" that began to afflict members of the Emergency Committee. Central Television's evening newscast, "Vremya," reported that Prime Minister Valentin Pavlov was suffering from high blood pressure and had been confined to bed. His ministerial responsibilities were reported to have been assumed by First Deputy Prime Minister Vitalii Doguzhiev.

Next to fall sick was USSR Foreign Minister Aleksandr Bessmertnykh (*CNN*, August 20). CNN cited Foreign Ministry employees as saying Bessmertnykh had been in his office the day before, in perfect health. This news was followed by persistent rumors, reported on August 20 by CNN and Western news agencies, according to which Kryuchkov and/or Yazov had resigned from the committee. These rumors were denied.

Attack on Russian White House Feared

As darkness fell, the military commandant of Moscow, General Nikolai Kalinin, announced on Central Television that a curfew was being declared in the capital, to begin at 11:00 P.M. (local time) and to last until 5:00 A.M. Members of the El'tsin government said they feared military action might be taken that night against the RSFSR Supreme Soviet building (*CNN,*, August 20). RSFSR State Secretary Sergei Stankevich appealed through a loudspeaker to women and children to leave the building, saying this would ease the task of those who might have to defend it. In a speech made available to RFE/RL's Russian service, Stankevich appealed to Soviet troops not to "spill the blood of your brothers and sisters." Western agencies said armored columns had been seen moving near the parliament building. Approaches to the building were barricaded, and, despite the pouring rain, hundreds of citizens prepared, for the second consecutive night, to keep watch outside the building.

Yanaev Tells El'tsin He Will Cancel Assault

Acting President Gennadii Yanaev was quoted as saying he would not permit any attack by the armed forces on the RSFSR parliament building. The parliament's press service said on August 20 that Yanaev had spoken by telephone that evening with El'tsin and assured him that, if orders for such an attack existed, he would cancel them (*AFP*, August 20). Later, during the night, El'tsin's close aide Gennadii Burbulis reportedly spoke twice by telephone to KGB Chairman Vladimir Kryuchkov (Western agencies, August 21). The organizers of the coup, it appeared, were becoming aware that they would be obliged, whether they liked it or not, to negotiate with El'tsin.

Coup Turns Deadly

Shortly before midnight, a brief burst of gunfire was heard near the Russian White House (*CNN*, August 20). Fighting between troops and demonstrators broke out at midnight on Moscow's Garden Ring Road. Buses were overturned and set alight; protesters lobbed concrete blocks and Molotov cocktails at tanks. The troops fired into the air in an effort to disperse the demonstrators, who responded with shouts of "Fascists, Fascists!" Three young men were shot or crushed to death when tanks tried to crash a barricade of trolley buses defending the RSFSR parliament building (*CNN, The Times*, August 21).

Troops in Tallinn

Over 100 armored vehicles were reported moving into Tallinn. Mayor Andres Kork told Estonian Radio, however, that the troops were returning to their barracks at Tondi, Kopli, and the Dvigatel' factory, and he called on Tallinn residents to avoid any actions that could be provocative.

Strike Committees in Estonia Support Coup Leaders

TASS reported that the strike committees in Estonia fully supported the new leaders in Moscow. "Only through joint and resolute action can we check the hunger, desolation, and civil war that are advancing on our multinational country," they said.

Governments-in-Exile Planned for Baltic States

Estonian radio reported that the three Baltic governments had authorized representatives abroad to form exile governments in case the elected governments found it impossible to function. Quoting the Baltic News Service, the radio said Estonian Foreign Minister Lennart Meri, Deputy Chairman of the Latvian Supreme Council Dainis Ivans, and Lithuanian Foreign Minister Algirdas Saudargas had been entrusted with forming exile governments. Meri was reported to be in Helsinki, Ivans in Stockholm, and Saudargas in Warsaw.

Lithuanian Customs Posts Attacked

Soviet military activity was extended to include attacks on Lithuanian customs posts, Radio Independent Lithuania reported. Soviet forces raided the Panemune post near the border with Kaliningrad Oblast. Troops also attacked and destroyed the Kybartai post on the same frontier. Troops drove up to the Lazdijai post on the Polish border and ordered its closure, but the order was ignored.

Casualties in Latvia

Radio Riga reported that Juris Bekeris had died of injuries sustained when Soviet troops seized the Riga radio building. Another man also died in a Riga hospital after his minibus collided with a Soviet armored vehicle. The first Latvian victim of the coup was Raimonds Salmins, a driver for the Latvian Writers' Association, who died after being hit by OMON bullets in Riga on August 19.

Estonia Ends Transition Period, Declares Independence

The Estonian Supreme Council declared full independence for the republic, thereby ending the transition period begun on March 30, 1990. The declaration called for the establishment of a Constitutional Assembly to write a new constitution, which would be put to a referendum. The assembly itself would be appointed jointly by the Supreme Council and the Congress of Estonia, a move that finally closed the gap between the two opposing movements. The declaration also called for elections to a new parliament in 1992.

The RSFSR was the first republic to recognize Estonian independence, the Estonian Foreign Ministry reported on August 21. Lithuanian Prime Minister Gediminas Vagnorius sent a congratulatory message to Estonian Prime Minister Edgar Savisaar.

On August 22, Estonian Foreign Minister Lennart Meri sent formal appeals to all the countries participating in the Conference on Security and Cooperation in Europe to recognize Estonia's declaration of independence.

THE USSR IN AUGUST, 1991

Wednesday, August 21

When dawn broke after a night of tension, it became clear that the expected siege of the Russian White House was not going to take place. That was the turning point in the coup. If the conspirators would not or could not use violence in order to terrorize the population, they could not enforce their will. From that night on, it was clear that the coup would fail. The only surprising element was the speed with which it disintegrated.

Coup Leaders Lose Their Nerve

Eventually, even the CPSU spoke out—obliquely—against the coup. A meeting of the CPSU Secretariat demanded that Acting President Gennadii Yanaev meet immediately with deposed President Gorbachev. The Party's demand was signed by Vladimir Ivashko, who, as deputy general secretary, was Gorbachev's second-in-command in the Party hierarchy. Ivashko was quoted as saying that, until the Party leadership met with Gorbachev and received guidance from him, it did not have the right to give "a political assessment" of his ouster (*TASS*, August 21).

Communist Party Enters the Fray

An emergency session of the RSFSR Supreme Soviet convened in the Russian White House (*CNN*, August 21). El'tsin told deputies that RSFSR Prime Minister Ivan Silaev and Vice President Aleksandr Rutskoi were preparing to leave for the Crimea with a team of medical doctors to meet with Gorbachev. El'tsin said he had been told by KGB Chairman Vladimir Kryuchkov that Gorbachev was being held at his villa on Cape Foros, south of Yalta. El'tsin added that the proposal for the visit had come from Kryuchkov, who had at first suggested that El'tsin should be the one to travel to meet Gorbachev in order to verify the claim of the Emergency Committee that Gorbachev was sick. Fearing a trap, the RSFSR government decided that El'tsin should remain in Moscow and that other high-level emissaries should lead the delegation instead.

RSFSR Supreme Soviet Holds Emergency Session

El'tsin told the RSFSR parliament that the eight members of the Emergency Committee were on their way to Moscow's Vnukovo Airport and were planning to leave Moscow by plane. He said their intentions were not clear. Khasbulatov suggested that they might be trying to go to the Crimea to negotiate with Gorbachev. Deputies called

Coup Leaders Try to Leave Moscow

on Muscovites to block roads to the airport, and El'tsin instructed the RSFSR KGB to arrest the coup leaders if they tried to flee the country. Later that afternoon, it was announced that the ringleaders had been arrested (Western news agencies, August 21).

Decrees Annulled, Gorbachev Reinstated as President

The Presidium of the USSR Supreme Soviet declared illegal the ouster of President Mikhail Gorbachev and the takeover of his duties by Vice President Gennadii Yanaev. It formally reinstated Gorbachev as president. In addition, the Presidium annulled all the emergency decrees passed by the Emergency Committee and lifted the curfews it had imposed (*TASS*, August 21). Soon after, troops and tanks began to pull out of the center of Moscow.

Press Restrictions Removed

Referring to an instruction of "the former Emergency Committee," the afternoon "Vremya" newscast carried a TASS dispatch saying all limitations imposed on the press by the coup organizers had been removed. Radio Rossii, Russian Television, and the radio station "Ekho Moskvy" all resumed regular broadcasting during the afternoon. Central Television's first channel went so far as to air an apology, saying its behavior during the coup had been caused by "the strict controls that existed over the past three days." Radio Mayak aired a call for "the removal of the discredited current heads of radio and television broadcasting."

El'tsin Places Enterprises under RSFSR Jurisdiction

In his speech to the RSFSR Supreme Soviet, broadcast on Moscow television on August 21, El'tsin said he had issued a decree placing all enterprises in the RSFSR under RSFSR jurisdiction. El'tsin justified his action by saying that Gorbachev had promised to do this once the Union treaty had been signed—the signing should have taken place on August 20. Gorbachev's promise had been a major factor in El'tsin's desire to sign the Union treaty as soon as possible.

Coup Leaders under Investigation

The USSR prosecutor-general opened a criminal investigation of the organizers of the coup, TASS reported. TASS quoted the Prosecutor's Office as saying that the members of the Emergency Committee were "illegally elected" and that their actions "showed signs of a state crime." On August 27, TASS added that the organizers were under investigation for high treason and that, if found guilty, could face the death sentence.

El'tsin Removes Kravchenko as Broadcasting Chief

El'tsin issued an edict placing the Soviet central radio and television network under the control of the government of the Russian republic (*TASS*, August 21). In addition, he removed Leonid Kravchenko from his post as chairman of the All-Union State Television and Radio Broadcasting Company. An appointment or dismissal at this level would normally have been the exclusive prerogative of the USSR president, but TASS noted that El'tsin's edict would stand until a ruling was made by Mikhail Gorbachev. TASS added that the RSFSR Prosecutor's Office was to make a legal assessment of Kravchenko's activities during his term as head of Soviet broadcasting.

On August 27, Gorbachev issued a decree appointing the chief editor of *Moscow News*, Egor Yakovlev, chairman of the All-Union State Television and Radio Broadcasting Company in place of Kravchenko. A decree also instructed Yakovlev and the RSFSR Minister for the Press and Information, Mikhail Poltoranin, to draw up proposals for reorganizing RSFSR Television.

Bessmertnykh Back at Work

USSR Foreign Minister Aleksandr Bessmertnykh, who disappeared from view during the coup, emerged at a Moscow press conference and declared that Gorbachev's ouster had been unconstitutional. Bessmertnykh explained his absence by saying he had been sick during the coup, Western agencies reported.

Protests in Ukraine

Radio Kiev reported on demonstrations organized in several Ukrainian cities by democratic forces in protest against the coup. In Ternopol' in Western Ukraine, a meeting called on the Ukrainian Supreme Soviet to convoke an extraordinary session of the republican parliament in order to declare Ukraine's secession from the USSR. The same demand was heard at a demonstration in Chernigov.

Karimov Rejects Coup

Uzbek President Islam Karimov, inclined at first to sympathize with the coup in Moscow, issued a decree declaring that all decisions of organizations and enterprises in Uzbekistan must be in accord with the laws of the republic and of the USSR and pronouncing invalid the orders of the Emergency Committee that violated those laws.

Niyazov Says Coup Decrees Invalid

Turkmen President Saparmurad Niyazov issued a decree saying that the decisions of "the putschists" were not valid in Turkmenistan, RFE/RL's Turkmen service was told by telephone from Ashkhabad. This was the first word from Niyazov on the coup.

Akaev Attacks Republican Communists

Kirgiz President Askar Akaev began to use the failed coup in Moscow to discredit the conservative Communist Party apparatus in Kirgizia. In an appeal to the people of the republic issued on August 21 and reported that day by Radio Moscow, Akaev said that all progressive forces in Kirgizia, but not the leadership of the Communist Party, had condemned the "military-Party putsch." Akaev also issued a decree banning organizations of political parties from all government offices (*TASS*, August 21). Central Television reported on August 23 that Akaev had followed up on this decree by nationalizing the building of the republican Communist Party.

Coup Organizers' Fatal Errors

Ultimately the coup failed because the conspirators made a number of fatal mistakes. Their first, tactical, error came when they placed Gorbachev under house arrest but allowed El'tsin to remain free: El'tsin immediately became the focal point for the resistance. The second error of the coup organizers was their failure to seal off the lines of communication. The independent press continued to function inside the USSR; domestic and international phone lines remained open; the correspondents of CNN and other Western media organizations were able to go on sending their reports out of the country; jamming was not reintroduced; and Western media, such as RFE/RL, were not prevented from broadcasting information back into the USSR. (Radio Liberty's stringers established an office inside the Russian White House itself and, by this means, El'tsin's edicts were no sooner promulgated than they were beamed back to the whole Soviet population.)

At first, commentators blamed bungling for the ultimate failure of the coup—the plotters, it was suggested, suffered a failure of nerve. But El'tsin told Russian Television on August 25 that the coup organizers had planned to storm the Russian White House and had ordered that the building should be seized regardless of what it cost in human life. That this did not happen was due not to bungling but to the fact that KGB officers refused to execute the order. The failure of nerve of the coup organizers followed. This highlighted the underlying reason for the coup's failure—namely, that the leaders of the coup misjudged the mood of the Soviet people. "Coups can fail," US President George Bush told newsmen, "if they run up against the will of the people" (*CNN*, August 19).

The USSR in August, 1991

Lithuania Bans Select Media Organs

The Lithuanian Ministry of Internal Affairs "temporarily halted the publication and distribution" of eighteen newspapers on Lithuanian territory, Radio Independent Lithuania reported. The ban invoked Article 3 of the new treaty between Lithuania and the RSFSR, under which both countries reserved the right to prohibit actions "seeking to destroy independence by force." The list included all the newspapers permitted to publish during the coup, including *Pravda, Izvestia, Krasnaya zvezda,* and *Sovetskaya Rossiya*; the local Lithuanian papers loyal to the old order, *Litva sovetskaya* and its Lithuanian-language counterpart *Tarybu Lietuva*; and the official newspaper of the anti-independence organization "Edinstvo," published in Lithuanian, Polish, and Russian. Directives ordering the lifting of the ban were issued on August 22 and 23.

Latvia Reaffirms Independence

The Latvian Supreme Council affirmed Latvia's independence, Radio Riga reported. The legislators, voting 111 to 13 with no abstentions, adopted what was called a "Constitutional Law" that modified the declaration of May 4, 1990, stating that Latvia was working towards the restoration of *de facto* independence. The new law declared: "Latvia is an independent democratic republic in which the sovereign power of the Latvian state belongs to the people of Latvia and whose internal legal status is defined by the Constitution of the Republic of Latvia of February 15, 1922."

Radio Riga Resumes Broadcasting

Radio Riga resumed regular broadcasts after the twenty-six Soviet paratroopers who had been occupying the building left it that morning, *Diena* reported. During the occupation of the building local radio stations had broadcast news and official announcements from the Latvian government and Supreme Council. Regular telephone and telegraph communications resumed in the evening.

Estonian Television Tower Taken Over

Some 50 to 60 paratroopers occupied the Tallinn television tower, Estonian radio reported. There were no reports of injuries to the troops or to some 100 people who turned out to protect the tower. Paratroopers allowed the tower director to enter the building and work in his office under guard. The attackers did not make any demands, saying they were waiting for further orders from superiors. Tallinn Mayor Andres Kork spoke to the troops but was unable to persuade them to leave the tower. Reception of television broadcasts was limited to Tallinn, but Estonian Radio continued to broadcast normally, and newspapers appeared.

As news of the coup failure reached the Baltic republics, troops occupying the Tallinn television tower withdrew, Estonian radio reported.

Landsbergis Comments In an interview with the RFE Lithuanian service, Lithuanian Supreme Council President Vytautas Landsbergis welcomed the failure of the coup, saying he hoped that "the situation will be much more suited to peaceful and democratic decisions." He warned, however, of further Soviet military action. He expressed concern over "military forces in the Baltic States and on the Baltic Sea that are in the hands of people who think in the old way." While new power and government relationships were being forged in Moscow, the situation "may be insufficiently defined," Landsbergis said. The Soviet forces "may take self-willed actions."

Lithuanian Killed near Parliament Late in the evening, four Soviet soldiers drove up to a checkpoint near the Lithuanian parliament building in a jeep and threw explosives, Radio Independent Lithuania reported. In the ensuing exchange of gunfire a Lithuanian security guard was killed and two National Defense Department members were injured, as was one of the Soviet soldiers (the other three escaped).

Thursday, August 22

Gorbachev Returns to Moscow USSR President Mikhail Gorbachev arrived back in Moscow early in the morning, Western agencies reported. He was accompanied by his wife, Raisa Maksimovna, who was said to be suffering from a nervous disorder that had paralyzed her left hand. Speaking to reporters at the airport, Gorbachev said nothing had come of attempts to "morally break" him and his family while they were in detention in the Crimea. Gorbachev looked tired, but he spoke vigorously. He was driven straight from the airport to his dacha outside Moscow, where he spent most of the rest of the day in consultations with his aides.

Most Coup Organizers Arrested; Pugo Commits Suicide The members of the Emergency Committee were placed under arrest. One of them, Minister of Internal Affairs Boriss Pugo, committed suicide; his wife was hospitalized after also attempting to kill herself. Defense Minister Dmitrii Yazov, Vice President Gennadii Yanaev, KGB Chairman Vladimir Kryuchkov, and industrialist Aleksandr Tizyakov were interrogated. Prime Minister Valentin Pavlov was still in the hospital. Peasants' Union Chairman Vasilii Starodubtsev and Deputy Chairman of the USSR Defense Council Oleg Baklanov were arrested later, after their parliamentary immunity as USSR people's deputies had been lifted (*Russian Television*, August 22).

El'tsin Orders Army's Party Cells Disbanded

El'tsin issued a decree ordering the disbanding of Communist Party cells in all army units located in the RSFSR, Western news agencies reported. "Party leaders in the armed forces directly supported the coup d'état," the decree said.

Moscow Celebrates Victory

El'tsin saluted a huge crowd of at least 150,000 people who gathered outside the Russian White House for "a rally of victors," which began at 12:00 noon (Moscow time). Broadcast live by Russian Television, the meeting also commemorated the three young men who lost their lives during the night of August 20–21. The crowd cheered and clapped when El'tsin proposed that the square in front of the Russian White House be renamed Square of Free Russia and that the RSFSR's mainly red flag of the Communist era should be replaced over the republican parliament by the tricolor of prerevolutionary Russia. The crowd roared its approval when El'tsin promised that one of the first steps of the Russian government in the aftermath of the coup would be a radical "departification" that would place the CPSU on an equal footing with other political parties and submit the army and police to democratic, parliamentary control.

Regarding the Union treaty, El'tsin said there should be no undue delay in signing the document but that, after the events of the past three days, there should be some amendments to the text. In particular, he repeated that the Russian republic must have its own National Guard. El'tsin said RSFSR Vice President Rutskoi would be charged with the implementation of this plan.

Acting Chairman of the RSFSR Supreme Soviet Ruslan Khasbulatov told the crowd that, in the wake of the failed coup, economic reforms would be accelerated and deepened (*Russian Television*, August 22).

In his address to the rally, Moscow Mayor Gavriil Popov called on Mikhail Gorbachev to resign from the CPSU. Popov called for an investigation into the role of the CPSU in the coup; other demands made by Popov included the appointment of a civilian as USSR minister of defense, the resignation of the Soviet government, the signing without delay of a new Union treaty, and the election of a new Soviet parliament. (*Russian Television*, August 22).

From the RSFSR parliament, the crowd streamed into Moscow's Red Square, where they continued to celebrate the defeat of the coup. The crowd shouted "El'tsin!" and "Down with the Communist Party!"

"Iron Feliks" Toppled

A crowd gathered outside the headquarters of the CPSU Central Committee in Moscow's Old Square, and some of those present tore up their Party cards. A crowd estimated at 5,000 demonstrated outside the headquarters of the KGB, where they attempted to topple the statue of Feliks Dzerzhinsky, founder of the Cheka, a forerunner of the KGB. Using trucks, the protesters draped cables over the statue and tried unsuccessfully to pull it down. Others threw white paint on the walls of KGB headquarters and painted "Hangman" on the statue. Police watched but did not intervene. Later the same evening, the fourteen-ton statue was removed on the orders of Mayor Gavriil Popov. A crowd of at least 10,000 people shouted "Down with the KGB!" and let off fireworks at 11:30 P.M. (Moscow time) when the huge statue was at last brought down. A nearby plaque dedicated to Yurii Andropov, who headed both the KGB and the CPSU, and who acted as mentor to Mikhail Gorbachev, was defaced by a swastika (*TASS*, Western agencies, August 22).

Gorbachev Holds Press Conference

Soviet President Mikhail Gorbachev held a long press conference in Moscow on the evening of August 22; it was broadcast live on Central Television. This was Gorbachev's first press conference since his release from house arrest, and he devoted considerable time to describing the circumstances of his detention. Gorbachev mentioned at one point that, although all the dacha's communications with the outside world were cut off, his aides had rigged up a homemade antenna that enabled him to receive the BBC, Radio Liberty, and The Voice of America and thus keep abreast of events. He paid tribute to all the people who supported him and praised "the leading role" of El'tsin. In insisting, however, on his determination "to do everything in order to purge the Communist Party of reactionary forces," Gorbachev shocked much of his audience, since it indicated that he had not yet come to the realization reached by many of his liberal supporters that the CPSU was unreformable.

The USSR in August, 1991

According to Western agencies, Gorbachev's first official act upon arriving in Moscow was to fire Deputy Defense Minister Army General Vladimir Govorov, who was responsible for civil defense. Govorov had not been mentioned as a conspirator, and he was reportedly being transferred to another post rather than arrested. His replacement was named as Colonel General Boris Pyankov, commander of the Siberian Military District since the spring of 1989.

Govorov Ousted; New Civil Defense Chief Appointed

Anatolii Luk'yanov, whose involvement in the abortive coup was under investigation, was suspended as chairman of the USSR Supreme Soviet, Radio Rossii reported. Gorbachev formally dismissed Valentin Pavlov as USSR prime minister, TASS reported.

Luk'yanov Suspended; Pavlov Dismissed

Gorbachev replaced Valerii Boldin, chief of staff to the president and longtime Communist functionary, with Grigorii Revenko, a former member of the defunct Presidential Council who had been advising Gorbachev on nationality relations (*TASS*, August 22). During the course of his press conference, Gorbachev revealed that Boldin had been among the emissaries of the Emergency Committee who delivered an ultimatum to him on the afternoon of August 18.

Gorbachev Replaces Chief of Staff

The CPSU Central Committee Secretariat denounced those members of the Central Committee who had participated in the failed coup (*TASS*, August 22). The Secretariat said the actions of such people had caused great damage to the Communist Party and the country. The Secretariat ordered the Central Control Commission to investigate Central Committee members who were involved in the coup and to "adopt appropriate decisions."

CPSU CC to Investigate Coup Participants

Journalists at Central Television held a meeting to demand the prompt implementation in their organization of El'tsin's edict of July 20 on the departification of the state sector in the RSFSR (*Russian Television*, August 22). The journalists called for an investigation of the role in the coup of the head of Central Television, Leonid Kravchenko, and his deputies.

Central TV Employees Demand Departification

Journalists on *Izvestia* voted to sack the newspaper's chief editor, Nikolai Efimov, and two of the members of the

Izvestia Staff Votes to Sack Editors

editorial board, Vladimir Sevruk and Dmitrii Mamleev, on the grounds that they had collaborated with the organizers of the coup (*Interfax*, August 22; *Izvestia*, August 23). (The staff had protested when the three men were appointed.) The staff also voted to dissociate the newspaper from the USSR Supreme Soviet, whose Presidium was registered as its official "founder."

Nazarbaev Leaves Politburo in Protest

Kazakh President Nursultan Nazarbaev announced that he was resigning from both the Politburo and the Central Committee of the CPSU. He also declared his intention of proposing to the Communist Party of Kazakhstan that it break with the CPSU and establish itself as an independent party (*TASS*, August 22). What had outraged Nazarbaev was an attempt made during the coup to get him, as a Politburo member, to sign a CPSU Central Committee declaration of support for the Emergency Committee. Nazarbaev declared that the Secretariat of the CPSU Central Committee had discredited itself during the crisis, and he revealed that he had resisted an attempt to summon an emergency plenum of the CPSU Central Committee on August 20. The aim of the plenum would have been to replace Gorbachev as Party leader and perhaps even to expel him from the CPSU (for further details, see the *Financial Times*, August 23).

Kazakhstan Depoliticizes

At the same time as resigning from his CPSU posts, Kazakh President Nazarbaev issued a decree ordering the immediate cessation of organized activity by political parties and mass movements in the republican prosecutor's office; law-enforcement and security agencies; judicial agencies, including the courts; and in the customs service. Like El'tsin's edict on departification, Nazarbaev's required law-enforcement officers to follow only the laws of Kazakhstan and prohibited discrimination on grounds of party membership or political activity (*TASS*, August 22). (On August 21, Kirgiz President Askar Akaev had issued an even wider-ranging depoliticization decree.)

Transcaucasian Leaders' Reactions to Coup

Armenian President Levon Ter-Petrossyan told reporters in Erevan that Gorbachev had facilitated the coup by making too many concessions to hard-liners. Ter-Petrossyan said he was pleased the coup had failed but cautioned the world against conferring on Gorbachev "laurels that only Boris El'tsin deserves" (*Radio Erevan*, August 22).

THE USSR IN AUGUST, 1991

Azerbaijani President Ayaz Mutalibov sent a telegram of congratulations to El'tsin (*Radio Moscow*, August 22). This did little to clarify Mutalibov's attitude towards the coup. On August 19, the Iranian news agency IRNA reported that Mutalibov supported the coup; on August 21, however, TASS quoted a statement by Azerinform denying that he supported it.

In a statement relayed by the Georgian presidential office to RFE/RL's Georgian service on August 22, Georgian President Zviad Gamsakhurdia called upon the West to recognize the independence of those republics that had refused to sign the Union treaty. Gamsakhurdia said the authorities in South Ossetia and Abkhazia, both of which opposed Georgian secession, had supported the coup.

Moldavia Suspends Communist Party Press, TASS Office

The Presidium of the Moldavian Supreme Soviet issued a decree suspending publication of the press organs in the republic that had supported the coup, RFE/RL was informed on August 22. The decree suspended, with immediate effect, the daily newspapers of the Moldavian Communist Party, *Cuvantul* and *Sovetskaya Moldova*, and a number of other Communist dailies and weeklies, including those of the would-be Dniester and Gagauz "SSRs." The Presidium found that these publications had printed the Emergency Committee's decisions and messages in support of the coup's organizers and that they had published misinformation about resistance to the coup. In addition, the decree suspended indefinitely the activities of the TASS office in Moldavia, which was accused of spreading disinformation favorable to the plotters.

Moldavian Victory Rally

The Moldavian leadership made a triumphant appearance at a farewell rally for tens of thousands of rural volunteers who headed for home after helping protect Kishinev against the threat of military intervention during the days of the coup. Thanking the volunteers, President Mircea Snegur, parliament Chairman Alexandru Mosanu, and Prime Minister Valeriu Muravschi urged them not to retaliate against those who had collaborated with the Emergency Committee but to let the judicial process take its course (*Moldovapres*, August 22).

Ukrainian Communists Condemn Coup

The Communist Party of Ukraine finally came out with an unambiguous statement against the attempted coup (*Radio Kiev*, August 22). A resolution of the Politburo of the Ukrainian Party condemned "the adventuristic attempted antistate coup" and criticized the CPSU Central Committee for failing to give a timely assessment of the coup. The Ukrainian Politburo urged the CPSU Central Committee to hold a plenum devoted to an evaluation of the situation as soon as possible. Finally, the resolution said that "giving real meaning" to Ukrainian sovereignty and leading society out of its profound crisis were the republican Party's "most important tasks."

Soviet Army Leaves Vilnius Television Tower

After more than seven months of occupation, the Soviet army left the Vilnius television studios and transmission tower, Radio Independent Lithuania reported. The withdrawal took place under the supervision of the newly appointed commander of the Vilnius garrison, Colonel Valerii Frolov. Broadcasts from the television facilities began later in the day.

Political Strike Ends in Latvia

Andris Zorgins, speaking on Radio Riga on August 21 and 22, thanked all those who had participated in the political strike and asked them to go back to work, since the immediate goals of the strike had been achieved. He added that the Strike Coordinating Council would continue its work until all the demands of the strikers had been met. These demands included the withdrawal of all troops from sites they were occupying, compensation for all damage done by those acting on behalf of the Emergency Committee, and the institution of legal proceedings against those guilty of criminal acts. Zorgins was deputy chairman of the Strike Coordinating Council.

Government Decree against OMON

Radio Independent Lithuania reported that the Lithuanian government had issued a decree ordering the Lithuanian Ministry of Internal Affairs to temporarily take control over the OMON troops based in Lithuania. The OMON troops were forbidden to leave their bases. OMON troops in Latvia were also told to stay in their bases by USSR Deputy Minister of Internal Affairs Boris Gromov.

Estonia Outlaws CPSU

The Estonian government outlawed the CPSU, saying the party was illegal in Estonia because it had not been registered. The government also ordered the prosecutor to begin investigations into the activities of the Estonian Communist Party (CPSU platform). No action was taken against the independent Estonian Communist Party.

Lithuanian Communist Party Outlawed

The Lithuanian parliament banned the Lithuanian Communist Party, Radio Independent Lithuania reported on August 23. It issued a resolution accusing the Party of having attempted to overthrow the government in January and of having followed the orders of the coup leaders on Lithuanian territory.

In accompanying legislation, the parliament passed a law "on the seizure of Lithuanian Communist Party property," Radio Independent Lithuania reported on August 23. In accordance with the law, "the property of the Lithuanian Communist Party and the CPSU illegally functioning on the territory of the Republic of Lithuania will be transferred without compensation to the Republic of Lithuania," and anyone attempting to obstruct its execution will be prosecuted.

Lithuania Demands Removal of Soviet Forces

The Lithuanian parliament passed a resolution on the military presence in Lithuania, Radio Independent Lithuania reported on August 23. It demanded that the USSR government remove as soon as possible all its army structures, paratrooper units, KGB, and MVD troops from the republic. The resolution based the demand on the clearly expressed will of the majority of Lithuania's population, noting that the continuing presence of the army "is a relic of World War II." The resolution asked the United States, Great Britain, and France resolutely to support the demand and appealed to UN member states to do the same.

On August 26, USSR Defense Minister Evgenii Shaposhnikov told RFE/RL that, for the time being, Soviet troops would remain in Estonia, Latvia, and Lithuania. He expected a USSR-Baltic agreement on the stationing of Soviet troops in the Baltic republics and added that after Moscow had reached accords with the United States on the reduction of strategic weapons and with Germany on the withdrawal of troops, it would be easier to reach agreement with Soviet republics that had declared their sovereignty.

Estonia to Punish Coup Supporters

Estonian Prime Minister Edgar Savisaar ordered Estonia's prosecutor-general to start criminal proceedings against those in Estonia who supported the coup "in words and deeds." According to the Estonian Foreign Ministry on August 23, an order signed by Savisaar ordered the sacking of the heads of several all-Union controlled factories, the punishment of municipal leaders in primarily Russian-speaking northeastern Estonia who supported the coup, and the closure of the Soviet navy-

"Intermovement" radio station "Nadezhda," which had carried broadcasts in support of the coup.

Friday, August 23

Gorbachev Addresses RSFSR Parliament

Gorbachev made his first official visit to the RSFSR Supreme Soviet where, earlier in the week, thousands of El'tsin supporters had gathered to oppose the coup. The event was shown live on Russian Television and on CNN. Gorbachev received a standing ovation when he opened his address by publicly thanking El'tsin for his role in foiling the attempted coup. Gorbachev went on to promise a reorganization of the KGB and to call for "a major regrouping of political forces" in the USSR.

During what turned into a very stormy session, Gorbachev responded to tough questions from members of parliament. His audience reacted negatively to his insistence that, while the leadership of the CPSU had been slow to condemn the coup, the ranks of the Communist Party contained millions of decent people and that calls for the outlawing of the CPSU would therefore result in "a witch-hunt." Gorbachev also argued in support of the USSR Supreme Soviet, despite the passivity shown by that body throughout the duration of the coup, and he irritated Russian parliamentarians by the amount of time he spent discussing his experiences in detention.

El'tsin shocked television viewers the world over by the heavy-handed way in which he forced Gorbachev to return to the subject and by his insistence that Gorbachev read aloud the minutes of a meeting of the USSR Cabinet of Ministers. (At that meeting, held on August 19, all but two of about twenty government ministers had either approved the coup or failed to oppose it.) When Gorbachev protested, El'tsin ordered him to "read it now."

El'tsin Suspends Activities of Russian Communist Party

Ignoring Gorbachev's strenuous protests, El'tsin went on, in full view of the cameras, to sign an edict temporarily suspending the activities in the RSFSR of the Russian Communist Party while that party's role in the coup was investigated (*Russian Television*, August 23). Gorbachev did say, however, that he would confirm in writing all the edicts El'tsin promulgated during the three-day crisis. Gorbachev strongly denied suggestions made by some deputies that he was himself involved in the coup attempt, or at least knew about it in advance and allowed it to happen in the expectation that his own stature would be enhanced when it failed. Gorbachev called such suggestions "a crude attempt to cast a shadow" on his leadership.

Gorbachev and El'tsin Agree on Power Transfer Procedures

Gorbachev revealed that he and El'tsin had agreed on a plan whereby each would assume the other's powers if one of them became unable to carry out his duties. Announcing this to the RSFSR Supreme Soviet, Gorbachev said a legal procedure had already been drafted that would in future apply in cases such as the coup attempt, during which Gorbachev was prevented from exercising his authority (*Russian Television*, August 23).

New Ministers Appointed

Gorbachev announced the appointment of new heads for the USSR Ministries of Defense and Internal Affairs and for the USSR KGB. The new appointees replaced the hard-liners named on a temporary basis by Gorbachev on August 22. All three new appointees were men of liberal views, and it was announced that Gorbachev had agreed the new appointments with RSFSR President Boris El'tsin and the government of the Russian republic (*TASS*, August 23).

Vadim Bakatin was named the new head of the USSR KGB. Bakatin had held the post of USSR Minister of Internal Affairs from October, 1988, to November, 1990, when he was sacked by Gorbachev on the insistence of the hard-line "Soyuz" group in the USSR Supreme Soviet. Bakatin's liberal record was, however, not without taint. He attended the two Politburo meetings in April, 1989, at which the decision to crack down in Tbilisi was made, and he was present in Baku in January, 1990; blood was shed on both occasions, and the lives of civilians were lost.

Named as the new USSR minister of defense was General Evgenii Shaposhnikov, who had previously headed the Soviet Air Force and who was one of a number of senior army officers who opposed the coup.

The new USSR minister of internal affairs was Viktor Barannikov, formerly minister of internal affairs of the Russian republic.

Foreign Minister Dismissed

Gorbachev fired USSR Foreign Minister Aleksandr Bessmertnykh (*TASS*, August 23). Bessmertnykh, who kept a very low profile during the coup and was subsequently criticized by Gorbachev for his "passivity," initially maintained he was out of action because of illness. On August 23, however, *Komsomol'skaya pravda* published an open letter to Bessmertnykh from Andrei Fedorov, in which the RSFSR deputy foreign minister accused Bessmertnykh of agreeing to distribute the Emergency Committee's appeal to foreign states and governments to Soviet embassies throughout the world. Fedorov said the USSR Ministry of Foreign Affairs had acted during the coup like "a political prostitute who is only interested in who will pay more." He went on to name several ambassadors who had supported the coup, notably Leonid Zamyatin, ambassador to Britain. Zamyatin and other ambassadors were subsequently recalled to Moscow (*The Independent*, August 27 and 29).

Fedorov also complained that USSR First Deputy Foreign Minister Yulii Kvitsinsky had issued an order "to stop the dispatch on B. N. El'tsin's instruction of a special telegram . . . to all USSR embassies and consulates abroad with an explanation of the Russian leadership's position and a condemnation of the coup d'état."

Bessmertnykh denied the charges of passivity and complicity both at the time of his dismissal and in a handwritten letter that he later submitted to members of the USSR Supreme Soviet (*AP*, August 27). In that three-page letter, Bessmertnykh said he had refused an invitation to join the plotters on August 18.

Pravda Adopts New Masthead, Appoints New Editor

The August 23 edition of *Pravda* described the newspaper as "a general political newspaper of the CPSU." Previously, the newspaper had identified itself as "the organ of the CPSU Central Committee." In a front-page statement, the paper's editorial board reviewed the daily's performance during the coup and opined that, "for the umpteenth time, unobjective and wishy-washy assessments" had appeared in the newspaper and fueled "the anti-Communist campaign now being launched." Saying that a prompt and resolute denunciation of the Emergency Committee by *Pravda* "could have altered the situation" during the coup, the newspaper promised to make staff changes within a few days. On August 29, Central Television announced that Gennadii Seleznev, who had been chief editor of *Komsomol'skaya pravda* until 1989, was replacing Ivan Frolov, a close associate of Mikhail Gorbachev, as chief editor of *Pravda*.

El'tsin Suspends *Pravda* and Five Other Communist Party Newspapers

RSFSR President Boris El'tsin adopted an edict ordering the suspension of *Pravda* and five other Communist Party newspapers—*Sovetskaya Rossiya*, *Glasnost'*, *Rabochaya tribuna*, *Moskovskaya pravda*, and *Leninskoe znamya*. He also ordered the dismissal of the heads of the TASS news agency, Lev Spiridonov, and of Novosti, Al'bert Vlasov, for spreading "disinformation" (*TASS*, August 23).

The USSR in August, 1991

Pravda resumed publication on August 31. On the front page, the daily appealed to readers for donations, saying that recent events had resulted in the loss of the newspaper's financial base.

El'tsin Strengthens His Executive Authority

In a further edict, El'tsin strengthened his own executive authority by decreeing that administrative leaders in krais and oblasts in the Russian Federation would in future be directly appointed by and accountable to the president of the RSFSR. The edict also gave El'tsin the power to dismiss regional leaders who had cooperated with the coup leaders or failed to put up enough resistance (*TASS*, August 23).

Luk'yanov Suspended from Chairing Supreme Soviet, Denies Coup Involvement

Anatolii Luk'yanov, chairman of the USSR Supreme Soviet, was suspended from chairing sessions of the parliament (*Radio Rossii*), August 23). Although not a member of the Emergency Committee that sought to oust Soviet President Mikhail Gorbachev, Luk'yanov was subsequently identified by both RSFSR President Boris El'tsin and RSFSR Prime Minister Ivan Silaev as the brains behind the coup.

On August 28, Luk'yanov denied the charge that he was the brains behind the abortive coup, adding that he had not participated in the plot. Luk'yanov told the Supreme Soviet that he could not have called a Supreme Soviet session either to approve or outlaw emergency rule in the USSR earlier than on August 26, a week after the coup. Luk'yanov said that the law required no less than two-thirds of each house to be present to make its decisions legal and that it always took at least five days to gather the deputies. According to Luk'yanov, he also wanted Gorbachev to be present at the session and claimed that he was "incapable of betraying the man whom I have known for over forty years." He failed, however, to explain why he had not convoked the body's Presidium, the members of which lived permanently in Moscow.

On August 29, the USSR Supreme Soviet consented to a request to lift Luk'yanov's immunity. USSR Prosecutor-General Nikolai Trubin told the legislators that Luk'yanov, while aware of the unconstitutional nature of the actions of Vice President Gennadii Yanaev, had attended a meeting of the junta the night before the coup was announced and had tried to justify its deeds "[holding] the Constitution in his hands." Luk'yanov had also promised the junta that the Supreme Soviet would approve of its actions, Trubin said. Trubin added that Luk'yanov faced

THE USSR IN AUGUST, 1991

a charge of "high treason" under Article 64 of the RSFSR Criminal Code.

Kryuchkov Interviewed

Former KGB Chairman Vladimir Kryuchkov said that, if he could turn the clock back, he would take "an entirely different course" from that which resulted in his arrest for his part in the coup against Soviet President Mikhail Gorbachev. A Soviet videotape of Kryuchkov in detention at an undisclosed location near Moscow was obtained and broadcast by CNN. His role in the failed coup apart, Kryuchkov said, "I do not think I have done anything in my life that my Motherland can hold against me."

Party Headquarters Sealed in Moscow and Leningrad

During the night of August 22, the Moscow City Soviet suspended the activities of the city's Communist Party organization and sealed its headquarters, Central Television reported on August 23. The offices of the CPSU Central Committee on Old Square in downtown Moscow were also sealed for a short period. The ban came after Soviet President Mikhail Gorbachev had identified Yurii Prokof'ev, leader of the Moscow City Party organization, as a supporter of the coup, and was carried out with Gorbachev's consent. The decree suspending the Communist Party's activities was signed by Moscow Mayor Gavriil Popov. The decree also suspended the activities of the Liberal Democratic Party, whose leader, Vladimir Zhirinovsky, had openly supported the coup (TASS, August 23). An aide to Popov was quoted as saying the main purpose of the order was to prevent Party leaders from destroying documents (*The Washington Post*, August 23).

Prokof'ev was detained at the city's Communist Party headquarters and investigated for his attitude during the coup; his detention came after the Moscow city authorities had lifted his immunity from prosecution as a member of the city soviet (*Interfax*, August 23).

Communist Party headquarters were also sealed in Leningrad on the orders of the mayor of the city, Anatolii Sobchak (*TASS*, August 23).

Komsomol Leader Quits CPSU Central Committee

The Buro of the Komsomol Central Committee issued a statement saying the coup had proved that "no further renewal or reform of the CPSU leadership is possible," and the Komsomol's first secretary, Vladimir Zyukin, resigned from the CPSU Central Committee (*TASS*, August 23). Originally set up as the youth arm of the

CPSU, the Komsomol had in the *perestroika* period become increasingly critical of the Communist Party.

Moldavian Communist Party Banned, Leader Quits CPSU

The Presidium of the Moldavian Supreme Soviet banned the activities of the CPSU and the Moldavian Communist Party on the territory of Moldavia, RFE/RL was informed by sources in Moldavia. The decree also ordered the nationalization of the Communist Party's property in the republic.

Moldavian Communist Party First Secretary Grigore Eremei resigned from the CPSU Politburo, citing the failure of the CPSU leadership to resist the coup against Gorbachev (*TASS*, August 23).

Lithuania Cracks Down on KGB, Orders Arrest of Party Leaders

The Lithuanian government issued a decree ordering an end to KGB activity in Lithuania and the creation of a commission made up of representatives of the Lithuanian government and the USSR KGB to coordinate the process. Later that day, Deputy Prime Minister Zigmas Vaisvila and Deputy Chairman of the KGB Valerii Lebedev signed an agreement establishing a thirty-day transition period, Radio Independent Lithuania reported. The KGB promised not to engage in any activities directed against the Republic of Lithuania, which, in turn, agreed to guarantee the social, political, and civil rights of KGB employees.

On August 25, Lithuanian Prosecutor Arturas Paulauskas sent a telegram to the USSR Defense Ministry requesting orders to be issued to Vilnius garrison commander Colonel Valerii Frolov to hand over to the Lithuanian authorities Lithuanian Communist Party leaders Mykolas Burokevicius and Algimantas Naudziunas, who were hiding at the army base in Vilnius, Lithuanian radio on reported August 26. Arrest warrants were also issued for Juozas Jermalavicius and other Party figures. Arturas also complained about the alleged burning of documents at the Lithuanian Party headquarters by officials under the protection of Soviet army troops.

Monuments to Lenin Removed

Thousands of people cheered as workers in Vilnius hoisted the thirty-foot statue of Lenin from its base, *The Times* reported on August 24. In Klaipeda, the monument to Lenin was also removed after Soviet soldiers who had been protecting it withdrew.

The giant statue of Lenin in Tallinn was torn down and hauled away amidst cheering crowds, according to RFE/RL's Estonian service. The statue, which stood in front of the Estonian Communist Party headquarters, was ordered dismantled by the city council.

Uzbekistan's Karimov Resigns from Politburo

Uzbek President Islam Karimov resigned from the CPSU Politburo (*TASS*, August 23). In a statement in support of his decision, the Buro of the republican Communist Party said it was motivated by "the cowardly and unprincipled position of the orthodox part of the leadership of the CPSU Central Committee and Secretariat," which had not only failed to condemn the actions of the Emergency Committee but had tried to "disorient" members of the Uzbek Communist Party and get them to support the coup.

Departification in Tajikistan

In reaction to the failed coup, Tajik President Kakhar Makhkamov banned the CPSU and other political parties from operating in the Tajik police, KGB, courts, and interior ministry (*TASS*, August 23).

Hundreds Arrested in Baku

Azerbaijani security forces arrested hundreds of people at a rally called by the Azerbaijani Popular Front in Baku (*Interfax*, August 23). The rally had been called to demand the resignation of Azerbaijan's Communist president, Ayaz Mutalibov, who, the popular front said, had supported the attempted coup.

On August 26, thousands of Azerbaijanis participated in a demonstration on Baku's central square organized by the Azerbaijani Popular Front and the "Independent Azerbaijan" faction to demand the lifting of martial law in Baku, the postponement of the presidential elections scheduled for September 8, the holding of new Supreme Soviet elections on a multiparty basis, and the declaration of Azerbaijan's independence, TASS reported.

Latvian CP Leader Arrested; Property Taken Over

After declaring the Latvian Communist Party unconstitutional, the Latvian Supreme Council endorsed the Supreme Court's proposal to bring criminal charges against Party leader Alfreds Rubiks. Shortly thereafter a Supreme Council committee took control of the Latvian Communist Party headquarters, and the local authorities started to claim Party property throughout Latvia. Rubiks and Secretary Ojars Potreki announced their resignation from the Latvian Communist Party and their desire to establish a new political party. This did not, however, stop the Latvian authorities from arresting Rubiks.

On August 27, Rubiks was charged with plotting to seize power from Latvia's democratically elected govern-

The USSR in August, 1991

ment. Rubiks was held in an isolation cell of the Latvian Ministry of Internal Affairs, Radio Riga reported.

Saturday, August 24

Gorbachev Quits as Party Chief

In a statement broadcast on Soviet television, CPSU General Secretary Mikhail Gorbachev announced his decision to resign as head of the Communist Party. "I believe that democratic-minded Communists . . . will stand up for the creation on a new basis of a Party capable of joining in the ongoing radical democratic transformations." He also nationalized Party property, called for the dissolution of the Central Committee, and banned Party cells in the armed forces, the KGB, and the police.

CPSU Secretariat Statement

The CPSU Secretariat issued a statement defending its actions during the coup and proclaiming that the Secretariat had no advance knowledge of the attempt to take power. The statement, which was carried by TASS on August 25, called for a plenum of the Central Committee to examine the question of disbanding itself.

RSFSR Takes Control of Economy, Communications, CPSU and KGB Archives

In a series of decrees carried by TASS on August 24, the RSFSR Council of Ministers moved to take operational and juridical control over all-Union economic ministries. The decrees transferred the property and responsibilities of the USSR State Committee for Material and Technical Supply and the USSR Ministry for Economics and Forecasting to RSFSR control. One decree also condemned "the active participation" of the USSR Cabinet of Ministers in the failed coup and imposed RSFSR leadership over all USSR economics ministries until a new cabinet was created.

El'tsin issued a decree putting under RSFSR control all types of government communication lines run by the KGB, including the Kremlin's secure communications channels. The decree transferred the entire system of the USSR Ministry of Communications to the jurisdiction of the RSFSR Supreme Soviet Committee for Communications, Computing, and Space, thus gaining control over the full spectrum of electronic communications media.

Further decrees transferred the CPSU and KGB archives to the control of RSFSR archive administration bodies. The decrees stated that these measures were necessary to prevent the illegal destruction of the archives and to enable scholars to gain access to the materials.

The USSR in August, 1991

Gorbachev Bans Political Activity in Armed Forces

In a decree broadcast on Central Television during "Vremya" on August 24, Gorbachev called for the cessation of political activity by all parties and movements within the USSR Armed Forces, the Ministry of Internal Affairs, and the KGB. Members of political parties and movements were ordered to practice politics outside these agencies and in their free time. Gorbachev's decree followed a similar order issued by El'tsin on August 22 that forbade political activities within the armed forces on the territory of the RSFSR.

Akhromeev Commits Suicide

At the age of sixty-eight, Marshal Sergei Akhromeev, Gorbachev's adviser on military affairs and the former chief of the Soviet General Staff, killed himself. While he had not been implicated in the coup attempt, Akhromeev had long been an outspoken opponent of liberalization. Reports varied on the details of the death, but apparently Akhromeev hanged himself after leaving a note saying everything he had devoted his life to was being destroyed.

Yakovlev Discusses Coup Leaders

In an eighty-minute interview broadcast by RSFSR television, Aleksandr Yakovlev said sources in the Kremlin apparatus had told him that members of the Emergency Committee had lost their nerve as early as late August 19. Yakovlev identified the leaders of the junta as Luk'yanov and Kryuchkov. He said that the junta's address to the Soviet people had been drafted by the CPSU Central Committee and KGB. Yakovlev also revealed that the Emergency Committee planned mass arrests and probably even executions of its opponents and added that he had a copy of a blank form for future deportations. He cited rumors that Stalin-era camps had been cleaned up for this purpose some time ago. Early on the morning of August 19, Yakovlev recalled, he had noticed two cars with KGB agents watching the entrances to his home. Thereupon Yakovlev had called El'tsin and escaped to the White House, where he had helped to organize the resistance.

Bakatin's Appeal to Muscovites

The new chairman of the USSR KGB, Vadim Bakatin, asked Muscovites not to extend their wrath against "a bunch of adventurists" to the entire KGB. Speaking on the television news program "Vremya," Bakatin asked that the takeover of KGB buildings and archives by persons who were pursuing "improper goals" be prevented. He expressed confidence that the KGB would have an opportunity to serve the interests of the people and would never be a weapon of "criminal policy."

The USSR in August, 1991

Latvia Starts Liquidation of the KGB

The Latvian Supreme Council decided to eliminate the Latvian branch of the KGB. Latvian police mounted a guard at the KGB headquarters in Riga, and local authorities elsewhere did likewise. Care was taken to prevent the destruction of archives.

On August 29, Latvian government and KGB representatives signed a protocol on mutual obligations of the Latvian Supreme Council Presidium and the USSR KGB. According to Radio Riga of August 29, the accord stipulated that the KGB would transfer its property (including control and communications systems and some archival materials) to Latvia. It was also reported that the KGB would operate in accordance with the laws of the Republic of Latvia.

Ukraine Declares Independence

An extraordinary session of the Ukrainian Supreme Soviet on August 24 adopted, by a large majority, a declaration proclaiming the independence of Ukraine, Radio Kiev and Western news agencies reported. The declaration was subject to approval by a republic-wide referendum scheduled for December 1. The Ukrainian parliament also decided to nationalize all-Union property in Ukraine and depoliticize the republican prosecutor's office, the KGB, the Ministry of Internal Affairs, state institutions, and radio and television.

Georgian National Guard in Conflict with Gamsakhurdia

Central Television reported that 15,000 members of the Georgian National Guard under the command of Tengiz Kitovani had left Tbilisi and announced that they were no longer subordinate to Georgian President Zviad Gamsakhurdia. Gamsakhurdia had issued a decree on August 20 abolishing the post of commander of the National Guard and subordinating the guard to the Georgian MVD in accordance with the decree issued by the Emergency Committee on August 18. The National Guard had distributed leaflets in Tbilisi condemning the republic's leadership for not denouncing the coup.

Sunday, August 25

CPSU CC Members Condemn Party

Seven members of the CPSU Central Committee, including Otto Latsis and Nail Bikenin, issued a statement carried by TASS in which they recommended that: the CPSU accept its moral responsibility not only for the coup but for the creation of the present political and state system as well; that the CPSU disband and relinquish its property; and that reformist members of the Party form a new party in cooperation with the Movement for Democratic Reforms, the Democratic Party of Communists of Russia, and others.

DPKR Calls On Untainted Communists

The Democratic Party of Communists of Russia (DPKR), led by RSFSR Vice President Aleksandr Rutskoi, issued an appeal calling on Communists who had not "tarnished their names by cooperating with the putschists" to leave the CPSU and join the DPKR, TASS reported. The DPKR expressed approval for El'tsin's decree suspending the activities of the RSFSR Communist Party but said that the rights of Communists "who remained true to the constitution" should be protected.

Commission to Select New USSR Cabinet

A commission was set up to nominate a new USSR Cabinet of Ministers, TASS reported. RSFSR Prime Minister Ivan Silaev would chair the commission, whose members included: Grigorii Yavlinsky, an economic adviser to El'tsin; Arkadii Vol'sky, head of the Scientific and Industrial Union; and Yurii Luzhkov, the deputy mayor of Moscow.

Kryuchkov's First Deputy Detained

Viktor Grushko, chief of the KGB's Second Main Administration for Counterintelligence, was detained on suspicion of involvement in the coup, TASS reported. Grushko was one of former KGB Chairman Vladimir Kryuchkov's closest associates and was responsible for the KGB's domestic activities.

Pavlov Pleads Ignorance

Former USSR Prime Minister Valentin Pavlov claimed that during the rule of the Emergency Committee, of which he was a member, he had no idea that he was involved in a plot. Pavlov was interviewed by "Vesti" on August 25 while under arrest. He asserted that former Vice President Gennadii Yanaev was also not fully informed of what had happened and had at first refused to sign decrees. Pavlov named Anatolii Luk'yanov as the person who knew better than others Gorbachev's circumstances. Pavlov said that had not "some fool" ordered tanks into the city, the committee would still be in power.

Shaposhnikov Orders Shake-Up of Soviet High Command

Defense Minister Evgenii Shaposhnikov said on Central Television that 80 percent of the High Command would be replaced, but on August 27 he told *Krasnaya zvezda* that his statement applied only to the Defense Ministry Collegium. Shaposhnikov also told German television on August 27 that making the Soviet army professional would be a long process.

Army's Chief Prosecutor Dismissed

In a decision taken jointly by Soviet and Russian judicial authorities, General Aleksandr Katusev was dismissed as the Soviet army's chief prosecutor for having been implicated in the attempted coup (*Central Television*, August 25).

OMON Units in Baltic Show Defiance

On August 25, special police (OMON) troops in Vilnius abandoned their barracks and the Lithuanian Police Academy building, which had been seized on January 12, and withdrew to the Soviet army base in the northern part of Vilnius. El'tsin told Supreme Council President Vytautas Landsbergis that OMON units in Vilnius were being dissolved and the men reassigned to units in the RSFSR, Radio Independent Lithuania reported on August 26.

On August 28, in discussions with Latvian and USSR authorities, members of OMON said that they did not want to be disbanded or to leave Latvia. Like their colleagues in Lithuania, the OMON unit in Latvia indicated on August 28 its willingness to withdraw if granted full amnesty for any crimes it had committed; it threatened bloodshed if this demand were not met. On August 29, in a written statement addressed to the leaders of European governments, Major Boleslaw Makutinowicz, the commander of the OMON unit in Vilnius, appealed for political asylum for eighty members of the unit, *The New York Times* reported on August 30. He said he would not apologize for any of OMON's actions in Lithuania, adding: "I am sorry about only one thing, which is that the USSR no longer exists." He said the unit's members "could be victims of lynch mobs" and doubted that Lithuanian courts would give them fair trials.

Further Repercussions of Coup in Estonia

The Estonian government outlawed several longtime pro-Soviet organizations because of their participation in the attempted coup, ETA reported on August 26. The "Intermovement," the Joint Council of Work Collectives, and the "worker brigades" of Kohtla-Järve and Narva were made illegal, and the government ordered criminal investigations of those organizations. The government also formally resumed control of the Narva border as of 11:00 P.M. on August 25.

Border under Lithuanian Control

The Lithuanian government issued an order that at midnight on August 26 Lithuanian customs officials would take over the functions of USSR customs in Lithuania. A coordinating committee of Lithuanian government and USSR customs officials was set up to settle "issues concerning the customs regulations of the USSR" and the situation of USSR customs employees during a one-month transitional period.

Western agencies reported on August 28, however, that although Lithuanian officials at Lazdijai had issued about 1,000 visas, Soviet border guards, formally under the command of the KGB, were not recognizing them and were demanding Soviet visas. Long lines of traffic formed on both sides of the border, and some foreign journalists from Warsaw tried in vain to enter Lithuania without Soviet visas.

No Nuclear Weapons in Lithuania

At a press conference broadcast by Radio Independent Lithuania, Vytautas Landsbergis said Boris El'tsin had told him that all the nuclear weapons that had been stored in Lithuania had been removed.

Baltic Military District Commander Replaced

Lieutenant General Valerii Mironov, formerly of the Leningrad Military District, was appointed commander of the Baltic Military District replacing Colonel General Fedor Kuz'min, who had supported the coup, Radio Riga reported.

Belorussia Declares Independence

The Belorussian Supreme Soviet adopted a law on the state independence of the republic, Belta-TASS reported. The Belorussian parliament also temporarily suspended the activities of the Communist Party of Belorussia and adopted a resolution ridding state bodies and institutions of political activity. The Belorussian parliament accepted the resignation of its chairman, Nikolai Dementei, whom opposition leaders had accused of supporting the coup.

Monday, August 26

USSR Supreme Soviet Extraordinary Session Opens

The session of the USSR Supreme Soviet originally intended to approve the Emergency Committee opened to evaluate the role of the CPSU and other parties in the coup. At least three members of the hard-line "Soyuz" group of deputies attempted to justify the coup. Poet

The USSR in August, 1991

Evgenii Evtushenko suggested that USSR Prosecutor Nikolai Trubin was unfit to investigate the case of the conspirators because, in the past, Trubin had justified the use of the army against civilians. The letter of resignation of former Supreme Soviet Chairman Anatolii Luk'yanov was read.

In his report to the Supreme Soviet, USSR President Mikhail Gorbachev said that the abortive coup was not unexpected. He said that he himself had been guilty of too great a tolerance of reactionary tendencies and of having ignored the warnings in the liberal press. He added that supporters of democratization had been divided.

Gorbachev said that, although the Union treaty was not perfect, there should be no delay in signing it. Regarding the republics that did not wish to sign, he said negotiations with them on independence should begin as soon as the treaty had been signed. He made no mention of the need to comply with the law on the mechanics of secession. At the same time, Gorbachev said that, since all fifteen Union republics were interested in maintaining economic links, work on an economic agreement should begin without delay.

Gorbachev said that on August 23 the leaders of the nine republics willing to sign the new Union treaty had agreed that, in the interim period before a new constitution was adopted, the Security Council should act as an authoritative organ making decisions on major questions of administration for the whole territory of the Union.

Gorbachev admitted to the Supreme Soviet that right-wing generals, including some in the Supreme Soviet, had long expressed their opposition to reform, foreshadowing the recent coup; he called for better constitutional control over the armed forces. Turning to the Union treaty, Gorbachev urged an agreement on the temporary disposition of military facilities in republics wanting to leave the Soviet Union. Gorbachev called for the removal of all obstacles to free enterprise and said that economic powers must be further delegated to the republics. He appealed to farmers and workers in the fuel and energy sector to continue working at least until the political situation in the country stabilized.

Acting Chairman of the RSFSR Supreme Soviet Ruslan Khasbulatov told the USSR Supreme Soviet that the Union treaty was a political, not a juridical document, and that juridical questions should be taken care of in the new constitution. At the same time, he insisted categorically that the republics of the RSFSR should sign the treaty as part of the RSFSR delegation. Tatarstan had still not agreed to do this on the eve of the coup, and Checheno-Ingushetia had said it would not sign until or unless the question of the return of the Prigorodnyi Raion of North Ossetia to Checheno-Ingushetia was resolved. In his speech, Khasbulatov said that the RSFSR authorities would disband the supreme soviets and remove the leadership of republics of the RSFSR that had supported the coup. For the Supreme Soviet proceedings, see *Izvestia*, August 27-31.

Value of CPSU Property Estimated at 4 Billion Rubles

Arkadii Vol'sky, a member of the new commission charged with managing economic affairs, told reporters in Moscow that CPSU property was worth about 4 billion rubles, Western news agencies reported. Vol'sky also said that banning Party cells from state enterprises and agencies would leave 150,000 people unemployed. Yurii Luzhkov, the deputy mayor of Moscow and also a member of the new commission, said on the news program "Vremya" on August 26 that nearly all of the Party's property had been seized, its assets frozen, and its buildings and offices sealed. "Vremya" also reported that journalists had "stormed" the CPSU Central Committee complex in Moscow and discovered the underground passageway leading from Old Square to the Kremlin.

RSFSR Claims Right to Challenge Borders of Seceding Republics

In an effort to discourage other republics from declaring independence, the RSFSR said that it reserved the right to raise frontier issues with republics—apart from the three Baltic republics—that declared their independence, TASS reported quoting El'tsin's press spokesman, Pavel Voshchanov. The republics most affected would be Belorussia, Ukraine, and above all Kazakhstan, most of whose northern part is inhabited overwhelmingly by Slavs.

Speaking at a press conference, Ukrainian Supreme Soviet Chairman Leonid Kravchuk said that "territorial claims are very dangerous." He also said that he had spoken with El'tsin and that the Russian leader had promised to clarify his press secretary's statement. "Rukh" issued a statement saying that the RSFSR's position on border questions "is an attempt to divide our Fatherland." On August 27, the Presidium of the Ukrainian Supreme Soviet issued a statement saying that Ukraine had no territorial claims with regard to the RSFSR or other republics, Radio Kiev and Ukrinform-TASS reported.

On August 27, Moscow's mayor, Gavriil Popov, expressed full support for El'tsin's statement. Popov told Central Television that republican parliaments had exceeded their authority by proclaiming independence and that this issue should be a matter of a referendum. Popov

The USSR in August, 1991

said that negotiations must be held on the territories of the Crimea, Odessa, the Dniester region, and northern Kazakhstan. He stressed that El'tsin's task was to defend Russians living outside the RSFSR. Popov rejected the idea that all republics should share the USSR's foreign debt.

On August 29, Council of Nationalities Chairman Rafik Nishanov reported that RSFSR Vice President Aleksandr Rutskoi was leading a delegation to Alma-Ata to calm Kazakh anger over the Russian statement. Interfax carried a similar report. Kazakh President Nursultan Nazarbaev asked El'tsin to send representatives to discuss the issue, citing growing public wrath in Kazakhstan.

KGB Special Force Refused to Obey Conspirators

It was revealed that the KGB antiterrorist force "Alpha" had refused orders to storm the RSFSR Supreme Soviet building during the attempted coup. This was the first time since its creation in 1974 that "Alpha" had disobeyed an order, its commander Mikhail Golovatov told TASS. The order to begin the attack was given by the former commander of the special forces, Major General Viktor Karpukhin, on the basis of "a government order"; the commanders of the units, however, refused to follow it, because they thought it could lead to civil war. Golovatov stressed that "the biggest part of the KGB, if not the main one," had not supported the plotters. He admitted, however, that "Alpha" had taken part in storming the Vilnius television center in January.

Shaposhnikov on Security Relations with the Republics

In sharp contrast to his predecessor, Dmitrii Yazov, Defense Minister Evgenii Shaposhnikov began immediate negotiations on August 26 with Latvia and Ukraine over the deployment, following independence, of troops and weaponry on their territories, Western agencies reported on August 27.

RSFSR Seeks Veto Power over Use of Nuclear Weapons

RSFSR Vice President Aleksandr Rutskoi told a news conference that the RSFSR was seeking joint control over the use of Soviet nuclear weapons, Western agencies reported. Rutskoi proposed that the approval of the Russian president be required before such weapons could be used.

KGB Troops Will be Transferred to Army

Speaking at the USSR Supreme Soviet emergency session, Gorbachev announced that KGB troops would be transferred to the command of the Soviet army. He also said that the new KGB chairman, Vadim Bakatin, was charged with preparing proposals for a quick reorganization of the KGB. Gorbachev stressed that provisions of the law on the KGB adopted in May should be revoked.

Sobchak against Senseless Dismantling of Central Structures

Speaking to the USSR Supreme Soviet, Leningrad Mayor Anatolii Sobchak rejected the idea of abandoning Soviet central structures and warned of catastrophic consequences for people in the Soviet Union and the world if the USSR as a state were senselessly dismantled. Sobchak criticized El'tsin's order to suspend the publication of six CPSU papers, including *Pravda*. Sobchak said that in closing down the periodicals legal regulations had not been observed.

Kruchina Commits Suicide

Nikolai Kruchina, head of the CPSU Central Committee's Administration of Affairs Department, committed suicide by jumping from the window of his seventh-floor apartment, TASS and Western news agencies reported. Kruchina, who was sixty-three, had not been implicated in the coup attempt. Kruchina was appointed to the Administration Department, which oversaw the Party's budget, finances, and property, in 1983.

Editorial Board of *Sovetskaya Rossiya* Resigns

The staff of *Sovetskaya Rossiya* issued a statement protesting against the suspension of the newspaper. The statement said that the paper had never called for a coup. (In fact, the newspaper had on numerous occasions published documents suggesting that there was a need to overthrow the legitimate power in the country.) The statement said that during the coup, the newspaper had had no choice but to publish resolutions of the Emergency Committee. The entire editorial board of the paper resigned "in order to save *Sovetskaya Rossiya* from complete closure," a Moscow journalist told RFE/RL on August 26.

Korotich Resigns from *Ogonek*

The editor of *Ogonek*, Vitalii Korotich, was in New York when the coup started on August 19. He reportedly decided to prolong his visit to the United States and not to return until the situation became clearer. Korotich's behavior was viewed very negatively by *Ogonek*'s staff, who demanded an explanation from the chief editor. In response, Korotich sent a telegram asking to be relieved of his duties, a Moscow journalist told RFE/RL on August 26. TASS reported the same day that Korotich's deputy, Lev Gushchin, had been made his successor.

The USSR in August, 1991

Novosti Protests against El'tsin's Accusation

Staff members of Novosti protested against El'tsin's decree of August 22, which accused Novosti of spreading disinformation during the coup. The staff members said that in fact their agency had given "objective information." (Indeed, Novosti's reports were relatively informative and objective during the coup.) In protest against El'tsin's accusation the staff members decided to suspend the distribution of Novosti material until the agency's name was cleared. The same day, Gorbachev issued a decree mandating the transfer of Novosti to RSFSR jurisdiction.

"Vremya" and "Vesti" Demand Independence

"TSN" reported that a group of journalists from Central Television had demanded that an independent news service be created within the All-Union State Television and Radio Broadcasting Company. The journalists appealed to Gorbachev, El'tsin, and the RSFSR Supreme Soviet for help in implementing the project. A similar proposal was put forward by journalists of the Russian Television news show "Vesti." Also on August 26, RSFSR Minister of the Mass Media and Information Mikhail Poltoranin supported a proposal by TASS employees to transform the state agency into an independent information service, "Vremya" reported.

Shevardnadze Not Interested in Resuming Office

In response to suggestions at the Supreme Soviet session that Eduard Shevardnadze return to his former post as foreign minister, Shevardnadze said in an Interfax interview, "Who needs a minister when there is no Soviet Union?"

Baltic Republics Win Diplomatic Recognition

Following RSFSR President Boris El'tsin's decree on August 24 recognizing Estonia's and Latvia's independence and calling for the restoration of diplomatic relations with the RSFSR, members of the international community one by one began the process of admitting the Baltic republics to the ranks of sovereign, independent nations. Iceland was the first to do so.

Ukraine recognized the independence of Lithuania, Latvia, and Estonia, Radio Kiev reported on August 26. The action was taken by the Presidium of the Ukrainian Supreme Soviet. The same day, Georgia formally recognized Estonia's independence on the basis of a vote by the republic's Supreme Council, TASS reported, quoting the official Georgian news agency Sakinform.

On August 27, Belgian Foreign Minister Mark Eyskens announced that the twelve nations of the European

Community had recognized Estonia, Latvia, and Lithuania as independent states.

Radio Riga reported that, when asked about international diplomatic recognition of the Baltic republics, Gorbachev had replied curtly that such moves were hasty.

On August 28, the Baltic foreign ministers traveled to Stockholm to reestablish diplomatic relations with Sweden. The same day, in ceremonies in Bonn hosted by Chancellor Helmut Kohl, German Foreign Minister Hans-Dietrich Genscher joined the Lithuanian, Latvian, and Estonian foreign ministers in signing documents formally reestablishing diplomatic ties, RFE/RL's correspondent reported.

On August 29, President Gorbachev again complained about international recognition of the Baltic States and told Italian radio that Estonia, Latvia, and Lithuania had not respected the USSR Constitution in declaring independence. Latvian Supreme Council President Anatolijs Gorbunovs sent a letter to Gorbachev proposing the prompt start of high-level talks between Latvia and the USSR. He noted that Latvia had affirmed its independence on August 21 and that this would be all the more reason for such talks. Radio Riga said on August 29 that about thirty countries had recognized the independence of Latvia.

Meanwhile, the Latvian Supreme Council authorized the Latvian government to take the proper steps to extend diplomatic recognition to Israel, Slovenia, and Croatia, Radio Riga reported.

The same day, French Foreign Minister Roland Dumas and his Lithuanian counterpart Algirdas Saudargas signed documents restoring formal diplomatic relations, the RFE Lithuanian Service reported. Saudargas had just returned from Helsinki, where he and his Baltic counterparts had signed similar agreements with Finland. Dumas said that France would give Lithuania back its gold.

"Ravnopravie" Faction Disintegrates

Radio Riga reported on August 26 that three members of the Latvian Supreme Council's opposition faction "Ravnopravie" had resigned. At the session of the Supreme Council on August 27, broadcast live by Radio Riga, the faction's leader Sergei Dimanis read an announcement indicating that the faction was breaking up; he said he would ask the members to sign his announcement. "Ravnopravie" deputies had hitherto advocated Latvia's remaining a part of the USSR.

Uzbekistan Moves to Break Away

Uzbek President Islam Karimov ordered the Presidium of the Uzbek Supreme Soviet to draft a law on the independence of the republic, which was to be debated at a special session of the republican legislature, TASS and Radio Moscow reported. He also issued a decree placing MVD and KGB structures functioning in Uzbekistan under republican jurisdiction and ordered that MVD troops stationed in Uzbekistan answer directly to him. The same decree ordered the depoliticization of law-enforcement agencies, judicial bodies, and units of the Turkestan Military District stationed in Uzbekistan.

Nazarbaev's Address to the Supreme Soviet

In his speech to the USSR Supreme Soviet, Kazakh President Nursultan Nazarbaev said that the USSR had no chance of remaining a federation and that a future confederation of republics would be based on economic ties. He asked for a treaty creating such a confederation to be signed as soon as possible. While each republic would have its own defense force, there would have to be a ministry of defense of the Union to protect common borders and control nuclear weapons and a central authority to coordinate communications and transport, he said.

Akaev Attacks Communist Party

The first deputy to comment on Gorbachev's report to the USSR Supreme Soviet on August 26 was Kirgiz President Askar Akaev, who compared the CPSU to a reactionary religious order of the Middle Ages and said the Supreme Soviet bore a great deal of the blame for the coup and should dissolve itself.

In an interview broadcast by Radio Rossii, Akaev explained his reaction, the most forceful of any Central Asian leader, to the Moscow coup. He said that the republican KGB, encouraged by the republican Communist Party's Central Committee, had attempted to take power and remove him as president. Akaev retaliated by firing the KGB chief and having El'tsin's appeal broadcast on republican television every two hours. Akaev said that his appeals to leaders of other republics to form a united front against the coup had failed for lack of coordination.

Tuesday, August 27

Gorbachev on Union Treaty

In his concluding remarks to the USSR Supreme Soviet, Soviet President Mikhail Gorbachev threatened to resign unless the republics agreed to preserve the country's unity by signing a Union treaty. In an impassioned speech he called on the leaders of all the republics to reflect again on what would happen if they refused to sign the treaty. He agreed that the text required amendment in the light of the attempted coup but said this should be done quickly. Gorbachev said he did not regard the recent declaration of independence by the Ukrainian Supreme Soviet as "having put a cross" on the Union treaty but rather that it was a reaction to the attempted coup.

Gorbachev met with RSFSR President El'tsin, Kazakh President Nazarbaev, Kirgiz President Akaev, and Aleksandr Yakovlev. The talks, which seemed to have been a response to the furor caused by Nazarbaev's call for a confederation without central organs and to El'tsin's demand for frontier reviews should republics declare independence, were reported by TASS on August 27 to have taken place in a spirit of frankness and full responsibility. The participants were said to have expressed their hopes that the Union treaty would be signed quickly. The creation of national armies, with the exception of individual national guards, was rejected, particularly in the light of the USSR's status as a nuclear power.

Gorbachev urged all fifteen Union republics to sign an economic agreement on "a common economic space." The agreement was discussed at Gorbachev's meeting with republican leaders. Akaev said the accord would be drafted and signed by Gorbachev and the three republican leaders present within ten days, according to Western agency reports. Akaev said the other republican leaders were not present at the meeting, because they were not in Moscow.

Reports of New Soviet Ballistic Missile TASS, citing *Nezavisimaya gazeta*, said that the USSR had completed work on the "Kur'er" program, which involved a new ballistic missile "similar to the US Minuteman missile" and with a flight range of 10,000 kilometers.

Silaev Sees No Future for Union RSFSR Prime Minister and *de facto* USSR Prime Minister Ivan Silaev told ABC Television that the role of the center would be "minimal" and that it would only handle the promotion of reforms and create a favorable climate for privatization and investment in those republics that wanted to cooperate economically. He said that the present center would disappear "if not in days, then in weeks."

Investigation of Leningrad Party Launched TASS reported that the Leningrad Prosecutor's Office had started criminal proceedings against the Leningrad Party organization in order to determine whether any of its members were involved in the coup. Meanwhile, a Leningrad journalist told RFE/RL that the head of the Leningrad Party organization, Boris Gidaspov, had demanded that his organization be given a new building in place of the famous Smol'nyi Institute, which had been nationalized.

RSFSR President El'tsin signed a decree saying the RSFSR would officially accredit RFE/RL correspondents and would allow the opening of an RFE/RL bureau in Moscow and offices in other parts of the RSFSR. The decree emphasized Radio Liberty's role in informing the Soviet population about events in their own country, especially during the coup attempt.

RSFSR to Accredit RFE/RL Correspondents

In an interview with Radio Rossii, the deputy chairman of the RSFSR Federation of Independent Trade Unions, Vasilii Romanov, said that *Rabochaya tribuna* had been reregistered and would be published under the auspices of its work collective and the trade union federation. Romanov cited the chief editor of *Rabochaya tribuna*, Anatolii Yurkov, as saying that the newspaper's staff was grateful to Radio Rossii and other democratic media for support during the days of its banning.

***Rabochaya tribuna* Reprieved**

Representatives of Estonia's Russian-nationalist antireform organization "Intermovement" claimed they had never obstructed Estonian independence, *Paevaleht* reported. Vladimir Vinogradov told reporters that the group had never fought Estonian state independence but that "we have only ever stood for the equal rights of Estonia's citizens."

Intermovement Protests Its Innocence

Ukrainian Supreme Soviet Chairman Leonid Kravchuk said that he was quitting the Communist Party, Western news agencies reported. Kravchuk said that he had made his decision on August 19, the day that the failed coup began. Kravchuk had resigned from the Party's leading organs on August 24.

Kravchuk Leaves the CPSU

Radio Kiev reported that the parliamentary opposition in Ukraine had evidence to show that the republican Communist Party was directly involved in the failed coup. Documents found in Lvov dated August 18 were said to show that instructions had been given to all oblast Party

Ukrainian CP Implicated in Coup

committees to support the coup. It was also revealed that Lvov Oblast Party Committee First Secretary Vyacheslav Sekretaryuk had flown to Moscow on August 18 where he held consultations with USSR Minister of Internal Affairs Boriss Pugo. Other documents revealed that Ukrainian Party First Secretary Stanislav Hurenko had issued orders in support of the coup leaders.

Moldavia Proclaims Its Independence

An extraordinary session of the Moldavian parliament unanimously adopted a declaration of independence, TASS and Western agencies reported. Deputies representing the Russian and Gagauz minorities did not attend the session. The declaration requested international recognition of Moldavia's independence and membership in the United Nations and the Conference on Security and Cooperation in Europe.

The Moldavian parliament urged the government to start talks on the withdrawal of Soviet troops from Moldavian territory and said it would debate the formation of a national guard. Prime Minister Valeriu Muravschi claimed that Moldavia could be economically viable because it produced more than it consumed. The parliament decided that the new national anthem should be "Romanians Awake," a nineteenth-century patriotic Romanian anthem declared Romania's national anthem following the fall of Nicolai Ceausescu. Several prominent speakers, including former Prime Minister Mircea Druc, said Moldavia's independence could only be "an intermediate stage in future unification with Romania."

The Moldavian parliament appointed a delegation headed by President Mircea Snegur to negotiate with Moscow Moldavia's secession from the USSR, Novosti reported.

Moldavian Minister of Internal Affairs Ion Kostash condemned the actions of militarized units on the left bank of the Dniester for trying to prevent left-bank Moldavians going to Kishinev to take part in the national rally on August 27 celebrating Moldavia's declaration of independence, TASS reported on August 28. A number of citizens were beaten up and the Moldavian tricolor desecrated.

Contention over Makhkamov

Tajik deputy Davlat Khudonazarov, head of the USSR Cinema Workers' Union, informed the USSR Supreme Soviet that Tajik President Kakhar Makhkamov had told a local journalist on August 19 that he supported the coup in principle. Khudonazarov said he feared that the planned separation of the Tajik Communist Party from

The USSR in August, 1991

the CPSU would be a cover for a regrouping of conservative forces in the republic under another name. Later in the session another deputy read out a telegram from Makhkamov denying that he had supported the coup.

In an appeal to the people of Tajikistan issued on August 27 and reported by TASS the same day, Makhkamov asked that there be no witch-hunts against individuals on grounds of their political affiliation, warning that it was not a time for society to split along political or religious lines. Makhkamov said that the cooperation agreements recently signed by the leaders of the five Central Asian republics should be put into effect as soon as possible in order to stabilize the economic and political situation in the USSR. Tajikistan was still willing to enter into a Union of sovereign republics but not to be pushed around.

Wednesday, August 28

First Deputy Prime Minister Vitalii Doguzhiev told the USSR Supreme Soviet that former Prime Minister Valentin Pavlov had been drunk at the crucial session of the Cabinet called to discuss the coup. *The Guardian* reported that Gennadii Yanaev, acting USSR president, was drunk at the beginning of the coup and at the moment of his arrest. "A catalogue of farce, drunkenness, gullibility, and incompetence emerges from accounts given by key sources close to the drama," *The Guardian* said, adding that advisers who remained loyal to Gorbachev during the coup had continued to operate from offices next to those of Emergency Committee members and kept the defenders of the Russian White House informed of the junta's plans.

"Farce, Drunkenness, and Incompetence" Reigned in the Coup

Soviet President Mikhail Gorbachev told the USSR Supreme Soviet that El'tsin's constant interference in all-Union affairs was not acceptable. In a speech broadcast by Central Television, Gorbachev stressed that it had been proper for El'tsin during the abortive coup to issue decrees that touched on the responsibilities of the center but now that it was over Russia and its president should stop direct involvement in all-Union affairs.

Gorbachev Warns El'tsin

Soviet and Western agencies said RSFSR President Boris El'tsin had ordered that all currency and financial transactions and transactions involving precious metals and

El'tsin Assumes Control of USSR State Bank, Ministry of Finance

stones be approved by the relevant RSFSR authorities. RSFSR agencies were taking over the entire network of the USSR Ministry of Finance, the USSR State Bank, and the Bank for Foreign Trade, according to the reports.

Egor Yakovlev Pledges to Rid State Television of KGB

The new chief of state television, Egor Yakovlev, promised to get rid of KGB employees working as journalists, Russian Television reported. He said that he had already discussed this topic with the new KGB chairman, Vadim Bakatin. According to Yakovlev, Bakatin had promised that, starting on August 29, KGB officers would be recalled to their regular jobs.

Government Reshuffle Continues

At a press conference, Arkadii Vol'sky, a member of the new commission charged with managing economic affairs, announced that Ivan Silaev's decision of August 26 to put RSFSR officials into top government positions had been revoked. Instead, the Soviet ministries' first deputy chairmen would do the jobs of their disgraced bosses. Viktor Gerashchenko was reinstated as chairman of the USSR State Bank, having been replaced by Andrei Zverev for three days. And Igor' Lazarev had reportedly not turned up at the USSR Ministry of Finance to take over from Vladimir Orlov. Evgenii Yasin was appointed to the economic reform team: his brief was Soviet industry and entrepreneurship, the *Financial Times* reported on August 29.

State Commission to Investigate KGB

Gorbachev issued a decree creating a state commission to investigate the KGB's involvement in the coup and to evaluate proposals for the KGB's reorganization and the imposition of legislative control on the state security organs. USSR MVD Colonel Sergei Stepashin, the chairman of the RSFSR Supreme Soviet Committee for Security, was to chair the commission.

Pankin Appointed Foreign Minister

Soviet President Mikhail Gorbachev issued a decree announcing the appointment of Boris Pankin as USSR foreign minister, TASS and Western agencies reported. Pankin, who had been Soviet ambassador to Czechoslovakia, was the only Soviet envoy to come out against the Emergency Committee in support of Gorbachev in the wake of the coup attempt.

On August 29, Pankin said in an interview with Central Television that his aim was for the USSR to join the community of "civilized nations." Pankin also gave an interview to RFE/RL in which he said that he would continue and develop Gorbachev's foreign policy. In light of recent events, Pankin said, changes in the top echelons of the Ministry of Foreign Affairs would be unavoidable. He also said that he saw no "special problems" in relations between the USSR ministry and republican foreign ministries and that the USSR ministry would set strategic priorities and coordinate all foreign political activities.

Ignatenko Appointed Director General of TASS

The head of the presidential press service, Vitalii Ignatenko, was made director general of TASS. Ignatenko replaced Lev Spiridonov, who was dismissed in the aftermath of the abortive coup.

"Vremya" Changes Its Name

The main Central Television news, "Vremya," was replaced by a new program entitled "TV Inform." An announcer reported that the nightly show was being reformed.

"600 Seconds" Ceases Transmission

The controversial show "600 Seconds" produced by Leningrad Television reporter Aleksandr Nevzorov would no longer appear, TASS reported. Chairman of Leningrad Television Boris Petrov stopped transmission of the program on the grounds that Nevzorov had been using Leningrad Television facilities without signing an official contract. Interviewed by TASS, Nevzorov said the suspension of his program was a political act, a punishment for his criticism of the Leningrad City Soviet.

New Chairman of USSR Writers' Union

According to "Vesti," the radical reformer Yurii Chernichenko was elected as the new chairman of the USSR Writers' Union, replacing poet Sergei Mikhalkov.

Movement for Democratic Reforms on Disintegration of the Union

The Political Council of the Movement for Democratic Reforms issued an appeal to Union and republican leaders calling for the Union to be maintained, while also welcoming the emergence and consolidation of sovereign republics, Radio Rossii reported. The statement noted that, given the critical state of the economy, the disintegration of the Union would be "a recipe for disaster."

El'tsin Orders Draft Law on Servicemen

El'tsin ordered the RSFSR Council of Ministers to prepare a draft law providing social guarantees for servicemen and veterans and spelling out the terms of alternative military service, Russian Television reported. They were also asked to develop, by the end of 1991, a housing program for discharged soldiers and to consider a proposal that would free servicemen in the RSFSR from obligations to pay income tax and several other taxes. A plan dealing with compensation and benefits for soldiers' wives was also ordered to be completed within a month.

Oil Production Continues to Plummet

The USSR minister of the chemical and petroleum refining industry, Salambek Khadzhiev, told the agency Info-Nova that his ministry's ability to supply fuel was not expected to improve in the foreseeable future. Khadzhiev listed several reasons, including a seemingly irreversible drop in oil production, the disintegration of economic linkages throughout the country, and a general lack of discipline in the economy and society, including the country's leadership organs.

USSR to Stop Conscripting Lithuanians

After a meeting in Vilnius with the new Soviet commander of the Baltic Military District, Lieutenant General Valerii Mironov, Lithuanian Supreme Council President Vytautas Landsbergis told reporters that the USSR had agreed to stop conscripting youths from Lithuania, Radio Independent Lithuania reported.

KGB Activities in Estonia to Be Halted and Local Control of Borders Resumed

President of the Estonian Supreme Council Arnold Ruutel and the newly appointed chairman of the USSR KGB, Vadim Bakatin, reached agreement to halt all KGB activities in Estonia, RFE/RL's correspondent reported from Tallinn. Ruutel and Bakatin also reached agreement on a step-by-step resumption of control of Estonia's borders and customs by the Estonian authorities.

State of Emergency Lifted in Azerbaijan

TASS reported that Azerbaijani President Ayaz Mutalibov had lifted the state of emergency declared in Baku in January, 1990, and issued decrees ordering the confiscation of some Communist Party buildings, the creation of independent military units "to safeguard Azerbaijan's territorial security," and the subordination to the republican government of all all-Union enterprises on Azerbaijani territory.

Ukrainian Declaration on Minorities

The Presidium of the Ukrainian Supreme Soviet issued a declaration, broadcast by Radio Kiev, announcing "a new era" in the development of interethnic relations in Ukraine in connection with its declaration of independence. It stated that the Presidium had assumed responsibility for guaranteeing that Ukrainian independence would in no way result in the violation of the human rights of anyone, regardless of nationality.

Ukraine Wants Diplomatic Ties

The permanent representative of Ukraine to the United Nations, Gennadii Udovenko, told a press conference that Ukraine wanted to establish diplomatic relations with the United States, Canada, Israel, and all the states with which it shared a border, Radio Kiev and TASS reported on August 29.

Kebich Resigns from CPSU

Belorussian Prime Minister Vyacheslau Kebich and his deputies announced their resignations from the CPSU, Radio Moscow reported. They cited the CPSU Central Committee leadership's behavior during the attempted coup as the reason for their move.

Diplomatic Recognition of Moldavia

Moldavian President Mircea Snegur and parliament Chairman Alexandru Mosanu told a press conference in Kishinev that Romania and Georgia had recognized Moldavia's independence. Romania and Moldavia signed an agreement on August 29 to exchange ambassadors, but TASS reported the same day that Romania's ambassador in Moscow, Vasile Sandru, had been told by USSR Deputy Foreign Minister Yulii Kvitsinsky that the question of Moldavia's independence was solely the business of the USSR.

Nazarbaev Gives Up Leadership of Kazakh CP

At a brief plenum, the Central Committee of Kazakhstan's Communist Party dissolved itself and Party committees at all levels. Republican President Nursultan Nazarbaev gave up his post as first secretary, calling on democratically minded Communists to set up a new party. Nazarbaev also issued a decree prohibiting state officials from holding posts in any political party.

Tajikistan's Economic Sovereignty

TASS reported that Tajik President Kakhar Makhkamov had issued a decree on the transfer to republican jurisdiction of enterprises formerly subordinate to all-Union ministries. Such enterprises could be privatized only with the permission of the Tajik government. Defense industries were not included. The Tajik government was to determine the republic's share in the USSR's gold and diamond reserves and national debt, and plans were being made for Tajikistan to set up its own gold and diamond reserves. TASS also reported that Tajikistan's president had issued a decree nationalizing the immovable property of the republican Communist Party, of which he was still the head.

Uzbek CP Breaks with CPSU A plenum of the Uzbek Communist Party resolved to break the Party's ties to the CPSU, TASS reported. Uzbek President and Communist Party First Secretary Islam Karimov also criticized Soviet President Gorbachev, saying a CPSU Central Committee plenum or Party Congress should decide the fate of the Party and its property.

Thursday, August 29

USSR President's Powers Curtailed The USSR Supreme Soviet voted 279 to 37, with 38 abstentions, to revoke the special powers vested in the USSR presidency by the USSR Congress of People's Deputies in 1990.

USSR Security Council Partially Constituted The USSR Supreme Soviet appointed leaders of nine republics to what was to be a new and strengthened Security Council headed by President Gorbachev. The nine republics—Russia, Ukraine, Azerbaijan, Belorussia, Kazakhstan, Uzbekistan, Kirgizia, Turkmenistan, and Tajikistan—were those that took part in the "Nine-plus-One" talks. Vadim Bakatin and Evgenii Primakov, members of the previous Security Council, would remain on the council. Gorbachev also proposed including Aleksandr Yakovlev, Gavriil Popov, Anatolii Sobchak, Yurii Ryzhov, Eduard Shevardnadze, and Grigorii Revenko. Shevardnadze later rejected the offer.

CPSU Suspended The USSR Supreme Soviet adopted a resolution suspending the activities of the CPSU across the USSR, TASS reported. The vote was 283 in favor, 29 against, with 52 abstentions. The resolution cited evidence of CPSU involvement in the coup as grounds for the suspension; it also froze the Party's financial assets and instructed the Ministry of Internal Affairs to make sure Party archives were not destroyed. The resolution ordered prosecutors to investigate the Party's actions during

The USSR in August, 1991

the coup and to turn the evidence over to the USSR Supreme Court. A motion to ban the CPSU altogether was defeated.

USSR Prosecutor Resigns

USSR Prosecutor-General Nikolai Trubin submitted his resignation to the USSR Supreme Soviet. Trubin said that although he had been abroad during the coup, he was answerable for the cooperation of his first deputy with the junta, as well as for the failure of his other deputies to control the actions of the KGB and the military. The parliament accepted Trubin's resignation but asked him to continue working until the USSR Congress of People's Deputies had chosen a successor.

More Personnel Changes in KGB

Air Force Lieutenant General Nikolai Stolyarov was appointed to replace Vitalii Ponomarev in the position of head of the USSR KGB Cadres Department, according to a USSR presidential decree published by TASS. KGB First Deputy Chairman Genii Ageev was also dismissed; Anatolii Oleinikov replaced him.

Bakatin Outlines Reform of KGB

KGB military counterintelligence organs, which monitor the Soviet Army and the MVD, were scheduled to be transferred to the respective institutions, USSR KGB Chairman Vadim Bakatin told Russian Television. Bakatin justified the need to preserve the Administration for the Protection of Constitutional Order (formerly the Fifth Main Administration), which investigated serious state crimes, on the grounds that having parallel organs in both the KGB and the MVD acted as a safeguard against an institutional monopoly. Bakatin supported suggestions that the KGB Main Archives be incorporated into a single organization but categorically rejected a proposal to make public the archives containing secret informants' reports.

El'tsin Meets Leaders of RSFSR Republics

The Soviet media carried a statement drawn up by the chairmen of the Supreme Soviets of ten of the sixteen autonomous republics of the RSFSR after they met with RSFSR President Boris El'tsin on August 28. The republics stressed their support for the integrity of the RSFSR and for the Union treaty, which they reaffirmed should be signed by them as part of the RSFSR delegation. Absent from the meeting were the leaders of Tatarstan, Checheno-Ingushetia, Buryatia, Kabardino-Balkaria, Tuva, and Karachai-Cherkessia. The leaders of the first four were under local pressure to resign because of their behavior during the abortive coup. Tatarstan still wanted to sign the Union treaty independently.

Authors of "A Word to the People" to Be Questioned

Prior to his resignation, Russian Television asked USSR Prosecutor-General Nikolai Trubin about the infamous "A Word to the People," written by twelve Russian conservatives and published in *Sovetskaya Rossiya* on July 23. Three of its signatories—Vasilii Starodubtsev, Aleksandr Tizyakov, and former First Deputy Defense Minister Valentin Varennikov—were arrested as coup leaders. Trubin said the remaining nine signatories were to be questioned by the prosecutors investigating the coup.

El'tsin Defends Army

In an address broadcast by Radio Rossii, RSFSR President Boris El'tsin praised the role of the Soviet Armed Forces in defending democracy during the coup. El'tsin said he would defend the army from unjustified criticism. El'tsin also said that the major role of a new center, to be created by the republics, would be control over nuclear weapons. He said there would be no large central bureaucracy and promised that the democrats now in power would not create a dictatorship.

Economic Reform Committee Meets

The four-man committee to study economic reform held its first session, TASS reported. The division of responsibilities was announced by Interfax on August 28. It was: Grigorii Yavlinsky—economic reform and integration into the world economy; Arkadii Vol'sky—the military-industrial complex, transportation, construction, and communications; Ivan Silaev—the KGB, defense, internal affairs, and the media; and Yurii Luzhkov—day-to-day foreign economic relations, food supplies, trade, and agriculture. On August 28, Vol'sky said that all fifteen republics had agreed to take part in the committee's work, the *Financial Times* reported on August 29.

Aid for the USSR

The Soviet ambassador to the European Community, Lev Voronin, appealed to the EC and the G-7 nations for increased food aid and more monetary assistance, RFE/RL's correspondent in London reported. After their meeting in London the same day, G-7 representatives restated the position adopted at the July summit meeting—namely, that large-scale cash aid to the USSR would be premature. Member-nations were prepared, however, to alleviate shortages of food and medicine during the coming winter. They also stressed the importance of intensifying links with the republics.

After his meeting with US President George Bush, British Prime Minister John Major listed six ways in which the West would help the USSR, Western agencies reported on August 29: (1) extending existing food credits; (2) assessing the need for food aid for the winter; (3) sending "lifeline" teams to help establish food-production and distribution systems; (4) implementing existing technical aid programs; (5) involving the International Monetary Fund and World Bank "urgently" in aiding structural reform programs; and (6) pushing for associate membership of the USSR in the IMF, with a view to full membership in the future.

Democratic Party of Communists of Russia Registered

The Democratic Party of Communists of Russia (DPKR) was registered by the RSFSR Ministry of Justice, TASS reported on August 30. Vladimir Lipitsky, a member of the party's organizing council, said the DPKR would not continue the cause of the CPSU.

Shaposhnikov Confirmed

USSR Supreme Soviet deputies voted overwhelmingly to confirm recently appointed USSR Defense Minister Evgenii Shaposhnikov, TASS reported. Addressing the assembly, Shaposhnikov urged the quick passage of a series of defense-related laws, including legislation that would prevent the armed forces being used for anything but national defense. He also said that the nuclear testing grounds at Semipalatinsk would be closed but spoke against a moratorium on Soviet nuclear tests.

General Refuses to Testify

The Russian Information Agency reported that Colonel General Viktor Samsonov, the commander of the Leningrad Military District, had refused to meet with a commission from the Leningrad City Soviet in order to discuss his actions during the coup. The report was broadcast by Radio Rossii. Samsonov cut a deal early in the coup with Leningrad's mayor, Anatolii Sobchak, and refused to order troops into the city's center. The radio report nevertheless pointed out that on the first day of the putsch Samsonov had appeared on Leningrad Television and announced the declaration of a state of emergency in the city.

***Pravda* Registered in RSFSR**

The RSFSR Ministry of the Mass Media and Information registered the former CPSU Central Committee daily

Pravda. El'tsin had already transferred the newspaper to RSFSR jurisdiction. TASS said that the newspaper was now being run by an organization made up of staff members. The report quoted the new editor in chief, Gennadii Seleznev, as saying the paper would be independent of any political party but would not change its name.

Sagalaev Appointed Deputy Chief of Central Television

The chairman of the USSR Journalists' Union and a former official at Central Television, Eduard Sagalaev, was appointed first deputy chairman of the All-Union State Television and Radio Broadcasting Company. Central Television quoted him as saying that his first task would be to give more independence to the television news service.

Mutalibov Resigns from CPSU, Denies Complicity in Coup

Addressing deputies of the Azerbaijani Supreme Soviet, Azerbaijani President and Communist Party First Secretary Ayaz Mutalibov resigned his CPSU membership and stepped down as republican Communist Party first secretary, Interfax reported. He further affirmed that the Azerbaijani Communist Party had split from the CPSU and called for an extraordinary Party congress. Mutalibov denied allegations by the Azerbaijani Popular Front that he had expressed support for the attempted coup and claimed that none of the demands made by the Emergency Committee had been implemented in Azerbaijan.

Belorussia to Form National Guard

Radio Moscow reported that Colonel General Anatolii Kostenko, the commander of the Belorussian Military District, had announced that Belorussia would form a national guard that would "defend the interests of Belorussians on their ethnic territory." There were no plans to form a republican army.

Ukrainian-Russian Agreement

Chairman of the Ukrainian Supreme Soviet Leonid Kravchuk and Vice President of the RSFSR Aleksandr Rutskoi signed an eight-point joint communiqué in Kiev pledging cooperation in order to prevent "the uncontrolled disintegration" of the Union state, Western agencies reported. The agreement envisaged setting up "interim structures" and invited "interested states that were subjects of the former USSR" to join them during this "transitional period" regardless of their current status. The two sides also agreed to recognize existing borders and exchange ambassadors. Leningrad Mayor Anatolii Sobchak, who took part in the negotiations, said the agreement meant that "the former Union no longer exists and that there can be no return to it." Rutskoi was quoted as saying that the term "former USSR" was being used for the first time and reflected existing reality.

The agreement had a substantial military dimension. As quoted by Western agencies, the joint communiqué said that the two republics concurred on "the special significance of military-strategic problems [and] consider it necessary to carry out a reform of the armed forces of the USSR and to create a system of collective security." Both sides agreed "not to adopt unilateral decisions on military strategic issues."

Ukrainian Defense Ministry Planned

Chairman of the Ukrainian Supreme Soviet Leonid Kravchuk met in Kiev with military commanders stationed in the republic, Western agencies reported. According to one of Kravchuk's spokesmen, Adam Voitovych, the meeting was "an initial step towards establishing our own Ministry of Defense." Voitovych said Kravchuk had sought advice from a number of military commanders on how best to set up and run a defense ministry.

Kravchuk also said that nuclear weapons located in the republic should be transferred back to the RSFSR, *The Washington Post* reported on August 30. He urged that Soviet nuclear forces continue to be controlled by the central government until the republics had decided on a new command structure. He added that some form of joint republican control should then be established. According to the same report, opposition leader Vyacheslav Chornovil said that Soviet military officers in Ukraine claimed to have received orders to begin transferring nuclear weapons to the RSFSR. He also voiced concern about Russian control of the nuclear arsenal and suggested that it be placed under United Nations control.

Tajik Opposition Demands Leadership's Resignation

Participants in a demonstration organized by opposition parties and movements demanded the resignation of Tajikistan's three top leaders, TASS reported. Speakers accused the republican leadership of having failed to condemn the Emergency Committee. While the demonstration was going on outside the Tajik Supreme Soviet building, opposition deputies at a special session of the legislature called for the leadership's resignation and criticized the absence of the Tajik delegation at the current session of the USSR Supreme Soviet.

On August 31, the Supreme Soviet of Tajikistan passed a vote of no confidence in the republic's president,

Kakhar Makhkamov, after which he resigned. (*Radio Moscow, Interfax*, August 31).

On September 4, Makhkamov, also resigned as first secretary of the republican Communist Party. The Central Committee plenum at which Makhkamov submitted his resignation called an extraordinary Party congress for September 21 (*TASS*, September 4).

Depoliticization in Turkmenistan

Turkmen President Saparmurad Niyazov issued a decree prohibiting political organizations in government agencies, military units, and educational institutions, Radio Moscow reported. RL's Turkmen service learned that several leaders of opposition groups had been arrested, and the Turkmen Committee of Afghan War Veterans had called on Gorbachev and El'tsin to intervene against "totalitarianism" in Turkmenistan.

Kirgiz CP Suspended for Six Months

Interfax reported on August 29 that the Kirgiz Ministry of Justice had suspended the activities of the Kirgiz Communist Party for six months. Communist Party organizations were forbidden to publish propaganda in the mass media or organize meetings, plenums, conferences, or congresses. TASS reported that the Kirgiz government had sealed all Party buildings and seized Party archives. The republican Communist Party reportedly attempted to overthrow president Askar Akaev at the time of the coup in Moscow.

Demands for Resignation of Tatarstan's President

Radio Rossii reported that more than 30,000 signatures had already been collected in Kazan' demanding the resignation of Tatarstan's president, Mintimer Shaimiev, for his alleged support of the Emergency Committee during the coup. It had earlier been reported that large meetings were taking place in Kazan', one organized by the "Sovereignty" committee supporting the republican leadership and moves for Tatarstan to sign the Union treaty independently, and the other by democratic forces demanding the resignation of the whole Communist leadership.

Dniester Republic Leader Arrested

Igor' Smirnov, leader of the self-proclaimed "Dniester SSR" in Moldavia was arrested, Western agencies reported. Moldavian Interior Minister Ion Costas said he had been arrested by Moldavian police in Kiev but declined to say whether this had taken place with the agreement of the Ukrainian authorities. The vice president of the

Dniester republic, Andrei Manoilov, said the arrest would fuel tension.

The Armenian parliament Presidium voted to nationalize all Armenian Communist Party property, including its headquarters in Erevan and bank accounts, Radio Erevan reported on August 30. The Armenian Party archives would be turned over to the Republic of Armenia.

Armenia Nationalizes CP Property

―――――――――――――――――――――― *Friday, August 30*

RSFSR President Boris El'tsin decreed the limiting of Russian defense contributions to the central Soviet budget beginning in 1992, Western news agencies reported. He also ordered the RSFSR Defense Committee to start working on military reform. The new RSFSR defense minister, Colonel General Pavel Grachev, also USSR first deputy defense minister, took over control of the former KGB special troops, according to Novosti.

El'tsin on Russian Defense

The political commentator of *Moscow News*, Len Karpinsky, was elected chief editor by the weekly's staff, Central Television reported. He replaced Egor Yakovlev, whom President Gorbachev had appointed to head the All-Union State Television and Radio Broadcasting Company.

New Chief Editor of *Moscow News*

The former chief editor of *Literaturnaya gazeta*, Fedor Burlatsky, complained in a letter read out on Radio Moscow on August 30 that accusations of his not having opposed the coup were unfounded. Burlatsky said that his ouster as chief editor had been arranged by his first deputy, not by the staff, as reported by *Izvestia*. He also stated that his first deputy had foiled his attempt to have the weekly published despite the junta's ban.

Burlatsky Complains of Unfair Treatment

A group of Soviet and foreign journalists was allowed to tour the archives of the CPSU Central Committee for the first time in Soviet history. Radio Rossii quoted the journalists as saying that the archives had the most sophisticated equipment, including special filing cabinets with shredders mounted inside. The shredders started working when people who did not know the appropriate codes opened the drawers. An independent Moscow journalist, Dmitrii Volchek, told RL on August 30

Journalists in Central Committee Archives

that some documents had already been destroyed by such filing cabinets.

USSR Defense Committee Dissolved

The Committee on Defense and Security was dissolved during an extraordinary session of the USSR Supreme Soviet, Interfax reported. The committee, which had long been criticized by liberals for its ineffectiveness, was accused of inactivity during the coup.

Pankin Implicates Foreign Affairs Officials

Speaking on Central Television, Foreign Minister Boris Pankin said the signatures of Aleksandr Bessmertnykh and Yulii Kvitsinsky were on orders issued under the Emergency Committee and received by Pankin while he was posted as ambassador to Czechoslovakia.

Azerbaijani Supreme Soviet "Restores" Independence

The Azerbaijani Supreme Soviet voted to restore the independent status the republic enjoyed from 1918 to 1920, TASS reported. Adherents of the Azerbaijani Popular Front were quoted by *The Guardian* (August 31) as arguing that the independence declaration was a political ploy by President Ayaz Mutalibov aimed at neutralizing political opposition within the republic prior to the presidential elections scheduled for September 8; Zardusht Ali-Zade, the only candidate running against Mutalibov for the presidency, announced on August 30 that he had withdrawn his candidacy, Interfax reported on August 31.

Saturday, August 31

OMON Troops Leave Latvia, Lithuania

OMON troops began withdrawing from Latvia. Those withdrawing and their families were flown to Pskov, from where they were expected to be taken to Tyumen' in Western Siberia. The OMON units agreed to leave only after the Latvian authorities had promised to grant them and their families safe passage out of Latvia and amnesty for those who had not been involved in killings. According to Latvian and Western media dispatches, about forty members of OMON were missing and one had been arrested. In Lithuania, parliament spokesman Audrius Azubalis said that the garrison commander in Vilnius, Colonel Valerii Frolov, had told him that forty-seven members of OMON in Vilnius had been disarmed and had left Lithuania, thirty-three had refused to leave, and another fifty had disappeared (*Radio Independent Lithuania*, August 31).

The USSR in August, 1991

More Generals Implicated in Coup Attempt

A special edition of the newspaper *Rossiya* identified several more members of the High Command who, it was claimed, had participated actively in the coup. They were Colonel General Nikolai Shlyaga, recently ousted as head of the Main Political Administration; Colonel General Aleksandr Ovchinnikov, first deputy head of the same organization; Colonel General Aleksandr Soshnikov, identified as a presidential aide attached to Oleg Baklanov; Lieutenant General Mikhail Surkov, secretary of the All-Army Party Committee; Colonel General Vladislav Achalov, a deputy defense minister; and Lieutenant General Soslan Guchmazov, identified as an aide to Prime Minister Valentin Pavlov (*Radio Moscow*, August 31).

Cabinet Changes

According to TASS, Soviet President Mikhail Gorbachev appointed three new deputy defense ministers: Colonel General Vladimir Semenov, to head the Ground Forces; Colonel General Viktor Prudnikov, as new commander in chief of the Air Defense Forces; and Colonel General Petr Deinekin, to head the Air Force. Semenov, who replaced the arrested General Valentin Varennikov, was a USSR people's deputy and a former member of the Communist Party Central Committee. He had served as commander of the Transbaikal Military District. Prudnikov succeeded Army General Ivan Tret'yak. He was also a Central Committee member and had been serving as commander of the Moscow Air Defense forces. Deinekin had been commander of Long-Range Aviation. Gorbachev also named Lieutenant General Evgenii Podkolzin as the new commander of Soviet Airborne Forces. He succeeded Pavel Grachev, who had been appointed a USSR first deputy defense minister and chairman of the RSFSR Defense and Security Committee.

Bakatin Joins Leadership of Movement for Democratic Reforms

Trud reported that the Political Council of the Movement for Democratic Reforms had several new members, including the new KGB chairman, Vadim Bakatin, and his deputy, Nikolai Stolyarov, as well as economist Pavel Bunich, USSR Journalists' Union Chairman Eduard Sagalaev, USSR Minister of the Chemical Industry Salambek Khadzhiev, and playwright Mikhail Shatrov.

Four Ministers Reinstated

Ivan Silaev reinstated four USSR ministers who had not supported the coup. They were Nikolai Vorontsov (environment), Nikolai Gubenko (culture), Salambek Khadzhiev (chemical industry), and Gennadii Yagodin (education) (*Komsomol'skaya pravda*, August 31).

Aftermath of Coup in RSFSR Republics

In the wake of the coup, "under pressure from democratic forces," the president and the whole leadership of Kabardino-Balkaria resigned, and its parliament was dissolved. In Checheno-Ingushetia demonstrations demanding the resignation of the leadership for supporting the coup entered their twelfth day, the Soviet media reported. The All-National Congress of the Chechen People proclaimed the dissolution of the Supreme Soviet and the creation of a temporary republican committee. In Buryatia, "Democratic Buryatia" picketed the government building and collected funds to send a delegation to RSFSR President Boris El'tsin to denounce the republican Supreme Soviet for its role during the coup. Democratic forces were also questioning the actions of the local leadership during the coup in Mordovia and North Ossetia ("TSN," *Central Television* and *TASS*, August 31).

Communist Party Banned in Ukraine

It was reported that the Presidium of the Ukrainian Supreme Soviet had banned the Communist Party of Ukraine on August 30. The decision was based on the findings of the Presidium's commission investigating the activities of public figures in connection with the attempted coup. The same day, a document from the Central Committee of the republican Communist Party was found in which Party organizations were instructed to support the coup leaders. The document was signed by Stanislav Hurenko, first secretary of the Ukrainian Communist Party, and other Central Committee secretaries (*Ukrinform-TASS*, *Radio Kiev*, Western agencies, August 31).

Communist Party Functionaries Arrested in Georgia

Georgian Communist Party Second Secretary Sergei Rigvava and the editor of the Party's daily newspaper, Otar Ioseliani, were arrested and their homes searched. Sixty-five Communist deputies to the Georgian parliament were removed from office on August 30; the opposition National Democratic Party called for a demonstration in Tbilisi that day to press for the resignation of Georgian President Zviad Gamsakhurdia (Western agencies, August 31).

The Month of September

Sunday, September 1

USSR Congress of People's Deputies Opens

The USSR Congress of People's Deputies opened with the reading by Kazakh President Nursultan Nazarbaev of a declaration addressed to the Congress by Soviet President Mikhail Gorbachev and the heads of ten republics (the signatories of the "Nine-plus-One" agreement and Armenia). It stated that the signatories had agreed on the need to draw up and sign a treaty on a Union of sovereign states, in which each of them "can autonomously determine the form of its participation in the Union," and on the need to have all republics conclude as soon as possible an accord on an economic union. The declaration went on to outline new structures for the transitional period: a council composed of twenty USSR and republican deputies from each Union republic that should decide "general questions of principle"; a State Council consisting of the USSR president and the heads of the republics, who should take joint decisions on domestic and foreign-policy matters of common interest; and an Interrepublican Economic Committee with equal representation for all republics (*Central Television*, September 1).

The Congress ended its session on September 5 with a number of legislative moves. It approved: (1) the creation of a new two-chamber USSR Supreme Soviet; (2) the creation of a State Council, made up of President Gorbachev and the leaders of the republics, which would assume executive power during the transition period; (3) the abolition of the post of USSR vice president and the establishment of new succession procedures aimed at preventing a repetition of the attempted coup; (4) the establishment of an Interrepublican Economic Committee; (5) the preservation of the parliamentarians' status and privileges; (6) the convening of the new USSR Supreme Soviet by October 2; (7) the empowerment of the new Supreme Soviet to make amendments to the constitution (theretofore the exclusive prerogative of the Congress). Gorbachev failed to get approval for only one measure: the Congress refused to dissolve itself but conceded that, in light of the Supreme Soviet's new powers to amend the constitution, there should be no further need to convene the Congress.

USSR and US Recognize Baltic States' Independence

In an interview with CNN, Soviet President Gorbachev said the independence of the Baltic States would be "consistent" with his approach to reform if it were "the final will of the people."

On September 2, US President George Bush announced that the United States had extended diplomatic recognition to the Baltic States. Bush said that he had been in contact with Gorbachev before making the announcement (Western agencies).

On September 4, the first act of the State Council, the new body governing the USSR, was to recognize the independence of Estonia, Latvia, and Lithuania ("TSN," *Central Television*, September 5).

Estonia Nationalizes Soviet Property

The Estonian Supreme Council voted on August 29 to nationalize USSR property on Estonian soil, according to a report published in *Rahva Haal* on September 1. According to the law, USSR property was defined as property that had been appropriated by the Soviet Union on June 16, 1940, and all other enterprises and organizations that were directed by, or under the administrative control of, USSR state organs. The law also stipulated that the Estonian government must come to an agreement over equipment belonging to, or being used by, the USSR Defense Ministry and its subordinate components.

Gagauz Republic Declares Independence

The Supreme Soviet of the self-proclaimed "Gagauz republic" declared that it was seceding from Moldavia but would remain a republic within the USSR, according to a Moldovapres report. The Supreme Soviet appealed to the USSR Congress of People's Deputies and the United Nations to send a commission to investigate allegations of the abuse of ethnic rights in Moldavia. The Gagauz action was taken in the absence of the president and vice president "Gagauz republic," who were in the custody of the Moldavian authorities charged with supporting the attempted coup.

Memorial Service for Victims of KAL Flight 007

A memorial service for those who died when the Soviet Union shot down a Korean Airlines plane in 1983 was held on the ship *Yurii Trifonov*. About 100 relatives of the victims and representatives of the ministries of foreign affairs of the USSR, RSFSR, and Republic of Korea attended. This was the first time that the victims had been so honored. The South Korean ambassador to the USSR spoke to the gathering and expressed hope that the circumstances of the tragedy would be cleared up (*TASS*, September 1).

The USSR in September, 1991

Changes at the Foreign Ministry

Deputy Foreign Minister Vladimir Petrovsky was promoted to first deputy foreign minister. Yulii Kvitsinsky, his predecessor appointed on May 15, 1991, was dismissed (*TASS*, September 1). The next day, Yurii Deryabin was elevated to deputy foreign minister (*TASS*, September 2).

Monday, September 2

Constitutional Supervision Committee Endorses New Structures

The USSR Committee for Constitutional Supervision endorsed the new institutional structures for governing the USSR proposed by Soviet President Mikhail Gorbachev and the leaders of the republics during the opening session of the Congress of People's Deputies. The committee noted that the creation of these new bodies required significant changes to the USSR Constitution that could only be carried out by the Congress (*TASS*, September 2).

TASS Editorial Board Resigns

In connection with the reforms under way at TASS, members of the news agency's editorial board submitted their resignations. The agency's new director general, Vitalii Ignatenko, accepted the resignations but asked all board members to continue to carry out their duties until new administrative bodies had been appointed. The TASS reform plan stipulated that the news agency be transformed from a governmental agency into an independent one (*TASS*, September 2).

More Personnel Changes in Soviet Military

Two new commanders of military districts were appointed. The new commander of the Transbaikal Military District was Valerii Tret'yakov, a fifty-year-old lieutenant general who had served since October, 1988, as first deputy commander of the same military district. The new commander of the prestigious Moscow Military District was Vladimir Toporov, a forty-five-year-old lieutenant general who had served since February, 1989, as chief of staff of the Far Eastern Military District (*TASS*, September 2).

Lobov on Student Conscription, Military Reform

Chief of the General Staff Vladimir Lobov announced that the armed forces would no longer conscript students. Reports that student deferments would be ended preceded the coup attempt. Lobov also said that he was working to end the draft altogether, with the institution of a professional army in prospect. He argued that the army had become overly politicized in the months before the coup and that "many generals and officers forgot their main purpose." Lobov fell out of favor in December, 1986, when, as commander of the Central Asian Military District, he refused to involve his troops in ethnic clashes in Alma-Ata (*Izvestia*, September 2).

Demonstrations in Western Ukraine

Thousands of people gathered in Ternopol' and Lvov to demonstrate in support of Ukrainian independence. The meeting in Lvov, organized by the Ukrainian Republican Party, was attended by an estimated 200,000 people (*Radio Kiev*, September 2).

Nagorno-Karabakh Declares Independence

Radio Moscow reported that a joint session of the oblast soviet of Nagorno-Karabakh and the local soviet of the adjacent Shaumyan Raion, both of which are inhabited predominantly by Armenians, declared the region the "Nagorno-Karabakh Armenian Republic," only three days after Azerbaijan had declared its independence from the USSR. The two soviets ruled that the USSR Constitution and laws were valid on the territory of the new republic.

Azerbaijani Popular Front Calls for Strikes

The Azerbaijani Popular Front called for a general strike beginning on September 3 to press for postponement of the presidential elections scheduled for September 8, in which the incumbent Ayaz Mutalibov was the sole candidate. Western agencies said later that most workers had ignored the strike call, but Interfax quoted a popular front spokesman who said that workers at more than seventy enterprises in Baku, Nakhichevan, Agdam, and Akstafa were striking (*Azerbaijan Assa-Irada*, September 2).

Tuesday, September 3

Makashov Dismissed

The newspaper *Ural'sky rabochii* announced the dismissal of Colonel General Al'bert Makashov as commander of the Volga-Urals Military District. Makashov's connection with the attempted coup remained unclear. Radio Moscow, meanwhile, reported that the Volga-Urals Military District had just completed the disbanding of more than 100 large Communist Party organizations. Some 30,000 Communists had reportedly been affected (*Russian Television*, "Vesti," September 3).

On September 5, TASS reported the appointment of Lieutenant General Anatolii Sergeev as the new commander of the Volga-Urals Military District. Sergeev, who was born in 1940, had served as chief of staff of the Odessa Military District since 1988.

NATO and the Baltic States

According to the BBC, Minister of State at the British Foreign Office Douglas Hogg said that NATO could not provide security guarantees for the Baltic States. Hogg suggested that Baltic security would be better served by developing relations with Moscow and the Soviet republics while protecting the rights of ethnic minorities.

El'tsin on Nuclear Weapons

RSFSR President Boris El'tsin called for a moratorium on underground nuclear weapons tests and for "the total elimination of nuclear weapons in Russia." El'tsin also said that nuclear weapons were being moved to Russia from Ukraine and Kazakhstan and that the RSFSR would demand control over the use of nuclear weapons. He added that the recent Strategic Arms Reduction Treaty had not gone far enough, but he cautioned that reductions of nuclear weapons had to be conducted on the basis of parity (*CNN, Los Angeles Times*, September 4).

Latvia Takes Over Banking

The Latvian Supreme Council adopted a decision to reorganize the banking system in Latvia and to take over those banking institutions hitherto under USSR jurisdiction, Radio Riga reported. The new president of the Bank of the Republic of Latvia was Einars Repse. Alfreds Bergs-Bergmanis, a man with many years of experience in the Latvian SSR banking system, was appointed vice president.

Ukrainian Defense Minister Appointed

The Ukrainian Supreme Soviet appointed Major General Konstantin Morozov as the first republican defense minister. Morozov, who had previously served as commander of a large air force unit in Ukraine, was voted in with only 3 dissenting votes (out of nearly 300). Morozov said he supported the idea of a Ukrainian army. He also said that the Ukrainian defense minister should be a civilian and offered to resign from the USSR Armed Forces (Western agencies, September 3).

Psychological Counseling for Deputies

TASS reported that an office for psychological consultations had been set up in the foyer of the Palace of Congresses in the Kremlin, where people's deputies who were suffering from stress could talk to a trained psychologist. Deputies were reportedly suffering from feelings of inadequacy caused by the abortive coup, from feelings of isolation and disorientation in the new political climate, or from stage fright at the thought of having to speak at the Congress. The office was also visited by many former Communist Party deputies.

Deputies' Opinions Polled The Institute of the Sociology of Parliamentarianism released the results of a poll of 994 USSR people's deputies. Some 46 percent of the respondents envisaged the USSR as a federation, 27 percent as a confederation, and 15 percent as "several independent states." Sixty-six percent considered RSFSR President El'tsin to be the country's true leader, 48 percent saw Leningrad Mayor Anatolii Sobchak in this role, while some 41.3 percent thought of Soviet President Mikhail Gorbachev as the nation's leader. Kazakh President Nursultan Nazarbaev was named by 37 percent, RSFSR Prime Minister Ivan Silaev by 22 percent, and former Soviet Foreign Minister Eduard Shevardnadze by 12 percent. The most popular candidate for USSR vice president was Aleksandr Yakovlev, with 19 percent; for USSR prime minister, Ivan Silaev, with 22 percent (*TASS*, September 3).

Akhromeev's Grave Desecrated Vandals dug up the corpse of the recently buried Marshal Sergei Akhromeev and stripped it of its military uniform. Akhromeev committed suicide after the failed coup. According to the report, the corpse of a colonel general, buried nearby, was treated in a similar fashion (*Russian Television*, September 3).

Progress in Moldavian-Dniester Talks Separatists in the self-proclaimed "Dniester republic" agreed not to cut off electricity and gas for Moldavia and pledged to try to end blockades of rail lines in the region. The separatists had been demanding the release of Igor' Smirnov, the president of the "Dniester republic" detained by the Moldavian authorities on a charge of having supported the coup (Western agencies, September 3).

Wednesday, September 4

Gromov Dismissed General Boris Gromov, who had been on vacation when the attempted coup took place, was dismissed. Gromov said that the putschists had asked him to join them on August 20 but that he had resolutely rejected their offer.

The USSR in September, 1991

He declared he would protest against his dismissal from the post of first deputy minister of internal affairs (*The Times*, September 4).

Sovetskaya Rossiya Is Back

Sovetskaya Rossiya, formerly the daily of the Russian Communist Party, resumed publication after an eleven-day break. *Sovetskaya Rossiya* returned as an "independent people's newspaper" with no further connection to the CPSU Central Committee (its former official "founder"—the equivalent of a proprietor). But, in a front-page announcement, the daily's journalists said the changes did not mean that *Sovetskaya Rossiya* would abandon "the noble aims avowed by the honest Communists of the Russian Federation." The journalists said they were now operating *Sovetskaya Rossiya* in partnership with a private company.

Communists, KGB Flee to China

The Japanese national newspapers *Nihon Keizai Shimbun* and *Sankei Shimbun* reported that several thousand CPSU members and KGB staffers had fled to China after the failure of the attempted coup. With one exception—that of a highly-placed Soviet official serving in the Soviet embassy in Peking—the Chinese Communist Party would provide asylum and support to the defectors. The Chinese government did not plan to release any information concerning the asylum-seekers.

Support for Coup in the Far East

The commander of the Far Eastern Military District said that half of all military personnel in the Soviet Far East had supported the attempted coup. Colonel General Viktor Novozhilov said that on the first two days of the coup the number of those opposed to the putsch and those supporting it was about equal. Novozhilov said that he had received orders from Defense Minister Dmitrii Yazov to "shut down news organs and deploy troops at strategic locations" but that he had ignored the instructions (*Le Monde*, September 3).

KGB Gives Wallenberg Documents to Sweden

TASS reported that KGB Chairman Vadim Bakatin had presented previously undisclosed documents to Sweden's embassy in Moscow concerning the case of Raoul Wallenberg, who saved many Jews from the Holocaust while a diplomat in wartime Hungary. Bakatin said that the material gave no new details but that the search for more information would continue. Wallenberg was arrested by Soviet forces in Budapest in 1945, and the

Soviet Union always maintained that he had died in jail in 1947. But there were strong grounds for believing that Wallenberg had been shot.

Executive Protection Reformed

The reformed Government Guard Administration (formerly the KGB's Ninth Administration for Government Protection) would be administratively independent of the KGB and responsible for the security of the presidents of the USSR and the RSFSR, according to the new head of the service, Colonel Vladimir Redkoborody (*TASS*, September 4). Redkoborody, formerly employed in the KGB's foreign intelligence, replaced Lieutenant General Yurii Plekhanov, who was arrested for his involvement in the failed coup. Soviet President Gorbachev's former bodyguard, Valerii Pestov, was appointed chief of the USSR President's Security Service.

Ukrainian Flags Flies over Parliament

The Ukrainian Supreme Soviet adopted a resolution recognizing the blue and yellow Ukrainian national flag along with the blue and red flag of the Ukrainian SSR, according to Radio Kiev. The resolution was adopted only after Supreme Soviet Chairman Leonid Kravchuk threatened to resign if it were not approved. Both flags were briefly hoisted atop the Supreme Soviet building in Kiev, but angry demonstrators outside succeeded in having the Soviet flag removed.

New Ukrainian Prosecutor

The Ukrainian Supreme Soviet suspended the activities of the Ukrainian Prosecutor's Office. It named people's deputy Viktor Shishkin the new republican prosecutor. The Ukrainian parliament also reinstated the parliamentary immunity of radical deputy Stepan Khmara, who was arrested in the Supreme Soviet building in November, 1990 (*Radio Kiev*, September 4).

Aliev to Chair Nakhichevan Supreme Soviet

Former Politburo member Geidar Aliev was elected chairman of the Supreme Majlis—the parliament—of Azerbaijan's Nakhichevan Autonomous Republic, according to a report passed by a Baku journalist to an RFE/RL correspondent. Aliev resigned from the CPSU in July, arguing that the Communist Party was trying to suppress the democratic movement in Azerbaijan.

Latvia to Restore Foreigners' Property

The Latvian parliament passed a bill that promised to return foreigners' property seized after the Soviet occupation in 1940. Companies whose factories were seized would be offered stocks in them with the hope that the former owners would invest in their modernization.

Akaev against Persecution of Communists

Kirgiz President Askar Akaev promised that he would not allow CPSU members to be persecuted (*TASS*, September 4). Akaev said that most Party members bore no responsibility for the policies of the leadership of the republican Communist Party and the CPSU and that every citizen of the republic must be guaranteed his rights, regardless of party affiliation.

Lithuania Recognizes Moldavia

The Supreme Council of Lithuania adopted a declaration extending official recognition to the Republic of Moldavia. The Lithuanian declaration added that "the integration of independent Moldavia into the international community of democratic states will constitute an event of historic importance" (*Moldovapres*, September 4).

Thursday, September 5

El'tsin Upgrades Role of Courts

RSFSR President Boris El'tsin signed a decree raising the status of the judiciary in the Russian Federation, according to a report by Radio Rossii. El'tsin's decree also stated that buildings confiscated from the CPSU after the abortive coup should be handed over to the RSFSR courts.

CPSU Documents Destroyed in Leningrad

In the period between August 21 and August 23, "all secret documentation" (apparently that related to the coup) was destroyed in the Leningrad Oblast Party Committee, according to a report by AP. The destruction of documents reportedly started after the local Party organization received a secret instruction from the CPSU Central Committee. The same day, deputy KGB chief Nikolai Stolyarov told a Moscow press conference that the agency would not for the present open the archives concerning Stalin's prison camps. He said not only the relatives of the victims were still alive but also those of the people who took part in the repressions (*Interfax*, September 5).

KGB Apparatus behind Coup

Among the KGB officials who were prime movers in the coup were the head of the KGB's Information and

Analysis Administration, Valerii Lebedev; Aleksandr Red'kin, head of the Interethnic Relations Department; and the senior officers of Administration "Z" (Protection of the Constitutional Order) Gennadii Dobrovol'sky, Aleksandr Kobyakov, Igor' Perfil'ev, Yurii Denisov, and Aleksandr Moroz. Administration "Z" controlled all aspects of domestic sociopolitical and economic activities, including monitoring of interethnic conflicts, riots, Soviet-Western joint ventures, and numerous cultural and charitable foundations, except those sponsored by the CPSU apparatus. Administration "Z" also had a network of agents in the mass media and public organizations, which allowed it to direct as well as monitor political processes in the country. Lieutenant Colonel Yurii Kichikhin, formerly of Administration "Z," described the KGB's involvement in *Novoe vremya* (No. 35).

KGB's Mission Redefined KGB Chairman Vadim Bakatin told a conference of republican KGB chairmen that one of the agency's main goals was a radical change in the structure of state security but that its intelligence-gathering, counterintelligence, and antiterrorism capabilities would be retained, TASS reported. According to a document on the division of functions between the central and republican security apparatuses that was presented to the conference, the all-Union KGB would keep its present role in personnel, financial, and technical issues. Sergei Stepashin, head of the state commission investigating the KGB's role in the coup, warned that disbanding the security services in some East European countries had seriously undermined their national security.

Ukrainian Representative to RSFSR The Presidium of the Ukrainian Supreme Soviet adopted a resolution creating a Ukrainian mission in the RSFSR. The mission was established in accordance with the Ukrainian-Russian treaty signed in November, 1990. People's deputy Volodymyr Kryzhanivs'kyi was named Ukraine's first envoy to the RSFSR (*Radio Kiev*, September 5).

Uzbekistan Declares Independence Uzbekistan declared its independence, claiming the right to determine its own state and administrative system, create its own ministry of defense and national guard, have its own currency, and establish diplomatic and consular relations with foreign states. It also guaranteed equal rights to all citizens regardless of nationality or religious affiliation and recognized Karakalpakistan's right to secede (*TASS*, September 5).

THE USSR IN SEPTEMBER, 1991

Friday, September 6

Azerbaijan Establishes Defense Ministry

Azerbaijani President Ayaz Mutalibov issued a decree establishing a republican ministry of defense. Lieutenant General Valeg Barshatly, an ethnic Azerbaijani who was appointed head of the Higher Combined Army Military Academy in Baku in the late 1970s and also served as deputy commander of the USSR's Western Group of Forces in Germany, was appointed minister (*TASS*, September 6).

Georgian Parliament Breaks Ties with USSR

Georgia formally broke ties with the USSR in protest over the failure of the USSR State Council to debate the question of recognizing Georgia's independence. Chairman of the Georgian parliament Akaki Asatiani affirmed that "any economic or defense-related agreements with the USSR are out of the question now" (*Interfax*, September 6).

Saturday, September 7

Shaposhnikov against Defense Cuts

USSR Minister of Defense Evgenii Shaposhnikov told CNN that Moscow faced no genuine external threat and that it was his aim to cut the number of military units but to increase the capability of those that were retained. He said that he opposed defense cuts but would reallocate existing funds in the military budget (Western agencies, September 7).

Soviet Ambassador to Britain Dismissed

Leonid Zamyatin, the Soviet ambassador to London, was dismissed after being accused of supporting the abortive coup. Zamyatin, who had held the post since 1986, was first recalled to Moscow and subsequently fired. According to the USSR Ministry of Foreign Affairs, he was not charged with any crime (*London Press Association*, September 7).

Ukraine and Poland to Establish Diplomatic Ties

Ukraine and Poland signed a joint communiqué in Warsaw, agreeing to establish diplomatic relations in the near future. The document was signed by Ukrainian Foreign Minister Anatolii Zlenko and Polish Foreign Minister Krzysztof Skubiszewski. Skubiszewski said that, after Ukraine's declaration of independence on August 24, there were no formal obstacles to an exchange of ambassadors between the two countries (Western agencies).

Plan to Storm RSFSR Parliament Derailed by Shaposhnikov

At the height of the abortive coup, helicopter gunships were prepared to storm the RSFSR Supreme Soviet building but refrained from doing so when Air Force General Evgenii Shaposhnikov, who was later named USSR minister of defense, threatened to scramble fighters to down the helicopters. The plan, which was devised by defense officials and the KGB, called for attacking the building on the night of August 20. Shaposhnikov, then commander of the air force, was present at the consultations and threatened to send up his fighter planes if the plan were put into effect (*Argumenty i fakty*, September 7).

Foreign Aid for the Soviet Union

French Economy and Finance Minister Pierre Bérégovoy, speaking at a press conference in Moscow, said that the G-7 industrialized countries and the European Community must form a mechanism to help reconstruct the Soviet Union's economy. Bérégovoy suggested that aid could come in a form similar to that received by Europe under the terms of the postwar Marshall Plan. Previously, Western leaders had backed away from the idea of drawing up such a plan (Western agencies, September 7).

Leningrad Becomes St. Petersburg

The Presidium of the RSFSR Supreme Soviet voted to restore the original name of St. Petersburg to the city of Leningrad. The decision was taken in accordance with the results of a referendum held on June 12, in which more than 50 percent of the city's residents favored the old name. The change was to take effect on October 1 (*TASS*, September 7).

Moldavia to Abandon Participation in Soviet Political Structures

Interviewed after returning to Kishinev from the USSR Congress of People's Deputies, Moldavian First Deputy Prime Minister Constantin Oboroc said that Moldavia would no longer be a part of Soviet political structures, nor would it be a part of the new ones being established. It would, however, participate in the Interrepublican Economic Committee and would continue its bilateral relations with the former republics (*Moldovapres*, September 7).

Sunday, September 8

Shevardnadze Warns of Dictatorship

Former USSR Foreign Minister Eduard Shevardnadze warned in an interview with French television that the threat of a dictatorship persisted in the Soviet Union

The USSR in September, 1991

because of the great instability in the country. With regard to the future structure of the country, he said that the republics should be individually represented in the United Nations and that the president of the USSR should be directly elected by popular vote (Western agencies, September 8).

Soviet Plea for Massive Foreign Aid

USSR Minister of Foreign Affairs Boris Pankin appealed for massive Western aid, saying that the recent upheaval in the Soviet Union affected the world at least as much as the Gulf war had.

Genscher Leaves for Moscow and the Baltic States

German Foreign Minister Hans-Dietrich Genscher began a five-day visit to Moscow and the three Baltic States. He was to hold talks with Gorbachev, El'tsin, and the Baltic leaders. Genscher would also take part in the opening of a human-rights meeting that was to be held under the aegis of the Conference on Security and Cooperation in Europe (Western agencies, September 8).

After meetings in Riga and Vilnius on September 12, Genscher said Germany supported the granting of associate membership in the EC to the Baltic States (*Radio Vilnius*, September 12).

Presidential Elections in Azerbaijan

Despite strikes and protests, presidential elections in Azerbaijan went ahead as planned. Ayaz Mutalibov, the incumbent, emerged victorious by a large majority. Mutalibov, who resigned from the CPSU after the failed coup, was the only candidate. He rejected widespread accusations that the elections had been rigged (Western agencies, September 8).

Lithuania Denies Rehabilitating War Criminals

Lithuania offered to open KGB archives to the public to disprove charges that its government had knowingly exonerated Nazi war criminals. Lithuanian Supreme Council President Vytautas Landsbergis claimed that Soviet intelligence organs might be spreading the disinformation in an attempt to discredit his country. *The New York Times* reported earlier in the week that Lithuania was exonerating thousands of people who had allegedly collaborated in the liquidation of Jews during the war (Western agencies, September 8).

On September 9, the Presidium of the Lithuanian Supreme Council issued a statement in which it proposed that joint Lithuanian-Israeli parliamentary groups be formed to examine cases involving charges of Nazi war crimes (Western agencies, September 9).

Monday, September 9

Bukovsky Discusses KGB with Bakatin

During a televised conversation, former dissident Vladimir Bukovsky urged Chairman of the KGB Vadim Bakatin to move towards gaining the trust of the world community by discarding the KGB's vast system of disinformation. Bukovsky asked that an international commission with access to KGB archives be created to clear up such mysteries as the backgrounds to the assassination of President John F. Kennedy and the attempt on the life of Pope John Paul II. Bakatin rejected the proposal (*Central Television*, September 9).

Soviet Ground Forces Commander on Future of Armed Forces

Colonel General Vladimir Semenov, the newly appointed commander in chief of Soviet Ground Forces, said that the structure of his branch of the armed forces would depend upon arrangements outlined in any future Union treaty. He did, however, urge that a unified army be retained, arguing that individual republics were unable to finance or train well-equipped ground forces. Only a strong central government, he argued, could maintain military forces capable of reliably ensuring the security of the Union (*TASS*, September 9).

Ukraine Adopts Law on Foreign Investment

The Ukrainian Supreme Soviet adopted laws protecting foreign investments and confirming the nationalization of all-Union institutions and organizations on the territory of Ukraine. The law on foreign investment allowed for the transfer abroad of profits in both rubles and hard currency (*Ukrinform-TASS*, September 10)

Tajikistan Declares Independence

The Supreme Soviet of Tajikistan adopted a declaration of independence that promised respect for human rights and the rights of all nationalities in the republic. It also called for the creation of a union of sovereign states, of which Tajikistan would be a member (*TASS*, September 9).

Russian Parliament Accuses Georgia of Human-Rights Violations

Members of several RSFSR parliamentary committees issued a statement expressing concern about human-rights violations in Georgia and proposing that a state of emergency be declared in Abkhazia, South Ossetia, and

The USSR in September, 1991

Tbilisi should the situation in those areas continue to deteriorate. Meanwhile, Georgian President Zviad Gamsakhurdia ordered the arrest of opposition leaders and those who had participated in demonstrations in Tbilisi the previous week (*TASS*, September 9).

Tuesday, September 10

Gorbachev on the Future Union

In his address to the Conference on Security and Cooperation in Europe meeting in Moscow, Soviet President Mikhail Gorbachev was fairly optimistic about the chances of a new Union's being formed. He said that there had been a realization in recent days that the attainment of independence by the republics was not a pretext for chaotic severing of historical ties but the basis for a solid Union of genuinely sovereign and truly independent states. The new Union, he argued, should be based upon the principles of independence and territorial integrity, with the right to join or secede (*TASS*, September 10).

El'tsin Cancels Some Decrees

RSFSR President Boris El'tsin annulled a series of decrees that he had issued during the failed coup and in its aftermath. Among these was the decree that suspended publication of several CPSU newspapers (*TASS*, September 10).

Lithuanian Poles Protest

Some 200 Poles demonstrated in Vilnius against the dissolution of two regional councils in predominantly Polish-inhabited areas of Lithuania. A member of one of the councils maintained that their dissolution was unjust because they had been legally elected. The leader of the Polish faction in the parliament said that some Poles felt threatened by Lithuanian independence. The councils were disbanded in connection with accusations that they had supported the coup attempt (Western agencies, September 10).

Yavlinsky Favors Return of Kurile Islands

Deputy Chairman of the Economic Management Committee Grigorii Yavlinsky said in a written response to questions from the Japanese Kyodo News Agency that the Soviet Union should return the disputed Kurile Islands to Japan. Yavlinsky said that the problem should be resolved in the near future and that the return of the islands should not be dependent upon Japanese aid to the Soviet Union (*TASS*, September 10)

The USSR in September, 1991

Latvia Bans Communist Party

The Latvian Supreme Council banned the Latvian Communist Party and its related organizations such as the Komsomol, the Council of Work Collectives, and the Council of War and Labor Veterans. The parliament had earlier suspended the activities of the Communist Party, ruling that it was an unconstitutional organization (*Radio Independent Lithuania*, September 10).

Wednesday, September 11

El'tsin Accused of "Usurpation of Authority"

A session of the interim Economic Management Committee, headed by RSFSR Prime Minister Ivan Silaev, heard accusations that RSFSR President Boris El'tsin had usurped authority and property both during and after the failed coup. Deputy Chairman of the committee Yurii Luzhkov proposed sending a letter to El'tsin asking him to review relevant decrees and legislative acts because they restricted the powers of the committee (*TASS*, September 11).

Primakov Stresses Soviet Role in Middle East

USSR envoy to the Middle East Evgenii Primakov said the Soviet Union intended to play an active role in a Middle East peace conference and would not be pressured into resuming diplomatic relations with Israel. He stressed his current tour of the region was not linked with Middle East peace negotiations (Western agencies, September 11).

On September 14, Primakov visited the United Arab Emirates, where he called for stronger ties between the USSR and the UAE. He also delivered a letter from Soviet President Mikhail Gorbachev to President Sheikh Zayid bin Sultan al-Nahayyan thanking him for his stance during the coup.

On September 15, Primakov arrived in Kuwait, where he met with Kuwait's Emir Sheikh Jabir al-Ahmad al-Sabah. He said that he would not ask for financial support but would discuss the improvement of economic relations, which Kuwait promised after the Gulf war, Western agencies and Interfax reported.

On September 17, Primakov flew to Teheran where he stressed that the USSR and Iran were "neighbors" developing "intensive relations," TASS reported.

On September 18, Radio Teheran quoted Iranian President Ali Akbar Hashemi-Rafsanjani as saying Iran would help "alleviate existing economic problems" in the USSR. Rafsanjani also said Iran did not wish to see Western countries in a position to exploit the situation in the USSR.

The USSR in September, 1991

On his return to Moscow, Primakov told TASS (September 21) that a number of Middle Eastern countries had given the USSR "serious" financial support, including credits for purchasing food and consumer goods. He did not quantify the aid. Primakov was quoted as saying the main task now was to make the necessary changes in the USSR to prevent the aid from "sinking through the sand." The Saudi special envoy in Moscow told US television on September 20 that his country would help provide food for the Soviet Union, Western agencies reported that day.

Demonstrators Call for Gamsakhurdia's Resignation; Arrests Made

Protests against Georgian President Zviad Gamsakhurdia spread from Tbilisi to other Georgian cities, including Batumi on the coast of the Black Sea. Some thirty opposition groups in Georgia were reported to have adopted a common program calling for Gamsakhurdia's resignation (Western agencies, September 11).

On September 16, some 10,000–20,000 people rallied in Tbilisi to demand Gamsakhurdia's resignation and new parliamentary elections. They subsequently marched on the Tbilisi television building, which Gamsakhurdia called on his supporters to defend; no clashes took place. Giorgi Chanturia, head of the National Democratic Party and one of the main organizers of the anti-Gamsakhurdia protests, was arrested while boarding a plane to Moscow, where he planned to hold a press conference, Western news agencies reported.

On September 17, hundreds of people demonstrated in Tbilisi to protest against the arrest on September 16 of four National Democratic Party members, including Chanturia, who were alleged to have been plotting together with former USSR Foreign Minister Eduard Shevardnadze to overthrow Gamsakhurdia. According to Gamsakhurdia's spokesman, Chanturia would be charged with "antisocial" activities.

Filmmaker Giorgi Khaindrava was arrested in Tbilisi on September 17, apparently for his support of the protests of the past two weeks. Georgian television employees repeatedly interrupted the screening on September 17 of an appeal by Gamsakhurdia to the population to converge on Tbilisi to defend the elected parliament. Busloads of Gamsakhurdia's supporters arrived in Tbilisi on September 18; police abandoned an attempt to remove barriers erected by anti-Gamsakhurdia protesters on the central avenue, Western news agencies reported on September 18.

On September 19, an emergency session of deputies from the Georgian parliamentary opposition prevented the expulsion of sixty Communist Party deputies suspended on September 15. Under pressure to modify his authoritarian style, Gamsakhurdia was reported by Western news agencies to have offered concessions to the opposition, including access to television.

The Tbilisi demonstrations continued on September 21. Members of the National Democratic Party were attacked by police, and several people were injured. Gamsakhurdia refused to talk to two representatives of the opposition. Opposition forces backed by National Guard troops occupied the Tbilisi television station early on September 22, and opposition forces clashed elsewhere in Tbilisi with police, who opened fire, killing two people. Pro- and antigovernment demonstrations were held on September 22. Gamsakhurdia met with Tedo Paatashvili, a former Roundtable ally now aligned with the opposition, who later said Gamsakhurdia had agreed to convene a session of parliament to discuss new parliamentary elections.

Pro- and anti-Gamsakhurdia demonstrations continued on September 23 at Tbilisi University. Rebel members of the National Guard reinforced the broadcasting center, which was being held by the opposition; shots were fired, but no one was injured. Talks on the opposition's demands for the withdrawal from Tbilisi of Gamsakhurdia supporters brought in from rural areas, liberalization of the press, and the release of political prisoners made no progress; a further round was scheduled for September 24 (Western news agencies, September 23 and 24). Two Georgian student groups called for sending international observers to Georgia. At the human-rights conference in Moscow, US delegate Max Kampelman criticized Gamsakhurdia for violations of human rights.

On September 24, Gamsakhurdia declared a state of emergency in Tbilisi to take effect the following day in response to what he termed "a military and civil putsch," Western news agencies reported on September 24. Gamsakhurdia said he would try to eject opposition forces occupying the Tbilisi television studios but ruled out further arrests of opposition figures. Gamsakhurdia refused to negotiate with the opposition, whom he called criminals whose actions were being orchestrated by Moscow. He threatened to impose presidential rule unless the opposition abandoned its efforts to compel him to resign.

Three Georgian policemen and two members of the rebel National Guard were killed in a shoot-out early on September 25, the circumstances of which were unclear. Talks between four government ministers and ex-Prime

The USSR in September, 1991

Minister Tengiz Sigua and National Guard commander Tengiz Kitovani on September 25 failed to yield an agreement. Opposition forces began live television broadcasts from the television center, which they continued to occupy (Western news agencies, September 25).

A Georgian military spokesman denied claims by Kitovani that four Georgian OMON troops had been killed in an attack on the National Guard camp at Shavnabada outside Tbilisi early on the morning of September 26, and he reported that shots had been fired later that day at the home of Gamsakhurdia, Western news agencies reported on September 26.

Talks on September 27 between the government and the opposition resulted in an unofficial cease-fire agreement.

Rutskoi's Party to Change Its Name

It was reported that the Democratic Party of Communists of Russia, headed by RSFSR Vice President Aleksandr Rutskoi, planned to drop the word "Communists" from its name. The recently formed party intended to abandon its Communist course and become an umbrella organization for people holding left-wing views (*Central Television*, September 11).

Head of Leningrad Television to Be Replaced

Radio Rossii reported that the director of the Leningrad Television and Radio Broadcasting Company, Boris Petrov, would be replaced by Viktor Yugin, the head of the RSFSR Supreme Soviet Commission on *Glasnost'* and the Media. Petrov had been accused of broadcasting the resolutions of the Emergency Committee on August 19.

Bush Meets with Baltic Envoys

US President George Bush met with envoys of the three Baltic States in Washington and pledged a package of measures aimed at beginning the process of reintegrating those states into the West. The package included the release of Baltic assets that had been kept in trust since 1940 (Western agencies, September 11).

Soviet Troops to Leave Baltic States in 1994

A Latvian defense official reported that Soviet troops were to withdraw from the Baltic States in 1994. Latvian officials were told of the deadline at a meeting with USSR Minister of Defense Evgenii Shaposhnikov in Moscow. Shaposhnikov said that a withdrawal would be possible only after all questions concerning Soviet troop withdrawals from Eastern Europe had been resolved.

Thursday, September 12

Nazarbaev Suggests Prunskiene as Head of Economic Management Committee

Kazakh President Nursultan Nazarbaev said that, in his view, a Russian should not head the interim Economic Management Committee. He suggested that former Lithuanian Prime Minister Kazimiera Prunskiene be appointed to the position (*Nezavisimaya gazeta*, September 12).

Further Changes at the KGB

Soviet President Mikhail Gorbachev dismissed Deputy Chairman of the KGB Valerii Lebedev, a close associate of former KGB Chairman Vladimir Kryuchkov. Also let go was Deputy Chairman of the KGB Gennadii Titov, who was on the state commission investigating KGB activities (*TASS*, September 12). Titov was replaced on September 15 by Fedor Myasnikov head of the KGB's Second Main Directorate and deputy chairman of the USSR KGB, according to TASS. KGB Chairman Vadim Bakatin was reported to have disbanded the Fourth Department of the KGB Administration for the Protection of Constitutional Order, which was responsible for monitoring religious organizations (*Izvestia*, September 13). Bakatin also recalled USSR KGB General Ivan Fedoseev from Lithuania, according to the Lithuanian government press office on September 15. Fedoseev had been overseeing the disbandment of the KGB in Lithuania. Radio Moscow said Bakatin had released Stanislav Tsaplin from his duties as deputy commander of the KGB in Lithuania.

Bakatin also approved the appointment of Evgenii Sevost'yanov as chief of the KGB Administration for the city of Moscow and Moscow Oblast, according to *Krasnaya zvezda* of September 12. Sevost'yanov—who was one of the organizers of Gavriil Popov's successful election campaign for the post of Moscow mayor—was nominated by Popov. Sevost'yanov was a member of the organizing committee of the Movement for Democratic Reforms and sat on the Coordinating Council of Democratic Russia. Sevost'yanov was also a close associate of the late Academician Andrei Sakharov.

On September 18, the commission investigating the activities of the KGB sent a proposal to the USSR State Council urging the replacement of the USSR KGB by an RSFSR Committee for State Security, according to Radio Rossii. Sergei Stepashin, chairman of the commission, called for some of the KGB's current divisions to be disbanded or transferred to the jurisdiction of other bodies. He said that the new RSFSR KGB would change its name to the Federal Security Service and would concentrate on protecting Russian economic interests and

THE USSR IN SEPTEMBER, 1991

fighting organized crime. Almost 50 percent of the territorial security apparatus and nearly 100 percent of human and electronic intelligence assets were in the possession of the RSFSR.

On September 20, Leonid Shebarshin, the head of the KGB's First Main Administration, in charge of foreign operations, resigned in protest over the reorganization conducted in the foreign espionage sector, Radio Mayak reported that day.

Lenin Monument Dismantled in Kiev

Workers began dismantling the gigantic Lenin monument on Kiev's Independence Square (formerly October Revolution Square). The decision was taken by the Kiev City Soviet (*Radio Kiev*, September 12).

Kravchuk Meets with Jewish Leaders

Chairman of the Ukrainian Supreme Soviet Leonid Kravchuk met with World Jewish Congress leader Edgar Bronfman and Nobel Peace Prize laureate Eli Wiesel in Kiev. The Jewish leaders, who were in Kiev to mark the fiftieth anniversary of the massacre at Babii Yar, requested that there be no statute of limitations on the prosecution of Nazi war criminals (*Ukrinform-TASS*, September 12).

Kazakhstan Creates Space Agency

Kazakh President Nazarbaev issued a decree creating a republican agency for space research. At the beginning of the year, Nazarbaev had met with Moscow officials to discuss the Baikonur launch site, which he complained did not bring any benefit to Kazakhstan (*TASS*, September 12).

New Central Asian Muslim Board

A group of imams from the Tashkent area were reported to have decided to create an alternative Muslim Religious Board for Central Asia. An attempt was made in July to remove the head of the existing board; he was accused of selling for profit Korans that had been donated by Saudi Arabia (*Interfax*, September 12).

Friday, September 13

US-Soviet Agreement on Arms Supplies to Afghanistan

The United States and the Soviet Union announced that they had agreed to halt weapons supplies to both sides in the Afghan conflict as part of an effort to arrange free elections in that country. The announcement was made in Moscow by US Secretary of State James Baker and

Soviet Minister of Foreign Affairs Boris Pankin. According to the statement, weapons supplies would end by January 1, 1992, and there would be no increase in supplies in the interim (Western agencies, September 13).

Soviet Defense Budget Figures

USSR Deputy Minister of Finance Vladimir Raevsky announced that of the 96 billion rubles planned for defense in 1991, 39.6 billion had been allocated for weapons; 12.4 billion for research, development, and design; 30.7 billion for maintenance; 6.3 billion for capital investment; 4 billion for pensions; and 3.2 billion for social provisions (*Interfax, Radio Rossii*, September 13).

Kobets Named RSFSR Defense Adviser

RSFSR President Boris El'tsin appointed Army General Konstantin Kobets to the position of RSFSR state defense adviser and confirmed him as a member of the RSFSR State Council. The previous week, Kobets had been named by USSR Minister of Defense Evgenii Shaposhnikov to head a temporary commission investigating the actions of military personnel during the attempted coup (*Interfax*, September 13).

Military Service in Kazakhstan

Kazakh President Nursultan Nazarbaev issued a decree subordinating military commissariats in Kazakhstan to the republican government. The decree also mandated that the republic's internal forces be composed of conscripts from within the republic (*TASS*, September 13).

Estonians Protest Draft Law on Citizenship

Hundreds of people protested in Tallinn against draft legislation that would grant automatic citizenship to all permanent residents of Estonia. The protest was organized by the Congress of Estonia, which regarded the draft legislation as unacceptable because it failed to provide legal continuity with citizenship in the interwar republic. The congress wanted people who were not either citizens of the interwar republic and their descendants to apply for citizenship rather than receive it automatically (Western agencies, September 13).

Saturday, September 14

Nuclear Weapons Code Taken from Gorbachev during Coup

Soviet President Mikhail Gorbachev's adviser Anatolii Chernyaev acknowledged that the communications code controlling the launch of nuclear weapons had been taken away from his boss during the coup. The *Los Angeles Times* quoted Chernyaev and another Gorbachev aide, Igor' Malashenko, as saying that during the coup the Soviet Union "had no retaliatory capability" and that the country's defense had been paralyzed. After the coup, a special committee to control nuclear weapons was set up under all-Union and RSFSR control.

USSR nuclear scientist Gennadii Pavlov said on September 25 that, although Gorbachev had had to relinquish his nuclear command briefcase to his deputy, Gennadii Yanaev, some Gorbachev loyalists had managed to "empty the briefcase" so that the putschists could not have used it. Western agencies quoted Pavlov as saying that, in addition to emptying Yanaev's briefcase, loyalist officers had also destroyed the links between the putschists and all nuclear launch control centers.

Changes at TASS and Central Television

The director general of TASS, Vitalii Ignatenko, told *Pravda* that his agency would no longer have two separate news services for foreign and domestic consumption. He said all desks publishing special news bulletins (known as "white TASS," which was distributed among top Soviet officials) had been closed down. Ignatenko also mentioned that cuts had been made in inefficient bureaus abroad.

On September 13, Soviet President Gorbachev and RSFSR President El'tsin signed an agreement dividing up the property of Central Television, TASS reported. The agreement stipulated that the second channel of Central Television would be given to the RSFSR.

Reorganization of the Soviet Military

USSR Defense Minister Evgenii Shaposhnikov said that he envisaged a Soviet army of some 3 million men during a "transitional" phase on the way to establishing a reformed and more professional force. The Soviet army currently has some 3.5 million men. Shaposhnikov stated that reshaping the armed forces could take up to six years, Western news agencies reported.

On September 16, TASS reported that nine of the seventeen members of the Defense Ministry Collegium had been removed since the August 19 coup. The report named only Dmitrii Yazov and Valentin Varennikov as having been fired for participation in the coup. It said that Mikhail Moiseev had been removed on account of illness and that Vladislav Achalov and Nikolai Shlyaga were also receiving medical attention. Ivan Tret'yak and Vladimir Govorov were reported to have been obliged to retire for reasons of age.

In a long interview published in *Sovetskaya Rossiya* on September 20, Shaposhnikov provided the most detailed description to date of planned military reforms. At the top he proposed a reconstituted USSR Defense Ministry staffed with more civilians. In the republics, Shaposhnikov proposed the creation of civilian Committees for Defense, to be headed by someone appointed jointly by the republican president and the USSR defense minister. The commander of Union troops in a given republic would be appointed by the USSR president with the approval of republican leaders and would be directly subordinated to the USSR president. The legal basis for stationing troop contingents in a given republic was to be defined by special agreements or treaties between the Union—through the Defense Ministry—and the republics. The troop contingents would be responsible for protecting external borders and would not interfere in the internal affairs of a republic. See also *Pravda*, September 25.

Reorganization of the Ministry of Foreign Affairs

USSR Foreign Minister Boris Pankin told Interfax that the Foreign Ministry Collegium would in future be made up of "modern, thinking people" whose actions were above reproach during the coup. He said that the Collegium would become the collective leadership organ of the ministry and would include deputy foreign ministers, department heads, and important public and political figures. The country's "supreme diplomatic body" was, however, to be the Council of Ministers of Foreign Affairs of the USSR and the Republics (CMFA), according to Radio Moscow.

Pankin revealed that an Executive Secretariat had been established by the Collegium that would allow close coordination of Union and republican foreign-policy activity. The Executive Secretariat of the CMFA was to be headed by Deputy Foreign Minister Valerii Nikolaenko.

On September 16, USSR Foreign Ministry spokesman Vitalii Churkin provided details of the ministry's newly created bodies. The Collegium's members included Foreign Minister Boris Pankin; First Deputy Foreign Ministers Anatolii Belonogov and Vladimir Petrovsky; and Deputy Foreign Ministers Aleksandr Belonogov, Yurii Deryabin, Viktor Karpov, Valerii Nikolaenko, Ernest Obminsky, Aleksei Obukhov, Igor' Rogachev, and Boris Chaplin.

One of the first actions taken by the Collegium was to restrict the duration of an ambassadorial assignment to five years. In addition, ambassadorial appointments were made subject to the endorsement of the CMFA, TASS reported on September 16.

THE USSR IN SEPTEMBER, 1991

The same day, Ruslan Khasbulatov, acting chairman of the RSFSR Supreme Soviet, called for a reduction in Soviet embassy personnel around the world, AFP reported on September 17. Khasbulatov said: "It is known that up to two-thirds of the employees in Soviet embassies are not at all involved in diplomatic work," suggesting that there was a large proportion of spies in Soviet missions.

On September 17, Churkin said that "a serious reorganization" would be carried out shortly in the missions of the USSR Foreign Ministry abroad. It would focus particularly on higher diplomatic appointments made for political reasons, "especially those made in 1991."

On September 18, Pankin said the USSR would reduce its KGB staff in embassies "to the lowest minimum required by our security interests." He added: "No KGB officers are now left in the sensitive Personnel Department of the Foreign Ministry."

Azerbaijani CP Disbands Itself; Uzbek CP Changes Name

The Azerbaijani Communist Party voted at an extraordinary congress to disband itself as thousands of people continued to demonstrate in Baku to demand the annulment of the results of the September 8 presidential election, TASS and Interfax reported.

The same day, the Communist Party of Uzbekistan voted at an emergency congress to change the party's name to the People's Democratic Party, TASS reported. The republican Communist Party had already broken with the CPSU. Congress delegates quoted by TASS said that a new party program, to be adopted at a founding congress, should offer a new ideology, but the Communist Party apparatus and membership remained intact.

Moldavian Leaders in Washington

Moldavian parliamentary Chairman Alexandru Mosanu and Popular Front Executive Committee Chairman Iurie Rosca completed a three-day visit to Washington. They discussed international recognition of Moldavia's independence with US Congressional leaders. The Lithuanian Embassy in the United States honored the Moldavian leaders with its first official reception since Lithuania recovered its independence. Moldavia was the first state entity anywhere to recognize Lithuania's independence, and Lithuania was in turn the first (apart from Romania) to recognize Moldavia.

Baker Tours Baltic States and Kazakhstan

US Secretary of State James Baker made stops in Tallinn, Riga, and Vilnius, where he talked with the Supreme Council presidents and prime ministers, *The New York*

Times reported. Baker promised the Baltic States 14 million dollars in financial aid for the fiscal year 1991-92, including 2 million dollars in medical supplies, animal feed, scholarships, a management training institute, a bank training center, programs for public administration, and advice on developing small businesses and efficient use of energy.

At a press conference broadcast by Radio Lithuania, Supreme Council President Vytautas Landsbergis noted that Baker had relayed a message from USSR Defense Minister Evgenii Shaposhnikov saying that the withdrawal of Soviet army troops would begin on January 1, 1994. He said the date could be moved forward if Lithuania helped build housing for the troops. Landsbergis noted that the Soviet army had taken Lithuania in two days and that he saw no reason why it could not withdraw in the same amount of time.

Following his trip to the Baltic States, Baker flew to Kazakhstan. During talks on September 16, Kazakh President Nursultan Nazarbaev presented Baker with specific proposals for trade relations between the two countries, including the creation of a US-Kazakh investment fund, TASS reported. Baker was quoted as saying that the United States was interested in developing cooperation with all republics and that the leadership of Kazakhstan inspired trust in him. Western agencies quoted Nazarbaev as saying he had reassured Baker about nuclear weapons in the republic, but a USSR Foreign Ministry spokesman said that Kazakhstan would not be allowed to control the nuclear weapons on its territory.

Sunday, September 15

Georgian Supreme Soviet Expels Communist Deputies

Most of the sixty-four Communist Party deputies to the Georgian parliament were expelled before it began its session on September 15. Some forty deputies from other parties walked out to protest against a decision not to televise the proceedings. The parliament declared the Soviet troops stationed in Georgia "an occupying force" and called for their immediate withdrawal. It further voted to nationalize all Soviet property and enterprises in Georgia, to call for UN recognition of Georgian independence, and to set up a Georgian customs service, according to Western news agencies.

Crisis in Checheno–Ingushetia

After three days of talks with an RSFSR delegation and the arrival in Groznyi of the acting chairman of the RSFSR

Supreme Soviet, Ruslan Khasbulatov, the Chechen-Ingush Supreme Soviet met in an extraordinary session and dissolved itself, TASS reported. All legislative power was passed to an interim council headed by USSR people's deputy Lechi Magomadov. The council was to organize and hold elections within two months. Khasbulatov congratulated the inhabitants of Checheno-Ingushetia on the victory of democratic forces and called for an end to meetings and demonstrations and the disbandment of armed formations.

Ukrainians Demonstrate for Independence

Thousands of people demonstrated in Kiev on September 14 for Ukrainian independence, Ukrinform-TASS and Western agencies reported. The demonstrators supported the Ukrainian declaration of independence, the immediate adoption of a new constitution, and the creation of a Ukrainian arm; they opposed the transfer of nuclear weapons to Russia. Speakers argued that nuclear weapons in Ukraine should be destroyed under the supervision of the appropriate international bodies.

RSFSR Delegation in Moldavia

A delegation of RSFSR Supreme Soviet deputies, headed by a Presidium member, Sergei Krasavchenko, visited Moldavia to meet with representatives of the Russian population and study its problems. In connection with the visit, Moldavian leader Mircea Snegur challenged the leaders of the self-proclaimed "Dniester SSR" to "show concrete evidence to support their allegations that ethnic rights are being impaired," Moldovapres reported. Snegur also urged the visiting RSFSR deputies to meet with Moldavians living on the left bank of the Dniester who had suffered discrimination.

On September 16, Moldovapres reported that, at a meeting with Russians in Tiraspol', the RSFSR deputies had met with disapproval because they judged the "Dniester SSR" to be illegal. On September 18, Krasavchenko asserted that his delegation "did not ascertain one single instance of violations of human rights by the Moldavian authorities," according to Central Television. The delegation found that it was local Russian leaders on the left bank of the Dniester who were violating the rights of Moldavians, including restricting native-language education, and chastised them for "a host of illegal actions, beginning with the proclamation of a 'Dniester SSR'."

At a news conference on September 19, the RSFSR delegation accused the "Dniester SSR" leaders of various violations of the law and of human rights and urged local Russians to repudiate these leaders. Concerning any possible autonomy of the area within Moldavia, the RSFSR deputies said that "any decision is for the entire people of Moldavia to make." Krasavchenko told a news conference that he had seen evidence that most "Dniester SSR" leaders had supported the coup and that "their political views and slogans in general ... are more right-wing than those of the Committee for a State of Emergency."

Nazarbaev on Control of Nuclear Weapons

Kazakh President Nursultan Nazarbaev told the Japanese newspaper *Tokyo Shimbun* that the RSFSR should not have sole control over nuclear weapons. He said that the plan to move all Soviet nuclear weapons to the RSFSR would involve great expense. Nazarbaev proposed that the arsenal be reduced to reasonable levels and placed under the control of the USSR State Council.

On September 20, USSR Defense Minister Evgenii Shaposhnikov suggested creating a Defense Council that would include the presidents of the republics where nuclear weapons were deployed. But he added that ultimate control over the weapons must remain with the center (*TASS*, September 20).

Monday, September 16

USSR State Council Reaches Tentative Agreement

The members of the USSR State Council agreed on the need to pursue a common food distribution plan for the coming winter and began considering the creation of a voluntary economic union, according to TASS.

Ukraine Calls for Own Army

The Times quoted Ukraine's new defense minister, Konstantin Morozov, as calling for the establishment of an independent Ukrainian army. Yurii Ryzhov, a leading democrat and new security adviser to Soviet President Gorbachev and RSFSR President El'tsin, told *The Washington Post* (September 17) that if the republics created their own armed forces, he foresaw an "Eastern NATO" with independent republican armies loosely controlled by an alliance headquarters in Moscow—comparable to NATO headquarters in Brussels. Ryzhov, who urged unified control over nuclear weapons, said he favored the creation of weak national guards and a strong, unified military. He pointed out that if Ukraine were to set up its own army, it would become a new European superpower with an army "bigger than that of Germany or France."

The USSR in September, 1991

The new commander in chief of Soviet Air Defense Forces, Viktor Prudnikov, said in *Krasnaya zvezda* on September 17 that the USSR's air defense system ought to remain unified. He warned against the Soviet republics' trying to take control of their own air space and said that a fracturing of the current air defense system would have negative effects both economically and in terms of defense capability.

Colonel General Pavel Grachev, recently appointed USSR first deputy defense minister and chairman of the RSFSR State Committee for Defense, told TASS on September 18 that Russia would only establish its own defense ministry in response to other republics' doing the same.

Revelations about Coup

In an interview with *Moscow News* (No. 36), KGB Chairman Vadim Bakatin recalled his encounter with the self-appointed "Acting USSR President" Gennadii Yanaev on the first day of the coup. According to Bakatin, Yanaev was frightened and made mysterious remarks about "a court-martial." Yanaev also told Bakatin that he had initially refused to join the Emergency Committee but that "they" had spent two hours convincing him and finally succeeded. When Bakatin asked him what was going on, Yanaev confessed that he did not know himself. In the same interview, Bakatin revealed some details of a statement condemning the Emergency Committee that had been issued by him and fellow USSR Security Council member Evgenii Primakov on August 20. According to Bakatin, Primakov asked then Foreign Minister Aleksandr Bessmertnykh to sign the letter as well, but Bessmertnykh refused. In turn, TASS refused to distribute Primakov and Bakatin's statement, but it was distributed by the independent news service Interfax.

Uzbekistan to Allow Only Limited Democracy

Uzbek President Islam Karimov told Western journalists that Uzbekistan would follow the Chinese model of economic reform because in his view the republic was not ready for full democracy or a market economy. He said privatization would take place primarily in the service sector. Karimov said his ban on political rallies in Uzbekistan was justified because they easily turned violent. Karimov expected elections early in 1992, but he said candidates could run only if they were nominated by a registered political party. The only registered parties were Karimov's People's Democratic Party (the Communist Party under a new name) and the small "Erk" Democratic Party. Karimov said that he doubted that the large popular front, "Birlik," would ever qualify for registration. The Islamic Renaissance Party, the other credible challenger to the Communists, remained prohibited by law.

On September 18, Karimov told a press conference that he had been misunderstood and that he did not favor the Chinese model of economic reform, because he knew nothing about it.

On September 30, the Central Television news program "TSN" reported that a group of deputies of the Supreme Soviet of Uzbekistan, which had just started a special session, planned to demand that Karimov resign.

Democratic Leader Critical of El'tsin

Vladimir Bokser, a leading member of the Democratic Russia movement, criticized Russian Television for allowing only views favorable to RSFSR President Boris El'tsin. Bokser accused El'tsin of monopolizing the media, Western news agencies reported. Bokser said Democratic Russia had adopted a resolution urging new city soviet elections throughout Russia because the former soviets had allegedly been elected in an undemocratic way. He did not specify whether he thought Gavriil Popov should be asked to stand for reelection as Moscow's mayor.

Proposal to Pay Non-Latvians Leaving Latvia; Controversy over Latvian Citizenship

Western agencies reported that Latvia's Immigration Department had proposed making financial payments to non-Latvians volunteering to resettle in the USSR. Its deputy director, Ugis Sulcs, said that the plan would be financed by selling the apartments of those who left.

On September 17, about 3,000 Latvian nationalists protested in Riga against proposals to allow Soviet immigrants the right to vote in Latvia, Western agencies reported that day. Speakers declared that only persons who had been citizens of Latvia in 1940 and their descendants should have that right. The former Communists were campaigning for everyone currently residing in Latvia to be given the right. Supreme Council President Anatolijs Gorbunovs wanted citizenship restricted to those who were residents when Latvia declared its independence in April, 1990, while some nationalist leaders of the Latvian Popular Front wanted it to apply only to ethnic Latvians and people who had been residents for more than ten years.

Baltic States Face Financial Problems

The deputy director of the Bank of Latvia, Alfreds Bergs-Bergsmanis, announced that his bank would no longer be able to complete cash transactions with banks in Estonia,

The USSR in September, 1991

Latvia, and the USSR, owing to a shortage of rubles, according to Radio Independent Lithuania. The problem was created by the refusal of the Soviet central authorities to ship rubles to Latvia after its independence was recognized.

According to a statement published in *Paevaleht* on September 13, the head of the Bank of Estonia, Rein Otsason, asked to resign following the passing of a foreign investment bill by the Supreme Council. Otsason objected to the September 11 bill on the grounds that Estonia's banking system was too weak to resist competition from foreign banks. By allowing foreign (mostly Soviet) banks to dominate, Otsason said, Estonia's young banking system would, in effect, be destroyed. Otsason said his major concern was not Western but Soviet banks, because Estonia still used the Soviet ruble.

Cossacks Raise Voices

The Urals Cossacks went ahead with the celebration of the 400th anniversary of their allegiance to Russia on September 14 and 15 in Ural'sk in Kazakhstan, despite strong objections by the local authorities, TASS and "Vesti" reported on September 16. Cossacks from the Don, the Kuban', the Northern Caucasus, the southern Urals, and Siberia came brandishing the Russian flag. Local students and representatives of the "Azat," "Zheltoksan," and Nevada-Semipalatinsk movements from Alma-Ata, Chimkent, Dzhambul, Aktyubinsk, and a number of other cities in Kazakhstan staged a protest that ended in minor clashes between the two groups.

On September 17, Kazakh President Nursultan Nazarbaev sent a personal message to RSFSR President Boris El'tsin complaining that the holding of the Urals Cossacks' celebration under the Russian flag had been interpreted by the population and public movements of Kazakhstan as a political action showing open disrespect for the republic's state sovereignty, Kaztag-TASS reported the same day. Nazarbaev said that it was only thanks to the efforts of the local authorities that events had not taken a more dramatic turn. Nazarbaev told El'tsin that a timely evaluation by the Russian leadership of the territorial claims being made by the Cossacks would have deterred the Cossack leaders from such actions.

On September 16, representatives of the Don, Kuban', Urals, and Terek Cossacks picketed the Russian parliament building demanding the creation of a national state in the RSFSR, TASS reported. Their demonstration was in anticipation of the session of the RSFSR Supreme Soviet starting on September 19, which was scheduled to discuss the rehabilitation of the Cossacks.

THE USSR IN SEPTEMBER, 1991

Lithuania Requests Membership of EBRD

Lithuania followed the example of Estonia and Latvia and made a request to become a member of the European Bank for Reconstruction and Development (EBRD), Western agencies reported. The bank said that it welcomed the application and would send a study mission to Vilnius. The same day the General Conference of the International Atomic Energy Agency in Vienna voted to admit Estonia, Latvia, and Lithuania as members.

Tuesday, September 17

Solzhenitsyn to Return to USSR

Russian writer Aleksandr Solzhenitsyn officially announced that he intended to return to the USSR, according to TASS. Solzhenitsyn made the announcement after he had been informed personally by USSR Prosecutor-General Nikolai Trubin of a ruling dropping the charge of state treason brought against Solzhenitsyn prior to his expulsion from the Soviet Union in 1974. Solzhenitsyn told NBC TV on September 14 that the fall from power of the CPSU and the KGB had prompted his decision to return. He said he had predicted the fall of communism a quarter of a century ago but that this prediction had met with disbelief in the West. He added that he would return following completion of a history of the October Revolution, adding that in Russia he would not have time to devote himself fully to writing.

International Recognition for Baltic States

The presidents of the three Baltic Supreme Councils made their maiden speeches to the UN General Assembly after taking their seats. Estonia's Arnold Ruutel said his country planned to maintain "absolutely friendly relations with the USSR"; Latvia's Anatolijs Gorbunovs said "we have returned from World War II at last"; and Lithuania's Vytautas Landsbergis said his country's "renunciation of fear" had proved stronger than tanks. Estonia and Lithuania named their ambassadors to the United Nations. Estonia appointed Ernst Jaakson, former consul general of Estonia in the United States with ambassadorial responsibilities. Lithuania named Anicetas Simutis, the long-time chief of the independent Lithuanian Consulate in New York.

On September 17, the Paris Court of Appeals held a closed session on appeals by Lithuania, Latvia, and Estonia for the return of prewar embassies that were taken over by the USSR, Western agencies reported that day.

On September 18, the bureau of the twenty-five-nation Council of Europe voted unanimously to grant the Supreme Councils of Estonia, Latvia, and Lithuania special guest status, Western agencies reported. Also on September 18, the International Olympic Committee Executive Board in Berlin decided that the Baltic States "are reintegrated into the Olympic movement with immediate effect," Western agencies reported that day.

Ukrainian Nationalists Protest against Economic Union

The draft economic union endorsed in principle by the leaders of ten republics was angrily rejected by Ukrainian parliamentarians, *The New York Times* reported on September 18. Upon his arrival in Kiev from Moscow, Supreme Soviet Chairman Leonid Kravchuk immediately had to face protests from radical deputies, who said Ukrainian independence had to be given "top priority over all other issues." Dmytro Pavlychko, chairman of the Supreme Soviet Committee on Foreign Relations, was quoted as saying that the Ukrainian parliament would never accept the economic union.

In an interview with Radio Liberty's Ukrainian service, Ukraine's plenipotentiary representative in the RSFSR, Volodymyr Kryzhanivs'kyi, expressed reservations about the proposed economic union. He said that Ukraine was willing to enter into arrangements of a purely economic nature but that the draft devised by economist Grigorii Yavlinsky was still too "centrist" and "political."

Lawyers of Putschists Go Public

The lawyers of the fourteen men arrested for having organized the August coup said they would base their defense on ambiguities in the law on high treason. In numerous media interviews and at a news conference, the lawyers argued that their clients' intentions did not correspond exactly with Article 64 of the RSFSR Criminal Code—"Betrayal of the Motherland." A remnant of the Stalinist era, Article 64 covers a wide range of offenses, from fleeing the country to conspiracy aimed at seizing power, and provides for penalties ranging from ten years of imprisonment to death. The lawyers argued that the accused had betrayed not the motherland but the USSR president, and they cited an official commentary on the law that defined treason almost solely as a crime against the Communist system.

Controversy over KGB Archives

TASS said half the archives of the Leningrad Administration of the KGB would be transferred to the RSFSR state archives. The agency quoted the head of the Leningrad Archival Administration, Nikolai Ponomarev, as saying that archival material of historical importance for the period before 1961 would be accessible to the public. The same day, Radio Rossii interviewed a member of the committee studying Moscow's Party and KGB archives, Boris Elisarov, who said that all the KGB archives should be taken out of that body's jurisdiction. He said card indexes on informers and KGB agents should be closely guarded to preclude the leaking of such information and its use in current political struggles.

Role of Military in Leningrad during Coup

The commander of the Leningrad Military District played an ambiguous role during the August 19 coup, while the military-political organs were its most solid supporters. These were the conclusions of a preliminary investigation by the Leningrad City Soviet broadcast by Radio Mayak. It also said that Leningrad's Air Defense Forces had "indirectly" supported the coup plotters, while naval and air forces had remained neutral. The leadership of the Northwest Border District and of local MVD forces resisted orders from the center.

Ukraine Abandons Socialism

The Ukrainian Supreme Soviet decided to eliminate the words "Soviet Socialist Republic" from the country's name and call the country simply "Ukraine" (*Radio Kiev*, September 17). The same day, all ideological determinants, such as the word "Socialist," were struck from the existing constitution of Ukraine.

Kazakhstan Starts Privatization

The privatization program approved by Kazakhstan's Supreme Soviet in June was finally published in the republican press (see *Kazakhstanskaya pravda*, September 17). A special commission was to be created by October 1 to determine how vouchers would be distributed to republican citizens to enable them to purchase state property, including housing. Under the plan, an individual who had worked for twenty-one years should receive enough vouchers to enable him to buy an apartment or house "of average cost."

Travkin Seeks to Strengthen His Party

Nezavisimaya gazeta reported that the Democratic Party of Russia (DPR) had set up a Political Council. Made up of seventeen people, the council included such liberals as Academician Evgenii Ambartsumov, philosopher Aleksandr Tsipko, and surgeon Svyatoslav Fedorov. Two-thirds of the council's members did not belong to the DPR, however. The Moscow branch of the DPR had declared its opposition to Moscow Mayor Gavriil Popov, accusing him of retreating from democratization and reestablishing an administrative-command system in the capital.

The leaders of the Democratic Party of Russia, the Christian Democratic Party, and the Constitutional Democratic Party of Russia—Nikolai Travkin, Viktor Aksyuchits, and Mikhail Astaf'ev, respectively—were visiting Bonn at the invitation of the Christian Democratic Union.

Vagnorius in Bonn

Lithuanian Prime Minister Gediminas Vagnorius flew to Bonn where he held talks with German Chancellor Helmut Kohl and Foreign Minister Hans-Dietrich Genscher. They agreed to expand cooperation in political, economic, and cultural areas. Vagnorius asked Germany for credits to purchase the production facilities and equipment of factories in former East Germany. A bilateral commercial treaty was scheduled to be signed that would promote free trade, including guarantees on investments.

Wednesday, September 18

Silaev Quits RSFSR Government

Ivan Silaev resigned from his post as RSFSR prime minister in order to concentrate fully on his tasks as head of the future Interrepublican Economic Committee, TASS reported. Silaev said that his appointment had been unanimously endorsed at the recent meeting of the USSR State Council.

Money Supply Increases

The managing director of the USSR State Bank's money supply department, Yurii Balagurov, told the *Financial Times* that the two state mints and two money printing centers were working round the clock. "The only limit to the money supply in the Soviet Union today is the capacity of the money presses," he said. The USSR State Bank had called five times for a wage and price freeze, but Balagurov doubted whether the authorities could enforce either. He called hyperinflation the greatest danger but declined to put a figure on the current rate. (Grigorii Yavlinsky had told Interfax the previous week that inflation was running at 2–3 percent a week).

Popov Pledges Reforms

Addressing several thousand members of the Democratic Russia movement in the former Comecon headquarters, Moscow Mayor Gavriil Popov called for the immediate introduction of sweeping reforms, Western agencies reported that day. Otherwise, he warned, the victory of reformers against the attempted coup could "turn into nothing." Popov called for a reorganization of the army and internal security apparatus and for the full legalization of a multiparty system. Most important, according to Popov, was the introduction of a competitive market economy and the privatization of land and the means of production. He also outlined his plans for the privatization of real estate in Moscow. Each family would be entitled to 12 square meters of housing space plus 18 square meters for each family member. Each resident would receive coupons to pay for his apartment after the housing stock had been valued. Those who wanted more space would be able to purchase it at market prices, while the few who had too much space could sell it at market prices. A similar arrangement was proposed for dachas, private plots, and stores. Popov also outlined a plan to sell at experimental prices surplus stocks of rationed goods such as sugar, tobacco, and vodka.

Shushkevich Elected Head of Belorussian Parliament

Stanislau Shushkevich won election as the new chairman of the Belorussian parliament, Central Television announced. He replaced Nikolai Dementei, a colorless figure who was discredited during the coup attempt. Shushkevich, a physicist by training and until the coup a Communist Party member, was regarded as a good centrist politician. His popularity plummeted during the workers' strikes in April, when, as first deputy chairman of the Supreme Soviet, he stated in public that the strikers' demands were unreasonable.

Reform Demands in Ukraine

Representatives of "Narodna Rada," the former opposition in the Ukrainian parliament, demanded the dismissal of members of the Presidium of the Ukrainian Supreme Soviet who supported the failed coup, Radio Kiev reported on September 19. They also called for the dismissal of individual ministers, chairmen of state committees, and the collegiums of the KGB and MVD and for structural reforms in the latter two institutions. It was also proposed that the December 1 presidential elections be postponed.

Aid to the USSR

US officials stated that aid to the USSR would be expedited to avoid winter food shortages. Head of the Interrepublican Economic Committee Ivan Silaev said meetings with US Treasury Secretary Nicholas Brady and Federal Reserve Chairman Alan Greenspan had yielded assurances that Washington would advance 375 million dollars in grain credits one month early. Brady said that the figure had not

The USSR in September, 1991

been fixed but that Washington's intention to give aid high priority was definite, Western agencies reported.

On September 19, USSR Deputy Prime Minister Yurii Luzhkov requested a total of 14.7 billion dollars in food and credits from the West, Western agencies reported that day. Luzhkov told members of the European Commission in Brussels that the USSR would like food gifts to the value of 2.2 billion dollars and credits amounting to about 5.2 billion dollars from the EC, with the balance coming from the rest of the international community. The new figure was nearly twice as high as the amount requested the previous week.

During a press conference at the European Bank for Reconstruction and Development on September 20, Leningrad Mayor Anatolii Sobchak appealed for the sale of surplus EC food to the USSR at cut-rate prices, Western agencies reported. He suggested that the surplus foodstuffs could then be sold within the Soviet Union "at a profit" (which assumed an unrealistic exchange rate) and the proceeds, together with income from privatizing housing and land, would reduce the ruble overhang. Sobchak warned that hyperinflation and declining living standards in the USSR could breed "National-Socialist feeling."

Thursday, September 19

Pankin in New York

USSR Foreign Minister Boris Pankin arrived in New York, where he was to address the UN General Assembly, participate in a conference on the Chernobyl' disaster, and meet with US officials. Pankin said his address to the United Nations would explain "what today's Soviet Union is, what its message to the world is, and what it expects from the international community." In a separate interview with a Western agency, Pankin said, "The message will be that we are a powerful nation that is in the critical stages of development."

Monitoring of AIDS Halted

Vadim Pokrovsky, the chairman of the USSR Anti-AIDS Association, told TASS that the Soviet health authorities were no longer able to monitor the spread of AIDS in the Soviet Union, because republican and regional authorities had stopped sending data on the virus to Moscow in the wake of recent ethnic tensions. Pokrovsky said that bank accounts used for purchasing medication from abroad had been frozen, and he warned that these factors could result in the "uncontrolled" spread of the AIDS virus in the USSR.

THE USSR IN SEPTEMBER, 1991

RSFSR Parliament Rejects Popov's Candidate for Moscow Police Chief

The RSFSR Supreme Soviet rejected Moscow Mayor Gavriil Popov's decision to appoint the former secretary of the Interregional Group of Deputies, Arkadii Murashov, as chief of the city's police force. "Vesti" reported that the RSFSR deputies supported the candidacy of General Vyacheslav Komissarov. The latter was appointed Moscow police chief in January but was later dismissed by former USSR Minister of Internal Affairs Boriss Pugo. Since then, the RSFSR parliament had fought for the reinstatement of Komissarov. Komissarov also received the support of the Moscow City Soviet, which objected to Popov's attempt to appoint an outsider to that post. On September 20, Popov backed down and replaced Murashov with Komissarov, "Vesti" reported.

USSR Joins Pacific Economic Group

Western agencies reported that the Pacific Economic Cooperation Conference (PECC) had admitted the Soviet Union into its ranks, Western agencies reported. The USSR applied to join the group in 1990 but was rejected. Although the effects of membership on the Soviet economy were unlikely to be noticeable for some time, participation in PECC was expected to provide the eastern region of the country in particular with contacts, potential business partners, and investors in the Pacific rim region.

USSR Starts Paying Latvia in Dollars for Oil Transportation

Latvian Deputy Energy Minister Ziedonis Blumbergs said the USSR had started to pay Latvia in dollars for use of its oil export terminal in Ventspils, Western agencies reported. He noted that about 19 million tons of oil would pass through the terminal in 1991; Latvia would receive 4–5 US dollars a ton for about half that amount and 4 rubles a ton for the other half.

Breakup of Party Rule in Tajikistan

Tajik Supreme Soviet Chairman Kadriddin Aslonov, who had been acting president of the republic since the resignation of Kakhar Makhkamov, announced his own resignation from the republican CP Buro and Secretariat, Radio Moscow reported. Aslonov explained that it would be improper for him to belong to any political organization. Demonstrators from opposition groups had been calling for his dismissal.

Soviet Arms Trade Continues

E. N. Vitkovsky, deputy minister of the defense industry, told the United Arab Emirates newspaper *Al-Ittihad* that "the Soviet Union will not withdraw from the international arms market." Vitkovsky said: "We will continue exporting arms, especially to the Middle East, unless there is an agreement with the United States to curb such exports to that region." Meanwhile, RSFSR Foreign Minister Andrei Kozyrev said in an interview with TASS that, while "the arms trade cannot be stopped either technically or economically," it should acquire a more "civilized character" so that it is not carried out for "ideological reasons."

Belorussia Becomes Belarus

News agencies reported that the Belorussian parliament had voted to change the official name of the republic to Belarus, dropping the adjectives "Soviet Socialist" and formalizing the Belorussian-language version of the country's name. The Supreme Soviet also voted to restore the traditional red-on-white flag. The national emblem known as Pahonia, depicting a white horseman with an upraised sword, would be the official symbol of Belarus.

Friday, September 20

Eye Surgeon Is El'tsin's Choice for RSFSR Premiership

The famous Soviet eye surgeon Svyatoslav Fedorov was asked by RSFSR President Boris El'tsin to become Russia's new prime minister after Ivan Silaev's resignation from the post (*Financial Times*, September 20). Fedorov was a USSR people's deputy and was one of the founders of the democratic movement in Moscow in 1989.

Gorbachev Accuses Luk'yanov of Coup Complicity

Soviet President Mikhail Gorbachev said that former KGB Chairman Vladimir Kryuchkov had played the key coordinating role in the putsch, but he also accused the former leader of the Soviet parliament, Anatolii Luk'yanov, of having plotted against him. TASS published excerpts from a private conversation Gorbachev had with journalists during which he said that Oleg Baklanov, another leader of the failed coup, had named Luk'yanov as a member of the Emergency Committee on August 18. Gorbachev asserted that Luk'yanov had remained in the shadows and had been planning to turn the Supreme Soviet against him. The USSR president stated his belief that the conservative USSR Congress of People's Deputies could have turned against him and elected a new leader.

Stankevich on Multiparty System in Russia

RSFSR State Councillor Sergei Stankevich foresaw a multiparty system developing in Russia. Western news agencies quoted him as saying that four categories of party would emerge: Communists, Social Democrats,

Liberal Democrats, and national fundamentalists. Stankevich said the CPSU would reconsolidate itself in the near future. He stressed that new parliamentary elections were needed because "the public no longer has faith in legislators elected only one or two years ago."

Saturday, September 21

Political Prisoners Released

In accordance with a request by the RSFSR Supreme Soviet Human-Rights Committee, RSFSR President Boris El'tsin and Kirgiz President Askar Akaev pardoned six political prisoners convicted either for attempted flight abroad or for attempted espionage. *Komsomol'skaya pravda* identified the prisoners as Aleksandr Goldovich, Valerii Smirnov, Anatolii Khobt, Aleksei Shcherbakov, Viktor Olisesnevich, and Valerii Yanin. In a related event, "Vesti" on September 20 interviewed an official from the office of the RSFSR prosecutor-general, who said that the office intended to exonerate all former prisoners of conscience.

El'tsin Brokers Nagorno-Karabakh Settlement

RSFSR President Boris El'tsin and Kazakh President Nursultan Nazarbaev were in Baku and Gyandzha on September 21 and in Stepanakert, Shusha, and Erevan on September 22 to discuss with local leaders various draft plans for a settlement of the three-and-a-half-year conflict over Nagorno-Karabakh. Negotiations began on September 23 in Zheleznovodsk in the RSFSR. *The New York Times* reported on September 23 that Armenia had agreed to renounce any territorial claim on Nagorno-Karabakh. Genrikh Pogosyan, former first secretary of the oblast Party committee of the Nagorno-Karabakh Autonomous Oblast, was quoted as stating that the main issue was cultural autonomy for the Armenian population. The El'tsin peace plan provided for free elections and full self-rule.

After twelve hours of talks in Zheleznovodsk, the leaders of Armenia, Azerbaijan, the RSFSR, and Kazakhstan signed an agreement to begin peace negotiations over Nagorno-Karabakh. The agreement called for an immediate cease-fire, the disarming of illegal ethnic militias, free local elections, the return to their homes of thousands of Armenian and Azerbaijani refugees, and the annulment of all executive and military decrees on Nagorno-Karabakh passed by the central government since early 1988, according to Interfax of September 23 and *The New York Times* of September 24.

The USSR in September, 1991

On September 27, thousands of people demonstrated in Baku to protest against the agreement, a Baku journalist told RFE/RL's Azerbaijani service on September 28. The Azerbaijani Popular Front considered the agreement to contravene Azerbaijan's interests and wanted to convoke a Supreme Soviet session to discuss the creation of a republican army. Also on September 27, a commission of the Armenian Supreme Soviet claimed Azerbaijan had already violated the cease-fire agreement by carrying out armed attacks and killing six people in Stepanakert and villages in Nagorno-Karabakh, TASS reported.

Armenia Votes for Secession

As anticipated, some 95 percent of the Armenian electorate participated in the referendum on secession; 99 percent of these voted in favor of Armenian independence (Western news agencies, September 22). A bipartisan US Congressional delegation monitoring the voting said that the referendum was conducted fairly and that it would urge US President Bush to recognize Armenian independence. On September 23, the Armenian parliament unanimously passed a declaration of independence that took effect immediately, TASS reported on September 23.

Talks with Cuba on Troop Withdrawal

Soviet Deputy Foreign Minister Valerii Nikolaenko met with Cuban First Deputy Foreign Minister Alcibiades Hidalgo in Havana on September 21 and 22 to discuss the withdrawal of Soviet troops from Cuba. (Gorbachev had announced on September 11 that Moscow intended to withdraw 11,000 Soviet troops from Cuba in the coming months.) An unidentified Soviet diplomat quoted by the Notimex news agency on September 22 characterized the talks as "slow and cold." Nikolaenko traveled to New York on September 23 to hold consultations with US officials on "the situation regarding Cuba" and ways to reduce tensions in Cuban-US relations, TASS reported that day. After his talks with Cuban officials, Nikolaenko said that, while Cuba would be justified in expecting the withdrawal of US troops from Guantanamo, the USSR would not link this issue to the withdrawal of its own troops, Radio Moscow, World Service, reported on September 23.

Cuban President Fidel Castro declared at a press conference in Havana on September 24 that he opposed the pullout of Soviet troops from Cuba. "We don't agree with the withdrawal of the [Soviet military training] brigade, just as we can't agree that Yankee troops should remain at Guantanamo" (Western agencies, September

25). Castro maintained that Cuba was not seeking to change its "links of friendship, tradition, and history" with the USSR, but his remarks—a day after the departure of Nikolaenko—underlined his clear displeasure with Cuba's erstwhile patron. At one point he asked, "Are you talking about the Soviet Union or what's left of the Soviet Union?"

Primakov Warns against Intervention in Iraq

Special presidential envoy Evgenii Primakov said at the end of a two-day trip to Turkey that the USSR opposed any new intervention by Allied forces in Iraq. He said Iraq must comply strictly with UN Security Council resolutions, Radio Moscow reported on September 22.

A Radio Moscow, World Service, commentary by Yurii Solton on September 24 chided Iraq for "deliberately provoking a new armed conflict in the region, evidently hoping at least morally to get revenge for the loss of the war." Solton, however, urged the United States to bide its time, saying "a well-balanced approach is necessary here."

Pankin on Foreign Policy

USSR Foreign Minister Boris Pankin said in an interview with *Izvestia* that the most important new initiative in Soviet foreign policy was the absence of any initiatives. "Almost throughout the history of Soviet diplomacy, we have bombarded the world with initiatives. Often we have done it just to be able to say afterwards: 'Look how full of initiative our foreign policy is.'" Pankin added, "We want to start speaking in the language of a new Union."

Tajik Communist Party Changes Its Name

The Tajik Communist Party changed its name to Socialist Party of Tajikistan at a special congress and declared itself the successor to the Communist Party, according to a TASS report. The former Communist Party Central Committee ideological secretary, Shodi Shabdolov, was named to head an organizing committee of the new party. Shabdolov played a somewhat more positive role in trying to pacify demonstrators during the violence in Dushanbe in February, 1990, than did other Party leaders.

Gorbachev Frees Balts of All Military Obligations

Soviet President Gorbachev issued a decree freeing citizens of the newly independent Baltic States from all military obligations, TASS reported. The decree said that all conscripts from the Baltic States would be released from the ranks of the Soviet Armed Forces in September or October. It also freed Balts from duty in the troops of the USSR Ministry of Internal Affairs, Border Troops, and railways. The decree noted that the Balts would no longer be drafted into the Soviet army. No mention was made of the release of Baltic citizens serving in the Soviet Armed Forces as officers.

Snegur Abjures Moldavian Reunification with Romania

Following a session of Moldavia's Higher Security Council, which discussed the situation on the left bank of the Dniester, Moldavian President Mircea Snegur issued a statement renewing assurances that Moldavia was not seeking reunification with Romania. Calling on left-bank Russian leaders to stop scaring local Russians with "inventions about a merger with Romania," Snegur reiterated that Moldavia's independence was his, and the government's, "unshakable political credo" (*Moldovapres*, September 21).

Sunday, September 22

Confrontation in Tajikistan

TASS reported that Tajik Acting President Kadriddin Aslonov had issued a decree ending the activities of the Communist Party in the republic and nationalizing its property. The decree was a response to demands by demonstrators outside the building of the republican Communist Party Central Committee the previous day (*TASS*, September 21). The demonstrators were protesting against the Communist Party's attempt to reorganize itself—in their opinion, the leaders of the Communist Party hopelessly compromised themselves during the August coup, and no reform could save the party. The reports left unclear whether Aslonov's decree prohibiting the Communist Party applied to the new party formed as its successor.

In response to the decree, the conservative Communist majority in the Tajik Supreme Soviet organized a demonstration against the ban on September 23 and forced the resignation of Aslonov. They also declared a state of emergency in the republic, but "TV Inform" reported that evening that the move would not be supported by the armed forces or by the USSR MVD or KGB, whose personnel would be needed to enforce it. The same day, the Tajik parliament elected a new chairman of the Supreme Soviet, who would also serve as acting president of the republic until the direct presidential election on October 27. The legislators' choice, according to TASS, was Rakhmon Nabiev, a former Communist Party leader who was pushed aside in 1985, apparently because Moscow felt he was not committed strongly enough to reform. Nabiev ran against his successor, Kakhar Makhkamov, for the newly created post of republican president in the fall of 1990 but received few votes.

Also that day, according to TASS reports, anti-Communist demonstrators in several cities pulled down Lenin monuments. The monument in Dushanbe was removed on the orders of Mayor Maksud Ikramov.

On September 24, the Union of Democratic Forces, composed of the three main opposition forces in Tajikistan, appealed to the republic's population to engage in civil disobedience in order to force the Tajik Supreme Soviet to dismiss Nabiev. TASS quoted Democratic Party Chairman Shomon Yusupov as saying that an estimated 10,000 people had joined demonstrations in Dushanbe. The democrats appealed to Gorbachev and Russian democrats for support in reversing the Supreme Soviet's "coup."

Western and Soviet news agencies reported on September 25 and 26 that demonstrators trying to force the resignation of the Supreme Soviet and the removal of Nabiev had settled in for a long stay on the square in front of the parliament building in Dushanbe. Minister of Internal Affairs Mamdaez Navdzhuvanov said that, as long as the demonstrators did not break the law, his forces would not intervene. Demonstrators reportedly greeted the appearance of Tajikistan's highest-ranking clergyman, Kazi Akbar Turadzhonzoda, with great enthusiasm, but both they and the kazi rejected hard-liners' charges that the opposition wanted to establish an Islamic state.

Western and Soviet news agencies reported on September 26 that 239 demonstrators had begun a hunger strike. A Tajik journalist said on "Vesti" that Nabiev had confirmed the ban on the Communist Party. Other sources reported that Nabiev had refused to resign, arguing that if he were to resign under pressure from demonstrators "the process would be endless."

TASS reported on September 26 that demonstrators and supporters of the republic's democratic parties were taking great pains to assure the Russian-speaking population of the republic that the anti-Communist demonstrations in Dushanbe were not directed against Russians. A delegation from the Democratic "Kyrgyzstan" movement arrived in Dushanbe on September 26 to support the Tajik demonstrators, as did representatives of the Uzbek Popular Front "Birlik."

Peaceful demonstrations continued in front of the Tajik Supreme Soviet building in Dushanbe over the weekend, according to Soviet news agency reports. Talks between officials and representatives of the opposition began on September 28. The opposition was demanding the holding of a special session of the republican Supreme Soviet to rescind the state of emergency declared on September 23. Radio Moscow reported on September 28 that hunger strikers on the square had been joined by six well-known Sufi leaders. A group of Russian and USSR Supreme Soviet deputies arrived in Dushanbe to assess the situation and told the demonstrators on September 29 that Russia and the center supported their demands.

On September 30, the Supreme Soviet of Tajikistan voted to lift the state of emergency, according to Western agencies. TASS reported that the session had begun with serious wrangling over an agenda that included the question of confirming a ban on the republican Communist Party. According to reports of correspondents in Dushanbe, some 10,000 demonstrators were still outside the Supreme Soviet building.

Ukraine and Canada signed a declaration on expanding contacts at all levels and on cooperation in political, economic, scientific, educational, and sporting matters, TASS and Radio Kiev reported on September 23. The declaration was signed on the first day of Chairman of the Ukrainian Supreme Soviet Leonid Kravchuk's three-day official visit to Canada. Kravchuk told a news conference in Ottawa that Ukraine wanted to be a neutral and nuclear-free state.

Ukrainian-Canadian Declaration

Soviet Foreign Minister Boris Pankin and his Finnish counterpart Paavo Vayrynen met in New York and agreed that negotiations should begin in October to scrap the forty-three-year-old Soviet-Finnish treaty and replace it with a new series of treaties, Western agencies reported on September 23. The provisions of the existing treaty of friendship, cooperation, and mutual assistance had obliged Finland to agree to prevent the use of its territory to attack the USSR and had prevented it from joining the European Community. Vayrynen commented, "It's a new age now, a new situation . . . and we need a new agreement."

Soviet-Finnish Treaty to be Replaced

Monday, September 23

The Moscow branch of the Movement for Democratic Reforms held a constituent session in Moscow at which it was scheduled to adopt statutes and elect delegates for a constituent congress of the movement, TASS reported.

Movement for Democratic Reforms Holds Conference, Forms Party

Speaking at the meeting, founding member Eduard Shevardnadze said that the country was in "political chaos." Another leading democrat, Aleksandr Yakovlev, warned that Stalinists still did not want to leave the political stage. Moscow Mayor Gavriil Popov urged the 1,000 participants in the meeting to form "at least two, and probably three parties" as a counterweight to the possible reemergence of the CPSU.

A group of participants in the Moscow session established a Party for Democratic Reforms of Russia (PDR), RFE/RL learned on September 24. The new party held its first congress on September 24. The most important leaders of the Movement for Democratic Reforms, Shevardnadze and Yakovlev, did not become members of the new party, however. The organizers of the new party said they had based their decision to establish a party on the results of an opinion poll that showed that almost 50 percent of the movement's members favored the creation of a party instead of a movement. The newly created Party for Democratic Reforms of Russia announced that it would become part of the Movement for Democratic Reforms, which also included the Republican Party of Russia and Communists for Democracy. The Democratic Russia movement was not a member of the Movement for Democratic Reforms.

On September 28, TASS quoted the members of the Political Council of the Movement for Democratic Reforms as expressing concern over the increasing conflict between executive (mayors' offices) and representative (local soviets) powers in Moscow and other areas of the Russian Federation. The council issued a statement on "the situation in Tajikistan," expressing concern over possible violence in the region. The council also announced that the movement's first congress would be held on November 30 and December 1.

Gorbachev Appoints New Press Secretary

Soviet President Mikhail Gorbachev appointed Andrei Grachev to head the presidential press service, TASS reported. Grachev replaced Vitalii Ignatenko, who became director general of TASS in the aftermath of the coup. Before this appointment, Grachev had been deputy head of the CPSU Central Committee International Department.

Yablokov Appointed RSFSR State Counselor

The ecologist and cofounder of the Interregional Group of USSR deputies, Aleksei Yablokov, was appointed RSFSR state councillor for science, education, and culture, USSR Supreme Soviet deputy Arkadii Murashov told the

The USSR in September, 1991

RFE/RL Research Institute. Yablokov (born in 1933) holds a doctorate in biological sciences and is a corresponding member of the USSR Academy of Sciences. In 1990, he became deputy chairman of the USSR Supreme Soviet's Committee for Ecology and the Rational Use of Natural Resources.

Silaev Supports Center

The chairman of the USSR Interrepublican Economic Committee, Ivan Silaev, raised a stir in the RSFSR government when he asked RSFSR President Boris El'tsin to rescind his decrees on Russian sovereignty, TASS reported. Silaev demanded that the central authorities regain control over Russian enterprises and energy resources that had been put under El'tsin's jurisdiction.

Kravchenko Says He Was A Victim

The former head of the All-Union State Television and Radio Broadcasting Company, Leonid Kravchenko, complained in an interview with *Pravda* that he had been the victim of a plot by the RSFSR leadership. He was dismissed in the aftermath of the coup. Kravchenko's policy of political censorship at Central Television was heavily criticized prior to the coup, and during it he followed the junta's line and dismissed El'tsin sympathizers from the broadcasting company. In the interview, Kravchenko said it had been difficult to assess the situation correctly on August 19 when he received instructions to broadcast the junta's resolutions from Politburo member Oleg Shenin.

Kirgiz President Opposes Economic Union

Kirgiz President Askar Akaev announced his opposition to the latest plan for an economic union (the Yavlinsky plan). TASS reported that Akaev had told the Japanese press that the Yavlinsky plan gave too much power to the center and that he supported "an economic community" of sovereign states of Europe and Asia instead. Akaev said Kirgizia would not sign an economic treaty that did not give its constituent members full authority in their economic affairs.

Uralmash to be Privatized

Postfactum reported that Uralmash in Ekaterinburg was to be privatized. The process was expected to take several years, and the complex, which employed some 40,000 workers, could be broken up during the sell-off. Uralmash was reported to be preparing a contract with a Moscow holding company for the issue of shares, some of which might be sold to foreign concerns.

Andreotti Meets with Gorbachev

Italian Prime Minister Giulio Andreotti met in Moscow with Soviet President Gorbachev, TASS reported. Gorbachev thanked Andreotti for his stance during the attempted coup and talked at length about the changes that had taken place in its wake. The two leaders also discussed international affairs, including arms reductions, the conflict in Yugoslavia, and efforts to convene a Middle East peace conference.

Deputy Alleges Illegal Nuclear Dumping

Andrei Zolotkov, a USSR people's deputy from Murmansk, charged that the USSR had dumped radioactive waste at sea for over twenty years in violation of international law. According to Western agency reports, Zolotkov told a Greenpeace seminar in Moscow that ships from the Murmansk commercial fleet had dumped nuclear waste in shallow waters of the Barents and Kara Seas off the USSR's northern coast from 1963 to 1986. During that time, the USSR claimed that the waste had been stored on land. Zolotkov disclosed that the damaged reactor core from the nuclear-powered icebreaker *Lenin*, which suffered a meltdown in 1966 or 1967, had been dumped at sea off Novaya Zemlya in the early 1970s.

Afghan Resistance Leader Invited to Moscow

The Soviet ambassador to Iran, Vladimir Gudev, was reported to have invited an Iran-based leader of the Afghan resistance to Moscow. According to Radio Teheran, Gudev met with Rahmatollah Mostafavi of the Islamic Unity Party, a Shi'ite group, and invited him to participate in talks on ending the civil war in Afghanistan. The previous week, the Afghan resistance based in Pakistan said it had accepted a Soviet invitation to send a high-level delegation to Moscow at an unspecified date.

Belorussia to Form Own Defense System

The Belorussian Supreme Soviet voted in favor of organizing Belorussia's own defense and national security system, TASS reported. The resolution said that, beginning in the fall, conscripts would serve on the territory of the republic, with service in the USSR Armed Forces to be carried out on a voluntary basis. The republican armed forces would be established for nonoffensive purposes, the resolution stressed, and would be conceived as an integral part of the common European security system.

Colonel General Anatolii Kostenko, commander of the Belorussian Military District, was quoted by TASS as expressing his satisfaction that the Belorussian Supreme Soviet had recognized the principle of keeping defensive nuclear capability under a single command. He said the emergence of two chains of command—a General Staff with headquarters in Moscow and a Belorussian army under republican jurisdiction—could "give rise to conditions for conflict."

Belorussian Border Controls

The Belorussian parliament voted to place border and customs controls under republican government jurisdiction, TASS said. The border with Poland, however, would still be recognized as a USSR state boundary.

New Belorussian Supreme Soviet Faction

The former Belorussian Communists for Democracy faction in the Supreme Soviet in Minsk, a liberal force opposed to the policies of the Central Committee, was reported to have reconstituted itself as the Democratic Reforms faction. TASS said that the faction's ranks had swollen following the abortive August putsch and the suspension of the activities of the Belorussian Communist Party. The Democratic Reforms group hoped to form a new political party and to lay claim to some portion of Belorussian Communist Party property.

Lithuania Commemorates Day of Jewish Genocide

The Lithuanian authorities designated September 23 as a day of annual commemoration of the genocide of the Jews in Lithuania. September 23 marked the end of the Nazis' liquidation of the Vilnius ghetto in 1943. On September 22, a commemorative meeting was held at a monument in Paneriai in Vilnius, at which members of the Lithuanian, Jewish, Polish, and Ukrainian communities spoke, as did Jewish representatives from many foreign countries. Similar commemorative meetings were held in many other places in Lithuania on September 22 and 23 (*Radio Lithuania*, September 23).

Landsbergis Criticizes Polish Media

Lithuanian Supreme Council President Vytautas Landsbergis accused the Polish media of running what he called "a propaganda campaign" against Lithuania and denied that Lithuania was mistreating its Polish minority. He specifically cited leaflets issued in Gdansk and Sopot and distributed in eastern Lithuania, which, he said, expressed Polish "nationalist and expansionist feelings."

On September 24, PAP reported that Polish government spokesman Andrzej Zarebski had rejected Landsbergis' criticism of the Polish media. Recalling that Poland had supported Lithuania's independence aspirations from the very beginning, he said that, while "continuing this policy we cannot forget the rights of the Polish minority in that country." Zarebski also expressed hope that the incidents would soon cease and would not harm further relations between the two countries.

Sverdlovsk and Zagorsk Regain Former Names

The Presidium of the RSFSR Supreme Soviet restored the former names of two Russian cities: Sverdlovsk again became Ekaterinburg, and Zagorsk regained the name of Sergiev Posad. TASS, in reporting the changes, said the name changes were in response to the wishes of the two cities' inhabitants.

Tuesday, September 24

Pankin Meets with Bush, Appeals for Aid

Soviet Foreign Minister Boris Pankin met in New York with US President George Bush and made an appeal for immediate humanitarian relief and "massive" long-term economic assistance. Bush said Pankin did not specify how much the USSR expected to receive, but Soviet officials had previously referred to a figure of 14.7 billion dollars in humanitarian aid that would be necessary to see the USSR through the winter, Western agencies reported.

Pankin Opposes UN Resolution on Zionism

Pankin called for the repeal of the UN General Assembly resolution of 1975 identifying Zionism with racism during his remarks to the General Assembly. He said the USSR had begun normalizing relations with Israel, Western agencies reported.

Yakovlev Interviewed

The new USSR state councillor for special assignments, Aleksandr Yakovlev, told Novosti that the KGB had been behind the events in the Baltic States in January and the attempt to oust Soviet President Mikhail Gorbachev at the CPSU plenum in April, 1991. He stressed that the KGB had conducted a campaign against him personally, providing journalists with information. Yakovlev also said he thought that most of the republics would be unable to survive on their own and would rejoin the Union. He excluded the Baltic States from this assessment.

***Pravda* Protests about Confiscation of Property**

A group of *Pravda* staffers sent an open letter to Soviet President Gorbachev and the State Council protesting the confiscation of all the daily's property and funds by the Moscow city authorities. The statement said that *Pravda* was ready to exist under conditions of open competition with other newspapers but that the confiscation of all its resources put it at a disadvantage vis-à-vis other periodicals. Strictly speaking, *Pravda* had never had its own property, since it was owned by the CPSU.

State Commission Opposes Disbanding KGB

TASS reported that the state commission investigating the activities of the KGB had concluded that the agency should not be disbanded, because it would not be possible to create a new security system. Instead, it suggested that the radical reorganization of the present system was in the interests of the republics and the Union as a whole. One of the main reform tasks would be the demonopolization and decentralization of the state security organization, with powers devolved to the republics.

Ukraine Replaces KGB with Own Security Service

TASS and Radio Kiev reported that the KGB of Ukraine had ceased to exist. In accordance with a decision made at a closed plenary session of the Supreme Soviet, the KGB's functions would be taken over by the Service of National Security of Ukraine (SNBU). The decision was announced at a press conference by Vasyl Durdinets, chairman of the Ukrainian parliamentary Commission on Defense and State Security, and Mykola Holushko, former chairman of the Ukrainian KGB and acting head of the SNBU. Employees of the former republican KGB would remain in place while the new service was being structured. KGB archives, with the exception of the latest operational documents, would be transferred to the Ukrainian state archive.

Kazakhstan and Ukraine to Pay Part of Soviet Debt

Kazakhstan pledged to cover its share of Soviet foreign debt, Western agencies reported. In a meeting with German Finance Minister Theo Waigel, Kazakh President Nursultan Nazarbaev said he favored dividing up Soviet foreign debt proportionally among the republics. Nazarbaev also stated that he did not want an economic divorce from the Soviet Union and favored a single currency. Kazakhstan was the second major Soviet republic after Ukraine to signal its willingness to cover a part of the Soviet debt.

Gorbachev Meets with German Finance Minister

German Finance Minister Theo Waigel met with Soviet President Gorbachev in the Kremlin and invited him to attend the next world economic summit, scheduled to take place in Munich in July, 1992, AFP reported on

September 25. He also visited Kiev and Alma-Ata and presented the Soviet Union with 7,000 trucks from the former GDR army. DPA said most of the trucks would be given to the central Soviet authorities, with 800 going to Ukraine and 500 to Kazakhstan. Gorbachev reportedly told Waigel that Germany had provided the greatest help for democrats in the USSR during the coup attempt. Waigel said Gorbachev had told him the Union would retain control over many aspects of foreign trade.

New Russian Newspaper in Latvia

A new Russian-language newspaper, *Russkyput'* (Russian Way) started publication in Latvia with a print run of 30,000 copies. The goal of the newspaper, published by the Russian Community of Latvia, was the unity of the Russian-speaking population in Latvia on the basis of Russian culture, the expansion of joint activities with the RSFSR, and a search for solutions to the problems of Russians in Latvia.

Lutheran Church of Russia Revived

The Independent Information Service reported on September 23 that the United Evangelical-Lutheran Church of Russia would be registered by the RSFSR Ministry of Justice on September 24. Protestant communities had already been registered in Leningrad, Moscow, Novgorod, Samara, and other cities.

Wednesday, September 25

Gorbachev Sets Up Consultative Council

Soviet President Mikhail Gorbachev set up a new Political Consultative Council. According to TASS, Gorbachev appointed former Foreign Minister Eduard Shevardnadze; his chief aide Aleksandr Yakovlev; KGB Chairman Vadim Bakatin; the mayors of Moscow and Leningrad, Gavriil Popov and Anatolii Sobchak; the chairman of USSR television and radio broadcasting, Egor Yakovlev; former economic adviser Nikolai Petrakov; Academician Evgenii Velikhov; and security expert Yurii Ryzhov as members of the council. The council would have an advisory role and not interfere directly in politics.

Demonstration in Defense of Moscow Mayor

A demonstration was held in defense of Moscow Mayor Gavriil Popov, who had been accused of an authoritarian style of leadership by deputies of the Moscow City Soviet. The demonstration was organized by the Moscow branch of the Democratic Russia movement, which called on Muscovites to resist "a campaign to discredit the first legally elected mayor and deputy mayor of Moscow." The constituent session of the Movement for Democratic Reforms and its leaders, Shevardnadze and Yakovlev, supported the demonstration. By contrast, the leaders of Democratic Russia, Yurii Afanas'ev and Tel'man Gdlyan, spoke against the demonstration, which they said would deepen the confrontation between democratic forces in Moscow, during a Central Television broadcast on September 24.

DPA reported that the demonstration, attended by more than 50,000 people, was addressed by Shevardnadze, who called on Muscovites to support Popov. Another speaker, Father Gleb Yakunin, called for the dissolution of the Moscow City Soviet, which opposed Popov.

New Credit Card Issued

A private bank in Moscow, Kredobank, was to issue credit cards commencing the following week, Western agencies reported. Holders would have to make an initial deposit with the bank of at least 10,000 dollars and keep a credit balance of at least $3,000. Card-holders would be charged 1 percent on all transactions, but merchants would not have to pay fees. The cards were to be issued in conjunction with Visa International.

El'tsin Issues Decree Opening Vladivostok

RSFSR President Boris El'tsin decreed that the Far Eastern port city of Vladivostok would be opened to foreigners as of January 1, 1992. Foreign ships would be permitted to use the city's port, and foreign citizens would be allowed to live in the city and "engage in entrepreneurial activity." According to *Komsomol'skaya pravda* of September 25, many foreign firms were ready to open offices in Vladivostok, and several countries planned to open consulates there. The report noted that the USSR Ministry of Defense had opposed the decree up to the last minute.

Georgia Applies for CSCE Observer Status

Georgia applied for observer status at the Moscow human-rights conference and in the Helsinki process. The Georgian request was supported by the official Soviet delegation but had to be approved by the other thirty-seven member-states. The only other state to have held observer status in the Helsinki process was Albania. Only independent sovereign states that supported the Helsinki process were eligible to become members.

On September 27, the Moscow human-rights conference rejected Georgia's application for CSCE observer status after NATO, the EC, and the nonaligned countries declined to consider it. The primary obstacle was reported to be Georgian President Zviad Gamsakhurdia's poor human-rights record. Speaking in Moscow the same day,, Gorbachev expressed concern that the situation in Georgia was "worsening" and rejected as "unrealistic" Gamsakhurdia's claims the Kremlin was supporting the opposition in Georgia, Western news agencies reported.

Armenian Prime Minister Resigns, Withdraws from Presidential Race

Radio Erevan reported that Armenian Prime Minister Vazgen Manukyan had submitted his resignation and withdrawn his candidacy for the Armenian presidential election scheduled for October 16. Manukyan, who resigned in June from the ruling Armenian Pan-National Movement to set up his own political party and whose government had been repeatedly criticized, argued that "the struggle to attain power" engendered by the presidential elections was destabilizing both political and economic life in Armenia.

Nazarbaev Visits Turkey, Meets with Ozal

Kazakh President Nursultan Nazarbaev met with Turkish President Turgut Ozal in Ankara and made progress on trade and economic agreements with Turkey. According to Western reports, Turkish spokesmen said the talks focused on establishing or improving waterway, rail, and air links between the two countries with the aim of facilitating trade. A Turkish-Kazakh satellite telephone link was also discussed, as were possible Kazakh exports of coal and natural gas. A formal Turkish-Kazakh trade pact was expected to be finalized during Nazarbaev's visit. Turkish officials, business people, and scholars had expressed interest in playing a significant role in the economic development of Azerbaijan and Central Asia.

Kravchuk Meets Bush

Chairman of the Ukrainian Supreme Soviet Leonid Kravchuk met with US President George Bush in Washington, Western agencies reported on September 26. The talks focused on Ukraine's economic needs and nuclear-weapons policy. Kravchuk told Bush that his country needed new technology for the production and export of grain and that he favored the transfer of nuclear weapons at present on Ukrainian territory to the central authorities. He also said that Ukraine wanted to participate in all US-Soviet arms agreements. No agreements were reached by the two leaders, but arrangements were made for further contacts.

The USSR in September, 1991

Kravchuk concluded his visit to Washington on September 26 after addressing the Heritage Foundation and the National Press Club, Radio Kiev and TASS reported. Kravchuk told reporters that the United States was ready to support Ukraine's movement towards democracy and independence. At the same time, the White House made it clear that the United States was not prepared to extend diplomatic recognition. With regard to relations with the center, Kravchuk stated that now there could only be economic relations between republics; the question of a political union, he asserted, was quite another matter.

Dniester Moldavian Town Besieged

Paramilitary detachments of Russian workers in eastern Moldavia stormed several administrative buildings in Dubasari and laid siege to the town's police headquarters overnight. A Moldavian MVD spokesman told TASS and AFP that three militants had been injured and sixty detained after attempting to seize a major bridge over the nearby Dniester. Side arms, firearms, and communications equipment taken from the attackers were shown on Moldavian television in the evening. Telephone and other communications with Dubasari were cut off by "Dniester SSR" supporters.

The attack on Dubasari capped recent efforts to persuade Moldavian police and other law-enforcement bodies to withdraw from the left bank of the Dniester or submit to the "Dniester SSR." Meanwhile, local Russian leaders continued enrollment in a "people's militia" of their own. Early on September 26, Moldavian President Mircea Snegur made a broadcast address to the residents and authorities of the Dniester area, appealing for calm and the observance of the law. The broadcast could not be received in most of the affected area, because the local Russian leadership had detached local radio and television networks from those of Moldavia.

Additional Russian "workers' detachments" arrived in Dubasari to reinforce the siege of the Moldavian police headquarters and other administrative buildings there, Moldavian Internal Affairs Minister Ion Costas told Radio Kishinev on September 26.

In an address to the Moldavian parliament on September 26, Moldavian President Snegur re-affirmed that Kishinev would rely solely on political means to resolve the situation on the left bank of the Dniester, Moldovapres reported. Noting the pressure put on the local Moldavian authorities by local Russian leaders, and particularly the threats against Moldavian policemen in six towns in the area, Snegur said he would rather resign than approve the use of force. In a message to the police stations in the six towns broadcast by Moldavian radio on September 25, Snegur said that force would be used only to ensure the physical safety of the policemen.

Moldavian police from the right bank were dispatched to the town of Dubasari on September 27 to defend the police besieged by the armed Russian "workers' detachments," which temporarily captured other government buildings there. Aided by unarmed Moldavian peasants, the police blocked the approaches to Dubasari to prevent the arrival of additional "workers' detachments."

Aggressive picketing of Moldavian police stations in the six raion centers on the left bank of the Dniester and physical intimidation of the policemen's families was persuading a growing number of policemen to quit or transfer allegiance to the Russian-led "Dniester SSR," which organized the picketing, law-enforcement sources in Kishinev told RFE/RL by telephone on September 27. While those defecting were as a rule ethnic Russian enlisted men, the ethnic Russian officers continued to obey the law.

On September 27, the Russian Communist leadership of the self-proclaimed "Dniester SSR" set up a Military Committee and began forming a professional "Republican Guard" in addition to the ordinary police and the "workers' detachments," sources in Tiraspol' told RFE/RL by telephone on September 28. Vladimir Rylyakov, deputy chairman of the Tiraspol' City Soviet and an activist of the Joint Council of Work Collectives, was appointed chairman of the committee, which was directly subordinated to the "Dniester SSR Supreme Soviet."

An inaugural meeting of officers and the first recruits of the "Republican Guard" was held at a plant subordinated to the all-Union authorities in Tiraspol'. A colonel of the Tiraspol' Civil Defense was appointed commander of the force, which consisted initially of 800 men. Training was to take place on military training grounds. The lowest ranks were to receive a tax-free monthly salary of 700 rubles.

Dniester Russians Establish Own Communist Party

Dnestrovskaya pravda, the main Russian-language newspaper on the left bank of the Dniester, published a statement from the organizing committee of a "Communist Party of the Dniester SSR," calling for the holding of a founding conference of the Party in the near future. The Moldavian Communist Party and *Dnestrovskaya pravda* had been banned by the Moldavian government for supporting the attempted coup in August, but they continued to operate in the Russian towns of the left bank.

The USSR in September, 1991

Gorbachev Appoints Delegation Leaders for Baltic Talks

Soviet President Gorbachev named prominent reformers to head the delegations for negotiations with the three Baltic States, TASS reported. Presidential adviser Aleksandr Yakovlev would lead the negotiating team for Latvia, Leningrad Mayor Anatolii Sobchak would head negotiations with Estonia, and former USSR Foreign Minister Eduard Shevardnadze would head the team for Lithuania. All three were members of Gorbachev's nine-member Political Consultative Council.

Turkestani Conference in Uzbekistan

An Uzbek journalist informed RFE/RL that the first International Conference of Turkestanis had been opened by Uzbek President Islam Karimov. The conference, which was being attended by 100 representatives of Central Asians living abroad, aimed to promote closer ties between Uzbekistan and Turkestani emigrants.

Thursday, September 26

Stankevich Attacks El'tsin; Sobchak Also Under Fire

RSFSR State Councillor Sergei Stankevich accused his boss, RSFSR President Boris El'tsin, of lacking statesmanship. Stankevich was quoted in *Der Wiener* as saying that El'tsin had no idea how to build a state and relied completely on old Communist Party apparatchiks. Stankevich complained that the old Party bureaucracy had "bought" El'tsin. Leningrad Mayor Anatolii Sobchak was also a target of criticism for having appointed three former KGB officials as leaders of city districts, *The Guardian* reported. Democrats also criticized Sobchak for moving his residence to the former Leningrad Communist Party offices in the Smolny Institute.

Fedorov on Russian Foreign Policy

RSFSR Deputy Foreign Minister Andrei Fedorov outlined Russia's foreign-policy aims at a conference on the Soviet Union sponsored by the Royal Institute of International Affairs in London. Fedorov said Russia had two separate foreign-policy programs, one based on Russia as part of a new confederation of sovereign states and the other envisaging Russia as a separate entity with an independent foreign policy. He said Russia did not want to be a superpower but did aspire to serve as a bridge between Europe and Asia.

Commenting on NATO, Fedorov said Russia did not view the organization as a threat. "I do not rule out that one day, and maybe quite soon, we will reach a situation where NATO will not be the North Atlantic Treaty

Organization but something like a European treaty organization, of which we can be a part." Fedorov's comments were reported by RFE/RL's London correspondent.

Lobov Briefs Foreign Military Attachés

General Vladimir Lobov, chief of the General Staff of the USSR Armed Forces, summoned about 100 military attachés from foreign embassies in Moscow to brief them on Soviet plans to restructure the Soviet army, Western news agencies reported. Lobov indicated that the Soviet Union might have a professional army by 1992. He also said the Defense Ministry would become a civilian institution and "a joint chiefs of staff" would be created to deal with strategy and logistics. Both bodies would be subordinated to the USSR president, who would have a "two-channel" command over the country's armed forces, according to Lobov.

New Baltic and Black Sea Fleet Commanders

Profiles of the new commanders of the Baltic and Black Sea Fleets appeared in *Krasnaya zvezda*. Vice Admiral Vladimir Egorov (born in 1938) was appointed commander of the Baltic Fleet. He had been its first deputy commander since 1988 and in 1990 graduated (as an external student) from the USSR Armed Forces General Staff Military Academy. Vice Admiral Igor' Kasatonov (born in 1939) was named the new commander of the Black Sea Fleet. Since 1988 he had been the first deputy commander of the Northern Fleet.

Enterprise Council Established

Soviet President Gorbachev issued a decree creating a twenty-eight-member Enterprise Council, TASS reported. Its declared functions were, inter alia, to further free enterprise activity, to form a market structure of economic links within the framework of a unified economic area, to protect the rights of businessmen, to counter monopolies, and to help promote fair competition. The vice president of the USSR Scientific-Industrial Union, Aleksandr Vladislavlev, was named to head the council; among its other members were Pavel Bunich and Konstantin Borovoi.

Soviet Savings Bank Invests in Eurasco

Western agencies reported that the USSR Savings Bank had invested some 2 million Swiss francs (1.35 million dollars) in Eurasco, Zurich, Western agencies reported. Eurasco is a financial company that obtains its capital from Eastern as well as Western sources. It is involved with Soviet banking partners in various programs aimed at reforming the outdated Soviet financial sector. Since gaining permission to undertake economic activities abroad in December, 1990, Soviet banks have invested a total of 30 million Swiss francs in Eurasco.

Gold Shipped Abroad

Reversing earlier denials of Western reports, TASS quoted a report in *Kuranty* as saying that gold worth 4 billion dollars had been shipped abroad secretly by the coup plotters in August. The purpose was to create a special reserve fund to purchase imports for Soviet industry in the expectation that Western credits would be cut off after the coup. Rumors of the gold shipment had caused London and Tokyo gold prices to decline in early September.

Mujahidin Seek Reparations from USSR

TASS reported that the Afghan Mujahidin Lawyers' Association, based in Peshawar in Pakistan, had written an appeal demanding that the USSR pay for the damage done to Afghanistan since the 1979 Soviet invasion. The group sent the appeal to the Afghan opposition delegation being formed to go to Moscow for talks on settling the Afghan conflict. It also wanted the USSR to make a full list of the damage done since 1979 and to send it to the United Nations and other international organizations. The appeal argued that, since Kuwait had demanded military reparations from Iraq, Afghanistan should be able to demand the same from the USSR. TASS said the Afghan opposition claimed that incomplete estimates of the damage ran to more than 644.8 billion dollars.

Mubarak in Moscow

Egyptian President Hosni Mubarak arrived in Moscow for "a short working visit," TASS reported. He was to hold talks on September 27 with Soviet President Mikhail Gorbachev and RSFSR President Boris El'tsin. Gorbachev's special Middle East envoy Evgenii Primakov, who met Mubarak at the airport, told TASS that the talks would focus on the proposed Middle East peace conference and on bilateral relations.

Ukraine and Kazakhstan Said to Hesitate over Missiles

Western agencies quoted RSFSR Deputy Foreign Minister Andrei Fedorov as saying in an address to the Royal Institute of International Affairs in London that Ukraine and Kazakhstan were backing away from previous offers to hand over to the RSFSR nuclear missiles located on the territory of their republics. Although the RSFSR would accept the missiles, Fedorov pointed out that transportation would be dangerous and that it would be cheaper to destroy the silos. He said missiles in Ukraine and Kazakhstan could be made the object of negotiations with the United States.

Democratic Crimea Warns of Ukrainian-Russian Conflicts

TASS, quoting sources in the Democratic Crimea opposition group, said the Communist authorities, who were still firmly in charge of the Crimean Peninsula, were attempting to pit Ukraine against Russia. According to Yurii Komov, a member of both Democratic Crimea and the Presidium of the Crimean ASSR Supreme Soviet, officials were gathering signatures on a petition to hold a referendum on whether to nullify the 1954 act on the transfer of the Crimea from the RSFSR to Ukraine.

Krauchanka Defines Belorussian Sovereignty

In an address to the UN General Assembly, Belorussian Foreign Minister Petr Krauchanka said his republic's goal was to achieve "real independence and sovereignty" through favorable political conditions that would lead to "a wave of diplomatic recognition." Krauchanka expressed the hope that the Conference on Security and Cooperation in Europe (CSCE) would look favorably on the republic's desire to join the Helsinki process when CSCE foreign ministers met in Prague in January.

Anti-Semitism Conference Concludes

The International Conference on Anti-Semitism ended in Moscow and issued a resolution calling for a ban on political parties and organizations that "ignite racial hatred" in the Soviet Union. The conference also called for Soviet and republican emigration laws to consistently adhere to international standards of human rights and commitments undertaken by the Soviet Union and urged that Jewish organizations be consulted in revising the laws. On September 25, the conference released a poll by the Moscow-based Jewish Scientific Center, which found that more than 50 percent of Soviet citizens wanted all Jews to leave the country. The poll, a sponsor said, reflected increasing anti-Semitism in the wake of growing economic uncertainty.

Nordic Council Meeting on Baltic States

Nordic Council parliamentarians held a meeting in Copenhagen with their Baltic counterparts, including Lithuanian Supreme Council President Vytautas Landsbergis, who gave an interview to the RFE Lithuanian service that day. Discussion at a meeting of the Nordic Council Secretariat focused on cooperation between the Nordic and Baltic Councils and the establishment of a Baltic Investment Bank with a proposed capital of 300 million ecus. The members of the secretariat also agreed to recommend to their governments that they support the immediate withdrawal of the Soviet army from the Baltic States.

Vagnorius on Lithuanian Economy

In a speech to the Lithuanian parliament broadcast by Radio Lithuania, Prime Minister Gediminas Vagnorius said the first economic priority for Lithuania was to convert to a market economy. The differences between market and state prices that were still in force for about 40 percent of goods had prompted many people to buy goods at state prices and resell them at market prices, resulting in shortages of goods at state prices. Vagnorius said that he hoped to free all prices by the end of the year. He noted that in October wages and other compensatory payments would be raised by about 30 percent.

Vagnorius said that existing ministries should be reorganized but without increasing the number of employees. The Ministry of Trade should be incorporated into the Ministry of Material Resources; the Department of National Defense should be made the Ministry of National Defense; and a new Ministry of International Economic Relations should be created whose primary purpose would be to increase Lithuania's international trade.

Vagnorius also proposed that the Bank of Lithuania should divest itself of all normal commercial accounts with enterprises and individuals by November 1, transferring them to commercial banks. The Bank of Lithuania should become a Central Bank (similar to the US Federal Reserve) that would regulate credit policies and the circulation of money (after Lithuania introduced its own currency). He hoped that an international bank would decide to establish a branch in Lithuania that would be a competitor and example for local banks.

Friday, September 27

Controversy over Size of Gold Reserves

Interviewed on Central Television, Grigorii Yavlinsky estimated that the USSR had sold off two-thirds of its gold reserves in 1990 and that holdings were now down to 240 tons, worth about 3 billion dollars at current world prices, Western agencies reported on September 28. He also disclosed that Soviet gold sales had been exceeding 400 tons a year for several years.

In an interview with a Western news agency on September 30, a deputy chairman of the USSR State Bank disputed Yavlinsky's estimate of the size of Soviet gold reserves. He asserted that "the balance of the monetary gold reserve remains at 374.4 tons," thereby restating the figure published in *Izvestia* on July 16.

Yavlinsky's figures were also challenged by *Izvestia* on October 3. The newspaper cited "well-informed sources" in the two Soviet gold-extracting organizations who "categorically" put the annual production at over 300 tons. *Izvestia* concluded: "Putting all the figures together, we come to the conclusion that, over the last three years, the government . . . with the approval of Gorbachev, has wasted for some unknown purpose gold worth 25–30 billion dollars. The Soviet foreign debt, at the same time, has grown by no less than 35 billion dollars. In any normal country, a parliament or a government commission would be demanding that the president and his prime ministers account for such fantastic embezzlement."

Sobchak Continues Appeal for Aid

Elaborating on calls he had recently made in London and Paris, Leningrad Mayor Anatolii Sobchak appealed to a banking conference in Frankfurt for sales of surplus EC foodstuffs to the USSR, Western agencies reported. Sobchak proposed that up to 10 billion dollars worth of surplus food be sold to the USSR on credit. This could then be sold to the Soviet population for up to 150 billion rubles, which would, in turn, be used for investment in the economy, including the creation of 100,000 new farms. He also invited unemployed or underemployed West European farmers to try their hand in the USSR.

Sobchak caused some consternation among his audience of German bankers when he mentioned that a search was on for the whereabouts of a 2.5-billion-mark loan received from West Germany in 1987. He said that no written trace could be found of the loan.

Shevardnadze and Bessmertnykh Form Think Tank

Izvestia reported that former Foreign Ministers Eduard Shevardnadze and Aleksandr Bessmertnykh were setting up a new foreign-policy think tank called the Center for Political Analysis. Bessmertnykh was to assume the position of director. He told *Izvestia* that he wanted to see "the structural integration" of the Soviet and Russian Foreign Ministries, Western agencies reported.

Another Kryuchkov Deputy under Arrest

The RSFSR Supreme Soviet approved the arrest of former USSR KGB First Deputy Chairman Genii Ageev, TASS reported. According to RSFSR Prosecutor-General Valentin Stepankov, Ageev was responsible for the isolation of

THE USSR IN SEPTEMBER, 1991

Soviet President Gorbachev during the coup. He also prepared plans for capturing the RSFSR Supreme Soviet building and for interning the active opponents of the junta, Stepankov charged.

Uzbek KGB Dissolved

TASS reported that a National Security Service directly subordinate to the president had been created in Uzbekistan to replace the republican KGB, which was dissolved on the orders of Uzbek President Islam Karimov. The new agency was to be responsible only for intelligence gathering, counterintelligence, and fighting organized crime; other departments of the former KGB were to be closed. The new agency would be headed by the former KGB chairman, Gulam Aliev.

Lithuanian-Latvian Diplomatic Relations

Lithuanian Supreme Council President Vytautas Landsbergis stopped in Latvia on his way back from Copenhagen, Radio Lithuania reported on September 29. He met with his Latvian counterpart Anatolijs Gorbunovs in Jurmala where they signed a joint communiqué on the reestablishment of formal diplomatic relations. The communiqué stressed the necessity of the immediate withdrawal of Soviet troops from their republics.

Poland Signs Economic Cooperation Agreement with Latvia

Poland and Latvia signed an intergovernmental commercial and economic cooperation agreement in Warsaw to promote trade between the two countries. The agreement included a most-favored-nation clause relating to customs tariffs, taxes, and sundry charges and opened the way for direct dealings between individual companies and banks, according to PAP.

Saturday, September 28

Komsomol Disbanded

The all-Union Komsomol voted itself out of existence at the organization's Twenty-second Extraordinary Congress, TASS reported. The central apparatus was to be dismantled over the next ten months, and a temporary coordinating council would oversee the activities of republican Komsomol groups. The thorny question of disposing of the Komsomol's assets was debated but not resolved: the congress appealed to the Presidium of the Russian parliament to settle the question of justly apportioning the all-Union Komsomol's property among republican Komsomol organizations. Delegates also urged the presidents of the

USSR, the RSFSR, and several other republics to halt "the forced confiscation" of the Komsomol's all-Union assets taking place in some republics.

USSR Academy of Sciences Opts for RSFSR Affiliation

The Presidium of the USSR Academy of Sciences was reported to have voted to transfer the main all-Union scientific body to RSFSR government jurisdiction. According to sources within the academy, the majority of all-Union academicians were eager to use the occasion to replace the academy's president, Gurii Marchuk. The USSR Academy would in future be called the Russian (Rossiiskaya) Academy, and new elections were planned.

Sakhalin Authorities Oppose Return of Kuriles

RSFSR Deputy Foreign Minister Georgii Kunadze told TASS the RSFSR was willing to study all aspects of the Kurile Islands dispute with Japan. He stressed that the Soviet population on the islands would be consulted and might even participate in the negotiations with Japan. Kunadze stressed that the RSFSR did not link the return of the islands with economic aid from Japan.

On September 30, authorities on the island of Sakhalin stated their opposition to any attempt to return the Kuriles to Japan. A TASS report, cited by Western agencies the same day, quoted Valentin Fedorov, head of the Sakhalin Oblast Soviet Executive Committee, as declaring his committee "a headquarters of struggle for the Kurile Islands."

A rally was held on October 4 in the town of Yuzhno-Sakhalinsk to protest against talks between Russian and Japanese officials on the status of the Kurile Islands, TASS reported that day. The event was organized by the Sakhalin Oblast Executive Committee.

Social Democratic Party of Russia Meets

The board of the Social Democratic Party of Russia opened a plenum in Moscow, TASS said. Addressed by the party's leaders Oleg Rumyantsev and Boris Orlov, the plenum discussed the participation of the party's candidates in the November elections for heads of local government in the RSFSR and the party's cooperation with the RSFSR leadership.

Travkin Voices Support for Russians in Moldavia

Russian Democratic Party leader and USSR Supreme Soviet deputy Nikolai Travkin visited Moldavia's Dniester area. Attending the founding conference of his party's branch in Tiraspol', Travkin spoke—as he had during his visit there in August—about the imperative of

The USSR in September, 1991

preserving "the Russian state" (*derzhava*) in the Dniester and other far-flung areas. "Our concept of Russia has always extended beyond its geographical boundaries," he told Radio Rossii on September 29. He maintained that "in the Dniester area all people who carry a Soviet passport consider themselves Russian" (*Russian Television*, September 29). Concerning the situation in Dubasari, where the Moldavian police station was being besieged by "workers' detachments," Travkin said he had talked to those people, "our compatriots," personally. He told them on a Central Television broadcast, "Boys, we shan't abandon you." (According to the Soviet census of 1989, the population on the left bank of the Dniester is 25.5 percent Russian and that of Dubasari Raion, 88 percent Moldavian.)

Sunday, September 29

Russia Mourns Coup Victims

Thousands of Muscovites gathered at the Russian White House to mark the fortieth day since the death of the three victims of the abortive coup (according to the Russian Orthodox faith, the souls of the dead leave the earth for the other world forty days after death). The meeting was addressed by RSFSR Vice President Aleksandr Rutskoi and other defenders of the RSFSR Supreme Soviet during the coup attempt.

Who Is a Jew?

Issue 35 of *Literator*, a weekly of the Leningrad Writers' Organization, reported on a new trend in the leaflets of the anti-Semitic "Pamyat'" society. In the past, "Pamyat'" leaflets, posted on a fence near Gostinyi Dvor, alleged that all liberals were Jews and even ascribed Jewish names to them. On August 26, *Literator* discovered on the same fence a "Pamyat" leaflet "unmasking" members of the Emergency Committee in the same way.

Sotsialisticheskaya zakonnost' to Change Name

In response to the change in the country's political climate, *Sotsialisticheskaya zakonnost'*, an organ of the USSR Prosecutor's Office, decided to change its name. It was announced in issue No. 8 of the journal that it would in future be called simply *Zakonnost'*.

Budget Deficit Exceeds 200–Billion Rubles

Izvestia reported that the Soviet budget deficit had already surpassed the 200-billion-ruble level. This figure was thought to include both the central government deficit and the combined deficits of the republics. The planned budget deficit for the entire year was originally set at 26.6 billion rubles.

Ukraine Objects to Moscow's Policy on Foreign Debt

Ukraine announced that it objected to Moscow's incurring increased "Union" debt without the express consent of the individual republics. Radio Moscow reported that Ukrainian Prime Minister Vitol'd Fokin had sent a letter to the Committee for the Operational Management of the USSR Economy in which he categorically protested against the Union's incurring new foreign debt without defining who would receive the money and who would pay for it. Without fulfillment of these conditions, Fokin said, his republic would not participate in the new Interrepublican Economic Committee and would pursue its own foreign debt policy.

Babii Yar Commemoration

Tens of thousands of people took part in a march in Kiev on September 29, the first day of a week-long commemoration of the massacres at Babii Yar that began on September 29-30, 1941, with the machine-gunning of nearly 34,000 Jews. The commemoration was attended by many Jewish leaders from Israel, Europe, and North America, according to Western and Soviet media. Shimon Samuels of the Simon Wiesenthal Center told Western agencies of his concern that Nazi collaborators might be among the 46,000 people who had been rehabilitated since April by the Ukrainian government in accordance with a new law on the rehabilitation of victims of Soviet political repression.

Monday, September 30

Solzhenitsyn on Gorbachev and El'tsin

In a rare interview, published in the Austrian newspaper *Der Standard*, Aleksandr Solzhenitsyn said he believed communism was now dead. He criticized Soviet President Gorbachev for failing to improve the country's economy and added that Gorbachev was "a dubious personality." He said that RSFSR President El'tsin had thus far "sold himself quite well" but that he too might fail to solve the country's economic crisis. Solzhenitsyn spoke out against the incorporation of Russia into the world economy because this would lead to inflation. He stressed the need for a spiritual revival in Russia and indicated that he was planning to return to his homeland.

The USSR in September, 1991

RSFSR Foreign Minister Andrei Kozyrev said at an international economic seminar in Rome that if political and economic reforms failed to be implemented in the following two or three months, another putsch by conservative forces might occur in the Soviet Union. TASS quoted him as saying that the West must help the USSR's democratic forces, because they were inexperienced and disorganized. He stressed that the West should control the distribution of its financial aid to the USSR to prevent its being diverted by conservative forces.

Kozyrev on Possibility of Another Putsch

The RSFSR State Council said it had received numerous reports of abuses in other republics of the rights of Russians and other peoples having ethnic ties to the nations of the RSFSR, according to TASS. A document of the State Council of the RSFSR president stated that the RSFSR intended to use all lawful means to protect the rights of Russians and members of other RSFSR nationalities living outside the RSFSR, TASS said. RSFSR deputy Aleksei Surkov, who was chairman of the RSFSR Supreme Soviet's Subcommission for Work with National Minorities and Ties with Fellow Countrymen Abroad, told Radio Rossii that he had recently participated in a roundtable of representatives of Russian-speaking communities in the republics, in the framework of the Conference on Security and Cooperation in Europe, where great concern had been expressed about the position of the Russian-speaking population.

RSFSR to Protect Rights of Natives of RSFSR Outside Republic

USSR Foreign Minister Boris Pankin met with a delegation of Afghan resistance leaders at the United Nations in New York to discuss the situation in Afghanistan. According to RFE/RL's correspondent in New York, a spokesman for the delegation termed their talks with Pankin on obstacles to settling the Afghan conflict "frank and open" and said "we think the Soviets are interested in movement" on the Afghan issue. He said that Pankin had invited them to Moscow to continue the dialogue.

Pankin Meets Mujahidin

TASS reported that Soviet President Gorbachev had appointed Academician Evgenii Primakov as head of KGB foreign intelligence and KGB first deputy chairman. Primakov, who said the appointment had not come as a surprise to him, declared his intention to separate the foreign intelligence service from the KGB and to create a new image for the organization. Primakov said he intended to use outside experts for analytical

Primakov Appointed Head of Foreign Intelligence

projects while at the same time continuing to adhere to traditional intelligence techniques, including "illegal" agents. Although TASS described the appointment of a "scientist" and "politician" to the KGB as a sensation, Primakov was alleged to have had ties to the agency since working as a *Pravda* correspondent in the Middle East in the early 1970s.

Official Response to Arms Offer

Responding to US President George Bush's offer to unilaterally reduce US nuclear arms in Europe and negotiate over further reductions with the Soviet Union, USSR Foreign Minister Boris Pankin said, "I think it's time to say farewell to so-called nuclear deterrence." Other Soviet officials also expressed enthusiasm for the US proposal. First Deputy Foreign Minister Vladimir Petrovsky said, "The Soviet side is ready to get down to the proposals made by President Bush constructively and without delay." Deputy Chief of Staff of the Soviet Armed Forces General Bronislav Omelichev described the US proposal as a "positive" step and said it paralleled proposals made by Mikhail Gorbachev in 1986, Soviet and Western news agencies reported on September 30.

Petrovsky also stressed that the issue of nuclear testing should be resolved, and he proposed the immediate resumption of negotiations on a nuclear test ban.

Kravchuk Addresses UN on Nuclear Arms

In his address to the UN General Assembly, Ukrainian Supreme Soviet Chairman Leonid Kravchuk hailed US President Bush's recent arms reduction initiative as "an important step towards a safe future" and added that Ukraine intended to be party to the Nuclear Nonproliferation Treaty. According to TASS and Western news agencies, Kravchuk stressed that "the liquidation" of the nuclear arsenal and bases located in Ukraine was "a matter of time."

Summarizing a report carried by *The Guardian* on September 30, TASS drew attention to Ukrainian reluctance to hand over nuclear weapons to the Russian Federation. Deputy Supreme Soviet Chairman Ivan Plyushch said that destruction of the weapons was too expensive a proposition for Ukraine but that he saw no reason to give them to Russia. He called for a joint interrepublican organ to exercise control over the nuclear arsenal. Supreme Soviet opposition deputies told *The Guardian* that fear of Russian territorial ambitions was prompting Ukraine to have second thoughts about disposing of its nuclear weapons.

The USSR in September, 1991

Popular Front Demonstration in Baku

The Azerbaijani Popular Front held a rally in Baku to call for the dissolution of the republic's Supreme Soviet, democratic elections, and "a mobilization of forces in order to ensure the security of the Azerbaijani population of Nagorno-Karabakh," "Vesti" reported.

Azerbaijani President Ayaz Mutalibov agreed on October 2 to begin talks with opposition leaders on dissolving parliament, holding new elections, and restructuring state bodies, an Azerbaijani journalist told RL's Azerbaijani service on October 3.

Disbanding of KGB in Baltic States

Deputy Chairman of the USSR KGB Nikolai Stolyarov told a press conference in Moscow after returning from a two-week visit to the Baltic States that the KGB would be dissolved in Estonia, Latvia, and Lithuania by early 1992, Radio Moscow reported. The KGB would have to abandon the buildings, equipment, and weapons it held in the three states.

The Month of October

Tuesday, October 1

Demonstrations Continue in Tajikistan

A TajikTA-TASS report of October 1 said that demonstrations, some in support of the Communist Party and some in support of the opposition, were taking place in cities and towns throughout the republic.

In its evening session on October 2, the Supreme Soviet of Tajikistan voted to suspend the activities of the republican Communist Party until the State Prosecutor's Office had completed an investigation of the Party's role during the August coup, TASS reported. The decision apparently had no effect on the demonstrators in front of the Supreme Soviet building, who continued to demand that the legislature dissolve itself, according to a Central Television report of October 3. The Supreme Soviet put off until its next session a decision on the legalization of the Islamic Renaissance Party, using the excuse that the law on freedom of conscience prohibited religious-based political parties.

On October 4, opposition rallies in Dushanbe continued to demand the resignation of the republic's Communist president, Rakhmon Nabiev, and the legalization of the Islamic Renaissance Party. Soviet President Gorbachev's envoys, St. Petersburg Mayor Anatolii Sobchak and presidential adviser Evgenii Velikhov, met with both government and opposition leaders to try to mediate a solution. Eight ministers of the republic's government threatened to resign unless elections were called, TASS reported. A Radio Moscow report of October 6 said that Nabiev, had resigned. The presidential election in the republic was deferred until November 24.

The text of an agreement worked out by representatives of the Tajik Supreme Soviet and the three opposition groups that had been staging demonstrations since late August was read on Radio Dushanbe. In addition to reimposing a ban on the Communist Party, the agreement scheduled a referendum to coincide with the presidential election on November 24 on whether or not to dissolve the Supreme Soviet. It also recommended that representatives of the Islamic Renaissance Party, Democratic Party, and "Rastokhez" Movement be added to election commissions and promised that all parties would have equal access to television and radio.

Sobchak told a press conference in Moscow that the agreement signed by the disputants was a small step, not a major victory, according to a TASS report of October 8.

Georgian Conflict Continues

On September 30, Georgian President Zviad Gamsakhurdia had stated that, if opposition forces surrendered their arms by noon on October 3, he would comply with their request to reconvene the parliament. He also undertook to lift the state of emergency in Tbilisi if they vacated the television center, which they had occupied for the previous ten days. Several thousand Gamsakhurdia supporters later followed his call at a rally in Tbilisi for a peaceful march to the television center, Western news agencies reported.

Western news agencies reported on October 2 that rebel National Guard leader Tengiz Kitovani had signed an agreement to withdraw his troops from Tbilisi over a period of two days beginning on October 3. TASS on October 3, however, quoted Kitovani as stating that he would merely redeploy his men elsewhere in Tbilisi and reserved the right to return if Gamsakhurdia again began reprisals against the opposition.

An exchange of fire on the outskirts of Tbilisi on October 4 between rebel national guardsmen and soldiers loyal to Gamsakhurdia left at least one dead and five wounded, Soviet and Western news agencies reported the same day. Following the shooting, thousands of supporters and opponents of the Gamsakhurdia government gathered outside the parliament building facing each other. The government announced the same day that it would accede to the opposition's demand to reconvene the parliament.

At least one person was killed and eighty were injured in clashes in Tbilisi during the night of October 4–5 between pro- and antigovernment demonstrators. There was further shooting during the morning of October 5, and many opposition supporters were arrested. Gamsakhurdia made a television appeal for an end to the violence and a peaceful solution to the crisis. Opposition leaders called for Gamsakhurdia's resignation at an emergency session of parliament on the evening of October 5. The parliament adopted an appeal to the population on October 6 to refrain from violence. A former ally of Gamsakhurdia claimed on October 7 to have blockaded the main road and rail links between Tbilisi and the Black Sea, Western news agencies reported.

On October 7, political groups supporting Gamsakhurdia called for the dissolution of parliament and the imposition of presidential rule; they also advocated the banning of opposition parties and organizations and the arrest of their leaders, as well as the revoking of the citizenship of opponents of the government, Western news agencies reported. Students began a sit-in at Tbilisi University to demand freedom of the press and the withdrawal of Gamsakhurdia's troops from Tbilisi, RIA reported.

On October 8, several hundred antigovernment protesters demonstrated outside the Georgian parliament, and sixty Communist deputies were banned from parliament on the grounds that the Communist Party was "illegal" in Georgia, Western news agencies reported. Former Soviet Foreign Minister Eduard Shevardnadze told *Nezavisimaya gazeta* that he was willing to mediate between Gamsakhurdia and the opposition but that he doubted his services would be welcomed. Kitovani was quoted by Interfax as stating that he would drop his demand for Gamsakhurdia's resignation if the opposition's other demands were met.

On October 13, TASS reported that the Georgian Supreme Soviet had amended the republic's constitution to limit the powers of the president; in future the president would have to seek the agreement of parliament for his nominations to senior government posts. To seek ways to defuse the ongoing conflict, the Supreme Soviet, according to an interview given by its chairman to "TV-Inform" on October 13, set up a commission that included several representatives of the opposition. A new opposition bloc, the Democratic Movement of Georgia, comprising five moderate Georgian groups, held its founding congress in Tbilisi on October 13. The same day, Shevardnadze again offered to mediate between the government and the opposition in Georgia, TASS reported.

Dniester Confrontation Defused

Moldavian government officials and representatives of Russian-controlled raions on the left bank of the Dniester signed two protocols designed to defuse the confrontation there. The compromise was reached after three days of talks, the final round of which was brokered by an RSFSR Supreme Soviet delegation headed by the progressive Nikolai Medvedev, chairman of the Supreme Soviet's Commission on Interethnic Relations. The provisions were summarized by Central and Russian Television and TASS on October 1.

The provisions included: the voluntary surrender of firearms by "civilian formations" (i.e., Russian detachments) in Dubasari simultaneously with the withdrawal of Moldavian MVD subunits "additionally deployed" there recently; the release of the three left-bank Russian leaders and one Gagauz leader remaining in Moldavian investigative custody on charges of supporting the August coup d'état; lifting of the blockade of Moldavian railroads (by left-bank Russians); strict observance of the law and renunciation of the use of force, economic strikes, "blackmail" picketing, and blockades (an indirect reference to methods repeatedly used by the left-bank Russian leaders); and the creation of a conciliation commission composed of officials of the Moldavian government and of left-bank raions to discuss further "normalization" steps.

USSR to Take Nuclear Missiles off Alert

In one of the first specific responses to US President George Bush's unilateral nuclear arms initiatives, Soviet presidential spokesman Andrei Grachev declared that the USSR would remove from alert status the intercontinental ballistic missiles earmarked for ultimate elimination under the terms of the Strategic Arms Reduction Treaty. His remarks were reported by TASS. Bush had announced on September 27 that the United States was taking such a step and had urged the Soviet Union to follow suit.

New Ambassador to Czechoslovakia

TASS reported that Gorbachev had appointed Aleksandr Lebedev to the post of ambassador to Czechoslovakia. Lebedev, a fifty-three-year-old career diplomat, had previously been a counselor at the Prague embassy.

Gorbachev Lowers Aid Request

The European Community's economic commissioner, Henning Christophersen, said that Soviet President Mikhail Gorbachev had lowered Moscow's aid request from 14.7 billion to 10.2 billion dollars, Western agencies reported. Christophersen was in the Soviet Union to discuss the country's economic problems and the possibility of the West's providing aid. He told reporters that the EC was ready to grant the Soviet Union humanitarian aid but did not want to provide cash merely to pay off Moscow's outstanding commercial arrears and short- and medium-term credits that were overdue or coming up for settlement.

Twelve Republics Sign Communiqué on Economic Treaty

The leaders of twelve present and former Soviet republics signed a communiqué in Alma-Ata proclaiming their intention to form "an economic community," TASS, Interfax, and Western agencies reported. The three Slav republics, the four Central Asian republics, and Kazakhstan said they intended to ratify the treaty by October 15, and three of them—Russia, Belorussia, and Kazakhstan—even said they were ready to ratify the treaty immediately. (TASS and the Russian Information Agency reported on October 2 that three republics—Belorussia, Kazakhstan, and Uzbekistan—had signed the treaty.) The reports said the three Transcaucasian republics and Moldavia would join the new economic community later, after supplementary agreements or consultations with their legislatures. Latvia, the only one of the Baltic States to attend the meeting, reserved the right to join the community as an associate member.

The draft treaty had proposed "an economic union," but Moldavian President Mircea Snegur suggested "an economic community of sovereign states" instead, a proposal that RSFSR President Boris El'tsin had earlier endorsed, according to Moldovapres. Reports said the agreement called for "an accelerated transition to market relations" and for the coordination of policies on money and credit and stipulated that, if republics wanted to issue their own currencies, that action should not further damage the ruble. The leaders also reportedly agreed to control nuclear weapons jointly from a single center in the interests of collective security.

El'tsin's Problems with the Regions

Fifty-seven local deputies from Gorbachev's home oblast of Stavropol' appealed to El'tsin to send a presidential envoy to the oblast in order to discipline hard-line local leaders who were openly sabotaging the policy of the RSFSR government, "Vesti" reported. In El'tsin's political home, Sverdlovsk, local authorities also voiced opposition to the RSFSR government, although for other reasons. They were protesting El'tsin's failure yet to fulfill his promise to transform Russia into a democratically governed republic, according to Radio Moscow.

Moldavian Officials Rule Out Reunification with Romania

Interviewed in *Die Welt* of October 1 in Bonn, Moldavian Deputy Foreign Minister Nicolae Osmochescu and the chairman of the Moldavian parliament's Foreign Relations Committee, Vasile Nedelciuc, said that reunification with Romania "is not on the table even in the long term." They named "lack of democracy, lack of resolve to privatize the economy. . . and the survival of Communist methods and structures" in Romania as "the chief obstacles to reunification in the future." Moldavia "wishes to become an internationally recognized member of the European home in its own right," they said. The Moldavian officials were received by German Foreign Ministry officials and senior parliamentarians.

THE USSR IN OCTOBER, 1991

Kazakh Demonstrators Call for Border Revision

"Vesti" reported that pickets outside the meeting of republican leaders in Alma-Ata had demanded the revision of Kazakhstan's borders—to the benefit of Kazakhstan. Members of opposition political groups and other Kazakh intellectuals have often reacted to demands for border changes from non-Kazakh inhabitants of the northern oblasts by calling for parts of neighboring oblasts of the RSFSR to be transferred to Kazakhstan on the ground that these regions were traditionally Kazakh lands.

Wednesday, October 2

Meeting of Political Consultative Council

Soviet President Gorbachev's new Political Consultative Council met under his chairmanship, TASS reported. The council discussed matters connected with the content of a new Union treaty and the prospects for concluding it. The latest draft, on which Gorbachev and El'tsin worked, was sent to members of the State Council for review. The council also discussed the food situation and recommended the removal of all barriers to radical reforms in the agrarian sector so as to increase agricultural production.

Sugar Riots in Perm

The "Vesti" news program of Russian Television reported that sugar riots had broken out in Perm. Residents of the city were said to have hijacked public transport vehicles and to have declared that they would retain them until sugar appeared in the stores.

Stankevich Attacks El'tsin

RSFSR State Councilor Sergei Stankevich was quoted in *The Philadelphia Inquirer* as saying he was so frustrated with El'tsin's failure to organize a cohesive Russian government that he might consider quitting and taking the job of ambassador to the United States. "We have a Russian government that is underdeveloped and a Union government that still exists and doesn't command any republic except Russia," he said. Stankevich severely criticized El'tsin for naming a former Sverdlovsk Party apparatchik—Yurii Petrov—as head of the presidential administration and for visiting Nagorno-Karabakh instead of troubled areas inside Russia.

Inhabitants of Saratov Demonstrate against German Autonomy

Inhabitants of Saratov Oblast, where a future Volga German Republic would be located, demonstrated outside the Saratov City Executive Committee against such a republic being reconstituted, Radio Rossii reported. The oblast soviet, which was meeting inside the building, included the question of German autonomy on its agenda and sent its decision to the USSR Supreme Soviet. Opposition in Saratov and Volgograd Oblasts presented the main stumbling block to the restoration of Soviet German autonomy.

North Ossetia Opposed to Return of Prigorodnyi Raion to Checheno-Ingushetia

The RSFSR law "On the Rehabilitation of Repressed Peoples" was the main topic on the agenda of the North Ossetian Supreme Soviet on October 2, TASS and Radio Moscow reported. The North Ossetian parliament made plain that it did not accept the law's implication that the Prigorodnyi Raion of North Ossetia should be returned to Checheno-Ingushetia, stressing that the boundaries of the republic's territory could only be changed with the consent of its people. Ingush deputies walked out of the session. A delegation from South Ossetia asked the North Ossetian parliament to raise the question of South Ossetia's transfer from Georgia to the RSFSR with the RSFSR parliament.

On October 3, the North Ossetian social and political movement "Adamon tsadis" sent an appeal to El'tsin requesting the restoration of the territorial and political integrity of Ossetia, divided in the 1920s into North and South Ossetia "against the will of the people" (*TASS, Radio Moscow,* October 3).

While he was in Groznyi on October 6 trying to defuse the crisis in Checheno-Ingushetia, RSFSR Vice President Aleksandr Rutskoi addressed the Third Congress of the Ingush People, which was in session at the time. He proposed that the question of the return of the Prigorodnyi Raion of North Ossetia to the Ingush be decided by a congress of elders of the Northern Caucasus. He said he would ask El'tsin to entrust him with the organization of such a congress, TASS reported. The Ingush congress decided to press for the immediate return of the Prigorodnyi Raion, which was given to North Ossetia when the Ingush were deported in 1944.

The decision of the Ingush congress caused great concern in North Ossetia, TASS reported on October 9. TASS said that demands were being made for the creation of a national guard in North Ossetia. According to "Vesti" of the same date, self-defense units and posts were already being created. An appeal to the USSR and RSFSR presidents from the Supreme Soviet and Council of Ministers of North Ossetia to take immediate steps to protect the population of North Ossetia was published in the North Ossetian press on October 10, TASS reported the same day. The appeal said it had been learned that on

THE USSR IN OCTOBER, 1991

October 12 the Ingush population would embark on acts of disobedience in order to further their claims to North Ossetian territory.

On October 16, Novosti reported that a decision had been taken to proclaim a Northern Ingush Republic, with the part of Vladikavkaz located on the right bank of the Terek River as its capital. Vladikavkaz is the capital of North Ossetia. The decision was announced by the chairman of the "Executive Committee of Ingushetia," Issa Kodzoev, who said the republic would be part of the RSFSR. An unofficial poll of Ingush living in the Prigorodnyi Raion of North Ossetia and on the right bank in Vladikavkaz was being conducted.

Belorussian Supreme Soviet Fails to Lift Ban on Party

The Communist-dominated Belorussian Supreme Soviet, meeting in a special session on October 2, defeated a proposal to lift the temporary ban on Communist Party activity. According to a report on October 3 by RFE/RL Minsk correspondent Syarhei Navumchyk, the reprieve was sought in order to allow the Communist Party of Belorussia to hold a congress at the end of the year to decide the Party's fate. Opposition deputies failed, however, to muster approval for a proposal for the Supreme Soviet to dissolve the Party and take control of its property.

Thursday, October 3

Fil'shin Becomes RSFSR Minister for Foreign Economic Relations

Interfax reported that Gennadii Fil'shin had been promoted to minister for foreign economic relations of the RSFSR. Fil'shin was already well known in the West as a fairly progressive, market-oriented economist. Fil'shin was implicated to some extent in the great "ruble scam" and was, as a result, removed from the post of RSFSR first deputy prime minister. After that he served as deputy minister for foreign economic relations. In his new post Fil'shin replaced Viktor Yaroshenko.

Obstruction of Work of RSFSR Constitutional Commission

Oleg Rumyantsev, secretary of the RSFSR Constitutional Commission, told journalists that three groups of RSFSR deputies—Communists of Russia, those representing the autonomous territories, and deputies who resented the fact that they had had no part in drawing up the new RSFSR Constitution—were blocking the work of the commission, TASS reported. Rumyantsev said that, if they continued to try to prevent the draft from being presented to parliament, RSFSR President El'tsin would exercise his right to submit it to a referendum, bypassing the Russian parliament.

Khasbulatov Defends El'tsin, Attacks Aides

At a press conference, Ruslan Khasbulatov, Acting chairman of the RSFSR Supreme Soviet, maintained that El'tsin was being unfairly attacked for the imperfect nature of some of the decrees he had adopted, TASS reported. Khasbulatov said the blame lay with State Secretary Gennadii Burbulis and RSFSR State Adviser for Legal Questions Sergei Shakhrai, and he argued that they should take responsibility for their actions and even resign. Khasbulatov reiterated that all the autonomous republics "will exist only as part of Russia." Khasbulatov expressed concern at the "Balkanization" of Russia, particularly of the Northern Caucasus.

Replying to Khasbulatov's criticism on October 6, Shakhrai acknowledged on Central Television that the decrees issued by El'tsin during the coup were faulty but maintained that El'tsin had not consulted him about them. Shakhrai stated that Khasbulatov's accusations were the result of nervous strain.

Stalemate in Karelia

An extraordinary session of the Karelian parliament, called to discuss the wait-and-see attitude of the local leadership during the abortive coup, adjourned without even discussing the matter, "Vesti" and TASS reported on October 2 and 3 respectively. A vote of no confidence in the Presidium of the republican Supreme Soviet had been demanded by the city soviets of Petrozavodsk and Kostomushka, but deputies refused to include the item on the agenda. In reply, eighteen deputies blocked the work of the session by refusing to vote on all other matters.

Tuva Changes Name, Will Elect President

The republican Supreme Soviet decided that the former Tuvinian ASSR would in future be called the Republic of Tuva. The republic would also shortly elect its own president (*Radio Moscow*, October 3).

Uzbekistan Prohibits Export of Cotton to Russia

An Interfax report quoted on "Vesti" stated that the Uzbek cotton-production authority had prohibited the shipping of cotton to the RSFSR.

Morozov Says Ukraine Should Have Black Sea Fleet

Ukraine's recently appointed minister of defense, Konstantin Morozov, told the newspaper *Narodnaya armiya* that Ukraine needed its own army and should

The USSR in October, 1991

take command of the Black Sea Fleet. Quoting from Morozov's interview, TASS said that a defense council and general staff were being formed that would oversee the transformation of Ukraine-based Soviet military units into a Ukrainian military force. Morozov also revealed that Ukrainian military academies would probably be set up in the near future.

Kravchuk Meets with Mitterrand

Returning to Kiev from his visit to North America, Ukrainian Supreme Soviet Chairman Leonid Kravchuk stopped over in Paris for a meeting with French President, François Mitterrand. Speaking afterwards to reporters, Kravchuk said Mitterrand had listened "very carefully" to his analysis of the situation in the USSR and Ukraine. Kravchuk told Mitterrand that Ukraine would not take part in any political union with Moscow and would restrict ties with other republics to the economic and collective security fields. Kravchuk said he opposed the transfer of nuclear arms from one country to another except for the purposes of destroying them.

Ukrainians in Moldavia Decry Russification

A delegation of Ukrainians from Moldavia's Dniester area brought to Kiev an appeal rejecting the label "Russian-speaking people" and complaining of the lack of Ukrainian schools and other cultural facilities in the area, Radio Kiev reported. The appeal said Ukrainians in the Dniester lived on friendly terms with the Moldavians. The appeal appeared to have been prompted by the fact that the Russian Communist authorities dominant on the left bank of the Dniester had blocked the introduction there of Kishinev's recent measures promoting the establishment of Ukrainian schools and cultural facilities.

Latvia Ends Participation in Union Bodies

Latvia's Supreme Council voted to end all participation in parliamentary bodies in the USSR, TASS reported from Riga. The decision withdrew all deputies from the USSR Supreme Soviet, Congress of People's Deputies, and other bodies. Following Latvia's declaration of independence, the deputies to these bodies had changed their status to that of observers. TASS quoted the Supreme Council's resolution as stating that the Latvian Foreign Ministry was thenceforth to be the sole agency representing Latvia in the USSR.

Yakovlev Says Another Coup Possible

Aleksandr Yakovlev, presidential adviser to Gorbachev, told the inaugural meeting of the Foundation for

Sociopolitical Studies in Moscow that economic hardships might prompt another coup attempt in the USSR, AP reported on October 4. Yakovlev, the foundation's honorary chairman, said the USSR was moving towards democracy and freedom but was "also making zigzags along the way."

Friday, October 4

Gorbachev Forsakes Referendum on Private Land Ownership

Gorbachev told a meeting of farm managers and agricultural ministry officials that the idea—which he had previously supported—of holding a Union-wide referendum on the question of private land ownership had been overtaken by events, Interfax reported. Gorbachev said the question could be decided by individual republics.

US to Build New Embassy in Moscow

The US Congress voted to build a completely new US embassy building in Moscow at an estimated cost of 220 million dollars, Western news agencies reported. The Congress also decided that the existing, unfinished embassy building, which had been heavily bugged by the Soviet authorities, could be used to house other, less sensitive offices. The Congressional action resolved a controversy dating back to 1985, when the partially built, eight-story building that was to have served as a new US embassy was found to be riddled with eavesdropping devices.

US Releases 400 Million Dollars in Export Guarantees for USSR

The US Agriculture Department released the last installment, worth 400 million dollars, of the 1.5-billion dollars in credit guarantees authorized by President George Bush to finance Soviet imports of agricultural commodities at the approach of winter, AP and an RFE/RL Washington correspondent reported.

US Air Force Chief Sees No Threat in Republican Forces

US Air Force Chief of Staff General William McPeak told Soviet military officials in Moscow that the United States would not worry if individual republics set up their own military forces, as long as nuclear weapons remained under central control, AP reported.

Rutskoi for Future USSR Membership in NATO

RSFSR Vice President Aleksandr Rutskoi suggested, after meeting with a NATO delegation in Moscow, that the USSR could be a member of a future "united armies of

THE USSR IN OCTOBER, 1991

NATO," AP reported. Such an expanded alliance could police various conflicts, he said.

Max Kampelman, the chief US delegate to the post-Helsinki conference in Moscow on the human dimension, told the conference's closing meeting that the United States was concerned about "excesses of violence and repression" in Georgia and had discussed the matter with other conference delegations including the USSR's, AFP reported. Kampelman added that the objections of the United States to Georgia's request to attend the conference as an observer were based on the view that Georgia had not yet committed itself to the human-rights provisions of the Helsinki accords.

United States Criticizes Georgia

TASS said that four people had been killed and several wounded on October 3 in fighting in an area adjacent to Nagorno-Karabakh. It added that the population of Nagorno-Karabakh was experiencing severe shortages of bread after supply lines to it had been cut. These actions threw into question the efficacy of the September 21 agreement between Azerbaijan and Armenia, brokered by RSFSR President Boris El'tsin and Kazakh President Nursultan Nazarbaev, to end the fighting.

In an open letter to El'tsin and Nazarbaev, made public by RFE/RL on October 4, Elena Bonner appealed to the two presidents to exercise the responsibility they had assumed and find a mechanism to ensure the implementation of the agreement on Nagorno-Karabakh. Bonner also called on them to go to South Ossetia to contribute to finding a settlement there. Bonner said that, in the ten days since the signing of the agreement on Nagorno-Karabakh, some 30 people had been killed, some 100 injured, several villages attacked, and more than 200 houses destroyed in the Armenian enclave. She also said residents feared renewed deportations.

Fresh Fighting around Nagorno-Karabakh

―――――――――――――――――― *Saturday, October 5*

On October 5, illegal armed formations (known as the National Guard) of the Executive Committee of the All-National Congress of the Chechen People (OKChN) seized the KGB building in Groznyi, *Izvestia* reported on October 7. The next day, a delegation consisting of RSFSR Vice President Aleksandr Rutskoi, RSFSR Minister of Internal Affairs Andrei Dunaev, and RSFSR KGB Chair-

Crisis in Checheno-Ingushetia

man Viktor Ivanenko held talks with the chairman of the OKChN Executive Committee, retired General Dzhakhar Dudaev. Rutskoi said he feared that a second Nagorno-Karabakh could develop in Checheno-Ingushetia. He reminded Dudaev that there were laws forbidding the storming of buildings and told him to stop politicizing the people, TASS reported on October 6.

On October 7, the Provisional Supreme Council of Checheno-Ingushetia handed Rutskoi an appeal to the RSFSR Supreme Soviet, Radio Mayak reported. (The Provisional Supreme Council was set up by the republican Supreme Soviet after the latter yielded to pressure from the OKChN and dissolved itself until new elections.) In its appeal, the Provisional Supreme Council complained that the OKChN Executive Committee was usurping its powers and asked to be recognized as the only legislative body in the republic.

On October 8, after hearing a report from Rutskoi on his visit, the Presidium of the RSFSR Supreme Soviet adopted a resolution on the situation in Checheno-Ingushetia, TASS reported. The resolution condemned the activities of unofficial armed formations; censured the OKChN Executive Committee for appropriating the powers of the organs of authority, stating that the only organ of legal state power in the republic was the Provisional Supreme Council; and ordered the armed formations to hand over their weapons by midnight on October 10.

Reacting sharply to the resolution, the OKChN Executive Committee on October 9 called for a general mobilization of the male population between the ages of fifteen and fifty-five, TASS reported. It also called for the National Guard to be in a state of combat-readiness. Interfax said Dudaev described the RSFSR Supreme Soviet Presidium resolution as "a virtual declaration of war on our republic."

The situation in Checheno-Ingushetia deteriorated further on October 10, according to various reports in the Soviet media. The Council of Ministers building in Groznyi was seized by the National Guard. Two hundred detainees in the local prison rioted, demanding to be released so as to enroll in the National Guard. Thirty escaped. Two of the escapees were shot, one fatally. A unit of MVD troops sent to strengthen the prison guard was turned back by a crowd. The republican prosecutor was arrested. Members of the Provisional Supreme Council either went into hiding in Groznyi or left the city. Meetings of supporters and opponents of the OKChN Executive Committee were held in adjacent squares in Groznyi on October 10 and 11, TASS reported.

Meanwhile, the crisis in Checheno-Ingushetia was discussed by a full session of the RSFSR Supreme Soviet.

The USSR in October, 1991

Rutskoi asked for special powers to deal with the situation. He said he had tried several times to discuss the matter with RSFSR President Boris El'tsin by telephone but had been unable to get through. The Russian parliament approved a resolution requesting that the Russian president and government take immediate steps to restore order. A delegation of RSFSR deputies headed by RSFSR Prosecutor-General Valentin Stepankov was dispatched to the republic.

In an interview on Central Television on October 10, Rutskoi said that Dudaev was being told that no action would be taken against him and that he could participate in the forthcoming elections if the National Guard handed in their weapons to the republican MVD. Rutskoi maintained that in the auls and in Groznyi itself armed formations were being organized that intended to act against Dudaev. Rutskoi further accused Dudaev of provoking hostility between the Chechen and Ingush peoples.

The same day, Acting Chairman of the RSFSR Supreme Soviet Ruslan Khasbulatov said on Russian Television that "literally thousands" of telegrams were being received appealing for order to be restored in the republic, if necessary with the use of force. Khasbulatov claimed that Dudaev "represents virtually no one apart from perhaps 200–300 desperate young men armed to the teeth."

As a result of negotiations with an RSFSR Supreme Soviet delegation, the All-National Congress of the Chechen People (OKChN) handed over to the MVD the Council of Ministers building and the television and radio studios, which had been occupied by units of the Chechen National Guard, Russian Television reported on October 14. Radio Moscow reported, however, that a thirteen-point agreement with the Executive Committee of the OKChN, which would include the disbandment of the National Guard, had been stalled because the RSFSR delegation would not recognize the authority of the Executive Committee, insisting that the Provisional Supreme Council of Checheno-Ingushetia—whose members were in hiding—was the sole legitimate power structure.

Dudaev told TASS on October 15 that the Executive Committee of the OKChN did not want to take over legislative or executive power but that events of the past few days had forced it to assume full responsibility for the situation. He said blame for the sharp deterioration in the situation lay with the leadership of the RSFSR, which had been meddling unceremoniously. Dudaev said that the Provisional Supreme Council, which the RSFSR was trying to present as the only legitimate organ of power, was operating virtually underground and that its orders appeared only in newspapers in Russian areas of the republic. He said reports that the Executive Committee had passed death sentences on Khasbulatov and Rutskoi and was preparing to attack North Ossetia were provocations.

In an interview with TASS on October 16, RSFSR Deputy Minister of Internal Affairs Anatolii Anikeev, who was in Groznyi, said that the situation in the republic was getting worse rather than better: members of the National Guard were still blockading the television and radio studios and a number of public buildings; supporters of the Executive Committee were continuing to hold meetings in the center of Groznyi; and the Executive Committee of the OKChN was refusing to disband the National and Home Guards. Vakha Ibragimov, the acting minister of internal affairs appointed by the Russian MVD, met with Dudaev. The Executive Committee did not recognize his status, but Anikeev said there was hope that these two people, the only ones with real power in the republic, might reach a compromise.

On October 15, Dudaev called on the population of Checheno-Ingushetia to prepare for war, Radio Rossii and Interfax reported on October 16. Speaking on local radio and television, Dudaev said there were troops, particularly in Dagestan and North Ossetia, who were ready to attack the republic. Dudaev said 62,000 people had joined the National and Home Guards.

On October 17, TASS reported that the situation in Checheno-Ingushetia was deteriorating by the hour. Preparations for the elections of the president and parliament, fixed by the rebel OKChN Executive Committee for October 27, were going ahead, but no one knew whether they would take place. Support among the population was divided between the Executive Committee and the constitutional authorities. The RSFSR parliamentary delegation headed by the prosecutor-general, Valentin Stepankov, addressed an appeal to the RSFSR president and Supreme Soviet in which it described the situation as "explosive."

On October 19, TASS reported that El'tsin had sent a message to the leaders of the Executive Committee of the OKChN demanding a halt to its illegal actions and asking that occupied buildings be freed, arms surrendered, and illegal armed groups dissolved. He also proposed elections to the Chechen-Ingush Supreme Soviet and a referendum on the region's state structure for November 17. El'tsin warned that, if his demands were not met within three days, the RSFSR would take measures to normalize the situation. The deputy chairman of the

The USSR in October, 1991

OKChN, Khusain Akhmadov, then appeared on local television in Groznyi to denounce El'tsin's message and earlier actions by the RSFSR leadership as "the last gasp of the Russian Empire" and as an attempt to crush democratic forces in the Chechen republic.

On October 21, TASS quoted a *Pravda* interview with Dudaev, who claimed that his organization was trying to normalize the situation in the republic. He said that representatives of the OKChN were in Moscow attempting to get the prosecutor-general to take action against Russian radio and television for spreading disinformation about the situation in Checheno-Ingushetia.

On October 22, rebellious Chechens rejected El'tsin's demand that they surrender their arms. A TASS report quoted a Chechen leader, Iles Arsanukaev, as calling El'tsin's demand an ultimatum and saying it was illegal.

On October 24, TASS reported that the RSFSR Supreme Soviet had declared elections scheduled for October 27 in Checheno-Ingushetia to be illegal and ordered the Provisional Supreme Soviet of the republic to ensure that future elections were conducted with proper legal guarantees. The same day, El'tsin named a personal representative to the Chechen-Ingush Republic. Although tensions were running high between proponents and opponents of elections in the republic, the chairman of the Defense Committee of the OKChN said that arms would be used only in the case of outside intervention and reiterated that El'tsin's demand that firearms be surrendered would be ignored.

The elections scheduled for October 27 went ahead as planned and Dudaev was declared the first president of the Chechen republic, "TSN" and TASS reported on October 28. *Izvestia* suggested that the results were invalid because special electoral commissions had not been set up in the raions, but the Executive Committee declared that they were valid regardless of how many people took part in the vote. Dudaev told TASS that the election of the president and a new parliament marked a qualitatively new stage in the life of the Chechen people. At the same time, he expected "political and economic blockades and provocations."

Organizers of the elections in Checheno-Ingushetia told TASS on October 30 that Dudaev had received 85 percent of the votes cast. It was claimed that 490,000 of the 640,000 ethnic Chechens eligible to vote had taken part in the elections. The Chechen Congress said it would not disband its National Guard, because of unconfirmed reports that the opposition was arming. In the meantime, Radio Moscow quoted the Provisional Supreme Council of the Chechen-Ingush republic as stating that the majority of voters had boycotted the elections and that therefore no decrees of the president or parliament of the Chechen republic should be obeyed.

Dudaev said at a press conference in Groznyi on October 28 that in foreign policy he favored equality and mutually beneficial collaboration with all republics and states, including the RSFSR, while in domestic policy he gave priority to civil peace, harmony, and the prosperity of people of all nations, TASS reported. Dudaev said he was a convinced supporter of a single and indivisible Checheno-Ingushetia and was sure the Ingush, "our blood brothers," who boycotted the elections, would agree. Earlier, Dudaev had appeared to sympathize with the desire of the Ingush to set up their own republic.

At the RSFSR Congress of People's Deputies on October 29, Khasbulatov said that only about 200,000 people had participated in the election of the president of the self-styled Chechen republic, TASS reported that day. Khasbulatov added that, in his view, this conflicted with the norms of democracy. At the time of the 1989 census, the population of Checheno-Ingushetia was 1,338,000, of whom 735,000 were Chechens. El'tsin's representative in Checheno-Ingushetia, Akhmed Arsanov, said that the elections had taken place "under the barrels of the machine guns" of the local National Guard.

At a press conference in the Kremlin on October 29, Khasbulatov accused the press of inflaming national enmities with its primitive and unskilled reporting on events in areas of tension. He said that the "criminal" regime of Dudaev in Checheno-Ingushetia had been encouraged by the perhaps involuntary support of the printed and electronic media.

Also on October 29, Russian Television's "Vesti" reported that an organizational committee to create a Party of the Independence of the Caucasus had been set up in Groznyi. "TV Inform" claimed, however, that Dudaev was already facing problems in his attempt to unite the peoples of the Caucasus. Not only did the Ingush want to remain part of the RSFSR but so did some of the Chechens.

Gorbachev Announces Nuclear Arms Cuts

In a televised speech reported by TASS and Western agencies, Soviet President Mikhail Gorbachev matched most of the nuclear arms initiatives announced earlier by US President George Bush and added some additional measures of his own. He declared that the USSR would cut its strategic nuclear arsenal to 5,000 warheads, or 1,000 fewer than the 6,000 allowed under the recently signed Strategic Arms Reduction Treaty, and announced a unilat-

The USSR in October, 1991

eral one-year moratorium on nuclear testing. In a major reversal in Soviet policy, Gorbachev said the USSR was willing to discuss US proposals on antimissile defenses and proposed a joint land- and space-based system to warn of nuclear missile attack. He also called on all the nuclear powers to renounce first use of nuclear weapons. Gorbachev confirmed that a further 700,000 personnel would be cut from the Soviet Armed Forces. (The previous week, USSR Defense Minister Marshal Evgenii Shaposhnikov had said that the armed forces would be reduced from 3.7 million to 3 million.) Gorbachev also suggested that the Strategic Rocket Forces, the Air Forces, and the Air Defense Forces be combined into one new military service.

Radio Rossii reported that RSFSR President Boris El'tsin had issued a new decree on measures for ensuring the state security of the RSFSR. The decree stated that the Russian KGB was the legal successor to the USSR KGB on the territory of the RSFSR and proposed that talks be held with the Union republics on the creation of a coordinating agency in the sphere of state security.

El'tsin Issues Decree on State Security

After some initial delay and confusion, documents certifying associate member status of the International Monetary Fund for the USSR were exchanged between Soviet President Mikhail Gorbachev and IMF Managing Director Michel Camdessus, Western and Soviet agencies reported. The agreement took effect immediately, and a team of IMF specialists was due to arrive in Moscow on October 7. Associate status involved three main elements: IMF review of the economy; Soviet compliance with IMF plans for economic reform; and technical assistance from the IMF.

USSR Granted Associate Membership in IMF

Customs officials in St. Petersburg were reported to have impounded European Community food aid to the value of 250 million ecus (about 300 million dollars) and to have demanded duty in hard currency before they would allow the food to be distributed (*The Independent*, October 5). About one-third of the food "disappeared" and was presumed to have been siphoned off to the black market.

Food Aid Impounded

During a visit to Syria, Patriarch of Moscow and All Russia Aleksii II met with Syrian President Hafiz al-Assad, TASS reported. He had earlier met with the head of Al-Azhar

Patriarch Aleksii in Syria

University in Cairo. The patriarch described his trip to the Middle East as cementing Orthodox unity in the region and initiating brotherly contacts with other Christian confessions and also with Muslim leaders.

Baltic States Demand Withdrawal of Soviet Troops

The Baltic Council adopted a joint statement in Vilnius demanding that the withdrawal of Soviet troops from the three Baltic States start immediately and that the troops be removed from the Baltic capitals by December 1, Baltfax and Western agencies reported.

On October 6, Lithuanian Radio reported an exchange of telegrams between Soviet Defense Minister Evgenii Shaposhnikov and the Lithuanian leader, Vytautas Landsbergis. In reply to a request from Shaposhnikov for a meeting with a Lithuanian delegation on October 8, Landsbergis said that all USSR troops must leave Lithuania by the end of 1991 and that other military issues should not even be discussed. Landsbergis complained that an assembly of Soviet officers stationed in Vilnius had informed the Lithuanian government they would not obey any order to withdraw without social guarantees.

The commander of the Baltic Military District, Lieutenant General Valerii Mironov, told TASS on October 7 that Baltic demands for Soviet troops to leave the three Baltic capitals by December 1 were unrealistic and must be negotiated.

On October 8, while on a visit to Britain, Landsbergis issued a new call for a swift withdrawal of Soviet forces from Lithuania, according to Western agency reports. He claimed there was a danger of another coup in Moscow and that it was imperative that the Soviet army leave Lithuania completely before it occurred. Landsbergis expressed concern that the USSR might be trying to legalize the presence of its troops in Lithuania and to alter the US-Soviet treaty on intermediate nuclear forces so as to make Lithuania a country where Soviet nuclear weapons could continue to be deployed. He said that British Prime Minister John Major supported his position and would press the Soviet Union on the issue.

At a meeting in Moscow between Shaposhnikov and Latvian Permanent Representative Janis Peters on October 9, it was agreed that the Baltic Military District headquarters would be withdrawn from Riga in early 1992.

USSR Foreign Ministry spokesman Vitalii Churkin said on October 10 that withdrawing Soviet forces from Eastern Europe was straining USSR resources, and he

The USSR in October, 1991

asked the Baltic leaders to be patient, Radio Moscow reported.

Latvian delegate Ojars Kalnins told the UN General Assembly the same day that the revival of the Latvian economy depended on the earliest possible withdrawal of Soviet troops from Latvia, an RFE/RL correspondent in New York reported. Kalnins added that a fair settlement of the USSR troops issue was critically important for advancing long-term security and cooperation in the region.

Ernst Jaakson, Estonian ambassador to the United Nations, told the UN General Assembly the same day that the presence of Soviet nuclear weapons and large contingents of "Soviet occupation forces" on its soil threatened the sovereignty of Estonia. Jaakson noted that, while Estonia understood that some time must be allowed for the removal of the Soviet troops, it should begin sooner than 1994—the date the Soviet Union had set.

Sunday, October 6

"Pamyat'" Bard Assassinated

The prominent pop singer Igor' Tal'kov was shot dead during a concert in St. Petersburg, the television news shows "Vesti" and "TSN" reported. Tal'kov's killer escaped, but "Vesti" said his identity was known to the police, adding that the killing could have been politically motivated. Tal'kov was well known for his controversial political views and had performed at meetings of the anti-Semitic "Pamyat'" Society. "Pamyat'" leader Dmitrii Vasil'ev counted the singer among "Pamyat's'" most ardent supporters.

Gorbachev and Kravchuk Denounce Anti-Semitism

A statement by Soviet President Mikhail Gorbachev condemning anti-Semitism was read by his representative, Aleksandr Yakovlev, at a ceremony commemorating the 120,000 Jews killed by the Nazis at Babii Yar during World War II, Western agencies reported. Gorbachev said that anti-Semitism had been used by "the Stalinist bureaucracy" to isolate the country from the outside world. He added that anti-Semitism existed in the USSR today and that it was being used by certain reactionary forces opposed to reforms. Gorbachev had previously been reluctant to denounce anti-Semitism, apparently for fear of upsetting Party conservatives.

Speaking earlier at the Babii Yar ceremonies, Chairman of the Ukrainian Supreme Soviet Leonid Kravchuk acknowledged that part of the blame for the tragedy lay with those in Ukraine who had failed to prevent the Nazis from carrying out the massacre. He vowed that such an atrocity would never happen again, the Western media reported.

Excerpts from Interrogations of Coup Leaders Published in *Der Spiegel*

The German news magazine *Der Spiegel* (No. 41) published excerpts from a video recording of the first interrogations of three of the leaders of the August coup. The excerpts included former Defense Minister Dmitrii Yazov calling himself a fool and appealing to Gorbachev not to put him on trial before a military court but simply to let him retire. Valentin Pavlov said he was completely drunk when the coup started. Former KGB Chairman Vladimir Kryuchkov insisted that he had counted on Gorbachev's eventually joining the coup and that "physically liquidating" the Soviet leader had never been considered. Yazov told an interrogator that one reason for the coup had been Gorbachev's break with the Kremlin tradition of collective leadership. He said Gorbachev had often failed to give an account of his foreign trips, which had aroused fears among the rest of the leadership that he was selling out to the United States. Yazov claimed that Kryuchkov had initiated the plot.

On October 10, TASS and Radio Mayak reported that Gorbachev had asked the USSR and RSFSR Prosecutor's Offices to conduct an immediate investigation into how the video tapes had reached *Der Spiegel.*

On October 17, V. Demin, an MVD official wrote in *Pravda* that the publication of the interrogation records of the leaders of the coup in *Der Spiegel* reflected the low level of the investigation but did not represent an attempt by political forces to influence the outcome of the legal proceedings. In contrast with *Pravda, Nezavisimaya gazeta* asserted on October 16 that the leaks were intended as a warning to those in charge of the investigation that more compromising material could be published on those participants in the coup whose role was played down. Meanwhile, KGB Chairman Vadim Bakatin said he had been assured that the records had been sold for profit, "TV Inform" reported on October 15.

Raisa Recalls Events in Crimea

Raisa Gorbacheva said during an interview on Central Television that the Gorbachev family and others who were detained with them in the Crimea from August 18 to 22 had discussed the possibility of escaping but in the end had rejected this option because of concern for

Gorbachev's safety. She remarked that she felt bitter when Soviet journalists portrayed the coup as a farce, because for her family it had been a tragedy. Raisa also revealed that the atmosphere in the Gorbachev home had become much gloomier since the coup.

Another CPSU Treasurer Jumps out of a Window

Georgii Pavlov, the eighty-one-year-old former administrator of affairs of the CPSU Central Committee, committed suicide by jumping from a window of his seventh-floor apartment, Soviet radio and television newscasts reported on October 8. The post that Pavlov held from 1965 to 1983 was believed to make its holder the only person who knew the whole truth about Party finances. Pavlov's successor in this post, Nikolai Kruchina, also reportedly threw himself from a window a few days after the decision was made to expropriate CPSU property. In *Literaturnaya gazeta* (No. 35), the widely respected legal columnist Arkadii Vaksberg, commenting on suspicious events following Kruchina's death, said the possibility could not be ruled out that somebody "wanted to eliminate those who knew too much."

Monday, October 7

EC Aid Package Approved

European Community finance ministers tentatively approved a 1.5-billion-dollar food and medical aid package for the USSR, Western agencies reported. The new credit was understood to be in addition to the 610 million dollars in credit guarantees and 300 million dollars in food donations approved by the EC in December, 1990. The ministers approved the sum on condition that similar amounts were forthcoming from the United States and Canada together and from Japan. Dutch Finance Minister Wim Kok said the credit facility was a contingency program and would be "put into practice when we are sure what the needs are."

Joint Military Structures in Europe Proposed

Representatives of the Russian State Committee for Defense suggested at an international conference of US and Soviet defense experts in Washington that the United States and the Soviet Union create joint military structures for security in Europe, according to an RFE/RL report from Washington on October 8. RSFSR President Boris El'tsin's military adviser, General Konstantin Kobets, said that "a single system unit for collective security" was needed.

THE USSR IN OCTOBER, 1991

New Administration Created in Russian KGB

"Vesti" interviewed Colonel Sergei Almazov, chief of the Russian KGB's newly created Administration for Fighting Organized Crime, who said that his main task would be to combat corruption at the government level. Almazov also stressed the need to fight economic crime. He said his administration would keep a close watch on cooperatives and joint ventures.

Soviet Merchant Ships Barred from Suez Canal

The Suez Canal authorities and maritime sources reported that twenty-four Soviet merchant ships were stranded at both ends of the canal because they could not pay the transit tolls in advance, Western agencies reported. The Aswan Maritime Agency, which handles Soviet vessels, said it had not received the dollar transfers from Moscow needed to pay the estimated 1 million dollars in transit tolls.

CPSU CC Resolution on Destruction of Archives

The RSFSR television news program "Vesti" reported that it had obtained a copy of instructions sent to the city of Ul'yanovsk showing that even before the attempted coup in August the CPSU Central Committee had issued a resolution addressed to all Party archives instructing them to destroy documents concerning the activities of Party officials. The instruction to the Ul'yanovsk Party archive was to destroy 300,000 of its 500,000 documents by September 1, 1991.

Ukraine Plans to Create Army of 450,000

The Presidium of Ukraine's Cabinet of Ministers approved a package of draft laws concerning the creation of a Ukrainian National Guard and army, Radio Kiev reported. The draft laws foresaw Ukraine's transformation into a neutral state and a nuclear-free zone in accordance with the principles enshrined in the republic's Declaration of State Sovereignty. It was envisaged that the size of the new Ukrainian army would not exceed 450,000 and that its role would be purely defensive. The activities of political parties and movements in the armed forces would be forbidden, and the language of the armed forces would be Ukrainian.

Lithuania Joins UNESCO and ILO

While visiting London, President of the Lithuanian Supreme Council Vytautas Landsbergis signed the UNESCO Constitution, Western agencies reported. Lithuania thus became UNESCO's 160th member. (Estonia and Latvia joined UNESCO on October 14.) On October 8, Lithuania became the 150th member of the International Labor Organization, TASS reported.

THE USSR IN OCTOBER, 1991

Japan Renews Diplomatic Relations with Baltic States

Lithuania and Japan formally reestablished diplomatic relations, Radio Riga and TASS reported. Notes to that effect were exchanged between Lithuanian Foreign Minister Algirdas Saudargas and Japanese Deputy Foreign Minister Muneo Suzuki during the latter's visit to Vilnius. According to a Kyodo dispatch of October 9, Japan reestablished diplomatic relations with Estonia when Suzuki visited Tallinn.

France Donates Building to House Baltic Embassies

Western agencies reported that, as a gesture of friendship, the French government had donated a building on Boulevard Montmartre in Paris to house the embassies of Estonia, Latvia, and Lithuania. The previous week, the Baltic States had asked a French court to expel Soviet diplomats from the embassies in Paris owned by the Baltic States prior to World War II; the court rejected the request, stating that no action could be taken, because the USSR enjoyed diplomatic immunity.

―――――――――――――――――――――――――――― *Tuesday, October 8*

Burbulis on Russia as Legal Heir of the USSR

RSFSR State Secretary Gennadii Burbulis told Interfax after returning from talks with RSFSR President Boris El'tsin in Sochi that El'tsin had reacted "normally" to his proposal to declare Russia the legal successor to the USSR. Burbulis said that this move would formally abolish the center and break all ties with the other republics. Soviet President Mikhail Gorbachev, Burbulis added, had reacted with "extreme anxiety" to the proposal.

RSFSR Deputies Must Observe RSFSR Constitution

The RSFSR Supreme Soviet adopted a resolution stipulating that deputies representing the RSFSR in the USSR Supreme Soviet must be guided by the constitution and laws of the RSFSR, TASS reported. The resolution set out the basis on which the RSFSR delegation would decide how to vote in the Council of the Republics, where each republic had only one vote. The resolution also stipulated that decisions of the USSR Supreme Soviet not supported by the RSFSR delegation must be examined immediately by the RSFSR Supreme Soviet or its Presidium.

Gavrilov Resigns in Protest over Russian Squabbles

RSFSR Deputy Prime Minister Igor' Gavrilov sent a letter of resignation to RSFSR President Boris El'tsin, TASS reported on October 8. Gavrilov criticized members of the RSFSR leadership for wasting their energies fighting a weakened center, neglecting Russia's economic problems, alienating other republics, and fighting among themselves. RSFSR Vice President Aleksandr Rutskoi echoed Gavrilov's criticism and warned of anarchy. He rejected the Alma-Ata agreement on economic union, saying it would make Russia "a milk cow" of the other republics. Rutskoi told Radio Rossii the same day that, instead of a broad economic union, he favored a political union with few republics. Rutskoi also expressed a desire to become Russia's next prime minister.

Majority of Republics Agree on Single Army

The USSR Ministry of Defense held its second meeting with republican representatives on military reform and the military budget, the Soviet media reported. Of the twelve remaining republics, only Ukraine did not attend. It was agreed that nuclear weapons must remain centrally controlled. The RSFSR, Belorussia, Kazakhstan, and the four Central Asian republics supported retaining a single army, while representatives of Azerbaijan, Armenia, and Moldavia expressed unspecified reservations. Invitations were sent to the Baltic States to attend, but, when President of the Lithuanian Supreme Council Vytautas Landsbergis protested, USSR Defense Minister Evgenii Shaposhnikov apologized, saying that the invitations should not have been sent, Radio Vilnius reported on October 7.

Republics Support Disarmament Proposal

Gorbachev's spokesman Andrei Grachev and USSR Deputy Foreign Minister Aleksei Obukhov said at a press conference that the RSFSR, Ukraine, Kazakhstan, and Belorussia—the four republics where the bulk of the USSR's nuclear weapons were deployed—had been consulted on Gorbachev's latest disarmament proposal and had voiced their support, *The New York Times* and *The Washington Post* reported on October 9. Grachev and other Soviet officials at the press conference sought to dispel concern in the West that Gorbachev's authority to negotiate arms reductions was eroding.

Japanese Aid Package Announced

Japanese government spokesmen disclosed details of an aid package for the USSR valued at 2.5 billion dollars, Western agencies reported. The package was said to consist of 1.8 billion dollars in trade insurance, 500 million dollars in credits for the purchase and transportation of foodstuffs and medicines, and 200 million dollars in export-import bank credits. An unidentified Japanese

The USSR in October, 1991

Foreign Ministry spokesman emphasized that the aid package had nothing to do with the Soviet-Japanese territorial dispute, and he denied that the size and timing of the package were in any way influenced by pressure from Japan's Western allies. The aid was "intended to support democracy and economic change in the USSR," he explained.

Gerashchenko on Liquidity and Rescheduling

Before leaving Moscow for the IMF annual meeting in Bangkok, Chairman of the USSR State Bank Viktor Gerashchenko told a Western agency that the USSR's foreign-exchange reserves were nearly exhausted. He acknowledged that it would take time for the USSR to obtain full membership in the IMF and thus qualify for credits from that institution, but he denied that his country would seek easier repayment terms for its foreign debt (estimated at 68 billion dollars, including commercial arrears). Gerashchenko called for foreign assistance to make the ruble convertible. He criticized Western investors for their reluctance to commit funds to projects in the USSR and Western bankers for holding back credit lines during the recent upheavals.

Solzhenitsyn on Independence Referendum in Ukraine

Trud carried an appeal by Aleksandr Solzhenitsyn in connection with the referendum on independence in Ukraine scheduled for December 1. It was Solzhenitsyn's first statement in the press since the appearance of his brochure "How Are We to Organize Russia?" in September, 1990. Solzhenitsyn welcomed the achievement of independence by the Soviet republics, adding that he did not believe that a confederation would be viable. Solzhenitsyn said the referendum in Ukraine was to be welcomed if it was scrupulously fair. He repeated his earlier call for the opinion of the residents of each oblast to be taken into account separately.

Cossack Volunteer Units to Maintain Order in Rostov Oblast

TASS reported that the executive committee of the Rostov Oblast Soviet had decided to create volunteer Cossack units (*druzhiny*) to maintain public order in the Don villages and cities, TASS reported. The Cossacks would help to patrol the streets; maintain order on public transport and at mass events; assist in the fight against hooliganism, drunkenness, moonshine, and drug addiction; and help the Prosecutor's Office, the courts, and the tax inspectorate. The Cossacks had been agitating for some time to be given an official role in the maintenance of law and order.

The USSR in October, 1991

Ukrainian Parliament Passes Liberal Citizenship Law

After a two-week break, the Ukrainian Supreme Soviet resumed its work and passed, at its second reading, a liberal law on citizenship. According to a report from Kiev from the Ukrainian information agency Ukrinform and TASS, the Ukrainian citizenship law had generated considerable controversy, and a compromise had to be worked out that would permit dual citizenship on the basis of bilateral agreements with other states.

Ukraine Set on Radical Economic Reforms

The chairman of the Ukrainian parliament's Commission on Economic Reform, Volodymyr Pylypchuk, told Western agencies that Ukraine planned to introduce its own currency by the middle of 1992 and to embark on a course of radical economic reform. He said Ukraine would guard its economic independence and would refuse "to allow any central monopoly on foreign economic activity, a single central bank, or any control by the center over foreign credits." Pylypchuk added, however, that, because of the poor harvest and the fragility of Ukraine's economy, strict "antimarket" measures—including tight limits on exports and a coupon system—would have to remain in force until the spring.

MVD Troop Withdrawal from Latvia and Lithuania

Quoting Latvian Minister of Internal Affairs Aloizs Vaznis, the Baltic News Agency reported that Soviet MVD troops were starting to withdraw from Latvia. Western news agencies reported on October 9 that Lithuania and the USSR had agreed that MVD forces would start to leave that country in March, 1992. About 10,000 MVD troops were stationed in the Lithuanian cities of Vilnius, Kaunas, Siaulai, and Snieckus. Lithuanians wanted them to complete the withdrawal in two years, but the Soviet authorities estimated that five years were needed.

Wednesday, October 9

Gorbachev Makes Formal Aid Request

Soviet President Mikhail Gorbachev met with US Secretary of Agriculture Edward Madigan and made a specific request for US assistance, Western agencies reported. Madigan declined to disclose details of the request, saying only that it included an element of humanitarian aid. Gorbachev was said to be enthusiastic about proposals to send US farm and food-processing experts to advise their Soviet counterparts and to set up "a model American farm." Madigan indicated that the United States planned to funnel most of its assistance through Gorbachev and

The USSR in October, 1991

the central government—apparently in an attempt to avoid the political and logistical headaches that might be encountered if aid were parceled out to republics.

Food Supply Agreement

The Committee for the Operational Management of the USSR Economy approved and sent to the State Council a draft agreement on the food supply, TASS reported. Grain procurements had so far reached only 54 million tons—the lowest level in half a century—and bread rationing had been introduced in sixteen territories. The draft envisaged a sharp contraction of the all-Union grain reserve. In future, this would provide only for the armed forces, labor colonies, prisons, and the inhabitants of Moscow. The draft allocated 10.4 billion dollars for imported foodstuffs—including 4.7 million tons of grain—although, in the opinion of specialists, 14.7 billion dollars would be needed to maintain the food supply at the 1990 level.

Saudi Humanitarian Aid Package

The Saudi Arabian ambassador to Washington told *The New York Times* that his country had agreed to send 1 billion dollars in emergency humanitarian aid to the Soviet Union during the fall. This was in addition to the 1.5 billion dollars in credits and aid pledged in the summer.

Saudi Arabia and Egypt to Send Imams to Muslim Republics

The New York Times said Saudi Arabia was working with Egypt on a plan to send Islamic preachers and scholars to the Muslim republics of the Soviet Union. The aim of the project was to head off Islamic fundamentalism and "revolutionary themes" coming out of Iran.

Tajik Employment Fund Established

A TadzhikTA-TASS item reported the creation of a state fund to promote full employment in Tajikistan. The republican Cabinet of Ministers ordered all employers, whether state or private, to contribute to the fund, which would also receive 4 percent of the republican budget. The fund was intended to help lessen the shock of the transition to a market economy in Tajikistan, where the unemployment rate was already one of the highest in the Soviet Union, by providing money for unemployment benefits, job creation, and development of the social infrastructure.

New Party in Kazakhstan

Radio Mayak reported that a new party, the Popular Congress of Kazakhstan, had held its founding congress in Alma-Ata. The objective of the new group was apparently to unite progressives, who had been scattered among a number of movements and groups. According to Radio Mayak, representatives of the antinuclear movement Nevada-Semipalatinsk, the Kazakh "Azat" Party (the largest non-Communist political party), the Russian "Edinstvo" group, the Kazakh Language Society, and others attended the congress, which elected Nevada-Semipalatinsk Chairman (and Writers' Union head) Olzhas Suleimenov and poet and political activist Mukhtar Shakhanov cochairmen of the new party. Kazakh President Nursultan Nazarbaev gave the new party his blessing.

USSR Reestablishes Diplomatic Relations with Lithuania, Latvia, and Estonia

USSR Foreign Minister Boris Pankin exchanged notes in Moscow with the foreign ministers of Lithuania and Estonia on the reestablishment of diplomatic relations at the ambassadorial level, Western agencies reported. Diplomatic relations with Latvia were reestablished on October 15.

RSFSR Supreme Soviet Discusses Economic Treaty

Opposing views were expressed at a joint session of the RSFSR Supreme Soviet devoted to the treaty on an economic community, TASS reported. Economist Grigorii Yavlinsky, the treaty's author, defended it and argued that it would not re-create the central bodies of control, as some of its opponents maintained it would. Deputy Prime Minister and Economics Minister Evgenii Saburov refuted suggestions that he had not been empowered to sign the relevant documents, saying that El'tsin had given him his personal blessing. First Deputy Prime Minister Oleg Lobov disagreed with Yavlinsky and Saburov, maintaining that the treaty was unacceptable in that it would infringe on the economic and political sovereignty of the RSFSR.

El'tsin-Silaev Exchange

"Vesti" reported an unfriendly exchange of letters between RSFSR President Boris El'tsin and his former prime minister, Ivan Silaev. The latter had asked El'tsin to return all-Union enterprises to the jurisdiction of the center. El'tsin said the Committee for the Operational Management of the USSR Economy headed by Silaev was unconstitutional, while Silaev described El'tsin's reaction as "too emotional."

Saburov Resigns

TASS reported that RSFSR Economics Minister Evgenii Saburov had resigned, complaining of the RSFSR government's inability to stabilize the economy and ensure the transition to a market economy. RSFSR Vice

The USSR in October, 1991

President Aleksandr Rutskoi had accused Saburov of initialing the treaty on an economic community in Alma-Ata without a proper mandate from his government.

Interfax Distributes Latest Union Treaty Draft

Interfax distributed as an express information issue the latest draft of the Union treaty circulated by Soviet President Mikhail Gorbachev to the republics at the beginning of October. *Nezavisimaya gazeta* of October 12 pointed to three significant innovations in the draft. First, the new Union would be called a Union of Free Sovereign Republics; second, the draft dropped the reference to a federation; and third, the concept of exclusive powers for the Union was absent. See also *Izvestia*, November 25.

Thursday, October 10

Radio Rossii on Crisis in Democratic Movement

Radio Rossii reported that various democratic parties in the republic were in crisis. The radio quoted Moscow Mayor Gavriil Popov as saying that the democratic movement had split into a liberal wing, which supported the introduction of a market economy but gave little heed to the creation of a social security net, and a social democratic wing, which was concerned with the latter. Radio Rossii added that the parties also disagreed about the future of the USSR: the Democratic Party of Russia and the Christian Democrats supported the creation of a viable federation on the territory of the USSR, while the Republican Party of Russia advocated a complete dismantling of the empire.

Conflict between RSFSR Vice President and KGB Chairman

RSFSR Vice President Aleksandr Rutskoi denounced RSFSR KGB Chairman Viktor Ivanenko as "lazy and incompetent and a danger to the state." According to the *Los Angeles Times* of October 11, Rutskoi told the RSFSR Supreme Soviet that he would demand Ivanenko's resignation. The conflict emerged after the KGB chairman had opposed demands by Rutskoi and the Acting chairman of the RSFSR Supreme Soviet, Ruslan Khasbulatov, for forceful action to bring the situation in Checheno-Ingushetia under control. Ivanenko had suggested a dialogue with the self-proclaimed leaders of the rebellious autonomous republic instead of the use of force.

UAE Aid on the Way

An aircraft carrying food and medical aid left the United Arab Emirates for the Soviet Union, Western agencies reported. A second shipment was due to leave on October 11. The aid shipments were ordered by the UAE president to help the Soviet people overcome economic hardships and pressures caused by the abortive August coup. The Emirates News Agency said the aid was also aimed at helping the economic reform process in the USSR and to thank the Soviet Union for its stance during the Gulf war.

High Court Rules That Hasidic Books Must Be Returned

TASS reported that the Supreme Arbitration Court of the RSFSR had ruled that the famous Shneerson Collection of Hasidic books and manuscripts, at present housed in the Lenin Library, must be handed over within a month to the Moscow Hasidic community, which had demanded its return. Members of the community staged a sit-in at the library to press their demand. The general director of the Lenin Library, Anatolii Volik, described the court decision as "a new attack on the national heritage" and claimed that ten years would be necessary to determine which books were part of the collection.

Poland and Belorussia Sign Friendship Declaration

Poland and Belorussia confirmed that their common border, established in 1945, would remain unchanged, Western agencies reported. The agreement came in a friendship treaty signed in Warsaw by Polish Prime Minister Jan Krzysztof Bielecki and Belorussian Prime Minister Vyacheslau Kebich. A Belorussian consulate was to open in Warsaw at the end of the year.

Azerbaijan Votes to Confiscate Soviet Military Hardware

The Azerbaijani Supreme Soviet voted to "nationalize" all Soviet military equipment on its territory to equip a new republican army, Western news agencies reported that day. Radical deputies said they would organize road blocks to prevent the transfer of arms back to the RSFSR. The parliament also approved the recall of 140,000 Azerbaijani conscripts currently serving in the Soviet Armed Forces.

Appeal for Postponement of Armenian Presidential Election

Interfax reported that four Armenian presidential candidates had appealed to the Armenian parliament to postpone the election, scheduled for October 16, in order to give them additional time for campaigning and to appoint a new electoral commission. The Armenian Supreme Court had recently overruled a decision by the existing electoral commission to bar the candidacy of USSR people's deputy Zori Balayan, who responded by demanding the resignation of the electoral commission members responsible.

Iran to Open Consulate in Turkmenistan

Iranian Foreign Minister Ali Akbar Velayati announced that his country would open a consulate in Ashkhabad and that Turkmenistan would open a representation office in Teheran. Velayati, who spoke to foreign journalists after talks with Turkmen President Saparmurad Niyazov, said that discussions had also touched on the establishment of a cross-border rail service. Niyazov arrived in Iran with a sixty-five-member delegation earlier in the week. The trip was part of his effort to establish Turkmenistan as an entity in its own right in the world community (Western agencies, October 10).

Moldavia Concerned about Russia's Ambitions

Moldavian President Mircea Snegur told a press conference in Kishinev that Moldavia was "perplexed and worried" by the positions of some RSFSR leaders concerning Russia's relations with other republics, TASS reported. Snegur focused on demands by RSFSR Vice President Aleksandr Rutskoi and others that the negotiation of an economic community be linked to, and preceded by, the conclusion of a political union and on plans for the RSFSR to become the legal successor to the USSR. Snegur said such demands were "categorically unacceptable" and that "there can be no question of any political union" as far as Moldavia is concerned.

Friday, October 11

Meeting of State Council

A meeting of the State Council under the chairmanship of Soviet President Mikhail Gorbachev was attended by representatives of ten of the remaining twelve republics (the absentees were Moldavia and Georgia), the Soviet media reported. The ten republics agreed to sign the treaty on an economic community by October 15 and approved the draft agreement on the food supply for 1992. Other topics of discussion were the latest draft of the Union treaty, the KGB, and greater access to central television for the republics. The members of the State Council also expressed their support for the US and USSR initiatives in the sphere of nuclear disarmament.

State Council Discusses Union Treaty

The members of the State Council decided that the republics should send in their comments on the latest draft of the Union treaty within ten days, after which the heads of state would put the finishing touches to it, TASS reported. During the discussion of the draft the question arose of Ukraine's decision to take no part in the political life of the country until after the independence referendum on December 1. On Gorbachev's initiative it was decided to appeal to the Ukrainian parliament to take part in the preparation of the treaty. Similar appeals were to be addressed to the parliaments of Armenia, Georgia, and Moldavia.

KGB to Be Abolished

The State Council decided to abolish the KGB and replace it with a central intelligence service, an interrepublican counterintelligence service, and a state committee for protecting the state frontier under the joint command of the Border Troops.

RSFSR Supreme Soviet on Economic Treaty

The RSFSR Supreme Soviet approved a resolution "On the Draft Treaty on an Economic Community, TASS reported. TASS said on October 13 that the resolution set up a working group to prepare the treaty for ratification. The resolution noted that decisions of Union and interrepublican bodies to which the RSFSR had not delegated powers would only have the force of recommendations in the RSFSR until approved by republican organs. It also called for an end to the financing by the RSFSR of Union and interrepublican organs in which the RSFSR was not a participant.

Constitutional Supervision Committee Recommends Abolition of *Propiska* System

The USSR Committee for Constitutional Supervision ruled that all laws and directives regulating the Soviet system of residence permits should be abolished by January 1, 1992, Sergei Alekseev, the chairman of the committee, told Central Television. He also noted that the committee would be issuing a statement criticizing recent departures from the basic principles of the USSR Constitution and condemning the dismissive attitude towards the "Brezhnevist-Stalinist Constitution" that currently prevailed among politicians and the public.

Stankevich Predicts New Union Centered on Russia

RSFSR State Councilor Sergei Stankevich repeated his former denunciation of the planned economic union. He was quoted in *The Washington Post* as saying that other republics were now asserting that "everything on our territory is ours: everything that is in Russia is common." He warned that the other republics would try to protect

The USSR in October, 1991

their markets by introducing their own currencies and then crush the Russian market with huge quantities of rubles. Stankevich stressed that Russia must become a real state and claim everything on its territory as its own. He forecast that other republics would in future unite around a strong Russia and that Russia would become the core of a future union.

Russian Orthodox Church Refuses Catholic Invitation

TASS reported that the leadership of the Russian Orthodox Church had declined a Vatican invitation to participate in a special assembly of European Roman Catholic bishops scheduled for November and December, 1991. The Russian Orthodox Church said participation would convey an incorrect picture of relations between the two Churches, and it criticized the Vatican's attitude to Orthodoxy in Western Ukraine. The response stressed, however, that the Russian Orthodox Church did not want to close the door to brotherly dialogue.

Chernobyl' Fire

A fire broke out at the Number 2 reactor of the Chernobyl' nuclear power plant, TASS reported on October 12. The fire was extinguished three and a half hours later. Nikolai Tenberg, head of the Ukrainian Nuclear Power Plant Inspectorate, said there had been no release of radiation and no injuries.

Henry Kissinger to Advise Ukraine on Its Foreign Policy

Radio Kiev announced that former US Secretary of State Henry Kissinger had agreed to act as "a consultant" to the Ukrainian government on the republic's new independent foreign policy. Kissinger recently met in the United States with Ukraine's foreign minister, Anatolii Zlenko, and intended to travel to Kiev in the near future.

Soviet Military Convoy Attacked in Armenia

TASS on October 12 quoted a USSR MVD press release stating that one of its convoys had been intercepted during the morning of October 11 near the Armenian town of Aparan by a crowd of 3,000 local residents and 200 armed guerrillas, who then seized eighteen vehicles, including tanks and armored personnel carriers. No one was injured during the attack, which was being investigated by the Military Prosecutor's Office.

Central Asians Agree on Water Resources

TASS and UzTAG reported that the water resources ministers of the five Central Asian republics had signed an agreement on the use of the region's water resources that should put an end to disputes over water use. A single plan for water use in the entire region was to be devised.

Conservatives Strike Back in Tajikistan

TASS reported that nineteen deputies of the Tajik Supreme Soviet and the USSR Supreme Soviet representing Tajikistan had issued a public protest against "unconstitutionality" in the republic. They objected particularly to the banning of the republican Communist Party and to the inclusion of representatives of the Islamic Renaissance Party in election commissions and claimed that the political crisis in Tajikistan was not the fault of "conservative Communist structures" but the result of disregard for the law and the lack of a strong executive power.

Moldavia for Economic Community without Political Ties

Moldavian President Mircea Snegur told Moldovapres that he had endorsed the Alma-Ata document on forming an economic community (see October 1) only on the basis of the "Twelve-plus-Zero" formula and the understanding it did not entail political ties. Snegur noted, however, that in the meantime the USSR president and some RSFSR leaders were seeking to use the document in order to "revive the obsolete central structures" and were linking the economic treaty to a political union. Terming that unacceptable to Moldavia, Snegur called for "an end to such political games undermining the economies of all republics."

Moldavian Communist Party Tries to Make a Comeback

In an open letter to the Presidium of the Moldavian parliament published in *Vechernii Kishinev*, the leader of the banned Moldavian Communist Party, Grigore Eremei, denied that the Party as such had supported the abortive Soviet coup d'état. He complained that the Presidium's decisions on August 23 to ban the Party and nationalize its property had been "overhasty." Eremei requested permission to hold a Central Committee plenum "to determine the Party's fate" and pleaded for "reconsideration" of the decision to nationalize the Party's property.

Saturday, October 12

Gorbachev Gives Television Interview

Central Television broadcast an interview with Soviet President Mikhail Gorbachev in which he expressed his satisfaction with the fact that the republics had agreed to sign the treaty on an economic community by October 15. (In fact the signing was postponed until October 18.) At the same time, he said an economic union could not function without a political union. He maintained that the latest draft of the Union treaty was innovatory and progressive. Gorbachev criticized the view expressed by some members of the RSFSR leadership that Russia was the legal successor to the Soviet Union. Gorbachev also again indicated his anxiety about the outcome of Ukraine's approaching referendum on independence. Implicitly criticizing Ukraine's declaration of independence and the Ukrainian Supreme Soviet's call for a referendum to endorse it, he expressed his confidence that the inhabitants of Ukraine would come out in favor of remaining in a new Union.

Gorbachev also said in the interview that, prior to the attempted coup, he had disclosed to close associates that he wanted to begin reforms in the KGB, the armed forces, the Ministry of Internal Affairs, and "the rest of the state structure" and that these plans had become known to the heads of those organizations. Gorbachev said that he had connected such reforms with the Union treaty, the signing of which was prevented by the coup.

Rutskoi on Russian National Guard

In an interview with *Argumenty i fakty* (No. 40), RSFSR Vice President Aleksandr Rutskoi said the size of the RSFSR National Guard would not exceed 3,000 in the first year. In the second year, the number of guardsmen would rise to 10,000, and later, as the budget deficit declined, to 66,000. Rutskoi said the first training center would be created on the base of the Dzerzhinsky Division in Balashikha. Recruitment would be on a competitive basis and would start after the law on the national guard had been approved.

Akaev Confirmed as Kirgiz President

Preliminary returns showed that Kirgiz President Askar Akaev had received about 95 percent of the votes in the first direct presidential election in Kirgizia (*TASS*, October 13). Akaev, who had gained a reputation in the Soviet Union as a convinced democrat and radical economic reformer, was quoted as saying he was distressed that no one had been willing to run against him. At a postelection press conference, Akaev described the vote, in which 90 percent of the electorate participated, as an endorsement of his program of reform and democratization. He added that Supreme Soviet elections should be deferred until the new political parties gained strength.

Western agencies reported on October 13 that Topchubek Turgunaliev, one of the leaders of Democratic Kyrgyzstan, the republic's largest non-Communist political group, was critical of the election of Akaev. Turgunaliev complained that potential opposition candidates had not been given enough time to gather the 25,000 signatures necessary to register.

Moldavian Delegation in Brussels

Moldavian Prime Minister Valeriu Muravschi and the chairman of the Moldavian parliament's Foreign Relations Committee, Vasile Nedelciuc, held talks in Brussels on October 9 to 12 with EC officials and business people, Muravschi told Moldovapres on October 14. The delegates informed the EC officials that Moldavia intended to "create the prerequisites for Moldavia's future integration into the EC." A group of EC experts was to be sent to Moldavia "soon" to evaluate the republic's economic situation, Muravschi said.

Sunday, October 13

Central Television Profiles Shevardnadze

Central Television profiled former USSR Foreign Minister Eduard Shevardnadze on its "Who's Who?" program. According to the moderator, the former head of Soviet television, Leonid Kravchenko, scotched an earlier plan to feature Shevardnadze on the program. During the show, Muscovites were asked what they thought of Shevardnadze, and all respondents said they approved of his foreign policy, particularly the withdrawal of Soviet troops from Eastern Europe. The program also included an interview with Shevardnadze, in which he commented on the events in the Baltic republics in January, 1991, and on the Gulf war.

G-7 Agreement on Aid to USSR

After two days of talks with the Soviet delegation in Bangkok, the Group of Seven issued a communiqué pledging closer cooperation with the USSR, Western agencies reported on October 13. The accord was widely interpreted as an implicit promise of further aid and of Soviet acceptance of more Western supervision over internal Soviet affairs.

On October 15, the *Los Angeles Times* reported that, at the meetings with the G-7 nations, the Soviet delegation had asked the West to commit as much as 20 billion dollars to a stabilization fund to underpin the internal convertibility of the ruble. The newspaper said it had obtained a copy of the USSR's proposal. At the G-7 summit meeting in London, the Soviet side had suggested a stabilization fund of 10–12 billion dollars.

The USSR in October, 1991

Yavlinsky Confirms Drop in Gold Reserves

On arrival in Bangkok, Grigorii Yavlinsky confirmed to Western reporters that total Soviet gold reserves were down to 240 tons. Chairman of the USSR State Bank Viktor Gerashchenko told Western journalists on October 13 that the Soviet Union was not seeking relief on its foreign debt. Other (unnamed) Soviet officials were reported to have told G-7 and IMF sources that the Soviet Union was indeed seeking relief on 5–10 billion dollars due for repayment in the next few months.

Pressure Increases in Tatarstan for Independence Declaration

The people of Kazan' commemorated those who fell when the city was captured by Ivan the Terrible 439 years ago, Russian Television reported on October 14. The Tatar Public Center, the "Ittifak" party, the "Azatlyk" youth organization, and the Muslim clergy used the occasion to hold a meeting, attended by about 5,000 people, at which it was demanded that the Tatarstan Supreme Soviet adopt a declaration of complete independence for Tatarstan when it opened its session on October 15.

On October 15, the Tatar Supreme Soviet agreed to put a declaration of independence on its agenda after a crowd attacked the building where it was sitting, TASS reported.

The same day, TASS reported clashes between members of the Kazan' branch of the Democratic Party of Russia and representatives of nationalist movements, which resulted in injuries. The Democratic Party of Russia issued a statement blaming local organs of power, the president, and the Supreme Soviet for the disturbances in Kazan'.

Radio Moscow reported on October 16 that the picketing of the Tatar parliament building by advocates of independence was continuing in spite of heavy rain. TASS reported on October 16 that a group of deputies of the Tatar Supreme Soviet had proposed that the session interrupt its work until the situation in Kazan' had stabilized. It was decided to hold no plenary sessions for the time being but instead to continue work in the committees and commissions.

On October 17, TASS reported that Tatar President Mintimer Shaimiev had signed a decree "on banning the creation and activity of public militarized associations and armed formations on the territory of the Tatar SSR." The decree said such units were to be disbanded from the moment the decree was published. Enrollment in home guard units subordinated to the Tatar Public Center had started about ten days earlier in reaction to a statement by Acting Chairman of the RSFSR Supreme Soviet Ruslan Khasbulatov (see *Sovetskaya Rossiya*, October 8).

The same day, the Executive Committee of the Democratic Party of Russia issued a statement condemning "irresponsible political forces" in Tatarstan who were insisting that the Supreme Soviet adopt a declaration of independence (*TASS*, October 17). The statement maintained that opinion polls had shown the population to be very skeptical about independence and called for a referendum to decide the issue.

Unsanctioned proindependence demonstrations continued in Kazan' on October 19, according to TASS. Shaimiev told a session of the republican Supreme Soviet that the former autonomous republics, including Tatarstan, still had not improved their state status but that this did not justify illegal demonstrations. Shaimiev's decree of October 17 forbidding armed groups was published in the local press, but an official of the republican KGB complained that the decree was being ignored and that the Tatar Social Center was setting up a national guard.

On October 23, the Supreme Soviet of Tatarstan continued debate on two draft declarations of independence and created a commission to resolve differences between the two documents, TASS and AFP reported. A Tatar journalist told RFE/RL the same day that troops were blocking the road from Kazan' to Naberezhnye Chelny, presumably to prevent proindependence forces from going to Kazan' to demonstrate during the debate.

On October 24, the Supreme Soviet of Tatarstan adopted a resolution on state independence that called for a national referendum on the status of the republic, Interfax reported. TASS said the resolution also called for public discussion of a new constitution, to be adopted when Tatarstan became an independent state.

Baltic States Aim for EFTA Membership

Lithuanian Prime Minister Gediminas Vagnorius said before leaving for the IMF conference that Lithuania, Latvia, and Estonia had already decided to form a free-trade area without customs duties and hoped to establish closer cooperation with the European Free Trade Association (*Reuters*, October 13).

Amnesty for Businessmen in Jail?

Soviet President Mikhail Gorbachev's newly established Council on Entrepreneurship proposed that all persons convicted of so-called "economic crimes" be amnestied. Gorbachev's adviser on entrepreneurship, Konstantin Zatulin, told "TV-Inform" on October 13 that some 127,000 people were currently serving prison terms for such "crimes" as "speculation" (the resale of goods for profit), "private entrepreneurship," and acting as a commercial middleman. Zatulin disclosed that decrees on an amnesty for such prisoners were to be prepared for signing by both USSR President Mikhail Gorbachev and RSFSR President Boris El'tsin.

Monday, October 14

Anatolii Aleinikov, first deputy chairman of the USSR KGB, said the Interrepublican Counterintelligence Service would be responsible for fighting corruption and organized crime and also for protecting the economic system and training personnel. It was to be modeled on the structure and functions of the FBI. Aleinikov's remarks were published in *Izvestia* on October 14. Aleinikov said the current changes provided a unique opportunity to remove superfluous functions from the KGB.

KGB Deputy Chairman on Reorganization of Agency

The USSR and Finland opened two days of talks in Helsinki to revise the treaty signed in 1948. The original treaty obliged Finland to protect the northwestern flank of the Soviet Union from attack by Germany or any German ally. The Finnish Foreign Ministry had described such clauses as obsolete (*Reuters*, October 14).

Revision of Treaty with Finland

Three days of talks between USSR Foreign Minister Boris Pankin and Japanese Foreign Minister Taro Nakayama opened in Moscow. The USSR reiterated its intention to reduce its troop strength on the Kurile Islands by one-third—an offer made originally by Soviet President Mikhail Gorbachev during his visit to Tokyo in April, 1991.

On October 16, Nakayama's visit ended inconclusively, but it left Japan with some hope of settling long-standing disputes.

On October 17, an unidentified Japanese Foreign Ministry official was quoted by AP as saying Japan would ask for repayment guarantees before releasing the 2.5-billion-dollar aid package it had announced on October 8.

Soviet-Japanese Talks

The RL Turkmen service received a copy of an appeal to Turkmen President Saparmurad Niyazov signed by sixty-nine Turkmen intellectuals in early September in reaction to the ambivalent attitude shown by the Turkmen government towards the Moscow junta. The appeal asked that the editors of the two republican dailies be replaced and

Turkmen Intellectuals Attack Government

the republican MVD chief removed and that opposition parties be registered in Turkmenistan. Niyazov had shown little inclination to grant any of these requests.

Tuesday, October 15

El'tsin Doubtful about Need for New Union Treaty

RSFSR State Secretary Gennadii Burbulis told Russian deputies on October 15 that RSFSR President Boris El'tsin had expressed doubts about the need for a new Union treaty in view of the forthcoming signing of an economic accord, Western agencies reported. Burbulis said El'tsin now believed that a Union of Sovereign Republics with its own constitution might be illusory. State Councilor Sergei Stankevich said El'tsin was particularly against the idea of direct popular election of the Union president—an idea that still figured in the latest draft of the Union treaty.

El'tsin Interviewed on "Vesti"

After the session of the RSFSR State Council on October 15, Boris El'tsin gave an interview to "Vesti." El'tsin said he would reorganize the RSFSR government as a government of national trust. So as to avoid a power vacuum, the present Council of Ministers would not resign. El'tsin would first appoint by decree an acting prime minister, who would start to put together a new Council of Ministers. He said that many of the present ministers would remain but that he intended to nearly halve the number of ministries. He revealed that he had three candidates in mind for the post of prime minister but that Vice President Aleksandr Rutskoi, who had expressed an interest in being premier, was not one of them. El'tsin said Rutskoi should first serve out his time as vice president.

El'tsin also said that the start of financial recovery lay in combating ruble intervention from other republics. He cited as an example the fact that the Baltic States were buying agricultural products in Russia at high prices and thus contributing to inflation. El'tsin said that to combat this Russia would start issuing its own ruble notes. Later the republic would go over to its own currency.

El'tsin Tries to Postpone Local Elections

El'tsin asked the RSFSR Supreme Soviet to review its decision to hold local elections during the fall, "Vesti" reported on October 15. Various reasons had been given in the Soviet media for this move—that the cost would be too high at a time of budget deficit, that it would paralyze constructive work at this juncture, and that any new local administrations, no matter what their political orientation, would be preoccupied with local concerns and thus make central administration nearly impossible. A major factor, though, was probably a recent study that showed that conservative administrations would be elected in most oblasts and krais.

The RSFSR Supreme Soviet rejected El'tsin's request, however. In protest against the Russian parliament's decision, one of El'tsin's top advisers, Sergei Shakhrai, resigned from his posts as chairman of the RSFSR parliament's legislation committee and as a member of its Presidium on October 18. He called the decision "suicide" for the parliament. Shakhrai told RFE/RL he would remain a deputy of the RSFSR Supreme Soviet in order still to have a voice in the Russian parliament.

On October 21, El'tsin sent a letter to the RSFSR Supreme Soviet explaining his veto of the republican law on "the election of heads of administrations," TASS reported. El'tsin said the elections, if held on December 8 as required by the law, would hamper the implementation of economic reforms in Russia. In response, the Presidium of the parliament said the dispute over elections should be clarified before the RSFSR Congress of People's Deputies started its session on October 28.

On October 25, the RSFSR Supreme Soviet agreed to a compromise under which local administrative elections would take place but the dates on which they were held could be staggered over a longer period, Interfax reported.

Gorbachev Mediates in Yugoslav Conflict

After talks with Soviet President Mikhail Gorbachev in Moscow on October 15, the leaders of Serbia and Croatia agreed to attempt another cease-fire. In a communiqué issued after the talks, the sides agreed to begin negotiations on all questions within "the next month." Gorbachev noted that "the Soviet Union has to deal with similar problems," adding, "this explains why recent events in Yugoslavia have aroused anxiety and concern in our country," Western agencies and TASS reported on October 15 and 16.

Cooperation between RSFSR KGB and CIA Discussed

Sergei Stepashin, chairman of the RSFSR Supreme Soviet Committee on Security, was quoted by TASS on October 15 as saying that a delegation of committee members who recently visited Washington had established good contacts with the US intelligence community—they met with the leadership of the CIA—and agreed to broad cooperation and an exchange of information between the RSFSR KGB and the CIA. US assistance was also proposed in the creation of an Analytical Administration in the Russian KGB. Stepashin said there had also been a proposal to create joint units of the two intelligence agencies in Moscow and Washington.

Kuriles Must Not Be "Sold," Deputies Say

Sergei Baburin and Nikolai Pavlov, deputies of the RSFSR Supreme Soviet, said that the Kurile Islands belonged to Russia and that the redrawing of frontiers was impermissible, TASS reported. The two parliamentarians stressed that it was unacceptable "to sell the motherland" or "to repeat the fate of the Meskhetian Turks and Crimean Tatars." They said they would seek state sovereignty for the Kuriles in the event of "a betrayal by Russia." The hard-line newspaper *Sovetskaya Rossiya* had recently published letters from Kurile Islands residents protesting about the fact that they had not been asked for their views on the future of the islands.

Belorussia and Czechoslovakia Agree to Establish Diplomatic Ties

TASS announced that Belorussia and Czechoslovakia had agreed to establish consular and diplomatic relations. The agreement was reached in Minsk during talks between Rudolf Slansky, Czechoslovakia's ambassador to the USSR, and Belorussian Deputy Prime Minister Uladzimir Zalamai.

New Belorussian Prosecutor Named

For the first time in Belorussian history, a new republican prosecutor-general was appointed not by Moscow but by the Supreme Soviet of Belorussia. He was Mikalai Ihnatovich, who became famous in the 1980s for his investigation of the so-called "Vitebsk Affair" involving the fabrication of criminal cases against fourteen innocent men on charges of serial killings. As a member of the USSR Supreme Soviet, Ihnatovich was also on the committee charged with establishing whether the group in the USSR Prosecutor's Office headed by Tel'man Gdlyan had used illegal investigative methods. Ihnatovich replaced Hryhor Tarnauski, whose term of office had run out. The new prosecutor was given the immediate task of investigating Belorussian Party support for the August coup.

Moldavian Leadership Approves National Army Blueprint

A session of Moldavia's Higher Security Council, chaired by Mircea Snegur, approved the outline of a plan to create "a national armed force," Moldovapres reported on October 16. The plan ruled out Moldavia's participation in "a common military space in a possible new Union" and defined the mission of the force as "defending the republic's independence and territorial integrity." The plan called for a negotiated withdrawal of USSR forces from Moldavia and the prompt transfer to the republic of all Moldavian military personnel currently serving in USSR forces outside Moldavia.

Moldavian Leadership against Reunification with Romania

At a meeting with Moldavian local officials from the left bank of the Dniester, Moldavian President Mircea Snegur reiterated the Moldavian leadership's opposition to reunification with Romania and criticized the popular front for pressing for reunification, Moldovapres reported on October 15. Snegur said that Moldavia sought "to consolidate its independence and have it recognized internationally" and that "any union with another state is out of the question".

At a general conference held on October 13, the Moldavian Popular Front resolved to go into opposition to President Snegur and the government. The conference resolutions, which were made public in Kishinev on October 15, accused Snegur of relying on a parliamentary majority of Communist holdovers, of coopting former Communist officials into the government, and of showing "inconsistency and lack of principle in relation to the USSR . . . thus jeopardizing Moldavia's independence." The front objected to holding a presidential election before the adoption of a new Moldavian constitution and reaffirmed its support for a parliamentary form of government rather than the presidential type of government favored by Snegur.

South Korea and Lithuania Establish Ties

South Korea formally established diplomatic relations with Lithuania, Western and Baltic media reported. Diplomatic relations between South Korea and Latvia were established on October 22.

Resolution on Latvian Citizenship

A resolution on citizenship was endorsed at its first reading by the Latvian Supreme Council, Radio Riga reported. The requirements for Latvian citizenship laid down by the legislation were: knowledge of the Latvian language, knowledge of the Latvian legal structure and laws, sixteen years' residence in Latvia, an oath of allegiance, and the renunciation of citizenship of another state.

The decision was criticized by two groups. The "Ravnopravie" group of deputies, which until recently had supported the idea of Latvia's remaining an integral part of the USSR, charged that the legislation would bring apartheid to Latvia and violate widely accepted norms of human rights. The Committee of Latvia, at the other end of the political spectrum, argued that the Supreme Council had no authority to pass such legislation, since it had been elected by Soviet citizens at a time when Latvia was not independent, according to *Diena* of October 16.

Estonian Legislation on Citizenship

On October 15 the Estonian Supreme Council discussed a draft law granting Estonian citizenship to those who held it before 1940 and their descendants and offering citizenship to those who had moved to Estonia after that date but who knew the Estonian language and had resided in Estonia for at least three years. The law proposed to provide free instruction in Estonian for applicants for citizenship. It also barred dual citizenship and gave Estonians living abroad one year to choose whether to renew Estonian citizenship or to retain foreign citizenship, according to Western agency and RFE Estonian service reports of October 16.

Baltic States Endorse Helsinki Final Act

Radio Riga reported that the heads of state of Estonia, Latvia, and Lithuania had arrived in Helsinki for the formal signing of the Helsinki Final Act, which was adopted on August 1, 1975.

In the speeches delivered at the signing ceremony, the Baltic leaders stressed the significance for the Baltic States' of being a part of the Helsinki process. They also reiterated their call for the prompt departure of Soviet troops from their countries (*Reuters, AP*, October 15).

Wednesday, October 16

Armenians Go to the Polls

Presidential elections took place in Armenia. On October 17, TASS quoted an Armenian government official as saying that Armenian Supreme Soviet Chairman Levon Ter-Petrossyan had received more than 80 percent of the votes cast. Paruir Airikyan, chairman of the Association for National Self-Determination, was in second place, and Sos Sarkisyan of the Armenian Revolutionary (Dashnak) Party came in third. A Central Electoral Commission official estimated voter turnout at more than 69 percent.

Soviet Economic Decline Accelerates

The report of the USSR State Committee for Statistics for the first nine months of 1991 showed that the decline in the country's economic situation was accelerating, Central Television and Western agencies reported. National income fell 13 percent; gross national product, 12 percent; industrial production, 6.4 percent; exports, 30 percent; and imports, 45 percent.

Kalmyk Territorial Claims

Chairman of the Kalmyk Council of Ministers Batyr Mikhailov said that, as a result of the RSFSR law on the rehabilitation of repressed peoples, Kalmykia was hoping that the material damage done to the Kalmyk people when they were deported in 1943 would be made good. It also wanted back two raions of Astrakhan Oblast and 215,000 hectares of Dagestan that were not returned when Kalmykia regained its autonomy in 1958.

Vaksberg Suggests Cover-Up in Coup Investigation

On the front page of *Literaturnaya gazeta* (No. 40), the well-known legal journalist Arkadii Vaksberg accused Mikhail Gorbachev of putting pressure on those responsible for the investigation of the August coup. Vaksberg said that there had been attempts to limit the number of those implicated in the coup and that the Soviet media had sought to whitewash the role of the junta. Vaksberg also suggested that the disbanded CPSU Central Committee Administrative Organs Department, which in the past had exercised the infamous "telephone justice" (instructions from above on how to administer justice), was trying to influence law-enforcement bodies by illegal means.

Ex-Communist Party Publishes Draft Program

Despite having been banned for a second time by the Supreme Soviet of Tajikistan, the republican Communist Party, renamed the Socialist Party of Tajikistan, published a draft program in the republican press, according to TASS.

Rehabilitation of "War Criminals" in Lithuania Suspended

According to Western media reports of October 17, the Lithuanian Supreme Court on October 16 suspended the rehabilitation of people sentenced by Soviet courts in postwar Lithuania on charges of war crimes, because some of the approximately 35,000 people exonerated were subsequently found to have been involved in the killing of Jews. Supreme Court Justice Genadius Slauta said: "We were trying to rehabilitate everybody as quickly as possible, but now we are sorry that we acted so rapidly. We see that serious errors were made."

On October 18, Rabbi Marvin Hier, Dean of the Simon Wiesenthal Center in Los Angeles, said the center would consider calling for congressional hearings on whether Lithuania should receive US aid if Lithuania did not review the cases of the people it had already exonerated. He said that his organization had found that eleven persons who had been exonerated had taken part in Nazi war crimes, Western agencies reported.

Thursday, October 17

Genscher in Alma-Ata and Kiev

KazTAG and TASS reported on the visit of German Foreign Minister Hans-Dietrich Genscher to Kazakhstan. At a press conference after one-to-one talks with Genscher, Kazakh President Nursultan Nazarbaev said that topics discussed included the opening of a Goethe Institute in Alma-Ata for the study of the German language, the establishment of consular relations, the starting of direct flights between Kazakhstan and Germany, and German technical assistance to Kazakhstan.

After his talks in Alma-Ata, Genscher traveled to Kiev, where he met on October 18 with Ukrainian Supreme Soviet Chairman Leonid Kravchuk and Foreign Minister Anatolii Zlenko. He also officially opened a week of German cultural events, Western agencies reported. During his talks with Ukrainian officials, Genscher did not conceal his disapproval of Ukraine's decision to refrain from signing the Soviet economic accord.

Ukraine Asserts Authority over Railroads and Civil Defense

The Presidium of the Ukrainian Supreme Soviet issued a decree giving Ukraine jurisdiction over the USSR military units in charge of railroads, government communications, and civil defense stationed on the territory of the republic, the Ukrainian media reported. The order extended to arms and technical equipment held by these units.

Pickets in Minsk Claim Baltic Territory

According to an RFE/RL stringer in Minsk, Russian-speaking residents of the Baltic States picketed near the Belorussian Supreme Soviet building to demand that Belorussia annex Vilnius and Klaipeda from Lithuania and three raions of Latvia. In March, 1990, in response to Lithuania's declaration of independence, the Presidium of the Belorussian Supreme Soviet had issued a statement asserting Belorussia's claim to Vilnius and other parts of Lithuania.

Friday, October 18

Treaty on Economic Community Signed

Eight of the twelve Soviet republics signed the Treaty on an Economic Community, which aimed at creating

The USSR in October, 1991

"a common economic space" in which the republics would cooperate on economic policy, trade, and other matters. The Soviet media said Ukraine, Azerbaijan, Moldavia, and Georgia had objections to the treaty and did not sign it. The treaty set up some central organs to regulate parts of the economy. Aides to Gorbachev said work on final details of the treaty was continuing even on October 18. The treaty would not take effect until ratified by the parliaments of the signatory republics.

Gorbachev presided over the signing ceremony in the Kremlin and also put his own signature to the document. He told correspondents afterwards that the signing of the treaty was "a tremendous event" that gave him personal satisfaction. The Soviet and Western media quoted Gorbachev as saying that he had talked to officials from Ukraine, Moldavia, and Azerbaijan and that he expected these three republics eventually to join the new economic union.

RSFSR President Boris El'tsin was quoted by TASS on October 18 as saying the signing of the economic treaty was "a very great event" that could help to stabilize the economy within a year. He said the treaty represented agreement on the need for a new structure in which most things would be controlled by interrepublican organs instead of by a rigid center. He said this was very important, especially in view of the country's move towards a market economy. El'tsin also expressed the hope that Ukraine, Azerbaijan, Moldavia, and Georgia would eventually join the new economic union. Both Gorbachev and El'tsin suggested that the signing of the treaty would help the USSR in its quest for Western aid.

On October 19, several Ukrainian officials said Ukraine's leaders supported the treaty in principle but wanted to reach separate bilateral accords with each of the other republics first (*TASS*, October 19). Ukrainian Minister of Energy and Power Development Vitalii Sklyarov said Ukraine's signing of the treaty was "only a matter of time," given the republic's need for uninterrupted supplies of fuel. Deputy Chairman of the Ukrainian Supreme Soviet Volodymyr Hryn'ov said the treaty was "badly needed," *Izvestia* reported.

RSFSR Law on Rehabilitations Passed

The RSFSR Supreme Soviet passed a law rehabilitating the victims of political repressions carried out during the Soviet period. The law stipulated financial compensation for many categories of those repressed. TASS reported that the parliament had also adopted a decree making October 30 an official day of commemoration of victims of political repressions. During the Brezhnev era, dissidents confined to labor camps declared October 30 the day of political prisoners. The parliament also adopted a separate decree rehabilitating Gleb Yakunin, a religious activist who spent a term in a labor camp under Brezhnev. Yakunin is now an RSFSR people's deputy.

USSR and Israel Restore Full Diplomatic Relations

Israel and the USSR restored full diplomatic relations, AP and Reuters reported. The announcement was made in a joint statement issued in Jerusalem by the Israeli and Soviet foreign ministers, David Levi and Boris Pankin. The Israeli embassy in Moscow was reopened on October 24.

Member of International Department Commits Suicide

A former sector chief of the International Department of the CPSU Central Committee, Dmitrii Lisovolik, committed suicide by jumping from a window of his twelfth-floor apartment in Moscow, AFP reported on October 18. TASS said it was not known why the fifty-four-year-old Lisovolik had killed himself. It was probable that, as a member of the International Department, Lisovolik had been involved in financial dealings between the CPSU and Communist parties abroad. These operations were being investigated by the USSR and RSFSR juridical bodies.

Sobchak Proposes Creation of Liberal Union

Leningrad Mayor Anatolii Sobchak called for the creation of an interparty union of liberal orientation, Radio Rossii reported on October 19. Sobchak said that if such a union were not created, neototalitarian groups would gain the upper hand in the RSFSR's political arena. He called on the Russian and Western media to propagate the idea of such a union.

Trade Ties with Cuba Shaky

Interfax reported that trade between the USSR and Cuba had fallen dramatically in 1991. According to information from an unidentified official at the USSR Ministry of Foreign Economic Relations, the termination of food supplies, especially grain, from the Soviet Union had hit Cuba the hardest. In an effort to solve the problem, Cuba had cut back on sugar supplies to the USSR in order to sell sugar for hard currency on the world market.

Azerbaijan Restores Independence

The Azerbaijani Supreme Soviet voted overwhelmingly not to sign the interrepublican economic treaty on the grounds that it did not accommodate the republic's interests, Interfax reported. The parliament also adopted a draft law "on the restoration of the state independence of the Azerbaijani Republic," which put into immediate effect the August 30 declaration of independence.

Land Law in Estonia

The Estonian Supreme Council passed a land law that returned nationalized land to its former owners, *Rahva Haal* reported. The law stipulated that current owners or occupiers of land should be compensated for land that was returned to those who lost it under Communist rule. The law did not specify who would provide compensation and exempted some plots smaller than two hectares (for the text of the law, see *Rahva Haal*, October 31).

_____*Saturday, October 19*

First Congress of Soviet Germans Held

RSFSR President El'tsin sent greetings to participants in the First Congress of Soviet Germans, TASS reported. El'tsin described the establishment of state independence for Soviet Germans as a process that would take place in several stages, the first of which would be the renewal of the infrastructure, the modernization of industry, and the improvement of social conditions in the former Volga German Republic.

On October 20, the congress adjourned, having passed a resolution that called on the RSFSR leadership to take the initiative by issuing a government decree guaranteeing the creation of an autonomous territory. The delegates suggested that such a decree should be issued prior to the adoption of the new RSFSR Constitution.

Former Ideology Chief in Volgograd Commits Suicide

TASS reported that another former Communist Party official, Sergei Klimov of Volgograd, had committed suicide. Klimov was ideology chief of the Volgograd Oblast Party Committee. According to the agency, he hanged himself.

_____*Sunday, October 20*

Poll Shows El'tsin Is Most Popular Politician

A public opinion poll conducted in the Russian Federation in connection with Boris El'tsin's 100th day in office showed the Russian president to be the most popular political figure in the country. Radio Moscow suggested that El'tsin's presidential term should be counted not from the date he was sworn in in June but from the day the coup collapsed—August 22.

Strikes and Demonstrations in RSFSR

Bus drivers went on strike in Petropavlovsk-Kamchatsky in the Soviet Far East. Radio Moscow said the drivers went back to work when they were promised higher wages and spare parts for their buses.

On October 21, 100,000 medical workers staged a two-hour strike in Kemerovo in Western Siberia to protest long working hours, low wages, and the shortage of medicines. The same day, inmates at a prison camp in Bashkiria began a hunger strike to demand legal reforms, while students in Novosibirsk and Moscow launched protests about accommodation problems, Russian Television's "Vesti" reported.

On October 23, thousands of people demonstrated in Moscow and St. Petersburg for higher wages, more food, and a minimum wage, Central Television and Western agencies reported. The protests were said to have been organized by the trade-union federations. The demonstrations continued outside the RSFSR parliament building on October 24. A Western news agency estimated the size of the crowd at around 30,000. One of the demands made was the full indexation of wages in the face of recent and anticipated retail price increases.

Sugar Riot in Moscow

A crowd broke into a bakery in the Perovo district of Moscow over the weekend in search of sugar, Western agencies reported on October 23 and 24. An official of the food department of the RSFSR State Committee for Statistics was quoted as saying that only 43 percent of sugar delivery quotas had been met by republics supplying the RSFSR.

Interrogations of Coup Plotters Aired on Russian Television

On October 20 and 21, Russian Television screened videotapes of the interrogations of Dmitrii Yazov, Vladimir Kryuchkov, and Valentin Pavlov. Russian Television obtained the tapes from the German weekly *Der Spiegel*, which had recently published excerpts from them. Former KGB Chairman Kryuchkov said, "We neither gave orders nor planned actions against the RSFSR government and Boris El'tsin, because we realized that no force could counter such tremendous support." Yazov said he regretted the deaths of the three young men killed during the coup.

Presidential Election in Kalmykia Inconclusive

Only two-thirds of the eligible voters turned out for the presidential election in the Autonomous Republic of Kalmykia. None of the three candidates received the majority necessary for election. TASS reported that a runoff election would take place in two weeks between the two candidates who received the most votes—the current chairman of the republican Council of Ministers, Batyr Mikhailov; and the chairman of the republican Supreme Soviet, Vladimir Basanov.

Monday, October 21

New USSR Supreme Soviet Convenes

The reorganized USSR Supreme Soviet opened its first session in Moscow, with deputies from only seven of the country's twelve republics participating. (The deputies who attended represented the RSFSR, Belorussia, Kazakhstan, Uzbekistan, Kirgizia, Turkmenistan, and Tajikistan.) Azerbaijan and Moldavia were represented only by observers. The two chambers, the Council of the Republics and the Council of the Union, met in separate sittings to consider lengthy agendas; discussion of some issues was postponed, however, in the hope that Ukraine would decide to send representatives.

Soviet President Mikhail Gorbachev addressed the opening session and called for faster democratization and "a decisive breakthrough" in the transition to a market economy, which he said should include radical agrarian reform. He told deputies that negotiations had resumed on "a treaty on a union of sovereign states" and that a draft was under consideration by members of the State Council. Gorbachev also rejected the notion of republican armies. His address included an appeal to Ukraine to participate in the Union treaty negotiations (*TASS*, October 21; *Izvestia*, October 21 and 22).

On October 22, Konstantin Lubenchenko was nominated as chairman of the Council of the Union, and, on October 24, a Kazakh writer, Anuar Alimzhanov, was nominated as chairman of the Council of the Republics.

On October 25, the deputies of both chambers issued an appeal to the four republics that had not signed the economic union agreement to become members of the new economic community, TASS reported. "Today, it is obvious to our peoples and to the whole world," the statement read, "that the complete, uncoordinated disintegration of the former Union might lead to further destabilization and aggravation of interrepublican relations." The same day, the Ukrainian Supreme Soviet decided to form a delegation to attend the USSR Supreme Soviet session as observers, although the resolution also stated that Ukraine considered it inappropriate to participate in any kind of interrepublican structure that could lead to its inclusion in another state, Ukrinform-TASS reported.

THE USSR IN OCTOBER, 1991

Communist Parliamentarians Still Active

Soviet historian and USSR people's deputy Roy Medvedev said that the Communist group within the USSR Supreme Soviet was continuing to work despite the ban on the CPSU, Radio Rossii reported. Medvedev said Communist deputies to the Supreme Soviet had met during the Supreme Soviet's first session and decided that the suspension of Communist Party activities did not apply to them.

Gorbachev Cancels Edict on Economic Sabotage

Soviet President Mikhail Gorbachev annulled his edict on economic sabotage and economic crimes ("TV Inform," October 21). The edict, which was issued on January 26, 1991, gave the KGB broad responsibilities in the economic field and led to the creation of the KGB Administration for Combating Corruption, Economic Sabotage, and Organized Crime. It authorized the police and KGB to enter all enterprises and organizations without the consent of the relevant officials and to seize documents and materials.

Vol'sky Comments on Economic Situation

In an interview with *Der Spiegel*, Arkadii Vol'sky, the president of the Scientific-Industrial Association of the USSR and a deputy chairman of the Committee for the Management of the USSR Economy, termed the food situation "chaotic" and warned of high unemployment and runaway inflation. Vol'sky estimated the grain harvest to be 170 million tons at best. He attributed the low figure to the refusal of many farmers to meet state orders and of republics to cooperate with the center. Because of the Ukrainian ban on food exports, meat cost ten times as much in Moscow as at a Ukrainian Kolkhoz market. He also predicted that 10–14 million people could be unemployed by the end of 1992.

Soviet Budget Deficit Reaches 120 Billion Rubles

Izvestia reported that the Soviet budget deficit for the first nine months of 1991 was 120 billion rubles—already four times the projected deficit figure. USSR First Deputy Finance Minister Vladimir Raevsky forecast in early October that the deficit would reach 300 billion rubles by the end of the year—100 billion rubles more than he had predicted just three weeks earlier.

Japan Offers New Economic and Technical Aid

Japanese Foreign Trade Minister Eiichi Nakao made new offers of economic and technical aid for the Soviet Union in a meeting with Soviet President Mikhail Gorbachev. TASS reported that Japan was prepared to assist the Soviet

The USSR in October, 1991

Union in oil and gas extraction, in the electrical engineering industry, and in the manufacture of consumer goods. Technical assistance in nuclear-power engineering and in organizing small- and medium-sized businesses was also discussed.

Another Writers' Union Established

Some 1,300 writers living in the RSFSR gathered in Moscow to announce the creation of the Union of Russian (*Rossiisky*) Writers, TASS reported. This union was intended as a counterweight to the RSFSR Writers' Union, which was headed by hard-liner Yurii Bondarev and which supported the attempted coup. The Russian Television news program "Vesti" noted that three writers' unions would now coexist in Moscow—the USSR Writers' Union, the RSFSR Writers' Union, and the Union of Russian Writers.

Norway Expels Soviet Diplomats

Eight Soviet diplomats were expelled from Norway for activities incompatible with their diplomatic status, the Norwegian Foreign Ministry said. Bjoern Blokhus, press spokesman for the Norwegian Foreign Ministry, said Norway did not expect the USSR to take retaliatory action, Western agencies reported.

German Minister Presses for Extradition of Honecker

German Justice Minister Klaus Kinkel flew to Moscow to request the extradition of former East German leader Erich Honecker. He met with RSFSR Justice Minister Nikolai Fedorov, USSR Justice Minister Mikhail Vyshinsky, and Gorbachev's adviser Aleksandr Yakovlev. Kinkel told reporters after the meetings that RSFSR officials had expressed an interest in helping Germany obtain Honecker's extradition but that the Soviet authorities were reluctant to let Honecker go, Western agencies reported. On October 22, USSR presidential spokesman Andrei Grachev said that the USSR's reluctance to return Honecker to the German authorities stemmed from a feeling of complicity in events in the GDR, RIA reported. On October 23, Fedorov indicated that Russia would be willing to extradite Honecker even if the Soviet authorities did not agree, TASS reported.

Ukraine Insists on Own Armed Forces

Soviet Defense Minister Evgenii Shaposhnikov's recent criticism of Ukraine's effort to establish its own army was rebuffed by Ukrainian Defense Minister Konstantin Morozov, Radio Kiev reported. Morozov rejected Shaposhnikov's insistence that military personnel in

Ukraine were bound to their oath of loyalty to the USSR Constitution, stating that Ukrainian soldiers would swear loyalty only to the constitution of independent Ukraine. Soviet President Mikhail Gorbachev, in his opening address to the USSR Supreme Soviet, also threatened to annul any legislation adopted by the Ukrainian parliament on the establishment of an independent army.

On October 22, in defiance of the Soviet central authorities, the Ukrainian Supreme Soviet adopted five draft laws covering the creation of a Ukrainian army, navy, air force, national guard, and border troops, Radio Kiev reported.

Meanwhile, amid increasing concern over the status of nuclear weapons in the Soviet republics, Deputy Chairman of the Ukrainian Supreme Soviet Vladimir Grinev said on October 23 that Ukraine had not "nationalized" nuclear weapons on its territory, Western news agencies reported. Grinev asserted that nuclear weapons stationed in Ukraine would remain under joint command and that there would be no separate Ukrainian nuclear weapons. The same day, US State Department official Richard Boucher said the United States took a positive view of Ukraine's determination to be a nuclear-free country, specifically its stand on nuclear arms, but he expressed concern over Ukraine's intention to establish independent armed forces (*TASS*, October 23).

On October 24, a Soviet military spokesman contradicted Gorbachev's position that republican armies were illegal. Lieutenant General Valerii Manilov, chief spokesman for the USSR Ministry of Defense, said Ukraine had the right to form its own armed forces, TASS reported. At the same time, Manilov maintained that Ukraine could not have nuclear arms or take over Soviet military bases. The same day, the Ukrainian Supreme Soviet adopted a statement on Ukraine's nonnuclear status, Ukrinform-TASS reported. "The existence of nuclear weapons of the former USSR on the territory of Ukraine is temporary," the statement said, adding, "These weapons are currently under the control of the appropriate institutions of the former USSR, but Ukraine insists on control over their nonuse. Further, Ukraine will conduct a policy aimed at the complete liquidation of nuclear weapons on its territory."

Dushanbe State of Emergency Ruled Illegal

Chairman of the USSR Constitutional Supervision Committee Sergei Alekseev said that the declaration of a state of emergency in Tajikistan in September was illegal, TASS reported. A ruling on the legality of the action had been requested by the Tajik Supreme Soviet, which had ordered the state-of-emergency declaration in reaction to demonstrations by opposition political groups demanding the restoration of a ban on the republican Communist Party. Alekseev commented that the declaration of a state of emergency to resolve a political conflict was impermissible.

Soviet Authorities Interfere with Baltic Airspace

The Soviet authorities turned away the Belgian Air Force plane bringing Belgian Foreign Minister Mark Eyskens to Riga. The plane was allowed to land in Riga only after the Latvian government intervened. According to a Belgian Foreign Ministry spokeswoman, the USSR was still in control of Latvian airspace and the incident occurred because the Soviet central authorities "had not been informed." The Belgian government would not issue a protest, she said, but the Latvian Foreign Ministry did protest to the USSR.

In a similar incident on October 22, Radio Vilnius reported that Soviet fighter planes had prevented a Danish plane carrying experts from the World Health Organization from landing in the Lithuanian capital. The plane was diverted to Warsaw, and the problem was settled after negotiations with the Soviet authorities. Lithuanian Deputy Prime Minister Zigmas Vaisvila telephoned USSR Minister of Defense Evgenii Shaposhnikov to protest against the Soviet interference. On October 24, Latvian Deputy Prime Minister Ilmars Bisers met with General Yurii Rulevsky of the USSR Baltic Military District to discuss the situation. To prevent the recurrence of such incidents, it was decided the Latvian Foreign Ministry would inform the Baltic Military District of foreign planes expected in Riga.

Tuesday, October 22

RSFSR Parliament Discusses Communist Party's Illegal Activities

Hearings took place in the RSFSR Supreme Soviet on the involvement of the CPSU and the Russian Communist Party in the attempted coup, TASS reported. During the hearings, RSFSR Justice Minister Nikolai Fedorov said that documents in his possession on the financial activities of the CPSU indicated that some of the Party's financial operations had been criminal. Western aid and hard-currency reserves were used to funnel aid to foreign Communist parties, TASS reported. A member of the RSFSR Supreme Soviet Committee on Links with Public Organizations and the Study of Public Opinion, Aleksandr Evlakhov, said that these activities had been conducted through the Fund for the Assistance of International Workers' Organizations set up by an order of the CPSU Central Committee Politburo. The CPSU Central Committee International Department was in charge of the distribution of money that was kept in the USSR's Foreign Trade Bank.

On October 23, Radio Rossii reported that 20 million dollars deposited with an Italian bank by the CPSU had recently been discovered. A Soviet journalist in Venezuela, Yurii Isaev, also described how the financing of the local Communist Party had been conducted. According to Isaev, every three months a representative of the Venezuelan Communist Party met with an employee of the Soviet embassy who provided the representative with a sum amounting to 250,000 dollars in cash. There were never any Soviet queries about how the money was spent, and Isaev claimed that the embassy employee often complained that the Venezuelan Communist Party leaders in fact used a good part of the Soviet aid to buy themselves villas and other property.

During the hearings on October 22, a member of the RSFSR parliamentary commission investigating the activities of the junta, Aleksei Surkov, announced that former Politburo member Egor Ligachev had probably been linked with the attempted coup. Surkov said that, according to documents in the possession of the commission, if the coup had been successful, Ligachev might have been appointed to replace Soviet President Mikhail Gorbachev as CPSU general secretary. Surkov also asked the parliament to insist that the CPSU hand over to the RSFSR Prosecutor's Office all documents concerning its illegal activities. Surkov alleged that, before the attempted coup, the former head of Gorbachev's personal secretariat, Valerii Boldin, had transferred all the most sensitive Politburo documents to a special presidential archive.

Ligachev and Gorbachev both responded to Surkov's claims. On October 23, in an interview with *Izvestia*, Ligachev denied the accusations leveled against him. The following day, in an interview in *Sovetskaya Rossiya*, Ligachev called the report "a malicious invention." He argued that he had been at a health resort outside Moscow during the coup and also noted that, even if he had wanted the job of CPSU general secretary, he would have been ineligible, because he was no longer a member of the CPSU Central Committee.

On October 24, in an interview with Interfax, Gorbachev's press secretary, Andrei Grachev, denied that sensitive documents were located in the presidential archives. He said the Soviet president was ready to hand over any documents from his archives relevant to the investigation of Communist Party activities.

State Council Suspends KGB Law

An official statement of the USSR State Council disseminated by TASS on October 22 ruled that the sovereign states composing the USSR had exclusive jurisdiction over their republican Committees for State Security. Three "central organs of government" would be created on the basis of the old KGB: the Central Intelligence Service, responsible for foreign intelligence "in the interests of the USSR and the republics"; an interrepublican Security Service to coordinate the activities of republican internal security services; and a Border Troops Committee under joint command. The State Council also suspended the law on the KGB but left some of its provisions in force.

On October 24, TASS reported that the number of KGB officers working in KGB central counterintelligence would be drastically reduced; Vadim Bakatin, the head of the new service, said that two months ago the number of officers was about 490,000 but that it would be reduced to 35,000–40,000 in the very near future.

St. Petersburg Mayor Interviewed by *Izvestia*

In an interview in *Izvestia*, St. Petersburg Mayor Anatolii Sobchak rejected as absurd speculation that the RSFSR parliament might adopt a law banning former KGB and Communist Party officials from occupying administrative positions. Sobchak said such a law would result in civil war. Sobchak also said that a famine in Russia was improbable, but he claimed that severe economic problems could be solved only if some kind of union existed between the remaining twelve republics.

KAL Wreckage Found

Izvestia reported on October 23 that the wreckage of KAL flight 007, which was shot down by the Soviet Union in September, 1983, had been found in the Tatar Strait on October 22. The discovery was aided by an autonomous diving apparatus referred to as "Tinro-2."

Kirgiz President Speaks at United Nations

Kirgiz President Askar Akaev told the UN General Assembly that the USSR as a state had ceased to exist, RFE/RL's UN correspondent reported. Akaev said that a confederation similar to the British Commonwealth would be an ideal solution for the former Soviet republics and that treaties among them would have to be based on international law. He added that Kirgizia had no immediate plans to join the UN.

Ban on Religious Parties Lifted in Tajikistan

The Tajik Supreme Soviet voted to lift the ban on religious parties that was contained in the republican law on freedom of conscience, TASS reported. This removed the main obstacle to the registration of the Islamic Renaissance Party, which had been functioning as a part of the democratic coalition and had forced a measure of liberalization in the republic but remained illegal. The Islamic Renaissance Party opened its founding congress on October 26.

Moldavia Bides Time on Economic Treaty

The Moldavian leadership sent Soviet President Gorbachev a telegram saying that it agreed "in principle" with the economic community treaty signed by eight republics on October 18 but that it objected to some of its provisions. Prime Minister Valeriu Muravschi told Moldavian television Moldavia would determine its position after further examination of the text and of the clauses to be negotiated. Muravschi also noted that Moldavia was heavily reliant on the USSR and Russia for fuel imports and as markets for Moldavian produce.

"Dniester SSR" Appeals for Recognition

The self-styled Supreme Soviet of the "Dniester SSR," proclaimed by Russian Communists in eastern Moldavia, appealed to the Supreme Soviets of the USSR and its constituent republics for acceptance as a constituent republic of the Union, TASS reported. Recalling that its territory was included in the Ukraine prior to World War II (as "the Moldavian ASSR") and had formed part of the Moldavian SSR ever since, the Dniester leaders said that the area could no longer be part of either Moldavia or Ukraine, since the two republics had declared their independence from the USSR.

On October 23, the Dniester Supreme Soviet resolved to boycott the Moldavian presidential elections scheduled for December 8 and to hold a popular election for a president of "the Dniester SSR," TASS reported. A referendum on the Dniester area's secession from Moldavia would be held concurrently.

Germany and Denmark to Aid Baltic States

Germany and Denmark decided to help the new Baltic democracies and called for urgent aid to the USSR, RFE/RL's correspondent in Bonn reported. The decision was announced in a joint statement following a

THE USSR IN OCTOBER, 1991

conference in Rostock of Danish and German envoys to countries of the Baltic region, Norway, and Iceland. German Foreign Minister Hans-Dietrich Genscher stressed that everything must be done to create decent living conditions to stem westward migration.

Wednesday, October 23

Addressing the USSR Supreme Soviet, USSR President Mikhail Gorbachev proposed an amnesty for military deserters and draft dodgers, Interfax and Central Television reported. The proposal specified that men would be eligible for the amnesty if they either returned to duty or presented themselves to the police within one month of the proposed legislation's taking effect.

Amnesty for Deserters and Draft Dodgers Proposed

The RSFSR Prosecutor's Office announced that all political parties and public associations on the territory of the republic that called for the violation of the RSFSR's territorial integrity were outlawed. TASS said the Prosecutor's Office was referring primarily to organizations that had voiced such calls in Tatarstan and Checheno-Ingushetia. Leaders and members of such parties would be subject to criminal investigation, and media organs promoting separatist tendencies would be closed. The USSR Law on Public Associations adopted in 1990 also forbade the creation of parties planning the violation of the USSR's integrity. This provision of the law had rarely been implemented, however.

RSFSR Prosecutor's Office to Take Measures against Separatists

A Western Jewish leader quoted Soviet Prosecutor-General Nikolai Trubin as saying that his office planned to exonerate and apologize to Jewish dissidents imprisoned in the 1970s. Trubin's assurance was given to Chairman of the World Jewish Congress Irwin Cotler at a meeting in Moscow earlier in the month, a Western news agency reported. Cotler said Trubin specifically referred to Natan Sharansky, Ida Nudel, and Iosif Begun among some twenty-five Jewish political prisoners whose sentences would be declared null and void.

Soviet Jewish Dissidents May Be Exonerated

A study conducted by the Control Department in the RSFSR President's Office indicated that more than 70 percent of the RSFSR's oblasts, krais, autonomous republics, autonomous oblasts, and autonomous okrugs had failed

Majority of RSFSR Officials Did Not Support El'tsin During Coup

to support RSFSR President El'tsin during the coup and had either sided with the junta or adopted a wait-and-see position. The remaining 29.5 percent of the territorial units in the republic declared their loyalty to the RSFSR, but only the local authorities in Moscow, Leningrad, and three oblasts gave active support to El'tsin. None of the Communist Party committees in the RSFSR supported El'tsin, *Moskovsky komsomolets* and *Nezavisimaya gazeta* reported. Instead, two-thirds of them supported the junta and one-third adopted a wait-and-see policy

Pankin Meets with Vietnamese and Chinese Leaders

In conjunction with the signing of the Cambodian agreement in Paris, Soviet Foreign Minister Boris Pankin met with his Vietnamese counterpart, Nguyen Manh Cam, to discuss bilateral relations and economic cooperation. The two ministers expressed the belief that Soviet-Vietnamese cooperation should continue. Pankin then met with Chinese Foreign Minister Qian Qichen to discuss the situation in the Soviet Union, bilateral relations, and international problems. The two ministers also agreed to hold wide-ranging talks during the visit of the Chinese foreign minister to the Soviet Union scheduled for March, 1992, TASS reported.

Presidential Decree on Foreign Trade Bank

Western agencies reported on a presidential decree dated October 19 concerning the Soviet Foreign Trade Bank. The decree stipulated that the bank was the sole agent responsible for servicing the country's foreign debt and for handling new credits and managing hard-currency resources in the interests of the Soviet Union and its republics. The bank was to maintain these functions in accordance with decisions of the USSR Supreme Soviet and the State Council.

Environmental Security Council Created

"Vesti" reported that the Soviet Foreign Policy Association headed by Eduard Shevardnadze had set up a Council for Environmental Security to carry out global environmental projects. Among the founders of the council were prominent scientists who had worked in the military-industrial complex: Academicians Andrei Avdevsky, Nikita Moiseev, and Jarmen Gvishiani.

RSFSR KGB Ready to Cooperate with Western Services

TASS quoted RSFSR KGB Chairman Viktor Ivanenko as saying the Russian KGB wanted to cooperate with Western secret services in combating terrorism, drug trafficking, and the proliferation of chemical and biological

THE USSR IN OCTOBER, 1991

weapons. His organization was interested not only in an exchange of information but also in the creation of joint operative units.

The chairman of Ukraine's Central Bank, Vladimir Matvienko, told Western agencies that his republic planned to begin replacing Soviet rubles with special coupons by the end of 1991, and possibly sooner. The coupons would be a step towards establishing a Ukrainian national currency. They would be on a par and wholly exchangeable with the Soviet ruble and would be valid for the purchase of services such as hotels, restaurants, and transportation.

Ukrainian Currency by Year's End

Thursday, October 24

Mass protests and strikes took place in Dagestan, "Vesti" reported. People were protesting against the appointment of Magomed Abdurazakov as head of the republic's Ministry of Internal Affairs. Abdurazakov had already demonstrated his inability to cope with growing criminality in Dagestan when he held the post of first deputy minister of internal affairs, "Vesti" said.

Protests in Dagestan over Appointment of Interior Minister

USSR Minister of Internal Affairs Viktor Barannikov said the ministry's personnel would be cut by 20 percent, TASS reported. He said the MVD was still needed but must be consolidated.

USSR MVD to Be Cut

Kazakh President Nursultan Nazarbaev told a group of supporters that the RSFSR had stopped shipping petroleum to Kazakhstan's Kustanai Oblast on October 22, an Alma-Ata journalist informed RFE/RL on October 24. Nazarbaev warned that, if the action were repeated, Kazakhstan would stop sending raw materials to the RSFSR. Nazarbaev also said he had sent a letter to RSFSR President Boris El'tsin about tensions between Kazakhs and Cossacks in northern Kazakhstan. Nazarbaev was critical of the RSFSR leadership, complaining that it was still trying to control everything.

Nazarbaev on RSFSR-Kazakhstan Friction

"Vesti" reported that young people in Alma-Ata had staged a demonstration against Kazakh President Nazarbaev. They tore up copies of his autobiography and

Demonstrations against Nazarbaev

claimed that he had participated in the suppression of nationalist demonstrations in Alma-Ata in December, 1986. In his book, Nazarbaev said he had led a group of demonstrators in 1986.

Moldavian President Launches Election Campaign

Moldavian President Mircea Snegur launched his election campaign and reaffirmed the Moldavian leadership's commitment to "full state independence." Stressing once again that "there can be no question of merging with another state," Snegur said the Moldavian leadership stood for close economic and cultural cooperation with former Soviet republics, Romania, and Western Europe and would redouble efforts to obtain recognition of Moldavia's independence.

Baltic States Admitted as Associate Members to North Atlantic Assembly

Estonia, Latvia, and Lithuania were admitted as associate members of the North Atlantic Assembly in Madrid, Radio Riga reported. The North Atlantic Assembly, founded in 1950, is a parliamentary body for NATO countries. East European countries are also associate members of the North Atlantic Assembly.

Estonian-RSFSR Relations Established

Estonian Foreign Minister Lennart Meri and his RSFSR counterpart, Andrei Kozyrev, signed a protocol in Moscow establishing diplomatic relations at the embassy level between their countries. The two sides also signed a protocol on talks between Estonia and Russia to work out as soon as possible an agreement on the rights and citizenship of the nonnative populations of the two states. It was also decided that, until an accord was signed, Estonia and Russia would maintain the status quo regarding their common border, Baltfax reported.

British Envoy Accredited in Riga

Richard Christopher Samuel was accredited as Britain's envoy to Latvia. Britain's decision to appoint a diplomatic representative to Latvia was viewed positively by the Latvian government, especially because in the prewar years one British diplomat had represented his country in all three Baltic States.

Friday, October 25

Soviet Foreign Minister on USSR's Nuclear Arsenal

Soviet Foreign Minister Boris Pankin told reporters in Paris that Soviet nuclear weapons were under the sole

The USSR in October, 1991

control of the central command, and only Soviet President Mikhail Gorbachev could operate them, Western agencies reported. He noted that the leaders of the republics where these weapons were located had a right to know how they would be used.

Kryuchkov Accused of Planning Coup

A senior official of the former KGB, Major General Anatolii Oleinikov, said former KGB Chairman Vladimir Kryuchkov had begun planning the coup d'état in 1990, Western agencies reported. Oleinikov said that Kryuchkov was the driving force behind the coup and that an internal KGB investigation had implicated at least six more top officials of the Soviet security service in the plot.

Soviet Nuclear Naval Disaster Revealed

A nuclear accident aboard a Soviet submarine in 1985 was covered up by Soviet military officials, *Trud* reported. The accident occurred in a naval shipyard near Vladivostok while sailors were replacing the core of a submarine's nuclear reactor. The core exploded, killing ten sailors, and sent radioactive debris over a large area. The Soviet newspaper called it the worst nuclear accident in the Soviet navy in the past thirty years, and local military commanders ordered that the blast be officially described as a thermal explosion.

Warning of Discontent among Discharged Troops

The chairman of the USSR Supreme Soviet Commission on National Security, Viktor Minin, warned of dissatisfaction among discharged servicemen in an interview published in *Krasnaya zvezda*. The reduction of the armed forces from 3.7 million to 3 million would worsen the country's housing and unemployment crises, he pointed out. "The army has become the sixteenth republic, hungry and unsettled, but well armed and trained." Minin spoke of the possibility of a social explosion that "could sweep away democracy and the market."

Global Strategic Security System Proposed

A joint US-Soviet space-based strategic security system might eliminate not only the risk of nuclear confrontation but also the danger of local conflicts, Academician Nikita Moiseev wrote in *Polis* (No. 5). Moiseev's system, called "Black Diamonds," would contain elements of the Soviet and US SDI programs; it would use a weapon based on new physical principles, which could make the nuclear arsenal of the superpowers obsolete by the third millennium.

The USSR in October, 1991

Kirgiz President Meets Bush Kirgiz President Askar Akaev met with US President George Bush in Washington, Western agencies reported. He delivered a letter from Soviet President Gorbachev and discussed Kirgizia's democratization program with the US president.

Defense Committee Created in Kazakhstan TASS reported that Kazakh President Nursultan Nazarbaev had issued a decree creating a republican State Committee for Defense. According to the report, the decree described the committee as intended to protect "the independence, territorial integrity, and vital interests" of the sovereign republic of Kazakhstan.

Saturday, October 26

Rutskoi's Party Holds First Congress The Democratic Party of Communists of Russia, headed by RSFSR Vice President Aleksandr Rutskoi, began its first congress in Moscow, TASS reported. Opening the congress, Rutskoi said the party was neither going to continue the political and ideological line of the Russian Communist Party nor become an instrument in the hands of the El'tsin leadership. On October 27, according to TASS, the congress confirmed the renaming of the party as the People's Party of Free Russia and elected Rutskoi its chairman. The congress also said that all CPSU property on the territory of the RSFSR should be transferred to the People's Party of Free Russia.

RSFSR Food Imports Cut At a meeting attended by representatives of the twelve remaining republics, RSFSR Deputy Prime Minister Gennadii Kulik said that regular imports of meat and other foodstuffs would be cut by as much as one-half because of the shortage of hard currency, TASS reported. He said that for this reason shortfalls in grain imports would amount to 7 million tons and that there was only enough grain to last until the end of the year in several regions of Russia.

Democratic Russia Criticizes El'tsin At a plenum of the Moscow branch of Democratic Russia, the movement's leaders said the RSFSR leadership had proved ineffective since Boris El'tsin was elected president on June 12. The movement expressed dissatisfaction with El'tsin for failing to introduce radical economic reforms more quickly. Western agencies quoted Professor Yurii Afanas'ev as saying the group

The USSR in October, 1991

might have to become an opposition movement if the Russian government did not take a "responsible" position towards solving problems.

Coup Leaders to Remain in Jail

A leading member of the group investigating the activities of the leaders of the attempted coup, Deputy USSR Prosecutor-General Evgenii Lisov, said the leaders of the failed coup should stay in jail. *Pravda* quoted him as saying that the alleged conspirators were still somewhat influential and could use their freedom to impede the criminal investigation. He also said members of the group might commit suicide if they were let out of jail. Lisov's comments came in response to a request by the defense lawyers of those arrested in connection with the attempted coup that their clients be let out of prison during the preliminary investigation.

Negotiations on Nagorno-Karabakh Open

Delegations headed by the first deputy chairmen of the Azerbaijani and Armenian parliaments met in Armenia's Idzhevan Raion for the first round of formal talks aimed at achieving a settlement of the Nagorno-Karabakh crisis, TASS reported. The talks were taking place within the parameters of the agreement brokered by RSFSR President Boris El'tsin in Zheleznovodsk in September. Both sides described the talks as encouraging but stressed that progress was likely to be slow. Participants adopted an appeal to the Armenian and Azerbaijani peoples to refrain from violence.

New "Social Progress" Party in Ukraine

Radio Moscow reported that former members of the banned Communist Party of Ukraine had formed a new party called the Party of Social Progress of Ukraine, Radio Moscow reported. A Radio Kiev report of October 28 said that 286 delegates had gathered in Kiev at the party's founding congress.

Turkmenistan Votes for Independence

Radio Moscow reported on October 27 that 94.1 percent of the population of Turkmenistan had voted for the independence of the republic in a referendum held on October 26. Accordingly, the Turkmen Supreme Soviet adopted a law on independence and proclaimed October 27 Independence Day. The declaration on which the voters cast ballots declared Turkmenistan to be a democratic state based on law, but opposition groups doubted the leadership's commitment to democratic principles.

Proposals for Belorussian National Guard Revealed

On October 25, the security and defense commission of the Belorussian Supreme Soviet revealed its draft proposals for a republican national guard. As summarized on October 26 in *Znamya yunosti*, the guard was to be formed on the basis of existing combat-ready and mobile units of the USSR Armed Forces. The guard would be trained in the spirit of "Belorussian military traditions and rituals," and its working language, after a period of transition, would be Belorussian. The force would number between 5,000 and 8,000 men.

Moldavia Still Refusing to Sign USSR Food Agreement

Moldavia was the sole republic withholding its signature from the interrepublican agreement on food deliveries, which had already been signed by eleven republics and was, in addition, being adhered to by the Baltic States as associates, TASS reported. Moldavian Prime Minister Valeriu Muravschi told TASS that Kishinev objected to the provisions committing Moldavia to supply foodstuffs to Union stocks while making the compensatory delivery of goods to Moldavia a subject of further, bilateral negotiations by Moldavia with the individual republics.

Moldavian Officers Summoned Home

The Moldavian Ministry of Internal Affairs called on Moldavian officers and NCOs serving with USSR border troops outside Moldavian territory to return home and join the republic's planned border guard (*Moldovapres*, October 26). The ministry also called on civilian reservists in Moldavia to join the republican border guard. The calls were issued in accordance with President Mircea Snegur's decrees of September 3 and 11, which ordered the formation of a Moldavian border guard, claimed exclusive Moldavian jurisdiction over the republic's borders and over USSR border troops and their assets in Moldavia, and initiated negotiations on the withdrawal of the troops.

Improving Belorussian-Lithuanian Relations

Belorussian newspapers published the text of a declaration on the principles of good-neighborly relations between Belorussia and Lithuania signed in Vilnius on October 24 by President of the Lithuanian Supreme Council Vytautas Landsbergis and Belorussian Supreme Soviet Chairman Stanislau Shushkevich. The two sides asserted their loyalty to the principle of the inviolability of borders, agreeing at the same time to set up a special commission to study the question of the Lithuanian-Belorussian border. Belorussia said it would not be part of any Soviet delegation in future talks between Lithuania and the USSR.

THE USSR IN OCTOBER, 1991

USSR Wants Lithuania to Finance Troop Withdrawal

Izvestia quoted USSR Deputy Minister of Defense Pavel Grachev as saying Lithuania must provide material and financial aid and help with the construction of new installations to house the Soviet troops being withdrawn from Lithuania. He also said that the USSR forces would not leave Lithuania completely until the end of 1994. Grachev noted that teams from both sides were trying to iron out the details of the withdrawal process and expressed regret that the negotiations were taking so long. On October 28, Grachev repeated his statement that Soviet troops would not be withdrawn from the Baltic States until those states could afford to relocate the soldiers, Western agencies reported. Grachev said the forces could not leave if there was no place to put them. When asked how the Baltic States could afford such a program given their severe economic problems, Grachev said the Soviet Armed Forces "will have to wait until [the Baltic States] become wealthy."

Russian Democrats Meet in Estonia

The Russian Democratic Movement of Estonia held its second congress in Tallinn, *Paevaleht* reported on October 27. The movement encompassed a broad spectrum of political thought ranging from former "Intermovement" supporters to democratically minded non-Estonians. Because the Russian Democratic Movement of Estonia was formed after the Estonian government outlawed "Intermovement" in the aftermath of the coup, some commentators suggested that the movement was an "Intermovement" front operation.

Sunday, October 27

Group of Seven Meets in Moscow

During the first day of meetings between officials of the Group of Seven leading industrialized nations and representatives of the USSR central authorities and of the twelve remaining republics of the USSR, Ukrainian Prime Minister Vitol'd Fokin proposed the creation of a special central bank to handle the payments of the Soviet Union's foreign debt, Soviet and Western agencies reported. His proposal was supported by nine of the twelve republics. The Western side was said to have warned of the adverse consequences of any reneging on the Soviet debt.

On October 28, the two sides agreed on a plan to share the USSR's foreign debt among the republics, TASS, Interfax, and Western agencies reported. A senior US official present described the talks as "highly active" and "very spontaneous." Fokin stormed out of the meeting, but returned later to sign the memorandum with a codicil stipulating that the Baltic States would also assume their debt obligations. A meeting in Kiev in November was proposed to discuss where the republics would obtain the necessary hard currency. Estonian Finance Minister Rein Miller said Estonia was prepared to assume its part of the Soviet foreign debt. There were no Baltic representatives at the G-7 meeting, but Miller nevertheless described the clause in the agreement pertaining to the Baltic States as "correct."

On October 31, RSFSR presidential adviser Sergei Stankevich said that the twelve republics had not yet reached final agreement on repaying the USSR's foreign debt, TASS and Interfax reported. Stankevich said that the republics still had to work out a payment mechanism, and he called earlier reports of an accord on the subject "very uncertain."

Successor Party to CPSU Founded in RSFSR

A new party was formed over the weekend to succeed the Communist Party in the RSFSR. The new party was called the Socialist Party of the Working People, TASS and Postfactum reported. Postfactum said it had been announced at the party's inaugural conference, which was attended by 300 delegates, that the aim of the organization was "to restore fairness and legality with regard to the CPSU." TASS called the Socialist Party of Working People "virtually a legal successor to the CPSU."

Protests against Removal of Lenin's Body

Nearly 300 people rallied in Moscow's Red Square to demand that Lenin's body not be disturbed, Western agencies reported. Several prominent democratic leaders, including St. Petersburg Mayor Anatolii Sobchak, had called for the removal of Lenin's body from the mausoleum and its burial.

Wealth Becoming Socially Acceptable?

A recent public opinion poll conducted by sociologist Boris Grushin suggested that Soviet citizens were growing more tolerant of wealth disparities. Eight months earlier, only 43 percent of those polled found it acceptable that some members of Soviet society should be richer than others, whereas 38 percent disapproved. But, when Grushin repeated the poll in September, he found that 75 percent thought the existence of rich people was acceptable and that only 13 percent disapproved ("TV Inform," *Central Television*, October 27).

THE USSR IN OCTOBER, 1991

Campaign to Transfer South Ossetia to RSFSR Continues

On October 27, the RSFSR Supreme Soviet voted to empower President Boris El'tsin to impose economic sanctions against Georgia in the campaign to transfer Georgia's South Ossetian Autonomous Oblast to the RSFSR, TASS reported. Meanwhile, artillery and missile bombardments continued near Tskhinvali, the South Ossetian capital, TASS reported on October 28. On October 29, however, USSR MVD forces claimed to have halted the bombardments of populated areas. The same day, USSR MVD troops were reported to have secured the release of twelve Ossetian hostages and two Georgian hostages. On October 31, the chairman of the South Ossetian Oblast Executive Committee, Znaur Gassiev, told reporters in Tskhinvali that his people would fight to the last man for the right to break free of Georgia and become part of the RSFSR.

Mass Demonstration in Baku

Some 100,000 people demonstrated in Baku to protest against Azerbaijani President Ayaz Mutalibov's support for the appeal issued on October 22 by the USSR Supreme Soviet to Ukraine to remain within the Soviet Union, Radio Rossii reported. The demonstrators also called for the publication of three resolutions adopted by the Azerbaijani parliament, including one on the creation of a republican army, and for the forthcoming session of parliament, scheduled to open on October 28, to be televised live.

Monday, October 28

El'tsin Proposes "Reformist Breakthrough" to RSFSR Congress of People's Deputies

The RSFSR Congress of People's Deputies opened a new session in Moscow, the RSFSR media reported. On the opening day, President Boris El'tsin proposed himself as Russia's new prime minister and asked for additional powers to conduct a policy that he called "a reformist breakthrough" (*reformistsky proryv*). In his speech to the Congress, El'tsin called for radical economic reform, including liberalization of prices, privatization, land reform, tightening of credit policies, and the possible introduction of a new currency in Russia. He stressed the need for the creation of a separate Russian army if the other republics created their own national armies. The proposed reform program foresaw the freeing of most prices and wages, with a rejection of total indexation; establishing a social safety net; privatizing small- and medium-sized enterprises, farms, and housing; monetary stabilization; tax reform; a single currency; and an appeal to the IMF and European Bank for Reconstruction and Development for help. He warned of short-term hardships but promised "real results by the fall of 1992."

Democrats and Communists in the RSFSR parliament welcomed El'tsin's proposal, TASS reported. Coleader of the Republican Party Vladimir Lysenko said El'tsin was the only politician who had the authority to convince the population of the necessity of introducing harsh new economic measures. Lysenko supported El'tsin's request for additional powers and his offer to take over the premiership, stressing that, for any other politician, assuming such a post would mean political suicide. El'tsin's proposal was also supported by the leader of the currently suspended Russian Communist Party, Viktor Stepanov, normally a El'tsin opponent.

On October 29, coleader of the Democratic Russia movement Yurii Afanas'ev told Western news agencies that his movement would support El'tsin. Nikolai Travkin, chairman of the Russian Democratic Party, emphasized that in El'tsin's speech the concept of a union had been put to rest. The same day, at a session of the Committee for the Operational Management of the Economy, Acting USSR Prime Minister Ivan Silaev praised the salient features of El'tsin's program, TASS reported that day. Silaev was quoted as declaring that the plan's provisions for price liberalization and rapid privatization would encourage the elaboration of a program for all the republics. He did not view El'tsin's blueprint as a threat to the economic community that had been tentatively agreed to by eight republics on October 18; "the success of reforms in the sovereign republics will largely depend on how fast and how successfully reforms go in Russia," he said. The same TASS dispatch cited USSR Deputy Minister for the Economy Vladimir Gribov as calling El'tsin's program hard to implement but necessary. Gribov emphasized that the freeing of prices must not be accompanied by the complete liberalization of salaries, as this would provoke rampant inflation. He advocated a reform of the tax system to draw in more revenues, stipulating higher profit taxes and the imposition of a 15-percent value-added tax on some goods. El'tsin appealed to the RSFSR Congress of People's Deputies on October 30 to grant him broad new political powers, Western agencies reported. He said he needed greater authority to enact economic reform and limit local political activity. He asked for extraordinary powers to rule by decree until the end of 1992, even if these contradicted Soviet and Russian laws, but he suggested that the RSFSR Supreme Soviet retain the right to overturn any presidential decree within a week of its being issued. He also asked for the power to ban any election in the RSFSR until the end of 1992. On November 1, the Congress overwhelm-

The USSR in October, 1991

ingly approved these measures, giving El'tsin and the RSFSR Supreme Soviet the right to override USSR laws that hindered reform. The Congress also approved El'tsin's proposed economic reform program, Western agencies reported.

Khasbulatov Elected Head of RSFSR Parliament

Ruslan Khasbulatov was elected chairman of the RSFSR Supreme Soviet ("Vesti," *Russian Television*, October 28). The post had been vacant since the election of El'tsin as RSFSR president in June. At the previous session of the RSFSR Congress, in July, Khasbulatov had failed to win a majority of votes. Several deputies had complained about his allegedly authoritarian style, but his firm stance during the coup boosted his popularity, and in the latest ballot 559 of the 873 deputies voted for him. Khasbulatov, a Chechen by nationality, had been first deputy chairman of the Russian parliament under El'tsin.

On October 29, Khasbulatov stressed the need to support El'tsin's radical economic program. He told TASS that the RSFSR parliament sought cooperation with the RSFSR executive. He warned that, following the dismantling of the Socialist bloc and the Soviet Union, the disintegration process had now reached the RSFSR.

Lubenchenko Elected Chairman of the Council of the Union

Konstantin Lubenchenko was elected chairman of the Council of the Union of the USSR Supreme Soviet—the chamber of the central parliament representing the Union. Lubenchenko, who belonged to neither the reformist nor the conservative faction in the parliament, was elected unanimously. Born in 1945 and Russian by nationality, Lubenchenko taught at Moscow State University until 1990. Since then, he had occupied the post of deputy chairman of the USSR Supreme Soviet Committee for Legislation.

El'tsin Creates Committee for Defense Conversion

RSFSR President Boris El'tsin decreed the establishment of an RSFSR State Committee for Defense Conversion (*Interfax*, October 28). The new body would offer posts for the best military specialists employed in the military-industrial complex. The aim of the new committee was to support El'tsin's reform program by supervising cuts in the military sphere and transferring army resources to civilian needs.

Churkin Rejects El'tsin Proposal on Foreign Ministry

USSR Foreign Ministry spokesman Vitalii Churkin criticized RSFSR President Boris El'tsin's proposal to strip the

USSR Foreign Ministry of most of its current functions. The consequence of such a move "would be that the Soviet Union as a single country would be no more," Churkin said. El'tsin had proposed that the Ministry of Foreign Affairs' funding be cut by 90 percent as part of an austerity program for the RSFSR. He suggested that the ministry limit its functions to coordinating the foreign policies of the Soviet republics, a Western news agency reported.

Gem Laboratory in *Pravda* Building In *Pravda* of October 28, the newspaper's former chief editor, Viktor Afanas'ev, confirmed that a jewel-cutting laboratory with computer simulation of diamond modeling had indeed existed in Room 626 of its editorial building. It had been set up by five scientists who were dismayed that Russia was selling uncut diamonds to the West at unrealistically low prices. Afanas'ev said former Party and state leaders, including Egor Ligachev and Lev Zaikov, had been aware of the operation of the laboratory and had visited it. Afanas'ev was responding to an article in the October 26 issue of *Moskovsky komsomolets*, which had alleged that *Pravda* was in the diamond business for the nomenklatura.

Uzbek-Ukrainian Agreement Uzbek President Islam Karimov and Chairman of the Ukrainian Supreme Soviet Leonid Kravchuk signed an agreement on economic cooperation between their two republics. A TASS report on the signing said that the ten-year agreement covered cooperation in science and technology as well as in economics and trade. A separate agreement was concluded on cooperation between the Ministries of Foreign Affairs of the two republics, providing for the Ukrainian delegation to the United Nations to represent Uzbekistan as well.

Turkmen Democrats Hold Congress in Moscow Radio Moscow reported that the Democratic Party of Turkmenistan had been invited by the Democratic Party of Russia to hold its congress in Moscow because it could not be held in Turkmenistan.

"Birlik" Forms Political Party The Uzbek Popular Front, "Birlik," proclaimed itself a political party at its congress, a Tashkent journalist told the RL Uzbek service. Cochairman of "Birlik" Abdurrakhim Pulatov was chosen to head the new party. According to the journalist, the republican authorities told "Birlik" to present a membership list by November 1 in order to qualify for registration. "Birlik" set up a Democratic Party of Uzbekistan in 1990, but it never gained official recognition. Earlier in 1991, Uzbek President Islam Karimov said he did not believe "Birlik" would ever qualify for registration.

Nazarbaev in Britain

On the first day of his visit to Britain, Kazakh President Nursultan Nazarbaev told a press conference that the main objective of his trip was the development of economic ties between Kazakhstan and Britain. Nazarbaev also said it was important for the republics that signed the economic union agreement on October 18 to establish a single market as quickly as possible (*TASS*, October 28).

On October 29, Nazarbaev met with British Prime Minister John Major to discuss the development of direct relations between Kazakhstan and Britain and Western assistance to the Soviet Union, TASS and Western news agencies reported. The Kazakh president also met with the president of the European Bank for Reconstruction and Development, Jacques Attali, and with former British Prime Minister Margaret Thatcher. In a speech to the Royal Institute of International Affairs, Nazarbaev explained his stand on nuclear weapons, saying that Kazakhstan did not want to take control of the nuclear weapons on its soil, much less use them, but insisted on having a say in the control of these weapons. Nazarbaev said that a single controlling body, comprising the defense ministers of all the republics, should oversee a single strategic weapons system. He also said that Kazakhstan wanted to participate in arms reduction talks affecting weapons on its territory.

USSR Rehabilitates Baltic Leaders

USSR Prosecutor-General Nikolai Trubin ordered the rehabilitation of two interwar Baltic leaders, TASS reported. Trubin signed the orders for the rehabilitation of former Estonian President Konstantin Pats and former Lithuanian Prime Minister Antanas Merkys, saying that both men, as the leaders of sovereign states, had been arrested unlawfully by foreign authorities. Pats and Merkys were arrested and deported to labor camps when the USSR forcibly annexed the Baltic States, and both died in imprisonment.

Sweden Signs Trade Accords with Baltic States

Swedish Foreign Minister Margaretha Af Ugglas signed agreements with her counterparts Lennart Meri of Estonia and Janis Jurkans of Latvia establishing most-favored-nation trade relationships between Sweden and the two Baltic States. A similar accord between Sweden and

Lithuania was endorsed in Vilnius on October 29 by Ugglas and Lithuanian Foreign Minister Algirdas Saudargas, Baltic news agencies reported on October 29 and 30.

Tuesday, October 29

USSR Budget Deficit and Defense Expenditure

USSR Deputy Finance Minister Vladimir Gribov told the Committee for the Operational Management of the Economy that the current budget deficit was 240 billion rubles, Interfax reported. One of the causes of the deficit, according to Gribov, was the republics' withholding of their contributions to the Union budget; he cited a figure of 29 billion rubles owed by the RSFSR. At the same meeting, the head of the committee's Defense Department, Soslan Guchmazov, put defense expenditure for 1991 at 173 billion rubles. He expected that figure to rise to 250 billion rubles in 1992, when price increases were taken into consideration.

Kazakh Elected Chairman of USSR Council of Republics

Anuar Alimzhanov, a Kazakh writer and journalist, was elected chairman of the USSR Council of the Republics, Radio Rossii reported. Representatives from seven republics participated in the election, which was carried out by secret ballot. The election had been delayed while an unsuccessful attempt was made to persuade Ukraine to send delegates. In the end, Ukraine decided to send only observers and only to the Council of the Union chamber.

Two RSFSR Supreme Soviet Deputy Chairmen Resign

Boris Isaev and Svetlana Goryacheva both asked to be relieved of their duties as deputy chairmen of the RSFSR Supreme Soviet, TASS reported. The two were known to be opponents of RSFSR President Boris El'tsin, and were among a group of deputies who had requested El'tsin's resignation in the spring.

Silaev on Fate of Union Ministries

In a statement in the latest issue of *Pravitel'stvennyi vestnik*, cited by TASS on October 29, Ivan Silaev, chairman of the Interrepublican Economic Committee, said that a Ministry of Finance was no longer necessary, since the budget would be formed on the basis of fixed contributions from the republics. Silaev said that the republics had agreed so far only to have a Union Committee of Culture and Ministries of Railways, Medium Machine-Building, and the Atomic Energy Industry.

The USSR in October, 1991

Silaev said that 37,000 employees of the central ministries and departments would be made redundant. He thought the majority would go into newly created RSFSR ministries.

RSFSR Foreign Aid

Acting RSFSR Minister for Foreign Economic Relations Gennadii Fil'shin told TASS that Russia would continue to invest in civilian projects in other countries, even though statements had been made about stopping all foreign aid. "This means that we will not support regimes for ideological purposes," Fil'shin remarked. He put the value of Russia's aid program at more than 10 billion hard-currency rubles a year.

US-Soviet Cooperation on Conversion

At a Moscow press conference, US Deputy Defense Secretary Donald Atwood said that the United States would act as "a catalyst" in the conversion of the Soviet defense industry to civilian production, Western agencies reported. Atwood was heading a delegation of US business and political figures touring Soviet military industrial complexes. At the same press conference, Viktor Protasov, a member of the Committee for the Operational Management of the USSR Economy, warned that the USSR's defense industry was threatened with disaster following the collapse of central power.

Bush and Gorbachev Hold Joint Press Conference

Soviet President Mikhail Gorbachev, who was in Spain for the opening of the Middle East peace conference, met with US President George Bush. At a luncheon meeting, Bush and Gorbachev discussed a wide range of subjects. Among them were arms control, the Middle East peace settlement, and US aid to the Soviet Union. Gorbachev said at a press conference that part of the meeting was devoted to the current internal situation in the Soviet Union, TASS reported.

At the same press conference, Bush said that the question of aid to the Soviet Union required further discussion. He did not provide details on the amount of aid discussed. On October 30, however, US Agriculture Secretary Edward Madigan said the USSR had requested 2.5 billion dollars from the United States in new agricultural credit guarantees and 1 billion dollars in humanitarian aid. The United States was considering up to 1.9 billion dollars in new agricultural credit guarantees and 1 billion dollars in humanitarian assistance, Madigan said (Western agencies, October 30 and 31).

Soviet Stance at Middle East Peace Conference

An unidentified aide to Mikhail Gorbachev said the Soviet Union would employ an evenhanded policy during the Middle East peace conference. According to a report in Israel's *Ma'ariv*, the aide said: "Our consistent support for the Arab side in the past stemmed mainly from our having been involved in a global conflict with the United States. Today we are no longer a superpower . . . . Our foreign policy is dictated by internal considerations and regional, rather than global, strategic interests . . . . We believe that, as long as the Arab-Israeli conflict remains unresolved, the chance of Islamic fundamentalism and instability spreading across our borders grows."

Ukrainian Supreme Soviet Votes to Close Chernobyl' as Soon as Possible

The Ukrainian Supreme Soviet appealed to the United Nations for technical assistance in shutting down the Chernobyl' nuclear power plant, according to TASS. Although Chernobyl' was due to be phased out of operation by 1995, the recent fire at the plant's second bloc led the Ukrainian parliament to vote for the immediate closure of that bloc and for the shutting down of the first and third blocs by no later than 1993.

Hunger Strikes in Crimea

Radio Kiev reported that Crimean people's deputy Yurii Meskhov, who headed the pro-Russian Republican Movement of Crimea, was continuing a hunger strike to gain support for annulment of the 1954 act that transferred the peninsula from RSFSR to Ukrainian jurisdiction. Three journalists from the newspaper *Krymsky komsomolets* were, however, staging "a counter-hunger strike" in protest against Meshkov's demands. The local Communist authorities had mounted a campaign to separate the Crimean ASSR from Ukraine, which was seeking independence.

Uzbeks Try to Retrieve National Heritage

Central Television's evening news show "TSN" reported that the authorities in Khorezm Oblast were trying to retrieve the throne of the khans of Khiva from the Hermitage in St. Petersburg. The historic city of Khiva is located in Uzbekistan's Khorezm Oblast. According to the report, the Uzbek request was rejected on the grounds that Khorezm lacked facilities to protect the throne and that it therefore might be stolen.

United States to Provide Economic Aid to Baltic States

US Vice President Dan Quayle and the three Baltic prime ministers—Edgar Savisaar of Estonia, Ivars

Godmanis of Latvia, and Gediminas Vagnorius of Lithuania—signed agreements in Indianapolis covering US economic aid to the Baltic States. Direct loans and loan guarantees to US companies seeking to participate in joint ventures and or make other investments in the Baltic States would be provided. In addition, US Peace Corps volunteers would provide English instruction, advice on environmental issues, and assistance in the development of business (RFE/RL correspondent's report, October 29).

EBRD Favors Baltic Membership

The directors of the European Bank for Reconstruction and Development (EBRD) recommended that Estonia, Latvia, and Lithuania be granted membership in the bank, Western agencies reported. Membership would entitle the Baltic States to aid from the bank.

Latvian Designated Language of Supreme Council

The Latvian Supreme Council decided that, as of November 1, the council's official documents and proceedings would no longer be translated into Russian. Deputies of the pro-USSR "Ravnopravie" faction opposed the decision, since many of them were not fluent in Latvian. The Russian-speaking deputies would, however, still be able to address the council in Russian and their speeches would be translated into Latvian.

Import/Export Easier in Estonia

The Estonian government approved a proposal to liberalize import/export regulations. According to *Paevaleht*, quoting Minister of State Raivo Vare, Estonia would eliminate quotas and licensing requirements and would not levy taxes on imported and exported goods purchased with hard currency. Certain categories of goods in short supply would still be subject to quotas, regardless of the method of payment.

Wednesday, October 30

El'tsin Sends Envoys to Explain Reform Program

RSFSR President Boris El'tsin sent special envoys abroad to explain his recently announced reform program and to ask for financial assistance, TASS reported. RSFSR Foreign Minister Andrei Kozyrev went to the United States, RSFSR Vice President Aleksandr Rutskoi to Italy and Britain, RSFSR State Secretary Gennadii Burbulis to Germany and France, RSFSR State Councilor Sergei Stankevich to Poland, adviser to the RSFSR President Galina Starovoitova to Finland and Sweden, and Chairman of the RSFSR Supreme Soviet Committee for Foreign Affairs and Foreign Economic Relations Vladimir Lukin to South Korea and Japan.

Gaidar Key Figure in El'tsin's New Cabinet

The *Financial Times* reported that RSFSR President Boris El'tsin planned to appoint the radical economist Egor Gaidar as RSFSR economics and finance minister and also to make him first deputy prime minister. Gaidar was regarded as the chief advocate of the idea that Russia should go its own way without the republics. This idea was at odds with that of another radical economist, Grigorii Yavlinsky, who stressed the need to preserve the Union. Gaidar would enter El'tsin's cabinet with his own staff of young economists from economic institutes in Moscow and St. Petersburg. The future RSFSR Cabinet of Ministers would consist of no more than twenty ministers.

RSFSR Forms Constitutional Court

Thirteen judges took their oath of office to serve in the new Russian Constitutional Court at the RSFSR Congress of People's Deputies, TASS reported. The judges were elected by the Congress and were empowered to judge the constitutionality of legislative texts and the actions of government officials. The court was also given the power to initiate proceedings to remove the RSFSR president if it decided the president had acted against the constitution.

Independent Trade Unions Warn El'tsin of Labor Unrest

The head of the parliamentary faction of the Russian Independent Trade-Union Federation, Kazbek Doev, warned that El'tsin's economic reform program could spark massive labor unrest, Interfax reported. Doev asserted that his group would only go along with the provision to end price subsidies if a 100-percent pay increase was first given to the 30–40 million Russian workers. Allowing prices to rise without wage compensation would lead to confrontation, Doev said, adding that the unions intended to press for the mandatory right to collective bargaining and for the funding of severance payments for those who lost their jobs.

Final Grain Harvest Figure

A spokesman for the USSR State Committee for Statistics told Western agencies that the grain harvest for 1991 totaled 165 million tons, or 160 million tons if the harvest in the Baltic States was excluded. This was the lowest

The USSR in October, 1991

recorded Soviet harvest since 1975 and was far below earlier, authoritative Soviet pronouncements and much lower than most Western estimates. It was possible, however, that farms and local authorities understated the amount of grain harvested, since in many instances they were unwilling to sell surplus grain for rubles.

200-Ruble Bank Notes in Circulation

The USSR State Bank announced that new 200-ruble bank notes would be in circulation starting on October 30, TASS reported on October 28. Prior to this, the largest denomination had been the 100-ruble note. The bank also planned to issue a 500-ruble note by the end of the year (see *Trud*, October 1, and *TASS*, October 3).

Tourism Declining

The number of tourists visiting the Soviet Union during the first half of 1991 declined sharply in comparison with the same period in 1990, Interfax reported. The biggest drop was recorded in visitors from Eastern Europe. Intourist, which used to hold a monopoly, saw its market share reduced to 38 percent.

Barannikov Expects Continued Emigration

USSR Minister of Internal Affairs Viktor Barannikov, addressing an international conference in Berlin on stemming illegal emigration, said he expected about half a million Soviet citizens to emigrate annually for the foreseeable future, Western agencies reported. In 1990, 453,700 Soviet citizens emigrated, but in 1991 the number of applications had fallen by about 9 percent, Barannikov noted.

Taxi Drivers Stage Protest against Violence

Moscow city officials threatened unspecified action against protesting taxi drivers who had blocked streets in parts of Moscow and attacked ethnic Transcaucasians, Western agencies reported. Soviet television reported that the protests had begun after two drivers were murdered and that the drivers blamed the Transcaucasians for bringing organized crime to Moscow. The taxi drivers were demanding life insurance, early retirement, and partitions in their taxis to deter attacks.

Statistics on Belief in God

Argumenty i fakty (No. 40) reported the results of an opinion poll carried out by the Center for Socioeconomic Research, in which 28 percent of respondents said they believed in God, 59 percent said they did not, and 13 percent did not know.

The USSR in October, 1991

Patriarch Aleksii II Criticizes Pope

Patriarch Aleksii II told a press conference at Lambeth Palace in London on October 30 that the pope was not welcome to visit Russia. The patriarch launched "a bitter attack" on the leadership of the Roman Catholic Church, *The Daily Telegraph* reported on October 31.

Republics Respond to El'tsin's Economic Reform Plan

Commenting on El'tsin's economic reform plan, the chairman of the Belorussian Supreme Soviet Stanislau Shushkevich said that conditions were different in Belorussia and Russia and that Belorussia's approach to the market would be more restrained, TASS reported. Many deputies in Minsk feared that a republic such as Belorussia, which lacks key natural resources, would be "brought to its knees" by El'tsin's proposals to conduct trade in world prices and eventually to introduce a Russian currency. Tajik Deputy Prime Minister Abduzhalil Samadov told *Izvestia* that unfreezing prices in one republic would have unequivocally negative consequences for all the republics, while Estonian Finance Minister Rein Miller said he was upset by El'tsin's statement that trade with republics that had not signed the economic treaty would be at world prices and in hard currency, when it had recently been stated that trade would be in rubles in 1992.

Ukrainian-Russian Talks

Ukrainian and RSFSR officials met in Kiev for talks aimed at working out common approaches to domestic and foreign policy, TASS reported. The delegations were led by the foreign ministers of the two republics, Anatolii Zlenko and Andrei Kozyrev. Also in attendance were Ukrainian Defense Minister Konstantin Morozov and Konstantin Kobets, chairman of the RSFSR Committee on Defense. The two sides agreed to work towards the speedy implementation of the Conventional Forces in Europe Treaty and the Strategic Arms Reduction Treaty of 1991. They also pledged mutual cooperation in gaining entry to international economic and financial organizations.

Azerbaijani Parliament Creates New Legislative Organ

After a stormy debate, the Azerbaijani parliament voted to create a new permanent legislative body, the National Council, which would have approximately fifty seats, TASS reported. Azerbaijani President Ayaz Mutalibov agreed to the creation of such a body, in which half the members would be chosen by him and half by the opposition, following protests organized by the Azerbaijani Popular Front earlier in the month.

The USSR in October, 1991

Tajikistan and Kirgizia Sign Economic Treaty

An economic agreement between Tajikistan and Kirgizia was signed in the Tajik capital, Dushanbe, TASS reported. It was agreed that mutual deliveries of food and consumer goods would amount to at least 70 percent of 1990 deliveries. It was also agreed to eliminate restrictions on direct transactions between enterprises in the two republics.

Western Shares Sold on the Baltic Stock Market

Shares from Western companies were sold on "The Baltic Fund" in Riga by fifteen firms of stock brokers. Shares in Eastman Kodak, Johnson & Johnson, Ford Motors, AT&T, PepsiCo, IBM, and other well-known US companies changed hands. The Baltic Fund's president, Valerii Belokop, told the Baltic News Service that among the buyers were businessmen from Russia, Kazakhstan, and Moldavia.

Rubiks—A Political Prisoner?

A press conference was organized in Riga by the pro-USSR faction of the Latvian Supreme Council to mark USSR Political Prisoners' Day, the Baltic News Service reported. Deputy Sergei Dimanis claimed that the independent Republic of Latvia was holding as political prisoners Alfreds Rubiks, head of the dissolved Latvian Communist Party; his aide, Vladimir Serdyukov; and Sergei Parfenov, a former member of the OMON unit stationed in Riga. Dimanis tried to persuade the press that the human rights of the three men, who were detained in Riga and accused of supporting the August coup, had been violated.

Thursday, October 31

Editor Concerned about Suppression of Press Freedom

Vitalii Tret'yakov, chief editor of the independent newspaper, *Nezavisimaya gazeta*, told the *Christian Science Monitor* that he was concerned about attempts by the RSFSR leadership to suppress the freedom of the press. Tret'yakov said that both his newspaper and *Moscow News* had recently received warnings from the RSFSR Ministry of the Mass Media and Information accusing them of violating the law on the press. Tret'yakov said he had been reprimanded for an interview with Ukrainian Deputy Prime Minister Konstantin Masik, in which the RSFSR ministry said it saw signs of war propaganda. Tret'yakov rejected the accusations as false and said the ministry had questioned the interview solely because it contained criticism of the policies of El'tsin's government. *Pravda* (November 1) also reported on the controversy.

Conflicting Views on Value of Western Aid

St. Petersburg Mayor Anatolii Sobchak said the West should stop sending humanitarian aid to the USSR, because it discouraged reform and "humiliates the individual." Speaking to Japanese Finance Minister Chino Tadao, Sobchak said that humanitarian aid "does not tackle the food problem" and only allows officials to postpone difficult decisions, Western agencies reported. The same day, Kazakh President Nursultan Nazarbaev told a news conference in London that the Soviet people might follow a dictator unless the West provided additional food aid to avert hunger during the winter.

Huge Increase in Price of Fuel Sold by RSFSR to Baltic States

Baltfax quoted Lithuanian Deputy Economics Minister Vytas Navickas as saying that the prices of oil, gas, and coal purchased from the RSFSR would increase by a factor of almost 100 starting on January 1. Navickas said that in return Lithuania had offered a list of twenty-six items, mainly machinery, engineering products, and electrical equipment, that it would sell for hard-currency.

Georgia Refuses to Sign Economic Treaty

The Georgian Supreme Soviet officially rejected Georgian participation in the new treaty on an economic union, which was signed by eight republics on October 18. TASS said the Georgian parliament had rejected Georgian participation in the treaty because the majority of deputies felt that the provisions of the treaty would infringe on Georgian sovereignty.

Seventeen Ecological Disaster Zones in the USSR

A study by the USSR Academy of Sciences Institute of Geography, published in Moscow News (No. 44), classified seventeen areas of the Soviet Union as "ecological disaster zones." Chernobyl', the cities of Moscow and St. Petersburg, the Donbass and Kuzbass coal-mining centers, and industrial areas in the Urals and in Azerbaijan were on the list, as was the area around the Aral Sea. The study found that 20 percent of the Soviet population and 40 percent of the urban population lived in badly polluted regions.

The Month of November

Friday, November 1

Pankin in Madrid, Foreign Affairs Ministry in Disarray

Interfax carried remarks from a "well-placed" Soviet Foreign Ministry staffer describing the frustration and dissatisfaction of ministry staff with Foreign Minister Boris Pankin. Staff were apparently bewildered that Pankin was spending so much time at the Madrid peace talks "while the fate of the USSR Foreign Ministry is being decided in Moscow," Interfax said.

Deputy Chairmen of RSFSR Supreme Soviet Elected

TASS reported that the RSFSR Congress of People's Deputies had elected the former secretary of the Presidium of the Russian parliament, Sergei Filatov, as first deputy chairman of the RSFSR Supreme Soviet. It also elected Yurii Yarov, Vladimir Shumeiko, and Yurii Voronin as deputy chairmen with special responsibilities for, respectively, work with local constituencies, economic reform, and control over the implementation of parliamentary decisions.

Moscow City Officials Bar November 7 Demonstration

The Moscow city authorities rejected a request by Communist and labor groups to mark the anniversary of the October Revolution with a demonstration on Red Square on November 7, TASS reported. City officials told the groups that they would have to hold their demonstration in the evening beyond the ring road circling the city.

Bashkiria Votes for Privatization and Presidential Rule

The Supreme Soviet of Bashkiria voted for privatization of property and the establishment of presidential rule, RFE/RL was informed. The Supreme Soviet also approved a rule requiring a new president to speak both Russian and Bashkir. Bashkiria had declared its independence earlier in the year.

Saturday, November 2

El'tsin Discusses Draft RSFSR Constitution

RSFSR President Boris El'tsin told the RSFSR Congress of People's Deputies that the newly drafted constitution contained "firm legal guarantees against totalitarianism, ideological control, and violence as a state policy," TASS reported. He said the new constitution would create a federal system with a strong executive branch and an independent judiciary and legislature. Despite assurances that the new constitution would let regions of the RSFSR retain their autonomous status, many deputies from regions demanding greater self-rule voiced strong opposition to the draft. The draft was referred to the RSFSR Supreme Soviet and to the Constitutional Commission, which was to report back to the Congress in March and April, 1992.

Interfax Judged to Be Best Soviet News Agency

The Center for the Study of Public Opinion, headed by Academician Tat'yana Zaslavskaya, asked 136 correspondents of Western press agencies, periodicals, and television and radio companies which Soviet press agency they regarded as the most professional. The Central Television news program "TSN" reported that 61 percent of those polled named the independent press agency Interfax. "TSN" also said that Interfax had recently opened a bureau in the United States.

Conference of Liberal Democratic Party of the USSR

The Liberal Democratic Party of the USSR, headed by Vladimir Zhirinovsky, held a conference over the weekend of November 2 and 3, TASS reported. The party had been criticized by the RSFSR's democratic forces for being neither liberal nor democratic. Addressing the conference, Zhirinovsky sharply attacked proclamations of independence by former Union- and autonomous republics. He also criticized Soviet President Gorbachev and RSFSR President El'tsin. Zhirinovsky ran unsuccessfully against El'tsin in the RSFSR presidential elections in June.

RSFSR People's Deputies on Minority Rights

The RSFSR Congress of People's Deputies adopted an appeal to the parliaments of the other fourteen erstwhile Union republics to speed up the conclusion of bilateral treaties guaranteeing the rights of minorities originating from the RSFSR, TASS reported. It also issued an appeal to the citizens of Ukraine, Belorussia, and Russia for the unity of the Slav republics and asked the RSFSR Supreme Soviet to adopt a law ensuring the territorial integrity of the RSFSR.

Crisis in Checheno-Ingushetia

The newly elected parliament of the self-styled Chechen republic met on November 2 and scheduled repeat elections for eight of the forty-one seats for November 12. According to the Russian Information Agency, in Groznyi and other towns self-defense units were being formed to oppose rebel leader Dzhakhar Dudaev's National Guard.

Meanwhile, the Provisional Supreme Council, recognized by the RSFSR as the sole constitutional authority, was going ahead with preparations for parliamentary elections. On November 4, however, Central Television's "TV Inform" reported that official elections of a new Chechen-Ingush Supreme Soviet and the referendum on whether Checheno-Ingushetia should be divided into two republics would be postponed from November 17 to December 8.

On November 5, the new parliament of the self-styled Chechen republic ratified the president's decree on the state sovereignty of the republic, declared Chechen and Russian the state languages, and banned the activities of the Provisional Supreme Council, Radio Moscow reported. The same day, a grand assembly of citizens in Ingushetia decided to hold parliamentary and presidential elections on December 22, the Russian Television news program "Vesti" reported. The Rostov newspaper *Utro* also published an appeal for support to the people of the Don from the Groznyi section of the Terek Cossacks, Radio Moscow reported..

The same day, the Committee for the Preservation of the Unity of the Chechen-Ingush Republic, headed by Akhmed Arsanov, El'tsin's representative in the republic, sent an appeal to the people and democratic parties and movements of Georgia, saying interference by Georgian President Zviad Gamsakhurdia and his emissaries in the internal affairs of Checheno-Ingushetia was leading to dissension and must be stopped, TASS reported on November 5. Dudaev had enlisted Gamsakhurdia's support in the spring, and Gamsakhurdia was one of the first to congratulate Dudaev on his election.

On November 7, the parliament of the self-styled Chechen republic nationalized all the enterprises, departments, and associations of Union and RSFSR subordination on its territory, Radio Moscow reported. Dudaev was also appointed head of the Cabinet of Ministers, and a national security service was set up instead of the KGB. The radio reported that the conflict between various groups, parties, and movements in Checheno-Ingushetia was intensifying.

On November 8, El'tsin issued a decree declaring a state of emergency in Checheno-Ingushetia for one month, beginning at 05:00 A.M. on November 9, the Soviet media reported. El'tsin called for a curfew, the banning of public rallies and strikes, and the handing in of all weapons. He also named an interim administration to be headed by Arsanov. The decree said that a state of emergency was being declared in connection with the acute deterioration of the situation in the republic.

In response to El'tsin's declaration, Dudaev on November 9 annulled the curfew and declared martial law "to defend the freedom of the people." He also called on Arsanov to resign by midday. TASS and Western agencies reported that thousands of demonstrators had poured into the streets of Groznyi and turned the city into "an armed fortress." Members of Dudaev's National Guard took control of several hundred MVD troops who had landed at a military base; on November 10, they were bussed out to North Ossetia. Airfield runways and roads were blocked, and rail traffic was stopped for twenty-four hours. RSFSR Vice President Aleksandr Rutskoi said that on no account was force to be used, and there was no sign of any attempt to implement the state of emergency.

El'tsin's decree also faced major opposition in the RSFSR Supreme Soviet on November 10, Radio Rossii and Western agencies reported. RSFSR KGB Chairman Viktor Ivanenko called the decree "a dramatic error," while Chechen deputy Aslanbek Aslakhanov, chairman of the Committee for Legality and Law Enforcement, criticized El'tsin for issuing the decree without consulting parliament. Rutskoi defended the decree, saying the state of emergency would not be lifted until all weapons had been laid down.

After heated debate, the RSFSR Supreme Soviet voted on November 11 not to endorse El'tsin's decree, the Soviet media reported. The resolution called on the RSFSR authorities to try to resolve the crisis by peaceful means. At the same time, it stressed the need to preserve the territorial integrity of the RSFSR. It was also decided that strict controls should be instituted to prevent the import of weapons into the republic and that an investigation should be launched to establish who had been responsible for the adoption of an insufficiently prepared decree.

The refusal of the RSFSR Supreme Soviet to endorse El'tsin's decree was greeted with rejoicing in Checheno-Ingushetia. Dudaev told reporters in Groznyi on November 12, however, that he would not negotiate with the RSFSR until it recognized him as the legitimate leader of Checheno-Ingushetia, Western agencies reported.

On November 13, El'tsin sacked Arsanov for allegedly having provided misinformation that was the basis for El'tsin's declaration of a state of emergency, TASS reported. Rutskoi had stated earlier that the state of emergency had been declared after receipt of a coded telegram from Arsanov, but Arsanov denied this charge.

The USSR in November, 1991

Against a background of reports that the situation was stabilizing in Checheno-Ingushetia, Dudaev held a press conference on November 13 at which he reiterated that negotiations with the RSFSR could only take place if the RSFSR recognized the sovereign Chechen republic and its legally elected parliament and president, TASS reported. He said that martial law would remain in force until the situation had completely normalized.

On November 14, Rutskoi told a Moscow press conference that a state of emergency should have been declared a month earlier in Checheno-Ingushetia and that an economic blockade might be imposed if the autonomous republic failed to hold a leadership referendum immediately. Meanwhile, Dudaev said that he would import food from Turkey through Georgia if a Russian blockade was imposed. *Izvestia* reported that the first loads of food supplies from Turkey had arrived.

The same day, TASS reported that the situation in Groznyi was returning to normal. There were hardly any armed men on the streets, the national guard had returned to barracks, and citizens were told to register their weapons within ten days.

On November 15, Radio Moscow reported that the Provisional Supreme Council, the only body in Checheno-Ingushetia recognized as legitimate by the RSFSR Supreme Soviet, had disbanded itself. The radio gave no reason for the move.

El'tsin's attempt to use force in Checheno-Ingushetia prompted extended debate and criticism. When asked by journalists to comment on the situation, Soviet President Mikhail Gorbachev said that all problems concerning the revival and self-determination of nations should be solved by political means (*TASS*, November 12). Without naming El'tsin, Gorbachev said "comrades" had "impermissibly overestimated the importance of force" in settling a complex problem. Galina Starovoitova, RSFSR State Council member and El'tsin's adviser on nationality affairs, told reporters during a visit to Finland the same day that El'tsin had been given poor advice.

Yurii Afanas'ev, a leader of the Democratic Russia movement, told a press conference in Moscow that he saw "dangerous imperialistic tendencies" in El'tsin (RL Russian service, November 12). He said the declaration of a state of emergency in Checheno-Ingushetia was only the latest example of tendencies that El'tsin had developed since the August coup attempt. Afanas'ev also said that Democratic Russia would cooperate with the present RSFSR leadership but did not want to be identified with it.

On November 16, First Deputy Chairman of the RSFSR Supreme Soviet Sergei Filatov said that preliminary agreement had been reached for the RSFSR and Chechen-Ingush delegations to meet without prior conditions. There was no sign, however, that Dudaev had abandoned his demand that the RSFSR first recognize the Chechen republic. TASS also reported that Dudaev had appointed Yaragy Mamodaev as prime minister. Mamodaev said countering a threatened economic blockade by Russia and ensuring food supplies for the winter were his priority concerns.

On November 18, Daud Akhmadov, aide to Dudaev, denied that Dudaev had agreed to drop his demand that the RSFSR recognize the president and parliament of the Chechen republic before he would start talks with the RSFSR, TASS reported. Akhmadov said that El'tsin's adviser on nationalities affairs had spoken on the telephone with Dudaev but that no agreement had been reached on the composition of the delegations and the time and place of the meeting. A final decision rested with the Chechen parliament, Akhmadov added.

On November 21, Dudaev issued a decree lifting martial law in the republic, TASS reported. The national guard was sent back to barracks. Radio Moscow reported the same day that an action had been planned to disarm the USSR MVD troops in the republic. Dudaev said he knew nothing of the move and promised to stop it, which he did.

On November 23, Dudaev told Baltfax that Tartu, Estonia, might be the venue for talks between himself and the RSFSR. Dudaev said he had rejected proposals for a meeting in St. Petersburg because he did not want the talks to take place on Russian soil. Dudaev commanded a strategic bomber unit outside Tartu before he resigned his post to lead the Chechen national movement.

On November 26, Dudaev said on Groznyi television that conscription for a Chechen army would start on November 27, Radio Rossii reported. Dudaev said the creation of an army was necessary to protect Checheno-Ingushetia from Russian intervention. Dudaev told *Krasnaya zvezda* on November 26 that Chechnya would negotiate with the Union for the transfer of the weapons and military equipment on the territory of the republic to the Chechen army. If no agreement were reached, weapons would be bought abroad, he said.

Officers for a Ukrainian Army

Seven hundred delegates took part in the Second Congress of the Union of Officers of Ukraine, held on November 2 and 3. RL's Ukrainian service learned that the congress was addressed by Defense Minister Konstantin

Morozov. The organization, which counted more than 10,000 members, was active in the movement to establish a Ukrainian army. Its first congress, held on July 28, was attended by only six officers, but membership as well as political clout expanded rapidly after the August coup.

Another independent association of officers was launched in Vinnitsa on November 1, Ukrinform-TASS reported. This, however, appeared to be "the military interfront" that Colonel Vilen Matirosyan, chairman of the Union of Officers of Ukraine, had warned about in a speech to a recent conference in Kiev on security issues and that he described as a "dangerous" development.

Burbulis on RSFSR Economic Plan

RSFSR State Secretary Gennadii Burbulis criticized El'tsin's decision to liberalize prices. The *Financial Times* of November 2 quoted him as saying that Russia "cannot free prices until at least some kind of dynamism in basic privatization is achieved." He pointed out that under conditions of economic monopoly freeing prices would not lead to real competition between producers.

In an interview with *Der Spiegel* on November 4, Burbulis expressed the hope that trade unions and political parties would form a bloc to support radical reform. He stressed that there was no time to adopt laws to regulate the transition to democracy and a market economy.

Conflict Continues over Independent Ukrainian Armed Forces

Chairman of the Ukrainian Supreme Soviet Leonid Kravchuk was reported to have received a letter from the USSR Ministry of Internal Affairs condemning his parliament's decision to set up a National Guard as "unconstitutional" and informing him that the issue would be raised at the next meeting of the USSR State Council. Radio Liberty's Ukrainian service was also informed on November 2 that as of November 1 the USSR Ministry of Internal Affairs had ceased funding its forces in Ukraine in order to protest against the decision to form a Ukrainian National Guard on the basis of existing MVD troops.

On November 3, USSR Defense Minister Evgenii Shaposhnikov expressed opposition to Ukraine's recent moves to place military units on its territory under republican jurisdiction, pointing out that such efforts went against Soviet law. Shaposhnikov said that he saw no reason to withdraw military units from Ukraine and that, instead, a collective defense concept should be devised in the near future. His comments appeared in *Moskovskie novosti* and were quoted by Radio Moscow.

On November 4, despite objections from Moscow, the Ukrainian Supreme Soviet gave final approval to laws creating a National Guard and border troops and defining the state border, Radio Kiev reported. The National Guard would consist of approximately 30,000 citizens of Ukraine and would initially be drawn from troops of the USSR Ministry of Internal Affairs. Its duties would include protection of Ukraine's sovereignty and territorial integrity as well as protection of the president, embassies, and government buildings. Members would enjoy medical and housing benefits and would have first priority in admission to Ukraine's higher military schools.

Ukrainians in Moldavia Hold Conference

The Society for Ukrainian Culture in Moldavia, which seeks to halt the Russification of Ukrainians and revive their language and culture, held its first republic-wide conference in Kishinev, Moldovapres reported. The conference discussed the society's activities and also urged Ukrainians not to heed calls by the leaders of the would-be "Dniester SSR" for a boycott of Moldavia's forthcoming presidential elections. The Moldavian government, reversing the policy of its Communist predecessors, has undertaken to create and subsidize Ukrainian cultural and educational institutions in Moldavia. Ukrainians are the largest nontitular ethnic community, forming 14 percent of Moldavia's population.

Sunday, November 3

Moldavian Popular Front Calls for Reunification with Romania

A rally by some 10,000 supporters of the Moldavian Popular Front, held in Kishinev and addressed by the front's leaders, demanded reunification with Romania and the immediate introduction in Moldavia of the Romanian currency (lei) in place of the ruble, TASS and Radio Bucharest reported. The participants also denounced Moldavian President Mircea Snegur for opposing reunification with Romania. Snegur had recently insisted that an overwhelming majority of Moldavians were opposed to reunification.

On November 7, more than 100 Moldavian deputies accused the parliament's Presidium of a gross violation of the constitution on the grounds that it had refused to hold an extraordinary session of the parliament, even though one had been requested by more than one third of the deputies, TASS reported. The extraordinary session was to discuss the referendum on the independence of

The USSR in November, 1991

Moldavia in connection with the demands for the unification of Moldavia and Romania.

The following day, Snegur asked the Presidium of the Moldavian parliament for protection from attacks by the extremist wing of the Moldavian Popular Front, which he feared because of his rejection of the idea of union with Romania, Radio Mayak reported. According to Radio Moscow, the Moldavian prosecutor asked parliament to sanction the arrest of a deputy who led a group of demonstrators shouting "Snegur is a traitor" outside Snegur's house, but the Presidium confined itself to condemning the unsanctioned demonstration.

On November 12 and 13, Moldavian Popular Front delegates, headed by Executive Committee Chairman Iurie Rosca, approached Romanian government and opposition leaders in Bucharest with the request that Romania grant the residents of its former provinces Bessarabia and Northern Bukovina the right to regain Romanian citizenship. At a press conference in Bucharest, broadcast on November 15, Romanian President Ion Iliescu disclosed that he had received the Moldavian delegates but turned down their request, considering it risky for Romania and inconsistent with Moldavia's independence. Rosca, however, told a Popular Front rally in Kishinev on November 17 that the matter would shortly be submitted to the Romanian parliament for consideration.

Snegur told an electoral rally on November 17 that the request for Romanian citizenship to be extended to Moldavians was unlawful and incompatible with Moldavia's independence. He said that Moldavians were interested in consolidating their statehood with all its attributes but not in merging with "any other state." Snegur commented that the popular front's recent policy of "rushing to unify" with Romania had cost the front a great deal of its former popularity.

Confederation of Mountain Peoples of Caucasus Proclaimed

The Third Congress of the Mountain Peoples of the Caucasus in Sukhumi ratified a treaty on a Confederative Union of the Mountain Peoples and a statute on the confederation's leading organs. A Kabardian, Yurii Shanibov, was elected president of the confederation on November 3, the Russian Television newscast "Vesti" reported on November 4. Yusup Soslambekov, the Chechen deputy chairman of the rebel Executive Committee of the All-National Congress of the Chechen People, was chosen as chairman of the Caucasian parliament, which included three representatives for each of the fourteen peoples signing the treaty. He also headed the

Defense Committee of the Caucasus. The congress came out unambiguously in favor of the independence of the peoples of the Northern Caucasus and Abkhazia and gave its support to the Chechen "revolution."

Post of President of Kalmykia Remains Vacant

The repeat elections for the post of president of Kalmykia on November 3 resulted in neither candidate's obtaining a majority, TASS reported on November 4. The prime minister of Kalmykia got 45.3 percent of the votes and the chairman of the Supreme Soviet, 40.4 percent.

Sovereignty Aspirations of Koryaks Arouse Opposition

A session of the Koryak Okrug Soviet decided that the Koryak Autonomous Okrug should secede from Kamchatka Oblast and become a republic of the RSFSR, Radio Moscow reported. The decision was said to have provoked an ambivalent reaction from the inhabitants of the peninsula.

Moldavia Arrests Members of OMON Unit Formerly in Latvia

Two members of the OMON unit formerly stationed in Latvia were arrested in Moldavia by the republican police, with assistance from the Latvian authorities, the Moldavian Ministry of Internal Affairs announced in a communiqué released through Moldovapres on November 3. The pair, who were ethnic Russians, confessed upon arrest that they and eight other members of their former unit had arrived in Moldavia in order to serve as instructors of the paramilitary units of the would-be "Dniester SSR" formed by Russian Communists in eastern Moldavia. The ten men had been accused of committing crimes in Latvia.

Diena reported on November 4 that the two members of OMON arrested in Moldavia, who were identified as Igor' Nikiforov and Vladimir Kozhavin, had been flown to Riga. Nikiforov was accused of armed robbery at the Dom Square in Riga on February 16, 1991, while Kozhevin was accused of shooting at guests in a Riga café while drunk on July 16. *Diena* also reported that the Latvian authorities were continuing their search in Leningrad, Moscow, and Tashkent for other OMON members thought to have committed crimes in Latvia.

Uzbekistan Nationalizes Gold Mines

Radio Moscow reported that a Kyzylkum state concern for valuable and rare metals had been set up in Uzbekistan. In the future, gold mined in Uzbekistan, which has one of the richest gold fields in the Soviet Union, would go into the republic's gold reserves.

The USSR in November, 1991

Monday, November 4

USSR State Council Begins New Session

The USSR State Council told economist Grigorii Yavlinsky to speed up the formation of an economic community, TASS reported. The council gave him one week to provide written proposals for implementing the twenty-two accords discussed by twelve republics on October 18 in Alma-Ata. Yavlinsky told the meeting that major differences still remained between republican and Union leaders on basic issues. He said that some republics continued mistakenly to believe that bilateral agreements could serve as a substitute for a treaty on an economic community.

The same day, the head of the Interstate Economic Committee (MEK), Ivan Silaev, outlined the structure of his institution to the USSR State Council. Silaev said the MEK would be subordinated to an assembly of government leaders of the republics that signed the economic treaty and would consist of five major sectors and fifteen departments, which would take over the role of the former ministries. Communications, industrial safety regulations, power, and atomic energy would continue to be controlled at the all-Union level under the auspices of the MEK.

Soviet President Mikhail Gorbachev addressed the State Council and criticized RSFSR President Boris El'tsin's radical economic plan for its failure to support the poorer members of the Soviet population. Gorbachev said that lifting restrictions on prices was impossible without taking other measures, such as dismantling state monopolies and adopting incentives to boost production. Gorbachev also criticized leaders of the republics for failing to take advantage of "the political capital" they had gained after the coup and faulted them for pushing the country further towards disintegration rather than trying to save it, TASS reported.

Also on November 4, the council agreed to maintain "united armed forces" until the republics signed a joint defense treaty. Aleksandr Yakovlev, a Gorbachev adviser, said that a time frame for signing this treaty had not been set, Interfax reported.

USSR to Build New Black Sea Naval Base

TASS reported that the Soviet navy intended to build a new base on the Black Sea in Krasnodar Krai because its former base in Sevastopol was now under Ukrainian jurisdiction. On November 5, however, First Deputy Commander in Chief of the Soviet Navy Ivan Kapitanets denied this report (_TASS_, November 5). Meanwhile,

Admiral Vladimir Chernavin, commander in chief of the Soviet navy, said at the start of his official visit to the United States (November 4) that his navy had scrapped more than 200 battleships over the past three years in an effort to have a smaller fleet with more modern equipment, Radio Rossii reported.

Demonstrations in Support of Coup Leaders

Some fifty friends and relatives of the arrested coup leaders demonstrated near the prison where they were being held, "Vesti" reported. The commentator noted that several such demonstrations had already taken place.

Investigation of CPSU Financial Operations

It was reported that more than 5 billion rubles and 14 million dollars previously belonging to the CPSU had been confiscated during the past month from various Soviet banks and organizations ("TV-Inform," *Central Television*, November 4). The same day, the Russian Television news program "Vesti" reported that the RSFSR Prosecutor's Office had initiated a criminal investigation into the CPSU leadership's alleged illegal financial operations. A special forty-member commission was established to investigate Communist Party financial operations.

Food Shortages in Moscow

In response to food shortages and some panic buying, the Moscow city government announced the introduction of rationing. A city government press spokesman told Radio Moscow that customers would be limited to about two kilograms of bread a day.

On November 5, Moscow Mayor Gavriil Popov announced on Soviet television that ration coupons would be issued beginning December 1 for bread, sausage, butter, cooking oil, and eggs. Vodka, sugar, and cigarettes had already been rationed for some time.

On November 26, however, Popov was reported to have told city employees that rationing would not be introduced in December after all (*Interfax*, November 26). No explanation for the cancellation of the rationing was given, and it was not clear whether the Moscow measures had been coordinated with RSFSR plans.

"Communists for Civil Rights" Movement Created

Another grass-roots organization of Communists, Communists for Civil Rights, was set up in St. Petersburg, Radio Moscow reported. At a press conference, the movement's leader, Evgenii Krasnitsky, a former member of the CPSU Central Committee and a deputy of the St. Petersburg City

Soviet, called for the re-creation of the RSFSR Communist Party. The movement united the former dissident Marxist Roy Medvedev and orthodox Bolshevik Nina Andreeva.

Chukchi Face Opposition from Magadan Oblast

Relations between Magadan Oblast and the Chukchi Autonomous Okrug deteriorated sharply after the Chukchi Okrug Soviet refused to hold a referendum on whether the okrug should secede from Magadan Oblast and become the Sovereign Chukchi Republic, Radio Mayak reported. (The Chukchi Okrug had already announced its intention to secede from Magadan Oblast and was afraid that Russians, who formed the majority of the oblast's population, would vote against such a move if a referendum were held.) The Chukchi authorities accused Magadan of infringing their sovereign rights, while Magadan accused the Chukchi authorities of nationalism, saying that they were ignoring the opinion of the Russian-speaking majority. In 1989 Chukchi constituted only 7 percent of the population.

Tuesday, November 5

Agreement Reached on Food Supplies

Representatives of twelve of the USSR republics reached an agreement designed to maintain food supplies in 1992. As reported by Radio Moscow, the agreement "recognizes the necessity of forming a unified market for food products as an important part of the economic space." The agreement gave the Interstate Economic Committee the right to conclude agreements with foreign partners on credits for and supplies of food. The Baltic States did not participate in the agreement.

New Ministry of External Relations

USSR Foreign Minister Boris Pankin expanded on plans for 30-percent cuts in personnel at the USSR Foreign Ministry, saying specific numbers of cuts in the 3,500-strong staff would be discussed at the November 14 meeting of the USSR State Council. Pankin said the November 4 meeting of the USSR State Council had yielded a new name for the Foreign Ministry—the Ministry of External Relations (*Ministerstvo vneshnykh snoshenii*), TASS reported.

Council of Defense Ministers of Sovereign States Created

The USSR State Council set up a Council of Defense Ministers of Sovereign States to coordinate military policy on the territory of the former Soviet Union ("Vesti,"

November 5). The council was scheduled to meet once a month in one of the capitals of the republics. USSR Defense Minister Evgenii Shaposhnikov said the USSR State Council had rejected republican claims for separate armies but agreed to hand over all civil defense functions, as well as military chairs at institutes and universities, to the republics for "a transitional period." He stressed that the republics could have their own national guards.

USSR Agrees to "Open Skies" The Soviet Union said it was ready to allow foreign reconnaissance planes to fly over its entire territory to verify military activity, Western agencies reported. Evgenii Golovko, chief Soviet delegate to the "open skies" conference in Vienna, said that the proposal could take effect in 1993 and that he hoped that an "open skies" treaty could be signed in Helsinki in March, 1992, at the scheduled meeting of the Conference on Security and Cooperation in Europe.

Navy Draft Time Reduced A Soviet defense official, Major General Gennadii Bochaev, said that compulsory service in the navy had been reduced from three years to two, *Krasnaya zvezda* reported. He also said that national service in the army would soon be shortened to eighteen months and that women would be eligible to participate in the new career army being planned.

CPSU International Department to Survive? The two agencies responsible for the Soviet Union's ties with international terrorists—the CPSU Central Committee's International Department and the First Main Administration of the KGB—"are in effect being united under a new label: the Central Intelligence Service" under the leadership of Evgenii Primakov, according to an article by International Department veteran Evgenii Novikov in *The Wall Street Journal*. Novikov, who defected to the United States in 1988, said that, despite the fact that the dismantling of the Soviet terrorist-training network was long overdue, "I will be surprised if it happens either voluntarily or soon."

RSFSR to Liberalize Foreign Trade The RSFSR government issued draft legislation liberalizing foreign-trade rules and regulations on its territory, TASS reported. The draft law provided for a convertible ruble that would replace all fixed exchange rates and for the removal of restrictions on hard-currency accounts. A simplification of import and export taxes was also covered. The law was aimed at increasing the potential for foreign trade and investment. The draft law was published in *Nezavisimaya gazeta*.

Yurii Petrov, head of the RSFSR Presidential Administration, told TASS that El'tsin was prepared to counter social unrest in Russia. A presidential food reserve had been set up for supplying the major industrial centers and an information service had been created under Petrov to monitor the effects of El'tsin's radical reform program. The information service would, if necessary, provide proposals for adjusting the situation if social tensions occurred. Petrov denied that there was friction within El'tsin's team.

El'tsin Prepared to Counter Social Unrest

The director of the All-Union Center for Hygiene and the Prevention of Children's Diseases, Galina Serdyukovskaya, called the state of children's health in the Soviet Union "catastrophic." Interviewed in *Argumenty i fakty* (No. 43), Serdyukovskaya said that 90 percent of all children suffered from vitamin deficiencies in 1990 because of food shortages and high prices. Fewer than one in ten school children showed normal physical development, and only about 15 percent of Soviet army conscripts could be considered healthy. Up to 35 percent of children had chronic illnesses, and 45 percent showed abnormalities that could develop into serious illnesses.

Health of Soviet Children Called "Catastrophic"

At the request of the Prosecutor's Office, the Georgian Supreme Soviet temporarily suspended the law on political parties (adopted on August 10), TASS reported. TASS commented that this in effect meant the end of democracy in Georgia. Factions representing the parliamentary minority did not take part in the vote.

Law on Political Parties Suspended in Georgia

The Lithuanian Supreme Council voted to start preparations for the introduction of the litas as Lithuania's official currency, Western agencies reported on November 6. Supreme Council President Vytautas Landsbergis, Prime Minister Gediminas Vagnorius, and Lithuanian National Bank Director Vilius Baldisius were appointed to head a committee that was to set the date for the introduction of the new currency and the official exchange rate against the ruble.

On November 6, Radio Riga announced that the Latvian Supreme Council had established a Monetary Reform Committee. Einars Repse, a member of the

Lithuania and Latvia to Introduce National Currencies

committee and president of the Bank of Latvia, said that the committee would oversee the introduction of the lats as Latvia's official currency and that the lats would be fully convertible.

Russia Restricts Gasoline Supplies to Latvia

Latvian Energy Minister Auseklis Lazdins told Radio Riga that since September, Russia had practically stopped sending gasoline to Latvia, forcing it to use its reserves. As of November 1, Russia decided to restrict its gasoline shipments to the Baltic States and to require special licenses. According to *Diena* of November 4, RSFSR Economics Minister Evgenii Saburov claimed that he had no information about the restrictions and asserted that "this is not an economic war" but merely a temporary interruption in the supply process.

Latvia Claims Property Occupied by Soviet Army

The Latvian Supreme Council adopted a resolution laying claim to all property occupied by the USSR Armed Forces, border guards, and Interior Ministry troops and invalidating any commercial transactions involving such property that took place after August 24, 1991, the Baltic News Service reported. According to deputy Talavs Jundzis, the Soviet Armed Forces occupy 234 plots of land (over 100,000 hectares) all over Latvia.

Wednesday, November 6

El'tsin Bans the Communist Party

On the eve of the seventy-fourth anniversary of the October Revolution, RSFSR President Boris El'tsin signed an edict banning the activities of the CPSU and Russian Communist Party on the territory of the Russian Federation, "Vesti" reported. The edict ordered the organizational structures of these parties to be disbanded. Following the abortive coup d'état on August 22, El'tsin and Soviet President Mikhail Gorbachev decreed that the activities of the CPSU be "suspended," pending the results of an investigation into Party involvement in the coup.

The unofficial committee "For the Union of Communists," set up on October 1, sent a formal statement to TASS protesting against El'tsin's decree. The statement said the decree was aimed at suppressing political opposition and establishing a new dictatorship in the RSFSR. In fact, the RSFSR leadership had taken no action against Communist groups that had been created in the RSFSR since the dissolution of the CPSU's ruling bodies.

The USSR in November, 1991

On November 8, RSFSR State Councilor Sergei Shakhrai defended El'tsin's edict on Russian Television. Answering charges that, under USSR law, a political party could be disbanded only by its own members or if it could be shown by the courts to have engaged in criminal activity, Shakhrai argued, not very convincingly, that neither the CPSU nor the Russian Communist Party was "a party in the civilized sense of the word" and that both had used illegal methods.

Gorbachev Approves New State Security Chiefs

Gorbachev formally appointed Vadim Bakatin as head of the Interrepublican Security Service, Evgenii Primakov as the director of the USSR Central Intelligence Service, and Il'ya Kalinichenko as the chairman of the Committee for Protection of the USSR State Border and the commander in chief of the Border Troops, TASS reported.

Reorganization of Soviet Interior Ministry Troops

USSR Minister of Internal Affairs Viktor Barannikov said that most of the 230,000 MVD troops would be subordinated to the republics, TASS reported. The Interior Ministry would retain jurisdiction over its rapid-intervention units—numbering 70,000 troops—and units guarding major facilities, while the MVD troops passing to republican control would include units guarding labor camps and police units that protected public order.

El'tsin Appoints Himself Prime Minister, Forms RSFSR Government

RSFSR President Boris El'tsin signed a decree appointing himself Russia's new prime minister and formally declaring the RSFSR Council of Ministers the RSFSR government. The position of first deputy chairman of the RSFSR government would be held by RSFSR State Secretary Gennadii Burbulis (*TASS*, November 6).

The government's twenty-four RSFSR ministries would be divided into four blocs—each headed by a government deputy chairman—with El'tsin himself assuming control of the RSFSR Ministries of Defense and Internal Affairs. Burbulis, as the new first deputy prime minister, would be in charge of organizing the work of the government and had the right to sign government decrees in the absence of El'tsin. RSFSR Vice President Aleksandr Rutskoi was put in charge of a newly created Center for Operational Control over Reform. El'tsin also decreed the formation of a Collegium of the RSFSR Government, which would consist of ten members—El'tsin; Burbulis; the three deputy prime ministers; the ministers of foreign affairs, internal affairs, and of the press and mass media; the RSFSR KGB chairman; and Rutskoi, TASS reported.

Ukraine and Moldavia Sign Economic Treaty

Ukrainian Prime Minister Vitol'd Fokin signed the economic union treaty but warned that he still had reservations about it, Western news agencies reported. This move came after the Ukrainian Supreme Soviet had voted on November 5, by a margin of 236–96, in favor of signing the economic treaty provisionally.

On November 8, Chairman of the Ukrainian Supreme Soviet Leonid Kravchuk told a press conference that Ukraine's signing the economic union treaty did not mean that "Ukraine is directly tied to implementing its statutes," Radio Kiev reported. According to the Ukrainian leader, lengthy negotiations would probably be needed to resolve twenty-five demands presented by Ukraine. The agreement itself, he said, could only be implemented after its ratification by the Ukrainian Supreme Soviet and the parliaments of all the other signatory states.

Moldavia also signed the economic union treaty on November 6. Moldavian Prime Minister Valeriu Muravschi told reporters after he had signed the document that the treaty made it possible to preserve the links previously established between the republics and thus stabilize the situation in the economy and in society as a whole, TASS reported. He foresaw possible problems, however, in drawing up the special agreements that accompanied the treaty. Muravschi reiterated that Moldavia was not planning to join any political or military union.

On November 8, Muravschi denied rumors that, in signing the treaty, Moldavia had caved in to pressure brought to bear on the republic by El'tsin, who had halted deliveries of oil products, "TSN" reported. Muravschi said the Moldavian move had been dictated by the reality that the West was not welcoming Moldavia with open arms. (Earlier in the week, Moldavian President Mircea Snegur had warned that the treaty "could become a political trap to restore the Soviet empire" [*TASS*, November 5].)

Ukraine's and Moldavia's decision to sign left Georgia and Azerbaijan as the only remaining former Soviet republics (apart from the Baltic States) that had not joined the economic union.

Treason Charges against Gorbachev Dropped

USSR Prosecutor-General Nikolai Trubin repealed the order to open treason proceedings against Mikhail Gorbachev in connection with the granting of independence to the Baltic States. Trubin dismissed the order as "a legally invalid manifestation of political extremism." The order had been issued by Viktor Ilyukin, USSR state prosecutor with responsibility for state security matters (*Pravda*, November 6). Ilyukin said Gorbachev had failed to uphold the USSR Constitution and violated his obliga-

THE USSR IN NOVEMBER, 1991

tion to defend the USSR's sovereignty and territorial integrity. Trubin then fired Ilyukin, "Vesti" reported on November 6.

Free Housing for Muscovites

Moscow Mayor Gavriil Popov told a press conference that apartments would be given to Moscow residents free of charge, TASS reported. He said the sale of apartments under economic reform might strip people of all of their money, which he called "inadmissible" in view of the imminent lifting of price controls. He said it also seemed unprofitable to sell housing at a time when the ruble was expected to decline in value. He announced that taxes on square meters of housing space exceeding the individual entitlement would be introduced later, after prices had stabilized.

On November 13, the head of Moscow's housing committee announced that occupants who were to be given their apartments free of charge would have to pay a new real estate tax that was likely to be higher than their current, subsidized rent, Western agencies reported.

Bovin to Become USSR Ambassador to Israel

Aleksandr Bovin, now *Izvestia*'s foreign-policy observer, was expected to become the USSR ambassador to Israel, "TV-Inform" reported. During the early years of Gorbachev's tenure, Bovin was the first Soviet journalist to argue publicly for Soviet reconciliation with Israel. Bovin also visited Israel earlier in the month, immediately after diplomatic relations were reestablished.

Soviet Troop Withdrawal from Mongolia to Be Complete in 1992

Western agencies cited a Soviet military officer in Ulan Bator as saying the last Soviet troops would leave Mongolia by September, 1992. According to the Mongolian government, there were some 2,500 Soviet troops in Mongolia, primarily in the area surrounding and north of the capital city.

Stock Exchange Congress on CPSU and KGB Property

The Congress of the Stock Exchange (an organization of about 200 Soviet brokerage firms) published a statement in *Moskovskaya pravda* claiming that capital, real estate, and other assets controlled by the CPSU and the KGB were being used in commercial operations in domestic and foreign markets. The volume of CPSU and KGB capital engaged in such operations well exceeded official figures, according to the congress. The congress expressed concern that various political parties were making claims on this property, arguing that distribution along partisan lines could lead to "a new ideologization" of the capital.

Ministry of Finance Said to Have Concealed Bank Accounts

Izvestia reported that government auditors had discovered 45.4 billion rubles in two accounts of the USSR State Bank that the USSR Ministry of Finance had not declared either to the USSR president or to the legislature. One of the accounts, containing 40 billion rubles, belonged to the USSR Ministry of Finance and was opened in 1939. *Izvestia* did not say who opened the other account. Acting USSR Finance Minister Vladimir Raevsky told *Izvestia* that he had been unaware of the accounts until recently. The chairman of the government Auditing Commission suggested transferring the money to the agricultural sector.

On November 12, Chairman of the USSR State Bank Viktor Gerashchenko said he was almost certain that the hidden funds had not been reserved for the CPSU but that they might have been set up as contingency funds for natural disasters or other emergencies (*TASS*, November 12).

Kuzbass Threatens Coal Embargo

A top official of the Kuzbass regional administration threatened an embargo on coal deliveries to other republics unless they fulfilled their obligations to supply food to the Kuzbass, in southern Russia, TASS reported. Deputy regional administrator Nikolai Krushinsky said that the food situation in the Kuzbass was serious and that the region was unable to feed itself, since industrial workers accounted for 97 percent of the working population.

Ukrainian-Russian Agreement

Ukraine and Russia signed a communiqué agreeing on the need for collective security and the formation of a common defense strategy, Radio Kiev and Western news agencies reported. The communiqué was signed by Chairman of the Ukrainian Supreme Soviet Leonid Kravchuk and RSFSR President Boris El'tsin. The same day, the two sides initialed a trade and economic agreement.

Intellectuals in Uzbekistan Concerned about Russian Exodus

Pravda Vostoka published an appeal to the presidents of Uzbekistan and Russia from a number of well-known scientists and journalists of Uzbekistan expressing concern at the continuing departure of the Russian-speaking population from Uzbekistan. The appeal called for the creation of an Uzbek-Russian Friendship Society to help stop the exodus.

The USSR in November, 1991

Azerbaijan passed a law renaming the KGB of that republic the Ministry of National Security (*Azerinform-TASS*, November 6). The ministry was made directly subordinate to the president of Azerbaijan rather than to the Cabinet of Ministers.

Azerbaijani KGB Changes Its Name

Uzbek President Islam Karimov and Belorussian Supreme Soviet Chairman Stanislau Shushkevich signed an accord in Tashkent governing bilateral ties between their two republics. The agreement covered cooperation on foreign policy, trade, and other issues, TASS said. Uzbekistan and Belorussia also recognized each other as sovereign states.

Uzbek-Belorussian Accord

The Estonian Supreme Council voted 64 to 14 to adopt the 1938 citizenship law, *Rahva Haal* reported on November 7. The Supreme Council also gave the government three weeks to come up with a draft law on how the 1938 law should be applied.

On November 22, the Baltic News Service reported that the government had announced its intention to "apply to the fullest extent" the law of 1938, which required a minimum three years' residence and a knowledge of Estonian for naturalization. The government move came after an opinion poll had shown overwhelming support among the population for a strict application of the law.

Estonia Adopts Citizenship Law

Thursday, November 7

Communists and anti-Communists held demonstrations in Moscow to mark the anniversary of the October Revolution, Soviet and Western media reported. Some 400 anti-Communist protesters gathered outside the Lubyanka headquarters to mourn victims of the Soviet regime, while several thousand Communists gathered near the Kremlin to mark the anniversary. Communists condemned RSFSR President Boris El'tsin's decree banning CPSU activities in Russia and denounced "the traitorous Gorbachev-El'tsin clique." Tens of thousands rallied in St. Petersburg to celebrate the victory of democratic forces and the restoration of the city's original name. Central Television devoted only ten minutes to the demonstrations.

Conflicting opinions on the significance of the anniversary were expressed in interviews with "TV-Inform." Academician Dmitrii Likhachev said it should not be the

Communists and anti-Communists Mark Revolution Anniversary

prerogative of a state to exercise ideological control, while historian General Dmitrii Volkogonov noted that the country's current problems were rooted in the October Revolution. Nina Andreeva, leader of the Bolshevik Platform in the CPSU, said the revolution was "the main point in Russia's history." She said that Gorbachev, El'tsin, and other leaders who had abandoned communism would be punished sooner or later.

In Kiev, the traditional holiday ended with scuffles between supporters and opponents of "the Socialist choice," Radio Kiev reported. Several hundred veterans of the Communist Party and its functionaries marched down Kiev's main thoroughfare and laid flowers at the statue of Lenin. This was followed by a meeting at the Republican Stadium, where a fight broke out.

In Minsk, a newly formed front organization for the suspended Belorussian Communist Party called "Workers of Belorussia for Democracy, Social Progress, and Justice" marked the holiday with a rally on Lenin Square in defiance of a ban imposed by the Minsk City Soviet, according to an RFE/RL correspondent in the Belorussian capital.

In Latvia, a few thousand people gathered in Riga's Victory Square to mark the October Revolution. Although the gathering was not sanctioned and November 7 was no longer a holiday in Latvia, the authorities took no action against the demonstrators.

East German Export Guarantees to Cease

The German Economics Ministry said the 100-percent government guarantee for East German exports to the USSR would cease to be provided after the end of 1991, Western agencies reported. Future exports would be subject to the terms that normally applied to German exports. As a result, Soviet customer enterprises would have to make a 15-percent down payment on products acquired from the former East German states, and Soviet firms would no longer receive other special credit terms.

Party of Businessmen Registered

The so-called Bourgeois Democratic Party became the first party of Russian businessmen to be officially registered in Moscow, "Vesti" reported. The party's leader, E. Butov, said the aim of the party was to defend the rights of small- and medium-sized businesses.

Gaidar Put in Charge of RSFSR Economics

RSFSR President Boris El'tsin appointed Egor Gaidar to head the economic section of the RSFSR government, TASS reported. Gaidar, a deputy prime minister, would coordinate the work of thirteen ministries responsible for implementing El'tsin's radical reform. Gaidar had previously worked as director of the Institute for Economic Policy and headed a group of young economists who prepared El'tsin's reform program.

On November 4, Gaidar was quoted by Western agencies as saying he believed that the Union was finished and that Russia should treat all other republics as sovereign states, charging them hard currency for its exports. He also proposed that the Russian Bank be transformed into a central bank issuing a Russian currency and that it assume responsibility for the total Soviet foreign debt, as it was the only republic capable of earning large amounts of hard currency.

Shokhin to Be Responsible for RSFSR Social Policy

RSFSR President Boris El'tsin appointed Aleksandr Shokhin as deputy prime minister in charge of the social policy section, TASS reported. Shokhin would coordinate the work of the RSFSR Ministries of Health, Labor, Education, Culture, and Social Security. Prior to this appointment, Shokhin had served as RSFSR minister of labor. Shokhin was one of the leaders of the Russian Social Democratic Party.

North Ossetia and Georgia Argue over South Ossetia

Chairman of the North Ossetian Supreme Soviet Akhsarbek Galazov said that, faced with the Georgian parliament's policy of solving "the Ossetian problem" by violent means, the North Ossetian parliament was forced to take measures to prevent the physical destruction of Ossetians in Georgia, TASS reported. Galazov was replying to a protest by Georgian President Zviad Gamsakhurdia about the North Ossetian parliament's having discussed South Ossetia's request for incorporation in North Ossetia.

Soviet MVD Property in Georgia Seized

Georgian President Zviad Gamsakhurdia ordered the Georgian Ministry of Internal Affairs to commandeer all weapons, equipment, and bases belonging to USSR MVD troops on Georgian territory. Gamsakhurdia's decree, broadcast by Radio Tbilisi, said that "they are now the property of the Republic of Georgia." Thousands of Soviet MVD troops were concentrated in South Ossetia, the scene of violent confrontations between Georgian forces and the local population. In addition, TASS carried a statement from the Presidium of the Georgian parliament saying that Georgia deserved to be compensated for the presence of Soviet troops on its territory.

Ukraine Names New National Security Chief

The Ukrainian parliament named Evgenii Marchuk as head of the republic's new National Security Service, the successor to the Ukrainian KGB, Interfax reported. Marchuk had been serving as Ukraine's state minister on questions of defense and security.

Baikonur Cosmodrome to Go Commercial

A spokesman for the Kazakhstan Space Research Agency told TASS that the Baikonur space center was to become a joint-stock company called International Spaceport. The company would compete with US and Chinese aerospace firms as well as with the European Ariane consortium in launching commercial payloads with Soviet rockets. The agency, along with major commercial banks and space rocket associations of the RSFSR and Ukraine would hold 80 percent of the shares.

Moldavian Parliamentary Presidium Outlaws Dniester Election

The Presidium of the Moldavian parliament said that plans by officials in the breakaway Dniester region to hold a presidential election and independence referendum in December were illegal, TASS reported. The Presidium accused the Russian-speaking region of continuing to provoke tension by its illegal activities and of hampering Moldavian efforts to resolve the Dniester issue.

Attack on Lithuanian Customs Post

Lithuanian Defense Minister Audrius Butkevicius told the Lithuanian Supreme Council on November 7 that an attack the previous night on the Lithuanian customs post on the border with Belorussia was a political act, but he did not elaborate. Three men drove up to the Sumska customs post and threw explosives, which injured one Lithuanian officer. Two of the three attackers were in custody in Vilnius, according to the RFE/RL Lithuanian service.

Friday, November 8

Belorussia Must Allow Price Increases

Belorussia's State Planning Commission said the republic must allow prices to rise two- or three-fold starting on January 1 in order to cope with the radical economic changes in the RSFSR. The committee recommended compensation for its citizens of up to 70 percent of the proposed price increases. The plan included doubling the prices for vodka and clothing; tripling apartment rents; and quadrupling the price of local transportation if all subsidies were withdrawn or doubling it if some subsidies were kept. Electricity would triple if some subsidies were maintained but increase sixfold if they were eliminated.

Sobchak Criticizes El'tsin Plan

St. Petersburg Mayor Anatolii Sobchak criticized El'tsin's plan to free prices, Radio Mayak reported. Sobchak said that prices should not be freed without real land reform and a program to supply food. He suggested that if prices for basic goods were not fixed this could lead to "a social explosion." The mayor also said that the state must prevent severe hardship and guarantee a social safety net.

Norwegian Export Guarantees

The Norwegian government offered to grant 277 million dollars in state export guarantees to Norwegian companies that sold on credit to the USSR, Western agencies reported. The guarantees would be offered through the country's State Guarantee Institute for Export Credit and would have to be approved by parliament.

Part of EC Loan for Triangular Trade

An unnamed European Community official told Western agencies that the USSR could spend one quarter of its 500-million-ecu EC loan on buying foodstuffs from East European countries. The loan was offered in December, 1990, but had yet to be used. Paris traders were quoted as saying that the money would be used for purchases of grain, meat, vegetable oil, and milk powder from East European countries and from the Baltic States.

Ukrainian Unity

Chairman of the Ukrainian parliamentary Commission on Questions of Defense and State Security Vasyl Durdinets told *Rude Pravo* that Ukrainian territory was indivisible, Radio Kiev and TASS reported. Durdinets rejected the statements of "certain right-wing forces" in the Czech and Slovak Federal Republic (CSFR) regarding the need to reexamine its eastern borders.

The same day, Radio Kiev reported that the independence referendum scheduled to be held in Ukraine on December 1 would be accompanied by a local survey in the Berehovo Raion of Transcarpathia regarding the formation of a Hungarian Autonomous District. (Transcarpathia borders on both Hungary and the CSFR.)

Kazakhstan Will Be Forced to Raise Prices

Kazakh President Nursultan Nazarbaev said that when the RSFSR raised its prices, Kazakhstan would be forced to follow suit, Radio Moscow reported. Otherwise,

Nazarbaev said, El'tsin's action would allow "sharp operators" from other parts of the USSR to buy up all Kazakhstan's food and industrial goods for resale at a profit.

Moldavia Seeks US Recognition

Moldavian Foreign Minister Nicolai Tsiu called on the United States to recognize Moldavia's independence, Western agencies reported on November 9. Tsiu, who was on a three-day visit to Washington, said that, as there was no Soviet Union any more, the West must deal directly with the republics.

Polish Envoy Protests about Latvia's Travel Restrictions

Jaroslav Lindenberg, Poland's envoy to Latvia, submitted a note to the Latvian government in connection with its recent decision to limit travel by residents of Latvia to Poland. The decision was intended to stop the sale of goods already in short supply in Latvia for hard currency in Poland. Lindenberg said the decision restricted free travel to Poland for about 60,000 Poles living in Latvia, and he urged Latvia to review it. Latvian lawmakers also criticized the decision on the grounds that it contravened the Helsinki accords (*Diena*, November 8).

"Ravnopravie" Forms Political Party

The Communist minority faction "Ravnopravie" in the Latvian Supreme Council was reported to have established a political party known as the Democratic Initiative Center. It was not clear when the party was formally founded, but the party's cochairman, Mikhail Gavrilov, told *Diena* on November 8 that since the Democratic Initiative Center had already functioned for several months as a political party, "this status should be affirmed *de jure*."

Saturday, November 9

Soviet Reaction to NATO Summit

USSR Minister of External Relations Boris Pankin said that NATO countries had taken "a step in the right direction" by calling for cooperation with former Warsaw Pact nations, Western agencies reported. His RSFSR counterpart, Andrei Kozyrev, expressed the view that NATO was "turning more and more into a potential and real partner" for the Soviet Union. Kozyrev stressed the need to create a political and military union of states of the northern hemisphere, in which Russia would occupy a leading position. He said that NATO should offer partnership first to Russia and the other sovereign republics and only then to the USSR.

THE USSR IN NOVEMBER, 1991

Accords Signed on Soviet-South African Consular Ties

Visiting South African Foreign Minister Pik Botha and USSR Foreign Minister Boris Pankin signed accords establishing consular ties, TASS reported. Pankin warned, however, that "a long road" lay ahead before full diplomatic ties could be reestablished. Moscow severed relations with South Africa in 1956 over Pretoria's racial policies.

Yavlinsky Discusses USSR Gold Reserves

In an interview on Central Television, Grigorii Yavlinsky stated that Soviet state coffers contained only 193 tons of gold and that the level was not expected to exceed 240 tons in 1991. He stressed that the 193 tons were virtually the entire gold stock of the country and said there were no secret hoards held by the CPSU, the army, or the KGB. He added that Uzbekistan and Kazakhstan had a few tons that they had refused to transfer to the state coffers.

Moscow News (No. 46) carried vital data issued by the Ministry of Finance on gold reserves for the past eight years, Western agencies reported on November 13. This showed that the highest level of reserves during that period was 850.4 tons in 1989. It also appeared to confirm Yavlinsky's disputed figure for gold reserves of 240 tons.

Armenia Declares Energy Emergency

Armenia declared a state of emergency in its energy sector, TASS announced. A resolution approved by the Armenian Council of Ministers ordered the suspension of operations at all Armenian enterprises, except for plants responsible for priority supplies to other republics and for meeting domestic orders. The measure included severe restrictions on the use of electricity. Armenia's energy production had fallen to only 40 percent of its electricity requirements, according to the head of its Fuel and Energy Resources Department.

Interfax reported on November 10 that Azerbaijan and Armenia had agreed to create a ten-kilometer buffer zone along their common border and that natural gas shipments to Armenia would resume. Armenian representatives denied the reports the following day, however. At a press conference in Moscow on November 11, Armenian Foreign Minister Raffi Oganesyan called on the Soviet republics to impose political and economic sanctions on Azerbaijan for refusing to restore gas supplies to Armenia (*AFP*, November 11).

Fuel Situation Critical in Moldavia

The director of Moldavia's Power and Electrification Production Association, Valerii Ikonnikov, said that because of a shortage of various fuels electricity consumption would have to be drastically reduced, TASS reported. Kishinev and other large cities would be divided into zones, which would receive electricity in turns. Hospitals, schools, and enterprises with a continuous production cycle would not be affected, but electricity for street lighting and advertising would be cut, and shops trading in manufactured goods would operate only in daylight hours. Ikonnikov said he had asked the government to cut television broadcasts.

Sunday, November 10

Split in Democratic Russia Movement

Three of the parties that made up the Democratic Russia movement—the Democratic Party of Russia, the Party of People's Freedom, and the Christian Democratic Movement–announced their break with the umbrella organization at the movement's second congress. TASS said the three parties disagreed with the willingness of the leaders of Democratic Russia to support the right of the RSFSR's autonomous republics to declare complete independence. The three breakaway parties announced their intention to set up their own "Coalition of Democratic Forces of Russia."

Sobchak Favors Political Union

St. Petersburg Mayor Anatolii Sobchak told the Portuguese weekly *Espress* that an economic union of former Soviet republics was not enough and that the emergence of small totalitarian states on the territory of the former Soviet Union could only be prevented by the formation of a political union. Sobchak said he thought a political union would be necessary to carry on the role of the Soviet Union in the international sphere.

Falin Denies Reports on CPSU Financial Operations

Former CPSU Central Committee Secretary for International Affairs Valentin Falin denied allegations that the CPSU Central Committee International Department had controlled the CPSU's financial aid to Communist parties abroad. Falin told TASS that when he was in charge of the department "not a single kopeck" had been given to foreign Communist parties. At the recent hearings on CPSU activities in the Russian parliament, republican officials quoted from documents kept in the CPSU Central Committee archives, showing that the International Department had conducted illegal financial operations.

THE USSR IN NOVEMBER, 1991

A delegation of the main Afghan resistance groups arrived in Moscow and on November 11 held talks with RSFSR Vice President Aleksandr Rutskoi, TASS reported. The delegation also met with relatives of Soviet servicemen who were listed as missing or were prisoners of war in Afghanistan.

On November 12, the delegation met with USSR Minister of External Relations Boris Pankin. Pankin said in a statement following their talks that the USSR was not insisting on any specific composition of a future government in Afghanistan and that the Soviet side was willing to hold talks with all Afghan resistance groups. He rejected a demand from the Afghan delegation to remove President Najibullah from power, but he said the USSR would accept an Islamic government in Kabul. Pankin also proposed the creation of a permanent Soviet working delegation in Peshawar to ensure a continuous dialogue, TASS reported.

On November 15, a joint communiqué was issued in which the Afghan delegation pledged to release the first group of Soviet prisoners by January 1, TASS reported. TASS also indicated that the USSR might cut off arms shipments to the Najibullah government sooner than planned, depending on the prisoner exchange. The document also included provisions for contacts between the USSR and Mujahidin groups and the establishment of a commission to ensure that the agreements would be fulfilled.

Afghan Resistance Delegation in Moscow

Monday, November 11

After a session of the Committee for the Operational Management of the USSR Economy, Acting Prime Minister Ivan Silaev told TASS that the situation regarding Soviet debt repayments was "extremely serious." He expressed the hope that the G-7 delegation due in Moscow on November 17 would agree to delay repayment of some of the Soviet debt "in order to ease the way for economic reforms . . . and to solve such problems as food supplies." Interfax reported that at the same session the Soviet external debt was given as 47.2 billion hard-currency rubles, with debts to former Socialist countries put at 17 to 18 billion and the debts of least-developed countries to Moscow valued at 94 billion hard-currency rubles.

USSR Debt Situation "Extremely Serious"

The post left vacant by the recall of Soviet Ambassador Nikolai Uspensky following the coup was filled by Oleg

Grinevsky Named Ambassador to Sweden

Grinevsky, formerly chief Soviet negotiator at the East-West disarmament talks in Vienna, Western agencies reported.

USSR Customs Duties Lowered

USSR head customs officer Nikolai Ermakov told a Moscow press conference about the easing of customs duties on imports and exports, Western agencies reported. He said that there would be no import duties on food, medicine, raw materials, or equipment for the food processing and light industry sectors; that enterprises would be able to import goods not only for production requirements but also for sale for rubles; and that parcels for individuals valued at less than forty dollars would be exempt from duty and would not, as a rule, be opened by customs. On the export side, he said that certain consumer goods could now be exported but that these would be subject to duties of 300–600 percent.

EC Extends Credit Guarantees

Some eleven months after the European Community decided to grant credit guarantees to the USSR, it finally gave approval for the extension of these guarantees to the value of about 620 million dollars, Western agencies reported. The delay was attributed to disagreement over the precise terms; the British representative blamed it on "sheer inertia and bureaucracy."

Soviet Defense Minister in Germany

Soviet Defense Minister Evgenii Shaposhnikov arrived in Bonn, where he met with German Chancellor Helmut Kohl and German Defense Minister Gerhard Stoltenberg, Soviet and Western agencies reported. Shaposhnikov assured Kohl that Soviet troop withdrawals from former East Germany would be completed as scheduled, by 1994. The meeting with Stoltenberg produced an agreement on closer cooperation between the two armies. Shaposhnikov also claimed in a TASS interview that both parties had agreed on the need "to maintain a single USSR defense space" to ensure domestic stability and international security.

On November 12, Shaposhnikov said the USSR had begun withdrawing nuclear weapons from some republics in order to scrap or destroy them, Soviet and Western agencies reported. He claimed that no republic had asked for control over nuclear weapons currently deployed on its territory but acknowledged that republican leaders had a right to information concerning the disposition of those weapons. He added that republican leaders had also approved the Soviet and US decision to destroy tactical nuclear weapons and said that no Soviet nuclear weapons remained in Germany.

Shaposhnikov also reiterated that the Soviet Union would honor agreements with other countries on arms control and troop withdrawals and said the USSR had no reason to demand more money from Germany for the pullout from that country than had been previously agreed upon. He nevertheless asserted that the Soviet Union should get a return on investments it had made in bases in Germany.

Shaposhnikov again raised fears that the creation of republican armies in what was the USSR would be destabilizing. He argued that economic constraints precluded the building of such forces and said that those advocating republican armies had departed from reason and realism. He told reporters that democratization would continue in the armed forces and, that the Ministry of Defense would become "self-financing" ("TSN," November 12).

Gaidar on El'tsin Program

In an interview with *Pravda*, Egor Gaidar discussed El'tsin's program for economic reform, of which he was the leading architect. He repeated El'tsin's assurances that prices and the market could be stabilized within one year but qualified the impression given in El'tsin's speech on October 28 that virtually all prices could be freed overnight. Before prices were liberalized, it would be necessary to change the tax system, limit wages, and provide for pensioners, he said. All this would take several months.

Khasbulatov Appeals to Karachaevo-Cherkessia

Chairman of the RSFSR Supreme Soviet Ruslan Khasbulatov issued an appeal to the peoples of the Karachai-Cherkess republic in the Northern Caucasus to engage in dialogue to solve their problems, TASS reported. His appeal followed a recent declaration of sovereignty by the Cherkess. Earlier the Karachai proclaimed their own republic—they had their own autonomous territory before they were deported in 1943—and the local Cossacks also proclaimed their own autonomous territory.

Ukraine Restricts Trade with Other Republics

The Ukrainian Cabinet of Ministers issued a decree that would restrict Ukrainian trade relations with the rest of the former USSR in 1992, TASS reported. The decree instructed the Ukrainian Ministry of Economics to present a list of goods and services for which trade (imports as well as exports) would be managed under a quota and license system. The Ukrainian Ministry of Foreign Economic Relations was instructed to determine the licensing processes and to inform foreign economic departments in other republics of proper licensing procedures. Ukrainian trade contracts that violated these regulations would not be honored and would be considered illegal.

El'tsin's Decree on Checheno-Ingushetia Gives Rise to Protests in Tatarstan

The Tatar Public Center, the "Ittifak" Party, and the Sovereignty Committee held a meeting in Kazan' to protest El'tsin's decree declaring a state of emergency in Checheno-Ingushetia, "Vesti" reported. Almost all those who took part in the meeting asserted that the decree was a dress rehearsal for the application of similar measures in Tatarstan if the national movement became active there.

Uzbekistan to Retain *Propiska* System

The Committee for Constitutional Supervision of Uzbekistan concluded that, until a political agreement had been reached on the fate of the USSR and the form of a future state structure, it would be premature to abolish the *propiska* system, Radio Moscow reported. The comparable all-Union body recently recommended that the system be abandoned because it contravened international law.

"Birlik" Registered

Tashkent reporters told RFE/RL that the Uzbek Popular Front, "Birlik," had been registered as an official organization exactly three years after it was founded.

Survey on Military Service in Moldavia

A poll of more than 12,000 draft-age Moldavian youth revealed that some 7,000 intended to serve in the ranks of the Soviet Armed Forces and that 60 percent of those were willing to serve anywhere in the USSR. Almost 5,600 of those surveyed said they would rather pursue alternative military service. The figures were provided by Major General Viktor Nazarov, the military commissar of Moldavia, according to a TASS report. Nazarov also noted growing rates of desertion among young men drafted to other parts of the USSR but said that investigations usually proved related claims of brutality to be without foundation.

G-24 Welcomes Baltic States

The Baltic States, along with Albania, were welcomed as the newest East European nations eligible for aid from the G-24 group of industrialized countries. According to

THE USSR IN NOVEMBER, 1991

Frans Andriessen, EC external relations commissioner, the group could help the Baltic States diversify their economies, reduce dependence, and play a role in the international economy, Western agencies reported. The G-24 was already providing direct aid to Hungary, Poland, Czechoslovakia, Bulgaria, and Romania.

Retail Price Increases in Lithuania

The retail prices for many food items rose in Lithuania. The price of meat rose by 50 percent and that of dairy products by 25 percent, Lithuanian Prime Minister Gediminas Vagnorius said that ration coupons would be issued to help people buy a minimum amount of the affected goods at fixed prices. The decision to raise prices in Lithuania was taken before RSFSR President El'tsin announced price liberalization in his republic.

The reaction in Lithuania to the increase in prices was generally calm, Western agencies reported. Many Lithuanians said they felt that the price increases were necessary to reduce state subsidies and institute a market economy. Vagnorius indicated that on November 15 price controls would be lifted on more goods. On November 14 the Baltic News Service reported that Lithuania would free prices on all manufactured goods on November 19.

_____ *Tuesday, November 12*

Gorbachev Gives Press Conference on Coup

At a press conference devoted to the publication of the Russian-language edition of his recollections of the August coup, Soviet President Mikhail Gorbachev confirmed that US President George Bush had warned him of the coup in advance (*Russian Television*, "Vesti," quoting *CNN*). Although Central Television devoted thirty minutes to the press conference, it omitted this admission from its report. Included were Gorbachev's remarks that the coup organizers had committed many errors and his explanation that he had always believed that "only a madman" could launch a coup in the Soviet Union. Gorbachev criticized the democrats, however, for not having learned the necessary lessons from the coup and for continuing to squabble, thus squandering the fruits of their victory.

Gorbachev Presses for New Union Treaty

At a meeting of the parliamentary committee investigating the role of the KGB in the coup, Mikhail Gorbachev repeated his threat to resign if no new Union treaty were signed, Western agencies reported on November 13. At a meeting on November 13 with leaders of the trade unions, Gorbachev said many of the country's problems could be solved only by preserving Union statehood, TASS reported. He pointed out that a recent opinion poll showed more support now for the Union than at the time of the referendum on the future of the USSR in March, 1991. Of those questioned, 80 percent in Moscow, 72 percent in Alma-Ata, and 60 percent in Kiev said they favored the preservation of the Union.

Bolshevik Party Restored

Stalinist Nina Andreeva announced the re-creation of the All-Russian Communist Party of the Bolsheviks, "Vesti" reported. In a manifesto signed by Andreeva, the party announced its adherence to "the dictatorship of the proletariat." Radio Rossii reported that Andreeva had been elected president of the new party by 150 delegates from hard-line Communist groups and that the party already had more than 15,000 members. The party intended to lay claim to all former CPSU property and take part in all parliamentary elections.

On November 14, the Central Committee of the Bolshevik Party called for a mass campaign to remove Presidents Gorbachev and El'tsin, Interfax reported. The committee said Gorbachev and El'tsin were leading the USSR into hopeless economic and military degradation.

Lenin's Unpublished Documents Stored in Party Archives

It was reported that some 4,000 unpublished documents by Lenin were being kept in the former Central Party Archives, (*TASS*, November 12; *Krasnaya zvezda*, November 13). A member of the RSFSR parliamentary commission set up to inspect the CPSU and KGB archives, Vladimir Ponomarev, said the documents had been kept secret because they did not fit the "idealized image" of the founder of the Soviet state. In October, historian General Dmitrii Volkogonov told RFE/RL that he was working on a book based on these unpublished documents.

Defense Ministry Opposes Transfer of Kuriles

Interfax said a two-page brief prepared by the USSR Defense Ministry for the RSFSR parliament had concluded that the transfer of the two southernmost Kurile Islands to Japan would grant Japan full control over the Strait of Catherine and "substantially reduce the combat stability" of Soviet strategic nuclear forces. The brief argued that, despite Soviet force reductions in the Far East, the Japanese had continued to strengthen their forces in the region.

THE USSR IN NOVEMBER, 1991

RSFSR Begins Controlling Border

The Baltic News Service reported that the RSFSR had begun restricting the outflow of goods by establishing its first border post with Estonia. On November 11, RSFSR authorities set up a checkpoint at Ivangorod, across the river from Narva. According to the director of the Estonian Border Authority, Andres Oovel, the RSFSR authorities were checking for forty-six categories of goods bound for Estonia, including gasoline and food.

Economic Treaty Debated in Ukraine

Ukraine's adherence to the economic cooperation agreement came in for harsh criticism. Radio Kiev reported that "Rukh" had issued a statement saying the agreement was, above all, a political document aimed at salvaging the Soviet empire. Presidential candidate Vyacheslav Chornovil also made clear his opposition to the treaty. Meanwhile, Ukrainian Minister of State Volodymyr Lanovyi said that, in effect, Russia had blackmailed Ukraine into validating the economic agreement by refusing to sign the Ukrainian-Russian bilateral agreement unless Kiev agreed to the economic union.

On November 13, Ukrainian Prime Minister Vitol'd Fokin defended Ukraine's decision to join the new economic union, TASS reported. "The economic treaty initialed by Ukraine on November 6 does not close off the republic's path to real independence," Fokin said, "but opens the way to fruitful cooperation between sovereign states—the former Soviet republics."

Georgia Claims Military Equipment

Georgian President Zviad Gamsakhurdia ordered his Cabinet of Ministers to begin negotiations with the USSR authorities over acquiring military equipment, weaponry, and other possessions currently belonging to Soviet military forces in the republic, TASS reported.

Ter-Petrossyan in United States

Levon Ter-Petrossyan, who was sworn in as Armenian president on November 11, arrived in Washington on November 12 for an official visit during which he met with US President George Bush and sought diplomatic recognition of Armenia's independence and US support for Armenian membership in the United Nations. The United States was continuing to withhold recognition of any Soviet republic until the USSR and the republics had worked out their relationships (Western agencies, November 14). Raffi Hovannisian, a US citizen who was formally instated as the Armenian foreign minister on November 11, accompanied Ter-Petrossyan.

Estonia to Establish Diplomatic Contacts with NATO

NATO General Secretary Manfred Wörner announced that Estonia would establish diplomatic contacts with the military alliance. Wörner made the statement after meeting with Estonian Foreign Minister Lennart Meri in Brussels (RFE Estonian service, November 12). A similar agreement was concluded with Lithuania on November 22.

Landsbergis Appeals to US and UN for Help with Problem of Soviet Troop Withdrawal

While visiting Detroit, Lithuanian Supreme Council President Vytautas Landsbergis said the United States should urge the USSR to withdraw its troops from Lithuania during the coming winter and should make the troop withdrawal a condition for aid, according to Western agencies. Landsbergis also said that fewer than half of the OMON troops stationed in Lithuania had left. The rest, Landsbergis said, had gone underground and appeared to be preparing to destabilize the Lithuanian government.

On November 13, Landsbergis met with UN Secretary-General Javier Perez de Cuellar and stressed the need for a speedy withdrawal of the approximately 100,000 Soviet army and special assault troops in Lithuania. At a press conference on November 14, he said that Lithuania would address the issue in an appropriate UN forum before the end of 1991 and that he expected the United Nations to help persuade Moscow to enter into substantive talks to resolve the problem (RFE/RL correspondent's report, November 14).

Wednesday, November 13

USSR Bank for Foreign Trade Faces Competition

The Journal of Commerce reported that the USSR Bank for Foreign Trade (Vneshekonombank) faced growing competition from the RSFSR Foreign Trade Bank (Rosvneshtorgbank). A Vneshekonombank official attributed the bank's liquidity crisis partly to the withholding by enterprises of the 40-percent remittance tax on hard-currency earnings. The bank's current commercial arrears were put at about 5 billion dollars. It was said to be paying companies only in countries that were lending money to the USSR. The Rosvneshtorgbank representative was confident that Russia would be able to repay its 60-percent share of the country's foreign debt but that this might take five to ten years.

Yavlinsky Warns of Final Collapse

Soviet President Mikhail Gorbachev's chief economic adviser, Grigorii Yavlinsky, warned republican leaders that the Soviet Union and its republics would face

THE USSR IN NOVEMBER, 1991

collapse if they did not quickly agree on cooperation in banking, finance, prices, and foreign-debt servicing, Western agencies reported. Yavlinsky said the Soviet Union would cease to function in 1992 if these problems were not solved soon. Yavlinsky's comments were made in documents presented earlier to State Council members.

In an interview with RFE/RL, Gorbachev's special adviser Aleksandr Yakovlev said he had met with the Soviet president the day he returned from detention in Foros and advised him on how to act. Yakovlev said that at that time Gorbachev did not fully understand how much the situation in the country had changed after the attempted putsch. According to Yakovlev, it was he who told Gorbachev that the CPSU was completely finished and advised him to resign as CPSU general secretary and order the dissolution of the Communist Party's ruling bodies.

Yakovlev Advised Gorbachev after Coup

Moscow city officials told a press conference that the city planned to privatize all its 4,500 retail stores by January 1, Western agencies reported. Stores with less than 500 square meters of floor space would be sold to their employees or auctioned, while larger stores would be turned into joint-stock companies. The city government would be prepared to sell stores to foreign investors provided they undertook to continue selling goods for rubles. It was also announced that Moscow residents would receive 60-ruble coupons valid at food stores to compensate for price increases.

All Moscow Stores to Be Privatized

The USSR Supreme Soviet angrily discussed an alleged betrayal of trust by President Gorbachev, the Ministry of Finance, and the USSR State Bank (Gosbank), TASS reported. It was alleged that, some time in mid-1991, Gorbachev had ordered Gosbank to begin issuing tens of billions of rubles to the Ministry of Finance in order to secretly finance certain government operations. This caused an overdraft of some 90 billion rubles in state finances that the Supreme Soviet neither agreed to nor knew about (some reports said the Supreme Soviet had agreed to an extra 5-billion ruble issue by Gosbank).

Financial Scandal Hits Gorbachev

Jane's Defense Weekly reported that a Soviet sales team was visiting Iran to display high-performance fighters and missiles, according to Western agencies. Agencies also

Soviet Arms Sales

reported that the Soviet Union had offered to sell sophisticated fighter aircraft and combat helicopters to Malaysia.

St. Petersburg Branch of Movement for Democratic Reforms Holds Inaugural Conference

The inaugural conference of the St. Petersburg branch of the Movement for Democratic Reforms was addressed by St. Petersburg Mayor Anatolii Sobchak, a leading member of the movement. Sobchak said the movement advocated a liberal-democratic line, adding that he hoped it would lead to the creation of several parties of democratic orientation and thus finally enable a multiparty system to emerge in Russia.

Soviet Troop Withdrawal from Cuba Discussed

A Soviet delegation arrived in Cuba to discuss the withdrawal of Soviet troops. Soviet special envoy Vyacheslav Ustinov, who led the delegation, told Interfax that the withdrawal of some 3,000 men stationed outside Havana would not be linked to the closing of the US naval base at Guantanamo Bay. Hours before the talks were scheduled to begin on November 15, Cuban President Fidel Castro said his country was absolutely opposed to a Soviet troop withdrawal as long as the United States retained a naval base on the island, Western agencies reported.

The previous week, USSR Defense Minister Evgenii Shaposhnikov had told Interfax that the timing of the Soviet withdrawal from Cuba "is first and foremost Cuba's concern." He added: "Our protracted military presence in various countries has brought us nothing but economic damage."

Patriarch Condemns Anti-Semitism

During an official visit to the United States, Patriarch Aleksii II met with representatives of the Jewish community in New York, TASS reported on November 14. The patriarch said in his address that Christians and Jews believed in one God, and he discussed the attitude of the Orthodox Church towards anti-Semitism. He declared that the hierarchy and the theologians of the Russian Orthodox Church openly condemned anti-Semitism and that it was the task of the Russian Orthodox Church to defeat this evil. Moscow's chief rabbi, Adolf Shaevich, who was present at the press conference, confirmed the statements made by the patriarch.

Gagauz in Moldavia Forming Armed Units

Following an armed raid by local black marketeers on a Moldavian customs checkpoint in which one attacker was killed, Gagauz residents in the raion center of Vulcanesti attacked the raion police station and courthouse with submachine guns and Molotov cocktails and burned down the two buildings. One Moldavian police officer was killed and three were injured. The police did not return fire. A "Gagauz self-defense unit commander" called Kishinev to demand that the recently established Moldavian customs service and the Moldavian police be withdrawn from the raion. On November 15, the self-styled "chief of the Gagauz SSR MVD" told "Vesti" that the Gagauz were forming "self-defense units" on the instructions of "the Gagauz Supreme Soviet."

Interviewed by Moldavian television on November 14, Prime Minister Valeriu Muravschi gave an account of the incidents in and around Vulcanesti based on a report by the Moldavian Prosecutor's Office. Commenting that the original incident at the customs point was a common crime by black marketeers that anti-Moldavian forces were trying to turn into an interethnic conflict, Muravschi also accused "forces among the central authorities" and "imperial circles" of "trying to turn Moldavia into another Karabakh." Calling for calm, Muravschi renewed assurances that "the Moldavian leadership categorically opposes any resort to force in solving nationality-related issues."

Karelia Changes Its Name

The Karelian Supreme Soviet decided to change the name of the republic to the Republic of Karelia (dropping "Soviet" and "Socialist"), TASS reported. It was the last of the former autonomous republics of the RSFSR to do so.

Protest in Bashkiria about Election Postponement

A group of young people, mainly students from nationalist organizations, tried to seize the television center in Ufa, "Vesti" reported. Eventually their representatives were allowed on the air to complain that the postponement of the presidential election by the Bashkir parliament was a violation of the republic's sovereignty and to demand the resignation of the Presidium of the Supreme Soviet and its chairman. The election had been scheduled for December 15 but was postponed indefinitely owing to the cost and the instability in the republic.

Ukraine and Uzbekistan Sign Cooperation Agreement

Ukraine and Uzbekistan signed a treaty in Tashkent on economic and cultural cooperation, Radio Moscow reported. Under the agreement, Ukraine would deliver iron, television sets, and other consumer goods in exchange for vegetables and fruits from Uzbekistan.

Turkmenistan to Raise Price of Raw Materials

Turkmen President Saparmurad Niyazov told the Turkmen Supreme Soviet that, in an effort to protect the republic's population and economy, he had sent a telegram to Soviet President Mikhail Gorbachev saying that Turkmenistan was planning to raise the price of its raw materials, TASS reported. Niyazov said that, despite the economic community treaty, other republics had without prior consultation raised the prices of goods that Turkmenistan imported. The Supreme Soviet approved Niyazov's decision. Turkmenistan is a major exporter of natural gas to the European part of Russia.

Nazarbaev Sole Presidential Candidate

Radio Moscow reported that Kazakh President Nursultan Nazarbaev would be the only candidate in the presidential election in Kazakhstan on December 1, Radio Moscow reported. The chairman of the National Democratic Party "Zheltoksan," Hasan Kozhakhmetov, was unable to register, because he could not produce the necessary 100,000 signatures. Interfax quoted Kozhakhmetov's press office as saying unidentified persons had stolen 40,000 signatures backing his candidacy.

Belorussian Opposition Calls on Government to Resign

Belorussian Popular Front deputies in the Supreme Soviet demanded the resignation of the republican government. In a statement carried by TASS, the deputies charged that Prime Minister Vyacheslau Kebich was incapable of creating the instruments of a market economy, including a national bank and Belorussian currency. The Council of Ministers, it continued, had been acting in the service of the former Communist Party apparatus. The opposition leaders called for the formation of "a government of the people's trust."

MVD Commander Says Troops Will Leave Baltic by 1992

The commander of Soviet MVD troops in the Baltic States said that all his forces guarding installations there would be withdrawn by January 1, 1992. General Arkadii Kramerev told Interfax that the troops could have been withdrawn earlier but that the Baltic authorities had delayed the move because they wanted to use the troops for an interim period as prison guards.

Thursday, November 14

Seven Republics Tentatively Agree on Union Treaty

At a meeting of the USSR State Council the leaders of seven republics—the RSFSR, Belorussia, Kazakhstan,

The USSR in November, 1991

Azerbaijan, Kirgizia, Tajikistan, and Turkmenistan—said they were ready in principle to sign the latest version of the Union treaty after it had been further reworked, the Soviet media reported. The treaty provided for a confederative union to be known as the Union of Sovereign States. The participants also agreed that the treaty itself should serve as the constitution of the new Union and that the Union should remain a single subject of international law. The draft would make the president of the Union of Sovereign States commander of the armed forces, including nuclear weapons, and the Union's representative in foreign relations (Western agencies, November 15).

Russia to Assume Total Soviet Foreign Debt?

In an interview with *Die Zeit*, RSFSR President Boris El'tsin reaffirmed that his republic would pay its share of Soviet foreign debt and would assume the debt burden of any other republic that refused to pay its share. Russia's motive in doing this would be to "save the good reputation" of the USSR. El'tsin's deputy finance minister, Andrei Zverev, told a Washington press conference on November 13 that the non-Russian republics were incapable of paying hard-currency debts and would default if asked to pay their share. It was therefore simpler for Russia to assume the whole burden and then seek other forms of compensation from the other republics, the *Los Angeles Times* reported on November 14.

USSR and Ukraine Accede to Human-Rights Protocol

The United Nations said that Ukraine and the Soviet Union had acceded to the optional protocol to the International Covenant on Civil and Political Rights. The protocol makes it possible for the UN Human-Rights Committee to consider complaints from individuals against their own governments.

Nishanov Named Gorbachev Adviser

Chairman of the Council of Nationalities of the former USSR Supreme Soviet Rafik Nishanov was appointed an adviser to Soviet President Mikhail Gorbachev, TASS reported. Nishanov told TASS that in assuming his new post he would be "performing the most varied missions connected both with interethnic and interrepublican relations and with international issues."

KGB Officers Said to Control Financial Capital

Senior officers of the KGB were reported to head many of the Soviet Union's stock, commodities, and financial exchanges (*TASS*, November 14; *Stolitsa*, No. 40). Examples given included: senior KGB officer Mikhail Boldyrev and another KGB officer, Igor' Chukhalntsev, who were said to be, respectively, vice president and financial director of an umbrella financial and banking alliance, the All-Russian Stock Exchange Center. This organization, 75 percent of whose staff was drawn from the state security officer corps, was also reported to control another organization, the All-Russian Immobility Stock Exchange. In addition, KGB officer Aleksandr Sumskoi was named as president of the Inventory Resources Stock Exchange. *Stolitsa* added that the KGB laundered its capital primarily in Eastern Europe, particularly Hungary.

On November 21, the Public Relations Center of the Interrepublican Security Service called the allegations "pure fiction" and said the security service would like to see an investigation into them.

Belorussia Moves towards Separate Currency

Belorussia decided to introduce special coupons to partially replace rubles as a first step towards establishing its own currency, Western agencies reported. The Russian Information Agency reported that the coupon system was due to go into effect at the beginning of 1992, when coupons would be paid as a proportion of salaries.

Uzbek Deputies Want Presidential Election in 1991

A group of Uzbek deputies sent a letter to the republic's parliamentary Committee on Questions of Legislation and Law and Order suggesting that the popular election of the republic's president should be held before the end of 1991, UzTAG-TASS reported. They said that the population did not understand why the parliament was dragging its feet over adopting the necessary law. The letter also said the popular election of the president would strengthen the republic's independence. Uzbekistan was the only Central Asian republic that had not yet either held or scheduled a popular presidential election.

On November 18, the Uzbek Supreme Soviet decreed that the popular election of the republic's president should take place on December 29, UzTAG-TASS reported. The same day, a referendum was to be held on the independence of the republic.

Moldavia Takes Over Soviet Army Property

A decree issued by Moldavian President Mircea Snegur declared all military equipment and assets of the Soviet army units stationed on Moldavian territory the property of Moldavia, TASS reported. The decree forbade the removal of any equipment from Moldavia. It said the step was necessitated by the need to create a material-technical base for the armed forces of Moldavia.

Friday, November 15

El'tsin Suspends Oil Exports

RSFSR President Boris El'tsin ordered the suspension of Soviet oil export licenses to protect domestic supplies for the winter, Western agencies reported. RSFSR Economics Minister Egor Gaidar told the Russian parliament that all export licenses had been suspended, while another El'tsin aide, Valerii Grishin, told reporters that some international export licenses remained in force.

RSFSR Takes Over Soviet Gold and Diamond Industries

RSFSR President Boris El'tsin signed a decree assuming full responsibility for the Soviet gold and diamond industries, Western agencies reported. El'tsin told the RSFSR parliament that the Soviet gold storage facility, Goskhran, had been abolished and would be replaced by RSFSR Goskhran.

USSR Prosecutor's Office Taken Over by RSFSR

The RSFSR Supreme Soviet passed a resolution establishing a single prosecutor's office under the jurisdiction of the RSFSR, TASS reported. RSFSR Prosecutor-General Valentin Stepankov told the Supreme Soviet that, since November 1, financing of the USSR Prosecutor's Office had ceased and that the department therefore did not have the means to ensure its continued existence. The USSR Prosecutor's Office employed 39,000 people, and Stepankov told RFE/RL that qualified specialists would get jobs in the RSFSR Prosecutor's Office.

RSFSR Parliament Endorses Draft Citizenship Law

The RSFSR Supreme Soviet gave preliminary approval to a draft bill on citizenship, the RL Russian service reported. Under the proposed law, all people living on the territory of the RSFSR who had not renounced Soviet citizenship would automatically acquire Russian citizenship. Dual citizenship would also be possible for people living in other republics who wanted to acquire Russian citizenship.

Yakovlev Appeals to the West

Soviet presidential adviser Aleksandr Yakovlev told businessmen and journalists in New York that the survival of democracy in the Soviet Union depended on the

West's welcoming the USSR as a full partner in the world economic system, Western agencies reported. Yakovlev said that, without the ability to trade equally with the West, and without emergency food and medical aid for the winter, the USSR could face uprisings and another coup attempt. He said, "We are not only talking about saving people but about saving democracy as well."

RSFSR Ministers Appointed

RSFSR President Boris El'tsin decreed the dissolution of the RSFSR State Council, Radio Rossii reported. RSFSR state councilors would become advisers in a Presidential Consultative Council—an institution that existed when El'tsin was head of the Russian parliament. Eduard Dunaev was appointed minister of education; Andrei Kozyrev, foreign minister; Boris Saltykov, minister of science; Mikhail Poltoranin, minister for mass media; Ella Pamfilova, minister of social security; Nikolai Fedorov, minister of justice; Viktor Ivanenko, KGB chairman; and Pavel Grachev, head of the Defense Committee.

Secret Gold Shipments?

TASS reported that the editorial board of *Izvestia* was examining documents it had received recently concerning secret shipments of gold, platinum, and other precious metals abroad over the last forty-five days, TASS reported. The documents indicated that the shipments (on Aeroflot planes destined for Paris, Frankfurt, Tokyo, and other major cities) totaled as much as 5,213 kilograms. The documents appeared to be fairly detailed, listing the flight number and type of aircraft used. The most recent shipment of 3,159 kilograms was reported to have been flown by Aeroflot to London. Who authorized the shipments was unclear.

On November 18, Evgenii Bychkov, an official of the USSR Ministry of Finance, denied reports by TASS and Western agencies that the USSR had secretly shipped precious metals to Switzerland. Bychkov did not dispute reports that shipments had gone to other countries but spoke of those shipments as though they were normal transactions. *Izvestia* reported that some 300 kilograms of palladium in ingots and in powder had been shipped from Moscow to Brussels on November 16.

Army to Privatize Its Baltic Property?

Representatives of Soviet troops stationed in the Baltic States told reporters that they intended to sell off military property in the region in order to finance their resettlement in the RSFSR, TASS and Western agencies reported.

The USSR in November, 1991

According to Captain Valerii Shorin—chairman of a Coordinating Council set up in the Baltic to represent the troops—the armed forces would sell off some 100 billion dollars in property, including port facilities and airports, to finance education, accommodations, buildings, and retraining programs for returning troops. Shorin claimed to have the tacit support of the USSR Defense Ministry for his plans.

El'tsin Appoints Representative to Kabardino-Balkaria

RSFSR President Boris El'tsin appointed Aziratali Akhmetov his plenipotentiary representative in Kabardino-Balkaria in the Northern Caucasus (*Radio Moscow*, November 15).

Gamsakhurdia Equates Opposition with Treason

Georgian President Zviad Gamsakhurdia reiterated in a televised address that Georgia would sign neither the new Union treaty nor the interrepublican economic treaty (*Interfax*, November 16). Gamsakhurdia further argued that market reforms served "only to impoverish the ordinary people and enrich corrupt dealers" and that, while opposition was acceptable in a rich country, it was "equal to treason" in Georgia as long as the country was "in a condition of collapse and war."

Saratov Newspaper on German Autonomy

The Saratov newspaper *Saratovskie vesti* carried an article saying that opposition in Saratov Oblast to the re-creation of German autonomy on the Volga had led to growing confrontation between the Russian and German populations in recent months, TASS reported. The newspaper suggested that the RSFSR government should bear in mind the feelings of the Russian population during El'tsin's upcoming visit to Bonn, when the question was expected to be finally decided.

Belorussia Establishes Defense Ministry

The Belorussian Supreme Soviet voted to establish a republican Ministry of Defense. The new ministry would be headed by a civilian, although a military officer would be appointed for a transitional period (Western agencies, November 17). The parliament voted against creating a National Guard for the time being.

Daugava River Contaminated

The Latvian authorities issued a public health warning after chemicals from a nearby plant in Belorussia escaped into the Daugava River, Radio Riga reported. The Daugava, Latvia's largest river, flows through Riga. The chemicals from the polymer plant at Novopolotsk in Belorussia were expected to reach Riga a day after the spill occurred. In 1990, acid from the same Belorussian plant got into the river, killing many fish.

Saturday, November 16

Lobov on National Armies

Chief of the General Staff Vladimir Lobov said that "the national question" was the most serious problem facing the Soviet Armed Forces, *Trud* reported. Lobov argued that a single, integrated armed forces remained the most effective way of ensuring security for each of the republics. He said that military reform and the creation of national military formations should be aimed at consolidating state power, not dividing it. He also proposed creating special organs at the center and in the republics that would oversee military spending.

Russian Communist Party Appeals to Constitutional Court of RSFSR

Leaders of the RSFSR Communist Party protested about RSFSR President Boris El'tsin's edict banning the activities of the Communist Parties of the Soviet Union and Russia and dissolving their structures in the RSFSR. According to *Sovetskaya Rossiya*, the former leaders of the RSFSR Communist Party took the dispute over the edict to the RSFSR Constitutional Court, asking it to review the edict to see whether it complied with the RSFSR Constitution and international law.

RSFSR and USSR Disagree over Honecker

Western agencies said the RSFSR government had decided former East German leader Erich Honecker should be expelled from the territory of the Russian Federation. RSFSR Justice Minister Nikolai Fedorov said the decision had been made on November 15 at a cabinet meeting headed by RSFSR President El'tsin. Meanwhile, an adviser to Soviet President Mikhail Gorbachev, Nikolai Portugalov, said Gorbachev's opposition to the return of Honecker was based on "a moral obligation" to the former leader.

The following day, amid reports that Honecker had applied for asylum in the USSR, Fedorov told reporters in Bonn that only Russian law applied to the former East German leader with regard to any such application and that no decision by the RSFSR government depended on the wishes of Soviet President Gorbachev.

Socialist Party of the Working Class Founded

The founding congress of Lenin's Socialist Party of the Working Class was held in Novosibirsk. TASS named

THE USSR IN NOVEMBER, 1991

forty-three-year-old Lyudmila Belousova as the new party's founder.

Sunday, November 17

El'tsin Issues Economic Decrees

RSFSR President Boris El'tsin issued ten decrees designed to assert greater control over the economy. Supplementing the measures announced on November 15 that asserted the RSFSR's control over oil exports and Soviet gold and diamond production, these decrees provided for salaries to be increased by up to 90 percent for many workers and a minimum wage of 200 rubles per month to be instituted with effect from December 1. The RSFSR would also take control of the printing of currency and the determination of foreign exchange rates. El'tsin ordered the cancellation of foreign exchange rates set by the USSR government as of January 1, 1992. All enterprises would be allowed to engage in foreign trade without special registration, and licensed banks would have the right to open hard-currency accounts for all citizens. Beginning on November 20, the RSFSR would stop funding some eighty central government ministries. The buildings and property of those agencies that ceased to exist would be transferred to the RSFSR government. No decree on freeing prices was issued, however (*TASS*, November 17).

Union of Cossack Republics Formed

The Great Council of Atamans of the Cossacks of Southern Russia, which was meeting in Novocherkassk, sent telegrams to the USSR and RSFSR presidents demanding the immediate adoption of a decree on the formation and arming of a Cossack National Guard in southern Russia, TASS reported. If no action were taken, the atamans said they would be forced to resolve the question themselves. They also demanded the creation of a presidential commission to deal with Cossack problems and decided to set up a Union of Cossack Republics of the South of Russia. Ataman of the Don Cossacks Sergei Meshcheryakov was elected ataman of the new union.

Anti-Cossack Meeting in Tselinograd

Radio Moscow reported that controversy over the Cossack question was not abating in Kazakhstan. The radio said a well-attended but unsanctioned meeting had taken place in Tselinograd to demand the suspension of the activity of the Union of Cossacks association registered by the local authorities on November 5. The participants at the meeting said the association's activities were anticonstitutional and liable to harm ethnic relations. Anti-Cossack feeling had been running high among the Kazakhs since the Ural Cossacks recently celebrated in Ural'sk, under the Russian flag, the 400th anniversary of their allegiance to Russia.

Monday, November 18

G–7 Holds Meetings with Republics on Soviet Foreign Debt

A meeting between officials of the G–7 countries and representatives of the twelve remaining republics adjourned in confusion over how to manage the USSR's 68-billion-dollar foreign debt, TASS and "Vesti" reported.

The meetings continued on November 19 and 20 without agreement. Republican leaders objected to a demand by the G–7 negotiators that Soviet gold (104 tons out of the estimated 240 tons of reserves) be deposited in Western banks as collateral for any loans or debt-deferment plan, Western agencies reported.

The meetings were extended for an unscheduled fourth day, and on November 21 an agreement was reached on a debt-relief package that included a loan of 1 billion dollars and deferment of 3.6 billion dollars in foreign debt payments, Interfax and Western agencies reported. The demand for Soviet gold was dropped, but the agreement made further aid conditional on implementation of radical economic reforms. Republican leaders who signed the accord committed themselves to sharp reductions in the Soviet budget deficit, curbing the inflationary growth of the money supply, ending state-controlled prices, and a further devaluation of the ruble. Eight republics signed the accord, and three of the four remaining (Ukraine, Azerbaijan, and Georgia) were expected to do so soon. Uzbekistan reportedly opposed the agreement and was insisting on paying separately.

The Baltic States did not sign the agreement, but, on November 16, Chairman of the Interstate Economic Committee Ivan Silaev met with Lithuanian Prime Minister Gediminas Vagnorius; Andris Gutnanis, an envoy of the Latvian prime minister; and Estonia's deputy chargé d'affaires Mehis Pilv. They reportedly agreed to send their respective countries' deputy foreign ministers as observers to the meetings in Moscow (*Interfax*, November 16). Lithuania also indicated on November 18 that it would be prepared to assume its share of the Soviet foreign debt, according to TASS.

In an interview on Central Television on November 22, Silaev said that the negotiations on the Soviet Union's foreign debt had been very difficult and "even to some extent humiliating" but that he did not understand the

The USSR in November, 1991

position of those republics that had not signed. Silaev warned that if the RSFSR paid their share of the debt they would receive no credits from abroad and would have to turn to the RSFSR, which would be able to dictate its terms.

Increase in Production of Natural Gas; Prices to Follow

An official of the Ministry of the Gas Industry said gas production from January to October in the USSR was 3.2 billion cubic meters more than in the same period in 1990. Demand for gas had also increased, and there were tentative plans to raise natural gas prices by 300 percent in the foreseeable future, TASS reported.

Inflation Rate Quadruples

The weekly *Kommersant* said the monthly inflation rate had quadrupled since the beginning of the year. The article said that cash in circulation had increased by some 35 billion rubles in the last two months. This put the increase of cash in circulation since the beginning of the year at some 83 billion rubles, or 63 percent.

Nonstate Economy Grows

The nonstate sector (cooperatives, leased firms, and joint ventures) of the economy produced some 15 percent of Gross Social Product in the first half of 1991, according to data provided by the analytical service TASTA in a survey entitled "The Nonstate Sector of the Soviet Economy: Results and Trends." As of July 1, 1991, there were about 4,200 joint ventures registered in the USSR with a capital base of more than 10 billion rubles. The total number of active joint ventures was much smaller, however.

Moscow Admits Downing Swedish Plane in 1952

In a statement broadcast by Central Television, the USSR Defense Ministry admitted that a Soviet fighter had shot down a Swedish military aircraft that disappeared over the Baltic Sea in 1952, Western agencies reported. The Defense Ministry admitted that the action was "an outright violation of . . . international law" and expressed its condolences to the families of the crew members who died in the attack.

New Data on Private Farming

New data released by the USSR State Committee for Statistics indicated that the share of agricultural output produced by the private agricultural sector in the USSR was increasing. There were reported to be some 38 million private farms in the USSR, plus some 12 million urban dwellers who cultivated gardens. There were a further 6.5 million families with smaller collective gardens. Nonstate agriculture produced about 22 percent of cattle, 33 percent of cows, 22 percent of pigs, and 35 percent of poultry in the USSR. The nonstate sector produced 31 percent of meat and 28 percent of milk. The largest problem, according to TASS's account of the published statistics, was that privatization of land was proceeding too slowly.

Kuwait Gives Loan to USSR

Kuwait announced at a press briefing given at its embassy in Moscow that it was granting a credit of 500 million dollars to the Soviet Union, DPA reported. Kuwait reportedly called on the USSR to help with the rebuilding of Kuwait and the freeing of Kuwaitis imprisoned in Iraq. Meanwhile, TASS reported that talks between Soviet President Mikhail Gorbachev and visiting Kuwaiti Emir Jabir al-Ahmad al-Sabah were held in an atmosphere of "mutual understanding and trust." The emir also met with RSFSR President Boris El'tsin.

Trade Unions Support El'tsin

Independent Russian trade unions welcomed RSFSR President El'tsin's radical reform program directed at the introduction of a market economy in Russia. The chairman of the Federation of the Independent Trade Unions of Russia, Igor' Klochkov, told TASS that El'tsin had fulfilled several of the trade unions' demands, such as raising the salaries of employees in cultural, scientific, and health organizations. Klochkov also welcomed the idea of establishing an organization attached to the RSFSR Ministry of Labor and Employment to arbitrate in labor disputes. Klochkov's only criticism was that the program lacked legal mechanisms for privatization of enterprises and housing.

Tatar Republic Repeats Call for National Guard

At a meeting in Kazan', called on the initiative of the Tatar Public Center, there were renewed calls for the creation of a National Guard of Tatarstan and armed struggle for the republic's independence, Central Television reported.

North Ossetia Creates Republican Guard

In an interview published in *Pravda*, the chairman of the North Ossetian Supreme Soviet, Akhsarbek Galazov, said that North Ossetia was forming a republican guard and self-defense committee, because the Ingush were persisting in asserting their territorial claims on North Ossetia.

Meanwhile, Ingush leaders and clergy had persuaded a thousands-strong rally of Ingush in Nazran to abandon their planned march on North Ossetia, TASS reported on

THE USSR IN NOVEMBER, 1991

November 17. "TV Inform" had reported the day before that the crowd, which had assembled for many days, had decided on November 7 to embark on a mass peaceful settlement of the territory if the RSFSR took no action to return the Prigorodnyi Raion of North Ossetia to them by November 16. The Ingush had been forbidden to settle there for several years. Although the participants in the rally abandoned their march, they vowed not to disperse until their demands were met.

Balkar Republic Proclaimed

The first congress of the Balkar people in Nalchik, the capital of the Kabardino-Balkar Republic in the Northern Caucasus, adopted a declaration on the national sovereignty of the Balkar people and the formation of a Balkar republic within the RSFSR, Central Television reported.

Harvest Failure in Kazakhstan

Because of severe drought, the 1991 grain harvest in Kazakhstan came to only 12.5 million tons, less than half that of 1990, *Izvestia* reported. This led to a critical situation in animal husbandry. The Kazakh cabinet was hoping to buy grain from abroad.

Withdrawal of Soviet Paratrooper Units Stalled

The chairman of Estonia's parliamentary Committee for State Defense said that the USSR had violated agreements regarding the withdrawal of two paratrooper units. Enn Tupp told the Baltic News Service that paratroopers scheduled to be withdrawn on November 3 had left Voru but simply gone to Tallinn and not left the country. A small unit had remained to guard the base, which should have been turned over to the Estonian authorities according to the terms of an agreement reached in September between Prime Minister Edgar Savisaar and USSR Defense Minister Evgenii Shaposhnikov. Tupp said the second paratroop unit in Viljandi had shown no signs of leaving.

New Chamber of Trade and Industry to Include Baltic States

Agreement was reached at a conference in Moscow to disband the Chamber of Trade and Industry of the USSR and create a Confederation of Trade and Industry in its place, according to TASS. Of the fifteen republics that formerly constituted the USSR, twelve were party to the agreement, including the three Baltic States; Georgia, Armenia, and Tajikistan failed to participate.

Estonia Passes Border Law

The Estonian Supreme Council passed a law regulating border traffic (*Rahva Haal*, November 19). The law specified that Estonia could be entered only at government checkpoints and that persons—rather than vehicles or cargo—would be controlled. The law aimed to reduce Estonia's soaring crime rate by clamping down on drug and other illicit traffic passing through Estonia's porous eastern border.

Pope Invited to Lithuania President of the Lithuanian Supreme Council Vytautas Landsbergis invited Pope John Paul II to visit Lithuania (Western agencies, November 18).

Tuesday, November 19

Shevardnadze Reappointed Foreign Minister Eduard Shevardnadze was appointed by presidential decree to head the new USSR Ministry of External Relations. His predecessor, Boris Pankin, was named ambassador to Britain, TASS reported. In an interview with *Komsomol'skaya pravda* on November 21, Shevardnadze said that he had agreed to run the ministry because the USSR was in a crisis, remarking: "If a man can do something useful, he has no right to stand aside." He also said that it had been more difficult to make the decision to come back than to resign in December, 1990. Shevardnadze said that one of his first actions would be to visit the capitals of the Soviet republics and hold negotiations with leaders there. He said he was open to dialogue with all his opponents (*Radio Rossii*, November 20).

Eight Ambassadors Leave Posts Soviet President Mikhail Gorbachev relieved three ambassadors of their posts: Aleksandr Baryshev (Guinea-Bissau), Leonid Zamyatin (Britain), and Lev Voronin (EC). Four more ambassadors—Yurii Dubinin (France), German Gventsadze (Ireland), Anatolii Slyusar' (Greece), and Nikolai Uspensky (Sweden)—were assigned to "other work" by Gorbachev on the same day, TASS reported. These ambassadors were recalled on suspicion of having sympathized with the coup's organizers. The same TASS report noted that Yurii Pavlov (Chile) had retired. Pavlov had recently "defected" to accept a teaching position at the University of Miami.

New Branch of Armed Forces Created *Rabochaya tribuna* reported that a new branch of the armed forces—the Strategic Deterrence Forces—had been created by presidential decree. It would incorporate the Strategic Rocket Forces, the missile warning and antimissile defense units of the Air Defense Forces, and organizations concerned with the military use of space. Strategic aviation and the navy's strategic nuclear forces would be under the operational control of the commander in chief of the new branch, Army General Yurii Maksimov, who previously headed the Strategic Rocket Forces. Gorbachev had announced that such a service would be created in his response to US President Bush's recent unilateral nuclear arms initiatives on October 5.

Volkogonov on Reform of Political Organs

Colonel General Dmitrii Volkogonov, appointed to head a commission overseeing the elimination of the army's military-political organs following the August coup, announced a series of measures aimed at transforming the Main Political Administration of the Soviet Army and Navy (MPA). According to "Vesti," 320 of 345 generals who served in the MPA would be discharged, while the corps of political officers as a whole would be cut by 40–45 percent. The number of military-political academies was also slated to be cut drastically.

Lopatin on Military Leadership

Colonel Vladimir Lopatin, a longtime critic of the USSR Defense Ministry and a leading military reformer currently serving in the RSFSR government, said that the Soviet military leadership was divided by an internal struggle for power, Western agencies reported. Lopatin also expressed concern over what he said was the continued presence in the High Command of a number of generals involved in the August coup.

Soviet Navy Unprepared for Battle?

A former Soviet nuclear submarine captain, Anatolii Gorbachev, said in *Nezavisimaya gazeta* that the Soviet navy was in such disarray that it would lose 85 percent of its fleet if war broke out. The captain also claimed that Soviet submarines were up to fifty times as noisy as their US equivalents and that their radars were one-tenth as effective.

El'tsin Appoints Envoy to United States

RSFSR President Boris El'tsin appointed Andrei Kolosovsky as Russia's envoy to the United States. Kolosovsky, an RSFSR deputy foreign minister, would work in the Soviet embassy in Washington with the rank of minister-counselor.

Newspaper Subscription Rates in 1992

Izvestia and Radio Moscow reported that *Komsomol'skaya pravda* and *Trud*, the two dailies with the highest circulation in the Soviet Union, had held their positions in the 1992 subscription campaign. The circulation of both newspapers was about 18 million. Subscriptions to *Literaturnaya gazeta* and *Ogonek* for 1992 were, however, reported to be 25 percent lower than in 1991. *Argumenty i fakty*, the weekly with the largest circulation outside the Soviet Union, was set to retain its record circulation of more than 30 million. Some former CPSU publications, such as *Rabochaya tribuna* and *Sel'skaya zhizn'*, had registered a 150-percent increase in subscriptions.

Metropolitan on Russian Orthodox-Vatican Split

Metropolitan Kirill of Smolensk and Kaliningrad, who is head of the Department of External Church Relations of the Moscow Patriarchate, said at a press conference in Bonn that representatives of the Russian Orthodox Church (Moscow Patriarchate) would not attend a synod of bishops of the Roman Catholic Church in Europe scheduled to begin at the end of November in Rome, TASS reported. The metropolitan sharply criticized the activities of the Vatican on the territory of the USSR.

Gamsakhurdia Disbands Georgian KGB

Georgian President Zviad Gamsakhurdia issued a decree transforming Georgia's KGB into a National Security Department under his personal supervision, TASS reported. The Georgian parliament was expected to pass a law specifying the functions of the new department.

Uzbekistan Opposes Latest Draft of Union Treaty

Addressing the Uzbek Supreme Soviet, Uzbek President Islam Karimov said that Uzbekistan would not sign the latest draft of the Union treaty, UzTAG-TASS reported. Karimov said the draft did not fully take into account the state independence of the republic; in his opinion, the Union republics should not only be members of the international community but also subjects of international law. He also complained that the draft did not make it clear that relations between the treaty participants should be based on the principles of equality and noninterference in one another's affairs. This omission could result in the continuation of the old division of "elder" and "younger" brothers, Karimov added.

Moldavia to Form Professional Army

The director general of the Moldavian Department for Military Affairs, Nicolae Chirtoaca, told TASS that Moldavia had decided to form a professional army of 12,000 to 15,000 men. Its mission would be defined in law as defending the republic's territorial integrity and constitutional order. The republic would also institute a general military draft that would require all young men to serve for six months and then take retraining courses on two or three subsequent occasions. This system would enable Moldavia to raise a volunteer force of a few hundred thousand men at short notice if necessary. Legislation on military service and on the social rights of servicemen was being drafted. (Moldavia had already enacted a law on conscientious objection.)

In a statement released through *Rompres*, Patriarch Teoctist, the head of Romania's Orthodox Church, called on the Romanian government to initiate talks with Ukraine on the return of Northern Bukovina and southern Bessarabia. The patriarch's call capped a series of statements by Romanian political parties and civic associations in connection with the impending referendum on Ukraine's independence. The Romanian parliament adopted a resolution making a similar call in June.

Romanian Orthodox Patriarch Calls for Return of Territories from Ukraine

Armenian and Azerbaijani delegations signed a protocol providing for the resumption of Azerbaijani gas supplies to Armenia, which were cut off by Azerbaijan on November 4, Radio Moscow reported. After the deadline of midnight on November 19 had passed, however, gas was still not flowing through the pipeline, TASS reported on November 20. On November 21, the news agency reported that Armenia had broken off talks with Azerbaijan on resolving the Nagorno-Karabakh dispute. The statement issued by the Armenian delegation said that talks would not resume until Azerbaijan had restored gas supplies to Armenia.

Armenian-Azerbaijani Dispute over Gas Supplies

―――――――――――――――――――――――*Wednesday, November 20*

Soviet President Mikhail Gorbachev addressed the USSR Supreme Soviet and appealed to the leaders of the twelve remaining Soviet republics to sign the new Union treaty, TASS reported. He said that the Soviet Union would face economic and political catastrophe if the Union was not renewed. He cited the growing budget deficit as the main reason for the USSR's economic decline, giving a figure of 300,000 million rubles for the combined Union and republican deficit for 1991. Gorbachev also said that representatives of the Union republics had agreed at a recent meeting of the State Council that the USSR presi-

Gorbachev Appeals to Republics to Sign Union Treaty

dent should be chosen by popular election "because all the presidents of the republics are elected by the citizens." Gorbachev noted that, if the president was chosen by the parliamentary assembly, he "would be more likely to be a puppet in its hands."

Army to Defend Its Property

In the face of mounting pressure from republican governments to dismember the armed forces, a USSR Defense Ministry spokesman was quoted in *The Washington Post* as saying that such efforts "cannot be tolerated any longer" and that "the armed forces have every [legal] right to defend themselves and their property." His remarks followed the issuing of a joint statement by the Defense and Internal Affairs Ministries on November 19 that denounced attempts to divide up army property and said that the armed forces were empowered to take all necessary steps, including force, to protect army property.

Members of USSR Defense Council Named

The members of the USSR Defense Council were named. They were: USSR President Mikhail Gorbachev; RSFSR President Boris El'tsin; the director of the Interrepublican Security Service, Vadim Bakatin; the chief of the General Staff, Vladimir Lobov; the USSR minister of external relations, Eduard Shevardnadze; and the USSR minister of defense, Evgenii Shaposhnikov, according to *Vedomosti Verkhovnogo Soveta* (No. 41). The council was chaired by Gorbachev.

MVD Personnel Cuts

Trud reported that USSR Minister of Internal Affairs Viktor Barannikov planned to cut his ministry's staff by 21 percent, beginning with the dismissal of 600 people in December. Barannikov said that seventy-eight departments would be eliminated despite the country's soaring crime rate. The reductions were a result of the RSFSR's decision to cut funding of central government ministries.

El'tsin Says He Will Resign in Event Reforms Fail

RSFSR President Boris El'tsin said in an interview on Central Television that both he and his new government team would resign if their reforms failed. In the same interview, he stressed the need to strengthen individual farms and said kolkhozes would no longer be subsidized. He added that harsh measures would be taken against criminals and corrupt elements. On the subject of the new Union treaty, El'tsin said that he expected no more than eight republics to sign it.

The USSR in November, 1991

Rationing in St. Petersburg

St. Petersburg Mayor Anatolii Sobchak told Interfax that rationing of all food in state stores would begin on December 15. He said that a coupon system would be introduced and that St. Petersburg residents would be able to use these coupons to purchase food only in certain shops near their homes. Sobchak noted that the city was receiving only 50 percent of its food requirements.

On November 23, Sobchak said the Baltic States and Ukraine had virtually halted food shipments to the city. According to the Japanese news agency Kyodo, Sobchak told a delegation of Japanese businessmen that St. Petersburg had only enough food stocks left for a few days.

Sabotage Suspected in Helicopter Crash in Nagorno-Karabakh

Azerbaijani officials claimed that the helicopter crash in Martuni Raion in Nagorno-Karabakh in which at least twenty-one people, including the Azerbaijani prosecutor and a deputy chairman of the Council of Ministers, were killed was caused either by a bomb or a missile attack. Initial TASS reports stated that the helicopter, carrying officials to a new round of talks on the Armenian-Azerbaijani dispute, had crashed in heavy fog. Later reports implied sabotage. Azerbaijani President Ayaz Mutalibov decreed three days of mourning and called for an emergency session of parliament to debate the matter.

Hundreds of thousands of people attended the funerals in Baku on November 22 of those killed in the crash. Mutalibov declared that "things have gone too far" and that "aggression against Azerbaijan will be stopped." The Armenian government called for an international investigation into the cause of the crash. According to the preliminary findings of the Azerbaijani Prosecutor's Office, the helicopter was shot down; other Soviet officials said on November 23, however, that the cause of the crash had not been established. They also said that the confiscation of material from the crash site by the Azerbaijani Prosecutor's Office was hindering the investigation and that the crash could have been caused by overloading.

International Economics Forum in Tallinn

Estonian government officials opened an international conference on Baltic economic development, "Mare Balticum '91," the Baltic News Service reported. Some 400 participants from the Baltic States and the USSR, along with 150 Westerners, gathered in Tallinn to discuss transportation development, investment and privatization, the establishment of a Baltic market, and other issues related to economic development. The same day, Estonian, Latvian, and Lithuanian representatives to the conference formed the Baltic Commercial Council. The director of Estonia's International Commercial Fund, Hillar Kala, told the Baltic News Service that the council would seek to increase cooperation between and unification of Baltic industries and to coordinate laws governing stock and commodity exchanges in the three states.

Thursday, November 21

El'tsin in Germany

RSFSR President Boris El'tsin met with German Chancellor Helmut Kohl on the first day of his three-day visit to Germany, TASS reported. Following their meeting, El'tsin and Kohl signed a statement pledging cooperation between the RSFSR and Germany, TASS reported. RSFSR Foreign Minister Andrei Kozyrev and his German counterpart Hans-Dietrich Genscher also signed a separate agreement calling for consultations between the two foreign ministries.

During his visit, El'tsin also met with the leaders of major political parties, President Richard von Weizsäcker, and leading businessmen. On the third day, he visited the Daimler Benz enterprises in Stuttgart and inspected the Western Group of Forces. El'tsin was accompanied by all the top Russian government officials, including Gennadii Burbulis, Egor Gaidar, Andrei Kozyrev, Pavel Grachev, and Yurii Petrov.

On November 22, El'tsin appealed to German businessmen and industrialists to involve themselves in the Russian economy, Western agencies reported. El'tsin said that tax and other incentives now existed for foreign investments, particularly in the areas of food and consumer-goods production, and that the time was right for a comprehensive accord on economic cooperation between Russia and Germany. El'tsin also suggested the formation of Russian-German joint ventures on former Soviet military bases in eastern Germany.

Gorbachev Visits Irkutsk

Soviet President Mikhail Gorbachev traveled to Siberia for informal meetings to promote economic reform and the new Union treaty, TASS and Western agencies reported. In Irkutsk, Gorbachev visited a military aircraft factory subject to conversion, a school, a children's hospital, and privately run food stores. He said that his primary task would be "to win the confidence of the people." In a speech broadcast by Central Television and in interviews with reporters, Gorbachev stressed the need to renew the Union. Gorbachev also warned that a situation not unlike that in Yugoslavia might arise if the republics did not stay together and that economic reform would be impossible without a political union (*Interfax*, November 21).

El'tsin Turns to Outside Advisers

Radio Moscow reported that El'tsin had invited leading economic specialists from Eastern Europe to a conference in Moscow in November. El'tsin also invited the head of the Swedish Institute for the Economy of Eastern Europe, Anders Aslund, to become his economic adviser. Aslund said that he had agreed to take the post but that his appointment had not yet been approved by the Russian government.

Murashov Wants Russian FBI

Moscow police chief Arkadii Murashov said that Russian KGB and MVD forces responsible for the fight against crime in the republic should eventually be merged into a single republican organization similar to the FBI in the United States, TASS reported. Since being put in charge of the Moscow police, Murashov had sought to make the city's police conform to Western standards and had urged police officers to study the English language. Murashov said that at present the expenses for the Moscow police force amounted to only 1 percent of the city's budget. Murashov expressed the hope that, after the recent wage increases, police service would become more prestigious.

Ukraine Wants Separate Ratification of CFE

German officials said in Bonn that Ukraine was refusing to join in the Soviet ratification of the Conventional Forces in Europe agreement but was considering a ratification act of its own, RFE/RL was told. The officials were reporting on a trip made to Kiev the previous week by disarmament experts of the German and French Foreign Ministries. Ukrainian authorities promised to abide by the USSR's arms control commitments, but they ruled out direct participation in a ratification vote by the USSR Supreme Soviet's Council of Republics, saying that such an act would conflict with Ukraine's goal of dissociating itself from the USSR.

Belorussia Sets Up Checkpoints on Baltic Borders

The Baltic News Service reported that the Belorussian government had ordered the republic's border authorities to establish temporary checkpoints with Latvia and Lithuania. The checkpoints, scheduled to be in place by December 1, were intended to stem the flow of goods out of Belorussia.

Moldavian Popular Front against Adherence to Soviet Debt Agreement

In a statement released through Moldovapres, the Moldavian Popular Front's parliamentary group contended that the Moldavian government's adherence to the Moscow memorandum on the sharing of USSR external debt obligations among republics was "reattaching our republic's economy to that of the empire for purposes of debt repayment." The deputies declared that there was no moral or legal justification for "forcing occupied peoples striving for independence to pay the debts of their conquerors."

Moldavia Declares Decisions of "Gagauz SSR" Unlawful

The presidium of the Moldavian parliament resolved to declare unlawful the decisions of the self-styled "Gagauz SSR" Supreme Soviet to hold presidential elections and a referendum on secession from Moldavia on December 1. Rejecting "any attempt to dismember the republic," the Moldavian Presidium termed the Gagauz decisions "immature games, lacking any legal basis and indulged in by politically shortsighted leaders," Moldovapres reported.

Latvia Creates Ministry of State and Defense Ministry

Diena reported that the reorganization of the Latvian government, in which two new ministries were created but six others abolished or combined, had been completed. Among other duties, the new Ministry of State, headed by Janis Dinevics, would be in charge of popularizing the work of the Latvian government and prime minister "among the masses." The new Ministry of Defense, headed by Talavs Jundzis, would run a self-defense force 8,000 to 9,000 strong drawn from volunteers and conscripts. Both of Latvia's new ministers were members of the Supreme Council.

Latvia to Free Prices

Latvian President Anatolijs Gorbunovs said that prices would be freed in the republic by December, Western agencies reported. Gorbunovs said that price reform was the only way to carry out the transition to a market economy.

Uzbek-Estonian Agreement

Uzbekistan agreed to sell Estonia 23–25 tons of cotton in 1992, the Baltic News Service reported. The agreement was the first step towards the conclusion of a general trade agreement between the two republics.

Lithuanian-Armenian Ties

TASS reported that Armenia and Lithuania had decided to establish diplomatic relations. The

Friday, November 22

RSFSR Parliament Takes Over Banks

The RSFSR Supreme Soviet voted to assume control of the USSR State Bank and the Bank for Foreign Economic Affairs with effect from January 1, 1992, TASS and Western agencies reported. The resolution stipulated that the Central Bank of Russia was the only body on Russian territory responsible for monetary, credit, and currency policy and would take over the issuing of currency until the creation of an interrepublican banking union. The RSFSR Supreme Soviet resolution was passed after deputies had rejected an earlier decree of RSFSR President Boris El'tsin's that placed the banking system under the control of the RSFSR president.

Abolition of Soviet Ministries to Begin on December 1

USSR Prime Minister Ivan Silaev announced that he would start disbanding USSR ministries on December 1, TASS reported. He indicated that a total of eighty ministries and departments would be abolished between December 1 and the end of January, 1992 but that the cuts would not affect the Ministries of External Relations, Defense, and Internal Affairs. The Ministries of Culture, Railways, and Atomic Energy and Industry would also be retained, along with the USSR Customs Service, the State Committee for Public Education, and the Committee for Ecology.

Few Take Advantage of Amnesty

USSR Defense Ministry spokesman Valerii Manilov told reporters that only a few draft dodgers and deserters had taken advantage of an official amnesty, TASS reported. Manilov said that only 200 of an estimated 6,000 deserters had so far presented themselves at local enlistment offices. The amnesty was due to expire on December 4.

Georgia and Iran to Open Consulates

TASS reported that Georgia and Iran had agreed to open consulates in Teheran and Tbilisi. The date for the opening of the consulates was not specified.

Latvian-Belorussian Economic Accord

Latvian and Belorussian officials signed a trade agreement under the terms of which Belorussia would supply Latvia with gasoline, fuel oil, and petroleum products, together with tires and other manufactured goods

(Baltic News Service, November 22). Deliveries to Latvia would start once Belorussia and Russia had coordinated their policies.

Saturday, November 23

Extraordinary Congress of Komi People

An extraordinary congress of the Komi people proclaimed itself and subsequent congresses to be the highest representative organ of the indigenous people and declared that the decisions of its executive must be taken into account by the parliament and administration of the Komi SSR, TASS reported. The congress outlined measures to consolidate the state sovereignty of the Komi SSR, including the conclusion of a bilateral treaty with the RSFSR, the dispatch of representatives to states and areas inhabited by Finno-Ugrian peoples, and the adoption of laws on citizenship, migration, and language.

Azerbaijan Tries to Abolish Autonomous Status of Nagorno-Karabakh

Negotiations between Armenia and Azerbaijan over the disputed territory of Nagorno-Karabakh were suspended after talks aimed at persuading Azerbaijan to restore gas supplies to Armenia broke down and several Azerbaijani and RSFSR officials were killed in a mysterious helicopter crash. USSR Minister of External Relations Eduard Shevardnadze called on both sides to show restraint, TASS reported. Demonstrations in Baku on November 24 called for reprisals against Armenia and for the resignation of Azerbaijani President Ayaz Mutalibov.

Meeting in special session on November 26, the Azerbaijani Supreme Soviet voted unanimously to abolish the autonomous status of the Nagorno-Karabakh Autonomous Oblast in response to popular demand for retaliation against Armenia, Western agencies reported. The name of Stepanakert (the capital of Nagorno-Karabakh) was changed to Khankendi. USSR people's deputy Galina Starovoitova called for the deployment of UN peacekeeping troops to prevent the outbreak of a full-scale war in the Transcaucasus (*The New York Times*, November 26).

The same day, the leaders of Armenia and Azerbaijan, Levon Ter-Petrossyan and Ayaz Mutalibov, flew to Moscow for talks with Soviet President Mikhail Gorbachev and other republican leaders aimed at preventing an escalation of the situation, Western agencies reported. The two leaders were summoned to Moscow by the USSR State Council after it had rejected Gorbachev's call for Soviet troops to patrol a ten-kilometer buffer zone along the Armenian-Azerbaijani border.

The USSR in November, 1991

At a session of the State Council on November 27, a resolution calling on Azerbaijan to restore the autonomous status of Nagorno-Karabakh was passed, TASS reported. The resolution also called for the abrogation of all legislation changing the oblast's juridical status, for a cease-fire, and for the withdrawal of all illegal armed formations from the conflict zone. The same day, deputies from Nagorno-Karabakh resolved to hold a referendum on the oblast's future in December, Russian Television announced.

On November 28, the Armenian Foreign Ministry asked Azerbaijan to seek ways of beginning a political dialogue between the two republics. Ter-Petrossyan stated that a new round of talks on Nagorno-Karabakh would begin the following week (*TASS*, November 28).

Gorbachev Visits Kirgizia

During his stay in the Kirgiz capital, Bishkek, Gorbachev visited a number of institutions and addressed a public meeting. In his remarks, he reiterated the need to continue *perestroika* and to preserve the Union. Interviewed by Central Television before his departure for Bishkek, Gorbachev said he liked the way Kirgiz President Askar Akaev had brought people together and removed the tension that threatened to split the republican Supreme Soviet and society. He said that the Kirgiz leadership was taking a positive attitude towards the presence of the 1 million Russians and more than 1 million representatives of other nationalities in the republic.

Kravchuk Again Says No to New Union Treaty

Ukrainian Supreme Soviet Chairman Leonid Kravchuk reiterated that Ukraine did not intend to join the new Union. "I will not take part in the Novo-Ogarevo process—that is, talks on signing a new Union treaty," he declared. According to Interfax, Kravchuk stressed that, "All allegations that I intend to join the treaty later are nothing but fiction."

Ukraine Criticizes Economic Agreements

Ukrainian Prime Minister Vitol'd Fokin reiterated that Ukraine was ready to pay its share of the Soviet debt but complained that it was being put under pressure by both Moscow and the Group of Seven to do so. Fokin told a press briefing in Kiev that Ukraine first wanted to know precisely how large the Soviet debt was and to work out ways of dividing both the debt and Soviet assets among the republics.

Ukrainian Supreme Soviet Chairman Leonid Kravchuk declared that the new treaty establishing a Soviet economic community was stillborn. Kravchuk argued that RSFSR President Boris El'tsin had torpedoed the economic accord by enacting a program of sweeping reforms without first consulting other republics as the treaty required (*Los Angeles Times*, November 23).

New Armenian Prime Minister Appointed

The forty-three-year-old economist and former head of an Armenian Communist Party Central Committee department Gagik Arutyunyan was appointed Armenian prime minister (*TASS*, November 23). Arutyunyan had been appointed a deputy chairman of the Armenian Supreme Soviet in August, 1990, and first deputy chairman in October, 1991.

Eighty Percent of Moldavians Said to Oppose Reunification with Romania

A Moldavian delegation, headed by an adviser to President Mircea Snegur and by a former popular front leader, told a press conference in Bucharest that "unification with Romania could end up in an explosion of discontent on the part of hundreds of thousands of people and would be a real disaster for our republic," TASS reported. Eighty percent of the people opposed reunification, mainly on economic grounds, they said.

Sunday, November 24

Tajikistan Holds Presidential Elections

Rakhmon Nabiev, chairman of the Tajik Supreme Soviet and former first secretary of the Tajik Communist Party, was elected president of Tajikistan (*TadzhikTA*, November 25). The republican electoral commission said Nabiev had received 58 percent of the votes cast, while his nearest rival, USSR people's deputy and Chairman of the USSR Cinema Workers' Union Davlat Khudonazarov, received just over 25 percent. Khudonazarov, who had the backing of the democratic and Islamic parties, accused the republican leadership of falsifying the results and claimed that he had video and photographic evidence of irregularities. TASS reports indicated that about 81 percent of the electorate voted. There were seven candidates. The voting was monitored by independent observers from other republics and from abroad.

Another Communist Party Created in RSFSR

Delegates from major cities, including Moscow, St. Petersburg, Ekaterinburg, and Tomsk, held a congress in Ekaterinburg to set up yet another Communist party. TASS said the new group would be called the Communist Workers' Party (CWP). The congress announced that its program was based on Marxist-Leninist principles and was directed at strengthening the power of the working class and its natural allies, the peasantry and the patriotic intelligentsia. The CWP was one of several Communist organizations established in the RSFSR since the attempted coup, and it was the third party in the republic to claim that it was the formal successor to the CPSU. TASS said the Ekaterinburg authorities had warned the organizers of the new party that action would be taken against them if they violated RSFSR President Boris El'tsin's decree of November 6 banning CPSU and Russian Communist Party activities on the territory of the Russian Federation.

Lithuanian Independence Party Chairman Linked to KGB

A meeting of the Lithuanian Independence Party approved the recommendation of its Control and Credentials Commission to discharge the party's chairman, Virgilius Cepaitis, for having cooperated with the KGB (RFE/RL Lithuanian service, November 24). Cepaitis had informed the commission on November 15 that the reports in the Lithuanian press about his working for the KGB under the code name "Juozas" were true but stressed that he had never signed a statement agreeing to be a KGB agent.

First Troops Leave Estonia

A signal battalion attached to the Soviet navy base at Paldiski became the first military unit to leave Estonian territory. Supreme Council State and Border Defense Department consultant Udo Helme told the RFE/RL Estonian service that twelve military vehicles had left Estonia at Narva. Another unit attached to the same base was due to follow later in the week.

Monday, November 25

New Union Treaty in Doubt

Leaders of several of the Soviet republics were expected to put the final touches to and initial the new Union treaty at a meeting of the USSR State Council, but the planned champagne ceremony had to be called off when republican leaders declined at the last minute to initial the Union treaty, Soviet and Western agencies reported. It was agreed that further revisions should be made to the draft, which would then be submitted to the republican parliaments. A dispirited Soviet president, Gorbachev, told a press conference that the republican leaders were under domestic pressure. The draft of the treaty was published in *Izvestia* on November 26.

Only seven republics were represented at the meeting—the RSFSR, Belorussia, Kazakhstan, and the four Central Asian republics. Gorbachev said Azerbaijani President Ayaz Mutalibov was unable to attend, because of the crisis in Transcaucasia.

The strongest objections to the draft came from RSFSR President Boris El'tsin. Soviet officials who were present said he wanted more powers for the RSFSR and fewer for the center (*Los Angeles Times*, November 26). One official, a Gorbachev supporter, said that El'tsin wanted Russia to be the political, economic, and strategic successor to the Soviet Union but that not everyone was prepared to hand over power to El'tsin.

The main bone of contention in the Union treaty discussions was whether the Union should be a confederative state or merely a Union, Soviet and Western agencies reported on November 26 and 27. In *Sovetskaya Rossiya* of November 26, the chairman of the Council of the Union, Konstantin Lubenchenko, said that the president of one republic he did not name had offered a surprise series of amendments. In the *Los Angeles Times* of November 27, RSFSR Deputy Prime Minister Gennadii Burbulis said that El'tsin had objected strongly to the draft when he found new elements in it. Burbulis said El'tsin had worked out his own draft.

German Delegation in Moscow to Discuss Volga Republic

A German government delegation arrived in Moscow to discuss the prospects for re-creating a German autonomous republic, RFE/RL reported. The Germans had been offered two areas. One was an area of relatively uninhabited territory where the Volga German republic existed until 1941; the other was the Kapustin Yar missile testing site on the RSFSR border with Kazakhstan. Heinrich Groth, chairman of the Soviet German Rebirth association, said that the Kapustin Yar site was an ecological disaster area.

Iranian Foreign Minister in Moscow

Iranian Foreign Minister Ali Akbar Velayati arrived in Moscow for a ten-day tour of the Soviet Union. USSR Minister of External Relations Eduard Shevardnadze welcomed Velayati's plans to visit Kazakhstan, Kirgizia, Tajikistan, Uzbekistan, Turkmenistan, and Azerbaijan, saying the development of relations between Iran and the Soviet republics was "a positive factor in Soviet-Iranian relations." Velayati said Iran was interested in opening consulates in some Soviet republics, TASS reported.

The USSR in November, 1991

On November 25, Velayati told the radio Ekho Moskvy that Iran would not recognize Azerbaijan's independence but that it intended to expand its relations with Azerbaijan within the framework of the Soviet Union.

On November 26, the RSFSR and Iran signed a Memorandum of Cooperation covering political, economic, cultural, and scientific cooperation. RSFSR Deputy Prime Minister Egor Gaidar, who signed the memorandum for the RSFSR, said, "We want to preserve ties existing between Iran and the USSR," TASS reported.

Military Reform Bill Again Rejected

The Council of the Union's Committee for Defense Matters again rejected a draft law on the status of servicemen prepared by the USSR Ministry of Defense (*Radio Moscow*, November 26). In a meeting on November 25, the committee decided that the draft law failed to reflect changes that had been taking place in the country since the August coup. The draft law, which proposed that a unified armed force should be retained, was rejected for the first time in the summer. A new working group was formed to resolve problems with the draft.

General Charges That Conservatives Remain

A leader of the movement Soldiers for Democracy told Radio Rossii that the potential existed for a second putsch in the Soviet Union because many of those associated with the first attempted coup had not been removed from positions of power. General Vladimir Dudnik charged that the commission investigating military complicity in the coup, headed by General Konstantin Kobets, had refused to act on evidence gathered by officers throughout the Soviet Union. He also claimed that the much-vaunted "depoliticization" of the armed forces was a charade and that hard-liners remained entrenched throughout the military high command.

Independent Army Newspaper Established

The RSFSR Ministry of Mass Media and Information said an independent all-Russian daily newspaper for servicemen called *Voiskovoi krug* had been registered. It was reportedly the first such publication in both the USSR and the RSFSR that was not subordinated to the military high command (*Moskovskie novosti*, No. 46).

Russian Economic Council Set Up

"Vesti" reported that a new Russian Economic Council had been set up to monitor and forecast economic developments in the RSFSR. In particular, the council would follow and analyze the results of El'tsin's economic reforms in the Russian periphery. The council would not be directly attached to the president's office or the Presidium of the RSFSR Supreme Soviet, as had been proposed by some legislators, but would act independently.

Centrist Bloc Offers Support to El'tsin

The Centrist Bloc of political parties announced that it was ready to fully support the new RSFSR government, "Vesti" reported. The bloc included a number of fringe organizations that enjoyed central government support prior to the abortive coup. Its members, whose main aim was the preservation of the empire at all costs, had been critical of El'tsin. Leaders of the bloc said that a drastic change in the bloc's policies was inevitable after the coup. They added, however, that the bloc still advocated a temporary ban on political parties and the creation in the RSFSR of a committee of national salvation (apparently to be headed by El'tsin).

Unemployment Figures and Projections

Director of the Moscow Labor Exchange Igor' Zaslavsky was quoted in *Pravda* as saying that women now made up 77 percent of the unemployed in Moscow. Most of the women who had lost their jobs were between forty-five and fifty, half of them had higher education, and they included scientists and former Communist Party officials. Zaslavsky said that preparations were under way to prohibit employers from firing women who were the sole breadwinners in their families.

RSFSR Deputy Prime Minister for Social Affairs Aleksandr Shokhin told the *Financial Times* of November 29 that up to 15 million people could become long-term unemployed over the next two to three years. He said that about 30 million could lose their jobs but that half of these should rapidly find new employment. Sixty percent of the unemployed would be in Russia, where much of the obsolete industry was located. Shokhin said Russia was seeking a 12-billion-dollar stabilization fund to help introduce internal convertibility of the ruble as well as further debt relief following the agreement with the G–7 nations.

Central Moscow Market Closed by Strike

The Central Market, the largest of the private markets in Moscow, was closed by a strike (Western agencies, November 27). An indefinite work stoppage was launched by eighty-four market workers to force the departure of the manager, Gazi Luguev. The strikers accused Luguev of trying to force price increases by restricting the number of sellers at the market.

The USSR in November, 1991

Situation in South Ossetia

Residents of South Ossetia appealed to the Soviet leadership to declare a state of emergency throughout the autonomous oblast immediately after the Georgian parliament had voted to lift the state of emergency declared a year earlier in Tskhinvali and in Dzhava Raion. They also called for talks to be opened with the USSR Ministry of Internal Affairs on withdrawing its troops from South Ossetia. A USSR MVD spokesman stated that its troops would remain in South Ossetia because they were the sole force capable of preventing an escalation of violence there.

Radio Moscow reported on November 26 that the South Ossetian Oblast Soviet had ordered the mobilization of all men between the ages of eighteen and sixty after it had heard rumors of an imminent attack on the region by Georgia. Georgian military units equipped with APCs, tanks, rocket launchers, and artillery were reported to be converging on the oblast capital, Tskhinvali. On November 28, the South Ossetian Oblast Soviet declared the disputed region a republic and declared a state of emergency on its territory, Radio Moscow reported.

New Demonstrations in Tbilisi against Gamsakhurdia

Thousands of students demonstrated outside the parliament building in Tbilisi to demand the release of opposition figures arrested by Georgian President Zviad Gamsakhurdia, Western agencies reported. Police monitored the demonstration, which was peaceful. Fifteen opposition groups had reportedly agreed to consolidate their efforts to oust Gamsakhurdia.

Ukrainian Presidium on Armed Forces

The Presidium of the Ukrainian Supreme Soviet issued a statement on the Armed Forces of Ukraine, saying that decisions of the USSR State Council taken earlier in the month on the preservation of unified Soviet Armed Forces and the USSR Defense Ministry's refusal to acknowledge Ukraine's sovereign right to have its own armed force were not in accordance with Ukrainian legislation. The contradiction could have a negative effect on morale and combat-readiness, the statement continued. The Presidium reiterated Ukraine's intention to establish its own armed forces as a defense against "an external military threat" and to protect state borders (*TASS*, November 26).

US Senate Urges Troop Withdrawal from Baltic States

The US Senate approved a resolution urging the USSR to promptly begin withdrawing its military forces from Estonia, Latvia, and Lithuania. The resolution stated that the continued presence of Soviet troops threatened the peace and independence of the Baltic States. Senator Orrin Hatch, the resolution's sponsor, said that Soviet military personnel in the Baltic States "unfortunately . . . seem to be making themselves right at home," RFE/RL reported.

Soviet Armed Forces Try to Sell Port in Estonia

The director of the Estonian State and Border Defense Department, Toomas Puura, said Soviet military commanders stationed on Estonia's largest island, Saaremaa, had informed the local authorities that the port there had been sold. Puura said the local leaders were not told the identity of the new owners.

The Estonian government reacted sharply to the announcement and issued a decree stipulating that the USSR Defense Ministry must consult with the Estonian government before bringing material into or out of Estonia. Although the move was prompted by the reported sale of the Saaremaa port, there had also been several instances of military units' sending their equipment out of Estonia in preparation for withdrawal. Under the terms of an agreement concluded between Estonian leader Edgar Savisaar and USSR Minister of Defense Evgenii Shaposhnikov in September, most material was supposed to remain in Estonia.

Lithuania Signs Trade Agreements with Three Republics

Lithuanian Economics Minister Albertas Simenas returned to Lithuania after signing trade agreements with Tajikistan, Azerbaijan, and Kirgizia, Radio Lithuania reported. The trade would be calculated in rubles, but alternative arrangements were made in case one of the signatories were to introduce its own currency. Lithuania would supply Tajikistan with paper and consumer goods, receiving in return metals, cotton, and agricultural machinery. Azerbaijan would send fruits, tires, and oil and receive electrical equipment, washing machines, fish, and light-industry products. Kirgizia would supply Lithuania with wool and other light-industry products.

Vagnorius in Tokyo

Lithuanian Prime Minister Gediminas Vagnorius arrived in Tokyo to attend a meeting of the financial leaders of the G-7 nations due to discuss problems of financial strategy and their policy towards the USSR, Radio Lithuania reported. Vagnorius also met with various Japanese government and business officials on November 26 and 27, Western agencies reported. Foreign Minister Michio Watanabe evaded Vagnorius' request for an agreement on protecting investments by replying that strengthening mutual understanding between the two nations should come first.

Lithuanian Deputy Prime Minister Zigmas Vaisvila sent a telegram to USSR Defense Minister Evgenii Shaposhnikov noting that he had been informed that the Soviet Armed Forces were planning to redeploy the surface-to-air missile forces defending the Ignalina atomic power plant, Radio Lithuania reported. Citing the importance of ensuring the security of the plant, he requested that such redeployments be made only by special agreement with the Lithuanian government.

USSR to Redeploy Surface-to-Air Missiles at Ignalina

Tuesday, November 26

RSFSR First Deputy Prime Minister Gennadii Burbulis met with RSFSR deputies and urged them not to hinder RSFSR President Boris El'tsin's radical reform program, "Vesti" reported. He appealed to the deputies not to spend their time revising El'tsin's decrees but to concentrate on their own sphere of legislation and adopt laws necessary for a smooth transition to the market system.

The RSFSR Supreme Soviet did not heed Burbulis' advice, however, and reportedly passed a law raising the minimum wage in all sectors of the economy to 342 rubles a month, Radio Moscow reported. The measure, which was to take effect on December 1, would also raise student stipends and establish a minimum pension for the elderly. This minimum wage was substantially higher than the 200 rubles per month included in a decree issued by El'tsin on November 17.

Conflict between RSFSR Government and Parliament

France announced that it was granting the USSR a 365-million-dollar credit for the purchase of French grain. On November 27, USSR Prime Minister Ivan Silaev signed credit guarantees for 630 dollars with the EC and looked forward to a further 1.6 billion dollars in credits for food purchases. The same day, both houses of the US Congress authorized 500 million dollars in aid to the Soviet Union; 400 million of this sum would be used to help dismantle nuclear and chemical weapons, and the remaining 100 million would pay for the transportation of emergency food and other aid from the United States to the Soviet Union. Also on November 27, the European Bank for Reconstruction and Development announced its first loans and technical assistance package for the USSR.

Latest Western Aid Commitments

The USSR in November, 1991

Shevardnadze Meets Japanese Businessmen

"Only economic reforms can alleviate the threat" of another coup, Minister of External Relations Eduard Shevardnadze said during talks with Japanese businessmen. He urged the Japanese to help the Soviet Union convert military industries to civilian use and develop Soviet oilfields and agriculture. Shevardnadze stressed that the biggest task facing the Ministry of External Relations was to "remove all obstacles" to developing relations with foreign countries, but Shevardnadze did not make any specific reference to the return of the disputed Kurile Islands to Japan (Western agencies, November 27).

New Envoy to Ireland

The Irish Foreign Ministry said Nikolai Kozyrev had been appointed Soviet ambassador to Ireland. He replaced German Gventsadze, one of the ambassadors recalled for questionable behavior during the coup attempt.

RSFSR KGB Reorganized

RSFSR President Boris El'tsin issued a decree transforming the Russian KGB into an Agency of Federal Security (*Agentstvo Federal'noi Besopasnosti*). The head of the RSFSR KGB, Viktor Ivanenko, was appointed director of the new agency (*Radio Moscow*, November 27). Ivanenko is a professional KGB officer who made his career in the Tyumen' region. In the 1980s, he worked in the central KGB apparatus; in 1991, he became head of the RSFSR KGB. Vladimir Podelyakin was appointed first deputy director of the Agency of Federal Security.

Union of Communists Holds Press Conference

The Union of Communists, which aimed to serve as an umbrella organization for all Communist and Marxist groups set up in the RSFSR since the attempted coup, held a press conference in Moscow. The union was headed by former CPSU Central Committee member Aleksei Prigarin, who used to be a leader of the Marxist Platform in the CPSU. Prigarin said that the union had been set up on the basis of the platform. TASS quoted Prigarin as saying that the country had embarked on the wrong political course in 1987 and that his organization's main aim was to restore "Soviet power" throughout the Soviet Union.

Rutskoi Pleads for Communists

RSFSR Vice President Aleksandr Rutskoi said some CPSU members were being thrown out of their jobs despite the fact that they had given years of honest work. In an interview with *Sel'skaya zhizn'*, Rutskoi said that the people responsible for firing them were acting under the

The USSR in November, 1991

influence of "the old system," with its lack of respect for human beings. Rutskoi said there could be no democracy without respect for every person's rights.

New Party Established in RSFSR

TASS reported that the Republican Humanitarian Party, headed by Moscow philosopher Yurii Bokan, had been set up in the RSFSR. One of the main aims of the new party was to find a solution to the problems of refugees and army draftees.

Lenin Library Closed

Western agencies reported that the Lenin State Library had been closed indefinitely owing to insufficient funds for mandatory repairs ordered by health inspectors. The library had been scheduled for renovation five years ago, and funds were supposed to come from the USSR Ministry of Culture's budget. *Kommersant* reported that the head of the Moscow city health service had warned the library repeatedly that it risked closure if repairs were not carried out.

Hanukkah to Be Celebrated in RSFSR

TASS quoted RSFSR Minister of Foreign Affairs Andrei Kozyrev as saying the RSFSR government supported the idea of celebrating the Jewish religious holiday Hanukkah on December 1.

MVD Troops Must Be under Ukrainian Command

In an interview with *Krasnaya zvezda*, Volodymyr Kukharets, commander of the newly established National Guard of Ukraine, asserted that all USSR MVD troops stationed in Ukraine must be transferred to republican command. Kukharets said that, during the first stage, the guard would be formed on the basis of operative and special mobilized police units and would have 30,000 members.

Belorussia and the Union Treaty

Meeting in Minsk with European parliamentary deputies, Belorussian Supreme Soviet Chairman Stanislau Shushkevich predicted that his republic would sign the Union treaty at the end of 1991 or early in 1992, BelTA-TASS reported. He said Belorussia could not deal either with the aftermath of Chernobyl' or with the current economic crisis on its own. Shushkevich told the deputies, however, that he took exception to the fact that his West European colleagues tended to deal only with Moscow. In connection with the recent establishment of a republican Ministry of Defense, Shushkevich reassured his guests that nuclear weapons would remain in central hands.

Belorussian Communist Party Resuscitated?

Mikalai Ihnatovich, the prosecutor-general of Belorussia, ruled that the temporary suspension of Belorussian Communist Party activities could not be lifted without a special Supreme Soviet resolution, BelTA-TASS reported. Nonetheless, Ihnatovich gave the go-ahead for a proposed congress of the Initiative Committee for the Renewal of Communist Party Activities, which was set to take place in early December. Ihnatovich said the congress must be considered legal, although participants were not allowed to use the funds or facilities of the suspended Communist Party.

Restrictions on Sales of Food and Consumer Goods in Baku

The Baku City Soviet decided to limit sales of food and consumer goods to holders of a Baku residence permit as of December 1 in order to prevent the export of such goods to other parts of the USSR, TASS reported.

Romanians in Northern Bukovina Form Political Movement

Rompres reported that representatives of the Romanian community in Northern Bukovina had set up a Christian-Democratic Alliance of Romanians in Ukraine. The inaugural conference in Chernovtsy defined the alliance as "a national movement for the protection of the legitimate rights and freedoms of Romanians in Northern Bukovina and other parts of Ukraine" (the other parts being southern Bessarabia and Ticevo Raion in Transcarpathia).

AIDS in the Baltic States

The head of the Lithuanian AIDS Prophylaxis Center, Saulius Cuplinskas, told The Voice of America that there were ten people in Lithuania known to be infected with the AIDS virus, two of whom were suffering from the disease. The Lithuanian Mathematics Institute estimated that about 100 people in Lithuania were carrying the AIDS virus. *Paevaleht* reported on November 27 that seventeen people in Estonia had tested HIV positive by the beginning of November. By the beginning of October, there were also fifteen known HIV carriers in Latvia.

Wednesday November 27

Military-Political Organs Dissolved

Pravda reported that the commission tasked with ending the activities of political organs in the armed forces had completed its work. The newspaper said 1,422 Party committees in the armed forces had been abolished, along with 2,000 CPSU control commissions and 29,328 primary Party organizations. Financial resources formerly devoted to these agencies would be redirected towards easing living conditions for military personnel, TASS said.

New State Secretary for Legal Affairs

The Soviet parliament approved Soviet President Mikhail Gorbachev's nomination of the chairman of the USSR Supreme Court of Arbitration, Veniamin Yakovlev, for the position of state secretary for legal affairs, TASS reported. Yakovlev would become the USSR's leading government authority on the interpretation of legal issues that fell outside the court system.

RSFSR Plans for Privatization

The deputy chairman of the RSFSR Privatization Committee, Oleg Kachanov, said that Russia aimed to sell off 70 percent of state property over the next decade. The immediate priority was to assert the RSFSR government's supervision over the privatization process following the collapse of central government ministries. In the absence of overall direction, local authorities had been conducting privatization on an *ad hoc* basis. This resulted in chaos in Moscow but was relatively successful in St. Petersburg (*Financial Times*, November 27).

MVD Anticorruption Chief Forced to Resign

Literaturnaya gazeta reported that the leadership of the USSR Ministry of Internal Affairs had forced the chief of the Sixth Administration for Combating Corruption and Organized Crime, General Aleksandr Gurov, to leave the agency. Gurov, who was also an RSFSR people's deputy, had introduced to the RSFSR Supreme Soviet a law banning people's deputies from engaging in business activities, but the law was rejected. Efforts to fight corruption had been blocked by the fact that many people in the political establishment were either connected with the criminal world or were being manipulated by it, Gurov told the newspaper. Gurov also said KGB Chairman Vadim Bakatin had offered him the position of deputy chief of the Main Administration for Combating Organized Crime within the newly created Interrepublican Security Service.

RSFSR Law on Mass Media Adopted

The RSFSR Supreme Soviet adopted at its first reading a law on the mass media, (*Radio Rossii*, November 28). The newly created Russian Association of Independent Broadcasting held a press conference on November 28 to criticize the draft law. Journalists strongly protested against a provision of the draft regulating the functioning of the mass media under a state of emergency. In accordance with this provision, members of "the organs of emergency power should be given unlimited access to radio and television."

Founding Congress of RSFSR Independent Miners' Trade Union

The founding congress of the Independent Miners' Trade Union opened on the island of Sakhalin, TASS reported. Delegates representing all coal-mining areas of the RSFSR met to discuss the main directions of their activity. The congress was expected to adopt union rules and elect leading bodies. The defense of workers' interests in connection with the shift to a market economy was one of the key issues on the agenda of the congress.

Russian Doctors Threaten to Strike

Chairman of the Central Committee of the Union of Health Service Workers Mikhail Kuzmenko announced that doctors would go on strike on January 25, 1992, in protest over the worsening situation in health care. The trade unions were demanding an annual allocation to the health-care sector of not less that 10–12 percent of the gross national product and the introduction of legislation "On the Protection of the Health of the Russian Population" by February 1.

Karachai Demand Immediate Restoration of Autonomy

A general meeting of the Karachai asked the RSFSR Supreme Soviet to adopt a decision on the complete rehabilitation of the Karachai, including the restoration of their separate autonomy, by December 1, Radio Moscow reported. The meeting decided that, if its demand were not met, the Extraordinary Congress of People's Deputies of Karachaya would resume work and create republican administrative structures. The Karachai, one of the deported peoples, had been agitating for some time for the separate autonomy they enjoyed before their deportation.

Poland Opens Border with Lithuania

Following talks between the two countries' foreign ministers, the border between Lithuania and Poland was opened, thus providing the first direct land route into the Baltic States from outside the Soviet Union, Western media reported.

Energy Crisis in Lithuania

The decrease in energy supplies from the USSR was reported to have created problems in Lithuania. Gasoline

The USSR in November, 1991

was being sold only on even-numbered days, and the prices for it had been raised, Radio Lithuania reported. Maximum room temperatures were not permitted to exceed 15 degrees centigrade.

Dual Citizenship for Exiled Latvians

Acting on the initiative of the newly formed "Satversme" (Constitution) faction, the Latvian Supreme Council voted to allow those Latvians (and their descendants) who were forced to leave Latvia and settle abroad between June 17, 1940, and August 21, 1991, to hold dual citizenship.

Thursday, November 28

USSR Supreme Soviet Fails to Approve Budget

The Soviet parliament failed to approve additional credits for the central state budget, TASS reported. Deputies in the Council of the Republics approved a credit of 90 billion rubles to be granted by the USSR State Bank to the USSR Ministry of Finance to cover the fourth-quarter deficit, but the move failed to be approved by the Council of the Union for lack of a quorum. USSR State Bank Chairman Viktor Gerashchenko said the USSR Ministry of Finance had 3 billion rubles left in its account, enough for only two or three days' budget expenditure.

USSR Bank for Foreign Trade Runs Out of Hard Currency

An aide to the chairman of the USSR Bank for Foreign Trade told Western and Soviet agencies that the bank had run out of hard currency and could not issue any more cash until December 3 at the earliest. This was subsequently qualified by the bank's press spokesman, who said that the failure to give foreigners cash was due to a misunderstanding by managers. Because of a liquidity crunch, he explained, they had been told to stop paying hard currency to Soviet state organizations and to Soviet citizens traveling abroad for private reasons

Law on Russian Citizenship Adopted

The RSFSR Supreme Soviet passed the long-expected Law on Russian Citizenship, which declared all people living in the RSFSR its citizens and superseded existing Soviet laws on citizenship. According to a report by Radio Rossii, the law also stipulated that Russian citizenship be granted to the 26 million ethnic Russians living outside the borders of the RSFSR and to the 20 million Russians who had left the USSR since the October Revolution. The law automatically granted RSFSR citizenship to the 400,000 recent émigrés who had been deprived of Soviet citizenship since 1967. The law also recognized dual citizenship.

Reform of Soviet Ground Forces

Krasnaya zvezda carried an interview with Lieutenant General Yurii Bukreev, identified as the new chief of staff of the Ground Forces, or "the Ground Defense Troops" as he preferred to call them. Bukreev said that there would be considerable cuts in these troops, since an attack on the Soviet Union from several directions at once was "unlikely." They would also change over to a corps and brigade structure from the existing division/army model.

RSFSR Approves Price Liberalization Law

A cabinet meeting presided over by RSFSR President Boris El'tsin adopted a draft law on price liberalization, TASS reported. After the meeting, RSFSR Deputy Prime Minister Egor Gaidar gave journalists a list of prices that would continue to be controlled. This included various types of bread, milk, cottage cheese, kefir, salt, sugar, cooking oil, vodka, liquors, matches, medicine, heating oil, gasoline, rents, communal services, and transportation.

Files on Deportees Opened

More than 600 files from the NKVD-MVD archives concerning the deportation under Stalin of people from the Crimea, the Northern Caucasus, Transcaucasia, and other parts of the USSR were reported to have been opened up. TASS announced that, according to one of the documents now available to scholars, 3.5 million people were deported from their homelands in the period between 1936 and 1956.

Mixed Reaction in Moscow to US Stance on Ukrainian Independence

A statement issued by Soviet President Mikhail Gorbachev's press office indicated surprise and irritation at the reported new readiness of the Bush administration to move towards recognizing Ukrainian independence. Some officials of the RSFSR parliament and government, however, welcomed the apparent shift in US policy. The chairman of a subcommittee on international affairs in the Russian parliament, Evgenii Kozhokin, commented that it represented "a natural process of reorientation" towards the "more important" republics and their leaders, (*Los Angeles Times*, November 29).

France Returns Gold to Latvia and Lithuania

Western agencies reported that France had returned to Latvia and Lithuania the gold those countries deposited with the Banque de France in the years 1932–36, before

The USSR in November, 1991

the Baltic States were annexed by the USSR. France returned 2.2 tons of gold to Lithuania and 1 ton to Latvia.

Friday, November 29

The USSR State Council was reported to have created a consultative body called the Defense Ministers' Council tasked with conducting a unified military policy and making decisions on defense matters, Chief of the General Staff Vladimir Lobov told Radio Moscow. Members would include defense representatives from the republics. In separate remarks reported by TASS, Lobov reiterated his call for unified armed forces that would permit the republics considerable input in military decision making and administration but would continue to subordinate strategic forces and general military forces to the center. He again urged that republican-controlled armed units be limited to national guard forces.

Defense Ministers' Council Created

Defense Ministry spokesman Valerii Manilov told Soviet television that tentative agreement had been reached to lower military spending for 1992 by about 3 percent. He said that spending on weapons procurement would be cut by around 30 percent and that these savings would be used to improve social conditions for soldiers.

Manilov on Military Budget for 1992

Aleksandr Vladislavlev was appointed first deputy minister of external relations. The ministry's spokesman, Vitalii Churkin, said one of Vladislavlev's priorities would be to eliminate "any obstacles to the development of market relations" and to create "maximum incentives for foreign investment."

New First Deputy Foreign Minister

The Georgian Supreme Soviet session that began on November 29 broke up amid scuffles between supporters of President Zviad Gamsakhurdia and the parliamentary opposition (*Radio Mayak*, November 30). The parliamentary chairman, Akaki Asatiani, reportedly asked to be relieved from his post owing to severe illness, and his deputy refused to chair the session, which was scheduled to resume on December 3.

Georgian Parliamentary Session Suspended

Nasirdin Isanov, prime minister of Kirgizia since January, was killed in an automobile crash, Soviet and Western

Kirgiz Prime Minister Killed

agencies reported. He had been traveling with an American businessman to the site of a gold mine. Isanov was one of the closest associates of Kirgiz President Askar Akaev in the latter's efforts to introduce economic reform in the republic.

Saturday, November 30

Russia Assumes Responsibility for Union Budget

After meeting with Soviet President Mikhail Gorbachev and Chairman of the USSR State Bank Viktor Gerashchenko, RSFSR President Boris El'tsin announced that Russia would assume responsibility for the Union budget through the end of the year, Central Television and Western agencies reported. El'tsin said that central government expenditure would be substantially reduced but that salaries would not be cut in military, scientific, cultural, or budget organizations. The move broke the deadlock over funding the Union budget for the last quarter of 1991 that arose when USSR deputies refused to approve additional credits of around 90 billion rubles.

Collective Security Treaty Drafted

The USSR Supreme Soviet was reported to have drawn up a draft treaty that would create a single security area for member-states of a new Union, establish a unified strategic force, and create nuclear-free republican armies. As reported by Radio Moscow, the draft also called for the elimination of tactical nuclear weapons and joint, proportional financing of the united forces by member-states.

Stolyarov to Head Defense Personnel Committee

The Defense Ministry Collegium met and named Major General (of Aviation) Nikolai Stolyarov chairman of the newly created Committee for Work with Military Personnel, (*TASS*, December 2). The committee was to take over many of the duties of the former Main Political Administration, and the Defense Ministry commission charged with dissolving that body reportedly agreed to Stolyarov's appointment. Stolyarov was a former political officer and an ex-member of the CPSU Central Committee. He supported RSFSR President Boris El'tsin during the attempted August coup and in its wake was appointed a deputy chairman of the USSR KGB.

Ukraine Affirms Wish for Own Armed Forces and Nonnuclear Status

Ukrainian Defense Minister Konstantin Morozov told a press conference that Ukraine's plan to establish its own armed forces would include a navy drawn partly from the

Black Sea Fleet, AFP reported. He also disclosed that defense officials from eleven of the twelve Soviet republics had met in Moscow on November 28 and 29 and had agreed on the right of the republics to set up their own armed forces independent of the USSR Armed Forces. Morozov acknowledged that talks with Moscow on the matter were crucial.

Disagreement over Planned Price Liberalization

RSFSR Vice President Aleksandr Rutskoi threatened to resign if Russia freed prices immediately, according to the Russian Information Agency. Rutskoi, who was on a tour of Siberian cities, said that the forthcoming liberalization of retail prices would inevitably lead to the impoverishment of the majority of the population and to "unpredictable social consequences." He argued that prices could not be freed before October, 1992, after foreign-trade liberalization and land and financial reforms had taken place, TASS reported. Rutskoi later withdrew his threat to resign (*TASS*, December 2).

Ingush Referendum

A referendum was held on the future of Ingushetia. Voters were asked whether they wanted to form an Ingush republic in the RSFSR with the right-bank portion of the North Ossetian capital, Vladikavkaz; as its capital and with land that had been taken from them illegally by Stalin returned, TASS reported. The organizers of the referendum maintained that RSFSR President Boris El'tsin had promised that this land would be returned to the Ingush if they voted to remain in the RSFSR. The referendum was opposed by the "Justice" party, by some of the Muslim clergy, and also by Chechen President Dzhakhar Dudaev.

Preliminary results of the referendum showed that 97.4 percent of those who voted were in favor of forming an Ingush republic in the RSFSR (*TASS*, December 2). According to the referendum commission, more than 70 percent of the adult Ingush population, voted.

Latvian Democratic Labor Party Holds Congress

At its third congress in Limbazi, the Latvian Democratic Labor Party elected deputy Juris Bojars as its leader; Bojars replaced Imants Kezbers, once the ideological secretary of the Latvian Communist Party. Most members of the Democratic Labor Party of Latvia were former liberal Communists who broke with the Latvian Communist Party in 1990 to form their own party. The congress discussed an economic program for Latvia and the party's strategy for the next parliamentary elections, Radio Riga reported.

The Month of December

Sunday, December 1

Ukraine Votes in Favor of Independence; Kravchuk Elected President

The official results of the referendum in Ukraine showed that just over 90 percent of voters had approved the Ukrainian independence declaration of August 24, Radio Kiev reported on December 2. Early reports indicated that in Kiev nearly 93 percent voted in favor of independence, while in Donetsk Oblast, Odessa, and the Crimea the figures were, respectively, 70, 75, and 54 percent in favor. In Lvov, in Western Ukraine, 80 percent of those who went to the polls voted for independence. In the presidential elections held at the same time, Chairman of the Ukrainian Supreme Soviet Leonid Kravchuk won 61.59 percent of the vote. Runner-up was Vyacheslav Chornovil, chairman of the Lvov Oblast Soviet, with 23.27 percent of the vote. He was followed by Vladimir Grinev (14.7 percent), Levko Lukyanenko (4.49 percent), Ihor Yukhnovskyi (1.74 percent), and Leopold Taburyanskyi (0.57 percent).

Reaction in the Soviet Union to the prospect of an independent Ukraine was mixed. RSFSR President Boris El'tsin said on Central Television the night before the vote he could not imagine a Union without Ukraine. The Russian leader also asserted that if Ukraine failed to sign a political treaty—i.e., a Union treaty—Russia would not sign either. Following the vote, El'tsin issued a statement recognizing the independence of Ukraine "in accordance with the democratic expression of the will of its people."

Soviet President Mikhail Gorbachev said even if Ukraine voted for independence this did not mean it would secede from the Soviet Union, Western news agencies reported. The remark was made during a telephone conversation with US President George Bush the day before the vote. In an interview carried by TASS, Gorbachev urged Ukraine to remain in the Union, implying that territorial claims would be raised if Ukraine seceded. Gorbachev's remarks elicited a strong response from Kravchuk, who said that such statements were "ill-considered" and constituted interference in Ukraine's referendum.

On December 4, however, Gorbachev sent a congratulatory telegram to Kravchuk, TASS reported. The message expressed Gorbachev's desire for close cooperation and mutual understanding in the common effort to implement democratic changes and "the formation of a union of sovereign states."

St. Petersburg Mayor Anatolii Sobchak told *Le Figaro* on December 4 that the RSFSR's reaction to Ukrainian independence was less important than the reaction of the Russian population of Ukraine. Sobchak decried what he called "the threat of forced Ukrainianization" in the Crimea, where there is a Russian majority, although upon further questioning he conceded that Kiev was permitting the use of the Russian language there. He warned that Russia would "immediately raise territorial claims" if Ukraine refused to join in a political union with Moscow. Sobchak stressed that the prospect of a conflict between the two republics was particularly threatening given the nuclear arms on their territories.

President of the Lithuanian Supreme Council Vytautas Landsbergis sent a telegram to Kravchuk congratulating him on his election as president of Ukraine and expressing hope for good relations, Radio Lithuania reported. He invited Kravchuk to visit Lithuania.

On December 4, the Lithuanian Supreme Council unanimously approved a statement recognizing Ukraine's independence. The Latvian Supreme Council voted to recognize Ukraine and authorized the government to seek to establish diplomatic relations, Radio Riga reported.

Western reaction to the Ukrainian vote was positive. The US ambassador to Moscow, Robert Strauss, told a US television news program on the day of the referendum that the United States would "acknowledge" Ukraine's vote for independence, Western news agencies reported. At the same time, Strauss said there would be no rush to extend formal recognition.

Poland became the first foreign country to recognize Ukraine as an independent state and establish diplomatic relations, Radio Kiev and TASS reported on December 2. The same day, Canada announced that it would recognize Ukraine and begin negotiations on diplomatic relations shortly; Czechoslovakia, too, said it was prepared to extend recognition. Several other West European states commented on the referendum and suggested that they would move towards establishing diplomatic ties (*TASS*, December 3).

Kravchuk was inaugurated as president of Ukraine at a ceremonial session of the Ukrainian Supreme Soviet on December 5 (*Radio Kiev*, December 5). In a speech outlining the domestic and foreign policy of "the new European state," Kravchuk said Ukraine intended to guarantee human rights and integrate its economy with the economies of the other republics, with priority given to private land ownership, conversion of military industries, the introduction of a national currency, and a system of social guarantees. He also stressed equal rights for all national minorities and said he was prepared to cooperate with all countries of the world and maintain friendly relations with all former Soviet republics, especially Russia.

The Ukrainian Supreme Soviet annulled the 1922 treaty that created the USSR and all the constitutional acts of the USSR that followed (*Radio Kiev* and *TASS*, December 5). The Supreme Soviet also chose Ivan Plyushch to replace Kravchuk as chairman of the Ukrainian Supreme Soviet. Plyushch was previously first deputy chairman.

Nazarbaev Confirmed as President of Kazakhstan

Kazakh President Nursultan Nazarbaev was confirmed in office in the first direct presidential election to be held in the republic, Soviet and Western agencies reported. Nazarbaev was first elected republican president by the Kazakh Supreme Soviet in 1990. Preliminary reports indicated that Nazarbaev had received around 90 percent of the vote; he was the only registered candidate. Some 87 percent of the electorate went to the polls.

On December 2, Nazarbaev told a postelection press conference that he interpreted his landslide win as a mandate for "more resolute measures in the economic field." Nazarbaev warned that there would be greater social tension during the transition to a market economy and that all political parties should work together to solve problems. He said that if any parties tried to act outside the framework of the law on public organizations, severe measures would be applied.

CPSU Gave US Communists 2 Million Dollars Annually

According to Aleksandr Drosdov, editor of *Rossiya*, the CPSU gave 2 million dollars annually to the Communist movement in the United States, with an occasional supplement of 1 million dollars. Drosdov, who was working on a book about CPSU allocations abroad, claimed that he had seen records dating back to the 1960s (*The New York Times*, December 1).

Protests in St. Petersburg over Banning of "600 Seconds"

In St. Petersburg 3,000 citizens rallied in support of the local television reporter Aleksandr Nevzorov, whose popular program "600 Seconds" had been taken off the air on the personal orders of the city's mayor, Anatolii Sobchak, Western agencies reported. Radio Moscow cited the chairman of the St. Petersburg Television and Radio Broadcasting Company, Viktor Yugin, as saying the main reason behind the action was Nevzorov's support

The USSR in December, 1991

for the attempted coup. RFE/RL also learned that Nevzorov, along with Colonel Viktor Alksnis, had set up a movement called "Nashi" to try to stop the disintegration of the Soviet Union.

On December 3, the management of St. Petersburg Television lifted the ban on "600 Seconds" in response to popular pressure, TASS reported. The agency revealed that many of Nevzorov's supporters had sent telegrams to RSFSR President El'tsin. One of the telegrams, according to TASS, was signed by Russian nationalist writer Vasilii Belov, who said by banning "600 Seconds" the television authorities had "buried freedom of speech in Russia."

Voting in Dniester and Gagauz "Republics" Marred by Displays of Force

The would-be "Dniester SSR" and "Gagauz SSR" in eastern and southern Moldavia held presidential elections and referendums on joining "the community of sovereign states." A senior official of the Moldavian Ministry of Internal Affairs told RFE/RL that armed Russian "workers' detachments" and uniformed Soviet troops had blocked access to the predominantly Russian towns where the elections were being held and had also been sent into Moldavian villages to intimidate residents into voting. Similar displays of force were reported from Gagauz areas. Officers in command of units blocking bridges over the Dniester told Moldavian officials that the units were subordinated to the "Dniester SSR."

On December 5, "the Dniester SSR Supreme Soviet" decided to replace village soviet chairmen in the region's Moldavian villages and to repeat voting in those villages, TASS and Moldovapres reported. The referendum was boycotted by the Moldavian villages, in which close to 40 percent of the area's population resides. The "Dniester SSR" leaders claimed a big "yes" vote. The Moldavian parliament declared the exercise null and void.

―――――――――――――――――――――――――――――――― *Monday, December 2*

Russia to Assume Responsibility for Budget

RSFSR Deputy Prime Minister Egor Gaidar told the RSFSR Supreme Soviet Presidium that Russia would assume responsibility for much of the Union budget provided that all republics undertook to cut their expenditures by at least 15 percent, Western agencies reported. A draft resolution on a joint Union and RSFSR emergency budget to cover the rest of 1991 was scheduled to be presented to the RSFSR Supreme Soviet on December 5. It stipulated that Russia would cover the expenditures of all the republics for defense, debt servicing, and other necessary items.

In what appeared to be a rejection of the agreement reached between Soviet President Gorbachev and RSFSR President El'tsin, deputies in the lower chamber of the USSR Supreme Soviet on December 3 approved credits from the USSR State Bank worth 90.5 billion rubles to cover the Union budget deficit, Western agencies reported. The assembly called on the USSR State Council to agree on a Union budget for 1992 by December 10.

Ruble Plunges against US Dollar

In the first day of almost unrestricted trading in Moscow, the exchange rate for the ruble plunged to around 80 to the US dollar, Western agencies reported. Exchange rate controls for foreign tourists visiting the USSR and for Soviet citizens traveling abroad had been largely lifted effective December 1. On December 3, the ruble fell even further, Western agencies reported. The USSR Foreign Trade Bank was said to be buying the dollar for 90 rubles and selling it for 99 rubles. On December 4, according to Interfax, the free-market rate of exchange fell to 130 rubles to the dollar.

USSR Releases "Prague Spring" Files

Soviet Ambassador to Czechoslovakia Aleksandr Lebedev was reported to have given the Czechoslovak authorities more than 200 pages of archival material—including previously classified cables that had passed between Moscow and the Soviet embassy in Prague—in an effort to shed light on the Soviet-led invasion of Czechoslovakia in 1968. The Czechoslovak authorities were particularly eager to see a letter allegedly written by Czechoslovak Communist Party officials inviting the Warsaw Pact intervention. According to the Soviet ambassador, "no letter of invitation is among the documents . . . . It is quite possible that it does not exist" (Western agencies, December 2).

No Progress in Talks on Withdrawal of Soviet Troops from Cuba

The first round of Soviet-Cuban talks on the withdrawal of Soviet troops from Cuba ended "with no concrete results," according to Interfax and the *Frankfurter Allgemeine Zeitung*. The newspaper reported that, although the Cuban side had agreed "in principle" to the Soviet withdrawal, it continued to insist on linking it to a US withdrawal from the Guantanamo Bay naval base. The Soviet negotiating team, led by special envoy Vyacheslav Ustinov, rejected such a linkage.

Russian Central Bank Short of Cash

Radio Rossii announced on November 30 that Russian banks would cease all payments in cash, except for salaries, effective December 2, and that salaries would be frozen. Bonuses and thirteenth-month wages would also be frozen. This move was said to stem from an RSFSR government resolution to curb the money supply. RSFSR Deputy Prime Minister Egor Gaidar went on Russian television later that evening to deny the report and assure viewers that "the Russian government guarantees that bank accounts will not be frozen."

On December 2, however, "TV Inform" reported that the Russian Central Bank was either withholding or delaying the payment to institutions and enterprises of funds for the thirteenth-month and long-service bonus payments traditionally due on December 1. Bank sources attributed the move to a shortage of cash but confirmed that money would be available for the payment of salaries, pensions, and stipends.

On December 3, Deputy Chairman of the USSR State Bank Arnol'd Voilukov told Central Television that the payment of traditional December bonuses would be delayed indefinitely.

Union of Cossacks of the Volga and Urals Formed

A constituent congress in Samara set up a Union of Cossacks of the Volga and Urals, Radio Moscow reported. The union embraced Cossack communities along the Volga from Astrakhan to Ioshkar-Ola, the capital of the Mari Republic, and two Cossack hosts, the Ural and the Orenburg. One of the chief aims of the union was to preserve the sovereignty and integrity of Russia in its historical frontiers. Colonel Gusev, a deputy of the Samara Oblast Soviet, was elected ataman.

Turkmen President in Turkey

TASS and Western agencies reported that Turkmen President Saparmurad Niyazov had begun a visit to Turkey. Niyazov was quoted as saying on his arrival that Turkmenistan was counting on "the fraternal assistance of the Turkish people" in instituting a market economy in the republic.

Tuesday, December 3

Ukraine Outlines Security Policies

At a press conference in Kiev, Ukrainian Foreign Minister Anatolii Zlenko outlined his country's military and security policies, Radio Kiev reported. He emphasized that Ukraine would take part in the implementation of all nuclear arms reduction treaties, including the 1991 START agreement, and that its ultimate goal was to be a neutral, nonnuclear state. The foreign minister maintained that Ukraine "does not have and does not wish to have control over the nuclear weapons on its territory," adding that control should be under the joint command of Ukraine, Russia, Kazakhstan, and Belorussia. Some Kiev-based diplomats noted, however, that Zlenko did not say anything about Ukraine's signing the Nuclear Nonproliferation Treaty (*Los Angeles Times*, December 4). Zlenko affirmed that Ukraine would take into account the Conventional Forces in Europe Treaty.

Gorbachev Pleads for Union Treaty

In an appeal to Soviet parliamentarians, which he read on Central Television, Soviet President Gorbachev pleaded with the remaining republics not to leave the USSR. He warned that the disintegration of the USSR would bring the threat of war and be a catastrophe for the world. This was not the first time Gorbachev had addressed the nation on the Union treaty, and his arguments for signing it were all familiar, but there was a greater sense of urgency in his remarks, although he made no direct reference to Ukraine.

In trying to marshal arguments for maintaining the integrity of the USSR, Gorbachev implied again that the Baltic States were discriminating against their minorities. He spoke of Baltic moves to deny state citizenship to residents of other nationalities and said this should serve as a lesson to other republics seeking independence. Noting that letters were pouring in from ethnic Russians in the Baltic States who feared they would be denied citizenship, Gorbachev said these people were calling on Moscow to defend them.

USSR Supreme Soviet Discusses Union Treaty

Both chambers of the USSR Supreme Soviet discussed the latest draft of the Union treaty (see *Izvestia*, November 24). Deputies in the Council of the Union agreed that a political union was vital but noted contradictions in the text, which they said were unacceptable in a document that was to replace the constitution, TASS reported. In the debate in the Council of the Republics, deputies from Kirgizia and the RSFSR said the formulation "confederative democratic state" was nonsense, and Sergei Shakhrai, speaking for the RSFSR delegation, called for a confederation, Radio Mayak reported. The Council of the Republics approved the draft in principle and appealed to the republican parliaments to debate it as soon as possible.

Cuts in Defense Spending

The USSR Defense Ministry claimed that spending on weapons and military technology procurement had been reduced by 23 percent in 1991 and that this rate of reduction would continue in 1992, Radio Moscow reported. The broadcast also quoted Defense Ministry figures claiming that the production of long-range missiles had declined by 40 percent, tank production by 66 percent, and warplane production by 50 percent.

Russian Oil Industry on the Brink of Bankruptcy

The president of Russia's Oil and Gas Corporation, Lev Churilov, told *Pravda* that the Soviet oil industry was on the brink of bankruptcy. He forecast that oil extraction in 1991 would total 500–505 million tons, down from 626 million tons in 1988. Churilov said that the country would hardly be able to satisfy its domestic requirements in 1992 and blamed what he called an unreasonable price policy for the crisis. The producer price for oil, according to Churilov, was only a twelfth of that for mineral water. The RSFSR Economics Ministry fixed "a starting price" of 400 rubles per ton of oil effective in 1992.

Moscow City Soviet Overturns Popov's Privatization Plans

The Presidium of the Moscow City Soviet asked Moscow Mayor Gavriil Popov to stop the planned privatization of trade, services, and restaurants that he had authorized the previous week, Radio Moscow reported. Later the same day, Popov announced that his decision on privatization was not affected by opposition from the city soviet and that the city government had already received applications to privatize about 3,000 Moscow stores (about half of all stores in the city). When asked about rumors of his resignation, Popov responded that, like any political figure, he did not rule out the possibility.

On December 4, the city soviet canceled Popov's order despite his refusal to withdraw the plan, TASS reported. The soviet also overturned Popov's decision to privatize housing and called on him to draft a privatization plan that complied with existing law and took greater account of the population's social problems.

Russia Asks for Environmental Aid

At a European environmental conference in Berlin, RSFSR Environment Minister Viktor Danilov-Danilyants asked the World Bank for money to help repair damage to the environment, Western agencies reported. A World Bank director, Harinder Kohli, said that the RSFSR could obtain such aid once it joined the bank but that it could take several years to be granted membership. He also noted that a 30-million-dollar credit for "technical support" had already been given to the USSR and that this could be used for environmental projects.

Karachai-Cherkess Soviet Wants Restoration of Separate Autonomy for Karachai

A session of the Karachai-Cherkess Soviet set up a commission to present to the RSFSR Supreme Soviet a statement justifying the restoration of Karachai autonomy as a necessary precondition for the complete rehabilitation of the Karachai people, TASS reported. The Karachai had been insisting on the restoration of the separate autonomy they lost as a result of their wholesale deportation. The session also appealed to the RSFSR Supreme Soviet to adopt a law on the complete rehabilitation of the Cossacks.

Armenia Appeals for Dispatch of UN Troops to Nagorno-Karabakh

Speaking in Paris, Armenian Foreign Minister-designate Raffi Hovannisian called for the immediate dispatch to Nagorno-Karabakh of UN peacekeeping troops. Hovannisian urged the world community to pay attention to the situation in Nagorno-Karabakh because "it is quite probable that there will be no Armenian population in Nagorno-Karabakh tomorrow." Hovannisian also stated that Armenia would recognize Ukraine's independence and was preparing to conclude cooperation treaties with Ukraine and Russia.

Romanian Territorial Claim Complicates Relations with Ukraine

On November 29 and December 3, respectively, the Romanian government and the Romanian Foreign Ministry each issued statements on Romanian claims to Ukrainian territory. (These followed a declaration by the Romanian parliament on November 28.) Acknowledging Ukraine's "inalienable right to self-determination," "greeting Ukraine's independence with sympathy," and expressing readiness to establish diplomatic relations with it, the Romanian government urged Ukraine to enter into negotiations with it under the provisions of the Helsinki accords for the peaceful change of borders in order to settle the question of Northern Bukovina, Hertsa District, Hotin County, and Southern Bessarabia. The Foreign Ministry added that "unquestionably, the Republic of Moldavia should participate in those negotiations."

Meanwhile, TASS reported on December 4 that Ukrainian Foreign Minister Anatolii Zlenko, who had been scheduled to arrive on an official visit to Romania on November 29, did reach the Romanian border that day but turned back on learning of the Romanian parliament's declaration raising territorial claims against Ukraine. TASS added that the sides had planned to sign during Zlenko's visit a declaration on the principles of Romanian-Ukrainian relations and had also agreed to establish diplomatic relations and to conclude a treaty of friendship, good-neighborliness, and cooperation.

THE USSR IN DECEMBER, 1991

Georgian President Zviad Gamsakhurdia ruled the previous week's call by the South Ossetian Oblast Soviet for a general mobilization void. Gamsakhurdia further ordered the Georgian prosecutor to take legal measures against those who had created the oblast parliament, Interfax reported.

Gamsakhurdia Declares Call for Mobilization in South Ossetia Void

Iranian Foreign Minister Ali Akbar Velayati and Azerbaijani Prime Minister Gasan Gasanov signed an agreement in Baku on political, economic, scientific, and cultural cooperation, TASS announced. Velayati also told reporters that a large Iranian bank planned to open a branch in Baku soon.

Azerbaijani-Iranian Cooperation Pact

_____*Wednesday, December 4*

The USSR and RSFSR presidents, Mikhail Gorbachev and Boris El'tsin, met behind closed doors to discuss the future of the Union treaty (*TASS*, December 5). Gorbachev told Central Television that, like El'tsin, he could not imagine a Union without Ukraine and that he was confident the majority of Ukrainians shared his view. He asserted that his role was now more important than ever before. Speaking on the same program, El'tsin said he had little hope for a new Union because of Ukraine's negative position. He indicated that he favored a Slavic economic union without the Central Asian republics.

Gorbachev and El'tsin on the Union

The USSR Foreign Trade Bank sent telexes to foreign banks saying that repayments on 3.6 billion dollars of commercial debt principal would be suspended until January, 1993, Western agencies reported. A spokesman said the bank would continue to make interest payments on its commercial debt. A deputy chairman of the bank, Eduard Gostev, was quoted as saying that this move was in line with the agreement on debt relief reached with the G-7 nations in November, although that agreement concerned government debts. This latest suspension appeared to be a unilateral measure made without the prior agreement of creditor banks.

Commercial Debt Repayments Suspended

Citing government sources in Kishinev and reports from eastern Moldavia, Radio Bucharest reported on December 4 and 5 that "a political-military putsch" was under way in the self-proclaimed "Dniester SSR." Lieutenant

Military-Political Putsch in "Dniester SSR"

General Gennadii Yakovlev, identified as commander of the Fourteenth Army stationed there, was reported to have accepted appointment as chief of the Directorate for Defense of the "Dniester SSR," which assumed political authority over the troops. Yakovlev was tasked with turning armaments and other property of the USSR Ministry of Defense in the area over to the "Dniester SSR." A number of USSR military units in the area had recently held assemblies and passed resolutions supporting the "Dniester SSR" and warned that they would resist any orders to withdraw from Moldavia.

Nicolae Chirtoaca, director-general of Moldavia's Department for Military Affairs, was cited by Radio Bucharest on December 5 as saying that the putsch in eastern Moldavia "may degenerate into civil war." Joint groups of armed "Dniester SSR" guardsmen and uniformed Soviet military personnel were reported to have taken over buildings belonging to the Moldavian police and other law-enforcement organs in several towns on the left bank of the Dniester on December 4 and 5 and in other areas of eastern Moldavia on December 6 and 8. Such piecemeal takeovers had been under way since September in the Dniester area, but these were the first with military participation. The armed detachments also continued to enter Moldavian villages to dissuade residents from voting in Moldavia's presidential election on December 8, and they closed down some polling stations. Army helicopters overflew Moldavian villages dropping leaflets urging residents not to vote. The military command in Kishinev was reported to have disclaimed involvement and to have assured the Moldavian government of its continued loyalty to the USSR Ministry of Defense.

On December 6, Moldavian President Mircea Snegur, parliament Chairman Alexandru Mosanu, and Prime Minister Valeriu Muravschi urged the United Nations to send observers to monitor the situation in eastern Moldavia. They said that paramilitary detachments of the would-be "Dniester SSR" and local Soviet army units had "launched overt aggression against Moldavia, occupying raion centers and settlements, and that they were being abetted by the USSR Ministry of Defense and other "central power structures." Snegur also told a news conference on December 6 that he had cabled USSR Defense Minister Evgenii Shaposhnikov and had sought to contact him by telephone in connection with the troop movements in eastern Moldavia but that Shaposhnikov had ignored both the cables and the calls. In spite of this, the Moldavian government received a message from Shaposhnikov demanding from Moldavia an allegedly overdue contribution of 1.2 billion rubles to the USSR military budget,

Snegur's press office informed RFE/RL. Since proclaiming independence in August, Moldavia had ceased contributing to the USSR military and space budgets.

First Deputy Commander of the Odessa Military District Lieutenant General Yurii Kuznetsov told Ukrinform-TASS that Yakovlev's agreement to take on the duties of defense chief of the would-be "Dniester SSR" was his own affair. The Moldavian Ministry of Internal Affairs meanwhile told Moldovapres that units of the Fourteenth Army were to become the regular army of the "Dniester SSR" by January, 1992.

Kuznetsov denied reports of a coup in the Dniester area backed by units of the Soviet Armed Forces. He claimed that paramilitary detachments of the "Dniester SSR" had dressed themselves in Soviet army uniforms they had obtained "we don't know where" and that they had "received their arms from the militia." Kuznetsov claimed that he had rejected Dniester leader Igor' Smirnov's request for military deployment in the Dniester area and dismissed Smirnov's subsequent threat to seize weapons from the armed forces.

The Romanian Foreign Ministry strongly condemned the Soviet army for its alleged arming of Russian separatists in order to disrupt the presidential election in Moldavia, the Romanian media and Western agencies reported. It issued a statement demanding "the immediate withdrawal from the territory of the Republic of Moldavia of armed forces that are jeopardizing its sovereignty."

On December 8, a delegation of the USSR Defense Ministry and the General Staff, headed by First Deputy Chief of the General Staff Colonel General Bronislav Omelichev, arrived in Moldavia at the invitation of the Moldavian government to look into "cases of officers of the Fourteenth Army interfering in Moldavia's internal affairs" (Moldovapres, December 9). Moldavian Prime Minster Valeriu Muravschi presented "incontrovertible evidence of the army's interference." Omelichev replied that the armed men in uniform "are not necessarily regular soldiers." The Defense Ministry also summoned Lieutenant General Yakovlev to Moscow to explain his actions.

On December 9, Moldavian law-enforcement officials and parliamentary deputies told RFE/RL that a detachment of more than 100 "Dniester SSR" armed guards and uniformed soldiers had besieged the police station in Bendery that day and given it an ultimatum to submit to the orders of the "Dniester SSR." The Bendery City Soviet served the ultimatum.

Meanwhile, the Moldavian press published intelligence information attesting that in Rybnitsa nearly 1,500 submachine guns had recently been handed over by the armed forces to the "Dniester SSR" on a single day. Also published was a facsimile of an army receipt recording the handing over by a military unit of twelve machine guns to a representative of a Russian "workers' detachment." A US Congressional observer of the presidential voting in the town of Comrat in southern Moldavia told journalists that the town was being patrolled by well-armed Gagauz militants.

The siege of the Moldavian police station in Bendery took a new turn on the evening of December 9 as Moldavian peasants from neighboring villages came to the aid of the police by forming a human wall around the building. The Moldavian police were under strict orders not to fire.

On December 10, at his first news conference after his election by popular vote, Moldavian President Mircea Snegur commented on "the political-military putsch" in the Dniester area. Snegur said that "if Moscow and the army want to bring us to our knees, I may again call for popular resistance to the putsch, as I did in August." Moldavia defied the attempted coup in August by organizing mass mobilization to stave off the threat of military intervention.

On December 13, paramilitary detachments of the "Dniester SSR" machine-gunned and overran a Moldavian police post on the Dniester bridge at Dubasari. For the first time in the recent series of such attacks, the police returned fire and recaptured the lost position as well as a police station lost earlier. The same day, "Dniester SSR" armed units seized the raion soviet building in Dubasari and the city soviet building in Bendery and renewed the siege of police stations in the two towns. The preceding night, at least four Moldavian policemen were picked off the street in Dubasari and were being held hostage. As in the preceding incidents, uniformed soldiers and officers of locally based army units were seen among the "Dniester SSR" detachments.

The Presidium of the Moldavian parliament issued a statement decrying the attacks on lawful authorities as an attempt by "the most reactionary forces of the agonizing empire to start a civil war in Moldavia." The Presidium appealed to the population for calm and cooperation in containing the conflict and urged that unlawfully held weapons be turned over to the authorities. The Presidium also charged that the clash had been "deliberately provoked" to torpedo the RSFSR's ratification of the Moldavia-RSFSR state treaty and President Snegur's talks with Boris El'tsin, Leonid Kravchuk, and Stanislau Shushkevich scheduled for December 12 through 15. Snegur broke off his official tour of the three Slavic capitals and returned home on December 13. Moldavian Prime Minister Muravschi and several members of the parliament's Presidium rushed to Dubasari to help defuse the conflict there.

In an appeal to the United Nations passed on by Moldavian President Mircea Snegur on December 14, a large group of Moldavian residents from raions on the left bank of the Dniester River decried "anti-Moldavian incitement by local [Russian-language] media" and discriminatory measures against Moldavians there "who form over 40 percent of the population." The appeal pointed to measures undertaken by the "Dniester SSR," including jamming Radio Kishinev broadcasts to the left bank, restricting the use of the Latin script in schools, and replacing "Moldo-Romanian" history with Soviet history on the curriculum of Moldavian schools.

The same day, following a decision to "provide any necessary help" to the "Dniester SSR," the self-styled "Gagauz republic" Supreme Soviet was reported to have "brought the Gagauz defense forces to a state of full readiness" (*TASS*, December 14). Volunteers from St. Petersburg and from the All-Russian Cossack Union arrived on the left bank of the Dniester "to defend the Slavs" there, Moldovapres and Western news agencies reported on December 15. The chief of staff of a Cossack host from southern Russia cabled the Moldavian government threatening to send more volunteers and military equipment to the left bank of the Dniester.

On December 15, members of a Conciliation Commission formed by Snegur the preceding day (comprising officials from Kishinev and the left bank of the Dniester) signed in the village of Dzerzhinskoe a protocol on the disengagement of opposing forces in the Dubasari area. The protocol provided for the forces to be returned to the bases where they were permanently stationed (*Moldovapres*, December 16).

Baltic States Admitted to EBRD

The board of governors of the European Bank for Reconstruction and Development voted unanimously to admit Lithuania, Latvia, and Estonia as members, Western agencies said. The three states had applied for membership in September and would now be allowed access to the bank's capital, which was about 10 billion ecus.

New Leader for Latvian Popular Front Faction

Radio Riga reported that Indulis Berzins had been elected to chair the Latvian Popular Front faction in the Latvian Supreme Council. He replaced Janis Dinevics, who became minister of state in November. Berzins received fifty-five of the seventy-two votes, while his opponent, Peteris Simpsons, received only twelve. Andrejs Pantelejevs was elected first deputy chairman of the faction. Radio Riga said that, although it had become smaller as members formed their own factions and groups, the Latvian Popular Front faction still remained the largest in the legislature.

Thursday, December 5

Coup Rumors Again Sweep Moscow

Dissension within the Soviet Armed Forces caused by abject living conditions, the breakdown of the economy, and political disintegration were once again raising the specter of a military-backed coup in the USSR, according to Western agency reports of December 5 and 6. As stated by *The Times*, NATO officials attending a recent conference in Moscow said that morale among junior and middle-level officers had plunged and that liberal officers were concerned about the failure of the current military leadership to remove hard-liners from top command positions.

On November 30, Major General Leonid Kozhendaev, identified as chief of a section of the General Staff, had warned in *Komsomol'skaya pravda* that the Soviet state had been destroyed and that the country was on the verge of civil war and anarchy. He called for immediate action, saying that the army was capable of helping politicians, but also warned that the army was becoming politicized and was "tired of being humiliated."

According to *The Washington Post* of December 6, suspicions were focusing increasingly on RSFSR Vice President Aleksandr Rutskoi as a potential leader of a hard-line coup. In what the newspaper described as "an extraordinary front-page article" in *Izvestia* on December 5, Rutskoi reportedly dismissed the coup rumors but suggested that "you cannot endlessly play with people who bear arms," because it "may end in disaster."

RSFSR Government and Trade Unions Reach Accord on Miners

Radio Moscow reported that the Russian government and the independent trade unions had signed an agreement on improving working conditions and raising the wages of miners. *Trud* reported that the working week for miners working underground must not exceed thirty hours; for surface workers the limit was forty hours. Overtime would be permitted only in extraordinary cases covered by Russian labor laws, and minimum wages for miners would be almost tripled by the beginning of 1992.

The USSR in December, 1991

Kuzbass Rail Workers Threaten to Strike

Railway workers in the Kuzbass region of Siberia threatened to launch warning strikes beginning on December 15 (RL Russian service, December 5). The workers were demanding higher wages and better living conditions. The chairman of the Kemerovo Oblast Soviet, Aman Tuleev, was reported to have written to RSFSR President El'tsin asking him to intervene and arguing a delay in addressing workers' demands could bring a railway strike affecting coal deliveries to other parts of the country.

Friday, December 6

Interrepublican Economic Committee at Work

In meetings held from December 4 to 6, the Interrepublican Economic Committee, under the chairmanship of Ivan Silaev, reached agreement on several key points (*TASS*, December 7). Among the most important were the establishment of a special committee to oversee the foreign-debt problem and agreements on coordinating price liberalization and economic reform measures.

A statement issued by the economic committee on December 6 said that the extraordinary economic conditions in the country dictated that the Bank for Foreign Trade could only make interest payments on the foreign debt (about 67 billion dollars) at this time. It was agreed that the committee on foreign debt would work with the IMF and other international organizations on questions of monetary and fiscal reform and debt repayment.

Gromov Resurfaces

Vechernyaya Moskva said Colonel General Boris Gromov had been appointed a first deputy commander in chief of Soviet Ground Forces. The last commander of Soviet forces in Afghanistan, Gromov subsequently headed the Kiev Military District and served as a first deputy minister of internal affairs. He was thought by many to have taken part in the August coup, but formal charges against him were never brought, and it was later reported that a slot was being sought for him in the Defense Ministry.

Minimum Wage Raised in RSFSR

The RSFSR Supreme Soviet agreed to raise the minimum wage to 342 rubles per month for workers in organizations financed by the state budget. The increase would take effect on January 1, 1992. Enterprises and organizations not financed by the state budget were instructed to introduce the same minimum wage in the first quarter of 1992. Radio Moscow carried the announcement, but made no mention of increases for pensioners, the unemployed, or the disabled, who were hit particularly hard by the current inflationary environment.

Nabiev Offers to Host Afghan Peace Talks

Newly elected Tajik President Rakhmon Nabiev told a Pakistani delegation that Tajikistan would be willing to host Afghan peace negotiations, Western agencies reported. The Pakistani delegation was touring all the Central Asian republics.

Saturday, December 7

Chief of General Staff Sacked

Only one day after concluding a high-profile visit to Britain, Army General Vladimir Lobov was removed as chief of the General Staff of the Soviet Armed Forces on Soviet President Mikhail Gorbachev's orders. Interfax cited "well-placed sources" as saying Lobov had been replaced "for reasons of health" and because of difficulties encountered in reforming the armed forces. A Defense Ministry spokesman called the firing "unexpected," and Interfax also mentioned unofficial reports that Lobov had resigned over developments in Ukraine and elsewhere that threatened the unity of the armed forces.

The commander of the Leningrad Military District, Colonel General Viktor Samsonov, was named to replace Lobov, Soviet and Western agencies reported. The fifty-year-old commander was best known for his role in the August coup, when, at the behest of Leningrad Mayor Anatolii Sobchak, he refused to send troops into the city.

On December 9, confusion continued to surround Lobov's dismissal. *Izvestia* quoted unnamed "military experts" as saying that Lobov's ideas on military reform were not consistent with those recently agreed upon by the USSR State Council. Lobov had been a strong proponent of a unified military structure.

Two New Military District Commanders Appointed

Decrees signed by Soviet President Mikhail Gorbachev on December 7 appointed two new military district commanders. The first, published in *Krasnaya zvezda* on December 13, named Lieutenant General Sergei Seleznev commander of the Leningrad Military District. Born in 1944, Seleznev had earlier served a short stint as chief of staff of the Leningrad Military District. He succeeded Colonel General Viktor Samsonov, who had been appointed chief of the General Staff. The second decree, published in *Krasnaya zvezda* on December 17, named Lieutenant General Georgii Kondrat'ev commander of the

The USSR in December, 1991

Turkestan Military District. He was born in 1944 and most recently served as first deputy commander of the same military district. Kondrat'ev replaced Colonel General Ivan Fuzhenko, who on December 7 was named chief of Rear Services.

Ligachev Is Back

Former Politburo conservative Egor Ligachev volunteered to be interviewed on the Russian Television program "Sovershenno sekretno" on December 7. Ligachev asserted that a popular movement aimed at reviving communism was gaining ground in the former Soviet Union and added that sooner or later "the Partocracy" would triumph. Asked about the August coup, Ligachev said that he sympathized with the aims of its organizers but disapproved of the anticonstitutional means employed to achieve them.

Silaev Blames Moscow Food Crisis on Russian Regions; Rationing Introduced

USSR Prime Minister Ivan Silaev complained that the food crisis in Moscow was the result of the failure of rural regions of Russia to meet their supply obligations. He told a news conference that the regions were only supplying about half of what they should be and that Moscow would begin bartering with them for increased supplies. Moscow had been authorized to use up to 15 percent of the goods produced in the city for these barter deals. The main reason farmers were not supplying the city was that they could get higher prices in their local markets (*TASS*, December 7).

On December 12, the Moscow City Soviet decided to introduce food rationing, Radio Moscow reported. Plans had been announced in November to ration meat, milk, butter, sausage, and eggs, but these were canceled by Mayor Gavriil Popov.

Elections to Russian Academy of Sciences

The first elections to the Russian Academy of Sciences took place, TASS reported. Thirty-nine newly elected academicians would join members of the USSR Academy of Sciences, which had been transferred to RSFSR jurisdiction earlier in the year. The election of 130 Russian academicians had been planned, but after the vote (conducted by members of the former USSR academy) the majority of positions remained vacant. Former all-Union academicians claimed that most of the candidates lacked proper scientific qualifications. TASS pointed out that many of those elected occupied high positions in the RSFSR state and government hierarchy. Among them was Chairman of the RSFSR Supreme Soviet Ruslan Khasbulatov.

Sunday, December 8

Slavic Leaders Establish Commonwealth of Independent States

At the end of a two-day meeting in a Belorussian village outside Brest, Russian President Boris El'tsin, Belorussian Supreme Soviet Chairman Stanislau Shushkevich, and Ukrainian President Leonid Kravchuk announced that they had agreed to establish a Commonwealth of Independent States comprising the three Slavic republics and open to all republics of the former USSR and other states sharing the Commonwealth's goals and principles. TASS issued a proclamation by the heads of the three Slavic states, a statement of the principles of the Commonwealth agreement, and a declaration on the coordination of economic policy. The three sides, as founding members of the USSR and signatories of the 1922 Union treaty, bore witness to the end of the USSR "as a subject of international law and a geopolitical reality." The new Commonwealth would strive for coordination in the sphere of foreign policy, the development of a common economic space, customs and migration policy, transport and communications, ecology, and crime fighting. The members pledged to take measures to reduce defense spending, eliminate nuclear weapons, and work towards neutrality.

Later the same day, TASS carried the text of the "Declaration by the Governments of Belorussia, the RSFSR, and Ukraine on Coordination of Economic Policy." Highlights were: the maintenance and development of existing close economic ties between the three states; the promised creation of fully fledged market mechanisms; the transformation of property relations; the retention of the ruble as a basis for economic relations, while introducing national currencies with mutual safeguards; the preservation of a unified economic space; and a pledge to agree on defense expenditure for 1992 within ten days.

The agreement stated that Minsk had been chosen as the official point of coordination for the organs of the new Commonwealth and that the activities of organs of the former USSR would become null and void in the states that had signed the Commonwealth agreement.

Moldavian Presidential Elections

Elections were held in Moldavia for the post of president. Of the 2.9 million eligible voters, 550,000 were unable to register for the vote owing to adverse pressures on the left bank of the Dniester and in the Gagauz-inhabited areas. Among the 2.35 million registered voters, the turnout was 83 percent. Incumbent President Mircea Snegur received 98 percent of the votes cast. The voting was monitored by observers from the United States, West and East European countries, the Baltic States, the RSFSR, Ukraine, and Romania.

Snegur told a news conference in Kishinev on December 10 that his overwhelming electoral victory confirmed that "the people's will today is for an independent Moldavia" (*Moldovapres*, December 11). Moldavia would continue to cooperate with Romania economically and culturally "but only under conditions of total independence for the Republic of Moldavia," Snegur said.

North Ossetia Demands Sanctions against Georgia

The North Ossetian parliament sent a telegram to RSFSR President Boris El'tsin and RSFSR Supreme Soviet Chairman Ruslan Khasbulatov calling for the imposition of sanctions against Georgia in an attempt to persuade Georgia to halt its military attacks on the disputed region of South Ossetia, TASS reported.

Energy Crisis in Central Asia

Central Television summarized the effects of the current energy crisis in Central Asia. In Kirgizia, kerosene for heating and cooking was in short supply, and flights had to be rescheduled because of lack of fuel at Bishkek airport. No gasoline or diesel fuel had been shipped to the republic, which was entirely dependent on outside sources for these products, since the beginning of December. In Uzbekistan many homes were receiving electricity for only a few hours a day, and in Tajikistan the supply of electricity to industry was cut by 15 percent, and street lighting was reduced. A TASS report attributed the power shortage in Tajikistan to lack of fuel for Uzbekistan's generating plants, which supplied the neighboring republic during the winter months.

Monday, December 9

Gorbachev's Reaction to the Commonwealth Agreement

Soviet President Mikhail Gorbachev, RSFSR President Boris El'tsin, and Kazakh President Nursultan Nazarbaev met in the Kremlin to discuss the new Commonwealth. El'tsin spoke on behalf of all three Slavic republics. Following the meeting, Gorbachev issued a statement, which was read on Central Television, saying that the agreement reached by the three Slavic republics had some positive aspects—namely, that Ukraine had taken part and that the agreement preserved a joint economic space and provided for cooperation in various spheres. While conceding that republics could secede from the USSR, Gorbachev said the three republics could not determine the fate of the multinational state. He maintained that the document had been signed in haste without a mandate from the population or parliaments of the three republics. He stated that both the draft Union treaty and the Minsk agreement should be debated by the republican and all-Union parliaments and that a session of the USSR Congress of People's Deputies should be called. He also said he would not exclude a referendum.

In a discussion on Radio Rossii the same day, RSFSR State Councilor and legal expert Sergei Shakhrai disputed Gorbachev's argument that the three Slavic republics had acted unconstitutionally in declaring that the Soviet Union had ceased to exist. Shakhrai said that the treaty of 1922 setting up the USSR had been signed by four republics—the three Slavic republics and the Transcaucasian republic, which had ceased to exist—and that in declaring their sovereignty and independence these republics were taking back the powers that they had transferred to the Union in 1922

On December 10, Gorbachev's press spokesman, Andrei Grachev, said that Gorbachev was open to any variant of a Union treaty that was arrived at constitutionally and democratically and that the Soviet president was not at present thinking of resignation, TASS reported. He said that Gorbachev was counting on the support of the public and of existing political and legislative structures and that if a referendum were held, it should take place in all twelve republics.

Gennadii Burbulis told RSFSR and USSR deputies on December 10 that Gorbachev's call for an extraordinary session of the USSR Congress of People's Deputies to discuss the future of the country would only lead to confrontation, TASS reported. At the same time, he said he did not exclude the idea of holding a referendum. At a press conference the same day he said that the Minsk agreement was not aimed at removing Gorbachev from political activity, and he suggested that his experience could be used constructively. Burbulis also pointed out that the text of the agreement did not say that the USSR "has ceased" to exist but "is ceasing to exist."

On December 12, in an interview published in *Nezavisimaya gazeta*, Gorbachev said it was time to say that he personally laid no claim to a role in the future structures of a successor state to the Soviet Union. He said that he just wanted it to be a Union state and that he would respect any decision if it were constitutional. He repeated that the Minsk agreement was unacceptable but that it would be a different matter if it were discussed and synthesized with the draft Union treaty.

The USSR in December, 1991

In a meeting with the press in the Kremlin the same day, Gorbachev seemed ready to bow to the inevitable and repeated his determination to resign if the Soviet state were destroyed, Soviet and Western agencies reported. Gorbachev said that the main work of his life was done and maintained that most other people would have given up long ago. At the same time, he warned that a situation was arising that could lead to dictatorship. He also expressed his resentment that RSFSR President Boris El'tsin had telephoned US President George Bush first about the Commonwealth agreement and only then did Belorussian leader Stanislau Shushkevich inform him.

Reaction of Ukrainian Parliament to Agreement on Commonwealth

At a press conference in Kiev, Ukrainian President Leonid Kravchuk had to justify his signing of the Minsk agreement. Radio Kiev said that day that people seemed to be reacting in one of three ways: some thought Kravchuk might have betrayed the interests of the nascent Ukrainian state; others welcomed the opportunity to create a European-style community of nations; and a third group wanted to know why Kravchuk had not consulted his parliament first. Kravchuk stressed that, with the exception of a few areas where joint action was needed, such as control over strategic weapons, the agreement guaranteed the jurisdiction of independent states.

Central Asian Reaction to Commonwealth

After his meeting with Mikhail Gorbachev and Boris El'tsin, Kazakh President Nursultan Nazarbaev complained to correspondents that an interstate structure based on ethnic affinity was a relic of the Middle Ages ("TV Inform," December 9). Nazarbaev added that an organ of coordination was needed for the republics to weather current difficulties and that such an organ could be headed by Gorbachev. Summaries of the press conference indicated that Nazarbaev was upset at having been excluded from the Minsk agreement and intended to continue supporting Gorbachev.

The presidents of the five Central Asian republics met in Ashkhabad on December 12 to discuss their reaction to the Commonwealth. On December 13, they issued a declaration, carried by TASS, indicating the willingness of their republics to join the Commonwealth of Independent States. They insisted, however, that the Central Asian republics should have equal rights with the three founding states, that the Commonwealth should not be based on ethnic or confessional considerations, and that existing borders should be recognized as inviolable. The Central Asians also called for unified control of nuclear weapons and unified command of strategic forces.

Lithuania and Latvia Welcome Commonwealth

President of the Lithuanian Supreme Council Vytautas Landsbergis told a press conference in Vilnius that he welcomed the creation of the Commonwealth of Independent States, Baltfax reported. He expressed confidence that the Commonwealth would become the successor to the USSR and that "Lithuania will surely benefit from that, especially in settling the problem of the withdrawal of Soviet troops from the Baltic States." Latvian Supreme Council President Anatolijs Gorbunovs, returning from Paris, told the press that Latvia's relations with the Commonwealth would be based on principles of bilateral relations between sovereign states, regardless of Gorbachev's views on these matters, *Diena* reported.

Lifting of Price Controls Delayed until January 2

RSFSR Deputy Prime Minister Egor Gaidar told Russian Television that his republic had agreed to delay lifting controls on most prices until January 2. This was requested by Ukraine and Belorussia at the weekend meeting in Minsk. All three republics would try to lift price controls simultaneously. Ukraine and Belorussia had appealed against the original target date of December 16, citing a shortage of rubles. In return for the postponement Ukraine and Belorussia agreed to increase deliveries of food and consumer goods to Russia.

EC Aid Arrangements Modified

Belgian Finance Minister Philippe Maystadt, speaking on behalf of the European Community, announced that the EC would change the mechanism for giving aid to the USSR, Western agencies reported. Instead of making credit guarantees available to Moscow for the purchase and distribution of food, these would now be offered directly to the cities where the food aid was needed. Individual republics seeking credit guarantees would have to honor their commitments to repay their share of the total external debt of the former USSR. The value of the EC credit package was put at 500 million ecus, or roughly 650 million dollars.

RSFSR to Import Medicines

RSFSR President Boris El'tsin signed a decree on the purchase of medicines from abroad, Interfax reported.

The USSR in December, 1991

Russia would allocate 1.35 billion hard-currency rubles to import essential medicines and the raw materials and equipment to produce medicines. The decree also stipulated that government proposals should be prepared within two weeks on raising the prices paid by citizens for medicines and health-care facilities and on compensation arrangements.

Estonia Recognizes Ukraine

The Estonian government voted to recognize Ukrainian independence, the Baltic News Service reported. The government had delayed recognition until the official results of the referendum on independence were published.

Ruutel and El'tsin Discuss Troops, Borders

President of the Estonian Supreme Council Arnold Ruutel and RSFSR President Boris El'tsin signed a joint communiqué in Moscow pledging a joint stand on troop withdrawals. According to the Baltic News Service, Ruutel told El'tsin that Estonia was willing to build housing in Russia for withdrawing troops. The two also discussed border questions, and Ruutel reportedly appealed to El'tsin to adjust borders drawn unilaterally by the USSR after World War II.

Rutskoi Demands Release of OMON Commander

RSFSR Vice President Aleksandr Rutskoi demanded that the Latvian authorities release Sergei Parfenov, deputy chief of the OMON detachment that was stationed in Riga before its transfer to Tyumen' Oblast at the end of August. Court proceedings were being prepared by the Latvian authorities against Parfenov in connection with his involvement in the August coup attempt. Parfenov was arrested by RSFSR officials, who then honored a Latvian request for extradition. Rutskoi claimed that it had not been legally correct to extradite Parfenov (*TASS*, December 9).

Controls Lifted on Food Prices in Latvia

Latvian Prime Minister Ivars Godmanis announced on Radio Riga a government decision to abolish controls on prices of basic foodstuffs and agricultural products as of December 10. He said that this decision was in line with Latvia's aim of establishing a market economy. Godmanis added that the step was also necessitated by the fact that similar measures had already been taken in Estonia and Lithuania and that Russia was also about to lift price controls. Godmanis told *Diena* that he expected the next two months to be the most difficult and that a special government commission would be following developments in Latvia closely.

Radio Riga reported that, as of December 10, lines in front of shops selling bread and dairy products remained long. One of the reasons for the lines was that the shops were afraid to order too much of a given item for fear of not being able to sell it at the higher price. People reacted stoically to the higher prices, especially for bread, saying that, while they were worried how they would make ends meet, they understood the need for freeing prices and the establishment of a market economy.

Tuesday, December 10

Military Reaction to the Commonwealth

Soviet President Mikhail Gorbachev met with senior military officers in Moscow, Western and Soviet agencies reported. According to a Defense Ministry spokesman, the gathering included senior commanders from the Defense Ministry, the General Staff, and all the commanders of military districts and fleets; military representatives from the republics also attended. He said that the meeting was an annual affair and had been scheduled far in advance. *Izvestia* reported on December 11 that Gorbachev had been expected at the Defense Ministry on December 9, but had failed to appear.

RSFSR President Boris El'tsin met with the same group of senior military officers on December 11. Reports after the meeting suggested that he had won tentative support for his Slavic Commonwealth from military commanders. Interfax quoted El'tsin as saying that a poll taken by Defense Minister Evgenii Shaposhnikov indicated that a majority of commanders were satisfied with El'tsin's program. A Radio Moscow commentary said that Gorbachev, by contrast, had been received coolly by the convocation. It added that one reason the officers supported El'tsin was that the majority of them were Slavs and were favorably disposed to a Slavic Commonwealth. *Izvestia* suggested that the officer corps would serve whoever supported it financially.

An unnamed participant in the meeting told *Komsomol'skaya pravda* on December 12 that El'tsin had proposed unified command over strategic forces. The republics would be allowed their own ground forces. Defense Ministry spokesman Valerii Manilov said that the Commonwealth would function on the principles of collective security with a united command of common armed forces. *The Independent* on December 12 suggested that El'tsin's trump card was his ability to raise military wages.

On December 11, Interfax cited unnamed military sources as saying Gorbachev had attempted "to split the armed forces" during his meeting with officers when he asked them to support the convocation of the USSR Congress of People's Deputies and a referendum on the Commonwealth agreement. Major General Aleksandr Tsalko told Interfax on December 11 that Gorbachev had called the army a factor for stability in the USSR and said he would not use it for political purposes, although he urged it to support the idea of a Union.

USSR Supreme Soviet Terms Commonwealth Illegal

Chairman of the USSR Supreme Soviet's Council of the Union Konstantin Lubenchenko distributed a statement saying that the Minsk agreement was completely illegal and that its political consequences could be dire, TASS reported. Lubenchenko said that under the present circumstances the USSR Supreme Soviet was one of the few forces that could in some way guarantee the integrity of the Union and added that it was the duty of deputies to carry this through to the end, regardless of the position adopted by the USSR president.

On December 12, the Belorussian legislature voted to change the status of its representatives in the USSR Supreme Soviet to that of observers. The same day, the RSFSR Supreme Soviet followed suit and recalled the republic's deputies from the USSR Supreme Soviet. Gorbachev issued a statement saying that such actions did not contribute to the stability of society at a time when the fate of the state was in question, and he called on the parliaments of both republics to reexamine the question, TASS reported. Gorbachev was to have addressed the legislature, but did not show up.

More Defense Ministry Officials Relieved of Their Posts

Deputy Defense Ministers Vladimir Arkhipov and Yurii Yashin were relieved of their duties, as heads continued to roll at the USSR Ministry of Defense. Western agencies reported that Arkhipov had been replaced by Colonel General Ivan Fuzhenko, formerly commander of the Turkestan Military District. No replacement for Yashin was named.

Slavic Republics Ratify Commonwealth Agreement

The Minsk Commonwealth agreement was ratified by the Supreme Soviets of Belorussia and Ukraine. The vote in Minsk was 263 in favor and only 1 against; in Kiev, 288 deputies out of 367 gave their approval.

On December 12, the RSFSR Supreme Soviet approved the Minsk agreement by 188 votes in favor, 6 against, and 7 abstentions, TASS reported. The RSFSR parliament also renounced the 1922 Union treaty. El'tsin described the parliament's decision as historic. In his speech to the Supreme Soviet he said the republics had been driven to this solution by Gorbachev's obstinate refusal to give up the idea of a strong center.

Unions Picket El'tsin and Popov

The Moscow Trade-Union Federation began picketing outside the Moscow City Soviet, the mayor's office, and the Russian "White House," TASS reported. The chairman of the trade unions, Mikhail Shmakov, said that the unions were demanding that El'tsin and Mayor Gavriil Popov stop price increases until social protection measures for Muscovites had been instituted and the food supply as well as law and order in Moscow was assured. The unions reportedly formed a strike committee.

Popov Threatens to Resign Again

Moscow Mayor Gavriil Popov said he might resign both for health reasons and because of differences with the Russian government over privatization of businesses and housing. In an interview with *Moskovsky komsomolets*, Popov noted that he had vowed to give land to the people but that the Russian government had done nothing but make promises for the past two years.

Nagorno-Karabakh Votes for Independence

TASS reported on December 11 that seven Armenians had been killed in clashes during the referendum on independence in Nagorno-Karabakh on December 10. Eighty percent of the electorate participated in the referendum, of whom 99 percent voted in favor of independence. The Azerbaijani population of the oblast apparently boycotted the referendum. Polling stations operated in Armenia to enable Armenian refugees from Nagorno-Karabakh to participate.

Kazakhstan Changes Official Name

The Supreme Soviet of Kazakhstan voted to drop "Soviet Socialist" from the republic's official name, according to a KazTAG-TASS report. According to "Vesti," a majority of deputies in Kazakhstan's legislature condemned Gorbachev's claim that five areas of the RSFSR were given to Kazakhstan during the Virgin Lands campaign of the 1950s.

The USSR in December, 1991

Wednesday, December 11

Tactical Nuclear Warheads Said to Have Been Removed

General Gelii Batenin, an adviser to the RSFSR Foreign Ministry, told RFE/RL that all tactical nuclear warheads had been removed from the Baltic States, Transcaucasia, and Central Asia. Until 1996 they would all be stored in Russia, he added. He said that only delivery vehicles for tactical nuclear weapons remained in these republics. Batenin further revealed that 70 percent of Soviet nuclear warheads had been disabled and that tactical nuclear weapons would be eliminated from the navy by 1992. He maintained that the KGB had lost its previous control over the warheads after the putsch and denied that Russia now had its finger on the nuclear button.

USSR Constitutional Supervision Committee Says Minsk Statement on End of USSR Has No Legal Force

The USSR Committee for Constitutional Supervision said that the statement in the Minsk agreement that "the USSR is ceasing to exist as a subject of international law and a geopolitical reality" had no legal force, TASS reported. Agreeing with Gorbachev's assessment, the committee said that individual republics could not make such a decision; nor were they empowered to say that the USSR organs had ceased to function on their territory. Committee members expressed serious concern about the statement that USSR norms no longer applied on the territory of the member-states of the Commonwealth.

Gorbachev's state counselor for legal policy, Veniamin Yakovlev, made many of the same points. He maintained that neither the three Slavic republics alone nor all twelve republics had the right to declare the 1922 Union treaty defunct, saying that, according to the treaty, only a congress of the USSR could change it and that this was why Gorbachev had been forced to raise the question of convoking a session of the USSR Congress of People's Deputies. Yakovlev also said that suddenly halting the functions of USSR organs and laws could have very serious consequences, since the legislation regulating the economy, the army, and many other spheres was primarily Union legislation, TASS reported.

Vneshekonombank Presses for G-7 Deal

Deputy Chairman of the USSR Bank for Foreign Trade Tomas Alibegov told the Interrepublican Economic Committee that his bank was running out of resources and had trouble even paying interest on the country's foreign debt, Interfax reported. Alibegov was said to have urged acceptance of the G-7 offer made in November. This provided for a loan of 1 billion dollars in return for collateral of 104 tons of gold. Alibegov was also quoted as saying that Soviet holders of accounts at his bank were transferring hard currency abroad in "an avalanche."

Germans Withhold Credit Guarantees

German government officials told RFE/RL that credit guarantees were now being given for Soviet deals only in a few urgent cases. The problem was said to be the lack of counterguarantees provided by the USSR Bank for Foreign Trade since the end of October and the inability of republican banks to replace the central foreign-trade bank in this function. (Bonn provides government guarantees for foreign credits only if a bank in the recipient country provides a guarantee that the necessary hard currency is available). Germany had so far provided credit guarantees for Soviet deals to the value of 26–27 billion deutsche marks.

Conflict over *Pravda*

The RSFSR Ministry of Information and the Mass Media told *Pravda*, which since the disbanding of the CPSU had been published as an independent newspaper, to vacate its office. The ministry said that the new *Pravda* was not the legal successor to the CPSU Central Committee daily to which the office belonged. Meanwhile, the "Pressa" publishing house, which printed *Pravda*, said the newspaper owed it 1 million rubles. Representatives of *Pravda* told a press conference that actions against them amounted to an attempt by the RSFSR government to silence an organ of the opposition, "Vesti" reported. Radio Moscow said on December 11 that telephone and electricity supplies had been switched off in *Pravda*'s main technical department. As a result, no issue of the newspaper appeared on December 11.

Georgia Delays Signing Black Sea Fleet Accord

TASS reported that Georgian President Zviad Gamsakhurdia had delayed signing an agreement giving the Soviet Black Sea Fleet access to Georgian ports in order to study more closely the terms of the accord, under which training would be provided for officers of a future Georgian navy in return for allowing the fleet access to Georgian ports and guaranteeing the safety of Soviet sailors and their families on Georgian territory.

Baltic States Appeal for Aid

Officials from Estonia, Latvia, and Lithuania met with the G-24 nations in Brussels, Western agencies reported. The Balts outlined medium-term needs for economic aid, stressing that their industrial infrastructure, run down

THE USSR IN DECEMBER, 1991

during fifty years of Communist rule, needed modernizing. The G-24 nations pledged to consider the request urgently.

Latvian Supreme Council Deputy Chairman Resigns

Dainis Ivans, first deputy chairman of the Latvian Supreme Council, announced his resignation, Radio Riga reported. The resignation was to go into effect on January 1, 1992. Ivans, who would remain a deputy, did not explain the reasons for his resignation but indicated that for some time he had felt that he had accomplished all he could as one of the chairmen of the legislature.

―――――――――――――――――――――Thursday, December 12

RSFSR Defense Budget

Interfax reported that the RSFSR defense budget for 1992 was expected to be 323.5 billion rubles. It said the USSR defense budget could amount to 529.4 billion rubles in 1992, with Russia's share constituting 61.3 percent. Calculations were reportedly made using 1992 prices.

Russia Gives Honecker Ultimatum

Izvestia reported that the Russian authorities had ordered former East German leader Erich Honecker to leave Russia by December 13 or else face deportation to Germany. According to *Izvestia*, Honecker protested against the Russian order and appealed to the USSR government for political asylum. Honecker then sought refuge in the Chilean embassy in Moscow.

Ukraine Recognizes Georgian Independence

Addressing a public meeting outside the Georgian government building in Tbilisi, Georgian President Zviad Gamsakhurdia stated that Ukraine had recognized Georgian independence, Radio Tbilisi reported.

Russia Will Not Sign Economic Accord with Georgia

RSFSR Deputy Prime Minister Egor Gaidar was quoted by TASS as affirming that Russia would not sign a 1992 economic agreement with Georgia until the situation in South Ossetia stabilized. Gaidar admitted that this was "a terrible sanction" but argued that it was warranted by the deteriorating situation in the region. TASS further quoted the deputy chairman of the South Ossetian Supreme Soviet as stating that Georgian blockades were preventing humanitarian aid from reaching Tskhinvali and that the town was without electricity, gas, and food.

Moldavian President Visits Moscow, Kiev, Minsk

Moldavian President Mircea Snegur began an official visit to Moscow, Kiev, and Minsk for talks with Boris El'tsin, Leonid Kravchuk, and Stanislau Shushkevich. Snegur was the first leader of a former Soviet republic to meet with the three founders of the Commonwealth of Independent States. Snegur was cited by Moldovapres on December 11 as expressing interest in a possible economic association with the Commonwealth. He also intended to discuss with the three leaders an early partial withdrawal of USSR troops from Moldavia.

IMF Creates New Baltic and Soviet Department

Michel Camdessus, managing director of the International Monetary Fund, announced that the IMF had created a new department to deal with the Baltic States and the former Soviet Union. The IMF was already providing technical help to the USSR and most of the republics individually (RFE/RL correspondent's report, December 13).

Lithuanian-Ukrainian Diplomatic Relations

Lithuanian Foreign Minister Algirdas Saudargas and his Ukrainian counterpart, Anatolii Zlenko, exchanged notes on the establishment of diplomatic relations, Radio Lithuania reported. The two countries agreed to establish offices in Kiev and Vilnius headed by chargés d'affaires to be appointed later. The ministers discussed cooperation in political, economic, ecological, and cultural areas. Saudargas also talked with Ukrainian President Leonid Kravchuk and Supreme Soviet Foreign Affairs Committee Chairman Dmytro Pavlychko.

Estonia Accedes to Human-Rights Protocol

Estonia acceded to the optional protocol to the International Covenant on Civil and Political Rights allowing people to report individual violations of human rights to the UN Human-Rights Committee, RFE/RL reported.

Friday, December 13

Kravchuk Decree Establishes Ukrainian Armed Forces

Ukrainian President Leonid Kravchuk issued a decree creating a national armed force out of former units of the Soviet army and Black Sea Fleet and appointing himself commander in chief. Western agencies also confirmed that the Supreme Soviet had added an amendment to the ratified Commonwealth agreement stating Ukraine's right to leave the Commonwealth's joint defense structure after the republic's nuclear arms had been eliminated.

The USSR in December, 1991

EFTA Expands Ties with Baltic States

Latvian Minister of State Janis Dinevics told Radio Riga that Estonia, Latvia, and Lithuania had signed in Geneva declarations that could pave the way for Baltic membership in the European Free Trade Association (EFTA). After the signing of the declarations on December 10, the EFTA chairman, Finnish Foreign Trade Minister Pertti Salolainen, told Western agencies that the declarations showed EFTA's recognition of the need to support political and economic reforms in the former Communist states. EFTA also pledged to provide aid to help the Baltic States, Bulgaria, and Romania join the process of European integration and build their own market economies.

Saturday, December 14

Gorbachev Fights for His Position

In a telephone conversation with US President George Bush on December 13, Soviet President Mikhail Gorbachev said he believed his task was to ensure that the changes in the Soviet Union occurred without confrontation and within a constitutional framework. Meanwhile, USSR Minister of External Relations Eduard Shevardnadze said that Gorbachev's resignation was not imminent and that both he and Gorbachev wanted "to facilitate the process of the formation of the Commonwealth" (*TASS*, December 14). On December 16, however, RSFSR President Boris El'tsin told Gorbachev in a private meeting to resign by the middle of January, according to Western agencies.

On December 18, Gorbachev told the chairman of Central Television, Egor Yakovlev, that he would resign when the era of the Soviet Union was finally over and that of the Commonwealth of Independent States had begun ("TV Inform," December 18). Gorbachev said that he intended to continue his political activity after he had retired. The Russian Information Agency reported that Gorbachev would dedicate himself to persuading the West to boost its aid to the member-states of the new Commonwealth, particularly Russia.

Shakhrai Appointed El'tsin's Deputy

Thirty-four-year-old Sergei Shakhrai was appointed RSFSR deputy prime minister in charge of the Ministry of Internal Affairs, the State Committee for Defense, and the Federal Security Agency (the former KGB). Interfax reported on December 14 that Shakhrai, who previously had worked as RSFSR state councilor for legal affairs, would also supervise the Ministry of Justice and the newly created State Committee for Nationalities Policy.

Movement for Democratic Reforms Holds Founding Congress

The Movement for Democratic Reforms held its constituent congress in Moscow on December 14 and 15. Established in the summer of 1991 in opposition to the CPSU, the Movement for Democratic Reforms emerged at its first congress as a liberal opposition to the anticommunist Russian government (*TASS, Central Television*, December 15). "TV Inform" quoted the movement's ideologist, Aleksandr Yakovlev, as saying that the democrats now in power might degenerate into a new authoritarian force. Other speakers, including Eduard Shevardnadze, Anatolii Sobchak, and Aleksandr Rutskoi, also expressed reservations about the RSFSR leadership. Nonetheless, the congress rejected a proposal calling for a compromise between the Minsk and Novo-Ogarevo agreements and passed a resolution endorsing the establishment of the Commonwealth of Independent States.

Third "Sajudis" Congress

About 1,000 delegates attending the third "Sajudis" congress on December 14 and 15 heard President of the Supreme Council Vytautas Landsbergis, Prime Minister Gediminas Vagnorius, and "Sajudis" Chairman Juozas Tumelis address the opening session. The congress discussed the need to change the "Sajudis" program, and many speakers expressed support for a referendum on establishing a Lithuanian presidency. The congress elected Landsbergis as honorary chairman of "Sajudis". On December 17 "Sajudis" issued a strongly worded demand for the departure of USSR troops from Lithuania by the end of the year, Western agencies reported. The Soviet servicemen sent a reply to Landsbergis saying that the demand was insulting and might provoke strong negative reactions from the Soviet military. Not being able to complete its work, the congress adjourned and was to continue on December 22.

Controversy over Soviet Foreign-Exchange Reserves

Russian Federation Deputy Prime Minister Egor Gaidar declared on December 14 that the USSR Foreign Trade Bank's balance on December 12 was down to 60 million dollars, according to TASS and Interfax reports of that same day. These declarations were, however, subsequently dismissed by the Interrepublican Bank Council as "rumors" and "incorrect interpretations" of the USSR's foreign-exchange reserves, according to a Reuters report of December 19. According to Gaidar, hard currency was no longer forthcoming from the West, and republics were no longer transferring part of their hard-currency earnings to the Foreign Trade Bank. Gaidar said that the Russian government was auditing loans given to former central

THE USSR IN DECEMBER, 1991

agencies and that Russia had sharply reduced its hard-currency spending, using hard currency exclusively to import food, spare parts, and equipment for the chemical and light industries.

Suspension of Soviet International Train Services Threatened

Ivan Shchirenko, the head of Moscow's international rail agency, told TASS on December 14 that the sale of international rail tickets had been suspended because the Railway Ministry could not pay debts of 150 million dollars to foreign companies. The ministry had also lost access to computers that were used to order international tickets. In addition, Shchirenko said that attempts to obtain help from the Russian Federation government and banking officials had yielded no results, and he warned that the ministry would soon be obliged to halt trains running to Europe and Asia.

Belorussia Substitutes Coupons for Rubles

TASS reported on December 14 that, as of January, 1992, citizens of Belorussia would receive 60 percent of their salaries in coupons and the remainder in rubles. Pensioners and students would get coupons only. The measures were taken to stabilize the flow of rubles in the republic.

Sunday, December 15

Commonwealth States on Control of Nuclear Weapons

Ukrainian President Leonid Kravchuk told Central Television that a new "political mechanism" should be worked out among the four states of the Commonwealth of Independent States—Ukraine, Belorussia, Russia, and Kazakhstan—where strategic weapons were deployed. The mechanism would define control over the use of the weapons. He said the four republics had already agreed to a mechanism under which there would be control over nonuse or a power of veto. Kravchuk stressed that the ultimate goal was total disarmament.

During his meeting with US Secretary of State James Baker, Kravchuk asked for the help of US experts in destroying the Soviet nuclear weapons based in Ukraine. Kravchuk said that he wanted to see all the strategic missiles, including those not scheduled for elimination under the terms of the START agreement, destroyed as quickly as possible (*TASS*, December 19).

In a statement read out on Russian Television on December 16, RSFSR President Boris El'tsin explained that control of nuclear weapons in the new Commonwealth would be in the hands of the leaders of the four nuclear republics, plus "the supreme commander in chief." They would consult with one another, but any launch order would come from "a unified center." El'tsin acknowledged that Ukraine and Belorussia would not transfer the strategic nuclear weapons on their territory to Russia but would insist that they be destroyed in place. He said that further talks would be held with Kazakhstan.

During his joint news conference with Baker on December 17, Kazakh President Nursultan Nazarbaev said that his republic would not give up all the nuclear weapons stationed on its territory as long as nuclear weapons remained in Russia (Western agencies, December 18).

At a press conference following Baker's visit to Belorussia on December 18, it was stated that the republic had confirmed its desire to be a nonnuclear neutral state, TASS reported.

Baker told a news conference in Brussels on December 19 that during his trip to the USSR he had been assured privately that Belorussia, Kazakhstan, and Ukraine had agreed to sign the Nuclear Nonproliferation Treaty as nonnuclear powers. This would mean they would not be able to keep any nuclear weapons on their territories. Western agencies also reported on December 20 that Ukraine and Russia had agreed to withdraw all tactical nuclear weapons from Ukraine in less than one year. Strategic nuclear bombers and their weapons would also be transferred to Russia, while Soviet strategic missiles in Ukraine would be taken off alert status. The agreement was disclosed by General Sergei Zelentsov of the USSR Ministry of Defense and confirmed by General Vadim Grechaninov, the deputy chief of staff of the Ukrainian Ministry of Defense.

An official of the Soviet nuclear arms complex was quoted in *The New York Times* of December 18 as saying it would take ten years and 2 billion dollars to destroy all Soviet tactical nuclear weapons. Viktor Mikhailov was addressing a conference in Moscow of Soviet and American experts studying the technical problems of warhead dismantlement. He urged that the 400 million dollars pledged in aid by the United States for this project be used to build a storage site for the fissionable material from the retired warheads, and he said that it should be under "joint control."

Popov Announces and Then Withdraws Resignation

Moscow Mayor Gavriil Popov announced his resignation during the founding congress of the Movement for Democratic Reforms in Moscow on December 15, Radio Moscow reported. Popov had been threatening to resign

THE USSR IN DECEMBER, 1991

since the Moscow City Soviet recently reversed his plans to introduce widespread privatization in Moscow. The mayor also indicated that he had reservations about El'tsin's economic reform program. Popov, elected mayor on June 11, 1991, said that bureaucratic opposition made it impossible for him to fulfill the promises he had made to the voters.

On December 17, the Moscow City Soviet appealed to Popov not to resign (*Radio Rossii*, December 17); and at a press conference on December 19, Popov said he would be willing to withdraw his resignation if he were sure that he would be able to carry out a privatization program without interference from the Russian government, Soviet and Western agencies reported.

On December 26, following a meeting between Popov and El'tsin, TASS reported that Popov had decided not to resign. El'tsin reportedly assured the Moscow mayor that he could rely on the complete support of the Russian government in carrying out economic reform plans in Moscow.

As of December 15 armed troops were supposed to be accompanying shipments of foodstuffs between warehouses and retail outlets in St. Petersburg, Radio Moscow reported on December 14. In addition, TASS reported on December 16 that Moscow bakeries were working at full capacity but that the needs of the population "could not be fully met." The news agency also reported that bread rationing had been introduced in parts of the Altai region, a major grain-growing area.

Food Shipments to Be Guarded in St. Petersburg

Monday, December 16

The Supreme Soviet of Kazakhstan adopted a declaration of independence on December 16, according to a KazTAG report. The declaration stated that the present boundaries of the republic were inviolable. Kazakh President Nursultan Nazarbaev proclaimed December 17 a Day of Democratic Renewal, according to Radio Moscow. It commemorated not only the independence declaration but also the Alma-Ata protests that began on December 17, 1986.

Kazakhstan Declares Independence

Soviet agencies reported the arrival in Turkey of an Uzbek government delegation led by President Islam Karimov. It was his first trip abroad since Uzbekistan declared its independence. The visit resulted in the signing of an

Uzbek and Kirgiz Leaders Visit Turkey

agreement between Uzbekistan and Turkey covering cooperation in the fields of transport, education, culture, science, and broadcasting (*TASS,* December 19).

On December 22, Kirgiz President Askar Akaev arrived in Ankara on an official visit and the following day signed bilateral economic, diplomatic, and cultural agreements, Western agencies reported.

Turkmen Communist Party Changes Name

The Communist Party of Turkmenistan voted at a special congress to dissolve itself and reconstitute itself as the Democratic Party of Turkmenistan (*TASS,* December 16).

Belorussia and Latvia Sign Accord

An official delegation from Belorussia headed by Supreme Soviet Chairman Stanislau Shushkevich arrived in the Latvian capital, Radio Riga reported. Shushkevich and Latvian Supreme Council Chairman Anatolijs Gorbunovs signed an accord on the principles of good-neighborly relations; accords on cooperation in specific areas were to follow.

Azerbaijan Nationalizes Soviet Forces

Azerbaijani President Ayaz Mutalibov decreed that all assets of the Soviet Armed Forces on his territory were now the property of Azerbaijan, Radio Moscow reported on December 16. The decree reportedly also applied to Nagorno-Karabakh.

Baltic States Ask UN to Help Remove Soviet Troops

In a joint letter addressed to United Nations Secretary-General Javier Perez de Cuellar, the ambassadors of the Baltic States asked for help in removing Soviet troops from their territory, Radio Lithuania reported on December 16. With the disintegration of the USSR, the ambassadors wrote, there was "a real possibility" that the center would be unable to control its troops in the Baltic, some of whose officers had "openly suggested the possibility of remaining despite orders to the contrary from Moscow." The letter asked the United Nations to monitor closely the situation in the Baltic States.

Fiat to Form Joint Venture with VAZ

Western news agencies reported on December 16 and 20 that the Italian automobile company Fiat was poised to acquire a 33-percent stake in VAZ, the largest automobile maker in the Soviet Union. RSFSR President Boris El'tsin announced on December 20 that the joint venture should be finalized "within a month." Thanks to investment by

The USSR in December, 1991

Fiat, which regards the former Soviet Union as a "market of top priority," production at VAZ was set to increase to almost 1 million cars per year. Fiat also hoped to develop a new car for the Russian market that would be competitive on Western markets as well. Reuters reported on December 23 that Russian automobile exports in 1992 could receive a boost from the Taiwan Lada company, which hoped to be the first seller of Russian cars in Taiwan. Ladas were scheduled to be displayed at the Taipei Motor Show on December 28.

Restrictions on Enterprises' Foreign Exchange Holdings

Russian Central Bank Chairman Dmitrii Tulin told TASS Russian enterprises had been ordered to refrain from keeping hard-currency accounts abroad. (Many firms had been refusing to pay the 40-percent tax levied on hard-currency earnings, which was one of the reasons for the liquidity squeeze.) Tulin said the RSFSR Supreme Soviet planned to adopt legislation later in the month to establish a Russian hard-currency reserve. The law would stipulate how much enterprises would have to pay into the reserve, which would be used to buy goods for the RSFSR.

Tuesday, December 17

Gorbachev and El'tsin Agree on Date for Official End of USSR

Soviet President Gorbachev and RSFSR President El'tsin agreed at a two-hour meeting on December 17 that the USSR would cease to exist on January 1, 1992, Western agencies reported. El'tsin's spokesman, Pavel Voshchanov, said Gorbachev had agreed that the process of transferring Union structures to the new Commonwealth would be finished by the end of the year. Gorbachev's press spokesman, Andrei Grachev, said the USSR would continue to exist until constitutional decisions had been taken about the creation of its successor, TASS reported.

Russia Claims Soviet Parliament Building

Meeting in Moscow, deputies to the USSR Supreme Soviet criticized moves by the RSFSR Supreme Soviet announced on December 16 to take over the USSR Supreme Soviet's Kremlin premises and appropriate its assets. As reported by TASS, Tajik deputy Bozorali Safarov called the move illegal and proposed appealing to an international court. But TASS also quoted RSFSR Supreme Soviet Chairman Ruslan Khasbulatov as saying the RSFSR parliament did not intend to declare itself the legal successor to the Soviet parliament and would share the assets with other former republics.

THE USSR IN DECEMBER, 1991

General Warns Republics Interviewed by the conservative newspaper *Sovetskaya Rossiya* on December 17, USSR Defense Ministry spokesman Lieutenant General Leonid Ivashov suggested that the army was being provoked to a dangerous degree in the Baltic area, the Transcaucasus, and the Northern Caucasus. He said the patience of servicemen was not infinite, criticized attempts to seize army property, and warned that any annexation of army facilities could destroy the defense and security system of the republics.

Ukrainian Official Views Commonwealth as Temporary Dmytro Pavlychko, chairman of the Ukrainian parliament's Foreign Affairs Committee, told journalists in Kiev on December 17 that Ukraine regarded the Commonwealth of Independent States as a temporary structure that would be abandoned after Soviet nuclear weapons had been destroyed (*The Chicago Tribune*, December 18). Pavlychko said the Commonwealth should play merely a transitional role as the Soviet republics consolidated their independence and developed economic relations.

Rutskoi Seeks Afghan Settlement RSFSR Vice President Aleksandr Rutskoi arrived in Iran on December 17 on the first leg of a trip aimed at forging a settlement of the conflict in Afghanistan (*The Independent*, December 17).

On December 19 Rutskoi concluded an agreement with Iranian-based Mujahidin on the release of two Soviet prisoners of war in exchange for a group of Afghan resistance prisoners held in Kabul. According to TASS, while in Teheran Rutskoi also signed an agreement to expand bilateral cooperation between the RSFSR and Iran. He then traveled on to Pakistan and Kabul.

Estonians Block Troops Entering Tallinn The authorities in Estonia denied entry into Tallinn to about 1,000 Soviet soldiers, according to Estonian and Western agency reports. Estonian home guards surrounded the central train station in Tallinn to keep the soldiers from entering the city. The Foreign Ministry formally protested to the USSR Foreign Ministry, pointing out that the troop transfer violated Soviet-Estonian agreements.

Agreements on Rescheduling and Division of Soviet Foreign Debt Representatives of the USSR Foreign Trade Bank, the Russian Central Bank, and a committee of Western creditor banks announced that agreement had been reached on rescheduling Soviet payments on principal due between December, 1991, and March, 1992, Western agencies reported that day. The amount involved was not disclosed but was believed to total about 8 billion dollars, including 3.4 billion dollars due in December. This rescheduling covered only debts contracted before January 1, 1991; it excluded government stocks, short-term loans from financial bodies, and bonds placed with private investors. The agreement of December 17 was followed by a preliminary agreement in Paris between representatives of seventeen creditor nations and Russia, Kazakhstan, Belorussia, Armenia, Turkmenistan, Tajikistan, Kirgizia, and Moldavia, RFE/RL's Paris bureau reported on December 21. The finance ministers of these republics reaffirmed their commitment to repay the Soviet foreign debt, and all parties agreed to meet again in Paris on January 3 to conclude "a final agreement."

Aeroflot Grounded

According to RSFSR Deputy Transport Minister Aleksandr Larin, about 2,800 of Aeroflot's fleet of 7,000 planes were grounded in mid-December because of shortages of spare parts and fuel. Political disputes over the control of airports and Aeroflot property in various republics added to the chaos. According to Western media reports, many aircraft had depreciated by 100 percent and Aeroflot's safety record had deteriorated; 33 crashes and 240 fatalities were reported in 1991. Flights into and out of Moscow in mid-December were running an average of seventy-two hours behind schedule. On December 17 Soviet Central Television announced that Aeroflot had canceled seventy-five flights and that eighty-seven airports had been closed. The program also gave a list of cities where no aviation fuel was available. Tens of thousands of would-be passengers were said to be stranded at airports around the country. In addition, a threefold increase in domestic fares was announced, while tickets for international flights were increasingly being sold for hard currency only.

Republics Sign European Energy Charter

Signatures or proxy signatures from all twelve former republics of the USSR were among the forty-five on the new European Energy Charter that was signed on December 17 in The Hague, Western agencies reported that day. RSFSR Energy Minister Vladimir Lopukhin told the meeting that the Russian Federation planned to establish up to twelve oil firms based on Western models within six months. Russia had already dismantled the central ministries that previously controlled oil and gas production.

Wednesday, December 18

Gorbachev Sends Letter to Alma-Ata Meeting

In a letter dated December 18 to the participants in the Alma-Ata meeting on the creation of the Commonwealth of Independent States, Soviet President Mikhail Gorbachev said that the transition from the USSR to the new Commonwealth was taking place under very difficult circumstances. He said any attempt to segment the system controlling the country's strategic weapons was dangerous. He also said that the Commonwealth should be recognized as an entity under international law and that it would be impossible to maintain a common strategic defense without a minimum of common foreign policy. Gorbachev also proposed establishing "Commonwealth citizenship" for a limited period in order to prevent ethnic conflicts and discrimination. He suggested that member-states abide by the economic community treaty and appealed for the transfer of power to be conducted with dignity and in accordance with the law (*TASS*, December 19).

USSR Supreme Soviet Tries to Coordinate Transition to Commonwealth

The Legislative Committee of the Council of the Union of the USSR Supreme Soviet drew up a draft law for the transformation of the Soviet Union into a Commonwealth, Interfax reported on December 18. The draft called for the retention of powers by the Union parliament until a new Commonwealth parliament had been created. It also recommended retaining the USSR Ministry of Defense, Ministry of Internal Affairs, and Ministry of External Relations, the USSR Supreme Court and Arbitration Court, state security agencies, and the USSR Prosecutor's Office during the transitional period.

Rutskoi Criticizes RSFSR Government

RSFSR Vice President Aleksandr Rutskoi termed RSFSR President Boris El'tsin's assumption of the post of RSFSR prime minister "a serious mistake." He told *Nezavisimaya gazeta* that El'tsin was facing "heart problems" and should not take "everything upon himself." He denounced the present RSFSR government, saying that the Russian White House had become "a place of intrigues." Rutskoi complained that El'tsin's closest entourage was denying him proper access to the president, and he charged that some "former lecturers in communism" were calling for "a witch-hunt" against Communists.

On December 26, Rutskoi said the RSFSR government was becoming completely uncontrollable. According to Interfax, Rutskoi complained that while El'tsin was in

The USSR in December, 1991

Italy, his deputy, Gennadii Burbulis, had signed a presidential decree limiting the powers of the vice president. Rutskoi reaffirmed that he did not intend to resign. He described the economic reform program of Burbulis's team as "another giant experiment on the country" and agreed with analyses forecasting a complete collapse of production in 1993.

New Economic Decrees

The RSFSR government approved eleven decrees on economic reform, welfare, and budget matters issued by El'tsin during the previous month, Radio Rossii and TASS reported that day. One decree set the new minimum wage at 342 rubles, starting in January, 1992. Another decree instituted indexation for certain levels of income, but details were not available. All eleven decrees would be submitted to the RSFSR Supreme Soviet for consideration.

RSFSR "Lost Control" of Oil Export Licenses

RSFSR Energy Minister Vladimir Lopukhin told the *Financial Times* and *The Journal of Commerce* that, in the confusion after the August coup, the RSFSR had lost control of its oil export licenses. The republic had committed itself to export up to thirty-one times as much fuel oil as was actually available. Similarly, in December the RSFSR expected to export about 51 million barrels of crude but had issued licenses for 245 million. The RSFSR reregistered some licenses and canceled others in mid-November.

Donbass Miners on Strike

Ukrainian Radio and Western agencies reported on December 18 that coal miners in the Donbass region had been on strike for three days in support of a demand for economic independence for their mine. Some 6,000 miners at the "Komsomolets Donbassa" mine went on strike on December 16, setting a one-week deadline for their demands to be met. The miners were also demanding that the Ukrainian government establish a commission to study the mine's finances.

Lithuania Seeks Extradition of Those Responsible for Killings

President of the Lithuanian Supreme Council Vytautas Landsbergis asked RSFSR President Boris El'tsin to extradite more than twenty people believed to have been involved in fatal clashes in Lithuania earlier in the year, Western agencies reported. The list included former USSR Defense Minister Dmitrii Yazov, former Soviet KGB Chairman Vladimir Kryuchkov, former Lithuanian

THE USSR IN DECEMBER, 1991

Communist Party leader Mykolas Burokevicius, and leaders of OMON. The Lithuanian authorities wanted to bring to justice those responsible for the killings of civilians in January, 1991, and the slaying of border guards in July.

Radio Riga reported that Lithuanian Prosecutor-General Arturas Paulauskas was seeking to bring to trial seven members of OMON held responsible for the slaying of seven border guards at the Medininkai customs post on July 31. According to information provided by the one border guard who survived the attack, some of the assailants came from the OMON base in Vilnius and others from the OMON base in Riga.

Thursday, December 19

El'tsin Takes Control of Central Structures

El'tsin issued decrees asserting Russian control over all Soviet structures on RSFSR territory except the USSR Ministry of Defense and Ministry of Nuclear Energy (*TASS*, December 19). Thus, the Kremlin, the USSR presidential apparatus, the USSR Ministry of External Relations, the Interrepublican Security Service (the former KGB), the Ministry of Internal Affairs, and all Soviet foreign-currency accounts would be taken over by the RSFSR. Soviet embassies would also come under Russian jurisdiction. "Vesti" also reported that the RSFSR had taken over all Soviet aviation equipment and airports on its territory.

Soviet Central Radio and Television were placed under jurisdiction of the RSFSR by a decree signed by El'tsin (*TASS*, December 27). The decree stated that the company would in future be known as the Russian Ostankino Television and Radio Company. Egor Yakovlev would remain in charge of these broadcasting entities.

El'tsin Tries to Merge KGB and MVD; RSFSR Supreme Soviet Suspends the Move

El'tsin issued an edict creating an RSFSR Ministry of Security and Internal Affairs comprising the USSR Ministry of Internal Affairs, the RSFSR Ministry of Internal Affairs, the Interrepublican Security Service, and the RSFSR Federal Security Agency ("Vesti," December 19). According to Radio Moscow, USSR Minister of Internal Affairs Viktor Barannikov was to head the new ministry.

El'tsin also decreed the takeover of the USSR Foreign Intelligence Agency by the RSFSR (*Interfax*, December 20). The agency had just become independent of the domestic wing of the KGB. El'tsin ordered that its property, buildings, information banks, and documentation be handed over to the newly created Russian Foreign

The USSR in December, 1991

Intelligence Service within a month. Evgenii Primakov would continue to head the service.

The provision of El'tsin's edict merging the internal affairs and state security agencies met with disapproval in the Supreme Soviet of the Russian Federation, which suspended the move ("Vesti," December 26). Opponents of the merger, including many KGB officers, argued that the consolidation might lead to a repetition of the state of affairs that had existed under the Stalinist NKVD, which had also brought internal affairs and state security under one umbrella. Barannikov said, however, that the measure was dictated by a need to "strengthen the potential of the law-enforcement agencies," improve the protection of human rights, and combat organized crime, corruption, and drug trafficking.

El'tsin in Italy

RSFSR President Boris El'tsin traveled to Italy on December 19 to inform the Italian government and business leaders about the Commonwealth agreement, to negotiate the release of a 6-billion-dollar credit line to the USSR, which was frozen in November, and to discuss Orthodox-Catholic tension with Pope John Paul II, Western news agencies reported.

Amnesty International to Open Moscow Bureau

Radio Rossii, citing the Russian Information Agency, reported that Moscow Mayor Gavriil Popov had signed orders granting permission to Amnesty International to open an information bureau in Moscow.

Widespread Fuel Shortages in Republics

Central Television and TASS reported fuel shortages in many parts of the Soviet Union, including the Donbass, Buryatia, the Northern Caucasus, and Armenia. According to the reports, the fact that producers were withholding fuel until prices were raised and that other suppliers were insisting on barter deals was a major reason for the shortages.

Unemployment Growing in RSFSR

There were more than 2 million unemployed in the RSFSR, and this figure was expected to increase fourfold or fivefold in the near future, according to the daily *Trud*. The article noted that people just below retirement age, professionals, and poorly qualified workers made up the majority of those affected. An allowance would reportedly be paid to those granted unemployment status but only for a period of up to twelve months.

Friday, December 20

Silaev Named Russian Representative to EC

RSFSR President Boris El'tsin appointed Ivan Silaev as Russia's representative to the EC, according to Interfax of December 20. Interfax on December 24 quoted Gennadii Burbulis as saying that Silaev's Interrepublican Economic Committee would cease to exist at the end of 1991.

Kazakhstan Adopts Citizenship Law

KazTAG reported that the Kazakh Supreme Soviet had adopted a law on citizenship. According to the report, the law guaranteed the equality of citizens regardless of nationality, religious confession, or political convictions.

Tense Polish-Lithuanian Relations

In comments to *Rzeczpospolita* published on December 20, Foreign Minister Krzysztof Skubiszewski indicated that tense relations over the Polish minority in Lithuania had postponed his long-contemplated visit to Vilnius. He criticized Lithuania for failing to call new local elections in two predominantly Polish areas that were dissolved after the attempted coup in the former Soviet Union in August. He also charged that district borders in the Vilnius area were being redrawn to the disadvantage of ethnic Poles. Skubiszewski's charge that the Lithuanian authorities had moved to discontinue Polish television programming was denied by Lithuania's chargé d'affaires in Warsaw.

Armenia to Reopen Nuclear Power Plant

Western agencies in Moscow quoted an Armenian government minister on December 20 as stating that Armenia's Medzamor nuclear power station, taken out of commission in 1989 following the earthquake in December, 1988, would be reactivated in 1992 to combat the republic's catastrophic energy shortage. By December 20 all industrial enterprises in Armenia had been closed because of fuel shortages caused by the energy blockade imposed by Azerbaijan.

Saturday, December 21

Further Eight Republics Join Commonwealth at Alma-Ata Meeting

At a meeting in Alma-Ata, the leaders of eight former Soviet republics (Armenia, Azerbaijan, Kazakhstan, Kirgizia, Moldavia, Tajikistan, Turkmenistan, and Uzbekistan) agreed to join the Commonwealth of Independent States

THE USSR IN DECEMBER, 1991

created by Russia, Belorussia, and Ukraine on December 8. One of the protocols stipulated that all signatory states enter the Commonwealth on an equal basis as cofounders; another recognized the independence and current borders of all signatory states; and a third asked the United Nations to give the USSR's seat on the Security Council to the RSFSR and obligated Russia, Belorussia, and Ukraine to seek admission to the United Nations for all Commonwealth members (Soviet and Western agencies, December 21).

The Commonwealth's Central Structures

In Alma-Ata the leaders of the eleven states forming the new Commonwealth issued a draft accord on its central structures (*TASS*, December 21). The supreme governing bodies would be a Council of Heads of State and a Council of Heads of Government that would meet twice a year to adopt basic policy decisions. The presidency of both bodies would be rotating. The accord also proposed setting up seven ministerial committees to coordinate policy on foreign affairs, defense, economics and finance, transport and communications, social protection for the population, internal affairs, and general policy. All Commonwealth members would participate in financing the central structures.

Ukraine Reaffirms Independence within Commonwealth

In a statement adopted on the eve of the Alma-Ata meeting, the Ukrainian parliament and president made it clear Ukraine would only participate in the new Commonwealth if this body remained a loose association and did not become a new state (*Radio Kiev*, December 21). At the meeting itself, Ukrainian President Leonid Kravchuk came out against the notions of "Commonwealth citizenship" and joint guarding of the Commonwealth's external borders (Western agencies, December 21).

Alma-Ata Agreement on Nuclear Weapons

The Agreement on Joint Measures regarding Nuclear Weapons signed by the leaders of the four former Soviet republics where strategic nuclear weapons were located showed that Kazakhstan remained at odds with the other three on this issue. As broadcast on Moscow television on December 21, the agreement indicated that all strategic nuclear weapons would be removed from Belorussia by July 1, 1992, and from Ukraine by an unspecified date. Those in Kazakhstan were not mentioned, nor was there any reference to Kazakhstan's planning to sign the Nuclear Nonproliferation Treaty, which Belorussia and Ukraine pledged to do. The agreement did imply that tactical nuclear weapons would be transferred from all three republics to Russia, where they would be dismantled "under joint supervision."

Georgia's Application for Membership in CIS Rejected

Georgia was represented at the Commonwealth conference in Alma-Ata by a deputy parliamentary chairman and a deputy prime minister but did not sign the Commonwealth Agreement (Western agencies, December 21).

On December 25, RSFSR President Boris El'tsin told the RSFSR parliament that the Commonwealth leaders had decided to reject the application for membership made by Georgian President Zviad Gamsakhurdia the previous day because of violations of human rights in Georgia and South Ossetia.

Shaposhnikov Named Interim Commander in Alma-Ata

USSR Defense Minister Evgenii Shaposhnikov was named interim commander in chief of the armed forces on December 21 in Alma-Ata, Soviet and Western agencies reported. The appointment of a permanent commander in chief, together with the resolution of a host of other defense-related issues, was postponed until December 30, when republican leaders were scheduled to meet in Minsk.

Socialist Workers' Party Holds Congress

On December 21 and 22, the Socialist Workers' Party, which considered itself to be the legal successor to the CPSU, held its first congress in Moscow, TASS reported. On the opening day, Roy Medvedev, a former dissident Marxist historian and a member of the party's organizing committee, noted that not one demonstration or rally had taken place to protest against the banning of the CPSU and that therefore a new party was necessary to reflect the people's wishes. The congress issued a resolution calling for the creation of a bloc of Socialist- and Communist-oriented parties.

Russian Newspapers Face Subsidy Cuts

Russian newspaper editors said that cuts in subsidies planned by the Ministry of Communications threatened the existence of the fledgling free press. "Vesti" reported on December 21 that government subsidies on newsprint, office rents, and printing costs would end on January 2 as part of the transfer to a market economy.

Nazarbaev Names New Foreign Minister

Kazakh President Nursultan Nazarbaev dismissed Foreign Minister Akmaral Arystanbekova and replaced her with

The USSR in December, 1991

Toleubai Suleimenov, Kazakh Radio reported on December 21.

Figures on Soviet Soldiers Seeking Asylum

More than 200 Soviet soldiers belonging to the Western Group of Forces requested political asylum in Germany in 1991, according to the December 21 issue of the German news magazine *Der Spiegel*. TASS on December 18 said that 164,000 soldiers and civilians would be withdrawn from Germany by the end of the year, 9,000 more than originally planned. This would put the year-end total of Soviet troops, civilian employees, and dependents at just over 380,000.

_____ *Sunday, December 22*

Demonstrations in Moscow and St. Petersburg

Under the banner of "march of the hungry queues," several thousand people demonstrated in Moscow against the end of the USSR and the introduction of uncontrolled capitalism. Speakers included the conservative hard-liners Viktor Alksnis and Vladimir Zhirinovsky, Soviet and Western agencies reported. Carrying Communist flags and portraits of Lenin and Stalin, the demonstrators marched to the Ostankino Television Center and demanded air time to voice their grievances. Meanwhile, in St. Petersburg demonstrations organized by various Communist groups took place in defense of workers' rights, TASS and Radio Moscow reported.

Georgian Opposition Launches Attack against Gamsakhurdia

Following demonstrations on December 20 and 21 by 10,000 people calling for the resignation of Georgian President Zviad Gamsakhurdia, fighting erupted in Tbilisi on December 22 between troops of the rebel National Guard and units loyal to the president, TASS and Western news agencies reported on December 22 and 23. Up to seventeen people were reported killed, and more than fifty injured. Both sides reportedly deployed tanks, rockets, and machine guns. A deputy interior minister was wounded, and the mayor of Tbilisi and a prominent Gamsakhurdia supporter were taken hostage by the rebels. A Georgian presidential press release of December 22 called for international observers to investigate the situation.

Following a lull in fighting and a temporary cease-fire on December 26, clashes continued on December 27. Georgian First Deputy Health Minister Merab Kvitashvili told TASS on December 26 that the death toll stood at

42, with 268 people injured. Western news agencies quoted rebel leader Tengiz Kitovani as claiming that gunmen from Checheno-Ingushetia had arrived in Tbilisi to fight for Gamsakhurdia.

The same day rebel forces stormed the KGB headquarters in Tbilisi and freed several prominent political prisoners. A first round of talks between pro- and anti-Gamsakhurdia forces on December 28 resulted in a cease-fire. A joint call for Gamsakhurdia's resignation and the transfer of presidential powers to the republic's parliament was issued after a second round of talks the same day. Several senior Gamsakhurdia supporters defected to the opposition. Fighting then resumed on December 29, and troops loyal to Gamsakhurdia drove out opposition forces from the parliament building who had penetrated it the previous day. TASS reported on December 29 that the civilian population was fleeing from central Tbilisi.

Sporadic fighting continued in Tbilisi from December 30 to January 1. On December 30, Gamsakhurdia arrested his deputy defense minister, Nodar Georgadze, after the latter had insisted that Gamsakhurdia negotiate with the opposition.

South Ossetia Declares Independence

A session of the South Ossetian Oblast Soviet passed a resolution proclaiming the oblast's independence and calling upon the parliaments of the constituent republics of the former USSR to recognize it, TASS reported. In response to rumors of a threatened Georgian attack on the oblast capital, Tskhinvali, the parliament also created a republican Committee for Self-Defense, which ordered a general mobilization of all men and women between the ages of eighteen and sixty (*TASS*, December 23). The text of the order was also circulated in North Ossetia. It stated that refugees in North Ossetia had to return home immediately to defend their homeland, otherwise they would be regarded as deserters (*TASS*, December 26).

Moldavian Popular Front against Joining Commonwealth

Moldavian Popular Front Chairman Iurie Rosca told the BBC that Moldavian President Mircea Snegur's decision to join the Commonwealth had the negative effect of delaying Moldavia's reunification with Romania. In that interview, cited by TASS the same day, Rosca also condemned Snegur's policy for purportedly "seeking to keep Moldavia tied to a Slavic bloc." At a rally in Kishinev on December 22, 3,000 supporters of the popular front chanted slogans accusing Snegur of "treason," Moldovapres reported. The front also called for a general strike in the

The USSR in December, 1991

republic. It was not heeded, however, and only 200–400 demonstrators gathered in Kishinev on December 23 and 24. In response to the front's protests, Snegur urged the Moldavian parliament to expedite the adoption of a law on referendums and challenged the front to put the issue of reunification with Romania to a popular vote.

Border Problems

Huge crowds of travelers hoping to enter Poland from Ukraine led the Polish authorities to consider "very drastic measures," including the imposition of entry visas, Deputy Internal Affairs Minister Jerzy Zimowski reported at a press conference. On December 22, Ukrainian officials in the Lvov area imposed a ban on the export of fifty-six categories of goods, including alcohol and food, in an attempt to limit congestion at the border. According to PAP, Ukrainian officials admitted to their Polish counterparts that corruption was prevalent among Ukrainian customs and border security personnel. Informal trading at Polish markets by travelers from the east was also reported to have become a serious problem. Polish officials estimated that Soviet "tourists" returned home from Poland with about 1 billion dollars in 1991, despite the fact that the sale of dollars to foreigners was illegal.

_____ *Monday, December 23*

Soviet Money Supply Grows in 1991; New Bank Notes in 1992.

TASS quoted "reliable sources" in the USSR State Committee for Statistics as saying that the amount of money circulating in the Soviet economy had increased from 132 billion to 211 billion rubles during the first ten months of 1991. The rapid growth in the money supply was a major cause of the triple-digit inflation rocking the former Soviet republics. Viktor Gerashchenko, the head of the USSR State Bank, offered to resign on December 24, according to Reuters of that day. Deputy Chairman of the RSFSR Supreme Soviet Commission on the Budget, Plans, Taxes, and Prices Aleksandr Pochinok told Western agencies the same day that 500-ruble notes would go into circulation on December 27 and that 1,000-ruble notes would be introduced in March, 1992.

Russia and Poland Sign Agreements

During a one-day visit to Moscow, Deputy Prime Minister Lezsek Balcerowicz discussed the withdrawal of Soviet troops from Poland with RSFSR President Boris El'tsin. According to Western and Polish media, they agreed that the deadlines for the Soviet troop withdrawal set earlier had to be observed. Later, after talks with RSFSR Deputy Prime Minister Egor Gaidar, Balcerowicz said the two countries had decided to establish a special hard-currency trading zone for certain important commodities.

Poland and the RSFSR signed a trade agreement on December 24 whereby each side would offer "strategic" commodities worth 1.4 billion dollars. Poland was to provide Russia with coal and sulfur, 500 million dollars in food, and 400 million dollars in medicines, according to a report in *Gazeta Wyborcza* on December 27. In return, Russia was to supply Poland with natural gas and oil. These deliveries were expected to cover all Poland's natural gas needs and half its oil needs in 1992.

Tuesday, December 24

Russian-Ukrainian Economic Friction

"Serious" disagreements surfaced at the meeting in Moscow of representatives of member-states of the Commonwealth of Independent States, according to TASS. RSFSR First Deputy Prime Minister Gennadii Burbulis reportedly claimed that Russia's economic reform program had been adopted as the basis for Commonwealth reform, and he confirmed that most Russian prices would be freed on January 2. Ukraine objected to this date, proposing January 15 instead. Ukraine also complained that Russia continued to control the mint and that it was refusing to supply other states with enough bank notes to meet the increased demand for money expected when most prices and wages were freed.

Wednesday, December 25

Gorbachev Resigns

Bowing to the inevitable, Soviet President Mikhail Gorbachev announced his resignation in a grim twelve-minute address to the nation broadcast on Central Television on December 25. He defended his reform course, saying that he had accomplished the historic task of leading a totalitarian country towards democracy. But he also stressed that he remained committed to the idea of a unitary multinational state and could not agree with the dissolution of the Soviet Union. He nevertheless promised to support the Commonwealth. Gorbachev appealed to his successors to continue on the path to democratization.

RSFSR President Boris El'tsin humiliated Gorbachev by depriving him of his state-owned Moscow apartment

The USSR in December, 1991

shortly after his resignation speech, Postfactum reported El'tsin decreed that Gorbachev's apartment be privatized. In a final blow, the Russian president moved into Gorbachev's office in the Kremlin on December 27, despite the fact that Gorbachev had supposedly been given several days to clean out his desk, *Izvestia* reported.

El'tsin Takes Control of Strategic Nuclear Arsenal

Immediately after announcing his resignation as president of the USSR, Mikhail Gorbachev handed the codes for the launch of nuclear weapons to RSFSR President Boris El'tsin (*TASS*, December 25). El'tsin stressed that he would have the only nuclear key but added that he could not fire the weapons without authorization from the presidents of Belorussia, Ukraine, and Kazakhstan. The same day, the RSFSR parliament ratified the Alma-Ata agreement on the creation of a joint military command of independent states. El'tsin also assumed formal command over the fractured Soviet Armed Forces, Western and Soviet sources reported on December 25. In a speech to the RSFSR Supreme Soviet, El'tsin emphasized that he now exercised primary control over the Soviet nuclear arsenal. The same day, the RSFSR Supreme Soviet ratified the Agreement on Joint Measures Regarding Nuclear Weapons signed by the leaders of the four republics possessing nuclear arms.

Russia Takes Soviet Seat in UN

El'tsin informed the UN secretary-general of Russia's assumption of the Soviet Union's seat in the UN, Western agencies reported. The republican leaders had agreed to this transfer of representation during the meeting in Alma-Ata on December 21. Ukraine and Belorussia had been members of the United Nations since 1945, and the Baltic States joined in September, 1991.

Controversial Russian Press Law Amended

At a meeting with editors of Russian newspapers, El'tsin promised to veto the republican press law adopted by the Russian Supreme Soviet a few days earlier (*Russian Television*, December 25). The Russian law was widely considered to be "three steps back" in comparison with the all-Union press law. While the latter required journalists to reveal their sources only to the courts, the Russian law required that journalists name their sources to prosecutors and the police. The law also allowed the police to search the offices of newspapers and journals and forbade secret filming.

El'tsin's veto turned out not to be necessary, since on December 27 the RSFSR Supreme Soviet amended the press law. The parliament repealed the passages ordering journalists to reveal their sources to the police and banning secret filming.

Recognition of Commonwealth States

Following the announcement by Russia, Belorussia, and Ukraine on December 8 of the creation of a Commonwealth of Independent States, a number of foreign countries moved to recognize the independence of individual former Soviet republics. On December 16, Turkey recognized all the former Soviet republics as independent states, Western agencies reported. On December 19, Sweden officially recognized Russia, Belorussia, and Ukraine (*TASS*, December 19), while Norway, which had already recognized the Russian Federation, was reluctant to extend recognition to other states until the Soviet Union had been officially dissolved.

The process of international recognition of the former Soviet republics was further accelerated by the meeting in Alma-Ata on December 21, at which eight more Soviet republics joined the Commonwealth of Independent States. The United States and the European Community (EC) announced that they would coordinate their recognition of the new independent states in the Commonwealth, while Romania officially recognized Belorussia. Bucharest had earlier recognized Russia, Armenia, and Moldavia (Western agencies, December 21). The same day, Afghanistan recognized Russia, Azerbaijan, Kazakhstan, Kirgizia, Tajikistan, Turkmenistan, and Uzbekistan; and on December 24, Belorussia and Ukraine were added to the list.

In anticipation of Gorbachev's resignation as USSR president on December 25, several countries extended recognition to some of the Commonwealth states. Iran recognized Russia and the six Muslim-populated republics. Britain, France, Germany, and Italy all recognized Russia as the legal successor to the Soviet Union, while the EC made a similar announcement immediately following Gorbachev's speech. Israel also announced its recognition of all former Soviet republics (Western agencies, December 25).

The day after Gorbachev's resignation the tide of recognition became a flood. The United States announced its intention to establish diplomatic relations with Russia, Ukraine, Armenia, Kazakhstan, Belorussia, and Kirgizia and acknowledged the independence of Moldavia, Turkmenistan, Azerbaijan, Tajikistan, Uzbekistan, and Georgia. Canada said it would establish immediate ties with Russia and Ukraine while recognizing the independence of the other states. Germany also confirmed its intention to establish diplomatic relations with Russia and was expected to recognize Ukraine as well. A German Foreign Ministry spokesman said that recognition of the other nine republics would follow when these states fulfilled the EC's conditions for recognition. Cuba also recognized all the former Soviet republics (Western agencies, December 26). TASS also reported that Belorussia had been recognized by Hungary, Mongolia, Bulgaria, and Lithuania.

On December 27, North Korea joined the world community in recognizing all the independent states of the Commonwealth. Japan and Greece acknowledged Russia as the legal successor to the USSR. Czechoslovakia recognized Russia, Belorussia, and Ukraine; and Albania expressed readiness to establish diplomatic relations with Russia and the other Commonwealth members. China also announced recognition of the Commonwealth member-states and Georgia and said the Chinese ambassador to the Soviet Union would switch his accreditation to Russia (Western agencies, December 27).

On December 28, Japan recognized the independence of the other ten former Soviet republics that signed the Commonwealth Agreement, having recognized Russia the day before. Also on December 28, Italy recognized Ukraine and said it would recognize the other republics once they met the criteria set by the EC, including respect for minorities, human rights, and internal borders. Syria and Bangladesh also announced recognition of the eleven Commonwealth member-states (Western agencies, December 28). On December 30, South Korea extended diplomatic recognition to the other ten Commonwealth member-states, having recognized Russia already. The same day Morocco and Oman made similar announcements (Western agencies, December 30). On December 31, the EC announced that its twelve member-states would recognize all CIS members except Kirgizia and Tajikistan. The EC repeated its willingness to recognize Kirgizia and Tajikistan once they had given assurances that they would comply with EC guidelines on such issues as human rights, disarmament, and nuclear nonproliferation (Western agencies, December 31).

Ban on Tajik Communist Party Lifted

The Tajik Supreme Soviet removed the ban it had placed on the activities of the republican Communist Party in October pending investigation of the party's actions during the August coup. The conservative legislature declared that no evidence had been found linking the Tajik Communist Party with the coup (*TASS*, December 25). The ban was first instituted in September by the chairman of the Supreme Soviet; its revocation shortly afterwards was one factor that provoked large anti-Communist demonstrations that continued until the ban was reimposed. But opposition forces in the republic suffered a setback with the November election of former Communist Party chief Rakhmon Nabiev as republican president.

Thursday, December 26

USSR Supreme Soviet Symbolically Dissolves Itself

Initially resisting the implications of the Alma-Ata Agreement, the USSR Supreme Soviet refused to dissolve itself until the republican parliaments had ratified the Commonwealth Agreement (*Radio Moscow*, December 24). Following Gorbachev's resignation on December 25, however, the deputies were left with no choice but to resign. Only about sixty deputies gathered in the parliament's upper chamber, the Council of the Republics, on December 26 to vote for its dissolution, far below the necessary quorum in the 173-seat chamber (*Radio Moscow*, December 26).

RSFSR Changes Its Name

The RSFSR Supreme Soviet voted to change the official name of the RSFSR to the Russian Federation (or Russia), Radio Moscow reported. The new title removed the words "Soviet" and "Socialist." The RSFSR was the last of the republics of the former Soviet Union to alter its official title.

Russian Constitutional Court Concerned about Violations

The Russian Federation's Constitutional Court expressed concern about violations of the republican constitution and laws, Russian Television reported on December 26. As examples, the judges cited the new republican law on the media, as well as El'tsin's edict merging the former USSR and RSFSR ministries of internal affairs and security services. The court also objected to the change in the republic's name on the grounds that only the Congress of People's Deputies, not the Supreme Soviet, was entitled to change the Russian Constitution.

Armenian Appeal for Nagorno-Karabakh

The Armenian parliament adopted an appeal to the other states of the Commonwealth to take immediate action to safeguard the population of Nagorno-Karabakh as Soviet troops withdrew. It characterized the situation there as "explosive" (*TASS*, December 26). El'tsin announced the

The USSR in December, 1991

withdrawal of Soviet troops on December 25, but Radio Rossii subsequently reported that it had been halted and that those troops still in the oblast would remain there until the leaders of the Commonwealth states met in Minsk on December 30.

Disagreement on Defense

Two days of talks in Moscow and a visit to Kiev (December 26) by USSR Defense Minister Evgenii Shaposhnikov failed to resolve sharp differences among members of the Commonwealth of Independent States (CIS) on security issues. Shaposhnikov told Russian television on December 27 that most CIS members had rejected his concept of a "unified" army in favor of, at best, a looser association of "joint" armed forces. The primary stumbling block was the determination of Ukraine, Moldavia, and Azerbaijan to create national armies. A Ukrainian official said Shaposhnikov had urged the retention of unified forces for at least a five-year transitional period but that he had left Kiev "disappointed."

Privatization Program for Russia Approved

The Russian government approved a privatization program for 1992, according to TASS and Interfax. Russian Minister of Science, Higher Education, and Technical Policy Boris Saltykov listed the following categories of enterprises: establishments to be privatized in 1992, including stores, restaurants, and small workshops; firms exempted from privatization, including banks, railways, airlines, and some armaments factories; and enterprises that may only be privatized with prior permission, including plants manufacturing medicines, alcohol, tobacco products, and baby food. Saltykov indicated that the privatization of Russia's economy would take three to five years to complete, and he estimated that revenue from privatization would amount to some 92 billion rubles in 1992 and about 300 billion rubles in 1993.

Estonian-Uzbek Agreement Signed

Estonia signed an economic and trade accord with Uzbekistan, BNS reported. Uzbekistan agreed to send Estonia nearly 18,000 tons of cotton in return for Estonian manufactured goods and paper products. The contracting parties would conclude a separate agreement in the event that either state introduced its own currency.

Treaty with Estonia Ratified by Russia

After nearly one year's delay, the Russian Supreme Soviet ratified the interstate treaty concluded in January, 1991, with Estonia, BNS reported on December 27. The parliament called on the government to begin talks with Estonia to resolve questions of borders and citizens' rights as well as other issues not addressed in the treaty. The Estonian Supreme Council had ratified the document in the spring of 1991.

Friday, December 27

Luk'yanov Not a Coup Plotter

The Russian parliamentary commission investigating the August coup told a press conference that Anatolii Luk'yanov, former USSR Supreme Soviet chairman, was not one of the original coup plotters. He would only have been given a key role if the coup had been successful (*TASS*, December 27).

Kuznetsov Joins Northern Fleet

The ship *Admiral of the Fleet of the Soviet Union Kuznetsov* (ex-*Leonid Brezhnev*, ex-*Tbilisi*) joined the Soviet Northern Fleet. A TASS report the following day said that the ship had docked at a specially built wharf in Murmansk. The USSR Ministry of Defense denied charges that the *Kuznetsov* was being moved out of the Black Sea to keep it out of the hands of the Ukrainian government, which had been reported to have taken over the shipyard where the ship had been built and had plans to seize the Black Sea Fleet to form its own navy (*Radio Moscow World Service*, in English, December 6). Interfax reported on December 27 that Ukraine had protested against the relocation of the *Kuznetsov*.

Saturday, December 28

Housing Problems for Withdrawing Troops

The commander of Soviet Forces in Germany, Colonel General Matvei Burlakov, said in *Die Welt* of December 28 that construction of housing by German firms for withdrawing Soviet troops was significantly behind schedule. In remarks summarized by Western agencies, Burlakov said none of the 36,000 apartments slated to be built had been received by the military. A government official in Germany said that the collapse of the Soviet Union had complicated plans for the construction and location of housing in a number of republics.

Kravchuk on Ukrainian Independence

Prior to the meeting of the Commonwealth of Independent States (CIS) in Minsk on December 30, Ukrainian

The USSR in December, 1991

President Leonid Kravchuk outlined Ukraine's priorities in the domestic and foreign spheres. He told Ukrinform that Ukraine intended to pursue its own independent foreign policy and would not agree to the CIS representing it at the international level. He noted with pride that Ukraine had been "the force" that had "destroyed the [Soviet] empire." Kravchuk explained that, as a democratic independent European state, Ukraine wanted to become a member of the European Community and was also especially interested in developing ties with countries where large numbers of Ukrainians had settled.

Following the Minsk meeting, Kravchuk told a news conference on December 30 that "no decisions interfering in the domestic and foreign policy" of the CIS states had been made, TASS reported. On their return to Kiev both Kravchuk and Ukrainian Foreign Minister Anatolii Zlenko said that Ukraine had received the go-ahead to create its own armed forces as of January 3, 1992, Radio Kiev reported on December 30 and 31. Kravchuk, who acknowledged that the negotiations in Minsk "had not been easy," also stated that Ukraine could not agree that only the Russian tricolor be raised over the embassies of the former USSR and said he had gained acceptance of his view that each of the members of the CIS had a right to a portion of "the former Soviet Union's property in other countries."

Land Privatization Decree

TASS and Interfax reported that Russian Federation President Boris El'tsin had issued a decree on the privatization of agricultural land. The decree called for the rapid reorganization of kolkhozes and sovkhozes and for the transfer of much of their land to private farmers before the spring planting. The measure apparently did not provide for a completely free market in land: it allowed only farmers (not the general public) to buy and sell land within prescribed limits. Sovkhozes were to be turned into holding companies, while kolkhozes were to become genuine cooperatives from which members would be free to withdraw their share of the assets. This was expected to lead to the dissolution of many sovkhozes and kolkhozes, and intense opposition from farm managers and rural bureaucrats was likely. According to a report in *The New York Times* of December 29, local officials could, however, be fined up to three months pay for obstructing land redistribution, and land reform commissions had been authorized to overturn local ordinances that impeded the privatization process.

Sunday, December 29

El'tsin on Russian National Guard and Military Budget

Russian Federation President Boris El'tsin announced that Russia would create a National Guard of between 30,000 and 40,000 men on the basis of Russian military traditions, TASS reported. According to *The Washington Post* of December 30, El'tsin also said that Russia would cut back sharply on spending for defense procurement in 1992.

Armenian-Russian Summit

At a one-day Armenian-Russian summit in Moscow, Russian Federation President Boris El'tsin and Armenian President Levon Ter-Petrossyan signed a treaty on friendship, cooperation, and mutual assistance that paid particular attention to human rights and economic cooperation, TASS reported.

El'tsin's Address to Russia

Russian Federation President Boris El'tsin appealed to Russians in a nationwide broadcast on Russian Television on December 29 to "start living in a new way." El'tsin blamed the legacy of communism for the country's problems and stressed that the forthcoming economic reforms, while painful and unpopular, were unavoidable. He appealed for endurance and promised that improvement would come by the summer of 1992. He congratulated his fellow countrymen on avoiding a civil war such as the one in Yugoslavia.

Azerbaijan Holds Referendum on Independence

A referendum was held in Azerbaijan to evaluate popular support for the law on Azerbaijani independence passed in October, TASS reported. On January 8, 1992, TASS reported that 3.75 million people out of a total population of 7 million had participated in the referendum and that more than 99 percent of them had voted in favor of Azerbaijani independence.

Election and Referendum in Uzbekistan

A presidential election and referendum on independence was held in Uzbekistan, Soviet and Western agencies reported. Contestants for the presidency were the incumbent, Islam Karimov, backed by the Popular-Democratic (formerly Communist) Party, and the poet Muhammad Salih, chairman of the small "Erk" Democratic Party. The opposition Popular Front, "Birlik," was not allowed to nominate a candidate. In a second ballot voters were asked to vote for or against Uzbekistan's independence, which was declared by the republic's Supreme Soviet on

The USSR in December, 1991

August 31. The results of the presidential ballot released by UzTag-TASS gave Karimov 86 percent of the vote, while Salih received slightly more than 12 percent. Voter turnout was high, with almost 95 percent of eligible voters participating. Independence was approved by more than 98 percent of those voting.

Russia banned the export of sixty categories of foodstuffs and consumer goods (*TASS* and Western agencies, January 9). The order for the ban was signed on December 29 by Russian First Deputy Prime Minister Gennadii Burbulis, and was to go into effect on January 10. The justification given was that "a few states, former members of the Soviet Union, have imposed restrictions on exports of consumer goods to the Russian Federation." The ban would not apply to members of the Commonwealth of Independent States that had not placed restrictions on trade with Russia. The states involved were not identified.

Ban on Export of Some Russian Goods

Monday, December 30

A meeting of the leaders of the new Commonwealth of Independent States (CIS) opened in Minsk to decide the future shape of the association and the direction that it would take. The leaders of the eleven states signed nine agreements, and the heads of government signed a further six, Soviet media reported. In addition to agreements on military matters, these included a temporary accord on establishing the Council of Heads of State and the Council of Heads of Government as the governing bodies of the CIS and agreements on the space program, the Aral Sea, Chernobyl', earthquake damage in Armenia, transport and tariffs, aviation, and the distribution of food bought with foreign credits.

CIS Leaders Hold Summit Meeting in Minsk

Although an accord was reached on command over strategic forces, security policy proved to be the most contentious issue at the Minsk meeting on December 30 (*TASS*, December 30). Republican leaders eventually signed an agreement on armed forces and border troops that confirmed the right of each member-state to create its own army. It also established a Council of Defense Ministers (subordinated to the Council of Heads of State) to oversee security issues. The agreement was clearly a concession to Ukraine, Moldavia, and Azerbaijan on the

CIS Leaders Stumble over Unified Army

921

issue of control over general purpose forces: each of these states was determined to create its own national army. At a press conference carried by Central Television on December 31, El'tsin suggested that the general purpose forces of the other eight republics would remain under a single command.

Minsk Agreement on Strategic Forces

The leaders of all eleven members of the Commonwealth of Independent States signed an agreement on strategic forces. According to the text, released by TASS on December 31, this agreement dealt with far more than just nuclear weapons and applied to virtually all the former Soviet Armed Forces except for ground forces. A decision to use nuclear weapons could be made by the president of the Russian Federation "in agreement" with the leaders of the other three republics where strategic nuclear weapons were based—Belorussia, Kazakhstan, and Ukraine—and "in consultation" with the leaders of the remaining republics. In an interview published by TASS on December 31, Ukrainian President Leonid Kravchuk said that he would have "special technical control" to prevent anyone using nuclear weapons on Ukrainian soil. Like the earlier nuclear agreement signed in Alma-Ata, the Minsk agreement spoke of the eventual removal of all nuclear weapons from Belorussia and Ukraine but was silent about those in Kazakhstan.

El'tsin Says No New Threat to US from Russia

Russian Federation President Boris El'tsin rejected a statement by US Secretary of Defense Richard Cheney that Russia was still producing strategic missiles for use against the United States (*TASS*, December 30). El'tsin stressed that Russia would abide by the START agreement and that by 1994 Ukraine and Belorussia would, with the assistance of Washington and Moscow, have destroyed all the nuclear weapons now on their soil.

Shevardnadze Suggests Gorbachev Join Movement for Democratic Reforms

USSR Foreign Minister Eduard Shevardnadze suggested that former USSR President Mikhail Gorbachev join the Movement for Democratic Reforms set up by Shevardnadze, Aleksandr Yakovlev, and other former Gorbachev associates in the summer of 1991. Shevardnadze told *Corriere della Sera* on December 30 that, although Russian President Boris El'tsin at present advocated democracy, one should not "construct a social system based on the qualities or flaws of men who are currently in power." Shevardnadze added that presidents could change.

The USSR in December, 1991

Tuesday, December 31

Addressing the people of Moldavia on December 31, Moldavian President Mircea Snegur said Moldavia "will cooperate [with the CIS] only in those areas where it is advantageous to do so and will participate only in those structures that do not impair Moldavia's sovereignty," Moldovapres reported on January 1. Snegur also renewed his insistence that Moldavia reserved the right to seek "to join other communities of states" (meaning the EC).

Moldavia Joins CIS with Reservations

The _Süddeutsche Zeitung_ reported on December 31 that the State Bank of Iran planned to open a branch in Ashkhabad. No date was given. The same report, which quoted the vice governor of Khorasan Province, added that the railroad link that was to be built as one of the first major cooperative ventures involving several Central Asian republics would connect with Khorasan. That province had already worked out a trade agreement with Turkmenistan.

Iranian-Turkmen Relations

Colonel General Dmitrii Volkogonov told Russian Television on December 31 that until 1989 he had headed the Psychological Warfare Administration of the former Main Political Administration of the Soviet army. Volkogonov, who is the author of books on Stalin and Trotsky, also said that he now considered himself a member of the democratic camp. He stressed that, as chairman of the Russian Federation committee charged with monitoring the transfer of Party and KGB archives to the Russian State Archive Administration, he deemed it his duty to protect from destruction documents concerning the foreign and internal policy of the Soviet state.

Volkogonov Was in Charge of Psychological Warfare

Name Index

Abalkin, Leonid, 196, 256, 322, 430
Abarinov, Vladimir, 205
Abdulatipov, Ramazan, 68, 329
Abdurazakov, Magomed, 759
Abisala, Aleksandras, 460–461
Abuladze, Tengiz, 35
Achalov, Vladislav, 627, 651
Advadze, Valerian, 363
Afanas'ev, Viktor, 770
Afanas'ev, Yurii, 288, 425, 442, 528, 768
   criticisms of reactionaries by, 42–43
   and demonstrations, 184, 211, 681
   and El'tsin, 762–763, 785
Agaev, Manaf, 306
Agamaliev, Fazail, 84
Agamirov, Karen, 151
Aganbegyan, Abel, 256
Ageev, Genii, 619, 690–691
Ahmedova, Elmira, 148
Aho, Esko, 533
Airikyan, Paruir, 306, 540, 742
Akaev, Askar
   and coup, 563, 572, 609
   and departification, 580, 586
   on economic issues, 80, 286, 538, 542
   foreign affairs, 115, 762, 898
   Gorbachev support for, 843
   and government restructuring, 52
   and Kazakh agreement, 124
   and land law, 399
   on political persecution, 637, 668
   presidential election, 733
   and RSFSR agreement, 486
   and Union issues, 286, 610, 675, 755–756
Akbulut, Yildirim, 82, 136
Akhmadov, Daud, 786
Akhmadov, Khusain, 713
Akhmadzhan, Kazi, 114
Akhmatov, Kazat, 100
Akhmetov, Aziratali, 825
Akhmetov, Nizemetdin, 194
Akhromeev, Sergei, 38, 89–90, 122, 416, 634
   and foreign affairs, 22, 43, 114, 261, 416
   and Moldavia, 174–175, 214
   suicide of, 598

Akhunov, Pulat, 502
Akihito, Emperor, 270
Aksenoka, Rita, 175–176
Aksyuchits, Viktor, 296, 663
Aleinikov, Anatolii, 737
Aleksandrov, Valentin, 436
Alekseev, Anatolii, 165
Alekseev, Sergei, 65, 69–70, 112, 409, 495, 730, 752–753
Aleksii II, Patriarch, 190, 375, 462, 818
   and coup, 560–561
   and Middle East, 221, 715–716
   and religious holidays, 13, 250
   and Roman Catholic Church, 489, 778
Alibegov, Tomas, 180, 889
Aliev, Geidar, 482, 636
Aliev, Gulam, 691
Alimzhanov, Anuar, 749, 772
Ali-Zade, Araz, 542
Ali-Zade, Zardusht, 542, 626
Alksnis, Viktor, 55, 134, 865, 909
   pressure on Gorbachev by, 57, 62, 68, 93, 278, 525
   and coup, 561
Allison, Graham, 403
Almazov, Sergei, 720
Amanbaev, Dzhumgalbek, 250, 290
Amanova, Maral, 573
Ambartsumov, Evgenii, 539, 662
Ametistov, Ernst, 172
Andreeva, Nina, 68, 407, 468, 793, 802, 814
Andreotti, Giulio, 353–354, 527, 676
Andriessen, Frans, 47, 392, 520, 813
Andropov, Yurii, 225, 584
Anikeev, Anatolii, 712
Antonchyk, Sergei, 354
Antonov, Vadim, 246
Antonov, Viktor, 357, 365
Aqazadeh-Kho'i, Gholam Reza, 407
Arafat, Yasser, 101, 325
Arbatov, Georgii, 22, 293
Arkhipov, Vladimir, 54, 887
Arsanov, Akhmed, 714, 783, 784
Arsanukaev, Iles, 713
Artemov, Vyacheslav, 448

925

Name Index

Arutyunyan, Gagik, 844
Arystanbekova, Akmaral, 908
Arzamastsev, Anatolii, 461
Asankulov, Dzhumabek, 572
Asatiani, Akaki, 266, 639, 859
Ashurov, Dadodzhon, 147
Aslakhanov, Aslanbek, 784
Aslonov, Kadriddin, 666, 671
Aslund, Anders, 839
Assad, Hafiz al-, 324, 325, 715
Astaf'ev, Mikhail, 663
Astakhov, Evgenii, 5
Attali, Jacques, 189, 395, 771
Atwood, Donald, 773
Avdevsky, Andrei, 758
Aziz, Tariq, 22, 118, 119–120
Azubalis, Audrius, 338, 340, 626

Bab'ev, Vladimir, 138–139
Baburin, Sergei, 740
Bad'zo, Yurii, 159
Bagirov, Tofik, 84
Bahrov, Mykola, 452
Bairamova, Favzia, 335
Bakatin, Vadim
 and coup, 657
 and Estonia, 215, 616
 KGB appointment, 591
 and KGB archives, 642
 and KGB reorganization, 598, 605–606, 614, 619, 638, 648, 755
 on leaks to press, 718
 and miners' strike, 154
 and Moscow administration, 208
 politics, *perestroika*, and, 39, 279, 386, 627, 680
 and RSFSR presidency, 327, 351, 374, 397
 and security and defense councils, 177, 618, 797, 836, 855
 and Wallenberg case, 635
Baker, James
 and Afghanistan, 649–650
 and arms control and nuclear weapons, 58, 192, 292–293, 505, 895, 896
 and Baltic republics, 58, 192, 224, 318, 415, 653–654
 and Middle East, 22, 58, 325, 192, 292–293, 508
 and rescue of Soviet citizens in Somalia, 7

 and US aid, 65–66, 367
 and US-Soviet bilateral agreements, 509
Baklanov, Oleg, 290, 554, 555, 573, 583, 667
Balagurov, Yurii, 299, 663
Balayan, Zori, 728–729
Balcerowicz, Lezsek, 911–912
Baldisius, Vilius, 795
Balebanov, Al'bert, 88
Barannikov, Viktor, 249, 591, 759, 777, 797, 836, 904, 905
Baranov, Lev, 57–58
Baron, Enrique, 267
Barshatly, Valeg, 639
Bar'yakhtar, Viktor, 353
Baryshev, Aleksandr, 832
Basanov, Vladimir, 749
Batenin, Gelii, 889
Batsanov, Sergei, 358
Beckman, Klaus, 321
Begun, Iosif, 757
Bekeris, Juris, 576
Belaev, Aleksandr, 449
Belokop, Valerii, 779
Belonogov, Aleksandr, 34, 38, 81–82, 172–173, 249, 652
Belonogov, Anatolii, 652
Belous, Grigorii, 166
Belousov, Igor', 18, 400
Belousova, Lyudmila, 827
Belov, Vasilii, 865
Belov, Yurii, 522
Belozertsev, Sergei, 434–435
Bérégovoy, Pierre, 640
Berezhnoi, Nikolai, 287
Berezin, Oleg, 348
Bergs-Bergmanis, Alfreds, 633, 658–659
Berzins, Indulis, 875–876
Bessmertnykh, Aleksandr
 and arms control, 505
 and Cabinet of Ministers, 138
 and Cambodia, 288
 and China, 228, 336
 and coup, 574, 579, 591–592, 626, 657
 election of, 32
 and Europe, 114, 131, 380
 and foreign-policy think tank, 690
 and France, 102
 and Germany, 195, 201, 400
 and Great Britain, 168, 202
 and Gulf crisis, 119, 121, 122

NAME INDEX

and Japan, 48
and Middle East, 82, 112, 324–325, 370–371, 508
and Poland, 245
republican foreign policy and, 112, 206
and Romania, 209
and Security Council, 176
and Syria, 79, 244
and US, 58, 192, 292–293, 488, 509
and Yugoslavia, 471–472
in Yugoslavia and Greece, 254
Bezaziev, Lentun, 418
Bichkov, Ivan, 103
Bickauskas, Egidius, 168
Bielecki, Jan Krzysztof, 245, 366, 728
Bigarov, Yurii, 281
Bikenin, Nail, 599–600
Birulis, Kostas, 24
Biryukova, Aleksandra, 400
Bisers, Ilmars, 262, 287, 510–511, 753
Bjoerk, Anders, 428–429
Blokhin, Yurii, 214, 234, 256, 277, 299–300, 408–409, 426, 471, 492
Blokhotin, Vladimir, 254–255
Blokhus, Bjoern, 751
Blumbergs, Ziedonis, 666
Bobkov, Filip, 20, 93
Bobylev, Aleksandr, 164
Bochaev, Gennadii, 794
Bocharov, Mikhail, 122
Bogdanov, Petr, 82, 207–208
Bojars, Juris, 861
Bokan, Yurii, 853
Bokser, Vladimir, 343, 658
Boldin, Valerii, 177, 554, 585, 754
Boldyrev, Mikhail, 822
Boldyrev, Yurii, 154
Bondarenko, Andrei, 426
Bondarev, Yurii, 147, 492, 541, 751
Bonner, Elena, 32, 346, 443, 528, 709
Boren, David, 211
Borodin, Oleg, 573
Borovoi, Konstantin, 686
Borovsky, Greg, 507
Botha, Pik, 807
Botha, Roelof, 142
Boucher, Richard, 752
Bovin, Aleksandr, 35, 799
Brady, Nicholas, 664–665
Brazauskas, Algirdas, 282

Brezhnev, Vladimir, 137
Bronfman, Edgar, 19, 649
Brumel', Aleksei, 313
Bucataru, Sorin, 13
Budaev, Choi Dorzhi, 164
Buka, Stanislav, 199
Bukovsky, Vladimir, 269, 642
Bukreev, Yurii, 858
Bunich, Pavel, 443, 498, 627, 686
Burbulis, Gennadii, 150, 721
and coup, 575
criticisms of, 706, 903
and economic reform, 787, 851, 912
and foreign affairs, 775, 838
and interrepublican issues, 882, 906, 921
RSFSR government positions, 487, 797
and Union treaty, 738, 846
Burca, Sergiu, 13
Buresova, Dagmar, 330
Burlakov, Matvei, 158, 294, 433–434, 918
Burlatsky, Fedor, 69–70, 465, 625
Burokevicius, Mykolas, 302–303, 422, 595, 904
Bush, George
and aid, 367, 394, 621, 678
and Armenia, 815
and arms control, 696, 701
and Baltic republics, 25, 224, 318, 513, 520, 547, 630, 647
and coup, 569, 580, 813
and El'tsin, 412, 883
and Georgia, 512, 530
and Gorbachev, 893
Gulf crisis and Middle East, 119, 120, 371
and Kirgizia, 762
and RSFSR, 397
and Shevardnadze, 319
and Soviet relations, 58, 269, 382–383, 507–508, 509–510, 773
and Ukraine, 517–518, 682
Bush, K., 75
Butkevicius, Audrius, 183, 203–204, 208, 339, 804
Butov, E., 802
Buzgalin, Aleksandr, 498
Buzulukov, Yurii, 274
Byambasuren, Dashiyn, 96
Bychkov, Evgenii, 824
Bykau, Vasil', 214

927

Camdessus, Michel, 367, 715, 892
Carlsson, Ingvar, 386
Carnogursky, Jan, 331
Castro, Fidel, 448–449, 509–510, 669–670, 818
Cepaitis, Virgilius, 845
Chanturia, Giorgi, 124, 645
Chapkin, Lev, 65
Chaplin, Boris, 652
Chastelain, John de, 328
Chebotarev, Gennadii, 244
Chekhoev, Anatolii, 162
Chemykh, Colonel, 565
Cheney, Richard, 922
Cheremnykh, Gennadii, 417
Chernavin, Vladimir, 499, 792
Chernenko, Konstantin, 173
Chernichenko, Yurii, 136, 197, 615
Chernousenko, Vladimir, 274
Chernovainov, Vyacheslav, 137, 138
Chernyaev, Anatolii, 650–651
Chernyshov, Yevhen, 118
Cheshenko, Nikolai, 238
Chirakabze, Archil, 227
Chirtoaca, Nicolae, 264, 834–835, 872
Chizik, Yurii, 353
Chornovil, Vyacheslav, 69, 518, 623, 815, 862
Christophersen, Henning, 701
Chubais, Anatolii, 463
Chubais, Igor', 85
Chukhalntsev, Igor', 822
Churaev, Evgenii, 220
Churilov, Lev, 869
Churkin, Vitalii
 and appointments, 859
 and arms sales, 404
 and Baltic republics, 26–27, 716–717
 and China, 428
 and East European Communists, 223
 and Ethiopia, 380
 and Foreign Ministry reorganization, 652, 653, 769–770
 and France, 102–103
 and Gulf crisis, 22, 34, 38, 43, 44–45, 120
 and INF treaty, 492–493
 and Iran, 112, 173
 and Iraqi Kurds, 254
 and Japan, 217
 and Latvian-Danish agreements, 203
 and NATO rapid deployment force, 450
 and South Africa, 142
 and Turkey, 185
 and US, 192, 508
Clark, Joe, 274
Costas, Ion, 624, 683
Costin, Nicolae, 424–425
Cotler, Irwin, 757
Cresson, Edith, 433
Cuplinskas, Saulius, 854

Danilov-Danilyants, Viktor, 869
Dashichev, Vyacheslav, 158
Daukshis, Valentin, 411
Deinekin, Petr, 627
Delors, Jacques, 298, 418
Dementei, Nikolai, 25, 73, 503, 602, 664
Demin, V., 718
Denisov, Yurii, 638
Deryabin, Yurii, 396, 631, 652
Dienstbier, Jiri, 35
Dimanis, Sergei, 165–166, 535, 608, 779
Dinevics, Janis, 840, 875, 893
Dmitrievsky, Anatol, 446
Dobravolskas, Algis, 473
Dobrovol'sky, Gennadii, 638
Doev, Kazbek, 776
Doguzhiev, Vitalii, 31, 73, 151, 210, 291, 574, 613
Dole, Robert, 33, 367
Dolin, Veniamin, 37
Domljan, Zarko, 523
Do Muoi, 322
Donii, Oles', 19
Doroshenko, Viktor, 45
Drach, Ivan, 518
Dregger, Alfred, 416
Drosdov, Aleksandr, 864
Druc, Mircea, 12, 135, 183, 355–356, 612
Dubcek, Alexander, 330, 346
Dubinin, Vyacheslav, 36
Dubinin, Yurii, 832
Dubynin, Viktor, 259, 370
Duchacek, Rudolf, 29
Duda, Janis, 517
Dudaev, Dzhakhar, 710, 711, 712, 713, 714, 783–786, 861
Dudnik, Vladimir, 847
Dumas, Roland, 102–103, 355, 402, 608
Dunaev, Andrei, 709–710

Name Index

Dunaev, Eduard, 824
Durdinets, Vasyl, 679, 805
Durnev, Vyacheslav, 146
Dzasokhov, Aleksandr, 8, 44, 55, 67, 79, 117
Dzerzhinsky, Feliks, 584

Eagleburger, Lawrence, 280
Efimov, Nikolai, 68, 394–395, 585–586
Egorov, Vladimir, 112, 686
Elisarov, Boris, 662
Elleman-Jensen, Uffe, 203
El'tsin, Boris
  agriculture and food, 21, 349, 919
  appointments by, 650, 802, 803, 833, 906
  and Armenian-Azerbaijani conflict, 307, 668, 709, 916–917
  and autonomous republics, 133, 215, 329, 619, 702, 738–739
  and Baltic republics, 26, 42, 46, 340, 419, 478, 505, 514, 601, 885
  and Checheno-Ingushetia, 712, 713, 783–784, 861
  and Chernobyl' disaster, 292
  and Commonwealth agreement, 880, 881, 886, 888, 922
  and RSFSR Congress of People's Deputies, 222–223, 237, 350
  and coup, 557, 558–559, 560, 563, 564, 567–568, 575, 577–578, 580
  and CPSU, 178, 257, 551–552, 796
  criticisms of, 41, 62, 68, 76, 89–90, 110, 251, 400, 469, 644, 658, 685, 694, 703, 762–763, 785, 844
  and Democratic Party of Communists of Russia, 529
  and departification, 483–485, 583, 598
  and dismantling of central government, 578, 675, 721, 726, 769–770, 823, 899, 904
  and Economic Treaty, 702, 745
  economy and economic reform, 110, 247–248, 287, 342, 534, 767–769, 795, 823, 827, 836, 898
  and education, 464
  and financial scandal, 243–244
  and financial sector, 613–614, 841
  foreign affairs, 14, 185, 267–268, 272, 317, 330–331, 398, 428, 517, 687, 775, 830, 838, 905, 911–912
  and funding central government, 6, 860
  and Gorbachev, 54, 116, 126–128, 141, 267, 327, 486, 495, 613, 883, 893, 912–913
  and interrrepublican relations, 31, 160–161, 486, 800, 862, 892, 920
  interviews, speeches, and television addresses, 212, 313–314, 391, 920
  and Jewish leaders, 19
  justice system, 637, 668, 737
  on Kaliningrad, 95–96
  and KGB, 90, 105, 316, 481–482, 852
  and media, 23, 29, 91, 193, 332, 391, 579, 611, 643, 651, 913
  and medicine imports, 884–885
  and miners' strike, 153, 157, 231, 233, 303
  and Movement for Democratic Reforms, 442
  and Novocherkassk memorial, 376
  and nuclear weapons, 633, 895–896, 913, 922
  and opening of Vladivostok, 681
  and political developments, 63, 181–182, 361, 429
  and Popov, 897
  postcoup action by, 583, 590, 591, 592, 593, 597
  and public opinion, 113, 239, 634, 747
  and RSFSR government, 52, 87, 189, 466, 487, 539–540, 705–706, 738, 781–782, 797
  and Russian defense and security, 625, 715, 904–905, 920
  and Russian Orthodox Church, 250, 375
  and Russian presidency, 167, 168, 198, 295, 352, 368, 374, 396–397, 461–462
  and Sakharov anniversary, 346
  salary of, 437
  Shevardnadze on, 922
  and Soviet foreign debt, 821
  and Soviet Germans, 747
  and Soviet military, 12, 54, 70–71, 615–616, 620
  support for, 134, 135, 136, 150, 157, 158–159, 183–184, 210–211, 303, 706
  and taxation, 492, 501, 510
  and territorial disputes, 604
  and Union issues, 359, 454, 528, 539, 543, 553, 610, 703, 738, 846, 871
  and US, 192, 411–413, 508–509, 569

El'tsin, Boris (*continued*)
  and USSR Defense Council, 836
  and Western advisors, 839
Eremeev, Yu., 100
Eremei, Grigore, 80, 132, 169, 290, 595, 732
Ermakov, Nikolai, 810
Esenov, Rakhim, 443
Evlakhov, Aleksandr, 753–754
Evstigneev, Aleksandr, 103
Evtushenko, Evgenii, 603
Eyskens, Mark, 607–608, 753

Fabius, Laurent, 419
Fahd, King, 325
Faisal, Saad Abdel Majid al-, 101
Falin, Valentin, 290, 808
Faminsky, Igor', 150
Fang Lizhi, 172
Fataliev, Ramiz, 246
Fedorov, Andrei, 591–592, 685–686, 687–688
Fedorov, Boris, 103, 107, 168
Fedorov, Nikolai, 483, 751, 753, 824, 826
Fedorov, Svyatoslav, 662, 667
Fedorov, Valentin, 692
Fedoseev, Ivan, 648
Fedulova, Alevtina, 128
Filatov, Sergei, 781, 785–786
Filatov, Viktor, 9, 145
Filatov, Vladimir, 497
Filippov, Petr, 223
Fil'shin, Gennadii, 66, 107, 123, 125, 244, 391, 532, 705, 773
Fischer, Stanley, 403
Fitzwater, Marlin, 26, 394
Fokin, Vitol'd
  and anticrisis program, 334, 452
  appointments proposed by, 357
  and Economic Treaty, 798, 815
  and energy, 109
  and foreign affairs, 191, 202, 402
  and interrepublican relations, 537, 540–541, 547
  and labor, 63, 106, 154
  and Soviet debt, 694, 765–766, 843
  and Ukrainian Church property, 358
  and Ukrainian control of Soviet enterprises, 387
  and Ukrainian coupon system, 447
Fomin, Ivan, 29
Frolov, Aleksandr, 205

Frolov, Arkadii, 130
Frolov, Ivan, 592
Frolov, Valerii, 588, 595, 626
Fronin, Vladislav, 90
Fur, Lajos, 35–36
Fuzhenko, Ivan, 879, 887

Gabrielyants, Grigorii, 137
Gaidar, Egor, 776, 802–803
  and economic reform, 811, 858, 884
  and foreign affairs, 838, 847, 912
  and foreign exchange reserves, 894–895
  and freezing bank accounts, 867
  and funding of central government, 865
  and oil exports, 823
  and sanctions on Georgia, 891
Gailitis, Karlis, 490
Galazov, Akhsarbek, 281, 803, 830
Gamsakhurdia, Zviad
  and Adzharia, 288
  and Black Sea Fleet accord, 890
  and central authorities, 15, 16, 27, 88, 268
  and Checheno-Ingushetia, 783
  and Commonwealth, 908
  and coup, 562, 571
  and economic issues, 315, 825
  and ethnic groups, 179, 480
  and foreign affairs, 192, 406, 512
  and Georgian citizenship, 431
  and Georgian independence, 146, 184, 257–258, 587
  Georgian National Guard and, 599
  and Georgian presidency, 265–266, 362–363
  and Georgian security force, 834
  and Georgian unrest and protests, 108, 123, 437, 628, 645–647, 699, 849, 909, 910
  and government appointments, 553
  and North Ossetia, 540
  and opposition groups, 643, 859
  and press harassment, 372
  and South Ossetia, 98, 160–161, 233, 234, 236, 314, 803, 871
  and Soviet military equipment, 803, 815
  and Ukraine, 891
Gasanov, Gasan, 84, 309, 396, 871
Gasisov, Rail, 239
Gassiev, Znaur, 767
Gavrilov, Igor', 721–722
Gavrilov, Mikhail, 806

Name Index

Gdlyan, Tel'man, 81, 155, 184, 348
Genscher, Hans-Dietrich
  and aid to USSR, 757
  and Baltic republics, 26, 608, 663
  in Kazakhstan and Ukraine, 744
  and Middle East, 121, 131
  and RSFSR, 838
  and Soviet nuclear weapons in Germany, 400
  and Soviet relations, 195, 201
  and Soviet troop withdrawal, 320, 321
  and Ukraine, 285
Georgadze, Nodar, 910
Gerashchenko, Aleksandr, 190
Gerashchenko, Viktor, 50, 553, 614, 800
  and debt rescheduling, 723, 735
  on EBRD, 219, 268
  and financing central government, 857, 860
  and Soviet financial status, 537, 911
Gerasimov, Gennadii, 179
Gidaspov, Boris, 369–370, 476, 498, 523, 561, 611
Girenko, Andrei, 86
Gismetdinov, Damir, 398
Gladush, Viktor, 154
Glazatov, Nikolai, 533
Glazov, Akhsabek, 540
Godmanis, Ivars, 190–191, 297, 317–318, 774–775, 885–886
Goldovich, Aleksandr, 668
Golembiovsky, Igor', 67
Golik, Yurii, 64, 76
Golikov, Vyacheslav, 229
Golovatov, Mikhail, 605
Golovko, Evgenii, 794
Golovkov, Gennadii, 29
Gol'ts, Aleksandr, 5
Golyshev, Boris, 107
Gonchar, Nikolai, 420
Goncharenko, Nikolai, 458, 515
Goncz, Arpad, 372
Gonzalez, Filipe, 560
Gorbachev, Anatolii, 833
Gorbachev, Mikhail
  agriculture and food, 6–7, 21, 243, 253, 413, 466, 708
  and all-Union referendum, 86, 185, 201
  and anniversaries, 285, 302, 325, 346, 421–422

  appointments by, 179, 336, 627, 674, 797, 832
  and Armenian-Azerbaijani conflict, 194, 305, 306, 311, 450, 842
  and arms control, 714–715
  and Baltic states, 21–22, 25, 26, 50, 62, 73, 80–81, 104, 166, 261, 340, 384, 433, 455, 513, 526, 608, 630, 670–671, 685
  and Belorussia, 141–142
  books by, 96
  and Bulgaria, 345
  and central government advisory and legislative bodies, 137–138, 176–177, 177–178, 464, 618, 680, 729
  charity donations, 245
  and Checheno-Ingushetia, 785
  and Chernobyl' disaster, 292
  and China, 336
  and Commonwealth agreement, 881–883, 886, 902
  and conservatives, 57, 87, 251, 256, 299–300, 386, 406, 409, 426, 438–439, 450, 458, 468, 471, 525
  and coup, 553–554, 560, 573–574, 577, 718–719
  and coup investigations, 667, 718, 743, 754, 813
  and CPSU, 169–170, 273, 436, 481, 497–498, 536, 551, 796
  criticisms of, 2–3, 9, 46, 51, 66, 68, 183–184, 259, 261–262, 278, 408–409, 425–426, 454–455, 586, 694
  and democrats, 42–43, 219, 225, 383
  and depoliticization, 30, 484, 495, 598
  documentary on, 164–165
  and economic issues, 49, 60, 166, 196–197, 204, 256–257, 263, 331, 334, 376, 686, 791
  and Economic Treaty, 732–733, 745
  and El'tsin, 54, 116, 126, 178, 212, 267, 327, 361, 412, 461–462, 486, 567–568, 613
  and European Community, 114
  and financial scandal, 817
  and Finland, 428
  and France, 102–103
  and G-7, 399–400, 456, 474
  and Georgia, 146, 682
  and Germany, 201, 421, 451–452, 679–680, 826

Gorbachev, Mikhail (*continued*)
  and Great Britain, 168, 202
  and Greece, 488
  and Gulf crisis, 38, 40, 43, 94, 118–119, 120
  and human rights, 401, 717
  and international banks, 189, 268, 715
  and Iran, 111
  and Italy, 353–354, 527, 676
  and Japan, 17, 48, 217, 270–271, 737, 750–751
  and Jewish leaders, 19
  and justice system, 3–4, 56, 64, 78, 85, 210, 737, 757
  in Kazakhstan, 367–368
  and KGB, 605–606, 614, 750
  in Kirgizia, 843
  and Kuwait, 830
  and labor issues, 153, 154, 156, 157, 229, 232, 294, 341, 344
  and media, 33–34, 74, 92, 314, 426, 579, 607, 651
  and Mexico, 450
  and Middle East peace, 687
  and military reform, 316, 833, 836
  and Moldavia, 11, 175, 435–436
  and Moscow, 207, 222
  and Movement for Democratic Reforms, 441, 922
  and Nine-plus-One agreement, 287, 297, 352, 403
  1990 Nobel Peace Prize for, 384
  and nuclear weapons, 13, 761
  and official end of USSR, 899
  and Poland, 245
  and political reform, 289, 418, 480–481, 629, 749
  position stability, 48, 180
  postcoup return and action by, 582, 584, 585, 590–592, 594, 597, 603, 817
  and public opinion, 113, 239, 634
  resignation of, 893, 912–913
  and RSFSR, 397, 721
  salary of, 437
  on secret privileges, 466–467
  and Shevardnadze, 194
  and South Korea, 10, 279–280
  and South Ossetia, 14–15, 160, 161
  and Spain, 460
  on state stability, 107, 300, 327
  support for, 20, 134, 220, 364, 494–495
  and Sweden, 386
  and Syria, 244
  and taxation, 113, 213–214, 246–247, 510
  treason charges against, 798–799
  and Turkey, 185
  and Ukraine, 752, 862–863
  and Union issues, 201, 266–267, 447, 475, 643, 887
  and Union treaty, 329, 359, 390–391, 410, 427, 490, 491, 519, 603, 609–610, 703, 727, 730, 813–814, 835–836, 838–839, 845–846, 868, 871
  and US, 192, 394, 488, 507–508, 569, 773
  and Vietnam, 322–323
  and Warsaw Pact, 293
  and Western aid, 701, 724
  and Yugoslavia, 517, 739
Gorbachev, Raisa, 185, 582, 718–719
Gorbunovs, Anatolijs
  and Armed Forces Day, 135
  and Belorussia, 898
  and Commonwealth agreement, 884
  and coup, 565, 566
  and European countries, 140, 264, 374
  and freeing prices, 840
  and independence, 165
  and Latvian citizenship, 658
  and Lithuania, 691
  and negotiations with center, 608
  and UN, 660
Gorgidze, Vakhtans, 97
Gorkovlyuk, Aleksandr, 275–276
Goryacheva, Svetlana, 127, 321, 772
Gostev, Eduard, 871
Govorov, Vladimir, 585, 651
Grachev, Andrei, 119, 674, 751, 882, 899
  and arms control, 701, 722
  and coup investigations, 754–755
Grachev, Pavel, 12, 625, 627, 657, 765, 824, 838
Granberg, Aleksandr, 196
Greenspan, Alan, 664
Gremitskikh, Yurii, 140, 253, 254
Gribov, Vladimir, 768, 772
Griffiths, Bryan, 104
Grigor'ev, Sergei, 39, 200
Grinev, Vladimir, 752, 862
Grinevsky, Oleg, 404, 809–810
Grishin, Valerii, 823

NAME INDEX

Gritsenko, Nikolai, 348
Gromov, Boris, 196, 634–635, 877
  and ethnic unrest in Northern Caucasus, 281, 160, 235
  and national-patriotic movement, 492
  and OMON troops in Baltic republics, 347, 588
  and RSFSR presidency, 328
Groth, Heinrich, 846
Grushin, Boris, 766
Grushko, Viktor, 7, 93, 104, 105, 600
Gubanov, Viktor, 83, 353
Gubenko, Nikolai, 365–366, 627
Guchmazov, Soslan, 627, 772
Gudev, Vladimir, 676
Gudinov, Sergei, 103–104
Gugushvili, Vissarion, 553
Gumbaridze, Givi, 212
Gunko, S., 163
Gurnov, Aleksandr, 523
Gurov, Aleksandr, 855
Guseinov, Ragim, 60
Guseinov, Vagif, 468
Gushchin, Lev, 606
Gutnanis, Andris, 828
Gventsadze, German, 832, 852
Gvishiani, Jarmen, 758

Hadjizedeh, Hikmet, 186
Hammadi, Saddoun, 118
Harutyunyan-Kozak, Bella, 308, 309
Hatch, Orrin, 850
Havel, Vaclav, 330, 493
Hel', Ivan, 12
Helme, Udo, 845
Hidalgo, Alcibiades, 669
Hier, Marvin, 743–744
Hogg, Douglas, 633
Holushko, Mykola, 679
Honcharik, Vladimir, 240–241
Honecker, Erich, 19, 195, 201, 370, 751, 826, 891
Hor Namhong, 288
Hovannisian, Raffi, 815, 870
Hryn'ov, Volodymyr, 745
Hurd, Douglas, 12, 202
Hurenko, Stanislav, 435, 480, 612, 628
Hussein, King (Jordan), 324
Hussein, Saddam, 30–31, 43, 101, 119–120, 159–160

Ibragimov, Mirzaolim, 400
Ibragimov, Vakha, 712
Ignatenko, Vitalii
  and Baltic republics, 8, 99, 166, 433
  and ban on political organs in RSFSR agencies, 484
  on declaring state of emergency, 278
  and foreign affairs, 120, 270, 280, 448, 471, 508
  and media, 260
  and Movement for Democratic Reforms, 441
  and TASS, 615, 631, 651, 674
  and Union treaty, 475
Ihnatovich, Mikalai, 400, 740, 854
Ikonnikov, Valerii, 807–808
Ikramov, Maksud, 672
Iliescu, Ion, 102, 245, 789
Il'in, Aleksei, 525
Ilyukin, Viktor, 798–799
Imnadze, Nodar, 300
Ioann, Metropolitan, 17
Ioseliani, Dzhaba, 123
Ioseliani, Otar, 628
Isaev, Boris, 344, 772
Isaev, Yurii, 754
Isakov, Vladimir, 212, 222
Isanov, Nasirdin, 52, 334, 859–860
Ivanenko, Viktor, 523, 727, 758–759, 824
  and Checheno-Ingushetia, 710, 784
  and RSFSR KGB, 316, 852
Ivanov, Nikolai, 155
Ivanov, Vitalii, 326
Ivans, Dainis, 311, 576, 891
Ivashenko, Oleksandr, 425
Ivashko, Vladimir, 65, 142, 261, 285, 289, 319, 577
Ivashov, Leonid, 900

Jaakson, Ernst, 660, 717
Jagminas, Jonas, 433
Jansons, Aris, 262
Jermalavicius, Juozas, 25–26, 595
Jiang Zemin, 142, 312, 336–337, 468
Joergensen, Anker, 140
John Paul II, Pope, 77, 194, 265, 385, 527, 549, 832, 905
Jovic, Borisav, 254
Jundzis, Talavs, 311–312, 796, 840
Jurkans, Janis, 388–389, 771

Kachanov, Aleksandr, 333
Kachanov, Oleg, 855
Kafarova, Elmira, 42, 84, 307, 308
Kaganovich, Lazar, 500
Kahn, Juri, 168
Kahveci, Adnan, 136
Kaifu, Toshiki, 270, 456, 469–470
Kala, Hillar, 838
Kalashnikov, Vladimir, 499, 516
Kalinichenko, Il'ya, 797
Kalinin, Mikhail, 318
Kalinin, Nikolai, 563, 574
Kalinin, Roman, 343
Kalistratov, Yurii, 220
Kalnins, Ojars, 717
Kalugin, Oleg, 225, 247
Kalyukin, Vitalii., 255
Kamalov, Sadikjan, 220
Kamenev, Al'bert, 125
Kampelman, Max, 646, 709
Kapitanets, Ivan, 73, 791
Karaev, Tamerlan, 84, 246, 309
Karamanlis, Constantine, 254
Karamanoukyan, Shahen, 311
Karamanov, Uzakbai, 334
Karasev, Valentin, 260
Karbainov, Aleksandr, 104, 105, 272
Karimov, Islam
  and coup, 563, 579
  and CPSU, 596, 618
  and independence, 178–179, 608–609
  and interrepublican relations, 770, 801
  and land reform, 83–84
  and politics, 657–658, 771, 920–921
  and Turkestani emigrants, 685
  and Turkey, 897–898
  and Union treaty, 111, 313, 834
  and Uzbek landslide, 316
  and Uzbek security, 477, 691
Karpinsky, Len, 625
Karpov, Viktor, 652
Karpukhin, Viktor, 605
Kartashov, Aleksandr, 358
Kasatkin, Valentin, 179
Kasatkin, Vladimir, 404
Kasatonov, Igor', 686
Kashakashvili, Guram, 212
Kasparov, Gary, 296, 425, 469
Katkus, Valdemaras, 396
Katusev, Aleksandr, 601

Katushev, Konstantin, 80, 96, 280
Katz, Julius, 47
Kazakov, Vasilii, 198
Kazaryan, Mikit, 311
Kebich, Vyacheslau, 132, 240, 243, 334, 338–339, 617, 728, 820
Keleti, Gyorgi, 134
Kendzior, Yaroslav, 12
Kezbers, Imants, 861
Khabuliani, Dilar, 16, 236
Khadzhiev, Salambek, 616, 627
Khaindrava, Giorgi, 645
Khamidoulin, Rashid, 499–500
Khandruev, Aleksandr, 196
Kharchenko, Viktor, 289
Khasbulatov, Ruslan
  and Checheno-Ingushetia, 654–655, 711, 714, 727
  and coup, 568, 577
  and economic reform, 583
  and Foreign Ministry, 653
  in Great Britain, 487
  and Karachaevo-Cherkessia, 811
  on military patrols in cities, 54, 222
  and politics, 279, 475, 706, 769
  and RSFSR army, 40
  on RSFSR as legal successor to USSR, 899
  and Russian Academy of Sciences, 879
  on Siberian republic, 546
  and Tatarstan independence demonstrations, 735
  on Union referendum and treaty, 168, 182, 603–604
Khitrov, Boris, 455
Khmara, Stepan, 96, 247, 264, 283, 302, 330, 479, 636
Khobt, Anatolii, 668
Khokhlov, Vitalii, 391–392
Khomenko, Yurii, 367
Khomich, Aleksei, 393
Khomyakov, Valerii, 444
Khoshtaria, Giorgi, 35, 97, 265, 553
Khudonazarov, Davlat, 612–613, 844
Kichikhin, Yurii, 638
Kinkel, Klaus, 751
Kireev, Genrikh, 228
Kirichenko, Vadim, 475–476
Kirill, Metropolitan, 834
Kirillovich, Vladimir, 313
Kirov, Sergei, 63

NAME INDEX

Kiselev, Evgenii, 196
Kissinger, Henry, 383, 731
Kitovani, Tengiz, 599, 647, 699, 700, 910
Klaczynski, Wladyslaw, 29
Klimov, Elem, 61
Klimov, Sergei, 747
Klochkov, Igor', 341, 830
Klyuchnikov, Igor', 180
Kobets, Konstantin, 71, 554, 564, 650, 719, 778, 847
Kobyakov, Aleksandr, 638
Kochetov, Konstantin, 135, 307, 347
Kodin, Mikhail, 67
Kodzoev, Issa, 705
Kogan, Evgenii, 256, 518–519
Kohl, Helmut, 36, 119, 451, 493, 810, 838
Kohli, Harinder, 869
Koivisto, Mauno, 428
Kok, Wim, 719
Koksanov, Igor', 137, 138
Kolesnichenko, Tomas, 59, 362
Kolesnikov, Mikhail, 216–217
Kolesnikov, Vyacheslav, 137
Kolosovsky, Andrei, 833
Komissar, Mikhail, 29
Komissarov, Vyacheslav, 82, 207, 249, 666
Komov, Yurii, 688
Komplektov, Viktor, 257
Konarev, Nikolai, 137, 322
Kondrashov, Stanislav, 2–3
Kondrat'ev, Georgii, 878–879
Konovalov, Vitalii, 343, 361–362
Konyakhin, Vasilii, 223
Korekovsky, B., 90
Kork, Andres, 575, 581–582
Kornienko, Georgii, 182–183
Korolev, Valentin, 440
Korotich, Vitalii, 606
Kostash, Ion, 612
Kostenko, Anatolii, 622, 676–677
Kovalchuk, Leonid, 230
Kovalenko, Yurii, 569
Kovalev, Mikhail, 414
Kovalev, Sergei, 42
Kovalev, Vladimir, 42
Kozhakhmetov, Hasan, 820
Kozhavin, Vladimir, 790
Kozhendaev, Leonid, 876
Kozhinov, Vadim, 45
Kozhokin, Evgenii, 858

Kozyrev, Andrei
  and arms trade, 667
  and foreign relations, 44, 775, 838
  and government-in-exile, 569
  and human rights, 349, 853
  and interrepublican relations, 760, 778
  and NATO, 806
  on possibility of second coup, 695
  and Presidential Consultative Council, 824
Kozyrev, Nikolai, 136, 852
Kramerev, Arkadii, 820
Krasavchenko, Sergei, 655–656
Krasin, Yurii, 417
Krasnitsky, Evgenii, 792–793
Krasnoshchekov, Nikolai, 109
Krastins, Andrejs, 165
Krauchanka, Petr, 418, 688
Kravchenko, Leonid
  and "600 Seconds," 456
  and censorship, 440
  and coup, 675
  crackdown on Central Television, 23
  criticisms of, 296, 479, 585
  and Journalists' Union, 61, 81, 263
  and Leningrad television, 426
  live phone-in with, 259–260
  and new broadcasting company, 92–93
  removal of, 579
  and RSFSR radio and television, 74, 193
  and "TSN," 196
  and "Who's Who?" 734
Kravchuk, Leonid
  and Babii Yar commemoration, 717–718
  and border disputes, 604
  and Commonwealth agreement, 880, 883, 907, 919
  and coup, 559, 562
  and Crimea, 47
  and economic union, 661, 798, 843–844
  on El'tsin, 126
  and food supplies, 479–480
  and foreign relations, 88, 185, 209, 285–286, 372, 402, 517, 673, 682–683, 707, 744
  and gold mining, 101
  and independence, 142, 636, 862
  and interrepublican relations, 92, 622, 770, 800, 892
  and Jewish leaders, 649
  and miners' strike, 156

Kravchuk, Leonid (*continued*)
  and nuclear weapons, 696, 895, 922
  resignation from CPSU, 611
  and Ukrainian Church property, 358–359
  and Ukrainian security, 623, 787, 892
  and Ukrainian presidency, 862, 863–864
  and Union treaty, 168–169, 424, 446, 457, 843
Krivosheev, Grigorii, 61–62, 266, 329, 479
Kruchina, Nikolai, 131, 467, 606, 719
Krushinsky, Nikolai, 800
Kryuchkov, Vladimir
  and Armenian-Azerbaijani conflict, 310, 451, 468
  Cabinet of Ministers and Security Council, 137, 176
  and coup, 555, 568, 574, 575, 577, 583, 594, 598, 667, 718, 748, 761
  criticisms of, 440
  and KGB, 93, 342
  libel suit against, 83
  and Lithuanian prosecution, 903
  and rallies, 134, 211
  and RSFSR KGB, 316
  and Union issues, 409
  and victims of Stalinist repression, 403
  on Western conspiracies, 422
Kryzhanivs'kyi, Volodymyr, 638, 661
Kudryavtsev, Gennadii, 137, 138
Kudryavtsev, Vladimir, 322
Kukharets, Volodymyr, 853
Kulik, Gennadii, 762
Kulikov, Viktor, 114, 347
Kulov, Feliks, 19, 552, 572
Kulumbegov, Torez, 16
Kuptsov, Valentin, 145, 524, 529
Kurchyukin, Viktor, 139
Kurginyan, Sergei, 416
Kurinnyi, Igor', 439
Kurkova, Bella, 260
Kutsenko, Viktor, 71
Kuvaldin, Aleksandr, 220
Kuzmenko, Mikhail, 856
Kuzmenok, Vladimir, 388
Kuzmickas, Bronius, 140
Kuz'min, Fedor, 1, 11, 276, 567, 602
Kuznetsov, German, 52, 480, 572
Kuznetsov, Yurii, 48, 873
Kvilitaya, Otar, 553
Kvitashvili, Merab, 909–910

Kvitsinsky, Yulii
  and coup, 592, 626
  on Eastern Europe, 203, 293
  and EC, 406
  and German reunification, 112–113, 145, 167
  and Iceland, 109
  and Moldavian independence, 617
  promotion and dismissal of, 337, 631
  and Yugoslavia, 453–454

Laanjarv, Olev, 214–215, 227
Lalumière, Catherine, 267
Lamont, Norman, 515
Landsbergis, Vytautas
  and Catholicism, 166, 832
  and central government negotiations, 261, 264, 389, 526, 722
  and Commonwealth agreement, 884
  and coup, 564, 582
  criticisms of, 422
  and customs post attacks, 276, 379, 513
  and foreign relations, 59, 188, 317–318, 345–346, 374, 419, 459–460, 677, 688
  and interrepublican relations, 258, 478, 505, 548, 691, 764, 863
  and justice system, 903–904
  and Lithuanian currency, 795
  and Lithuanian independence, 81, 186
  and military action in Lithuania, 25, 28, 203–204, 208, 291–292, 377, 433, 470, 601
  and nuclear weapons, 429, 602
  public opinion of, 461
  and "Sajudis," 894
  and Soviet military service, 616
  and Soviet troop withdrawal, 654, 716, 816
  and UN, 660, 720
Lanovyi, Volodymyr, 815
Lapienis, Saulius, 208
Laptev, Ivan, 67–68, 443, 444
Larin, Aleksandr, 901
Latsis, Otto, 498, 599–600
Laverov, Nikolai, 31, 73, 341–342, 393
Lazar', Father, 3–4
Lazarev, Igor', 614
Lazdins, Auseklis, 796
Lazutkin, Valentin, 217, 220
Lebedev, Aleksandr, 701, 866
Lebedev, Valerii, 595, 638, 648
Lenin, 244, 284–285, 766, 814

Name Index

Leont'ev, V., 515
Levi, David, 324–325, 746
Levin, Andrei, 405
Levin, Ariel, 5
Ligachev, Egor, 87, 173, 279, 406, 754, 770, 879
Likhachev, Dmitrii, 569, 801–802
Lindenberg, Jaroslav, 806
Lintner, Eduard, 359–360
Li Peng, 195, 228, 312
Lipitsky, Vladimir, 528, 621
Lisov, Evgenii, 763
Lisovolik, Dmitrii, 746
Litvov, V., 20
Liu Guangzhi, 228
Lobov, Oleg, 726
Lobov, Vladimir
    appointments and dismissals, 227, 322, 836, 878
    and Gulf war, 114
    and military reform, 631–632, 686
    on need for military strength, 434
    and nuclear codes, 554–555
    on unified versus republican armies, 826, 859
Loenning, Inge, 186
Loginov, Vladlen, 285
Lohan, Helmut, 388
Lomakin, Vladimir, 23
Loncar, Budimir, 254
Lopatin, Vladimir, 833
Lopukhin, Vladimir, 901, 903
Löschnak, Franz, 65
Lubenchenko, Konstantin, 749, 769, 846, 887
Lubitsky, Evsei, 8
Lubkivs'kyi, Roman, 452
Lucinschi, Petru, 64, 80
Luguev, Gazi, 848
Lukhovsky, Vsevolod, 139
Lukin, Vladimir, 776
Lukyanenko, Levko, 862
Luk'yanov, Anatolii
    and Moscow's role in Baltic attacks, 399
    and conservatives, 9, 278
    and coup, 18, 557, 566, 567, 573–574, 585, 593–594, 598, 600, 667, 918
    democrat lawsuit against, 434–435
    on departification, 495
    and foreign affairs, 14, 121, 400
    and Georgia, 98, 179
    and May Day, 302
    and media restrictions, 34
    and miners' strike, 153
    on Shevardnadze, 8–9
    support for Gorbachev from, 220
    and Supreme Soviet session, 121
    and Union referendum and treaty, 200, 352, 390–391, 465–466, 556
Lushchikov, Anatolii, 179
Lushchikov, Sergei, 37–38, 65, 137, 138, 156, 484, 544–545
Lushev, Petr, 227, 293
Luzhkov, Yurii
    and CPSU property, 604
    and economic issues, 56, 620, 644
    and Moscow police chief appointment, 249
    and Oktyabr'sky Raion Soviet, 532
    and pro-El'tsin rally, 211
    on restoration of churches, 123
    USSR committee appointment, 600
    and Western aid, 665
Lyashko, Aleksandr, 360
Lysenko, Vladimir, 554, 768
Lyubachivs'kyi, Cardinal, 77, 226, 358–359, 363, 398
Lyubimov, Aleksandr, 217
Lyubimov, Mikhail, 440

McPeak, William, 708
Madigan, Edward, 724–725, 773
Magomadov, Lechi, 655
Magomedov, Magomedali, 179
Major, John, 168, 399–400, 621, 716, 771
Makarov, Konstantin, 502
Makarovich, Vladimir, 73
Makashov, Al'bert, 326, 328, 351, 382, 397, 541, 632
Makhkamov, Kakhar, 106, 255, 281, 502, 542, 596, 617–618
    and coup involvement, 612–613
    resignation of, 624
Makhov, Evgenii, 67, 293
Maksimov, Yurii, 833
Maksumov, Akbar, 502
Makutinowicz, Boleslaw, 341, 433, 601
Malashenko, Igor', 509, 651
Malei, Mikhail, 376
Maleki, Abbas, 101
Malinov, Valerii, 12

Malishevsky, Grigorii, 261–262
Mal'tsev, Igor', 554
Mamedov, Aydin, 246
Mamikonyan, Feliks, 130, 309, 491
Mamleev, Dmitrii, 586
Mamodaev, Yaragy, 786
Manaenkov, Yurii, 261, 524
Manilov, Valerii, 312, 546, 752, 841, 859, 886–887
Manoilov, Andrei, 625
Manucharian, Arshot, 308
Manukyan, Vazgen, 192, 309, 519, 546, 682
Marchuk, Evgenii, 804
Marchuk, Gurii, 692
Margiani, Avtandil, 124
Marjasa, Ruta, 205
Markov, Georgi, 225, 247
Markov, Yurii, 395
Markovic, Ante, 254, 453, 517
Markovsky, Frants, 12–13
Martirosyan, Vilen, 196, 787
Martynov, Aleksandr, 323
Martynov, Vladlen, 269, 322
Masaliev, Absamat, 250, 290
Masel'sky, Aleksandr, 357
Masik, Konstantin, 357
Maslennikov, Arkadii, 427
Maslennikov, Nikolai, 94
Maslyukov, Yurii, 31, 51–52, 195, 366, 465, 486
Masyk, Konstantyn, 49
Matlock, Jack, 12
Matvienko, Vladimir, 759
Matyukhin, Georgii, 195–196, 258
Matyukhin, Leonid, 322
Matzke, Richard, 371
Maystadt, Philippe, 884
Mazalov, Anatolii, 494
Meany, George, 172
Meciar, Vladimir, 191
Medvedev, Nikolai, 1, 700
Medvedev, Roy, 750, 793, 908
Medvedev, Vadim, 197
Melkov, Gennadii, 103
Mel'nikov, Ivan, 499
Men', Aleksandr, 3
Mendelson, Toomas, 208
Meri, Lennart, 165, 224, 469, 576, 760, 771, 816
Merkys, Antanas, 771
Meshcheryakov, Sergei, 827
Mesic, Stipe, 448

Meskhov, Yurii, 774
Mezun, Vyacheslav, 356
Michelis, Gianni de, 114
Migiladze, Jani, 124
Mikhailov, Arkadii, 370
Mikhailov, Batyr, 743, 749
Mikhailov, Viktor, 896
Mikhal'chenko, Aleksandr, 137, 138
Mikhalkin, Vladimir, 190
Mikhalkov, Sergei, 615
Miller, Rein, 766, 778
Miloslavsky, Leonid, 76
Minchenko, Anatolii, 357
Mindolin, Vladimir, 458, 484–485
Minin, Viktor, 761
Mirikov, Nikolai, 72
Mironov, Valerii, 602, 616, 716
Mirsaidov, Shukurulla, 423
Misiukonis, Marijonas, 399
Mitkova, Tat'yana, 196
Mitsotakis, Constantine, 488
Mitterrand, François, 268, 355, 419, 707
Mlynnik, Cheslav, 315
Mock, Alois, 65
Moiseev, Mikhail
  and arms control treaties, 499, 504
  and Armed Forces Day, 134
  and Baltic republics, 12, 73, 383, 476–477
  dismissal of, 651
  and foreign relations, 320, 328, 488
  on security, 249
  and World War II, 415–416
Moiseev, Nikita, 758, 761
Molchanov, Vladimir, 440
Möllemann, Jürgen, 106–107, 343, 363–364
Molukov, Marat, 118
Moroz, Aleksandr, 638
Moroz, Oleksandr, 435
Morozov, Ivan, 33
Morozov, Konstantin, 633, 656, 706–707, 751–752, 778, 786–787, 860–861
Mosanu, Alexandru, 333, 435–436, 570, 587, 617, 653, 872
Mosbacher, Robert, 280
Moskovchenko, Nikolai, 103–104
Mostafavi, Rahmatollah, 676
Mostovoi, Anatolii, 42
Mrill, Aleksandr, 229
Mubarak, Hosni, 325, 687
Mukhazhanov, Bulat, 151

Name Index

Mukhin, Georgii, 241
Murashov, Arkadii, 211, 262, 296, 425, 666, 674–675, 839
Muravschi, Valeriu, 356
  and coup, 587
  and Dniester putsch, 872, 873, 875
  and EC, 734
  and economic agreements, 543, 756, 764, 798
  and Gagauz unrest, 819
  and Moldavian independence, 612
  and Romanian agreement, 530–531
  on Union treaty, 375
Murdoch, Rupert, 314
Murnieks, Roberts, 2
Mutalibov, Ayaz
  and Armenian-Azerbaijani conflict, 42, 276, 305, 306, 308, 310, 450–451, 535, 837, 842
  and Azerbaijani Defense Ministry, 639
  and coup, 562, 587, 596
  CPSU resignation of, 622
  and government restructuring, 84, 778
  and independence, 616, 626
  and Iran, 550
  and Nine-plus-One agreement, 362
  and politics, 435, 697
  and Soviet military property, 898
  and Union issues, 171, 767, 846
Myasnikov, Fedor, 648
Myasnikov, Valerii, 44
Myasnikovich, Mikhail, 241

Nabiev, Rakhmon, 671–672, 698, 844, 878, 916
Nagle, David, 275
Nahayyan, Zayid bin Sultan al-, 644
Nakao, Eiichi, 750–751
Nakayama, Taro, 47–48, 737
Namdar-Zangeneh, Bijan, 396
Nastase, Adrian, 209, 535
Naudziunas, Algimantas, 164, 200, 595
Navdzhuvanov, Mamdaez, 672
Navickas, Vytas, 780
Navumchyk, Syarhei, 414, 705
Nazarbaev, Nursultan
  appointments by, 908–909
  and Commonwealth agreement, 881, 883
  and Cossacks, 659
  and coup, 563, 571–572
  and CPSU, 586, 617
  criticisms of, 759–760
  and defense, 762
  and economic issues, 217–218, 284, 323, 368, 547, 648, 805–806
  and foreign affairs, 115, 185–186, 468–469, 508, 654, 682, 744, 771
  and independence, 897
  and Kazakh presidency, 820, 864
  and Kirgiz agreement, 124
  and military service, 650
  and miners' strike, 151, 155
  and Nagorno-Karabakh, 668, 709
  and nuclear weapons, 656, 896
  and political groups, 442, 726
  and postcoup interrepublican negotiations, 609, 610, 629
  and public opinion, 634
  and RSFSR relations, 605, 759
  and Semipalatinsk site closure, 525
  and Soviet foreign debt, 679
  on Soviet and Russian leadership, 126, 259
  and space program, 649
  and taxation system, 510
  and transfer of Union enterprises, 411
  and Union treaty, 101, 427, 447, 491, 546, 553
  and Western aid, 780
Nazarov, Viktor, 812
Nechaev, Evgenii, 183
Nedelciuc, Vasile, 702, 734
Neiland, Nikolai, 268–269
Nemtsov, Boris, 90
Nenashev, Mikhail, 316, 417, 466, 498
Nerubailo, Viktor, 345
Neskoromnyi, Evgenii, 90
Nevzorov, Aleksandr, 27, 175, 176, 422, 455–456, 615, 864–865
Nguyen Manh Cam, 758
Nguyen Van Linh, 323
Nicholas II, 421
Nikiforov, Igor', 790
Nikiforov, Valentin, 396
Nikolaenko, Valerii, 280, 652, 669
Nikolaev, Leonid, 63
Nikol'sky, Boris, 511–512
Nishanov, Rafik, 73, 138, 143, 480, 605, 821
Nixon, Richard, 318, 517
Niyazov, Saparmurad, 92, 130–131, 239, 624, 737–738, 820

Niyazov, Saparmurad (*continued*)
  and coup, 573, 579–580
  and foreign affairs, 111, 729, 867
Nogradi, Pal, 253
Novikov, Evgenii, 794
Novodvorskaya, Valeriya, 108, 486–487
Novozhilov, Viktor, 372, 635
Nudel, Ida, 757
Nugis, Ulo, 567
Nurmammedov, Nurberdi, 91
Nurmyradov, Shiraly, 91–92
Nurtazin, Marash, 91
Nysanbaev, Ratbek, 536

Obminsky, Ernest, 358, 416, 652
Oboroc, Constantin, 640
Obukhov, Aleksei, 652, 722
Odilov, Akhmadzhon, 188, 275
Oganesyan, Raffi, 807
Oganesyan, Gevork, 371
Ogarkov, Nikolai, 41
Oleinik, Boris, 18, 53, 98, 322
Oleinikov, Anatolii, 619, 761
Olisesnevich, Viktor, 668
Omanidze, Murman, 553
Omelichev, Bronislav, 115, 504, 696, 873
Ominami, Carlos, 423
Oovel, Andres, 815
Orlov, Aleksandr, 248, 342
Orlov, Andrei, 59
Orlov, Boris, 692
Orlov, Gennadii, 176
Orlov, Vladimir, 137, 138, 198–199, 200, 224, 614
Orlov, Yurii, 232
Osipyan, Yurii, 322
Osmochescu, Nicolae, 702
Ostroumov, Georgii, 179
Otsason, Rein, 659
Ovchinnikov, Aleksandr, 107, 108, 627
Ovesen, Eric, 239
Ovezberdev, Saparmurad, 126
Ozal, Turgut, 136, 185–186, 682
Ozawa, Ichiro, 217
Ozceri, T., 82
Ozherel'ev, Oleg, 112, 221, 239–240
Ozolas, Romualdas, 461

Paatashvili, Tedo, 646
Pakalniskis, Vytautas, 139

Pakhomov, Nikolai, 545
Pamfilova, Ella, 824
Panasyutin, Nikolai, 133–134
Pankin, Boris
  and Afghanistan, 650, 695, 809
  appointments, 614–615, 832
  and arms control and nuclear control, 696, 760–761
  and Baltic republics, 726
  and coup, 626
  criticisms of, 781
  and Finland, 673
  foreign ministry reorganization and postcoup policy, 652–653, 670, 793
  and Israel, 746
  and Japan, 737
  and NATO, 806
  and South Africa, 807
  and UN, 665, 678
  and US aid, 678
  and Vietnam and China, 758
Panov, Aleksandr, 404–405
Pantelejevs, Andrejs, 876
Panyukov, Boris, 345
Parfenov, Sergei, 779, 885
Pastukhov, Boris, 220
Patrikeev, Valerii, 108, 307
Pats, Konstantin, 771
Paulauskas, Arturas, 338, 514, 595, 904
Paul'man, Valerii, 430–431
Pavlov, Gennadii, 651
Pavlov, Georgii, 719
Pavlov, Nikolai, 740
Pavlov, Valentin
  and anniversaries and holidays, 250, 285, 421
  and anticrisis program, 256, 283–284, 409, 492
  and Baltic republics, 191, 340
  and Cabinet of Ministers, 129, 206
  and China, 336
  and coup, 555, 574, 583, 600, 613, 718, 748
  criticisms of, 251
  and Cuba, 520
  and East European countries, 176, 191, 245, 345, 517
  and economic issues, 50, 73, 110, 122, 189, 196, 248, 324, 329, 369, 394, 413, 447, 544
  firing of, 585

Name Index

and government restructuring, 133
and international banking conspiracy, 104, 384–385
and Israel, 271
and labor issues, 152, 155, 156, 228, 341, 398, 453, 543–544
and media, 314
and Mongolia, 96
and politics, 31, 127, 210–211, 290, 405–406, 408–409, 426
and Security Council, 176
on Union treaty, 543
on Western aid, 326
and West European countries, 102, 107, 297–298, 353, 363–364, 533
and women's issues, 248
Pavlov, Yurii, 832
Pavlychko, Dmytro, 661, 892, 900
Paznyak, Zyanon, 214, 263, 432, 449, 503
Penyagin, Aleksandr, 129
Pepse, Einars, 795–796
Pereira, Cesar, 225
Perez de Cuellar, Javier, 382, 391, 816
Perfil'ev, Igor', 638
Pestov, Valerii, 636
Peters, Janis, 166, 168, 716
Petkel, Vladimir, 262
Petrakov, Nikolai, 35, 39, 57, 112, 256, 257, 279, 441, 680
Petrauskas, Antanas, 204
Petrov, Boris, 426, 615, 647
Petrov, Sergei, 44
Petrov, Yurii, 41, 221, 529, 703, 795, 838
Petrovsky, Vladimir, 631, 652, 696
Petrunya, Vladimir, 78
Petrushenko, Nikolai, 41, 158
Petukhov, Nikolai, 216
Pilv, Mehis, 828
Pilyuto, Vladislav, 241
Pirozhkov, Vladimir, 93
Pithart, Petr, 176, 330, 331
Pitin, Andrei, 314–315
Plekhanov, Yurii, 554, 636
Plyushch, Ivan, 116, 424, 527, 696, 864
Pochinok, Aleksandr, 122, 123, 911
Podelyakin, Vladimir, 191, 852
Podgorbunsky, Sergei, 332
Podkolzin, Evgenii, 627
Pogosyan, Genrikh, 668
Pogosyan, Stepan, 337, 375

Poher, Alain, 419
Pokrovsky, Vadim, 665
Pokrovsky, Valentin, 147–148
Pokutny, Pavel, 285
Politkovsky, Aleksandr, 23
Polozkov, Ivan, 147, 167–168, 173–174, 237, 289, 351, 420, 528
Poltoranin, Mikhail, 6, 192, 579, 607, 824
Polyanichko, Viktor, 535
Ponomarev, Lev, 287
Ponomarev, Nikolai, 661–662
Ponomarev, Vitalii, 619
Ponomarev, Vladimir, 814
Poos, Jacques, 89, 114
Popov, Dimitar, 345
Popov, Gavriil
  and Amnesty International, 905
  and coup, 583–584
  criticisms of, 141, 511–512, 662–663
  and food rationing, 792
  and housing, 799
  and May Day, 302
  and Moscow, 405, 426, 666
  and Political Consultative Council, 680
  and politics, 184, 218–219, 349, 397, 420, 439, 441, 485, 594, 674, 680–681, 727
  and price increases, 238
  and privatization, 869, 888, 896–897
  and reform, 52, 279, 663–664
  and Security Council, 618
  and territorial disputes, 604–605
  and US, 65–66, 192
Portugalov, Nikolai, 826
Potoben'ko, Mykhailo, 264
Potreki, Ojars, 596
Powell, Colin, 488
Pozner, Vladimir, 259, 296
Prigarin, Aleksei, 852
Primakov, Evgenii
  and Central Intelligence Service, 794, 797
  and coup, 657
  and foreign intelligence, 695–696, 905
  and Middle East, 30–31, 100–101, 119, 159–160, 644–645, 670, 687
  rumors about, 63–64
  and Security Council, 177, 618
  and US aid, 367
Prokhanov, Aleksandr, 147, 545
Prokof'ev, Yurii, 79, 134, 420, 481, 493–494, 498
  and coup involvement, 594

Prostyakov, Igor', 211
Protasenko, Yurii, 528
Protasov, Viktor, 773
Prudnikov, Viktor, 627, 657
Prunskiene, Kazimiera, 4, 282, 648
Pryakhin, Georgii, 112
Pugo, Boriss
  and AIDS, 420
  and Armed Forces Day, 134
  and Baltic republics, 26, 28, 186, 215, 291, 339, 340, 379, 510–511, 513
  and Cabinet of Ministers, 138
  and coup, 555, 612
  and CPSU, 293
  and crime and law enforcement, 54, 77, 125, 359–360, 372
  and Moscow police chief, 207, 249
  and Party Control Commission, 67
  and *perestroika*, 279
  and politics, 42–43, 211, 425–426
  and Security Council, 176
  and South Ossetian unrest, 16, 98
  suicide of, 582
  and Union issues, 409
Pukhova, Zoya, 128
Pulatov, Abdurrakhim, 387, 502–503, 770
Puscasu, Victor, 125, 255
Puura, Toomas, 850
Pyankov, Boris, 585
Pylypchuk, Volodymyr, 432, 724

Qadhafi, Muammar, 40–41
Qian Qichen, 228, 336, 758
Qin Jiwei, 312
Quayle, Dan, 774–775

Raevsky, Vladimir, 650, 750, 800
Rafsanjani, Ali Akbar Hashemi-, 82, 396, 550, 644
Rainis, Janis, 303
Rakhimova, Bikhodzhal, 341
Rasosnykh, Viktor, 355
Rasputin, Valentin, 492
Razumau, Mikalai, 369, 526–527
Reagan, Ronald, 318
Red'kin, Aleksandr, 638
Redkoborody, Vladimir, 636
Reinieks, Andris, 514
Repse, Einars, 633
Reshetov, Petr, 23

Revenko, Grigorii, 200–201, 329–330, 391, 410, 501, 585, 618
Reznik, Genri, 111
Rhundadze, Kudzha, 98
Rigvava, Sergei, 628
Rodionov, Igor', 525
Rogachev, Igor', 4, 9–10, 246, 288, 652
Roman, Petre, 102, 530–531
Romanov, Vasilii, 156–157, 484, 611
Rosca, Iurie, 653, 789, 910
Rostov, Yurii, 75, 196
Rostovtsev, Aleksandr, 124
Rubiks, Alfreds, 262, 565, 596–597, 779
Rudalov, Valerii, 24
Rudev, Petr, 338
Rudis, Audrius, 224
Rulevsky, Yurii, 753
Rumyantsev, Oleg, 296, 692, 705–706
Rutskoi, Aleksandr
  and Center for Operational Control over Reform, 797
  and Checheno-Ingushetia, 704, 709–710, 711, 784, 785
  and control of nuclear weapons, 605
  and coup, 577, 693, 876, 622–623
  criticisms of, 469, 729
  and departification, 484
  and Economic Treaty, 727
  expulsion from CPSU, 528, 529
  and foreign affairs, 708–709, 775, 809, 900
  and KGB inaction, 727
  and Latvia, 885
  and political groups, 237, 334, 371–372, 441, 444, 521, 600, 647, 762, 894
  and politics, 494–495, 852–853, 902–903
  and price liberalization, 861
  and RSFSR National Guard, 68, 583, 733
  and Russian premiership, 722, 738
  and territorial disputes, 605
Ruutel, Arnold
  and coup, 567
  on El'tsin, 419
  and Estonian leadership, 419
  and Europe, 374, 429
  and independence, 165
  and KGB in Estonia, 616
  and Nordic countries, 140, 264
  and Soviet troop withdrawals, 885
  and UN, 660
  and US, 224

Name Index

Ruzimuradov, Shovruk, 477
Ryabchenko, Sergei, 352, 409
Ryabev, Lev, 138, 152
Ryaboshapka, Svetlana, 424
Rybas, Stanislav, 262
Rylyakov, Vladimir, 571, 684
Ryzhkov, Nikolai, 31, 57, 251
   and RSFSR presidency, 295, 322, 327, 374, 381, 396, 397
Ryzhov, Yurii, 618, 656, 680

Sabah, Jabir al-Ahmad al-, 644, 830
Saburov, Evgenii, 467, 726–727, 796
Safarov, Bozorali, 899
Sagalaev, Eduard, 81, 622, 627
Saidov, Abdrashid, 58
Saikin, Valerii, 467
Sakalas, Aloyzas, 315
Sakharov, Andrei, 172, 331, 346–347
Sal'e, Marina, 63
Salih, Muhammad, 442–443, 920–921
Salinas, Carlos, 450
Salmins, Raimonds, 576
Salolainen, Pertti, 893
Saltykov, Boris, 824, 917
Salykov, Kakimbek, 151, 217
Samadov, Abduzhalil, 778
Samaras, Antonios, 254
Samsonov, Viktor, 561, 569, 621, 878
Samuel, Richard Christopher, 760
Samuels, Shimon, 694
Sandru, Vasile, 617
Sarkisyan, Aram, 375
Sarkisyan, Sos, 742
Sarkisyan, Tigran, 307
Sattar, Zakhir, 136
Saud al-Faisal, Prince, 325
Saudargas, Algirdas, 429, 576, 608, 721, 772, 892
Savisaar, Edgar, 50, 137, 204, 215, 340, 419, 576, 831
   and coup, 567, 589–590
   and US, 317–318, 774–775
Schlueter, Poul, 140
Schneier, Arthur, 527
Schwarzkopf, Norman, 207
Scowcroft, Brent, 280, 412
Sedov, Valerii, 432
Sekretaryuk, Vyacheslav, 612
Seleznev, Gennadii, 442, 592, 622

Seleznev, Sergei, 878
Semenov, Vladimir, 627, 642
Semenov, Yurii, 137
Senchagov, Valentin, 204
Sen'ko, Fedor, 138, 216
Serdyukov, Vladimir, 779
Serdyukovskaya, Galina, 795
Sereda, Gennadii, 413
Sergeev, Aleksandr, 228–229
Sergeev, Aleksei, 281, 328
Sergeev, Anatolii, 632–633
Sevost'yanov, Evgenii, 648
Sevruk, Vladimir, 395, 586
Shabad, Anatolii, 306
Shabdolov, Shodi, 670
Shaevich, Adolf, 188, 818
Shafarevich, Igor', 45
Shaimiev, Mintimer, 398, 463, 573, 624
   and departification decree, 23, 523
   and Tatarstan independence demonstrations, 735, 736
Shakhanov, Mukhtar, 726
Shakhnazarov, Georgii, 48, 63–64, 379
Shakhrai, Sergei, 539, 706, 739, 797, 868, 882, 893
Shaki, Avner, 221
Shamir, Yitzhak, 271, 324
Shanibov, Yurii, 789
Shapirov, Vyacheslav, 151–152
Shaposhnikov, Evgenii
   appointments, 591, 836, 908
   and Baltic republics, 589, 605, 647, 654, 716, 753, 831, 850, 851
   and Commonwealth of Independent States, 886, 917
   and coup, 640
   and Cuba, 818
   and Dniester putsch, 872–873
   and interrepublican military issues, 722, 751–752, 787, 794
   and military cuts, 639, 715
   and nuclear weapons, 555, 656
   and reorganization of military, 600–601, 651–652
   on role of military, 621
   and withdrawal from Germany, 810–811
Shapovalenko, Vyacheslav, 126
Shara, Farouq al-, 244, 324
Sharansky, Natan, 757
Sharin, Leonid, 347

Shatalin, Stanislav, 35, 39, 51, 79, 279
 and CPSU, 131, 290
 and political opposition groups, 69–70, 257, 381, 441, 445
Shatalin, Yurii, 215, 306, 308
Shatrov, Mikhail, 627
Shchadov, Mikhail, 152, 156, 411
Shchekochikhin, Yurii, 462
Shchelkanov, Aleksandr, 132
Shcherbak, Yurii, 117, 274, 418
Shcherbakov, Aleksei, 668
Shcherbakov, Vladimir, 138, 277, 284, 302, 341, 524, 543
 and anticrisis program, 334, 492
 and economic reform, 403, 531–532
Shcherbakov, Vyacheslav, 561
Shcherbitsky, Vladimir, 360
Shchirenko, Ivan, 895
Shebarshin, Leonid, 649
Sheinis, Viktor, 238
Shemyatenkov, Vladimir, 336
Shenin, Oleg, 65, 261, 458, 554, 675
Shevardnadze, Eduard
 and Armenian-Azerbaijani conflict, 381–382, 842
 and Baltic negotiations, 685
 on Bessmertnykh appointment, 32
 and coup, 568
 and CPSU, 450, 464
 criticisms of, 90–91, 114, 183, 347, 406
 on defense and security councils, 618, 836
 and environmental council, 758
 and foreign affairs, 48, 192, 193–194, 260, 319–320, 846, 852
 foreign-policy associations, 94, 128, 690
 and Georgia, 173, 645, 700
 and Gorbachev resignation, 893
 and Political Consultative Council, 680
 and political opposition groups, 257, 392, 441, 443, 444, 485, 674, 894, 922
 and pro-Popov rally, 681
 public opinion and, 634
 reappointment as foreign minister, 607, 832
 and reform, 279, 395–396, 489
 resignation of, 2–3, 8–9, 39
 and RSFSR presidential election, 397
 on state stability, 180, 212–213, 236–237, 300, 552, 640–641
 television profile of, 734
 on troops in Moscow, 225

Shilov, Ivan, 207–208, 249, 310, 334, 529–530
Shilov, Viktor, 419
Shimko, Vladimir, 137, 138, 411
Shishkin, Viktor, 636
Shlyaga, Nikolai, 627, 651
Shlykov, Serafim, 78
Shmakov, Mikhail, 230, 888
Shmelev, Nikolai, 50, 256
Shokhin, Aleksandr, 803, 848
Shorin, Valerii, 825
Shul'ha, Mykola, 442
Shumeiko, Vladimir, 781
Shushkevich, Stanislau, 241, 664, 778, 853–854, 880, 883
 and interrrepublican relations, 764, 801, 892, 898
Shushpanov, Pavel, 152, 229
Sidorov, S., 213
Sidorov, Vitalii, 458, 515
Sigua, Tengiz, 94, 553, 647
Silaev, Ivan
 and anticrisis program, 334
 appointments, 600, 906
 appointments by, 627
 and coup, 577, 593
 and CPSU, 461
 and economic committees, 644, 726, 791, 877
 and economic reform, 46, 219, 222–223, 477, 620, 768
 and financial scandal, 243–244
 and foreign affairs, 136, 176, 191, 280, 345, 664, 851
 and miners' strike, 155, 157, 231
 and Moldavian agreement, 543
 and Moscow food shortage, 879
 and political opposition groups, 159, 441, 444
 and postcoup political structure, 610, 772–773, 841
 and price reform, 110
 and public opinion, 634
 and RSFSR government, 466, 663
 and Russian sovereignty, 675
 and Siberian republic, 546
 and Soviet debt, 809, 828–829
Silins, Elmars, 191
Simenas, Albertas, 850
Simpsons, Peteris, 876

Name Index

Simutis, Anicetas, 660
Sitaryan, Stepan, 431
Sklyarov, Vitalii, 745
Skokov, Yurii, 155, 304, 487
Skoryk, Larisa, 425
Skrypnikov, Viktor, 255
Skubiszewski, Krzysztof, 639, 906
Sladkevicius, Cardinal, 348, 385
Slansky, Rudolf, 740
Slauta, Genadius, 743
Slyun'kov, Nikolai, 414
Slyusar', Anatolii, 832
Smirnov, Igor', 449, 624–625, 634, 873
Smirnov, Valerii, 668
Smirnov-Ostashvili, Konstantin, 294
Snegur, Mircea
   and Commonwealth agreement, 923
   and Consultative Council, 147
   and coup, 562, 570–571, 587
   and Dniester, 655, 683, 872, 874–875
   and EC, 388
   and Economic Treaty, 702, 732, 798
   and elections, 760, 880–881
   and Jewish culture, 552
   and leadership controversy, 355–356
   and Moldavian army and border guard, 740, 764
   and Moldavian independence and recognition, 135, 332–333, 431–432, 617
   and Moldavian National Bank, 383–384
   and Moldavian Popular Front, 910–911
   resignation of, 132
   and reunification with Romania, 671, 741, 788–789
   and Romania, 102, 125, 209, 531
   on Russian ambitions, 729
   and Soviet military in Moldavia, 190, 389, 822–823, 892
   and Union issues, 86, 174, 436, 538
Snegurets, Anatolii, 153
Soares, Mario, 346
Sobal, Mikhal, 241
Sobchak, Anatolii
   and Baltic negotiations, 685
   and coup, 562, 569, 621
   and crime, 472
   criticisms of, 685
   death threats to, 8
   on dismantling central structures, 606
   and economic reform plan, 545, 805
   and food supplies, 426, 837
   and foreign affairs, 168, 192, 336–337, 360, 364
   and government restructuring, 52, 407
   and Leningrad CP, 594
   and Lenin's tomb, 766
   and media, 426, 864
   and Political Consultative Council, 680
   and political opposition groups, 257, 441–442, 746, 818, 894
   and politics, 126, 132, 397
   and public opinion, 634
   and Security Council, 618
   and Soviet military, 37, 54
   and stability, 110
   and Tajik unrest, 698–699
   and Ukrainian independence, 863
   and Ukrainian-Russian postcoup agreement, 622–623
   and unity issues, 86–87, 755, 808
   and USSR Supreme Soviet, 464
   and Western aid, 665, 690, 780
Sobol', Mikhas', 226
Sokolov, Sergei, 326, 347
Solomatin, Viktor, 55
Solomentsev, Mikhail, 406
Solomin, Yurii, 521
Solton, Yurii, 670
Solzhenitsyn, Aleksandr, 331, 660, 694, 723
Soshnikov, Aleksandr, 627
Soslambekov, Yusup, 789–790
Spassky, Igor', 402
Spinei, Gheorghe, 260
Spiridonov, Lev, 592, 615
Spiridonov, Yurii, 217
Stalin, 8, 63
Stankevich, Sergei
   and conservatives, 59, 525
   and coup, 554, 574–575
   criticisms by, 685, 703
   and Easter service, 250
   as foreign envoy, 775
   and military patrols of cities, 54–55
   as Moscow advisor, 510
   on multiparty system, 667–668
   and pro-El'tsin rally, 184
   and Sakharov memorial, 347
   and Soviet debt, 766
   and Union issues, 730–731, 738
Stankevicius, Ceslovas, 433

Starodubtsev, Vasilii, 181, 555, 583, 620
Starovoitova, Galina, 78, 363, 425, 775–776, 785, 842
Stavenhagen, Lutz, 345
Steinbrik, Bruno, 470
Stepankov, Valentin, 149, 189, 690–691, 711, 712, 823
Stepanov, Viktor, 768
Stepashin, Sergei, 95, 113, 149, 316, 614, 638, 648, 739–740
Steponavicius, Julijonas, 166
Stercken, Hans, 345
Sterlikov, Vladimir, 354
Stetten, Wolfgang von, 346
Stoltenberg, Gerhard, 294, 810
Stolyarov, Nikolai, 498, 619, 627, 637, 697, 860
Stoyanov, Dimitar, 225
Strauss, Robert, 382–383, 863
Streibl, Max, 285
Sturua, Melor, 465
Sulcs, Ugis, 658
Suleimenov, Olzhas, 525, 726
Suleimenov, Toleubai, 909
Sumskoi, Aleksandr, 822
Surkov, Aleksei, 695, 754
Surkov, Anatolii, 194
Surkov, Mikhail, 290, 294–295, 520, 523, 627
Susha, Ales', 242
Suslov, Mikhail, 285
Süssmuth, Rita, 345
Suzuki, Muneo, 721
Syadou, Valerii, 460
Syskovets, Oleg, 411, 413
Systsov, Apollon, 404

Taburyanskyi, Leopold, 862
Tadao, Chino, 780
Tae-Woo, Roh, 279–280
Tahirzade, Adalat, 171
Talas, Mustafa, 79–80
Tal'kov, Igor', 717
Tamkevicius, Sigitas, 348
Tarasenko, Sergei, 120
Tarasov, Artem, 85, 158, 243
Tarasov, Boris, 87–88, 360
Tarazevich, Georgii, 27, 28, 73, 352, 478
Tarnausky, Ryhor, 449
Tashaliev, Ataman, 205
Tashmuhammadov, Bekjan, 294

Tenberg, Nikolai, 731
Teoctist, Patriarch, 102, 835
Terekh, Kondrat, 211
Terekhov, Vladislav, 188, 434
Ter-Petrossyan, Levon
  and Armenian-Azerbaijani conflict, 288–289, 305, 306, 307, 309–310, 451, 468, 842, 843
  and Armenian elections, 742
  and Armenian genocide commemoration, 291
  attack on family of, 439
  and Baltic republics, 25, 548
  and coup, 562, 586
  and Dashnaks, 463
  and France, 355
  and Nine-plus-One agreement, 362
  and Russian cooperation agreement, 920
  and Union treaty, 490–491
  and US, 815
Thatcher, Margaret, 364, 771
Timoshishin, Mikhail, 385, 536
Tishin, Vitalii, 196
Titov, Gennadii, 93, 226, 648
Tiu, Nicolae, 102, 209
Tizyakov, Aleksandr, 555, 583, 620
Tkachenko, Aleksandr, 357
Tkachou, Mikhas', 468
Tolkushkin, Vladimir, 231
Topal, Stepan, 11, 169
Töpfer, Klaus, 399, 400
Toporov, Vladimir, 631
Travkin, Nikolai, 184, 210, 381, 444, 549, 663, 692–693, 768
Tret'yak, Ivan, 651
Tret'yakov, Valerii, 631
Tret'yakov, Vitalii, 779
Trizno, Oleg, 242
Trubin, Nikolai
  and Baltic military actions, 340–341, 376–377
  and Chernobyl' investigation, 83
  and El'tsin, 182, 391
  and Jewish dissidents, 757
  and postcoup investigations, 593–594, 603, 620
  and rehabilitation of Baltic leaders, 771
  resignation of, 619
  and Solzhenitsyn, 660
  and Tarasov immunity, 158, 243

Name Index

and Tbilisi massacre, 173
and treason charges against Gorbachev, 798–799
and Union referendum, 170
Tsagalov, Kim, 373
Tsalko, Aleksandr, 887
Tsaplin, Stanislav, 648
Tsipko, Aleksandr, 662
Tsiu, Nicolai, 806
Tsvetov, Vladimir, 259
Tsyganenko, Igor', 447
Tuleev, Aman, 327, 397, 877
Tulin, Dmitrii, 899
Tumanov, Oleg, 251
Tumelis, Juozas, 315, 894
Tunaitis, Juozas, 348
Turadzhonzoda, Akbar, 672
Turgunaliev, Topchubek, 733–734
Tutwiler, Margaret, 66, 104–105, 377
Tyssovsky, Yurii, 471
Tyul'kin, Viktor, 541

Udovenko, Gennadii, 617
Ugglas, Margaretha Af, 771–772
Umalatova, Sazhi, 181
Ungureanu, Ion, 521
Uoka, Kazimieras, 172
Urbsys, Juozas, 301
Urdze, Andrejs, 188–189
Uskhopchik, Vladimir, 25, 378
Usmanov, Anvar, 132
Uspensky, Nikolai, 832
Ustinov, Vyacheslav, 818, 866

Vagnorius, Gediminas
 and economic issues, 350, 689, 736, 795, 813
 and Estonia, 576
 and foreign affairs, 274–275, 473, 547, 663, 775, 850–851
 and "Sajudis," 894
 and Soviet debt, 828
 and Soviet military action in Lithuania, 333, 338–339, 357
Vahidov, Erkin, 503
Vaisvila, Zigmas, 187, 379, 595, 753, 851
Vaksberg, Arkadii, 719, 743
Valoshka, Yas, 527
van den Broek, Hans, 114
Vardanyan, David, 305

Vare, Raivo, 775
Varennikov, Valentin, 73, 347, 492, 554, 620, 651
Vartazaryan, Artak, 371
Vasil'ev, Dmitrii, 717
Vasil'ev, Georgii, 532
Vayrynen, Paavo, 673
Vazgen I, Catholikos, 291
Vaznis, Aloizs, 457, 724
Velayati, Ali Akbar, 82, 111, 396, 550, 729, 846–847, 871
Velichko, Vladimir, 31
Velikhov, Evgenii, 443, 680, 698
Venkevicius, Romualdas, 195
Verdine, Hubert, 268
Vershkov, Vladimir, 72
Vilkas, Eduardas, 461
Vinogradov, Aleksei, 314–315
Vinogradov, Vladimir, 611
Visockis, Algimantas, 548
Vitkovsky, E. N., 666–667
Vladislavlev, Aleksandr, 443, 686, 859
Vlasov, Al'bert, 592
Vogel, Dieter, 195, 321, 489
Voilukov, Arnol'd, 867
Voitovych, Adam, 623
Volchek, Dmitrii, 535, 625–626
Volik, Anatolii, 728
Volkogonov, Dmitrii, 95, 126, 222, 416, 802, 814, 833, 923
Volkov, Vyacheslav, 144
Vol'mer, Yurii, 137
Volodin, Eduard, 545
Voloshchuk, Semen, 128
Voloshka, Yas, 6
Vol'sky, Arkadii, 525, 600, 604, 614, 620, 750
 and Movement for Democratic Reforms, 441, 444
Voronin, Lev, 98, 336, 400, 520, 620, 832
Voronin, Vladimir, 51, 89, 116, 181, 282
Voronin, Yurii, 781
Vorontsov, Nikolai, 627
Vorontsov, Yulii, 225, 471
Voroshilov, Kliment, 17
Vorotnikov, Valerii, 386
Voshchanov, Pavel, 110, 523, 563, 604, 899
Vrba, Jan, 176
Vvedensky, Sergei, 484
Vyshinsky, Mikhail, 751

Waigel, Theo, 679–680
Walesa, Lech, 3, 172
Wallenberg, Raoul, 635–636
Watanabe, Michio, 317, 850–851
Weizsäcker, Richard von, 285, 360, 838
Wiesel, Eli, 649
Wormsbächer, Hugo, 188
Wörner, Manfred, 816
Wurth, Hubert, 406

Yablokov, Aleksei, 206, 674–675
Yachenkov, Vladimir, 184
Yagodin, Gennadii, 139, 481, 627
Yakovlev, Aleksandr, 39, 63–64
    and Babii Yar commemoration, 717
    and Baltic negotiations, 685
    and conservatives, 57, 438–439
    and coup, 568, 598, 817
    and CPSU, 438, 536, 550–551, 552
    criticisms of, 324, 334
    on Gorbachev, 197–198, 383, 551
    and government restructuring, 7–8
    and Honecker case, 751
    and ideology, 278–279, 501–502, 520
    and integrating into global economy, 823–824
    and joint defense treaty, 791
    and KGB, 678
    media and public opinion on, 552, 634
    and Moscow City Assembly, 453
    and Movement for Democratic Reforms, 441, 444, 674, 894, 922
    and Political Consultative Council, 680
    and postcoup republic negotiations, 610
    and pro-Popov rally, 681
    and Security Council, 177, 618
    stabilization accord and Transcaucasus violence, 362
    on state stability, 551, 707–708
Yakovlev, Egor, 61, 579, 614, 625, 680, 893
Yakovlev, Gennadii, 872, 873
Yakovlev, Veniamin, 855, 889
Yakunin, Gleb, 136, 681, 746
Yanaev, Gennadii
    and coup, 554, 555–556, 559–560, 562–563, 567, 575, 577, 583, 600, 613, 657
    and election irregularities, 17, 129
    and Japan, 48
    and Lenin birthday ceremonies, 285
    and miners, 94, 151

and minister appointments, 4
and pro-El'tsin rally, 211
on progress of reform, 70
and Security Council, 176
and Soviet Germans, 143
and Union treaty, 567
Yanin, Valerii, 668
Yaremenko, Yurii, 322
Yarov, Yurii, 781
Yashin, Yurii, 887
Yasin, Evgenii, 614
Yavlinsky, Grigorii
    and anticrisis program, 256, 491–492
    and appointments, 14, 600
    and economic reform, 403, 408, 430, 620
    and economic union, 661, 726, 791
    and gold reserves, 689–690, 735, 807
    on inflation, 663
    and Kurile Islands, 643
    resignation of, 107
    and Union issues, 776, 816–817
Yazov, Dmitrii
    and anniversaries, 134, 421
    on army's problems, 422–423
    and Cabinet of Ministers, 137
    and CFE agreement, 257
    and Cossack army units, 326
    and coup, 555, 568, 574, 583, 635, 651, 718, 748
    on CPSU in military, 225
    demonstrations against, 42–43
    and education minister, 481
    and foreign affairs, 79–80, 168, 201, 312, 364, 400, 488
    and Gulf War lessons, 207
    and Lithuanian prosecution, 903
    and military in Baltic republics, 25, 187, 393
    and military patrols in cities, 54
    and military reductions, 496
    on national security, 326
    and nuclear codes, 554
    on professional army, 226
    and Security Council, 176
    and Soviet air defense, 121
    and Union issues, 409
    and World War II historiography, 416
Yoo Chong Ha, 10
Yugin, Viktor, 647, 864–865
Yukhnovskyi, Ihor, 457, 862

Name Index

Yuldashev, Shavkat, 400
Yurkov, Anatolii, 611
Yusupov, Shomon, 672

Zaikov, Lev, 770
Zalamai, Uladzimir, 740
Zalygin, Sergei, 217
Zamyatin, Leonid, 592, 639, 832
Zaramensky, I., 522
Zarebski, Andrzej, 677–678
Zaslavskaya, Tat'yana, 35, 782
Zaslavsky, Igor', 848
Zaslavsky, Il'ya, 504, 532
Zatulin, Konstantin, 736–737
Zavgaev, Doku, 215
Zeile, Valentina, 368–369
Zelentsov, Sergei, 896
Zhelev, Zhelyu, 345
Zhirinovsky, Vladimir, 542, 546, 782, 909
 and coup, 561, 594
 and RSFSR presidency, 282, 351, 380–381, 397, 400
Zhitnikov, Aleksandr, 203–204
Zhivkov, Todor, 247
Zhivotnyuk, Anatolii, 481
Zhukovets, Gennadii, 413–414
Zimowski, Jerzy, 911
Zlenko, Anatolii, 286, 418
 and foreign affairs, 639, 731, 744, 870
 and Lithuania, 892
 and RSFSR, 778
 and Ukrainian security, 867–868, 919
Zolotkov, Andrei, 676
Zorgins, Andris, 588
Zverev, Andrei, 614, 821
Zyuganov, Gennadii, 324, 522
Zyukin, Vladimir, 594

Subject Index

Abkhazia, 258, 475, 587
Abortion, 438
Academy of Sciences,
  USSR, 692
  Russian, 879
Accidents
  automobile, 90, 859–860
  Chernobyl' fire, 731. *See also* Chernobyl' nuclear accident
  helicopter crash in Nagorno-Karabakh, 837
  nuclear submarine, 402, 761
  Donbass mining, 440
  industrial, 388
Adzharia, 288, 425
Aeroflot, 20–21, 901
Afghanistan
  accidental bombing by, 385
  arms supplies to, 649–650
  conflict in, 676, 695, 878
  and damage reparations from USSR, 687
  natural gas from, 7
  and recognition of CIS republics, 914
  and Soviet aid, 28, 220
  and Soviet POWs, 136
  See also Mujahidin
AFL-CIO, 152, 153, 172
Agriculture
  grain harvest, 253, 385, 544, 776–777
  harvest failure in Kazakhstan, 831
  and Moldavia, 515
  and reform, 197, 703, 829–830, 836. *See also* Land reform
  state of, 109, 245
  and Tajikistan, 502
  terms of trade for farmers, 413, 521, 536–537
  See also Food
"Agzybirlik," 91–92, 573
Aid
  appeals for Western, 326, 391–392, 678, 690, 756–757, 824
  and EBRD, 189
  and EC, 89, 297–298, 358, 388, 392, 701, 719

  environmental, 869
  and G-7, 469, 470, 474, 734
  from Germany, 451
  and Harvard plan, 402–403, 430
  and Japan, 271, 456–457, 722–723, 750–751
  mishandled and stolen shipments, 36
  for Nagorno-Karabakh, 252
  from RSFSR, 486, 773
  from Saudi Arabia, 725
  from South Korea, 51
  Soviet foreign, 28, 136, 220
  from United Arab Emirates, 727–728
  and US, 32–33, 367, 421, 509, 724–725, 773
  US, to Baltic republics, 109–110, 654, 774–775
  Western, 202, 362, 374, 620–621, 640, 664–665, 745, 780, 828, 851
  and Western reaction to intervention in Baltic republics, 25, 26, 28, 47, 88–89
  See also Credit; Training
AIDS. *See* Health
Albania, 31, 146, 345, 812, 915
All-Army Communist Party conference, 225
All-Latvian National Salvation Committee, 2
All-National Congress of the Chechen People (OKChN), 709–714, 789
All-Russian Communist Party of the Bolsheviks, 814
All-Russian State Radio Company, 74
All-Ukrainian Association of Solidarity with Workers, 425
All-Union Council of Soldiers' Mothers, 485
All-Union Islamic Renaissance Party, 60–61
All-Union State Television and Radio Broadcasting Company
  and air time policies, 193
  calls for independent media, 607
  criticisms of, 296
  as successor to Gosteleradio, 92–93
  and Leningrad media, 178, 426
  personnel changes, 579, 622
  and RSFSR television, 220
  "TSN" staff purges, 196
  and "Vzglyad," 217
  See also Media; Television

Altai Krai, 21, 427
Amnesty International, 905
Amoco, 402, 435
Anticrime Coordination Committee, 64
Anti-Semitism, 688, 693, 717–718, 818
Appointments
  central government, 211, 260, 322, 341–342, 466, 585, 591, 614–615, 622, 627, 631, 674, 797, 821, 832, 855, 860
  CPSU, 67, 112, 179, 290, 293, 375
  Foreign Ministry, 179, 257, 280, 337, 345, 701, 799, 809–810, 832, 852, 859
  military, 833, 877, 878–879, 908
  Moscow, 82, 207–208, 249, 504, 511–512, 666
  Soviet representative to EC, 336
  TASS, 615
  See also individual republics
Aral Sea, 124, 151, 246, 780
Archives
  coup attempt and CPSU order to destroy, 720
  CPSU, 618, 625–626, 637
  on deportees to Urals, 145
  KGB, 619, 642, 661–662, 679
  Latvian KGB, 599
  Lenin documents in CPSU, 814
  NKVD-MVD, 858
  presidential, 754–755
  RSFSR takeover of, 597, 923
  See also Historiography
Argumenty i fakty, 834
Armenia
  and all-Union referendum, 199
  appointments, 844
  and coup attempt, 562, 586
  environmental issues, 273
  and France, 355
  and independence, 151, 482, 669
  and Iraqi Kurds, 253–254
  and Lithuania, 548, 840–841
  and media, 371
  and Nagorno-Karabakh, 668–669, 842–843, 916–917
  nationalization of CPSU property, 272–273, 625
  and political groups, 146, 463, 519. *See also individual groups*
  presidential election, 431, 540, 682, 728–729, 742

and RSFSR, 920
and Soviet military, 11, 72
state of emergency lifted, 550
and ties with other republics, 130
and Union treaty, 366, 490–491, 546
and US, 815
See also Armenian-Azerbaijani conflict
Armenian-Azerbaijani conflict
  and appeal for UN peacekeeping troops, 870
  blockade of Armenia, 265, 807, 835, 906
  and human rights abuses, 288–289, 401, 487
  proposals to mediate, 381–382, 535
  violence, 251–252, 305–312, 362, 468
  See also Nagorno-Karabakh
Armenian Communist Party, 273, 309, 337, 375
  nationalization of property, 272–273, 625
Armenian National Army, 255
Armenian National-Democratic Union, 519
Armenian Pan-National Movement, 273, 361
Armenian Republican Party, 306
Armenian Union for National Self-Determination, 306
Arms control
  British on, 202
  El'tsin on, 633
  Soviet decisionmaking and authority in, 115, 722, 811
  nuclear missiles off alert, 701
  and nuclear test ban, 696
  Soviet military dissatisfaction over, 502
  START Treaty, 504, 507, 778
  and Ukraine, 867–868
  US accusations of treaty violations, 492–493
  US-Soviet negotiations, 58, 59, 192, 505, 696, 714–715
  See also Conventional Forces in Europe treaty; Nuclear weapons
Arms sales, 18, 404, 666–667
  to Afghanistan, 649–650
  to China, 206, 336
  and Middle East, 173, 407, 817–818
  to Nicaragua, 4–5
  See also Weapons
Arrests and detentions
  and antispeculation law, 319
  and Armenian-Azerbaijani conflict, 308–309, 310

Subject Index

Belorussian, 432, 460
and coup involvement, 594, 600, 628, 690–691, 779
of coup leaders, 577–578, 582–583
of Democratic Union leader, 486–487
and demonstrations in Baku, 596
of Dniester leader, 624–625, 634
and Georgia, 123–124, 645
and Khmara, 479
of Latvian CP leader, 596–597
and Lithuanians, 103–104, 203–204, 595
and OMON members, 790
opposition groups in Turkmenistan, 624
and Ukrainians, 19–20, 118, 247
See also Court proceedings; Investigations; Justice system
Association of Southeast Asian Nations (ASEAN), 464–465, 500
Austria, 65
Autocephalous Orthodox Church, 288
Avtrokon, 437
Awards
AFL-CIO human-rights, 172
1990 Nobel Peace Prize, 384
Norwegian award to Landsbergis, 186
"Azat" movement (Kazakhstan), 443, 726
Azerbaijan
and all-Union referendum, 148, 171, 199
Baku commodities exchange, 60
and Central Asian republics, 547
and coup, 562, 587
curfews and states of emergency, 276, 450
defense and security issues, 639, 728, 801
demonstrations in, 596, 697, 767
and Economic Treaty, 745
government restructuring in, 778
and helicopter crash in Nagorno-Karabakh, 837
and independence, 616, 626, 746–747, 920
and Iran, 169, 396, 550, 847, 871
Nagorno-Karabakh negotiations, 668–669, 842–843
political groups, 148, 171, 435, 482, 622, 653. See also Azerbaijani Popular Front
presidential election, 435, 542
and Soviet military property, 898
Supreme Soviet session, 84–85

and Turkey, 186
and Union treaty, 427, 487
See also Armenian-Azerbaijani conflict; Nagorno-Karabakh
Azerbaijani Communist Party, 482, 622, 653
Azerbaijani Popular Front, 84, 171, 186, 632, 669
and postcoup demonstration, 596, 697

Babii Yar, 110–111
Baku, 45, 60, 276, 854. See also Azerbaijan
Baltic Communist parties, 297
Baltic Council, 213, 264
Baltic republics
and AIDS, 854
and all-Union referendum, 199
calls for presidential rule in, 89
and central government negotiations, 73, 165, 396, 685
and Council of Europe, 208–209, 428–429
criticism of Western position on, 446
and CSCE, 365–366, 415
customs post incidents, 378–379, 470. See also Border, post incidents in Baltic republics
and defense, 633
and diplomatic recognition, 607–608, 630, 726
and EBRD, 775, 875
and EC, 406, 459–460
economic sanctions against, 366
economy and financial sector, 658–659, 779, 837–838
and energy, 780
and European countries, 168, 188–189, 202, 239, 721
and free trade, 736, 893
G-7 and G-24 groups, 473, 812–813, 890–891
and Gorbachev, 50, 384
and Helsinki process, 742
and Icelandic mediation, 264
and KGB, 697
military action in, 11–12, 62, 393, 399
mistreatment of Soviet servicemen in, 108
and minorities, 178, 744, 868
MVD troop withdrawal, 820
and Nordic countries, 140, 148, 688–689, 771–772
and North Atlantic Assembly, 760

953

Baltic republics (*continued*)
  and plans for governments-in-exile, 576
  proposed commission on military-civilian tensions, 476–477
  reactions to military action in, 41, 46–47, 48, 58–59, 114
  and republican mutual-support treaties, 31
  and Soviet foreign debt, 766, 828
  Soviet interference in airspace, 753
  and Soviet military service, 670–671
  Soviet troop withdrawal from, 647, 716–717
  and UN, 459, 660–661, 898
  and US, 192, 317–318, 421, 509, 513, 520, 547, 647, 653–654, 774–775
  on Western aid for USSR, 374
  See also Estonia; Latvia; Lithuania
Bangladesh, 915
Bank(s)
  Belorussian hard-currency accounts, 6
  EBRD and reforming, 189
  and economic crime, 456
  Estonian, 659
  and hard-currency shortage, 866–867, 889–890
  investing in Eurasco, 686–687
  joint Saudi-Soviet, 401
  Kazakhstan peasant, 64
  in Latvia, 633
  Moldavian National, 383–384
  nationalization of Georgian, 550
  new Soviet investment, 395
  republican-central dispute, 537
  RSFSR takeover of central, 841
  Soviet Foreign Trade, 758, 816, 857
  suspension of commercial debt payments, 871
  and Western credit blockade, 384–385
  See also Financial sector
Bashkiria, 191, 239, 247, 454, 781, 819
Bavaria, 285–286
Belarus. *See* Belorussia
Belgium, 753
Belorussia
  and all-Union referendum, 199
  appointments and leaders in, 664, 740
  and Baltic republics, 399, 744, 764, 841–842, 898
  border controls, 677
  and central politics, 127, 141–142, 887
  and Chernobyl', 75–76, 139, 292, 414
  and Commonwealth of Independent States, 880, 887–888
  and Czechoslovakia, 740
  defense and security, 622, 676–677, 764, 825
  and economic reform, 778, 804–805, 884
  financial sector, 6, 822, 895
  government restructuring in, 131–132
  and independence, 503, 602
  and interrepublican exports, 839
  justice system, 369, 432, 449, 526–527
  and labor, 240–243, 332, 354–355, 369, 414, 526–527
  and Lithuanian border post incidents, 338–339, 340
  name change for, 667
  and nuclear weapons, 896, 907
  and Poland, 728
  political groups in, 158, 214, 414, 468, 602, 677, 705, 820, 854
  presidency for, 420–421
  and RSFSR border disputes, 604
  and UN, 688
  and Union treaty, 853–854
  and Uzbekistan, 801
Belorussian Communist Party, 602, 705, 854
Belorussian Communists for Democracy, 677
Belorussian Confederation of Labor, 226
Belorussian Popular Front, 158, 214, 468, 820
Bessarabia, 436
"Birlik" (Uzbek Popular Front), 111, 294, 502–503, 672
  and official registration, 657–658, 812
  as political party, 770–771, 920
Bishkek, 85
Black Berets. *See* OMON units
Black market, 50, 334, 392, 715
Black Sea Fleet
  Georgian accord and, 890
  and Ukraine, 861, 918
Blockade(s)
  of Armenia, 265, 906
  and Checheno-Ingushetia, 785
  and Dniester-Moldavian dispute, 634, 701
  and Georgia, 234, 437, 699, 891
  of Klaipeda during coup, 565
  threat of Baltic economic, 318

SUBJECT INDEX

Border
  Afghan resistance and Tajik, 543
  and Armenian-Azerbaijani unrest, 251–252
  Belorussian controls on, 677, 839
  calls for Kazakh revision of, 703
  and Commonwealth agreement, 907
  crossing between Poland and Kaliningrad, 183
  Czech-Ukrainian, 191
  Estonian controls on, 601, 616, 831–832
  Estonian-RSFSR, 760, 885
  Lithuanian-Belorussian, 764
  Lithuanian control of, 602
  Moldavian customs and border guard, 515, 764
  opening of Lithuanian-Polish, 856
  Polish-Belorussian, 728
  Polish-Ukrainian, 911
  post incidents in Baltic republics, 338–341, 378–379, 503–504
  and Romania, 246
  RSFSR challenges, 604–605
  RSFSR controls on, 815
  Sino-Soviet, 228, 312, 336, 428, 459
  Tajik-Kirgiz, 501
  See also Territorial disputes
Bourgeois Democratic Party, 802
Buddhism, 139–140, 164
Bukovina, 436
Bulgaria, 345, 893, 915
Buryatia, 37, 137, 139–140, 619–620, 628
Business
  Apple computers, 507
  Central Moscow Market, 848
  conference on entrepreneurship, 430
  and foreign exchange holdings, 899
  free enterprise zones, 388, 463, 477
  and free market oil sales, 335
  joint-stock Kazakh hydroelectric station, 506–507
  Kazakh commercial data bank, 130
  and Kazakh reform, 218
  platinum marketing, 486
  political party for, 802
  Pravda diamond, 770
  private ownership of, 21
  restrictions on and interference in, 133, 319, 366
  and RSFSR reform plan, 223, 449
  and space payloads, 804
  and taxes, 213, 394, 462
  Volga auto plant, 496
  See also Financial sector; Industry; Joint ventures

Cabinet of Ministers, USSR
  and calls for state of emergency, 544
  and economic and social issues, 166–167, 283, 427, 495–496
  political action by, 210, 295
  and coup attempt, 557, 590
  and cuts in Soviet ministries, 415
  and miners' strike, 156, 229
  nominating members of, 137–138, 600
  role of, 129, 206
  RSFSR condemnation of, 597
  and Union treaty, 552–553
Cambodia, 288
Canada, 274–275, 328, 673, 863, 914
Caspian Sea, 402, 435
Censorship
  and Central Television, 53, 82–83, 263, 440
  and coup, 556, 557, 569
  and coverage of RSFSR Supreme Soviet, 21
  in Georgia, 405
  GUOT closure, 445
  law on KGB functions and postal, 363
  new agency for, 532–533
  and "TSN" staff purges, 196
  by using economic sanctions, 411
  See also Media
Central America, 508
Central Asian republics
  agreements among, 546–547
  and agricultural policy, 502
  and Commonwealth agreement, 883–884
  democrats in, 328, 386
  reaction to Movement for Democratic Reforms, 443
  and water resources, 731–732
  See also individual republics
Central government
  abolition of ministries, 772–773, 841
  appointments in, 211, 260, 322, 341–342, 591, 614–615, 627, 674, 797, 821, 855, 860. *See also* Foreign Ministry, USSR, appointments

955

Central government (*continued*)
deficits, 283, 299, 334, 359, 430, 693–694, 750, 772, 835. *See also* Debt
dismantling of, 606, 904
financing, 857, 860, 865–866
1991 budget, 28
personnel cuts, 415
postcoup proposals on, 609, 610
and presidential powers, 618
republican payments to, 6, 190–191, 224, 248, 256, 284, 297, 368–369
and Union treaty, 390–391
See also Soviet Union; *individual bodies and structures*
Central Intelligence Agency (CIA), 422, 739–740
Central Intelligence Service, 755, 794
Centrist Bloc, 51, 89, 116, 181, 282, 848
CFE. *See* Conventional Forces in Europe treaty
Checheno-Ingushetia
conflict and divisions in, 389–390, 709–714, 782–786
Cossacks in, 298
elections and referendums, 186, 198, 654–655
"Justice Day," 335
and postcoup events, 628
and Prigorodnyi Raion, 704–705
and RSFSR leaders, 215, 727
and Union treaty, 603–604, 619–620
Chernobyl' nuclear accident
and aid from central government, 141
compensation, 139, 319, 382
and court cases, 208
death toll, 273–274
fifth anniversary of, 292
impact and health effects, 75–76, 83, 128, 353, 418
international aid, 399, 519
investigations, 125, 414
securing site, 274
tours to, 80
Ukrainian aid, 148
"Chernobyl'" organization, 382
Chernobyl' Union, 193
Chevron Corporation, 300, 371, 547–548
Chile, 79, 423
China
and arms purchases, 206

and ASEAN, 464–465
credit from, 195
ideology, 521
and Kazakhstan, 468–469
as political asylum for coup supporters, 635
and recognition of CIS republics, 915
and Soviet relations, 142, 312, 336–337, 459, 758
transfer of Damansky Island, 428
Chinese Communist Party, 420
Christian Democratic Party, 663, 727, 808
Chukchi Autonomous Okrug, 793
Churches
Cathedral of the Mother of God, Ufa, 266
Catholic cathedral in Odessa, 549
restoring Kitai Gorod, 123
St. Casimir, 166
Sofia Cathedral, 548
See also individual Churches; Religion
CIA. *See* Central Intelligence Agency
Cities
league of RSFSR, 293
living standards in RSFSR, 417–418
renaming, 67, 85, 147, 678
renaming Leningrad to St. Petersburg, 369–370, 398, 640
Citizenship
"Commonwealth," 907
and Estonia, 650, 742, 801
fees related to Soviet, 506
and Georgia, 431
and Kazakhstan, 906
and Latvia, 658, 741–742, 857
and Lithuania, 389, 505
Moldavian law on, 385
and RSFSR, 823, 857–858
Tajik, 437
and Ukraine, 724
Civil war
dangers of, 381, 383
predictions of, 62, 128, 141, 219
See also Soviet Union, and stability
CNN, 558, 568, 580, 590, 594
Comecon, 7, 431
Commemorations and memorials
anniversary of German invasion, 421–422
Armenian-Azerbaijani, 45, 142, 291
Babii Yar, 110–111, 694, 717–718
Chernobyl' disaster, 292
for coup victims, 693

Subject Index

for deportees in Latvia, 218
for Holocaust victims, 452, 677
Kazan' and Ivan the Terrible, 735
for Novocherkassk massacre, 375–376
and Tajikistan violence, 106
for victims of KAL Flight 007, 630
for victims of political repressions, 745–746
See also Holidays and celebrations
Committee for Constitutional Supervision, USSR
and banning rallies, 210
and Commonwealth agreement, 889
on constitutionality of Emergency Committee, 560
and departification, 495, 526
and police and army patrols, 65, 76, 112, 244–245
and postcoup transitional structures, 631
and *propiska* system, 730
and referendums, 92, 170
and state of emergency in Tajikistan, 752–753
and Union treaty, 457
See also Justice system
Committee on Cooperation with the Baltic States, 459
Committee for Coordination of the Work of the Law-Enforcement Organs, 77
Committee on Defense and Security, 626
Committee of Soviet Women, 128, 248
Committee of Wives and Mothers, 13–14
Commonwealth of Independent States
Baltic republics and, 884
Central Asian reaction to, 883–884
central structures of, 907, 921
foreign recognition of republics, 914–915
formation of, 880, 906–907
and Georgia, 908
and Gorbachev, 881–883, 902
military reaction to, 886–887
and Moldavia, 892, 910–911, 923
and nuclear weapons, 895–896, 907–908, 913
ratification of, 887–888
and security and defense issues, 917, 921–922
and Ukraine, 883, 900, 907, 918–919
USSR Committee for Constitutional Supervision on, 889
and USSR Supreme Soviet, 887, 902

Communications, 169, 433, 566, 580, 597, 682
Communist Initiative Movement, 438–439, 458
Communist Party of the Soviet Union. *See* CPSU
Communists
anticapitalism demonstrations, 909
for Civil Rights, 792–793
congress of orthodox, 438–439
discrimination against, 445, 637, 852–853
and El'tsin departification decree, 483–485
new political movement of, 844–845, 879
and October Revolution anniversary, 801–802
and postcoup USSR Supreme Soviet, 750
and RSFSR presidential campaign, 327–328
Soviet-Vietnamese, 323
and Ukrainian presidency, 435
Union of, 852
See also Conservatives; CPSU; *individual republican Communist parties*
Communist Workers' Party, 845
Compensation
for Chernobyl' accident, 139, 319, 382
and Estonian land law, 747
for farms, 349
from Germany for victims of Nazism, 489
for invalid care, 427
and low-income people, 344
for nuclear testing site, 524–525
and price increases, 204, 214, 331, 776, 804, 817
and repressions during Soviet period, 745
See also Rehabilitations; Subsidies
Confederation of Jewish Organizations, 52–53
Confederation of Trade and Industry, 831
Confederation of Trade Unions, USSR, 248, 284, 388
Conference on Nuclear Disarmament, 549
Conference on Security and Cooperation in Europe (CSCE)
and Baltic republics, 28, 188–189, 213, 317, 365–366, 514, 576
and Belorussia, 688
coup attempt and appeals to, 564
and crisis mediation measures, 415
and Gorbachev, 643
and Ukraine, 88

Congress of Democratic Forces, 57
Congress of People's Deputies, USSR
  postcoup action by, 629
  and Union treaty, 427, 464, 465–466
Congress of Repressed Peoples, 446
Congress of Soviet Germans, 187–188
Congress of the Stock Exchange, 799–800
Conservatives
  in Belorussia, 503
  Bolshevik Platform, 68, 468
  call for patriotic front, 492
  and coup, 620
  democrats on, 480
  demonstration in Leningrad of, 99–100
  and emigration, 268–269
  and foreign policy, 20
  and Gorbachev, 57, 405–406, 450, 458
  and government instability, 9, 237, 429, 695
  in military, 434, 847, 876
  and purging CPSU of reformists, 551
  in RSFSR regions, 702
  RSFSR Supreme Soviet factions, 210, 280–281, 360
  and Soviet Armed Forces Day demonstration, 134–135
  and Tajikistan, 671–673, 732
  and Union treaty, 409, 491
  in Uzbekistan, 502–503
  See also Centrist Bloc; Communists; "Soyuz"
Constitutional Democratic Party of Russia, 407–408, 663
Consultative Council of the Democratic Congress, 481
Consumer goods
  customs duties on, 524
  decree on supplies, 521
  and joint ventures, 264
  promised to farmers, 470, 480
  republican exports of, 540–541, 810, 921.
    See also Trade
  restrictions on sales of, 146–147, 854
  shortages, 201
  and taxes, 352
  See also Prices
Conventional Forces in Europe (CFE) treaty
  alleged Soviet violations of, 20, 202, 257
  and arms control talks, 115
  negotiations, 192, 403–404

  Soviet ratification of, 249, 499
  and Ukraine, 839, 868
  Ukrainian-Russian talks on, 778
  US ratification, 293
Corruption, 85, 466–467, 855
  and Russian KGB role, 720
  and Ukrainian border officials, 911
Cossacks
  and Dniester conflict, 875
  in Karachaevo-Cherkessia, 811
  in Kazakhstan, 659, 827–828
  and law-enforcement units, 213, 326, 422, 723
  leadership, 223
  and rehabilitation, 870
  Union of Cossack Republics, 827
  Union of Volga and Ural, 867
  and unrest in Checheno-Ingushetia, 298, 323
  and Zelenchuk-Urup territorial Okrug, 76–77
Council of Europe, 131, 208–209, 428–429, 660–661
Council of the Federation
  economic agreements by, 4
  and Georgian human rights violations, 383
  and military action in Baltic republics, 25, 73
  and Union treaty, 73, 180, 411
Council of Ministers for Foreign Affairs, 206
Council of Nationalities, 170
Council of Workers' Collectives (Latvia), 175
Coup d'état
  arrest of leaders, 577–578, 582–583
  and Baltic republics, 564–567, 581–582, 588
  and Cabinet of Ministers, 557
  causes of, 556
  and Central Asia, 562–563, 571–572, 573, 579, 586, 609
  and Committee for Constitutional Supervision, 560
  control of nuclear weapons during, 554–555, 650–651
  and CPSU, 585, 586, 595, 596, 597
  and Dniester, 656
  and El'tsin, 558–559
  and Foreign Ministry, 626
  gold shipments prior to, 687
  Gorbachev press conference on, 813

Subject Index

Gorbachev return, 582, 584, 817
Gorbachev under house arrest, 553–554, 560, 718–719
and KGB, 605, 637–638, 761
and Komsomol, 568–569
leaders of, 553–554, 555, 593–594, 598, 600, 613, 620, 627, 657, 667, 718, 748, 763, 792
and Leningrad, 561–562, 569–570, 621, 662
and media, 557–558, 559
military planning for, 640. *See also* Military
and Moldavia, 562, 570–571
and Moscow stand-off, 558, 563, 564, 567–568, 574–575
predictions and warnings of, 7–8, 38, 48, 103, 117, 300, 383, 551. *See also* Soviet Union, and stability
reasons for failure of, 580
and RSFSR regions, 573, 757–758
and Russian Orthodox Church, 560–561
state of emergency declared, 555–556, 559–560
support for, 561, 563, 565, 571, 573, 575
and Transcaucasus, 562, 571, 586–587, 599
and Turkmenistan, 579–580
and Ukraine, 559, 562, 570, 579, 587–588, 611–612
and Union treaty, 567
unraveling of, 574, 577
Western reaction to, 569
See also Investigations, postcoup

Court proceedings
and Armenian-Azerbaijani conflict, 310
and Azerbaijan, 542
and Belorussian deputy's immunity, 432, 449
and Belorussian labor leaders, 369, 526–527
and charges against Bashkir poet, 194
and Chernobyl' accident, 208
against coup supporters, 589–590
espionage case, 71
Khmara trial, 330
libel and slander suits, 78, 108, 111, 176, 196
and OMON commander in Latvia, 885
Osh affair, 205
and RSFSR deputy's immunity, 158, 243
and Shneerson Collection of Hasidic books, 728
against Soviet harassment of democrats, 434–435
suit against KGB chief, 83
and Tbilisi massacre, 173
and Turkmen writer, 91–92
Uzbek cases, 188, 275, 477
See also Arrests and detentions; Investigations; Justice system

CPSU
appointments, 67, 112, 179, 290, 293
archives, 625–626, 814
bans and suspensions, 588, 594, 618–619, 796–797
Bolshevik Platform, 68, 468
cells in police departments, 172
Central Committee plenums, 67, 289–290
China on, 521
and coup, 574, 577, 583, 585, 586, 588, 590, 597, 753
criticisms and calls to disband, 454–455, 476, 584, 599–600
on democrats and opposition parties, 87, 145, 174, 271, 442, 522
and departification decree, 495, 498, 523, 524. *See also* Depoliticization
documents destroyed, 637, 720
on economic crimes, 456
and El'tsin, 110, 178
expulsions from, 528, 529, 532
financial problems within, 131, 534–535
and Gorbachev, 141–142, 261–262, 450, 551, 584, 597
harassment of nationalist groups by, 64–65
and illegal financial operations, 753–754, 792, 808
internal divisions, 237, 319, 371–372, 481, 522
and Kishinev Lenin monument, 424–425
and Komsomol, 594–595
and Lithuanian military action, 27
and media, 411, 551–552
and military, 37, 107, 225, 244–245, 294–295
and Molotov-Ribbentrop Pact, 436
nationalization and confiscation of property of, 272–273, 467, 589, 595, 596, 599, 604, 618, 625, 654, 671

CPSU (*continued*)
  Program, 436, 497–499, 534
  property and Bolshevik Party, 814
  property and People's Party of Free Russia, 762
  purge of reformers from, 551, 552
  registration of, 115, 260–261, 470–471, 544–545
  resignations from, 450, 461, 465, 482, 493–494, 586, 595, 596, 611, 617, 622
  and Shatalin, 131
  and Shevardnadze, 392, 464
  and Soviet unity, 145, 169–170
  and US Communists, 864
  and Yakovlev, 438, 520, 536, 550–551
  See also Communists; Conservatives; Socialist Party of the Working People; *individual republican Communist parties*
Credit
  blockade by Western banks, 384–385
  cards issued, 681
  from China, 195
  and EBRD, 268, 395
  and EC, 805, 810
  from France, 103
  and Germany, 107, 890
  and Japan, 354, 496
  from Middle East, 52, 645, 830
  and Norway, 805
  opposition leaders and Western, 177–178
  from South Korea, 226, 272
  from Turkey, 205
  from US, 18, 275, 318, 394, 708
  Western food, 664–665, 690
  See also Aid
Crime
  attacks on individuals, 315–316, 439
  bomb explosions, 166, 175–176, 195, 183
  "cotton affairs," 130–131
  currency deal, 66
  death threats, 8
  desecration of graves, 634
  and Estonia, 832
  increase in, 125, 334, 425–426, 529–530
  murders, 3–4, 29, 78, 254–255, 717
  stolen food aid, 36
  vandalism in oil fields, 343
  See also Arrests and detentions; Black market; Court proceedings

Crimea
  and autonomy, 47, 105–106, 438
  draft constitution for, 490
  hunger strikes in, 774
  and 1954 transfer to RSFSR, 688
  and Union treaty, 452
Crimean Tatars, 105–106, 418–419, 530
Croatia, 522–523, 608
CSCE. *See* Conference on Security and Cooperation in Europe
Cuba, 28, 41, 915
  and Soviet trade, 221, 395, 448–449, 746
  Soviet troop withdrawal from, 669–670, 818, 866
  and US, 509–510, 520
Curfews
  and Armenian-Azerbaijan conflict, 30, 276
  in during coup attempt, 561, 574
  lifted in Dushanbe, 4
  See also State(s) of emergency
Cuvantul, 587
Czechoslovakia
  and Belorussia, 740
  on dismantling Warsaw Pact, 35
  files on 1968 invasion of, 866
  and KGB, 218
  and recognition of CIS republics, 915
  and RSFSR, 330–331
  and Soviet relations, 176, 191
  Soviet troop withdrawal from, 29, 365
  and Ukraine, 805, 863

Dagestan, 58, 338, 759
Dagestanis, 179
Dashnak Party, 463
Debt
  and anticrisis program, 410
  figures on foreign, 392
  and monetary policy, 511
  payments, 37, 180, 765–766
  rescheduling, 496, 723, 735, 809, 848, 877, 900–901
  republican share of payments on foreign, 334, 679, 694, 803, 821, 840, 843, 884, 901
  Russian, 816
  suspension of payments on commercial, 871
  See also Central government, deficits; Credit

Subject Index

Defense
  budget, 28, 639, 650, 772, 868–869, 891
  and CFE, 499
  Commonwealth agreement on, 917, 921–922
  concerns about NATO, 249, 320, 326, 450
  and European stability, 203, 219, 719
  global strategic security system, 761
  interrepublican agreements on, 791, 800, 860
  and Kola Peninsula military base, 170
  lessons from Gulf War, 121, 207
  "open skies" treaty, 794
  RSFSR spending on, 920
  threats to USSR, 226, 502
  and USSR State Council, 793–794, 859
  See also Military
Defense Council, USSR, 836
Defense Ministry, USSR
  and army property, 836
  and Dniester, 872, 873
  and downing of Swedish plane, 829
  enforcing military draft, 11–13. *See also* Military service
  and Finland, 545–546
  and media, 34
  and military peacetime deaths, 413–414
  postcoup shake-up, 591, 601, 627, 651, 686, 887
  and RSFSR presidential campaigning, 381
  and transfer of Kuriles, 814
  See also Defense; Military
Demilitarization, 441
Democratic Bloc of Azerbaijan, 148, 171
Democratic Congress, 158–159
Democratic Crimea, 688
Democratic Kyrgyzstan movement, 100, 572, 733–734
Democratic Movement of Communists, 528
Democratic Movement of Georgia, 700
Democratic Party of Communists of Russia, 444, 481, 521–522, 528, 600, 621, 647, 762. *See also* People's Party of Free Russia
Democratic Party of Russia
  as all-Union opposition party, 549
  and decree banning political organs, 484
  and Democratic Russia movement, 210, 808
  Kazan' branch, 735, 736
  internal divisions, 296
  and Movement for Democratic Reforms, 444
  Political Council for, 662–663
  registration of, 193
  and Shatalin, 381
  and Union issues, 727
Democratic Party of Tajikistan, 137, 463, 698
Democratic Party of Turkmenistan, 770, 898
Democratic Party of Ukraine, 60, 439
Democratic Russia movement
  and Armenian-Azerbaijani conflict, 305–306
  criticisms of, 262
  and Democratic Congress, 158
  and economic issues, 287, 768
  and El'tsin, 181, 183–184, 762–763, 785
  explosion at headquarters, 343
  and media, 111, 658
  and Movement for Democratic Reforms, 442
  and Oktyabr'sky Raion, 532
  organizational structures of, 85, 95
  and Popov, 511–512, 680–681
  prodemocracy rallies, 43, 134, 210–211
  registration of, 291
  RSFSR presidential candidate, 295
  split in, 425, 808
  and unity issues, 144, 448
Democratic Ukraine, 60
Democratic Union, 250–251, 258, 486–487
Democratic Union of All Romanian Associations in Ukraine, 390
Democrats
  and Azerbaijani abuse of Armenians, 487
  and Bolshevik Platform, 468
  calls for broad-based party of, 392, 439
  and central government, 426
  criticisms of, 813
  and forming coalitions, 282, 328, 386–387
  harassment of, 381, 434–435
  and May Day rally, 302
  and Popov, 511–512
  and postcoup action in RSFSR autonomous republics, 628
  splits in, 727
  and support for Gorbachev, 494–495
  and unity issues, 454, 481
  and Western help, 695
  See also individual democratic groups

961

"Demokraticheskaya Moldaviya," 99
Demonstrations and protests
  Adzharia and religious, 288
  in Azerbaijan, 596, 653, 697, 767
  banning, 221–222, 256, 283
  in Bashkiria, 819
  of conservative groups in Leningrad, 99–100
  and coup, 556, 558, 561, 562, 568, 569–570, 570–571, 579
  against CPSU and KGB, 584
  in Dagestan, 759
  in Georgia, 108, 645–647, 849
  against Gulf War, 13–14, 58, 120–121
  in Kazakhstan, 759–760
  and Leningrad television, 479, 864–865
  in Lithuania, 282, 315, 538–539
  by Meskhetians, 512
  by military draftees, 24
  against military action in Baltic republics, 31–32, 42–43
  in Moldavia, 788–789
  Moscow taxi drivers, 777
  and Nagorno-Karabakh, 100, 130, 669
  in North Ossetia, 97
  and October Revolution anniversary, 801–802
  against price increases, 21, 41–42
  pro-Communist, 909
  prodemocracy, 134
  pro-El'tsin, 136, 183–184, 210–211, 295
  pro-Popov, 680–681
  for release of Novodvorskaya, 486–487
  and Soviet Armed Forces Day, 134–135
  and strikes, 231, 232, 240–241, 242, 748
  student, 232
  supporting coup leaders, 792
  in Tajikistan, 623–624, 672–673, 698–699
  for Tatar sovereignty, 251, 736
  in Ukraine, 96, 283, 632, 655
  and Union treaty, 423–424
  Uzbek ban on, 657
  See also Unrest
Denmark, 140, 203, 239, 514, 756–757
Depoliticization
  and Belorussia, 602
  El'tsin decrees on, 523–524, 583
  and Georgia, 654
  Gorbachev and, 597, 598
  in Kazakhstan, 586, 617

  and Kirgizia, 552, 580
  and military, 632
  and RSFSR justice system, 526
  in Tajikistan, 596, 666
  and Turkmenistan, 624
  and Ukraine, 599
  and Uzbekistan, 609
Deportations
  from Nagorno-Karabakh, 310, 311, 439–440, 477
  RSFSR law on, 323
  under Stalin, 858
Deutsche Bank, 37
Dictatorship. See Political system
Dniester
  and central government coup, 571
  Communist Party in, 684
  elections in, 804, 865
  leader arrested, 624–625
  military-political putsch in, 871–875
  and Moldavian independence, 612
  Moldavian negotiations with, 634, 700–701
  and recognition, 756
  and RSFSR delegation, 655–656
  siege of Dubasari, 683–684
  and sovereignty measures, 11, 531
  and Soviet unity, 86, 449, 475
  jurisdiction over all-Union enterprises, 550
  support for Russians in, 542, 692–693
  Ukrainians in, 707
"Do i posle polunochi" (Before and after Midnight), 61, 225, 440
Dominican Republic, 204–205
Donbass region
  and coup, 569
  environment, 106, 780
  miners' strikes, 151, 152, 154–155, 156, 229, 230, 903
Donetsk, 230, 303–304
Dukhobors, 448
Dushanbe, 4, 472, 542

Eastern Europe
  Communists in, 223, 445
  Soviet nuclear weapons in, 492–493
  Soviets and anti-Communist movements in, 260
  and Soviet security, 293
  and Soviet trade, 392
  See also individual countries

Subject Index

EBRD. *See* European Bank for Reconstruction and Development
EC. *See* European Community
Economic agreements
  and Comecon, 7
  and Commonwealth of Independent States, 880
  by Council of the Federation, 4
  interrepublican, 115, 139, 543, 547, 603, 610, 620, 770, 800, 816–817, 819, 841–842, 850, 917. *See also* Republics, cooperation and mutual-support agreements
  and stabilization, 287, 290, 297, 313–314, 326, 352, 362, 403, 448
  See also Economic Treaty; Trade
Economic Management Committee, 644, 648
Economic reform
  and Baltic republics, 689, 837–838
  and Belorussia, 131–132
  and conservatives, 281, 405–406
  criticisms of El'tsin plan, 776, 778, 787, 791, 805, 844
  and El'tsin, 412, 767–769, 811
  European Bank on, 189
  Gorbachev advisors on, 39, 239–240
  Gorbachev on, 196–197
  Harvard plan, 402–403, 408, 409, 430
  and housing, 799
  and independent trade unions, 830
  and institutional change, 133, 418
  interrepublican councils on, 129, 284, 620, 686
  and Kazakhstan, 218, 323
  Kirgiz plan, 538
  and law enforcement, 372
  models for, 79
  progress of, 195–196, 221, 544, 583, 664, 749
  and RSFSR, 219, 222–223, 342, 467, 847–848, 851
  and social unrest, 795. *See also* Demonstrations; Unrest
  and trade organizations, 150
  trusting supply and demand, 324
  Ukrainian progress in, 118, 724
  and unemployment, 390
  and Western aid, 202, 367, 392, 828
  See also Business; Financial sector; *Perestroika*; Prices

Economic Treaty
  appeals to nonsignatories of, 749
  and Azerbaijan, 746
  communiqué on, 701–702
  criticisms of, 722, 727
  and Georgia, 780, 825
  Gorbachev on, 732–733
  implementing, 791
  and Kirgizia, 675
  and link to political union, 732
  and Moldavia, 756, 798
  and RSFSR, 726, 730, 730–731
  signing of, 744–745
  and Ukraine, 661, 798, 815, 843–844
Economy
  anticrisis program, 256–257, 333–334, 409–410, 460, 491–492
  and domestic economic relations, 141
  figures on, 55, 248, 276, 337, 475–476, 548, 742–743
  Gorbachev on, 177
  growth of nonstate, 829
  integrating into global, 823–824
  management conference on, 447
  and miners' strike, 156, 248
  republican jurisdiction over all-Union enterprises, 387, 542, 549, 550, 578, 616, 617
  and RSFSR, 69, 247–248, 388
  stabilizing, 364, 394
  Ukraine and anticrisis program, 452–453
  US public view of Soviet, 504
  See also Economic agreements; Economic reform; Trade
"Edinstvo," 68, 236, 500, 581
  and congresses, 280, 407, 726
  and May Day, 302
  popularity of, 478
  and RSFSR presidency, 326
  and Shevardnadze, 90–91
Education
  Jewish summer school, 469
  minister of, 481
  RSFSR plan for, 464
  for Soviet Greeks, 254
  teachers' strike, 139
  university for humanities, 288
EFTA. *See* European Free Trade Association
Egypt, 325, 687, 715–716

Ekaterinburg. *See* Sverdlovsk
"Ekho Moskvy," 557, 578
"El," 494
Elections
  Adzhar parliamentary, 425
  Armenian presidential, 431, 540, 682, 728–729, 742
  Azerbaijani presidential, 435, 626, 632
  calls for new Russian parliamentary, 668
  in Checheno-Ingushetia, 654–655, 713–714, 783
  in Dniester and Gagauz, 865
  Georgian presidential, 266, 362–363
  investigations of irregularities in, 17, 129
  in Kalmykia, 748–749, 790
  Kazakh presidential, 820, 864
  Kirgiz presidential, 733–734
  for Leningrad mayor, 397
  Moldavian presidential, 756, 760, 880–881
  for Moscow mayor, 349, 397
  protest over RSFSR presidential, 400
  RSFSR ban on, 768
  RSFSR local, 738–739
  RSFSR presidential, 237–238, 282, 295, 322, 326, 327–328, 335, 337, 396–397
  RSFSR presidential campaigns, 368, 374, 380–381, 381, 382, 391
  Tajik, 698, 844
  Tatarstan presidential, 398
  Ukrainian presidential, 453, 862
  USSR Supreme Soviet, 31, 32
  in Uzbekistan, 400, 657–658, 822, 920
Emigration
  figures on, 57, 276, 777
  to Finland, 10
  Jewish, 325, 370, 688
  stalling of law on, 268–269
  US on free, 370
Energy
  Armenian-Azerbaijani dispute over supplies, 807, 835
  concession to exploit gas reserves, 541
  European Energy Charter, 901
  foreign development of oil fields, 70, 174, 300, 371, 402, 478, 547–548. *See also* Joint ventures
  hydroelectric station in Kazakhstan, 506–507
  incentives for oil and gas production, 335, 526
  investment in oil and gas infrastructure, 398
  Iranian-Soviet oil and gas cooperation, 407
  Latvian oil export terminal, 666
  natural gas from Afghanistan, 7
  natural gas production, 345, 829
  oil industry and bankruptcy, 869
  oil production, 59–60, 312, 446, 476, 616
  power blockades in South Ossetia, 96–97, 98, 235
  prices, 534, 780
  RSFSR oil export licenses, 903
  RSFSR suspension of oil exports, 796, 823
  shortages, 49, 109, 544, 807–808, 856–857, 881, 905
  shortages and miners' strike, 153, 154
  and Tatar oil fields, 343
  and Western investment, 329
  See also Nuclear power
Enterprise Council, 686
Environment
  aid for, 869
  and Aral Sea, 151
  and Armenia, 273
  Bashkiria pollution, 191
  and bombing of Iraq, 117
  and Chernobyl' accident, 83. *See also* Chernobyl' nuclear accident
  Council for Environmental Security, 758
  criticism of Ecology Commission, 217
  damage to Poland by Soviet troops, 370
  Daugava River contamination, 825–826
  and Donbass region, 106
  ecological disaster zones, 206, 780
  formation of Green Party, 365
  illegal nuclear dumping, 676
  Kuzbass region, 159
  and Leningrad dam project, 376
  mining pollution, 75
  and 1989 nuclear submarine accident, 402
  pollution at Soviet bases in Germany, 313
  radiation pollution, 23, 128–129
  Romanian-Moldavian accord on, 181
  Soviet military effect on Mongolian, 356
  and Tajik aluminum plant, 116–117
  and Tajik-Kirgiz border dispute, 501
  Ukrainian minister for, 418
  and World Conservation Union, 312
  See also Nuclear weapons

Subject Index

"Erk" Democratic Party, 442–443, 657, 920
Estonia
  and all-Union referendum, 185, 199
  anniversary of Republic of, 137
  and border control, 616, 831–832
  border post incidents, 339, 378, 514
  and citizenship, 650, 742, 801
  Congress of, 198
  and coup, 566–567, 575, 581–582, 589–590
  economic reform, 204, 506, 747
  and foreign affairs, 224, 469, 721
  and human rights, 892
  and independence, 86, 165, 187, 576
  leadership, 419
  and May Day, 303
  and Moldavia, 227
  and NATO, 816
  outlaw of CPSU in, 588
  political groups in, 266, 361, 601, 765
  and RSFSR, 760, 885, 917–918
  Soviet military in, 72, 717, 831, 845, 900
  and Soviet military property, 630, 850
  and Soviet military service, 214–215
  special status for northeastern, 497
  and trade, 775
  and Ukraine, 885
  and Uzbekistan, 840, 917
  See also Baltic republics
Estonian Popular Front, 266, 361
Ethiopia, 220, 380
Ethnic groups
  Buryat people, 137
  Chechen people, 389–390
  congress of peoples of the North, Siberia, and Far East, 323–324
  Cossacks, 76–77, 298, 659. *See also* Cossacks
  Crimean Tatars, 105–106, 418–419, 530
  and human rights, 349, 868. *See also* Human rights
  Ingush in North Ossetia, 281
  Kalmyk people, 743
  Karachai, 856
  Komi people, 842
  Kurds, 253–254
  Latvian law on minority rights, 205
  Meskhetians, 480, 512
  in Moldavia, 655–656, 707, 788. *See also* Dniester
  Poles in Lithuania, 475, 643, 677–678, 906
  and republican foreign ministries, 206
  Romanians in Ukraine, 390, 854
  RSFSR on minority rights, 782
  Russians in Baltic republics, 680, 744
  Russians outside RSFSR, 695
  Slavs in Kirgizia and Kirgiz in RSFSR, 486
  Soviet Arabs, 286
  Soviet Germans, 74, 143, 187–188, 360, 427, 428, 747
  Soviet Greeks, 254, 488
  Tatars, 118
  and Ukrainian declaration on minorities, 616–617
  and Union treaty, 475
Europe
  and RSFSR, 267
  security issues, 219, 249, 380, 415, 719
European Bank for Reconstruction and Development (EBRD), 103, 189, 268
  aid from, 189, 665, 851
  and Baltic republics, 660, 775, 875
  and G-7 summit, 474
  and new Soviet investment bank, 395
  Soviet membership in, 219
European Community (EC)
  aid from, 202, 297–298, 358, 388, 392, 620–621, 640, 665, 690, 701, 719, 851, 884
  and Baltic republics, 25, 26, 28, 47, 406, 419, 459–460, 607–608
  credit from, 805, 810
  and European security issues, 380
  foreign ministers in Moscow, 114
  and Georgia, 406
  media criticisms of, 88
  and Moldavia, 734
  and recognition of CIS republics, 914, 915
  Russian representative to, 906
  and Soviet cooperation, 418
  Soviet representative to, 336
  and technical cooperation, 520–521
European Free Trade Association (EFTA), 736, 893
Evangelical-Lutheran Church, 468, 490, 680
Experimental Creative Center, 416–417

Financial sector
  and Baltic republics, 633, 658–659, 689, 795–796

Financial sector (*continued*)
  Baltic stock market, 779
  commodities exchanges, 60, 499
  convertibility of ruble, 176, 326, 734
  enterprise hard-currency holdings, 899
  and Eurasco, 686–687
  exchange rates, 238, 392, 506, 866
  foreign-exchange market, 150
  foreign-exchange reserves, 723, 857, 894–895
  gold reserves, 689–690, 735, 807
  and government deficits, 299
  KGB control of Soviet capital, 821–822
  Leningrad stock exchange, 180, 358
  and membership in EBRD, 219
  and membership in international banks, 491
  Moldavian law on, 547
  new currency denominations, 777
  and RSFSR, 613–614, 738, 827
  state of Soviet, 473–474, 537
  and Ukraine, 759
  See also Business; Economic reform; Money supply
Finland
  independence of, 545–546
  and recognizing Baltic republics, 608
  Soviet emigration to, 10
  and Soviet relations, 673, 737
  and Soviet trade, 428, 533
Food
  aid impounded, 715
  aid from Saudis, 645
  aid from West, 620–621, 664–665, 690
  credits from US, 47, 708
  crisis and Kirgiz land reform, 286
  and Cuba, 746
  distribution problems, 656, 750
  and EC loan, 805
  grain procurements, 275, 470, 536–537
  imports cut, 762
  interrepublican agreements on, 764, 793
  and Kuzbass region, 800
  mishandled and stolen aid shipments, 36
  and Polish surplus, 264
  prices, 41–42, 239, 281, 423, 885–886
  production and land reform, 83–84. *See also* Land reform
  rationing, 56, 837
  restrictions on sales of, 854

  RSFSR-Czech deal, 331
  Russian ban on exports, 921
  shortages, 154, 216, 217–218, 792, 879, 897
  and South Ossetian unrest, 162, 163
  sugar riots, 703, 748
  supplies, 21, 80, 109, 166–167, 309, 344, 426, 521, 558, 725
  Tajik control of border trade in, 538
  Ukraine on grain harvest, 479–480
  See also Agriculture
Foreign affairs
  Afghanistan, 136, 385, 649–650, 676, 687, 695, 809
  Albania, 31, 146
  Asia-Pacific region, 246, 270, 312, 404–405, 464–465, 486, 499–500, 666
  Baltic republics, 726
  Bulgaria, 345
  Cambodia, 288
  China, 142, 228, 312, 336–337, 428, 459, 758
  coordination of republican foreign ministries, 206
  Council of Europe, 131, 428–429
  CSCE, 415
  Cuba, 41, 520, 866
  Czechoslovakia, 29, 176, 191
  Denmark, 203
  discussions on policy, 2–3, 5, 32, 87, 90–91
  Dominican Republic, 204–205
  Eastern Europe, 203, 293, 445
  East-West relations, 320
  EC, 114, 418, 520–521
  Ethiopia, 380
  Finland, 673, 737
  France, 102–103
  Germany, 19, 112–113, 144–145, 167, 195, 201, 257, 321–322, 342–343, 363–364, 416, 421, 451, 489, 679–680, 751, 826
  Great Britain, 168, 202
  Greece, 254, 488
  G-7, 399–400
  Guatemala, 6
  Gulf crisis, 8. *See also* Gulf crisis
  Honduras, 33
  Hungary, 134, 253
  Iceland, 109
  India, 536

SUBJECT INDEX

Iran, 81–82, 100–101, 111–112, 172–173, 407, 846–847
Iraq, 101, 173, 471, 670
Iraqi Kurds, 253–254
Israel, 5, 19, 271–272, 678, 746
Italy, 353–354, 676
Japan, 14, 47–48, 217, 270–271, 317, 469–470, 643, 737, 852
Mexico, 450
Middle East, 249, 324–325, 370–371, 644–645, 687, 774
Mongolia, 96, 193
NATO, 806
Nicaragua, 4–5
North Korea, 4, 269–270
Norway, 751
Panama, 225
Poland, 3, 29, 133–134, 245, 365–366
postcoup policy, 670
and recognition of Commonwealth states, 914–915
Romania, 209, 245–246
RSFSR support for Soviet policy, 20
Shevardnadze associations, 94, 128, 690
South Africa, 142, 807
South Korea, 9–10, 193, 272, 279–280
Spain, 460
Sweden, 5, 386
Syria, 79–80, 244
Turkey, 82, 185–186
Ukrainian-Russian talks on, 778
United States, 4, 7, 18, 58–59, 109–110, 141, 192, 292–293, 367, 394, 507–508, 509, 773, 858
Vietnam, 322–323, 758
Yugoslavia, 254, 436–437, 448, 453–454, 471–472, 517, 739
See also individual republics; Republics, and foreign affairs; Warsaw Pact
Foreign Ministry, USSR
appointments, 179, 257, 280, 337, 345, 614–615, 701, 799, 809–810, 859
and coup, 626
and Lithuania, 396, 510
postcoup personnel shake-ups, 591–592, 631, 639, 832, 852
postcoup reorganization of, 652–653
proposal to cut, 769–770, 781, 793
See also Foreign affairs; Ministry of External Relations, USSR

France
aid from, 851
and Armenia, 355
and Baltic republics, 419, 608, 721, 858–859
discussions on Gulf crisis, 102–103
recognition of CIS republics, 914
and RSFSR, 268
and Ukraine, 402, 707
Frunze, 85
Future of Lithuania Forum, 282

Gagauz
conservative support for, 542
and coup, 571
cultural celebration of, 525
and Dniester putsch, 875
elections, 865
and independence, 11, 630, 840
and Union issues, 86, 169, 475
unrest in, 818–819
General Agreement on Tariffs and Trade (GATT), 299
Georgia
and all-Union referendum, 69, 184, 199
antigovernment unrest, 599, 645–647, 699–700, 849, 859, 909–910
antimilitary protests in, 108
and Black Sea Fleet accord, 890
and call for mass civil disobedience, 268
and Checheno-Ingushetia, 783
and Commonwealth of Independent States, 908
Communists arrested in, 628
and coup, 562, 571, 587
creation of National Guard for, 66
and Dagestanis, 179
deal for weapons, 94
departification in, 654
earthquakes in, 298, 405
economic blockade of, 437
and economic reform, 825
and economic sanctions, 366, 881, 891
and Economic Treaty, 745, 780
energy shortage in, 49
and foreign policy, 406
government restructuring, 66–67, 202
and human rights, 383, 642–643, 681–682, 709
and independence, 35, 146, 184, 227, 257–258, 265, 639

Georgia (*continued*)
  and Iran, 841
  law on citizenship, 431
  leadership shakeups, 212, 553
  and media, 372, 405
  and Meskhetians, 480, 512
  nationalization of banks in, 550
  new powers for president, 512
  and North Ossetia, 540
  political parties in, 124, 425, 700, 795
  presidential elections, 265–266, 362–363
  prices and taxes in, 315
  and rail transport, 265
  recognition of republics by, 607, 617
  and Slovenia, 542
  and South Ossetia, 14–17, 88, 96–99, 160–163, 233–236, 314–315, 767, 803, 871
  and Soviet military action in Baltic republics, 27
  and Soviet military draft, 11
  and Soviet military patrols, 55, 72
  and Soviet military property, 803, 815
  transforming KGB in, 834
  and Tskhinvali Raion, 296
  and Ukraine, 891
  and United States, 530
  unrest in, 123–124
Georgian Communist Party, 425
Georgian Independent Communist Party, 124
Germany
  aid and training from, 61, 399, 451
  and Baltic republics, 608, 756–757
  and Bashkiria, 239
  conservatives' criticisms of, 476
  cooperation agreement on crime, 359–360
  credit and export guarantees, 802, 890
  Honecker case, 19, 195, 201, 751
  and housing for Soviet troops, 321–322, 420, 918
  and Kazakhstan, 428, 744
  and Lithuania, 345–346, 419, 663
  recognition of CIS republics by, 914–915
  and RSFSR, 360, 838
  and Soviet military affairs, 257, 294, 299, 313, 395, 530, 909
  and Soviet relations, 167, 201, 363–364, 416, 421, 679–680
  and Soviet trade, 37, 106–107
  Soviet troop withdrawal from, 36, 39, 56, 113, 158, 167, 238–239, 320, 433–434, 505, 810–811, 909
  Soviet weapons in, 400, 462–463
  and Ukraine, 285–286, 744
  and Wismut uranium mines, 342–343
  World War II compensation from, 144–145, 489
Gosplan. *See* State Planning Committee, USSR
Government Guard Administration, 636
Great Britain, 168, 202, 487, 515, 760, 771, 914
Greece, 254, 488, 915
Green Party, 365
Group of Seven (G-7)
  and aid, 447, 474, 620–621, 640, 734, 889–890
  and Gorbachev, 399–400, 456
  and Soviet foreign debt, 765–766, 828–829
  and Soviet policy, 469–470, 473, 850
Group of Twenty-four (G-24), 812–813, 890–891
Guatemala, 6
Gulf crisis
  calls to avert war, 22, 34
  citizen reports on, 57
  demonstrations against, 13–14, 58
  detention of Soviet freighter, 18
  and Gorbachev, 40, 94, 141
  media reactions to war, 44–45, 114, 145
  officials' reactions to war, 38–39, 40, 43–44, 58, 79, 81–82, 108, 114–115, 122
  policy discussions, 8, 30–31, 103, 111–112, 128, 131
  postwar reports on, 159–160
  Soviet cease-fire efforts, 101, 118–121
  Soviet citizens in Iraq, 22
  and Soviet weaponry, 207, 226

Harvard reform plan, 402–403, 408, 409, 430
Health
  AIDS, 20, 56, 147–148, 315, 420, 665, 854
  and Aral Sea pollution, 151
  and Chernobyl', 75–76, 353, 399
  children's, 795

Subject Index

disease outbreaks, 5, 130, 506
and doctors' strike, 856
and environmental pollution, 206. *See also* Environment
medicine imports, 884–885
prenatal care and infant mortality, 100
psychological counseling for deputies, 633–634
and unrest, 162
workers' strike, 748
Helsinki process, 681–682, 742. *See also* Human rights; CSCE
Helsinki Watch Group, 45, 542
Historiography
  Katyn massacre, 205
  Kirov case, 63
  Lenin, 285, 766, 814
  murders near Khar'kov, 540
  1968 invasion of Czechoslovakia, 866
  political repressions, 23, 403, 858
  riots in Novocherkassk, 295
  Romanov remains, 479
  Stalin, 8
  throne of khans of Khiva, 774
  Wallenberg case, 635–636
  World War II, 415–416
  See also Archives
Holidays and celebrations
  anniversary of Sakharov's birth, 346–347
  Belorussian, 503
  Cossack 400th anniversary of Russian allegiance, 659
  Dniester celebration of Moldavia's annexation, 449
  Easter, 250
  Estonian, 137
  Gagauz cultural celebration in Moldavia, 525
  Hanukkah, 853
  Lenin's birthday, 284–285
  Lithuanian, 186, 455
  May Day, 302–303
  Moldavian-Romanian festival, 408
  October Revolution anniversary, 781, 801–802
  Orthodox Christmas, 13
  postcoup celebrations, 583–584, 587
  Soviet Armed Forces Day, 134–135
  Tajik religious, 255
  Ukrainian, 45–46, 414
  Victory Day, 325–326
  World Youth Day, 549
  See also Commemorations and memorials
Honduras, 33
Housing
  economic reform and Moscow, 799
  privatization of, 449, 662, 664, 869
  for troops returning from Germany, 39, 321–322, 364, 420, 422, 434, 918
  and troop withdrawal from Baltic republics, 765, 885
Human rights
  abuses against Armenians, 401, 477, 487
  and Azerbaijan, 186
  discrimination against Communists, 445, 637, 852–853
  discriminatory decrees annuled, 170
  and Estonia, 892
  and Georgia, 383, 642–643, 646, 681–682, 709, 908
  international conference on, 346
  Lithuanian right of nonviolent resistance, 148–149
  and minorities, 349
  and Moldavia, 655
  prison conditions, 460
  of Romanians in Ukraine, 390
  and UN protocol, 821
  and voting, 200
  See also Anti-Semitism
Hungary
  recognition of CIS republics by, 915
  and Soviet military agreement, 35–36
  Soviet troop withdrawal from, 134, 253, 419
  and Ukrainian accords, 372

Iceland, 99, 109, 264, 514, 607
Ideology
  and arms sales, 667
  and China, 521
  and CPSU, 516
  Gorbachev on, 497–498
  public opinion on, 113
  and RSFSR foreign aid, 773
  and Ukrainian constitution, 662
  USSR name change, 379
  views on capitalism, 476
  warnings against radicalism, 278–279
  Yakovlev on, 502, 520

Subject Index

ILO. *See* International Labor Organization
IMEMO. *See* World Economics and International Relations Institute
IMF. *See* International Monetary Fund
Immigation, 260. *See also* Emigration
Income. *See* Wages
Independence
  Armenian, 151, 306, 482, 669
  and Azerbaijan, 626, 746–747, 920
  Baltic, 140, 188–189, 213, 264
  Belorussian, 214, 602
  and Checheno-Ingushetia, 714
  and economic reform, 263
  Estonian, 137, 165, 187, 266, 576
  and Gagauz, 630
  Georgian 146, 184, 227, 257–258, 265
  Gorbachev on republican, 201
  and Jewish Autonomous Oblast, 346
  and Kazakhstan, 897
  and Kishinev Forum, 361
  Latvian, 165–166, 297, 581
  Lithuanian, 80–81, 99, 315, 461, 534
  Moldavian, 135, 332–333, 375, 431–432, 478, 612
  and Nagorno-Karabakh, 632, 888
  and referendum on preserving USSR, 138. *See also* Soviet Union
  republican cooperational efforts, 250. *See also* Republics, cooperation and mutual-support agreements
  and Russian autonomous republics, 247
  South Ossetian, 910
  and Tajikistan, 642
  and Tatarstan, 735–736
  and territorial disputes, 604–605
  and Turkmenistan, 763
  Ukrainian, 116, 599, 723, 733, 862–864
  and Uzbekistan, 608–609, 638, 920–921
Independent Azerbaijan Democratic Bloc, 435
Independent Moldavian Communist Party-Democratic Platform, 255, 332
India, 536
Indonesia, 486
Industry
  autonomy in, 331
  conversion of defense, 197, 256, 439, 496, 531–532, 769, 773
  pollution and chemical, 273
  privatizing, 376

  production, 166–167, 221, 231, 476, 548, 743
  and supplies, 263
  Ukraine and defense, 365
  See also Business; Economy; Mining
Inflation, 432, 663, 750, 768, 829, 911. *See also* Prices
Ingush, 281, 323, 830–831, 861
Intellectuals, 34–35, 99, 480, 737–738, 800
Intelligence
  abolition of KGB, 730
  foreign Muslim, 262
  KGB East European network, 65
  reorganization of foreign, 695–696
  Russian Foreign Intelligence Service, 904–905
  Union treaty and US, 409
  and Uzbekistan, 691
  Western-RSFSR cooperation in, 739–740, 758–759
  Western step up in, 105, 226
  See also KGB
Interfax, 29, 657, 782
"Interfront," 165, 175
"Intermovement," 601, 611, 765
International Bank for Reconstruction and Development, 491
International Conference of Turkestanis, 685
International Development Association, 491
International Finance Corporation, 491
International Front of Latvian SSR Workers, 1–2
International Labor Organization (ILO), 390, 720
International Monetary Fund (IMF), 367, 451, 474, 491, 621, 715, 892
Interregional Council of Estonia, 475
Interregional Group of Deputies, 35, 43, 117, 352, 409
Interrepublican Council for Safety in Industry and Atomic Energy, 431
Interrepublican Counterintelligence Service, 737
Interrepublican Economic Committee (MEK), 629, 640, 663, 791, 793, 877, 906
Interrepublican Security Service, 822, 904–905

Subject Index

Investigations
  into arms transfers to Salvadoran rebels, 4–5
  and Chernobyl' accident, 83, 353
  of coup, 578, 585, 601, 610–611, 614, 618–619, 620, 628, 650, 662, 743, 761, 847, 918
  by CPSU, 438
  and CPSU finances, 746, 753–755, 792, 808
  into currency deal, 66, 123
  into election fraud, 17
  into Estonian Communist Party, 588
  of former ministers, 400
  of KGB spying on El'tsin, 90
  into leaks to press, 718
  of military action in Baltic republics, 376–377, 401, 433, 455, 513
  of military peacetime deaths, 316, 413–414
  into shooting of Pope, 527
  into Tajik unrest, 69
  into threats against RSFSR official, 321
  See also Court proceedings; Crime; Justice system
Investment, foreign
  anticrisis program and, 256, 334
  in Bashkiria, 239
  and Eurasco, 686–687
  foreign uncertainty and need for, 202, 329, 406, 489, 723
  and Japan, 270, 271
  and Latvian return of foreigners' property, 637
  legislation on, 369, 452–453
  and oil and gas industry, 70, 398, 446. See also Energy
  privatization and, 467
  and RSFSR, 223, 838
  Ukraine and, 88, 642
  and US companies, 775
  Volga auto plant and, 496
  See also Joint ventures
Iran
  and Azerbaijan, 169, 396, 550, 871
  and Georgia, 841
  oil and gas cooperation, 407
  recognition of CIS republics by, 914
  and RSFSR, 900
  and Soviet relations, 81–82, 100–101, 111–112, 172–173, 644, 846–847
  and Turkmenistan, 729, 923

Iraq
  and Kurds, 253–254
  nuclear capacity of, 117–118, 471
  and Soviet conservatives, 518–519
  and Soviet relations, 101, 173
  and UN resolutions, 670
  See also Gulf crisis
Islam
  Islamic institute, 64
  Kirgiz Muslim Center, 220
  Muslim Religious Board on military service, 148
  new Central Asian Muslim Board, 649
  and religious parties, 58, 143. See also Islamic Renaissance Party
  Saudi and Egyptian Imams to Muslim republics, 725
  state of, in Kazakhstan, 536
  Sunnah publication, 140
  and Tajik holidays, 255
  unrest over pilgrimage expenses, 401–402
Islamic Democratic Party, 58
Islamic Renaissance Party, 463, 658, 698, 756
Israel
  and Baltic republics, 608
  consulate opening in Moscow, 5
  potential arms sales to, 407
  recognition of CIS republics by, 914
  and Russian Orthodox Church, 221
  and Soviet relations, 19, 271–272, 324–325, 746
  See also Middle East
Italy, 119, 193–194, 905
  recognition of CIS republics by, 914, 915
  and Soviet relations, 353–354, 676
Izvestia
  banning of, 581
  and Chechen republic elections, 713
  coup reporting, 559
  expulsion from North Korea, 180–181
  and Georgian censorship, 405
  and gold reserves, 690
  and Gulf crisis, 119
  and INF treaty violations, 493
  and secret gold shipments, 824
  on secret organs of power in Ukraine, 360
  staff problems, 67–68, 394–395, 585–586

Japan
  aid from, 456–457, 722–723, 737, 750–751
  and Baltic republics, 721, 850–851
  credit from, 354, 496
  and Kurile Islands dispute, 85, 217, 270–271, 469–470, 509
  recognition of CIS republics by, 915
  and Soviet military threat, 501
  and Soviet relations, 14, 47–48, 270–271, 317, 852
  transportation services, 60, 313
Jehovah's Witnesses, 288, 487
Jewish Autonomous Oblast, 346
Jews
  anti-Semitism and emigration, 688. *See also* Anti-Semitism
  congresses, 19, 52–53, 188
  exonerating dissidents, 757
  Holocaust commemorations, 452, 677, 694
  Hanukkah, 853
  international Israeli organization, 541
  Moldavian support for, 552
  schools for, 469, 527
  Shneerson Collection of Hasidic books, 728
  and Ukraine, 649
Joint Council of Work Collectives (OSTK), 102, 571, 601
Joint ventures
  and aviation, 190
  Baltic-Danish, 239
  and Bavarian firms, 286
  British Gulf and Gulf Canada, 478
  and Caspian offshore oil fields, 435
  concession to exploit gas reserves, 541
  Fiat-VAZ, 898–899
  figures on, 829
  Ford dealerships, 548
  and free economic zones, 477
  German-Soviet bus factory, 437
  gold mining in Africa, 24
  Romanian-Moldavian, 375
  Russian-German, 838
  Saudi-Soviet bank, 401
  and taxes, 462
  Tengiz oil fields, 300, 371
  Tokyo trading firm and aluminum, 264
  and US companies, 775
  in Uzbekistan, 143, 423
  See also Business; Financial sector

Jordan, 324
Journalists
  calls for independent media, 585, 607
  criminal charges and Leningrad, 176
  firing of TASS staff, 38
  firing of "TSN" staff, 196
  harassment in Georgia of, 372
  and *Izvestia*, 394–395, 585–586
  resignations of, 259
  Seventh Congress of Union of, 81
  See also Media; Television; Union of Journalists, USSR
Justice system
  and amnesty for some economic crimes, 736–737
  and coup leaders, 661, 763
  and enforcing central legislation, 273
  Georgian, 203
  interrepublican agreements concerning, 500
  and legal searches, 56
  political prisoners released, 668
  RSFSR, 189, 467, 526, 637, 776, 826
  and Russian constitutional violations, 916
  statistics on death sentences, 37–38, 417
  treason charges against Gorbachev, 798–799
  and war criminals in Lithuania, 743–744
  See also Arrests and detentions; Committee for Constitutional Supervision, USSR; Court proceedings; Crime

Kabardino-Balkaria, 619–620, 628, 831
Kaliningrad, 1, 95–96, 183, 370, 490, 540
Kalmykia, 743, 748–749, 790
Karachai-Cherkessia, 619, 811, 856, 870
Karelia, 454, 533, 706, 819
Katyn massacre, 205
Kazakh Communist Party, 525, 617
Kazakhstan
  appointments, 908–909
  border issues, 604, 605, 703
  and China, 468–469
  and citizenship, 906
  and Cossacks, 659, 827–828
  and coup, 562–563, 571–572
  defense, 762
  demonstrations and protests in, 41–42, 759–760
  and departification, 586, 617

Subject Index

and economic reform, 218, 275, 323, 662
financial sector, 64, 130
food supplies and harvest, 109, 217–218, 831
and Germany, 744
Gorbachev visit to, 367–368
and Great Britain, 771
hydroelectric station, 506–507
and independence, 897
joint ventures in, 300, 401, 547–548
and Kirgizia agreement, 124
military service in, 650
and miners' strike, 151–157
name change for, 888
and nuclear testing site, 91, 524–525
and nuclear weapons, 687–688, 896, 907–908
political groups in, 386–387, 442, 443, 525, 617, 725–726
presidential elections, 820, 864
price rises in, 805–806
religion in, 536
RSFSR relations, 604, 605, 759
and Soviet debt, 679
space program in, 77, 649
and Turkey, 185–186, 682
and Ukrainian treaty, 132–133
and unity issues, 101, 199, 411, 427, 519, 553
and US, 654
KGB
abolition of, 730
appointments and firings, 37, 93, 591, 619, 648
archives, 642, 661–662
and Armenian-Azerbaijani conflict, 308, 311
and Baltic attacks, 104, 183, 462, 470, 522, 616, 678
and Baltic republics, 595, 599, 697
and Bashkiria pollution, 191
budget, 28
collaborators, 440, 845
control of army units by, 9
and control of nuclear weapons, 889
control of Soviet capital by, 821–822
and Czechoslovakia, 218
departification of, 523, 598
disbandment of Uzbek, 691
and eavesdropping on El'tsin, 90

in Foreign Ministry, 653
in Kirgizia, 609
and Markov case, 225, 247
and police and MVD coordination, 64, 77
postcoup appeals from, 598
public protests against, 584
and Radio Liberty, 251
regulating, 342, 363, 750
and rehabilitation of Stalin victims, 403
reorganization of, 590, 605–606, 619, 638, 648–649, 679, 695–696, 737 755
repression of reform and nationalist groups, 64–65, 78
role of, 105, 448, 481–482
role in coup of, 580, 605, 614, 637–638, 761
RSFSR, 95, 316, 715, 720, 852
RSFSR, and cooperation with Western secret services, 739–740, 758, 758–759
and RSFSR merger of security organs, 904–905
and security issues, 8, 36, 226, 262, 386
and state television, 272, 614
support for Gorbachev, 20
and Ukraine, 332, 679
See also Interrepublican Counterintelligence Service
Khudzhand, 147
Kiev
Communists in, 261–262
Gorbachev in, 451
Lenin monument in, 649
and May Day, 302
and October Revolution anniversary, 802
rallies and strikes, 134, 231, 232, 263–264
Kirgiz Communist Party, 250, 552, 580, 624
Kirgizia
appointments in, 19
and coup, 563, 572
and departification, 552, 580
economic and land reform, 286, 388, 399, 402, 538
and economic union agreement, 675
energy crisis in, 881
food production, 80
Gorbachev in, 843
government reform, 52
Islamic center in, 220
jurisdiction over all-Union enterprises in, 542

973

Kirgizia (*continued*)
  justice system, 205
  and Kazakhstan agreement, 124
  political groups in, 5–6, 100, 480, 572, 733–734. *See also* Kirgiz Communist Party
  presidential election, 733–734
  prime minister killed, 859–860
  and RSFSR agreement, 486
  and Tajikistan, 501, 779
  and Turkey, 898
  and Turkmenistan, 474
  Ukrainian agreement, 547
  and Union issues, 135–136, 199, 286, 427, 755–756
  and US, 762
  and Uzbekistan treaty, 194
Kishinev, 303, 424–425
Kishinev Forum, 361
Klaipeda, 287, 565, 595
Kola Peninsula, 170
Komi Autonomous Republic, 217, 842
Komsomol, 568–569, 594–595, 691–692
Komsomol'skaya pravda, 9, 34, 90, 279, 295, 502–503
  and coup, 569
  subscription rates, 833–834
Korean Airlines incident, 10, 630, 755
Koryak Autonomous Okrug, 790
Krasnaya zvezda, 40, 41, 214, 219, 347, 581
Kuibyshev, 67
Kurds, 253–254
Kurile Islands, 85
  as block to Japanese aid, 456, 509, 643
  and defense issues, 814
  El'tsin on, 14, 212, 398
  and G-7 summit meeting, 469–470
  negotiations on, 48, 217, 270–271
  and RSFSR, 692, 740
  Soviet troop withdrawal from, 372, 737
Kuwait, 52, 644, 830. *See also* Gulf crisis
Kuzbass Council of Workers' Committees, 126–127
Kuzbass region
  and Democratic Union, 250–251
  environment in, 159, 780
  and food supplies, 800
  free economic zone in, 477
  and miners' strikes, 151–155, 157, 229, 230–233, 303–304

  and rail strike, 877
  strikes and coup, 559, 569
"Kyrgyzstan," 135–136, 672

Labor
  Belorussian response to strike demands, 414
  demands in Ukraine, 106
  and economic reform, 776
  for harvest, 253
  laws on strikes, 348–349
  law on work safety, 388
  and Moldavian immigration, 260
  and RSFSR legislation, 277
  unrest and shortages, 166–167
  See also Strikes; Trade unions
Land reform
  Estonian, 747
  and farm production, 830
  and freeing prices, 805
  Gorbachev on, 466, 708
  and Kazakhstan, 217–218
  and Kirgizia, 286, 399
  Lithuanian, 500
  Moldavian, 53
  and Movement for Democratic Reforms, 441
  and Peasant Party of Russia, 197
  and redistribution of farmland, 6–7, 243
  and RSFSR, 258, 919
  and Ukraine, 215
  Uzbek, 83–84
  See also Agriculture; Property ownership
Language
  and Bashkiria, 781
  and "Dniester SSR," 531
  and Latvian Supreme Council, 775
  RSFSR bill on, 417
  Ukrainian program, 49
Latvia
  and Armenian-Azerbaijani conflict, 311–312
  and Belorussian agreements, 841–842, 898
  casualties during coup attacks, 576
  and central government, 262, 510–511, 707
  and Chernobyl' victim conpensation, 382
  and citizenship, 658, 741–742, 857
  commemoration for deportees, 218
  and Commonwealth agreement, 884

SUBJECT INDEX

contributions to center from, 190–191, 297, 368–369
and coup, 565, 566, 588
and CPSU, 596
customs post incidents, 339, 378–379, 457–458, 514, 541
and Denmark, 203
and Economic Treaty, 702
and energy supplies, 796
environment, 825–826
explosions in, 175–176, 476
financial sector, 499, 633, 795–796
freeing prices, 840, 885–886
government restructuring, 840
and Great Britain, 760
and independence, 165–166, 581
justice system, 205, 411, 779, 885
and KGB, 599
and language, 775
leadership, 891
and Lithuania, 25, 691
and May Day, 303
media in, 680
military and OMON troops in, 1–2, 72, 433, 588, 601, 605, 626, 717, 724
and military property, 796
and October Revolution anniversary, 802
oil export terminal in, 666
and Poland, 691
political groups in, 320, 608, 806. See also *individual groups*
and property ownership, 250, 286–287, 636–637
and Soviet economic pressure, 388–389
and Soviet military service, 383, 517
travel restrictions in, 806
and Ukraine, 863
and Union issues, 175, 199, 535
See also Baltic republics
Latvian Communist Party, 262, 286–287, 320, 443–444, 565
ban on, 596, 644
Latvian Democratic Labor Party, 303, 565, 861
Latvian Popular Front, 153, 262, 297, 361, 658, 875–876
Latvian Social Democratic Workers' Party, 303
Law enforcement
and anticrisis program, 256

committees on, 64, 77
Cossack police squads, 213, 723
CPSU on economic crime, 456
and economic transition, 372
El'tsin on, 482, 836
and joint police-military patrols in Leningrad, 472
and law on security agencies, 342
MVD directorate on, 78
reorganization of, 839
and Russian KGB role, 720
Soviet and Western collaboration, 7, 359–360
See also Justice system; Police
Leadership
Cabinet of Ministers, 137–138
concerns about Russian, 894
criticism of RSFSR, 685
criticisms of Soviet, 71, 126–128, 251, 259, 269
elections for prime minister, 31
El'tsin address to people, 920
Estonian, 419
Gorbachev on, 177, 219, 368, 480–481
Gorbachev-El'tsin power transfer procedures, 591
Gorbachev resignation, 893, 912–913
Latvian, 891
military, 833, 877, 878–879, 908
and Moldavia, 355–356
Moscow, 896–897
postcoup shakeups in, 585, 591, 614, 634–635
and public opinion, 113
resignations, 2, 8–9, 39, 107, 124
RSFSR, 797
shakeup in Georgia, 553
Ukrainian, 357, 418
USSR people's deputies on, 634
See also Appointments; *individual republics*; Political power
Left-Centrist Bloc of Political Parties, 167
Legislation
Armenian, on political parties, 146
ban on political strikes, 271
on Cabinet of Ministers, 129, 206
and Chernobyl' accident, 139, 148, 319
consumer rights, 144, 356–357
contradictions between Union and republican, 65, 273

975

Subject Index

Legislation (*continued*)
currency regulation, 150
and dissolving Union, 889
on foreign investment, 369, 452–453, 642
on incomes indexation, 430–431
Kazakh, on food production, 109
labor, 294, 277, 348–349, 388
Latvian law on minority rights, 205
law on referendum, 198
law on weapons, 533
on police and security agencies, 144, 172, 342, 363
on postcoup military role, 621
privatization and land reform, 53, 92, 275, 445, 449, 500
on railways, 269
on recalling people's deputies, 321, 380
republican, on citizenship, 385, 431, 437, 801, 823, 857–858, 906
RSFSR, on Constitutional Court, 467
RSFSR, on deportation, 323
RSFSR, on emergency measures, 344
RSFSR, on media, 855–856, 913–914
RSFSR, on presidency, 290–291, 350–351, 351–352
RSFSR price and trade liberalization, 794–795, 858
RSFSR, on rehabilitations, 745–746
Soviet copyright law, 494
Tajik, on defaming president, 472
tax, 113–114, 462
on travel, 348
Ukrainian employment, 88
Ukrainian, on religion, 288
on Ukrainian presidency, 435
Leninabad, 147
Leningrad
and all-Union referendum, 200
committee for defense of city soviet, 63
and coup, 561–562, 569–570, 570, 621
demonstrations in, 99–100, 801
El'tsin in, 212
and El'tsin-Gorbachev controversy, 126, 150
and food supplies, 426, 837, 897
free enterprise zone in, 463
joint police-military patrols in, 72, 472
leadership, 132, 449
living standards and environment, 417, 780

May Day, 302
mayoral elections, 397
media in, 53, 178, 426, 455–456, 479
name change for, 369–370, 398, 640
Party organization and coup, 594, 610–611
and privatization, 545
protection for Sobchak, 8
restructuring city soviet, 407
and Soviet Armed Forces Day, 134
stock exchange, 180, 358
strikes in, 232, 453
suit against journalist in, 176
Leningrad Television and Radio Broadcasting Company, 647
Leninist Workers' Party, 407
Lenin's Socialist Party of the Working Class, 826–827
Lenin State Library, 853
Liberal-Conservative Union, 425
Liberal Democratic Party, 261, 400, 544, 545–546, 561, 594, 782
Liberal Forum, 258
Libertarian (Radical) Party of the USSR, 31–32, 343
Literaturnaya gazeta, 625, 834
Lithuania
anniversaries, 186, 302–303, 422, 455
and anticrisis program, 350
and Armenia, 548, 840–841
ban on procoup media organs, 581
and Belorussia, 399, 764, 915
budget for, 224
building occupations, 93, 175, 261, 291–292, 333, 343, 347, 473, 588
and Canada, 274–275
casualties during coup, 582
commemoration of Jewish genocide, 77, 677
and Commonwealth agreement, 884
control of borders, 602
and coup, 564
crackdown on KGB, 595
and Croatia, 522–523
currency for, 795
customs post attacks, 276, 338–341, 378–379, 401, 503–504, 512–514, 576, 804
Defense Department, 299
demonstrations and strikes in, 282, 287, 315, 538–539

Subject Index

and Denmark, 140
detention of defense director, 203–204
diplomatic recognition of Moldavia by, 637, 653
and EBRD, 660
and EC, 419
and economic reform, 143, 204, 367, 500, 689, 813
economic and trade agreements, 4, 850
energy shortage in, 856–857
and Germany, 345–346, 663
and Gorbachev, 21, 21–22, 80–81
and Ignalina atomic power plant, 851
investigations of military action in, 376–377, 462
and Japan, 721, 850–851
justice system, 903–904
and Latvia, 691
leadership, 473
military action in, 24–28, 72, 103–104, 357
minorities in, 643
National Independence Front, 534
nationalization of CPSU property, 589
negotiations with central government, 396, 460–461, 526
and Nuclear Nonproliferation Treaty, 429
OMON troops in, 187, 208, 432–433, 470, 601, 626
persecution of nationalist groups in, 65
and Poland, 677–678, 856, 906
political parties in, 143–144, 315. *See also individual groups*
public opinion in, 86, 99, 461
reactions to military action in, 31–32, 34–35, 588, 589
and rehabilitation of war criminals, 743–744
and right of nonviolent resistance, 148–149
and Roman Catholic Church, 385, 832
and RSFSR, 478, 505, 564
and Slovenia and Croatia, 510
and South Korea, 741
and Soviet citizenship law, 389
Soviet damage to, 430
and Soviet military service, 548, 616
and Soviet troop threat to parliament building, 377–378
and Soviet troop withdrawal, 654, 716–717, 724, 765, 816, 894

and Ukraine, 139, 863, 892
and UNESCO, 720
and Union issues, 164, 199–200, 429
and US, 317
Lithuanian Communist Party, 143–144, 164, 166, 303, 315, 589, 595
Lithuanian Independence Party, 845
Lithuanian National Salvation Committee, 24, 25–26
Lithuanian Social Democratic Party, 315
Lithuanian Workers' Union, 153
Living standards, 535

Magadan Oblast, 17, 793
Media
and all-Union referendum, 198
in Armenia, 371
and Armenian-Azerbaijani conflict, 311
attacks on El'tsin in, 41
calls for independent news, 607
charges for air time, 179
congress of Journalists' Union, 81
and coup, 557–558, 559, 570, 573, 580
and coup investigation, 743
coverage of Baltic events, 26, 27, 61
coverage of Supreme Soviets, 122, 321
criticisms of coverage, 29, 79, 91, 93, 161, 163, 242–243, 714
decree on Gosteleradio, 92–93
and democratic coalition, 159
downscaling of central newspapers, 9
ELTA-PAP agreement, 459
formation of Press Association, 275–276
and Gorbachev, 220, 813
on Gulf War, 44–45
independent army newspaper, 847
independent newspaper in Turkmenistan, 126
independent radio station in Khabarovsk, 105
information minister, 466
and international tycoon, 314
Leningrad independent, 53, 178
lifting of restrictions after coup, 578, 581
Lithuanian, 175
new Communist-sponsored newspaper, 541
newspaper subscription rates, 833–834
newspaper subsidy cuts, 908
Nordic news for Baltic republics, 148

Subject Index

Media (*continued*)
  postcoup personnel shakeups, 579
  republican banning and suspension of procoup, 571, 581, 587, 592, 643
  restrictions on and suppression of, 22–23, 29, 33–34, 35, 38, 53, 67–68, 74, 90, 411, 532–533
  and RSFSR, 144, 779, 855–856, 913–914
  RSFSR television, 192–193, 220
  seizures of Baltic centers, 565, 566
  taxes and paper shortage, 316–317, 357–358, 515
  Turkish television, 124
  and Ukraine, 452
  See also Censorship; Television; Union of Journalists, USSR
MEK. *See* Interrepublican Economic Committee
Mercedes-Benz, 437
Meskhetians, 480, 512
Mexico, 450
Middle East
  and Gulf War, 122. *See also* Gulf crisis
  peace negotiations, 185, 192, 202, 249, 271, 293, 324–325, 511, 774
  Primakov visit to, 644–645
  US-Soviet roles in peace conference, 508
  weapons in, 173, 370–371
Military
  appointments, 877, 878–879, 908
  in Armenia, 731
  and Armenian-Azerbaijani conflict, 305–312, 468
  and Asia-Pacific region, 404–405, 457, 499–500, 501
  and Baltic airspace, 753
  crackdown in Baltic republics, 24–28, 41, 333, 393, 588
  in Baltic republics during coup, 565, 566, 567, 575, 576, 581–582
  and Baltic customs post incidents, 276, 339, 378, 379
  base on Kola Peninsula, 170
  and Canadian-Soviet pact, 328
  and Commonwealth agreement, 886–887
  conservatives in, 434, 603, 847
  Cossack units in, 326
  cuts and budget, 190, 496, 715, 769, 859
  departification and CPSU, 37, 98, 523, 107, 225, 244–245, 294–295

dissatisfaction and protests within, 24, 62, 100, 761, 876
and El'tsin, 70–71, 391, 567–568, 620, 913
equipment auctioned, 54
equipment moved beyond Urals, 20, 257, 403–404
in Estonia, 900
and Georgia, 16–17, 654, 815
in Germany, 299, 313
and Gorbachev, 2–3, 300, 603
harvest and use of, 470
independent army newspaper, 847
investigations and commissions on Baltic crackdown, 376–377, 476–477
KGB control of army units, 9
leadership, 833
in Leningrad during coup, 561–562, 662
in Lithuania, 357, 377–378, 589
in Moldavia, 189–190, 531, 871–875
in Moscow during coup, 558, 563, 564, 574–575, 577, 578
murders within, 458–459
and Nagorno-Karabakh, 163, 393, 916–917
patrols in Soviet cities, 54–55, 65, 69, 72, 112, 472. *See also* OMON
peacetime deaths, 215–216, 316, 413–414, 483, 485
political officers on Gulf War, 108
and political organs, 833, 854–855
postcoup personnel shake-ups, 600–601, 602, 631, 632–633
professional force, 226, 329, 631
property and republics, 796, 822–823, 824–825, 836, 850, 898, 900
reform and reorganization, 261, 651–652, 686, 847, 858
republics on deployment of, 605, 623
role in coup of, 635, 640
and RSFSR, 113, 583
strength, 213, 488
Strategic Deterrence Forces, 832–833
unwarranted use of military transport, 347
in Ukraine during coup, 570
unified versus republican, 642, 656–657, 722, 791, 826, 859, 861
withdrawal from Baltic republics, 647, 654, 716–717, 724, 765, 816, 831, 845, 894

Subject Index

withdrawal from Cuba, 669–670, 818
withdrawal from Czechoslovakia, 29, 365
withdrawal from Germany, 36, 39, 56, 113, 133–134, 134–135, 158, 167, 238–239, 320, 433–434, 505, 810–811, 909
withdrawal from Hungary, 134, 253, 419
withdrawal from Kurile Islands, 372
withdrawal from Mongolia, 356, 799
withdrawal from Poland, 29, 36, 245, 259, 370, 911–912
Yazov on problems of, 422–423
See also Defense; Defense Ministry, USSR; Military service; Ministry of Internal Affairs (MVD) troops; Navy
Military-industrial complex, 22. *See also* Industry, conversion of defense
Military service
　amnesty for deserters and draft dodgers, 757, 841
　decree freeing Balts from, 670–671
　desertions, 98–99, 163, 294, 395, 530
　draft figures, 266, 479
　draft problems, 1–2, 11–13, 61–62
　draft regulations, 545, 631, 794
　Estonia on, 214–215
　and Kazakhstan, 650
　and Latvia, 383, 517
　and Lithuania, 548, 616
　and Moldavia, 39, 171–172, 264, 812, 835
　Muslim clerics on, 148
　and navy, 329
　republics and withholding conscripts, 422–423
　social services for servicemen, 138–139, 373, 615–616
　and volunteers in areas of unrest, 1, 380
　See also Military; Russian All-Army Union
Miners
　agreements with, 63, 876
　and coup, 559, 569
　demands of Ukrainian, 106
　and independent trade union, 482, 856
　promises to, 94
　strikes, 33, 151–157, 228–233, 903
Mining
　Donbass mine fire, 440
　gold and diamond industries, 101–102, 790, 823
　July performance, 548
　mine closures, 341, 413

and pollution, 75
RSFSR jurisdiction over, 303–304
transfer of German uranium mines, 342–343
See also Miners
Ministry of Defense, USSR. *See* Defense Ministry, USSR
Ministry of External Relations, USSR, 793, 832, 852, 859. *See also* Foreign Ministry, USSR
Ministry of Finance, USSR
　and hidden accounts, 800
　State Bank loan to, 364. *See also* State Bank, USSR
　See also Financial sector
Ministry of Foreign Affairs, USSR. *See* Foreign Ministry, USSR
Ministry of Internal Affairs (MVD)
　anticrime directorate for, 78
　and Bakatin, 386
　and Baltic negotiations, 510–511
　departification of, 598
　and Moscow appointments, 82. *See also* Moscow, police chief appointment
　personnel cutbacks in, 759, 836
　postcoup leadership, 591
　property seized in Georgia, 803
　and RSFSR merger of security organs, 904–905
　and Ukrainian army, 787
　See also Ministry of Internal Affairs (MVD) troops
Ministry of Internal Affairs (MVD) troops
　in Baltic republics, 1–2, 26, 203–204, 291–292, 340, 347, 820
　in Checheno-Ingushetia, 784, 786
　coordination with KGB, 77
　in Kishinev, 424–425
　patrols in Soviet cities, 54–55
　reorganization of, 797
　and soldiers from Estonia, 214–215
　in South Ossetia, 16–17, 161, 233–236, 314–315, 767, 849
　in Transcaucasus, 42, 252, 255, 305–312
　in Ukraine, 853
　in Uzbekistan, 609
　See also OMON units; Police
Ministry of Material Resources, USSR, 263
Minsk, 240–243, 802
Mkhedrioni group, 123–124

979

SUBJECT INDEX

Moldavia
  army and border guard for, 515, 740–741, 764, 834–835
  ban on procoup media, 571, 587
  and citizenship, 385
  and Commonwealth agreement, 892, 923
  Consultative Council, 147
  and consumer goods coupons, 146–147
  and coup, 562, 570–571
  and CPSU, 595
  and Dniester-Gagauz referendums, 865
  and Dniester region, 10–11, 449, 531, 624–625, 634, 683–684, 700–701, 804, 871–875
  and EC, 734
  and Economic Treaty, 745, 756, 798
  energy shortage in, 807–808
  and Estonia, 227
  financial sector, 183, 383–384, 547
  food agreement, 764
  and Gagauz, 10–11, 525, 818–819, 840
  and Georgia, 617
  government restructuring, 171, 350, 640
  immigration quota, 260
  and independence, 33, 375, 431–432, 612
  and Jews, 452, 552
  leadership, 132, 135, 355–356
  and Lithuania, 27, 637, 653
  morals police in, 472–473
  political groups in, 99, 255, 332, 477–478. *See also individual groups*
  presidential elections, 760, 880–881
  and property reform, 53
  and reunification with Romania, 533, 671, 702–703, 741, 788–789, 844
  and Romania, 102, 125, 181, 187, 209–210, 375, 408, 530–531, 617
  and RSFSR delegation on Dniester, 655–656
  and RSFSR relations, 521, 729
  and Soviet army property, 822–823
  Soviet military and OMON troops in, 11–13, 55, 72, 189–190, 389
  and Soviet military service, 39, 171–172, 264, 812
  Supreme Soviet, 332–333
  and trade-union agreement, 300–301
  Ukrainians in, 788
  and Union issues, 86, 102, 125–126, 169, 174–175, 199, 214, 366, 435–436, 538, 732
  and United States, 653, 806

Moldavian Communist Party
  and all-Union referendum, 86, 174
  ban on, 595, 732
  and Dniester, 684
  elections, 80
  and leadership struggle, 132
  popularity of, 478
  split in, 64, 255
Moldavian Popular Front, 303, 477–478, 741, 840
  and Kishinev Forum, 361
  and Romania, 245–246, 788–789
  and Union issues, 62, 102, 910–911
Molotov-Ribbentrop Pact, 33, 246, 435–436
Money supply
  and currrency reform, 49–50, 73–74, 104–105
  and freeze on bank accounts, 866–867
  growth in, 663, 911
  tightening, 511
  in Ukraine, 912
  and Uzbekistan, 129
  wage freeze and, 544
  See also Financial sector
Mongolia, 96, 193, 356, 799, 915
Monuments, 595–596, 649, 672
Morocco, 915
Moscow
  Armenian genocide commemoration, 291
  City Assembly, 453
  and coup, 563, 564, 567–568, 574–575, 577
  and CPSU, 467, 594
  demonstrations in, 42–43, 134, 136, 183–184, 210, 295, 801
  elections and referendums, 200, 349, 397
  environment and living standards, 417, 780
  food supplies, 56, 558, 748, 792, 879
  government restructuring in, 426
  housing and residence permits, 503, 799
  human-rights conference, 681–682
  joint police-military patrols in, 72
  Kitai Gorod, 123
  leadership and appointments, 420, 504, 511–512, 896–897
  May Day and October Revolution, 302, 781
  police chief appointment, 82, 207–208, 249, 666

Subject Index

postcoup celebration, 583–584
and price liberalization, 888
privatization in, 664, 817, 869
strikes and protests, 139, 153–154, 777
transportation in, 405
Moscow Federation of Trade Unions, 230
Moscow News, 557, 625
Moscow Workers' Union, 485
Moskovskaya pravda, 592
Mountain Peoples of the Caucasus, 789–790
Movement for Democratic Reforms
  conferences and formation, 441–445, 673–674, 818, 894
  and CPSU, 529, 551
  and democrats, 481
  members of, 627
  as opposition party, 501–502, 536, 922
  and pro-Popov rally, 681
  and Shevardnadze, 489, 552
  and Union issues, 615
Mujahidin, 543, 687, 695, 809, 900
Muslim Religious Board for the Northern Caucasus, 121
Muslims. *See* Islam
MVD. *See* Ministry of Internal Affairs

Nagorno-Karabakh
  and all-Union referendum, 171
  appeal for UN peacekeeping troops, 870
  Armenian appeals concerning, 916–917
  and Azerbaijani government helicopter, 246, 837
  and Azerbaijani Supreme Soviet, 84–85
  demonstrations in, 130
  deportations from, 439–440, 477
  and escalation of Armenian-Azerbaijani conflict, 306–312
  and Gorbachev, 194
  and independence, 632, 888
  media coverage of, 93
  military protest in, 100
  and negotiations, 381–382, 668–669, 763, 842–843
  unrest in, 30, 42, 142, 163–164, 252, 393, 450–451, 709
  See also Armenian-Azerbaijani conflict
Nakhichevan ASSR, 298, 636
Narodnaya pravda, 541
National Democratic Party (Georgia), 124
National Independence Front, 534

Nationalization. *See* CPSU, nationalization and confiscation of property of
National Movement of Crimean Tatars, 418–419
National salvation committees, 50, 51, 116, 159, 204
NATO
  and Baltic republics, 25, 26, 633, 816
  call for dissolution of, 416
  concerns about Soviet High Command, 434
  and European stability, 219
  and rumors of second coup, 876
  Russian views on, 685–686
  Soviet concerns about, 203, 249, 261, 293, 320, 326
  and Soviet membership, 708–709, 806
Natural disasters
  floods, 296
  Georgian earthquakes, 298, 347, 405
  landslide in Uzbekistan, 316
Navy, 329
  and Asia-Pacific region, 404–405
  and Black Sea base, 791–792
  Kuznetsov to Northern Fleet, 918
  leadership, 686
  nuclear submarine accidents, 402, 761
  state of, 354, 499, 833
  Ukraine and Black Sea Fleet, 706–707
  See also Military
Nevada-Semipalatinsk, 365, 726
Nevskoe vremya, 570
Nicaragua, 4–5
Nordic Council, 140, 688–689
Nordic countries, 148. *See also individual countries*
North Korea, 4, 180–181, 269–270, 333, 915
North Ossetia
  and Georgia, 540, 881
  and Ingush, 830–831
  and Prigorodnyi Raion, 704–705
  and RSFSR Congress of People's Deputies, 351
  and RSFSR referendum on presidency, 160, 167, 198
  and South Ossetian refugees, 93
  and South Ossetian unrest, 96, 97, 803
  unrest and tension in, 15–16, 281, 335
Norway, 419, 751, 805, 914
Novocherkassk, 375–376

Novosti, 592, 607
Nuclear Nonproliferation Treaty, 429, 696, 868, 896, 907
Nuclear power
  Armenian, 49, 273, 906
  Chernobyl' station, 30, 731, 774
  increasing reliance on, 361–362
  moratorium in Ukraine, 109
  safety concerns, 57–58, 431
  Soviet-South Korean agreement on, 272
  worker error and plant shutdowns, 494
  See also Chernobyl nuclear accident; Energy
Nuclear weapons
  and Belorussia, 854
  and Commonwealth agreement, 884, 895–896, 907–908, 913, 922
  control during coup of, 554–555, 650–651
  discussions on control of, 620, 656, 722, 760–761
  and Economic Treaty, 702
  environmental contamination and production of, 129
  in Estonia, 717
  in Germany, 400, 811
  and Iraq, 117–118, 471
  and Kazakhstan, 91, 654, 687–688, 771
  and Kola Peninsula military base, 170
  in Lithuania, 602, 716
  and North Korea, 269–270
  in Poland, 259
  RSFSR control over, 605, 633
  in South Korea, 51–52
  Soviet movement and destruction of, 810–811, 889
  testing, 13, 30, 365, 368, 621
  and uranium mine, 343
  US on, in Eastern Europe, 492–493
  See also Arms control

Obshchaya gazeta, 557
OECD. *See* Organization for Economic Cooperation and Development
Ogonek, 111, 606, 834
Oil. *See* Energy
OKChN. *See* All-National Congress of the Chechen People
Oktyabr'sky Raion, 532
Oman, 915

OMON units
  and all-Union referendum, 175
  and Armenian-Azerbaijani conflict, 312, 451
  arrests and attempted prosecutions of members, 790, 904
  and Baltic customs post incidents, 338–341, 378–379, 457–458, 503–504, 513–514, 541
  detachments of "Dniester SSR," 531
  and Latvia, 1–2, 134–135, 315–316, 510–511, 566, 588, 601
  and Lithuania, 72, 187, 208, 347, 432–433, 455, 470, 588, 601, 816
  in Moldavia, 389
  oversight body for Baltic forces, 515
  withdrawal from Baltic republics, 626
Opinion polls
  and Armenian independence, 482
  on capitalist issues, 319, 403, 504, 766
  on departification decree, 523–524
  on El'tsin and Gorbachev, 239, 747
  and Estonian citizenship, 801
  on ideology and leadership, 113, 634
  on Lenin, 244
  and Lithuanian independence, 461
  on media, 434, 782
  on military service, 812
  Moldavian, 477–478, 533
  and religious beliefs, 777
  on Russian presidency, 66
  and Union issues, 138, 182, 814
Organization for Economic Cooperation and Development (OECD), 474
Organization for International Economic Cooperation, 7
OSTK. *See* Joint Council of Work Collectives
"Otchizna," 360
"Otechestvo," 13–14

Pacific Economic Cooperation Conference, 666
Pakistan, 136, 262
Palestine Liberation Organization (PLO), 325, 511
"Pamyat'," 294, 302, 375, 693, 717
Panama, 225
Party of Democratic Rebirth of Ukraine, 60
Party for Democratic Reforms of Russia, 674

Subject Index

Party of the Independence of the Caucasus, 714
Party of People's Freedom, 808
Party of Social Progress of Ukraine, 763
Pavlogradugol Association, 154
Peasant Party of Russia, 197
People's Party of Free Russia, 762
People's Party of Russia, 184
Perestroika, 7–8, 279, 384, 489, 563
   See also Economic reform; Political reform
PLO. See Palestine Liberation Organization
Poland
  and Belorussia, 728
  food offer from, 264
  and Kaliningrad Oblast, 490
  and Latvia, 691, 806
  and Lithuania, 459, 677–678, 856, 906
  and RSFSR, 183, 911–912
  and Soviet barter agreement, 493
  and Soviet relations, 3, 365–366
  Soviet troop withdrawal, 29, 36, 245, 259, 370
  and troop withdrawal from Germany, 133–134
  and Ukraine, 639, 863, 911
Police
  besieged in Moldavia, 683–684, 872–874
  and coordination with KGB, 64
  expansion of powers, 76
  harassment of political parties by, 60–61
  and Interpol, 244
  and joint military patrols in Moscow and Leningrad, 72, 472
  law on, 172
  Moldavia and morals, 472–473
  in Moscow, 31–32, 211, 839
  Nagorno-Karabakh chief attacked, 42
  OMON troops and Latvian, 457
  political organs in, 480
  RSFSR on role of, 144
  See also OMON units
Polis, 416–417
Political asylum
  and Armenian-Azerbaijani conflict, 310
  for coup supporters in China, 635
  for East European Communists, 223
  in Europe for Lithuanian OMON units, 601
  and Honecker case, 370, 826, 891
  and Soviet soldiers in Germany, 395, 530, 909

Political Consultative Council, 650, 703
Political organs
  and coup, 662
  dissolution of military, 854–855
  El'tsin departification decree, 483–485
  and Gulf War, 108
  and police departments, 172, 480
  Psychological Warfare Administration, 923
  reform of, 833
  transfer of jurisdiction for, 30
  See also Depoliticization
Political parties and movements
  Armenian law on, 146
  call for national-patriotic movement, 492
  calls for centrist party, 141–142, 485
  calls to create opposition party, 218–219, 236–237, 257, 269, 392, 439, 549
  conference for united Russia, 147
  coup and ban on activities of, 556
  CPSU on consultations with, 289–290
  and CPSU-KGB assets, 799–800
  and creation of interparty liberal union, 746
  democratic coalitions, 57, 60, 158–159, 181, 213, 282, 328
  formation of Movement for Democratic Reforms, 441–445
  and Georgia, 795
  government consultations with, 295
  harassment of, 60–61, 118, 294, 352–353
  "Independent Russian Alliance," 258
  Islamic, 143
  and racism, 688
  registration of, 3, 260–261, 544–545
  RSFSR, 193, 407–408, 545
  RSFSR government posts and leaders of, 189
  RSFSR on separatist, 757
  social democratic, 70
  structure of, 85
  total number in USSR, 145
  and Uzbekistan, 657–658
  See also Communists; CPSU; Democrats; *individual groups*
Political power
  calls for restructuring, 71
  conservative pressures, 57, 90, 236–237, 386

Political power (*continued*)
  El'tsin and postcoup, 593, 768–769
  Gorbachev-El'tsin struggle, 68, 126–128, 133–134, 134–135, 136, 150, 613
  and reformists, 361
  rescinding special USSR presidential, 618
  Shevardnadze on "shadow power," 180
  transfer to republics of, 358. *See also* Republics
  Ukrainian secret organs of, 360
  and Union treaty, 543
  and USSR prime minister, 408–409
  See also Leadership
Political reform
  Azerbaijani government restructuring, 778
  Belorussian presidency, 420–421
  calls for, 51, 663–664
  and Georgian government, 66–67, 202, 265–266
  and Harvard plan, 430
  and instability, 327
  Kirgizia government structure, 52
  Latvian government restructuring, 840
  and Lithuania, 689
  military on, 22, 261
  Moldavian, 171, 350
  progress of, 70, 94, 364
  restructuring central government, 7–8, 133
  RSFSR, 52, 290–291, 487, 539–540, 738, 781–782
  and security organs, 72–73
  Ukrainian government restructuring, 332
  and US aid, 367
  See also Economic reform; *Perestroika*
Political system
  call for authoritarian rule, 93
  confederation proposals, 144, 255, 375, 609
  democratic coalition on, 159
  dictatorship proposal, 116
  Gorbachev on dictatorship of law, 107
  multiparty, 3, 667–668, 818
  opinion poll on, 634
  postcoup transitional structures, 629
  presidential system, 2
  and Russian presidency, 66, 89, 222
  and Union treaty, 359, 846, 868. *See also* Union treaty
  United States, 395–396
  See also Commonwealth of Independent States; Soviet Union

Popular Congress of Kazakhstan, 725–726
Popular Unity, 480
Population, 56–57
Portugal, 179
Pravda
  and Armenian-Azerbaijani conflict, 311
  and Baltic republics, 34, 446
  bans and suspensions of, 581, 592–593
  and Central Television, 91
  confiscation of property of, 678–679
  and coup, 559, 718
  diamond business, 770
  and El'tsin, 127, 391
  and Gulf crisis, 119, 159
  libel suit against, 78
  and Middle East peace talks, 511
  and miners' strike, 231
  and Moldavia, 214
  and Movement for Democratic Reforms, 442
  registration of independent, 621–622
  staff of, 592, 890
"Pravda" publishing house, 411
Press Association, 275–276
Prices
  Belorussian increases, 804–805
  El'tsin on increases, 110, 116
  energy, 63, 526, 534, 780, 829, 869
  food and agricultural produce, 413, 885–886
  and Georgia, 315
  and health care, 85
  Kazakh increases, 41–42, 805–806
  Latvian freeing of, 840
  liberalizing, 110, 122, 177, 204, 238, 256, 257, 476, 787, 805, 811
  Lithuanian increase, 143, 689, 813
  Moscow liberalization of, 888
  nickel, 157
  and press expenses, 316, 357–358
  protests and strikes over rising, 21, 230, 240
  RSFSR liberalization of, 423, 858, 861, 884
  Tajik, 218, 281, 330
  Turkmen increase on raw materials, 820
  Ukrainian objections to Russian freeing of, 912
  women and increases in, 248
Prisoners of war, 136, 809, 900

Subject Index

Privatization
  and agriculture and food supplies, 344, 830
  and anticrisis program, 256, 333–334
  Armenian, 310
  and Bashkiria, 781
  and foreign ownership, 453
  Gorbachev advisor on, 240
  and Kazakhstan, 217–218, 275, 662
  and Kirgiz reform plan, 538
  Leningrad dispute over, 545
  and liberalizing prices, 787
  Lithuanian law on, 367
  in Moscow, 664, 817, 869, 888, 897
  and Movement for Democratic Reforms, 441
  and RSFSR, 219, 376, 449, 467, 855, 917, 919
  and sale of country dachas to officials, 467
  Soviet law on, 445
  and Uralmash, 675
  and Uzbekistan, 657
  See also Property ownership
Productivity, 276, 476. *See also* Industry, production
Property ownership
  and agriculture, 6–7, 243. *See also* Land reform
  and CPSU confiscations, 792, 799–800. *See also* CPSU, nationalization and confiscation of property of
  and foreign investment, 453. *See also* Investment, foreign
  Gorbachev on, 466
  and Latvia, 250
  Moldavian law on, 53
  and Moscow shops and cafes, 21
  and production, 258
  public opinion on, 504
  and scientific and intellectual discoveries, 393
  Ukrainian law on, 92, 215
  and the Union, 447
  See also Privatization
Prosecutor's Office, USSR
  investigations of Baltic violence, 376–377, 401
  and miners' strike, 152
  and nuclear power concerns, 57–58
  and political groups, 352–353
  RSFSR takeover of, 823
  and social unrest, 48–49
  Trubin resignation, 619
Publications
  ban on Lithuanian Communist Party, 143–144
  by Gorbachev, 96
  History of the Great Patriotic War, 416
  on Katyn massacre, 205
  Ligachev memoirs, 173
  Polis, 416–417
  Sunnah in Russian, 140
Public opinion. *See* Opinion polls
"Pyatoe koleso" (The Fifth Wheel), 259–260

Rabochaya tribuna, 592, 611, 834
Radio and Television Broadcasting Council. *See* All-Union State Television and Radio Broadcasting Company
Radio Free Europe/Radio Liberty, 251, 262, 580, 611
Radio Mayak, 557, 578
Radio Riga, 566, 581
Radio Rossii, 74, 181, 317, 578
"Rastokhez" Movement, 69, 698
"Ravnopravie" faction, 166, 205, 535, 608, 741–742, 775, 806
Referendum(s)
  all-Union, 18, 36–37, 62, 69, 80, 86–87, 89, 92, 111, 117, 132, 135–136, 137, 138, 142, 144, 145, 151, 159, 164, 168–169, 170, 171, 174–175, 184, 185, 189–190, 197–198, 198–200, 200–201
  on Armenian independence, 491, 669
  on Armenian nuclear energy, 273
  on Azerbaijani independence, 920
  calls for, on CPSU property, 467
  on Crimean autonomy, 47
  on Dniester secession from Moldavia, 756, 865
  on Gagauz secession from Moldavia, 840, 865
  on Georgian independence, 146, 184, 202–203, 227
  on Hungarian Autonomous District in Ukraine, 805
  on Ingushetia, 861
  on Leningrad name change, 369–370, 398
  on Moldavian independence, 333, 431–432

Referendum(s) (*continued*)
  Moscow, on mayor, 200
  on Nagorno-Karabakh independence, 888
  on private land ownership, 708
  proposed, on South Ossetia status, 236
  on RSFSR presidency, 160, 167–168, 186, 197–198, 198
  on Tajik Supreme Soviet, 698
  on Tatar independence, 736
  and Turkmenistan independence, 763
  on Ukrainian independence, 357, 599, 723, 733, 862
  on Uzbek independence, 822, 920–921
  and Western Ukrainian oblasts, 116
  See also Elections
Refugees
  and Armenian-Azerbaijani conflict, 310
  Iraqi Kurds, 254
  official figures on, 338
  political party on, 853
  South Ossetian, 160, 162, 910
Rehabilitation
  of Cossacks, 870
  and interwar Baltic leaders, 771
  RSFSR law on, 745–746
  of victims of Stalinist repression, 403
Religion
  beliefs, 777
  demonstrations against religious discrimination, 288
  first congress of Dukhobors, 448
  Protestants, 468, 487, 490, 680
  Soviet unity and leaders in, 190
  Ukrainian legislation on, 288
  Vatican appointment of bishops, 265
  See also Islam; Jews; *individual Churches*
Republican Humanitarian Party, 853
Republican Party of Russia, 85, 193, 439, 444, 727, 768
Republics
  and all-Union referendum, 138
  and anticrisis program, 284, 333–334, 409–410, 460
  armed forces in, 62, 326, 506, 610, 656–657, 811, 921–922
  and central budget contributions, 224, 248, 256, 284, 297, 359, 772
  and confederation proposals, 125–126.
  See also Political system

  cooperation and mutual-support agreements, 31, 46, 100, 124–125, 194, 227, 250, 283, 399, 474, 478, 486, 546–547, 548, 801, 920
  cultural agreements, 521
  defense agreements, 800
  and establishing relations, 132–133, 505, 898, 917–918
  and export restrictions, 263
  and food supply agreement, 793
  and foreign affairs, 65–66, 112, 206
  and Gorbachev, 177, 456
  and independence, 178–179, 201, 263
  laws contradicting USSR Constitution, 48, 65, 273
  and Soviet debt, 765–766
  and trade wars, 528
  and Union treaty, 256, 277, 359, 387
  and US aid, 32–33. *See also* Aid
  See also Economic agreements; Trade; *individual republics;*
Research, 190, 285, 393, 439, 472
Residence permits, 730
Roman Catholic Church
  bishops appointed, 265
  cathedral returned, 549
  and Lithuania, 348, 832
  and Russian Orthodox Church, 731, 778, 834
Romania
  and Dniester putsch, 873
  and EFTA aid, 893
  and Moldavia, 102, 125, 181, 209–210, 375, 530–531, 617
  recognition of CIS republics by, 914
  and reunification with Moldavia, 535–536, 789
  and Soviet relations, 209, 245–246
  Soviet travel to, 186–187
  and Ukraine, 835, 870
Roundtable/Free Georgia coalition, 268, 300, 361, 425
Royal Bank of Canada, 104
RSFSR. *See* Russian Soviet Federated Socialist Republic
"Rukh"
  attacks on, 262
  and Babii Yar, 110–111
  and coup, 559
  and Crimean autonomy, 105–106

Subject Index

and Democratic Congress, 158
and Economic Treaty, 815
and independence, 283
and RSFSR border issue, 604
and Unity day, 45
and unity issues, 92, 423
and US, 518
"Rus' monarkhicheskaya" (Monarchist Russia), 313, 407, 421
Russian All-Army Union, 334–335, 444
Russian Association of Independent Broadcasting, 855–856
Russian Association of Victims of Political Repressions, 23
Russian Christian Democratic Party, 258, 296
Russian Communist Party
  and China, 420
  and CPSU, 454–455
  and El'tsin reform plan, 768
  and Movement for Democratic Reforms, 444
  new newspaper for, 541
  plenums, 334, 528–529
  and RSFSR presidency, 327–328
  split in, 237, 371–372
  suspension of, 590, 796–797, 826
Russian Democratic Movement of Estonia, 765
Russian Democratic Party, 692–693, 768
Russian Federation. *See* Russian Soviet Federated Socialist Republic (RSFSR)
Russian Federation of Independent Trade Unions, 97, 156–157, 231, 232, 341, 482, 776
Russian Information Agency, 78
Russian Orthodox Church
  on anti-Semitism, 818
  and Christmas celebration, 13
  and coup, 560–561
  and Middle East, 221, 715–716
  returned property, 123, 266, 375, 548
  and Roman Catholic Church, 489, 731, 778, 834
  and Romanovs, 421, 479
  and Ukrainian Catholic Church, 363
Russian Party of the RSFSR, 346
Russian People's Party, 348
Russian Popular Front, 374–375
Russian Social Democratic Party, 296, 803

Russian Soviet Federated Socialist Republic (RSFSR)
  appointments, 14, 149, 510, 529, 674–675, 705, 776, 802–803, 824, 825, 833, 893, 906
  and autonomous republics, 207, 247, 276–277, 329–330, 338, 454, 619–620, 628, 782
  Checheno-Ingushetia, 710–714, 727, 782–786
  and coup, 573, 757–758
  draft federal treaty, 68
  and central government, 721
  funding, 6, 224, 359, 860, 865–866
  as legal successor to USSR, 721
  and Soviet debt, 821
  takeover of property and offices, 823, 827, 841, 899, 904
  and USSR Supreme Soviet, 887
  cities, 293, 417–418
  citizenship, 823, 857–858
  and coup, 569, 573, 577, 590, 757–758
  economic issues
    economic reform, 219, 222–223, 342, 467, 477, 767–769, 847–848, 851, 903
    economy, 69, 247–248, 388
    financial sector, 537, 613–614
    food, 344
    land reform, 197, 258
    and oil exports and leases, 70, 823, 903
    price liberalization, 122, 858, 861, 884
    privatization, 376, 855, 917
    takeover of economics ministries and all-Union enterprises, 578, 597
    taxation, 342, 492
    trade liberalization, 794–795
  education, 464
  ethnic issues, 695, 782
    Cossacks, 659
    Jews, 853
    language bill, 417
    law on deportation, 323
    Soviet Germans, 74, 747
  foreign affairs, 685–686, 775–776
    Czechoslovakia, 176, 191, 330–331
    Europe, 267–268
    Finland, 428
    Germany, 360, 751, 826, 838, 891
    Great Britain, 487
    Israel, 272

RSFSR (*continued*)
  foreign affairs (*continued*)
    Iran, 847, 900
    Italy, 905
    Japan, 14, 317, 692
    Poland, 911–912
    Russian foreign aid, 773
    Turkey, 136
    United Nations, 391
    US, 280, 411–413, 508–509
    and USSR foreign policy, 20
  health and environment, 128–129
    and Chernobyl', 292
    medicine imports, 884–885
  interrepublican and unity issues
    all-Union referendum, 89, 199
    Armenia, 920
    ban on exports to republics, 921
    Commonwealth of Independent States, 880, 888
    Economic Treaty, 726, 730, 730–731
    Estonia, 576, 760, 885, 917–918
    Georgia, 93, 160–161, 767, 891
    Kirgizia, 486
    Lithuania, 478, 505, 564
    Moldavia, 521, 543, 655–656, 729
    republican mutual-support treaties, 31
    Supreme Soviet reaction to Baltic action, 46–47
    Transcaucasus conflict, 42, 311, 535
    Ukraine, 622–623, 778, 800, 912
    Union treaty, 182, 247, 427, 454, 519, 528, 539, 553
    Uzbek justice system agreement, 500
  justice system, 467, 526, 637, 776, 826, 916
    law on rehabilitations, 745–746
  labor issues, 748, 876, 877
    miners' strikes, 152, 155, 157, 230–233, 303–304
    minimum wage, 277, 877–878
    unemployment, 905
    wage freeze proposal, 543–544
    Workers' Union, 63
  and media, 74–75, 78, 144, 192–193, 220, 317, 321, 331–332, 779, 855–856, 913–914
  name change for, 916
  politics and government
    appointments, 14, 149, 510, 529, 674–675, 705, 776, 802–803, 825, 833, 893, 906
    and ban on rallies, 210
    Congress of People's Deputies, 221–223, 237–238, 350–352, 781
    conservatives in, 360
    constitution, 705–706, 781–782
    departification, 189, 483–485, 498, 523–524, 583
    government restructuring, 52, 487, 539–540, 738, 797
    leadership, 107, 125, 126–128, 461–462, 466, 475, 667, 685, 902–903, 920
    local elections, 738–739
    political groups in, 193, 291, 365, 371–372, 407–408, 746, 757, 796–797. *See also individual groups*
    presidency, 167–168, 197–198, 222, 237, 290–291, 350–351, 351–352
    presidential campaigns and election, 282, 295, 322, 326, 327–328, 337, 368, 374, 380–381, 382, 391, 396–397
    Presidential Consultative Council, 824
    Supreme Soviet Advisory Council, 87
    Supreme Soviet elections, 769
    Supreme Soviet factions, 210, 237, 280–281, 360, 371–372, 414
  security and defense, 625, 650, 657, 715
    army for, 40, 41, 62, 70–71, 95
    borders, 183, 604–605, 815
    Committee on Defense and Security, 71, 87–88, 95
    control of nuclear weapons, 605
    defense budget, 891
    KGB, 316, 363, 852
    law on emergency measures, 344
    National Guard for, 568, 583, 733, 920
    police role, 144
    reform of security organs, 72–73, 904–905
    Soviet military, 54–55, 113
Russky put' (Russian Way), 680

St. Petersburg. *See* Leningrad
"Sajudis," 262, 315, 361, 377, 538, 564, 894
Samara, 67
Sanctions
  against Georgia, 767, 881, 891
  press censorship using economic, 411
  against republics not signing Union treaty, 366, 388–389
Saudi Arabia, 325, 401–402, 645, 725

Subject Index

Scandals and accusations
　and Armenian-Azerbaijani conflict, 252, 305, 309–310, 362, 837
　Chernobyl' official misdeeds, 414
　and coup, 754–755. *See also* Coup d'état
　and CPSU, 482, 719, 864
　of Dagestani expulsions from Georgia, 179
　against democrats and radicals, 141, 173–174, 271
　and economic conspiracies, 104–105, 133, 243–244, 384–385, 824
　against El'tsin, 110, 391, 644
　against Gorbachev, 63–64, 116, 126, 438–439, 590–591, 817
　and government embezzlement, 690
　and KGB, 183, 522, 821–822
　and Moldavia, 214, 355
　secret organs of power in Ukraine, 360
　against Shevardnadze, 406
　and Tajik election irregularities, 844
　against the West, 422
　against Yakovlev, 324
Scientific-Industrial Union, 443
Secession. *See* Independence
Security Council, USSR, 176–177, 618
Sel'skaya zhizn', 834
Semipalatinsk, 13, 30, 124, 365, 368, 524–525, 563, 621
Sergiev Posad. *See* Zagorsk
"Shield," 43, 103–104, 522
Siberia, 174, 323–324, 534, 546, 838
　and miners' strike, 151–157, 229–233
Sierra Leone, 24
"600 Seconds," 455–456, 615, 864–865
Slovenia, 542, 608
Smena, 570
Social Democratic Party, 70, 193, 692
　in Moldavia, 478
Socialist Party of Tajikistan. *See* Tajik Communist Party
Socialist Party of the Working People, 766, 908
Social programs
　and labor agreements, 284
　public works, 511
　and servicemen, 373, 615–616
　unemployment benefits, 402, 445
"Soglasie," 465
"Sokhnut," 541

"Solidarity," 269
Somalia, 7
Sotsialisticheskaya zakonnost', 693
South Africa, 142, 486, 807
South Korea
　aid and credit to Soviet Union, 51–52, 226, 272
　aviation agreement, 193
　and Korean Airlines incident, 10, 630, 755
　and Lithuania, 741
　nuclear energy agreement, 272
　and recognition of CIS republics, 915
　and Soviet relations, 9–10, 279–280
South Ossetia
　campaign to transfer to RSFSR, 704, 767, 803
　and central government support, 88
　and coup, 587
　earthquakes in, 347, 405
　and Georgian independence declaration, 258
　and independence, 910
　mobilization of population in, 849, 871
　and Union treaty, 475
　unrest in, 14–17, 96–99, 160–163, 233–236, 314–315
　violations of human rights, 383
Sovereignty
　and Balkar people, 831
　and Chukchi, 793
　and Crimea, 438
　and Dagestan, 338
　defining, 65
　Gagauz and Dniester, 11
　and Georgia, 35
　and Koryaks, 790
　and Moldavia, 33
　and republics, 31, 178–179, 183
　and RSFSR, 350, 675
　and South Ossetia, 14–17
　and Tatarstan, 251, 326–327
　and Ukraine, 199
　and Union treaty, 73, 179
　See also Independence
Sovetskaya Moldova, 587
Sovetskaya Rossiya, 343, 635, 740
　attacks on politicians by, 41, 391, 406, 438, 442
　bans and suspensions, 581, 592, 606
　and coup reporting, 559
　and Gulf War, 40, 114

Soviet Far East, 635
Soviet Germans
   autonomy for, 74, 427, 703–704, 747, 825, 846
   and central government, 143
   congress of, 187–188
   and Germany, 201, 428
   resettlement in Leningrad of, 360
Soviet Greeks, 488
Soviet Union
   and confederation, 755–756. *See also* Political system
   discussion over preserving, 101, 190, 327, 383, 465, 493, 615, 643, 727. *See also* Referendum(s), all-Union
   dissolving, 899, 919
   name change for, 379
   need for political union, 808, 838–839
   opinion polls on Union, 182
   possibility of second coup, 707–708, 876
   and stability, 81, 110, 128, 173–174, 178, 194, 212–213, 225, 327, 429, 640–641, 816–817. *See also* Civil war; Coup d'état
   stability and Western aid, 447
   and Ukrainian-Russian cooperation agreement, 622–623
   as Union of Sovereign States, 821
   warnings of dictatorship, 300, 640–641, 883
   as world military power, 40–41, 213
   See also Central government; Commonwealth of Independent States
"Soyuz,"
   attacks on El'tsin, 41
   and conservative action, 35, 93, 134, 216, 277–278, 408–409, 471, 525
   and coup, 561, 573–574, 602
   democrats' reactions to, 282
   and emigration, 269
   and Iraq, 518–519
   and RSFSR presidency, 327
   and South Ossetian unrest, 234
   support for Gorbachev, 299–300
   and Union issues, 175, 256, 390, 426, 465–466
   and Yazov, 423
Space program, 77, 439, 649, 804
Spain, 460
Sports, 105

State Bank, USSR, 238, 299, 473–474, 537
   and money supply, 511, 663
   RSFSR control of, 613–614, 841
State Committee for the State of Emergency in the USSR, 554, 555. *See also* Coup d'état
State Council, USSR, 629, 791
   Defense Ministers' Council, 859
   and food distribution plan, 656
   and KGB, 730, 755
   recognition of Baltic independence, 630
   republican armies versus unified forces, 793–794, 849
   and Union treaty, 729–730
State(s) of emergency
   Armenian, 550, 807
   Azerbaijani, 450–451, 616
   calls for, 259, 277–278
   and Checheno-Ingushetia, 783–784
   and coup, 555–556, 559–560, 561, 563
   laws and decrees concerning, 344, 544, 856
   in Makhachkala, 401
   in North Ossetia, 281
   and South Ossetia, 98, 160, 233, 235, 314, 849
   in Tajikistan, 671–673, 752–753
   in Tbilisi, 646
State Planning Committee, USSR (Gosplan), 133
Stepanakert, 130, 142, 163, 291, 309
Strategic Arms Reduction Treaty (START). *See* Arms control
Strike(s)
   in Azerbaijan, 84
   bans and moratoriums on, 256, 271, 283, 287, 341, 556
   in Belorussia, 240–243, 354–355, 526–527
   and Central Moscow Market, 848
   Cheboksary steelworkers, 500
   and coup, 558–559, 564, 567, 569, 569–570
   and dockworkers, 287, 453
   doctors', 856
   general, 230, 232, 234, 236, 263–264
   hunger, 175, 335, 382, 672, 673, 774
   laws on, 348–349
   miners', 33, 151–157, 228–233, 303–304, 413, 903
   and pro-Soviet forces, 282, 320
   in RSFSR, 748

Subject Index

teachers', 139
threats in transportation industry, 344–345, 877
Students, 5–6, 19–20, 232, 545, 748, 849
  and draft, 545, 631
Subsidies, 122, 908
Suicides, 719, 746, 747, 763
Supreme Soviet, USSR
  and all-Union referendum, 184, 200
  and Armenian-Azerbaijani conflict, 307–308
  ban on demonstrations, 210–211
  Cabinet of Ministers, 206
  Commission for Links with Public, 18
  and Commonwealth agreement, 887, 902
  Council of the Republics, 772
  Council of the Union, 769, 847
  and coup, 557, 578, 590, 593–594, 602–604
  dissolution of, 916
  and economic issues, 144, 150, 283–284, 356, 393, 409–410, 445, 462
  elections within, 31, 32
  environmental issues, 217, 319
  foreign affairs, 43, 79, 167
  and foreign investment, 369, 452–453
  labor issues, 155, 156, 294, 348–349, 388, 430–431
  law on entry and exit, 348
  and Lithuanian military action, 27
  and media restrictions, 33–34
  and politics, 126, 181–182, 220, 380, 408–409, 466–467, 750
  and security agencies, 172, 342
  sessions, 121–122, 749
  and South Ossetia, 98, 160, 233
  suspension of CPSU by, 618–619
  and Union treaty, 352, 464, 465, 868
Sverdlovsk, 23, 157, 200, 228, 678, 702
Sweden, 5, 386, 635–636, 829, 914
  and Baltic republics, 608, 771–772
Swiss Bankers' Association, 104
Syria, 79–80, 244, 324, 325, 715, 915

Tajik Communist Party, 115, 670, 743
  ban on, 671, 698, 915–916
Tajikistan
  and Afghanistan, 385, 543, 878
  and agriculture, 502
  citizenship law, 437
  commemorations in, 106
  conservative-democrat confrontation in, 472, 612–613, 623–624, 671–673, 698–699, 732
  control of cross-border trade, 538
  departification in, 596, 666
  employment, 725
  energy crisis, 881
  environment, 116–117
  and foreign Muslim infiltration, 262
  and independence, 617–618, 642
  investigation of unrest in, 69
  and Kirgizia, 501, 779
  legality of state of emergency in, 752–753
  political groups in, 137, 463, 698, 756
  presidential elections, 844
  and prices, 218, 281, 330
  and religious holidays, 255
  and Union issues, 137, 199, 427
Tallinn, 303, 318, 595–596
Tariffs, 524, 775, 810
TASS, 78, 587, 651, 657
  personnel changes, 38, 592, 615, 631
Tatar Public Center, 118, 735, 736, 812, 830
Tatarstan
  constitutional changes, 276–277
  and coup, 573, 624
  and departification decree, 523
  National Guard for, 830
  oil fields in, 343
  and RSFSR presidency, 168, 198, 335, 398
  and sovereignty, 247, 251, 735–736, 812
  and taxation, 492
  and Union treaty, 326–327, 329, 454, 463, 603, 619–620
Taxation
  agreement on federal system of, 501, 510
  and anticrisis program, 352, 452, 460
  and creative unions, 113–114
  and economic reform, 394, 462, 768
  and Georgia, 315
  Gorbachev decrees on, 213–214, 246–247
  and print media, 357
  RSFSR, 223, 248, 342, 492
  and Tatarstan, 463
  and Ukraine, 118, 300, 432
Tbilisi massacre, 173
Television
  and air time for El'tsin, 91
  boycott of, 82–83

Television (*continued*)
  calls for departification of, 585
  and censorship, 263, 440
  and coup, 555–556, 559–560, 578, 748
  coverage, 321, 484, 493, 590, 658
  CPSU seizure of, 551–552
  criticisms of, 91, 286, 296
  documentaries, 164–165, 251
  firing of "TSN" staff, 196
  and KGB, 251, 272, 614
  Kravchenko phone-in, 259–260
  Leningrad, 53, 178, 426, 479, 647
  and Minsk strike committees, 240, 241
  and Moldavia, 214
  opinion poll on, 434
  reorganization of, 615, 651, 622
  RSFSR channel, 192–193, 220, 331, 331–332
  RSFSR jurisdiction over Central, 904
  "Siberia," 174
  "600 Seconds", 455–456
  Turkish, 124
  and "Vzglyad", 217
  "Who's Who," 525, 734
  See also All-Union State Television and Radio Broadcasting Company; Media
Territorial disputes
  Belorussia and Baltic republics, 744
  and Cossacks, 659
  Ingush-North Ossetian, 215, 351
  and Kalmyk, 743
  RSFSR border challenges, 604–605
  RSFSR-Kazakh, 888
  Tajik-Kirgiz, 501
  Ukrainian-Czechoslovak, 805
  and Ukrainian independence, 863
  Ukrainian-Romanian, 835, 870
  See also Border
Terrorism, 343, 386, 794
"Tomaris," 549
Trade
  and anticrisis program, 410
  Baltic republics and free, 736, 893
  Black Sea free-trade zone, 185
  central government and republican, 183, 366, 387
  and Chile, 423
  and Cuba, 221, 395, 448–449, 746
  with Eastern Europe, 31, 176, 392, 493, 691, 912
  and Estonia, 775
  and Finland, 428, 533
  and GATT, 299
  and Germany, 106–107, 239, 802
  interrepublican agreements on, 115, 779, 840, 917. *See also* Economic agreements
  interrepublican export restrictions, 263, 538, 540–541, 706, 811–812, 839, 921
  interrepublican trade wars, 28, 528
  and Mongolia, 193
  and North Korea, 333
  organizations as independent companies, 150
  RSFSR and, 778, 794–795, 912
  Soviet-South Korean, 280
  statistics, 276, 298, 743
  Turkish-Kazakh, 682
  Ukrainian-Bavarian, 285–286
  and US, 269, 370, 494, 509, 520
  See also Arms sales
Trade unions
  agreement with central government, 284
  air traffic controllers agreement, 518
  and Belorussia, 226, 332
  and decree banning political organs, 484
  economic reform and, 830, 888
  law on, 294, 348
  and miners, 153, 156–157, 304, 482, 856, 876
  Moldavian agreement with, 300–301
  and RSFSR strikes and demonstrations, 748
  and Ukraine, 303–304, 425
Training, 61, 461
Transportation
  air, 20–21, 60, 75, 193, 408, 901
  and air traffic controllers dispute, 344–345
  bus strikes, 748
  Japanese-Soviet ferry service, 313
  miners' strike and, 229–230, 235
  and Muscovites, 405
  new rail lines, 183, 485, 923
  railway problems, 75, 242, 243, 265, 877, 895. *See also* Blockades
  railways law, 269
  railways minister, 322
  shipping, 289, 370, 270
Travel
  to Chernobyl', 80
  and currency exchange, 238
  and Kaliningrad, 1, 540

SUBJECT INDEX

and Kurile Islands, 270
Latvian restrictions on, 806
laws on, 268–269, 348
opening of Magadan Oblast, 17
opening of Vladivostok, 681
passport and visa fees, 505–506
restrictions on opposition leaders, 177–178
Romania and visa requirements, 186–187
tourism figures, 777
Treaty on an Economic Community. *See* Economic Treaty
Treaty on German Reunification, 112–113, 145, 167, 238
Trud, 833–834
Tskhinvali, 15, 16, 96, 97, 98, 162–163, 233–236, 314
"TSN," 35, 62, 196, 484, 658
Turkey
 credit from, 205
 and Kazakhstan, 682
 NATO rapid deployment force in, 450
 and recognition of CIS republics, 914
 and RSFSR economic talks, 136
 and Soviet relations, 82, 185–186
 television transmission from, 124
 and Turkmenistan, 867
 and Uzbek and Kirgiz relations, 143, 897–898
Turkmen ili, 126
Turkmenistan
 "cotton affairs," 130–131
 and coup, 573, 579–580, 737–738
 depoliticization in, 624
 foreign relations, 111
 and independence, 763
 and Iran, 729, 923
 and Kirgizia, 474
 oil leases to foreigners, 70
 political groups in, 91–92, 443, 573, 770, 898
 and price increases on raw materials, 820
 and Turkey, 867
 and Union issues, 199, 216
 and Uzbekistan, 239, 283
Tuvin Autonomous Republic, 198, 619, 706
"TV Inform," 615

UAE. *See* United Arab Emirates
Udmurt ASSR, 454

Ukraine
 central government relations, 749
  contributions to central budget, 359
  control over Soviet enterprises, 387, 744
  and coup, 562, 570, 579, 587–588
  and Soviet debt, 679, 694
  Soviet military in, 11, 12, 605
  and Soviet military service, 483
 commemorations and celebrations, 45–46, 110–111, 414
 economic issues
  anticrisis program, 452
  coupon system, 447, 541
  decree on industrial supplies, 263
  defense industries, 365
  economic reform, 118, 215, 724, 884
  financial sector, 101–102, 759
  food supply, 479–480
  law on foreign investment, 642
  property reform, 92, 215
  taxes, 118, 300, 432
 energy, 109
 ethnic issues
  Crimean autonomy, 47, 105–106
  declaration on minorities, 616–617
  Jews, 649
  and language, 49
  Romanians in, 390, 854
 foreign affairs, 88, 617, 731
  Canada, 673
  Conventional Forces in Europe treaty, 839
  East European countries, 191, 209, 372, 639, 835, 870, 911
  France, 402, 707
  Germany, 285–286, 744
  G-7 summit, 474
  Israel, 541
  Turkey, 185
  US, 517–518, 682–683, 858
  volunteers for Slovenia and Croatia, 497
 health and environment
  Chernobyl', 148, 292, 774
  diphtheria outbreak, 130
 interrepublican affairs
  and all-Union referendum, 116, 142, 168–169, 199
  Armenian-Azerbaijani conflict, 309
  Baltic republics, 85, 139, 607, 892
  Commonwealth agreement, 880, 883, 887–888, 900, 907, 918–919

993

Ukraine (*continued*)
  economic issues (*continued*)
    Economic Treaty, 661, 745, 798, 815, 843–844
    Georgia, 891
    and independence, 116, 599, 723, 733, 862–864
    interrepublican trade restrictions, 540–541, 811–812
    Kazakhstan treaty, 132–133
    Kirgizia agreement, 547
    and RSFSR, 604, 622–623, 638, 778, 800, 912
    and Union treaty, 423–424, 446, 457, 527–528, 537, 730, 843
    Uzbekistan, 770, 819
  justice system, 247, 479, 636
    and human rights, 821
    law on religion, 288
  labor issues, 106, 263–264, 304–305, 425
    law on employment, 88
    miners' strike, 151–157, 229–233, 303–304
  and media, 452
  politics and government
    citizenship, 724
    demonstrations on, 96, 283, 632, 655
    departification, 599
    government restructuring, 332, 435
    leadership, 357, 418
    name change and flag for, 636, 662
    political groups in, 60, 439, 442, 664.
      See also individual groups
    presidential election, 453, 862
    secret organs of power in, 360
    and "Soyuz," 278
    unity of, 805
  security and defense, 867–868
    armed forces for, 76, 506, 656, 706–707, 720, 751–752, 786–787, 787–788, 849, 860–861, 892, 919
    and Black Sea Fleet, 918
    Defense Ministry, 623, 633
    and KGB, 679
    National Security Service, 679, 804
    and nuclear weapons, 687–688, 696, 895, 896, 907
    republican command of MVD troops, 853
  Western oblasts, 69, 116, 168–169

Ukrainian Autocephalous Orthodox Church, 17
Ukrainian Catholic Church, 288, 358–359, 363, 777
  return of Cardinal Lyubachivs'kyi, 226, 398
Ukrainian Communist Party, 490, 524, 587–588, 628
  and coup involvement, 611–612
  See also Party of Social Progress of Ukraine
Ukrainian Interparty Assembly, 118
Ukrainian People's Democratic Party, 118
Ukrainian Republican Party, 60, 83, 96
Ukrainian Students' Union, 19–20
Unemployment
  benefits, 88, 402, 445, 461
  and defense industry conversion, 531–532
  and departification, 604
  and economic reform, 390
  figures and projections, 750, 848, 905
  funds and schemes for unemployed, 511, 725.
Union Bank of Switzerland, 104
Union of Communists, 852
Union of Democratic Forces (Tajikistan), 672
Union of Journalists, USSR, 263, 343, 411
Union of Officers of Ukraine, 786–787
Union of Russian Writers, 751
Union treaty
  and all-Union referendum, 200. *See also* Referendum(s), all-Union
  and Armenia, 490–491, 546
  and Belorussia, 853–854
  and central government, 352, 390–391, 447, 464, 465–466, 552–553, 703, 868
  conservatives on, 256, 278, 409, 426, 491, 543
  constitutionality of, 457
  and coup, 556, 567
  and Crimea, 452
  democrats on, 448, 487
  economic sanctions for nonsigning republics, 256, 277, 366, 387
  El'tsin on, 583, 738, 836
  and ethnic groups, 475
  and Georgia, 146, 825
  Gorbachev on, 384, 519, 603, 609–610, 813–814, 835–836, 838–839, 868

Subject Index

and Kazakhstan, 124, 427, 553
and Kirgizia, 124, 286
Latvian opposition faction on, 535
March and June drafts, 179–180, 410–411
and Moldavia, 102, 375, 478, 538
negotiations, 73, 177, 359, 629, 820–821, 845–846
and Nine-plus-One agreement, 287, 297
October draft, 727, 729–730, 733, 749
and RSFSR, 182, 207, 247, 454, 528, 539, 553
and RSFSR autonomous republics, 328–329, 329–330, 454, 619–620
and Tatarstan, 326–327, 463
and Turkmenistan, 216
and Ukraine, 423–424, 432, 446, 457, 527–528, 537, 843, 862, 871
and USSR name change, 379
and Uzbekistan, 111, 313, 834
and West, 530
Union of Veterans of the Afghan War, 193
United Arab Emirates (UAE), 644, 727–728
United Democratic Party of the USSR, 481
United Nations
appeals for peacekeeping troops, 870
and Armenian-Azerbaijani conflict, 309, 310
and Asian-Pacific security, 246
and Baltic republics, 98, 315, 459, 660, 816
and Belorussia, 688
and call for convention on minorities, 349
and Chernobyl', 292, 519
and Commonwealth agreement, 907
on control of nuclear weapons, 623
and Dniester, 872, 875
and Georgia, 160, 406
and human rights, 821, 892
Pankin address to, 665
and RSFSR, 267, 391, 913
and Yugoslavia, 454
and Zionism, 678
United States
aid, 18, 32–33, 367, 421, 664–665, 678, 724–725, 773, 851
aid to Baltic republics, 109–110, 774–775
ambassador to Moscow, 382–383
and Armenia, 815
arms control issues, 30, 492–493, 696, 896, 922

and arms supplies to Afghanistan, 649–650
and Baltic republics, 26, 27, 47, 224, 317–318, 377, 433, 509, 513, 520, 547, 630, 647, 653–654, 816, 849–850
bilateral agreements, 509
and converting defense industries, 773
and coup, 569
and Cuba, 509–510, 669
embassy, 223, 708
and Georgia, 530, 709
grain credits, 275, 394, 708
and Gulf crisis, 18, 114–115, 119, 120
and Kazakhstan, 654
and Kirgizia, 762
and Middle East peace process, 325, 370–371
military power of, 213
and Moldavia, 653
most-favored-nation trading status, 370, 494, 509
and North Korean ties, 4
opinion poll on Soviet economy, 504
political system of, 395–396
and Popov, 65–66
recognition of CIS republics by, 914
and republican military forces, 708
rescue of Soviet citizens in Somalia, 7
and RSFSR, 280, 397, 411–413
Shevardnadze in, 319–320
and Soviet emigration law, 269
and Soviet hostages in Ethiopia, 220
on Soviet military, 12, 488
and Soviet relations, 58–59, 141, 192, 292–293, 773
summit meeting, 58–59, 507–508
and Ukraine, 517–518, 682–683, 752, 858, 863
and Vietnam, 500
Unrest
Armenian-Azerbaijani conflict, 251–252, 305–312, 731, 842–843
attack in Sadarak, 298
Checheno-Ingushetia, 298, 323, 709–714, 782–786
Cossacks in Kazakhstan, 659
and currency reform, 50
discharged troops and possible, 761
Dniester, 871–875
and economic reform, 795

995

Unrest (*continued*)
  explosion at Democratic Russia headquarters, 343
  explosions on Baku-bound trains, 371, 451
  in Georgia, 96–99, 123–124, 645–647, 699–700, 909–910
  international mediation for ethnic crises, 478
  in Kashino, 453
  in Latvia, 2, 476
  Lithuanian, 208
  Moldavian, 356, 683–684, 818–819
  Muslims in Makhachkala, 401
  and Nagorno-Karabakh, 30, 42, 142, 163–164, 246, 252, 393, 451, 709
  and North Ossetia, 281
  Prosecutor's Office on, 48–49
  and South Ossetia, 14–17, 160–163, 233–236, 314–315
  statistics on casualties of, 349–350
  sugar riots, 703
  and Tatarstan independence, 735–736
Uralmash, 675
USSR. *See* Soviet Union
USSR State Committee for Television and Radio Broadcasting (Gosteleradio), 29, 53, 74, 91, 92–93. *See also* All-Union State Television and Radio Broadcasting Company
Uzbek Communist Party, 618, 653. *See also* People's Democratic Party
Uzbekistan
  and Belorussia, 801
  and coup, 562–563, 579
  democracy in, 502–503
  economic issues, 83–84, 129, 423, 657–658, 706
  energy crisis, 881
  environment, 116–117
  and Estonia, 840, 917
  ethnic issues, 286, 494, 800
  gold mines in, 790
  and independence, 608–609, 638, 920–921
  justice system, 188, 477, 500
  and Kirgizia treaty, 194
  landslide in, 316
  leadership, 400
  National Security Service, 691
  political groups in, 60–61, 143, 442–443, 618, 653, 657, 920
  and presidential election, 822, 920–921
  propiska system, 812
  and Turkey, 143, 897–898
  and Turkmenistan, 239, 283
  and Ukraine, 770, 819
  and Union issues, 111, 132, 199, 313, 519, 834
Uzbek Popular Front. *See* "Birlik"

Vatican, 385, 489. *See also* Roman Catholic Church
Venezuelan Communist Party, 754
"Vesti," 400, 434, 484, 552, 607
Vietnam, 322–323, 404–405, 499–500, 758
Vilnius, 134, 175, 195, 379, 432–433, 595
Vilnius Communist Party, 367
Vladikavkaz, 97, 281
Vladivostok, 75, 134, 681
Voenno-istoricheskyi zhurnal, 9, 111
Voiskovoi krug, 847
Volga German Republic, 703–704, 747, 825, 846. *See also* Soviet Germans
Vorkuta region
  and coup, 569
  and miners' strikes, 152, 153, 154, 155, 157, 229, 231, 232, 233, 304
Vote Counting Commission, 129
"Vremya," 181, 286, 316–317, 434, 452, 607, 615
  and Armenian-Azerbaijani conflict, 311
  and coup reporting, 557–558, 560, 574, 578
  and departification of state agencies, 484
  and Georgian censorship, 405
"Vzglyad," 22–23, 53, 217, 259, 554, 560

Wages
  and air traffic controllers, 344–345
  freeze proposal, 543–544
  and government-trade union agreement, 284
  indexation of, 204, 344, 430–431, 748
  of leaders, 437
  and Leningrad dockworkers, 453
  and Lithuanian reform, 689
  and medical workers, 135
  miners', 229
  and minimum consumer budget, 495–496

oil and gas workers', 398
and RSFSR, 277, 827, 851, 877–878, 903
teachers', 139, 464
and Ukraine, 304–305
Warsaw Pact, 3, 35–36, 203, 219, 227, 293, 322
Water supply, 162, 163, 246, 506, 731–732
Weapons
biological, in Iraq, 44
and Checheno-Ingushetia, 784, 786
chemical, 358, 462–463
curbing spread in Middle East of, 370–371
and Dniester putsch, 873–874
Georgian deal, 94
and illegal groups, 386
internal movement of, 20
"Kur'er" program, 610
law on control of, 533
MiG-31s exhibition, 404
military confiscation of, 216–217
and OMON raids in Vilnius, 433
production, 190, 391
and South Ossetia, 97
supplied to North Korea, 51
See also Arms sales; Nuclear weapons
West
and coup, 571
criticisms of and accusations against, 422, 446
economic help and advisors from, 362, 515, 839
and integrating Soviet economy, 823–824
and Lithuanian military action, 25, 26, 28
radio broadcasts during coup from, 557, 580, 584
and recognizing independent republics, 265, 587, 607–608
and stability of the Union, 447
See also Aid; Group of Seven
Women, 248, 438, 848
"Word to the People, A," 620
Workers' Union of Belorussia, 240
World Bank, 367, 474, 621, 869
World Conservation Union, 312
World Economics and International Relations Institute (IMEMO), 509
World Health Organization, 567
World Jewish Congress, 19
World War II, 270, 271, 415–416
Writers' Union, 615, 751

Yakutia, 247, 549
Yugoslavia
conflict in, 436–437, 446, 448, 452, 493, 497
Soviet mediation in, 453–454, 739
and Soviet relations, 254, 517
and summit meeting, 508
warning against intervention in, 471–472

Zagorsk, 678
Zhurnalist, 411
Zionism, 678

About the Book
and Editors

This last volume in the annual series chronicles the developments that led up to the abortive August coup, the disintegration of the Soviet Union, and the establishment of the Commonwealth of Independent States.

The book is arranged as a day-by-day chronology with boldface headlines identifying individual topics. Among the highlights are analyses of the crackdown in the Baltic republics, the miners' strikes, and the ongoing ethnic warfare in the Transcaucasus; the referendum on the future of the USSR and the prolonged negotiations between the center and the republics over the Union treaty; the emergence of Russia as an alternative center of power; and the banning of the Soviet Communist Party. The volume also documents in depth the failed coup and the political realignment that followed, the disastrous state of the economy, and the discussion of potential future cooperation among the newly independent republics.

Vera Tolz is an assistant director of the RFE/RL Research Institute's Analytic Research Department, and **Melanie Newton** is an editor of the *RFE/RL Research Report*, a weekly publication of the institute.